# THE BLACK
# AMERICAN
# REFERENCE
# BOOK

# THE BLACK AMERICAN REFERENCE BOOK

Edited by MABEL M. SMYTHE

SPONSORED BY THE PHELPS-STOKES FUND

PRENTICE-HALL, INC.  Englewood Cliffs, New Jersey

*The Black American Reference Book*
Edited by Mabel M. Smythe
Copyright © 1976 by Prentice-Hall, Inc.
Printed in the United States of America
Prentice-Hall International, Inc., London
Prentice-Hall of Australia, Pty. Ltd., Sydney
Prentice-Hall of Canada, Ltd., Toronto
Prentice-Hall of India Private Ltd., New Delhi
Prentice-Hall of Japan, Inc., Tokyo

10 9 8 7 6 5 4 3 2 1

**Library of Congress Cataloging in Publication Data**
Main entry under title:
The Black American reference book.

   Previous ed., by J. P. Davis, published in 1966
under title:   The American Negro reference book.
   Includes bibliographical references and index.
   1.   Afro-Americans.   I.   Smythe, Mabel M.
II.   Davis, John Preston, 1905-1973, ed. The American
Negro reference book.   III.   Phelps-Stokes Fund.
E185.D25   1976   301.45'19'6073   75-26511
ISBN 0-13-077586-X
Some material in Chapter 22 reprinted with the permission
of the following:
Farrar, Straus & Giroux, Inc., from *Ceremonies in Dark Old
Men* by Lonne Elder, copyright © 1965, 1969 by Lonne
Elder, III.
Bobbs-Merrill Company, Inc. and William Morris Agency,
from *No Place To Be Somebody* by Charles Gordone.

# PREFACE

*The Black American Reference Book* brings together in one volume a comprehensive view of the world of black Americans: history; personality pressures; social and economic status; political activities; involvement in and contribution to arts and letters; participation and treatment in the popular media, sports, and the armed forces; and other matters related to these categories. These themes, developed by a distinguished group of scholars and specialists, offer a balance of historical and current material designed to give the reader depth and perspective.

The *Reference Book* can be used in many ways. Viewed as a unit, "The Black American in Agriculture," "The Black Worker," and "The Black Role in the Economy," comprise a handbook on the economic life of black Americans. The chapters on "The Black Population in the United States," "The Black Family," "The Black Woman," "Young Black Americans," "Educating Black Americans," and "Prejudice: A Symposium," offer broad insights into social status. The sections dealing with "Afro-American Music," "Afro-American Art," "The Popular Media," "Black Influences in the American Theater," and "The Black Contribution to American Letters," taken together, provide a wealth of cultural insights and understanding. Such chapters as John Hope Franklin's "A Brief History," and Dr. Charles A. Pinderhughes' "Black Personality in American Society," are in themselves complete and provocative introductions to the subjects treated. Judge Constance Baker Motley's "The Legal Status of Black Americans," with interpretive commentary by Judge Robert L. Carter, stands as a succinct handbook of civil rights cases.

Since in an age of precipitous change it is impossible for the statistics presented in a work of this scope to remain current for more than a few months, emphasis has been placed on trends and interpretation rather than on the specifics of the moment.

The sponsorship by the Phelps-Stokes Fund of the *Reference Book* grows out of a commitment of more than sixty years to increasing the understanding of black Americans on the part of others, along with a concern for research in the area of black education, development, and culture in the United States and abroad. In the past, the fund has sponsored more than fifty publications of research studies and reports, ranging in coverage from Thomas Jackson Woofter, Jr.'s *Negro Migration, Changes in Rural Organization and Population of the Cotton Belt* (1920) to W. E. B.

v

DuBois and Guy B. Johnson's *Encyclopedia of the Negro—Preparatory Volume* (1945). The fund is currently preparing *The American Indian Reference Book*, a companion volume related to its commitment to another American minority. Ultimately the fund expects to develop a Phelps-Stokes Reference Shelf of publications, for which *The Black American Reference Book* provides the nucleus. Subjects treated will be related to the fund in such areas of interest as: the education of black and Indian Americans, Africans, and poor whites; housing; and the development of understanding of its target groups.

The thirty-eight authors who have contributed to the *Reference Book* are listed with brief pertinent background information regarding their scholarly interests on page xix. The manuscript has been read by a variety of specialists who have offered valuable suggestions; other consultants have also been helpful in providing information and assistance at various stages of the work. They are not, however, responsible for the final text. A profound debt is owed to them all; we wish to acknowledge their professional assistance here: Frederick S. Arkhurst, formerly Ghana's Ambassador to the United Nations and later Vice President for African Programs, the Phelps-Stokes Fund; Joyce Cooper Arkhurst, librarian and writer; Darwin Bolden, President, Pan-African Business Information Center; the late Horace Mann Bond, retired Dean of the School of Education, Atlanta University, and President Emeritus, Lincoln University (Pa.); Robert S. Browne, Director, Black Economic Research Center; James E. Cheek, President, Howard University; Kenneth B. Clark, Chairman, Department of Psychology, the City College, City University of New York; Mamie Phipps Clark, Director, Northside Center for Child Development; Alice T. Curran, Vice President, Encyclopaedia Britannica Educational Corporation; James Curtis, M.D., Associate Dean, Cornell University Medical College; Dan Davis, Special Assistant to the Executive Director, National Urban League; John A. Davis, Chairman, Department of Government, the City College, City University of New York; Lloyd C. Elam, M.D., President, Meharry Medical College; William Gordon, United States Information Agency; the late Percy Ifill, architect; Nell Jackson, Professor of Physical Education, University of Illinois; the staff of the Schomburg Center for Research in Black Culture, particularly Ernest Kaiser; John Henrik Clarke, Professor of Black Studies, Hunter College; Carlton Molette, Professor of Drama, Spelman College; Annelle Murray, of the research staff of Encyclopaedia Britannica Educational Corporation; Moran Weston, pastor, St. Phillip's Episcopal Church; Ida Wood, Vice President for Scholarship and Exchange Programs, the Phelps-Stokes Fund.

In paying tribute to those who have made this work possible, a special word is due to four of our authors who did not live to see this edition completed. The first of these is the renowned Langston Hughes, whose lively presentation of black involvement with the American theater appeared in *The American Negro Reference*

*Book* (1966). The second is the distinguished scholar, Gordon W. Allport, whose thoughtful statement on prejudice is also retained from the first book. The third, Arna Bontemps, the eminent writer, completed the revision of his chapter, "The Black Contribution to American Letters: Part I," only four days before his death. Finally, the stalwart sociologist, Joseph H. Douglass, lived long enough to read and approve the co-authored chapter on the family, based on his earlier work.

The editor would like to pay tribute to the foundation laid for the present work by *The American Negro Reference Book*, edited by the late John P. Davis. Thanks are due to the trustees and officers of the fund for their encouragement and unwavering support, especially the Chairman of the Board, I.N.P. Stokes, Elmo R. Zumwalt, Jr., and President Franklin H. Williams. Judith Miles, Toni Trent Parker, and Monique C. Clark have done invaluable work in research and management of the project. Other present and former members of the staff who have contributed in special measure are Charlotte T. Morgan, Rose Mary Rudden, Normine Thompson, Gloria Allen, June Yearwood, Josephine Barnes, and William H. Thompson. We are also indebted to Harry S. Murphy for preparation of charts and graphs and to Robert Palmer for assistance with the index. Additional staff members and friends of the fund and others too numerous to mention have been more helpful than they know in responding to our many requests for information and guidance. Finally, Mariana Fitzpatrick, the late Nancy Roodenburg, John Walsh, Rudolph V. Lawrence, Pamela Smythe, and Shirley Stein, have carried much of the burden of preparing the manuscript for publication.

*The Editor*

# CONTENTS

# A NOTE ON TERMINOLOGY

The intellectual arguments for and against various styles of nomenclature to designate a category of people mean little in situations involving group identity. Those who, for whatever reason, have a strong emotional reaction to a given term, however acquired, are unlikely to be persuaded by an academic approach to language usage or by explorations of the historical development of specific terms. Moreover, psychological interpretations of the choice are unlikely to be welcomed.

The overriding fact is that *black*, regardless of its accuracy or inaccuracy as a description of the actual skin color of persons so described, was once a despised term and has now been rehabilitated. The identification with *black* had been rejected by darker Americans who, tragically, sought to escape the burdens and inconveniences of discrimination by accepting white values as their own, adopting white manners and morals and standards of beauty. They courted the illusion that they could thus be accepted for themselves, without regard to color.

Perhaps this hope explains why *brown* was not popular years ago as a term of greater accuracy. Instead, adopting *Negro*, a capitalized form of the Spanish word for black, may have seemed to its sponsors to reduce the sense of the importance of skin color, since in English *Negro* is not seen as a color but rather as a designation for a total ethnic group. *Negro* included all persons of African descent, of whatever class or color; the term had no social or ideological connotation. In fact, for decades the most militant members of the group were leaders in the movement to promote the term *Negro*. It was the label associated with pride, and southern whites were reluctant to use it as a replacement for *black* or *nigra*.

Those who were part of the campaign in the 1920s and 1930s to be called *Negro* (capital *N* to parallel the capital in *Caucasian*), at the same time seeing themselves as *brown* Americans (lower case *b* in parallel with *black*, *white*, *red*, and *yellow*), viewed *Negro* as the term of respect which they had to force whites to accept. The declaration by some militants of the 1960s that *Negro* was a slavery term (as a matter of fact, lower-case *negro* and *black* were interchangeable during slavery) rallied many poorer young blacks to the idea of a new name and identity. The proclamation of *black* as the new label provided a sense of a fresh start which may well have served on a number of levels to develop the sense of self which was initiated by young militants. Middle-class youth soon joined in the movement toward proclaiming a new group name.

There still remains some confusion concerning nomenclature. In a number of communities in the South, on some college campuses, and in some churches, *Negro* seems to come more comfortably to the lips. In cities, among young activists, and in most publications, *black* (often with, sometimes without a capital) is preferred.

The term *African-American* appears to be generally acceptable; there are some, however, who are convinced that New World identity should not have to look to Africa for its validity. In any case, *African-American* is perhaps too lengthy a label to become truly popular and the slightly abbreviated *Afro-American* has not done notably better.

Some of the resistance to *black*—and some remains, although it seems to be decreasing as the new terminology becomes more commonplace—arose from the attack on *Negro* as a slave-related term associated with accommodation to segregation and discrimination (it has even been written without the capital letter by some militants who perceive the capital as a mark of prestige on an anti-black level). There has been perhaps enough feeling of guilt on the part of more educated self-styled *Negroes* who traditionally concentrated on getting ahead to make this association strike home, as well as enough inaccuracy and error to arouse resentment (mostly silent) as well.

Nevertheless, there is reason to believe that the American descendants of Africans may by now have, as a people, worked things through to the point that *Negro*, *Black*, and *black* are all widely used. Scholars are comfortable with *black* as a generic term to be used opposite *white*. Nevertheless, language does not necessarily follow consistency and logic, and when a substantial number of people are clear in their own minds as to what they want to be called, convention respects their preferences.

A 1972-73 Phelps-Stokes study of forty-six publications addressed primarily to American audiences of African descent was informative as an indication of current modes of address in popular publications. Editors were asked four questions:

1. As a matter of policy, which label(s) does your publication use?
2. If a writer uses a term different from those designated, is it changed before publication?
3. Has your policy changed in recent years?
4. What would be your *personal* preference if there were no pressure to use any particular term?

Of the forty-six publications replying to the first question, twenty-two confined themselves to a single term (see Table I). Of these, fourteen or 63.6 percent, used *Black*; and eight or 36.4 percent, *black*. All of those using two or more terms employed *Black* or *black* alone (five used *only* these two) or in combination with *Negro, Afro-American,* or *African-American.* No publication preferred *African-American* or *colored,* a term widely used forty or fifty years ago; those using either were tolerant of a variety of other labels as well.

There is no responding publication which does not use a form of *black.* Of the forty-six publications, thirty-six or 78.2 percent, use *Black;* twenty-one or 45.7 percent, *black;* fifteen or 32.6 percent, *Negro;* nine or 19.6 percent, *Afro-American;* four or 8.7 percent, *African-American;* and three or 6.5 percent, *colored.*

Twenty publications answering the second question indicated that if a writer used a term different from that (or those) officially preferred, it would be changed; three responded that they might change it, depending on circumstances. Eighteen publications, on the other hand, indicated that they would not edit a writer's preference of labels.

Twenty-nine of the forty-six publications responding indicated that they had changed their policy on which term to use in recent years.

**TABLE I**—NOMENCLATURE PREFERRED BY 46 PUBLICATIONS ADDRESSED TO PERSONS OF AFRICAN DESCENT, 1973

| | Approved Terms | | | | | | | |
| --- | --- | --- | --- | --- | --- | --- | --- | --- |
| | One Only | | Two | | Three or More | | Total | |
| | Number | Percent | Number | Percent | Number | Percent | Number | Percent |
| Total Publications | 22 | 100.0 | 18 | 100.0 | 6 | 100.0 | 46 | 100.0 |
| Terms Used: | | | | | | | | |
| Black | 14 | 63.6 | 16 | 88.9 | 6 | 100.0 | 36 | 78.3 |
| black | 8 | 36.4 | 7 | 38.9 | 5 | 83.3 | 21 | 45.7 |
| Negro | — | | 8 | 44.4 | 6 | 100.0 | 15 | 32.6 |
| Afro-American | — | | 5 | 27.8 | 4 | 66.6 | 9 | 19.6 |
| African-American | — | | — | | 4 | 66.6 | 4 | 8.7 |
| colored | — | | — | | 3 | 50.0 | 3 | 6.5 |

Note: Some predominantly white publications, including *The New York Times,* employ *Negro* or *black,* according to the writer's preference.

The personal preference of the editors contacted followed much the same pattern, except that a majority (thirty-seven) preferred one term (see Table II). Although fewer than half of these (sixteen) preferred *Black,* if *black* were added a clear majority (twenty-four) favored the color designation. *Negro* (seven) and *Afro-American* (six) were the only other sole preferences.

Where respondents indicated two or more personal labels, *Black* (eight) and *Negro* (five) led the list; *black, Afro-American,* and *African-American* were designated by two persons each. Taking the respondents as a whole, twenty-four preferred

*Black*; twelve, *Negro*; ten, *black*; eight, *Afro-American*; and two, *African-American*. No one listed *colored* as a preference.

**TABLE II**—PERSONAL PREFERENCE OF NOMENCLATURE OF 46 RESPONDENTS*

|  | One choice | Two or more choices† | Totals |
|---|---|---|---|
| Black | 16 | 8 | 24 |
| black | 8 | 2 | 10 |
| Negro | 7 | 5 | 12 |
| Afro-American | 6 | 2 | 8 |
| African-American | 0 | 2 | 2 |
| colored | 0 | 0 | 0 |

*Editors or others replying to the questionnaire for publications.
†Each approved term is counted once for each publication using it.

It is for these reasons—and despite the acknowledged interrelationship between the first and second editions of this reference book—that the title has been changed to conform with the current trend toward a color designation. The present work, *The Black American Reference Book* is thus the second edition of *The American Negro Reference Book* (1966). The label *black* is widely used in the book, along with *Negro* and an occasional *Afro-American*. Some authors have shown a preference for one rather than the other. Our own preference for *black* over *Black* stems from standard reference form rather than ideology, and we have avoided the special complication (preferred by a few) of *Black* as a noun, *black* for adjectival use.

In spite of some remaining differences of opinion, we look forward to eventual consistency regarding labels.

# A NOTE ON SEX EQUALITY

The rapid change in awareness of subtle sex discrimination during the period in which *The Black American Reference Book* was prepared has made us frustratingly conscious of the pervasiveness of bias; e.g., government statistics on the two-parent family arbitrarily assume a male head. Some of the quoted material in the book uses sexually-slanted terminology. Editing to eliminate bias in the text may have fallen short of perfection; but the reader is assured that, however faulty the implementation, editorial intent has been to correct such aberrations.

# CONTRIBUTORS

**Gordon W. Allport** (deceased). Professor of Psychology, Harvard University. Past President, American Psychological Association; recipient of Gold Medal from the American Psychological Foundation (1963). Author: *The Nature of Prejudice, Personality and Social Encounter,* and other works.

**David Baker.** Award-winning composer, instrumentalist. Chairman, Department of Jazz, University of Indiana Conservatory. Author: *Black Music Now—A Source Book for the 20th Century* (in progress).

**Calvin L. Beale.** Head, Farm Population Analysis Section, Economic Research Service, U. S. Department of Agriculture. Winner of the Superior Service Award of the Department of Agriculture for writings on the farm population. Coauthor (with Donald J. Bogue): *Economic Areas of the United States.* Contributor to numerous government and social science bulletins and magazines.

**Arna Bontemps** (deceased). Novelist, playwright. Author: *American Negro Poetry, The Story of the Negro, Black Thunder, God Sends Sunday,* and other works. Coauthor: (with Langston Hughes) *The Poetry of the Negro*; (with Countee Cullen) *St. Louis Woman* (a musical play); (with W. C. Handy) *Father of the Blues*; (with Jack Conroy) *They Seek a City*; other works.

**Robert Hughes Brisbane.** Chairman, Department of Political Science, Morehouse College. Consulting Editor, *Encyclopaedia Britannica.* Author: *The Black Vanguard; The Black Revolution.*

**Robert L. Carter.** United States District Judge (Southern District of New York). Formerly General Counsel, NAACP; former partner, Poletti, Freidin, Prashker, Feldman & Gartner; former columnist, *Black Enterprise.*

**Christine Philpot Clark.** Attorney, CBS, Incorporated. Formerly Consulting Dean and Lecturer in Law, Bryn Mawr College. Coauthor (with Sheila Rush): *How to Get Along with Black People*; other writings.

**Joseph H. Douglass** (deceased). Sociologist. Formerly Executive Director, Presidential Committee on Mental Retardation (1971-72); Staff Director, 1970

White House Conference on Children and Youth. Author: *The Negro Family's Search for Economic Security*, and other studies.

**G. James Fleming.** Professor (retired) of Political Science, Morgan State College. Author: *An All-Negro Ticket in Baltimore 1960, Why Baltimore Failed to Elect a Negro Mayor in 1971*, and other studies.

**John Hope Franklin.** John Matthews Manly Distinguished Service Professor of History, University of Chicago. Past President, Southern Historical Association, Organization of American Historians; former Chairman of the Executive Committee, American Historical Association. President, United Chapters of Phi Beta Kappa. Author: *From Slavery to Freedom: A History of Negro Americans*; *The Militant South*; *An Illustrated History of Black Americans*, and other works.

**Edmund B. Gaither.** Director/Curator of Museum, National Center of Afro-American Artists; Chairman, Visual Arts Program, Elma Lewis School of Fine Arts, Boston. Consultant, Museum of Fine Arts, Boston.

**Regina Goff.** Professor of Education, University of Maryland. Former United States Assistant Commissioner of Education. Author of articles in professional journals; contributor to several books in professional education.

**Edwin Bancroft Henderson.** Retired Director of Health, Physical Education, Athletics and Safety, Washington, D. C., school system. Elected to the National Black Sports Hall of Fame in 1973 for outstanding achievement in the field of athletics. Author: *The Negro in Sports,* and other works.

**Langston Hughes** (deceased). Poet, playwright, author, lecturer. Author: *Selected Poems, The Big Sea, Pictorial History of the Negro, Troubled Island* (opera, with William Grant Still), *Mulatto*, and numerous other works.

**Luther P. Jackson, Jr.** Associate Professor, Columbia University Graduate School of Journalism. Former reporter, Newark *Record*, New Jersey *Herald News*, Baltimore *Afro-American*, Newark *Evening News*, and Washington *Post*.

**Helen Armstead Johnson.** Professor of English, York College of the City University of New York; Director, The Helen Armstead-Johnson Afro-American Theater Museum; theater columnist, *Encore*.

**Vernon E. Jordan, Jr.** Executive Director, National Urban League. Former Executive Director, United Negro College Fund.

**Ernest Kaiser.** Bibliographer, essayist. Consultant, Schomburg Center for Research in Black Culture, New York Public Library. Associate Editor, *Freedomways*. Coeditor (with Harry A. Ploski), *The Negro Almanac* (revised 1971 edition). Contributor: *William Styron's Nat Turner: Ten Black Writers Respond*. Coauthor (with Warren Halliburton): *Harlem: A History of Broken Dreams*.

**Richard A. Long.** Director, Center for African and African-American Studies, Atlanta University. Former Visiting Lecturer in Afro-American Studies, Harvard University. Coeditor: *Negritude: Essays and Studies*; *Afro-American Writing: Prose and Poetry*.

**Constance Baker Motley.** United States District Judge (Southern District, New York). Former President, Borough of Manhattan, City of New York. Formerly Associate Counsel, Legal Defense and Educational Fund, National Association for the Advancement of Colored People; formerly member of the Senate of the State of New York.

**Larry Neal.** Visiting Lecturer in Literature and Creative Writing, Yale University. Author: *Black Boogaloo*; coeditor (with LeRoi Jones-Baraka): *Black Fire.*

**Dorothy K. Newman.** Director, Black Americans in Their Country. Former Director of Research, National Urban League. Past President, District of Columbia Sociological Society. Author: *The Negroes in the United States: Their Economic and Social Situation,* Bureau of Labor Statistics, Bulletin No. 1511, June 1966.

**George E. Norford.** Vice President, General Executive and Director, Westinghouse Broadcasting Company. National Coordinator, Broadcast Skills Bank. Chairman of the Communications Commission, American Foundation for Negro Affairs.

**Thomas Fraser Pettigrew.** Professor of Social Psychology and Sociology, Harvard University. Author: *Racially Separate or Together?*, *A Profile of the Negro American*, *Epitaph for Jim Crow*, and other studies. Editor: *Race Discrimination in the United States.*

**Charles A. Pinderhughes, M.D.** Professor of Psychiatry, Boston University School of Medicine; Director of Clinical Training for Psychiatry Service, Bedford Veterans Administration Hospital; Lecturer on Psychiatry, Harvard Medical School. Author: "Racism and Psychotherapy," in *Racism and Mental Health*, and other studies.

**Inez Smith Reid.** Associate Professor of Political Science, Barnard College. Former Executive Director, Black Women's Community Development Foundation. Author: *"Together" Black Women*, and other works.

**Harry V. Richardson.** President Emeritus of the Interdenominational Theological Center, Atlanta, Georgia; former President, Georgia Council of Churches. Author: *Dark Glory.*

**Elliott P. Skinner.** Franz Boas Professor of Anthropology and International Relations, and Chairman, Department of Anthropology, Columbia University.

Former United States Ambassador to Upper Volta. Chairman, African-American Scholars Council. Author: *The Mossi of the Upper Volta, Peoples and Cultures of Africa, African Urban Life: The Transformation of Ouagadougou.*

**Hugh H. Smythe.** Professor of Sociology, Brooklyn College and the Graduate Center, City University of New York. Former United States Ambassador to the Syrian Arab Republic and to Malta. Associate Editor, *Journal of Asian and African Studies.* Coauthor: *The New Nigerian Elite* (with Mabel M. Smythe), and other studies.

**Mabel M. Smythe.** Vice President, Phelps-Stokes Fund. Economist; author; lecturer. Consultant, Encyclopaedia Britannica Educational Corporation. Editor, *The Black American Reference Book, Curriculum for Understanding* (with E. S. Bley). Author or contributor, other works.

**Richard J. Stillman, II.** Chairman, Public Administration Program, California State College, Bakersfield. Public Administration Fellow and Special Assistant to the Deputy Attorney General, U. S. Department of Justice. Author: *The Integration of the Negro in the U. S. Armed Forces, A Preface to Public Administration,* and other works.

**Carl B. Stokes.** Former Mayor of Cleveland, Ohio. News analyst, National Broadcasting Corporation; former First Vice President, National League of Cities; Steering Committee, National Urban Coalition; Advisory Committee, Urban American, Inc.

**Alma F. Taeuber.** Research Associate, Institute for Research on Poverty, University of Wisconsin. Coauthor (with Karl E. Taeuber): *Negroes in Cities: Residential Segregation and Neighborhood Change.*

**Karl E. Taeuber.** Professor of Sociology and Fellow, Institute for Research on Poverty, University of Wisconsin. Author: numerous studies of residential segregation and black population trends.

**Ernestein Walker.** Professor and Chairperson of History, Morgan State College. Author: articles in *Journal of Social Science Teachers* and *Journal of Higher Education.*

**Wendell Whalum.** Fuller E. Callaway Professor of Music, Morehouse College. Coproducer of Scott Joplin's opera, *Treemonisha,* 1972.

**Robin M. Williams, Jr.** Henry Scarborough Professor of Social Science, Cornell University. Past President: American Sociological Association, Sociological Research Association. American Academy of Arts and Sciences. Author: *American Society: A Sociological Interpretation, Strangers Next Door,* and other works.

**Nathan Wright, Jr.** Professor of Urban Affairs, State University of New York, Albany. Chairman, National and International Conferences on Black Power, 1967 and 1968. Black Media Award, 1975, for excellence in scholarship applied to black public policy. Author: *Black Power and Urban Unrest* (Media Workshop Book Award, 1967), *Let's Face Racism*, and other works.

# LIST OF TABLES

## Chapter 7 · The Black American in Agriculture

## Chapter 8 · The Black Family

## Chapter 9 · The Black Woman

## Chapter 10 · Young Black Americans

## Chapter 11 · Educating Black Americans

## Chapter 12 · The Black Professional

## Chapter 14 · Afro-American Religion

## Chapter 17 · The Black Role in American Politics: Part I, The Present

## Chapter 18 · The Black Role in American Politics: Part II, The Past

## Chapter 29 · Black Participation in the Armed Forces

## Chapter 30 · The Black American in Sports

# THE BLACK
# AMERICAN
# REFERENCE
# BOOK

# 1

## *A Brief History*

### *John Hope Franklin*

## NEW WORLD ADVENTURE

### African Pioneers in the New World

It is significant that the first Negroes in the New World were not from Africa but from Europe. Their involvement in the European exploration of the New World in the fifteenth and sixteenth centuries is an important commentary on the connection between Europe and Africa by that time. As early as the fourteenth century, if not before, Europeans began to bring Africans into Europe. As the Spanish and Portuguese made contacts with the coast of Africa, going as far as the Gulf of Guinea, they began to appreciate the possibility of using Africans as an important source of labor for European ports, businesses, and homes. Thus they took Africans to Europe and made servants of them, justifying this invasion of human rights by declaring that Africans would thereby have the opportunity to cast off their heathenism and become Christians.

It was not long before Europeans were selling Negro servants in their home markets along with other African wares, and the slave trade soon came to be accepted as an important part of European commerce. Spanish and Portuguese traders appreciated the economic advantages afforded by such trading and by the time Portugal's remarkable Prince Henry died in 1460 this infamous commerce had become more than a passing fancy. Europeans were becoming accustomed to having Negroes do their work; and already they were looking into the possibility of using them in other ways. It was only natural, therefore, that as Europeans turned their eyes toward the New World they would "enlist" the services of the Africans both to further the cause of Christianity and to assist Spain, Portugal, France, or whatever country it might be, to exercise its sovereignty in the New World.

There was never a time in the Europeans' exploration and exploitation of the New World when they were without the services of black Europeans. The claim that Pedro Alonso Niño of the crew of Columbus was a Negro has never been disproved; and if he was indeed a black explorer he performed more than yeoman service for the Admiral of the Ocean Sea. In 1501 Spain lifted her ban on the taking of Africans to the New

World, and thereafter Africans almost invariably accompanied the Spanish explorers and settlers. There were at least thirty Negroes with Balboa when he discovered the Pacific Ocean in 1513. When Hernando Cortes conquered Mexico in 1519, he had several in his ranks, one of whom planted and harvested the first wheat crop in the New World. Alvarado, the intrepid explorer of Equatorial South America, was accompanied by 200 Negroes when he arrived at Quito; and in his Peruvian expedition Pizarro took several along. Indeed, they were the ones who bore their leader into the cathedral after he was murdered.

When the Spanish and Portuguese explorers moved into what is now the United States, Negroes were at their sides. They accompanied Narvaez on his expedition in 1527 and were with Cabeza de Vaca in the exploration of the Southwest. Perhaps the outstanding black explorer was Estevanico, Little Stephen, who penetrated deep into the interior of the Southwest. When he encountered hostile Indians, he insisted that he was the emissary of the white men; but they killed him, believing him to be an imposter. Even so, he had paved the way for the conquest of the Southwest by the Spaniards.

The French also were accompanied by Negro servants when they undertook their explorations of the New World. In the Canadian expeditions, Negroes stood side by side with the Jesuit missionaries. As the French opened up the Mississippi Valley in the seventeenth century, blacks assisted in the settlement of the region. At the places later to be known as St. Louis and New Orleans, French Negroes helped to plant the flag of France and to establish the culture that was to make an indelible mark on the interior of the United States.

Exploitation of the rich natural resources of the New World was the primary aim of the Europeans. For this they needed an abundance of labor. Soon it became obvious that Indians were not the solution. The great susceptibility of the aborigines to the diseases of the Europeans, their firm commitment to a much simpler economic system, and their determination to escape the wrath and inhumanity of the Europeans ruled them out as a permanent and satisfactory source of labor. Europeans not only wanted more tractable servants, but they wanted them in greater quantities than the Indians could provide. Indians were utilized to the extent possible, but the Europeans early turned to other potential sources.

Europeans did not at first regard Africans as the answer to their labor problem, however. The poorer Europeans were their initial choice. In the first half of the seventeenth century, these landless, penniless whites were brought over in considerable numbers. Some were voluntary indentured servants, others were prisoners working out their fines, still others were simply kidnapped and sold into servitude. Europeans, especially the English, never knew when they would be swept up and taken to the New World against their will. In *Capitalism and Slavery*, Eric Williams has suggested that the horrors the poor whites of Europe experienced during this era were as great as those experienced by any group in the later years of the African slave trade.

It gradually became apparent, however, that white servants would not do. When whites became restive and ran away, it was extremely difficult to identify them as servants bound to a particular master. Some of them, conscious of their rights as Englishmen, began to sue their masters for illegal detention. Even if they worked well, their terms of service were not indefinite; and the task of recruiting new white workers was at best irksome. Englishmen soon came to realize that Africans presented few of the difficulties they were encountering with whites. They could be purchased outright, and their years of servitude would be unlimited. They were cheaper in the long run as well, since they could be purchased once and for all. Since they came from a pagan land, moreover, with no exposure to the principles of Christian brotherhood, they could be subjected to the most rigid discipline with impunity. Here again, the masters could rationalize their actions by reminding themselves they were offering their slaves the advantages of Christianity to which they would not otherwise be exposed.

## The Beginnings of the Slave Trade

In 1517 the great Spanish bishop Bartolomé de Las Casas took a step that greatly encouraged the establishment of slavery in the New World. He had noticed with apparent horror the wholesale destruction of the Indians by the Spaniards in the effort to force them to work. Convinced that the Indians could never become good slaves but hoping, all the same, that they could be converted into good Christians, he persuaded Charles V to encourage additional immigration to the New World by permitting Spaniards to import twelve slaves each. This step may be regarded as the formal opening of the slave trade to the New World; and the bishop would later regret it. In subsequent years an increasing number of Africans were imported into the Spanish colonies, at times by Dutch traders, at other times by Portuguese, French, or English. Soon the trade had become a huge, profitable enterprise. By 1540 the annual importation of Negro slaves into the West Indies had reached 10,000.

The trade continued, and by the seventeenth and eighteenth centuries it was largely in the hands of Dutch, French, and English companies. In 1621 the Dutch West India Company was organized, with a monopoly both of the African trade and trade with the Dutch colonies in the New World. It then challenged the right of the Portuguese to trade on the coast of Africa, and by the middle of the century it had gained a substantial foothold on the coast of West Africa. Soon the Dutch slavers were visiting the ports of almost all the American colonies, and were even engaged in trade with the French and Spanish colonies.

The trade was so profitable that the English were not content to see the Dutch reap all the benefits. The Dutch wars with France and England, moreover, weakened the position of the leading slave-trading power generally, thus giving the English an opportunity to make a bid for at least a portion of the lucrative trade. The French would also make an effort to enter the picture, but they were never a match for the English.

English interest in Africa and the slave trade was by no means new when she made a bid for leadership in the second half of the seventeenth century. Before the end of the reign of Henry VII in 1509, traders from Britain were establishing connections along the Guinea coast and at other important points in Africa. England contented herself with trading in gold, ivory, and spices until 1562, when Captain John Hawkins broke the Portuguese monopoly in Africa and the Spanish monopoly in the New World by taking slaves from Portuguese Africa to Spanish America. It thus became easy for James I in 1618 to grant a charter to the Company of Adventurers of London, giving them control over the trade on the west coast of Africa. In 1631 Charles I granted a group of traders a thirty-one-year monopoly of the trade in Guinea, Benin, and Angola. Governmental aid in the form of franchises, permits, and concessions became the pattern by which the English eventually claimed a large share of the African trade in human flesh.

Competition for the slave trade was keen not only among nations but also among trading companies within countries. In England, for example, many individuals and organizations, including the powerful East India Company, were interested in the African slave trade. As the demand for slaves in the New World increased and as conditions in Europe remained unsettled, it seemed that any group might have a chance to reap some benefits from the slave trade. In 1672 the king chartered the Royal African Company, which held a monopoly for a decade, and which dominated the slave trade for another fifty years. It assumed the responsibility for driving the Dutch and the French out of West Africa, and its efforts were crowned with much success. It held sway until 1731, when, with its margin of profits in the slave trade dwindling, it began to devote its attention to ivory and gold dust.

## Slave Trading as Big Business

In the eighteenth century the African slave trade became an important economic institution; and since the English had come to dominate it, their slave trading practices became standard. Slavers left European ports laden with goods to be used in the trade: cotton textiles, brass, pewter, beads, gunpower, and whisky, brandy, and rum. They proceeded to the trading posts maintained by the company or the country, where the factors or managers maintained contacts with key Africans. The factors secured permission from the chief who was plied with gifts to trade on his domain. From this point on it was not too difficult to round up some Africans—slaves of the chiefs or captives in war—to be sold. The price varied, of course, depending on the age and condition of the slave, the period of trading, and the location of the post.

It was not at all unusual for a slaver to make calls at a number of posts before a full complement of slaves was secured for the voyage to the New World. Once that was done, the captain of the slaver had to make certain that he had sufficient provisions to make the crossing to America. Foodstuffs, water, and medicines were indispensable to a successful voyage. If any room was left, spices and ivory were regarded as certain to bring extra revenue which the captain might not even have to report to the company that had engaged him.

Perhaps the most poignant aspect of this heartless transaction was the resistance that the slaves put up to their forced sale and incarceration on the floating prison. Fierce wars broke out between tribes when the members of one sought to capture members of another for the purpose of selling them to traders. Even after the slaves were sold and chained, it was necessary to guard them heavily lest they make a futile attempt to escape and injure or kill themselves in the process. One trader remarked that the Negroes were "so wilful and loth to leave their own country that they have often leap'd out of the canoes, boat and ship, into the sea, and kept under water till they were drowned." They preferred a watery grave or to be devoured by sharks to enslavement in some faraway land.

Mankind has experienced few tortures so ghoulish and uncivilized as the transportation of slaves from Africa to the New World, known as the Middle Passage. The men were chained two by two, the right wrist and ankle of one to the left wrist and ankle of another. They were then sent to the hold or to the "house" that the sailors had built on deck. On some ships the women and children were allowed to wander about almost anywhere during the day, the women being regarded as fair prey for the sailors; but at night they were sent to rooms other than those occupied by the men. There were two schools of thought among captains of slavers regarding the loading of slaves. The "loose packers" believed that by giving the slaves a bit more room and better food, they reduced the mortality rate and could get a better price for healthier slaves that arrived in the New World. The "tight packers" argued that although the loss of life might be greater if they started out with larger numbers, they were likely to arrive with more and thereby get a larger profit from the cargo.

Regardless of the point of view of the captains, most ships transported many more Africans than could be adequately accommodated; and this is undoubtedly responsible for the high incidence of disease and death during the middle passage. Usually they were packed in closely with not even the room to sit upright during the entire voyage. Remarking on a situation such as this, one contemporary said, "The poor creatures, thus cramped, are likewise in irons for the most part which makes it difficult for them to turn or move or attempt to rise or to lie down without hurting themselves or each other. Every morning, perhaps, more instances than one are found of the living and the dead fastened together."

Because of the enormous profits made by some slavers the "tight loaders" gained the ascendancy. Despite death from a variety of maladies, it was not unusual for a ship carrying 250 slaves to net as much as £7,000 on one voyage. Profits of 100 percent were not uncommon for Liverpool merchants. As a result there emerged in England, and to a lesser extent on the Continent, a class of wealthy men whose new position was firmly based on the trade in men. They gained not only economic power but political influence, and were in a position to resist for many years the efforts of the humanitarians to control the slave trade and, ultimately, to put a stop to it.

There is no way of knowing how many Negroes were taken in Africa and sent on their way to slavery in the New World. In the years between 1783 and 1793, Liverpool traders alone were responsible for sending out some 300,000 slaves, while in the following decade they were certainly responsible for as many if not more. It has been estimated that 2,760,000 were sent in the seventeenth century, 7,000,000 in the eighteenth, and 4,000,000 in the nineteenth. Millions died en route, and millions of those who arrived were permanently disabled. Millions more were successfully sold into slavery. Whatever the total number, whether ten or fifteen million or more, the figures are a remarkable commentary on the profitableness of the trade as well as on the brutality and ruthlessness of those Europeans who were willing to enjoy the luxury and wealth afforded by such an operation.

## Early Slave Practices

Negroes were first used as slaves on the tobacco plantations of the Caribbean islands. Then, as the European tobacco market became glutted, the Caribbean planters turned to sugar and other staples for their money crops. With the emergence of sugar as a major crop, the importation of Africans into the Caribbean began in earnest. In 1640 there were only a few hundred blacks in Barbados. By 1645, after the new sugar plantations had proved themselves, there were 6,000 slaves there. By the middle of the century the Negro population had increased to 20,000. A similar growth in the slave population could be seen on the other Caribbean islands. Indeed, the importation of slaves accelerated to such a degree that by the end of the century, although the demand for slaves on the islands was actually declining, the importation not only continued but in some cases increased.

There were few humanizing influences on the institution of slavery in the West Indies in the seventeenth century. The slaves were "black gold" as their labor produced the profits that made the islands the favorite colonies of the European powers. Many of the landlords were in London or some other European city; and their only interest was in the profits that were increasing annually. The islands were not a place of residence, but merely a source of wealth; and the slaves were not human beings, but merely a factor in production. Overseers and plantation managers were expected to perform any task that increased profits, and this included getting work out of slaves by whatever method seemed necessary. Slaves who offered resistance were to be "broken in"—and this meant flogging or any other form of torture that would get results.

Since the black population tended to exceed that of the white, the laws governing the conduct of Negroes were designed to provide a maximum of security for the whites as well as to make the blacks effective workers. Slaves had few, if any, rights in the English colonies, and the French colonies, though recognizing slaves as persons with souls, were scarcely better. But however stringent the laws, they did not succeed in creating a tractable, docile slave population. There were uprisings in Jamaica, Barbados, Saint Domingue, and elsewhere. Fugitive slaves organized into groups called Maroons and defined the whites' attempt to subjugate them. On more than one occasion it became necessary for the whites in the Caribbean to resort to the force of arms to keep the slaves in line.

By the end of the seventeenth century the Caribbean was no longer the principal source of wealth for Europe in the New World. The Portuguese now had Brazil as their main New World colony, while the Spaniards had annexed numerous important colonies in North and South America. The British were turning their attention more and more to their mainland colonies that extended from the Carolinas to Massachusetts. Englishmen began importing slaves directly to these mainland holdings and shipping many of those blacks already on the islands to join them. Gradually the European powers realized they could vastly increase their profits by utilizing the experience they had gained in the island colonies to establish an infinitely more elaborate system of plantation slavery in Virginia, the Carolinas, and similar mainland colonies. If there was disappointment over the decline in Jamaica, there was hope for unlimited expansion in Maryland. More and better slaves would make the difference.

## COLONIAL SLAVERY

### Virginia and Maryland

The twenty Africans who were put ashore at Jamestown in 1619 by the captain of a Dutch frigate were not slaves in a legal sense. And at the time the Virginians seemed not to appreciate the far-reaching significance of the introduction of Africans into the fledgling colony. The new arrivals were simply twenty more indentured servants who happened to be black. They were listed as servants in the census counts of 1623 and 1624; and as late as 1651 some Negroes whose periods of service had expired were being assigned land in much the same way that it was being assigned to whites who had completed their indenture. During its first half-century of existence, Virginia had many Negro indentured servants; and the records reveal an increasing number of free Negroes.

Only after Virginia had failed to satisfy her labor needs with Indians and indentured servants did she give serious thought to the "perpetual servitude" of Negroes. She began to see what her neighbors in the Caribbean had already seen, that black men could not easily escape without being identified, that they could be disciplined, even punished, with impunity since they were not Christians, and that the supply seemed inexhaustible. Black labor was precisely what Virginia needed in order to speed up the clearing of the forests and the cultivation of larger and better tobacco crops. All that was needed was the legislative approval of a practice in which many Virginians were already involved.

The actual statutory recognition of slavery in Virginia came in 1661. The status of Negroes already there was not affected if they had completed their indenture and were free. Indeed, the recognition was almost casual and was first indicated in a law that was directed at white servants: "That in case any English servant shall run away in company with any negroes who are incapable of making satisfaction by addition of time . . . that the English so running away . . . shall serve for the time of the said negroes absence as they are to do for their owne. . . ." In the following year Virginia took another step toward slavery by indicating in her laws that children born in the colony would be held in bondage or would be free according to the condition of the mother. Some mitigation to the duress of slavery was intended by the law of 1667 which provided that slaves could be baptized as Christians. In order to protect the institution of slavery, however, the law continued, "the conferring of baptisme doth not alter the condition of the person as to his bondage or freedome." Thus, "diverse masters, freed from this doubt, may more carefully endeavour the propagation of christianity."

At first the Negro population of the colony grew quite slowly. In 1625 there were only 23 Negroes there; and as late as the middle of the century scarcely 300 could be counted. With the chartering of the Royal African Company in 1672, however, the shipment of slaves into the colony was accelerated. By the end of the century blacks were being brought in at the rate of more than 1,000 per year. Then in the eighteenth century the Negro population shot up at what some Virginians began to view as an alarming rate. In 1708 there were 12,000 Negroes and 18,000 whites. By 1756 there were 120,156 Negroes and 173,316 whites, with blacks outnumbering whites in many Virginia communities.

Although Virginians greatly appreciated the importance of Negro slave labor in the development of the colony, they soon became apprehensive about having such large numbers of Negroes living among them. Already whites and blacks were mixing, and a mulatto population was emerging. There were, moreover, the persistent rumors of conspiracies aimed at rebellion; and many whites feared for their lives. Those who were apprehensive took the lead in attempting to control the importation of slaves, but the commercial interests fought off these attempts with all the resources at their command. For the time being they were successful.

But the fears of insurrection were not groundless. Within two years after the first statutory recognition of slavery, the Negroes of Virginia were showing clear signs of dissatisfaction and began to plot rebellion against their masters. In 1687 a group of slaves in the Northern Neck planned an uprising during a funeral, but it was discovered before it could be carried out. Rumors continued, and plots of varying sizes were uncovered. Where there were no plots, there was general disobedience and lawlessness. By 1694 the Virginia slaves had become so ungovernable that Governor Andros complained that there was insufficient enforcement of the code which, by that time, had become elaborate enough to cover most of the black man's activities and relationships.

The Virginia slave code, borrowing heavily from practices in the Caribbean and serving as a model for other mainland codes, was comprehensive, to say the least. No slave was allowed to leave the plantation without the written permission of his master. Slaves wandering about without such permits were to be taken in and returned to their masters. Slaves found guilty of murder or rape were to be hanged. For major offenses such as robbing a house or a store, slaves were to receive sixty lashes and be placed in the pillory where their ears were to be severed from their heads. For petty offenses such as insolence and associating with whites or free Negroes, they were to be whipped, maimed, or branded. The docility of which their masters boasted was thus achieved through the enactment of a comprehensive code containing provisions for punishment designed to "break" the most irascible blacks in the colony. With the sheriffs, the courts, and even the slaveless whites on their side, the masters should indeed have had little difficulty maintaining peace among their slaves.

Although slavery in Maryland was not recognized by law until 1663, the first Negroes introduced into the colony were sold into slavery immediately. As early as 1638 there was reference to slavery in some discussions in the legislature; and by 1641 the governor himself owned a number of slaves. The colonists had no difficulty, therefore, when they turned their attention to the problem of the status of Negroes and concluded that legislation should be enacted to fix their status as slaves. The law of 1663 was rather drastic. It undertook to reduce to slavery all Negroes in the colony even though some were already free, and it sought to impose the status of slaves on all Negroes to be born in the colony regardless of the status of their mothers. It was not until 1681 that the law was brought in line with established practices by declaring that Negro children of white mothers and children born of free Negro mothers would be free.

The slave population of Maryland was slow to increase, not because of any disinclination on the part of the colonists to own slaves but because they were not in ample supply during the early years of the colony. This is the principal reason why, during the Restoration period, laws were enacted to encourage and facilitate the importation of slaves. In 1671 the legislature declared that the conversion of slaves to Christianity would not affect their status. Masters now felt that they could import African heathens, convert them to Christianity, and thus justify the act of holding them in slavery. By the end of the century the importation of slaves was increasing steadily. In 1708 the governor reported that six or seven hundred had been imported during the preceding ten months. By 1750 there were 40,000 blacks in the colony, as compared with 100,000 whites.

As in Virginia, the Negroes of Maryland early showed resentment against their status as slaves. In several instances white masters died at the hands of their slaves; and there was more than one case of a Negro cook poisoning her owner. In 1742 seven Negroes were executed for the murder of their master. Others were convicted for committing such acts of sabotage as arson, stealing of property, and the brutal treatment of livestock.

The increase in the black population and the fear on the part of the whites for their own safety led to the enactment of stringent laws covering the conduct and activities of Negroes. In 1659 legislation was enacted relating to the return and treatment of fugitive slaves. Soon there were laws forbidding slaves to deal in stolen goods and liquor as well as legislation providing for the punishment of free Negroes and slaves found guilty of murder, arson, larceny, association with whites, insolence, and going about without permission. Punishment ranged from death to branding and whipping. Enforcement was rigorous, but clemency was not unusual. There are numerous examples of intervention on the behalf of accused slaves by masters who, while approving the strict enforcement of the law, would want "on just this occasion" a bit of leniency.

## The Carolinas and Georgia

It was a foregone conclusion that slaves would be introduced into the Carolinas as soon as was feasible. After all, four of the proprietors of the colony were members of the Royal African Company and fully appreciated the profits that could come from the slave trade. By 1680, moreover, the example of Virginia and Maryland led influential Carolinians to believe that the colony could become prosperous through a system of plantation slavery. Perhaps John Locke had these things in mind when, in his *Fundamental Constitutions*, he wrote "every freeman of Carolina shall have absolute power and authority over his negro slaves, of what opinion or religion soever." This sanctioned slavery and protected it against any possible destruction that might have come through the conversion of slaves to Christianity.

Negroes were in the Carolina colony virtually from the beginning. This was undoubtedly the result of the deliberate encouragement of the importation of slaves by the proprietors themselves. In 1663 they offered to the original settlers twenty acres for every Negro man slave and ten acres for every Negro woman slave brought into the colony in the first year. Somewhat smaller incentives were offered for the importation of slaves in subsequent years. Twenty years after the original settlements, the Negro population in the Carolinas was equal to the white population. By 1715 the Negroes led the whites with 10,500 to 6,250. In 1724 there were three times as many Negroes as whites, and the growth of the Negro population was to continue for decades thereafter.

As in the other colonies the growth of the Negro population led to the enactment of legislation concerned with its control. As early as 1686 the Carolina colony forbade Negroes to engage in any kind of trade, and enjoined them from leaving their masters' plantations without written authorization. In 1722 white justices were authorized to search Negroes for guns, swords, and "other offensive weapons" and to confiscate them unless the Negro could produce a permit less than one month old authorizing him to carry such a weapon. Patrols were given authority to search Negroes and to whip those deemed to be dangerous to peace and good order. Punishments for offenses by slaves were summary and severe.

The Carolinians had not established their controls any too soon, for as early as 1711 there were rumors that the Negroes were getting out of hand. In 1720 several slaves were burned alive and others were banished because of their implication in a revolt near Charleston. In subsequent years there were other revolts or rumors of revolts. In 1739 the well-known Cato conspiracy twenty miles west of Charleston threw the countryside into a state of terror. After slaves killed two guards in a warehouse and secured arms, they went on a full-scale drive to destroy slavery in the region. The uprising was quickly put down, but not before thirty whites and forty-four blacks had lost their lives. Later in the century other uprisings occurred, and the general state of affairs led to a full-scale revision of the slave code. Before the Revolution, South Carolina, now divided from North Carolina, had enacted one of the most stringent sets of laws governing slaves to be found anywhere in the New World.

Georgia was the only important New World colony established by England in the eighteenth century. In several significant ways it was different from the others: it was to grant no free land titles, prohibit the use of alcoholic beverages, and allow no slavery. From the time of its establishment in 1733, however, each of these proscriptions was subjected to enormous pressure on the part of the settlers themselves. One by one they fell. It was in 1750 that the third petition of the colonists brought about the repeal of the hated prohibition against slavery. From that point on the Negro population grew, and slavery flourished. By 1760 there were 6,000 whites and 3,000 Negroes in the colony. In the last estimate before the War for Independence, made in 1773, the white population had increased to 18,000, while the Negro population numbered some 15,000.

Much of Georgia's slave code, adopted in 1755, was taken from the South Carolina code, and it reflected South Carolina's experience rather than Georgia's. For example, the interdiction against more than seven Negroes being out together without a white chaperon indicated South Carolina's general fear of Negro uprisings. Between Saturday evening and Monday morning, not even those slaves who were authorized to possess firearms were permitted to carry them on their persons. Under no conditions were Negroes to be taught to read and write.

If the slaves of colonial Georgia did not erupt into rebellion, they resisted their enslavement by other means: sabotage and running away to Florida. Strangely enough, Georgia displayed a relative indifference to insurrection by subjecting her slaves to service in the militia. Perhaps the service which Spanish Florida rendered as an escape value for the more discontented Negroes made possible the paradoxical practice of using Negroes as Georgia militiamen in the colonial period.

## The Middle Colonies

Although the Dutch were primarily interested in the slave trade and made great profits from transporting their human wares to various colonies, they did not neglect their own New World settlements. Large Dutch plantations flourished in New Netherland, particularly in the valley of the Hudson River, and by 1638 many of them were cultivated largely by slave labor. The institution of slavery as practiced by the Dutch in the New World was relatively mild, however, with slaves receiving fairly humane treatment and many considerations regarding their personal rights. The Dutch slave code was not elaborate, and manumission was not an uncommon reward for long or meritorious service. Although the demand for slaves always exceeded the supply, the number imported by the Dutch never reached such proportions as to cause serious apprehension or difficulty during the period of Dutch domination.

The character of the institution of slavery in the region changed, however, when the English took over New Netherland in 1664. In 1665 the colonial assembly recognized the existence of slavery where persons had willingly sold themselves into bondage; and in the statute of 1684 slavery was recognized as a legitimate institution in the province of New York. As a result the Negro population of New York grew. In 1698 there were only 2,170 Negroes in a total population of 18,067, while in 1723 the census listed 6,171 slaves. By 1771 the Negro population had increased to 19,883 in a total population of 168,007.

The slave code of New York became further defined early in the eighteenth century. In 1706 a law was enacted stating that baptism of a slave did not provide grounds for the slave's claim to freedom. A further significant provision was that a slave was at no time a competent witness in a case involving a freeman. In 1715 the legislature enacted a law providing that any slave caught traveling forty miles above Albany, presumably bound for Canada, was to be executed upon the oath of two credible witnesses. Meanwhile, New York City was enacting ordinances for the better control of slaves. In 1710 the city forbade Negroes to appear "in the streets after nightfall without a lantern with a lighted candle in it."

The concentration of an increasing number of slaves in the city of New York brought with it increased dangers to the white population. Negroes defied authority and disobeyed the laws. In 1712 the ungovernable temper of New York Negroes flared up into a fully organized insurrection in which twenty-three slaves armed with guns and knives met in an orchard and set fire to a slaveholder's house. In the melee that followed, nine whites were killed and six were injured. In the ensuing trial of the accused Negroes, twenty-one were found guilty and executed. Later, in 1741, there was rumor of an even larger insurrection. After a series of fires, word spread that blacks and poor whites were conspiring to destroy law and order in the city and seize control. After the city offered generous rewards for the apprehension of the conspirators, almost two hundred whites and blacks were arrested and prosecuted. At least one hundred Negroes were convicted, eighteen were hanged, thirteen burned alive, and seventy banished. Four whites, including two women, were hanged. There were no more serious outbursts during the colonial period, and by the time of the Revolution, New York had begun to recognize the moral and economic undesirability of holding men in bondage.

South of New York, the colonies of New Jersey, Pennsylvania, and Delaware each in its own way subscribed to the institution of slavery. After the English came to dominate New Jersey, they encouraged slavery in every way. Soon the black population there was growing steadily: 2,581 in 1726, 3,981 in 1738, and 4,606 in 1745 out of a total population of 61,000. In Pennsylvania the growth was not so rapid, due largely to the opposition to slavery by the Quakers. In 1688 the Germantown Quakers issued their celebrated protest, and in 1693 George Keith remonstrated with Pennsylvanians for holding men in perpetual bondage. But in 1685 no less a person than William Penn himself expressed the view that black slaves were better than white servants; and this had the effect of greatly encouraging slavery in some quarters. In 1721 the black population of Pennsylvania was estimated at between 2,500 and 5,000. Thirty years later there were about 11,000 Negroes in the colony. In 1790 this number had fallen to 10,274, of whom 3,737 were slaves and 6,537 were free. Meanwhile, as early as 1636 slavery existed on the right bank of the Delaware River. Since Delaware was a part of Pennsylvania until 1703, the laws of the latter colony applied here as well. After that date Delaware was on her own, and the slave population increased at a somewhat more rapid rate than that of Pennsylvania. As this occurred, Delaware drifted away from her mother colony and identified more and more with the interests of her southern neighbors.

Slavery was never really successful in the Middle Colonies. Their predominantly commercial economy, supplemented by subsistence agriculture, did not encourage any large-scale employment of slave labor; and many of the slaves who were cleared through the New York and Pennsylvania ports were later sent into the southern colonies. Even where there were extensive agricultural enterprises, there was no desire for slaves; for the Dutch, Swedes, and Germans cultivated their farms with meticulous care and seemed to prefer to do it themselves. There were those, moreover, who had definite moral scruples against using slaves. Thus many in the Middle Colonies welcomed the arguments against slavery that became increasingly pronounced during the Revolutionary period.

## Negroes in Colonial New England

Although New England's primary interest in slavery was in the trade itself, Negroes were early introduced into Massachusetts and Connecticut. In 1638 a Salem ship unloaded several Africans in Boston, and during the following year Negroes appeared in Hartford. Before a decade had passed black labor was used to construct houses and forts in Connecticut. By the middle of the century the refugees who founded Rhode Island were employing Negroes to help establish that colony. While the status of these early New England Negroes was rather uncertain, it gradually became clear throughout the New England colonies that slavery was a legitimate institution.

Whether slaves landing in New England were to be settled there or shipped to other colonies, they became important to the commercial life of the area. New England slave traders competed in the trade, although they were at a serious disadvantage with the powerful European trading companies. After England secured a monopoly of slave trade to the New World in 1713 she welcomed New England merchants, for there was more than enough for her own traders to handle. In the first half of the eighteenth century the New England traders thrived. Boston, Salem, Providence, and New London bustled with activity as ships laden with rum, fish, and dairy products set out to sea, and Negroes, molasses, and sugar were unloaded from incoming vessels. Until the War for Independence the slave trade was vital to the economic life of New England.

The Negro population in New England grew slowly. In 1700, when the total population of the entire region was approximately 90,000, there were only 1,000 Negroes there. In the eighteenth century the growth was more rapid. Massachusetts led with 2,000 Negroes in 1715 and 5,249 by 1776. Connecticut was second, with 1,500 Negroes in 1715 and 3,587 by 1756. The largest percentage of Negroes was to be found in Rhode Island where in 1774 there were 3,761 Negroes to 54,435 whites. The number in New Hampshire remained negligible during the entire colonial period.

New England slavery needed little legal recognition for its growth and development. When the codes emerged late in the seventeenth century, slavery had already become well-established. In 1670 Massachusetts enacted a law providing that the children of slaves could be sold into bondage, and ten years later it began to enact measures restricting the movement of Negroes. In 1660 Connecticut barred Negroes from military service, and thirty years later it restrained them from going beyond the limits of the town without a pass. The restrictions against the education of slaves, however, were not as great as in other regions, and frequently Negroes learned to read and write without opposition.

Since the number of slaves remained relatively small throughout the colonial period, there was not the same fear of insurrections in New England as in some other colonies. Nevertheless, many slaves indicated their dislike of the institution by running away. Others attacked their masters and even murdered them. Still others plotted to rebel. In 1658 a group of Negroes and Indians in Hartford decided to make a bid for freedom by destroying several of their masters' houses. In the eighteenth century a number of rebellions were plotted in Boston and other Massachusetts towns. The situation became so serious in Boston in 1723 that the selectmen found it necessary to take precautionary measures—slaves were forbidden to be on the streets at night and had to refrain from "idling or lurking together."

Negroes in New England enjoyed a relatively unique position in colonial America. They were not subjected to the harsh codes or the severe treatment that blacks received in the colonies to the south. But it is possible to exaggerate the humanitarian aspects of their treatment. Masters in New England held a firm grip on the institution of slavery and gave little consideration to the small minority that argued for the freedom of the slaves. Although the New Englander took his religion seriously, he did not permit it to interfere with his appreciation of the profits of slavery and the slave trade. At the same time, he was careful not to glut his home market with slaves and increase their number to the point where he would be fearful for the safety of himself and his family. One seems to glimpse a characteristic Yankee shrewdness in the New Englander's assessment of the importance of slavery to his economic and social life.

## SLAVERY AND THE RIGHTS OF MAN

### Slavery and the American Revolution

By the middle of the eighteenth century slavery had become a very important part of the evolving economy of colonial America. Certain individuals and groups had reservations, of course. As we have seen, the Quakers seriously questioned the right of one man to hold another in perpetual bondage. Other colonists objected to the indefinite expansion of the slave system lest the slaves engulf the whites in a bloodbath of resentment and revenge. Yet another group persisted in the Christian belief that there was a fundamental contradiction between the principles of Christian brotherhood and the enslavement of one's brother. None of these reservations prevailed, however; and the colonists, preoccupied with critical economic and social problems, either tolerated slavery as unavoidable or embraced it with enthusiasm as indispensable.

When England revised her colonial policy at the end of the French and Indian War in 1763, she paved the way for a new approach to slavery in the colonies. If the colonists were to object to the new stringent policies imposed by England, they felt also compelled to speak out against the holding of slaves. John Woolman, the New Jersey Quaker, and Anthony Benezet, the Philadelphia Huguenot, had begun their antislavery activities even before the controversy between England and her colonies flared into the open. But when England imposed new laws on the colonists, such as the Sugar Act of 1764 and the Stamp Act of the following year, the colonists began to reflect upon their dual roles as oppressed and oppressor. Soon their leaders were denouncing not only England's new imperial policy but slavery and the slave trade as well.

It is not surprising that the colonists saw a connection between the problem of slavery and what they regarded as their oppression by England. When James Otis penned his eloquent protest on the *Rights of the British Colonies*, he affirmed the slave's inalienable right to freedom. "Does it follow that it is right to enslave a man because he is black?" Otis asked. Negroes themselves sensed the dilemma of their masters and began to press for emancipation. Addressing the Massachusetts General Court in 1774, several of them said, "We have in common with all other men a natural right to our freedoms without Being depriv'd of them by our fellow men as we are a freeborn Pepel and have never forfeited this Blessing by any compact or agreement whatever."

For the time being the General Court could not be moved to act. But neither the members of the General Court nor the other citizens of Massachusetts could soon forget the incident a few years earlier in which a Negro, according to the black historian George Washington Williams, became the "first to pour out his blood as a precious libation on the altar of a people's rights." The presence of British soldiers in Boston in 1770 had excited the indignation of the people, and many wondered what could be done about it. On the fifth of March, a crowd of colonists began to taunt a group of British soldiers under the command of Captain Thomas Preston. When one of the soldiers received a blow from the unruly mob, the soldiers began to fire. One of the patriots, a mulatto named Crispus Attucks, "had hardiness enough to fall in upon them, and with one hand took hold of a bayonet, and with the other knocked the man down." But Attucks had been fatally struck, and the first blood in the struggle against England had been shed. The colonists may well have been shaken by the realization that their fight for freedom had been waged by one who was not as free as they.

In the years that followed the Boston Massacre, as the incident was called, the colonists frequently spoke out against slavery and British colonial policy at the same time. In 1774 Abigail Adams wrote to her husband John, "It always appeared a most iniquitous scheme to me to fight ourselves for what we are daily robbing and plundering from those who have as good a right to freedom as we have." This feeling of inconsistency was reflected in the act of the Continental Congress that provided that after December 1, 1775, no slaves would be imported into the colonies. One might have assumed from this that the colonists' stand against slavery and the slave trade had become unequivocal and irrevocable.

The real test of the colonists' position on slavery, however, came in their reaction to the Declaration of Independence submitted to the Continental Congress by Thomas Jefferson. Most of the draft was acceptable, but one of the arraignments against the king was not. In part it declared that the king had "waged cruel war against human nature itself, violating the most sacred rights of life and liberty in the persons of a distant people who never offended him, captivating and carrying them into slavery in another hemisphere, or to incur miserable death in their transportation thither." Such acts were described as piratical warfare, and they were vigorously denounced by the Declaration. This accusation was unacceptable to the southern delegation at the Continental Congress, however, and it was stricken from the final draft of the Declaration. Thus the status of the Negro remained but vaguely connected with the philosophy of freedom for all men.

There was no uniform policy among the several colonies on the use of Negroes as soldiers when hostilities broke out in April 1775. In Massachusetts, slaves as well as free Negroes fought in the battle of Bunker Hill. Peter Salem, who had been a slave in Framingham, won the plaudits of his fellows when he shot down the British Major Pitcairn. Another, Salem Poor, a soldier in a company of soldiers who were largely white, distinguished himself by behaving "like an experienced officer as well as an excellent soldier." There were other Negroes who, like Poor and Salem, fought bravely at Bunker Hill: Caesar Brown of Westford, who was killed in action; Titus Coburn and Alexander Ames of Andover; and Prince Hall, later an abolitionist and leader of the Masons.

The performance of Negroes at this early stage of the Revolutionary struggle did not settle their status as soldiers in the War for Independence. Shortly after George Washington took command of the Continental Army in 1775 an order was issued to recruiting officers instructing them not to enlist "any deserter from the ministerial army, nor any stroller, negro, or vagabond, or person suspected of being an enemy of the liberty of America nor any under eighteen years of age." In October of that year Washington's council of war agreed unanimously to reject all slaves and, by a large majority, to reject Negroes altogether. This remained the policy until the end of the year.

It was British policy that finally forced the Americans to change their regulations with regard to enlisting Negroes in the Continental Army. When Lord Dunmore, the governor of Virginia, invited Negroes into the British army in November 1775, General Washington seemed to realize that he had made an error in turning down black volunteers. Later that year he learned that Negroes, slave and free, were rallying around the British flag. Wherever the British armies went they attracted many Negroes with their promise of freedom to those who would serve. On December 31 Washington reversed his policy and, with the approval of Congress, ordered the enlistment of free blacks. In the ensuing months the policy was liberalized further, so that before the end of the war all Negroes were permitted to enlist in all states with the exception of Georgia and South Carolina.

Of the 300,000 men who saw service in the cause of American independence, some 5,000 were black. They served in the navy as well as the army; some volunteered, while others were forced to substitute for whites. Most of them served in outfits that were predominantly white, but there were a few predominantly black fighting units, including two companies in Massachusetts, one in Connecticut, and one in Rhode Island. Negroes saw action all over the country: at Lexington, Concord, Ticonderoga, Bunker Hill, Trenton, Princeton, Brandywine, Saratoga, Savannah, Eutaw Springs, and Yorktown. Most of them remain anonymous, as far as military exploits are concerned. Indeed, as Benjamin Quarles points out in *The Negro in the American Revolution*, many Negroes who enlisted were enrolled without specific names. They were "A Negro Man," or "Negro by Name" or "A Negro name not known."

Some Negroes distinguished themselves by the services that they rendered. Two of them, Prince Whipple and Oliver Cromwell, were with Washington when he crossed the Delaware on Christmas Day, 1776. Lemuel Haynes, who was later to have a career as a minister to white congregations, joined the expedition to Ticonderoga to stop the inroads of Burgoyne's northern army. The victory of Anthony Wayne at Stony Point in 1779 was made possible by the spying of a black soldier named Pompey. At the siege of Savannah in 1779 more than 500 blacks from Haiti were with the French forces that helped save the day. Among them and perhaps the youngest was Henri Christophe, "who one day would become King of Haiti, but was then a bootblack and messboy, not yet out of his teens."

### The First Antislavery Movement

Early in the seventeenth century colonists here and there began to speak out against slavery. It was not until the Revolutionary period, however, that a full-scale, organized opposition to the institution of slavery emerged. In a sense it was nurtured by the same sentiments that fostered the movement for independence. In Rhode Island the Reverend Samuel Hopkins made a house-to-house canvass urging masters to liberate their slaves. In Pennsylvania Anthony Benezet, who has been called "the foremost antislavery propagandist of his day," was writing and speaking against the practice that was "repugnant to humanity" and "inconsistent with the Bible." He joined with others, like Benjamin Rush, in organizing the Society for the Relief of Free Negroes Unlawfully Held in Bondage. In 1785 the New York Society for Promoting the Manumission of Slaves was organized with John Jay as President. In Delaware a similar society was set up in 1788; and by 1792 there were antislavery societies in every state from Massachusetts to Virginia.

Negroes began to take heart, both from the efforts of the whites and from the congenial climate produced by arguments for the rights of man. In 1777 a group of Massachusetts blacks asked for a law against slavery, declaring that a life of slavery was "far worse than Nonexistence." Two years later a group of nineteen Negroes in New Hampshire requested the state to enact a law whereby they might regain their liberty "and that the name of slave may not more be heard in a land gloriously contending for the sweets of freedom." Throughout the country individual blacks and groups of blacks were seeking legislation that would bring an end to slavery.

States slowly began to respond to the pressure. In 1777 the Massachusetts legislature would no more than consider a bill for "preventing the practice of holding persons in Slavery," but by 1780 the new Massachusetts constitution had stated that "all men are born free and equal." This was the beginning of the end of slavery in that state. New Hampshire legislators debated the question of abolishing slavery in 1780, but postponed action to a "more convenient opportunity." While some states equivocated, however, Pennsylvania took decisive action. On March 1, 1780, it passed a law providing that when children of slaves reached twenty-eight years of age, they would become free.

Manumission acts were passed in New York in 1785 and in New Jersey in 1786, although effective legislation was not achieved in these states until 1799 and 1804 respectively. Finally, Congress in 1787 indicated its interest in the antislavery movement by enacting a law providing that in the Northwest Territory neither slavery nor involuntary servitude should exist.

## Slavery and the Constitution

The antislavery leaders experienced only limited success during and after the War for Independence. Resistance to the abolition of slavery intensified in the southern states, where much capital was invested in slaves and where, during the postwar years, a new economic importance was attached to slavery. Nowhere was the resistance to abolition reflected better than in the convention that wrote a new Constitution for the United States in 1787. In the debates over representation in Congress, the question arose as to how the slaves should be counted. Most of the northern delegates regarded slaves as property and therefore not deserving of representation. Southerners were loud in their demands that slaves be counted as people, in which case the slave states would gain in the number of members they would have in Congress. Despite the objection on the part of some antislavery delegates to recognizing slavery in the Constitution, the compromise finally agreed upon permitted states to count each slave as three-fifths of a person.

By 1787 several states, including such slave states as Virginia, North Carolina, and Georgia, had taken action to prevent the importation of slaves. Opponents of the slave trade hoped that the convention would put an end to the trade in all parts of the United States. When the matter came before the convention, it was debated with such vehemence that some feared a disruption of the entire proceedings. One southerner said that his own state, South Carolina, could never accept a Constitution that prohibited the slave trade. After much acrimonious debate, the members agreed on a compromise that provided that the slave trade "shall not be prohibited by the Congress prior to the Year one thousand eight hundred and eight, but a Tax or duty may be imposed on such importation, not exceeding ten dollars for each Person."

Runaway slaves had always been a problem in the colonies; so it is significant, but not surprising, that there was almost no opposition to the proposal that states give up fugitive slaves to their owners. When Roger Sherman of Connecticut declared that he saw "no more propriety in the public seizing and surrendering a slave or servant, than a horse," he found little support, even among his New England colleagues. Thus the provision was written into the Constitution calling for the rendition of fugitive slaves "upon Claim of the Party to whom such Service or Labour may be due." In these several ways the new Constitution not only recognized the institution of slavery but offered the resources of the Government of the United States in its protection and support.

## Negroes in the New Nation

When the new Constitution went into effect, there were approximately three-quarters of a million Negroes in the United States. Almost 90 percent of them were slaves in the South Atlantic states, while some 60,000 free Negroes were scattered all over the country. The Negro population was essentially rural. Here and there one found a slight concentration in the cities. New York City with 3,252, Philadelphia with 1,630, and Baltimore with 1,578. Nowhere was the Negro population dying out; indeed, there were signs of significant increase, especially in the slave states. In the North the only significant development was the increase in the number of free Negroes. By 1790 all of Boston's 761 Negroes were free.

Nor were the black Americans altogether anonymous, even at this early date. There was, for example, Phillis, the personal maid of Mrs. Susannah Wheatley of Boston. She early developed an interest in writing poetry, and in 1770 her first poem, "On the Death of Reverend George Whitefield," appeared. Three years later she published a collection of her verse, *Poems on Various Subjects, Religious and Moral*. During the war she composed a tribute to "His Excellency General Washington," which the general acknowledged by declaring that the poem was "striking proof of your great poetical talents." Then there was Paul Cuffee, the Massachusetts Negro who built and sailed his own ships. He owned a sixty-nine-ton schooner, the *Ranger*, two brigs, and several smaller vessels. When settlers refused to do so, he built a school in Westport, Massachusetts, and gave it to the community. He also helped build a meetinghouse for the Society of Friends to which he belonged. In 1780 he presented a petition to the Massachusetts legislature asking to be relieved from paying taxes since he and the Negroes who joined him in signing the petition had "no voice or influence in the election of those who tax us." As businessman, philanthropist, and petitioner he won grudging recognition among his fellow citizens in Massachusetts.

Perhaps the most significant of the Negroes in the new nation was Benjamin Banneker, mathematician, astronomer, and political philosopher. In 1791 this Maryland free Negro published his first almanac, a worthy undertaking which lasted until 1802. Thomas Jefferson, to whom Banneker sent a copy of his first almanac, was greatly impressed and told Banneker that it was a work that justified the Negroes' resentment against the claims that they were intellectually inferior. At the suggestion of his friends George Ellicott and Jefferson, Banneker was appointed by Washington to serve with the commission to define the boundaries of and lay out the new capital, the District of Columbia.

There were also several Negro religious leaders who became well known for their initiative and courage in the early days of the new nation. George Liele founded a Baptist church in Savannah in 1779 before quitting the United States and settling in Jamaica. In Philadelphia, Richard Allen founded the African Methodist Episcopal Church after he was thrown out of the St. George Church because he refused to accept segregation. Soon branches of Allen's church sprang up in Baltimore, Wilmington, and various Pennsylvania and New Jersey towns. Able colleagues such as Absolom Jones, Daniel Coker, and Morris Brown helped to promote this branch of Methodism among Negroes in the South as well as in the North. In New York in 1796, Negroes under the leadership of Peter Williams, James Varick, and Christopher Rush withdrew from the John Street Methodist Church and organized the African Methodist Episcopal Zion Church. Before the beginning of the nineteenth century, Negro Baptist and Methodist churches had been established in all the states of the union.

If there were no outstanding Negro leaders in the field of education, it did not prevent a movement for the education of Negroes from getting under way. In 1798 a separate school for black children was established by a white teacher in the home of Primus Hall, a prominent Boston Negro. In 1800 the Negroes of Boston asked the city to establish a school for Negroes, but the request was not granted. Not until 1820 did the city open the first school for black children. The first school for Negroes in New York City was established in 1787 by the Manumission Society. By 1820 the school had more than 500 children. New Jersey began educating her Negro children in 1777. Soon there were schools in several New Jersey towns. Philadelphia, which began Negro education in 1787, had seven schools for Negroes before the end of the century. In the other states the beginnings were not as auspicious and the task was more difficult, but even in Virginia and the Carolinas schools for Negroes were founded. The insurrection of 1800 in Richmond frightened many slaveholders, who feared that Negroes were reading incendiary literature. From that point on it became increasingly difficult to establish and maintain schools for Negroes in the slave states.

## SLAVERY IN YOUNG AMERICA

### Growth of an Institution

By the beginning of the nineteenth century there were unmistakable signs of profound economic and social changes taking place in the United States. The commercial activities of the new nation were expanding; and there were those who already were beginning to think in terms of promoting industrial development similar to that which was occurring in England and on the continent. Beyond the areas of settlement, rich new land was beckoning settlers who could plant staple crops and enjoy the freedom offered on the frontier. In 1803 the United States purchased the vast Louisiana Territory, and although it would be many years before the entire area was settled, Americans and European immigrants were rapidly moving beyond the Allegheny mountains. The greater portion of the people who moved from the Atlantic seaboard were committed to the institution of slavery, and if they had any slaves they took them along.

Not even the War of 1812, in which several thousand Negroes fought, could halt the march of Americans and slavery into the new West.

When peace came in 1815 the movement westward accelerated. The men of the South and West, who had been the most enthusiastic supporters of the war, felt they had earned the right to move on to even better lands. Into the gulf region went large numbers of settlers to clear the rich lands and cultivate extensive crops of cotton and sugar. Louisiana had become a state in 1812; Mississippi and Alabama became states in 1817 and 1819 respectively. By 1820 the gulf region had about 200,000 inhabitants, and twenty years later there were almost a million people there. The increase of the white population, coupled with the tremendous growth of the black population, largely slaves, is essentially the story of the emergence of the cotton kingdom.

The rise of the cotton kingdom was America's response to the growing demand for cotton brought on by the industrial revolution in England. Methods of producing cotton textiles were undergoing revolutionary changes, and with the invention of spinning and weaving machinery the cost of the manufacturing process was so drastically cut that the market for cotton goods was greatly stimulated. The demand for cotton fiber to feed the newly developed machinery seemed limitless, and the cotton farmers of the United States undertook to profit from this fact. Already they had made two significant steps toward increasing productivity. First, they put into use a type of cotton, the short-staple variety, that could be grown almost anywhere in the South. Secondly, they made greater use of the cotton gin, a device that had been developed by a Connecticut schoolteacher, Eli Whitney. Within a few years the South was on its way toward making the economic transition that these new developments induced.

As the planters expanded their operations, the need for additional labor became urgent. By now they were committed to Negro slavery, but the supply of slaves was not abundant. The African slave trade had officially closed in 1808, but even after that date American capital, American ships, and American sailors were carrying on an extensive slave trade between Africa and the New World. The long, unprotected east coast of the United States, a sure market for their wares, and the prospect of huge profits were enough to tempt many Americans. W. E. B. DuBois, in his *The Suppression of the African Slave Trade*, asserts that thousands of slaves were smuggled into the country each year from the time of the closing of the trade down to the outbreak of the Civil War. It was the domestic slave trade, however, that constituted the principal means by which the farmers of the cotton kingdom secured the slaves that they needed.

Even before 1800 the domestic slave trade in Maryland and Virginia was well-developed. As tobacco cultivation tended to decline and as the farmers of the upper South diversified their economic activity, they discovered that there was a ready market for the surplus of slaves they had on hand. Slave-trading firms like Woolfolk, Saunders, and Overly of Maryland and Franklin and Armfield of Virginia did a lively business in purchasing slaves in the upper South and selling them "down the river" to planters in Mississippi and Louisiana who desperately needed them. Traders made individual deals with planters or attended estate auctions or sales by the sheriff of bankrupt estates. At times planters sold off incorrigible slaves—habitual runaways or those who refused to work—and the traders in turn sold them to unsuspecting planters in some faraway community. Baltimore, Washington, Richmond, Norfolk, and Charleston were principal trading centers in the older states; while Montgomery, Memphis, and New Orleans were the major marketplaces in the newer areas.

The domestic slave trade involved some of the most sordid practices to be developed in the grim business of slavery. Slave families were ruthlessly divided, with mothers frequently being sold away from their children or vice versa. In his journal William Reynolds, an itinerant merchant, recorded this account of the sale of twenty-three slaves at auction in Memphis: "One yellow woman was sold who had two children. She begged and implored her new master . . . to buy her children, but it had no effect. . . . She then begged him to buy her little girl, about five years old, but all to no purpose." In the states of the Upper South, owners encouraged the breeding of slaves in order to increase profits. As early as 1796 a South Carolina slaveholder declared that the fifty slaves he was offering for sale had been purchased for breeding purposes. In 1832 Thomas R. Dew admitted that Virginia was a "Negro-raising state" and that she was able to export 6,000 slaves per year because of breeding. Moncure Conway of Fredericksburg, Virginia, boldly asserted that the "chief pecuniary resource in the border states is the breeding of slaves. . . . "

Because of the foreign slave trade, the illicit foreign slave trade after 1808, slave breeding, the normal excess of births over deaths among slaves, and a booming domestic slave trade, the Negro population grew steadily in the first half of the nineteenth century. In 1790 there were 604,000 slaves. By 1808, when the foreign slave trade officially closed, there were about 1,000,000. In 1830 there were 2,156,900; and by 1860 the number had increased to 3,953,760. In 1860 Virginia continued to lead in numbers with 549,000, followed by Georgia with 465,000, and Alabama and Mississippi with approximately 435,000 each. The most significant increase was in the states of the cotton kingdom—Georgia, Alabama, Tennessee, Mississippi, Arkansas, Louisiana, and Texas—where by 1860 there were approximately 2,000,000 slaves, more than half of the entire Negro population.

There were 384,000 owners of slaves in 1860, and this means that since the white population of the South numbered around eight million, fully three-fourths of the southern white families had neither slaves nor any immediate economic interest in slavery. Most of the slaveowners had only a few slaves; 200,000 owners had five slaves or less; while 338,000 owners, or 88 percent, held less than twenty slaves. Nevertheless, the institution came to dominate the political and economic thinking of the entire South. The vast majority of the staple crops was produced on those relatively few plantations employing large numbers of slaves (2,000 planters had more than 100 slaves each in 1860), thus giving such owners an influence far out of proportion to their numbers. Even those who had no slaves hoped that some day they would; and they took on the habits and patterns of thought of the slaveholders. Too, in the context of a slave society in which all slaves were black people, the color of the whites became a badge of superiority in which *all* whites took pride.

## The Slave Codes

Slaves were a special kind of property, not quite like houses or beasts of burden, but not quite like people either, within the meaning of the law. A special set of laws was therefore designed to protect the owners of such property and to shield all whites against such dangers as might arise from the presence of so many slaves. These codes began to develop in the seventeenth century, and long before the Civil War they were fully refined. From time to time it was necessary to modify them, and they differed from state to state; but in important particulars they were quite similar. Since they were designed to achieve due subordination of the slaves, they were frankly repressive, a fact for which the white planters and legislators made no apologies.

A slave had no standing in the courts. He could not be a party to a suit at law; and he could not offer legal testimony except against another slave or a free Negro. Since he had no legal responsibility, his oath was not binding. Thus, he could not make a contract, and his marriage was not a legal contract. His children were not legitimate. The ownership of property by slaves was generally forbidden, and although some states permitted them to possess certain types of holdings, there was no legal basis for even this concession. A slave could not strike a white person, even in self-defense; but the killing of a slave, however malicious, was rarely regarded as murder. The rape of a female slave was a misdemeanor when it involved trespassing on the property of another person. Slaves could not leave the plantation without the permission of their master; and any white person encountering a slave who was away from the plantation without permission could take him up and turn him over to the public officials. Slaves could not possess firearms and, in Mississippi, they could not beat drums or blow horns. Laws generally forbade the hiring out of slaves, but many owners ignored this proscription.

Slaves could not purchase or sell goods or visit the homes of whites or free Negroes. They were never to assemble unless a white person was present; and they were never to receive, possess, or transmit any incendiary literature calculated to incite insurrections. They were not to be taught to read or write or cipher; and any white person or free Negro found guilty of violating this law was to be subjected to severe punishment of fine or imprisonment or both. Slaves guilty of petty offenses were to be punished by whipping, but the more serious offenses drew severe punishments such as branding, imprisonment, or death. Arson, rape of a white woman, and conspiracy to rebel, for example, were capital crimes in all the slaveholding states. Since slaves were always regarded with suspicion and since they could not testify against a white person who accused them, many of them were found guilty of crimes they did not commit and against which they were unable to defend themselves.

Despite the elaborateness of the slave codes and the machinery of enforcement, there were numerous infractions that went unpunished altogether. When times were quiet the laws were disregarded, and slaves could get away with a great deal. But when there were rumors of revolts among the slaves, the white community became apprehensive and tended to enforce the codes with unusual zeal. Slaveowners, moreover, did not generally pay much heed to the slave codes where their own slaves were concerned. The planter conceived of himself as a valid source of law and justice and he preferred to take all matters involving his own slaves into his own hands and mete out justice in his own way. He was certain that he could handle his own slaves, if only something could be done about those on the neighboring plantation. Such an attitude was obviously not conducive to the uniform, effective enforcement of the slave codes.

## Slaves at Work

A great deal has been written about the institution of slavery as "a matrimonial bureau," "a chapel of ease," and the like. All too often the planter is described as a patrician who, as a great Christian humanitarian, maintained his establishment largely as a civilizing institution. Such descriptions hardly square with the facts. Slavery was essentially an economic institution; and the primary concern of the slaveowner was to get work out of his slaves. This work was largely agricultural. In his study of urban slavery, Richard Wade has pointed out that only some 400,000 slaves lived in towns and cities in 1850 and that slavery in the urban areas was largely unsuccessful. Of the 3,200,000 slaves in the United States in 1850, approximately 2,800,000 were on farms and plantations. Some 1,800,000 of these were on cotton plantations, while the remainder worked in tobacco, sugar, and rice fields. In agricultural units with only a few slaves, as was the case in a vast majority of instances, the slaves and their owners worked together in the fields at a variety of tasks. On the larger plantations, where organization and the division of labor were elaborate, there was extensive supervision by the owner or his overseer or both. In such instances there might be two distinct groups of slaves, the field hands and the house servants.

The cultivation of a crop was a most demanding activity; and the entire future of both slaves and owners depended on the success of the undertaking. It was generally believed that one slave was required for the successful cultivation of three acres of cotton. The planting, cultivation, and picking of the cotton required little skill, but a great deal of time. Men, women, and children could be used to do this work and, indeed, they all were. Other duties included clearing new land, burning underbrush, rolling logs, splitting rails, carrying water, mending fences, spreading fertilizer, and breaking the soil. Small wonder that many slaves worked not merely from sunrise to sunset, but frequently long after dark.

On some plantations, slaves were assigned a certain number of daily tasks; and when they had completed these, their day was done. Much more common, however, was the gang system in which gangs of slaves were taken to the field and put to work under supervision. Where there was not watchful supervision little was likely to be accomplished. Slaves felt no compulsion to extend themselves, since their benefits were more or less the same, regardless of effort, except on the few plantations where systems of bounties and rewards were developed. Masters complained loudly about the idleness and laziness of slaves. If slaves felt overworked, they frequently feigned illness or simply walked off for a day or two or, perhaps, forever. The constant evasion of work on the part of slaves was one reason why planters always felt the need for more slaves in order to increase productivity.

In order to get work out of slaves the lash was frequently used. There was a general belief, born of a naïve defense of the institution of slavery, that blacks were a childlike race and should therefore be punished just as children were punished. The excessive use of the lash was one of the most flagrant abuses of the institution of slavery. As Thomas Jefferson pointed out in his *Notes on Virginia*, the whole master-slave relationship was "a perpetual exercise of the most boisterous passions, the most unremitting despotism on the one part; and degrading submissions on the other. . . . " The dominion over the slave that the master enjoyed all too frequently brought out the worst in the master and stimulated a brutality in treatment that seemed to be inherent in the relationship. Excessively cruel treatment at the hands of the planter or the overseer, together with their natural aversion to enslavement, explain the tendency of slaves to run away or, worse still, to revolt against their masters.

### An Ignoble Existence

Except for some house servants who may have had special advantages and opportunities, slaves generally lived at a near-subsistence level. Many planters were so preoccupied with growing staple crops that they gave little attention to growing foodstuffs for their slaves. Numerous plantations were compelled to purchase food and other supplies for the slaves and for the plantation family. The standard meal-and-meat diet, infrequently supplemented by potatoes, peas, and syrup, was not particularly exciting fare. Some slaves had their own gardens and chickens, but they ran the risk of incurring the disfavor of the owner by devoting too much time to them. It would be unrealistic to suppose that slaves seriously resisted the temptation to take food from the owner's larder if the opportunity presented itself. As far as clothing was concerned, no more was provided than was absolutely necessary. Housing was especially poor and uncomfortable. When Frederick L. Olmsted toured the South he was shocked to see the small, dilapidated cabins on some of the plantations he visited.

Generally, slaves had little time that they could call their own. Even though they could generally expect to be free from work on Saturday afternoons and Sundays, there was little available to them in the way of enjoyment or satisfaction during their leisure moments. Plantations were isolated, and slaves were not free to come and go at will. Hence, unless the plantation was large enough to have sufficient slaves to provide their own social diversions, recreation was extremely limited. At Christmas time and on a few other holidays, the rules of the plantation were relaxed, additional food was provided, and slaves were permitted to dance and sing. Some were even allowed to hunt and fish on special occasions. But on the whole, theirs was a depressingly drab existence.

As long as the proper precautions were taken there was little opposition to some form of religious activity among the slaves. After the Nat Turner revolt of 1831, some states banned black preachers and required slaves to attend the churches of their masters. Generally, however, Negro congregations flourished in the towns and on certain plantations, supported by groups of neighboring planters. Toward the end of the slave period black churches became generally frowned upon; and planters were encouraged to permit religious services for slaves only when some responsible white person was present. If this was not possible, slaves were expected to worship in white churches. The earliest examples of the segregation of blacks are to be found in the practices of the white churches. In one instance the white congregation constructed a partition several feet high to separate the masters from the slaves.

Even if the slave enjoyed some sort of social life and was permitted to attend church, he could never escape the fact that he was a slave and that his every movement was under constant surveillance. This created a restiveness among some and a sense of despair among others. If a slave found it possible to rise above his obviously ignoble existence, it was because he possessed a remarkable capacity for accommodation or he was totally ignorant of the depth of his degradation.

The prevailing notion in the antebellum years was that the slave was docile, tractable, and happy, a view that has persisted in some quarters. Advocates of the institution defended it on these very grounds, pointing to the attitude of many slaves to support their contention. In fact, slaves developed many techniques to mislead the owner regarding their real feelings. In the process of adjustment they learned how to escape work as well as punishment; and they were not above obsequiousness and meekness when it served their purposes. What was to be gained by revealing their true sentiments concerning their enslavement, sentiments of resistance and protest as old as the institution of slavery itself? Resistance to slavery exists wherever slavery exists, and Negro slavery in the United States was no exception. There are examples of kindness and understanding on the part of the owner as well as docility and tractability on the part of the slave;

but these can hardly be regarded as typical of a system based on the exploitation of one group by another.

Slaves reacted to their status in various ways. Some sang songs and expressed the hope that their burdens would be relieved in the next world. As long as they were in this world, they attempted to make the most of an unwelcome situation by loafing on the job and feigning illness in the fields and on the auction block. Others engaged in active sabotage, destroying farming tools, driving animals with a cruelty that suggested revenge, and when possible damaging crops, burning forests and homes, and destroying their masters' property in other ways. Still others resorted to self-mutilation and suicide. Slaves were known to cut off their toes and hands in order to render themselves ineffective as workers. A final group attempted violence to the master class. Poisoning was always feared, and with reason. As early as 1761 the Charleston *Gazette* remarked that the Negroes had "begun the hellish act of poisoning." On occasion slaves even murdered their masters by stabbing, shooting, and choking.

Running away began the first year that slavery was established in the New World and continued until emancipation. There was federal and state legislation to assist in the recovery of runaway slaves, but many of them nevertheless escaped forever. Long before the Underground Railroad became an efficient operation under the abolitionists, slaves were running away: men, women, and children, alone or in pairs or groups. Some disguised themselves; others, armed with counterfeit passes, claimed that they were free. If they were apprehended, they would do it again. One woman in North Carolina fled from her master's plantation no less than sixteen times. While there is no way of even approximating the number of runaways, it is obvious that it was one of the most effective means of resisting slavery. Neither the fugitive acts of 1793 nor 1850 could put an end to it.

Revolting against the whites was the slaves' most desperate form of resistance. To Negroes, it was "carrying the fight to the enemy." To the whites, it was a mad, sinister act of desperate savages who had no appreciation for the benign influences of slavery. There were numerous revolts, large and small. And there were even more numerous rumors of revolts. Whether real or fancied, the merest suggestion of an uprising threw the white community into a paroxysm of fear and led it to adopt desperate measures to prevent a bloodbath. In 1800 a thousand slaves, led by Gabriel Prosser, attempted to march on Richmond and destroy the town and their masters. A violent storm and betrayal by two slave informers brought a tragic end to the attempt. In 1822 the slaves and free Negroes of Charleston planned a revolt, under the leadership of Denmark Vesey. The word leaked out, and it was aborted. In 1831 the blacks of Southampton County, Virginia, under Nat Turner, were almost successful in their bid for freedom through revolt. They began by killing Turner's master and his family and several other white families. Within the first day some sixty whites had been killed, and the revolt was spreading rapidly when the main body of black revolutionaries were met and overpowered by state and federal troops. More than a hundred slaves were killed immediately, and within a few weeks Turner himself was captured and executed. Right down to the Civil War, slaves demonstrated their violent antipathy to slavery by attempting to rise against it, but their successes were few.

## Free Negroes, South and North

In 1790 there were some 59,000 Negroes in the United States who were not slaves, a considerable increase over the twenty black indentured servants who landed in Jamestown in 1619. By 1830 there were 319,000; and by 1860 there were 488,000, of whom 44 percent lived in the South and 46 percent in the North. Some had been set free by their masters. Others had purchased their freedom. Some were born of free mothers, white and black. Others had run away and made good their bid for freedom. In the South the existence of a large number of free Negroes proved to be a source of constant embarrassment to the slaveholders, since their existence undermined the very foundation on which slavery was built. Southerners carried on a campaign of vilification against free Negroes and undertook a program of legislation designed to keep them in their place.

A free Negro's existence, even in the North, was precarious. A white person could claim, however fraudulently, that the free Negro was his slave; and the heavy burden of proof that he was not rested on the accused. There was the danger, moreover, of his being kidnapped, as often happened. In the South the chances of being reduced to servitude or slavery by court decree were also great. All southern states required free Negroes to have passes and certificates of freedom. Some states, such as Virginia, Tennessee, Georgia, and Florida, required registration; some others compelled free blacks to have white guardians.

The controls which the state and community exercised over free Negroes increased year by year. In no southern state could a free black move about as he wished, and in some northern communities it was dangerous to try. Some states forbade free Negroes to possess or carry firearms without a license. By 1835 the right of assembly had been taken away from almost all blacks in the South, and their contact with others was, by law, kept to a minimum. Many proscriptions interfered with their making a living. In 1805 Maryland prohibited free Negroes from selling corn, wheat, or tobacco without a license. In 1831 North Carolina required all black traders and peddlers to be licensed, while most states required free Negroes to work and show visible means of support.

In the nineteenth century Negroes steadily lost their various citizenship rights. In 1800 they could vote almost everywhere. By 1835 they could vote in no southern state, with Pennsylvania and Indiana confining the franchise to whites in 1838 and 1851 respectively. Seldom did they enjoy protection at the hands of the state or local government. In cities such as Pittsburgh, Philadelphia, and New York they were attacked with impunity by mobs; their homes and churches were destroyed, and they were run out of the community. It was this kind of treatment, North and South, that caused Fanny

Kemble to say, "They are not slaves indeed, but they are pariahs, debarred from every fellowship save with their own despised race. . . . All hands are extended to thrust them out, all fingers point at their dusky skin, all tongues have learned to turn the very name of their race into an insult and a reproach."

In the face of all this, however, there were free Negroes who not only survived but did relatively well in a variety of fields. Some even managed to accumulate considerable wealth. Individual cases of affluence include the wealthy Thomy Lafon, who amassed an estate in New Orleans of more than a half-million dollars, and prosperous James Forten, the Philadelphia sailmaker, who built up a fortune of more than $100,000. Schools for black children increased in the North during the nineteenth century; and in some communities, such as Boston and New Bedford after 1855, they were permitted to attend school with the whites. In the South, where teaching of free Negroes was generally outlawed after 1830, many blacks received private instruction. There are examples, moreover, of free Negroes going to the North, to Canada, and to Europe for an education during the antebellum period. Some northern free Negroes were attending colleges and universities. Amherst was the first college to graduate a Negro when Edward Jones received his degree there in 1826. After that time Bowdoin, Oberlin, Harvard, and other institutions received free Negroes.

Negroes were becoming articulate and expressed their views in various ways. They held conventions, beginning in 1831, and in the resolutions and positions that sprang from such meetings, they indicated their feelings and aspirations. They published newspapers: *Freedom's Journal*, the *North Star*, and the *Anglo-African*. They wrote books: Frederick Douglass and a host of former slaves wrote autobiographies; J. W. C. Pennington wrote a history of the Negro people; George Moses Horton published a book of verse; and William Wells Brown published numerous works, including a novel.

Perhaps the most important work performed by free Negroes was the general assistance they gave to the antislavery movement, which gained considerable momentum after 1830. Negroes were among the most enthusiastic supporters of William Lloyd Garrison when he began to publish his *Liberator* in 1831. Many joined the American Antislavery Society and the regional and state societies when they were organized. Frederick Douglass was the best known of a larger number of writers and speakers in the antislavery cause. Others were Charles Remond, Charles B. Ray, Henry Highland Garnet, David Ruggles, Sarah Remond, Frances Harper, Sojourner Truth, and Harriet Tubman. In their militant bitterness the Negro abolitionists equaled and sometimes surpassed their white colleagues. Perhaps not even Garrison reached the intensity of feeling against slavery that David Walker attained in 1829 in his *Appeal in Four Articles*. Many Negro leaders, moreover, counseled violence if no other approach against slavery was successful. In 1854 the Negro convention adopted a resolution that represented the views of an increasing number of Negroes. In part, it declared that "those who, without crime, are outlawed by any government can owe no allegiance to its enactments. . . . we advise all oppressed to adopt the motto, 'Liberty or Death.'" This was five years before John Brown attacked Harper's Ferry.

## CIVIL WAR AND RECONSTRUCTION

### The Evolution of Federal Policy

The unequivocal stand that white and black abolitionists took against slavery in the 1850s made compromise difficult, if not impossible, just as the dogmatic defense of slavery by white southerners ruled out any possibility of concessions on their part. This impasse was further accentuated by the positions of the leading political parties: the southern Democrats held that the election to the presidency of a pro-black Republican such as Abraham Lincoln was wholly unacceptable to them and that they would rather secede than remain under abolitionist rule. The Republicans would not concede that slavery should be permitted in the territories, and while they would permit slavery to continue where it existed, they were determined to pursue a policy of containment. When Lincoln was in fact elected, the southern leaders concluded that secession was their only recourse. And when the new president went on to decide that the secessionists were not entitled to federal forts, post offices, and other properties in the South, the war broke out.

When Lincoln issued a call for 75,000 volunteers in April 1861, Negroes rushed forward to offer their services. Frederick Douglass expressed the sentiments of many when he said, "Standing outside the pale of American humanity, denied citizenship, unable to call the land of my birth my country. . . and longing for the end of the bondage of my people, I was ready for any political upheaval which should bring about a change in the existing condition of things." Indeed, as the Negro historian Joseph T. Wilson recalled, "at the sound of the tocsin at the North, Negro waiter, cook, barber, bootblack, groom, porter, and laborer stood ready at the enlisting office." In many parts of the country— Boston, Providence, Philadelphia, Cleveland, Battle Creek—Negroes organized themselves into military corps and offered their services. In every instance their services were declined. The Secretary of War was curt and firm: "This Department has no intention to call into the service of the Government any colored soldiers."

Blacks were critical of the government for rejecting them, and so were many whites. Horace Greeley, after the fiasco at Bull Run in the summer of 1861, was bitter in his denunciation, as were some other antislavery editors. But the Lincoln government wanted to be careful not to convey the impression that the war was one for freedom. There were many northerners, including some soldiers, who feared that it would become one. "We don't want to fight side by side with the nigger," said a young soldier from

New York. "We think we are too superior a race for that." But if Negroes could not fight, they would help in other ways. Many southern blacks offered to help the Confederacy, although it had rejected their services as soldiers. Northern Negroes offered money, goods, and other support to the Union, which they served as cooks, teamsters, hospital attendants, and body servants.

At some point early in the war, perhaps in the first year, blacks even in the South began to believe that their freedom might be bound up with the war. This led them not only to take a greater interest in the struggle but also to do whatever they could to promote a Union victory. Slaves who were close enough began to leave the plantations and join the Union lines. Loyalty, about which masters boasted, became the exception rather than the rule, according to Bell Irvin Wiley in his *Southern Negroes, 1861–1865*. When the slaves of Georgetown, South Carolina, sang "We'll fight for liberty" in 1861, they were thrown in jail. By the second year of the war, slaves were leaving the plantations in such large numbers that the whites became apprehensive not only because of the loss of labor but also because they feared uprisings and acts of revenge.

President Lincoln was under severe pressure from a powerful sector in Congress not only to permit Negroes to enlist but to issue a proclamation setting all Negroes free. Charles Sumner, United States Senator from Massachusetts, was one of the leaders to urge such a policy upon the President. But the President was adamant. He feared, he said, that if blacks were set free and given arms, thousands of white soldiers from the border states would lay down their weapons. In his newspaper Frederick Douglass urged a policy of emancipation, declaring that the "Union cause would never prosper till the war assumed an Anti-Slavery attitude, and the Negro was enlisted on the loyal side." But the President would not be moved.

Some of the Union generals were moving fast, however, much to the embarrassment of the President. In May 1861, the daring, flamboyant Benjamin Butler, in command at Fort Monroe, refused to give up three slaves and, in effect, set them free as contrabands of war to be employed by the Union forces there. In August 1861, General John C. Frémont proclaimed martial law in Missouri and declared as free all slaves who had been confiscated from persons resisting the authority of the United States. Lincoln promptly ordered Frémont to show leniency as to martial law and to modify the emancipation order to conform to existing law. In March 1862, General David Hunter, in command of the Department of the South, began to issue certificates of emancipation to all slaves who had been employed by the Confederacy. In the following month he declared slaves free throughout the Department of the South. This was too much for Lincoln. On May 19 he countermanded the Hunter proclamation, making it clear that neither Hunter nor any other commander had been authorized to emancipate the slaves.

Even the Congress was on the move. In August 1861, it passed the first Confiscation Act, providing that when slaves were engaged in hostile military service, the owners' claims to the labor of such slaves were forfeited. In April 1862, Congress abolished slavery in the District of Columbia; and in the following June it abolished slavery in the territories. Congress took its boldest step toward emancipation when it passed the Second Confiscation Act in July 1862. The act provided that if anyone committed treason, his slaves were free. It further provided that the slaves of all persons supporting rebellion should be "forever free of their servitude, and not again held as slaves." Perhaps now it was time for the President to act.

While Lincoln was unequivocally opposed to slavery, he firmly believed that blacks and whites could not live together once blacks were free. He therefore looked toward the colonization of Negroes outside the United States—in Africa or in the Caribbean area. He attempted to enlist the support of Negroes as well as influential members of Congress in his colonization schemes, but he was totally unsuccessful. The President also believed that there would be less controversy over emancipation if the owners of slaves were compensated for their losses. It was at his insistence that Congress wrote into the act setting slaves free in the District of Columbia a provision for the compensation of their owners. But he was unable to persuade any considerable number of people of the wisdom of such a policy.

Early in the second year of his administration, Lincoln decided that he should emancipate the slaves. It was not only just and right, he was later to say, it was also good policy that would hasten the end of the war. In the late spring of 1862 he began to draft a proclamation setting the slaves free. After the Second Confiscation Act was passed, he rewrote his draft and read it to a meeting of the Cabinet on July 22, 1862. Some members did not like it at all; others advised that he wait until a propitious moment to issue it. This he decided to do. Meanwhile, he was attacked by numerous persons for not issuing such a proclamation. Five days after the Battle of Antietam, he issued the preliminary Emancipation Proclamation, declaring that slaves in states still in rebellion on January 1, 1863, would be set free.

Reaction to the proclamation was mixed. The President's critics said that it was an act of desperation calculated to incite the slaves against their masters. His supporters greeted the proclamation with enthusiasm. Even the abolitionists, while not entirely satisfied, regarded it as a good beginning. When the President issued the final Emancipation Proclamation on January 1, 1863, he cited the states and portions of states where it was applicable. He also invited Negroes to enlist in the armed service of the United States "to garrison forts, positions, stations, and other places, and to man vessels of all sorts in said service." As he put his signature to the proclamation, the President said, "I never in my life felt more certain that I was doing right than I do in signing this paper."

### Negroes Fighting for Freedom and Union

Even before Lincoln issued the Emancipation Proclamation, the War Department had authorized the enlistment of Negroes in the Department of the South, "not exceeding five thousand"; and Ben Butler in Louisiana and Jim Lane in Kansas were receiving Negroes into the army. Early in 1863, black enlistment accelerated. In the North, leading

Negroes like Frederick Douglass acted as recruiting agents, while in the South white soldiers were assigned the task of enlisting slaves. Rallies were held at which speakers urged blacks to enlist; and in Boston, New York, and Philadelphia Negroes flocked to the recruiting stations in large numbers. By the end of the war more than 186,000 blacks had enrolled in the Union army. From the seceded states came 93,000; from the border slave states, 40,000; and from the free states, approximately 53,000. It is possible that the total figure was larger, for some contemporaries insisted that many mulattoes served in white units without being designated as Negroes.

While some whites declined to command the men serving in the group designated as "United States Colored Troops," others were pleased to do so. Among them were such distinguished leaders as Colonel Thomas Wentworth Higginson, of the First South Carolina Volunteers; Colonel Robert Gould Shaw, of the Fifty-Fourth Massachusetts Regiment; and General N. P. Banks, of the First and Third Louisiana Native Guards. There were several outstanding Negro officers as well, among them Captain P. B. S. Pinchback and Major F. E. Dumas of Louisiana; and Major Martin Delany and Captain O. S. B. Wall of the One Hundred and Fourth Regiment. Black hospital surgeons included Charles B. Purvis and John Rapier, while Henry M. Turner, James Underdue, and other Negroes served as chaplains. At the beginning there was discrimination in pay, and the Negro soldiers were understandably bitter in their denunciation of this practice. Finally in 1864 they were successful in their drive to secure equal remuneration.

Negroes saw action in every theater of operation. They were at Milliken's Bend in Louisiana, Olustee in Florida, Vicksburg in Mississippi, and at the siege of Savannah. They took part in the taking of Petersburg and were at the surrender at Appomattox Court House. Many of them were cited for gallantry. Four men of the Massachusetts Fifty-Fourth earned the Gilmore Medal for heroism in the assault on Fort Wagner in which their commanding officer, Colonel Shaw, lost his life. George Washington Williams, in his *History of the Negro Troops in the Rebellion*, says that Negroes saw action in more than 250 skirmishes and that the "roll of honor is luminous with the names of Negro soldiers who, by deeds of personal valor, won the applause of the commanding generals and the Congress of the United States."

Blacks served in other ways. They organized raiding parties, went through Confederate lines to destroy fortifications and supplies, built bulwarks along the coasts and up the rivers, and served as spies and scouts. Some women, such as Harriet Tubman, spied for the Union army. More than 38,000 black soldiers lost their lives in the war, their rate of mortality being about 40 percent greater than that of the white soldiers. It would be difficult for later critics to say that Negroes did not fight for their freedom, just as it was unrealistic for white soldiers to object to participating in the struggle on the grounds that they were not anxious to risk their lives to set idle Negroes free.

If the end of the war marked a victory for the theory of the indestructibility of the Union, it was a signal victory for the cause of freedom as well. The end of the war brought to a close a period of enslavement that had lasted for some 250 years. The desire for freedom had been kept alive throughout that grim and desperate era by those Negroes who demonstrated by their conduct that freedom and the right to it transcended racial lines. The ultimate victory was won, in part, by the black man's struggles through the centuries as well as by his service in the final battles.

## An Uncertain Peace

As the war progressed, Lincoln made many plans. One of them had to do with the settlement of the problems of war once the hostilities ceased. In December 1863, in his Proclamation of Amnesty and Reconstruction, he spelled out his solutions. The spirit was one of leniency. Only a few of the leaders of the Confederacy were not to be restored to the full enjoyment of their rights as citizens, and when 10 percent of the 1860 electorate in a given state had taken the oath of allegiance, the government would be restored. This meant, of course, that the government would be exclusively white. But Lincoln also had plans for Negroes. He hoped that they would be given the franchise; and in 1864 he suggested to the Governor of Louisiana that at least those Negroes of education and property should be permitted to vote. He also hoped, through the Freedmen's Bureau and otherwise, that adequate educational opportunities for Negroes would be provided. On more than one occasion toward the end of the war, he indicated that Negroes should receive the same treatment as other citizens.

The former Confederate states that were restored by Lincoln and, after April 1865 by Johnson, were dominated by former Confederate leaders. They had no intention of extending any semblance of equality to their former slaves. Indeed, they had little enthusiasm for the Thirteenth Amendment that was being ratified during the summer and fall of 1865. It is not surprising, therefore, that the policies formulated by these governments were colored by the view that the blacks were inferior and should be kept subordinate. The new black codes, passed by the southern legislatures in 1865 and 1866, demonstrate this clearly. Negroes could now own and dispose of property, could make contracts and enter into marriage, and were competent witnesses in cases involving Negroes. But the vagrancy laws, authorizing the arrest of Negroes with no visible means of support, were a thinly disguised plan to exploit the Negro working force. Some states forbade Negroes to purchase farmland, while others subjected them to curfew laws, forbade them to possess liquor and firearms, and outlawed acts of insolence on their part. Not one southern state provided for the education of Negroes at the time when schools for whites were being established throughout the South.

When Congress met in December 1865, it was greeted with the news of the black codes and of the domination of the southern state legislatures by former Confederates. Congress refused to seat members of Congress from these states, and many members began to talk openly of the necessity of punishing traitors. Early in the following year the Joint Committee that had been set up by Congress recommended the continuation of the policy of excluding southern members and the enactment of legislation to protect freedmen.

One piece of legislation growing out of these recommendations was the Civil Rights Act of 1866, which guaranteed the rights of all citizens regardless of race. Another was the extension of the Freedmen's Bureau, which was vetoed by the President but finally passed over his veto. A third was the passage of a resolution that incorporated the provisions of the Civil Rights Act and became in 1868 the Fourteenth Amendment. News from the South put Congress in an even more uncompromising mood. The Freedmen's Bureau was helping destitute whites as well as Negroes and was providing schools for the latter where the whites had neglected to do so; but it was being bitterly opposed in virtually every southern community. White northern teachers who had been engaged by the bureau or by religious groups to teach blacks were not only ostracized by the whites, but were in some cases run out of the community. Negroes, moreover, were being subjected to numerous forms of intimidation and terror. In their conventions in 1865 and 1866 they passed resolutions asking the President and Congress for protection. In the spring and summer of 1866 race riots in Memphis and New Orleans confirmed the North's worst fears. A reign of terror was sweeping the South. Something would have to be done.

It was in March 1867 that Congress took over from the President the task of Reconstruction. It reimposed military rule on the South, disfranchised all former Confederates who had voluntarily taken up arms against the United States, called for new governments based on the suffrage of all loyal men regardless of race, and required the ratification of the Fourteenth Amendment as a condition for readmission to the Union. No provisions were made for the economic rehabilitation of the former slaves, no "forty acres and a mule" that some had believed they would receive. Political power lay in the hands of the northern whites who had taken up residence in the South, southern whites who could take the oath that they had not voluntarily fought against the United States, and the Negroes. Economic power, however, remained with the former Confederates who, although restricted momentarily to the sidelines, stood ready to attack and oppose everything that the new political leaders sought to establish.

In the constitutional conventions called to write new organic laws for the former Confederate states, blacks were in the majority only in South Carolina. In Louisiana the forty-nine Negro delegates were equal in number to the whites. In some states, such as Georgia, Alabama, and North Carolina, native whites outnumbered blacks. In others, including Texas and Arkansas, the number of Negroes in the conventions was small. Even so, the conventions were ridiculed as "Ethiopian minstrelsy" and "Ham radicalism." Much more was said about how the delegates looked than about what they did.

The conventions gave the southern states the best constitutions they had ever had. The new documents forbade any race or color distinctions in their suffrage provisions. They provided for free common school systems, although only in South Carolina and

Louisiana were integrated schools attempted. The rights to travel, to a proper trial, and to the fair administration of justice were provided. They eased the burdens of the debtors, but did not provide for the confiscation and redistribution of the land. In each state the black codes were either repealed outright or superseded by new laws. By the summer of 1868 all states except Virginia, Texas, and Mississippi had been readmitted to the Union and their representatives in Congress seated. By 1870 all states were back in the Union.

The period that followed has been described as one of "Negro rule." Yet Negroes were not in control of the state governments at any time anywhere in the South. They held public office and at times played important parts in public life, but only in South Carolina did they ever have a numerical majority in the lower house of the legislature. (See Table I.) From the outset, whites controlled the upper house of that state, and at all times the governor was white. There were other leaders. Negroes were lieutenant governors in 1870 and 1872. From 1868 to 1872 Francis Cardozo was secretary of state, and from 1872 to 1876 he was state treasurer. The situation was not so favorable for Negroes elsewhere in the South, however. In Mississippi, "of seven state officers, only one, that of secretary of state, was filled by a colored man, until 1873 when colored men were elected to three of the seven offices." In some states, very few Negroes held positions of prominence.

TABLE I—RACIAL COMPOSITION OF SOUTHERN LEGISLATURES,
LOWER* HOUSES, 1870–71**

| State | Whites | Negroes |
|---|---|---|
| Alabama | 73 | 27 |
| Arkansas | 71 | 9 |
| Georgia | 149 | 26 |
| Mississippi | 77 | 30 |
| North Carolina | 101 | 1 |
| South Carolina | 49 | 75 |
| Texas | 82 | 8 |
| Virginia | 116 | 21 |

*The upper houses were all predominantly white.
**The Negro Year Book, published by Tuskegee Institute, Tuskegee, Alabama (1921–1922 edition), p. 176.

The Negroes who stood out were largely men of education and experience. Cardozo of South Carolina had been educated at the University of Glasgow and in London. Hiram Revels, elected to the United States Senate from Mississippi, had been educated in a seminary in Ohio and at Knox College in Illinois. James T. Rapier, Negro member of Congress from Alabama, had been sent by his father to school in Canada. Jonathan J. Wright had been educated in Pennsylvania and was a member of the Pennsylvania bar before he migrated to South Carolina, where he became a member of the state supreme court. Some, however, were self-made, like Robert Smalls, who had won fame during the Civil War by piloting the Confederate ship *Planter* out of Charleston harbor and delivering it to Union officials. He was later to sit in Congress. Or, like John R. Lynch, speaker of the House in Mississippi and later a member of Congress, who had sat outside the window of a white schoolhouse and learned everything its students were being taught.

Sixteen Negroes served in Congress between 1869 and 1880. Two of them, Hiram Revels and Blanche K. Bruce, represented Mississippi in the Senate. South Carolina sent six Negroes, the largest number from a single state, to the House of Representatives; but they were not all in the House at the same time. Alabama sent three, while Georgia, Florida, Mississippi, North Carolina, and Louisiana sent one each. Their responsible conduct moved James G. Blaine, their contemporary, to observe, "The colored men who took their seats in both Senate and House did not appear ignorant or helpless. They were as a rule studious, earnest, ambitious men, whose public conduct . . . would be honorable to any race."

It cannot be said that the Reconstruction governments or the Negro leaders were any more corrupt than their contemporaries in other parts of the country. There was some graft in connection with railroad construction, printing contracts, public works, and the like, but wherever there was corruption, it was marked by the participation of all segments of society: former Confederates as well as northern whites and blacks. Corruption was bisectional, bipartisan, and biracial.

If no race or party had a monopoly on public immorality, it can be said that no group was the sole keeper of the public conscience. In the South, however, the groups that opposed Reconstruction tried to assume this role, insisting that "Negro rule" had brought on evils and sufferings and must be destroyed. This viewpoint is what stimulated the growth of the Ku Klux Klan and similar groups after 1867. Rumor had it that the Union League, which had been organized during the war, was teaching blacks not only to be faithful to the Republican party but to regard themselves as the equals of whites in every respect. The Klan lost no time in assailing the league as the enemy of the South. It began to attack white and black members, destroy their property, and whip and sometimes murder them. Politically minded Negroes and so-called Negro militia units were the special objects of attack by Klansmen. Despite the fact that very few troops had ever been in the South after the Civil War, the Klan used any and all armed Negroes as an excuse to attack Negroes generally. Murders, lynchings, drownings, and other hazards faced blacks and whites who had played any part in the rebuilding of the South.

Reconstruction had no chance for success in the South because it did not provide for even a semblance of economic security and independence for Negroes. Although Negroes could vote, they remained at the mercy of those bitterly opposed to their exercising the franchise. It is remarkable that Negroes were able to gain any economic security, but some of them did. By 1866 the freedmen in Florida had secured homesteads covering 160,000 acres of land; and by 1874 the Negroes of Georgia owned more than 350,000 acres. Those with some skills, moreover, such as tailors, caulkers, blacksmiths, and cabinetmakers, were able to secure employment. But the vast majority of Negroes had neither the means nor the skills to achieve economic independence. Most of them were employed by their former masters who could simply threaten them with starvation if they persisted in voting. Meanwhile, northern financiers and industrialists were gradually moving in to establish economic control over the South. Negroes were excluded altogether from the new opportunities; and they could hold their old jobs only if they obeyed the command of their employers to stay out of politics. The economic stranglehold that the whites held over blacks was enough to put an end to Reconstruction.

Indeed, Reconstruction was over in some places almost before it began. If one measures the time from the readmission of the reconstructed states to the time of Democratic victories, one is impressed with how short the period was. While these periods varied from state to state, they were less than a decade, except in Florida, South Carolina, and Louisiana. Even during the time it existed, Reconstruction was not very radical. Segregated schools and laws against intermarriage persisted. There was no confiscation and redistribution of the land. The military occupation was brief and ineffective, and Negroes did not dominate any state governments. The Fourteenth Amendment was pretty much a dead letter; and the Fifteenth Amendment was not being enforced by the Federal Government. In realistic terms, Negroes were only slightly better off than they had been when war came in 1861.

## EARLY STRUGGLES FOR CITIZENSHIP

### Loss of Civil Rights

When chattel slavery was abolished in 1865, some interested observers made dire predictions about the future of the freedmen. Such forebodings reflected serious doubts about the Negro's capacity to survive in his new role. Ignoring the fact that the incredible suffering that took place at the end of the war made little distinction between the races, these observers saw in the destitution and disease among Negroes a portent of their complete extinction. An eminent white southerner, Dr. C. K. Marshall of Mississippi, echoed this view when he said in 1866, "In all probability . . . on the morning of the first of January, 1920, the colored population in the South will scarcely be counted." While most Americans were uncertain about the future of Negroes in the United States, they were not nearly as pessimistic regarding numbers as Dr. Marshall. Most of them seemed to agree that the Negro American would at least survive; and many entertained the hope that he could be utilized, if not exploited, in the advancement of American civilization. In fact, Negroes not only survived, but demonstrated a remarkable capacity to thrive even in an atmosphere where their freedom was continually compromised. When the war came in 1861 there were approximately 4,441,830 Negroes in the United States, of whom 3,953,000 were slaves. By 1900 the Negro population had virtually doubled.

While the problem of survival was early solved once and for all, the problem of the status of blacks was a continuing one. Toward the end of Reconstruction, as the collapse of the enforcement of federal laws deprived Negroes of their opportunity to vote, their enjoyment of other rights was also being challenged. Congress made one last effort to protect them. In May 1870, Senator Charles Sumner introduced the most far-reaching civil rights bill that was to be considered by Congress until 1963. The bill provided for equal accommodations in railroads, steamboats, public conveyances, hotels, licensed theaters, houses of public entertainment, common schools, all institutions of learning authorized by law, churches, cemetery associations, and juries in federal and state courts. For a time the bill's fate remained uncertain. When it finally became law in 1875, it declared that the United States should "mete out equal and exact justice to all, of whatever nativity, race, color, or persuasion, religious or political." From the beginning the climate in the country was not favorable to the enforcement of the act, which had already been watered down by the deletion of the provision to desegregate the schools. During its eight years of life the act provided little protection for Negroes because of the general failure of the Federal Government to enforce it.

That the act would ultimately be tested in the courts was a foregone conclusion; and its unhappy fate was almost as certain. Of the incidents involved in the cases that came to the Supreme Court under the Civil Rights Act, one involved the use of a parlor car by a Negro in Tennessee, another involved the denial of hotel accommodations for Negroes in one northern state, others involved the use of public facilities in Missouri, California, Kentucky, and New York. In handing down the decision, Mr. Justice Bradley, speaking for the majority, held the relevant provisions of the act unconstitutional. Congress could enact legislation to meet the exigency of state action adverse to the rights of citizens as secured by the Fourteenth Amendment, he said. But Congress could not properly "cover the whole domain of rights appertaining to life, liberty, and property, defining them and providing for their vindication."

The Court's limitation of the scope of the Fourteenth Amendment as set down in the civil-rights case decision seemed to assure that there could be no significant advancement of Negroes toward full citizenship. Negroes greeted the ruling with discouragement, remembering that the Court had never been a source of strength, as far as they were concerned. The Dred Scott decision in 1857 had declared that Negroes were not citizens. The decisions in the Reese and Cruikshank cases in 1876 indicated that Congress could not enact legislation to protect the rights guaranteed in the Fifteenth Amendment. Now, in the civil-rights cases, the Fourteenth Amendment was rendered ineffective. Small wonder that blacks saw this as a reversal in the march toward equality, if not a step backwards toward slavery. T. T. Allain, a Negro leader in Louisiana, said that the civil-rights decision showed that whites of the North and South had allied "to leave the Negro to fend for himself." T. Thomas Fortune, a Negro journalist, said that Negroes felt that they had been "baptized in ice water." John Mercer Langston, who in 1889 would become the only Negro ever elected to Congress from Virginia, called the decision "a stab in the back."

The attitudes of vast numbers of the country's influential white people had as much to do with defining the status of the Negro as anything that the Supreme Court or any other branch of the Federal Government was doing. The dark cloud of assumed racial differences became more ominous than ever, bespeaking a new, frightening conclusion that many white Americans had reached: that racial differences were normal and natural and the Negro American was a classic example of the hopeless inferiority of a whole race of people. This belief in Anglo-Saxon superiority was an offshoot of Darwinism and obsessed many whites in the last quarter of the nineteenth century. Whites were in a dominant position because they were the superior race; they were the fittest. Primitives such as Negroes were in an arrested stage of childhood or adolescence and could never gain the full stature of manhood. Distinguished white scholars argued that it was absurd to attempt to change the natural order of things. As early as 1876 William G. Sumner advocated the restoration of "home rule" in the South because Reconstruction had attempted the impossible in trying to reverse the natural course of things in which superior whites ruled over inferior blacks.

The leading and most-respected literary journals of the country reflected the view that blacks were inferior and did not possess rights which should be protected by government. In the last two decades of the nineteenth century such journals as *Harper's, Scribner's* and the *Atlantic Monthly* strained their own ample ingenuity by portraying blacks in the most unfavorable light. In an exhaustive study of the period, *The Negro in American Life and Thought*, Rayford W. Logan has shown that every possible insulting term was used by these journals in reference to Negroes. They were made to appear ludicrous by the bestowal of absurd titles upon them. Invariably they were described as ugly. In articles, stories, anecdotes, poems, and cartoons, Negroes were portrayed as superstitious, dull, stupid, imitative, ignorant, happy-go-lucky, improvident, lazy, immoral, and criminal. White southern writers helped to further these views. In his *The Leopard's Spots: A Romance of the White Man's Burden* and in other works, Thomas Dixon, Jr. described in vivid terms the "base" character of Negroes. This, he argued, justified almost any degradation they received at the hands of their white superiors.

It followed that if Negroes were as undesirable and unequipped for civilization as the writers of the North and South claimed, they were not fit associates for white people and should be segregated. There had been some segregation, both in law and in practice before and during Reconstruction. But, as C. Vann Woodward has pointed out in *The Strange Career of Jim Crow*, it was not nearly as extensive as it later became. The major Protestant churches were not only divided as between North and South even before the war, but within the South there were separate white and Negro Protestant churches. From the first, the public schools of the South were segregated with few exceptions. The armed services were segregated during the Civil War and remained so during the following years. The first state segregation statutes were those of Mississippi and Florida in 1865. The Tennessee Law of 1881, sometimes referred to as the first Jim Crow Law, directed railroad companies to provide separate cars or portions of cars for first-class Negro passengers, instead of relegating them to second-class accommodations, as had been the custom.

In the ensuing twenty years, the enforced separation of blacks and whites on public carriers and almost everywhere else became a major preoccupation of many southern legislators, although opposition on the part of some articulate whites, such as George W. Cable, continued until the end of the century. By 1892 six southern states had joined Tennessee in segregating blacks on public carriers—Texas, Louisiana, Alabama, Arkansas, Georgia, and Kentucky. In some states, such legislation met with substantial opposition on the part of blacks and their white supporters. In Louisiana a Negro representative declared that the segregation law would humiliate Negroes and "make them appear before the world as a treacherous and dangerous class of people." In Arkansas a Negro member of the legislature sought to ridicule a segregation bill's supporters by insisting that if whites did not want to associate with blacks, there should be laws to divide the streets and sidewalks so that blacks could go on one side and white people on the other. "He would like to see an end put to all intercourse between white and colored people by day, and especially by night."

As the pattern of segregation took shape in some states, pressure for various forms of segregation mounted in other states. South Carolina passed a law segregating blacks and whites on railroads in 1898. North Carolina and Virginia enacted similar legislation in 1899 and 1900 respectively. When Oklahoma entered the union in 1907 every conceivable form of segregation had already been provided for. Segregation was spreading to other areas relating to transportation. In 1888 the railroad commission of Mississippi was authorized to designate separate waiting rooms for blacks and whites. By 1893 the railroad companies, on their own initiative, were doing the same thing in South Carolina. By 1907 segregation had been enacted into law in all southern states on streetcars, in penitentiaries, county jails, convict camps, institutions for the blind and deaf, hospitals for the insane, and other institutions.

While the southern states were in the process of enacting laws to separate the races, the Supreme Court in the decision of *Plessy v. Ferguson* gave their cause a significant boost. In 1890 Louisiana had enacted a law providing that "all railway companies carrying passengers in their coaches in this state, shall provide separate but equal accommodations for the white and colored races." When Plessy, whose appearance was as white as that of any person in New Orleans but who was known to have Negro blood, boarded a coach reserved for whites, he was ordered to the "colored" coach. When he refused to move, he was arrested and charged with violating the law. Plessy argued that the Louisiana statute was in conflict with the Thirteenth Amendment abolishing slavery and the Fourteenth Amendment, which prohibited certain restrictive legislation on the part of the states. The Supreme Court did not agree. Speaking for the Court, Mr. Justice Bradley interpreted the statute as intending to enforce "absolute equality of the two races before the law" while recognizing fundamental distinctions between them. Thus the doctrine of "separate but equal" became the law of the land and gave moral as well as legal support to those who were engaged in enacting segregation statutes.

Meanwhile, the southern states had undertaken to disfranchise Negroes in order to make certain that they would not have the political strength to resist the move to make permanent their status as second-class citizens. Advocates of disfranchisement had to be certain that they did not contravene the Fifteenth Amendment or antagonize illiterate, poor whites. As early as 1886, sentiment in Mississippi, where a majority of the population was Negro, was strong for constitutional revision. A convention met in 1890 for the primary purpose of disfranchising the Negro. A suffrage amendment was written which imposed a poll tax of two dollars, excluded voters convicted of bribery, burglary, theft, arson, perjury, murder, and bigamy, and also barred all who could not read any section of the state constitution, or understand it when read, or give a reasonable interpretation of it. Before the convention convened, Negroes from forty counties met and protested to President Harrison their impending disfranchisement. The President did nothing; and since the new constitution was never submitted for ratification but simply put into effect, its opponents had no chance of working to defeat it.

South Carolina followed Mississippi by disfranchising Negroes in 1895. Ben Tillman, who had initiated the campaign for disfranchisement, left the United States Senate and returned to the convention in South Carolina to push through the desired revision of the constitution. The new clause called for two years' residence, a poll tax of one dollar, the ability to read and write the constitution or the ownership of property worth $300, and the disqualification of convicts. Negro delegates bitterly denounced the move. In answer to Tillman's charge that Negroes had done nothing to demonstrate their capacity for government, Thomas E. Miller, a leading Negro in the state, replied that Negroes were largely responsible for the "laws relative to finance, the building of penal and charitable institutions and, greatest of all, the establishment of the public school system." The story was essentially the same in Louisiana, where in 1898 a new device, the "Grandfather Clause," was written into the constitution. This called for an addition to the permanent registration list of the names of all males whose fathers or grandfathers were qualified to vote on January 1, 1867. At that time, of course, no Negroes in Louisiana were qualified to vote. Blacks, but not whites, therefore had to comply with the educational and property requirements. By 1910 Negroes had also been effectively disfranchised in Virginia, Georgia, North Carolina, Alabama, and Oklahoma.

By the end of the century Negroes had lost most of the civil rights they had ever enjoyed, however fleetingly. They had been denied the use of public accommodations, they had been disfranchised, and the concept of "separate but equal" had given the whites an opportunity to reduce black schools to a level of total inadequacy. In South Carolina, where Negroes constituted 61 percent of the school population, they received 21 percent of the school funds. Already separation seemed to be a guarantee not only of inequality in education but of a permanently inferior status in American life.

## Out of the Mainstream

The end of Reconstruction brought little improvement in the social and economic status of Negroes. There was one small glimmer of hope, however. While southern whites were not willing to appropriate very much for the education of blacks, they seemed less opposed than formerly to the support of Negro education by northern philanthropic and religious organizations. At the same time, many blacks viewed education as their greatest single opportunity to escape the indignities and proscriptions of an oppressive white South. Negro parents thus sent their children to school in increasing numbers at great sacrifice to themselves; and while the schools were not excellent, they did provide the rudiments of an education. Religious groups such as the American Missionary Association and the Freedmen's Aid Society of the Methodist Church continued the work of the defunct Freedmen's Bureau. Philanthropic agencies such as the George Peabody Fund, the Anna T. Jeanes Fund, and the Rockefeller's General Education Board gave attention to special problems of Negro education such as teacher training and vocational education. Since many of the grants made by philanthropists were on the condition that local school boards and agencies would match their gift, they had the effect of stimulating a limited amount of local support for Negro education.

Negroes themselves were contributing substantially to the support of their own schools and colleges. At the Sixth Atlanta Conference for the Study of Negro Problems in 1901 it was reported that between 1870 and 1899 Negroes paid a total of $25,000,000 in direct school taxes, while the indirect taxes they paid amounted to more than $45,000,000. Negroes also had paid more than $15,000,000 in tuition and fees to private institutions. The report concluded, "It is a conservative statement to say . . . that American Negroes have in a generation paid directly forty millions of dollars in hard-earned cash for educating their children." The institutions, meanwhile, had done much to sustain themselves. The Fisk Jubilee Singers had gone out in 1871 and had raised more than enough money to construct the first important building at that young university. Other institutions had sent out speakers, demonstrators, and others in the effort to gain support. Self-help became an important principle in the early days of Negro schools and colleges.

The results of the efforts of Negroes to secure an education were gratifying. In 1900 there were 28,560 Negro teachers and more than 1,500,000 Negro children in school. Thirty-four institutions for Negroes were giving collegiate training; and more Negroes were entering the institutions of higher education in the North. There were four state colleges for Negroes—in Virginia, Arkansas, Georgia, and Delaware. By 1900 more than 2,000 Negroes had graduated from institutions of higher learning, while more than 700 were in college at the time. As Negroes manifested an avid interest in education, there were some whites who questioned the wisdom of their securing an education to live in a society in which they were not part of the mainstream.

Even among Negroes there was no agreement as to the amount and type of education Negroes should seek. Booker T. Washington, who founded Tuskegee Institute in 1881, thought that Negroes could be most effective and would be acceptable in the southern communities if they sought to provide many of the services and much of the produce that the white community needed. He emphasized the intelligent management of farms, ownership of land, proficiency in mechanics, domestic service, and the professions. On numerous occasions, and especially in his celebrated speech at Atlanta in 1895, he assured the whites that the blacks were their friends, that they did not seek social equality but merely an opportunity to serve. His advocacy of vocational education for blacks was hailed by whites in the North and in the South. They came to regard him as the wisest and most reliable spokesman of his race.

Some blacks, however, preferred to speak for themselves. Among them was William Edward Burghardt DuBois, a young Negro trained at Fisk, Harvard (where he received the degree of doctor of philosophy), and Berlin. In books, essays, and addresses DuBois criticized what he viewed as the narrow educational program of Washington, which he considered too predominantly economic in its objectives. He accused Washington of preaching "a gospel of Work and Money to such an extent as apparently almost completely to overshadow the higher aims of life." DuBois also criticized the manner in which Washington ignored or winked at the white South's denial of civil rights for blacks. It was this kind of conciliation, he insisted, that had resulted in the disfranchisement of the Negro and the enactment of discriminatory legislation of many kinds. Despite such criticisms, Washington remained the most important and indeed the most powerful Negro in the United States until his death in 1915. It was during his ascendancy, however, that lynchings of blacks reached a new high, and that Negroes were effectively disfranchised and systematically excluded from American industry and American labor unions.

In 1880 some 75 percent of the Negroes in the United States were still in the former Confederate states and were primarily engaged in agricultural work. Most of them were without capital with which to purchase land and were compelled to engage in various forms of tenancy and sharecropping. As farm workers their incomes were meager. In 1902 agricultural laborers in South Carolina were receiving ten dollars per month, while those in New York were receiving twenty-six dollars per month. Some, however, accumulated enough capital to purchase farms. In 1890 Negroes owned 120,738 farms; by 1910 they owned 218,972 farms, with the average size less than ten acres. Booker Washington, through the farmers' conference at Tuskegee, sought to eliminate "the evils of the mortgage system, the one-room cabin, buying on credit," and the like; but it was a difficult task in the face of persistent hostility from the white community.

When industry first came to the South, Negroes for the most part were excluded from the job market. The iron industry was growing in Tennessee and Alabama, cloth was being manufactured in the Carolinas, and the business of transporting manufactured goods to the southern consumer was becoming a major economic activity. In 1891 some 196 industrial employers of the South were using only 7,395 Negroes, largely as menials. Ten years later the number had increased substantially, and some were employed in cottonseed-oil mills, sawmills, and furniture factories. By 1910 Negro factory workers had increased to more than 350,000. Prejudice against the black worker and the refusal of many whites, North and South, to work with blacks served to exclude many Negroes from labor unions. Manufacturers thus had two excuses to justify their exclusion of Negroes from greater employment: they were temperamentally unfit, according to no less an authority than *The Manufacturer's Record*, and whites would not work with them.

But Negroes were, in some instances, contributing to the growing industrialization of the United States. Jan E. Matzeliger, a Negro from Dutch Guiana, invented the shoe-lasting machine which was purchased by the United Shoe Machinery Company of Boston. In 1884 John P. Parker invented a "screw for tobacco presses," and through his own company made many presses. Elijah McCoy patented fifty different inventions relating principally to the automatic lubrication of machines. Granville Woods made significant contributions in the fields of electricity, steam boilers, and automatic air brakes. Several of his inventions were assigned to the General Electric Company, the Westinghouse Air Brake Company, and the American Bell Telephone Company.

Many Negroes concluded that since they were excluded from the mainstream of American economic life, they should organize and promote businesses of their own. It was with this in mind that Booker Washington called a group of Negro businessmen together in 1900 in Boston and organized the National Negro Business League. Washington urged Negroes to enter a wide variety of business fields. Either in response to Washington's urging or because they already realized the importance of such moves, many Negroes set up their own commercial ventures. They operated grocery and merchandise stores, they were restaurant operators, caterers, bakers, tailors, builders, and contractors. Some operated shirt factories, cotton mills, rubber-goods shops, lumber mills, and carpet factories. They were also engaged in cooperative enterprises; and some accumulated considerable wealth. Madam C. J. Walker founded a hair-and-skin-preparation business and made a fortune. Negro banking and insurance companies in Richmond, Atlanta, Washington, Birmingham, and Montgomery achieved both stability and respect.

Such scattered signs of progress and prosperity were not enough for many Negroes who remained dissatisfied with their lot in their communities. Their political and social degradation had not been relieved by their meager economic gains, and some of them decided to leave the South for other parts of the country. In 1879 and 1880 thousands of Negroes left the lower South and took up residence in the North and West, a trend that continued for the next several decades. In spite of the hostility and rejection they met at the hands of northern labor unions and industrialists, they continued to believe that their opportunities were greater anywhere than in the South. Neither the findings of a congressional investigation into the causes of black migration nor promises by southern whites of good treatment and high wages could dissuade them. They were in search of an entrée into the mainstream of American life, which seemed more and more like a will-o'-the-wisp.

## The Black World

Whites in the South and in the North maintained a discreet distance from blacks and excluded them from all areas of their social activities. Negroes were thus compelled to work out their own means of survival in a hostile world, and this led to the creating of institutions and activities that, in turn, created a black world. One of the mainstays in the process of building up group spirit and promoting self-help was the Negro church. Seeing that they were not welcome among the white Baptists, Negroes organized the National Baptist Convention in 1886. Soon the National Baptist Publishing House began to circulate Sunday School and other religious literature among Negroes. The older black denominations, African Methodists and Colored Methodists, continued their activities; and in the cities the churches worked to help Negroes adjust to their new environment. In New York, Detroit, Chicago, St. Louis, and other metropolitan areas, the Negro churches established employment bureaus, maintained schools for domestic training, and organized various clubs for boys and girls. In Atlanta Dr. H. H. Proctor's Congregational Church organized a day nursery, kindergarten, gymnasium, and school of music; while in Springfield, Massachusetts, Dr. W. N. DeBerry led his Congregational members in the establishment of a home for working girls and a welfare league for women.

Fraternal organizations with auxiliary activities such as insurance and burial societies became numerous during the period. The Knights of Pythias and the Knights of Tabor competed for membership among Negro men. Others, such as the Independent Order of St. Luke and the Order of True Reformers, were open to both men and women. Out of some of these organizations came the founders of important insurance companies. S. W. Rutherford left the True Reformers and organized the National Benefit Life Insurance Company of Washington, D. C. In Durham, North Carolina, John Merrick, who had also been a True Reformer, joined several other businessmen to establish the North Carolina Mutual Life Insurance Company. These and similar businesses grew into important social and economic institutions, providing a variety of benefits for the black community.

As Negroes became better educated and more articulate they began to write extensively, and most of their writings dealt with their being blacks in a white world. Frederick Douglass and Booker T. Washington wrote their autobiographies. Henry O. Flipper wrote of his experiences as a Negro cadet at West Point. In the effort to refute the arguments of some whites that Negroes had contributed nothing to American civilization, several writers published histories of the Negro in the United States. In 1883 George Washington Williams published his *History of the Negro Race in America* in two volumes.

Histories by E. A. Johnson, W. H. Crogman, and Booker T. Washington soon followed. In 1896 W. E. B. DuBois brought out his *Suppression of the African Slave Trade*, which became the first work in the Harvard Historical Studies. Negroes were also writing about "the Negro problem," as is evidenced by T. T. Fortune's *Black and White* in 1884 and *The Negro in Politics* in 1885. Meanwhile, Charles W. Chesnutt rose to prominence as a novelist with such works as *The House Behind the Cedars, The Marrow of Tradition*, and *The Conjure Woman*. Perhaps no Negro writer of the period had a greater impact than Paul Laurence Dunbar, whose poems won the critical acclaim of such people as William Dean Howells, and whose *Lyrics of the Lowly* and *Oak and Ivy* were widely read at the turn of the century.

Throughout this period Negro newspaper editors remained preoccupied with the problem of fighting for a larger place for Negroes in American life. Magazines like the *Southern Workman*, published at Hampton Institute, and the *A.M.E. Review*, begun in 1884, were concerned primarily with educational, literary, and religious matters. In 1900 there were three black daily newspapers—in Norfolk, Kansas City, and Washington—and 150 weekly newspapers. Some were widely read and provoked considerable discussion. In Boston, George Forbes and Monroe Trotter were publishing the *Guardian*, which led the fight against Booker Washington. In the nation's capital, the Washington *Bee* was vigorous and outspoken, and in New York City *The Age*, edited by T. Thomas Fortune, was outstanding.

Nothing suggests the extent to which the Negro was still outside the mainstream of American life more than the attention given to the Negro problem by conferences and conventions of whites and blacks during this period. At the Lake Mohonk Conference on the Negro Question in 1890, white citizens discussed the educational and economic problems affecting Negroes. The Hampton Conference, conducted in part by Negroes, dealt with similar problems, as did the Capon Springs Conference. There were, moreover, the Tuskegee Conference, conducted by Booker Washington, and the Atlanta University Conferences on the Negro Problem, conducted by W. E. B. DuBois. Out of some of them, such as the Atlanta Conferences, came significant published studies. Out of all of them came much talk. Out of none of them came any effective solutions to the many problems that beset Negro Americans at the turn of the century.

## NEW PATTERNS OF RACIAL ADJUSTMENT

### Urban Problems

Writing shortly after the turn of the century, W. E. B. DuBois said that the problem of the twentieth century would be the problem of the color line. It was the experience of the closing years of the nineteenth century that prompted DuBois to make this observation. It was not merely the Supreme Court decision in the Plessy case, or the 1898 riot in Wilmington, North Carolina, or the increase in the number of lynchings each year. It was also the employment of the total political and legal apparatus of many of the states for the purpose of making impossible full citizenship for blacks. It was meek acquiescence of the Federal Government in the South's so-called "legal" disfranchisement of Negroes through state constitutional amendments that were as transparent as they were specious. It was the use of law-enforcement officers to sanction the denial of the rights of Negroes. It was the perfection of the machinery of segregation and discrimination in many parts of the country. It was the determination to frustrate those Negroes who, like so many other Americans, believed that their major problems could be solved in the cities to which they flocked in ever-increasing numbers.

The trickle of Negroes northward that began in the late 1870s was almost a steady stream by 1900. The stimulus was not only the depressing conditions of the South but the opportunities that Negroes thought they would have in the North. Agents of northern employment offices or northern factory owners went to southern farms as well as southern towns to lure Negro workers to the North. As long as these agents could evade hostile local police or other authorities, their task was not very difficult. Thousands of Carolina and Georgia Negroes migrated to the industrial Northeast. Similar groups from the middle South states—Alabama, Mississippi, and Louisiana—went to Ohio, Indiana, Michigan, and Illinois cities. Those who did not dare venture so far went to Atlanta, New Orleans, Louisville, and other thriving southern cities.

By 1900 only 27.7 percent of the Negro population was urban, but this represented a significant increase over the situation in 1860, when approximately 16 percent of the nation's Negroes were living in cities. In 1900 there were seventy-two cities with more than 5,000 Negroes, while six cities—Philadelphia, New York, Baltimore, Washington, Memphis, and New Orleans—each had more than 50,000. There were several cities of moderate size, all in the South, where Negroes outnumbered the whites. Among them were Charleston, Savannah, Jacksonville, Montgomery, Shreveport, Baton Rouge, and Vicksburg.

As the Negro urban population grew, its problems multiplied. There was no longer the stultifying control by the southern plantation owner, and the opportunities for education were somewhat improved. But labor unions were as hostile to blacks as they were to other newly arrived groups. Most of them excluded blacks from membership; and when Negroes accepted employment to break a strike, labor leaders accused them of not understanding the principles of trade unionism. Likewise, blacks arriving in the city fresh from the country discovered that all but a few sections of the city were closed to them for housing. And when they crowded into the few areas that were open to them, where housing was often already substandard and falling apart, they were accused of destroying property values and running down the neighborhood. It was this attitude that led to the passing of the first housing-segregation law in Louisville, Kentucky, in 1912. The law provided that city blocks containing a majority of whites were designated as white blocks; and those with a majority of blacks were black blocks. No blacks could move into the white blocks, and vice versa. Other cities, including Baltimore, Richmond, and Atlanta, followed Louisville's lead; and Negro ghettos, sanctioned by law, became well-established in many parts of the country.

One of the most characteristic manifestations of the problem of Negro assimilation in the urban community at the beginning of the century was the race riot. Lynchings and burnings were rural fare; but rioting, on an even larger scale than had occurred in Philadelphia and New York before the Civil War, became the typical expression of resentment against the urban Negro of the twentieth century. While there were outbreaks in numerous small southern towns in the first decade of the century, the Atlanta riot of 1906 was the largest southern disturbance of the period. For months the city had been lashed into a fury of race hatred by loose talk and by the movement to disfranchise blacks. In September Atlanta newspapers told of four successive but entirely unsubstantiated assaults on white women by Negroes. The country people, in town on the last Saturday of that month, joined the urban element in creating an outraged, semihysterical mob. Whites began to attack every black they saw. Many innocent persons were beaten; others were dragged from vehicles. For several days rioting continued; factories were closed and all transportation stopped. Many Negroes were killed, and there was a substantial destruction of Negro property. When it was all over, the whites confessed their shame and condemned the rioters. But a scar remained on black-white relationships in the fastest-growing city of the South.

Rioting in northern cities was equally common. Springfield, Ohio, alone had two riots within a few years—in 1904 and 1906. The northern riot that shook the entire country, however, occurred in Springfield, Illinois, in August 1908. A white woman claimed that she had been dragged from her bed and raped by a Negro, who was then arrested and jailed. Later, before a special grand jury, the woman admitted that she had in fact been severely beaten by a white man whose identity she refused to disclose and that the black defendant had no connection whatever with the incident. By this time, however, feeling was running high. Mobs gathered, raided stores, secured guns and other weapons, and began to destroy Negro businesses and drive Negroes from their homes. Before order was restored by more than 5,000 militia, two Negroes had been lynched, four white men killed, and more than seventy persons injured.

Thus in the early decades of the twentieth century Negroes found scant acceptance in the American urban community. They were unable to impose their claim to equal treatment in the labor market; and in the laissez-faire atmosphere that prevailed, the Government declined to come to their rescue. Indeed, in 1894 Congress had repealed much of the Civil Rights Act of 1866 that might have been invoked for the protection of Negroes. Theodore Roosevelt, who had become President in 1901 and on whom many Negroes had pinned their hopes, had proved a great disappointment. He talked repeatedly about justice, but did little for the Negro aside from inviting Booker T. Washington to dine at the White House. Negroes had already come to the conclusion that Harold Laski was to reach much later: that Roosevelt had great "verbal audacity" but "a relative caution in action." Black citizens continued to suffer numerous political disabilities and enormous personal indignities, including living in ghettos, and they were lucky to escape with their lives from the violent attacks of white mobs. What little relief they got came from organized groups of whites and blacks who could no longer tolerate the conditions that prevailed.

The tragic events of the early years of the century caused many blacks to lose faith in government at every level. They no longer felt that any whites could be trusted to act in their behalf. As one Negro put it, "In the degree that the southern people stand by in silence and see the Negro stripped of his civil and political rights by a band of unscrupulous men . . . they compromise their own civil and political freedom. . . . If by a mere technicality one class of citizens can be deprived of their rights and immunities . . . what is to prevent any other class from sharing the same fate?" It was at this point that some blacks began to think in terms of an action program capable of formulating specific plans to secure full citizenship for all Americans, black and white. Soon groups as far apart as the New England Suffrage League and the Georgia Equal Rights League had resolved to press for equal rights for blacks.

## New Organizational Efforts

The most articulate spokesman in this new drive for full citizenship was W. E. B. DuBois, who in 1905 called a conference of Negro leaders to meet in Niagara Falls, Canada, to formulate a program. After discussing their numerous problems, the delegates drew up a "Declaration of Principles," which stated, among other things:

> We believe that Negroes should protest emphatically and continually against the curtailment of their political rights. We believe in manhood suffrage; we believe that no man is so good, intelligent, or wealthy as to be entrusted wholly with the welfare of his neighbor.

The group demanded equal economic opportunity, equal education, a fair administration of justice, and an end to segregation. For the next three years members of the group, now calling itself "The Niagara Movement," met and renewed their protests against injustice. By 1908 the group had won the respect and support of large numbers of Negroes, including the Equal Suffrage League, the National Association of Colored Women's Clubs, and college and high school students. And it had begun to challenge the constitutionality of some of the Jim Crow laws of the southern states. By now, however, several of its leading members had become involved in another movement which was soon to eclipse the Niagara Movement.

The Springfield riot of 1908 plunged blacks into the deepest despair and shocked the sensibilities of many whites. In a widely read article, "Race War in the North," William English Walling deplored the conduct of the white people of Springfield and called on the responsible whites of the country to make amends. In 1909, in response to Walling's call, a small group met and formulated plans for an organization to fight for the rights of Negroes. May 1910 marked the birth of the National Association for the Advancement of Colored People (NAACP). It was a group composed of prominent whites as well as distinguished blacks; and it pledged itself to work for the abolition of all forced segregation, equal education for black and white children, and the enforcement of the Fourteenth and Fifteenth Amendments. Moorfield Storey of Boston was its first president, and DuBois became director of publicity and research, and editor of its house organ, the *Crisis*.

In its first year of existence the NAACP launched a program aimed at widening industrial opportunities for Negroes, seeking greater police protection for Negroes in the South, and launching a crusade against lynching and lawlessness. Instrumental in carrying out this program were the *Crisis* and the Legal Redress Committee, of which a New York lawyer, Arthur B. Spingarn, was chairman. White and black attorneys worked closely with Spingarn, and within a short time plans were made to test the constitutionality of state laws and state constitutions discriminating against Negroes. Spingarn's committee reasoned that even if the Supreme Court was hostile to efforts by Congress to implement civil rights—as was inferred from the decision in the Civil Rights cases of 1883—perhaps it could be persuaded to frown upon the efforts of states to eliminate Negroes from consideration as citizens.

The NAACP contended that the Negro's best opportunity to protect his rights lay in his exercise of the franchise. It was fitting, therefore, that the organization's first efforts would be against franchise restrictions. In 1910 it began its attack on the Grandfather Clause of the Oklahoma state constitution, assailing that provision which stated that "no person who was, on January 1, 1866, or who was at any time prior thereto, entitled to vote under any form of government . . . and no lineal descendant of such persons shall be denied to register and vote because of his inability to read and write" any section of the state constitution. In 1915 the United States Supreme Court, in its decision in *Guinn v. United States*, pronounced as unconstitutional the suffrage provision of the Oklahoma constitution. "We seek in vain," Chief Justice White declared, "for any ground which would sustain any other interpretation but that the provision . . . was adopted . . . to make [those conditions] the basis of the right to suffrage conferred in direct and positive disregard of the Fifteenth Amendment." In another case two years later, *Buchanan v. Warley*, the Supreme Court outlawed the city ordinances requiring blacks and whites to live in separate blocks in the city.

Fair administration of justice was one of the most serious obstacles to the Negro's enjoyment of full citizenship. The NAACP was determined to put an end to the abuse of the Negro's rights in the courts; and it found ample opportunity to launch its crusade in Elaine, Arkansas. During a riot that occurred after a group of white men fired on an assemblage of blacks in a church, one white man was killed. In the days that followed, Negroes were hunted down and slaughtered like animals. During the melee, another white man was killed, for which crime several Negroes were arrested and charged with murder. The Negroes were tried in the midst of a surging, unruly mob. They had no opportunity to consult with counsel, and witnesses were not called. The trial lasted forty-five minutes; the jury deliberated less than five. The verdict was murder in the first degree. When the NAACP took the case to the Supreme Court on the ground that the defendants had been denied due process of law, the Court agreed. Justice Holmes was appalled by the flagrant denial of the rights of the five defendants; and the decision of the state court was reversed and a new trial ordered.

The NAACP also sought to combat, head-on, the violence against Negroes that was increasing almost everywhere. Toward this end, it organized a parade in New York City protesting the terrorization of the Negro community during the riot in East St. Louis, Illinois, in 1917. Two years later it held a national conference on lynching, at which the chief speaker was Charles Evans Hughes. Shortly thereafter, it embarked on a campaign to secure the passage of a federal antilynching law. In 1921 a Missouri representative, L. C. Dyer, introduced such a bill in the lower house of Congress, and it passed by a vote of 230–119. When it reached the floor of the Senate, however, the southern members succeeded in organizing a filibuster that ultimately prevented a vote on the measure.

Economic opportunities for Negroes were even less certain, if such was possible, than their enjoyment of their civil rights. Their situation as farm employees and share-croppers was deteriorating; and in the new southern industries exclusion or discrimination continued. Migration to the cities often aggravated their problems. Employment opportunities were fewer than the number of people moving to urban areas; and Negroes found great difficulty in securing anything except the more onerous and less attractive jobs, if they were lucky enough to secure anything at all. They continued to live around the "ragged edge of industry" with organized labor evincing a pronounced hostility. Only the Cigarmakers' International Union and the United Mine Workers of America seemed to welcome Negroes, although some other unions had Negro members. The situation was somewhat better for Negro women who found employment as maids and household servants; and this caused a larger number of women than men to come to the cities. The implications of this situation in terms of family disorganization, juvenile delinquency, and other problems were considerable.

Although the NAACP included in its program a plan to widen industrial opportunities for Negroes, it had neither the time nor the resources to do much in this area. More and more it concentrated on the question of civil rights. The need for organized effort in the economic and social spheres was urgent, however. In 1905 two organizations were established in New York to deal with the major economic and housing problems facing Negroes. They were the Committee for Improving Industrial Conditions of Negroes in New York City and the National League for the Protection of Colored Women. Soon the two began working together; and in 1911 they created the National League on Urban Conditions, commonly known as the National Urban League. The new organization undertook to open up new opportunities for Negroes in industry and to assist newly arrived Negroes in their problems of adjustment in the cities. Branches were established in many of the larger metropolitan areas, with programs for meeting the migrants, directing them to jobs and lodgings, and offering information on how to live in the city. It also did an effective job in bringing the employer and employee together and easing the difficulties of mutual adjustment.

There were numerous other efforts on the national and local levels to assist Negroes with their problems. The Young Men's Christian Association and the Young Women's Christian Association began to organize Negro branches and provide recreational as well as religious opportunities in the Negro community. Civic clubs for Negro men and women took on special projects designed to raise the Negro's level of aspiration. Some of them fostered civic pride by encouraging home improvement, while others grappled with the more serious problems of crime and juvenile delinquency. In some northern communities Negro political groups were already attempting to capitalize on the concentration of Negroes and elect Negroes to local offices.

## Making the World Safe for Democracy

Negroes had never been wholly politically inactive, despite the concerted efforts of the southern whites and some of their northern friends to make them so. During the Roosevelt and Taft administrations, blacks made themselves felt in some sectors of the Republican Party, but their disillusionment deepened when neither Roosevelt nor Taft did much to help them secure their civil rights. In 1912 they were willing to turn to any group that might advance their cause. To some blacks, Woodrow Wilson offered a glimmer of hope when he said during his campaign that he wished to see "justice done to the colored people in every matter; and not mere grudging justice, but justice executed with liberality and cordial good feeling." Shortly after Wilson's inauguration, however, it became clear to most Negroes that they could not rely on Wilson or his party for support. Soon, segregation was reintroduced in the nation's capital and in the offices of the Federal Government.

The experience of Negroes during World War I pointed up the painful fact that nowhere, not even in the armed services of the United States, did Negroes enjoy full citizenship. Under the Selective Service legislation 2,290,525 Negroes registered and 367,000 of them were called into the service. But there was discrimination everywhere. In the newly organized Air Force, Negroes were rejected outright. In the United States Navy they were used only as menials; in all other branches of the service they were segregated. The war was well under way before the War Department made some grudging arrangements for the training of Negro officers at Fort Des Moines, Iowa. Few if any communities were pleased to have Negroes in training camps nearby, and there were numerous incidents of clashes between black soldiers and white civilians. Negro soldiers complained, moreover, that they were constantly subjected to insults at the hands of their white officers.

Overseas, the situation was not much better. Negro combat troops were placed in various divisions of the French army, and they were naturally faced with numerous problems of adjustment. They were taunted by the Germans, who reminded them that they were fighting for the benefit of "Wall Street robbers" and others and not for their own freedom. Meanwhile, the French soldiers and citizens were warned by white United States Army officials not to treat black soldiers as equals. Despite all this, Negroes fought loyally and gallantly. Hundreds of them received the Croix de Guerre and other citations from the French Army, but none received the Medal of Honor from the United States.

During the war Negroes rushed to northern industrial communities in the hope of finding employment in wartime industries. More than 300,000 Negroes left the South and settled in the North and West in the war decade. Consequently, urban problems became more acute than ever. In 1916 the National Urban League held a Conference on Migration and issued recommendations and advice to employers and migrants. But the hostility directed against Negroes made it clear to the newcomers that they were not welcome. The riot in East St. Louis, Illinois, in which forty Negroes lost their lives, was merely the worst of a series of racial clashes arising from the resentment of whites toward Negro workers, yet in spite of it all, many Negroes secured the best jobs they had ever had. Blacks were engaged in the manufacture of ammunition and iron and steel products. They were employed in the meat-packing industries, and large numbers found work in the new automobile industry. They held jobs in the coal mines, on the railroads, and in the shipbuilding yards.

Some articulate Negroes cried out over the treatment that their race was receiving. For their article, "Pro-Germanism among Negroes," in which they severely criticized the policy of the United States, the editors of *The Messenger*, A. Philip Randolph and Chandler Owen, were sentenced to jail for two and a half years and their second-class mailing privileges revoked. More influential among Negroes, however, was the editorial in July 1918 by W. E. B. DuBois, entitled "Close Ranks." In it he said, "Let us not hesitate. Let us, while this war lasts, forget our special grievances and close our ranks shoulder to shoulder with our white citizens and the allied nations that are fighting for democracy."

## The Reaction

Talk of democracy during the war had raised the hopes of most Negroes, and they were optimistic about the future. But their hopes were soon dashed by the events that followed the end of the war. Already the Ku Klux Klan had been revived and had adopted a broad program "for uniting native-born white Christians for concerted action in the preservation of American institutions and the supremacy of the white race." Within a ten-month period shortly after the close of the war, the Klan made more than two hundred public appearances in twenty-seven states. Soon the Klan and other anti-Negro groups were terrorizing the Negro population in a variety of ways. Returning black soldiers discovered that neither they nor their fellows had won a semblance of equality or decent treatment for themselves. More than seventy Negroes were lynched during the first year of the postwar period. Ten black soldiers, several still in their uniforms, were lynched. Mississippi and Georgia mobs murdered three black veterans each. Fourteen Negroes were burned publicly; and eleven of them were burned alive. In despair a black editor in South Carolina cried out, "There is scarcely a day passes that newspapers don't tell about a black soldier lynched in his uniform. Why do they lynch Negroes anyhow? With a white judge, a white jury, white public sentiment, white officers of the law, it is just as impossible for a Negro accused of crime or even suspected of crime to escape the white man's vengeance or his justice as it would be for a fawn to escape that wanders accidentally into a den of hungry lions."

With the summer of 1919 came the riots, twenty-five of them, North and South. In Longview, Texas, a black school principal was flogged on the streets, and several leading black citizens were run out of town. In Washington, D.C., mobs consisting primarily of white sailors, soldiers, and marines ran amok through the streets for three days, killing several blacks and injuring scores of others. In Chicago, when a Negro attempted to swim in a part of Lake Michigan that whites had reserved for themselves, a riot began that lasted for thirteen days. Thirty-eight persons were killed—fifteen whites and twenty-three blacks—and more than five hundred were injured. More than a thousand families, largely Negroes, were homeless due to the burning and general destruction of property.

The racial strife of the postwar years indicated that Negroes were willing to fight and die for their own causes as well as for democracy in Europe. It was no longer a case of one race intimidating another into submission. Now it was war in the full sense of the word, and Negroes were as determined to win as they had been in Europe. And even if they could not win in an obviously one-sided struggle, they sought to make a good showing. They loudly protested against what they termed injustice and oppression. But soon they realized that protests were not enough; not even fighting back was enough. Intelligent planning and action were needed. The following years would be characterized by their efforts to do precisely that.

## THE RESTORATION OF SELF-RESPECT

### The New Negro

The migration of blacks from their ancestral homes on the plantations to urban America that began during the war placed the Negro's destiny more squarely in his own hands than ever before. And the forces that touched off this wave of migration gave way to other factors in the years following the war that continued to stimulate migration down to the present day. The urban North was becoming increasingly attractive, while the South, even as it became industrialized, gave every indication that it had no intention of revising its views regarding the inferior position of the black. In 1910 no city in the United States had as many as 100,000 Negroes. By 1920 there were six such cities; and by 1940 there were eleven: New York, Chicago, Philadelphia, Detroit, Washington, Baltimore, New Orleans, Memphis, Birmingham, St. Louis, and Atlanta. Meanwhile, scores of thousands of Negroes were moving into urban communities where, up to that time, the Negro population had been negligible, if indeed it existed at all.

This extensive urbanization of Negroes had a profound effect upon their status and especially on their self-esteem. The black man developed a sense of responsibility and a self-confidence that he had not previously known. During the war Negroes learned from no less a person than their President of the promise of freedom, and on the battlefield some of them had served their country. Now, as they began to see the discrepancies between the promise of freedom and their experiences in their own country, they became defiant, bitter, and impatient. Congregating in the cities in large numbers, they were no longer afraid as they had been on the southern plantation. And many of them were more than willing to speak out against injustices. It was not the timorous, docile Negro of the past who said, "The next time white folks pick on colored folks, something's going to drop—dead white folks."

Negroes were achieving, moreover, a degree and kind of articulation that made it possible for them to state their feelings clearly and forthrightly. Despite their intense feelings of hatred and hurt, they possessed sufficient restraint, if not objectivity, to use their materials artistically but no less effectively. The new Negro was sufficiently in touch with the main currents of American literary development to adapt the accepted forms to his own materials and therefore gain a wider acceptance. The result was the emergence of a remarkable crop of Negro writers who made up what was later called "The Harlem Renaissance." Through poetry, prose, and song they cried out against social and economic injustices. They protested against segregation and lynching; and they called for better conditions of work. In their demands they were almost unanimous in their efforts to secure justice within the framework of the existing economic and political structure.

There was a sense of satisfaction among Negroes as they insisted that they were on the right side of the country's professed ideals. As Alain Locke said in his volume, *The New Negro*, published in 1925, "The Negro mind reaches out as yet to nothing but American wants, American ideas. But this forced attempt to build his Americanism on race values is a unique social experiment, and its ultimate success is impossible except through the fullest sharing of American culture and institutions. . . . We realize that we cannot be undone without America's undoing. It is within the gamut of this attitude that the thinking Negro faces America, but with variations of mood that are, if anything, more significant than the attitude itself." Articulate Negroes sensed the moral advantage that they possessed, and they used it in every way possible.

The number of Negroes who now came forth in the 1920s to write about the plight of their race was itself an indication of the intellectual achievement so many of them had made. DuBois continued his creative writings, bringing out several novels, two volumes of poems and essays, and other works. James Weldon Johnson, who had published his *Autobiography of an Ex-Colored Man* in 1912 and in the following year his poem "Fifty Years," commemorating the anniversary of the Emancipation Proclamation, was even more prolific in the years following the war. His book of *American Negro Poetry* and his own volume of folk poems, *God's Trombones*, placed him in the mainstream of American writers. Claude McKay, regarded by many as the leading poet of the Harlem Renaissance, was also one of the most caustic in his strictures of American life. His *Harlem Shadows* and *Home to Harlem* intensively examined the Negro ghetto in poem and prose. Countee Cullen published his first volume of poems, *Color*, in 1925, when he was only 22 years old. In succeeding works such as *The Ballad of the Brown Girl* and *Copper Sun*, he demonstrated his capacity for imagination as well as critical insight into the problems that beset the Negro American. There were others: Jean Toomer, whose *Cane* displayed a rare talent; Langston Hughes, whose most significant work belonged to a later period; Jessie Fauset, who captured the problems of the middle-class Negro to a remarkable degree; and Walter White, whose studies of lynching did much to dramatize the nature of American violence. These and many more gave ample evidence that the new Negro was not only deeply sensitive but extremely articulate.

There were other even more dramatic manifestations of the new Negro. The NAACP was not only carrying on its campaign against lynching, under the leadership of James Weldom Johnson and Walter White, but it was also attempting to abolish the practice of southern states of excluding Negroes from Democratic primaries. It succeeded, in the case of *Nixon v. Herndon* (1927), in having the Supreme Court of the United States declare null and void a Texas statute which excluded Negroes from the Democratic primaries in that state. When the Texas legislature enacted a law giving the executive committee of the party the authority to fix the qualifications for party membership, the NAACP in *Nixon v. Condon* (1932), succeeded in having the law nullified by arguing that the statute had set up a party committee and made it a state agency with certain power and duties. It suffered a setback, however, in 1935 when, in *Grovey v. Townsend*, the Court refused to interfere with the exclusion of Negroes from the Democratic primaries when such an exclusion had been effected by a resolution of the state convention of the party. It was not until 1944 that the NAACP recovered its lost ground when, in *Smith v. Allwright*, the Court decided that the exclusion of Negroes from the Democratic primary was a clear violation of the Fifteenth Amendment. Although these decisions were to prove insufficient to destroy the resistance to Negroes voting in the South, they were important steps toward the enjoyment of political participation.

The concentration of Negroes in urban centers in the North had much to do with another manifestation of the New Negro, namely, political regeneration. As early as

1915 a Negro, Oscar DePriest, was elected alderman from the densely populated South Side of Chicago. In 1917 black New Yorkers sent E. A. Johnson to the state assembly. In the years that followed they became increasingly aware of their political strength and took advantage of it. By 1928 some Negroes were turning their backs on the Republican Party to support Alfred E. Smith, a Democrat, for the presidency, because they thought he would do more for them than Herbert Hoover, the Republican candidate. That same year they sent Oscar DePriest to Congress, the first Negro to serve there since 1901. And in 1930 they used their political influence to block the confirmation of John J. Parker for the Supreme Court, because they regarded him as an enemy of Negroes. By the time that Franklin D. Roosevelt ran for President in 1932 on the Democratic ticket, Negroes were in a position to use their political strength to force greater consideration on the part of the major parties.

At the same time, the New Negro was becoming more militant in the economic sphere. In 1929 the National Negro Business League, more certain than ever that white businesses and labor unions were passing Negroes by, organized the Colored Merchants Association which undertook to establish stores and to purchase their wares cooperatively. Shortly thereafter a "Jobs-for-Negroes" movement began in earnest in St. Louis, where the Urban League led a boycott against a white-owned chain store whose trade was almost exclusively Negro but employed no Negroes. The movement spread to Pittsburgh, Chicago, Cleveland, and other midwestern cities, and many blacks found employment because of the pressure brought on white employers in Negro sections. Even during the Depression such movements continued. In New York City in 1933, the Reverend John H. Johnson organized the Citizens' League for Fair Play and attempted to persuade white merchants to employ black clerks. When their first efforts failed they resorted to picketing the stores and appealing to Negroes with the motto, "Don't Buy Where You Can't Work." The campaign resulted in the employment of hundreds of Negroes in the white stores of Harlem and in such public utilities as the telephone, electric, and bus companies.

There were some Negroes, bitter, defiant, and frustrated, who believed that practical programs to achieve equality were unfeasible. The strain and stress of living in hostile urban communities had left them completely disillusioned and willing to accept more drastic solutions to their problems. That is why so many blacks were eager and ready to embrace the Universal Negro Improvement Association, organized by Marcus Garvey during the war. Garvey insisted that the Negro had no future in the United States, and he declared that the only hope for Negro Americans was to flee America and return to Africa to build up a country of their own. "Wake up Ethiopia," he cried out; "Wake up Africa! Let us work toward one glorious end of a free, redeemed, and mighty nation. Let Africa be a bright star among the constellation of nations." To inculcate a sense of self-esteem among Negroes, Garvey exalted everything black. He insisted that black stood for strength and beauty, not inferiority.

The movement grew rapidly and Garvey claimed that he had six million followers in 1923. That was an exaggeration, of course; but even his severest critics conceded that he had perhaps a half-million members, which was more than the NAACP had at any time during this period. His Universal African Legion, Black Eagle Flying Corps, Black Star Steamship Line, and numerous orders of African nobility captured the imagination of many Negro Americans. Although his many projects came to naught, they gave many frustrated blacks a sense of hope and dignity that had long been denied them. It was the first real mass movement that Negroes had embraced; and its momentary success bears testimony to the extent to which Negroes entertained doubts about ever gaining first-class citizenship in the country of their birth.

Perhaps even more bizarre was the movement led by George Baker, commonly known as "Father Divine," who promised his followers a veritable heaven on earth. Beginning with a small group on Long Island in 1919, this remarkable leader built up a following within the next two decades that amused some observers and perplexed others. Although his followers deserted their churches and began to call their leader "God," it was as much a social movement as a religious development. By 1930 Father Divine was holding open house and feeding thousands in buildings that came to be known as "heavens." In many eastern cities and in some midwestern communities Father Divine had large followings. The movement became interracial as early as 1926, and within a few years had attracted a considerable number of white members, some of whom were wealthy. That such a movement could flourish suggests a variety of social ills and a large scale frustration among whites as well as Negroes.

**The New Deal**

Despite the growing political sophistication of the Negro American, it is doubtful that large numbers of them turned away from the Republican Party to support Franklin D. Roosevelt when he was elected to the Presidency in 1932. But once in office, Roosevelt quickly gained a large following among Negroes and other minority groups. He was the first President to appoint Italian-Americans and Negroes to the federal bench. He frequently received Negro visitors, and it was widely reported that he listened to suggestions and advice from certain powerful Negro politicians. Mrs. Roosevelt, moreover, was active in a variety of social programs that involved the improvement of disadvantaged groups, including Negroes. On several occasions during his first year in office, the President denounced lynching and mob violence. His Secretary of the Interior, Harold L. Ickes, had been president of the Chicago branch of the NAACP, thus becoming the first American cabinet officer to have been so intimately associated with the struggle for Negro rights. The President appointed Negroes as "advisers" in several executive departments; and it was assumed that they were in a position to state the case for the economic and political equality of Negroes. In some sectors of the Federal Government the racial segregation that had been established by the preceding Democratic President, Woodrow Wilson, was abolished by Roosevelt.

While there was no civil rights legislation during the period of the New Deal, the relief-and-recovery legislation helped somewhat to improve conditions among Negroes as well as the rest of the population. Under such agencies as the Agricultural Adjustment Administration, the Rural Electrification Administration, and local production credit associations, Negroes received benefits, though not in proportion to their numbers and needs. They were substantially aided by the Farm Security Administration, which insisted that there be no discrimination between white and black farmers. The Civilian Conservation Corps and the National Youth Administration provided employment for thousands of young Negroes. By 1939 more than one million Negroes owed their living to employment under the Works Progress Administration. Even some of the writers, actors, and musicians who had gotten their start during the period of the Harlem Renaissance found an opportunity to continue their creative work under the WPA. There was still widespread discrimination against Negroes, particularly in the local administration of New Deal agencies in the South and in some areas of the North. But the old patterns of discrimination that had existed for decades were weakened to some extent during the New Deal period.

The New Deal was particularly favorable to labor, although not necessarily to Negro labor. The Wagner Act of 1935 gave permanency and strength to the National Labor Relations Board which enjoyed wide power in handling labor disputes and in settling strikes. It was labor's "bill of rights," but it did not break the barriers which excluded Negroes from the unions. The Fair Labor Standards Act of 1938 established the principle of a minimum wage and a maximum work week. Better than a million Negroes were affected by the act, but several million were not. The act meant little to Negroes if they were unable to secure employment in those industries it covered. There were few unions like the United Mine Workers, which brought together in one union all the workers of the industry and which, since its organization in 1890, had encouraged the organization and participation of Negro workers. Most of the principal unions in the American Federation of Labor either barred Negroes or accepted their membership only on a segregated basis.

It was the so-called industrial bloc in the American Federation of Labor that gave the black worker his first real opportunity in organized labor. Led by John L. Lewis of the United Mine Workers, the bloc organized the Congress of Industrial Organizations (C.I.O.) and left the American Federation of Labor. Soon the C.I.O. was organizing the mass production industries; and the Amalgamated Clothing Workers, the International Ladies Garment Workers, and the Steel Workers gave Negro members something resembling an equal opportunity to participate in union affairs. The C.I.O. became active in the political sphere as well and sought equal opportunities for Negroes through its Committee to Abolish Racial Discrimination and its Political Action Committee.

Meanwhile, the Brotherhood of Sleeping Car Porters, under the leadership of A. Philip Randolph, successfully pressed for better working conditions for its members and proved that Negroes, when given the opportunity, could adhere to the principles of organized labor.

In spite of such advances, the Negroes' patience in waiting for justice through the courts and for equity at the hands of government leaders—including those of the New Deal—was wearing thin. They had to fight for their rights, many began to insist. As one Negro wrote to President Roosevelt's Attorney General, "It strikes us that the time is just about at hand when we must cast aside our Bible, stop offering so many solemn addresses to the Supreme Being and fight for our rights. . . . We would prefer death in lieu of remaining here on earth and having our manhood trampled upon." Such views were provoked by the persistence of the denial of the rights of Negroes, even when so much was being said about the protection and support of the disadvantaged elements of the American population. Consequently, Negroes sought to mobilize their intellectual and political resources for the purpose of pressing for their rights. Even as they supported Roosevelt in 1936 and 1940 they made it clear that they reserved the right to give their support to whatever political organizations were most sensitive to their needs. In organizations such as the Joint Committee on National Recovery, the National Negro Congress, and the Southern Negro Youth Congress, they came together and formulated plans for pressing even more vigorously for full citizenship. Even if these groups accomplished little, they developed approaches and techniques that were to be most valuable in the decades ahead.

## The New Negro Community

The inability of Negroes to become part of the mainstream of American urban life not only added to their disillusionment but forced them to rely heavily on institutions of their own making. The almost universal discrimination in employment, difficulty in securing adequate housing, and absence of equity in the administration of justice contributed significantly to family disorganization among Negroes. Yet at the same time, as E. Franklin Frazier pointed out in his *The Negro in the United States*, there was an increase in stability within the Negro urban family in the post-World War I years. With the growth of the Negro middle class and the improvement of educational opportunities, the Negro family as well as other institutions reflected a capacity to provide a measure of strength and stability for the Negro community.

The practice of forcing blacks into ghettos and of barring them from participation in the life of the white community helped to create a new emphasis on the perpetuation of the Negro's world. In a nation dedicated to the idea of the essential equality of mankind and in which there was general commitment to the fusion of races and cultures, the existence of a separate Negro community constituted one of the truly remarkable social anomalies of the twentieth century. This situation created innumerable problems of a political, social, and economic nature that confounded any thoughtful observer of the American scene.

The most powerful institution in the Negro's world was the church. More and more, as he found himself rejected by the white churches and by the white community in general, the Negro turned to the church for self-expression, recognition, and leadership. Nothing in his world was so completely his own as the church, whether it was one of the more common branches like Baptist or Methodist, or one of the more exotic institutions like the Apostolic Overcoming Holy Church of God or the Kodesh Church of Immanuel. The Negro church stimulated pride and preserved the self-respect of many who had been humiliated in their efforts to adjust themselves to American life. By the middle of the twentieth century, thirty-four all-Negro denominations claimed a membership of more than 5,000,000 Negroes, more than 35,000 churches, and property valued at $200,000,000. This period also marked the first steps toward a move to reintegrate American religious institutions. Roman Catholics insisted that they could not countenance segregation in the churches, while even the Methodists began to take steps to unite the Negro and white branches. The Negro church remained completely intact, however.

In the new Negro community the press played an increasingly important part. The white press of the South ignored the black community except to publicize crimes allegedly committed by Negroes, while the white press of the North paid scant attention to their activities. The Negro press thus became the medium for the dissemination of information among Negroes and a powerful voice in expressing the black man's aspirations. It was during World War I that the Negro press became powerful and prosperous. It encouraged Negroes to move to industrial centers in search of work and to support the war effort, but it also led the fight for complete equality of Negroes in American life. Newspapers such as the Baltimore *Afro-American*, the *Chicago Defender*, the Norfolk *Journal and Guide*, and the *Pittsburgh Courier* made rapid strides both in circulation and influence. In later decades the number of Negro newspapers, primarily weeklies, increased enormously, while weekly and monthly periodicals such as *Jet* and *Ebony* provided brief pictorial summaries of Negro life in modern America.

The emergence of a free, separate Negro community provided great stimulation for the rise of Negroes in the professions. The new Negro world needed teachers, clergy, physicians, dentists, pharmacists, nurses, attorneys, social workers, recreation leaders, morticians, and many others to minister to its needs. These professionals constituted the most highly trained group in the Negro community and formed the basis for the Negro middle class. Preoccupied though they necessarily were with their own training and service and the maintenance of high standards, black professionals were also aggressive in the advocacy of full citizenship for all. They were compelled to organize their own associations for their protection and mutual assistance, but it would not be accurate to suggest that they thereby neglected the important role of leadership in the Negro community. Many Negro attorneys and physicians and members of the clergy served as officials in civil rights organizations, realizing, of course, that segregation and discrimination were, in the last analysis, as oppressive to them as to the least-advantaged member of their race.

The education of Negroes remained a separate enterprise, for the most part. Almost nowhere did Negroes enjoy equal educational opportunities, although the white community was scrupulously careful in seeing to it that such opportunities remained separate. In the South separate schools were maintained by law. In the North they were maintained by the Negro ghetto. In the South a wide disparity between the money spent on the education of white children and that spent for the education of black children prevailed throughout the first half of the twentieth century. In 1935–36 the current expenditures per black pupil in ten southern states averaged $13.09, while such expenditures per white pupil averaged $37.87. While separate books were not kept for ghetto schools in the North, even a most cursory observation of buildings, equipment, and facilities indicated considerable disparity.

It is not possible to measure precisely the effects that separate and unequal education had on both white and black populations in the areas where it was maintained. Separate schools were one of the strongest supports of the concept of white supremacy in the South. They contributed, moreover, to the perpetuation of a leadership devoted not only to separate education but to the maintenance of economic and political inequalities between the white and black populations of the South. In the face of these difficulties, however, the number of Negro schools, colleges, and universities increased, while the Negro student population virtually exploded in the years following World War I.

In spite of the confused pattern of education available to Negroes, there emerged a body of highly trained men and women who were scholars by any criteria. While almost all of them, until quite recently, received their graduate and professional training in northern and European universities, many of them were products of separate schools on the lower level and most had attended Negro colleges. There was, of course, the usual complement of Negro clergy, teachers, physicians, and attorneys; but to these were added, in more recent years, an increasing number of scholars in various scientific fields, history, sociology, political science, and the humanities. Negro scholars became increasingly articulate, contributing articles to learned journals and publishing numerous books. Many of them devoted much of their talents and energies to studying and describing the place of Negroes in American life. The Association for the Study of Negro Life and History, founded in 1915 by Carter G. Woodson, went so far as to promote the works of Negro scholars and, indeed, of white scholars who were concerned with reassessing the role of Negroes in American history. The association's *Journal of Negro History* soon became a respected periodical in the most scholarly circles, while the *Journal of Negro Education*, published at Howard University, joined in the vigorous efforts of Negro scholars and their friends to restore Negro Americans to a place of respect in the larger community.

# GLOBAL WAR AND AFTERMATH

### Fighting for the Four Freedoms

Negroes were among the first Americans to advocate intervention against the aggression of the fascist powers. As early as 1935 they were bitterly protesting the Italian invasion of Ethiopia. In many communities they raised funds for the defense of the African kingdom. In New York the International Council of Friends of Ethiopia was organized, and one of its founders, Willis N. Huggins, pleaded before the League of Nations for support of the African nation. The Pittsburgh *Courier* sent a reporter, J. A. Rogers, to cover the war; and upon his return he published *The Real Facts About Ethiopia* and lectured to many black and white groups. As they witnessed the rape of Ethiopia by Italian fascists and the slaughter of Jews by German Nazis, many blacks concluded that racism, whether in Europe or America, was inimical to their best interests.

When Europe was plunged into war in September 1939, the armed services of the United States were in a low state of preparedness. The army in 1940 consisted of some 230,000 enlisted men and officers, of whom less than 5,000 were Negroes. Only the four Negro units in the standing army, the 24th and 25th Infantries and the 9th and 10th Cavalries, were up to their full strength. Some other Negro units were activated: among them quartermaster regiments, antiaircraft battalions, and corps of engineers. But blacks generally had little interest in the armed services in the years between the wars; and few were, therefore, ready to participate in the first stages of building up a large fighting force.

Under the Selective Service Act of 1940 more than 3,000,000 Negro men registered for service. In the first year, while hope remained that the United States could stay out of the war, only 2,069 Negroes were drafted. In 1941 more than 100,000 entered the service, while in 1942 approximately 370,000 joined the armed forces. In September 1944, when the Army was at its peak, there were 700,000 Negroes in that branch of the service alone. Approximately 165,000 served in the Navy, 5,000 in the Coast Guard, and 17,000 in the Marine Corps. The total number of Negroes in all branches of the armed services during World War II was approximately 1,000,000 men and women.

At the beginning of the war the armed services were generally segregated, and there was considerable discrimination. But Negroes had a much greater opportunity to serve their country than in any previous war. They were in the infantry, coast and field artillery, cavalry, tank battalions, transportation units, signal corps, engineer corps, and medical corps or well as other branches in which they had previously served. When the Women's Auxiliary Corps was organized, Negroes were received; and before the end of the war more than 4,000 women had enlisted. In 1940 the War Department announced that Negroes would be trained as aviation pilots at Tuskegee, Alabama. While some Negroes vociferously objected to the Air Force's segregation of Negroes into special training units, others looked upon the acceptance of Negroes as candidates for officer-pilot training as a step forward. Late in 1941 the 99th Pursuit Squadron was ready for organization into a fighting unit, and other groups of Negro fighter pilots were undergoing training. Approximately 600 Negro pilots had received their wings before the end of the war.

In June 1940 there were 4,000 Negroes in the Navy, most of them serving as mess men. Since World War I Negroes had had no opportunity either to learn the many trades provided in naval training or to become combat seamen. Then, in April 1942, the Secretary of the Navy announced that the Navy would accept the enlistment of Negroes for general service and as noncommissioned officers. Soon a program for the training of Negroes as officers was launched, and Negro women were permitted to enlist in the WAVES. At the same time it was announced that Negroes would be received in the Marine Corps, a break with a tradition as old as the corps itself. The Army, meanwhile, had established a policy of training black and white officer candidates in the same schools. Despite considerable resistance on the part of some white officers of the regular Army, Negroes received their commissions, and with pressures brought by William H. Hastie, the Civilian Aide to the Secretary of War, and others, they received advanced training that made them eligible for promotion.

Approximately a half-million Negroes saw service overseas during World War II. Most of them were in separate outfits, more frequently than not commanded by white officers. After D-Day in 1944, more than 50,000 Negro engineers erected camps, tents, and buildings, cleared debris, rebuilt cities, and performed other important services. Twenty-two Negro combat units participated in the ground operations in the European theater. Negro fighter squadrons participated in the air operations over Italy, Romania, and Austria. In January 1945, the War Department announced that black troops would be integrated with white troops in an experimental unit in the European theater. Negroes everywhere were elated at the news of the experiment and were delighted to learn that the mixed units were a success. Meanwhile, Negro troops were becoming more active in the war in the Pacific and the Orient. Negro combat units saw action against the Japanese in the New Georgia Islands, the Solomons, the Philippines, and elsewhere.

The problem of maintaining high morale among Negroes in the service was a difficult one, however. Time after time, white officers and white civilians subjected blacks to indignities and humiliations. In Durham, North Carolina, a white bus driver was found not guilty of murder after he left his bus in July 1944, and killed a black soldier with whom he had argued on the bus. In the South Negro soldiers were refused food in places where German prisoners of war were eating and enjoying American hospitality. In Kentucky three Negro WACS were beaten by civilian police when the women did not move promptly from the white waiting room in a railroad station when asked to do so. In South Carolina a white policeman gouged out a black soldier's eyes in an altercation. On military posts the situation was scarcely better. At many camps black soldiers were forced to wait until white soldiers had boarded the buses, then, if any room was left, they could ride. When the War Department issued an order in 1944 forbidding racial segregation in recreational and transportation facilities at all army stations, the Montgomery *Advertiser* said, "Army orders, even armies, even bayonets cannot force impossible and unnatural social relations upon us."

If whites were resisting moves toward the equal treatment of Negro soldiers, Negro newspapers and leaders were constantly protesting against all forms of segregation and discrimination. They protested the Red Cross practice of separating black and white blood in the banks that had been established for the relief of wounded servicemen. They were quick to point out that there would, perhaps, have been no blood banks at all without the work of a Negro, Dr. Charles Drew. They also criticized the USO when that organization banned Ruth Benedict's *The Races of Mankind* in its clubs. While Negroes were willing to serve their country in war as well as in peace, most of them insisted that the Four Freedoms and the other noble sentiments expressed in the war aims should be practiced at home as well as abroad. The Pittsburgh *Courier* launched a vigorous "Double V" campaign: Victory at home as well as abroad.

## Problems of Employment

As the United States began to put itself on a war footing, Negroes wondered where they would fit in as far as defense and war industries were concerned. It soon became apparent that they would face serious difficulties in securing employment in these areas. The first benefits they derived from the boom in defense industries were in securing the jobs deserted by whites who were attracted by higher wages to plants making weapons of war. The Federal Government made several gestures to discourage such discrimination. The Office of Education declared that in the expenditure of funds in the defense training program there should be no discrimination based on race, creed, or color. In August 1940, the National Defense Advisory Committee issued a statement against the refusal to hire Negroes in defense plants. These actions brought few satisfactory results, however, and discrimination continued. As Negroes saw wages skyrocket in plants holding huge defense contracts, they saw few signs that the rigid anti-Negro policy in industry was undergoing any change. All too typical of industry was the statement by a West Coast aviation factory which said, "We will receive applications from both white and colored workers. However, Negroes will be considered only as janitors and in other similar capacities. Regardless of their training as aircraft workers, we will not employ them."

Such positions indicated to Negro leaders the need for a program of drastic action. In January 1941, A. Philip Randolph, president of the Brotherhood of Sleeping Car Porters, advanced the idea of fifty to one hundred thousand Negroes marching on Washington and demanding that their government do something to insure their employment in the defense industry. The idea was received with enthusiasm by many Negroes, while federal officials viewed the prospect as most regrettable. Soon a full-scale March-on-Washington Movement had developed, and it was supported by the heads of all the major Negro organizations. The President sought to head off the movement by speaking out against discrimination, but Negroes felt that he was not doing enough. Mrs. Roosevelt and Mayor LaGuardia of New York also attempted to persuade the Negro leaders to abandon the idea of the march, insisting that it would do more harm than good. Finally the President himself appealed to Randolph and his colleagues to call off the march, but Randolph remained adamant.

In late June 1941, Negroes all over the United States—many thousands, if not a hundred thousand—were making preparations to entrain for Washington to be ready to march to the Capitol and White House on July 1. As the day drew near, governmental officials became increasingly desperate. Finally, after several conferences, the President said that if Randolph would call off the march, he would issue an order prohibiting discrimination in employment in defense industries. Randolph agreed, and on June 25, 1941, the President issued his famous Executive Order 8802, saying, "There shall be no discrimination in the employment of workers in defense industries or Government because of race, creed, color, or national origin. . . . And it is the duty of employers and labor organizations . . . to provide for the full and equitable participation of all workers in defense industries, without discrimination because of race, creed, color, or national origin. . . . " Later a Fair Employment Practices Committee was established, and this was the beginning of the involvement of the Federal Government in programs to improve the economic status of blacks. Undoubtedly, many employers persisted in their discriminatory practices, but even if the commitment of the Federal Government to fair employment may have appeared lukewarm, it created a generally improved climate in which Negroes could seek employment.

In another way, however, the climate was deteriorating. The migration of large numbers of Negroes to the North and West raised anew the difficult question of how blacks and whites could live together peacefully in communities where the patterns of race relations were not clearly defined. Within the five-year period between 1940 and 1945 the Negro population of Los Angeles County increased from 75,000 to 150,000. Negroes were also moving in large numbers to Oakland, Detroit, Cleveland, Chicago, and other industrial centers. The lack of housing, the presence of race-baiters and demagogues, the problem of organizing the newly arrived workers, and the impotence of local governments created an ideal atmosphere for the emergence of racial violence.

Consequently, as blacks and whites were fighting the Germans, Italians, and Japanese abroad, they were fighting each other at home. In June 1943, the most serious race riot of the war period broke out in Detroit. Months of racial tension were climaxed on June 20 when a fist fight occurred between a black man and a white man. Soon several hundred persons were involved, and blacks and whites were fighting in various parts of the city. Nothing effective was done to bring order out of chaos until President Roosevelt declared a state of emergency and sent 6,000 troops to patrol the city. After thirty hours of rioting, twenty-five blacks and nine whites had been killed; and property valued at several hundred thousand dollars had been destroyed. There were other racial clashes on a smaller scale in New York, Los Angeles, Chicago, and several southern cities. No city wanted to become another Detroit, however, and numerous efforts were made after the summer of 1943 to prevent the recurrence of such violence.

## Postwar Breakthrough

After Harry S Truman took office upon the death of President Roosevelt in April 1945, it became clear that the new President would be an active exponent of a greater enjoyment of equality for Negroes. In an address to the annual meeting of the NAACP in 1947, he said, "As Americans we believe that every man should be free to live his life as he wishes. He should be limited only by his responsibility to his fellow countrymen. If this freedom is to be more than a dream, each man must be guaranteed equality of opportunity. The only limit to an American's achievement should be his ability, his industry, and his character." Already the President had taken steps to provide this equality of opportunity. Late in 1946 he created the President's Committee on Civil Rights "to inquire into and determine whether and in what respect current law enforcement measures and the authority and means possessed by federal, state, and local governments may be strengthened and improved to safeguard the civil rights of the people." After surveying every aspect of American life involved in the problem of civil rights, the committee published its report under the title, *To Secure These Rights*. The report made comprehensive and far-reaching recommendations calling for concrete measures to improve the administration of justice, to protect the exercise of the franchise, and to eliminate segregation in American life. In the same year the President appointed another interracial committee to look into the problem of higher education. In its report the committee recommended not only the elimination of inequalities in educational opportunities but the abandonment of all forms of discrimination in higher education.

The move toward integration in the armed services that had been inaugurated in the closing years of World War II was accelerated by President Truman. In 1948 he appointed a committee to study the problem, and its report, *Freedom to Serve*, was a blueprint of the steps by which integration was to be achieved. In Korea in 1950, there were new opportunities to test military integration under battlefield conditions. Between

May and August 1951, the percentage of integrated troops in the field in Korea jumped from 9 percent to 30 percent. A special army report declared that the integration of Negroes had resulted in an overall gain for the army. At long last Negro Americans had become a vital and integral part of the military manpower pool of the nation.

In February 1948, President Truman sent a special message on civil rights to Congress, the first such message that any President had ever sent. He called for the establishment of a permanent Commission on Civil Rights, federal legislation against lynching, the establishment of a permanent Fair Employment Practices Committee, the prohibition of discrimination in interstate transportation facilities, and the strengthening of existing civil-rights statutes. Congress did nothing to implement the demands of the President or the recommendations of his several commissions, but the President's stand was a historic one. After Truman, no President could turn his back on this important problem.

While Congress paid little attention to the matter of civil rights, the Supreme Court dealt with the issue in a variety of cases. Indeed, there was scarcely an area of American life in which the rights of citizens were jeopardized that escaped the Court's attention in the years following World War II. In 1946, in a case coming up from Virginia, *Morgan v. Virginia*, the Court held unconstitutional a Virginia law that segregated passengers traveling across state lines. In 1948 the Court held that racially restrictive covenants in the conveyance of real property could not be enforced in the courts. The decision in this case, *Shelley v. Kraemer*, was the first significant assault on segregation and discrimination in housing since the ordinance requiring whites and Negroes to live in separate blocks was outlawed in 1917. In 1950 the Court, which in 1938 had already required states to provide professional training for blacks if it was provided for whites, held that such facilities not only must be equal but must, indeed, be the same. To many white southerners, this was a frightening departure from the "separate but equal" doctrine laid down in the Plessy case in 1896. It seemed clear that in time the Court would open all public institutions of higher education to Negroes. Many whites hoped that the Court would not desegregate primary and secondary schools.

In the hope that the Court would not disturb the system of separate schools at the lower levels, the southern states made a desperate effort to equalize Negro primary and secondary schools. In the late forties and early fifties they spent millions of dollars to improve segregated Negro schools. The more they spent the more they seemed to convince themselves that this was the best—indeed, the only—solution to the problem of segregated education in the South.

The assault on segregated schools was part of a larger drive to eliminate segregation throughout the United States. It could be seen in the emergence of new groups that joined with the older ones to challenge segregation laws and practices. In the Midwest the American Council on Race Relations was active. In the North the Anti-Defamation League, the American Jewish Congress, the C. I. O. Committee to Abolish Racial

Discrimination, the National Lawyers Guild, the American Veterans' Committee, and the Workers Defense League represented a wide variety of interests working for the elimination of segregation. In the South the Southern Conference of Human Welfare and the Southern Regional Council began to take action. In Washington the National Committee on Segregation in the Nation's Capital was working. In 1948 it described Washington, D. C. as the "capital of white supremacy," and called for the elimination of all practices of segregation and discrimination. Early in 1949 the white Washington hotels began to accept black guests. Soon some theaters and motion-picture houses took steps to desegregate. In 1953 the Supreme Court, invoking a law that had been passed in 1873, declared that restaurants in Washington could not refuse to serve "well-behaved and respectable persons."

The move to desegregate Washington schools was a part of the move to desegregate schools in other parts of the country. Taking cognizance of the efforts of many southern states to make their segregated schools equal as far as facilities were concerned, the NAACP and its supporters began to argue that segregated education, regardless of equal facilities, was per se unconstitutional. They set forth this position in the five cases arising in Kansas, South Carolina, Virginia, Delaware, and the District of Columbia. Numerous organizations entered briefs in behalf of the position of the Negroes. The Attorney General of the United States asked the Court to strike down the doctrine of "separate but equal." Racial discrimination, he said, furnishes "grist for the communist propaganda mills, and it raises doubt even among friendly nations as to the integrity of our devotion to the democratic faith." The decision of the Court on May 17, 1954, in *Brown v. The Board of Education*, was the most significant breakthrough of the twentieth century. It was unequivocal in outlawing segregation in public schools. Speaking for a unanimous court, Chief Justice Warren said, "Separate educational facilities are inherently unequal." There was no doubt, therefore, that Negro children who were segregated in public schools had been deprived of the equal protection of the law guaranteed by the Fourteenth Amendment. The implications of the decision were far-reaching, and they would not be fully appreciated for many years to come.

There were those, however, who understood from the first what the decision meant to them. A Richmond editor denounced the Court as "that inept fraternity of politicians and professors" who had "repudiated the Constitution and spat upon the Tenth Amendment." More than a hundred southern members of Congress issued a manifesto saying, "The unwarranted decision of the Supreme Court . . . is now bearing the fruit always produced when men substitute naked power for established law. We regard the decision as a clear abuse of judicial power." But one white editor in Knoxville, Tennessee, said, "No citizen, fitted by character and intelligence to sit as a justice of the Supreme Court, and sworn to uphold the Constitution . . . could have decided this question other than the way it was decided." A group of leading Negro educators said simply, "It was the right and moral thing to do."

# FROM THE CIVIL RIGHTS STRUGGLE
## TO THE BLACK REVOLUTION

## An Improved Climate

Many factors and forces led to the creation of a better climate for Negroes in the years following World War II. The assumption by the United States of a position of leadership in world affairs made the country particularly vulnerable regarding the position of its black population. As one of the chief builders of the United Nations and as its host country, it became increasingly embarrassing to speak out against the denial of human rights in faraway lands while admitting that there were flagrant denials of those rights in many parts of the United States. Other nations would naturally doubt the sincerity of America's professions regarding the rights of all peoples. The United States became sensitive to the discrepancies in its domestic human relations and sought to make amends by appointing Negroes to the delegations to the United Nations and to commissions dealing with international problems. Such moves, however, did not cover up the housing and employment problems that Negroes experienced and that even the casual visitor could see; nor did it obscure the numerous practices of segregation and discrimination that were mentioned all too frequently in the Russian press.

The emergence of independent states in Africa added to America's distress, in a sense. Beginning with Ghana in 1957, one African state after another gained its independence, and as they did so they inadvertently contributed toward the changing of the racial climate in the United States. Psychologically, black Americans immediately identified with the new African nations and pointed with pride to the accomplishments of their brothers. They also reminded white Americans that Negro states in Africa were living proof of the Negro's ability to assume responsibilities at the highest level; and this living proof stimulated the Negroes of the United States to press a bit harder for their own rights. Equally important was the presence in the United States of an increasing number of African representatives to the United Nations and ambassadors to the United States. In the cold war with Russia, the United States felt that it was most important to win over the African nations. But it was most difficult for the United States to accomplish this feat in the face of insults and indignities heaped upon African diplomats by white Americans. It became a major concern of the United States, therefore, not only to treat the Africans with dignity and respect but also to assure them that such treatment should be accorded Americans of dark skins. As this problem came to be a major concern of the President of the United States and the Secretary of State, they used their power and prestige to seek to correct some of the racial practices in the United States. In so doing, they contributed to the improvement of the racial climate.

The extensive urbanization of Negro Americans during and after World War II greatly contributed to the improvement of the political climate as far as the Negro was concerned. Between 1940 and 1970 the Negro population outside the old Confederacy increased two and a half times. By 1970 more than half the black population was living in the North and West. Most of this growth outside the South was in the central cities of the twelve largest metropolitan areas of the United States: New York, Los Angeles, Chicago, Philadelphia, Detroit, San Francisco-Oakland, Boston, Pittsburgh, St. Louis, Washington, Cleveland, and Baltimore. By 1970 more than one-third of all black Americans lived in these areas; and it was in such areas of concentration that they began to wield considerable influence.

Ironically, one of the very significant results of herding Negroes into urban ghettoes in the North was an enormous increase in their political power. Negroes began to sit in lawmaking bodies in every northern state that had large cities with a concentrated Negro population. They served as state and municipal judges, city commissioners, corporation counsels, and in a variety of other important elective and appointive public offices. Negroes were elected to the school boards of Atlanta and Houston, to the state senate in Georgia, and to the councils of many southern cities. They became mayors of such major cities as Cleveland, Newark, and Gary. They won state-wide elections, with, for example, the election of Edward Brooke first as state attorney general and then as U. S. Senator from Massachusetts, and the voting-in of Otis Smith as auditor general of Michigan. It was the large metropolitan areas that sent twelve Negroes, including the first black woman, to the House of Representatives in 1970.

The growing political strength of Negro Americans was also reflected in important presidential appointments. These began with Truman's appointment of William H. Hastie to the United States Court of Appeals for the Third Circuit and were continued by President Eisenhower in his appointment of J. Ernest Wilkins as Assistant Secretary of Labor, Scovel Richardson as Chairman of the United States Parole Board and later to the United States Customs Court, E. Frederic Morrow to the White House staff, and Clifton Wharton as Minister to Romania. President Kennedy also made numerous appointments of Negroes to important posts: Robert Weaver as Administrator of the Housing and Home Finance Agency, Clifton Wharton as Ambassador to Norway, Carl Rowan as Ambassador to Finland, Thurgood Marshall to the United States Circuit Court, and several others as judges of the U. S. District Court and as U. S. Attorneys. Among his numerous appointments, President Johnson assigned Carl Rowan to be Director of the United States Information Service, Wade McCree to the U. S. Circuit Court, and Mrs. Frankie Freeman to be a member of the United States Commission on Civil Rights; his most important black appointments were Thurgood Marshall to the U. S. Supreme Court, Robert C. Weaver to the Cabinet post of Secretary of Housing and Urban Development, and Andrew Brimmer to the Federal Reserve Board as Governor. President Nixon, continuing the policy of his predecessors, sent several Negroes to ambassadorial posts and appointed blacks to the White House staff, to the Federal Trade Commission, and to several sub-cabinet posts.

There were other manifestations of change in the racial climate in the United States. Both political parties, for example, came out strongly for civil rights in their 1960 platforms. In every section of the country, including the South, white citizens began to be active in the civil-rights struggle; and religious bodies—Protestant, Catholic, and Jewish—began speaking out for racial equality. Numerous white local and national groups that heretofore had excluded blacks from membership opened their doors to all qualified persons. In most litigations involving civil rights from 1950 to 1970 numerous groups—law school professors, religious organizations, civic groups, and educational societies—presented briefs as friends of the court asking that segregation laws and discriminatory practices be outlawed.

The change in the manner in which the rest of the population viewed the entrance of Negroes into areas of American life previously closed to them was a measure of the improved climate in the years following World War II. When Jackie Robinson entered organized baseball in 1947 as a member of the Brooklyn Dodgers, he created a sensation. Within a few years virtually all the baseball teams in the two major leagues had Negro players, and the signing of an additional Negro team member was no longer newsworthy. Despite the long tradition of Negro singers performing creditably on the concert stage, the announcement in 1955 that Marian Anderson, one of the world's greatest contraltos, would have a small part in a production at the Metropolitan Opera, was sensational news. Within five years Negroes were singing leading roles, and in 1961 Leontyne Price sang a title role on opening night. For many years blacks played only stereotyped roles as clowns and servants in motion pictures and on the stage. In recent years, however, such actors and actresses as Sidney Poitier, Harry Belafonte, Ossie Davis, Ruby Dee, Diahann Carroll, and Richard Roundtree have gained acceptance on the basis of their skills and talents in spite of their color. Before 1970 large and small universities that had previously given no attention to the possibility of hiring black professors had begun actively to seek them out, partly from pressure by black students and partly from pressure by the Department of Health, Education, and Welfare.

In 1950 there were virtually no blacks in major posts in the American business community. Soon, however, they were receiving appointments to positions related to "special markets," meaning markets among blacks, and by the 1960s there were black presidents or vice-presidents of banks, both black and white, in several cities. They were also receiving appointments to executive positions in major industrial and merchandising firms. Major corporations such as Pan American Airways, Trans World Airlines, General Motors, and International Business Machines appointed Negro Americans to their boards of directors.

## The Involvement of Government

The involvement of government at every level in the movement to improve the condition and status of Negroes in the United States was a significant development of the postwar period. Although many states in the North and West had civil rights statutes dating back to the period before World War I, many of these had been universally disregarded. In the 1950s, however, there was a move to revive and enforce such statutes and, in many cases, to strengthen them. By 1964 twenty-one states had enacted enforceable fair employment practice laws. New York took the lead in 1945, and the number of such states had increased to eight by 1950. In 1955 three states—Michigan, Minnesota, and Pennsylvania—enacted fair employment practice laws; and in each succeeding year new states passed such legislation. By 1964 nineteen states and fifty-five cities had barred discrimination in some area of housing. Eleven states, the Virgin Islands, and three cities adopted fair housing laws which applied to privately financed as well as governmentally aided housing. Meanwhile, many volunteer fair housing groups were organized in several sections of the country. After 1964 federal legislation reduced the need for civil rights legislation on the state and local levels.

The courts, especially the federal judiciary, continued to support the general principle of equality. In 1955, one year following the Supreme Court's decision in the school segregation cases, the Court remanded the cases to the courts of origin and indicated that it expected the lower courts to require states to make a prompt and reasonable start toward full compliance with the decision of May 1954. From that point on, the district and circuit courts had the responsibility for examining the compliance measures of the several states. In numerous cases the judges of the lower federal courts carried out the decision of the Supreme Court by refusing to countenance techniques and devices developed by the several states to render ineffective the historic Supreme Court decision.

For almost twenty years following the decision in *Brown v. The Board of Education* the lower courts had to cope with numerous ingenious schemes of local communities to evade desegregation of the schools. In 1964 less than 2 percent of the Negro students in the eleven states of the former Confederacy were in desegregated schools. When the Civil Rights Act of 1964 and the Education Act of 1965 proposed to withhold federal support from school districts that had no plans to comply with the decision, a flurry of activity began. While the percentage of children in desegregated schools began to increase, there was bitter resistance on the part of many whites and some blacks to some techniques of desegregation, such as busing. Meanwhile, the problem of desegregation had begun to plague boards of education in cities outside the South, as parents and civil rights groups began to attack *de facto* segregation and as the Federal Government began to withhold funds until it was satisfied that local authorities were making efforts to desegregate the schools. Consequently, some northern cities began to transport children by bus, and they, too, ran into the fierce opposition of parents. Although the Supreme Court in 1971 upheld the constitutionality of busing to achieve desegregation, the opponents of busing were encouraged in their stand when President Nixon expressed opposition to the use of federal funds to transport school children by bus for that purpose. In signing the multibillion-dollar education act in 1972 the President went on to scold the Congress because the antibusing amendment to the act was not as strong as he wished.

The decision in the school desegregation cases sped up action in other areas. Even after the Morgan decision in 1946 there had been numerous efforts to segregate Negroes in interstate, as well as intrastate transportation. After hearing a variety of cases on the subject over the years, the Supreme Court seemed exasperated in 1962 when it stated in *Bailey v. Patterson*, "We have settled beyond question that no state may require segregation of interstate or intrastate transportation facilities. . . . The question is no longer open; it is foreclosed as a litigable issue." The Court also upheld the argument advanced by Negro litigants that tax-supported public institutions, including parks, golf links, and swimming pools, could not be segregated. In 1964 it ruled unconstitutional the separate-but-equal provision of the Hill-Burton Act, which provided federal funds for hospital construction.

Even the Congress reacted favorably to the winds of change that were sweeping over the United States in the 1950s and 1960s. In 1957 it passed a civil rights act, the first such legislation since 1875. Among other things the act created a Civil Rights Commission as a continuing agency concerned with the enforcement of civil rights, and enlarged and strengthened the civil rights section of the Department of Justice. It also authorized the Department of Justice to institute injunction proceedings against persons conspiring to deprive citizens of their rights. The act was neither revolutionary, as many southern members of Congress claimed, nor was it merely a sham, as Senator Wayne Morse of Oregon declared. It served the definite purpose of focusing attention on the Government's responsibility in the area of civil rights in a way never done before. Negroes of Tuskegee now had a national agency to which they could relate the manner in which they had been gerrymandered out of the city limits and denied the right to vote. Negroes in Louisiana could now tell of acts of violence and intimidation against them if they attempted to vote. And the reports of the Civil Rights Commission would constitute a significant body of information that could be used in the protection of civil rights in the future.

Having broken its silence regarding civil rights after so many years, in 1960 Congress took another step. Opposition had not been stilled, and only after one of the longest and bitterest debates in the nation's history did the rather mild 1960 civil rights bill become law. The rash of bombings of black churches and of synagogues led Congress to single out for punishment any person or persons defacing or damaging synagogues, churches, or other buildings. All election officials were required to keep registration and other records for twenty-two months and make them available, upon request, to the Attorney General or his representative. If a court found a pattern or practice of denial of the right to vote by reason of race or color, any Negro within the affected area would be entitled to vote upon proof of qualification. Court-appointed referees could receive applications, take evidence, and report the findings to the court. The Attorney General hailed the new law as having "historic significance" by making it clear "that all branches of the Federal Government firmly support the proposition that the Fourteenth and Fifteenth Amendments to the Constitution are not to be considered mere promises but must become realities for all citizens in all areas of the country." No dramatic changes stemmed from the laws of 1957 and 1960, but the logjam had been broken. Perhaps it would not be quite so difficult to secure the enactment of civil rights legislation in the future.

The executive branch of the Federal Government was also active in promoting equality in American life. The work begun by Truman and continued by Eisenhower was carried forward with vigor by Presidents Kennedy and Johnson. During the campaign of 1960, candidate Kennedy indicated that he fully appreciated the significance of the civil rights struggle. When the civil rights leader, Dr. Martin Luther King, Jr., was jailed in Georgia, Kennedy called Mrs. King, expressed his sympathy, and offered to do whatever he could to help. Although many factors contributed to the Kennedy victory in the closest presidential contest in years, there can be no doubt that that one telephone call swung thousands of votes to Kennedy in states he otherwise would have lost. Once in office he would have an opportunity to demonstrate what he contended during the campaign, that the office of the President of the United States was "a place of moral leadership."

It appeared for a time, however, that the new President would not provide the kind of leadership in this area that many hoped for and others expected and still others feared. He took the position that no additional civil rights legislation was needed, except perhaps to protect voting rights. At the same time, however, he and his brother Robert, the Attorney General, worked quietly with southern railroads and southern municipal governments in a largely successful effort to eliminate segregation in interstate transportation facilities. In September 1961 he issued a personal plea for the ending of segregation and discrimination in restaurants and other places of public accommodation. He took the initiative in promoting fair employment by creating the President's Committee on Equal Employment Opportunity, with Vice President Lyndon B. Johnson as chairman. At that time he said, "I have dedicated my administration to the cause of equal opportunity in employment by the Government or its contractors. The Vice President, the Secretary of Labor, and the other members of this committee share my dedication." For the next three years the committee took steps to eliminate discrimination in employment in Government and in the private sector.

Meanwhile the Kennedy administration, through the Department of Justice, the Federal Bureau of Investigation, and the several executive offices, sought to implement the stated commitment of the administration to equality. The Department of Justice participated in abundant litigation for the protection of civil rights. The Federal Bureau of Investigation not only looked into numerous complaints regarding discrimination and the denial of civil rights, but in the interest of a better administration of justice conducted numerous schools and institutes for law-enforcement officers. In November 1962 the President signed the long-awaited order prohibiting discrimination in federally assisted housing. During the campaign two years earlier, he had taunted President Eisenhower by saying that he could have done this "with the stroke of a pen." When later asked why he himself had waited so long, President Kennedy replied that he had always intended to issue the order at the right time, and now the right time had come.

The President was not so slow to act in emergencies, however. In September 1962, when the state of Mississippi in defiance of a court order attempted to prevent the enroll-ment of James Meredith at the University of Mississippi, the President acted promptly by sending in federal troops, as President Eisenhower had done in Little Rock in 1951, to protect Meredith in the exercise of his rights. When the Birmingham demonstra-tions were at their height in April 1963, he sent in 3,000 federal troops to protect the rights of Negroes. In June 1963, when it appeared that the governor of Alabama would prevent the enrollment of three Negroes at the University of Alabama, the President ordered federal officials to the university to assist in enforcing the court order to admit the black students. He then addressed the American people and warned them that there was "a rising tide of discontent that threatens the public safety"; and he declared that "the events in Birmingham and elsewhere have so increased the cries for equality that no city or state or legislative body can prudently choose to ignore them."

## Achieving Civil Rights

One of the most significant chapters in the recent history of Negro Americans has been the development of new techniques to achieve old goals. In the 1960s many people —white and Negro—began to consider the possibility of taking matters into their own hands by direct action. They had seen violent direct action at work in the emergence of the white citizens' councils and the revival of the Ku Klux Klan to fight, with every means at their disposal, the enforcement of desegregation decisions. It now occurred to some Negroes that they might accelerate the enjoyment of their rights through non-violent direct action. In 1956, a year before the passage of the Civil Rights Act, the Negroes of Montgomery, Alabama, began to boycott the bus lines of the city to protest the abuse of Negro passengers by white drivers, including Mrs. Rosa Parks, who had refused to move to the back of the bus. They called for a more satisfactory seating practice on the buses and the employment of Negro drivers on buses serving predomi-nantly Negro sections of the city.

As the boycott continued, the white community became outraged. Some ninety Negroes were indicated under a 1921 anti-union law forbidding conspiracy to obstruct the operation of a business. Their leader, the Reverend Dr. Martin Luther King, Jr., was the first to be tried. He was found guilty. Immediately he served notice of appeal, while the bus company frantically sought to settle the problem before it became bank-rupt. The Montgomery Negroes finally won their battle; and the effective weapon of boycott gained in popularity as Negroes of Tallahassee, Atlanta, and Nashville success-fully put it to the test.

Soon other organizations were committing themselves to direct, nonviolent action. Within the next few years numerous groups, most of them interracial, became active. Among them were the Congress of Racial Equality (CORE), the Southern Christian Leadership Conference, and the Student Nonviolent Coordinating Committee (SNCC). These were backed up by other groups who gave aid and comfort to those involved in direct action. Among them were the NAACP, the National Urban League, the Southern Regional Council, numerous religious groups, and labor and civic organizations.

On February 1, 1960, four students from the Negro Agricultural and Technical College of Greensboro, North Carolina, entered a variety store, made several purchases, and sat down at the lunch counter and ordered coffee. When they were refused service because they were black, they remained in their seats until the store closed. This was the beginning of the sit-in movement, which spread rapidly through the South and to some places in the North. In the spring and summer of 1960 thousands of young people, white and black, participated in similar peaceful forms of protest against segregation and discrimination. They sat in white libraries, waded into white beaches, and slept in the lobbies of white hotels. Many of them were arrested for trespassing, disorderly conduct, and disobeying officers who ordered them off the premises. A southern journalist labeled the sit-ins "the South's new time bomb," and observed that young Negroes were infused with a new determination to risk violence to acquire some of the rights they believed were due them. When Negro students were criticized for their actions, they placed a full-page advertisement in the white *Atlanta Constitution*, in which they said, "We do not intend to wait placidly for those rights, which are already legally and morally ours, to be meted out to us one at a time." Black students and their white colleagues were on the march to secure their rights. As a result, literally hundreds of lunch counters across the South began to serve Negroes; and other facilities began to open up. Whenever their efforts were not successful, they boycotted white businesses or engaged in "selective purchasing," thus bringing to bear another effective weapon to secure their rights.

In May 1961 an even more dramatic attack on segregation and discrimination was undertaken by CORE. It sent Freedom Riders through the South to test segregation laws and practices in interstate transportation. In Alabama an interracial team was attacked at Anniston and Birmingham. Although Attorney General Robert Kennedy was obviously somewhat annoyed by the aggressiveness of these unorthodox fighters for civil rights, he ordered the Federal Bureau of Investigation to look into the matter and made it clear that the Freedom Riders would be protected. In the summer of 1961 the jails of Jackson, Mississippi, and other southern communities were virtually filled with Freedom Riders who had been arrested for alleged violation of the law. The Federal Government kept a sharp eye on these proceedings, sending some 400 United States marshals to Alabama to restore order, and securing an injunction to prohibit any attempt to stop, by force, the Freedom Riders from continuing their test of bus segregation.

At about the same time the Negroes of Albany, Georgia, began to protest their plight by marching through the streets and holding large mass meetings. Hundreds were arrested, and the white officials of the city were adamant in their refusal to discuss the situation with black leaders. In the two years that followed, marching, picketing, and public demonstrations were taken up by Negroes in Atlanta; Danville, Virginia; Cambridge, Maryland; and many other communities. In March 1963, for example, the Negroes of Leflore County, Mississippi, began to march in order to dramatize a voter registration drive sponsored by the SNCC. In April 1963, Dr. King inaugurated forty days of marching in Birmingham, Alabama, during which more than 2,500 Negroes were arrested. The Birmingham marches inspired scores of others in the North and South, some of which were attended by violence and rioting. These demonstrations also served the purpose of focusing attention on the Nation of Islam (Black Muslims), who used the marches as a means to point out one of the basic tenets of their position: that the United States would never grant equality to Negroes. Negroes, therefore, should reject any semblance of cooperation with whites and turn their attention to the development of their own culture as well as their own political and economic institutions. While the Nation of Islam was not large in numbers, it gained both popularity and respect, even among many who rejected its program.

In the year of the centennial of the Emancipation Proclamation the first stage of the civil rights revolution reached its peak. The numerous successful demonstrations and marches suggested to the leadership that one massive march on Washington might dramatize to the nation and to the world the importance of solving the problem of the status of the Negro in the United States once and for all. Preparations were made to carry out the march on August 28, 1963. All of the major Negro organizations joined in formulating the plans, and they were joined by scores of other organizations, white and black. A wide-eyed world watched as a quarter of a million blacks and whites converged on Washington from all over the United States, by every conceivable mode of transportation and under every conceivable auspices.

Washington had never seen such a day as this. The businesses in the downtown area closed, not out of respect to the marchers but because of the fear of rioting and looting. Most of the federal employees took the day off, some to participate in the march, others to get as far from the center of things as possible. Before the impressive memorial to Abraham Lincoln the civil rights leaders spoke: Whitney Young, Roy Wilkins, Martin Luther King. From his jail cell in Louisiana, James Farmer, Director of the Congress of Racial Equality, sent a message. Mahalia Jackson sang. Ministers, movie stars, radio commentators, college students, thousands of organizations, and ordinary citizens participated. The President of the United States cordially received the leaders, while other marchers called on their representatives and senators. The nation looked on via television, and the entire world would later see in the newspapers and on the newsreels the most remarkable testimony in behalf of the equality of mankind ever made in this or any other country. One important figure was absent. Fifty-odd years earlier he had assumed the leadership in the fight for equality. On the eve of the march, W. E. B. DuBois, now a citizen of Ghana, had passed away in Accra.

Two months before the march, President Kennedy had asked Congress to enact laws that would provide a legal guarantee to all citizens of equal access to the services and facilities of hotels, restaurants, places of amusement, and other establishments engaged in interstate commerce; empower the Attorney General to start school segregation suits when requested by someone unable to do so; authorize broad federal action to stop discrimination in federal jobs and activities financed wholly or in part with federal funds; create a Community Relations Service to act as a mediation agency in communities with racial tension; and make it clear "that the Federal Government is not required to furnish any kind of financial assistance to any program or activity in which racial discrimination occurs."

The President's message of June 19, 1963, is not only a historic document, a veritable landmark in the history of the drive for equality. It is also the best available summary of the unfinished business of democracy in 1963. In it, President Kennedy deplored the fact that Negroes did not have equal access to public accommodations and facilities. "No one has been barred on account of his race from fighting or dying for America— there are no 'white' and 'colored' signs on the foxholes and graveyards of battle. Surely, in 1963, one hundred years after emancipation, it should not be necessary for any American citizen to demonstrate in the streets for the opportunity to stop at a hotel, or to eat at a lunch counter in the very department store in which he is shopping, or to enter a motion picture house, on the same terms as any other customer." With regard to segregated schools, he said, "Many Negro children entering segregated grade schools at the time of the Supreme Court decision in 1954 will enter segregated high schools this year, having suffered a loss which can never be regained. Indeed, discrimination in education is one basic cause of the other inequities and hardships inflicted upon our Negro citizens."

Those who marched on Washington in August 1963 were doing what they could to emphasize the importance of enacting the legislation the President had called for. More than that, they were expressing their continuing faith in the efficiency of democratic institutions in righting the wrongs of centuries as well as giving themselves a new lease on life through a process of self-purification. But those who marched were under no illusions and were not blindly optimistic. As soon as they returned to their respective homes, they continued their fight. In New York and Chicago they urged an end to *de facto* segregation in the schools. In Birmingham they called for some tangible indication of good faith on the part of the city administration. In Placquemine Parish, Louisiana, they called for obedience of the law regarding the rights of citizens to register and vote.

When President Kennedy was assassinated on November 22, 1963, many civil rights leaders as well as ordinary citizens thought that the cause of civil rights had suffered a permanent setback; and many were disconsolate. The manner, however, in which the new President, Lyndon B. Johnson, counseled with Negro leaders, the numerous instances during his early days in office in which he pledged himself to fight for equality, and his unequivocal stand in favor of a strong civil rights bill without crippling amendments was a source of considerable optimism. With the Senate Majority Whip, Hubert H. Humphrey, in charge of the bill and with strong bipartisan support, Congress proceeded to enact the strongest civil rights bill that had ever been passed. The very process of enactment was historic, in that a majority of the members of both parties supported the bill, thereby making it possible for the Senate to invoke cloture and cut off the bitter-end marathon filibuster conducted by a bloc of southern senators.

It was a great day of rejoicing, therefore, when President Johnson signed the new civil rights bill on July 2, 1964, in the presence of congressional and civil rights leaders. The chances for the enforcement of the bill were substantially increased when several prominent southern senators who had fought its passage called for southerners to obey the new law. The appointment of Leroy Collins, former Governor of Florida, as the first director of the Community Relations Service, was widely hailed as an auspicious beginning in the effort to gain acceptance of the law, despite the fact that one prominent southerner called him a "renegade Confederate." As expected, there was vigorous initial opposition to the bill in some quarters, but the prompt declaration by a federal district court that the bill was constitutional and the refusal of Supreme Court Justice Black to suspend its enforcement contributed to the decrease of such resistance. Consequently, Negroes began to eat in restaurants and register in hotels in many parts of the South where hitherto they had not found it possible to secure service.

Perhaps it was the general improvement of the climate of race relations that brought about other desegregation steps in the months following the enactment of the civil rights bill of 1964. The summer had witnessed some ugly manifestations of racial unrest as rioting erupted in New York City, Philadelphia, Chicago, and several New Jersey cities. But civil rights leaders were quick to point out that these were not civil rights riots but the angry outbursts of poverty-stricken, jobless people living under intolerable conditions in the city slums. There had also been numerous incidents of violence in the South—including the mysterious murder of three civil rights workers in Mississippi and the brutal slaying in Georgia of a Negro educator returning from reserve-officer training to his home in Washington. But the process of desegregation continued. Segregated public facilities in many parts of the country bowed to the new law, and the pace of school desegregation began to increase noticeably.

The issue of civil rights became an important matter in the presidential campaign of 1964. While the civil rights bill that year had received generous bipartisan support in Congress, the man who became the Republican nominee for the presidency, Senator Barry Goldwater, had voted against the bill on the ground that he regarded certain parts of it as unconstitutional. This gained him strong support in many parts of the South, but it alienated virtually all Negroes—even those who had been lifelong Republicans—from the Republican nominee. If the votes of the so-called white backlash—those opposed to the Negro's vigorous drive for equality—drifted to the Republican party, there were those that President Johnson and his supporters called the frontlash—supporters of civil rights—who joined the Democratic ranks.

The breaking down of racial barriers in hotels and coffee shops did not bring with it the sense of satisfaction and fulfillment that some had expected. Not even the passage of the Civil Rights Act of 1964 or the Voting Rights Act the following year succeeded in inspiring real hope and optimism among Negro Americans. The places that opened their doors to serve them were inordinately slow in modifying their employment policies to provide jobs above the menial category for blacks. The enforcement machinery of the Department of Justice seemed, at times, helpless in the face of the stern opposition of local whites to any change in voting patterns. Indeed, where Negroes gained the vote and even public office, the acceptance of change on the part of whites was often grudging and without grace. Eight years after the passage of the Civil Rights Act, moreover, there was conclusive evidence of racial discrimination as high up as in some of the federal cabinet offices. Small wonder that many black Americans concluded that there was no serious intention on the part of white Americans to commit themselves or the nation to racial equality.

A major source of dissatisfaction and pessimism was the grinding poverty that most blacks experienced in a land of superabundance. Even as employment opportunities opened for some, the unemployment rate among Negroes was still pitifully high. In 1970 unemployment averaged 7 percent among blacks, versus 3.8 percent among whites. In 1968 the average black high-school graduate earned less than the average white with no high-school training. A black with four years of college had a median annual income of $7,744, compared with $8,154 for the average white who had completed only high school.

Poverty was the lot of millions of black sharecroppers who remained in the rural areas as well as those who came to the city. But urban poverty seemed more painful as well as more visible in the rat-infested, dilapidated slum tenement, the vain search for employment, the delinquency of the young, and the temptation toward crime on the part of the elders. The cost of 13.2 billion dollars for public welfare in 1971 was a dramatic reminder of the persistence of poverty in the United States. While far more whites than blacks were on welfare, most discussions of the problem seemed to make the erroneous assumption that only blacks were involved to any considerable extent.

Many racial confrontations of the early 1960s were surprisingly peaceful, although groups like the White Citizens Councils and the Ku Klux Klan frequently instigated a measure of violence. It was a hit-and-run form of violence marked by snipings that tried the patience of even the more conservative elements of the black communities. Many civil rights workers in the South, black and white, were the victims of snipers' bullets. Scores of Negro churches and other meeting places were bombed, sometimes with loss of life. In the later years of the 1960s the conditions of life in the northern and western ghettos slowly pushed blacks to the breaking point of despair. Rioting, accompanied by looting, burning, and loss of life, erupted in many places, notably in Los Angeles and Rochester in the summer of 1965 and in Detroit and Newark two years later.

While the Black Muslims were among the first to state categorically their disillusionment with white America, they were soon joined by others. Young blacks who had worked with CORE and SNCC became convinced of the pervasive nature of American racism and wondered if the door of opportunity had not been permanently closed to them. Soon many of them began to challenge the United States and its institutions. It was this mood that led Stokely Carmichael, Chairman of SNCC, to propound in 1966 the doctrine of Black Power. In its most positive sense, Black Power meant the promotion of black self-determination, self-respect, and full participation in all decisions affecting black people. Carmichael insisted that only the full use of Black Power would force whites to deal with blacks on a basis of equality.

Emotions of despair, frustration, and defiance merged to produce a new, fierce breed of black militants no longer willing to compromise in the fight for freedom and equality. Indeed, many were no longer interested in equality in the white man's world. Directing their attention to the masses of blacks, the militants urged their fellows to reevaluate the theory and practice of American law and convention, since these, they insisted, had worked so poorly for them. Theory and practice were white; values in American society were white; and the goals of American democracy were white. Blacks, they argued, should begin to search for their own identity, not among white groups and institutions, but among darker peoples wherever they could find them.

Some black Americans began to focus more attention on Africa and began to think and speak of it as their home. Many of them adopted African dress and wore their hair "natural." Some followed the lead of Malcolm X and other Black Muslims and adopted African or Arabic names, or used an X in place of their surname to show that they had broken all connections with white America. Some rejected the term *Negro*, arguing that it was a relic of slavery, and expressed a strong preference for *Black* (often capitalized) or *Afro-American*. They began to demand control of the institutions in the black community, including the schools; and in some communities, such as the Ocean Hill-Brownsville section of New York City, moves to seize this control led to conflict among blacks as well as with whites. In 1970 some sixteen million blacks belonged to various Christian denominations, but many of them were moving away from a religion of a white Madonna and a white Christ to one more consonant with their pride in race.

The literary manifestations of the new militant mood were wide-ranging, indeed. In the fifties, such prize-winning writers as novelist Ralph Ellison, poet Gwendolyn Brooks, and essayist and novelist James Baldwin had been concerned with the difficulties that black Americans experienced as they confronted American society in general. But if their analyses suggested an urgency they seldom approached desperation. In the sixties, such writers as Eldridge Cleaver, Don Lee, and LeRoi Jones would be more unsparing in their indictment of American society and more far-reaching in their suggestions for solutions. The new mood called for the total control of the black man's destiny by black men and went on to propose the complete remaking of American institutions.

As the professional writers concentrated on the problems of Negroes in American society, they joined the swelling ranks of those who were calling for greater attention to studies of the black man's past and present. Negroes had been systematically excluded from the study of history, they argued. Thus virtually nothing was known of their past contributions, while conventional approaches had rationalized the exclusion of blacks from the enjoyment of citizenship and full equality. Now, as they demanded equality of opportunity in American life, they demanded that schools and colleges introduce courses in black history, black literature, black sociology, and the like. Soon large numbers of educational institutions at every level were responding to the demands of students, parents, and leaders and were establishing programs of black studies of varying degrees of quality and effectiveness.

As Negro Americans made a strong bid to focus on—even to glorify—the history and traditions of darker peoples, many began to reject American values, institutions, and practices. Some saw in government, the police, and the armed services the symbols of their own oppression. As the United States became more deeply involved in the war in Vietnam, blacks began to denounce the conflict as a war against darker peoples and a diversion of national resources that could better be used to wipe out poverty and racial discrimination. Conflicts between white and black soldiers in Southeast Asia and Europe confirmed their view of the armed services as a racist institution. When Cassius Clay, the heavyweight boxing champion, took the Black Muslim name of Muhammad Ali and refused induction into the armed forces in 1967, he was convicted for refusing the draft and was stripped of his title. This embittered many Negro Americans who viewed it as further evidence of racism. In 1971 the United States Supreme Court reversed the draft conviction; but by that time Muhammad Ali had lost millions of dollars because he was unable to defend his title and had suffered untold humiliation. It was not until October 1974 that Ali enjoyed some vindication upon regaining his title by knocking out George Foreman in Kinshasa, Zaire.

The assassination of Martin Luther King, Jr., on April 4, 1968, not only shocked and saddened many Americans, but it proved once again to most Negroes that some whites would go to any lengths, including murder, to frustrate legitimate black aspirations. Since 1955 King had been the central figure in the struggle of black Americans for equality and dignity. In 1968 he went to Memphis to assist the sanitation workers of that city in their quest for higher wages and better working conditions. As he stood on the balcony of his motel room he was struck down by a rifle shot. The news of King's death sent young blacks into the streets in more than a hundred cities in what one commentator called "a widespread convulsion of disorder." There were several days of rioting, looting, and burning in Washington, Chicago, Baltimore, Kansas City, and many other places. Before it was over some 55,000 troops had been called out and 46 persons had died.

In March 1968, a month before King's death, the National Advisory Commission on Civil Disorders had observed that "our nation is moving toward two societies, one black, one white—separate and unequal." King's death and its aftermath seemed to confirm that somber observation. The capture of James Earl Ray, an escaped convict, and his confession that he had murdered Dr. King, perhaps could have eased the tension. But Ray's swift trial and sentencing to life imprisonment, with no attempt to determine whether others were involved, merely contributed to the Negro Americans' lack of confidence in the fair, even-handed administration of justice.

The assassination of presidential candidate Robert F. Kennedy in June 1968 was another severe blow to black America. Both major parties had appeared to be softening their earlier stands on civil rights, but Kennedy had won enormous support in the black community by his hard-hitting attacks on poverty and racism. When the Democrats nominated Hubert Humphrey as their standard-bearer, most blacks supported him, for they had no enthusiasm for Richard Nixon, the Republican candidate; and they were repelled by the raucous segregationist stand of George Wallace.

Negro Americans were generally disappointed with the new Republican administration. President Nixon's efforts to aid the development of "black capitalism" seemed half-hearted. Blacks criticized his welfare program as inadequate. They were disappointed with many of his appointments and were especially appalled by his nomination of Florida's G. Harrold Carswell to the Supreme Court; and they were among those who successfully fought the nomination. They were angered by the Nixon administration's move to repeal important provisions of the Voting Rights Act of 1965 and by the President's opposition to busing children to break down school segregation. When he waited for more than a year to comply with the request of the entire Negro membership of the House of Representatives to meet with him, many blacks regarded it as a studied insult to the whole Negro community.

By this time many Negroes were blaming not merely the President or the Federal Government for existing conditions, but the entire system. Even when they played by the rules of the political game and won, whites refused to abide by the rules. When Richard Hatcher was elected mayor of Gary, Indiana, some all-white sections investigated the possibility of seceding. When Charles Evers became mayor of Fayette, Mississippi, whites began to leave the town. When the leading challenger in the Los Angeles mayoralty race turned out to be a black city council member with an impeccable record of public service, whites rallied to the support of the white incumbent whom they had bitterly criticized, and returned him to office. The system seemed not to work for blacks as it did for whites.

The bitterest indictment of existing racial practices was made by a new group, the Black Panther party, which had been founded on the West Coast by two young men, Huey P. Newton and Bobby Seale. Newton declared that the only culture worth holding on to "is revolutionary culture." In his best-selling *Soul on Ice*, and other writings, Black Panther leader Eldridge Cleaver denounced American racism and the system that produced it. Panthers urged full employment, decent housing, black control of the black community, black studies in the schools and elsewhere, and an end to every form of repression and brutality. In the ghettos the Panthers established centers to provide food and health services for the poor, including hot breakfasts for school children.

Soon the Black Panthers were involved in numerous encounters with the police. In the public mind their possession of arms and their willingness to countenance violence overshadowed everything else. Several leaders, including Newton and Cleaver, were charged with killing policemen. Newton was sent to prison, but in 1970 the conviction was set aside; and Cleaver left the country while out on bond. Meanwhile, public officials seemed determined to deal more harshly with the group, and the Director of the Federal Bureau of Investigation, J. Edgar Hoover, pronounced the Panthers to be dangerous and subversive. There were numerous shoot-outs and other bloody encounters. In 1968 a number of off-duty policemen assaulted several Panther party members who had come to a Brooklyn courthouse to observe a trial involving other members. In December 1969, two party leaders were killed in Chicago in a predawn raid by police who were looking for arms. When it became known that only one shot came from within, it was clear that the raid was less than a shoot-out, and charges against other Panthers present were dropped.

In many parts of the country it appeared that public officials had overextended their fight against the Panthers; consequently, many charges against the latter did not hold up. In May 1971 several Panthers in New York were cleared of a bomb plot, while in the following month twelve were cleared of charges of murdering a New York policeman. In New Haven murder charges against Bobby Seale and a local Panther leader were dismissed. In Oakland charges of murder against Huey Newton were dropped after two juries were unable to reach a verdict.

Even if more members of the Black Panther party were winning their freedom in the courts, many blacks remained unconvinced that it was possible to secure justice in or out of the courts. In 1970 Angela Davis, a former teacher at the University of California at Los Angeles and an admitted communist, was charged with implication in a courtroom shoot-out in California. Many blacks insisted that Miss Davis was the victim of harassment for her political views, and she became something of a heroine before her trial and acquittal in 1972. George Jackson, the best known of the trio charged with murdering a guard in Soledad prison, was killed in an alleged attempt to escape prison, but the others were later acquitted. Large-scale violence such as occurred at the Attica prison in New York, where almost forty black inmates were killed in 1971, was an indication to many that racism was as rampant in the administration of prisons as in the administration of justice.

It was the deep feeling of disappointment and frustration in the Negro American's quest for equality that sparked the calling of the National Black Political Convention that met in Gary, Indiana, March 10 to 12, 1972. From every part of the country Negro Americans came to Gary to exchange views on the strategy for improving the condition of their fellows. The meeting had the endorsement of the Black Political Caucus, composed of the Negro members of the House of Representatives, the Southern Christian Leadership Conference, and People United to Save Humanity (PUSH), the Southern Christian Leadership Conference's breakaway group, headed by the Reverend Jesse L. Jackson. With LeRoi Jones and Mayor Richard Hatcher assuming leading roles, the group canvassed virtually every facet of economic, social, and political life in the United States. Even when the group had difficulty in reaching agreement regarding the means by which they could best achieve their goals, they manifested a remarkable unity in the manner in which they condemned "rampant racism" in the United States.

The "Political Coming of Age," as *Ebony* magazine described the posture of Negro Americans in 1972, was seen in the determination of the Black Political Convention to ignore party labels in supporting candidates. It could also be seen in the presence of 209 Negro Americans sitting in 37 state legislatures (by April 1974 the figures were 236 and 41, respectively) and pressing for the enactment of laws designed to improve the condition of blacks. And it could be seen in the action of Shirley Chisholm, the first Negro woman member of Congress, in seeking the Democratic presidential nomination by competing in several state primaries. Finally, it could be seen in the realization of black political leaders that their role could be decisive in the national election, and in their resolution to use that role as a lever to bring about significant improvement in the status of their people.

After the 1974 elections, black members sat in 45 state legislatures and their number in Congress had risen to sixteen in the House, four of them women; the lone black Senator had retained his seat. The national television exposure in 1974 of Representative Barbara Jordan of Texas, John Conyers of Michigan, and Charles Rangel of New York—all Democrats—in the House Judiciary Subcommittee hearings on Watergate confirmed the new image of black political figures as active participants on issues unrelated to race.

In spite of the claims to improvements made since World War II, racial inequities in American life remained persistent and flagrant. The period of affluence, during which minority gains appeared possible without apparent cost to the white community, disappeared into accelerating inflation and a deepening recession in the midseventies; and even the hope of improving life in the urban slums seemed to fade. The growing unemployment, as in earlier periods, was much higher among blacks than among whites; and recent efforts to increase minority employment in industry, on university faculties, and in executive recruitment programs, were increasingly being undone by seniority rules and reduction of force. Antiblack violence seemed not to subside, and antiwhite violence among blacks seemed to be on the increase. For any group at any level to resolve the conflicts that had such a long history and so much tragedy appeared extremely difficult. Relations between the races continued to be the most critical domestic problem of the twentieth century. Black people hoped for a better future, but in view of the disappointments of the past they looked with apprehension toward that future.

# BIBLIOGRAPHY

Bennett, Lerone, *Before the Mayflower.* Chicago, Johnson Publishing Company, 1971.

Butcher, Margaret J., *The Negro in American Culture.* New York, Alfred A. Knopf, Inc., 1956.

Cruse, Harold, *Crisis of the Negro Intellectual.* New York, William Morrow & Co., 1967.

DuBois, William E. B., *Black Reconstruction.* New York, Harcourt Brace, 1935.

Fishel, Leslie and Quarles, Benjamin, *The Negro American: A Documentary History.* Glenview, Scott, Foresman, and Co., 1967.

Franklin, John Hope, *From Slavery to Freedom: A History of Negro Americans.* New York, Alfred A. Knopf, Inc., 1967.

Frazier, E. Franklin, *The Negro in the United States.* New York, The Macmillan Co., 1957.

Huggins, Nathan and others, *Key Issues in the Afro-American Experience.* New York, Harcourt Brace Jovanovich, 1971.

Huggins, Nathan, *Harlem Renaissance.* New York, Oxford University Press, 1971.

Jordan, Winthrop, *White Over Black.* Chapel Hill, University of North Carolina Press, 1968.

Logan, Rayford, *The Betrayal of the Negro.* New York, Collier Books, 1965.

McPherson, James and others, *Blacks in America, Bibliographical Essays.* New York, Doubleday, 1971.

Meier, August, *Negro Thought in America.* Ann Arbor, University of Michigan Press, 1963.

Parsons, Talcott and Clark, Kenneth B., *The Negro American.* Boston, Beacon Press, 1966.

Quarles, Benjamin, *The Negro in the American Revolution.* Chapel Hill, University of North Carolina Press, 1961.

Toppin, Edgar A., *A Biographical History of Blacks in America Since 1528.* New York, David McKay Company, Inc., 1971.

# 2

## The Legal Status
## of the Black American

### Constance Baker Motley

**FOREWORD** *by Robert L. Carter*

Close on the heels of Lee's surrender to Grant at Appomattox, signaling final victory for the Union cause, three amendments were added to the Constitution of the United States. The basic purpose of these provisions was to harvest the victory won on the battlefield by ending slavery and granting freedom and citizenship status to the former bondsmen.

The first of these Civil War Amendments, the Thirteenth, outlawed slavery and was intended to serve as a permanent prohibition against future resurrection of that infamous practice in this country. The second, the Fourteenth, overturned the *Dred Scott* decision by making blacks citizens and sought to insure that the newly created citizens could not be victimized by differentiation between blacks and whites on racial grounds. The third and last, the Fifteenth, was intended to guarantee the full participation of blacks in the political process as a means of enabling them to protect themselves against the imposition of discriminatory laws or regulations. Between 1866 and 1875, national implementing civil rights legislation was enacted to give effect to the newly adopted constitutional provisions.

Today, more than a century later, however, the promised transmutation from hobbled slave to unfettered freeman which the Thirteenth, Fourteenth, and Fifteenth Amendments sought to effectuate remains unaccomplished. After more than a century, the Constitution has proved largely ineffective in protecting blacks against social, political, and economic deprivation. Indeed, the attempt of black Americans to complete the break with their slave heritage has proved to be an extraordinarily difficult, stubbornly resistant, and seemingly never-ending process. Vestiges of slavery seem to endure, and although modified in form from time to time, the unchanging and relentless result is to keep blacks mired and shackled in ways that in many respects are akin to their old slave status.

Before the turn of the century the high hopes blacks held of being "free at last" in the immediate aftermath of their release from slavery were soon dashed. The United

States Supreme Court restricted the scope and reach of the Fourteenth Amendment guarantee against racial differentiation to discrimination imposed by state authority, and held that the separate-but-equal doctrine enunciated in *Plessy v. Ferguson*[1] was consistent with the mandate of equal opportunity. Thus within less than three decades after its adoption the Fourteenth Amendment, far from being the Magna Charta of black freedom, provided no protection to blacks against private, as opposed to public, discrimination and condoned apartheid, white supremacy, and black subordination. Indeed, well into the third decade of the twentieth century the original purposes of the Fourteenth Amendment were well-nigh forgotten as it became a protective bastion for the development and spread of corporate power.

The validation of laws imposing stringent residential requirements, early registration, and the payment of a poll tax as prerequisites to the exercise of the right to vote in effect nullified the Fifteenth Amendment. However neutral the terms of these statutory provisions, they were specifically designed to disenfranchise blacks, being addressed to their basic contemporary characteristics—their poverty, ignorance, lack of sophistication, and residential transience. Since the courts refused to look at the racist purposes behind these laws, the aforesaid legal restrictions had accomplished the wholesale disenfranchisement of blacks by the early twentieth century. When the statutory barriers did not suffice, terror and violence were utilized.

The Thirteenth Amendment's prohibition against slavery was also blunted. Outright slavery did not survive, but for many years blacks were effectively chained to the land and required to work exclusively for a particular white landowner. Peonage and serfdom became lawful substitutes for slavery.

The United States involvement in World War I caused domestic convulsions which shook the foundations of the old order. The insatiable needs of northern industry for labor caused by the war's demands lured blacks out of the rural South. Thus began the mass migration of blacks to the metropolitan areas of the North, and with this movement northward the meanness of Negro life, the extent of the deprivation to which blacks were subjected because of their color, and the depth and pervasiveness of racism in this country were revealed for all to see. The Negro question became a focus of national and international attention.

Out of this new awareness came the movement to return the Civil War Amendments to their original purposes. The chapter that follows discusses the case law and statutes which were spawned by court litigation, marches, sit-ins, lobbying, and protest which the movement produced. This civil rights activity culminated in the 1954 United States Supreme Court decision in *Brown v. The Board of Education*[2] outlawing racial segregation in the nation's public schools, in the passage of the United States Civil Rights Act of 1964, and the Voting Rights Act of 1965. As a result, the Fourteenth and Fifteenth Amendments now give strong support to black claims to equal treatment and equal opportunity in all facets of American life.

In the cases discussed in the ensuing chapter the courts have held that racial discrimination and differentiation are forbidden under law; that blacks are entitled to and guaranteed equal citizenship status in all aspects of American life. These holdings set forth binding legal standards applicable and enforceable throughout the United States. Separate but equal has been overturned; racial discrimination in all of its manifestations has been declared to be legally impermissible.

*Brown v. The Board of Education* was the high point of the campaign to secure freedom through law. In mandating effectuation in real life of the constitutional guarantees of equality, *Brown* is one of the peaks of American constitutional adjudication. In assuming that the nation can function more or less routinely in conformity with the highest ethical considerations, *Brown* espouses the highest values of the society and will forever remain a historic statement of American law. Paradoxically, perhaps, the *Brown* decision brought to a close an era in which blacks were confident of the efficacy of the law in the quest for equal citizenship status in American life.

While the law established the blacks' right to equality, nonetheless the previous patterns of white supremacy persisted. Even though *Brown* ordered the elimination of the dual school system pursuant to its "all deliberate speed" decree of implementation in 1955, southern communities succeeded in preventing *Brown*'s actual enforcement except on a very small scale, at least until passage of the Civil Rights Act of 1964. With the more effective administrative-enforcement machinery established under the act, the pace of school desegregation quickened, but full compliance with *Brown* is not as yet an accomplished fact.

Although *Brown* must be adjudged a failure in respect to outlawing school segregation in the United States—indeed, there is more school segregation, both *de facto* and *de jure*, than existed when *Brown* was decided—*Brown*'s impact, nonetheless, was extremely significant. In holding, in effect, that blacks were the equal of whites under law, *Brown* and cognate cases altered the whole syndrome of race relations in this country. Blacks shed their passivity and quiet acceptance of their inferior status; under law they had been adjudged entitled to equality. They had the right to demand full vindication of their rights. Thus they became more aggressive, assertive, and impatient in their struggle for equality.

While the pace of change quickened and doors heretofore closed to blacks were now ajar, a great mass of the black poor remains trapped in an inferior status of deprivation and discrimination. And with the seemingly unyielding persistence of racial discrimination and the successful resistance of the white community to full implementation of the ban on school segregation, housing or job discrimination, blacks began to lose faith in the law. The belief grew that freedom would be obtained only when blacks were able to make strategic and judicious use of whatever levers of social, political, or economic power they possessed. This led to a politics of black and white confrontation, to increasing interracial tensions and polarization. The more genteel style which had generally prevailed in interracial dealings was replaced by open and cacophonous declarations of mistrust.

Heretofore the South had been viewed as the battleground on which the campaign for equality would be won or lost, but the aftermath of *Brown* revealed that racial discrimination was a national, not a regional, phenomenon. The patterns of discrimination were somewhat less rigid and more subtle than the raw racism of the South, but measured against a standard of full equality under law, it was soon manifest that racial discrimination was as widely practiced to the north as to the south of the Mason-Dixon line. Indeed, *Brown*, by outlawing segregation, considered it merely a symptom of white supremacy—the disease that afflicts American life and has kept blacks imprisoned in a lower-caste status. When faced with the obligation of giving effect to the egalitarian standard which the law since *Brown* has required, fierce resistance by the white community became nationwide.

Northerners condemned southerners for opposing school desegregation in the wake of *Brown* and the Civil Rights Act of 1964, but northerners themselves engaged in bitter battles to maintain *de facto* school segregation by means of neighborhood schools of black and white concentration. Moreover, in the face of the possible wide-scale use of busing as an effective means of accomplishing school desegregation in the urban North and South, northerners have joined with southerners in creating a climate of near-hysteria over the question.

Bills have been enacted by both the Senate and the House to restrict the power of the courts to order busing to accomplish school desegregation. Before his resignation, President Nixon proposed that the Congress order a moratorium on busing, and there has been strong sentiment in the Congress backed by public opinion for a constitutional amendment to bar busing for the purpose of school integration. The antibusing view was supported by President Ford's reaction to the disorders in South Boston accompanying the integration of schools with bused-in black pupils. Thus blacks face the enactment of some form of legal restriction to prevent full vindication of their constitutionally guaranteed right to equal educational opportunity.

The controversy over busing for integration will probably dissipate whatever faith remains in the black community that freedom can be secured through law. It is clear that busing is a false issue; the real question is white America's failure of will to give full implementation to the constitutional requirement that blacks be accorded equal educational opportunity, if school integration must follow. The Chief Justice of the United States, Warren Burger, in an opinion approving busing to remedy the denial of equal educational opportunity, pointed out that busing "was perhaps the single most important factor in the transition from the one-room schoolhouse to the consolidated school. Eighteen million . . . public school children, approximately 38 percent [of the nation's public-school population] were transported to their schools by bus in 1969–70 in all parts of the country."[3] Moreover, statistics of the United States Department of

Transportation show the rise in the cost of busing in the nation's public-school system from 1.5 billion during the 1970–71 school term to 1.7 billion in the 1971–72 school term, only 1 percent of which can be attributed to busing for integration.[4]

While the fears of white parents are real, private anxieties must give way to constitutional necessities. The Constitution calls for equal treatment. If equal education is denied, courts must have full authority to fashion a remedy, else the constitutional provision becomes a meaningless abstraction. The proposed antibusing laws would limit court authority to remedy a violation of what the Constitution requires. Such laws would appear to be patently unconstitutional. Further, if these laws are validated by the courts or are adopted in the form of a constitutional amendment, basic principles of equality and justice will have been greatly compromised, and the whole concept of American democracy as a system of equal rights and equal justice for all, of course, will be badly tarnished. Whatever reservations blacks may themselves have about busing, they will all certainly interpret the adoption of antibusing legislation or constitutional amendment as evidence that the white majority will not allow the law to become the vehicle through which blacks secure first-class citizenship in this country.

Moreover, it has become evident that our criminal justice system, like all other American institutions, is riddled with racism; that blacks are treated more harshly from the moment of their initial contact with the criminal justice system; the police are more likely to arrest or mistreat blacks than whites; the prosecution is more likely to decide to bring blacks to trial than whites; the jury is more inclined to find guilt and to recommend a harsher penalty and the judge more often than not metes out heavier sentences. Once in prison, the black convict, as in the outside world, is subjected to discrimination in respect to the amenities of prison life, as is true of probation as well. Thus blacks run afoul of the law because they are black; they are more likely to be brought to trial, are consistently given harsher sentences, demeaned, and brutalized in prison life and are less likely to be given the benefit of the doubt by parole officers—all because they are black. One need not attempt to show innocence or lack of justification in respect to violation of the criminal law by blacks. Granting the criminal infractions, what can no longer be disputed is that the penalty imposed is likely to fall more heavily on the black criminal deviant than on the white.

Thus while the following chapter shows that under law almost all legal disabilities against blacks are no longer operative, a wide gap between legal equality and equality in fact still remains. Trust in the law as the key to fulfillment of the country's promise of a free and open society has been eroded at all levels of American society. Cynicism about the fairness and objectivity of the law and our legal institutions is prevalent among the young, blacks, and other underprivileged groups. The nature, depth, and extent of racism in American life and the way in which it affects American institutions, attitudes, and practices has long been the subject of serious scholarship. Three brilliant studies have added new dimension to current knowledge on the subject.[5] Racism has prevented full fruition of the victories over racial discrimination won in the courts and in legislative halls, which are discussed in this chapter. Yet what is important is that while the law against racial discrimination may not be effectuated—that enclaves of power may yet frustrate its implementation—blacks have won the campaign for legal equality. When they secure sufficient political and economic muscle, they will at last have the power to insist that the gap between what the law ordains and what real life establishes be closed, and that the black citizen's real status conform to his or her legal status.

Robert L. Carter

## PARTICIPATION IN GOVERNMENT*

In the years immediately following the Civil War, blacks were emancipated from slavery by adoption of the Thirteenth Amendment and were granted both national and state citizenship by the Fourteenth Amendment; yet the former slaveholding states where they resided in large numbers excluded them from participation in the body politic by denying them the right to vote. This led to adoption of the Fifteenth Amendment in 1870, prohibiting both the state and the national governments from denying the right to vote because of race, color, or previous condition of servitude.

The Enforcement Act of 1870, enacted to enforce the Fifteenth Amendment, made it a crime for a public official or private person to interfere with the right to vote.[1] The next year, the law was amended to make possible federal supervision of the entire electoral process in former Confederate states, from registration of voters to the certification of election returns.[2] However, in 1894 most of these provisions were repealed,[3] for the North had lost interest in the race problem by then and the former slaveholders were back in control of southern state governments. What remained of the Enforcement Act was seldom enforced.[4]

In addition to the use of outright intimidation through such groups as the Ku Klux Klan, the southern states adopted a number of more sophisticated stratagems for disenfranchising blacks. These included grandfather clauses, white primaries, poll taxes, and literacy tests for voter applicants. The grandfather clause typically provided for continued registration of former voters and their lineal descendants. More stringent

---

*Other chapters have dealt in some depth with the social, political, and economic realities which provide the background for the body of court cases that constitute the legal history of the black American. This chapter is thus limited to a lay discussion of the developments which now define the current legal status of black Americans and dismantlement of the legal framework which supported the segregated society—one of the more significant revolutions of the twentieth century. Space limitations permit discussion of only the major cases in each area bearing directly upon the rights of black Americans. Cases involving broader areas of civil liberties, such as free speech and the whole range of criminal cases which affect blacks in common with other members of society will not be dealt with here.    —M.M.S.

regulations were applied to the registration of new voters. The white primary was a whites-only party primary election to select candidates for the general elections. The poll tax made annual payment of a capitation tax a prerequisite to voting. The literacy test imposed a high standard of literacy to be judged by the registrar of voters. The registrar's judgment was largely uncontrolled. Generally, a voter registration statute required that an applicant be able to read, write, understand, and explain a constitutional provision to the satisfaction of the registrar.

Oklahoma, for example, used the literacy test combined with the grandfather clause. After Oklahoma's admission to the Union, its constitution was amended and the state's otherwise valid voting provisions were altered to include a required literacy test. All those who were qualified to vote on January 1, 1866, or lineal descendants of such persons, were exempt from the test, but since few blacks, if any, were qualified voters in 1866, most Negroes were required to take it. In 1915 the Supreme Court invalidated this clause as a device discriminatory against Negroes.[5] Oklahoma then provided that persons who had voted in the general election of 1914 would remain qualified. All others who could qualify were required to register during a twelve-day period from April 30, 1916, through May 11, 1916. The Court held this a continuation of the grandfather clause. It ruled with respect to the brief registration period that the Fifteenth Amendment "nullifies sophisticated as well as simpleminded modes of discrimination."[6]

The white primary was challenged in 1927 in Texas and 1948 in South Carolina. Prior to 1927, Texas law had provided that "in no event shall a negro [sic] be eligible to participate in a Democratic party primary election held in the state of Texas." In Texas, as in most southern states at that time, the Democratic party was the only party of any significance. Thus, election in the primary was tantamount to election in the general election. The Supreme Court held the Texas enactment a direct violation of the Fourteenth Amendment.[7] The Texas legislature immediately declared an emergency and substituted another statute. This time the state executive committee of a party was given power to determine qualifications of voters in a party primary. The Democratic party executive committee quickly adopted a resolution that only white Democrats could vote in its primary. This action was likewise held to violate the Fourteenth Amendment.[8] The Court said: "The 14th Amendment, adopted as it was with special solicitude for the equal protection of members of the Negro race, lays a duty upon the court to level by its judgment these barriers of color." Without any further statutory enactment, Texas then permitted the Democratic party state convention to determine the qualifications of voters in the party primary. The convention simply adopted the same resolution which the executive committee had adopted. The Supreme Court upheld this action in 1935.[9] It ruled there was no state action involved in this decision and, consequently, no violation of the Federal Constitution.

Then the Supreme Court held in *United States v. Classic*, 313 U.S. 299 (1941), that Congress had the power to regulate primaries where the primary is made by state law an integral part of the machinery of federal elections. The *Classic* case provided a new legal theory for attacking the white primary in Texas. The Democratic party primary was obviously an important part of the Texas election process. Consequently, in *Smith v. Allwright*, 321 U.S. 649 (1944), the Court found that in Texas the primary was, by law, an integral part of "the machinery for choosing officials, state and national." To this state function the Court applied the proscriptions of the Fifteenth Amendment.

South Carolina, another white-primary state, then took up the fight. After *Smith v. Allwright, supra,* South Carolina repealed all of its laws governing the primary. This bold attempt to avoid the impact of the Fifteenth Amendment was likewise nullified in 1948 by the federal courts.[10] South Carolina's Democratic party then tried to bar blacks from its primaries by requiring of party members an oath supporting segregation and opposing fair employment practices. This device for denying the franchise was also invalidated.[11]

Another Texas white-primary device was struck down by the Supreme Court as late as 1953. In that case, the Jaybird Party in Texas, a purported private club, excluded blacks. The club elected persons who then ran in the primaries and general elections. These candidates were invariably elected. The Supreme Court held that blacks could not be excluded.[12]

Beginning in 1957 the Congress once again acted to protect the right to vote. At that time, it authorized the Attorney General of the United States to seek injunctions against public and private interference with voting rights.[13] The Civil Rights Act of 1960 authorized making the recalcitrant states themselves parties to lawsuits brought by the Government, gave the Attorney General access to local voting records, and permitted the registration of voters by courts.[14] The Civil Rights Act of 1964 expedited the hearing of voting cases before three-judge federal courts, forbade the arbitrary disposition of applications by blacks to register in federal elections, and made a sixth-grade education prima facie evidence of literacy in such elections.[15]

The poll tax was finally eliminated as a requirement for voting in federal elections by the Twenty-fourth Amendment to the Constitution in 1964. The Voting Rights Act of 1965 excuses those made eligible to vote, by application of that law to a particular state or a part thereof, from paying accumulated past poll taxes for state and local elections. In 1966 the Supreme Court finally held poll taxes as applied to state and local elections a violation of the equal-protection clause of the Fourteenth Amendment. *Harper v. Virginia Board of Elections*, 383 U.S. 663.

In 1965, after the march from Selma to Montgomery, Alabama, led by Martin Luther King, Congress finally and forthrightly came to grips with the undeniable fact that after almost a century blacks were still being denied the right to vote in most southern states or parts of these states. Consequently, the Congress provided, once again, with the Voting Rights Act of 1965, for federal supervision of elections where necessary. When the 1965 law was enacted, the states of Alabama, Georgia, Louisiana, Mississippi, North Carolina, South Carolina, and Virginia were still using the literacy test as a device to restrict black voting. The act suspended the use of these literacy tests in those states for five years. South Carolina unsuccessfully challenged this and other provisions of the law in the Supreme Court *South Carolina v. Katzenbach*, 383 U.S. 301, 310 (1966).[16] Suspension of the use of literacy tests was found justified by the fact that although the discriminatory application of such tests had been previously held unconstitutional, the tests were still being widely used in the South as an effective device for limiting black voting strength.[17]

In addition, the act provides, *inter alia*, for: 1) suspension of any *new* voting regulations pending review by federal anthorities; 2) the assignment of federal examiners to list qualified applicants who are thereafter entitled to vote in all elections; 3) the appointment of federal poll-watchers in places to which federal examiners have already been assigned; 4) balloting by persons denied access to the polls in areas where federal examiners have been appointed; 5) strengthening existing provisions for bringing lawsuits; 6) facilitating constitutional litigation challenging the imposition of all poll taxes for state and local election; and 7) civil and criminal sanctions against interference with the right to vote.[18] The act was extended for another five-year period by the Congress on June 22, 1970.[19]

In upholding the constitutionality of those provisions of the act which South Carolina had attacked, the Court said: "The constitutional propriety of the Voting Rights Act of 1965 must be judged with reference to the historical experience which it reflects. Before enacting the measure, Congress explored with great care the problem of racial discrimination in voting. . . . At the close of these deliberations, the verdict of both chambers was overwhelming."[20] The Supreme Court's affirmation of the constitutionality of the provisions was equally clear-cut, although Mr. Justice Black dissented in part. He was of the view that Congress had exceeded its power under the Fifteenth Amendment to enforce its provisions by providing in the act that a covered state could not amend its constitution or laws relating to voting without first receiving federal approval.[21] However, the majority held: "This may have been an uncommon exercise of congressional power, as South Carolina contends, but the Court has recognized that exceptional conditions can justify legislative measures not otherwise appropriate."[22]

The act applies to those states, or any part thereof, where the Attorney General finds: 1) on November 1, 1964 the state maintained a "test or device"; and 2) the Director of the Census has determined that less than 50 percent of the state's voting-age residents were registered on November 1, 1964, or voted in the presidential election of November 1964. These findings are not reviewable in any court.

In addition to validating the sweeping remedies provided by the act, the Court has given a liberal construction to its provisions. In *Hadnott v. Amos*, 394 U.S. 358 (1969), for example, the Court held a 1967 Alabama statute, which prohibited certification of any person who failed to file an official declaration of intention to become a candidate for public office by March 1 of the general election year, a new law within the contemplation of the act and therefore subject to federal review and approval. Then, in *Allen v.*

*State Bd. of Elections*, 393 U.S. 544 (1969), the Court held alterations in the laws of Mississippi and Virginia which tended to dilute the effectiveness of black voting power by substituting at-large voting, as within the contemplation of the act. It next refused to permit North Carolina to reinstate its suspended literacy tests, on the broad ground that recent fair application of other state laws had not been sufficient to eliminate voting discrimination and remedy the educational handicaps of blacks resulting from inferior segregated schools. *Gaston County v. United States*, 395 U.S. 285 (1969).

The Court previously had barred the use of racial designations of candidates on ballots.[23] And it had voided a blatant racial gerrymander employed in Tuskegee, Alabama, to dilute black voting power.[24] Consequently, after enactment of the Voting Rights Act of 1965, blacks turned their attention to voter-apportionment schemes which also dilute the effectiveness of their votes. The Supreme Court has ruled that such schemes are subject to challenge where the circumstances of a particular case operate to minimize or cancel out black voting strength. *Fortson v. Dorsey*, 379 U.S. 433 (1965). However, proving such discrimination to the satisfaction of a majority of the Supreme Court has been extremely difficult. In 1971, for example, the Supreme Court reversed a federal trial-court conclusion that multimember district voting in Indiana (as opposed to single-member district voting) diluted the effectiveness of black votes in the ghetto area of the Marion County district. The majority of the Court was of the view that the blacks had failed to prove an invidious discrimination in Indiana's scheme for electing state legislators. *Whitcomb v. Chavis*, 403 U.S. 124 (1971).

## ACCESS TO PUBLIC FACILITIES

The Supreme Court has divested "Jim Crow" of all legal status in the public domain by construing the equal-protection clause of the Fourteenth Amendment as a prohibition against state-enforced racial exclusion or segregation in any facility owned or operated by the state.[25] In a case involving courthouse segregation, it held the issue no longer open to question.[26] This revolution in law occurred in the decade 1954–64. The Civil Rights Act of 1964 authorizes the Attorney General of the United States to bring suits to desegregate state-owned or -operated facilities at the request of an individual otherwise unable to bring suit.

The Court has also applied the Fourteenth Amendment's proscription to state-owned facilities leased to private persons or corporations for operation for the benefit of the public,[27] and to private facilities, such as hospitals, where there is significant state involvement.[28] However, in 1972 the Court failed to find significant state involvement in a case where a private club which held a liquor license from the state of Pennsylvania refused to serve black guests of white members. *Moose Lodge No. 107 v. Irvis* 407 U.S. 163 (1972).

Where the state has required segregation in a privately owned place of public accommodation, the Court has interposed the amendment's prohibition as a bar to the owner's discriminatory acts. In such cases the state is significantly involved and the owner's wish is constitutionally indistinguishable from the state's command. This the Court held in 1963 in a group of sit-in cases involving convictions of black college students who sought food service at dime-store lunch counters in several southern communities.[29]

On June 22, 1964, the Supreme Court decided another significant group of sit-in cases without deciding by a majority vote the crucial constitutional issue raised.[30] These cases posed a question which, if decided in the affirmative, would have opened all privately owned places of public accommodations to blacks. The question was whether the prohibitions of the Fourteenth Amendment or any other constitutional provisions preclude state court enforcement of state trespass laws against blacks who, over the owner's objections, persist in peacefully seeking equal treatment in places of public accommodation. Three members of the court (Chief Justice Earl Warren, Mr. Justice Douglas, and Mr. Justice Goldberg) answered this question in the affirmative. Three other justices (Black, Harlan, and White) answered the question in the negative. Three other justices (Brennan, Clark, and Stewart) avoided decision of the issue. They found other less far-reaching constitutional grounds on which to reverse the trespass conviction in those cases.[31] The Chief Justice and the two who agreed with him on the major issue concurred in the reversal of the convictions on these lesser grounds in order to form a six-member majority for reversal.

However, ten days after the Court's decisions in these cases, the Congress on July 2 enacted the Civil Rights Act of 1964. Title II of the act makes unlawful racial discrimination in a place of public accommodation "if its operations affect commerce, or if discrimination or segregation by it is supported by state action." The words "affect commerce" operate to make most places of public accommodation subject to the act.[32] It was held constitutionally valid under the commerce clause of the Federal Constitution (Article I, Section 8) by a unanimous Supreme Court on December 14, 1964 in *Heart of Atlanta Motel v. United States*, 379 U.S. 241 (1964) and in *Katzenback v. McClung*, 379 U.S. 294 (1964). On the same day the high Court, in a five-to-four decision, barred further proceedings in thousands of prosecutions commenced in state courts against those who had peacefully sought service in segregated establishments through sit-in demonstrations. The Court held Title II also "prohibits the application of state laws in a way that would deprive any person of the rights granted under Act." *Hamm v. City of Rock Hill*, 379 U.S. 306 (1964).

The attack upon public accommodations discrimination which resulted in Title II of the Civil Rights Act of 1964 began in 1960. In that year, black college students in Greensboro, North Carolina, silently sat at a department-store lunch counter reserved for white customers.[33] This was the birth of the sit-in movement which mushroomed throughout the South.[34] The sit-in movement succeeded in desegregating many privately owned lunch counters without resorting to the courts.[35] Violence ensued in several localities;[36] but in virtually every instance the "sit-inners" were arrested. They were charged with breach of the peace, disorderly conduct, refusing to obey an officer, trespass, or some similar misdemeanor. Thousands of these cases were pending in southern state courts at the end of 1963.[37]

In the North prior to 1964 public accommodations discrimination had been prohibited by state law. Thirty-one states and the District of Columbia in 1964 had laws prohibiting discrimination against blacks in such privately owned places.[38] The number and types of facilities covered varied from state to state. The only border states with such laws were Delaware and Maryland.[39]

The Civil Rights Act of 1964 takes these state statutes into account and provides for suit by an aggrieved party in a federal court thirty days after seeking relief as provided by state law. In such cases the Attorney General of the United States may intervene. The court, upon application of an aggrieved party, may appoint counsel; authorize commencement of the suit without payment of fees, costs, or security; and allow the prevailing party reasonable attorney fees.

When suit is commenced in a state having no protective legislation, the court *may* refer the matter to the Community Relations Service established by the Civil Rights Act of 1964 (Title X). This may be done, where the court believes there exists a reasonable possibility of obtaining voluntary compliance, for a period not exceeding 120 days. Suits may also be commenced by the Attorney General against any person or group of persons "engaged in a pattern or practice of resistance to the full enjoyment of any rights secured" by the public-accommodations section of the law.


## FREEDOM TO TRAVEL


Travel by common carrier is a notably important kind of use of public facilities, with a distinct history of its own. By the end of 1961 the courts and the Interstate Commerce Commission had outlawed all segregation in transportation, and racial restrictions in interstate transportation had virtually disappeared. The "Jim Crow" railroad car is no more; segregation on intrastate carriers has been outlawed; travel is now legally free of all racial restrictions; yet some blacks still ride in the back of local buses and others continue to gather in the waiting rooms once marked "Colored." These practices carry with them the habits of a century of segregation. Fear of local reprisals is also a factor.[40]

Segregation in transportation was first challenged in the Supreme Court by Homer Adolph Plessy. Mr. Plessy was a Negro as defined by Louisiana law, because he had "one-eighth African blood." He had been charged with refusing to occupy a seat in the "colored coach" of a local railroad. Plessy brought suit to enjoin his prosecution for violating the Louisiana statute requiring railroad-car segregation. The Supreme Court in

1896 ruled against him. The case, *Plessy v. Ferguson*, 163 U.S. 537, was the Supreme Court's first sanction of the "separate but equal" doctrine. The doctrine remained inviolate as it applied to transportation for half a century.

In 1941, the Supreme Court construed the Interstate Commerce Act to require Pullman companies to provide equal accommodations for blacks.[41] In 1946, the first successful and far-reaching attack upon the doctrine of "separate but equal" as applied to transportation was made. The Supreme Court held a Virginia statute requiring segregation of blacks on interstate buses an unreasonable burden on interstate commerce.[42] Then in 1950 the Supreme Court forced an end to dining-car segregation.[43] It required railroads to permit blacks to occupy any empty seat on the diner. The custom had been to partition off a small part of the dining car for service of blacks. When this small portion became filled, a black customer had to wait. The Court held this a violation of the Interstate Commerce Act.

The Interstate Commerce Commission in 1955 ordered an end to passenger segregation on eleven southern interstate railroads. The suit had been filed by the National Association for the Advancement of Colored People on behalf of its members. Individual persons who had been segregated on railroads also joined in the suit.[44] On the same day, the commission required an end to segregation on interstate buses.[45] Railroad terminals and bus depots, however, remained segregated. The Montgomery, Alabama, bus boycott movement led to a Supreme Court decision barring segregation in intrastate travel in 1956.[46] In 1960, the Interstate Commerce Act was again construed by the Supreme Court. This time it required restaurants in depots utilized by interstate carriers to serve the carriers' black passengers.[47]

It was largely to test the extent of compliance with this decision that the Freedom Riders set out on their freedom journey in 1961. In the summer of that year, approximately 300 persons from northern communities traveled by bus to Jackson, Mississippi.[48] When these Freedom Riders arrived in Mississippi, each was arrested. They were charged with disorderly conduct. Most spent time in jail. Appeals were taken in many of the cases. (Three years later the bulk of these cases were still making their way through the Mississippi courts.) The attendant wide publicity and aroused public opinion caused the Attorney General of the United States to request an order of the Interstate Commerce Commission banning segregation in train terminals and bus depots. Such an order was issued and became effective November 1, 1961. It also took a Supreme Court decision and subsequent court action to desegregate transportation facilities in Jackson, Mississippi.[49] Shortly thereafter, the Supreme Court held racial segregation unconstitutional in an airport restaurant in Memphis, Tennessee, which had been leased to a private company.[50] Memphis had previously removed signs designating separate rest rooms for black and white passengers in the terminal. Airlines were the only carriers which did not pursue a passenger segregation policy and southern state laws did not require such segregation.

# FREEDOM OF RESIDENCE

Housing in urban centers is still largely segregated. This racially divisive pattern has resulted not only from private prejudice but from governmental action and inaction as well. The role of government in the past in initiating and sustaining residential segregation has been a pervasive one. Notwithstanding the Fourteenth Amendment and a federal statutory bar, southern cities enacted housing segregation ordinances. These were held unconstitutional, however, by the Supreme Court. The first case arose in Louisville, Kentucky,[51] in 1917. There the Court ruled the "separate but equal" doctrine inapplicable to property rights. The Court's exemption of property rights was predicated upon the express protection of property in the due-process clause of the Fourteenth Amendment. The decision was also based on the Civil Rights Act of 1866 which guaranteed Negroes the same rights as white persons with respect to real property. Nevertheless, a residential segregation ordinance was still being enforced in Birmingham, Alabama, in 1949. Its enforcement was enjoined the following year by a federal appeals court.[52] A similar ordinance was being enforced in Palm Beach, Florida, as late as 1958.[53] And in 1963, Atlanta, Georgia was still enforcing residential zoning segregation.[54]

In both northern and southern cities, all-white residential communities were created by private builders and individual homeowners. Such communities were perpetuated either through voluntary adherence to, or court enforcement of, racially restrictive covenants. These covenants were contained in the deeds to individual lots. Court enforcement of these agreements between white property owners not to sell to blacks or other racial and ethnic groups proved most effective. The Supreme Court in 1948 held such agreements unenforceable by state[55] and federal[56] courts. The Court held that state court enforcement of such agreements violated the equal protection clause of the Fourteenth Amendment to the Federal Constitution. Such enforcement was also declared to be contrary to the terms of the Civil Rights Act of 1866. Federal court enforcement of such covenants was held to violate the public policy of the United States, since the Fourteenth Amendment barred enforcement by the states. However, these decisions did not affect voluntary adherence to such agreements. The agreements, per se, were not held illegal.

Since most blacks are poor or low-middle-income wage earners, their exclusion from the better housing areas is readily effected by subtle economic devices such as two-acre zoning requirements, refusal of local authorities to authorize construction of low-income housing, and by the construction of high-rental housing in urban renewal areas. Economic devices of this kind have thus far escaped court disapproval.[57]

For many years the Federal Government played a major role in initiating housing segregation. In 1934 the Federal Housing Administration (FHA) was established by an act of Congress.[58] Its purpose was to stimulate the construction of new housing by insuring repayment of mortgages on housing meeting certain requirements. FHA's *Underwriting Manuals*, the 1935, 1936, 1938, and 1940 editions, advocated exclusion of blacks and other minorities and mandated adoption of racially restrictive covenants for new construction.[59] The 1948 decision precluding governmental enforcement of such agreements forced deletion of these proposals from the 1949 edition. Thereafter, the agency announced an ambiguous policy: it would refuse to insure mortgages where restrictive agreements were "recorded" after February 15, 1950.[60] But FHA steadfastly refused to *require* builders securing bank FHA mortgage-insurance commitments for their developments to sell to blacks. This alleged government neutrality continued until 1962. Then President Kennedy signed his promised Executive Order.[61] The order barred future government insurance where builders refused to affirm in writing a policy of nondiscrimination.[62]

Housing erected by state agencies with public funds has also been largely segregated, in the North and South alike. Construction of this kind provides an easy legal target, however, and numerous court decisions have held that the Fourteenth Amendment prohibits segregation in public housing projects.[63] The President's Executive Order permitted the Attorney General to sue to desegregate public housing aided financially by the Federal Government.[64] Prior to the order, the Federal Government's Public Housing Administration, which furnished funds to local public agencies, approved separate units for black tenants.[65]

By 1964 a number of states and cities had laws protecting against discrimination in some area of housing. California was one such state, with laws prohibiting discrimination in publicly aided housing and private housing containing more than four units. Opponents of fair-housing legislation sought to counteract this legislation by proposing an amendment to the state's constitution which was submitted to the voters for approval in a state-wide election in 1964. The citizens of California approved the amendment, known as Proposition 14. It denied power to the state to limit in any way the ability of an individual to sell, lease, or rent real property. But the Supreme Court affirmed the judgment of the state's highest court that the amendment authorized racial discrimination in violation of the equal protection clause of the Fourteenth Amendment and therefore could not stand consistently therewith. *Reitman v. Mulkey*, 387 U.S. 370 (1967). A similar attempt by the city of Akron, Ohio, to repeal a fair-housing ordinance and to prevent any future antidiscrimination ordinance by requiring approval of same by the voters in a referendum was also voided by the Supreme Court. *Hunter v. Erickson*, 393 U.S. 385 (1969).

The most difficult housing areas to attack legally have been areas of mixed public and private involvement. The federal urban renewal program exemplifies such a situation. That program involves federal and city funds, municipal planning, land clearance and use of the power of eminent domain. Under this program a private developer often contracts with the local public agency to redevelop a cleared area for residential or commercial use in accordance with a municipally approved plan. However, the Housing Act of 1968 has made it unlawful to refuse to sell or rent any housing owned or operated by the Federal Government or aided in any way by the Federal Government.[66] The act also prohibits discrimination in all private housing except the sale or rental of a single-family house by its owner. The owner cannot own more than three such single family homes at any one time if he is to be exempt from the law's coverage. The exemption also applies only with respect to one sale by an owner within any twenty-four-month period. The act provided that after December 31, 1969, the sale or rental of any such single family house by its owner is exempt from coverage only if such house is sold or rented without the aid of a real estate broker and without the publication of any advertising banned by the act.[67] Rooms or units in dwellings containing living quarters occupied or intended to be occupied by no more than four families living independently of each other are also exempt from coverage if the owner actually maintains and occupies one such unit as his residence.[68] The law thus appeared to exempt a large part of suburban and rural America, which is mainly composed of single-family homes, from its coverage. But the ban against use of the services of real estate brokers and discriminatory advertising seems to have minimized the effectiveness of the exemption. The act makes it unlawful to publish any advertisement with respect to sale or rental of a dwelling that indicates a preference concerning race, color, religion, or national origin.[69] It also outlaws discrimination by real estate agents, "blockbusting" by real estate salesmen and others,[70] and discrimination by financing institutions such as banks.[71] Religious organizations are exempt from coverage provided membership in the religion is not restricted on racial grounds.[72] Private clubs not in fact open to the public are also exempt if as an incident to their primary purpose they provide lodging to members or give preference to members.[73]

The Secretary of Housing and Urban Development has the responsibility for administering the act. Complaints must be filed with the Secretary within 180 days after the alleged discriminatory act prohibited by its terms and the Secretary must investigate the complaint within 30 days and inform the aggrieved party whether he intends to resolve the complaint. If he so decides, the Secretary must then proceed to resolve the complaint by informal conference. If within 30 days after a complaint is filed with the Secretary, voluntary compliance has not been obtained, the aggrieved person may, within 30 days thereafter, file a complaint in the appropriate United States District Court.[74]

In states or cities with comparable fair-housing laws, the Secretary must notify the appropriate agency of the filing of any complaint with him which appears to violate any such state or local law. The Secretary is then barred from taking further action if the state or local agency acts within 30 days.[75] Also, in cases where an aggrieved person may bring an action in a state court under a state law providing rights and remedies substantially equivalent to those provided by the federal law, he may not bring an action in a federal court as set forth above.[76] If an action is brought in a federal court, it may enjoin the respondent from engaging in the act prohibited or order such affirmative action as may be appropriate. It may also award actual damages and up to $1,000 in punitive damages.[77]

In addition to providing an aggrieved person with a legal as well as administrative remedy, the act empowers the Attorney General of the United States to bring suit. He may bring an action in a federal district court whenever he has reasonable cause to believe that any person or group of persons is engaged in a pattern or practice detrimental to the full enjoyment of any of the rights accorded by the act. He may also bring such an action when he has reasonable grounds to believe that any group of persons has been denied any rights granted by the act and such denial raises an issue of general public importance.[78] The act, by authorizing suits by the government, itself, to enforce its many prohibitions, embodies one of the more salient features of the Civil Rights Act of 1964 and the Voting Rights Act of 1965.

Shortly after the 1968 enactment, the Supreme Court rendered its momentous decision in *Jones v. Mayer*, 392 U.S. 409 (1968). In that case the Court held Congress' first "fair-housing" act, the Civil Rights Act of 1866, applicable not only to racial discrimination in housing enforced by public authorities but applicable also to private racial discrimination in the sale and rental of real property. It further held that a Negro refused the right to buy or lease a house by a private person solely because of race, could sue in a federal court to enjoin such discrimination.[79] In its decision, the Court noted that soon after the Thirteenth Amendment to the Constitution was adopted, Congress undertook its historic task of giving substance to a constitutional proclamation of freedom. It enacted a number of laws which were intended to guarantee freedom in fact to a people newly freed from slavery. One of the incidents of slavery was that slaves could not own, lease, or inherit real or personal property. Consequently, Congress declared in the Civil Rights Act of 1866 that: "All citizens shall have the same right, in every State and Territory, as is enjoyed by white citizens thereof to inherit, purchase, lease, sell, hold, and convey real and personal property."

Although the 1866 statute had long been held applicable to the states, it had never before been held applicable to private racial discrimination. As construed by the Court in *Jones v. Mayer*, *supra*, the Civil Rights Act of 1866 reaches housing previously exempted from coverage by the 1968 Act; i.e., single-family and owner-occupied dwellings, if the refusal to sell or rent is *racially* motivated. The Court held that the 1866 law encompasses every racially motivated refusal to sell or rent and cannot be confined to officially sanctioned segregation in housing. The 1866 act was reenacted in 1870, two years after adoption of the Fourteenth Amendment. The Court pointed out that some members of Congress voted to adopt the Fourteenth Amendment in order to eliminate doubt as to the applicability of the 1866 act to the states. "But," said the Court, "it certainly does not follow that the adoption of the Fourteenth Amendment or the subsequent readoption of the Fourteenth Amendment or the subsequent readoption of the . . . act were meant somehow to *limit* its application to state action." The Court then went on to hold that the power vested in Congress to enforce the Thirteenth Amendment by appropriate legislation includes the power to enact laws operating directly upon the private racially discriminatory acts of individuals whether or not sanctioned by state legislation. This conclusion, the Court stressed, stems from the fact that the amendment not only prohibits state laws from establishing or upholding slavery but prohibits all slavery. Most significantly the Court held that Congress has the power by virtue of the amendment's enabling clause to pass laws necessary and proper for abolishing all badges and incidents of slavery. The Court then added these words which point the way to outlawing all racial discrimination: "Surely Congress has the power under the Thirteenth Amendment rationally to determine what are the badges and the incidents of slavery, and the authority to translate that determination into effective legislation." Then, as if it intended to end a century of litigation, the Court said: "And when racial discrimination herds men into ghettos and makes their ability to buy property turn on the color of their skin, then it too is a relic of slavery. . . . At the very least, the freedom that Congress is empowered to secure under the Thirteenth Amendment includes the freedom to buy whatever a white man can buy, the right to live wherever a white man can live. If Congress cannot say that being a free man means at least this much, then the Thirteenth Amendment made a promise the Nation cannot keep."

## EQUAL OPPORTUNITY IN EDUCATION

An equal opportunity to obtain education afforded by the state without discrimination because of race is the right of every person in the United States. This right is guaranteed by the equal-protection clause of the Fourteenth Amendment to the Constitution of the United States.

The struggle to secure equal educational opportunities for blacks preceded emancipation of the slaves. In 1831 Prudence Crandall, a Quaker school teacher, began operating a private school for girls in Canterbury, Connecticut.[80] She decided to admit a free Connecticut Negro girl in 1833, causing enraged local residents to threaten to withdraw financial support. Miss Crandall then decided to dismiss all her white students and recruit free black girls from other states. The townsfolk who had engaged Miss Crandall to conduct their school for young ladies vehemently opposed the idea of educating free blacks to a status of equality with whites. A campaign of persuasion and harassment failed. The opposition then secured the enactment of a law by the Connecticut legislature making it a crime to admit a nonresident Negro to a school in the state. Miss Crandall was convicted of violating the law. Instead of deciding the question whether free out-of-state blacks were citizens within the contemplation of the U. S. Constitution and therefore entitled to the privileges and immunities of free citizens of Connecticut as guaranteed by Article 4, Section 2, of the Constitution, the state's highest court voided the conviction on a technicality.[81] Nevertheless, the campaign of harassment continued. After the ground floor of the school was destroyed by a mob, Miss Crandall finally abandoned it and left the state.

The Crandall case was followed by a struggle against segregated public schools for Negroes in Boston. In 1849 in *Roberts v. City of Boston*, 5 Cush. (Mass.) 198 (1849), a separate school for black children was unsuccessfully challenged. The circumstances leading to this case were as follows: In Boston, an abolitionist stronghold, Negroes were at first excluded from public schools. Then in 1845 a state law conferred on any person unlawfully excluded a right to recover damages,[82] and a separate school for blacks was established. One of the leading lawyers in Boston of that day, Charles Sumner, acted as one of the attorneys for the black children. A black lawyer, Robert Morris, was associated with him. Sumner argued that blacks had a right under the Massachusetts Constitution not to be segregated in public schools. The Massachusetts courts disagreed with Sumner. The losing of the case resulted in a state law securing this right.[83]

After the Civil War, when Sumner was leading the fight in the United States Senate for equal rights, he remembered his defeat in the courts. He proposed, in 1871, an amendment to a bill which would have secured the rights of blacks in the public schools.[84] Equal treatment on common carriers, in inns, theaters, other places of public amusement, and in cemeteries was also sought. This law was finally enacted. It became the Civil Rights Act of 1875.[85] However, before its passage, schools and cemeteries were stricken from the bill. The public accommodation provisions of the 1875 law were declared unconstitutional in 1883 by the Supreme Court in the *Civil Rights Cases*, 109 U.S. 1 (1883).

This early retreat from vigorous federal enforcement of equality in the public domain was followed by further retrenchment in 1896. At that time, the Supreme Court in *Plessy v. Ferguson*, 163 U.S. 537, in an eight-to-one decision, sanctioned the "separate but equal" compromise of the Fourteenth Amendment. There the Court upheld a Lousiana statute requiring segregation on railroad cars. This, in short, gave "Jim Crow" legal status. The lone dissenter in the *Plessy* case predicted: ". . . the judgment this day rendered will, in time, prove to be quite as pernicious as the decision . . . in the Dred Scott case."[86]

A legal assault which was to prove fatal to the doctrine of "separate but equal" commenced in 1946 when a Negro, Herman Marion Sweatt, sought admission to the University of Texas Law School. He claimed it was impossible to secure an equal education in the law school hastily set up for blacks in the basement of a building, and he asserted the state's inability to duplicate intangible benefits accruing to those enrolled at the long-established University Law School. Four years later, in *Sweatt v. Painter*, 339 U.S. 629 (1950), the Supreme Court agreed with this contention and, for the first time in its history, ordered admission of a Negro to a previously all-white educational institution.[87]

In September of 1962, federal troops were required to enforce a federal court order directing the admission of James Meredith to the University of Mississippi.[88] In January

1963 a law suit ended in the admission of Harvey Gantt to South Carolina's Clemson College.[89] South Carolina was the last state to maintain an all-white college and university system. In every other southern state except West Virginia and Arkansas it had been necessary to bring suit to secure the admission of the first black to a state college or graduate or professional school.[90]

In *Brown v. The Board of Education of Topeka, Kansas*, 347 U. S. 483 (1954), and four related cases, the Supreme Court finally held that the states could not educate blacks in separate educational institutions. These cases involved the elementary and high-school levels. Unanimously, the Court ruled state-enforced racial segregation in public education unconstitutional. It found such segregation inherently unequal because state-enforced racial segregation denotes the inferiority of the black race. This, in turn, inflicts psychological harm upon black children which interferes with their ability to learn. Such harm, inflicted by the state, deprives such children of equal educational opportunities because white children are not subjected to similar harm. In so holding, the Court relied upon a finding of fact made by a United States District Court in Kansas. The Kansas court had found as a fact that:

> Segregation of white and colored children in public schools has a detrimental effect upon the colored children. The impact is greater when it has the sanction of the law; for the policy of separating the races is usually interpreted as denoting the inferiority of the Negro group.

The court also found that:

> A sense of inferiority affects the motivation of a child to learn. Segregation with the sanction of the law, therefore, has a tendency to [retard] the educational and mental development of Negro children and to deprive them of some of the benefits they would receive in a racial[ly] integrated school system.

Segregation of black children by the Federal Government was prohibited in a companion case, *Bolling v. Sharpe*, 347 U. S. 497 (1954). The Court held that although the Fourteenth Amendment did not apply to the Federal Government, the Fifth Amendment to the Federal Constitution does. That Amendment contains a clause prohibiting federal deprivation of "life, liberty, or property without due process of law." The Court held that:

> Liberty under law extends to the full range of conduct which the individual is free to pursue, and it cannot be restricted except for a proper governmental objective. Segregation in public education is not reasonably related to any proper governmental objective, and thus it imposes on Negro children of the District of Columbia a burden that constitutes an arbitrary deprivation of their liberty in violation of the Due Process Clause.

The Court's 1954 decisions in the *Brown* and *Bolling* cases were followed in 1955 by a supplemental *Brown* decision, *Brown v. The Board of Education of Topeka*, 349 U.S. 294. This decision delegated to the federal trial courts the task of deciding whether desegregation in a particular school district should occur immediately or "with all deliberate speed" predicated on the resolution of enumerated administrative problems. By the end of

1970 there still had been a largely minimal compliance in the deep South with the new decision. This resulted in part from unrelenting public and private resistance to integration, but also from the debilitating effect of the "all deliberate speed" doctrine. Some southern school officials, faced with the problem of unifying the long-established dual school systems, viewed the doctrine as license for delay. A number of so-called desegregation plans were offered by recalcitrant officials and their legislative partners. Grade-a-year plans starting with either the first grade and proceeding up or the twelfth grade and proceeding down were one type of scheme. Individual pupil assignments pursuant to numerous vague criteria were another variety. Freedom-of-choice which purported to allow parents the right to choose the school which their children would attend was still another device. After more than a decade of such schemes, the Supreme Court finally barred employment of the "with all deliberate speed" doctrine in 1969. *Alexander v. Holmes County Board of Education*, 396 U.S. 19 (1969). Earlier the Court had upheld the view that the *Brown* decision requires faculty as well as pupil integration. *Rogers v. Paul*, 382 U.S. 198 (1965) and *Bradley v. School Board of Richmond*, 382 U.S. 103 (1965).

By 1972, however, the nation was convulsed by a new school desegregation crisis resulting from court approval of desegregation plans which included extensive busing. In 1971 the Supreme Court approved a plan for the city of Charlotte, North Carolina, which included city-wide busing. *Swann v. Charlotte-Mecklenburg Board of Education*, 402 U.S. 29 (1971). Then the United States District Court for the Eastern Districts of Virginia ordered into effect a plan which would desegregate the overwhelmingly black Richmond schools by merging them with the schools of Henrico and Chesterfield counties, both of which adjoined the city of Richmond. *Bradley v. School Board of City of Richmond*, 338 F. Supp. 67 (E. D. Va., 1972). The adverse reaction to the Richmond case was so great that President Nixon urged the Congress to declare a moratorium on court-ordered busing plans and to propose a constitutional amendment prohibiting busing to achieve racial balance. The Congress responded by attaching a rider to the Higher Education Act Amendments of 1972. Senate Bill 659, Public Law 92-318, June 23, 1972. The rider provides that no court order seeking to *achieve racial balance* through busing of public school children can go into effect until all appeals have been exhausted or the time within which to appeal has expired. This provision expired January 1, 1974. However, it came in time to affect an order by a federal district court in Detroit, Michigan, in June 1972 which had ordered that city's schools desegregated by a merger of more than fifty school districts within the city. *Bradley v. Milliken*, 345 F. Supp. 914 (E. D. Mich., 1972). Then the Court of Appeals for the Fourth Circuit reversed the decision of the federal district court in Richmond. 462 F. 2d 1058 (4th Cir. 1972).[91]

At the end of its term in June 1972 the Court blocked attempts by city schools to secede from county school districts of which they were a part and set up separate school districts when the effect would be to hinder or frustrate attempts to dismantle dual school systems. *United States v. Scotland Neck City Board of Education*, 407 U.S. 484 (1972), *Wright v. Council of the City of Emporia*, 407 U.S. 451 (1972).

THE LEGAL STATUS OF THE BLACK AMERICAN

One of the unexpected developments following the *Brown* decision was the attack
upon segregated schools in the North.[92] Such schools result largely from residential
segregation. However, several cases have developed evidence of intentional segregation
of black children in communities where no law required it.[93] In New Rochelle, New
York, for example, the school authorities in 1963 finally tore down the Lincoln Elementary School. It was 94 percent black. For thirty-three years it had been the center
of controversy. In 1961, a federal court had ruled that the New Rochelle school board
had segregated black pupils in the Lincoln School through its refusal to alter that school's
zone lines over the years.[94] It required the board to devise a plan of desegregation. The
board's plan permitted the Lincoln School pupils desiring to do so to transfer to other
schools in the city.[95] Continuing controversy led to the school's demise.[96] The New
Rochelle case spurred a rash of similar cases in northern communities.

The United States Supreme Court declined on May 4, 1964, to review a northern
school segregation case from Gary, Indiana. There a federal district and appellate court
had denied a claim that the *Brown* decision requires remedying the effects of residential
segregation.[97] Similar suits asserting a constitutional duty to integrate *de facto* segregated
schools have been filed in other northern communities.[98] In a case filed in Pasadena,
California, the state court ruled that the school authorities were under a duty to desegregate *de facto* segregated schools.[99] In another development, the highest court of the State
of New York upheld the voluntary action of the Board of Education of the City of New
York in drawing school zone lines to promote integration against a challenge by white
parents. The United States Supreme Court likewise declined to review this decision.[100]
It would seem there is nothing in the Constitution which prevents a state from taking
action to remedy the effects of housing segregation on public education.

## EQUAL OPPORTUNITY FOR EMPLOYMENT

Racial discrimination with respect to employment by any federal agency is prohibited by statute,[101] and would be clearly violative of the due-process clause of the
Fifth Amendment to the Federal Constitution.[102] The federal Civil Service Commission
now has the function of promoting equal opportunity in federal employment.[103]
Discrimination because of race by any state agency would violate the equal protection
clause of the Fourteenth Amendment. Invoking the equal protection clause, black
teachers in 1940 won the right to equal pay which they had been denied in most of the
separate school systems of the southern states.[104]

Southern state segregation policies have included laws which curtailed equal opportunity to earn a living in one's chosen business or profession solely because of race
and color. These statutes have been struck down by the courts on Fourteenth Amendment grounds. In Louisiana, for example, such a statute prohibited mixed professional

boxing matches between black and white boxers.[105] A similar statute was held constitutionally void by a Texas court.[106] A Georgia court invalidated an ordinance prohibiting black barbers from serving white women or children.[107]

The fair employment practices section of the Civil Rights Act of 1964 (Title VII) bars discrimination in employment and union membership, which affects commerce, and provides, for the first time, federal remedies against discrimination in employment by employers, employment agencies, and labor unions.[108] The first remedy provided is the opportunity to file charges with the Equal Employment Opportunity Commission established by the law. This commission was originally empowered to redress the charges strictly through informal methods. However, by 1972 the Congress had amended the act to empower the commission, which had sought the power to enforce its own orders, to do so by resorting to the courts.[109]

Presently, charges arising in a state which already has a fair employment practices law may be filed with the federal agency sixty days after the aggrieved party has sought relief at the state level. A charge may also be filed by a member of the federal commission. Except where a complaint must first be filed at the state level, a federal complaint must be filed within ninety days of the discriminatory act charged. Failure of the commission to eliminate the discriminatory practice complained of within thirty days may be followed by suit instituted by the aggrieved party in a federal court within thirty days thereafter. The court, upon application by the aggrieved party, may appoint counsel and may authorize commencement of the action without payment of fees, costs, or security. The court may also permit the Attorney General to intervene in such cases. If the court finds discrimination, it may enjoin the employer, employment agency, or labor union from pursuing such action now declared by the statute to be unlawful. The court may also order reinstatement or hiring with or without back pay. Reasonable attorneys' fees may also be allowed by the court to the prevailing party's counsel. If an employer, employment agency, or labor union fails to comply with a court order, the federal agency may commence proceedings to compel compliance. The Attorney General may also institute suit whenever he "has reasonable cause to believe that any person or group of persons is engaged in a pattern or practice of resistance to the full enjoyment of any of the rights secured" by the act.

The fair employment practices provisions of the 1964 Civil Rights Act did not become effective until one year after enactment. During the first year after the effective date, the law applied to employers of one hundred or more employees, during the second year seventy-five or more, and during the third year fifty or more.

The Supreme Court has recently upheld the right of black railroad employees to go immediately into a federal court with a complaint alleging discrimination by the railroad and the union with respect to promotions of Negro personnel without first exhausting any contractual or administrative remedies where it appeared that exhaustion of such remedies would be futile or the administrative agency would be powerless to act. *Glover v. St. Louis–San Francisco Ry. Co.*, 393 U.S. 324 (1969).

Labor-union discrimination has seriously complicated the private-employment problem for the black worker. There are two basic discriminatory practices. Negroes are sometimes barred from union membership or segregated in powerless auxiliaries.[110] They also have been purposefully discriminated against by unions authorized by law to bargain for the nonunion black members of a bargaining unit as well as the white members of the unit who have been admitted to union membership.[111] According to common law, unions had the right to exclude Negroes from membership.[112] In most of the states with fair employment practices laws, however, discrimination by unions is prohibited. New York was the first state to prohibit discrimination in union membership in 1940. In 1945 a union unsuccessfully challenged the law as unconstitutional in the Supreme Court.[113] That same year the courts protected the right to work in a closed shop when union membership has been denied because of race or color.[114]

The Supreme Court since 1944 has required unions authorized by law to act as the exclusive bargaining agent for all members of a bargaining unit, whether union members or not, to represent nonunion black members fairly and "without hostile discrimination against them."[115] Applying this principle, the lower federal courts have enjoined enforcement of contracts which discriminated against Negroes. And they have awarded damages against both the unions and the employers who were parties to such agreements.[116]

The National Labor Relations Board (NLRB) now enforces the duty of fair representation in its adjudications. Between 1944 and 1962 NLRB failed to construe a violation of the duty as a violation of the National Labor Relations Act (NLRA).[117] On July 1, 1964, however, one day before the enactment of the Civil Rights Act of 1964 prohibiting discrimination in union membership and outlawing the segregated local (Title VII), the NLRB rendered a decision which so construes a violation of the duty and curbs union membership discrimination.[118] NLRB ruled that a union's failure to fairly represent black workers violates provisions of the NLRA prohibiting unfair labor practices by labor unions. This ruling had been foreshadowed, as the decision notes, by a ruling in a nonracial 1962 case recognizing the NLRB's power to enforce the duty of fair representation in construing the NLRA. The duty, it further ruled, bars discrimination and segregation in union memberships. Unexpectedly, NLRB ruled that when this duty is violated a defaulting union is subject to a revocation of its NLRB certification as the exclusive bargaining agent for the employee unit involved. For the first time the board said: "Where a union segregates members or excludes or denies full membership status to applicants on racial grounds, it is violating its duty of fair representation to all members of the unit and should not be permitted to hold a certified status." A federal appellate court has since held that a company which refuses to bargain in good faith regarding racial discrimination violates duties and obligations imposed upon an employer by the NLRA. *United Packinghouse etc. Workers v. NLRB*, 416 F. 2d 1126 (D.C. Cir. 1969).

A long-neglected civil rights statute, Title 42 U.S.C.A. Section 1981, has recently been invoked by black workers against private employers. That statute provides in pertinent part as follows:

> All persons within the jurisdiction of the United States shall have the same right in every State and Territory to make and enforce contracts . . . as is enjoyed by white citizens. . . . .

The above statute was enacted originally in 1866. Relying upon the Supreme Court's decision in *Jones v. Mayer*, discussed, *supra*, in the section on housing, black plaintiffs have successfully argued that Section 1981 applies to both private discrimination in making and enforcing employment contracts and to discrimination by labor unions in denying union membership or referral status.[119] More recently the Supreme Court ruled in *Griggs v. Duke Power Co.*, 401 U. S. 424 (1971), a case presenting a challenge to the use of psychological and formal educational requirements as employment criteria which result in exclusion of blacks seeking employment, that use of such criteria when not related to the employer's jobs is violative of Title VII of the Civil Rights Act of 1964.

## PROTECTION AGAINST INTERFERENCE WITH THE EXERCISE OF CIVIL RIGHTS

Since their emancipation from slavery, blacks have encountered both public and private resistance to their efforts to exercise their rights as citizens and members of the American community. Such resistance has often been violent. It has sometimes resulted in the death of Negroes involved in attempts of this kind as well as those seeking to help them. Such resistance has frequently stemmed from conspiracies between public officials and private citizens. During the past two decades as Negroes, particularly in the South, have sought to exercise newly affirmed rights (such as the right to vote, to attend "white" schools, and to take advantage of places of public accommodation), they and their supporters have been subject to violence, threats of violence, and intimidation. In order to deter such unlawful acts, prosecutions of private persons and public officials became necessary. In bringing such criminal prosecutions, the Government had to rely on civil rights statutes enacted during Reconstruction. There were two such statutes which made it a crime to interfere with the exercise of civil rights.

One of these statutes, Title 18 U.S.C.A., Section 241, is a felony statute. First enacted in 1870 to enforce the provisions of the Fourteenth Amendment, it was directed primarily against the activities of private persons and groups such as the Ku Klux Klan. This law makes it a crime for two or more persons to conspire or to go in disguise upon the highway or upon the premises of another to interfere with rights secured by the Constitution and laws of the United States or to injure, oppress, threaten, or intimidate any persons for having exercised any of these rights. It provides for imprisonment up to ten years and fines up to $5,000 upon conviction.

The other statute, Title 18 U.S.C.A., Section 242, first enacted in 1866, is a misdemeanor statute. It is aimed at the actions of state officials. It makes it a crime for any person, acting under color of state law, to willfully subject an inhabitant of any state to the deprivation of any rights secured by the Constitution and laws of the United States. Maximum imprisonment of one year and a fine up to $1,000 are possible.

The first statute had been construed by some Supreme Court justices in 1951 as applicable only to those rights and privileges conferred directly upon citizens by the Federal Government and not merely by means of prohibitions against state action.[120] However, as the Court later ruled in *United States v. Price*, 383 U. S. 787 (1966), in sustaining indictments against Mississippi officials and private citizens charging a violation of Section 241, this law had been enacted to protect all of the rights and privileges secured to citizens by the Constitution, including the prohibitions of the Fourteenth Amendment. In the *Price* case the Court further held that it is possible to secure indictments against private persons who conspire with police or other state officials to deny Negroes their civil rights in violation of Section 242, since the general federal conspiracy statute, Title 18 U.S.C.A. Section 371, makes it a crime for any person to conspire with public officials to violate a federal statute. The indictments in the *Price* case arose out of the murders of three young civil-rights workers in Philadelphia, Mississippi, in the summer of 1964. These workers, Michael Schwerner and Andrew Goodman, two white youths from New York, and James Chaney, a black Mississippian, had been detained by Deputy Sheriff Cecil Price in the Neshoba County jail as they were on their way to Philadelphia. He later released the three workers in the dark of night. When the three left in their automobile, they were allegedly intercepted by the deputy sheriff and taken to a place on an unpaved road. Their bodies were found some months later in an earthen dam nearby. The deputy sheriff, the sheriff, a policeman, and fifteen individuals were subsequently indicted and charged with violating Section 241 and conspiring to violate Section 242. Since state officers were alleged to be involved in the conspiracy, and since the indictment alleged that the object of the conspiracy was to deny the victims a right secured by the Federal Constitution—the Fourteenth Amendment right not to be summarily punished by persons acting under color of law without due process of law—Section 241 was clearly applicable.

The Court, on the same day, in *United States v. Guest*, 383 U. S. 745 (1966), upheld the indictments of private persons under Section 241 who had been charged with conspiring to deny blacks equal access to state-operated facilities in Athens, Georgia, with possible active connivance by state officials. And in addition, a majority of the Court held that under Section 5 of the Fourteenth Amendment, Congress has the power to enact laws punishing all conspiracies which interfere with the exercise of Fourteenth Amendment rights, whether or not state officers are involved.

Then in 1968 the Supreme Court sustained indictments against private persons who had been charged by the government with conspiring to injure blacks who exercised the rights conferred upon them by a federal law, i.e., the public accommodations provisions of the Civil Rights Act of 1964. *United States v. Johnson*, 390 U. S. 563. There the government relied upon the anti-Ku Klux Klan statute, Section 241. The Civil Rights Act of 1964 had provided for the civil remedy of injunction by an aggrieved person or the government against the owner of a public accommodation who refused to serve persons because of race and against persons who resort to the use of violence against persons seeking to exercise the right to service. Defendants in the *Johnson* case were outsiders or nonowners who were charged with inflicting violence upon three blacks for having received service at a restaurant. The decision was five to three, one judge not participating. The dissenting justices held the injunctive remedies under the 1964 act to be the exclusive remedies in this situation.

That same year, about two weeks after the decision in the *Guest* case, and three days after the decision in the *Johnson* case, Congress took action. It provided as part of the Civil Rights Act of 1968 for federal criminal prosecutions of both public officials and private persons, whether or not acting under color of law, who by force or threat of force willfully injure, intimidate or interfere with federally protected civil rights activity, including peaceful protest against discrimination. Congress also declared it a crime to so interfere with anyone who seeks to aid or encourage others to take advantage of any civil right.[121] If bodily harm results, the convicted defendant may be sentenced to prison for ten years and fined up to $10,000; if death results, there may be imprisonment for any term of years or for life; otherwise, the maximum term of imprisonment which may be imposed is one year and a fine up to $1,000.[122]

Other Reconstruction statutes provide for civil suits for injunctions and damages. One, Title 42 U.S.C.A., Section 1983, provides for civil suits against public officials who, acting under color of state law, deprive any persons of their civil rights as defined by federal law. It is the civil parallel of Section 242. The other, Title 42 U.S.C.A., Section 1985, provides for such actions against private persons who conspire to interfere with the exercise of civil rights. It is the civil counterpart of Section 241. The first statute has been regularly invoked in civil rights cases against state officials. Federal district courts have been given jurisdiction to hear and determine such cases.[123] The second statute has been seldom invoked.[124] Federal courts now have jurisdiction in all civil rights actions.[125]

## UNFAIR CRIMINAL PROCEDURES

There was a time when the lynching of black males accused of crimes was commonplace. They were plainly and simply denied all due process of law. Lynching generally took the form of hanging a Negro accused of crime from a tree by a rope around his neck until dead. This form of mob violence has virtually disappeared. To illustrate: in 1882, 49 blacks were lynched; that number rose to 113 in 1891; in 1892, it was 161; but by 1902, the number of Negroes lynched decreased to 85; by 1912, it was 61; in

1922, it was 51; in 1932, it was 6.[126] Since 1952, the number has been no more than one per year.[127] Today, however, lynching might take the form of the police shooting a black person accused of a crime. Specific federal anti-lynching statutes have been proposed since the turn of the century,[128] but as the problem seemed to be receding they were not pushed actively until the recurrence of anti-civil rights violence in the 1960s.

Prior to 1968, federal protection of blacks from bodily harm was negligible. There were only four federal statutes which bore directly upon the problem, including the two federal criminal statutes discussed in the preceding section.[129] One statute, Section 242, in effect condemns participation in lynchings by state officers. When read in connection with the general federal conspiracy statute,[130] this federal enactment applies to private citizens acting in concert with officers. There is also a federal statute which prohibits inducing or procuring the commission of a crime.[131] When read with Section 242, that statute outlaws private attempts to secure willful police cooperation with lynchings. The other federal criminal statute, Section 241, has been held to cover a mob which seizes a prisoner from a federal marshal. Such action deprives the victim of federal protection.[132] It would also now be read to apply to a prisoner seized from state authorities by a mob.

There are also two federal civil statutes applicable here.[133] These allow suits for damages against state officers and private citizens for participation in lynching. Insofar as police brutality is concerned, the same statutes would apply in a suit against a police officer for such brutality.

Many states have statutes condemning lynchings or mob violence. Some of these laws cover mob violence generally. Others merely govern seizing a prisoner who is in jail. They have resulted in few prosecutions and even fewer convictions. No convicted lyncher has ever been sentenced to death.[134] Those states which have statutes forbidding lynchings are: Alabama, California, Georgia, Illinois, Indiana, Kansas, Kentucky, Minnesota, Nebraska, New Jersey, New York, North Carolina, Ohio, Pennsylvania, South Carolina, Tennessee, Texas, Virginia, and West Virginia--nineteen in all.[135] Some states, such as New York, allow civil suits in state courts against municipalities for police brutality.[136] However, most states, pursuant to theories of sovereign immunity, have not recognized the cause of action.

When a defendant in a criminal case comes before the bar of justice to be tried for the commission of a crime, his liberty is always in jeopardy. His life is likewise in jeopardy where the state law provides the death penalty for the offense charged. Slaves were not permitted to serve on juries or to be witnesses in court against a white person.[137] Slaves were also subject to more severe punishments for crimes.[138] Consequently, after adoption of the Fourteenth Amendment, Congress acted to enforce it by legislation removing these burdens and disabilities.[139] A law was enacted in 1870 securing the right of Negroes to be witnesses in court.[140] The same statute provides that all persons "shall be subject to like punishment, pains, penalties, taxes, licenses, and exactions of every kind, and to no other."

In 1875 Congress passed another civil rights law. One section made it a crime, punishable by a fine of up to $5,000, to exclude Negroes from service on either the grand or petit jury.[141] On March 1, 1880, the Supreme Court upheld a federal indictment against a Virginia state-court judge for violation of this section.[142] But it appears there have not been any federal indictments sought or procured since that time. "That case has been allowed to stand as solitary and neglected authority for direct enforcement of the Negro's right to sit on juries."[143]

It also appears that a long-neglected civil remedy is available.[144] The civil statute which permits blacks to sue any state official who subjects any person to a deprivation of rights secured by the Federal Constitution and laws may be employed.[145] Relying upon this provision, a Negro brought suit in a federal district court in Kentucky in 1956. The Kentucky court agreed that blacks were entitled to a federal court injunction against such discrimination by the courts of a state.[146]

Although the civil and criminal remedies have been neglected, black criminal defendants have succeeded, on numerous occasions, in getting their convictions reversed because of jury discrimination. Reversals of convictions have been secured whenever blacks have been systematically excluded from the grand jury which indicted the defendant or the petit jury which tried the case under whatever device for discrimination the state had utilized. The first Supreme Court reversal of such a conviction came on March 1, 1880, the same day on which the court upheld the indictment against the Virginia judge.[147] The most recent decision came on the last day of the Court's term in June 1972, when it reversed the conviction of a white man who challenged the exclusion of Negroes from the grand jury which indicted him and the petit jury which tried him.[148]

Black criminal defendants were responsible for establishment of the constitutional principle that no conviction may be predicated upon a coerced confession.[149] Convictions secured through the introduction into evidence of such forced confessions violate the due process clause of the Fourteenth Amendment to the Federal Constitution. This, of course, is a principle now relied upon not only by black criminal defendants but white criminal defendants as well.[150]

Constitutional protection against sham trials resulting from mob domination of the courtroom was also judicially affirmed as a result of an appeal to the nation's highest tribunal by black criminal defendants.[151]

The right to counsel in a capital case is another great precept of American constitutional law established by Negro criminal defendants. In the famous Scottsboro case, *Powell v. Alabama*, 278 U. S. 45 (1932), the Supreme Court for the first time had occasion to rule that denial of counsel in a capital case violated the due process clause of the Fourteenth Amendment to the Federal Constitution. Now conviction of a defendant in any case for which he can be imprisoned and where he has been denied the right to counsel may now be reversed.[152]

Aside from the 1954 school desegregation decision, the most revolutionary legal development of this century occurred in June 1972 when the Supreme Court held, five to four, that state statutes which leave to the discretion of judge or jury the determination of whether the death penalty should be imposed on a defendant violate both the Fourteenth and Eighth Amendments to the Federal Constitution. *Furman v. Georgia*, 408 U. S. 238 (1972).[153] The Court left open the question whether absent such discretion, a mandatory death penalty is unconstitutional. The decision recognized the fact that blacks convicted of capital crimes are sentenced to death far more frequently than whites similarly convicted. It is also true that a black man convicted of any crime is more likely than not to receive a longer sentence than a white man convicted of the same crime.[154] Thus the long-range impact of the death-penalty decision may well be not only to make our society more humane but may also eliminate this shameful disparity in sentencing.

## OFFICIAL RACISM OUTLAWED

Segregation of Negroes was predicated upon the notion that they were members of an inferior order of beings unfit to associate with the white race on a basis of equality (See *Dred Scott v. Sandford\**, 19 Howard 393, 15 L. ed 691 [1857].) In the southern states where segregation was long officially decreed and sanctioned, commitment to the doctrine of white supremacy was reflected not only in the network of laws which segregated the Negro from birth to death but in the practices of public officials. Where no law specifically required it, segregation was often instituted and enforced as a matter of policy. State officials also regularly declined to accord to blacks the common courtesies one human being owes to another. They almost uniformly refused to address blacks as Mr. or Mrs. and referred to them by their first names even in official transactions. When Miss Mary Hamilton appeared in an Alabama court as a witness, the state's attorney refused to address her as Miss Hamilton. She in turn refused to answer until so addressed. When ordered to answer by the judge, she again refused and was convicted of contempt of court. Her conviction was reversed by the Supreme Court without argument or opinion in *Hamilton v. Alabama*, 376 U. S. 650, in 1964. The date is significant. This was 100 years after Lincoln freed the slaves.

American racism was expressed most pointedly in state statutes prohibiting marriages between whites and Negroes. In 1964 nineteen states had such laws; two, Indiana and Wyoming, were nonsouthern states. The seventeen southern states involved had a history of state-decreed racial segregation in several areas.[155]

At least eighteen other states had similar laws.[156] These statutes have been repealed.[157]

The Supreme Court has now ruled upon the constitutionality of antimiscegenation laws. In *Loving v. Virginia*, 388 U. S. 1 (1967), the Court finally held such laws violative

\*The official record misspelled Sanford.

of both the due process and equal protection clauses of the Fourteenth Amendment. This decision, too, came more than 100 years after the adoption of the Thirteenth Amendment abolishing slavery.

In 1954 and again in 1956 the Court had declined to pass upon the issue of interracial marriages and state interdictions when presented by two cases. The first case arose in Alabama;[158] the other case came up from Virginia.[159] But by 1967, more than a decade after the Supreme Court's 1954 school desegregation decision, the Court was ready to act on this issue and to wipe out the remaining indicia of official racism.

In 1883, in *Pace v. Alabama*, 106 U. S. 583, the Supreme Court had upheld a state statute imposing a greater penalty for adultery or fornication when committed by members of different races.[160] The Supreme Court, on appeal by a black man and a white woman, reversed convictions for violating a similar Florida statute in 1962.[161] The Florida statute of which the couple was convicted provided:

> Any Negro man and white woman, or any white man and Negro woman, who are not married to each other, who shall habitually live in and occupy in the nighttime the same room shall be punished by imprisonment not exceeding twelve months, or by fine not exceeding five hundred dollars.[162]

Florida did not also make criminal the same conduct when both parties were of the same race as was true in the case in Alabama. Florida also prohibited marriages between Negroes and whites. Its statute was typical of those still on the statute books in 1964. Florida law proclaimed:

> It is unlawful for any white male person residing or being in this state to intermarry with any Negro female person; and it is in like manner unlawful for any white female person residing or being in this state to intermarry with any Negro male person; and every marriage formed or solemnized in contravention of the provisions of this section shall be utterly null and void, and the issue, if any, of such surreptitious marriage shall be regarded as bastard and incapable of having or receiving an estate, real, personal, or mixed, by inheritance.[163]

Also typical was Florida's statute defining who is a Negro. The state's definition was an essential element of the crime charged in the Florida and similar cases.

> The words *negro, colored, colored person, mulatto*, or *person of color*, when applied to persons, include every person having one-eighth or more of African or negro blood.[164]

These state definitions, however, are still on the books.

The United States Supreme Court's reluctance to strike down state barriers to interracial marriages was not matched by the states. The Supreme Court of California in 1948 had held that state's antimiscegenation law violative of the Fourteenth Amendment to the Federal Constitution.[165] It ruled such statutes unreasonably restrict the choice of one's mate.

Once the United States Supreme Court had ruled out on constitutional grounds all other restrictive state statutes and policies predicated wholly upon race, the constitutional demise of these antimiscegenation and anticohabitation laws was inevitable. And since these particular laws were the most difficult to challenge because of their emotional and psychological origins, their demise is no minor revolutionary achievement, although long overdue.

## Notes (Foreword)

1. 163 U. S. 537 (1896).
2. 347 U. S. 483 (1954).
3. *Swann v. Charlotte-Mecklenburg Board of Education,* 402 U. S. 29 (1971).
4. See *The New York Times,* Wednesday, April 12, 1972, p. 11.
5. See D. Davis, *The Problem of Slavery in Western Culture,* Cornell University Press, 1966; W. Jordan, *White Over Black: American Attitudes Towards the Negro, 1550–1812,* University of North Carolina Press, 1968; G. Frederickson, *The Black Image in the White Mind: The Debate on Afro-American Character & Destiny,* Harper & Row, 1971. These and other studies may bring a fuller understanding of the reasons and basis for the pervasiveness of racism in society.

## Notes (Chapter)

1. 16 Stat. 140.
2. 16 Stat. 433.
3. 28 Stat. 36.
4. 42 U.S.C.A. 1971 before its amendment in 1957.
5. *Guinn v. United States,* 238 U. S. 347 (1915).
6. *Lane v. Wilson,* 307 U. S. 268 (1939).
7. *Nixon v. Herndon,* 273 U. S. 536 (1927).
8. *Nixon v. Condon,* 286 U. S. 73 (1932).
9. *Grovey v. Townsend,* 295 U. S. 45 (1935).
10. *Rice v. Elmore,* 165 F. 2d 387 (4th Cir. 1947); *cert. den.,* 333 U. S. 875 (1948).
11. *Brown v. Baskin,* 80 F. Supp. 1017 (E.D.S.C. 1948); *affirmed* 174 F. 2d 391 (4th Cir. 1949).
12. *Terry v. Adams,* 345 U. S. 461 (1953).
13. 71 Stat. 634.
14. 74 Stat. 86.
15. 78 Stat. 241.
16. The Supreme Court invited all of the states to participate by filing briefs because of the importance of the issues and because the law's application was not limited to the southern states. A majority of the states responded. Seven states in addition to South Carolina argued orally; the others filed briefs.
17. In 1949, for example, the Alabama test had been held unconstitutional in *Davis v. Schnell,* 817 Supp. 872 (S. D. Ala. 1949); aff'd, 336 U. S. 933, on the ground that the registrar of voters had been given uncontrolled discretion to determine who could read, write, understand, and explain a provision of the Federal Constitution. The Court also noted in that case that State Senator Boswell, author of the law known as the Boswell Amendment, had advocated its adoption as a device for eliminating Negro applicants. The Court had also invalidated Louisiana's literacy test. *Louisiana v. United States,* 380 U. S. 145 (1965).

18. 42 U.S.C., Section 1973.

19. *Ibid.* 84 Stat. 315.

20. *South Carolina v. Katzenbach,* 383 U. S. 301, 308–309 (1966).

21. *Ibid.* at 356.

22. *Ibid.* at 334.

23. *Anderson v. Martin,* 375 U. S. 399 (1964).

24. *Gomillion v. Lightfoot,* 364 U. S. 339 (1960).

25. *Johnson v. Virginia,* 373 U. S. 61 (1963) (court houses); *Watson v. City of Memphis,* 373 U. S. 526 (1963) (public parks, playgrounds, tennis courts, etc.). *Dawson v. City of Baltimore,* 220 F. 2d 386 (4th Cir. 1955); *aff'd,* 350 U. S. 877 (1955) (public beaches); *Holmes v. City of Atlanta,* 350 U. S. 879 (1955), *vacating* 223 F. 2d 93 (5th Cir. 1955) (public golf courses). The Supreme Court let stand, by refusing to review, a Supreme Court of California decision holding racial segregation in public housing violative of the equal protection clause. *Banks v. Housing Authority of City and County of San Francisco,* 120 Cal. App. 2d 1, 260 P. 2d 668 (1953); *certiorari denied,* 347 U. S. 974 (1954).

26. *Johnson v. Virginia, supra.*

27. *Turner v. City of Memphis,* 369 U. S. 350 (1962) (municipally owned airport restaurant); *Burton v. Wilmington Parking Authority,* 365 U. S. 715 (1961) (municipally owned parking lot restaurant); *Muir v. Louisville Park Theatrical Ass'n,* 347 U. S. 971 (1954), *vacating and remanding* 202 F. 2d 275 (6th Cir. 1954) (municipally owned amphitheater).

28. *Burton v. Wilmington Parking Authority, supra.* See also *Simkins v. Moses H. Cone Memorial Hospital,* 323 F. 2d 959 (4th Cir. 1963), *certiorari denied,* 376 U. S. 938 (1964).

29. *Petersen v. City of Greenville,* 373 U. S. 244 (1963); (trespass conviction); *Lombard v. Louisiana,* 373 U. S. 267 (1963) (criminal mischief conviction); *Gober v. City of Birmingham,* 373 U. S. 374 (1963) (trespass). For an explanation of the charge in the *Gober* case, see *Shuttlesworth v. City of Birmingham,* 373 U. S. 262 (1963). In October 1961, the first of the sit-in cases was argued in the United States Supreme Court. Baton Rouge, Louisiana, college students were arrested by a police officer who peered in a drug store window and saw them sitting unmolested at the lunch counter. They were charged with disturbing the peace. The Court reversed their convictions. It held there was no evidence to support the charge. In *McCain v. Davis,* 217 F. Supp. 661 (E. D. La. 1963), a Louisiana statute providing for hotel segregation was voided by a three-judge federal court.

30. These cases were: *Griffin v. State of Maryland,* 378 U. S. 130 (1964); *Barr, et al. v. City of Columbia,* 378 U. S. 146 (1964); *Bouie v. City of Columbia,* 378 U. S. 347 (1964); *Bell, et al. v. Maryland,* 378 U. S. 226 (1964); *Robinson, et al. v. Florida,* 378 U. S. 153 (1964).

31. The *Griffin* case convictions were reversed on the ground that the arresting officer, a deputy sheriff, was simultaneously a private policeman and a state officer, thus making his action state action. The Columbia, South Carolina cases were reversed on the ground that there was no evidence in the first case to sustain a conviction for breach of the peace and on the ground that the trespass statute upon which the second-case convictions were based was too vague to have given the sit-ins notice that remaining in the drug store after being requested to leave would constitute a crime. The *Bell* case was sent back to the Supreme Court of Maryland for further proceedings on the ground that after the convictions Maryland enacted a public accommodations statute which might change the state court's result in that case. The Florida case was reversed on the ground that Florida has a state health regulation requiring restaurants to provide separate toilets for blacks and whites, thus significantly involving the state in the private owner's decision to exclude Negroes.

32. The act applies to: "(1) any inn, hotel, motel, or other establishment which provides lodging to transient guests, other than an establishment located within a building which contains not more than five rooms for rent or hire and which is actually occupied by the proprietor of such establishment as his residence; (2) any restaurant, cafeteria, lunchroom, lunch counter, soda fountain, or other facility principally engaged in selling food for consumption on the premises including but not limited to, any such facility located on the premises of any retail establishment; or any gasoline station; (3) any motion picture house, theater, concert hall, sports arena, stadium, or other place of

exhibition or entertainment; and (4) any establishment (A) (i) which is physically located within the premises of any establishment otherwise covered by this subsection, or (ii) within the premises of which is physically located any such covered establishment, and (B) which holds itself out as serving patrons of such covered establishment." 42 U.S.C.A. Section 2000a.

33. *Southern School News*, 6, No. 9 (March, 1960), p. 3.

34. *Ibid.*

35. *The New York Times*, April 10, 1964, pp. 1, 22.

36. *Southern School News, Ibid.*

37. NAACP Legal Defense and Educational Fund, *Annual Report*, 1963, p. 9. (New York, N. Y.).

38. Alaska, Calif., Colo., Conn., Del., D. C., Idaho, Ill., Ind., Iowa, Kansas, Maine, Md., Mass., Mich., Minn., Mont., Neb., N. H., N.J., N. Mex., N.Y., N. Dak., Ohio, Ore., Pa., R.I., S. Dak., Vt., Wash., Wisc., Wyo. *Summary of 1962–1963 State Anti-Discrimination Laws*, prepared by American Jewish Congress (mimeographed booklet), December 31, 1963, p. 3.

39. In some southern states the law permitted owners of places of public accommodation to exclude blacks via broadly worded nonracial statutes. In Florida, for example, a group of blacks and whites seeking to eat together were asked to leave the Shell City Restaurant in Miami. They refused. They were charged with a misdemeanor. The statute making their refusal to leave a misdemeanor was a new variety adopted by southern states after the sit-in movement commenced. It provided that a place of public accommodation may exclude one who, "in the opinion of the management, is a person whom it would be detrimental for it any longer to entertain." Florida Statutes Annotated, Section 509.141. *Robinson, et al. v. Florida*, 378 U. S. 153 (1964).

40. For a compilation of state statutes which required transportation segregation, see Jack Greenberg, *Race Relations and American Law* (New York: Columbia University Press, 1959), pp. 116–17, Appendix A.1.

41. *Mitchell v. United States*, 313 U. S. 80 (1941).

42. *Morgan v. Virginia*, 328 U. S. 373 (1946).

43. *Henderson v. United States*, 339 U. S. 816 (1950).

44. *NAACP v. St. Louis and San Francisco Railroad Co.*, 297 I.C.C. 335 (1955).

45. *Keys v. Carolina Coach Co.*, 64 M.C.C. 769 (1955).

46. *Gayle v. Browder*, 142 F. Supp. 707 (M. D. Ala. 1956), aff'd 352 U. S. 903 (1956).

47. *Boynton v. Virginia*, 364 U. S. 454 (1960).

48. *Southern School News*, 8, No. 2 (August 1961), p. 15.

49. *Bailey v. Patterson*, 369 U. S. 31 (1962), 323 F. 2d 201 (5th Cir. 1963); *certiorari denied*, 376 U. S. 910 (1964). For the story of the first Freedom Rider see Allan F. Westin, "Ride In," *American Heritage*, 13, No. 5 (August, 1962), pp. 57–8.

50. *Turner v. City of Memphis*, 369 U. S. 350 (1962).

51. *Buchanan v. Warley*, 245 U. S. 60 (1917).

52. *City of Birmingham v. Monk*, 185 F. 2d 859 (5th Cir. 1950); *certiorari denied*, 341 U. S. 940 (1951).

53. *Holland v. Board of Public Instruction of Palm Beach County*, 258 F. 2d 730, 731 (5th Cir. 1958).

54. *L. K. Googer, et al. v. City of Atlanta, et al.*, Case No. A97697, Fulton Superior Court, March 1, 1963. State Court ordered a wall erected by the city to keep Negroes out of a residential area demolished.

55. *Shelley v. Kraemer*, 334 U. S. 1 (1948).

56. *Hurd v. Hodge*, 334 U. S. 24 (1948).

57. See, e.g., *James v. Valtierra*, 402 U. S. 137 (1971). *Kennedy Park Homes Association v. City of Lacka-wanna*, 436 F. 2d 108 (2nd Cir. 1970). *Certiorari denied* 401 U. S. 1010 (1971).

58. Title 12, U.S.C.A., Sections 1702, *et. seq.*

59. Charles Abrams, *Forbidden Neighbors*, (New York, Harper and Brothers) pp. 229–33.

60. Charles Abrams, *Ibid., supra*, p. 224; B. T. McGraw, "Desegregation and Open Occupancy Trends in Housing." *Journal of Human Relations* (Fall, 1954), pp. 59–61.

61. Executive Order No. 11063, 27 Federal Register 11527.

62. *Ibid.*, Section 302, p. 11528.

63. These cases are collected in Jack Greenberg, *op. cit., supra*, p. 290 ftn. 71.

64. *Ibid.*, ftn. 81, Section 303, p. 11529.
65. See *Heyward v. Public Housing Administration*, 238 F. 2d 689 (5th Cir. 1956).
66. Title 42, U.S.C.A. Section 3603(a). The law applied upon enactment to housing aided by the Federal Government pursuant to contracts entered into after November 20, 1962, unless payment due has been made in full prior to April 11, 1968. After December 31, 1968 the law applies to all such housing.
67. Title 42, U.S.C.A. Section 3603(b)(1).
68. Title 42 U.S.C.A. Section 3606(b)(2).
69. 42 U.S.C.A. Section 3604(c).
70. "Blockbusting" is the practice of moving a black family into an all-white block for the purpose of inducing white homeowners to sell to the real estate operator out of fear that Negroes moving into the area will reduce property values. If it works, the white owners sell out of fear. The real estate operator then has additional properties to sell to Negroes in the block at higher prices than he paid the panicky white owners. Since housing in such areas is desperately sought by Negroes who cannot buy elsewhere, the tactic often works.
71. 42 U.S.C.A. Sections 3604, 3605 and 3606.
72. 42 U.S.C.A. Section 3607.
73. *Ibid.*
74. *Ibid.* Section 3610.
75. *Ibid.*
76. *Ibid.*
77. *Ibid.* and Section 3612.
78. *Ibid.* Section 3613.
79. Suits have been brought successfully in federal courts since the decision. See for example *Smith v. Sol D. Adler Realty Co.*, 436 F. 2d 344 (7th Cir. 1970); *Baker v. F & F Investment*, 420 F. 2d 1191 (7th Cir. 1970), *certiorari denied* 400 U. S. 821. *Lee v. Southern Home Sites Corp.*, 429 F. 2d 290 (5th Cir. 1970), 444 F. 2nd 143 (5th Cir. 1971). But see *Trafficante v. Metropolitan Life Insurance Co.*, 446 F. 2d 1158 (9th Cir. 1971); *certiorari granted*, 400 U. S. Law Week 3398, Feb 2, 1972.
80. Eugene Rachlis, "The Magnificent Martyrdom of Prudence Crandall." *Coronet*, 50, No. 2 (June 1961), pp. 172–76.
81. *Crandall v. State*, 10 Conn. 339 (1834).
82. Massachusetts Acts 1845, Section 214.
83. General Laws of Mass., c. 256 Section 1 (1855).
84. Cong. Globe, 42nd Cong., 2nd sess., 244 (1871).
85. 18 Stat. 335.
86. John Marshall Harlan dissenting, at p. 559.
87. Prior to the *Sweatt* decision, in 1948, a less determined attack had been made on the doctrine. This occurred in the case of a young black woman, Ada Lois Sipuel, who desired to attend the University of Oklahoma Law School. *Sipuel v. Board of Regents*, 332 U. S. 631 (1948). Oklahoma had failed to provide a separate law school for Negroes despite the Supreme Court's ruling in 1938 in *Missouri* ex rel *Gaines v. Canada*, 305 U. S. 337. There, Missouri had offered to pay the difference between what it would cost Lloyd Gaines to go to a law school outside the state that would accept him, and what it would cost at the state's university. The Court held this out-of-state scholarship plan a denial of the equal protection of the laws. It said that the state could only guarantee equal protection within its borders. Missouri then built a separate law school for Negroes at its previously established black college.

    When the *Sipuel* case was before the Supreme Court, the Court ruled that blacks were not required to demand of the state the erection of separate facilities for them before they could claim a denial of equal protection. The Court put its first significant pressure on the doctrine of "separate but equal" by ruling that under the Fourteenth Amendment the state's duty was to provide "equal protection" for Negroes "at the same time" it provided such protection for other citizens. The practical result of this appeared to be that since the state had failed to set up a separate law school for Negroes, Miss Sipuel was entitled to immediate admission to the state's only law school.

This conclusion was reinforced by the fact that the Court ruled quickly after argument. Its ruling came shortly before a new semester at the university commenced.

The plaintiff's argument was also bolstered by the fact that in 1935, another black, Donald Murray, had been admitted to the University of Maryland Law School within the separate-but-equal context. There, Maryland had failed to provide a separate law school for the education of its black citizens. Consequently, the highest court of the state ruled that under the separate-but-equal doctrine Mr. Murray was entitled to admission in the state's only law school.

Prior to 1935, the Supreme Court had opportunities to strike down the doctrine as applied to education in several cases but failed to do so. One was *Gong Lum v. Rice*, 275 U. S. 78 (1927). Chinese children living in Mississippi objected to being classified as "colored" for school purposes without attacking the "separate but equal" concept. Their desire to be classified as "white" was denied. In the Berea, Kentucky, College case, in 1908, the Court upheld a state prohibition against corporations teaching white and Negro pupils in the same institution. *Berea College v. Kentucky*, 211 U. S. 45 (1908). It suggested such a prohibition might be invalid as to individuals. Negro children in a Georgia county sought to enjoin the maintenance of a white high school. None had been provided for Negroes. The Court denied this indirect assault on segregation in *Cumming v. Richmond County Board of Education*, 175 U. S. 528 (1899). It pointed to other remedies available to the complainants for securing a school facility for themselves.

88. Fifteen thousand federal soldiers and six hundred United States marshals secured Meredith's admission. *Southern School News*, 9, No. 4 (October 1962), p. 1.

89. *Gantt v. The Clemson Agricultural College of South Carolina*, 320 F. 2d 611 (4th Cir. 1963); *certiorari denied*, 375 U. S. 814.

90. Suit was also necessary in Florida, Georgia, Alabama, Virginia, North Carolina, Maryland, Texas, Tennessee, Kentucky, Delaware, Oklahoma, Missouri, and Louisiana.

91. The Supreme Court on January 15, 1973 agreed to review the Fourth Circuit decision, 41 U. S. Law Week 3388.

92. The attack on segregated schools in the North immediately following the 1954 decision was not a planned, coordinated attack such as the attack in the South had been.

93. E.g., *Walker v. Board of Education of City of Englewood, N. J.*, 1 Race Relations Law Reporter 255 (1956); *Clemons v. Board of Education of Hillsboro, Ohio*, 228 F 2d 853 (6th Cir. 1956); *certiorari denied*, 350 U. S. 1006; *Taylor v. Board of Education of City of New Rochelle*, 294 F. 2d 36 (2d Cir. 1961), *affirming* 191 F. Supp. 181 (S.D.N.Y. 1961); *certiorari denied*, 368 U. S. 940; *Blocker v. Board of Education*, Manhasset, N. Y., 226 F. Supp. 208 (E.D.N.Y. 1964).

94. *Taylor v. Board of Education of City School District* (S.D.N.Y. 1961), 191 F. Supp. 181. There were blacks in ten of the eleven other elementary schools in the district.

95. *Taylor v. Board of Education of City School District*, 294 F. 2d 36 (2d Cir. 1961).

96. *Standard Star*, New Rochelle, New York, November 16, 1963, p. 1.

97. *Bell v. School City of Gary, Indiana*, (N. D. Ind. 1963), 213 F. Supp. 819, 324 F. 2d 209 (7th Cir. 1963); *certiorari denied*, 377 U. S. 924 (1964).

98. *Southern School News*, 8, No. 10 (April 1962) p. 10.

99. *Jackson v. Pasadena School District*, 59 Cal. 2d 876, 382 P. 2d 878 (1963).

100. *Balaban v. Rubin*, 250 N. Y. Supp. 2d 281, 20 A. D. 2d 438; *aff'd* 14 N.Y. 2d 193; *certiorari denied*, 379 U. S. 881 (1964).

101. Title 5, United States Code, Annotated Section 1074.

102. See *Bolling v. Sharpe*, 347 U. S. 497 (1954), barring racial discrimination by the Federal Government in public education.

103. Executive Order No. 11246, 30 Federal Register 12319 (1965).

104. *Alston v. School Board of City of Norfolk*, 112 F. 2d 992 (4th Cir.); *certiorari denied*, 311 U. S. 693 (1940).

105. *Dorsey v. State Athletic Commission*, 168 F. Supp. 149 (E.D. La. 1958); *affirmed*, 359 U. S. 533 (1959).

106. *Harvey v. Morgan*, 272 S.W. 2nd 621 (1954).

107. *Chaires v. City of Atlanta*, 164 Ga. 755, 139 S.E. 559 (1927).

108. 42 United States Code Annotated 2000e, *et seq.*

109. Public Law 92961, Mar. 24, 1972.

110. Clyde W. Summers, *The Right to Join a Union*, 47 Columbia Law Review 33, 34 (1947).

111. *Steele v. Louisville and Nashville R.R.* 323 U. S. 192 (1944).

112. *Mayer v. Journeymen Stonecutters Association*, 47 N.J. Eq. 519, 20 Atl. 492 (Ch. 1890).

113. *Railway Mail Association v. Corsi*, 326 U. S. 88 (1945).

114. *James v. Marineship Corp.*, 25 Cal. 2d 721, 155 Pac. (2d) 329 (1945). See Clyde W. Summers, *op. cit.*, *supra* ftn. 143 pp. 44–45 for citation of other cases.

115. *Steele and Louisville and Nashville R.R.*, *supra* at 203; *Syres v. Oil Workers International Union*, 223 F. 2d 739 (5th Cir. 1955); reversed *per curiam*, 350 U. S. 892 (1955).

116. See, e.g., *Central of Georgia Railway v. Jones*, 229 F. 2d 648 (5th Cir. 1956); *certiorari denied*, 352 U. S. 848 (1956); *Rolax v. Atlantic Coast Line Railroad*, 186 F. 2d 473 (4th Cir. 1951).

117. Michael I. Sovern, *The National Labor Relations Act and Racial Discrimination*, 62 Columbia Law Review 563 (1962).

118. *Independent Metal Workers Union, Local No. 1 and Local No. 2 and Hughes Tool Company*, 147 NLRB 1573 (1964).

119. See, e.g., *Caldwell v. National Brewing Co.*, 443 F. 2d 1044 (5th Cir. 1971); *certiorari denied*, 405 U. S. 916 (1972); *Waters v. Wisconsin Steel Works*, 427 F. 2d 476 (7th Cir. 1970); *certiorari denied*, 400 U. S. 911 (1970); *Saunders v. Dobbs House, Inc.*, 431 F. 2d 1097 (5 Cir. 1970); *certiorari denied*, 401 U. S. 948 (1971).

120. *Williams v. United States*, 341 U. S. 70, 73, 77 (1951). In *Logan v. United States*, 144 U. S. 263 (1892), the Court held the statute applicable to a mob which had seized a prisoner from a federal marshal on the ground that the prisoner had thereby been deprived of federal protection while properly in federal custody.

121. 18 U.S.C.A. 245 (b).

122. *Ibid.*

123. *Monroe v. Pape*, 365 U. S. 167 (1961); 28 U.S.C.A. Section 1343(3).

124. See, e.g., *Collins v. Hardyman*, 341 U. S. 651 (1951).

125. 28 U.S.C.A. Section 1343(4).

126. Jessie Parkhurst Guzman, *Negro Yearbook*, (New York: William H. Wise & Co., 1952), p. 278.

127. Jack Greenberg, *op. cit.*, *supra*, p. 320.

128. See Maslow and Robison, *Civil Rights Legislation and the Fight for Equality* (1862–1952), 20 Chicago Law Review 363, 380–85 (1953).

129. Title, 18 U.S.C.A. Sections 241 and 242. For examples of the difficulty in securing convictions of police officers guilty of brutality against Negroes see *Screws v. United States*, 325 U. S. 91 (1945); *Williams v. United States*, 341 U. S. 97 (1951).

130. Title 18, U.S.C.A. Section 371.

131. Title 18, U.S.C.A. Section 2(a).

132. *Logan v. United States*, 144 U. S. 263 (1892).

133. Title 42, U.S.C.A. Section 1983 and Section 1985(3).

134. Maslow and Robison, *op. cit.*, p. 383.

135. For short descriptions of these statutes, see Jack Greenberg, *op. cit.*, *supra*, 374 Appendix A25.

136. See, e.g., *McCrink v. City of New York*, 296 N.Y. 99, 71 N.E. 2d 419 (1947).

137. *Civil Rights Cases*, 109 U. S. 3, 22 (1883).

138. *Ibid.*

139. The Fourteenth Amendment to the Federal Constitution, among other things, conferred citizenship on the former slaves.

140. Title 42, U.S.C.A. Section 1981.

141. Title 18, U.S.C. Section 243.

142. *Ex parte Virginia*, 100 U. S. 339 (1880).

143. *Cassell v. Texas*, 339 U. S. 282 (1950), Mr. Justice Jackson dissenting at p. 303. See also *Justice*, Report of the United States Commission on Civil Rights (1961) pp. 89–103.

144. *Ibid.*

145. Title 42, U.S.C. Section 1983. This statute is invoked to enjoin school segregation and other forms of state discrimination based on race. See, e.g., *Brown v. The Board of Education of Topeka*, 347 U. S. 483 (1954).

146. *Brown v. Rutter*, 139 F. Supp. 679 (W. D. Ky. 1956).

147. *Strauder v. West Virginia*, 100 U. S. 303 (1880). For citation of a number of these cases see Jack Greenberg, *op. cit., supra*, pp. 323–29. See also Justice, *op. cit., supra*, ftn. 175.

148. *Peters* v. *Kiff*, 407 U. S. 493 (1972).

149. *Brown v. Mississippi*, 297 U. S. 278 (1936).

150. *Ashcraft v. Tennessee*, 322 U. S. 143 (1944).

151. *Moore v. Dempsey*, 261 U. S. 86 (1923).

152. *Gideon v. Wainwright*, 372 U. S. 335 (1963); *Argersinger v. Hamlin*, 407 U. S. 25 (1972).

153. This decision was rendered on June 29, 1972, long after this chapter was written. However, because of the importance of the case this brief paragraph was inserted before printing.

154. Memorandum from United States Attorney, Southern District of New York, to Judges of Second Circuit and Southern District dated January 10, 1973 in regard to disparities in sentencing.

155. These seventeen antimiscegenation states were: Alabama, Arkansas, Delaware, Florida, Georgia, Kentucky, Louisiana, Maryland, Mississippi, Missouri, North Carolina, Oklahoma, South Carolina, Tennessee, Texas, Viginia, and West Virginia.

156. Arizona, California, Colorado, Iowa, Kansas, Massachusetts, Michigan, Montana, Nebraska, Nevada, New Mexico, North Dakota, Ohio, Oregon, Rhode Island, South Dakota, Utah, Washington.

157. Jack Greenberg, *op. cit., supra*, p. 344, 398.

158. *Jackson v. State*, 37 Ala. App. 519, 72 So. 2d 114 (1954); *certiorari denied*, 260 Ala. 698, 72 So. 2d 116 (1954); *certiorari denied*, 348 U. S. 888 (1954).

159. *Naim v. Naim*, 197 Va. 80, 87 S.E. 2d 749 (1955); *judgment vacated*, 350 U. S. 891 (1955); *judgment reinstated*, 197 Va. 734, 90 S.E. 2d 849 (1956); *appeal dismissed*, 350 U. S. 985 (1956).

160. See Jack Greenberg, *op. cit, supra*, p. 396, for a collection of such statutes.

161. *McLaughlin and Hoffman v. The State of Florida*, 379 U. S. 184 (1964). Opinion of Supreme Court of Florida reported in 153 So. 2d 1 (1963).

162. Florida Statutes Annotated Section 798.05.

163. Florida Statutes Annotated Section 741.11.

164. Florida Statutes Annotated Section 101. For a collection of similar laws see: Pauli Murray, *States' Laws on Race and Color*, (New York Woman's Division of Christian Service, Board of Missions and Church Extension, the Methodist Church 1950), *passim*.

165. *Perez v. Lippold*, 32 Cal. 2d 711, 198 P. 2d 17 (1948).

# 3

## Black Personality
## in American Society

*Charles A. Pinderhughes*

### THE SEARCH FOR UNDERSTANDING

Twentieth-century relationships between blacks and whites in the United States have been fashioned by the dynamic interplay of human forces during generations of life in America, Europe, and Africa. Despite the diversity and complexity of such relationships, many attempts have been made over the years to analyze and reduce the nature of black-white interaction to simple terms. This can be done, however, only at the risk of resorting to half-truths and stereotypes.

Persons and agencies attempting to promote either ethnic development among blacks or integration of blacks and whites have thereby been on the lookout for new ways to achieve a more comprehensive insight into black-white relationships. One technique which has proved its validity is the setting up of discussion groups possessing diverse theoretical frameworks, skills, experiences, and cultural backgrounds who attack the complexities of racial interaction as realistically as possible. New insights and understandings have evolved from such groups, black and integrated alike, which from coast to coast have been exploring the effects of being black or white upon one's personality, role relationships, personality development, family dynamics, and community dynamics. As the discussants gather together and communicate through a process of open dialogue known as "rapping," conflicting belief systems, myths, and stereotypes frequently give rise to confrontation. In the hands of experienced leaders, such clashes can be channeled toward the achievement of greater understanding and insight within the group.

### The "Rap" Session

The following partial transcript of one such meeting, involving a group of white and black personnel in a clinic, illustrates how the rap session works. Discussion was opened with the question: "Are there definitive points in the growth process in black children which are different from those in white children?"

Discussant 1:    "There are some nodal points which probably are determined more by biological factors than cultural ones, such as starting to walk. Others, like going to school, may be culturally defined."

Discussant 2:    "One study indicated that black children bypassed certain latency-age features that white children experienced. Latency-age (6 to 12 years old) black children did not perceive themselves as students as white children of the same age did. Instead, the black children very quickly perceived themselves in work roles. This may mean that school and student roles hold less meaning for some black children."

Discussant 3:    "That need not be a negative finding. Rather, it seems to be related to African cultural patterns in which the family and neighbors serve as the principal educators in an apprentice learning process rather than a more artificial and contrived school situation. Even the older children help the younger ones and instruct them."

Discussant 4:    "It is possible that the slavery experience reinforced the use of the naturally available teachers rather than the use of contrived educational systems."

Discussant 5:    "If maturity is measured by prevailing cultural standards, if adulthood means holding a job, how can we reinforce self-esteem and a sense of adulthood in blacks who can't get jobs? How can we give emotional support when our cultural standards and social structures favor some and victimize others?"

Discussant 6:    "Here in the clinic, black children assume helping roles with other black children or with white children as often as white children assume helping roles. Yet blacks, especially males, are often stereotyped as helpless or undependable."

Discussant 7:    "Black mothers have often been stereotyped as more oppressive to black male children. As representatives of a culture oppressive to black males, the mother helped prepare them for survival in it by oppressing them to fit the system."

Discussant 5:    "Black women may be trying to redefine their role in relation to black males; are there cultural supports for this?"

Discussant 8:    "We should develop ideas of successful black adaptation which take into consideration the experience of blacks in their special circumstances. We are prone to conceptualize normality in the framework of our own group's experience, and to consider a different experience as abnormal. Distrust, sacrifice of individual goals, etc., may be healthy and adaptive under some circumstances. What constitutes adequate development should be related to the life realities of a given child."

Discussant 5:    "I am ambivalent about institutions that end up defining terms and values for a community. What is adequate for a given child? A particular personality may seem comfortable and adequate for the child, but will it fit the demands of the group he lives in? Or will it fit the demands imposed by the school group or work group into which he moves? The concept of fitting in is important for defining satisfactory development, and this in turn implies some flexibility and multiple potentials."

Discussant 9:    "We are not even sure what constitutes our community. Do we mean the white as well as the black residents? Do we include those who come here to work but live elsewhere?"

Discussant 10:   "Identity and who I am is the issue. What does it mean to a child to establish an identity of being black? What are the responsibilities and expectations the child feels and how can we help the child to feel it as positive?"

Discussant 11:   "We're still defining what happens with individuals and this may not jibe with institutions. A black child may develop an identity which he feels as positive and which we may define as positive but can meet a world that defines him differently. How can he cope when he's told and then feels he's crazy?"

(At this point several black participants presented examples of the kinds of outside social pressures that push blacks to reject what feels comfortable and is functional in a strictly black environment.)

Discussant 12:   "You are leaving the parents and their conflicts out of the discussion of identity development."

Discussant 11:   "The problem is not in the home. Black children are not supported by our social institutions."

Discussant 12:   "I can cite two children who developed nicely until they moved out into the world, where they rapidly began to feel negatively about themselves."

(Three black discussants gave examples from their personal life experiences dealing with surprising racist behavior encountered when they entered predominately white schools.)

Discussant 13:   "Puerto Ricans and Chicanos clash with institutions that don't support their homes. We're talking about what happens when a child defined one way at home meets up with institutions that define him differently."

Discussant 8:    "Let's get back to what we were talking about."

Discussant 1:    "When you say, 'what *we* were talking about,' you imply that in this room there are some 'we' people talking about one thing and some 'they' people talking about other things. We have noted adversary relationships and arguments with divisions occurring along four different lines. During the discussion 'we' and 'they' divisions have been occurring among us according to race, class, power, and ideology. Some confrontations have occurred between whites and blacks, some between supervisors and lower-echelon staff members, and some between those who prefer to focus on intrapsychic factors and those who prefer to focus on societal factors."

Discussant 8:    "I'd like to underline the importance of awareness of processes to be encountered and the need to prepare people for them. We help children to be aware of and prepared for certain experiences with their parents, but are children prepared for the endless rebuffs from society beyond the family?"

Discussant 3:     "I won't deal with that. We are undervaluing the black parents and the preparation they give. I was confirmed at age 12 and had many experiences which defined me as a woman at various points in my teens. But there were always contradictions in our society. I was a woman at 18 in New York, but had to wait to be 21 in the next state I worked in."

Discussant 8:     "In many ways your preparation was inadequate and irrelevant to the experiences you encountered."

Discussant 14:    "My 11-year-old son was repeatedly beaten when we lived in a white neighborhood until I sent him to judo school. That proved to be relevant preparation."

(Discussants 2 and 6 described ambivalence in black parents about the society around them and then pointed out how ambivalent all people are.)

Discussant 6:     "Black children are being reared differently now. Black mothers used to say, 'accommodate, be good, be passive.' Now they say, 'be aggressive.' How can we talk about this kind of preparation in black families when we can't get society to support it?"

Discussant 10:    "The examples given are useful. They show that there are dangers to be dealt with in the world, that kids can be helped to deal with the real dangers, that kids will have ambivalence and conflict within them, and kids have to be prepared to face and deal with that also."

Discussant 15:    "How can we hope to change? There's still conflict between the way we prepare our children and the messages they find in school which are so tough on them."

Discussant 5:     "Our focus here is on how we address ourselves to problem feelings in people and to the real problems they encounter. We, ourselves, are part of the problem. Right here in this group, for example, we listen more to some than to others. What some individuals say needs no validation. When others speak, some upper-status person needs to validate or invalidate what they have said. Subtle differences in the way we behave with different people reflects our irrationality and discrimination."

(Several personal experiences were described.)

Discussant 11:    "I grew up in the South. Are we talking about parents preparing children for the world as it is, or about more adaptive survival? Do we prepare people to take insults or to change the world which is so filled with them?"

Discussant 12:    "Throughout our discussion blacks have been talking about the black experience while whites talk about their own. We must develop more back-and-forth interaction involving more understanding and acceptance."

From this point on in the dialogue, there was greater agreement between white and black and between upper- and lower-echelon personnel. It was generally agreed that no matter what identity black children develop, American society as a whole sends back discouraging messages to them about themselves.

The group then went on to discuss how individual identity cannot be developed without some conflicts with family, with institutions, and with the psychic institutions within parents and siblings. It was further pointed out that even within an individual personality, conflict is inevitable and is usually resolved by the dominance of one component over the rest. Resultant behavior is likely to fall into one of two basic categories: initiative or accommodative. Mastery and manipulation are associated with the former mode and slavery or sacrifice are associated with the latter.

### Separation-Individuation and Liberation

The majority of black people today make it clear that they will no longer be defined by someone else. Since the formation of a viable group requires the subordination of individual interests to those of the larger entity, this means that certain contemporary concepts of blackness and black experience function in opposition to black group development. On the one hand, blacks want to join ranks, or build a "nation"; but at the same time they want to retain "soul," being faithful to their individual selves, with each person defining what constitutes "good" and what constitutes "bad" in his or her experience.

Participants in the dialogue quoted earlier noted that greater success had been achieved in finding group targets of aggression than in developing a common binding ideology and loyalty. Although numerous black religious groups and diverse organizations with nationalistic goals were emerging, there was no sign of a significant move toward unification in 1971–72. Blacks during this period had a common object of projection, however—whites—whom they perceived as the embodiment of evil and destructiveness. This, along with political expediencies, constituted the principal basis for such federations as occurred among diverse black groups.

A close look at the above transcript reveals a constant focus upon black experience, even though whites made up almost half of the group. Several persons suggested during the dialogue that equal focus upon white experience might lead to a more balanced perspective.

### The Black Individual, the Black Family System, and the White Social System

What constitutes preparation of a child and a parent for their interaction with one another? How can both parties through their engagements and confrontations during the growing process achieve mutually satisfying role relationships and identity formation? And how do we prepare an individual and his society for mutual interaction and optimum growth?

In each case active effort is required on both sides. Both the child and his parents must practice a subtle policy of give and take. The same is true with the individual and his society, who must work to mesh with one another. Only by such a process of mutual adaptation can the dynamics of power, domination, and enslavement of one party by the other be avoided.

All over America black groups and black-and-white groups were working with questions like these during the late 1960s and early 1970s. Although the dialogue quoted earlier was held on a sophisticated level, this had not always been the case. Earlier rap sessions tended to be more polarized and more emotional, with whites taking more initiative in defining the needs of black people, and blacks assisting them. In later stages blacks took more initiative and were assisted by whites.

## Corrective Black Activism

Many of the issues facing black people are illustrated by the above dialogue. How do blacks, descendants of slaves, identify and rid themselves of the destructive coercive slave and segregation cultures which have shaped them? How can they successfully manage the antigroup behavior imposed upon them from both within and without? How do they form supportive and constructive groups which fit black individual needs on one hand and the surrounding culture on the other? To accomplish this, a human engineering process of monumental proportions has been set in motion. It has constituted a most important force for constructive social change, initiating and spearheading the activation of oppressed individuals and groups throughout the country. Activists have progressed from dissent processes to demonstration processes, to the active use of nonviolent confrontation, and finally to the development of power for concerted action and defense. Throughout the spectrum of the integration movement, the Black Power movement, and subsequent ethnic development, confrontation processes have been mastered and employed with remarkable courage and skill in hundreds of American institutions.

Black caucuses and Afro-American societies became typical instruments of black-group formation, confrontation, and constructive social change. These instruments made possible concerted action within a framework which allowed for multiple points of view and for specialized and diversified responses.

During 1970–72 one could find examples of every stage of black development in the United States. Some black people had become liberated to a remarkable degree, some remained powerless and virtually enslaved, and the condition of others ran the entire gamut between these two extremes.

## The Oppressed Begin to Move in Concert

Persons who participate in social movements have their behavior shaped to some degree by their experiences in those movements, with different movements reinforcing different patterns.

During the early 1960s Dr. Martin Luther King was the principal spokesman for a civil rights movement based upon the highest national and religious ideals and upon a mature psychology which stressed mutual consideration, respect, sharing, and equality. The mass-communications media, especially television, played a decisive role in the development and course of this movement. Audience appeal at that time was determined by the degree to which excitement and emotional involvement could be generated. When large numbers of people gathered, demonstrated peacefully against oppression and discrimination, and sang freedom songs in unison, there was widespread interest among that group which looked favorably upon racial desegregation and racial integration.

Those persons, however, who felt threatened by desegregation and opposed to integration experienced aggressive responses and viewed the civil rights movement as a threat. Associated with their images of a repressed unacceptable people rising and entering what they considered to be their exclusive domain was a sense that evil forces were rising to destroy them. In the unconscious thinking processes of many whites, the repressed black people were associated with all the characteristics of human behavior which should be repressed to prevent it from overwhelming and destroying society.

Most whites viewed the integration movement as a dangerous intrusive invasion—an attack. Malcolm X at this time was vigorously portraying whites as exploitative and destructive to black people, as a kind of devil who had altered their natures, destroyed their families, groups, culture, morality, and threatened their basic humanity. Malcolm X did not advise attacking the enemy, however, but on the contrary encouraged separatism, self-rehabilitation, and self-development. He felt that a constructive culture to support a more adaptive black identity should be developed by black people to replace the slave culture which had been imposed upon them and passed on from generation to generation.

For most whites Malcolm X symbolized their own unconscious sexual and sadistic fantasies and their fears of their own undesirable impulses. In Malcolm they saw an external object who could be feared in place of an internal one, and their own hatred could be mobilized consciously against Malcolm and the evils they imputed to black people. Many whites could not show anger and vent their wrath at Dr. King because he represented and was living out their most cherished ideals and ethics. The fear and outrage they unconsciously experienced as a response to the integration movement was therefore directed at Malcolm, who seemed to be attacking them. With Malcolm symbolizing black people, arousal to rage and retaliation seemed justified. One might say that unconscious white fears engendered by Dr. King were diverted to Malcolm X, who became a target of white rage, some of which then spilled over to Dr. King. By attacking Dr. King and his demonstrations, whites not only disrupted demonstrations, but attached the stigma of violence to such gatherings in the minds of some people so that demonstrations became repressed and discredited in the thinking of many whites. By 1965 an overflow of white hostility led to the emergence of an oppressive white power movement referred to as the "White Backlash," which neutralized the integration movement and made it ineffective as an avenue for improving the lot of black people. Blacks had approached whites with love and whites had responded with hate.

## Television and Social Movements

The extent to which television was both consciously and unconsciously used to bring about this turn of events will never be fully known. What is clear is that Dr. King and his movement were portrayed on television only when a large demonstration was being mobilized. Malcolm X was portrayed on television far more frequently in 1963 and 1964 although he had only a handful of followers compared to Dr. King.

It appeared to whites that Malcolm was attacking them, thus their enraged response toward him and his black following seemed justified. In the eyes of blacks, Malcolm was describing their historical past and offering a prophecy that since whites could not be trusted, blacks would have to separate from whites and develop themselves. Television was the principal instrument used to disperse and plant the seeds of this ideology in the minds of the nation's black population. Television was also the principal tool used to incite rage and rejection among whites at a time when most blacks and some whites were trying to unify and integrate this country. Because conflict is more emotionally involving and attracts larger audiences than harmonious and peaceful processes, the mass-communications media directed itself to the former, escalating conflict and polarization by communicating that which was most arousing and most likely to attract the largest audiences.

By misinterpreting the integration movement, and by disseminating Malcolm's prophecy and message across the country and then neutralizing integration efforts through the White Backlash, whites blocked the road to collaboration, instituted the ethics and processes of competitive group strength, and projected polarizing processes into dominance.

## The Black Power Movement, Liberation, and Social Revolution

At this point, many blacks who had formerly trusted, relied upon, and been favorably disposed toward whites turned against them. At the same time, many middle-class blacks who had been positively disposed toward whites and negatively disposed toward blacks underwent a reversal in their feeling. The response to white rage and white power was black rage and group formation aimed at the development of black power, since whites had defined group power as the basis for consideration and participation.

For the first time many blacks began to identify with one another and to form positive emotional bonds with other blacks. They fantasied themselves to be "Soul Brothers" and "Soul Sisters" and responded as a group to any attack or unnecessary force used by a white against a black. Aggressive group responses to instances of police brutality led to frequent confrontations and many riot interactions between citizens and city officials. Confrontations between blacks and whites occurred at every level.

As blacks gained self-esteem and respect for themselves, whites became increasingly sensitive and respectful of their needs. Some whites, however, defended their own supremacy by invoking and organizing more power, which caused blacks, in turn, to mobilize themselves for forceful, skillful, but nonviolent confrontations. Blacks were ready to defend their integrity, their homes, and their "territory." Their efforts to increase community control reflected the desire to gain control over their persons, their families, and their communities. Intense efforts were devoted by blacks to defining themselves and their own values, and to the rejection of the definitions and manipulative forces of white individuals and white institutions. This dynamic activity on the part of blacks spread to other oppressed groups, including Puerto Ricans, Mexican-Americans, Indians, the poor, women, and prisoners, and the thrust of these liberation movements initiated many changes.

The shift from an accommodating role to an active participatory and initiating role involves a shift in feeling tone, in attitude, in the quality and quantity of emotion experienced, and in behavior.

Some blacks who assumed initiating roles became aware that aggressive feelings and distrust of others were associated with this stance, whereas affiliative feelings and trust were apt to be associated with accommodating roles. In American culture a higher value has regularly been assigned to initiating roles and a lower one to those of accommodation.

In our society whites, males, and "upper" economic-political-educational-social echelons have always been accorded the most power, organization, rewards, status, privileges, and value. Blacks, females, working classes, and "lower" economic-political-educational-social echelons have traditionally lagged behind.

## The Crisis of Maximal Polarization

During 1967 and 1968 the continuing polarization of blacks and whites and increased group formation among blacks and whites alike resulted in an alarming number of confrontations and encounters in which violent interactions occurred.

Blacks, in these confrontations, were expressing many things. They were letting it be known that they no longer accepted the prowhite, antiblack racist dogma and psychology which, under coercion, they had shared with whites. They were letting it be known that henceforth they would not passively accommodate to racist oppression, but would stand up for their rights, defend themselves, retaliate if mistreated, and protect with vigilance their interests and welfare in a racist society.

As the black-white relationship moved toward greater equality, there was increasing conflict; conflict is inherent in all equal relationships. Whenever two persons are talking at the same time there is conflict. Mutuality, alternation of roles, and give-and-take relationships represent the synchronizing and harmonizing of equal roles which might otherwise conflict.

Generally among human beings, as among other primate animals, as we shall see later, conflict between equal parties is resolved by struggles for dominance in which one party submits to domination by another and sacrifices self-interest to the interests of the dominant party. This results in grossly unequal, unfair relationships and in exploitation of the more submissive party. Men have done this with women, whites with blacks, and upper classes with lower classes.

## Mutuality, Sharing, and Identification With Victims as Well as With Aggressors

Most human beings recognize that they are capable of identifying with the weak as well as with the strong, with victims as well as with aggressors. However, in all encounters between individuals, the strongest one can, if he chooses, impose his interests or punish or even destroy the weaker. By forming groups people can gain enough power to exceed the power of any one individual although this does not often occur. More often groups have so many inert or loosely organized persons among them that persons who use power may, through socioeconomic and political power processes, use the groups for personal rather than group interests.

Thus the behavior of a group and its leaders may be in conflict with and opposed to the ideals and ethics avowed by the group members. The United States was established as a land of freedom and equality, yet through the social, economic, and political dynamics of power, a slave state defined by Stanley Elkins as the most coercive society in history was established here. Where power dynamics are operative, people can remain human in their thinking and behavior toward themselves yet be quite inhuman in their thinking and behavior toward others.

It is for this reason that once a group of people defines their ethics, moral codes, and laws, great care must be taken to see that these are upheld. When conflicts arise, there should be a search for reliable processes, ethics, and guidelines for resolving the conflicts to prevent recourse to power dynamics.

However, should one party use power, the other must be prepared to take a strong stand and provide the confrontations needed to bring the power-wielder to the realization that he must employ more humane and more adaptive methods.

When blacks used group formation, power, and confrontation methods in the 1960s, the use of power and polarization by whites accelerated with violent and sometimes tragic results. After a series of assassinations of prominent nonviolent champions of the oppressed (Medgar Evers, Malcolm X, John F. Kennedy, Martin Luther King, Robert Kennedy, plus some sixteen less well-known civil rights workers and leaders), an escalation of white fear and guilt led to a wave of integrative activity in white institutions, along with the invocation and organization of more power to control violence and subtler, less-physical methods of maintaining oppressed people in a powerless state.

Integration occurred increasingly at points of contact between blacks and whites. Amid much conflict and emotional turmoil some institutions began to take affirmative action to recruit blacks. At this point whites were confronted with the harvest of 200 years of enslavement of blacks followed by continuing segregation of blacks to perpetuate the slave culture cast of white superiority and black inferiority. All too often there were "no qualified blacks" to be found for openings. Instead of perceiving that the imposed slave culture had put most blacks on tracks which insured that they would be excluded and unqualified, the shortage of qualified blacks was assumed by many whites to be evidence of their inferiority.

While most white persons have focused upon the modest amount of integration occurring in some institutions, the majority of blacks are becoming increasingly aware of the number of black people being programmed *not* to fit into those institutions.

One area where the lack of fit between black people and white institutions has been difficult to understand and remedy is in the school systems.

In many instances African educational systems of the past used the readily available family and tribal structure and apprenticeship methods for conveying an education, which helped students to fit well with their families and with their wider culture.

The slave-training system disrupted tribal and family structure and used apprenticeship methods to educate blacks not to fit into a basically white system except in servile roles. Most black children were fitted into this maladaptive educational system which programmed them for their slave status.

After slavery and under segregation, black children continued to be trained and educated not to fit basically white systems. The training system involved both family structure and community structure as well as public schools. Both home and school structure worked together to train black children for their oppressed low-status roles. All but a few children were fitted into this educational system.

Under slavery most blacks had been segregated in the South. Under segregation this pattern continued. During the twentieth century increasing migration of blacks to the North and West occurred. Every northern city developed a colony of blacks who had migrated from the South in search of more freedom and opportunity. In the massive migration of individuals and segments of families, further disruption, depression, and suffering occurred. In most cases those who moved North left poor but relatively stable communities in which there was little opportunity. Blacks moving to the North found themselves encountering other recently displaced, often lonely, frightened, depressed, and disorganized persons. They were often victimized; and the black communities usually had no group structure to turn to and could expect only grossly inadequate services from city agencies. Social instability, continuing segregation, reduced opportunities, increasing population density, increasing victimization, higher prices, higher morbidity rates, increasing medical and mental health needs, and increasingly deficient services characterized many northern communities of black poor people.

There was seldom organized group support in the neighborhood for the families and all too often families lacked sufficient organization and resources to meet the needs of family members. Antigroup behavior and antisocial behavior received reinforcement on the streets which undermined parental efforts at home. All too often depressing experiences left parents discouraged, disorganized, and less effective than they might have been in more supportive circumstances.

The public educational system into which black ghetto children went after migration northward or after integration was often part of that white system into which blacks had been programmed not to fit for so long. In these situations the school personnel were often separate from and sometimes at odds with the pupils.

Under integration more black children were being educated to fit basically white institutions, and more were also being educated neither to fit, nor to serve, nor to find any acceptable role in the wider culture because of the inadequate schools and lack of adjustment to pupils' needs.

Present educational problems, while basically traceable to the programming which took place under slavery and segregation, involve far more than schools and pupils. In their solution, attention should be directed at the same time to schools, to students, to families, and to communities in order to develop education which is relevant and not isolated, and which fits the student and family, student and culture, and student and community, to one another adaptively. Educators and family members need to find more ways to work in harmony with mutual support and trust to bridge the gaps that exist in life styles, goals, values, and culture.

## The Oppression of Non-Elites in an Elitist Society

Every society contains a relatively powerful, aggrandized, more highly rewarded elite and a less powerful, devalued, poorly rewarded, and often dehumanized non-elite.

Conflict and sometimes violence occur in interactions between these two groups, but even more evident is the inevitably destructive effect that elites unconsciously have on non-elites.

Beliefs about the specialness and superior nature of elites are promoted in both elites and non-elites. This is based upon the former's conspicuous possession or acquisition of selected resources or attributes. Institutions and social structures are developed to reinforce or program the elites toward these selected resources and attributes and to program the non-elites away from them.

All aspects of human functioning are subjected to these programming influences; and parents, families, schools, churches, and other institutions coordinately "track" people toward elite or non-elite roles in various relationships and institutions. Differing standards of physical behavior, verbal behavior, clothing, and beliefs about self and about others are maintained for elites and non-elites; and in a given society the institutions for producing elites are carefully separated from those which produce non-elites.

Such calculated social realities express and further reinforce beliefs that elites are superior and non-elites inferior. The appearance and behavior of people seem to confirm these beliefs, and most people are unaware of the contrived nature of social structures.

## The Contrived Nature of Social Realities

The contrived and imposed nature of social realities is not easy for some persons to perceive and acknowledge. Persons who are imposing their "system" on the system of another person, thereby getting the other person to accommodate and conform to them, are seldom aware of the manipulatory and aggressive nature of their behavior or of the destructive effects upon accommodating persons. Even when they acknowledge that they are the decision-makers, initiators, or bosses, they rationalize their behavior and use preexisting contrived social realities as a justification for their actions.

An individual in an initiating role is uniquely unable to identify with the person in the accommodating role. Individuals in accommodating roles are generally subjected to the power and authority vested in and assumed by the initiator and dependent upon the initiator for resources and for direction. Careful study of the history of these relationships reveals that where initiating roles are relatively fixed, each relationship has been brought about and maintained by use of power and bribery, punishments and rewards. The one who mobilizes and organizes power most effectively prevails and determines roles, beliefs, processes, and structures for each party to the relationship.

The organization and institutionalization of one party's position by means of laws, codes of behavior, belief systems, governments, schools, churches, and associated agencies can create an organized power system and an alignment of rewards and punishments that insure a favored role for one party and a disadvantaged role for another. Particular styles of appearance, speech, training, clothing, behavior, relationships, beliefs, and other aspects of background may be conscious or unconscious requirements for admission and participation. Institutionalized racism, classism, sexism, and other patterns of social discrimination have these institutionalized as well as personalized aspects.

In such a social system it is easy for one in an elite family to be conditioned toward an elite track and painful for that individual to function in non-elite directions. It is difficult for persons in non-elite families to be conditioned toward an elite track and may be painful as well. Persons who move from one group to another often experience painful criticism from those they leave behind as well as from those they join. Identity conflicts and painful isolation often result. The family and community into which one is born, as well as all the surrounding educational, religious, political, and economic institutions have been structured by those with the ability to mobilize and organize power. Upward mobility for black citizens has thus been seen as a desertion by less fortunate blacks, and an intrusion by whites in more favorable circumstances.

## A General Systems Concept of Black-White Relationships

If one takes care to interview white people in a manner which does not direct them or influence the content of what they say, it soon becomes evident that every white person has certain body parts, body products, body processes, sounds, ideas, words, and acts of which he is critical and even views as bad or evil. Invariably these are associated with blackness and darkness.

Careful study will also reveal that the "black" aspects of each white person's body, body products, sounds, ideas, words, and acts are those which are disruptive to their social groups and which each group member is trained to repress in order not to unduly excite or disturb his fellows.

Every white person has "black" aspects which are renounced by his or her groups and which must be repressed, renounced, and excluded from group social behavior. This is one basis for the repression of certain "black" aspects of mental life in white people. Those characteristics of bodies and behavior which are openly welcomed and highly valued in group life are invariably viewed as good and as white.

The universal use of blackness as a symbol for all which is excluded, renounced, or evil seems related to the experiences which all humans have with night and day. Sun and light are associated with access to the persons and objects one loves and needs, and with knowledge, perception, awareness, understanding, competence, and mastery which are not present when the sun and light are gone. The dark is thereby associated primarily with a sense of loss, gloom, uncertainty, unknown, foreboding, threat, fear, disruption, and evil. Occasionally, one may find that secondary meanings may be developed under special cultural circumstances in which white may be associated with mourning in a kind of warding-off behavior, or where dark becomes identified positively with one's self and white with threat as may happen among blacks who are oppressed by whites.

If one takes care to interview black people in a manner which does not direct them or influence the content of what they say, it soon becomes evident that each black person also has some body parts, body products, body processes, sounds, ideas, words, and acts of which they are critical and which they view as bad or evil. Invariably these too are associated primarily with the black and the dark.

Careful study reveals once again that the "black" aspects of each black person's body, body products, sounds, ideas, words, and acts are those which are disruptive to their groups and which each group member is trained to repress in order not to unduly excite or disrupt his fellows.

Every black person, like every white person, then, has "black" aspects which are renounced by his or her groups and which must be repressed, renounced, and excluded from group social behavior.

Each and every black individual and each and every white individual has both a free, rewarded, group-approved, aggrandized "white" side and a renounced, group-censored, excluded, and repressed "black" side to their personalities, behavior, and identity. "White" people and "black" people exist in every human system, whether it be a one-person system, a two-person system or a multiple-person system. Dynamics of power define which will be white and dominant and which will be black and repressed.

Whenever differential value is assigned to two aspects of any human system, the more highly valued aspect is symbolized by white and the lesser-valued aspect by black. This happens with regard to physical systems of the body, to emotional systems, to psychological systems, to two-person systems, and to multiple-person systems.

The inclination to perceive the world in dichotomies is itself anchored in the nature of human physiology and body structure. The basic body processes involving such dualities as tensing-relaxing, opening-closing, extending-flexing, putting out-taking in, affiliating-aggressing, all have physiological correlates. Good-bad, right-wrong, up-down, light-dark, constructive-destructive, life-death, peace-war, and other dualisms which characterize percepts, concepts, and beliefs are associated with subsystems of physiological patterns in which there is corresponding dualism.

By rewarding some persons to be open, affectionate, dependent, trusting, and self-sacrificing and to serve others we may condition them to have pleasant feelings associated with affiliative physiology and accommodating roles. By rewarding others to be aggressive, independent, self-actualizing, self-trusting, and self-serving, we may condition them to have pleasant feelings associated with aggressive physiology and initiating roles.

In some cultures higher value may be placed upon accommodating to others, serving others, and being dependent. In other cultures, higher value may be placed upon initiating roles. Regardless of the value which is or seems to be accorded these roles, it is the initiating role which is the principal determinant of structure. Initiators project their views, their structures, their processes upon accommodators who accede, and the outcome is defined by dynamics of power.

## Dominance Behavior in Primates and Humans

The dynamics of struggles between individuals, between nations, between races, between social classes, between generations, between other human groups, and combinations of the above have some similarities to dominance behavior among primates.

If several male Rhesus monkeys who have never had contact with one another are placed in a limited space, they engage in fights with one another for a brief period; and within minutes an entire hierarchy of rank is clearly established. This status arrangement is subsequently respected except for occasional conflicts and modifications. In each encounter the dominant monkey elevates his tail and the subordinate one lowers his tail. The dominant monkey's interests and initiative are given primary attention. The lower-ranked monkey accommodates, accedes, and sacrifices self-interest while assuming a complementary role which resolves conflict and reduces destructiveness among the monkeys. Once rank is defined, there is no equality, but there is dependable order with the subordinate party reliably identifying with the interests of the dominant party.

The behavior of human beings differs notably in several ways. Dominance behavior results in less rigid, less fixed order. Subordinate parties must have lengthy consistent, intense conditioning in order to identify dependably with the aggressor's interests. A greater capacity for identifying with self-interest, plus a strong capacity to identify with the behavior and methods of the aggressor results in more conflict, as repressed parties try to overthrow repressors under certain conditions. Dominant individuals or groups try to stabilize roles by organizing power, resources, laws, and people into institutions which maintain relationships and handle conflict with firmness and assurance. These institutions often have built-in hierarchical dominance systems with relatively fixed rank order.

Human animals appear to have more strongly developed capacities to identify with victims and subordinate persons as well as with aggressors and dominant persons than primates have. Yet although most individuals have this capacity, they are able to use it only when they have opportunity for frequent informal human contacts with persons on lower social-economic-political-educational echelons. Where institutions prescribe disparate formal roles and build in distance and disparity of experience for the decision-making dominants on one hand and accommodating subordinates on the other, there is reduced opportunity for mutual identification. Kiss-up, kick-down ethics in which each person affiliates with and identifies with interests of those above, while aggressively imposing himself or herself upon those below, characterize hierarchical social structures and bureaucratic systems. These generally lack feedback mechanisms and imply idealization of those in upper roles and devaluation or dehumanization of those in lower roles.

In hierarchical social institutions many pressures prevent people from identifying with people designated as above or below their own rank, position, or salary level. People on each level tend to function as an exclusive group, pressing their associates to be loyal, to share in beliefs of that level, and to refrain from or prohibit fraternization with persons from more distant levels.

As a result, formal behavior in hierarchical institutional contexts presses human beings to function with those behavior patterns that we have seen to be characteristic of primate animals while undermining human capacities for more considerate behavior and mutual identification. Segregation has thus served to inhibit white empathy with black feelings.

## Origins of the White-Over-Black Relationship

In his book, *White Over Black*, historian Winthrop Jordan has documented some of the early developmental course and dynamics of American racism. He gathered and creatively organized his data so that it shows how sixteenth-century European whites, upon encountering blacks, imputed to the blacks all the group-threatening characteristics which the whites were attempting to renounce and repress in themselves. The English and other white Europeans purged and purified their image of themselves by the psychological mechanism of projection, imputing their own undesirable characteristics to blacks, and thereby creating a prowhite, antiblack paranoia. Role relationships, philosophies, economies, politics, and all other aspects of culture and social structure were then altered to support and to conform to these false beliefs which aggrandized whites and denigrated blacks and led to untold destructive effects upon the personalities, families, group structure, and culture of blacks who were enslaved or descended from slaves.

Sixteenth-century England was caught up in a conflict between liberating forces seeking greater freedom and the repressing-controlling forces of Puritanism. Conflicts over licentiousness, freedom of movement, and aggression were common. In fact, the exploration and colonization movements which brought white people into large-scale interactions with black, yellow, brown, and red people were expressions of increasing mobility and aggression.

In this connection, Shakespeare may be credited with a perceptive interpretation of seventeenth-century social dynamics in the play "Othello," in which he has the crafty white Iago systematically undermine and destroy the dignity, manhood, confidence, initiative, self-esteem, capacity for love and trust, and eventually the life of the black Othello.

## The Reinforcement of Conflict in Descendants of Slaves

Slavery in the United States has been described as the most coercive and most destructive form of slavery ever devised because of its effects upon family and group structure. Once the colonies succeeded in winning freedom from England in the American Revolution, they were at liberty to develop their institutions as they saw fit without the approval of the mother country. Whites could do what they pleased to blacks in a land which was rejecting the traditional authority of church and government.

In South America, however, where church and European governmental influences prevailed, the family structure of slaves was preserved. Other ethnic groups who have been enslaved at some point in their history were also permitted to retain their family and group structure and their culture during their period of enslavement. Retention of culture, family, and group structure by such groups as Jews, West Indian Negroes, African Negroes, Irish, Italians, Chinese, and others, has meant that their ghettos have generally provided more support and sanctuary to the residents than have some ghettos of black descendants of slaves in the United States.

Among such descendants of slaves, antigroup behavior and antigroup culture coercively introduced under slavery is associated with great difficulty in organizing and maintaining groups or gathering people for orderly, concerted action. Moreover, these slaves were drawn from relatively diverse cultures with different languages, in the first place. In addition to the many factors that encouraged and reinforced conflict among them, they lacked consensus about sexual-role definition and conflict management, which are commonly found in ethnic groups that have defined their own culture over several generations.

With power and resources concentrated in the hands of white authorities, control was easily exercised over blacks by whites, using blacks against blacks in many instances. As whites withdrew and became lax in exercising control in black communities, they left powerless, resourceless black ghettos open to victimization by blacks and whites alike. Many black descendants of slaves found it difficult to form supportive communities in the absence of the factors necessary for grouping behavior and socialization. (These factors will be discussed in the following section of this chapter.)

In urban communities of black descendants of slaves outside the South today, migration-mobility-turnover and separation-depression-discouragement-disorganization compound and magnify the effects of continuing racial oppression. The relative inadequacy of support and organization coupled with the magnitude of interpersonal and intergroup conflict create conditions under which conflict escalation toward crises may not be dealt with by agreed-upon standardized group or community mechanisms for processing conflict. This often leads to fruitless debate about "who is right and who is wrong" instead of the questions, "What is the best method of resolving conflict between points of view when each view is considered legitimate by someone?" and "How can conflict be resolved without degrading, oppressing, or annihilating one party?"

Situations of this kind are common in family settings. Take the example of a family that employs a rigidly defined gathering device to increase the family unity and stability which all family members desire, in this case the device of attending church together each Sunday. The following occurred: One Sunday, two days after the family dog had had puppies, one puppy which appeared to be dying was repeatedly rejected by the mother dog. It was pushed aside again and again. One child in the family put milk in a baby bottle and in various ways attempted to revive the dying puppy. The parents exercised authority on the family's church agreement, kept calling the busy child to change clothes and get ready for church. Repeatedly, the child refused and said he was not going to change but would remain with the puppy. All the other family members expressed their belief that the puppy was practically dead, and could not be saved in view of the mother dog's behavior. They pointed out that two other puppies in the litter of twelve had died without individual attention and without disruption of the family. Enough pressure was brought to bear on the child for him to reluctantly leave with the family. As they left the house, his crying and obvious bitterness so affected two of the other children that they refused to go to church. This precipitated open conflict between parents and children.

In this situation power and authority were used in an attempt to settle a conflict between two legitimate interests. One interest was the group interest involving unity of the family and the other was the individual interest of the child. In a discussion of this conflict somewhat later, eight possible solutions could be seen as options which might have been considered. Some of these might have been uncomfortable or awkward (like having all the family members go to church and take the puppy with them). In a subsequent discussion, family members recalled that the child who resisted had always been sensitive about being neglected or pushed aside by parents or siblings, and they began to understand the extent to which the child had identified with the rejected puppy. They even concluded that the rejection of the puppy was a more important element to the child than the dying of the puppy. Here the debate over who was right and who was wrong, or about which course was right and which course was wrong proved to be less important than having some suitable mechanism for resolving conflict. It would have been better if a parent or child could have said, "Let us call everyone together, examine the nature of this conflict, consider our options, agree upon some way of arriving at a decision, and decide how to deal with these perfectly legitimate interests without doing harm to either."

When families, neighbors, communities, nationalities, or races have been free to develop their own cultures and have lived in one place for generations, they develop ways of dealing with conflict which become standardized over time. Whenever power dynamics are employed in the resolution of conflict, there remains an oppressed party which is inevitably the seed of subsequent conflict. The more powerful party sometimes attempts to use total destruction in an effort to prevent future uprisings. Even here, however, there are always those among the destroyers who identify with the ones destroyed so that conflict remains in any case.

Black descendants of slaves, in the absence of opportunities to develop their own culture and having to rely upon the authority and power of outsiders to settle their conflicts, have developed relatively few agreed-upon approaches to conflict resolution. The antigroup factors have operated to prevent development here as well as in other areas. As a result, blacks find themselves more commonly struggling to define which person is right and which wrong and which direction is right and which wrong. They have come intellectually to accept the fact that diversity of interests is legitimate; however, in each human being when emotion rises, action-oriented and power-oriented dynamics are activated. Where reliable group methods of conflict resolution are absent, conflict involves so much frustration and emotion that individual persons, unable to find assisting mechanisms in the social structures around them, experience more and more feeling until they "blow their cool" and take whatever action they believe needs to be taken.

Black descendants of slaves under oppression for a long time seem to go through an initial stage of liberation involving initiating activity. Patterns of assuming individual responsibility have been associated with action-taking. In the verbal sphere, this has been manifested by a remarkable number of authoritative pronouncements, sometimes referred to as "rhetoric." It is much easier to get a large number of persons to begin to assume individual initiative and responsibility than it is to help them develop methods of coordinating their individual interests or even of subordinating individual interests to group interests.

## GROUPING BEHAVIOR AND SOCIALIZATION

In order for human beings to live in social groups, the group members must find ways to develop affiliative ties to one another and to exclude behavior which is disruptive to the group. Individual group members must suppress in themselves those elements of behavior which are disruptive to their groups if groups are to cohere.

In the social context of the group, hostile behavior, sexual arousal, elimination of body wastes, disquieting excitement, and disrespect for group values must be repressed and excluded from direct expression. Repressions of this kind constitute a part of the learning, conditioning, socializing, and acculturating processes in the life of each social individual.

Group formation is encouraged by the development of a common target on which to focus and impute renounced, repressed aspects of the group members. Another group is often chosen as the common target. In the absence of this a scapegoat within the group may serve as an outlet for aggressive feelings and thereby protect other group members from disruptive hostility.

Groups discourage higher brain functions which lead to individualized behavior and favor the reinforcement of more primitive paranoid patterns associated with conformity and stereotyped thinking and behavior. In fact, paranoid thinking and behavior, aggrandizing group members and denigrating outsiders, is essential for maintaining exclusive groups.

Persons who share belief systems made up of false components are not sick paranoids. Group-related paranoia is not pathological; it simply indicates the capacity of group members to trust and identify with one another. Individual paranoid beliefs, held by persons who are unable to trust and identify with others, are pathological in that they are not shared. Pathological paranoia interferes with social bonds while group-related nonpathological paranoia facilitates social bonds. Ideologies, religions, schools of thought, ethnocentric perceptions, and even shared points of view represent group-related paranoias. They guide behavior and are followed and clung to as infants cling to mothers and lollipops. The ties that bind man to belief systems and to other aspects of his culture seem to be displaced from and derived from the dependence of infants upon parents. Our sense of identity and of emotional and physical integrity is linked to cherished beliefs which are shared with others.

Every well-established group which is constructive for its members programs and promotes:

1. Trust of group members, distrust of outsiders.
2. Affiliative bonds (and associated physiology) with group members.
3. Aggressive bonds, criticism, and derogation toward an outside target.
4. Value system which supports self-esteem.
5. Good fit with institutions of broader culture.
6. Good fit with family members and culture mates.
7. Efforts toward mastery.
8. Success.
9. Initiative rather than accommodation.
10. Competence for mastery.
11. Development of culture and institutions by group members.
12. Centralized internal power to control, protect, and help group members to meet needs, resolve conflicts, and deal with problems.
13. Distinctive common religion, language, ideology, or territory around which group members can rally.

## Antigrouping Behavior of American Descendants of Slaves

Under our especially destructive slave system prowhite, antiblack paranoid beliefs were expressed by altering realities to fit beliefs. Social structures were devised to fit false beliefs and to produce programmed "white" blacks who conformed to white superiority-black inferiority beliefs. The products of racist institutions appear to validate the beliefs, if one forgets the pervasive coercive system which programmed behavior, contrived life conditions, and tracked most whites into institutions and participation in American society and tracked most blacks out.

Black mothers were used as the principal programming instruments. As representatives of a white world that used harsh absolute authority on any blacks who failed to accommodate, black mothers had to assume a nonnegotiating absolute position with their children, and especially with male children. Black females more often had initiating and controlling roles in both black families and white ones than did black males. Parents, families, churches, schools, and other institutions programmed slaves and their descendants not to fit white institutions. The institution of segregation, *de jure* and *de facto*, has perpetuated many characteristics of the imposed slave culture by the same processes through which Catholics, Protestants, Jews, Europeans, Orientals, and Africans pass on beliefs, codes, styles of behavior, and institutions for as many generations as they live in separation without cultural diffusion.

Most people are unaware of the many ways in which the culture and group structure of American descendants of slaves differ from the culture and group structure of all other ethnic groups, including West Indian and African blacks.

American descendants of slaves constitute the only people whose white-imposed culture and group structure have traditionally programmed the group members toward all of the following:

1. Trust of (white) outsiders, distrust of (black) selves.
2. Affiliative bonds (and associated physiology) with (white) outsiders.
3. Aggressive bonds, criticism, derogation (and associated physiology) toward (black) selves.
4. Value system which undermines and destroys self-esteem.
5. Poor fit with institutions of broader culture except in typically servile roles.
6. Poor fit with family members and culture mates.
7. Self-sacrifice rather than mastery.
8. Defeat rather than success.
9. Accommodation rather than initiative.
10. Incompetence rather than competence.
11. Culture and group structure developed by outsiders and imposed by outsiders.
12. Systematic prevention of development of internal power to control, protect, and meet needs of group members, while needed resources and power of government have been withheld or used in disorganizing ways.
13. Absence of a distinctive common religion, language, ideology, or territory around which the group can rally.

All of the above characteristics are the exact opposite of those mentioned earlier as important for group formation and necessary for constructive effects upon group members. It should be recognized, however, that these thirteen characteristics are never present or absent in all-or-none ways. All people have some group-promoting and some antigroup factors within and among them.

American black descendants of slaves continue to struggle with a destructive culture which programs them toward antigroup behavior. Some of the destructive antiperson and antiproperty behavior in disorganized and disruptive black ghettos can be traced to this antigroup behavior which was imposed and ingrained in the process of unhinging blacks from each other while bonding and enslaving blacks to whites. On the other hand, African blacks, West Indian blacks, and other blacks with supportive groups have as many group-promoting characteristics as white ethnic groups.

Black descendants of slaves who have constructive religious, community, or social organizations can develop effective group behavior, but these seldom involve a single community homogeneously.

Where homogeneous group structure with coordinating authority exists, black communities are as stable as white ones. Often this structure is absent in portions of black urban communities, with the result that predatory, aggressive, sadistic, exploitative persons of any color can victimize the residents. Other black ghettos may be as organized, as orderly, as clean, as safe as any ghetto of other ethnic groups.

In some instances, blacks have formed groups which share the value systems, behavior styles, and aspirations of some white middle-class groups. Persons from these "black bourgeoisie" groups have been integratable into white institutions more easily than others.

With the advent of the black ethnic-development movement, some white-oriented blacks reoriented themselves toward other black people, thereby producing cultural strains and conflicts with their white friends and associates. Black middle-class children, who were more compliant than their white middle-class counterparts a generation ago, became militant or aggressive promoters of social change. Strains developed between them and blacks who continued to support often-hypocritical white middle-class styles of behavior (which verbalized ethics of freedom and equality while supporting a racist, classist, sexist society). Some black religious groups adopted white middle-class Protestant, Catholic, and Jewish ethics.

Other black groups developed philosophies very similar to that of Zionist Jews, sought separation, and asked to be given territory of their own to which they might journey and around which they might rally. Some whites who strongly advocated this course for their own groups vigorously criticized this goal for black descendants of slaves.

## Psychodynamics of Dissent

Oppressed human beings repeatedly seek understanding and assistance from their oppressors. However, oppressors rarely identify with the oppressed and seldom spontaneously institute reforms which might reduce their own rewards, status, or privileges.

When oppressors do identify with the oppressed, it is more apt to happen in the wake of some emotion-laden confrontation in which the human feelings and qualities of both parties interact.

Quite commonly, when oppressed parties fail in their quest to have the oppressors identify with them and respond to their needs, those oppressed begin to identify with the behavior of the aggressors. Dissent is registered in the context of shared values. It is reinforced by demonstrations, often with passive resistance manifested toward aggressors. If there is inadequate response to this resistance, more active forms of dissent and demonstration may occur, in gradations that lead all the way up to the sometimes violent interactions of militant confrontation.

This sequence is most apt to occur during some period when there are rising expectations for constructive change and when undue oppressive authority and force are not being invoked in response to dissent. Repression of dissent and of militant activists and demonstrators for civil rights can quickly undermine movements toward reform or toward social revolution. At such times oppressive government officials are ambivalent, wanting to live up to their avowed principles and to maintain their idealized perception of themselves, but also to hold on to their power. Individual liberties, freedom of speech, freedom of the press, peaceful demonstrations and other "rights" may be reinforced or curtailed depending upon the ideological and political positions of persons in power. It is for this reason that persons incarcerated during social movements are looked upon by many as political prisoners. Those who do not identify with activists who are incarcerated often see them as guilty of crimes for which there should be punishment without consideration of the political context. Those who identify with the social-reform goals of the incarcerated ones may perceive the acts as oriented toward constructive change and required by existing sociopolitical factors.

When repressed-accommodating parties become aggressive and attempt to employ initiative or kinds of nonnegotiable demands ordinarily made only by initiators, the hostile response of persons in authority may be unduly vigorous. Violent interaction is most commonly associated with a needless overresponse on the part of authorities who become enraged at the thought of having their territory invaded or their prerogatives usurped.

When aggression in a human system has been repressed and directed within that system, endemic destructive effects may be observed in that system. In the process of liberation, increased expression of hostility may occur initially within the system in accordance with the basic program described.

Persons emerging from depression may show increased inclination toward suicidal activity. People in oppressed social groups appear to attack what they perceive as enemies within them or within their community in actions which exclude "outsiders" and promote group solidarity. In subsequent stages authority may be variously organized and applied in numerous institutions.

The behavior of the more powerful party eventually determines the course of relationships between oppressing and oppressed forces. At times, the repressed can overthrow oppressors in psychic systems, in interpersonal role relationships, in intergroup relations, and in international relations.

This may be called an irruption or a revolution. The process may be rapid, narrowly defined, with little effect on basic institutions, or it may be slower, but more pervasive, with dynamic changes in intergroup, interpersonal, and intrapsychic institutions. The present and ongoing American social revolution is of the latter variety. There is greater understanding of the nature of conflicts, of the humanity of all parties. Continuing dehumanization and continuing oppression is a source of continuing stress that motivates repetitive cycles of oppression → liberating social change → resistance → backlash → counterbacklash → increased repression → liberating social change, etc. The pattern evolves gradually toward behavior which is more consistent with the national and religious beliefs, laws, and codes.

## Forces Perpetuating Racism

Concepts of property rights lead people to identify with "their property" as much or more than with "their people." Whatever gets imprinted in one's nervous system as "one's own" is not given up easily. The mental representation is associated with mental representations of body parts and processes. At times, to give up anything which is "one's own" is as difficult as giving up part of one's body.

Those who have the power and influence to initiate broad-based reforms are usually the ones whose power, influence, property, possessions, income, and status are dependent upon or involved with existing institutions and prevailing conditions. As a result, persons with the capacity to alter institutions and conditions on a broad scale are seldom motivated to do so. When individual persons or organizations do try to depart from the status quo they may find themselves out of phase with their society, scapegoated, and at a competitive disadvantage economically and politically.

Thus persons who desire political power often cater to the influential persons who want to maintain all of their advantages, status, and exclusiveness as elites although it may mean continued unnecessary disadvantages such as low status and exclusion for their non-elite associates.

Meanwhile, persons with motivation to make constructive change lack the organization, resources, influence, and power to bring it about.

The magnitude, pervasiveness, and destructiveness of racism in America have given rise to many questions concerning the nature and origins of racism. A closer look at *White Over Black*, Winthrop Jordan's careful study of white American and English attitudes toward blacks prior to 1812 mentioned earlier, clearly delineates the paranoid nature of racism. His material discloses a sequence of several stages: (1) readiness to use the psychological mechanism of projection at the time of initial white-black encounters; (2) white denial in themselves and false imputation to blacks of a monopoly of those human characteristics which they do not wish to acknowledge in themselves; (3) elaboration, rationalization, and justification of the false beliefs; (4) alteration of reality to fit the false beliefs; (5) transmission of the false beliefs and the contrived reality along with and as part of other elements of culture; (6) ongoing dynamic conflict within individuals and between them over the morality or adaptive value of the beliefs or the realities created in their image; and (7) scapegoating with sacrifice of a part to save the main body of paranoid beliefs, paranoid behavior, and paranoid social order. (Eliminating the slave trade for example, took the heat off opposition to slavery and emancipation of slaves was followed by continuing segregation and inhumane treatment of blacks by whites.)

## Similar Dynamics of Psychological and Social Repression

The "white-over-black" phenomenon, slavery, and other patterns of social discrimination can be viewed as examples of a large class of interactions in which persons with more power and resources assign lower value to and repress persons with less power and resources. This has happened under feudal and manor systems, under caste and class systems around the world, and occurs as well in virtually every institution, organization, and family the world over despite the noble efforts of many persons to develop democratic patterns with equality, justice, and mutual consideration for all.

When we rid ourselves of a feudal system, why are we apt to replace it with another repressive social pattern which grants more status, privilege, opportunity, reward, and power to some than to others? Collective dissent, social movements, revolutions, and wars manifest this issue. We can observe similar dynamics in the interactions between men and women, rich and poor, management and labor, college administrators and students, whites and blacks, colonial powers and their colonies, and adults and children.

Could it be that there are common dynamics to be found wherever interactions take place between repressing forces and the repressed in any human system, be it a somatic system, psychological system, or social system? Might this explain why the black psychoanalyst Franz Fanon in the twentieth century and the white humanist Juan Luis Vives in the sixteenth century could arrive at the same conclusions regarding the inevitability of uprising of repressed people?

### The Projection of Body Image Into Human Perception

The neurophysiological patterns in the central nervous system containing impressions of all past behavior and experiences give meaning to all which is perceived or created by human beings. In the development of the images imprinted in the central nervous system the representations of body parts and body processes constitute the earliest impressions and provide a basis for relating to subsequent impressions. Representations in the mind of objects in the environment become fused with representations in the mind of the body's parts and processes. The varying values which become associated with various body parts are also assigned to the object representations associated with each part respectively.

With minor exceptions due to unusual cultural variants, the same body parts and processes are aggrandized and the same ones denigrated in societies throughout the world. Upper parts are aggrandized and lower ones denigrated. Free, unrestricted, and known parts are aggrandized while restricted, hidden, and unknown parts are denigrated. The front is aggrandized and the behind denigrated, the near aggrandized and the distant denigrated. These values are projected into perception and into the products, ideas, and social structure which men create. The heavens are always above and the hells are below, the upper parts of buildings are decorated while lower parts, i.e., basements, remain neglected and unadorned. Fronts are decorated while rears remain neglected. Upper aspects of social structure are accorded more worth, privilege, resources, and power while lower parts go neglected.

In societies where all parts of the body are well accepted, the clothing, social structure, and culture tend to be simple. In societies where renunciation of some body parts and idealization of others occur, the clothing, social structure, and culture are more differentiated and complex. Differentiation starts with the body parts and processes. For social structure to loosen, clothing and bodies must loosen also. As a result miniskirts, nudism, more open speech, and relaxation of restrictions in other areas occurred in association with the loosening and attempt to liberate various repressed segments of our society.

The differential value associated with various body parts and processes which is projected into perception and into the creation of social structure is easy to relate to the origins of racism. (A phenomenon similar to racism can be discerned in such relationships as the older persons versus youth, men versus women, middle class versus poor persons, management versus labor.) Certainly we shall be unable to develop societies without racism so long as we continue to create societies in the image of our bodies. Moreover, it seems unlikely that we shall cease doing this until somehow we can become aware of this universal unconscious tendency.

## The Two Divergent Processes of Understanding Associated With Racism

We are much more primitive in our thinking and behavior than many people would like to believe. We understand some persons immediately by introjection if we perceive them as members of our own group. On the other hand, we understand others immediately by projection if we perceive them as outsiders. Thus some persons we understand by taking them in or by taking in what they offer while we understand others by dumping upon them things we renounce within ourselves. Wherever a white person and a black person experience conflict in "white-racist" structure, the white is understood by introjection and is presumed to be right, while the black person is understood by projection and is presumed to be wrong. A ghetto tends to be understood by projection while the rest of the city tends to be understood by introjection.

Since group members understand one another by introjection, and understand outsiders by projection, the members of any group have affectionate bonds with aggrandizement for one another and aggressive bonds with denigration for outsiders.

Thus each group member searches on one hand for objects of affection in other group members, and for objects of projection in outsiders. What is projected is always that which one renounces and which one unsuccessfully struggles to remove from oneself. In the struggle it is repressed from consciousness, but it repeatedly presses to reenter conscious thinking and behavior.

When the repressed content can be associated with some outside person, it can reenter consciousness bound tightly to the image of the outsider, and there seems to exist an opportunity concretely to control, repress, or rid oneself of the repressed badness in oneself by controlling, repressing, and getting rid of the outsider.

Despite our lack of knowledge about the nature and origins of racism and other group-related paranoias, we have developed many techniques for changing them favorably. However, attempts to modify them evoke so much resistance, conflict, and often violence, that better understanding of the nature of these processes is needed to reduce resistance to change. More understanding could also inhibit the production of new maladaptive forms which spring up as our reforms and revolutions alter old ones.

## Clarifying the Meanings

One of Langston Hughes' most provocative poems, written in 1926, was entitled "Cross":

> My old man's a white old man
> And my old mother's black.
> If ever I cursed my white old man
> I take my curses back.
>
> If ever I cursed my black old mother
> And wished she were in hell,
> I'm sorry for that evil wish
> And now I wish her well.
>
> My old man died in a fine big house.
> My ma died in a shack.
> I wonder where I'm gonna die,
> Being neither white nor black?

Succinctly and graphically the poem refers to white and black skin, to white and black culture, and to white and black psychology. The implied rage and curses are associated with thoughts of the parents in hell. They are defined as evil and by implication black. Also present are remorse, good wishes, and affection. The conflict in the poet's feelings about his parents and about his identity are as clear as the differences in white skin and black skin, father and mother, and fine house and shack.

Ordinarily people live out their lives trapped in illusions and delusions to varying degrees. Descriptive adjectives and labels are symbols associated with objects to convey ideas and feelings associated with the object. Some ideas conveyed with each label are apt to be false. While the reader may have seen human skin in a variety of shades from quite light to quite dark it is doubtful that he ever saw skin the color of this paper or the color of the printing thereon. Actually human skin does not come in white or black and our labels are at best approximations which carry piggyback many false meanings.

The words father and mother are commonly associated with meanings which are often as antithetical as the words male and female. Yet mothers and fathers may be very much alike, or one may receive fathering from mother and mothering from father. Mother may be "hard" and father "soft" or vice versa. In both social and sexual roles each human being has both masculine and feminine attributes.

Likewise "fine big house" and "shack" convey many false meanings. One implies pleasure, comfort, and happiness while the other implies deprivation, discomfort, and sadness. The facts are that pleasure, deprivation, comfort, discomfort, happiness, and sadness occur in every fine big house and in every shack. They also occur in every man, woman, and child regardless of race, culture, or family. Langston Hughes' poem communicates several messages about the dialectical processes in every reader.

All human beings struggle with opposing and conflicting aspects of themselves. They are destined to live in the divided houses they refer to as their personalities. For many persons the conflicts are so painful that they take actions or hold beliefs designed to clarify whether they are male or female, assertive or passive, up or down, right or wrong, good or bad, when in fact every personality contains a mixture of all of these.

From a psychological standpoint, racism may be looked upon as an attempt to deal with the uncertainty, ambivalence, and mixed identity each human being possesses. The white-racist culture creates an illusion about who is low and defective and who is high and exemplary by reserving the symbols of low defective status for blacks and the symbols for high and exemplary status for whites wherever possible. Once established, this illusion can be maintained only by keeping the blacks and whites from getting to know each other well. In the course of forcing people into accommodating roles they may be trampled, deprived, excluded, and debased; but their capacity for warmth, consideration, caring, thoughtfulness, tenderness, and love continues and may even be intensified in the process. The aggression and hate required to institute or maintain racism and segregation tend to reinforce intolerance, lack of consideration, intellectualization, and coolness. This cluster of qualities has been associated with whites and with directing roles; warm, caring qualities have been associated with blacks and with service roles. With desegregation and integration processes in which people come to know each other well, however, all aspects of each person's personality may be acknowledged, affirmed, and organized in a manner appropriate to each circumstance.

In a racist society cultural, social, and psychological rewards and punishments induce most people to manage their lives and behavior in a manner which expresses racist illusions and delusions.

Only in a world contrived by power and filled with delusions and illusions can it successfully be maintained that Caucasians are good and Negroes bad, that whites are superior and blacks inferior, that Caucasians are "head" people and Negroes "body" people. No one has described the "white condition" and the "black condition" more succinctly than Eldridge Cleaver, who has stated that in the master-slave relationship the Caucasian lost his body while the Negro lost his mind. According to Cleaver, in the corrective interaction the master must regain and reaffirm his body and the slave must regain and reaffirm his mind.

Acceptance of and belief in negative connotations for the word "black" is characteristic of delusional, primitive thinking processes and indicates an absence or loss of accurate, realistic thinking. Likewise belief in positive connotations for the word "white" characterizes delusional primitive thinking and is inaccurate and unobjective. The manipulation of myths and structuring of reality into alignment with these delusions creates the illusion that such primitive thinking has validity. White and black people who accept and believe these illusions, myths, and stereotypes have lost their capacity for mature thinking and, in this sense, truly have "lost" their minds.

## Note: Addendum

Material in this chapter is based upon that in the bibliography which follows. The basic thesis has been offered between 1967 and 1975 in presentations at various universities, at regional meetings of psychiatric societies, at annual meetings of the National Medical Association, the American Psychiatric Association, the American Psychoanalytic Association, the Association for the Advancement of Psychotherapy, the Association for the Study of Negro Life and History, and the American Historical Society.

# BIBLIOGRAPHY

Barbour, F., *The Black Power Revolt*. Boston, Porter Sargeant Publishers, 1968.

Brain, W., *Mind, Perception and Science*. Springfield, Ill., Charles C. Thomas, 1951.

Butts, H. F., "White Racism: Its Origins, Institutions, and the Implications for Professional Practice in Mental Health." *Internat. J. Psychiat.* 8: 6: 914, December, 1969.

Cannon, W. B., *Bodily Changes in Pain, Hunger, Fear and Rage*. Boston, Charles T. Branford Company, 1929.

Carmichael, S. and Hamilton, C., *Black Power*. New York, Vintage Books (Random House), 1968.

Clark, K., *Dark Ghetto: Dilemmas of Social Power*. New York, Harper and Row, 1965.

Cleaver, E., *Soul on Ice*. New York, McGraw-Hill Co., 1968.

Comer, J., "Some Parallels Between Individual and Afro-American Community Development," read at the convention of the National Medical Association, St. Louis, Mo., August 11, 1967.

Deutsch, F., *On the Mysterious Leap from the Mind to the Body*. New York, International Universities Press, 1959.

Elkins, S. M., *Slavery*. University of Chicago Press, 1959.

Erikson, E., *Childhood and Society*. New York, Norton, 1963.

Fanon, F., *The Wretched of the Earth*. New York, Grove Press, 1963.

Franklin, J. H., *From Slavery to Freedom*. New York, Random House, 1969.

Frazier, E. F., *The Negro in the United States*. New York, Macmillan Co., 1949.

Freud, S., "On the Mechanism of Paranoia," in *Collected Papers*, Vol. 3. London, Hogarth Press, 1948.

Grier, W. and Cobbs, P., *Black Rage*. New York, Basic Books, Inc., 1968.

Hess, W. R., *The Biology of Mind*. Chicago, University of Chicago Press, 1964.

Hughes, L., *The Big Sea*. New York, Hill and Wang, 1940.

Jordan, W. D., *White Over Black*.
   Maryland, Penguin Books, 1968.
Kardiner, A. and Ovesey, L., *The Mark
   of Oppression*. Cleveland and New York,
   The World Publishing Co., 1951.
Mendelsohn, J., *The Martyrs*. New York,
   Harper and Row, 1965.
Pinderhughes, C., "Understanding Black
   Power: Processes and Proposals."
   *Amer. J. Psychiat.*, 125: 11, 1969.
Pinderhughes, C., "The Universal

Resolution of Ambivalence by Paranoia
   with an Example in Black and White."
   *Amer. J. Psychother.*, 24: (4) 597–610, 1970.
Pinderhughes, C., "Somatic, Psychic, and
   Social Sequelae of Loss." *J. Amer.
   Psycho-Anal. Assn.*, 19: (4) 670–696, 1971.
Pinderhughes, C., "The Psychodynamics of
   Dissent." In Masserman, J., ed., *The
   Dynamics of Dissent*, New York, Grune &
   Stratton, 1968.

# 4

## The Black Population
## in the United States

### Karl E. Taeuber and Alma F. Taeuber

Blacks and whites both originally came to North America as immigrants, and the history of their settlement is only a few hundred years old. Most of the white immigrants came in search of an increased measure of freedom and enlarged opportunity. Most of the black immigrants came in bondage to others. Both groups participated in the settling of a continent and the creation of a gigantic urban and industrial nation out of a small number of agricultural colonies. In this chapter many of the social transformations that accompanied this period of growth are traced with the aid of population statistics from a long series of national censuses.

Data from the censuses tell a story of increasing numbers of blacks and whites, and of expanding black settlement first in the South, then in the cities of the North and West. Other data tell of the characteristics of blacks today, their social and economic status, their housing, the rates at which they give birth and the rates at which they die. The charts and tables that illustrate this story are, like pictures, worth thousands of words. By studying them closely, the reader will find far more information than can be conveyed in the text, and will be able to form his own conclusions.

A few words of introduction to census data may help the reader of this chapter and several later chapters to evaluate the statistical material provided. The category "Negro" as used in census publications is a peculiar one. It is arbitrarily designed for simple application and does not convey any biological, anthropological, or legal meanings. A person who appears to be or claims to be white is so listed. Everyone else is automatically classified according to "race" as Negro, Indian, Japanese, Chinese, etc. Taking a census is a massive operation, and it is not possible to make finer distinctions. The color-race classification used by the census is merely a rough estimate of the person's social identity in his local community.

In this volume, attention is centered on the black population. Sometimes, however, data will be presented for nonwhites. In 1970 blacks made up 90 percent of all nonwhites in the country. Except for a few areas (mainly in the West) containing large numbers of Indians, Orientals, or other nonwhites, figures for nonwhites may be regarded for practical purposes as referring to blacks.

FIGURE 1—REGIONS AND GEOGRAPHIC DIVISIONS OF THE UNITED STATES

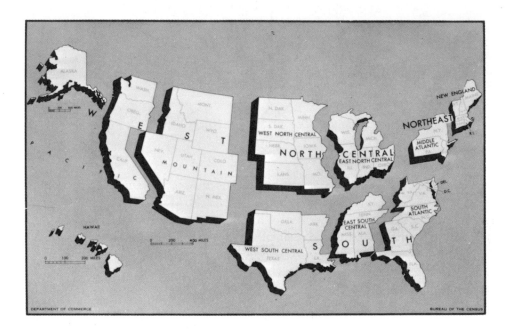

Many people attribute too much accuracy to statistical data. It is important to realize that a census is taken by tens of thousands of enumerators, administrators, and other personnel, and perfect accuracy is not possible. Although the 1970 census reported a total black population of 22,578,273, nobody would claim that the last few digits are precise. Furthermore, it is not important whether they are or not. To know that there were about twenty-three million blacks in 1970 is sufficient for almost any purpose.

There are many ways of dividing the country into North, South, and West. Census data are usually presented for four geographic regions, or nine geographic divisions, as portrayed in Figure 1. In this chapter, "the South" refers to all those states in the three southern divisions; the "West" refers to those states in the Mountain and Pacific divisions; and "the North" refers to all other states. The term "conterminous United States" refers to the first forty-eight states, excluding Alaska and Hawaii.

# GROWTH AND DISTRIBUTION
# OF BLACK POPULATION

The history of black population developed out of the slave heritage of southern rural residence and depressed social and economic status. In the decades since emancipation, the black population has been approaching a pattern of distribution and of social characteristics in many ways similar to that of the white population. At the time of our first national census in 1790, the total population of the new nation was about four million: 3.2 million whites and 757,000 blacks. Nearly all of the blacks were slaves, and nearly all lived in the South. On the eve of the Civil War the situation of the black population was not greatly different. Although there were about 4.4 million blacks in the United States in 1860—more than the total national population at the time of the first census—nearly 90 percent were slaves and more than 90 percent still lived in the South. In the one hundred years since emancipation, however, there have been dramatic changes. The black population increased to twenty-three million in 1970, of whom eleven million lived outside the South and seventeen million lived in metropolitan areas.

## The Spread of Slavery

Many of the current features of black population distribution are the product of patterns laid down before the Revolutionary War. The southern colonies developed as suppliers of agricultural commodities to Britain, and plantation agriculture proved to be an efficient means of exploiting some of the rich resources of the region.

The first ship bringing blacks to the colonies reportedly arrived in Virginia in 1619. This marked the beginning of an agricultural system utilizing slave labor which gradually developed and expanded. Slaves were used in the raising of tobacco in Virginia and Maryland before 1700, and the practice spread into South Carolina and Georgia with rice cultivation after 1700. Cotton was not a major crop until later, but once it took hold in South Carolina and Georgia, it spread rapidly. The invention of the cotton gin in 1793 led to an increase in the efficiency of slave labor. With the depletion of much of the land in the eastern portions of the South, there was a westward expansion of cotton and tobacco cultivation and with these, of slavery. The maps in Figure 2 clearly reveal this westward movement along with the heavy concentrations of Negro slaves in selected agricultural areas of the South, and their virtual absence from other areas—particularly the Appalachians and the Ozarks.

The slave trade was legally abolished in 1808. According to rough estimates, fewer than 400,000 slaves were imported between 1619 and 1808. Historians disagree as to whether substantial numbers entered illegally after 1808 to meet the continuing demand for agricultural labor.

Because of the constitutional provision that slaves counted only three-fifths as much as free persons in determining congressional representation, the 1790 census and subsequent censuses up until 1860 made separate tallies for the Negroes who were slaves and those who were free. Although manumission became increasingly difficult as various southern states enacted legislation discouraging it, the free black population grew, being added to by births occurring to free parents, by the legal abolition of slavery in northern states and by the escape of slaves into freedom. In 1790 a mere 8 percent of Negroes were free. In 1830 this figure rose to about 14 percent, but during the decades before the Civil War the growth of the free black population slowed and by 1860 the percentage had slipped back to 11.

The slave population was very heavily concentrated in the South. In fact, after 1830 slavery outside the South was found almost exclusively in Missouri. Free Negroes, on the other hand, were more equally divided between North and South, with about 40 percent living in the North. At a time when only a small portion of the white population and an even smaller portion of the slave population lived in cities, many free blacks found that large cities offered greater freedom and wider opportunities for earning a living. Sizable free black colonies developed in several cities of the South—Baltimore, Washington, New Orleans, Charleston, Richmond, and Petersburg. In the North, black population (virtually all free) was concentrated in Boston, New York, Chicago, Cincinnati, and Philadelphia. Despite discrimination and restrictive legislation, free blacks in cities held a variety of skilled jobs and in many cases owned property and voted. In general, however, free blacks lived in precarious economic circumstances, whether in large cities or in rural areas.

### Growth of White and Black Population

The population of the colonies in 1650 included an estimated 1,600 blacks and 48,768 whites. During the next three centuries, both groups grew rapidly, although their periods of rapid and slow growth did not always coincide. The patterns of growth from 1650 to 1970 are portrayed in Figure 3.

The relative proportions of blacks and whites in the population have varied considerably throughout our history. This is shown in Figure 4. During the colonial period, when there was little new immigration of Europeans but continued importation of slaves, black population grew at a faster rate than white population, and the percentage of blacks in the total rose from 1.3 percent in 1630 to a peak of 21.4 percent in 1770. During the next fifty years, both blacks and whites gained population largely due to natural increase (the excess of births over deaths) and the percentage of blacks remained close to 20.

The black population has increased very little due to immigration since the Civil War. The white population, however, embarked upon a period of very rapid growth

FIGURE 2—GEOGRAPHIC DISTRIBUTION OF SLAVE POPULATION,
1790, 1800, 1830, AND 1860

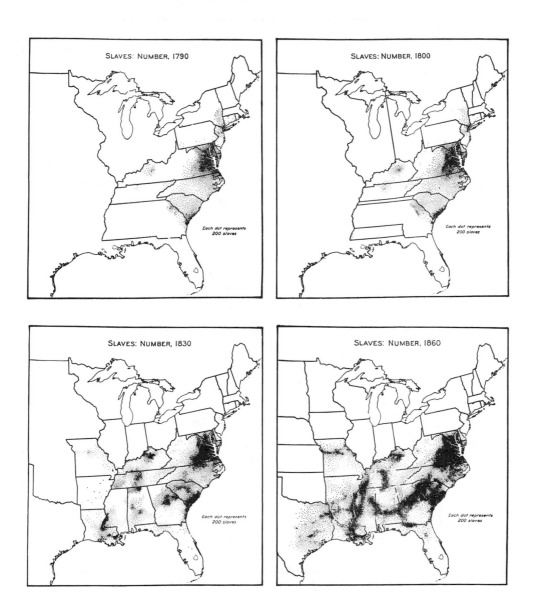

Source :   E. Franklin Frazier, *The Negro in the United States* (New York : The Macmillan Company, 1957), Maps II, III, IV, and V.

FIGURE 3—POPULATION OF THE UNITED STATES BY RACE, 1650–1970

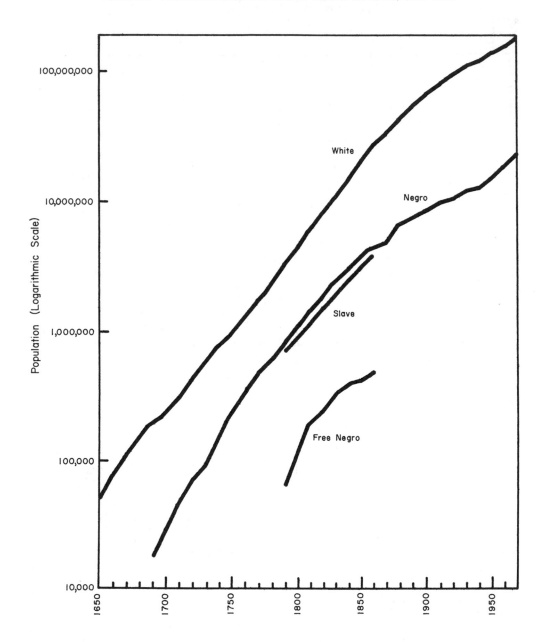

Source :   1650–1950 from U. S. Bureau of the Census, *Historical Statistics of the United States, Colonial Times to 1957;* 1960–1970 from U. S. Bureau of the Census, *Census of Population: 1970.*

as the great period of migration from Europe began in the late 1800s. Millions of immigrants were added to a high rate of natural increase. This caused the percentage of blacks to decline, reaching a low point of 9.7 in 1930. With restrictive legislation choking off the flow of immigrants from Europe in the early 1920s, both white and black populations in recent decades have grown mainly by natural increase. During this period, blacks have been increasing at a slightly faster rate than whites, and their share in the population has been rising slowly. By 1970, blacks constituted 11.1 percent of the United States population, a figure which may increase slowly in the years to come. Nonetheless, blacks will undoubtedly continue to comprise a smaller percentage of the population than at the time of the founding of the country.

## Regional Distribution

Although many free Negroes and a small share of the slave population lived in the North, the overwhelming bulk of black population until recently was concentrated in the South. According to every census from 1790 to 1900, at least 90 percent of the black population of the United States lived in the South (Figure 5). In 1910, this was still true for 89 percent of all blacks but the percentage fell in succeeding decades, to 85 percent in 1920, 77 percent in 1940, and 53 percent in 1970. The reverse pattern, of course, is apparent for northern and western states. Prior to 1900, states outside the South never contained more than 10 percent of the black population, but by 1920 they contained 15 percent; by 1940, 23 percent; and by 1970, 47 percent.

It is clear that the last few decades have been a time of great migrations. Millions of blacks made the long journey from the South to the North or West. After more than a century of relative stability in the regional distribution of Negro population, amazingly rapid and profound changes have taken place within the last sixty years.

For nearly fifty years before 1910, blacks had the freedom to move. This freedom was granted with emancipation, and there are many reports of newly freed slaves testing their new-found rights by moving to another farm, village, county, or state. During the decades following the Civil War, there was a continued westward settlement within the South itself carrying increasing numbers of blacks as well as whites into new agricultural areas in Louisiana and Texas. Within the North there was also westward movement into Ohio, Michigan, and Illinois, with a few blacks accompanying the many whites settling these states. During the Civil War and its aftermath, thousands of blacks migrated to Washington, D.C. and a few thousands even farther north, but hundreds of thousands remained near where they had lived as slaves. All in all there was relatively little movement of blacks from South to North in the fifty years that followed emancipation.

The explanation for the stability of black population during this period lies in the failure of emancipation to bring with it any organized programs to provide blacks with new means of earning a livelihood. Many plans were considered, and some were attempted on a small scale, but for a variety of reasons the Reconstruction programs

**FIGURE 4**—PERCENT BLACK OF TOTAL POPULATION
IN THE UNITED STATES, 1630–1970

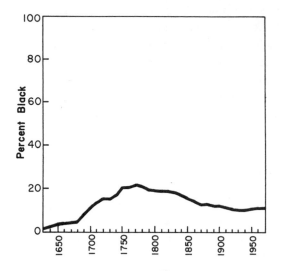

Source :    Donald J. Bogue, *The Population of the United States* (New York : The Free Press of
Glencoe, 1959). Table 7–2 ; U.S. Bureau of the Census, *Historical Statistics of the United
States, Colonial Times to 1957;* and U.S. Bureau of the Census, *Census of Population:
1970.*

**FIGURE 5**—PERCENT DISTRIBUTION BY REGION FOR NEGROES, 1790–1970

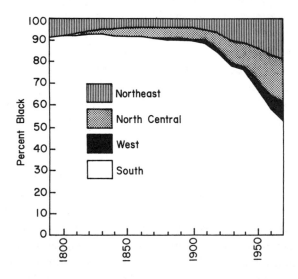

Source :    1960 and 1970 from U.S. Bureau of the Census, *Census of Population;* 1790–1950 from
U.S. Bureau of the Census, *Historical Statistics of the United States, Colonial Times to
1957.*

never included any major effort to alter the economic circumstances of blacks. Colonization abroad was discussed during the post-Civil War period as in later times, but never undertaken on a large scale. Utilization of blacks in the expanding industrial cities of the North was ruled out by prejudice, inertia, and the continuing availability of millions of European immigrants. No government programs were initiated to provide large quantities of land for black agricultural settlement on new farmlands in the North and West or to facilitate black land ownership in the South. Neither did the newly freed black find many new economic opportunities in southern cities, where he had to eke out an existence earning wages in competition with whites and with skilled and experienced blacks who had been free before Emancipation. Furthermore, after the war the high price of cotton eased the process of southern economic recovery. Hence blacks continued to labor on white-owned farms and plantations, under new forms of tenancy. One result of the general economic situation was a high degree of stability in black population distribution.

Each of the major regions of the country has its own distinct pattern of change in black population. In 1860 blacks comprised 37 percent of the total population of the South. In 1970 they comprised 19 percent. In Kentucky the change was from 20 to 7 percent, while in Mississippi it was from 55 to 37 percent. Full data on the black population in each state in 1860, 1910, and 1970, as well as the exact percentage of blacks at each date, are given in Table I. Differences between states in their response to school desegregation and many other aspects of race relations can be traced in part to such differences in population as are found between Kentucky and Mississippi.

Southern states with high percentages of blacks may have some counties in which blacks form a vast majority of the population, and others where they make up only a small percentage. Similarly, those states with small percentages of blacks may nonetheless have some counties with a highly concentrated black population. In 1880 there was a belt of about 300 mainly contiguous counties in the rich agricultural area of the central South in which blacks constituted more than half of the population. The number of "black belt" counties has been steadily declining, however, numbering 264 counties in 1910, 138 in 1960, and 103 in 1970; several southern states (Delaware, Kentucky, Maryland, Oklahoma, and West Virginia) have no counties in which blacks are in the majority. By 1970, the "black belt" had pretty much been dissipated by the continued movement of blacks out of many rural areas.

A new development in the composition of the black population is for a number of cities to have a black majority. In 1970 this was the case in three large cities—Washington (71 percent), Newark (54 percent), and Atlanta (51 percent). Four cities with a population size of 25,000 to 100,000 also had black majorities—Compton, California; East St. Louis, Illinois; East Orange, New Jersey; and Gary, Indiana. Among large cities that were more than 40 percent black in 1970 there are three that showed sharp increases in black percentage during the 1960s and that may have reached the 50 percent level by now—Baltimore, Detroit, and St. Louis.

TABLE I—BLACK POPULATION AND PERCENT BLACK BY STATES,  1860, 1910, AND 1970

| State | Black Population | | | Percent Black | | |
|---|---|---|---|---|---|---|
| | 1860 | 1910 | 1970 | 1860 | 1910 | 1970 |
| NORTH | 340,240 | 1,027,674 | 8,913,687 | 1.7 | 1.8 | 8.4 |
| New England | 24,711 | 66,306 | 388,398 | 0.8 | 1.0 | 3.3 |
| Maine | 1,327 | 1,363 | 2,800 | 0.2 | 0.2 | 0.3 |
| New Hampshire | 494 | 564 | 2,505 | 0.2 | 0.1 | 0.3 |
| Vermont | 709 | 1,621 | 761 | 0.2 | 0.5 | 0.2 |
| Massachusetts | 9,602 | 38,055 | 175,817 | 0.8 | 1.1 | 3.1 |
| Rhode Island | 3,952 | 9,529 | 25,338 | 2.3 | 1.8 | 2.7 |
| Connecticut | 8,627 | 15,174 | 181,177 | 1.9 | 1.4 | 6.0 |
| Middle Atlantic | 131,290 | 417,870 | 3,953,739 | 1.8 | 2.2 | 10.6 |
| New York | 49,005 | 134,191 | 2,166,933 | 1.3 | 1.5 | 11.9 |
| New Jersey | 25,336 | 89,760 | 770,292 | 3.8 | 3.5 | 10.7 |
| Pennsylvania | 56,949 | 193,919 | 1,016,514 | 2.0 | 2.5 | 8.6 |
| East North Central | 63,699 | 300,836 | 3,872,905 | 0.9 | 1.6 | 9.6 |
| Ohio | 36,673 | 111,452 | 970,477 | 1.6 | 2.3 | 9.1 |
| Indiana | 11,428 | 60,320 | 357,464 | 0.9 | 2.2 | 6.9 |
| Illinois | 7,628 | 109,049 | 1,425,674 | 0.5 | 1.9 | 12.8 |
| Michigan | 6,799 | 17,115 | 991,066 | 0.9 | 0.6 | 11.2 |
| Wisconsin | 1,171 | 2,900 | 128,224 | 0.2 | 0.1 | 2.9 |
| West North Central | 120,540 | 242,662 | 698,645 | 5.6 | 2.1 | 4.3 |
| Minnesota | 259 | 7,084 | 34,868 | 0.2 | 0.3 | 0.9 |
| Iowa | 1,069 | 14,973 | 32,596 | 0.2 | 0.7 | 1.2 |
| Missouri | 118,503 | 157,452 | 480,172 | 10.0 | 4.8 | 10.3 |
| North Dakota | —a | 617 | 2,494 | —a | 0.1 | 0.4 |
| South Dakota | —a | 817 | 1,627 | —a | 0.1 | 0.2 |
| Nebraska | 82 | 7,689 | 39,911 | 0.3 | 0.6 | 2.7 |
| Kansas | 627 | 54,030 | 106,977 | 0.6 | 3.2 | 4.8 |
| SOUTH | 4,097,111 | 8,749,427 | 11,969,961 | 36.8 | 29.8 | 19.1 |
| South Atlantic | 2,058,198 | 4,112,488 | 6,388,496 | 38.4 | 33.7 | 20.8 |
| Delaware | 21,627 | 31,181 | 78,276 | 19.3 | 15.4 | 14.3 |
| Maryland | 171,131 | 232,250 | 699,479 | 24.9 | 17.9 | 17.8 |
| District of Columbia | 14,316 | 94,446 | 537,712 | 19.1 | 28.5 | 71.1 |
| Virginia | 548,907 | 671,096 | 861,368 | 34.4 | 32.6 | 18.5 |
| West Virginia | — | 64,173 | 67,342 | — | 5.3 | 3.9 |
| North Carolina | 361,522 | 697,843 | 1,126,478 | 36.4 | 31.6 | 22.2 |
| South Carolina | 412,320 | 835,843 | 789,041 | 58.6 | 55.2 | 30.5 |
| Georgia | 465,698 | 1,176,987 | 1,187,149 | 44.1 | 45.1 | 25.9 |
| Florida | 62,677 | 308,669 | 1,041,651 | 44.6 | 41.0 | 15.3 |
| East South Central | 1,394,360 | 2,652,513 | 2,571,291 | 34.7 | 31.5 | 20.1 |
| Kentucky | 236,167 | 261,656 | 230,793 | 20.4 | 11.4 | 7.2 |
| Tennessee | 283,019 | 473,088 | 621,261 | 25.5 | 21.7 | 15.8 |
| Alabama | 437,770 | 908,282 | 903,467 | 45.4 | 42.5 | 26.2 |
| Mississippi | 437,404 | 1,009,487 | 815,770 | 55.3 | 56.2 | 36.8 |
| West South Central | 644,553 | 1,984,426 | 3,010,174 | 36.9 | 22.6 | 15.6 |
| Arkansas | 111,259 | 442,891 | 352,445 | 25.6 | 28.1 | 18.3 |
| Louisiana | 350,373 | 713,874 | 1,086,832 | 49.5 | 43.1 | 29.8 |
| Oklahoma | — | 137,612 | 171,892 | — | 8.3 | 6.7 |
| Texas | 182,921 | 690,049 | 1,399,005 | 30.3 | 17.7 | 12.5 |

TABLE I—(Cont.)

| State | Black Population | | | Percent Black | | |
|---|---|---|---|---|---|---|
| | 1860 | 1910 | 1970 | 1860 | 1910 | 1970 |
| WEST | 4,479 | 50,662 | 1,694,625 | 0.7 | 0.7 | 4.9 |
| Mountain | 235 | 21,467 | 180,382 | 0.1 | 0.8 | 2.2 |
| Montana | — | 1,834 | 1,995 | — | 0.5 | 0.3 |
| Idaho | — | 651 | 2,130 | — | 0.2 | 0.3 |
| Wyoming | — | 2,235 | 2,568 | — | 1.5 | 0.8 |
| Colorado | 46 | 11,453 | 66,411 | 0.1 | 1.4 | 3.0 |
| New Mexico | 85 | 1,628 | 19,555 | 0.1 | 0.5 | 1.9 |
| Arizona | — | 2,009 | 53,344 | — | 1.0 | 3.0 |
| Utah | 59 | 1,144 | 6,617 | 0.2 | 0.3 | 0.6 |
| Nevada | 45 | 513 | 27,762 | 0.7 | 0.6 | 5.7 |
| Pacific | 4,244 | 29,195 | 1,514,243 | 1.0 | 0.7 | 5.7 |
| Washington | 30 | 6,058 | 71,308 | 0.3 | 0.5 | 2.1 |
| Oregon | 128 | 1,492 | 26,308 | 0.2 | 0.2 | 1.3 |
| California | 4,086 | 21,645 | 1,400,143 | 1.1 | 0.9 | 7.0 |
| Alaska | — | — | 8,911 | — | — | 3.0 |
| Hawaii | — | — | 7,573 | — | — | 1.0 |
| U.S. TOTAL | 4,441,830 | 9,827,763 | 22,578,273 | 14.1 | 10.7 | 11.1 |

ᵃDakota Territory.

Source:   1860 and 1910 from U.S. Bureau of the Census, *Negroes in the United States, 1920–32;* 1970
from U.S. Bureau of the Census, *Census of Population: 1970.*

These percentages, of course, refer to the total black population, whereas for certain social problems or prospects it is more appropriate to consider only certain age groups. For voting purposes one might prefer to examine the percentage of the population over age 18 that is black, or the percentage of registered voters over age 18 that is black. In almost every city the second percentage will be substantially below the first, and the first will be less than the corresponding percentage for all age groups. For assessment of racial aspects of a school system, one might need to know the percentage black among a district's children age 6-18. This is typically 10 or more percentage points higher than the figure for all ages, and may be 20 points higher if the comparison is restricted to children of school age enrolled in the public schools. Space does not permit a full presentation of such data for these large cities, nor of equivalent data for smaller cities, counties, congressional districts, or school districts. Readers are urged to consult the census volumes for their states to obtain specific information on such local variations.

## PATTERNS OF MIGRATION, 1870-1970

If the early history of black population is linked with the development of southern agriculture, its current history is part and parcel of the history of the entire nation. Millions of blacks have left the South to seek new opportunities in the cities of the North, and to join with whites in the ever-increasing migrations to the West. The volume of these movements during certain decades has been nearly unbelievable, especially when it is recognized that such movement often involves radical transformations in the way of life of the black migrant.

## The Evidence of Migration

A population in a given area can grow through an excess of births over deaths (natural increase) or by an excess of in-migrants over out-migrants (net migration). Thus in the absence of migration, population growth in a region occurs within a fairly narrow set of biological limits. The extremely rapid increases in northern black population in the last fifty years are the product of large-scale population movements. Had these migrations not occurred, the black population would still be 90 percent southern.

During the first fifty years after emancipation, the relative stability in black residential distribution was disrupted only by some movement to new agricultural areas in the western portion of the South. Although the movement of whites to cities in the North and South was already gaining momentum, the rural southern character of the black population remained substantially intact. In the decades since 1910, however, black migrations, rural-to-urban and South-to-North, have been proceeding at a rapid and at times incredible pace, completely altering the patterns of distribution which would have resulted in the absence of migration.

From 1870 to 1910 the black rural population of Georgia increased steadily from 500,000 to 952,000, but despite a continuing excess of births over deaths, this population diminished to 400,000 in 1970. The same pattern is true of black rural population in many other states. At the same time, the black urban population of New York State, which numbered 118,000 in 1910, multiplied tenfold in fifty years, numbering more than 1,000,000 by 1960. In fact, in 1960 for the first time a northern state, New York, had a larger black population than any southern state. This trend continued during the 1960s. By 1970 New York State had more than 2,000,000 blacks, Illinois and California had 1.4 million each, and Texas with just under 1.4 million had more than any state in the traditional Deep South.

That continuing massive migrations of blacks have been taking place in the past half-century is obvious from these facts of population redistribution. Unfortunately, direct information is lacking on the numbers involved, the characteristics of migrants, the paths they follow and the forces which impel them to leave their homes. In the United States, anyone can move from one part of the country to another without notifying the Government and without any records being kept. Data on migration come indirectly. The fact of out-migration, for instance, becomes apparent only when the census counts fewer blacks in Mississippi in 1970 than in 1960, and records a near-doubling of the black population of California in the same period.

Statistics for immigration from abroad are drawn from the decennial census questions on place of birth. Blacks have proved to be an overwhelmingly native population. Since the days of the slave trade, there has been only a tiny stream of black immigration. At no time during this century have foreign-born blacks comprised as much as 1 percent of the total black population. In 1900 the census recorded only 20,000 blacks as born abroad. During the next fifty years, this number increased, primarily as a result of immigration from the West Indies. By 1950, of a total of 114,000 foreign-born blacks, 67,000 or three-fifths were from the West Indies.

## Migration from South to North, 1910 to 1970

The general patterns of black migration during each decade from 1910 to 1970 can be seen from the data in Table II. This table presents the estimated net gain or loss from migration for geographic divisions and selected states. Northward movement of blacks was large between 1910 and 1920, and increased to even larger numbers during the 1920s. During the Depression decade, migration into the north continued at a diminished pace. The volume of migration picked up sharply during the war decade of 1940–1950; it was nearly 75 percent greater than the volume of the 1920s. To the traditional direct northward movement to the Middle Atlantic and East Central states were added an augmented flow to New England and a massive flow to the West (mainly to California). The volume of black net migration to the North and West reached peak levels in the 1950s and dropped slightly in the 1960s. During the 1960s most of the major destination states in the North and West gained fewer migrants than during the preceding decade. New York State was the major exception, as black migration, primarily to New York City, reached a record-breaking level.

Trends in black movement out of the South mirror those of black migration into the North and West. Net migration out of the South grew from very low levels before 1910 to nearly half a million persons in 1910–20 and three-quarters of a million in 1920–1930. Following the slowdown during the Depression, net out-migration from the South continued at extraordinarily high levels for three successive decades. The volume was about 125,000 net out-migration each year during the 1940s, 146,000 each year during the 1950s, and 138,000 each year during the 1960s. The thirty-year total was a net movement of more than four million blacks out of the South.

## Causes of Migration*

There is still no scholarly agreement on the precise causes of these massive population movements. Their timing, however, provides some insight into the factors involved. The major northward migration of southern blacks appears to have started about 1915

*See also Chapter 7, "The Black American in Agriculture."

and to have continued at a high rate during most of the next ten years. In discussing causes of migration, it is helpful to distinguish between those causes of dissatisfaction in the local community which "push" people out, and those attractions at the place of destination which "pull" people in.

TABLE II—ESTIMATED NET INTERCENSAL MIGRATION OF BLACKS, FOR GEOGRAPHIC DIVISIONS AND SELECTED STATES, BY DECADE, 1910–1970

| Area | 1960–70 | 1950–60[a] | 1940–50 | 1930–40 | 1920–30 | 1910–20 |
|---|---|---|---|---|---|---|
| **Geographic Division** | | | | | | |
| New England | 72,000 | 70,000 | 24,900 | 5,200 | 7,400 | 12,000 |
| Middle Atlantic | 540,000 | 472,000 | 386,800 | 165,700 | 341,500 | 170,100 |
| East North Central | 356,000 | 521,000 | 493,800 | 107,700 | 323,700 | 200,400 |
| West North Central | 26,000 | 37,000 | 35,000 | 20,100 | 40,300 | 43,700 |
| Mountain and Pacific | 302,000 | 385,000 | 304,300 | 49,000 | 36,100 | 28,400 |
| South Atlantic | −538,000 | −542,000 | −424,100 | −175,200 | −508,700 | −161,900 |
| East South Central | −560,000 | −620,000 | −484,600 | −122,500 | −180,100 | −246,300 |
| West South Central | −282,000 | −295,000 | −336,000 | −49,800 | −60,200 | −46,200 |
| **Selected States** | | | | | | |
| Pennsylvania | 25,000 | 77,000 | 89,600 | 20,300 | 101,700 | 82,500 |
| New York | 396,000 | 282,000 | 243,600 | 135,900 | 172,800 | 63,100 |
| Illinois | 127,000 | 189,000 | 179,800 | 49,400 | 119,300 | 69,800 |
| Michigan | 124,000 | 127,000 | 163,300 | 28,000 | 86,100 | 38,700 |
| Ohio | 45,000 | 133,000 | 106,700 | 20,700 | 90,700 | 69,400 |
| California | 272,000 | 354,000 | 258,900 | 41,200 | 36,400 | 16,100 |
| District of Columbia | 36,000 | 54,000 | 61,200 | 47,500 | 16,000 | 18,300 |
| Florida | −32,000 | 101,000 | 7,200 | 49,900 | 54,200 | 3,200 |
| Virginia | −79,000 | −70,000 | −30,600 | −36,900 | −117,200 | −27,200 |
| North Carolina | −175,000 | −207,000 | −127,300 | −60,000 | −15,700 | −28,900 |
| South Carolina | −197,000 | −218,000 | −159,000 | −94,400 | −204,300 | −74,500 |
| Georgia | −154,000 | −204,000 | −191,200 | −90,300 | −260,000 | −74,700 |
| Alabama | −231,000 | −224,000 | −165,400 | −63,800 | −80,700 | −70,800 |
| Mississippi | −279,000 | −323,000 | −258,200 | −58,200 | −68,800 | −129,600 |
| Arkansas | −112,000 | −150,000 | −116,100 | −33,300 | −46,300 | −1,000 |
| Louisiana | −163,000 | −92,000 | −113,800 | −8,400 | −25,500 | −51,200 |
| Texas | −4,000 | −27,000 | −67,200 | 4,900 | 9,700 | 5,200 |

Note:   A minus sign indicates net out-migration; no sign indicates net in-migration.
 [a]Figures for 1950–60 refer to nonwhites and were estimated by a different procedure from that used for the 1910–50 and 1960–70 estimates.
Source:   U. S. Bureau of the Census, *Historical Statistics of the United States, Colonial Times to 1957;* and *Current Population Reports,* Series P-25, No. 460.

Among the push factors it might be thought that discrimination, segregation, and injustice would be the most important. However much these factors contributed to a general willingness to move, there is no evidence that oppression was any worse during 1915–25 than in preceding years. This is not to deny that many blacks leaving the South before 1915 as well as later were seeking better social conditions. But the causes of the change in volume of migration must also include certain precipitating factors not present in earlier periods, such as the severe devastation of southern agriculture caused by the combination of the boll weevil and a series of bad crop years. Conditions had often been depressed, but the devastation and depth of the agricultural depression in many counties were greater than ever before. Out-migration increased greatly from many of the hardest hit areas.

A change in certain pull factors inducing migration is also clearly evident. Immigration of Europeans to the United States, which had been bringing more than a million persons a year to northern industrial cities, was cut off by the war in Europe. At the same time, the war, even before direct U. S. involvement, brought new demands upon northern manufacturing industries. Thanks to the ensuing need for labor, despite widespread prejudice and concern about the "suitability" of blacks as industrial laborers, some firms found that blacks could do the work. Labor recruiters encouraged blacks to come North and promised them jobs (sometimes, it seems, as temporary strikebreakers). Many blacks who made the move encouraged friends and relatives to join them, and the move became easier with the knowledge that there was someone at the other end to help find a place to live and a job. After the first world war, immigration from Europe briefly resumed, only to be cut back permanently by restrictive legislation in the early 1920s. Blacks have retained a position in the northern industrial labor force ever since, but that position has remained as tenuous and controversial as its origins suggest.

## Migration Rates and Their Social Impact

The impact of migration, on both the community where the migrants originate and the community which is their destination, can be better appreciated if the number of migrants is related to the number of people left behind or the number already at the destination. When expressed in such terms, the black migrations imply tremendous upheavals in both northern and southern communities. For instance, between 1910 and 1920, Alabama lost one-tenth of its black population by out-migration. Between 1940 and 1950, Mississippi lost over one-fourth of its blacks by out-migration. Were it not for the continual replenishment of population by natural increase, these states would by now have few blacks left.

Migration is a highly selective process. Young adults are usually much more eager to give up the old for the new than are those with families, homes, and attachments to customary ways of earning a living. The black migrations show no exception to this rule, for they have always drawn most heavily from those in the young adult ages. Some of the migration rates shown in Table III for young black males are spectacular. Consider black males in Georgia who were between the ages of 15 and 34 in 1920. Out-migrants among this group during the 1920–30 decade numbered *forty-five* out of every *one hundred* average population in Georgia. Similarly, between 1940 and 1950, Mississippi lost nearly *one-half* of its young black adults by out-migration, principally to northern states. The impact of migration on the black population in some northern states was also large. In 1920, 1930, and 1950, from one-third to one-half or more of the young adult blacks in such states as Michigan, Illinois, and New York had moved there within the preceding ten years.

TABLE III—NET INTERCENSAL MIGRATION FOR BLACK MALES AGE 15–34 AT BEGINNING
OF DECADE, BY DECADES FOR SELECTED STATES, 1870–1950

| Intercensal Period | Southern States | | | Northern States | | |
|---|---|---|---|---|---|---|
| | Alabama | Georgia | Mississippi | Illinois | Michigan | New York |
| 1870–80 | −20.9 | −4.6 | 4.0 | 37.1 | 12.5 | 23.9 |
| 1880–90 | −8.8 | 2.9 | −4.1 | 28.7 | — | 32.1 |
| 1890–00 | −12.5 | −7.6 | −2.6 | 53.9 | 10.5 | 55.2 |
| 1900–10 | −10.1 | −5.0 | −5.5 | 33.3 | 25.0 | 44.4 |
| 1910–20 | −22.1 | −16.7 | −23.3 | 67.4 | 138.4 | 53.6 |
| 1920–30 | −21.3 | −44.7 | −14.2 | 65.5 | 88.4 | 79.3 |
| 1930–40 | −11.7 | −13.5 | −9.8 | 14.5 | 19.0 | 29.8 |
| 1940–50 | −32.3 | −30.9 | −47.0 | 59.0 | 81.5 | 54.3 |

Note:   A minus sign indicates net out-migration; no sign indicates net in-migration.

Source:   Everett S. Lee, Ann Ratner Miller, Carol P. Brainerd, and Richard A. Easterlin, *Population Redistribution and Economic Growth, United States, 1870–1950, I. Methodological Considerations and Reference Tables* (Philadelphia: The American Philosophical Society, 1957), Table P-1.

Dramatic as some of these figures are, they do not tell the full story as they refer only to net migration—the balance of in- over out-migration or out- over in-migration. Not all blacks who move from one state to another go from South to North. Many who have been in the North move back to the South. Many others move from one southern state to another or from one northern state to another. Thus, in-migration and out-migration are both heavy, and the figures shown in the tables indicate the extent to which one movement predominates over the other. But it must be remembered that gross movement is always higher, usually much higher, than net movement.

Large-scale movement of people between farm and town, village and city, South and North, necessarily entails a circulation of ideas, of life styles, of money and of knowledge. Thus each process of social change increases the possibility of further evolution.

The impact of migration is watered down by using states as units. There are reports of special trains taking away virtually the entire black population of small southern communities, but such dramatic population shifts are not directly reflected in state-wide statistics. Similarly, the dramatic impact of black migration on New York City's Harlem or Chicago's South Side is obscured when data are presented for entire states.

The social results of these migrations are extraordinarily diffuse and are difficult to calculate. High rates of natural increase among rural southern blacks have not led to a piling up of black population in depressed agricultural areas. Rather, the continuing migrations have transferred much of the increase in black population from the South to the North. To an extent, this out-migration helps alleviate economic problems, for in its absence the South would have been confronted with the need to provide jobs and housing for a great many additional blacks. Out-migration, however, is not an unmitigated blessing. The South's investment in food, clothing, housing, and schooling required to raise children from birth to an age when they are ready to begin productive employment is lost when these youths migrate. Hundreds of thousands go North to add to the productive labor force there rather than functioning in the region which raised and educated them. The remaining southern rural blacks are a population with many dependent children and aged persons, with depleted numbers of young and middle-aged adults to support them. In northern cities a rapid rate of in-migration not only brings about a rapid expansion in the number of those seeking productive employment, but also augments housing shortages, accelerates overcrowding, complicates the task of providing suitable jobs for all those seeking work, and adds to the need for city social and welfare services.

As economic opportunities outside of agriculture increase in the South, and as the number of rural and village blacks decreases, it seems unlikely that the volume of net out-migration from the South will continue at the same high levels as in the recent past. The impact of black in-migration on northern cities should also change. As the black population has increased in the North, a given number of new in-migrants forms a smaller percentage of the population already there. In the past, migration accounted for a high proportion of black population increase in most northern and western cities. More recently the share of population growth attributable to natural increase has been moving rapidly upward. Births are now the major source of black population growth in many cities.

Despite the high rates of black migration from South to North during the past half-century, well over one-half of blacks living in the North today were born there. Many northern blacks have never been in the South. A high proportion of these northern-born blacks are children, but there are already many in the adult ages, and this number is increasing rapidly. If these people are inadequately trained and educated, northern politicians cannot legitimately blame the South.

## Residential Mobility and Short-Distance Moving

Mobility is a prominent feature of an urban industrial society. People in the United States are frequent movers, and blacks are no exception. They move from one community to another or from one house or apartment to another with high frequency. In March 1971, the Bureau of the Census asked a large sample of the population where they were living one year earlier. Of blacks, 21 percent were in a different house, compared to 18 percent for whites. Every year about one of every five families, white and black, changes residence. This rate of mobility has been observed each year since data collection began in 1948. The 1960 census reported that only 11 percent of blacks and 14 percent of whites had lived in their present housing unit since 1940.

Sociologists sometimes split residential mobility into "migration," referring to moves involving a change of community, and "local movement," referring to moves within a single community. The Bureau of the Census makes a similar distinction by referring to persons moving from one county to another as "migrants," and to persons whose move is entirely within a county as "local movers." Most of the people who move each year are local movers rather than migrants. In 1970–71, for blacks, 17 percent of the population were local movers and 4 percent were intercounty migrants. Of the migrants, roughly one-half moved to a different county within the same state, and one-half moved to a different state.

An urban industrial society is a changing one, and it could not function in the absence of residential mobility. Not only is the freedom to move necessary for the adjustment of people to changing situations and changing opportunities, but it is a basic liberty of blacks and whites alike. Each year in the United States about one in five persons moves, with about two-thirds of movers shifting residence within a county and the remaining one-third migrating to a different county.

It is misleading to view "local moving" as being without social consequences. A move from one neighborhood to another can entail as many changes in the lives of a family as a move from one city to another. The consequences for urban planning are likewise just as important for the short move as for the long. When one-fourth, one-third, or even more of the populace (as is true in many city-apartment areas) has lived for less than a year in a neighborhood, can there be a sense of community identification? Under such circumstances, can there be effective local participation in planning, in school administration, in neighborhood governance? Those who advocate decentralization and community control must devise new social mechanisms that can endure in the face of continual residential turnover.

## URBANIZATION OF THE BLACK
## POPULATION, 1910–1970

One simple piece of information from the 1970 census summarizes the profound change in the status of the Negro population that has taken place during this century. In 1970 blacks were significantly more urban than whites. Of the black population, 81 percent lived in cities, as compared to 72 percent of the white population. Not only has the movement of blacks from South to North been a movement to cities, but within the South itself blacks have been moving from rural areas to urban centers. Civil rights struggles in Birmingham and Little Rock, Atlanta and Richmond, shared headlines with those in Chicago, Detroit, and New York. Although there are still hundreds of thousands of blacks living in poverty in the rural South, the stereotyped picture of the American black as a southern sharecropper is long outdated.

## Urbanization before 1910

The United States began as a rural nation, with most of its people dependent on agriculture for their livelihood. Her rise to world power, however, depended not only on a bountiful agriculture, but on becoming an urbanized and industrialized nation. Cities have always played an important part in national life. Boston, New York, Philadelphia, Charleston, and other urban centers were centers of commerce, trade, politics, and culture in the eighteenth century. Even the largest cities of those days, however, would be considered small by today's standards. It was not until the nineteenth century that American cities, paced by New York, increased by leaps and bounds to truly large size. The urbanization of America was accelerated after the Civil War by rapid industrial growth and the construction of the nationwide rail transportation network. By 1910 most of the large cities of today had already reached large size. Yet in 1910 fewer than 50 percent of Americans lived in cities. The movement of people to cities has continued in the twentieth century.

Black participation in the urbanization of America was slight during the early stages. The concentration of free blacks in cities has been discussed above, but their numbers were never large relative to the total population of the cities in which they lived. Within the South, black slaves were utilized in greatest numbers in agriculture, and they lived in mainly rural areas and villages. Rural settlement was also characteristic of the white population. The southern urban population included its proportionate share of black population but the numbers were small.

From 1860 to 1910 the movement of blacks from the South to northern cities was very slight. Within the South, what black migration occurred was primarily in response to changing opportunities in agriculture, particularly the westward movement of cotton. As of 1910, just over one-fourth of blacks and just under one-half of whites in the United States lived in cities. These national figures mask considerable regional variation. Within the South, blacks and whites were equally urbanized, with about one-fifth living in cities. Within the North and West, blacks, with 77 percent in cities, were significantly more urbanized than whites. These patterns are portrayed in Figure 6. In 1910, nearly all blacks lived in the South. Despite the high percentages of northern blacks designated as urban, the numbers involved were small and the national average reflected primarily the pattern in the South. For whites the national percentage urban was an average of the high figure in the North and West, and the low figure in the South.

## Urbanization since 1910

During the sixty years from 1910 to 1970, urbanization proceeded rapidly among both whites and blacks in every region. Within regions, however, the differences between whites and blacks remained relatively stable. In the South, despite a period of particularly rapid urbanization beginning in 1940, blacks and whites maintained nearly identical

FIGURE 6—PERCENT URBAN BY RACE AND REGION, 1900–1970

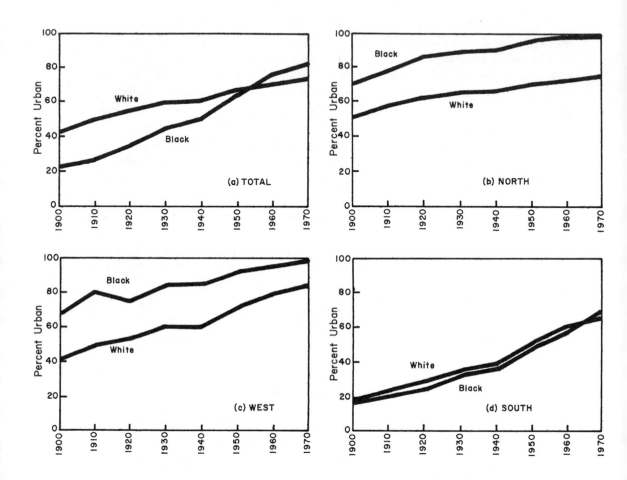

Note:   Definition of "urban" not fully comparable throughout this period.

Source:   U. S. Bureau of the Census, *Census of Population: 1920, 1940, 1950, 1960, and 1970.*

proportions in cities. In 1970, 67 percent of southern blacks and 64 percent of southern whites lived in cities. In the North and West, blacks continue to be more highly urbanized than whites. In 1970, the percentages living in cities were, in the North, 97 for blacks and 74 for whites, and in the West, 97 for blacks and 83 for whites.

On a national basis, there has been a convergence between whites and blacks in percentage urban. This is portrayed in the graph for "Total" in Figure 6. Note that this graph differs from each of the regional graphs. Within each region, the differences between blacks and whites in urbanization (or lack of differences in the South) remained about the same throughout the sixty-year period. Yet when all regions are grouped together into the total United States, the picture is one of the percentage urban among blacks catching up to and surpassing the figure for whites. This peculiar difference between urbanization when viewed within regions and urbanization when viewed for the total United States results from the massive shift of black population from South to North during this half-century. Blacks in the South have always been as urbanized as whites in the South, but they have been much less urbanized than blacks in the North and West. As hundreds of thousands of blacks have moved from the South to the North and West, they have taken on the urban residential distribution of the North and West. In 1910, 89 percent of blacks in the United States lived in the South and the percentage urban for blacks for the total United States was very close to the percentage for the South alone. In 1970, 52 percent of blacks lived in the South and the percentage urban for the total United States was midway between the figure for the South and the figure for the North and West.

## Cities with Large Numbers of Blacks

In 1910 there were fewer than 1,000,000 blacks living in all cities in the North and West. In 1970, New York City and Chicago each had more than 1,000,000 blacks. Sixty years ago there were a few northern cities with large black populations, but most urban blacks lived in southern cities. The twenty-five cities with the largest black populations in 1910 and 1970 are listed in Table IV.

In 1910 no single city had as many as 100,000 black residents, but in 1970 all twenty-five cities which led in black population were above this level. In 1910 there were eight northern and no western cities on the above list. In none of these northern cities did blacks comprise as much as 10 percent of the population. There were few large cities in the South, and even though blacks often comprised 30, 40, or 50 percent of the population, only a dozen or so southern cities had as many as 20,000 black residents.

The rapid urbanization since 1910, and particularly the pronounced movement to northern and western cities, is evident in the changes in the list of the twenty-five leading cities in black population between 1910 and 1970. New York, Chicago, Detroit, and Philadelphia lead the 1970 list, and Los Angeles and Cleveland also appear in the top ten. Fifteen of the twenty-five cities are in the North or West. In all of these cities, blacks comprised more than 10 percent of the population. In contrast to sixty years earlier, when blacks were but a very small segment of most northern and western cities, in several cities blacks now comprise one-fourth to one-half of the population. In only eight of the twenty-five are blacks less than one-fourth of the population.

TABLE IV—THE TWENTY-FIVE LEADING CITIES IN BLACK POPULATION, 1910 AND 1970

| City | 1910 Black Population (000) | Percent Black | City | 1970 Black Population (000) | Percent Black |
|---|---|---|---|---|---|
| Washington | 94 | 28 | New York | 1,667 | 21 |
| New York | 92 | 2 | Chicago | 1,103 | 33 |
| New Orleans | 89 | 26 | Detroit | 660 | 44 |
| Baltimore | 85 | 15 | Philadelphia | 654 | 34 |
| Philadelphia | 84 | 5 | Washington | 538 | 71 |
| Memphis | 52 | 40 | Los Angeles | 504 | 18 |
| Birmingham | 52 | 39 | Baltimore | 420 | 46 |
| Atlanta | 52 | 33 | Houston | 317 | 26 |
| Richmond | 47 | 37 | Cleveland | 288 | 38 |
| Chicago | 44 | 2 | New Orleans | 267 | 45 |
| St. Louis | 44 | 6 | Atlanta | 255 | 51 |
| Louisville | 41 | 18 | St. Louis | 254 | 41 |
| Nashville | 37 | 33 | Memphis | 243 | 39 |
| Savannah | 33 | 51 | Dallas | 210 | 25 |
| Charleston | 31 | 53 | Newark | 207 | 54 |
| Jacksonville | 29 | 51 | Indianapolis | 134 | 18 |
| Pittsburgh | 26 | 5 | Birmingham | 126 | 42 |
| Norfolk | 25 | 37 | Cincinnati | 125 | 28 |
| Houston | 24 | 30 | Oakland | 125 | 35 |
| Kansas City | 24 | 9 | Jacksonville | 118 | 22 |
| Mobile | 23 | 44 | Kansas City | 112 | 22 |
| Indianapolis | 22 | 9 | Milwaukee | 105 | 15 |
| Cincinnati | 20 | 5 | Pittsburgh | 105 | 20 |
| Montgomery | 19 | 51 | Richmond | 105 | 42 |
| Augusta | 18 | 45 | Boston | 105 | 16 |

Source:   1910 data: U. S. Bureau of the Census, *Negro Population 1790–1915;* 1970 data: U. S. Bureau of the Census, *Census of Population: 1970.*

## Sources of Urban Population Growth

Migration from the South to northern cities and within the South from rural areas to cities has been taking place at a rapid rate during much of the last sixty years. Migration, however, is not the only source of growth of urban black population. As we have seen, the excess of births over deaths contributes to population growth even in the absence of migration. Migration brings to cities large numbers of young couples and young persons about to form families. As compared to a population with a larger share of older persons, a city population heavily augmented by migration contains many couples in the childbearing ages. Birth rates are therefore high, and in the absence of a large older population, death rates are low. The difference between high birth rates and low death rates results in a high rate of natural increase. Urban black populations, therefore, are increasing rapidly not only because of in-migration, but also because of natural increase.

The large volume of natural increase among urban black populations is further altering the old stereotypical picture of blacks as southern sharecroppers. In a more up-to-date version of this stereotype, northern urban blacks are pictured as recent migrants from the rural South, lacking in knowledge of the manners and niceties of city living. The census documents that in fact more than half of northern blacks are northern-born. Of the migrants from the South, many come from southern cities rather than rural areas. A survey in 1967 showed that 7 million urban blacks aged 17 and over grew up in cities. Of the total 9.1 million urban black adults, only 2.1 million, less than one-fourth, were of rural origin.

## BLACKS IN METROPOLITAN AREAS

As the urbanization of the United States has progressed, the society has increasingly come to be organized around the large cities. The sphere of influence of a large city extends far beyond its boundaries. A very large city such as New York has economic and cultural ties with every part of the country and with much of the world. Other cities do not have such an extensive range of influence, but there is always a high degree of interdependence between each large city and its surrounding area. Although the political boundaries of large cities have not expanded to encompass the entire population that is socially and economically integrated with the city, the entire suburban area of a large city, together with much of the close-in rural area, can be considered together with the central city as comprising a single metropolitan area.

Consideration of the changing distribution of black population is incomplete without an indication of the position of Negroes in the metropolitan system of the country. To permit analysis of metropolitanization, the Federal Government has recognized, for statistical purposes, a number of "Standard Metropolitan Statistical Areas" (SMSAs). Each SMSA consists of at least one city of 50,000 inhabitants or more, together with the county (or counties) in which the city is located, and as many contiguous counties as are essentially metropolitan in character and socially and economically integrated with the central city. The metropolitan area concept is quite distinct from the concept of urban population. Cities are politically incorporated units. A metropolitan area includes at least one large city, a number of nearby large and small cities, and some outlying rural population, both farm and nonfarm.

Both black and white population movement has been largely to the cities and suburbs of metropolitan areas. Cities outside of metropolitan areas have not participated to the same degree in the urbanization of the population. The increasing concentration of blacks and whites in metropolitan areas over the period 1900 to 1960 is shown in Table V. In 1900, 44 percent of whites and 27 percent of blacks lived in metropolitan areas, then by 1960 the figure was 63 percent for whites and 65 percent for blacks. For the 1970 census 243 metropolitan areas were delineated; they contained 64 percent of whites and 71 percent of blacks.

TABLE V—PERCENT OF BLACKS RESIDING IN METROPOLITAN AREAS BY
RACE AND REGION, 1900–1970*

| Race and Year | Conterminous United States | Region | | |
|---|---|---|---|---|
| | | North | West | South |
| BLACK | | | | |
| 1970 | 71 | 94 | 90 | 52 |
| 1960 | 65 | 93 | 93 | 46 |
| 1950 | 56 | 92 | 91 | 39 |
| 1940 | 45 | 89 | 86 | 32 |
| 1930 | 42 | 87 | 83 | 30 |
| 1920 | 34 | 82 | 68 | 26 |
| 1910 | 29 | 72 | 72 | 23 |
| 1900 | 27 | 66 | 67 | 22 |
| WHITE | | | | |
| 1970 | 64 | 68 | 72 | 52 |
| 1960 | 63 | 67 | 72 | 49 |
| 1950 | 60 | 66 | 67 | 42 |
| 1940 | 56 | 64 | 62 | 35 |
| 1930 | 56 | 64 | 61 | 33 |
| 1920 | 51 | 60 | 52 | 29 |
| 1910 | 48 | 56 | 51 | 26 |
| 1900 | 44 | 51 | 47 | 24 |

*Metropolitan Areas as defined in 1960.

Source :   Compiled from data in U. S. Bureau of the Census, *Historical Statistics of the United States, Colonial Times to 1957*, and *Censuses of Population: 1960* and *1970.*

## Regional Trends in Metropolitanization

Because the population movements to urban areas have been principally to urban centers within metropolitan areas, regional differences in the patterns for blacks and whites resemble those already noted for overall urbanization. In the South, both blacks and whites have participated about equally in metropolitan concentration, with just under one-fourth of each group in metropolitan areas in 1900 and over one-half in 1970.

In the North and West, blacks have always been more concentrated than whites in metropolitan areas. In 1970, 94 and 90 percent respectively of blacks in these regions were metropolitan dwellers, as compared to 68 and 72 percent of whites.

A large proportion of metropolitan population lives in the very large metropolitan areas—in 1970, 56 percent of metropolitan whites and 65 percent of metropolitan blacks were in areas of over 1,000,000 total population. Large metropolitan areas are principally located in the North and West, and blacks moving North have been particularly attracted to these centers. In the South, however, metropolitan blacks and whites are similarly distributed among areas of each size. One out of every twelve blacks in the country in 1970 lived in the New York metropolitan area. Seven metropolitan areas in the North, each with more than 300,000 black residents, together contained two-thirds of all northern blacks (Table VI). Two metropolitan areas in the West contained two-thirds of that region's black population. In the South thirteen metropolitan areas, each with more than 100,000 black residents, together contained one-third of the region's black population.

#### TABLE VI—METROPOLITAN AREAS WITH 100,000 OR MORE BLACKS IN 1970

| Metropolitan Area | Black Population (000) | Metropolitan Area | Black Population (000) |
|---|---|---|---|
| New York | 1,883 | Miami | 190 |
| Chicago | 1,231 | Pittsburgh | 170 |
| Philadelphia | 844 | Norfolk-Portsmouth | 168 |
| Los Angeles | 763 | Cincinnati | 152 |
| Detroit | 757 | Kansas City | 151 |
| Washington | 704 | Indianapolis | 137 |
| Baltimore | 490 | Richmond | 130 |
| Houston | 384 | Boston | 127 |
| St. Louis | 379 | Greensboro* | 118 |
| Newark | 348 | Jacksonville | 118 |
| Cleveland | 333 | Mobile | 113 |
| San Francisco | 330 | Gary† | 112 |
| New Orleans | 324 | Tampa-St. Petersburg | 109 |
| Atlanta | 311 | Buffalo | 109 |
| Memphis | 289 | Milwaukee | 107 |
| Dallas | 249 | Columbus | 106 |
| Birmingham | 218 | Louisville | 101 |

*Greensboro-Winston Salem-High Point Metropolitan Area
†Gary-Hammond-East Chicago Metropolitan Area
Source:   U. S. Bureau of the Census, *Census of Population: 1970.*

Regional differences in the course of black metropolitanization have many causes. In the South, blacks were an integral part of the initial settlement of the region and have always been distributed similarly to the white population. Both races there are now responding in similar fashion to the social and economic forces which are producing a metropolitan society. Both races started as predominantly rural and the process of urbanization since 1900 has been eroding their common rural heritage. In the North and West, on the other hand, blacks represent a new group (similar in this respect to the white immigrants of the past) which is being superimposed upon established metropolitan settlement patterns.

## Black Migration to Metropolitan Areas

The United States has experienced a massive redistribution of population during its second hundred years. The creation of a predominantly metropolitan black population heavily concentrated in the North and West as well as the South came about through the migration of millions of persons. These individuals and families left an accustomed place and set off for another for much the same reasons that make migrants of nearly all Americans at least once during their lives. The dominant reason has been the search for a better living in the midst of a rapidly industrializing and urbanizing society. The loss of old ways of life and the willingness to seek out new ways are at least as characteristic of the black population as of the white. The demise of sharecropping, the shifting patterns of demand for agricultural labor, the rise and subsequent fall of domestic service work in cities, the expansion and leveling off of jobs in manufacturing industries, the growth of other blue collar jobs and eventually of lower-level white collar jobs have all played a part. The rapidly increased availability of education, even if segregated, the interregional circulation of newspapers, radio shows, and television programs have contributed to the knowledge of new worlds and dissatisfaction with old ones. The development of civil rights—to travel, to serve in the armed forces, to obtain public services, to vote—has been a distinctive aspect of the changing character of black migration.

Much of what we know about the period from 1910 to 1950 is based upon fragmentary sources and the reports of observers. Most accounts assert that blacks moving to cities were of lower social and economic status than were those blacks who were long-term city residents. Considerable friction was generated between the two groups and between these groups and whites. Increased racial tension was commonly blamed upon the heavy influx of blacks of low socioeconomic status.

Redistribution of black population from the rural South to northern cities appears to have often been an indirect process. Some blacks moved directly from southern farms to Chicago or New York, but farmers, croppers, or laborers were more likely to move first to a nearby southern city. Later they or their children moved to one of the northern cities. Such "stage migration" has often encompassed a number of moves, from farm to village to town to city to metropolis. Some migrants, of course, skipped all or most of the intervening stages. Others moved only one or two stages, and still others, few in number, moved in the reverse direction, from North back to South, or from large place to small.

The individual migrant, in his efforts to maintain continuity and lessen the shock of adjustment, tended to choose a destination about which he knew something, where friends or kin could provide information and assistance. Hence paths of migration tended to follow paths of transportation, especially the North-South rail lines.

Black migrants to metropolitan areas in the Northeast (Newark, New York, Philadelphia, and Pittsburgh) came primarily from the Atlantic seaboard states. Metropolitan areas in the North Central region (St. Louis, Detroit, Cleveland, Cincinnati, and Chicago) received substantial shares of their black in-migrants from the states of the middle South. Los Angeles and San Francisco drew from the states along the western edge of the South and from the Midwest. Migrants to metropolitan areas of the South have most often come from nonmetropolitan areas in the same or neighboring states.

As the black population in metropolitan areas has grown, the movement of blacks between metropolitan areas has been added to the earlier rural-to-urban movement. This intermetropolitan movement is an increasingly important component of total migration. Once resident in a metropolitan area, blacks are much more likely to move to other metropolitan areas than back to the rural areas and small towns of the South. In a society which is overwhelmingly metropolitan, the predominant movement is clearly intermetropolitan rather than rural-to-urban. Most black newcomers, particularly to northern metropolitan areas, have already had considerable experience with metropolitan living.

Old patterns of migration change, but public perceptions often lag. The 1960 and 1970 censuses each had a question asking where people lived five years before. Comparison of current with previous residence provided the basis for a number of special migration reports. Analyses just now being reported from the 1970 census data confirm and extend findings made from the 1960 data. Black migrants to cities are no longer (and probably never were entirely) drawn from the most rural, poorest, and least educated segments of the southern black population. Indeed, recent black migrants from the South to northern cities are less likely than northern-born blacks to be on welfare. The recent migrants have higher rates of participation in the labor force and higher incomes than the northern blacks.

Any large-scale and long-continued migration carries the seeds of its own destruction. As young adults are transferred by moving from one locality to another, much of the next generation of natural increase occurs in the new locale. The flow of young people off farms is now but a trickle and the total rural to urban flow has diminished in size. It has been expected that the southern to northern flow would soon diminish, and that eventually the pace of metropolitanization would have to slow down. The latest data from the periodic national surveys conducted by the Bureau of the Census suggest that these expected changes in migration pattern have arrived quite suddenly. From March 1970 to March 1973, there was a net migration flow of whites toward the South from other regions and for the first time in a century no net outflow of blacks from the South. Even more startling in these data was the evidence of a net outflow of whites from metropolitan to nonmetropolitan places. For blacks there was a sharp shift, but not a reversal, in the pace of metropolitan movement: in-movement to metropolitan areas compared to out-movement from metropolitan areas dropped to a ratio of 3 to 2.

A group that occupies a narrow position in the social and economic structure of a nation is likely to display highly specific migration patterns. The westward drift of slaves across the rural South is one example; the flocking of newly freed persons to Washington in the mid-1860s is another. As a group expands its role in the economy and occupies an increasing number of social roles, its migration patterns become more complex. Contemporary American society is noted for its high rates of geographic mobility and for the complexity of its migratory interchanges. Blacks have become more widely dispersed in American geography, on the regional dimension, on the rural-urban dimension, and in the number of urban centers with sizable black populations. It is no longer easy to typify "black migration," for blacks are as diverse in their social settings and patterns of mobility as are whites. The principal migration currents in which blacks are not, as yet, participating in substantial numbers are those involving suburbs—city to suburb, suburb to suburb, nonmetropolitan location to suburb. Is it likely that we shall soon see a sharp change in patterns of black suburbanization?

## Blacks in Suburbs

A metropolitan area can conveniently be divided into two parts—the central city (or cities) which gives it its name, and the surrounding suburban "ring." The extent of suburbanization can then be measured by the percentage of a metropolitan area's population which resides in the suburban ring. The use of this measure shows that blacks and whites have not shared equally in the movement to the suburbs. Although there is a higher concentration of blacks in metropolitan areas, within metropolitan areas they are grouped in the central cities to a much greater extent than are whites (Table VII). Three out of every five metropolitan whites live in the suburban ring as compared to only one out of every five metropolitan blacks. This underrepresentation of blacks in suburban areas occurs within each region.

Since 1900 the concentration of metropolitan blacks in central cities has increased, in contrast to the rapid suburbanization among the white population (Table VIII). This has affected the racial composition both of cities and of suburban rings. In the North and West, both suburban rings and central cities increased in percent black during 1900–70, indicating that the black population in both components of metropolitan areas was increasing more rapidly than the corresponding white population (Table IX). The percent black in cities, however, rose to much higher levels than in rings. In southern metropolitan areas the percent black in the rings has declined rapidly, while the color composition of the cities has remained about the same.

**TABLE VII—METROPOLITAN DISTRIBUTION BY RACE AND REGION, 1970**

| Residence | Population (000) | | Percent Distribution | |
|---|---|---|---|---|
| | Black | White | Black | White |
| **UNITED STATES** | | | | |
| Metropolitan | 16,122 | 113,628 | 71 | 64 |
| In Central City | 12,586 | 45,088 | 55 | 25 |
| In Ring | 3,536 | 68,540 | 16 | 39 |
| Nonmetropolitan | 6,685 | 63,802 | 29 | 36 |
| **NORTH** | | | | |
| Metropolitan | 8,310 | 65,545 | 94 | 68 |
| In Central City | 6,995 | 26,115 | 79 | 27 |
| In Ring | 1,315 | 39,430 | 15 | 41 |
| Nonmetropolitan | 567 | 31,282 | 6 | 32 |
| **WEST** | | | | |
| Metropolitan | 1,511 | 22,646 | 90 | 72 |
| In Central City | 1,087 | 8,194 | 65 | 26 |
| In Ring | 424 | 14,452 | 25 | 46 |
| Nonmetropolitan | 176 | 8,572 | 10 | 28 |
| **SOUTH** | | | | |
| Metropolitan | 6,301 | 25,438 | 52 | 52 |
| In Central City | 4,504 | 10,780 | 37 | 22 |
| In Ring | 1,797 | 14,658 | 15 | 30 |
| Nonmetropolitan | 5,942 | 23,947 | 48 | 48 |

Source:   U. S. Bureau of the Census, *Current Population Reports,* P-23, No. 37.

**TABLE VIII—PERCENT OF METROPOLITAN POPULATION RESIDING IN CENTRAL CITY BY RACE AND REGION, 1900–1970**

| Race and Year | United States* | Region | | |
|---|---|---|---|---|
| | | North | West | South |
| **BLACK** | | | | |
| 1970 | 78.1 | 84.2 | 71.9 | 71.5 |
| 1960 | 79.5 | 84.9 | 72.5 | 74.6 |
| 1950 | 77.2 | 83.5 | 69.9 | 72.0 |
| 1940 | 74.6 | 81.1 | 78.3 | 69.5 |
| 1930 | 72.8 | 79.8 | 79.8 | 67.3 |
| 1920 | 67.2 | 78.0 | 83.8 | 61.1 |
| 1910 | 60.4 | 72.1 | 81.7 | 55.7 |
| 1900 | 54.5 | 68.6 | 80.3 | 49.5 |
| **WHITE** | | | | |
| 1970 | 39.7 | 39.9 | 36.2 | 42.4 |
| 1960 | 47.8 | 47.6 | 43.0 | 52.5 |
| 1950 | 56.6 | 58.1 | 49.6 | 57.3 |
| 1940 | 61.6 | 62.5 | 57.7 | 60.6 |
| 1930 | 63.9 | 64.4 | 61.5 | 63.6 |
| 1920 | 65.9 | 66.8 | 66.8 | 61.0 |
| 1910 | 64.9 | 66.4 | 65.3 | 56.0 |
| 1900 | 62.8 | 64.7 | 62.3 | 51.8 |

*Data for 1900–1960 use the 1960 metropolitan area definitions and exclude Alaska and Hawaii.

Source:   U. S. Bureau of the Census, *Census of Population: 1960; Current Population Reports,* P-23, No. 37.

**TABLE IX**—BLACK POPULATION AS PERCENT OF TOTAL IN CENTRAL CITY
AND SUBURBAN RING BY REGION, 1900–1970

| Residence and Year | United States* | Region | | |
|---|---|---|---|---|
| | | North | West | South |
| **TOTAL METROPOLITAN** | | | | |
| 1970 | 12.3 | 11.2 | 5.9 | 19.8 |
| 1960 | 10.8 | 9.1 | 5.1 | 19.6 |
| 1950 | 9.4 | 6.9 | 3.9 | 20.4 |
| 1940 | 8.0 | 5.0 | 1.7 | 22.4 |
| 1930 | 7.5 | 4.4 | 1.4 | 22.9 |
| 1920 | 6.8 | 3.1 | 1.1 | 24.6 |
| 1910 | 6.7 | 2.4 | 1.1 | 27.4 |
| 1900 | 7.4 | 2.4 | 1.0 | 30.7 |
| **CENTRAL CITY** | | | | |
| 1970 | 21.5 | 21.0 | 10.9 | 29.4 |
| 1960 | 16.8 | 15.1 | 8.2 | 25.8 |
| 1950 | 12.4 | 9.6 | 5.4 | 24.3 |
| 1940 | 9.6 | 6.4 | 2.3 | 24.8 |
| 1930 | 8.4 | 5.5 | 1.8 | 23.9 |
| 1920 | 6.9 | 3.6 | 1.5 | 24.6 |
| 1910 | 6.3 | 2.6 | 1.3 | 27.5 |
| 1900 | 6.5 | 2.5 | 1.3 | 29.6 |
| **RING** | | | | |
| 1970 | 4.9 | 3.2 | 2.7 | 10.9 |
| 1960 | 4.6 | 2.8 | 2.5 | 11.6 |
| 1950 | 5.2 | 2.8 | 2.4 | 14.3 |
| 1940 | 5.5 | 2.6 | 0.9 | 18.2 |
| 1930 | 5.7 | 2.6 | 0.7 | 21.0 |
| 1920 | 6.5 | 2.1 | 0.5 | 24.5 |
| 1910 | 7.5 | 2.0 | 0.5 | 27.4 |
| 1900 | 8.9 | 2.1 | 0.5 | 31.7 |

*Data for 1900–1960 use the 1960 metropolitan area definitions and exclude Alaska and Hawaii.

Source:  U. S. Bureau of the Census, *Census of Population: 1960; Current Population Reports,* P-23, No. 37.

Recent gains in the black population residing in certain suburban rings, although small, have been hailed by some as the beginning of large-scale suburbanization. Such an interpretation may possibly be correct, but a closer look at actual trends prompts a more cautious view. Take the example of the Chicago metropolitan area. Among Chicago's many suburbs are several with considerable industry and a large supply of old, urban-type housing. Nine such suburbs, listed in Table X, had small black populations in residentially segregated neighborhoods as far back as 1950. The addition of black population in these suburbs was accomplished by the expansion of these segregated neighborhoods, in a manner exactly the same as the absorption of additional black population in the city of Chicago and in other central cities. From 1950 to 1970, the black population in the total Chicago suburban area increased by approximately 85,000 persons. Nearly two-thirds of this increase was centered in the black neighborhoods of these nine industrial suburbs. Another one-fourth of Chicago's growing black suburban population went to "black suburbs," entire communities or separate sections of existing suburbs in which new housing developments were constructed expressly for blacks. Five black suburbs are identified in Table X. Altogether the nine industrial suburbs and five black suburbs absorbed 89 percent of the increase in Chicago's black suburban population. During the twenty-year period only 9,414 blacks were added to the rest of the Chicago suburban area, an area that in 1970 contained more than 3,000,000 whites.

Suburbanization of black population has been occurring in a number of metropolitan areas. But the growing numbers of blacks in the suburbs are still small compared to the growing numbers of whites in the suburbs. The types of suburban neighborhoods into which blacks are moving tend to be, as in the Chicago area, older portions of industrial suburbs or segregated developments for blacks only. The suburbanization of blacks is seen to be simply the spilling-over of residential patterns from central cities to suburbs. Suburbanization of blacks has not entailed any major increase in racially integrated housing.

**TABLE X—BLACK POPULATION IN SELECTED CHICAGO SUBURBS, 1950–1970**

| Place | Black Population | | | | Percent Black, 1970 |
|---|---|---|---|---|---|
| | 1950 | 1960 | 1970 | Change 1950–70 | |
| Chicago City | | | 1,102,620 | | |
| Total Suburban Area | 43,640 | 77,517 | 128,299 | 84,659 | 4 |
| Industrial Suburbs | | | | | |
| Aurora | 1,151 | 2,227 | 4,867 | 3,716 | 7 |
| Chicago Heights | 4,109 | 6,529 | 7,100 | 2,991 | 17 |
| Elgin | 768 | 1,595 | 2,671 | 1,903 | 5 |
| Evanston | 6,994 | 9,126 | 12,849 | 5,855 | 16 |
| Harvey | 1,010 | 1,986 | 10,711 | 9,701 | 31 |
| Joliet | 1,950 | 4,638 | 9,507 | 7,557 | 12 |
| Maywood | 2,500 | 5,229 | 12,416 | 9,916 | 41 |
| North Chicago | 832 | 4,577 | 7,836 | 7,004 | 17 |
| Waukegan | 2,313 | 4,485 | 8,421 | 6,108 | 13 |
| Black Suburbs | | | | | |
| Dixmoor | 554 | 1,855 | 3,071 | 2,517 | 65 |
| East Chicago Heights | 1,190 | 2,794 | 4,855 | 3,665 | 97 |
| Markham | 66 | 2,505 | 7,981 | 7,915 | 50 |
| Phoenix | 1,461 | 2,744 | 3,151 | 1,690 | 88 |
| Robbins | 4,729 | 7,410 | 9,436 | 4,707 | 98 |
| Total Specified Suburbs | 29,627 | 57,700 | 104,872 | 75,245 | 19 |
| Rest of Suburban Area | 14,013 | 19,817 | 23,427 | 9,414 | 1 |

Note:   The designation of a suburb as "industrial" is based upon data for manufacturing establishments and employment and amount of commuting to Chicago to work, as described in the suburban histories of the Kitagawa and Taeuber volume cited below.

Source:   Evelyn M. Kitagawa and Karl E. Taeuber, *Local Community Fact Book Chicago Metropolitan Area 1960* (Chicago: Chicago Community Inventory, University of Chicago, 1963); U. S. Bureau of the Census, *Censuses of Population: 1950, 1960, and 1970.*

**Urban Residential Segregation**

A high proportion of the nation's blacks dwell in the central cities of large metropolitan areas. Not only are blacks virtually absent from most of suburbia, but they are virtually absent from many residential neighborhoods within these central cities. Individual city neighborhoods throughout the country tend to be occupied either by blacks or by whites, with few areas of sustained residential intermixture. Civil rights struggles for open occupancy, against school segregation and against a variety of other forms of segregation in parks, libraries, and other public facilities, have called attention to the prevalence of racial residential segregation in many cities. The prevalence of residential segregation has been documented by the data amassed concerning individual city blocks in the 1940, 1950, and 1960 censuses.

Preliminary work with 1970 data indicates that these earlier patterns continue. If race were not a factor in where a person lives, and whites and blacks had similar socioeconomic characteristics, every city block might be expected to have the same proportion of white and black residents as every other block. In fact, the data reveal very clearly that blocks tend to be occupied by whites or by blacks, with relatively few blocks having a high degree of intermixture. With these data it is possible to demonstrate that residential segregation is not only characteristic of northern cities or of southern cities. *Every* city with a sizable black population displays a high degree of residential segregation, regardless of region or size, regardless of whether it is a manufacturing center, a trade center, or a suburb. Sometimes groups protesting housing discrimination in a city contend that their city is the most segregated in the country. Examination of the census data, however, indicates that this type of segregation is found in all American cities.


# HOUSING AND THE BLACK POPULATION


**Trends in Home-ownership**

Today more than 2.5 million black families are homeowners. Owners make up more than 40 percent of black households, but blacks lag far behind whites in home-ownership. Trends in home-ownership in the United States, pictured in Figure 7, tell a surprising story. From 1890 (the earliest date for which reliable statistics are available) until some time after World War II, a minority of Americans were homeowners. For whites, the home-ownership rate stood at about 50 percent until 1940. It was only during the postwar period of economic prosperity, accompanied by high levels of accumulated savings, high rates of marriage and household formation, and extensive governmental programs to facilitate home-ownership, that the balance was finally tilted strongly in favor of ownership. In the decades from 1940 to 1970 (and mainly in the fifteen years from 1945 to 1960) home-ownership among whites climbed from a low of 45 percent of households to 65 percent. The levels of home-ownership among blacks have always been much lower than among whites, but the overall trend has been rather similar. From 1900 to 1940, the percent owners among blacks remained steady at 24 to 25, increasing sharply to 38 percent in 1960 and then to 42 percent in 1970.

FIGURE 7—PERCENT OWNER-OCCUPIED BY COLOR: UNITED STATES 1890–1970

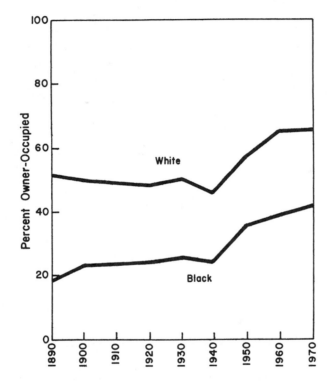

Note:   Data for 1910 not available.
Source:   U. S. Bureau of the Census, *Censuses of Housing: 1960* and *1970*.

For both blacks and whites, the first thirty years of this century were a period of increasing income and wealth, which should have been reflected in augmented home-ownership. These years were also a time of rapid urbanization, however, and the move to cities inhibited the growth of ownership which otherwise would have occurred. Prior to the days of mass automobile ownership and easy transportation over long distances, cities tended of necessity to be settled very densely. Under such circumstances, multiple-dwelling units predominated over single-family dwellings. In addition, millions of the immigrants from Europe and white and black migrants from rural America came to cities in search of economic opportunities. Despite considerable improvement in the economic well-being of many of these migrants over their former circumstances, their incomes were not high in relation to the cost of urban housing.

The prevalence of home-ownership varies greatly with regions of the country, types of areas, cities, and even parts of a single city. To a great extent these variations are determined when an area is first built up, for single-family detached dwellings are usually for purchase, and multiple-unit dwellings are for rent. Old units which were once owned may be converted into rental units, but the reverse seldom happens.

For blacks in 1970, 35 percent of housing units in metropolitan areas of the North were owner-occupied. These blacks live chiefly in the old central portions of cities that were built up in the dense tenement pattern prevailing many decades ago. In the South this type of housing has always been less prevalent, and 43 percent of metropolitan blacks are owners. Outside of metropolitan areas in the South, building codes are not as strict, inexpensive units are more common, and 52 percent of the units are owner-occupied. Among whites, the levels of ownership are much higher: 62 percent in northern metropolitan areas, 65 percent in southern metropolitan areas, and 72 percent in the small towns and rural areas of the South.

## Housing Characteristics of Whites and Blacks

Whether they are renters or owners, the housing obtained by blacks is less adequate or less desirable in many respects than the housing obtained by whites. Black households are more likely to live in substandard housing, more likely to be overcrowded, less likely to be in new housing, and less likely to have such amenities as air conditioning or an automobile. Telephones are not available to 31 percent of black households as compared to 11 percent of white households (Table XI).

There is considerable controversy over the question of whether because of segregation and discrimination blacks get less housing value than they should for what they pay. In their careful study of the situation in Chicago in 1956, *Housing a Metropolis—Chicago*, Beverly Duncan and Philip M. Hauser came to the conclusion that for roughly equivalent housing, blacks had to pay about fifteen dollars a month more than whites. To the extent that blacks, by virtue of residential segregation, have access to only a limited amount of housing, despite rapidly increasing numbers, the laws of supply and demand operate in black residential areas to raise housing prices in relation to housing quality. Unfortunately there is no way to determine what values and rents would be in the absence of discrimination. In some northern cities blacks pay nearly as high rents, on the average, as do whites (Chicago, 1970, blacks $107, whites $109; Cleveland, 1970, blacks $77, whites $80). There can be no doubt that in these cities blacks are poorly treated in the housing market.

TABLE XI—SELECTED HOUSING CHARACTERISTICS BY METROPOLITAN
LOCATION, 1970

| | | United States | Metropolitan Areas | | Outside Metropolitan Areas |
| --- | --- | --- | --- | --- | --- |
| | | | Central Cities | Suburbs | |
| Occupied housing | Black | 6,180 | 3,838 | 907 | 1,435 |
| units (000) | White | 57,270 | 17,544 | 21,574 | 18,152 |
| Owner-occupied | Black | 42 | 35 | 54 | 52 |
| (percent) | White | 65 | 51 | 71 | 72 |
| Owner-occupied: | Black | $10,600 | $12,100 | $13,000 | $6,300 |
| Median value | White | $17,400 | $17.000 | $20,900 | $12,400 |
| Renter-occupied | Black | 58 | 65 | 46 | 48 |
| (percent) | White | 35 | 49 | 29 | 28 |
| Renter-occupied: | Black | $71 | $76 | $78 | $32 |
| Median rent | White | $92 | $94 | $115 | $66 |
| Crowded | Black | 25 | 22 | 25 | 33 |
| (percent) | White | 8 | 9 | 7 | 9 |
| Lacking some | Black | 17 | 5 | 17 | 49 |
| plumbing facilities | White | 6 | 3 | 3 | 11 |
| (percent) | | | | | |
| Telephone not | Black | 31 | 26 | 26 | 47 |
| available (percent) | White | 11 | 11 | 7 | 15 |

Source:   U.S. Bureau of the Census, *Census of Housing: 1970.*

Blacks usually spend a high proportion of their low incomes on housing. In 1960 nearly one-third of black renters, as compared to one-fifth of white renters, paid out more than 35 percent of their annual income on rent. Interpretation of these figures can lead to very subtle questions of economic theory, but it is clear that the income gap between blacks and whites is much greater than the difference in amounts actually spent on housing, and that the housing obtained by blacks is much inferior to that obtained by whites.

The new homes and apartments which were built in the last three decades to house the rapidly growing American population were located principally in the suburbs. The black population, because of residential segregation and to some extent because of lesser economic status, has not gained much access to new suburban housing. Instead, the black city-dwellers have had to make do with the older housing stock.

The housing stock of a city or a nation is not simply a static supply of aging and deteriorating structures. It is rather an inventory subject to continual change, to renewal as well as to aging. Particularly during periods of housing shortage and low vacancy rates, additional housing units are created by adding partitions and plumbing facilities or otherwise subdividing existing units. Nonresidential structures such as garages and lofts may be converted to residential use. Deterioration, if not aging, of older units can be controlled through programs of maintenance and rehabilitation. Countering these processes are others that subtract from the total housing supply. Demolition may be accidental, as from fire or storm, or it may be planned as part of a program of highway construction, urban renewal, or other purpose. Two or more small units may be merged into a lesser number of large units. Housing units may be converted to nonresidential use. The continual operation of these processes produces continual change in the housing stock, even aside from new construction.

Numerous controversies testify to the close linkage between these processes of change in the housing stock and the growth and location of black populations in the central cities. But neighborhood change in the cities has assumed social importance more for its racial than for its physical aspects. Hundreds of thousands of housing units which remained physically more or less the same over a period of years were transferred from white to black occupancy. This racial turnover occurred in highly systematic patterns so as to sustain the patterns of racial residential segregation already discussed. The urban renewal and highway construction programs complicated this pattern of change and aggravated the problems associated with it, but it was the persistent day-in day-out channeling of whites to certain residential areas and blacks to other residential areas that produced the current racial geography of the American metropolis. It is only in this larger context of the social structure of the metropolis that the specific comparisons of housing characteristics of blacks and whites can be understood.

## SOCIAL, ECONOMIC AND HEALTH CHARACTERISTICS OF BLACKS

Blacks today are confronted with a wide variety of social problems, some of them the heritage of slavery, all of them a reflection of their current position in American society. At the time of emancipation, most blacks were illiterate, lived in the rural South, worked in agriculture (primarily as laborers), and received little cash income. Sanitary conditions were often bad, medical and hygienic knowledge slight, and death rates high. A major trend in black history since emancipation has been absorption into a changing industrial society. As concerns many of the characteristics which have distinguished blacks from whites, the century since emancipation has been marked by a gradual but not yet completed convergence of the races.

The topics touched upon in this section are especially difficult to discuss briefly. Several of them are subject to more extensive analysis in other chapters. Here the attempt is to emphasize the mutual interrelations, omitting many of the technical complexities and regional variations.

## Educational Attainment

In 1870, about 80 percent of nonwhites were illiterate. Fifty years later the figure was down to 23 percent. Not until 1959, however, was illiteracy down to 7.5 percent, a level attained by whites seventy years earlier. Although blacks have to a considerable degree caught up with whites in insuring that their children receive at least a primary education, there is still a large lag at the higher educational levels.

Virtually all children between the ages of 7 and 13, white and black, are enrolled in school. The percentage enrolled, however, falls off faster for blacks than for whites. At ages 16–17, the enrollment in the fall of 1970 was 86 percent for blacks, 91 percent for whites. At ages 18–19, beyond the ages of compulsory attendance, the percentages dropped to 40 and 49 percent, respectively, and at ages 20–24, to 14 and 22 percent. (See Chapter 10, "Young Black Americans.")

School attendance, of course, is not a valid measure of education actually received. There are substantial differences in the extent of grade retardation. For example, of 17-year-olds enrolled in school in 1970, two-thirds of the whites but less than one-half of the blacks were high school seniors. Quality of education is more difficult to measure. If it is related to the educational attainment of teachers and the per capita expenditure on schooling, then nearly all southern blacks and the great bulk of northern blacks who attend predominantly black schools receive inferior education.

By age 25 most persons have completed their schooling. Trends in the median years of school completed for whites and nonwhites in the 25–29 age group suggest convergence between the two groups during the last thirty years (Table XII). While the figure for white males advanced from 10.5 school years in 1940 to 12.7 in 1970, the figure for blacks increased from 6.5 to 12.1. Blacks in the North and West report higher levels of education than do those in the South, while levels in the urban South greatly exceed those in the rural South. As blacks have moved in large numbers from the rural South to the cities of all regions, they have improved their educational opportunities and attainment.

Educators have long recognized that a person's family background, even in a society which provides free public education, affects whether the child attends school and how far he progresses in school. A recent special survey by the Bureau of the Census revealed that college attendance is much more frequent among children of high school and college graduates than among children of parents with only a grade school education. Black children are much more likely than white children to come from those families which send few children on to college. In fact, among families at each educational level, blacks were less likely to have children enrolled in college than whites. Unless a high percentage of black children surmount this handicap, they will become yet another generation of parents who are poorly educated, and whose children in turn may be handicapped by lack of a family background encouraging educational attainment. (See Chapter 11,

"Educating Black Americans.") Formal education takes place early in life, and is seldom continued after a person first leaves school. By the time a person reaches age 25, therefore, he has reached the educational level which he will retain throughout the rest of his life. Even if blacks now reaching ages 25–29 matched the educational achievements of whites, it would be more than a generation before educational level in the total black adult population caught up with those in the white population.

TABLE XII—MEDIAN YEARS OF SCHOOL COMPLETED BY PERSONS 25–29 YEARS OLD, BY COLOR AND SEX, 1940–1970

| Date | Male | | | Female | | |
|---|---|---|---|---|---|---|
| | White | Black | Percentage, Black of White | White | Black | Percentage, Black of White |
| April, 1940 | 10.5 | 6.5 | 61.9 | 10.9 | 7.5 | 68.8 |
| March, 1957 | 12.3 | 9.4 | 76.4 | 12.3 | 10.3 | 83.7 |
| March, 1962 | 12.5 | 11.0 | 88.0 | 12.4 | 11.4 | 91.9 |
| March, 1970 | 12.7 | 12.1 | 95.3 | 12.5 | 12.2 | 97.6 |
| Increase, 1940–70 | 2.2 | 5.6 | | 1.6 | 4.7 | |

Source:    1962 and 1970 from U.S. Bureau of the Census, *Current Population Reports,* Series P-20, No. 121; and Series P-23, No. 37 ; 1940 and 1957 from U.S. Department of Labor, *The Economic Status of Negroes in the United States*, Bulletin S-3, Revised 1962.

## Occupation and Income

The legacy of lower educational levels among the black population would be expected to be reflected in a concentration in the lower occupational levels. At each level of educational attainment, however, blacks obtain a smaller proportion of upper-level jobs than do whites with the same amount of education. For persons with little formal education, few occupations are open, whether the person is white or black. At the college-graduate level, blacks do fairly well in terms of broad occupational categories— perhaps because of the many outlets for professional employment within the black community as teachers, clergymen, doctors, and lawyers serving a black clientele. (See Chapter 12, "The Black Professional.")

Some of the advancement in occupational status which has occurred for blacks derives from an increase since 1940 from 214,000 to over 1,000,000 blacks employed in federal, state, and local governments. Much advancement in occupational levels, like that in educational levels, has resulted from the migration of blacks from areas with few economic opportunities to the rapidly growing metropolitan focal points of the expanding national economy.

The chief source of income for most black families is the wages received for their labor. With the twin disadvantages of lower educational attainment and lower occupational levels at each educational level, blacks fare much worse than whites in the amount of income they receive. Adjusting for changes in the cost of living, median family income for white families rose from $5,200 in 1947 to $7,300 in 1962 and $12,600 in 1973. Income for nonwhite families rose from $2,700 to $3,300 to $7,600 at the same dates. Median income for black families increased from 52 percent to 55 percent to 58 percent of the figure for whites. During the second world war, the income of nonwhites increased faster than the income of whites. Changes in the income ratio during the 1950s were mainly due to the regional migration of blacks from low-wage areas to high-wage areas. Incomes for blacks are particularly low in the South (Table XIII). (See Chapter 6, "The Black American Worker.")

Basic to an individual's ability to get along in an industrial society is his training and education, which fit him for an occupation. A job, in turn, provides his principal source of income and largely determines the style of life he will be able to maintain for himself and his children. The preceding discussion shows that at several critical junctures in their life history, blacks have been unable to keep pace with whites. In comparison with whites, blacks complete less formal schooling, obtain poorer jobs than do whites with comparable levels of education, and are rewarded by receiving lower earnings than do whites with similar educations and occupations. Census Bureau estimates show blacks with four years of college have smaller lifetime earnings than whites who did not go beyond the eighth grade. The relationships among education, occupation, and income indicate that reduction in racial discrimination might have a cumulative impact on the economic welfare of blacks.

**TABLE XIII—MEDIAN INCOME OF FAMILIES BY REGION AND COLOR, 1973**

| Region | White | Black | Percentage, Black of White |
|---|---|---|---|
| U.S. Total | $12,595 | $7,269 | 58 |
| Northeast | 13,230 | 7,762 | 59 |
| North Central | 13,128 | 9,109 | 69 |
| South | 11,508 | 6,434 | 56 |
| West | 12,661 | 8,233 | 65 |

Source: U. S. Bureau of the Census, *Current Population Reports,* P-23, No. 48, p. 17.

## Family and Fertility

Under slavery there was little security for blacks in the bond of marriage or parenthood. Fertility must have been high, for death rates were high, and yet the black population increased by more than the number of slaves imported. There is evidence that at least since 1850 birth rates among blacks have been higher than among whites. Although these historical trends are very difficult to document, the data in Figure 8 for years since 1920 are fairly reliable.

Various aspects of population distribution and social structure are related to fertility patterns. Farm families and other rural families, for instance, tend to have more children than city families. Part of the high fertility among blacks in earlier years could be attributed to their population concentration in the rural South. Since 1910 blacks have been leaving the rural South in great numbers and moving to cities where they have tended to display a lower rate of childbearing. Whites were also moving from high-fertility areas to low-fertility areas, however, and the racial difference persisted. During the 1920s and the first half of the 1930s, birth rates among both blacks and whites fell rapidly, and rates for both races rose sharply during World War II and the postwar "baby boom." During this period of rapidly declining fertility, those with higher social and economic status tended to produce fewer children, while those with lower status tended to have larger families.

During the 1950s, birth rates among whites averaged only slightly higher than in the late 1940s. For blacks, the postwar upward trend continued through the 1950s. This happened despite rapid urbanization. Students of fertility trends are uncertain why this divergence between white and black birth rates occurred. One interpretation emphasizes improved health among the black population. Historically, blacks in comparison with whites had much more childlessness among married couples. Their higher fertility arose from the fact that many couples did not practice any form of birth control and tended to have larger families than were common among the white population. Hence much of the childlessness among black couples would seem to have been involuntary. According to this interpretation, malnutrition (particularly as manifested in the disease of pellagra) and venereal disease may have greatly limited childbearing. Following World War II, both categories of disease were largely brought under medical control and many couples who in the past would have remained childless from disease were able to bear children. Since these diseases were much more common among the black population, their elimination had a much more stimulating impact on fertility among blacks than among whites. During the years of the "baby boom" of the 1950s the proportion of women never marrying declined among both blacks and whites, as did the proportion of married women remaining childless. Childbearing in the teens and early twenties became much more prevalent. Both whites and blacks developed a pattern of youthful marriage and early childbearing.

Since 1957 both races have experienced rapidly declining fertility. This downward trend appears to be continuing in the early years of the 1970s. Few scholars predicted that such a decline would occur so rapidly, and few would be so rash as to predict trends for the future. Many would agree that fertility among both races is now determined largely by the choices of individual parents as to family size and that disease and "fate" are no longer major factors. Some feel that the rapid spread of new contraceptive tech-

**FIGURE 8**—BIRTHS PER 1,000 FEMALES AGED 15–44 YEARS,* BY COLOR, 1920–1970

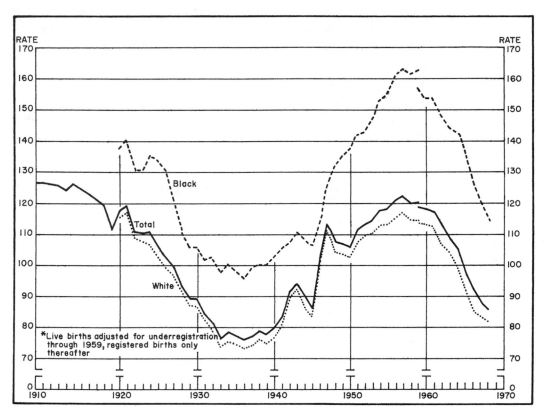

Note:   1969 and 1970 figures are for "Negro and other races."

Source:   U. S. Department of Health, Education, and Welfare, *Health, Education, and Welfare Indicators,* March, 1963; *Vital Statistics, 1968,* and *Statistical Abstract of the United States, 1974,* p. 54.

nology has wrought a permanent change in the ability of young couples to plan their families and their lives, and that there is little likelihood of a return to the increased childbearing pattern of the 1950s, after the reversal in these patterns during the 1960s and early 1970s. Birth rates have dropped to record low levels. If this is an enduring social change it will greatly alter the magnitude and character of such formerly major social problems as teen-age pregnancy, illegitimacy, large families among the poor, single-parent households, the rapid growth of welfare payments for dependent children, crowding in schools, and so on through a long list of population-related phenomena.

Distinguishing the more enduring social changes in marriage and fertility from the short-run fluctuations is a task which still challenges sociologists. Of the many factors affecting marriage and fertility, urban and rural residence, levels of economic welfare, and social status are among the most important and most easily measured.

Now that knowledge of family planning has spread throughout society and some degree of family limitation characterizes couples at all social and economic levels, the former class and ethnic differentials in fertility seem to have diminished, and even to have been partially reversed. A detailed analysis cannot be undertaken here, but some of the complexities can be indicated.

Social scientists have seldom been successful in their attempts to explain reproductive behavior. It is clear that among blacks, just as among whites, individuals vary widely. Their behavior in childbearing depends on their background, their education, their family status, the current occupation of husband and wife, and similar social factors. Race is significant mainly as it involves the concentration of individuals with particular characteristics which are associated with high or low fertility.

## Mortality and Health

Poverty and illness are intertwined in complicated ways. Sustained periods of illness may hamper a person in his efforts to earn a livelihood, and place a limit on his income. Sustained periods of low income, in turn, can lead to overcrowding, inadequate nutrition, a low level of preventive medical care and an increased incidence of ill health. That many blacks in the United States are economically less well off than most whites has been demonstrated above. In addition, blacks see physicians less often than do whites, make less use of hospitals, and have fewer of their hospital bills paid by insurance. That blacks suffer from higher death rates is an expected consequence.

Perhaps the best single measure of the general level of health among a population is the expectation of life at birth. This figure summarizes the death rates prevailing among people of all ages during a given year. It indicates the average length of life a newborn child can expect, given the current patterns of mortality. In 1900 white males in the United States had an expectation of life of 47 years, black males 32 years. In industrial societies the figures for women tend to be higher than those for men. Among females the white figure, 49 years, was nearly half again as large as the black figure, 34 years.

Death rates in the white population had already been falling for many decades prior to 1900, and continued to fall in succeeding years. The trend in expectation of life has been upward, with much annual fluctuation and a large interruption during the influenza epidemic of 1917–18 (see Figure 9). The figures for nonwhites have followed somewhat the same path, but have shown an even sharper rate of increase. With improvements in levels of living, in hygienic knowledge and nutrition, in public health and general medical care, the gap between whites and blacks was considerably narrowed. In fact, by 1967 black females had nearly caught up with white males in expectation of life, 67.8 versus 68.2 years.

Despite the remarkable trend toward convergence of death rates, a gap still exists. In 1967, white babies had about seven more years of life to look forward to than did black babies. Many of the missing years of life for blacks are lost within the first year after birth. In 1967 about 20 of every 1,000 white babies did not survive their first year. The figure was much higher for black babies, 36 per 1,000. Infant mortality rates, shown in Figure 10, have declined tremendously during this century. During the 1950s and 1960s there was much concern at the failure of infant mortality rates to continue in rapid decline. The reasons for the plateau in the chart are not fully known, but in the last few years the decline in rates for both blacks and whites has resumed.

Very little of the racial difference in mortality can be attributed to innate or genetic attributes of the races. There is currently much public discussion of sickle-cell anemia, a genetically linked and often fatal disease occurring primarily among blacks. But most of the excess black mortality, above the rates prevailing for whites, is from such causes, common to both groups, as heart disease, influenza and pneumonia, accidents, cancer, tuberculosis, and so on.

Many of these causes of death are correlated with social and economic circumstances of life. Persons of poor education and low income, of whatever race, are far more likely to fall ill and die from these causes than are persons of greater affluence. For the years 1964–1966 the National Center for Health Statistics conducted a survey of births and infant deaths. Infant death rates were found to be 50 to 100 percent higher in the lowest socioeconomic groups than they were in the middle and upper groups. This comparison suggests that the nation has the medical and public health knowledge to prevent many of the infant deaths occurring in families in the lower socioeconomic group. Indeed, the study estimated that nearly half of the infant deaths in this lower group are preventable, and that about one-fourth of *all* infant deaths are, in this sense, preventable. Black infants are far more likely than white infants to be born to parents of low education or income. The study documented that one-half of all black legitimate live births occurred in families with incomes of less than $3,000. This study and others examining deaths at older ages confirm that most of the high mortality among blacks is a reflection of their social and economic situation and of inequitable distribution of medical care.

FIGURE 9—EXPECTATION OF LIFE AT BIRTH, BY COLOR AND SEX, 1900–1967

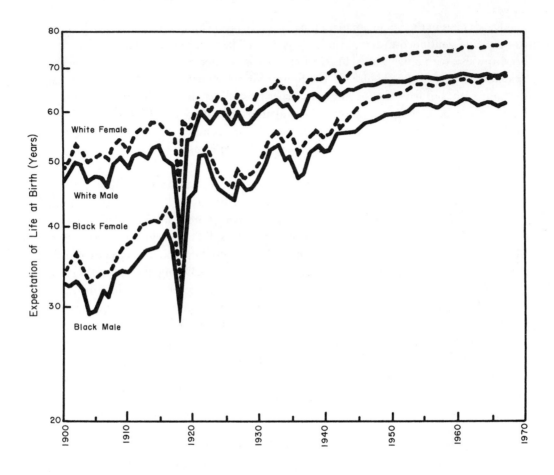

Note:   Data include Alaska beginning with 1959 and Hawaii beginning with 1960. Data refer
to the death registration area, which did not include the total United States, until 1933.

Source:   U. S. Bureau of the Census, *Historical Statistics of the United States, Colonial Times to 1957;* U. S. Department of Health, Education, and Welfare, *Vital Statistics of the United States, 1961* and *1967.*

**FIGURE 10**—INFANT MORTALITY RATE PER 1,000 LIVE BIRTHS, BY COLOR, 1915–1967

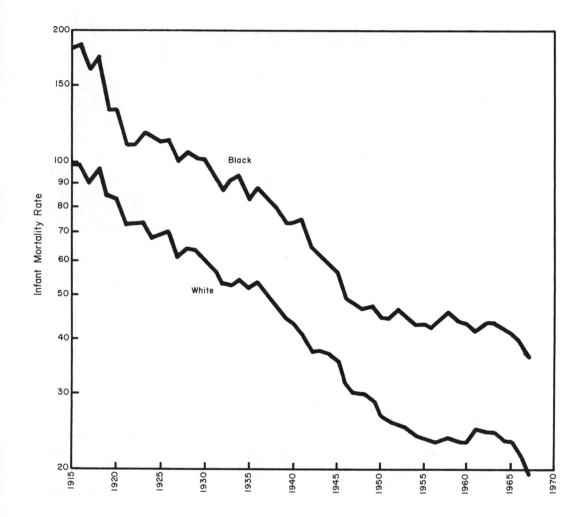

Note: Data refer to the death registration area, which did not include the total United States until 1933.

Source: U. S. Bureau of the Census, *Historical Statistics of the United States, Colonial Times to 1957;* U. S. Department of Health, Education, and Welfare, *Vital Statistics of the United States, 1960* and *1967.*

## THE FUTURE BLACK POPULATION

Forecasting the future is at best a tricky business, and the latest projections published by the U. S. Bureau of the Census show not one but four different estimates. According to these figures, the total population of the nation may increase from 205 million in 1970 to 240–258 million in 1985 and 271–322 million in the year 2000. If a major depression or war occurs, or some other factor produces radical changes in rates of birth, death, or immigration, the actual figures in the future might well fall outside these limits.

The latest official projections do not include separate estimates for whites and blacks. In 1960 blacks constituted 10.6 percent of the total population, and in 1970, 11.1 percent. Since the rate of increase of the black population has been greater than that of the white population, it is likely that this percentage will slowly rise, perhaps to about 12 percent by 1985. The black population would then be about 30 million, as compared with 23 million in 1970. By extrapolation of recent trends in the distribution and composition of population, guesses can be made about what changes to expect in where blacks will be living and what their characteristics will be.

Changes in population distribution during past decades have already moved us beyond the position where problems of race relations can be regarded as regional, and the future will see a further spread of black population throughout the nation. The black population increase will probably accrue mainly to cities. Although regional patterns of migration are changing, it may happen that by 1985 a majority of the nation's black population will be living in northern cities. Blacks may then comprise a majority or near-majority of the population in a dozen large cities. There is no basis in the past to project any rapid change in the concentration of most metropolitan blacks in segregated areas of central cities. The southern rural black population should continue to decrease in size, despite its high fertility. Out-migrants from this population may be numerous, but they will be a diminishing share of all black migrants.

As we have seen, large-scale migrations produce unusual age distributions in both the place of origin and that of destination. Age distributions are further distorted by fluctuations in fertility rates. For example, many of the blacks who moved to cities in the early 1940s were young adults in the childbearing ages. There would have been sharp increases in the number of black children in these cities even without the aforementioned postwar "baby boom." Barring major catastrophes, it is obvious that if many more babies were born from 1955 to 1960 than from 1940 to 1945, many more children will have reached age 18 from 1973 to 1978 than from 1958 to 1963. In many cities, problems such as those of school dropouts and the provision of jobs for new entrants to the labor force are rapidly becoming more difficult, in large part because the number of people in the relevant ages is growing.

Anticipating changes in the age distribution of a population is relatively easy. Anticipating changes in socioeconomic characteristics is more difficult. Educational advancement seems fairly certain to continue at a rapid pace, with high school graduation becoming increasingly common and college graduation more frequent. Just how rapidly improvements in educational background can be translated into rising occupational and income levels depends on the business cycle, actions of the Federal Government, and other unpredictable factors.

Social change is continuous, and with change comes a diminution in the importance of old social problems and a rise in the importance of new ones. For example, although the problems of the illiterate sharecropper newly arrived in a northern industrial city are perhaps more acute than ever, the number of such migrants is small and diminishing. In contrast, continued growth of urban black populations if combined with maintenance of a high degree of residential segregation can only aggravate the many problems already attributable to racial segregation. How effectively these problems will be dealt with we cannot predict. They can certainly be better met if the social transformations of the past sixty years are recognized and if we update our perspectives and policies to take account of continuing rapid change.

## BIBLIOGRAPHY

Davie, Maurice R., *Negroes in American Society*. New York, McGraw-Hill Book Co., 1949.

Farley, Reynolds, *Growth of the Black Population. A Study of Demographic Trends*. Chicago, Markham, 1970.

———, "The Changing Distribution of Negroes within Metropolitan Areas: The Emergence of Black Suburbs." *American Journal of Sociology*, 75, No. 4 (January 1970), 512–529.

Frazier, E. Franklin, *The Negro in the United States*, rev. ed. New York, The Macmillan Co., 1957.

Hamilton, C. Horace, "The Negro Leaves the South." *Demography*, 1 (1964), 273–295.

Hare, Nathan, "Recent Trends in the Occupational Mobility of Negroes, 1930–1960: An Intracohort Analysis." *Social Forces*, 44, No. 2 (December 1965), 166–173.

*Journal of Negro Education*, XXXII, No. 4 (Fall, 1963).

Kiser, Clyde V., "Fertility Trends and Differentials Among Nonwhites in the United States." *The Milbank Memorial Fund Quarterly*, XXXVI, No. 2 (April 1958), 149–97.

Kiser, Clyde V., Wilson H. Grabill, and Arthur A. Campbell, *Trends and Variations in Fertility in the United States* (a Vital and Health Statistics Monograph). Cambridge, Harvard University Press, 1968.

Price, Daniel O., *Changing Characteristics of the Negro Population*, (a Census Monograph). Washington, U. S. Government Printing Office, 1969.

Taeuber, Irene B., "Change and Transition in the Black Population of the United States." *Population Index* 34, No. 2 (April–June 1968), 121–151.

Taeuber, Irene B., and Conrad Taeuber, *People of the United States in the 20th Century* (a Census Monograph). Washington, U. S. Government Printing Office, 1971.

Taeuber, Karl E., and Alma F. Taeuber, *Negroes in Cities: Residential Segregation and Neighborhood Change*. Chicago, Aldine, 1965.

U. S. Bureau of the Census, *Negro Population 1790–1915*. Washington, U. S. Government Printing Office, 1918.

———, *Negroes in the United States 1920–32*. Washington, U. S. Government Printing Office, 1935.

———, *Historical Statistics of the United States, Colonial Times to 1957*. Washington, U. S. Government Printing Office, 1960.

———, *The Social and Economic Status of Negroes in the United States, 1970* (Current Population Reports, Series P-23, No. 38). Washington, U. S. Government Printing Office, 1971.

———, *The Social and Economic Status of the Black Population in the United States, 1971* (Current Population Reports, Series P-23, No. 42). Washington, U. S. Government Printing Office, 1972.

U. S. Department of Labor, "A Century of Change: Negroes in the U. S. Economy, 1860–1960." *Monthly Labor Review* (December 1962), 1359–65.

# 5

## The Black Role
## in the Economy

### Mabel M. Smythe

Throughout America's history the black man has played an essentially passive role in the economy. His labor made possible the cotton economy of the South, but his voice was not heard in its councils. The neighborhoods he has inhabited have not traditionally made economic policy, even for themselves. Much of the current movement toward black self-determination reflects an awareness of the subtle or open exclusion practiced in the past.

In few aspects of American life is failure more conspicuous than in the preparation of blacks ostensibly for full participation in the economy. As workers, as consumers, as investors, as managers, as entrepreneurs, black citizens have been educated to perform typically up to only a part of their potential. The difficulties they encounter cannot be blamed altogether on education, but stem as well from society's uncertainty as to its commitment to having black Americans work or manage aggregations of capital or prosper in the same circumstances which bring affluence to whites. Society has developed a network of socioeconomic pressures which make it impossible for the above economic roles to be fully realized. As we shall see, blacks historically have been programmed *not* to thrive in the American economy.

### The 1900s: A Survey

A brief look at some of the significant historical trends of the twentieth century is helpful in understanding the economic role and potential of the black American today.

As the black population left the farms and small towns at the turn of the century, the future for these newcomers to the cities was bleak. Not only did they lack the capital, skills, and education to compete successfully in the job market, but the rapid replacement of unskilled labor by mechanization offered them little prospect of better times to come. Still, jobs in town appeared to be the only possibility for the displaced farm workers, despite a policy of exclusion of blacks by many unions, and in World Wars I and II burgeoning employment in war plants caused significant migrations to key areas from other cities as well as from the farms and small towns.

Migration was further encouraged by visitors returning home from the cities; these were likely to be persons who had done comparatively well. Often they were part of the slowly growing black middle class of professional, skilled, and (to a smaller degree) businessmen and women who sent their children to high school, encouraged them to get a college education, and saw the need for expanding the economic horizons of the Afro-American community. Members of the rising black bourgeoisie were able to tell their rural or semirural friends about elite professionals or business leaders who had prospered as employees or owners of black newspapers, insurance companies, and mortuaries. They could describe homes with pianos and elegant furnishings, even though the average black consumer was plagued by higher prices, poor access to credit, and limitations on his or her use of places of public accommodation, particularly before the 1950s.[1] In later years they could even speak of a handful of black millionaires.

At the other extreme, of course, there was urban poverty as cruel as any in the rural districts; but since in cities, in the South as well as the North, black Americans typically lived in black enclaves, they were protected from some of the more immediately humiliating forms of racism and could maintain an illusion of well-being in a white world.

So the migration to the cities continued, fueled primarily by the promise of available jobs and by the growing desperation of the rural poor, caught between a declining demand for their services and the prospect of no place to work or even to live, since sharecropping and tenant farming involved housing as well as employment. However, not all the movement to the cities and to the North was inspired by desperate poverty or the decline of farming. As mentioned above, World War I, which coincided with the boll weevil farm recession (see Chapter 7), stimulated a sudden and massive increase in industrial production, and it became clear that staffing the plants would require the use of black as well as white manpower. Old restrictions on hiring gave way to new patterns of recruitment, and black workers were lured to the centers of production, sometimes in larger numbers than were actually required.

Some of the younger blacks followed broader employment or educational opportunities, settling where semiskilled, skilled, white-collar, or professional employment was most promising. Their new neighborhoods increasingly contained neat or even, for a few, relatively luxurious homes; and the black child of a generation ago could hope for a better life than his parents if he planned carefully and worked hard.

Such hopes fared poorly in the depression of the 1930s. The traditional "black" jobs, such as bellhop, waiter, and elevator operator, became "white" in some establishments, under the pressure of widespread unemployment. It did not cheer the black worker to discover that poor whites shared his sense of helplessness, since he constantly encountered special handicaps which put him at a disadvantage in the competition with whites, and since experience had taught him that they would have priority whenever and wherever opportunities developed. Racism was everywhere; even in the predominantly black neighborhoods, stores selling chiefly to its residents refused to hire them, companies supplying such establishments employed only white salespersons, and lily-white unions fought to monopolize jobs and to organize the unorganized—so long as they were not black.

In 1935, the Committee for Industrial Organization, later to become the Congress of Industrial Organizations, undertook to form industrial unions of workers, regardless of race, and the traditional black attitude of distrust of unions began to change. A new black union for baggage porters (redcaps), the United Transport Service Employees of America, joined the older Brotherhood of Sleeping Car Porters in protecting black workers who were still excluded from the white railroad brotherhoods.[2]

Black leaders, concerned and frustrated, confronted economic problems with a strategy which can be documented as far back as 1879 and which emphasized patronizing black-owned business, thus building independence and black pride at the same time (the doctrine of the "double-duty dollar"). During the 1930s a corollary to this doctrine was added: "Don't buy where you can't work," thus suggesting a triple-duty dollar which at one and the same time bought goods, supported employment, and developed a sense of independence and black pride. Similar campaigns, which today include programs like People United to Save Humanity (PUSH), have confronted racism directly; however, they have never been sufficiently comprehensive for their success to assure economic equality.[3]

Throughout American history the obstacles to black business success, even given the loyal and united support of the black community, have been immense. Before the 1960s capital was all but impossible to obtain; and since the black would-be borrower could not offer collateral or a record of responsible stewardship in business, he could not qualify for loans even if his color had not already automatically disqualified him in the eyes of most banks and conventional lenders. Opportunities for gaining experience in management before going into business were generally restricted to the segregated service industries (barber and beauty shops, laundries, mortuaries), "hustling" (such ghetto-related operations as selling stolen property, bootlegging, operating numbers games, or the only slightly more respectable selling of dream books), or developing religious or other organizations. There were some black newspapers and magazines, black insurance companies, a few black banks and savings and loan associations, and (by the latter 1940s) even one or two black-owned radio stations; but the general view was one of extremely narrow choice.[4]

At the time of World War II there had already been considerable industrial experience among black workers, and the clear need for manpower in industries with war contracts softened old scruples about employing blacks. The call for patriotic sacrifice explicitly urged giving up race and sex prejudices in hiring. Changing old ways was difficult, however.[5] Workers were by then no longer being drawn mainly from the farms; many were already in urban areas, living on the margin of employment, where jobs were unstable and income minimal.

Wartime employment not only opened up new opportunities and geographically reshaped black population patterns; its emergency nature forced operational flexibility and innovations in employee training. Traditional selection and apprenticeship either did not suit new kinds of skills or were too restrictive and prolonged. Customary trades were, in some instances, divided into component skills which could be shared among several workers, each of whom could master his portion more quickly than he could the whole.[6] These solutions to wartime needs provided fresh approaches to manpower development which have broad applicability today.

Since the 1950s, the development of the American economy, coupled with the continuance of racial discrimination in subtle new forms, has posed fresh threats to the black citizen, even as unprecedented prosperity and the end of legal supports for racism have provided new areas of hope. The movement of white population, followed by industry, from central cities to the suburbs has made many potential jobs geographically inaccessible to black workers. Their poverty makes it difficult for them to live in or get to these outlying areas, even if there were more willingness to sell or rent homes to blacks, or to finance their purchases of real estate.[7] Moreover, new technology increasingly has made obsolete unskilled and semiskilled jobs, thus worsening the prospects of adjustment for black workers, who have been concentrated in these categories. At the same time, the tight union control of skilled jobs in such crafts as the building trades and on the railroads long effectively excluded blacks.[8] It remains for the 1970s to demonstrate that the will to democratize unions can be backed up by the power to do so.

Nevertheless, in the irregular advance of prosperity in the 1950s and the 1960s, blacks were carried along with the tide. In the flush of economic expansion, many whites ceased viewing black advancement as threatening to their own security; there were jobs for all—all, that is, except the undereducated, unskilled, poorest blacks. This group remained outside the great economic surge in a backwater of their own, not comprehending why they could achieve no foothold in the economy. The welfare program, which had been viewed originally as an emergency arrangement, now had the status of a permanent niche for the unwanted, the nonparticipants; and society insisted upon viewing these unfortunates as if they were the designers of their own misery, who by a mere act of will could become self-supporting, "contributing" members of society.

Those in a position to benefit from this period of increasing prosperity and liberalism were the better educated, the skilled, those whose background and outlook had prepared them to take advantage of new opportunities—in short, the middle class. They seized the chance to benefit from gradually opening new jobs, bought better homes, occasionally invested in sometimes promising new ventures, persuaded greater numbers of banks to lend them money, and became increasingly consequential as consumers. Their children went to college—often on scholarships to Ivy League colleges and Big Ten universities; NAACP lawyers won them state-supported educational opportunities, equal teacher's salaries, and the right to use hotels and restaurants. Few of these rights and opportunities, however, meant much to the poorly educated recent migrant to the city, unable to work except as a laborer, unprepared for higher education, lacking the means to use dining cars or hotels, unqualified for training as a manager or computer programmer.

Thus the vista of expanding economic opportunity, so clear to the rising middle class, was obscured from the eyes of the poor—and the poor constituted roughly half the black population at the end of the 1950s.[9]

Black poverty, reinforced by racial isolation, insured the continued subjugation of this least advantaged group. The tendency in American cities toward growing class isolation reinforced the situation in which the poor and "unsuccessful" typically associate only with each another, thus providing few alternatives to models of economic failure for the young. Until recently, comprehensive housing as a concept was virtually unknown, nor had the general public even in the mid-70s become aware of its possibilities. Those who climbed to a higher socioeconomic status were expected to move to middle-class neighborhoods; indeed, in government-subsidized housing, those whose incomes exceeded a predetermined level were generally required to relinquish their rented quarters.[10]

Exploitation of the black poor is widespread. Their housing is expensive. Their helplessness, lack of information, and restriction of choice to "black" neighborhoods have given landlords quasi-monopoly power in establishing rentals. Even when they have had money, the poor have been forced to pay more than others for food—slum stores typically charge more for inferior goods—and without home freezers or other storage arrangements secure against vermin and spoilage, the poor would be unable to take full advantage of sales or bulk prices even if they had the money or credit to do so.[11] On the farms, the extreme shortage of cash and the system of landlord-owned living quarters and food stores for years insured that most farm tenants would remain in debt, and lack of credit still handicaps the declining number of farmers in this category. Owners of small farms, also unable to obtain adequate credit, have typically lived close to the poverty level. Both in cities and in rural areas, black consumers have been poorly informed concerning alternate sources of supply; many have no idea where they might buy goods at a discount.[12]

Increased housing opportunities for the black poor in the suburbs have been negligible; here again, fortune has favored those with money and education over the neediest.

Although federal mortgage-guarantee programs have encouraged the growth of the suburbs, new communities have typically erected such barriers to low-income housing as zoning for lots of an acre or more, building codes which preclude certain cost-saving innovations, and prohibitions against multifamily dwellings.

As growth of population in the central city has been accelerated by rising mobility and the resulting in-migration, a new generation of black urban dwellers has grown up without a solution to the basic problem of finding a place in the economy. The economy has not only failed to include this group in its manpower needs; those needs are constantly revised to eliminate more workers in the unskilled and low-skilled categories. There are now second- and third-generation welfare recipients whose prospects of fitting into the economy depend upon sporadic and underfinanced job-training programs and similar piecemeal efforts which leave the burden of adjustment primarily on the disadvantaged individual.

Black poverty diminished noticeably in the 1960s; while nearly half the black population (47 percent) fell in that official category in 1960, only 31.9 percent were so classified in 1973.[13] Nevertheless, over a quarter of the black population continues to live in grinding misery, although we have demonstrated our ability to reduce their numbers. For those who remain in that group, the dramatic progress of the past offers little encouragement when they see no change in their own circumstances.

The frustration of the hard-core poor can be expected to mount even further as the high expectations of the 1960s are forgotten in the less prosperous and more conservative seventies, and as those at the bottom of the socioeconomic scale see the momentum of economic development slowing to a halt just before it reaches them.

## Income

Table I, which compares all nonwhite, black, and white median family incomes over a period of 24 years, shows a steady trend toward higher incomes for all three groups, along with a gradually increasing ratio of black and other nonwhite income to white. That ratio has slipped back in the 1970s, as economic prosperity and political liberalism have slowed down. Equally disturbing is the irony that while the black/nonwhite incomes tend to gain proportionately on their white counterparts, the gap between the two in absolute dollars has widened as all incomes have risen. In 1950 the median nonwhite income of $1,869 was 54 percent of the corresponding white figure of $3,445; the absolute difference between them was $1,576. In 1973 the black median of $7,269 was 60 percent of the white median of $12,595; the absolute difference between them was $5,326.

Obviously, black incomes must continue to grow at a faster rate than white incomes if they are to overtake the latter; however, that rate must be accelerated significantly if the gap in absolute dollars is not to increase in the meantime under conditions of even moderate inflation; and a still greater growth in black incomes will be required to wipe out the differential in absolute dollars and reach the goal of equality within a decade or even a quarter of a century.

One of the difficulties with breaking the poverty cycle is that there are so many determinants of incomes: amount and quality of education, race discrimination, quality of health, geographic location, access to capital and credit, access to the labor market, availability of information regarding employment and business opportunities, and the like. The attempts in the 1960s to fight poverty and bring about greater equality of income between black and white emphasized increased access to education (in both amount and quality) and job training. There were efforts to end discrimination in labor unions and to provide access to business capital and credit; but some powerful unions are still far from providing equality by any reasonable definition, and full participation by black citizens in business management and ownership may be even further from realization.[14]

TABLE I—MEDIAN INCOME OF FAMILIES: 1950–1973

(In current dollars)

| Year | Race of head | | | Ratio: Nonwhite to white | Ratio: Black to white | Black-white Dollar gap |
|------|----------|-------|-------|------|------|------|
| | Nonwhite | Black | White | | | |
| 1950........ | $1,869 | (NA) | $3,445 | 0.54 | (NA) | $1576 |
| 1951........ | 2,032 | (NA) | 3,859 | 0.53 | (NA) | 1827 |
| 1952........ | 2,338 | (NA) | 4,114 | 0.57 | (NA) | 1776 |
| 1953........ | 2,461 | (NA) | 4,392 | 0.56 | (NA) | 1931 |
| 1954........ | 2,410 | (NA) | 4,339 | 0.56 | (NA) | 1929 |
| 1955........ | 2,549 | (NA) | 4,605 | 0.55 | (NA) | 2056 |
| 1956........ | 2,628 | (NA) | 4,993 | 0.53 | (NA) | 2365 |
| 1957........ | 2,764 | (NA) | 5,166 | 0.54 | (NA) | 2402 |
| 1958........ | 2,711 | (NA) | 5,300 | 0.51 | (NA) | 2589 |
| 1959........ | 3,161 | $3,047 | 5,893 | 0.54 | 0.52 | 2846 |
| 1960........ | 3,233 | (NA) | 5,835 | 0.55 | (NA) | 2602 |
| 1961........ | 3,191 | (NA) | 5,981 | 0.53 | (NA) | 2790 |
| 1962........ | 3,330 | (NA) | 6,237 | 0.53 | (NA) | 2907 |
| 1963........ | 3,465 | (NA) | 6,548 | 0.53 | (NA) | 3083 |
| 1964........ | 3,839 | 3,724 | 6,858 | 0.56 | 0.54 | 3134 |
| 1965........ | 3,994 | 3,886 | 7,251 | 0.55 | 0.54 | 3365 |
| 1966........ | 4,674 | 4,507 | 7,792 | 0.60 | 0.58 | 3285 |
| 1967[1] ...... | 5,094 | 4,875 | 8,234 | 0.62 | 0.59 | 3359 |
| 1968........ | 5,590 | 5,360 | 8,937 | 0.63 | 0.60 | 3577 |
| 1969........ | 6,191 | 5,999 | 9,794 | 0.63 | 0.61 | 3885 |
| 1970........ | 6,516 | 6,279 | 10,236 | 0.64 | 0.61 | 3957 |
| 1971* ...... | 6,714 | 6,440 | 10,672 | 0.63 | 0.60 | 4232 |
| 1972* ...... | 7,106 | 6,864 | 11,549 | 0.62 | 0.59 | 4685 |
| 1973* ...... | 7,596 | 7,269 | 12,595 | 0.60 | 0.58 | 5326 |

(NA) Not available. The ratio of black to white median family income first became available from this survey in 1964.

Dollar gap computed by subtracting median black (nonwhite in years when black was not available) from median white income.

*Based on 1970 census population controls; therefore, not strictly comparable to data for earlier years.

Source:   U. S. Department of Commerce, Social and Economic Statistics Administration, Bureau of the Census. Current Population Reports, Special Studies Series P-23, No. 48, p. 17.

Table II shows clearly the relationship between education and income: more than a quarter of black families whose heads had completed less than 8 years of education had access to less than $3,000 of annual income, while close to half (46 percent) of the black families whose heads had 4 or more years of college enjoyed incomes of $15,000 or more.

It should be noted also that the effect of education falls short of assuring comparable incomes for blacks, since white family heads with less than 4 years of high school education receive $10,000 or more in 53.8 percent of the cases, whereas blacks with 1 to 3 years of college education have this much family income in only 52.3 percent of the families. Black family heads with 4 or more years of college receive $10,000 or more in 71.8 percent of the families; whites with this high level of education receive $10,000 or more 85.3 percent of the time.

Since black families are less likely to send their sons and daughters to college, the influence of education on income suggests that until educational parity is achieved the differential between black and white will tend to widen rather than to narrow. When undereducated young people establish their own families, their incomes, like those of their parents, can be expected to be low; their children in turn will be under pressure to go to work to help support the family instead of finding the path to higher education easy and natural.

It should also be noted that the irregularity of employment experienced by many blacks, especially men, takes a heavy toll in income: layoffs or periods between jobs, greater difficulty in finding work, lower seniority in higher-level positions, and the reversal of equal opportunity and affirmative action in times of recession, when the last hired are first fired. These as well as limited education and experience tend to multiply the disadvantages faced by black workers.

Judging by the past, the relatively rapid increase in secondary and higher education in the last decade should result in higher black incomes as median education rises and the group with less than a high school education shrinks.

Although black income as a percentage of white has gradually increased, parity is not yet in sight. A black college graduate in 1972 still earned less, at the median, than a white high school graduate, and at all educational levels, blacks earned less than whites.

Nowhere is the imbalance between black and white family income reflected more dramatically than in the gap in opportunities which qualify children as future earners; thus poverty tends to be self-perpetuating unless the opportunities and stimulation normally provided by more fortunate families can somehow be made available to the poor.

As can be seen from Table III, 72 percent of 1971's black college students came from families with incomes under $10,000, a circumstance which offers considerable hope for further improvement in the economic viability of the next generation of adults, in view of the correlation between education and income. The relatively small percentage of black students from higher-income families can be assumed to reflect in part the much smaller number of black families in the upper categories.

**TABLE II—MONEY INCOME: FAMILIES WITH HEADS 25 YEARS OLD AND OVER, BY INCOME LEVEL, BY RACE OF HEAD AND YEARS OF SCHOOL COMPLETED: 1972**

| Race of Head and Years of School Completed | Number of families (1,000) | Percent Distribution by Income Level | | | | | | Median income |
|---|---|---|---|---|---|---|---|---|
| | | Under $3,000 | $3,000– $4,999 | $5,000– $6,999 | $7,000– $9,999 | $10,000– $14,999 | $15,000 and over | |
| White families ........ | 44,880 | 5.4 | 8.1 | 9.1 | 15.9 | 27.4 | 34.1 | 11,943 |
| Elementary school, less than 8 years ...... | 4,926 | 15.8 | 20.8 | 15.7 | 18.1 | 17.5 | 12.1 | 6,689 |
| 8 years.............. | 5,183 | 8.6 | 15.5 | 15.9 | 18.9 | 23.4 | 17.8 | 8,595 |
| High school, 1-3 years ...... | 6,967 | 6.1 | 9.8 | 10.8 | 19.4 | 29.1 | 24.7 | 10,587 |
| 4 years............. | 15,272 | 3.5 | 5.1 | 7.7 | 17.2 | 32.7 | 33.8 | 12,426 |
| College, 1-3 years ...... | 5,435 | 2.7 | 3.8 | 6.4 | 13.2 | 30.1 | 43.9 | 13,987 |
| 4 years or more...... | 7,099 | 1.7 | 1.9 | 2.8 | 8.2 | 21.8 | 63.5 | 18,479 |
| Negro and other families ...... | 5,297 | 16.4 | 17.0 | 14.3 | 17.3 | 18.5 | 16.6 | 7,352 |
| Elementary school, less than 8 years ...... | 1,285 | 25.8 | 24.8 | 14.8 | 14.6 | 11.9 | 8.3 | 4,958 |
| 8 years............. | 546 | 18.2 | 17.5 | 19.1 | 18.7 | 15.3 | 11.2 | 6,419 |
| High school, 1-3 years ...... | 1,248 | 17.4 | 20.4 | 15.3 | 18.6 | 16.8 | 11.6 | 6,612 |
| 4 years............. | 1,372 | 11.5 | 12.8 | 13.1 | 20.3 | 22.5 | 19.7 | 8,893 |
| College, 1-3 years ...... | 420 | 10.2 | 9.2 | 15.1 | 13.5 | 27.6 | 24.7 | 10,379 |
| 4 years or more...... | 425 | 3.4 | 4.0 | 6.6 | 14.3 | 25.8 | 46.0 | 14,158 |

Source: U. S. Bureau of the Census, *Current Population Reports*, series P-60 No. 90.

TABLE III—FAMILY MEMBERS 18 TO 24 YEARS OLD, BY COLLEGE ENROLLMENT
STATUS AND FAMILY INCOME: 1971

| Enrollment status and race[1] | Total[2] (thousands) | Percent of total | | | | |
|---|---|---|---|---|---|---|
| | | Under $3,000 | $3,000 to $9,999 | $10,000 and over | | |
| | | | | Total | $10,000 to $14,999 | $15,000 |
| **BLACK** | | | | | | |
| Enrolled in college .......... | 408 | 12 | 60 | 27 | 16 | 11 |
| Not enrolled in college ...... | 1,102 | 25 | 59 | 16 | 11 | 6 |
| High-school graduate ...... | 635 | 21 | 60 | 19 | 12 | 7 |
| Not high-school graduate .. | 467 | 31 | 57 | 12 | 8 | 4 |
| **WHITE** | | | | | | |
| Enrolled in college .......... | 3,889 | 2 | 27 | 71 | 31 | 41 |
| Not enrolled in college ...... | 5,053 | 7 | 43 | 49 | 29 | 20 |
| High-school graduate ...... | 3,970 | 5 | 39 | 56 | 32 | 24 |
| Not high-school graduate .. | 1,082 | 18 | 58 | 24 | 17 | 7 |

[1]Excludes family heads and wives and other family members who are married, spouse present.
[2]Based on persons reporting on family income.

Source: U. S. Department of Commerce, Social and Economic Statistics Administration, Bureau of the Census, Series P-23, No. 42, p. 87.

TABLE IV—COLLEGE ENROLLMENT IN FAMILIES WITH MEMBERS 18 TO 24 YEARS
OLD, BY RACE AND FAMILY INCOME: 1971
(Numbers in thousands)

| Family income | Black | | | White | | |
|---|---|---|---|---|---|---|
| | Total | One or more members attending college full time | Percent of total | Total | One or more members attending college full time | Percent of total |
| Total[1] .............. | 1,260 | 288 | 23 | 8,272 | 3,341 | 40 |
| Under $3,000 .......... | 298 | 33 | 11 | 429 | 68 | 16 |
| $3,000 to $4,999 ...... | 299 | 61 | 20 | 623 | 134 | 22 |
| $5,000 to $7,499 ...... | 250 | 64 | 26 | 1,036 | 306 | 30 |
| $7,500 to $9,999 ...... | 141 | 43 | 30 | 1,288 | 427 | 33 |
| $10,000 and over ...... | 193 | 69 | 36 | 4,279 | 2,167 | 51 |
| $10,000 to $14,999 .. | 124 | 42 | 34 | 2,236 | 953 | 43 |
| $15,000 and over .... | 69 | 27 | 39 | 2,043 | 1,214 | 59 |

Note: Families with members 18 to 24 years old. Excludes families whose only members 18 to 24 years old are the head, wife, or other members who are married, spouse present.
[1]Includes income not reported, not shown separately.

Source: U. S. Department of Commerce, Social and Economic Statistics Administration, Bureau of the Census, Series P-23, No 42, p. 86.

As Table IV shows, at every income level a smaller percentage of black families sent their members to college. Even where family income was $15,000 or over, 39 percent of black families, as compared with 59 percent of white ones, had members enrolled in colleges.

Table V shows the extent to which black incomes tend toward the lower half of the distribution: black families are much more heavily concentrated below the $5,000 mark than are whites; they are more than three times as likely as whites to have incomes below $3,000, and more than twice as likely to fall below the $5,000 mark. At the top level, black families have only one-sixth as much chance as white ones of attaining incomes of $50,000 or above, less than half as much chance of having incomes in excess of $15,000. Nearly half (48 percent) had incomes below $7,000 in 1973.

**TABLE V—DISTRIBUTION OF FAMILIES BY INCOME IN 1965, 1969, AND 1973**
(Adjusted for price changes in 1973 dollars. Families as of the following year)

| Income | Negro | | | White | | |
|---|---|---|---|---|---|---|
| | 1965 | 1969 | 1973 | 1965 | 1969 | 1973 |
| Number of families..thousands.. | 4,424 | 4,774 | 5,440 | 43,500 | 46,023 | 48,919 |
| Percent ................... | 100 | 100 | 100 | 100 | 100 | 100 |
| Under $3,000 ............... | 24 | 16 | 16 | 8 | 6 | 5 |
| $3,000 to $4,999 ............. | 22 | 16 | 18 | 9 | 8 | 8 |
| $5,000 to $6,999 ............. | 17 | 15 | 14 | 10 | 9 | 9 |
| $7,000 to $9,999 ............. | 18 | 20 | 17 | 20 | 17 | 15 |
| $10,000 to $11,999 ......... | 8 | 10 | 9 | 14 | 12 | 11 |
| $12,000 to $14,999 ......... | 6 | 10 | 10 | 15 | 17 | 15 |
| $15,000 and over ............. | 6 | 13 | 16 | 23 | 33 | 38 |
| Median income ............... | $5,510 | $7,280 | $7,269 | $10,210 | $11,869 | $12,595 |
| Net change over preceding date: | | | | | | |
| Amount ................... | (X) | $1,770 | $−11 | (X) | $1,659 | $726 |
| Percent ................... | (X) | 32.1 | −0.2 | (X) | 16.2 | 6.1 |

(X) Not applicable.

Source: U. S. Department of Commerce, Social and Economic Statistics Administration, Bureau of the Census. Special Studies Series P-23, No. 48, p. 19.

Yet it should be noted that while in 1965 24 percent of black families had incomes under $3,000, in 1973 only 16 percent were in this group; similarly, in 1965 only 6 percent had incomes of $15,000 or over, but in 1973 16 percent fell in this category. In 1973 more than a third of all black families (35 percent) had incomes of $10,000 or more, as compared with only 18 percent eight years earlier.

In 1972, the last year for which data were available before publication, 2.1 percent of black families, as compared to 8.0 percent of white families, had incomes of $25,000

**TABLE VI**—MONEY INCOME OF FAMILIES—RACE AND REGION BY INCOME LEVEL: 1972

(As of March 1973. Based on Current Population Survey.)

| Race and Region | Total (1,000) | Percent Distribution, by Income Level | | | | | | | | | | Median Income |
|---|---|---|---|---|---|---|---|---|---|---|---|---|
| | | Under $1,000 | $1,000–$1,999 | $2,000–$2,999 | $3,000–$3,999 | $4,000–$4,999 | $5,000–$6,999 | $7,000–$9,999 | $10,000–$14,999 | $15,000–$24,999 | $25,000 and Over | |
| All families[2] | 54,373 | 1.3 | 2.2 | 3.7 | 4.5 | 4.9 | 10.2 | 16.8 | 26.1 | 23.0 | 7.3 | $11,116 |
| White ........... | 48,477 | 1.1 | 1.7 | 3.1 | 4.1 | 4.5 | 9.7 | 16.7 | 27.0 | 24.2 | 8.0 | 11,549 |
| Northeast ...... | 11,599 | 0.7 | 0.8 | 2.8 | 3.7 | 3.8 | 8.5 | 16.3 | 27.6 | 26.6 | 9.2 | 12,307 |
| North Central .. | 13,708 | 0.9 | 1.5 | 2.6 | 3.6 | 4.1 | 9.0 | 16.2 | 28.6 | 26.1 | 7.4 | 11,947 |
| South .......... | 14,508 | 1.4 | 2.8 | 3.9 | 4.9 | 4.9 | 11.6 | 18.1 | 25.8 | 19.8 | 7.1 | 10,465 |
| West .......... | 8,661 | 1.4 | 1.3 | 3.2 | 3.9 | 5.2 | 9.7 | 15.7 | 26.2 | 25.2 | 8.3 | 11,724 |
| Black .......... | 5,265 | 2.8 | 6.7 | 9.3 | 9.4 | 8.7 | 14.1 | 17.4 | 17.5 | 12.2 | 2.1 | 6,864 |
| Northeast ...... | 1,007 | 1.5 | 4.1 | 7.2 | 9.6 | 8.1 | 14.1 | 17.5 | 21.7 | 13.9 | 2.3 | 7,816 |
| North Central .. | 1,077 | 2.4 | 4.2 | 8.1 | 8.2 | 7.0 | 12.3 | 16.4 | 22.8 | 16.4 | 2.4 | 8,318 |
| South .......... | 2,676 | 3.6 | 9.2 | 10.6 | 10.4 | 9.9 | 14.6 | 18.0 | 12.9 | 9.1 | 1.8 | 5,763 |
| West .......... | 505 | 2.3 | 3.8 | 8.5 | 5.8 | 7.4 | 15.6 | 15.7 | 21.7 | 16.4 | 2.7 | 8,313 |

[2]Includes races not shown separately.

Source: U. S. Department of Commerce, Bureau of the Census *Statistical Abstract of the United States, 1974, p. 385.*

or more (see Table VI). Thus a white family was nearly four times as likely as a black one to achieve this level of prosperity. Black families in the West had a better chance (2.7 percent) to be in this category; those in the South were least likely (1.8 percent) to do so.

Much of the increase in black incomes has been made possible by improvement in the earnings of wives (see Table VII), a larger proportion of whom in middle-income black families work, as compared to those in similar white families. Continued gains in black family incomes will require significant growth in the earnings of black men as well, if income equality is to be achieved.

**TABLE VII**—MEDIAN INCOME IN 1969 AND 1972 OF HUSBAND-WIFE FAMILIES BY AGE OF HEAD, EARNING STATUS OF HUSBAND AND WIFE, AND REGION

| Race and earning status of husband and wife | Total | | | Head under 35 years old | | |
|---|---|---|---|---|---|---|
| | United States | North and West | South | United States | North and West | South |
| *1969* | | | | | | |
| Black, total[1] .................... | $7,329 | $9,142 | $5,944 | $7,488 | $8,859 | $6,286 |
| Husband only earner ............. | 5,574 | 6,681 | 4,341 | 5,792 | 6,500 | 5,059 |
| Husband and wife both earners .... | 8,954 | 11,064 | 6,998 | 8,423 | 10,130 | 6,670 |
| White, total[1] ................. | 10,217 | 10,598 | 9,192 | 9,384 | 9,703 | 8,649 |
| Husband only earner ............. | 8,992 | 9,402 | 8,108 | 8,805 | 9,137 | 7,927 |
| Husband and wife both earners .... | 11,711 | 12,139 | 10,681 | 9,926 | 10,267 | 9,227 |
| Black as a percent of white | | | | | | |
| Total[1] ...................... | 72 | 86 | 65 | 80 | 91 | 73 |
| Husband only earner ............. | 62 | 71 | 54 | 66 | 71 | 64 |
| Husband and wife both earners .... | 77 | 91 | 66 | 85 | 99 | 72 |
| *1972* | | | | | | |
| Black, total[1] ................. | $9,165 | $10,870 | $7,547 | $9,420 | $10,573 | $8,679 |
| Husband only earner ............. | 6,949 | 7,954 | 5,401 | 6,984 | 7,563 | 6,375 |
| Husband and wife both earners .... | 11,566 | 13,716 | 9,513 | 10,611 | 12,300 | 9,420 |
| White, total[1] ................. | 12,121 | 12,578 | 10,929 | 11,042 | 11,414 | 10,333 |
| Husband only earner ............. | 10,750 | 11,155 | 9,661 | 10,175 | 10,630 | 9,055 |
| Husband and wife both earners .... | 14,095 | 14,660 | 12,895 | 11,834 | 12,170 | 11,228 |
| Black as a percent of white | | | | | | |
| Total[1] ...................... | 76 | 86 | 69 | 85 | 93 | 84 |
| Husband only earner ............. | 65 | 71 | 56 | 69 | 71 | 70 |
| Husband and wife both earners .... | 82 | 94 | 74 | 90 | 101 | 84 |

[1]Includes other combinations not shown separately.

Source: U. S. Department of Commerce, Social and Economic Statistics Administration, Bureau of the Census. Special Studies Series, P-23, No. 48, p. 25.

As can be seen from Table VII, the incomes of black husband-wife families compare more favorably with similar white families than do undifferentiated black families as a whole. As we saw above, median black family income in 1973 was only 58 percent of median white family income; in 1972 the corresponding figure was 59 percent. In husband-wife families, black median income was 76 percent of that of whites and 82 percent where both husband and wife worked. Even more striking, such families with a head less than 35 years old garnered 85 percent as much income as similar white families. Young families in which both husband and wife worked had 90 percent of the income of whites, and in the North and West 101 percent in 1972.

Because economic statistics so consistently confirm the inequality of blacks, much has been made of the finding that this one black income sub-group—young husband-wife families in the North and West—has had for several years a median income which exceeds slightly the corresponding white figure. However, where only the husband worked, black income for the same geographic and age group was $7,563, as compared to $10,630, only 71 percent of white income.[15] In considering the above figures it must also be taken into account that the income advantage cited is apparently within the limits of the standard error for the material and might reflect ordinary statistical inaccuracy. It is also possible that a significantly greater number of young white husbands and wives are in colleges and universities and that their earnings come from student employment, thus temporarily minimizing white income in that group, but preparing them for an advantage later on. The most persuasive possibility, however, is that blacks in the North and West are significantly more likely than whites to live in metropolitan areas where money incomes are higher. Black wives are also more likely to work full time than their white counterparts. If the figures compared white and black city dwellers not now in colleges and universities, then one could expect a substantially different result.

It is also possible that the figures are accurate as they stand and that for the first time in America a group of blacks have attained income equality with whites.[16] Even if the importance of this achievement is somewhat exaggerated, it would come as welcome news. Adequate income brings with it the chance for educational and cultural advantages which can prepare the next generation in turn to achieve a higher level of income.

Table VIII makes clear that working black wives contribute substantially to family income and that in those regions of the country where family income is higher, the percentage contributed by the wife's earnings is greater. On the whole, white working wives contribute about a fourth (25.5 percent) of white family income; black wives contribute about a third (32.4 percent). In both black and white families whose incomes stem from white collar occupations, the contribution of wives is proportionately greater than for all occupations in general. Black white-collar wives earn just under two-fifths (38.0 percent) of total family income; in white families the proportion is under three-tenths (28.9 percent). By a small margin, the greatest contribution to family earnings for both white and black wives is in the South, where white-collar wives contribute 39.0 percent of the family income in black families and 29.6 percent in white ones. For both whites and blacks the importance of wives' earnings declined between 1959 and 1972.

The amount contributed to the family budget by wives is smaller than it would be if all wives were full-time employees who earned salaries equal to those paid men. Even

**TABLE VIII—WIFE'S CONTRIBUTION TO FAMILY INCOME—FAMILIES WITH HUSBAND AND WIFE WORKING, BY RACE OF HUSBAND: 1959 AND 1972**

(Workers as of April 1960, and March 1973)

| Race, Region, and Current Occupation Group of Wife | 1959 | | | | 1972 | | | |
|---|---|---|---|---|---|---|---|---|
| | Husband-wife families, both Working (1,000) | Average (mean) family income | Earnings of wife | | Husband-wife families, both working (1,000) | Average (mean) family income | Earnings of wife | |
| | | | Average (mean) | Percent of family income | | | Average (mean) | Percent of family income |
| All white workers ......... | 12,282 | $7,814 | $2,097 | 26.8 | 19,103 | $15,432 | $3,932 | 25.5 |
| North and West ...... | 9,040 | 8,112 | 2,144 | 26.4 | 13,068 | 15,986 | 4,023 | 25.2 |
| South ................ | 3,242 | 6,986 | 1,967 | 28.2 | 6,035 | 14,231 | 3,737 | 26.3 |
| White collar workers[1] ...... | 5,420 | 9,064 | 2,819 | 31.1 | 10,003 | 17,488 | 5,059 | 28.9 |
| North and West ...... | 3,950 | 9,314 | 2,878 | 30.8 | 6,849 | 18,023 | 5,163 | 28.6 |
| South ................ | 1,470 | 8,392 | 2,682 | 32.0 | 3,154 | 16,327 | 4,832 | 29.6 |
| All black workers ......... | 1,273 | 4,769 | 1,323 | 27.7 | 1,817 | 12,387 | 4,014 | 32.4 |
| North and West ...... | 514 | 6,237 | 1,804 | 28.9 | 865 | 14,052 | 4,723 | 33.6 |
| South ................ | 759 | 3,776 | 998 | 26.4 | 952 | 10,872 | 3,370 | 31.0 |
| White collar workers[1] ...... | 167 | 7,397 | 2,879 | 38.9 | 626 | 15,329 | 5,956 | 38.9 |
| North and West ........ | 91 | 7,557 | 2,692 | 35.6 | 368 | 15,557 | 6,032 | 38.8 |
| South ............. | 76 | 7,206 | 3,104 | 43.1 | 258 | 15,004 | 5,848 | 39.0 |

[1]Includes professional, managerial, clerical, and sales workers.

Source: U. S. Bureau of the Census, *Current Population Reports*, series P-23, No. 39 and series P-60, No. 90.

**TABLE IX—MONEY INCOME: PERCENT DISTRIBUTION OF RECIPIENTS, BY INCOME LEVEL, BY SEX: 1950 TO 1972**

(Covers persons 14 years old and over as of March of following year.)

| Sex, Year, and Race | Total Persons | | Persons with Income—Income Level | | | | | | | | | Median income |
|---|---|---|---|---|---|---|---|---|---|---|---|---|
| | With income | Without income | Under $1,000 or less | $1,000–$1,999 | $2,000–$2,999 | $3,000–$3,999 | $4,000–$4,999 | $5,000–$5,999 | $6,000–$6,999 | $7,000–$9,999 | $10,000 and over | |
| MALE | | | | | | | | | | | | |
| 1950............ | 90.1 | 9.9 | 20.7 | 16.4 | 21.6 | 20.9 | 9.6 | 4.6 | 2.0 | 2.0 | 2.0 | $2,570 |
| 1955............ | 92.1 | 7.9 | 18.2 | 12.8 | 13.2 | 16.5 | 15.8 | 10.3 | 5.4 | 5.1 | 2.9 | 3,354 |
| 1960............ | 91.4 | 8.6 | 16.2 | 11.3 | 10.3 | 11.1 | 12.0 | 12.7 | 8.9 | 11.3 | 6.1 | 4,081 |
| 1965............ | 91.5 | 8.5 | 13.5 | 10.3 | 8.6 | 8.6 | 8.9 | 10.6 | 9.8 | 18.1 | 11.8 | 5,023 |
| 1970............ | 92.1 | 7.9 | 10.4 | 8.3 | 6.9 | 6.8 | 6.2 | 6.7 | 7.0 | 21.0 | 26.7 | 6,670 |
| 1972, total...... | 91.7 | 8.3 | 8.9 | 7.1 | 6.8 | 6.3 | 5.0 | 6.0 | 6.1 | 18.2 | 34.5 | 7,450 |
| Nonwhite ...... | 84.4 | 15.6 | 13.2 | 11.7 | 9.0 | 8.7 | 8.8 | 8.0 | 6.5 | 18.4 | 15.4 | 4,824 |
| FEMALE | | | | | | | | | | | | |
| 1950............ | 43.2 | 56.8 | 51.8 | 23.6 | 18.1 | 4.5 | 1.2 | 0.3 | 0.1 | 0.2 | 0.2 | 953 |
| 1955............ | 49.3 | 50.7 | 47.3 | 20.6 | 15.8 | 10.7 | 3.4 | 1.2 | 0.4 | 0.4 | 0.3 | 1,116 |
| 1960............ | 56.0 | 44.0 | 44.4 | 18.4 | 14.0 | 11.1 | 6.7 | 3.1 | 1.2 | 0.9 | 0.2 | 1,262 |
| 1965............ | 59.4 | 40.6 | 38.4 | 18.6 | 13.0 | 11.1 | 7.8 | 5.1 | 2.6 | 2.4 | 0.8 | 1,521 |
| 1970............ | 66.5 | 33.5 | 27.6 | 19.2 | 11.8 | 10.3 | 8.8 | 6.9 | 4.9 | 7.5 | 3.0 | 2,237 |
| 1972, total...... | 67.4 | 32.6 | 22.9 | 18.5 | 13.0 | 10.1 | 8.4 | 7.1 | 5.5 | 9.6 | 5.1 | 2,599 |
| Nonwhite ...... | 72.1 | 27.9 | 20.0 | 22.0 | 14.6 | 11.3 | 8.8 | 6.7 | 4.9 | 8.2 | 3.7 | 2,502 |

Source:  U. S. Bureau of the Census, Statistical Abstract of the United States, 1974, p. 389.

after adjusting for hours worked, women are paid significantly less than men, on the average. Table IX sets forth the tendency for men's individual incomes to be higher than those of women who are heavily concentrated in low-income categories, with less than ten percent in any category exceeding $4,000 per year. Clearly, families headed by women suffer a special economic handicap. Men were considerably less likely to fall in the categories below $4,000 and were much more heavily concentrated in the categories above $7,000 per year. In 1972, when only 5.1 percent of women had incomes of $10,000 or more, 34.5 percent of men, or nearly seven times as many, had achieved this level.

In view of the persistent inequalities in black economic status it is small wonder that over 40 percent of black men in 1972 had incomes under $2,000 and another 26.5 percent earned $2,000–$4,999, with a median income for the year of $4,824. In comparison, 69.9 percent of black women earned under $2,000 and 34.7 percent $2,000–$4,999, with a median income of $2,502. While 33.9 percent of black men earned $7,000 or more, only 11.9 percent of black women achieved this level; even fewer (3.7 percent) women, compared with 15.4 percent of black men, earned $10,000 or more.

## Welfare

In examining the welfare program in the United States one should keep in mind the falsity of the popular assumption that all the poor whose incomes fall below an officially defined minimum are receiving public assistance of some kind. In fact, the majority of black as well as white families and individuals whose incomes are below the poverty level are *not* welfare recipients (see Tables X and XI).

TABLE X—AID TO FAMILIES WITH DEPENDENT CHILDREN (AFDC) 1971 AND 1973

| | 1971 | | | 1973 | | | Percent of Low-Income Families Receiving AFDC in 1973 |
|---|---|---|---|---|---|---|---|
| | Low Income Families | AFDC Number | Percent | Total No. of Low Income Families | AFDC Number | Percent | |
| Total AFDC families | | 2,524,000 | 100.0 | — | 2,990,000 | 100.0 | — |
| White | 3,751,000 | 1,219,000 | 48.3 | 3,219,000 | 1,402,000 | 46.9 | 43.6 |
| Black | 1,484,000 | 1,093,000 | 43.3 | 1,527,000 | 1,369,000 | 45.8 | 89.7 |
| Other | (X) | 212,000 | 8.4 | (X) | 218,000 | 7.3 | (X) |

(X) Not available

Source: Statistical Abstract of the United States, 1974, p. 300; Bureau of the Census, Special Studies Series, P-23, No. 48, p. 31.

Two groups for whom public assistance is vitally important are the very young and the aged. As can be seen in Table X, families whose low incomes would justify public assistance are not necessarily receiving it; 89.7 percent of such black families were receiving Aid to Families with Dependent Children. Despite the low wages earned by most elderly blacks throughout their lives, only 31.8 percent were on Old Age Assistance in 1970 (Table XI).

**TABLE XI—OLD-AGE ASSISTANCE—1970**

|  | Population over 15 | Receiving Assistance | | Percent Receiving OAS |
|---|---|---|---|---|
|  |  | Number | Percent |  |
| Total recipients | — | 2,033,000 | 100.0 | — |
| White | 19,196,000 | 1,454,000 | 71.5 | 7.6 |
| Black | 1,539,000 | 496,000 | 24.4 | 31.8 |
| Other and unknown | 176,000 | 85,000 | 4.2 | 48.3 |

Source:   Statistical Abstract of the United States, 1974, pp. 33, 301.

The phenomenon of welfare benefits for persons who, temporarily or permanently, are unable to earn a living in the American economy, sprang from the expectation that emergency assistance until such time as the economy could absorb the unemployed would take care of most of the nonproducing poor. Unfortunately, there is a growing need for permanent or long-term arrangements for categories of citizens who, in most cases, will not develop into self-supporting workers in the short or intermediate term: dependent children, the aged, the disabled, the chronically ill, the mentally ill, the retarded. Added to these categories are the increasingly visible "hard-core" unemployed, who have not developed currently salable skills and attitudes toward work.

In a humanitarian society which cannot permit helpless people to starve, the welfare system, developed for a great economic depression emergency, has been allowed to continue in the absence of some other plan for incorporating the nonproductive poor into a distribution system traditionally tied to productivity or the ownership of productive resources. Welfare payments transfer wealth from "productive" components of society to "nonproductive" ones, thus providing insecure income to which the recipient has no "right" if the legislature chooses to reduce or even withdraw its appropriation. Welfare does not provide a permanent niche for the needy; it is essentially an *ad hoc* response to a problem which does not disappear.

Some efforts have been made by the National Welfare Rights Organization, the Movement for Economic Justice, and others to provide a dignified role for dependent persons in American society, but the popularity of the work ethic and of the notion that prosperity results from merit confuse the issue so that three-year-old orphans or blind adults are assumed somehow to have brought poverty upon themselves.

Black American citizens have a larger proportion of nonproductive persons to support than does the white community, since the number of children below working age is high; poor health and medical care standards increase the number of disabled or physically under-par persons, as well as reduce the number who live to complete their working years; and poverty, racism, and lack of communication have limited black access to education, apprenticeship, and job opportunities.[17] Older black workers who have reached retirement age generally lack the resources for even modest self-support, since so many have worked in poorly paid jobs which afford little opportunity for saving or for building up rights to retirement funds. Incomes from land or capital are unavailable to most of these elder citizens. For working relatives to support nonproducers and their dependents, as the employed ones struggle against economic and other barriers, severely strains ties of family and charity.

In the 1970s federal policy has tended to favor cash assistance over the provision of services, apparently in the expectation that putting purchasing power in the hands of welfare recipients will make their motivations more compatible with those of the economy as a whole. Obviously, no amount of motivation can transform the aged, the severely disabled, small children, or the grossly retarded into productive workers. Moreover, the funds put into the hands of the black poor have been so small and have been drained out of the community so quickly that their impact has been minimal. This is due in part to the fact that welfare funds are spent typically on rent to absentee landlords and on groceries and other goods sold in markets owned by persons who live outside the community, and on clothing and other goods produced elsewhere. At best, welfare rewards are unrelated to productivity or shrewdness in handling funds; in fact, a good case could be made that the feckless receive more than others.

Yet the principle of cash assistance could conceivably be applied more effectively. More adequate benefits could be issued without increasing the overall welfare budget if regulations were changed to offer incentives for working and encouragement to learn skills and assume responsibility for as much of one's life as is possible. The involvement of welfare workers in the detailed expenditures of each family might be replaced, in most cases, by sound consumer education and training in nutrition, home maintenance, and other skills which could increase the family standard of living without increasing the budget. Our current prevailing philosophy of benefits too small to maintain minimum health standards discourages a sense of worth and reduces the ability of recipients to strive for self-sufficiency. Basically, however, the majority of persons on welfare are marginal at best as prospective producers in the short or intermediate run; and the incentive to work provided by meager support and by bureaucratic insensitivity to the need for dignity on the part of welfare recipients is ineffective in the short run even with those who might be trained to work.

There is evidence from our World War II experience and some more recent experiments that hard-core unemployables, hired under training programs which are geared to their needs and which respect them as persons, can develop the skills required for productive employment on the job. Unaccustomed to the routines and discipline required, they are able to learn these social skills along with the production skills needed, as they gain confidence in their ability to meet the requirements of the job and sense the rewards in doing so. Too often, however, training programs have fallen short because the understanding required for this process is not communicated effectively, the time allowed is insufficient, or the growing independence and skills of the trainees are inadequately recognized and rewarded.[18]

The hopelessness and discouragement of the hard-core group, developed after years of reinforcement of society's evaluation of them as inadequate and unsuccessful, lies behind much black poverty. Reversing this process is difficult; it requires that America's social, educational, and economic systems insure that the current generation of children have ample access to the kind of education, motivation, and opportunities which can lead them into rewarding roles in the economy. Perhaps the most encouraging development in this direction is the above-mentioned effectiveness of rethinking job requirements and designing job specifications to fit the job-seekers, rather than the other way around. But getting this flexibility into the average employer's way of operating would be a formidable task; it has been tried in only a few experimental situations. In these approaches, some employers have begun to perceive that if job requirements do not bend to accommodate workers whose life styles are already different from those of traditional employees, the increasing number of alienated and jobless black citizens must threaten the economy itself, already under oblique attack on many fronts by those who question its values, motivations, and effect on ecology, as well as on humanity.

## Costs of Crime

The economic cost of crime in the black community was estimated in 1970 as up to three billion dollars a year—over 8 percent of aggregate black family income in 1970, more than half again the 5 percent it costs the population as a whole.[19]

The population of the black slums which breed crime falls constant prey to vandalism, petty thievery, and other crimes against persons and property. Assaults and homicides account for significant loss of income and incur extra medical expenses. Crimes against business have hit black neighborhoods with such force that owners are unable to obtain adequate insurance—a problem only partly met by government-sponsored insurance pools for entrepreneurs. Fire and theft insurance for automobile and home have long cost more for residents of the black slums.[20]

The latest available statistics on business losses due to crime (see Table XII) indicate clearly that the burden is heaviest in the slums of the central city where black population tends to concentrate. Except for offenses involving checks, with which poor blacks have less general experience, all categories of crime are significantly higher there than in every other type of location listed.

Such levels of crime not only drive up the cost of doing business in typical black neighborhoods and raise prices to the consumer; they drive out business establishments which serve local residents and further reduce potential employment and the tax base.

The above-mentioned accumulated individual costs hardly measure the total economic impact of crime. The exploitation of black inner-city residents by organized crime

**TABLE XII—BUSINESS LOSSES DUE TO CRIME, BY TYPE OF CRIME: 1967–1968**

(Money figures in millions of dollars.)

| Type of Crime | Losses by Size of Business[1] | | | | | | Businesses Victimized, by Location—Percent | | | | |
|---|---|---|---|---|---|---|---|---|---|---|---|
| | Total | Percent | Under $100,000[2] | $100,000–$1,000,000 | $1,000,000–$5,000,000 | Over $5,000,000 | Total | Ghetto | Non-ghetto[3] | Sub-urbs | Rural |
| Total ......... | 3,049 | 100 | 990 | 1,198 | 844 | 217 | (X) | (X) | (X) | (X) | (X) |
| Burglary ......... | 958 | 31 | 338 | 381 | 200 | 39 | 14 | 28 | 18 | 16 | 9 |
| Robbery ......... | 77 | 3 | 37 | 22 | 17 | 1 | 2 | 9 | 3 | 2 | 1 |
| Vandalism ...... | 813 | 27 | 242 | 259 | 223 | 89 | 15 | 37 | 18 | 17 | 9 |
| Shoplifting ..... | 504 | 17 | 142 | 278 | 61 | 23 | 15 | 24 | 14 | 15 | 15 |
| Employee theft .. | 381 | 12 | 89 | 150 | 116 | 26 | 8 | 11 | 10 | 9 | 4 |
| Bad checks ..... | 316 | 10 | 142 | 108 | 27 | 39 | 37 | 30 | 33 | 31 | 36 |

(X) Not applicable.   [1]Size based on gross receipts.   [2]Includes "not reported."   [3]Central city.

Source: U. S. Small Business Administration, *Crime Against Small Business*, Senate Document 91–14, 1969.

through loan sharking, narcotics, and gambling is so great that substantial economic development is unlikely to be achieved unless some way of plugging this drain of community resources is found. In the black slums of New York City, in a recent year the revenues of organized crime from narcotics and gambling alone exceeded the state welfare bill in those areas by $70,000,000.[21]

## Public Finance

Public finance in the black community also presents problems. As the more prosperous whites move out of the cities, the tax base changes; fewer well-to-do taxpayers remain, but the economically dependent blacks and whites persist and their proportions increase. Having only a marginal role in the economy, they typically must eke out a precarious living in low-wage, low-profit industries. Public services, fiscally anemic, deteriorate as increasingly crowded schools falter before the job of educating children for whom the traditional curriculum is at best ill-suited; public transportation systems combine rising fares and declining standards of service; hospital clinics serve ever larger numbers whose health falls well below the standards of citizens in other modern nations.[22]

Caught between the rising demand for public services and a declining tax base, the cities face fiscal crisis and the prospect of spreading blight in the black neighborhoods, where the drain of capital is visible in deteriorating housing. Black homeowners often work hard to maintain their houses; but too many have fallen victim to speculators who have refurbished old housing and resold it at inflated prices shortly before its inadequacies have proved to require extensive repairs. Government agencies which have guaranteed loans for such housing have found themselves holding title to substandard city housing, along with assuming a measure of responsibility for abandoned residential buildings which fail to meet standards for occupancy but cannot economically be restored to useful life as rental property.[23]

## Black Capitalism

At various times in history there have been campaigns to encourage patronage in black enterprises, and much hope has been attached to the role of the black entrepreneur. One of the major emphases of the Nixon Administration in dealing with black poverty was encouragement of minority businesses by the Small Business Administration. *Minority-Owned Businesses: 1969*,[24] the first comprehensive statistical study of black and other minority businesses, revealed that in 1969 black enterprisers owned 163,073 businesses with receipts of nearly $4.5 billion (Table XIII). While 38,304 of these businesses had paid employees, 124,769, or nearly 77 percent, had none, with that latter group accounting for only 18 percent of the gross receipts of black businesses; 155,280, or 95 percent, had fewer than five paid employees each and accounted for less than 53 percent of the total receipts. (Only 19 percent of white businesses have fewer than ten employees.)

The 7,793 establishments with five or more paid employees had gross receipts of $2,112,101,000, or 47 percent of the total, as compared with $1,541,262,000, or 34 percent of the total, for the 30,511 firms with one to four employees.

TABLE XIII—COMPARISON OF BLACK FIRMS BY RECEIPTS
AND NUMBER OF PAID EMPLOYEES, 1969

| Number of Paid Employees | Number of Firms | Gross Receipts* | Average Receipts per Firm* |
|---|---|---|---|
| No paid employees | 124,769 | $ 820,828,000 | $ 7,000 |
| With paid employees | 38,304 | 3,653,363,000 | 95,000 |
| 1–4 paid employees | 30,511 | 1,541,262,000 | 50,000 |
| 5–9 paid employees | 4,923 | 665,570,000 | 135,000 |
| 10–19 paid employees | 1,894 | 482,325,000 | 254,000 |
| 20–49 paid employees | 779 | 483,368,000 | 620,000 |
| 50–99 paid employees | 156 | 248,651,000 | 1,593,000 |
| 100 or more paid employees | 41 | 232,187,000 | 5,663 000 |
| Total | 163,073 | $4,474,191,000 | $ 27,000 |

*Rounded off to nearest 1,000

Source: U. S. Department of Commerce, Bureau of the Census, *Minority-Owned Businesses: 1969*, MB-1, Issued August, 1971, pp. 16, 144.

The tendency of minority businesses to be extremely small excludes them from the advantages of large-scale purchasing, processing, delivery, and use of such outside services as accounting and legal advice. A third of them grossed under $10,000 in 1969, and only 2 percent grossed over a million dollars, as compared with 9 percent of white-owned businesses (see Table XIV).

TABLE XIV—SIZE DISTRIBUTION OF MINORITY-OWNED* BUSINESSES
By Gross Receipts, 1969

| Gross Receipts $ (000) | Minority-Owned Percent | Other Percent |
|---|---|---|
| 0– 9.9 | 33 | 19 |
| 10– 19.9 | 15 | 12 |
| 20– 49.9 | 19 | 19 |
| 50– 99.9 | 14 | 15 |
| 100–999.9 | 17 | 26 |
| 1,000 and over | 2 | 9 |

*Includes black, Spanish-speaking, Oriental and other minorities.
Source: U. S. Department of Commerce, Small Business Administration, 1969.

Eighty-two percent of all black firms were in four major groups of industries: services, retail trade, transportation and other public utilities, and contract construction (see Table XV).

**TABLE XV**—MOST IMPORTANT INDUSTRY GROUPS OF BLACK-OWNED
FIRMS IN ORDER OF RECEIPTS, 1969
(with details of chief components)

| Industry Group | Number of Firms | Gross Receipts (000 omitted) |
|---|---|---|
| Retail Trade | 45,220 | 1,932,363 |
| Automotive dealers and service stations | 6,380 | 631,321 |
| Food stores | 11,268 | 438,492 |
| Eating and drinking places | 14,125 | 359,975 |
| Liquor stores | 1,300 | 103,745 |
| Selected Services | 56,077 | 663,236 |
| Personal services (laundry, dry cleaning, funeral services, beauty and barber shops, etc.) | 33,906 | 287,663 |
| Miscellaneous business services | 6,497 | 103,578 |
| Contract construction | 16,235 | 464,343 |
| Wholesale trade | 1,660 | 385,039 |
| Groceries and related products | 240 | 95,247 |
| Manufacturers | 2,981 | 302,648 |
| Lumber and wood products, textiles, chemicals, printing and publishing, etc. | | |
| Finance, insurance, and real estate | 7,612 | 287,471 |
| Insurance carriers | 104 | 133,314 |
| Transportation and other public utilities | 16,733 | 210,808 |

Source: U. S. Department of Commerce, Bureau of the Census, *Minority-Owned Businesses: 1969,* MB-1 Issued August, 1971, pp. 16-21.

**TABLE XVI**—INDUSTRY DISTRIBUTION OF BLACK-OWNED AND WHITE-OWNED
BUSINESSES, WITH PERCENTAGE OF EACH INDUSTRY OWNED BY
BLACKS, 1969

| Industry | Black-Owned Businesses | White and Other Businesses | Industry Owned by Blacks |
|---|---|---|---|
| | (%) | (%) | (%) |
| Personal Services | 29.9 | 7.3 | 8.4 |
| Other Services | 12.3 | 20.3 | 1.4 |
| Construction | 10.4 | 9.0 | 2.6 |
| Manufacturing | 3.5 | 6.9 | 1.2 |
| Retail Trade | 29.9 | 34.9 | 1.9 |
| Other Industries | 14.0 | 21.6 | 1.4 |
| All Industries | 100.0 | 100.0 | 2.3 |

Source: National survey of U. S. business, Small Business Administration, 1969.

In an analysis of the participation of black-owned businesses in all industries, the Small Business Administration found that in personal services, blacks owned 8.4 percent of the industry (see Table XVI). In only one other industry—construction—did blacks own as much as 2 percent.

## Financial Institutions

One consistent measure of the poverty and weakness of the black community has been the paucity and inadequacy of financial institutions devoted to its service. A severe shortage of capital, whether for investment or for operations, has traditionally explained much of the inability of black business institutions to take root and flourish; even if there had been sound experience in management and equal access to services, supplies, and personnel, the inability to finance business adequately would have raised costs and vitiated the possibility of competing effectively for the consumer's dollar.[25]

The importance of black financial institutions and resources has been exemplified by the greater tendency of black businesses to develop and succeed in communities like Atlanta, Georgia, which has had black banks and insurance companies, along with a substantial number of black professionals with savings which could contribute to the capital needs of the surrounding community.

Segregation and discrimination, which kept white financial institutions from hiring black employees or admitting black members to such relevant business associations as the Mortgage Bankers Association or National Association of Real Estate Boards, also made white insurance companies reluctant to write insurance on black lives and property and discouraged white banks from lending to black businessmen.

Shrewd black businessmen have long realized the necessity for better financial services. Slowly and painfully they have developed a modest but growing nucleus of black-controlled banks and insurance companies which have supplied needed services, provided opportunities for developing leadership and management skills, and demonstrated the ability of black citizens to build and succeed in business, despite obstacles and failures along the way.

Once black insurance companies had demonstrated the profitability of black business, white interest became attracted to this potentially rich market; black success led to a loss of their exclusive market as powerful white insurance companies increasingly sent competing salesmen into black neighborhoods to do business. In time white insurance agencies began to employ black salesmen in response to civil-rights pressure and a growing realization that an all-white employment policy could be a liability in doing business with blacks.

Still the forty-six black-owned insurance companies reported in January 1971 controlled only two-tenths of 1 percent of the total assets of the industry; and all of them together are smaller than the sixtieth-largest white-owned insurance company.[26] Table XVII lists the eleven which had assets in excess of $10,000,000.[27]

TABLE XVII—LARGEST MEMBERS OF THE NATIONAL INSURANCE ASSOCIATION, 1971

| Founded | | Assets |
|---|---|---|
| 1889 | North Carolina Life Insurance Company | $94,111,428 |
| 1905 | Atlanta Life Insurance Company | 69,952,133 |
| 1919 | Supreme Life Insurance Company of America | 35,066,067 |
| 1922 | Universal Life Insurance Company | 32,014,797 |
| 1925 | Golden State Mutual Life Insurance Company | 28,921,786 |
| 1927 | Chicago Metropolitan Mutual Assurance Co. | 21,913,923 |
| 1915 | Mammoth Life & Accident Insurance Company | 18,568,893 |
| 1898 | Pilgrim Health & Life Insurance Company | 13,388,321 |
| | Great Lakes Mutual Life Insurance Company | 12,260,667 |
| 1922 | Protective Industrial Insurance Co. of Alabama | 11,924,463 |
| 1901 | Afro-American Life Insurance Company | 11,559,293 |

Source:   National Insurance Association, *Golden Anniversary Membership Roster 1971.*

The black banking community, which had no exclusive preserve in which to operate, found its path to success exceedingly difficult. White banks were happy to accept black savings accounts, so building up capital was subject to heavy competitive pressures; on the other hand, white banks left to their black counterparts the most risky and poorly secured loans. Squeezed between slow accumulation of funds and high-risk opportunities for lending, it was small wonder that a number of infant black banks failed, discouraging savers from entrusting to these weak institutions their pitifully small nest eggs. Government, which before the 1960s did not generally champion minority ventures, deposited its funds in strong white-run banks whose owners had political as well as economic influence. Other sources of substantial funds, the lifeblood of commercial banking, were likewise inaccessible to black banks. The pressure to maximize the return on savings pushed black savers toward the more profitable white banks and further restricted the access of black institutions to even small accretions of capital.

It has been only since the 1960s that the federal government, foundations, and a few large commercial concerns have recognized a moral responsibility to deposit in black financial institutions a share of the funds they have heretofore kept in white banks.

The 1972 announcement that the Office of Economic Opportunity stimulated additional deposits of $17,000,000 in thirty-seven minority-owned banks, twenty-nine of them black-controlled, was an encouraging step in the direction of including black financial institutions among repositories of significant government funds. It will not be until such government, institutional, and corporate deposits become routine that black banks can grow to their full potential.[28]

As in the case of black insurance companies, the thirty black banks are very small in comparison with their mainstream competitors. The largest among them, the Freedom National Bank in Harlem, which had total assets of $53,871,473 as of March 31, 1972[29] did not rank as one of the 1,000 largest banks in the United States.[30]

Mortgage banking, which has been aided extensively by the Federal Government since the 1930s, was until recently exclusively white. The Mortgage Bankers Association (MBA), founded in 1941, had no black members in 1960, after almost a quarter-century of federal home-loan mortgage insurance and well over a decade of experience with veterans' mortgage guarantees under the G.I. Bill of Rights. The 1971 Directory of the MBA listed only three black firms as members.

The United Mortgage Bankers of America (UMBA) was incorporated in 1962 to develop black participation in mortgage banking.[31] The organizing committee, formed in 1961 to work out plans for the UMBA, had only one member approved by the Federal Housing Administration (FHA) as a mortgage lender; in 1972, fourteen of the fifty members of UMBA were FHA-approved mortgagees. Although the MBA is now open to black members, UMBA is continuing its work of training black mortgage bankers and brokers, bringing pressures for the selection of black mortgage-banking firms by white institutions doing business in the black community, serving as consultant for federal housing legislation, encouraging the commitment of the life insurance industry toward black economic development, and helping black families to qualify for mortgage loans. Its very presence in the industry has been influential in increasing the hiring of blacks in mortgage banking and in getting funds from large institutions directed into the hands of black mortgage bankers. Since commitments of substantial funds are necessary to make viable operations possible, this last function can be of crucial importance to the black sector of the industry.

Comparative figures in mortgage banking are revealing. There are 3,020 white-owned mortgage-banking institutions, as compared to 50 owned and operated by blacks. Thus blacks control only 1.6 percent of the businesses in the industry.

Since black-owned business in the industry is small, black mortgage banks account for substantially less than 1.6 percent of the servicing volume: 120 million dollars out of a mortgage-banking industry total of 75 billion, or .16 of 1 percent. The average white mortgage banker does ten times as much business as his black counterpart, a circumstance partially explained by the fact that the Federal National Mortgage Association was the only major continuous market available to black mortgage bankers until the insurance industry program of the late 1960s declared its intention to put a billion dollars into black economic development.[32]

## The Role of Small Business

Governor Andrew Brimmer of the Federal Reserve System has pointed out that in times like these, small business is unlikely to be the answer to the problem of black economic development, since small business in general is declining in America.[33] Indeed, opportunities for real success require far more capital and larger markets than are contemplated by small business. An entrepreneur who must limit his horizons bears a far greater risk of failure than his larger, better-financed, less circumscribed competitors.

At the same time, until there is greatly increased black ownership of business there cannot be a fair share of the profits and of business control in the hands of black people. Various solutions have been proposed to achieve this end, including transferring to blacks considerable stock ownership in existing corporations, fostering schemes for lending black investors the money to purchase stock, and turning over sizable corporations, one at a time, to black owners.[34] For the present, there is not much expectation of wholesale transfers of this kind; in the meantime, when black entrepreneurs wish to go into business, they should have fair and equal access to the capital and management assistance they need so as to give them a more equitable chance at such business opportunities as exist.

To this end the Interracial Council for Business Opportunity, Grass Roots, and other agencies have enlisted experienced executives to advise black businessmen who need help in learning the details of merchandising, purchasing, keeping records, and the like, or in implementing a promising business idea. The First Harlem Securities Corporation began as a branch of the brokerage firm of Shearson, Hammill and Company; a black supermarket chain started by purchasing a supermarket from a white-owned chain whose president assisted with organization and management advice.[35]

Other groups, such as the Presbyterian Economic Development Corporation, other local development corporations, and the Small Business Administration, provide funding for minority enterprises. The Opportunity Funding Corporation, a private nonprofit agency funded by the Office of Economic Opportunity, is committed to finding innovative ways of attracting private capital for minority economic development.

**Mainstream Business Activity**

If black capitalism is not the most promising avenue to black economic development problems, what can be hoped for in the way of integrated participation in American business as a whole?

As the exclusion of blacks from employment and other roles in American business began to lessen, the differentiation between "white jobs" and "black jobs" narrowed, changing first at the lower levels and moving up on the scale of desirability. One of the major advances for the black worker in World War II was the opening up of more jobs on the production line; after the war, as white-collar jobs multiplied, offices, banks, and shop counters increasingly hired blacks along with whites in the lower white-collar categories. As prosperity spread, the level of work available to blacks inched upward, and here and there a daring or especially liberal manager might employ a black supervisor. Yet few were bold enough to suggest that integration might go all the way to the executive suite and the board room.

The 1960s passed before there was a successful black bid for a seat on the New York Stock Exchange;[36] not until 1964 was a black director, Samuel R. Pierce, Jr., elected by a national corporation (U. S. Industries). In 1970 it was still possible for the chairman of General Motors to be caught unprepared when, at the annual meeting, a stockholder inquired as to why there were no black directors of the corporation.[37]

In a 1970 survey of fifty of America's largest corporations (the twenty-three largest industrial corporations, the six largest commercial banks, the six largest life insurance companies, the five largest retailing corporations, the six largest transportation concerns, and the four largest utilities), the lack of integration at the top was demonstrated with shocking clarity.[38] Of 3,182 senior officers and directors in the fifty corporations, *three* were black. In the twenty-three largest American industrial companies, *not one* of the 880 top executives and 238 other directors was black; of the 836 senior officers and 118 other directors of the six largest blanks, *one* was black; the six largest insurance companies had *two* black directors; *none* of the 104 senior executives and 39 other directors of the nation's five largest retailers was black, nor was a single one of the 251 top executives and 86 directors of the six largest transportation companies, nor of the 96 senior officers and 53 other directors of the four largest utilities.

Since that survey was made, some of those fifty corporations have taken steps to have at least token black membership on the board. Table XVIII lists black directors of these and a few smaller corporations. Because of the tendency to look to widely known persons in selecting candidates, prominent black directors often hold seats on more than one board. In 1972 it was announced that Jerome H. Holland, a former college president and, more recently, United States Ambassador to Sweden, had been elected a director of the New York Stock Exchange. By October of that year Mr. Holland was said to hold more directorships than any other black American: American Telephone and Telegraph Company, General Foods Corporation, Manufacturers Hanover Corporation, Union Carbide Corporation, and Continental Corporation are some of them. At the top of the list of others who have held multiple corporate directorships are Hobart Taylor, Jr., a Washington lawyer (Westinghouse Electric, Standard Oil of Ohio, the Great Atlantic and Pacific Tea Company, and Aetna Variable Annuity Life Insurance Company); William T. Coleman, a Philadelphia lawyer before he joined the Ford Cabinet as Secretary of Transportation (Pan American, First Pennsylvania, Penn Mutual, Western Savings Bank); Patricia Roberts Harris, Washington lawyer and former United States Ambassador to Luxembourg (Chase Manhattan, International Business Machines, Scott Paper, National Bank of Washington); and Reverend Leon H. Sullivan, Philadelphia minister and leader in the movement for economic advancement (General Motors, Girard Trust, Philadelphia Savings Fund Society). The pressure to select women as well as blacks may account in part for the popularity of able Mrs. Harris, who has been said to hold more major directorships than any other American woman.[39]

Still, the membership of blacks on industrial and commercial boards of directors, while proportionally far beyond what it was in 1970, has a long way to go before it represents a fair share of existing positions.

TABLE XVIII—A PARTIAL LIST OF BLACK DIRECTORS IN CORPORATIONS, 1975

| | |
|---|---|
| Aetna Life and Casualty | Hobart Taylor, Jr. |
| Aetna Variable Annuity Life Insurance | Hobart Taylor, Jr. |
| Amalgamated Trust and Savings Bank of Chicago | Chauncey Eskridge |
| | Louis E. Martin |
| American Broadcasting Company | Mamie Phipps Clark |
| American Stock Exchange | William T. Coleman, Jr. |
| American Telephone and Telegraph | Jerome H. Holland |
| Bankers Trust | Vernon E. Jordan, Jr. |
| Boston Edison Co. | Kenneth I. Guscott |
| Bowery Savings Bank | Robert C. Weaver |
| Burroughs Corporation | Clifton R. Wharton, Jr. |
| Celanese Corporation | Vernon E. Jordan, Jr. |
| Chase Manhattan Bank | Thomas A. Wood |
| | Patricia Roberts Harris |
| Chemical Bank | Franklin H. Williams |
| Chesapeake & Potomac Telephone Company | Belford Lawson, Jr. |
| | Roy D. Hudson |
| Chrysler Corporation | Jerome H. Holland |
| C.I.T. Financial Corporation | Christopher F. Edley |
| Chicago City Bank and Trust Co. | Louis E. Martin |
| Coca Cola | William W. Allison |
| Columbia Broadcasting System | Franklin A. Thomas |
| Commonwealth Edison | George E. Johnson |
| Consolidated Edison | Franklin H. Williams |
| Continental Bank (Philadelphia) | Ragan A. Henry |
| Continental Corporation | Jerome H. Holland |
| Dollar Savings Bank | James A. Colston |
| Dreyfus Third Century Fund | Vernon E. Jordan |
| Dukor Modular Systems | Cecil F. Poole |
| Empire Savings Bank | Frederick W. Eversley |
| Equitable Life Insurance Company of Iowa | James S. Thomas |
| Equitable Life Assurance Society | Clifton R. Wharton. Jr. |
| Equitable Trust (Baltimore) | Raymond V. Haysbert, Sr. |
| Fidelity National Bank | Carl B. Hutcherson |
| First National Bank of Washington | James E. Cheek |
| First National City Bank of New York | Franklin A. Thomas |
| First Pennsylvania Corporation | Henry G. Parks |
| | William T. Coleman, Jr. |
| First Plymouth National Bank | Joyce Hughes |
| Ford Motor Company | Clifton R. Wharton, Jr. |
| General Foods | Jerome H. Holland |
| General Motors | Rev. Leon H. Sullivan |
| Gino's, Inc. | Robert Evans |
| Girard Trust | Rev. Leon H. Sullivan |
| W. T. Grant | Asa T. Spaulding |
| Great Atlantic & Pacific Tea Co. | Hobart Taylor, Jr. |
| Hamilton International Corp. | Esque Crawford |
| Harcourt, Brace & Jovanovich | Daniel A. Collins |
| Hubbard & Company | Gerard M. Peterson |
| Illinois Bell Telephone Company | John Hope Franklin |
| International Business Machines | Patricia Roberts Harris |

**TABLE XVIII**—(Cont)

| | |
|---|---|
| International Paper | Samuel R. Pierce, Jr. |
| Jewel Companies | Jewel Stradford Lafontant |
| John Hancock Mutual Life Insurance | Mary Ella Robertson |
| Kraftco Corp. | Lloyd C. Elam, M. D. |
| Levi Strauss & Company | Cecil F. Poole |
| Liggett & Myers Tobacco Company | Earl C. Graves |
| Lilli Ann | Cecil F. Poole |
| Lincoln Savings Bank (New York) | Kenneth B. Clark |
| Lockheed Aircraft Corp. | Leslie N. Shaw |
| Arthur D. Little | Alonzo S. Yerby |
| Macrodyne-Chatillon Corporation | Henry G. Parks |
| Magnavox Company | Henry G. Parks |
| Manufacturers Hanover Trust Company | Jerome H. Holland |
| Manufacturers National Bank of Detroit | William T. Patrick, Jr. |
| Marine Midland Bank | Ulric St. Clair Haynes |
| Michigan Bell Telephone | Delores D. Wharton |
| Metropolitan Life Insurance Co. | Robert C. Weaver |
| | George E. Johnson |
| Michigan Consolidated Gas | Alfred M. Pelham |
| Midwest Federal Savings & Loan | Cecil Newman |
| Miller Brewing Co. | Thomas B. Shropshire |
| Mountain States Bell Telephone Co. | Sebastian C. Owens |
| National Bank of Washington | Patricia Roberts Harris |
| | William S. Harps |
| | Marjorie M. Lawson |
| | Charles T. Duncan |
| | William Lucy |
| National Broadcasting Co. | William J. Kennedy, III |
| National Corporation for Housing Partnerships | John H. Wheeler |
| | Mabel M. Smythe |
| | Abraham S. Venable |
| New York Bank for Savings | Cornelius C. McDougald |
| New York Life Insurance Company | Franklin A. Thomas |
| New York Stock Exchange | Jerome H. Holland |
| Pan American World Airways | William T. Coleman, Jr. |
| Penn Mutual Life Insurance Company | William T. Coleman, Jr. |
| Peoples Gas Company | Millard D. Robbins, Jr. |
| Philadelphia Savings Fund Society | Rev. Leon H. Sullivan |
| Philip Morris | Margaret Young |
| Post-Newsweek Stations | Tyrone Brown |
| Potomac Electric Power | Theodore R. Hagans |
| Prudential Insurance Co. | Samuel R. Pierce, Jr. |
| Public Service Electricity and Gas | Samuel R. Pierce, Jr. |
| RCA Corporation | William J. Kennedy, III |
| Rich's, Inc. | Jesse Hill, Jr. |
| J. Schlitz Brewing Co. | Willie D. Davis |
| Scott Paper | Patricia Roberts Harris |
| Standard Oil of Ohio | Hobart Taylor, Jr. |
| Teachers Insurance and Annuity Assn. | Luther H. Foster |
| | Vivian W. Henderson |
| | Charles Z. Wilson |

TABLE XVIII—(Cont)

| | |
|---|---|
| Trans World Airlines | Jewel Stradford Lafontant |
| | Emmett J. Rice |
| Twentieth Century-Fox | John H. Johnson |
| Union Carbide | Jerome H. Holland |
| URS Systems | Franklin H. Williams |
| Union National Bank | Marion E. Officer |
| U. S. Industries | Samuel R. Pierce, Jr. |
| Western Savings Bank | William T. Coleman, Jr. |
| Westinghouse Broadcasting | George E. Norford |
| Westinghouse Electric | Hobart Taylor, Jr. |

Note :   Where there are two or more black directors, they are listed in order of appointment.

Sources :   *Black Enterprise,* September 1971, p. 18 ; September 1973, pp. 17–28 ; December 1973, p. 8 ; May 1974, p. 9 ; and December 1974, p. 10 ; *Negro History Bulletin,* November 1971, p. 166 ; *The New York Times,* June 25, 1972, Section F, p. 3 ; Milton R. Moskowitz, "The Black Directors : Tokenism or a Big Leap Forward ?" *Business and Society Review,* Autumn, 1972, No. 3, pp. 73–80, at p. 77 ; N.C.H.P. Annual Report, 1975.

## Executives

Black senior executives are even less numerous than black directors relative to their proportions in the population; and the highest rank held by a black officer in any major corporation is vice president.[40]

In the 1960s, American business was subjected to increasing demands for black participation in management. The initial response was feeble and defensive, producing a mere trickle of appointments. But as these reaped favorable publicity and resulted in gratifying experience with sometimes highly qualified black personnel, other concerns took courage and made appointments of their own or promoted black employees who had previously been overlooked.

Some prospective employers found it easier to accept the concept of black executives, or to sell the idea to others in the company, when the appointee had a special assignment related to race; hence a good many of the trail-blazing positions of the 1950s and early 1960s dealt with the nonwhite market, recruitment of minority employees, and urban affairs or community relations. This way of "integrating" management without admitting blacks to the exercise of power or the making of policy seemed to blacks to apply to a majority of what were billed as executive opportunities.

As time progressed, however, a small but growing number of black holders of the Master of Business Administration degree and others with training and experience suited to management rebelled against such "ghettoization." They turned down the "specialist in minority affairs" assignments and called for positions leading to promotion to the top levels of corporate responsibility.

At the present time, several organizations are working toward the development of management abilities and the integration of genuine management jobs. The Interracial

Council for Business Opportunity (ICBO) helps develop management skills by bringing together white businessmen and aspiring black entrepreneurs who wish to develop and improve their businesses; the Association for the Integration of Management (AIM) encourages "white" companies to plan for integration and to set schedules for achieving specific objectives in terms of number and level of positions and the provision of training and assistance to black personnel. The Council of Concerned Black Executives (CCBE) opposes this approach; it prefers to abandon special programs in favor of equal treatment for blacks and whites, with the same chance at promotions, apparently believing that the black executive will receive more solid acceptance and benefit from a sense of having made it on his own.[41] Opportunities Industrialization Centers (OIC) prepare black employees for positions up to and including executive levels. All four organizations agree that full equality is a desirable goal, but AIM favors leading management to establish forward movement since management does not show sufficient progress on its own. (It seems easy for executives to believe mistakenly that integration is now common in other companies like theirs, and that the all-white management of their own company is an exception.[42])

The National Urban League sponsors a Business Executive Exchange Program which sends black executives to black colleges to interest students in business careers and to conduct workshops. Training for business managment at the black colleges is still weak; the Atlanta University Center is among very few with a history of such programs more than ten years old. This can be partly explained by the fact that until executive positions were available there was obviously little point in training for them.

Business training in white institutions, which saw few black applicants for the M.B.A. degree a decade ago, has grown to the point where in 1972 Harvard graduated fifty blacks with this degree, Columbia 27, and Chicago 25. This evidence of a nucleus of well-prepared black candidates for executive positions may be reflected in the student bodies of a good many smaller institutions as blacks become aware of the possibilities in business careers. This training comes none too soon, since at present less than 3 percent of the line managers and officers in American industry are black.

A number of black executives are uncomfortable or rebellious in their role. They see promotions as extra-difficult for blacks; they see whites as reluctant to give them a fair chance; finally, they tend to feel apprehension about a loss of identity under the insistence of the corporate world that they conform to its ways concerning dress, manners, interests, and values. More than the rebelliousness familiar among today's young whites is involved here; black pride and identity are at stake.

Despite the weaknesses of the black position in the economic mainstream, black officers are coming gradually within observation distance of the seats of power and are thus slowly gaining exposure to the working of large-scale business. Since the lack of such experience has severely restricted the development of black business competence in the past, this opportunity can hardly fail to provide greater motivation toward business careers and some of the skills and sophistication required to achieve them. There is as yet, however, little evidence that white business is ready to welcome black management talent in significant numbers.[43]

The ownership of stock in mainstream enterprises is another area in which blacks lag behind, because of the lower income and capital accumulation levels among black citizens. Yet ownership is essential to full participation in policy-making as well as in gaining a share of the profits. In investments, a small but growing number of black account executives suggests that a rise in black income will be accompanied by increased awareness among black investors of the importance of active participation in stock and bond ownership. Already a growing number of prosperous professionals and business men are investing in securities, as well as in the more traditional real estate.

## The Black Consumer

In 1969, when Macmillan published D. Parke Gibson's *The $30 Billion Negro*, it gave formal recognition to what advertising agencies were already tacitly acknowledging: the growing importance of the aggregate income of black Americans, particularly in recent years. In 1965 only 20 percent of black families had incomes of $10,000 (adjusted for 1973 prices) or more. Since 1969, a third of black families have had incomes of $10,000 or more, as compared to about three-fifths of their white counterparts. In 1973, 42 percent of black families and 66 percent of white families in the North and West were in this category, although in the South only 28 percent of blacks and 58 percent of whites could boast of this level of security. The marked discrepancy between the two racial groups was maintained in the 1970s and seemed unlikely to decrease as economic expansion gave way to growing unemployment and decline. (See Table XIX.)

In 1973, when there were 5,440,000 black families with a mean income of $8,667,[44] aggregate black personal income could be estimated as exceeding $47 billion. Since this figure does not include black-controlled churches, schools and colleges, businesses, social agencies, organizations, and other such institutions, it clearly and substantially underestimates the potential influence of black purchasers in the marketplace. Beyond doubt institutional buyers account for the bulk of black purchases of office supplies, technical equipment, and other goods suited to other than personal or home use; a substantial portion of expenditures for travel, communications (telephone and telegraph, postage), hotel and group meals is institutional.

Systematic studies of the spending habits of the black population are rare; much of the information on which advertising agencies base their conclusions is superficial, outdated, limited to one geographical area, or otherwise deficient.

Raymond Oladipupo's 1969 report for the advertising firm of Ogilvy and Mather[45] offers several insights into black consumer expenditures. First, black housewives in cities tend to spend from 2 percent to 12 percent more on food than do white housewives in the same income category. Some of the reasons for this discrepancy are as follows: (1) black households are larger (the per capita expenditure is usually smaller); (2) since more black wives work, they cannot give as much time to comparison shopping; (3) food prices tend to be higher in the black community, where limitations on credit and on information concerning alternative sources of supply make the consumer a weak bargainer vis-à-vis the seller; (4) higher crime and insurance costs in black urban neighborhoods tend to drive up costs beyond those in white residential areas, even though the average income is higher in the latter.

TABLE XIX—PERCENT OF FAMILIES WITH INCOMES OF $10,000 OR MORE AND $15,000 OR MORE, BY REGION: 1965, 1969, 1972, AND 1973

(Adjusted for price changes in 1973 dollars. Incomes of $10,000 and $15,000 in 1973 were equivalent in purchasing power to about $7,100 and $10,650, respectively, in 1965)

| Area and year | Black | | White | |
|---|---|---|---|---|
| | Income of $10,000 or more | Income of $15,000 or more | Income of $10,000 or more | Income of $15,000 or more |
| UNITED STATES | | | | |
| 1965............................ | 20 | 6 | 52 | 23 |
| 1969............................ | 33 | 13 | 61 | 33 |
| 1972............................ | 35 | 16 | 63 | 36 |
| 1973............................ | 35 | 16 | 64 | 38 |
| SOUTH | | | | |
| 1965............................ | 10 | 3 | 41 | 17 |
| 1969............................ | 22 | 8 | 54 | 27 |
| 1972............................ | 27 | 12 | 56 | 30 |
| 1973............................ | 28 | 11 | 58 | 33 |
| NORTH AND WEST | | | | |
| 1965............................ | 31 | 10 | 56 | 25 |
| 1969............................ | 44 | 18 | 64 | 35 |
| 1972............................ | 43 | 20 | 65 | 38 |
| 1973............................ | 42 | 21 | 66 | 40 |

Source: U. S. Department of Commerce, Social and Economic Statistics Administration, Bureau of the Census, Special Studies Series P-23, No. 48, p. 20, Issued July 1974.

The Oladipupo study concluded that middle-income blacks and whites follow roughly the same patterns of expenditure, except for clothing and home and automobile ownership. Blacks owned significantly fewer homes and automobiles than did whites, a phenomenon logically explainable by the great difference in access to credit, an essential component in the majority of such purchases. Gibson's study indicates that blacks spend larger percentages of their incomes on shelter than do whites, a finding which confirms the monopoly effect of restricted housing choices: higher prices for equivalent housing. As for the distinctly higher clothing costs in black families, part of the explanation probably lies in the greater size of black families and the poorer access of black families to a variety of stores selling good-quality merchandise at reasonable prices. The factor of necessity buying applies less to house furnishings, however, since one can do without specific items if one must, whereas one's clothing and appearance at work or at school may be crucial to fulfilling one's function there. A high regard for clothing may also have developed in a community where other purchases associated with recreation may be more expensive or less accessible.

Since there is a tendency toward rapid expansion in middle- and upper middle-income black groups,[46] there is already a substantial black consumer group in the category of incomes which allow for discretionary expenditures beyond basic requirements. Accordingly, active and potential travel and leisure expenditures have been growing. Gibson asserts that urban blacks spend more than $541,000,000 for vacation travel each year—and would spend more if they did not fear exposure to segregation and discrimination at American resorts.[47]

Statistics concerning acquisition of durable equipment reflect this need to economize. Table XX shows that of every 100 households, blacks purchased 22.6 washing machines between 1968 and 1972 as compared with 29.2 for whites; 7.0 clothes dryers (whites purchased 21.7, over three times as many); 1.4 dishwashers (as against 11.2); and 9.7 room air conditioners, little more than half the 17.0 bought by white households. In the same five-year period, new car purchases were 27.4 for blacks, 66.1 for whites. Only in the purchase of kitchen ranges and black and white television sets did black households purchase as many or more than did whites. Color television sets were bought by whites at a rate more than 50 percent beyond that of blacks. For poor black families, television sets, which are available on deceptively "cheap" installment purchase plans, may substitute for travel, vacation homes, theater tickets, hobbies, magazine subscriptions, and even a family car.

**TABLE XX—NUMBER OF CARS AND SELECTED OTHER DURABLES PURCHASED PER 100 HOUSEHOLDS, FIVE-YEAR TOTAL: 1968 TO 1972**

| Selected durables | Total | Black | White |
|---|---|---|---|
| Cars: | | | |
|    New | 62.5 | 27.4 | 66.1 |
|    Used | 107.3 | 72.9 | 110.8 |
| Selected appliances: | | | |
|    Washing machines | 28.5 | 22.6 | 29.2 |
|    Clothes dryers | 20.1 | 7.0 | 21.7 |
|    Kitchen ranges | 17.9 | 18.0 | 17.9 |
|    Refrigerators and freezers | 32.7 | 29.1 | 33.1 |
|    Dishwashers | 10.3 | 1.4 | 11.2 |
|    Room air conditioners | 16.1 | 9.7 | 17.0 |
| House entertainment items: | | | |
|    Black and white television sets | 29.6 | 36.8 | 28.5 |
|    Color television sets | 36.4 | 23.7 | 37.6 |

Source: U. S. Department of Commerce, Social and Economic Statistics Administration, Bureau of the Census.

## Home Ownership

The trend toward increased home ownership among blacks is a gradual one; the percentage who own their own homes has gradually increased until it now equals about two-thirds the corresponding white percentage. In 1960, 38 percent of nonwhites and 64 percent of whites were homeowners; in 1970 the corresponding figures were 42 and 65 percent. By region the largest proportion (47 percent) of black homeowners lived in the South in 1970—a change from 1960 when the West had that distinction. (See Table XXI.)

**TABLE XXI**—TENURE OF OCCUPIED HOUSING UNITS BY REGION: 1960 AND 1970
(Numbers in thousands)

| Area | Black | | | | White | | | |
|------|-------|-------|---------|---------|-------|-------|---------|---------|
| | Total | Owner-occupied | | Renter occupied | Total | Owner-occupied | | Renter occupied |
| | | Number | Percent of total | | | Number | Percent of total | |
| **1960** | | | | | | | | |
| United States .... | 5,144 | 1,974 | 38 | 3,171 | 47,880 | 30,823 | 64 | 17,057 |
| Northeast ......... | 875 | 236 | 27 | 639 | 12,648 | 7,352 | 58 | 5,295 |
| North Central ...... | 947 | 339 | 36 | 607 | 14,432 | 9,968 | 69 | 4,464 |
| South ............. | 2,756 | 1,146 | 42 | 1,610 | 12,747 | 8,467 | 66 | 4,280 |
| West ............. | 567 | 253 | 45 | 314 | 8,053 | 5,035 | 63 | 3,018 |
| **1970** | | | | | | | | |
| United States .... | 6,205 | 2,578 | 42 | 3,627 | 57,212 | 37,284 | 65 | 19,928 |
| Northeast ......... | 1,279 | 365 | 29 | 913 | 14,183 | 8,543 | 60 | 5,640 |
| North Central ...... | 1,284 | 540 | 42 | 744 | 16,253 | 11,383 | 70 | 4,871 |
| South ............. | 3,136 | 1,470 | 47 | 1,666 | 16,111 | 10,971 | 68 | 5,140 |
| West ............. | 507 | 203 | 40 | 303 | 10,665 | 6,387 | 60 | 4,278 |

Note:  In this table, 1970 data are presented separately for "black" households and for households of "white and other races"; 1960 data are presented separately for "white" households and for households of "black and other races."

Source:  U. S. Department of Commerce, Bureau of the Census, Series P-23, No. 42 (1971).

## Consumer Education

The movement toward better consumer education is still in its infancy in the black community. As the amount and quality of schooling rises, however, effective consumer instruction can be accomplished more easily. Until then the sharp practices, the usurious contracts, the shoddy goods outlasted by their time payments, the withering vegetables and decaying meats in supermarkets serving blacks, and the higher prices on days when welfare checks are paid can be expected to continue, pending more energetic enforcement of consumer protection laws. Increasingly, the families with rising incomes are leaving the neighborhood stores for those which serve a broader or richer clientele.

Consumer education need not be a function of education and incomes. Just as before 1900 blacks tried to use their consumer power by patronizing black business establishments,[48] the Montgomery Bus Boycott in 1955 was a use of consumer power to withhold expenditure and force a desired outcome. PUSH, formerly Operation Breadbasket, and the Selective Patronage Program in Philadelphia are contemporary demonstrations of the use of the economic power of consumers to force employment of black workers in businesses selling to the black community. That power is made considerably more effective by the concentration of the black population in metropolitan areas today.

The multiplicity of economic problems faced by black Americans has made it difficult for a strong consumer movement to gain the support it deserves. Nevertheless, the economic potential already at hand in the wallets of the black population is enormous. Effectively organized, it has forced open jobs, lowered prices, and slowed down the drain of capital out of the black community by concentrating purchasing power on those establishments which hire local people and buy from local producers.

## Strategies for Change

Given the conditions, problems, and circumstances described above, what do America's black citizens want?

Quite simply, they want what everyone else wants: economic prosperity, a fair share of the nation's wealth and resources, a voice in the decisions that govern their destinies. They want the assurance that jobs or opportunities will be color-blind, that their children can aspire to any economic role on the basis of merit, and that the chance fully to realize their potential is as great for blacks as for anyone else.

Black strategists take a hard look at proposals to better the economic conditions in the black community, evaluating the extent to which these programs are likely to achieve the goals of (1) greater income, (2) sufficient economic power to influence significant decisions affecting the welfare of blacks, and (3) equality of participation in the total economy as workers, managers, consumers, owners of real estate, borrowers, entrepreneurs, directors, stockholders, and general policy-makers. Not until these goals are in sight can there be stable and widespread contentment among black citizens.

Since the goals are so broad, it is clear that the strategies for change must be equally comprehensive. Given the interdependence of social and economic conditions, economic strategies must take into account social and educational considerations if they are to achieve real progress. Black critics are quick to observe that large-scale training programs fail if jobs are controlled by a union which excludes black workers, or by companies which are reluctant to advance black employees in accordance with their growing skill, seniority, and competence. Similarly, compensatory hiring policies must be backed up by the machinery to prepare workers for the jobs they want. Furthermore, the "black capitalist" strategy of promoting small-business ownership cannot alone produce significant economic advance in a society dominated by ever-larger corporations and conglomerates which leave the multitude of small businesses, white as well as black, little room to wield influence.[49]

Nevertheless, current strategies for change are numerous, varied, and sometimes highly imaginative, including the simplistic and the sophisticated, the specific and the diffuse, the radical and the conservative, the realistic and the visionary.[50] Most of them take as a point of departure the present makeup of the United States economy, assuming that the black population will continue to be part of a larger mass which must at least acquiesce in the projected changes. There are, as well, occasional plans for a separate geographic enclave with its own economy, with black farms and factories supplying the needs for a largely self-sufficient "nation," usually organized on socialist or semisocialist lines; these are not generally put forward by black economists, however, and are not set forth in sophisticated terms. There are also plans which contemplate a black economy within the larger economy, with numerous points of contact but a large area of internal autonomy.

Since the world has not yet demonstrated its ability to bring about rapid development for poor, powerless nations with inadequate natural resources (despite an occasional success in nations with special power potential like Israel, postwar Germany, and Japan, all of which had literate populations with skills and industrial experience), it is hardly surprising that the results of the past ten years of accelerating effort to boost black economic development have been disappointing. No experiment has yet been made on a scale large enough to provide a dramatic demonstration of its effectiveness. Moreover, strategies have not been coordinated or consistent in approach, and they have therefore often worked at cross-purposes. Finally, sentimentality and political and social objectives have frequently taken center stage, while economic considerations have been minimized or even overlooked. As a result, there has been emphasis on helping individuals establish small proprietorships or cottage industries like quilting or tie-dyeing at a time when small business has a poor chance of success; job-training centers have sometimes emphasized training for jobs whose futures are unpromising at best; the emphasis has not been put upon the tough, basic problems of housing and transportation and economic resources and power.

## Reparations

The concept of payment due to Afro-Americans for their unpaid labor during slavery has a persuasive logic. In view of the reluctance of many whites to recognize the necessity for more-than-equal treatment until black Americans overcome the heritage of past injustice, the reparations idea makes a good deal of sense. Other whites, who understand the handicaps which have prevented blacks from being as ready as whites to grasp advantages when they appear, are uncomfortable with the notion that equal opportunity from now on is enough. Reparations would seem compatible with the attitudes of both kinds of people.

The "Black Manifesto," presented in 1969 by James Forman at the first meeting of his National Black Economic Development Conference (NBEDC) in Detroit, proposed that the conference be given as reparations $500,000,000 by white churches and synagogues; this figure, calculated originally at $15 per black American, was later revised to $3,000,000,000.

Despite the overtone of hostility in the initial presentation and subsequent reaction, as well as questions as to the appropriateness of the NBEDC as custodian of the money, several church groups saw merit in the general idea. In the two years since the manifesto was published, NBEDC has collected a little more than $300,000; however, the idea of reparations has been more successful than this figure suggests. There is no question but that churches and church-related organizations[51] have visibly increased their expenditures for programs which aid blacks or which seek to ameliorate the economic, social, educational, psychological, or other handicaps which prevent "equality of opportunity" from being a reality.

It may well be that the concept of reparations has helped to spur public support for such programs as the Office of Economic Opportunity and Upward Bound, the Urban League Street Academies, private school and college scholarships, and a spurt in the training and hiring of black executives. However, at this writing, any undeclared commitment to reparations is impossible to estimate.

As the above analyses and tables amply demonstrate, the sometimes considerable progress which has been made in economic development in the black community falls far short of anything approaching economic equality. It must be remembered, however, that black economic status and opportunity have always lagged behind educational progress and, in some ways, political opportunity; and that a black citizen's right to education and the ballot have been accepted as part of the American creed in a sense that the right to prosper has not.

Initial access to the control of wealth, particularly the means of production, is difficult to achieve by recourse to legal approaches. Precedent is still being built up for an economic Bill of Rights. Meanwhile, much economic control is in the hands of persons who have neither interest in nor commitment toward a more equal opportunity for black citizens; indeed, many of them see little obligation to the poor of any ethnic or racial background.

The weapons for the battle for economic equality are still being fashioned. Although it is a contest as old as human history, the circumstances of this current phase are complicated by the forces of racism. But the fight for economic freedom and equality must go on, since it aims at the very center of the target: a full and unfettered life for America's black citizens.

## Notes

1. Howard J. Samuels, "Prejudice in the Marketplace," in Charles Y. Gluck and Ellen Siegelman, eds., *Prejudice, USA* (Praeger, New York, 1969), pp. 150–168; Ben B. Seligman, *Permanent Poverty, An American Syndrome* (Quadrangle Books, Chicago, 1968), pp. 42–45.
2. John Hope Franklin, *From Slavery to Freedom* (Knopf, New York, 1956), pp. 484–5, 529.
3. John H. Bracey, Jr., *Black Nationalism in America* (Bobbs-Merrill, New York, 1970), pp. 237, 372–75.
4. Theodore L. Cross, *Black Capitalism: Strategy for Business in the Ghetto* (New York, 1969), pp. 14 ff; Ulf Hannerz, *Soulside: Inquiries into Ghetto Culture and Community* (Columbia University Press, New York, 1969), pp. 139–142.
5. Irving Kovarsky and William Albrecht, *Black Employment* (University of Iowa Press, Ames, 1970), p. 59; Herman D. Bloch, *The Circle of Discrimination* (New York University Press, New York, 1969), pp. 111–112.
6. Daniel R. Fusfeld, "The Basic Economics of the Urban and Racial Crisis," *Review of Black Political Economy*, Vol. 1, No. 1, Spring/Summer 1970, pp. 63–64; *see also* Charles A. Valentine, *Culture and Poverty* (University of Chicago Press, Chicago, 1968), p. 158.
7. Eli Ginzberg, ed., *Business Leadership and the Negro Crisis* (McGraw-Hill, New York, 1968), pp. 15–16.
8. Herbert Hill, "Racial Inequality in Employment," in Murphy & Elinson, *Problems and Prospects*, pp. 86–108; *see* Herman D. Bloch, *op. cit.*, especially pp. 124–151.
9. U. S. Department of Commerce, Bureau of the Census, *The Social and Economic Status of Negroes in the United States*, 1970; p. 37.
10. *The New York Times*, January 19, 1973, pp. 1, 66.
11. Seligman, *op. cit.*, p. 44.
12. Cross, *op. cit.*, p. 25.
13. U. S. Department of Commerce, Bureau of the Census, *op. cit.*, p. 37; also, U. S. Department of Commerce, Bureau of the Census, *Current Population Reports*, Series P-23, No. 48 (1974), p. 29.
14. Kovarsky and Albrecht, *op. cit.*, pp. 77–105.
15. U. S. Department of Commerce, Bureau of the Census, *Statistical Abstract of the United States*, 1974, p. 385.
16. According to Daniel P. Moynihan in "The Schism in Black America," *The Public Interest*, Spring 1972, pp. 10–11, sources of possible bias were checked, and this finding is a genuine measure of progress.
17. "Manpower Report of the President," *Monthly Labor Review*, May 1970, p. 50.
18. Valentine, *op. cit.*, pp. 157–159.
19. *The New York Times*, September 27, 1970, pp. 1, 85.
20. *Ibid.*; see also Andrew F. Brimmer, "An Economic Agenda for Black Americans," Remarks at Atlanta University, October 16, 1970.
21. *The New York Times*, September 27, 1970, pp. 1, 85.
22. Fusfeld, *op. cit.*, pp. 58–83, especially pp. 60, 66–67.
23. Joseph P. Fried, *Housing Crisis, U.S.A.* (Praeger, New York, 1971).
24. U. S. Department of Commerce, Bureau of the Census, MB-1, issued August 1971.
25. Carl E. Haugen, "Short-Term Financing," in Ginzberg, *op. cit.*, pp. 95–105.
26. *The New York Times*, January 10, 1971, p. 39.
27. Thirty-four additional companies had assets below $10,000,000 in 1968. The oldest black insurance company is Southern Aid Life Insurance Company, Richmond, Virginia, with assets in 1968 of $3,974,404. National Insurance Association, Fiftieth Anniversary brochure, Richmond, (Virginia, 1970).
28. "OEO Funded Agencies Deposit $17 Million in Minority-Owned Banks," Office of Economic Opportunity, April 2, 1972.

29. Freedom National Bank of New York, *Interim Report, First Quarter*, 1972.
30. Ginsberg, *op. cit.*
31. Dempsey J. Travis, President of UMBA, supplied the information in this section.
32. Andrew F. Brimmer, "Desegregation and Negro Leadership," in Ginzberg, *op. cit.*, p. 39. Apparently this was not net, but included existing levels of investment in limited income housing and similar programs.
33. Andrew F. Brimmer and Henry S. Terrell, "The Economic Potential of Black Capitalism," a paper delivered before the American Economic Association, December 29, 1969. *See also* Thaddeus H. Spratlen's review of Theodore L. Cross, *Black Capitalism: Strategy for Business in the Ghetto, The Review of Black Political Economy*, Vol. I, No. 1, Spring/Summer 1970, pp. 94–97; and Vivian W. Henderson, "Education and Training," in Ginzberg, *op. cit.*, pp. 150–51.
34. Richard F. American, Jr., "What Do You People Want?" *The Review of Black Political Economy*, Spring/Summer 1971, pp. 45–57.
35. Grass Roots has enlisted such companies as F. W. Woolworth Company, J. C. Penney Company, Columbia Broadcasting System, and the Great Atlantic and Pacific Tea Company to cooperate with black-owned businesses. *The New York Times*, January 1, 1972, pp. 25, 30.
36. *The New York Times*, May 23, 1972, p. 57.
37. *Washington Post*, July 10, 1970. The Reverend Mr. Leon Sullivan has since been named to the Board of Directors.
38. By John Egerton for the Race Relations Information Center and the Community News Service.
39. "Room at the Top," in *Black Enterprise*, Vol. 2, No. 14, September 1971, p. 18; *Negro History Bulletin*, November 1971, p. 166, *The New York Times*, June 25, 1972, Sec. F, p. 3.
40. Clarence C. Finley, Executive Vice-President, Burlington House Products Group of Burlington Industries, Inc., and former President of Burlington's Charm Tred carpet division is said to be the highest-ranking black executive in terms of actual functions and responsibility in a national corporation. Frederick D. Wilkinson, a vice-president of R. H. Macy, is close behind Finley in the ranks of black executives directly participating in top management. Other vice-presidents with responsibility are:
    Hughlyn Fierce, vice-president, Chase Manhattan Bank, in charge of a group of commercial-loan specialists.
    Walter Clarke, Senior Vice-President, First Federal Savings and Loan Association, Chicago.
    Richard Jackson, vice-president for engineering, Gits Brothers, Chicago.
41. Ernest Holsendolph, "Black Executives in a Nearly All-White World," *Fortune*, September 1972, pp. 140–151.
42. *Ibid.*
43. *The New York Times*, April 29, 1971.
44. U. S. Department of Commerce, Bureau of the Census, Current Population Reports, Series P-23, No. 48 (July 1974) pp. 19, 21.
45. Raymond O. Oladipupo, *How Distinct is the Negro Market?* (Ogilvy and Mather, Inc., New York, 1972).
46. Department of Commerce, Bureau of the Census, Series P-23, N. 42 (1971), p. 30.
47. D. Parke Gibson, *The $30 Billion Negro* (Macmillan, New York, 1969), p. 214.
48. Bracey, et al, *op. cit.*, pp. 372–73.
49. *The New York Times*, April 6, 1972; Whitney M. Young, Jr., "Domestic Marshall Plan," from *The New York Times Magazine*, October 6, 1963, Reprinted in Murphy and Elinson, *Problems and Prospects of the Negro Movement* (Wadsworth, 1966) pp. 45–49. *See also* John Seder and Berkeley G. Burrell, *Getting It Together: Black Businessmen in America* (New York, 1971), *passim*.
50. In addition to those already cited, *see* James Boggs, "The Myth and Irrationality of Black Capitalism," in *The Review of Black Political Economy*, Vol. I, No. 1, Spring/Summer 1970, pp. 27–35; James Forman, "*The Black Manifesto*," *Ibid.*, pp. 91–93; Theodore L. Cross, *op. cit.*; "Program Like Foreign Aid Urged for Black Business," in *The New York Times*, September 29, 1971, p. 42. Summaries and analyses of a variety of strategies are found in William C. Haddad and

G. Douglas Pugh, eds., *Black Economic Development* (Prentice-Hall, Englewood Cliffs, New Jersey, 1969) and Valentine, *op. cit.*

51. Among them are the United Presbyterian Church, the Episcopal Church, the United Methodist Church, the Christian Church (Disciples of Christ), the U. S. Catholic Bishops' Campaign for Human Development, the Fund for Social Justice of Riverside Church in New York. *Time,* May 3, 1971, pp. 51–52.

# BIBLIOGRAPHY

America, Richard F., Jr., "What Do You People Want?" *The Review of Black Political Economy*, Vol. I, No. 1, Spring/Summer 1970, pp. 45–57.

Bloch, Herman D., *The Circle of Discrimination: An Economic and Social Study of the Black Man in New York.* New York, NYU Press, 1969.

Bracey, John H., Jr., August Meier & Elliott Rudwick, eds. *Black Nationalism in America.* Indianapolis and New York, The Bobbs-Merrill Co., 1970.

Brimmer, Andrew F., "An Economic Agenda for Black Americans," Remarks at the Charter Day Convocation Celebrating the 105th Anniversary of Atlanta University, Atlanta, Georgia, October 16, 1970 (unpublished).

Brimmer, Andrew F. and Harriett Harper, "Economists' Perception of Minority Economic Problems: A View of Emerging Literature." *Journal of Economic Literature*, Vol. VIII, No. 3, September 1970, pp. 783–806.

Brimmer, Andrew F. and Henry S. Terrell, "The Economic Potential of Black Capitalism," a paper presented at the 82nd Annual Meeting of the American Economic Association, New York, N. Y., December 29, 1969.

Cross, Theodore L. *Black Capitalism: Strategy for Business in the Ghetto.* New York, Atheneum, 1970.

Franklin, John Hope, *From Slavery to Freedom.* New York, Knopf, 1956.

Fried, Joseph P., *Housing Crisis USA.* New York, Praeger, 1971.

Ginzberg, Eli, ed., *Business Leadership and the Negro Crisis.* New York, McGraw-Hill Book Co., 1968.

Glock, Charles Y. and Ellen Siegelman, eds. *Prejudice U.S.A.* New York, Praeger, 1969.

Haddad, William C., and G. Douglas Pugh, eds., *Black Economic Development.* Englewood Cliffs, New Jersey, Prentice-Hall, 1969.

Hannerz, Ulf, *Soulside: Inquiries into the Ghetto Culture and Community.* New York and London, Columbia University Press, 1969.

Holsendolph, Ernest, "Black Executives in a Nearly All-White World." *Fortune*, Vol. LXXXVI, No. 3, September 1972, pp. 140–151.

Jones, Edward H., *Blacks in Business.* New York, Grosset and Dunlap, 1972.

Kain, John F., ed., *Race and Poverty: The Economics of Discrimination.* Englewood Cliffs, New Jersey, Prentice-Hall, 1969.

Murphy, Raymond J. and Howard Elinson, *Problems and Prospects of the Negro Movement.* Belmont, California, Wadsworth, 1966.

"Reparations up to Date," *Time*, Vol. 97, No. 18, May 3, 1971, pp. 51–52.

*A Report on the Black Population Characteristics, Product and Media Usage*, prepared by Media Research Department, Ogilvy and Mather, Inc., May 1972.

*The Review of Black Political Economy,* Vols. I–V, 1970–74.

Ross, Arthur M. and Herbert Hill, eds., *Employment, Race and Poverty*. New York, Harcourt, Brace and World, 1967.

Seligman, Ben B., *Permanent Poverty, An American Syndrome*. Chicago, Quadrangle Books, 1968.

Theobald, Robert, ed., *Committed Spending: A Route to Economic Security*. Garden City, New York, Doubleday & Co., 1968.

U. S. Department of Commerce, Bureau of the Census, *Minority-Owned Businesses: 1969*. MB-1, Issued August 1971.

———, ———, Special Studies, *The Social and Economic Status of Negroes in the United States, 1970*. BLS Report No. 394, Current Population Reports, Series P-23, No. 48, July 1974.

———, Small Business Administration, *Special Catalog of Federal Programs Assisting Minority Enterprise*. Summer 1971. Washington, D.C.

Valentine, Charles A., *Culture and Poverty: Critique and Counter-Proposals*. Chicago, University of Chicago Press, 1968.

# 6

## *The Black American Worker*

### *Dorothy K. Newman*

Much is owed those young black students of the 1960s who insisted on introducing black studies into American education. Now, long out-of-print scholarly works on black economic history by George Haynes, Charles Wesley, Frederick Douglass, W. E. B. DuBois, Mary Ovington, and many others are once more available; at last, white as well as black students are undertaking serious study of black history.

Since some contemporary writers have not taken these scholarly works into account, their analyses of the economic plight of black Americans today are subject to substantial reassessment—especially in discussing the gaps between blacks and whites in employment and unemployment, and in earnings and family income. Government questionnaires and reports, and studies in economic and econometric analysis require fresh conceptualization to avoid assumptions based only on the recent past. The stereotype of the disadvantaged black worker must be examined on the basis of documented social and economic history.

### The Skilled and Creative Black Worker—Slave and Freed

American history and analysis of studies, surveys, and censuses dating from the seventeenth century to early in the twentieth century illustrate the skill diversity among black workers—slave and free, black, mulatto, and octoroon. Slaves were not field hands alone. They did mechanical, structural, and creative work on farms and plantations. As industry developed, slaves were either hired out or bought to work in many different occupations because of their skills. Industrial and commercial enterprises often owned many slaves. Freed blacks practiced the crafts they had learned while slaves, or learned skills on the job.

Both slaves and freedmen and women were cabinetmakers, tailors, dressmakers, bakers, chefs, weavers, shoemakers, carpenters, printers, clerks, bookkeepers, tanners, millers, coopers, brickmakers, masons, plasterers, wheelwrights, blacksmiths, mechanics, and artisans. They built, maintained, and operated facilities associated with households, land holdings, and commercial and industrial enterprises. Slaves were credited with significant inventions and in some cases patented them in the course of their work.

After being freed by their masters before emancipation, many former slaves became prosperous. A number entered the professions. This period saw the emergence of black doctors, teachers, ministers, research scientists, writers, historians, and social libertarians, some of whom led movements for freedom, collective bargaining, and economic cooperation.

In his classic work *Negro Labor in the United States, 1850–1925*,[1] Charles Wesley, on coming to emancipation and the Reconstruction period, repeats the then popular question "Will the Negro work?" (meaning without direction and goading by a master). Wesley's findings and those of other scholars document unequivocally that the real question, rather, was whether whites, suddenly confronted with a newly expanded labor force free of their control and free to search for work, would accept black workers as equals in a society called free. It was at this point that the current stereotype of the so-called disadvantaged worker or, more honestly, the less-desired worker, came into being.

Before emancipation, neither slaves nor freedmen and women were seen as serious competitors to white workers. Slaves who were hired out represented a cheap and tractable labor pool. Masters received most of their pay. But when all black Americans entered the free labor force, fear, greed, competition, and habits of thinking and acting in a caste society induced sharp discrimination in hiring, employment, and working conditions. New laws were passed explicitly excluding blacks from specified occupations, barring them from holding land or engaging in certain types of contracts, or requiring special licenses for undertaking certain types of businesses. Restrictions on their economic life became so harsh that blacks were gradually excluded from many occupations, especially in the South.

Slave holding had prevailed in the North as well as the South but not to the same degree. Reports indicate that many of the northern abolitionists were motivated more by the wish to equalize the cost of labor between North and South than by a moral stance against slave holding.

Large numbers of black people began migrating to the northern cities in the mid-1860s in search of jobs and improved living conditions. They moved mostly to escape depressed economic conditions in the South and to profit from emerging northern industries. They were met by intense resistance, particularly from the wave of white immigrants who had arrived in large numbers beginning in about the mid-1880s. Competition erupted into conflict in a number of large northern cities, leading to riots started usually by white workers, often immigrants. The riots of the 1860s were more numerous and bloody than those of the 1960s.

Henry Ward Beecher is quoted as saying as early as 1862 that "The only chance for the colored man North nowadays is to wait and shave,* and they are being driven

*I.e., be a waiter or barber.

from that as fast as possible."[2] Nevertheless the migration stream intensified, in spite of the hardships of resettlement.

The migration of blacks from the South is the most extensive movement of a single group in American history. The motivation was largely economic, accompanied by hopes for improved living conditions. Blacks have made greatest advances in employment and incomes in the North and in the western cities, which have been their most recent destinations. George Haynes's theme, in his study *The Negro At Work in New York City*,[3] emphasizes that black people have merely traveled the route of white immigrants and other whites in reaching out for better jobs, more amenities, and a higher level of living. (See Figure 1.)

The most urbane of present economists and econometricians admit the complexities of the phenomena they seek to explain—the gap between white and black achievement in terms of employment, occupation, and income.[4]

Without knowledge of history and a grasp of its importance it is impossible to deal sensibly with today's results. Econometric models and analysis of all the available texts and data cannot apportion how much of the present black disadvantage in the job market results from what causes. Scholars need to place much greater emphasis than in the past on the cultural, social, psychological, geographic, and economic processes involved, including the role of race prejudice.

## Occupations and Earnings

From being expected to do virtually everything until the mid-1800s, most black people were thwarted from doing anything but the most menial work during much of the next one hundred years. By the late 1950s and during the 1960s and early 1970s, however, this situation had changed greatly because of the aspiration, hard work, persistence, and pressure by blacks themselves who took advantage of opportunity or created it whenever they could.

Although federal and state civil rights commissions and committees have made employers self-conscious, direct government efforts dating chiefly from 1941 have not been as effective in moving blacks into better positions as have other influences. White employers' most powerful incentives have been labor shortages in major economic upturns, especially during World War II and the Korean War.

Executive orders and the laws on the books specific to equal employment rights have not been enforced vigorously even when enforcement rather than conciliation machinery has been provided.[5] Few government agencies have challenged the policies of important corporate enterprises in the courts. The Federal Government's record has been less imposing than that of such private groups as the National Association for the Advancement of Colored People (NAACP) and the American Civil Liberties Union.

FIGURE 1— BLACKS HAVE MIGRATED TO THEIR BENEFIT

## 1970

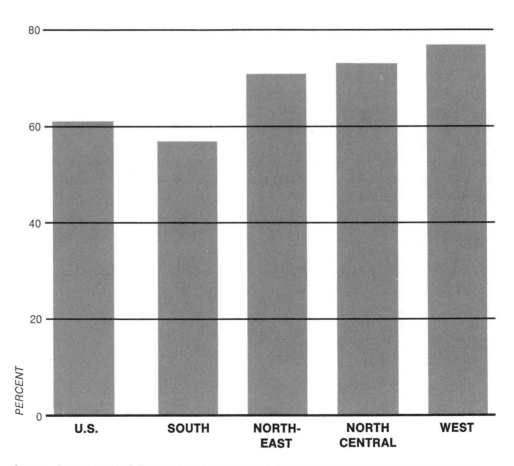

Source:   Derived from U. S. Bureau of the Census and U. S. Bureau of Labor Statistics, *Current Population Reports*, P-23, No. 38 and BLS Report No. 394, "The Social and Economic Conditions of Negroes in the United States, 1970," Table 18.

Legal suits through any agency require the commitment, time, and money necessary to use, test, and improve laws or regulations on the books.

The most important "equal opportunity" employment agency, the Equal Employment Opportunity Commission (EEOC) created by the Civil Rights Act of 1964, received enforcement powers for the first time in 1972, but without its own binding cease-and-desist orders. The EEOC must still go to the federal courts for enforcement. To date, almost all procedures under the EEOC, the office of Federal Contract Compliance, and the Civil Rights Commission have been through reports, hearings, and conciliation. The push for equality has been difficult and tortuous.

One of the most effective methods for advancing occupational attainment was through the generous educational provisions under the Servicemen's Readjustment Act of 1944—the GI Bill of Rights—which provided vocational and college educational assistance adequate to support a student and his or her family, as well as to pay tuition. A larger portion of blacks than whites took advantage of this provision of the GI Bill,[6] and they, their families, and the country are reaping the benefits today. World War II and Korean veterans entered schools of their choice, and graduated qualified to undertake a variety of skilled and professional jobs, even when judged by discriminating employers. Educational advancement and good jobs helped black veterans and have given their children an important leg up in meeting their own school and job competition. This significant piece of legislation, which was provided to all veterans, accounts partly for the substantially greater proportional advancement into college training by blacks than whites in recent decades. (See Figure 2.)

Prosperity or an expanding economy; the push for equality which instigated equal employment opportunity orders, committees, and commissions; the degree to which enforcement has been vigorous; and many other related and seemingly unrelated activities and conditions account for recent changes in the occupational distribution of black Americans. To understand the meaning and nature of the occupational shifts requires careful disaggregation of averages and medians—by age and sex, by industry, and by location and the economic history of regions, areas, and cities.

What are some of the changes? According to the accompanying tables, showing occupational distribution for black and white men and women for selected years since 1958, substantial increases among black men and women have occurred in generally preferred types of jobs (including many well-paid operative jobs in industry). Major declines took place in occupations bringing lowest pay (mostly laboring, farm work, and domestic service). Occupational distributions usually change slowly, so that the shifts reflected in these data from the U. S. Bureau of Labor Statistics are actually more impressive than the numbers themselves show. The proportions in professional and technical work more than doubled for both black men and women, amounting to about a quarter of a million people in each case and about one-fourth of the change in black employment between 1958 and 1971.

FIGURE 2 — BLACK SONS HAVE MUCH MORE EDUCATION THAN THEIR FATHERS

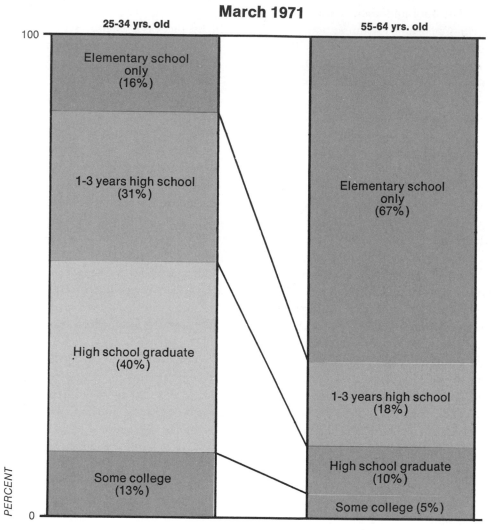

**March 1971**

25-34 yrs. old

55-64 yrs. old

100

Elementary school
only
(16%)

1-3 years high school
(31%)

Elementary school
only
(67%)

High school graduate
(40%)

1-3 years high school
(18%)

Some college
(13%)

High school graduate
(10%)

Some college (5%)

PERCENT

0

Source:   Derived from U. S. Bureau of the Census, *Current Population Reports*, P-60, No. 80, "Income in
1970 of Families and Persons in the United States," Table 28.

**TABLE I**—PERCENTAGE DISTRIBUTION OF MEN BY OCCUPATION AND RACE, SELECTED YEARS 1958–1971

| Occupation | Black* | | | | White | | | |
|---|---|---|---|---|---|---|---|---|
| | 1958 | 1963 | 1968 | 1971 | 1958 | 1963 | 1968 | 1971 |
| Total | 100 | 100 | 100 | 100 | 100 | 100 | 100 | 100 |
| Professional & technical | 3 | 5 | 7 | 8 | 11 | 13 | 14 | 14 |
|   Medical | ↓ | 1 | 1 | 1 | 1 | 1 | 1 | 1 |
|   Teachers | 1 | 1 | 1 | 1 | 1 | 1 | 1 | 2 |
|   Other | 2 | 3 | 5 | 6 | 9 | 10 | 11 | 11 |
| Managers | 3 | 3 | 4 | 5 | 15 | 15 | 15 | 16 |
|   Salaried | 1 | 1 | 2 | 4 | 7 | 9 | 11 | 12 |
|   Self-employed—retail | 1 | 1 | 1 | 1 | 3 | 3 | 2 | 2 |
|   Self-employed—other | 1 | 1 | 1 | 1 | 4 | 4 | 2 | 2 |
| Clerical | 5 | 5 | 7 | 7 | 7 | 7 | 7 | 7 |
|   Stenographers & secretaries | ↓ | ↓ | ↓ | ↓ | ↓ | ↓ | ↓ | ↓ |
|   Other | 5 | 5 | 7 | 7 | 7 | 7 | 7 | 7 |
| Sales | 1 | 2 | 2 | 2 | 6 | 6 | 6 | 6 |
|   Retail | 1 | 1 | 1 | 1 | 2 | 2 | 2 | 2 |
|   Other | ↓ | 1 | 1 | 1 | 4 | 4 | 4 | 4 |
| Craftsmen & foremen | 9 | 11 | 13 | 13 | 20 | 20 | 21 | 21 |
|   Carpenters | 1 | 1 | 1 | 1 | 2 | 2 | 2 | 2 |
|   Other construction | 2 | 3 | 3 | 4 | 4 | 4 | 4 | 4 |
|   Mechanics | 3 | 3 | 4 | 3 | 5 | 5 | 6 | 5 |
|   Metal | 1 | 1 | 1 | 1 | 3 | 3 | 3 | 2 |
|   Other craftsmen | 2 | 2 | 2 | 3 | 4 | 4 | 4 | 4 |
|   Other foremen | ↓ | 1 | 1 | 1 | 3 | 3 | 3 | 3 |
| Operatives | 24 | 25 | 28 | 26 | 19 | 20 | 19 | 17 |
|   Drivers & deliverymen | 8 | 8 | 7 | 7 | 5 | 5 | 5 | 5 |
|   Other | 16 | 18 | 21 | 19 | 14 | 15 | 14 | 13 |
|     Durable goods mfg. | 6 | 7 | 10 | 10 | 6 | 6 | 7 | 7 |
|     Nondurable goods mfg. | 4 | 4 | 5 | 5 | 4 | 4 | 3 | 3 |
|     Other industry | 7 | 6 | 6 | 4 | 5 | 4 | 4 | 3 |
| Nonfarm laborers | 24 | 21 | 18 | 18 | 6 | 6 | 6 | 7 |
|   Construction | 6 | 5 | 4 | 4 | 1 | 1 | 1 | 1 |
|   Manufacturing | 7 | 6 | 6 | 5 | 2 | 2 | 2 | 2 |
|   Other industry | 11 | 11 | 8 | 8 | 3 | 3 | 3 | 4 |
| Private household | 1 | ↓ | ↓ | ↓ | ↓ | ↓ | ↓ | ↓ |
| Service | 15 | 16 | 14 | 15 | 5 | 6 | 6 | 7 |
|   Protective | 1 | 1 | 1 | 2 | 2 | 2 | 2 | 2 |
|   Waiters | 2 | 3 | 3 | 2 | 1 | 1 | 1 | 1 |
|   Other | 12 | 12 | 10 | 11 | 3 | 3 | 3 | 4 |
| Farmers & farm managers | 6 | 3 | 2 | 1 | 7 | 5 | 4 | 4 |
| Farm laborers & foremen | 9 | 8 | 5 | 4 | 3 | 2 | 2 | 3 |

*Black and other races
↓ Less than half of one percent

Source: Derived from *Employment and Earnings,* December 1971; and unpublished tabulations of the U. S. Bureau of Labor Statistics.

**TABLE II**—PERCENTAGE DISTRIBUTION OF WOMEN BY OCCUPATION AND RACE, SELECTED YEARS 1958–1971

| Occupation | Black* | | | | White | | | |
|---|---|---|---|---|---|---|---|---|
| | 1958 | 1963 | 1968 | 1971 | 1958 | 1963 | 1968 | 1971 |
| Total | 100 | 100 | 100 | 100 | 100 | 100 | 100 | 100 |
| Professional & technical | 5 | 8 | 10 | 11 | 13 | 13 | 15 | 15 |
|   Medical | 1 | 2 | 2 | 2 | 4 | 4 | 4 | 4 |
|   Teachers | 3 | 5 | 5 | 5 | 6 | 6 | 6 | 7 |
|   Other | 1 | 2 | 3 | 3 | 4 | 4 | 5 | 4 |
| Managers | 2 | 2 | 2 | 2 | 5 | 5 | 5 | 5 |
|   Salaried | ↓ | 1 | 1 | 2 | 2 | 3 | 3 | 4 |
|   Self-employed—retail | 1 | 1 | 1 | 1 | ↓ | 1 | 1 | 1 |
|   Self-employed—other | ↓ | ↓ | ↓ | ↓ | 1 | 1 | 1 | 1 |
| Clerical | 7 | 10 | 18 | 22 | 33 | 34 | 36 | 36 |
|   Stenographers & secretaries | 2 | 3 | 5 | 6 | 12 | 12 | 13 | 13 |
|   Other | 5 | 7 | 13 | 16 | 22 | 22 | 23 | 23 |
| Sales | 2 | 2 | 2 | 3 | 9 | 8 | 8 | 8 |
|   Retail | 1 | 1 | 2 | 2 | 8 | 7 | 7 | 7 |
|   Other | ↓ | ↓ | ↓ | ↓ | 1 | 1 | 1 | 1 |
| Craftsmen & foremen | 1 | 1 | 1 | 1 | 1 | 1 | 1 | 1 |
|   Carpenters | ↓ | ↓ | ↓ | ↓ | ↓ | ↓ | ↓ | ↓ |
|   Other construction | ↓ | ↓ | ↓ | ↓ | ↓ | ↓ | ↓ | ↓ |
|   Mechanics | ↓ | ↓ | ↓ | ↓ | ↓ | ↓ | ↓ | ↓ |
|   Metal | ↓ | ↓ | ↓ | ↓ | ↓ | ↓ | ↓ | ↓ |
|   Other craftsmen | ↓ | ↓ | ↓ | 1 | ↓ | 1 | 1 | 1 |
|   Other foremen | ↓ | ↓ | ↓ | ↓ | 1 | ↓ | ↓ | ↓ |
| Operatives | 14 | 14 | 17 | 15 | 16 | 15 | 15 | 13 |
|   Drivers & deliverymen | ↓ | ↓ | ↓ | ↓ | ↓ | ↓ | ↓ | ↓ |
|   Other | 14 | 14 | 17 | 15 | 15 | 15 | 15 | 13 |
|     Durable goods mfg. | 2 | 2 | 4 | 4 | 4 | 4 | 5 | 4 |
|     Nondurable goods mfg. | 6 | 5 | 8 | 7 | 8 | 8 | 8 | 6 |
|     Other industry | 6 | 6 | 5 | 4 | 3 | 3 | 2 | 2 |
| Nonfarm laborers | 1 | 1 | 1 | 1 | ↓ | ↓ | ↓ | 1 |
|   Construction | ↓ | ↓ | ↓ | ↓ | ↓ | ↓ | ↓ | ↓ |
|   Manufacturing | ↓ | ↓ | ↓ | ↓ | ↓ | ↓ | ↓ | ↓ |
|   Other industry | 1 | 1 | ↓ | 1 | ↓ | ↓ | ↓ | 1 |
| Private household | 37 | 34 | 22 | 16 | 1 | 5 | 4 | 3 |
| Service | 22 | 22 | 25 | 27 | 13 | 15 | 14 | 16 |
|   Protective | ↓ | ↓ | ↓ | ↓ | ↓ | ↓ | ↓ | ↓ |
|   Waiters | 5 | 5 | 6 | 5 | 5 | 6 | 6 | 6 |
|   Other | 17 | 18 | 19 | 22 | 1 | 8 | 9 | 10 |
| Farmers & farm managers | 1 | 1 | ↓ | ↓ | 1 | 1 | ↓ | ↓ |
| Farm laborers & foremen | 9 | 6 | 2 | 1 | 3 | 2 | 2 | 1 |

*Black and other races
↓ Less than half of one percent

Source:  Derived from *Employment and Earnings,* December 1971 ; and unpublished tabulations of the U. S. Bureau of Labor Statistics.

Black men gained in all fields in which wages are relatively the highest, and lost ground in all in which wages tend to be lowest. (The median wage for full-time work in the major occupation groups are shown in order of rank in Table III.) Women, whether white or black, are concentrated in fewer kinds of work than are men, and in work bringing much less income. Among black women the greatest gain was in clerical work, in which about a fifth of all black women workers were employed in 1971 compared to less than a tenth in 1958. This change of about 600,000 women amounted to 60 percent of the increase in black women's employment in the 1958–71 period. Clerical jobs rank slightly above the median in earnings for full-time workers. Employment dropped sharply in private household work, in which almost 40 percent of all black women worked in 1958, compared to fewer than 10 percent in 1971. Domestic workers' earnings for those working full-time year-round are the lowest among all jobs for which we have data. They average close to the poverty level for one person and considerably below the poverty level for a family of four.

Services other than domestic work require a special word because they are a mixed group often presented as a single statistical unit without explanation. The group properly should be analyzed by occupation and reassessed for possible reclassification. The services group includes police and firemen (protective services), airline stewards or stewardesses, business and repair service occupations, and some paraprofessional jobs, such as practical nurses and dental assistants. It includes barbers, hairdressers, and beauticians also, in addition to all restaurant workers, from the chef to the dishwasher. Many employees in such services have highly esteemed positions and earn relatively high wages. The economy is growing in the direction of needing and providing more openings in the better-paying service fields and both black and white women have found increasing opportunities in these services. The group as a whole, however, is weighted heavily with intermittent workers and low earners.

The 1958–71 shifts in occupational structure are striking, but did not create equality. Black men and women were far from being as occupationally successful as whites by 1971. What is more, within each occupational group black workers earn less than whites. The specific job the black worker does in the occupation group may pay less; the black worker may not be promoted as readily; he or she may be getting less for the same job; or black workers may live in areas or work in businesses in which the pay is less, regardless of the job or who holds it.

Studies so far have not fully quantified or identified the conditions leading to occupational inequality. Among those studies which are least convincing are those which use the technique of assigning the precise proportion of blacks in the labor force to occupation groups for measuring equality. It is inconceivable that blacks or any other group should be expected to occupy each occupation in precisely the proportion they are found in the population, for many reasons, including personal preferences, individual differences, group ideologies, and local or regional economic needs where large numbers of the group may live.

**TABLE III—MEDIAN EARNINGS OF YEAR-ROUND FULL-TIME WORKERS BY OCCUPATION, SEX, AND RACE, 1970**

| Occupation | Men | | | Women | | | Ratios | | | |
| --- | --- | --- | --- | --- | --- | --- | --- | --- | --- | --- |
| | | | | | | | Black to White | | Women to Men | |
| | All Races | Black | White | All Races | Black | White | Men | Women | Black to Black | White to White |
| Self-employed professionals | $20,031 | ↓ | $20,320 | ↓ | ↓ | ↓ | ↓ | ↓ | ↓ | ↓ |
| Salaried manager | $12,597 | $9,216 | $12,657 | $6,885 | ↓ | $6,811 | 73 | ↓ | ↓ | 54 |
| Salaried professional | 11,937 | 8,558 | 12,078 | 7,856 | 7,685 | 7,871 | 71 | 98 | 90 | 65 |
| Teachers—elem. & second. | 9,883 | ↓ | 9,969 | 7,856 | 7,975 | 7,826 | ↓ | 102 | ↓ | 71 |
| Sales | 9,765 | ↓ | 9,851 | 4,174 | ↓ | 4,167 | ↓ | ↓ | ↓ | 42 |
| Craftsmen & foremen | 9,253 | 7,353 | 9,349 | 4,955 | ↓ | 4,942 | 79 | ↓ | ↓ | 53 |
| Clerical | 8,652 | 7,668 | 8,763 | 5,539 | 5,575 | 5,529 | 88 | 101 | 73 | 63 |
| Self-employed managers | 7,767 | ↓ | 7,781 | 3,611 | ↓ | 3,642 | ↓ | ↓ | ↓ | 47 |
| Operatives (not in mfg.) | 7,753 | 5,932 | 8,012 | 3,342 | 3,693 | 3,905 | 74 | 95 | 62 | 49 |
| Durable goods operatives | 7,710 | 6,941 | 7,877 | 5,055 | 4,497 | 5,114 | 88 | 88 | 65 | 65 |
| Nondurable goods operatives | 7,292 | 5,882 | 7,523 | 4,242 | 3,847 | 4,309 | 78 | 89 | 65 | 57 |
| Services (except domestic) | 6,964 | 5,670 | 7,388 | 3,875 | 3,786 | 3,898 | 77 | 97 | 67 | 53 |
| Nonfarm laborers | 6,462 | 5,410 | 6,796 | 4,375 | ↓ | 4,389 | 80 | ↓ | ↓ | 65 |
| Farmers and farm managers | 3,881 | ↓ | 3,175 | ↓ | ↓ | ↓ | ↓ | ↓ | ↓ | ↓ |
| Farm laborers and foremen | 3,355 | ↓ | 3,741 | ↓ | ↓ | ↓ | ↓ | ↓ | ↓ | ↓ |
| Domestic workers | ↓ | ↓ | ↓ | 1,990 | 2,054 | 1,863 | ↓ | 110 | ↓ | ↓ |
| Median | 7,152 | 6,368 | 9,223 | 5,323 | 4,447 | 5,412 | 69 | 82 | 70 | 59 |

Note:   Data are for workers 14 years old and over; few full-time workers are less than 16 years old.
↓  Base too small

Source:   Derived from U. S. Dept. of Commerce, Bureau of the Census, *Current Population Reports*, P-60, No. 80, "Income in 1970 of Families and Persons," Tables 56 and 58.

In the early 1970s more than a fifth of all Japanese-American or Chinese-American men were in the professions, compared to 14 to 15 percent of Polish, Italian, and Irish-origin men, two-fifths of whom are craftsmen or other kinds of industrial workers.[7] Polish, Italian, and Irish men represent between 2 and 7 percent of the male labor force. The Japanese and Chinese-American men are even smaller groups. What does proportional representation possibly accomplish? (See Figure 3.)

Actually, the economy's employment requirements dictate an occupational distribution which changes with the demands of industry, trade, and the professions. In 1971 about 14 percent of all working men were in professional or technical work, 14 percent were managers, and 20 percent each were craftsmen or operatives. The white ethnic ratios correspond roughly to the distribution of American working men as a whole. Among black American men, who are 11 percent of the total male labor force, 8 percent were in professional or technical types of jobs in 1971, 5 percent were managers, 13 percent were in the crafts, and 26 percent were operatives. This picture suggests that substantial numbers of black men had not yet been permitted to contribute their talents to facets of the American economy requiring professional, technical, and managerial competence, or craftsmanship in the skilled trades. Some economists have tried to measure the dollar cost of this occupational discrimination.[8] The cost in productivity, effects from rebuff and humiliation, and experience lost, leading to reductions both in material and human capital, are not easily measured, if indeed they can be measured at all.

The effect of the occupational mix of black men and women workers is reflected in their relative earnings. (See Table III.) Black men who are full-time workers earn about 70 to 80 percent of the salary of white men. The ratios are lowest in the better-paying occupation groups. Black women who work full-time earn (at the median) about 80 percent of white women's full-time earnings. They earn about as much as or a little more than white women in a few occupation groups, such as elementary and secondary school teaching, clerical work, and in services. Both black and white women in each occupation group earn substantially less than either black or white men. (See Figure 4.)

A more important key to the relative disadvantage of black workers, however, is the level of earnings. Black men who worked full time all year in 1970 averaged about $6,500, compared to about $9,225 for white men who were full-time workers. Since a substantially larger proportion of blacks than whites live in large cities it is fair to use the Bureau of Labor Statistics budgets for a metropolitan-area family of four to test the adequacy of a $6,500 annual income. (About half earned less than this and about half earned more, of course.)

In the spring of 1970 it cost over $7,000 in metropolitan areas to live at a lower-than-intermediate budget. This budget incorporates a food plan used widely to estimate money allowances for food in public assistance programs, that is, for the very poor. The Bureau of Labor Statistics (BLS) itself states that "Although families can achieve nutritional adequacy from the low-cost plan, it has been estimated that only about a

FIGURE 3 — THE SIZE OF ETHNIC GROUPS BEARS NO RELATION TO
PROPORTION OF EACH IN EACH OCCUPATION

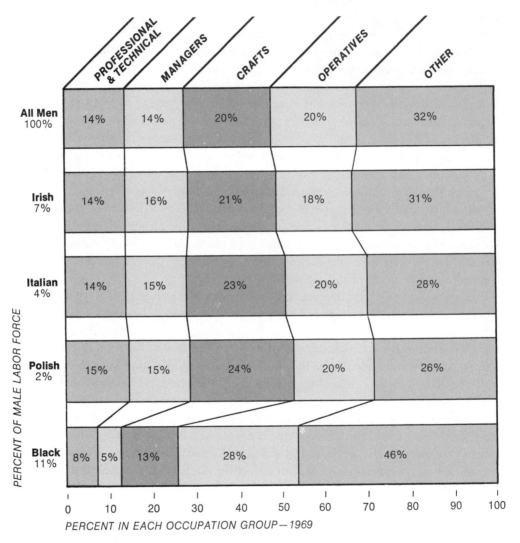

Note:   Data are for ethnic origin; blacks are "Negroes and other races."

Source:   Derived from U. S. Bureau of Labor Statistics, unpublished tabulations; U. S. Bureau of the
Census, *Current Population Reports,* Characteristics of the Population by Ethnic Origin,
November 1969, P-60, No. 221, Table 15.

FIGURE 4 — BLACK WOMEN ARE POOR; BLACK MEN ARE BETTER OFF THAN WHITE WOMEN

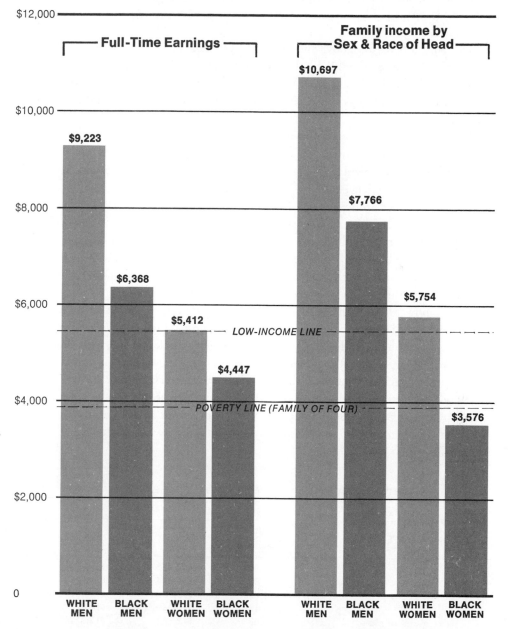

Source:   Derived from U. S. Bureau of the Census, *Current Population Reports,* P-60, No. 80, "Income in 1970 of Families and Persons in the United States," Tables 17 and 52, and P-60, No. 81, "Characteristics of the Low-Income Population, 1970," Table N; and U. S. Bureau of Labor Statistics, *Three Budgets for an Urban Family of Four Persons, 1969-70,* Table A-1.

fourth of those who spend amounts equivalent to the cost of the plan actually have nutritionally adequate diets. Menus based on this plan will include foods requiring a considerable amount of home preparation, as well as skill in cooking to make varied and appetizing meals."[9]

The $6,500 is $2,500 above the officially estimated 1970 poverty level of almost $4,000 for a family of four. If black women's average earnings alone are considered (about $4,445), families living at or below this level have no leeway for discretionary expenditures for such things as special education, recreation, and social and community participation.

The earnings cited, moreover, are for full-time all-year workers. Many cannot count on full-time employment, especially in recession years, and many are unable to work full time either because of disabilities, their age, household responsibilities, or school or college attendance.

Because earnings are low, black family income depends more heavily than white family income on supplementary earnings, usually those of the wife. Black wives are much more likely than white wives to be in the paid labor force. When the wife, as well as her husband, is a full-time wage earner, the black woman contributes about 37 percent to family income, compared to 33 percent by the white man's working wife. The wife's share varies somewhat by age. It is a little higher when the family is young and earning power in general is less than in the prime working years. It took two earners among black families in 1970 to achieve an income almost as high at the median ($8,430) as in one-earner white families ($8,713). (See Figure 5.) Black families with even more earners (three, four, or more) had less income than two-earner white families. (Table IV.) When the wife was not in the paid labor force in 1970 the black family's median income was $5,961, about $600 below the BLS lower-than-intermediate budget for metropolitan areas, and $2,000 above the poverty level for a four-person family. It was 63 percent of the white median income of $9,254 in a family in which the wife remained at home also.

### TABLE IV—MEDIAN FAMILY INCOME BY NUMBER OF EARNERS AND RACE, 1970

| Number of Earners | All families | Black | White |
|---|---|---|---|
| 0 | $ 3,289 | $ 2,235 | $ 3,489 |
| 1 | $ 8,352 | $ 4,844 | $ 8,713 |
| 2 | $11,190 | $ 8,430 | $11,450 |
| 3 | $14,438 | $10,000 | $14,795 |
| 4 or more | $16,688 | $11,112 | $17,311 |

Source: Derived from U. S. Dept. of Commerce, Bureau of the Census, *Current Population Reports,* P-60, No. 80, "Income in 1970 of Families and Earners," Table 29, p. 67.

FIGURE 5 — BLACK FAMILIES WORK HARDER AND GET LESS

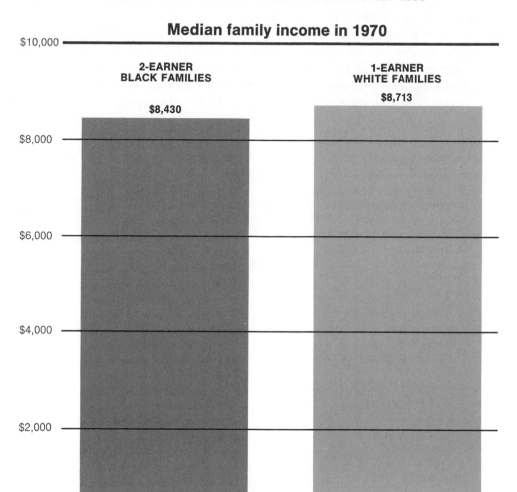

## Median family income in 1970

| | | |
|---|---|---|
| **2-EARNER BLACK FAMILIES** | | **1-EARNER WHITE FAMILIES** |
| $8,430 | | $8,713 |

$10,000

$8,000

$6,000

$4,000

$2,000

0

Source:   Derived from U. S. Bureau of the Census, *Current Population Reports*, P-60, No. 80, "Income in 1970 of Families and Persons in the United States," Table 29.

One of the myths of recent economic literature is that black women have higher earning power and greater employment potential than black men. If further documentation on this point is needed after the discussion above, a special study of industry occupation distributions by sex and race can be cited. The study used 1969 data for fifteen industries reporting (under law) to the Equal Employment Opportunity Commission. The number of persons in each industry, by sex and race for nine major occupation groups, were weighted by 1969 earnings. The earnings weights were refined statistically to reflect type and class of job by sex and race within the broad major groups. The following results (converted to index numbers) illustrate concisely the place of black men and women relative to white (other than Spanish-American) men and women in relative occupational attainment. (See Table V.)

TABLE V—OCCUPATIONAL ATTAINMENT INDEXES BY INDUSTRY, RACE, AND SEX, 1969 (WHITE[1] MEN = 100)

| Industry | White[1] Men | Black Men | White[1] Women | Black Women |
|---|---|---|---|---|
| All Industries | 100 | 70 | 68 | 62 |
| Steel | 100 | 76 | 70 | 64 |
| Metal products | 100 | 75 | 67 | 64 |
| Office machines | 100 | 71 | 59 | 57 |
| Motor vehicles | 100 | 76 | 70 | 67 |
| Aircraft | 100 | 71 | 63 | 59 |
| Meat products | 100 | 79 | 68 | 66 |
| Knitting mills | 100 | 84 | 69 | 67 |
| Commercial printing | 100 | 82 | 68 | 64 |
| Plastics | 100 | 70 | 65 | 61 |
| Petroleum refining | 100 | 69 | 62 | 58 |
| Trucking | 100 | 80 | 73 | 68 |
| Intercity transport | 100 | 74 | 70 | 63 |
| Telephone | 100 | 71 | 62 | 56 |
| Radio & TV | 100 | 67 | 58 | 55 |
| Department stores | 100 | 67 | 71 | 64 |

[1] Excluding those of Spanish origin.
Source:   From an unpublished study of the Research Department of the National Urban League, "Occupational Attainment of Ethnic Groups and Women in 15 Industries, 1971."

Invariably black women take last place. On the other hand, black men exceed white women in occupational attainment in almost every case. They nevertheless were far from equalling the occupational attainment of white men in any of the industries studied. Studies which have not related men and women's earnings on a continuum by race and occupation, have omitted an important dimension of analysis. It is anachronistic, but unfortunately common practice, to relate men's occupations and earnings only to those of men, and women's only to those of women.

The influences on equality in the job market are legion. Only some are touched upon in this chapter. A few important conditions relate to location (region, size of place, and whether in or outside of a central city or metropolitan area), the earning power of the family head, and the breadth and equity of the income distribution within each race. All of these are affected by access to jobs. Some of these influences are discussed briefly below.

## Family Income

By 1970 black family income was two and a third times its 1947 level (in constant dollars). White family income had almost doubled, but from a much higher base. Thus the ratio of black to white family income rose only 10 points, from about 50 to 60 percent, during a whole generation—23 years. (See Table VI.) In 1970 median black family income was $6,279 (including all forms of income and the earnings of all family members), compared to $10,236 for white families. Thus half of all black families had incomes close to or below the lower budget level in metropolitan areas, and not far from the poverty level for a family of four. Many, therefore, were near-poor or poor. (See Figure 6.)

TABLE VI—MEDIAN FAMILY INCOME BY RACE, 1947, 1950, 1958–1970
(in constant 1970 dollars)

| Year | Income | | Ratio | | Index (1947 = 100) | |
|------|--------|-------|-------|-------|--------|-------|
| | Black | White | Black to White | | Black* | White |
| | | | Including other races | Black only | | |
| 1947 | $2,807 | $ 5,478 | 51 | NA | 100 | 100 |
| 1950 | $3,014 | $ 5,601 | 54 | NA | 107 | 102 |
| 1958 | $3,645 | $ 7,118 | 51 | NA | 130 | 130 |
| 1959 | $3,883 | $ 7,517 | 52 | NA | 138 | 137 |
| 1960 | $4,236 | $ 7,664 | 55 | NA | 151 | 140 |
| 1961 | $4,147 | $ 7,783 | 53 | NA | 148 | 142 |
| 1962 | $4,273 | $ 8,009 | 53 | NA | 152 | 146 |
| 1963 | $4,401 | $ 8,307 | 53 | NA | 157 | 152 |
| 1964 | $4,806 | $ 8,590 | 56 | 54 | 171 | 157 |
| 1965 | $4,930 | $ 8,935 | 55 | 54 | 176 | 163 |
| 1966 | $5,591 | $ 9,341 | 60 | 58 | 199 | 171 |
| 1967 | $5,978 | $ 9,628 | 62 | 59 | 213 | 176 |
| 1968 | $6,249 | $ 9,972 | 63 | 60 | 223 | 182 |
| 1969 | $6,568 | $10,362 | 63 | 61 | 234 | 189 |
| 1970 | $6,516 | $10,386 | 64 | 61 | 232 | 187 |

NA = not available
*Black and other races

Source:  Derived from U. S. Dept. of Commerce, Bureau of the Census, *Current Population Reports,* P-60, No. 80, "Income in 1970 of Families and Persons in the U.S.," Table 8, p. 22 and Table 11, p. 24. Also, from U. S. Dept. of Commerce, Bureau of the Census and U.S. Dept. of Labor, Bureau of Labor Statistics, *Current Population Reports,* P-23, No. 38 and BLS Report No. 394, "Social and Economic Status of Negroes in the U. S., 1970," Table 16, p. 25.

FIGURE 6 — MOST BLACK FAMILIES ARE AT THE LOWER END OF THE INCOME  SCALE

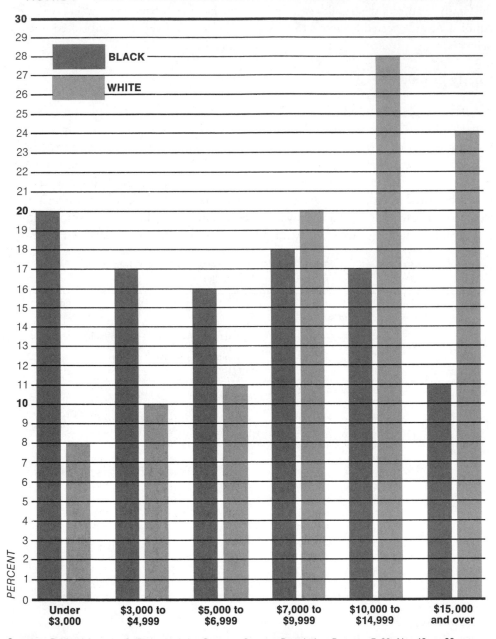

Source:   Derived from U. S. Bureau of the Census, *Current Population Reports,* P-23, No. 42, p. 30.

This was especially true in the South, where median black family income was $5,226 in 1970, only 57 percent of the white median. In the West and North Central regions, black family income was about three-fourths of the white. (See Table VII.)

TABLE VII—MEDIAN FAMILY INCOME BY REGION AND RACE, 1970

| Region | Family Income | | Ratio Black to White |
|--------|-------|-------|----------------------|
|        | Black | White | |
| United States | $6,279 | $10,236 | 61 |
| Northeast | $7,774 | $10,939 | 71 |
| North Central | $7,718 | $10,508 | 73 |
| South | $5,226 | $ 9,240 | 57 |
| West | $8,001 | $10,282 | 77 |

Source: Derived from U. S. Bureau of Census and U. S. Bureau of Labor Statistics, *Current Population Reports,* P-23, No. 38 and BLS Report No. 394, "Social and Economic Conditions of Negroes in the U.S., 1970" Table 18, p. 27.

Some of these disparities can be explained by where the families live inside each region. In each occupation group, black earnings were higher in the central cities of metropolitan areas than in small places where wages are not as high. Family income was highest of all in metropolitan areas of 1,000,000 or more population. Black people are more urban than whites, and more of the largest urban centers are located in the North than in the South. In addition, wages are higher in cities of the North than in the South.

The fact remains, however, that wherever they are and whatever the circumstances, middle income is much lower for black than white families. Only a fourth of black families were at or above white median income in 1970. Most black families had less than $8,000 and most white families had more. Yet expectations for life style and levels of living are often imposed similarly. The degree to which black families live up to these expectations, especially in educating their children beyond high school, reflects an extraordinary push for achievement.

Since 1947 little change has taken place in the reported share of their aggregate income that black or white families receive. The top 5 percent of black families had 15 percent of black income in 1970; 14 percent in the case of white families. In contrast, the lowest fifth of black families had about 5 percent of black aggregate income; 6 percent among white families. The figures in between, at each fifth of family income, appear if anything to make the income distribution among blacks somewhat less equitable than among whites.

Income alone, however, is an inadequate measure of the capacity to consume and prosper. It does not take account of assets, fixed taxes on wages or sales, tax benefits, deferred investment income, lines of credit from which blacks are often barred, and pension and welfare benefits to which only persons in particular industries, occupations,

or unions are entitled. Black workers are much less likely than whites to have the resources or monetary cushion which these benefits confer. On the other hand, they are
more likely to pay a higher percentage of their income in taxes. Because more of them
are poor, they can afford less for health care and other human resources, and have a
shorter total life span and working life. If all assets were taken into account—all tangibles
and the as yet unmeasured intangibles—that contribute to a broad concept of total
wealth, there is little doubt that white families, even at similar levels of income, would
be much richer than black families. It is likely also that disparity among whites would
be greater than among blacks, whose limited outside resources even at relatively high
incomes prevent accumulating great wealth. There are very few black millionaires.

## The Working Poor

Over 7.5 million black people, or one-third of the black population, was poor in
1970 by official standards. (One-tenth of the white population was poor, or 17.5 million.) Over half of the black poor were children, a larger proportion than among whites.
Of the adults, proportionately more blacks than whites were working—about 2,000,000,
including 1,000,000 women. Well over half a million of the black adults who were
poor worked at least forty weeks in 1970 and still had incomes below the poverty level.

TABLE VIII—WEIGHTED AVERAGE THRESHOLDS AT THE POVERTY LEVEL
IN 1970, BY SIZE OF FAMILY

| All Families | $3,580 | 5 Persons | $4,654 |
|---|---|---|---|
| 2 Persons | 3,507 | 6 Persons | 5,212 |
| Head Under 65 | 2,569 | 7 Persons or More | 6,407 |
| Head 65 or Over | 2,328 | Unrelated Individuals | 1,947 |
| 3 Persons | 3,080 | Under 65 | 2,005 |
| 4 Persons | 3,944 | 65 or Over | 1,552 |

Source : U. S. Department of Commerce, Bureau of the Census, *Current Population Reports,*
"Characteristics of the Low-Income Populations, 1970," Table N, p. 20.

Among those on welfare, a larger proportion of blacks than whites worked. According to a Social Security Administration survey of recipients of Aid to Families with
Dependent Children (AFDC), the largest public-assistance program, 30 percent of the
black mothers were working, in training, or seeking work or training in 1969, compared
to 22 percent of the white mothers.

## Employment, Unemployment, and the Labor Force

The facts clearly show, then, that black people, just as others, aspire to better conditions through effort. They have adhered to the American work ethic. What are the

results? In 1971 they were 11 percent of the labor force, 18 percent of the unemployed, and 19 percent of those unemployed fifteen weeks or more or working part-time although wanting full-time work.[10]

The unemployment rate of black people has never fallen to the first Nixon administration's "interim" target level of 4 percent in any year on record (1940–71). Yet this target was judged inadequate as an eventual national goal by President Nixon in 1972. The lowest black rate on record was 4.5 percent in 1953 during the Korean War. It was highest in the recession of 1961—12.4 percent. Except during the Great Depression, the white rate has rarely equalled the black, regardless of the year or the state of the economy. Even in the best of times, unemployment rates for blacks are substantially higher than for whites. (See Table IX.)

Averages of the total number unemployed relative to the civilian labor force require detailed analysis to be understood. They reflect, for instance, trends in the American population and its composition, and shifts in the economy.

Whereas black unemployment rates are far higher than white rates, the ratio of black to white rates does not invariably rise in bad times and decline in good times. The ratio has been over 2 to 1 in times of recession, such as in 1958 and 1961. It was below the 2 to 1 rate in good times and bad, such as during the Korean War and in the recession of 1970–71. (See Figure 7.)

One explanation for this and other trends or relationships in unemployment rates are concurrent trends within the labor force and, to some extent, the population distribution from which the labor force is drawn. Historical data show that teenagers and youth have the highest unemployment rates in the labor force and that both black and white women, especially in the decade of the 1960s, have higher unemployment rates than men. A larger proportion of the labor force was composed of these higher-risk groups in 1970 than in 1960. (See Table X.)

As a result of the baby boom of the fifties, more youth, black and white, are available and looking for jobs today, but white youth find work much more easily than the black. Whether white or black, young people are more apt to leave jobs, experiment with vocations, and work part-time at various times and at odd jobs while attending high school and college. Such sporadic activity, or turnover, adds to their unemployment rate. However, white youth are more readily and more quickly accepted than black youth into usual avenues of employment. Black youth could be working and earning but at intermittent and varied types of work which they or the household informant might interpret as not being a real job, or as looking for work. Therefore the statistics on employment may not include many young blacks in marginal or odd jobs. In reality the youth may be earning and seeking employment, but may not be successful in working arrangements normally considered permanent or desirable, even though by Census and Labor Department definition, all paid activity places one in the labor force.

**TABLE IX—UNEMPLOYMENT RATES OF TOTAL LABOR FORCE, 1929–48, AND BY RACE AND SEX, 1949–71, WITH RATIOS OF BLACK TO WHITE AND WOMEN TO MEN[1]**

| 1929–48 | | 1949–71 | | | | | | | | | | |
|---|---|---|---|---|---|---|---|---|---|---|---|---|
| Total Labor Force | | | | Black* | | | White | | | Ratios | | |
| Year | Rate | Year | Total | Total | Men | Women | Total | Men | Women | Black to White | Black Women to Black Men | White Women to White Men |
| 1929 | 3.2 | 1949 | 5.9 | 8.9 | NA | NA | 5.6 | NA | NA | 1.6 | NA | NA |
| 1930 | 8.7 | 1950 | 5.3 | 9.0 | NA | NA | 4.9 | NA | NA | 1.8 | NA | NA |
| 1931 | 15.9 | 1951 | 3.3 | 6.3 | NA | NA | 3.1 | NA | NA | 1.7 | NA | NA |
| 1932 | 33.6 | 1952 | 3.0 | 5.4 | NA | NA | 2.8 | NA | NA | 1.9 | NA | NA |
| 1933 | 34.9 | 1953 | 2.9 | 4.5 | NA | NA | 2.7 | NA | NA | 1.7 | NA | NA |
| 1934 | 21.7 | 1954 | 5.5 | 9.9 | 10.3 | 9.3 | 5.0 | 4.8 | 5.6 | 2.0 | 0.9 | 1.1 |
| 1935 | 20.1 | 1955 | 4.4 | 8.7 | 8.8 | 8.4 | 3.9 | 3.7 | 4.3 | 2.2 | 1.0 | 1.2 |
| 1936 | 16.9 | 1956 | 4.1 | 8.3 | 7.9 | 8.9 | 3.6 | 3.4 | 4.2 | 2.3 | 1.1 | 1.2 |
| 1937 | 14.3 | 1957 | 4.3 | 7.9 | 8.8 | 7.3 | 3.8 | 3.6 | 4.3 | 2.1 | 0.9 | 1.2 |
| 1938 | 19.0 | 1958 | 6.8 | 12.6 | 13.8 | 10.8 | 6.1 | 6.1 | 6.2 | 2.1 | 0.8 | 1.0 |
| 1939 | 17.2 | 1959 | 5.5 | 10.7 | 11.5 | 9.4 | 4.8 | 4.6 | 5.3 | 2.2 | 0.8 | 1.2 |
| 1940 | 14.6 | 1960 | 5.5 | 10.2 | 10.7 | 9.4 | 4.9 | 4.8 | 5.3 | 2.1 | 0.9 | 1.1 |
| 1941 | 9.9 | 1961 | 6.7 | 12.4 | 12.8 | 11.8 | 6.0 | 5.7 | 6.5 | 2.1 | 0.9 | 1.1 |
| 1942 | 4.7 | 1962 | 5.5 | 10.9 | 10.9 | 11.0 | 4.9 | 4.6 | 5.5 | 2.2 | 1.0 | 1.2 |
| 1943 | 1.9 | 1963 | 5.7 | 10.8 | 10.5 | 11.2 | 6.0 | 4.7 | 5.8 | 2.2 | 1.1 | 1.2 |
| 1944 | 1.2 | 1964 | 5.2 | 9.6 | 8.9 | 10.6 | 4.6 | 4.1 | 5.5 | 2.1 | 1.2 | 1.3 |
| 1945 | 1.9 | 1965 | 4.5 | 8.1 | 7.4 | 9.2 | 4.1 | 3.6 | 5.0 | 2.0 | 1.2 | 1.4 |
| 1946 | 3.9 | 1966 | 3.8 | 7.3 | 6.3 | 8.6 | 3.3 | 2.8 | 4.3 | 2.2 | 1.3 | 1.5 |
| 1947 | 3.9 | 1967 | 3.8 | 7.4 | 6.0 | 9.1 | 3.4 | 2.7 | 4.6 | 2.2 | 1.5 | 1.7 |
| 1948 | 3.8 | 1968 | 3.6 | 6.7 | 5.6 | 8.3 | 3.2 | 2.6 | 4.3 | 2.1 | 1.5 | 1.7 |
| | | 1969 | 3.5 | 6.4 | 5.3 | 7.8 | 3.2 | 2.5 | 4.2 | 2.0 | 1.5 | 1.7 |
| | | 1970 | 4.9 | 8.2 | 7.3 | 9.3 | 4.5 | 4.0 | 5.4 | 1.8 | 1.3 | 1.4 |
| | | 1971 | 5.9 | 9.9 | 9.1 | 10.8 | 5.4 | 4.9 | 6.3 | 1.8 | 1.2 | 1.3 |

NA—Not available

*Black and other races

[1]Data before 1949 are for persons 14 years old and over; from 1949 they are for persons 16 years old and over.

Source: Derived from *Employment and Earnings*, January 1972, Tables A-1 and A-3. U. S. President, *Second Manpower Report*, April 1971, Table A-12. U.S. Bureau of the Census (*Current Population Report*, P-23, Vol. 38) with U.S. Bureau of Labor Statistics (BLS Report No. 394) "The Social and Economic Status of Negroes in the U.S., 1970." July 1971. Table 36.

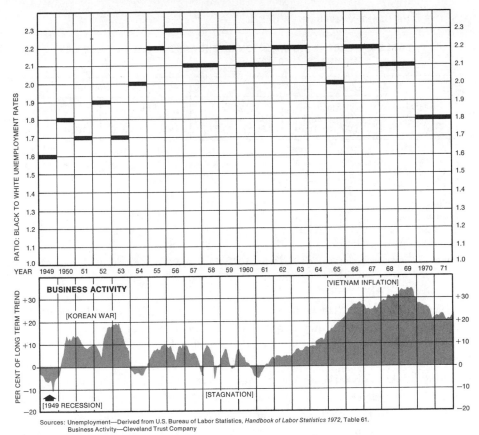

**FIGURE 7—** THE RATIO OF BLACK TO WHITE UNEMPLOYMENT RATES DOES NOT FOLLOW THE BUSINESS CYCLE

Sources: Unemployment—Derived from U.S. Bureau of Labor Statistics, *Handbook of Labor Statistics 1972*, Table 61.
Business Activity—Cleveland Trust Company

**TABLE FOR FIGURE 7—**RATIO BETWEEN BLACK AND WHITE
UNEMPLOYMENT, 1949–1971

| Year | Unemployment Ratio |
|------|--------------------|
| 1949 | 1.6 |
| 1950 | 1.8 |
| 1951 | 1.7 |
| 1952 | 1.9 |
| 1953 | 1.7 ........... Prosperity |
| 1954 | 2.0 ........... Recession |
| 1955 | 2.2 |
| 1956 | 2.3 |
| 1957 | 2.1 ........... Prosperity |
| 1958 | 2.1 ........... Recession |
| 1959 | 2.2 |
| 1960 | 2.1 ........... Recession |
| 1961 | 2.1 ........... Recession |
| 1962 | 2.2 ........... Recession |
| 1963 | 2.2 |
| 1964 | 2.1 |
| 1965 | 2.0 |
| 1966 | 2.2 |
| 1967 | 2.2 ........... Prosperity |
| 1968 | 2.1 ........... Prosperity |
| 1969 | 2.0 |
| 1970 | 1.8 ........... Recession |
| 1971 | 1.8 ........... Recession |

273

TABLE X—PERCENT DISTRIBUTION OF THE LABOR FORCE BY AGE, SEX, AND RACE, 1960–1970

| Age | Men | | | | Women | | | |
|---|---|---|---|---|---|---|---|---|
| | Black* | | White | | Black* | | White | |
| | 1960 | 1970 | 1960 | 1970 | 1960 | 1970 | 1960 | 1970 |
| Total | 100 | 100 | 100 | 100 | 100 | 100 | 100 | 100 |
| 16–19 | 8 | 9 | 6 | 8 | 7 | 9 | 9 | 11 |
| 20–24 | 12 | 16 | 9 | 13 | 11 | 16 | 11 | 15 |
| 25–54 | 65 | 60 | 67 | 61 | 69 | 63 | 62 | 57 |
| 55–64 | 12 | 11 | 14 | 13 | 11 | 10 | 13 | 14 |
| 65 and over | 3 | 3 | 5 | 4 | 2 | 3 | 4 | 3 |

*Black and other races.

Source: *Employment and Earnings,* January 1971, Table A-1; U. S. President, *Second Manpower Report,* April 1971, Table A-3.

Many more black than white young people, therefore, may not be counted in the labor force at all although they may be earning and keeping on the lookout for greater earning potential. The effect of not counting such black youth in the labor force would be to maximize the effect of youth unemployment among white youth and minimize it among blacks. This raises a technical question to which answers are not easy. Studies are needed that delve with understanding and insight, and perhaps with participant observation, into the working and earning ways of young people, white and black, in different settings, to cast more light on this matter. An enigma exists when almost all data point to effort and aspiration among black youth, while official labor force figures indicate a sharp decline in their labor force participation, and, therefore, in job seeking. Are all these young people in fact "discouraged" workers, as they have been called in the 1970–71 recession, or are a large number actually "different" workers, many of them doing odd jobs, especially in recession periods? Their labor force participation could well be much larger at all times than the data show.

Turning to women, those in the prime working years were a smaller proportion of women's total population in 1970 than in 1960. Although the population of young working women 25 to 44 years old rose comparatively little, especially relative to the younger groups, their entry into the labor force increased substantially, particularly among white women. (See Table XI.) Labor-force participation among white women far exceeded expectations at all normal working-age levels, looking at population changes alone. This phenomenon greatly increased the vulnerability to unemployment of the white labor force as a whole, because of women's higher unemployment rates relative to those of men.

The combination of influences, therefore, of 1) more youth and women in the black than the white labor force as a regular situation, and 2) the more sharply increasing participation of white women in recent years, and 3) the apparent drop in black youths' participation, has brought the official unemployment rates of white and black workers a little closer together in the recession years 1970–71 than they were in the late sixties, but at very high levels. It would seem, therefore, that the black to white ratio, while still expressing a large gap in employment opportunity, cannot be depended on by itself to trace the trend in opportunity. It is affected too extensively by the characteristics and changes in the age and sex composition of the population and of the labor force in the groups being compared.

**TABLE XI**—PERCENTAGE CHANGE IN THE WORKING AGE POPULATION AND IN THE LABOR FORCE, BY AGE, SEX, AND RACE, 1960–1970

| Age | Men | | | | Women | | | |
|---|---|---|---|---|---|---|---|---|
| | Population | | Labor force | | Population | | Labor force | |
| | Black* | White | Black* | White | Black* | White | Black* | White |
| Total | | | | | | | | |
| (16 years and over) | 23 | 15 | 14 | 11 | 26 | 17 | 30 | 37 |
| 16–19 | 63 | 39 | 37 | 39 | 61 | 38 | 70 | 56 |
| 20–24 | 66 | 55 | 56 | 49 | 56 | 53 | 84 | 92 |
| 25–34 | 16 | 10 | 12 | 9 | 11 | 10 | 28 | 39 |
| 35–44 | 1 | −1 | −1 | −6 | 8 | −7 | 9 | 13 |
| 45–54 | 11 | 11 | 6 | 10 | 22 | 15 | 21 | 28 |
| 55–64 | 14 | 16 | 10 | 11 | 27 | 20 | 27 | 42 |
| 65 and over | 18 | 11 | 3 | −12 | 32 | 25 | 24 | 9 |

*Black and other races

Source:   Derived from U. S. President, *Second Manpower Report,* April 1971, Table E-4.

The trend and level of the unemployment rates themselves are more significant as a measure of relative disadvantage. Important also are the higher proportions of black than of white married men who are unemployed since they are most numerous among all groups in both races and are expected to support families. Another barometer is the degree to which black workers are unemployed for lengthy periods, employed part-time when wanting full-time work, or on short hours or reduced overtime. In all these key situations, black workers tend to suffer relative to white workers. Yet they have fewer resources to fall back on in times of crisis.

## Especially Handicapped Groups

Whether in a recession or in the best of times, those groups which have little bargaining power in the job market or are entering the job market for the first time suffer most.

Among the most vulnerable are *those living in the lowest-income areas* of large cities under the poorest housing and neighborhood conditions. This is not because residents of low-income neighborhoods lose their capacity to achieve, but because those able to move out do so as soon as they can, leaving behind those most susceptible to unemployment, underemployment, and poverty. The population has been declining in the poorest neighborhoods. Although ghettos continue to include persons and families at many income levels, an increasing proportion of the poor or near-poor live in them. These changes have led to changes in the demography of the ghetto. The black lowest-income ghettos in America's largest cities now include an increasing proportion of women having to raise a family on their own and of the elderly who can no longer work hard and steadily.

Such neighborhoods and groups of people, in their relative isolation and obvious vulnerability, have the highest incidence of employment handicaps. It is doubtful, actually, whether employment is always the best solution for the problems some working-age people face in these lowest-income neighborhoods. Some should not be required or considered to be in the labor force at all. The young might better have the choice of remaining in school when they are still in their teens and early twenties. Others might prefer attending to home responsibilities such as school-age children. Still others might best have the choice of retiring after a lifetime of hard work or because of disabilities. Such choices would be possible under a human-resources program which would permit free education and adequate income under a dignified, anonymous, income-maintenance system at decent levels of living.

A new group of vulnerable workers is the *Vietnam-era war veterans*, whose unemployment rates were substantially higher than for other groups in 1969–71. The rates were especially high among black veterans 20 to 24 years old. Many young veterans are married and have dependents. All have had substantial training in fields useful in civilian life, if only in discipline itself. Skills learned in military service include repair of electronic equipment, medical-aide specialities, construction crafts, administrative and clerical work, electrical and mechanical equipment operation and repair, leadership, and interracial cooperation.

Many, however, are new entrants into the civilian labor force in a time of recession, and thus are doubly handicapped. Unlike the women, children, and aged of the low-income ghettos discussed above, many of whom are unable or should not be expected to work except by choice, most Vietnam-era war veterans are able and want to work. Yet they have failed to find jobs as quickly as nonveterans of the same age although many have more to offer the job market. Some of the explanation may stem from veterans' entitlement to unemployment insurance, subject to the regulations of their state. Veterans may use a period of time to shop around for work commensurate with their skills and suited to their interests. However, unemployment benefits are relatively small, averaging about $52 weekly in 1971. This provides little incentive for indulging in idleness. By 1971 about three in ten of all veterans 20 to 29 years old had been out of work fifteen weeks or more. The figure is even higher for black veterans.[11]

Reemployment rights under the military Selective Service Act of 1967 (as amended by P. L. 90–491 in 1968) have helped many—especially those in state and Federal Government services who have points added to a passing score in competitive exams. Black veterans especially have benefitted. Twice as large a proportion of black than of white veterans were in government service in 1971—24 percent compared to 12 percent.[12]

Another group of potential workers handicapped in the job market are *those who have not completed secondary school training or attended college*. The less schooling, the more difficult it is—especially for blacks—to get a job, and particularly one which pays as well as the jobs whites get. On the other hand, the greater one's schooling, the lower the unemployment rate and the higher the ratio of black to white income. Among young adults in the prime working ages of 25 to 34, most of whom would have completed their schooling, the ratio of black to white family income was lowest among the family heads who were high school dropouts (63 percent) and highest among those with some college education (93 percent).

The substantial strides in education made by black youth during the 1960s should improve their competitive position in the job market in the 1970s. Comparing fathers and sons who were heads of black families in 1970 (those 55 to 64 years old versus those 25 to 34 years old) the sons were more than three times as likely to have completed high school and about three times as likely to have had some college training. (Refer to Figure 2.)

College enrollment, however, was not as great as among whites at all family income levels in 1970. Considering the need for immediate earners and the extra effort required in black families to provide the family income at each level, the proportion aspiring to higher education is substantial. Over 20 percent of all black families with 18- to 24-year-olds had one or more of these young people attending college full-time in the 1970–71 school year. (The corresponding proportion in white families was about 40 percent.)[13] A sizable number of black families, about 40,000, had more than one child attending college full-time, and half of these were in families with less than $10,000 income.

Another handicapped group are *those who, on the job, must act alone in bargaining with management*. Thus, in cases of discriminatory practices or any other grievance, they cannot appeal through a union agent under a collective-bargaining agreement. Nor are they protected by seniority rules, deferred wage increases, health and welfare benefits, and other conditions which make unionized workers more secure as both employees and consumers. Black workers are more likely than white workers to be in occupations in which union membership is most common—in industrial and laboring work—but they are only just about as likely to belong to a union. (See Figure 8.)

Actually, only a fifth of all workers belonged to a union in 1970. This is a fact often overlooked or not understood, for the influence of organized labor goes far beyond its actual strength in numbers. A larger proportion of men than women were organized. Even so, only 30 percent of black men worked under collective bargaining agreements in 1970, and 28 percent of white men.[14]

FIGURE 8— BLACK WORKERS ARE AS LIKELY TO BE IN UNIONS AS WHITE
WORKERS, MEN MORE THAN WOMEN

## Percent in unions—1970

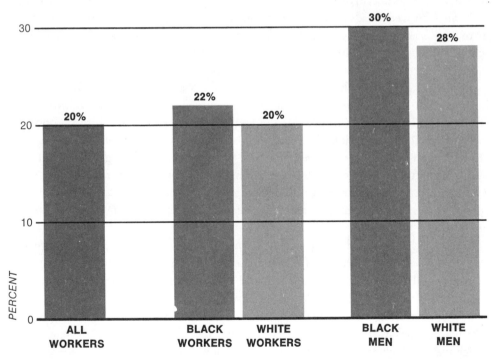

Source:    Derived from U. S. Bureau of the Census, *Current Population Reports*, P-60, No. 81,
"Characteristics of the Low-Income Population, 1970," Table 10.

In those occupations most commonly organized—the crafts and operatives jobs—not even half the men, black or white, belonged to a union. Fewer than 10 percent of the working poor of either sex were union members, whatever the type of work.

Considering the degree to which collective action has proven effective in institutional change and in providing cash benefits, and the extent to which black workers are in fields in which unions are the most common, public policy directed toward spreading collective bargaining generally and combating restrictive practices would substantially benefit black workers.

## Government as an Equal-Opportunity Employer

Lester C. Thurow, in his study, *Poverty and Discrimination*, concludes that poverty among blacks can be overcome only by eliminating discrimination, and that the main implementation lies in the hands of local, state, and Federal Government. He writes that "Eliminating discrimination in all levels of government may be one of the most effective means of eliminating the effects of discrimination throughout the economy."[15]

Enormous though such a task would be, one is nevertheless struck by the logic of Thurow's conclusion. After all, it is only reasonable to expect one's government to set an example in its own employment practices. Even if institutional arrangements and the effects of coercion and clout of the white community continue to affect private arrangements for some time to come, the Federal Government certainly, and state and local governments hopefully, should be expected to lead in the employment of black men and women.

Examination of the data available on government employment practices is not reassuring, however. From 1969–71, about 11 percent of all employees in General Schedule federal employment were black, only slightly better than for all business and industry together, as reported to the Equal Employment Opportunity Commission. Some sectors of private industry, such as motor vehicle production, for instance, do better.

About 20 percent of the other federal employees were black, including the Postal Field Service and Wage Board workers, but almost all of these services—half of all federal full-time employment—were outside of policy making, professional, or administrative work. In any event, most of the black workers in these services earned less than $8,000 in 1970.

The General Service group, which covers most executive departments of the Federal Government, includes a wide variety of professional and administrative work and many policy positions. However, in 1971 most black employees (82 percent) were below the GS-9 level (in a salary scale from GS-2 to GS-18), and therefore were not even in middle management, much less in key professional jobs or at the policy shaping level.

The Federal Civil Service does not collect or publish its data, so it is impossible to determine the degree to which men or women among minority personnel occupy any given grade level. The special survey on women's employment alone, however, shows that two-thirds or more of everyone in jobs below GS-6 were women in 1970. It is reasonable to conclude that men occupied most of the jobs held by blacks at the GS-15-to-18 level, and also those paying $35,000 or more in the Postal Field Service. These high-level federal jobs held by blacks totaled fewer than 600 nationwide in 1970, or less than 2 percent of all federal positions in the $25,000-or-over category. Analysis should be made further into how many of the 600 highly placed blacks in the federal service hold positions that are substantive to the agency's work, as against those employed to provide assistance with minority employment, or with enforcing the various civil rights acts. The latter jobs, while important, are nevertheless not germane to the main function of the agencies in which these highly paid black men or women are employed. Although many high-level black federal employees hold so-called equal-opportunity jobs only, no count is readily available.

State and local governments by and large have an even less creditable rating, according to a study of the U. S. Civil Rights Commission.[16] Some state and local governments, however, equal or surpass the Federal Government in minority employment—for instance New York State. In addition, New York State collects its data by sex, so that the ratio of women to men at all grade levels can be determined. About 15 percent of all New York State employees in 1970 were black. Twice as many were women as men, and the women were almost entirely concentrated at very low grades. About 70 percent of all the women were at grades paying less than $6,100 in 1970, compared to 50 percent of the men. While distributed into a wider range of grades, however, only 1 percent of black men employed by New York State had jobs paying over $22,000 in 1970. Black men outnumbered black women by 3 to 1 in jobs paying $13,000 or more.

Government is indeed a disappointment as a pace setter for equal employment within its own ranks. Its initiative in placing legislation on the books and issuing Executive Orders and Resolutions is much better. The force and will with which the laws and regulations are carried out is reflected in the employment record of each place.

The predominantly white establishment has been slow to move vigorously and affirmatively toward assuring black workers their rightful place in the economy. Cautious optimism finds support in the growing black determination to have a fair chance, in the increasing education of black youth, and growing experience of black workers with new fields and new levels of responsibility. This optimism engenders rising expectations, a strong thrust to push for a rightful place in the economy, and greater acceptance by more employers.

Along with the growth of black pride has come increasing community participation, an expanded electorate, and growing sophistication and success in politics. By 1972 there were 2,264 elected officials, two-thirds more than in 1970. Of the black officials in 1972, only one was a senator, 13 were congressmen, 86 were mayors or vice-mayors, 37 were state senators, 169 were state representatives, and 132 were county commissioners. The numbers are still proportionally small, but have grown rapidly at the local level. These officials are chosen and employed to represent their total constituency, white and black alike. They, as do all representatives, bring with them sensitivity to particular issues. The issue of equal economic rights, long denied the largest minority population in America, is one to which they can give strong advocacy.

Ultimately the black worker must have a total commitment from employers, unions, and fellow workers of all races to move from the present status to equal participation in America's work and rewards. Such a commitment requires continued pressure in both the private and public domain. Any reduction of that pressure risks the momentum already built up, paving the way for inertia and even the condoned assertion of forces hostile to black progress.

## Notes

1. Charles H. Wesley, *Negro Labor in the United States, 1850–1925*, New York, Russell and Russell, 1925.
2. *Ibid.*, p. 101.
3. George E. Haynes, *The Negro at Work in New York City*, Arno Press and *The New York Times*, 1968, from the first edition by Columbia University, New York, 1912.
4. See, for instance, Albert Wohlstetter and Sinclair Coleman, *Race Differences in Income*, Santa Monica, California, Rand, October 1970 p. 65:
   "These examples suggest how hard it is to disentangle the effects of current discrimination in the marketplace from the various results of multiple past discriminations that may in turn have made it unlikely that a minority can compete currently on equal terms. While the fact of current as well as past discrimination is clear enough, the precise magnitudes involved are not clear; and, it appears to us, given our present state of knowledge, they are likely to resist exact determination. The proportion of the current income differences that is attributable to current discrimination in the marketplace is extremely difficult to determine, and in spite of several attempts, it does not seem to us to have been measured convincingly."
5. See U. S. Commission on Civil Rights, by the Brookings Institution, *Jobs & Civil Rights*, April 1969; and U. S. Commission on Civil Rights, *For All the People . . . By All the People*, 1969, for analysis of Federal, state, and local government efforts to improve racial equality in employment.
6. The present benefits to veterans scarcely pay college tuition, much less living expenses. For evidence of the employment effects of the earlier provisions, see U. S. Department of Labor, Bureau of Labor Statistics, *The Negroes in the United States, Their Economic and Social Situation*, BLS Bulletin 1511, June 1966, p. 45 and pp. 235–238.
7. U. S. Department of Commerce, Bureau of the Census, Current Population Reports, *Characteristics of the Population by Ethnic Origin*, November 1969, Table 15.
8. See Lester C. Thurow, *Poverty and Discrimination*, Washington, D.C., Brookings Institution, 1969, p. 134.
9. U. S. Department of Labor, Bureau of Labor Statistics, *Three Standards of Living*, BLS Bulletin No. 1570-5, 1969, p. 9.
10. In discussing employment, unemployment, and the labor force, the data are for "Negroes and other races," but persons in the "other races" are less than 10 percent of those not classified as white.
11. Precise data are not available.
12. U. S. Department of Labor, Bureau of Labor Statistics, *Employment Situation of Vietnam Era Veterans, 1971*, Special Labor Force Report 137, September 1971.

13. U. S. Department of Commerce, Bureau of the Census, Current Population Reports, *School Enrollment*, October 1970, Series P-20, No. 222, Table 13.

14. U. S. Department of Commerce, Bureau of the Census, Current Population Reports, *Characteristics of the Low-Income Population, 1970*, Series P-20, No. 81, Table 10.

15. Lester C. Thurow, *Poverty and Discrimination*, Washington, D.C., Brookings Institution, 1969, p. 159.

16. U. S. Civil Rights Commission, *For All the People . . . By All the People: A Summary Report on Equal Opportunity in State and Local Government Employment, 1969.*

# BIBLIOGRAPHY*

Ashenfelter, Orley, "Changes in Labor Market Discrimination Over Time," *Journal of Human Resources*. Fall 1970, pp. 403–30.

Baker, Henry E., *The Colored Inventor, or a Record of Fifty Years*. New York, Crisis Publishing Co., 1913.

Bergmann, Barbara R., "The Effect on White Incomes of Discrimination in Employment," *Journal of Political Economy*. March/April 1971, pp. 294–313.

Brimmer, Andrew F., "Economic Agenda for Black Americans Over the Decade of the 1970s," *Black Politician*. January 1971, pp. 12ff.

Browne, Robert S., "Barriers to Black Participation in the American Economy," *Review of Black Political Economy*. Autumn 1970, pp. 57–67.

Ferman, Louis A., Kornbluh, Joyce L., and Miller, J. A., eds., *Negroes and Jobs*. Ann Arbor, University of Michigan Press, 1968.

Goode, Kenneth G., "Query: Can the Afro-American Be an Effective Executive?", *California Management Review*. Fall 1970, pp. 22–26.

Haynes, George E., *The Negro at Work in New York City*. New York, Arno Press, 1968. Reprint of 1912 ed. by Longmans, Green & Co.

Hiestand, Dale L., *Economic Growth and Employment Opportunities for Minorities*. New York, Columbia University Press, 1964.

Jacobson, Julius, ed., *The Negro and the American Labor Movement*. Garden City, New York, Doubleday and Co., Inc., 1968.

*Journal of Negro History, 1916—.* Washington, D.C., Association for the Study of Negro Life and History.

Nathan, Richard P., *Jobs and Civil Rights*. Prepared for the U. S. Committee on Civil Rights by the Brookings Institution, Washington, D.C., GPO, 1969.

Newman, Dorothy K., "The Negro's Journey to the City," *Monthly Labor Review*. May and June 1965, pp. 502–507, pp. 644–649.

Ovington, Mary W., *Half a Man: The Status of the Negro in New York*. New York, Longmans, Green & Co., 1911.

*This bibliography is only illustrative of the wide variety of studies available about black American workers. Readings may be inconsistent in approach and findings.

Palmore, Erdman, and Whittington, Frank J., "Differential Trends Toward Equality Between Whites and Nonwhites," *Social Forces.* September 1970, pp. 108–117.

Tabb, William K., "Perspectives on Black Economic Development," *Journal of Economic Issues.* December 1970, pp. 68–81.

Thurow, Lester C., *Poverty and Discrimination.* Washington, D.C., Brookings Institution, 1969.

U. S. Bureau of Labor Statistics, *Black Americans: A Chart Book.* Washington, D.C., GPO, 1971. (BLS Bulletin 1699).

U. S. Bureau of Labor Statistics. *Black Americans: A Decade of Occupational Change.* Washington, D.C., GPO, 1972. (BLS Bulletin 1731).

U. S. Bureau of Labor Statistics, *Employment and Earnings.* (monthly).

U. S. Bureau of Labor Statistics, *The Negroes in the United States, Their Economic and Social Situation.* Washington, D.C., GPO, 1966. (BLS Bulletin 1511).

U. S. Bureau of Labor Statistics, Special Labor Force Reports. (Issued periodically. Reprints from *Monthly Labor Review.*)

U. S. Bureau of the Census and U. S. Bureau of Labor Statistics, *The Social and Economic Status of Negroes in the U. S., 1970.* Washington, D.C., GPO, 1971. (Current Population Reports, Series P-23, No. 38, BLS Report 394).

U. S. Commission on Civil Rights, *For All the People . . . By All the People: A Summary Report on Equal Opportunity in State and Local Government Employment, 1969.* Washington, D.C., GPO, 1969.

U. S. President, *Manpower Report of the President and a Report on Manpower Requirements, Resources, Utilization, and Training By the Department of Labor.* Washington, D.C., GPO, 1971.

Wesley, Charles H., *Negro Labor in the United States, 1850–1925.* New York, Russell and Russell, 1967. Reprint of 1927 edition by Vanguard.

Wohlstetter, Albert, and Coleman, Sinclair, *Race Differences in Income.* Prepared for the U. S. Office of Economic Opportunity, Santa Monica, California, Rand, 1970. (R-578-OEO).

Woodson, Carter G., *A Century of Negro Migration.* New York, Russell and Russell, 1969. Reprint of 1918 edition by The Association for the Study of Negro Life and History.

Wright, Richard R., *The Negro in Pennsylvania: A Study in Economic History.* Philadelphia, A.M.E. Book Concern, 1912.

# 7

## *The Black American in Agriculture*

### *Calvin L. Beale*

In the reams of material written about black Americans in recent years there is little concerning the black farmer and farmhand. This may be traced to the fact that the dominant trend in black affairs since the beginning of the second world war has been the wholesale flight of people to the cities—the big cities—and a rising concern over the problems that face them there.

With this emphasis on urbanization, rural life is considered by many as *déclassé*, an unpleasant reminder of the miseries of the past that have been shaken off and exchanged for the hope of the metropolis. Nor is the study of a society in decline an attractive subject for most research workers. Yet the black rural population still numbers nearly a fifth of all black Americans, and many of the problems which beset blacks everywhere occur in their most severe, undiluted, and least hopeful settings in the countryside. Thus to the diminishing extent that rural areas continue to be a seed bed for the cities, the problems of the rural minority continue to have serious implications for all black Americans.

### Former Concentration of Blacks in Agriculture

Agriculture was the prime mover in the importation of Negroes into the American colonies as slaves. Some blacks were used as domestic servants and to a limited extent others were employed in industry in the South, but only in agriculture were they used on a large scale. Free blacks who moved North often settled in the cities but their numbers were few compared with the farm workers still held as slaves.

Emancipation did not radically alter black dependence on the land. Comparatively few blacks moved to the North, except from the border states, and these did not usually find themselves welcome. In the South there was some initial rush to the towns, but urban work was scarce and cotton was still king.

An entirely new system of relations had to be worked out between the freed blacks and their former owners. With rather rare exceptions, the freedmen were not provided land by the Federal Government and the monopoly land ownership of the planters was not broken. At first efforts were made to hire the former slaves for wages. These efforts were not very successful, however, for cash was scarce for the average planter, the freedom-sensitive Negroes no longer responded well to the demands of gang work, and hiring made for an unreliable supply of workers. Soon a system of renting evolved in which a family was assigned to work a particular piece of land and receive a share of the crop as wages. This system proved to be more stable and guaranteed that a family would remain until the crop was in.

This arrangement was financed by a system of credit in which the tenants were "furnished" with supplies on which to live during the year by a merchant or by the planter (who was himself usually operating on credit). As security for the credit, the tenant mortgaged his share of the forthcoming crop and repaid his debts after the harvest.

In the absence of land reform and a program of federal intervention, this system provided many opportunities for abuse. The rates of interest charged the tenants were usually very high and the goods they received were often overpriced. Illiterate blacks were unable to detect sharp practices. At the end of a season they were lucky if any cash was left after the bills were paid. Some of the most diligent and fortunate earned enough to buy a small farm of their own or to obtain tools and work animals and rent a farm for cash, but for the majority the share-tenant system seemed to encourage improvidence. The once-a-year payday led to unrealistic debts during the year and to quick dissipation of earnings in the fall.

It was during this period, when tenancy was becoming the prevailing way of life, that the seeds of agricultural education for blacks were first sown. There was much to do since although many Negroes aspired to knowledge, they were mostly attracted by professional training and the classics. After years of servitude in the cotton fields, there was little incentive to learn to farm.

Formal training aimed at producing agricultural leaders began with the opening of Hampton Normal and Agricultural Institute at Hampton, Virginia, in 1868, under the auspices of the American Missionary Society.

A decade later Hampton had trained Booker T. Washington, whose ideas dominated black agricultural thinking for at least two generations thereafter. Washington established Tuskegee Institute in Alabama in 1881. Here in the years that followed he saw the need for demonstration work in the field, for scientific research at the institute and for the organization of farmers. Tuskegee hired the man who was to become his generation's foremost black scientist, George Washington Carver, in 1896, and sponsored the first black demonstration specialist, T. M. Campbell, in 1906. In the 1890s the Tuskegee Farmers Conference became an annual event with a South-wide influence in the shaping of programs and thought for black farm families; similar conferences were developed by other states. Unfortunately these never led to an organized, economically effective organization of black farmers.

## The Beginning of Change

Twenty-five years after the Civil War, the census of 1890 showed that over 60 percent of all employed blacks were farmers or farm laborers. In the South the figure was about 65 percent.

During the late nineteenth and early twentieth centuries, considerable westward movement took place as new lands were drained in the Mississippi Valley or cleared farther west. In certain older areas, the role of Negroes in farming declined, with the collapse of rice farming along the South Atlantic States and the renunciation of agriculture by black farmers in such border ex-slave states as Kentucky and Missouri. By and large, however, the increase in farmers in expanding areas offset the losses elsewhere.

During the first world war, thousands of Negroes took the opportunity to enter industrial work in the North,[1] despite opposition from landlords and creditors, as foreign immigration was cut off and many white workers were diverted into military service. This led to the establishment of lines of family communication with the North which have served the millions who have since followed.

In the same era, the menace of the boll weevil was reaching its climax. This beetle, which lays its eggs in cotton bolls and whose larvae consume the cotton, had entered southern Texas from Mexico in the 1890s. It gradually penetrated into the areas heavily settled by Negro farmers, and by 1921 had spread over the entire Cotton Belt. For a few years the boll weevil wrought panic, heavily damaging millions of acres of cotton. In some sections, cotton never regained its prominence, and thousands of Negroes emigrated as the landlords turned to livestock and dairying.

In the rolling Piedmont country of Georgia and South Carolina, severe erosion and soil depletion impelled additional thousands of blacks to leave or look for industrial work. Thus, in general, the time between World War I and the Depression was a time of upheaval and receding activity in farming for Negroes in the old Cotton Belt. In less severely affected areas, means of limiting the damage by weevils were devised after a few years, and cotton expanded northward into safer areas. But the old pattern of black farming was never the same. Black owners, a number of whom lost their land or gave up farming, were particularly affected. The developing opportunities in the fertile Delta country were mostly for tenants. Hundreds flocked in to work the large plantations on shares.

## The Depression and the New Deal

It is difficult to say whether the great economic depression of the 1930s hit black farmers any harder than it did whites. It was nightmarish for both. With his already precarious financial position and limited possessions, however, perhaps the typical Negro had less room to fall.

The bottom dropped out of the cotton market. The number of black farmers declined and the number of white tenants rose rapidly. It was now that the New Deal introduced an entirely new level of Federal Government activity in agriculture: widespread relief and welfare measures, cheap credit for farmers, and help with buying land. Plantations heavily in debt were acquired by the Government, then subdivided and sold in family-farm sizes to former tenants. Writing of a Black Belt county in Alabama, Morton Rubin has said, "The number of Negroes who have become operators (owners) without the help of the Federal Government and its agencies is a small proportion of the total."[2]

At the same time, the idea of farmers agreeing by majority vote to institute programs such as limitations of crop acreage in return for certain federal price and other benefits was put into practice. Some argued that these programs often worked to the ultimate disadvantage of the small farmer, who found himself restricted to a very small allotment of acreage. But for many black farmers such programs offered an opportunity to do something that they had never been able to do before—vote.

# WORLD WAR II TO THE PRESENT

## Mechanization of Cotton

In the years just before Pearl Harbor the future character of cotton farming in the United States became discernible. In the northern part of the Mississippi Delta country scores of tenant people were being "tractored off" the cotton plantations. As mules were replaced by tractors, families were displaced to camp along the roadside until publicity and aroused public opinion induced some efforts to help them.

In the same period it became obvious that it was only a matter of time before the mechanical cotton picker would be perfected. The coming of the war, however, delayed the practical introduction of the picker, although in the drier cotton areas of Oklahoma and west Texas, where relatively few black farmers lived, efforts were made to harvest cotton mechanically during the war. After the war the mechanical harvesters began slowly but surely to replace hand picking and snapping. In the 1950s the final technical hurdle to complete elimination of hand field labor became possible through several developments in planting and weed control. The triple triumph of tractors, pickers, and weed control released thousands of tenants—the majority of them black, who could not have been spared until all aspects of cotton cultivation were mechanized or chemicalized. Mechanical picking is now the standard method of harvesting throughout the southeastern states. The following table shows the progress of mechanical harvesting. From 8 percent of the crop in 1950, the proportion picked or snapped by machine rose to 51 percent in 1960 and 98 percent in 1970. (See Table I.)

**TABLE I—PERCENTAGE OF COTTON HARVESTED BY MACHINE AND BY HAND**

| Area | 1970 | 1965 | 1960 | 1950 |
|---|---|---|---|---|
| United States | | | | |
|   Machine | 98 | 85 | 51 | 8 |
|   Hand | 2 | 15 | 49 | 92 |
| California | | | | |
|   Machine | 100 | 98 | 87 | 34 |
|   Hand | 0 | 2 | 13 | 66 |
| Texas and Oklahoma | | | | |
|   Machine | 99 | 90 | 58 | 11 |
|   Hand | 1 | 10 | 42 | 89 |
| South, except Texas and Oklahoma | | | | |
|   Machine | 96 | 77 | 31 | 1 |
|   Hand | 4 | 23 | 69 | 99 |

Source: Economic Research Service and Agricultural Marketing Service, U. S. Department of Agriculture.

Another trend of equal importance for the black cotton farmer in the last generation has been the growth of cotton cultivation under irrigation in the West. Until after World War I comparatively little cotton was grown in areas where there were few black farmers. However, it was found that with irrigation, bumper yields of cotton could be harvested in the high plains of Texas and in parts of California, Arizona, and New Mexico. These western farms did not inherit the southern tenant system and often were developed by people with the capital and zeal to operate under conditions of high labor productivity. Western cotton areas soon were producing cotton at a lower price per bale than all but the most productive sections of the old Cotton Belt. The proportion of all cotton raised in Arizona, California, New Mexico, and west Texas rose from 2 percent in 1919 to 34 percent in 1959.

The changes in methods and location of cotton cultivation, combined with the poverty of most black farmers, worked both to push Negroes out of farming and to make the attractions of city life irresistible. As a result the number of nonwhite farmers growing cotton in the South plummeted from 482,000 in 1945 to 110,000 in 1964, a decline of 77 percent in slightly less than twenty years. Some of this loss was converted into an increase in hired hands, but most of it was not. The shift was particularly acute in the Mississippi Delta lands where the large plantations were concentrated. Although the decline was greatest for tenants, it also affected black owners.

Adding to the problem has been the steady erosion of the market for cotton, caused by competition from other fibers and increased production abroad. Marketing difficulties, coupled with increased yields per acre, have caused farmers to vote every year since 1954 to restrict the acreage planted. When a cut in acreage allotments has occurred, as in 1955 and 1956, the black farmer with his predominantly tenant position has been most likely to find himself forced out because there has simply not been enough acreage to support as many tenants per landlord as before.

## Diversification

With the decline of cotton acreage in the South since the mid-1920s, some of the land has been put to other agricultural uses and some has been taken out of farming altogether. Naturally the least productive and suitable lands have been the most likely to go out of cultivation and converted to other uses. The theme of diversification has been preached to black farmers just as it has been to white ones. In the South its greatest single source has been cattle raising. Since 1945 the number of black owner-operators who raise cattle for sale has been stable, despite the general decline in the total number of black-owned farms. But the average number of cattle and calves sold by Negro owners was only five animals per farm in 1964, up from three per farm in 1945. Thus although there has been some gain in cattle raising, it has not been of a generally significant nature. Furthermore, in 1954 the average value of cattle sold by black farmers was less than $70 per animal. Either because of a higher proportion of calves or lower quality of animals, this was 30 percent below the average for southern white farmers.

In crop production, an easy means of diversification has been to grow soybeans. The crop offers several advantages. It can be produced in many states under a wide range of conditions. The market for the beans for use in oleomargarine, cooking oils, and other commodities has expanded rapidly, and the price has remained good. Furthermore, there are no restrictions on the acreage that a farmer may plant.

With these incentives the number of farmers growing the crop has increased in the South as elsewhere. Generally, soybeans are well adapted to those sections of the South where black farmers are located—in the Coastal Plain and the Mississippi Delta. Many black farmers grow soybeans as a supplement to their other crops, although their full number is not known.

## The Increased Importance of Tobacco

During and after the first world war the rise in cigarette smoking unquestionably intensified the role of Negroes in American agriculture. Cigarettes were not new, but for a variety of reasons, among them urbanization, the growing number of women smokers, a rise in personal income, and the invention of cigarette-making machinery, the consumption of cigarettes soared. Much of the tobacco used was grown only in the South. The result was a steady expansion of tobacco farming throughout the Coastal Plain from North Carolina to northern Florida—predominantly in sections where many black farmers were already present.

The black farmer was well suited to tobacco, which was cultivated strictly by hand and animal labor, making good use of the plentiful work pool provided by large families. And tobacco was well suited to the black farm owner, since it did not require much land. Between 1910 and 1945 the number of nonwhite, tobacco-growing southern farmers— both owners and tenants—rose from 42,000 to 91,000 in a period when the net change in cotton farmers was down. The increase in the economic importance of tobacco was much greater than the mere change in number of farmers raising it. In 1910 hundreds of farmers in the Deep South were raising only small patches for home use, whereas almost all of the farms in the latter period were producing for sale.

The growth of the cigarette-tobacco industry continued with little slackening until the middle 1950s. At that time, bumper yields, new methods which used less tobacco per cigarette, and a near halt in the growth of per capita consumption produced conditions that led to severe cutbacks in acreage allotments per farmer. A decline in number of farms raising tobacco has now set in, but not so rapidly as with cotton. Thus tobacco has continued to increase in its relative importance to the black farmer.

The proportion of southern nonwhite farmers who grew any tobacco at all was less than 5 percent in 1910, but rose to 14 percent in 1945 and 25 percent in 1964. In relation to cotton there was one black farmer growing tobacco in 1910 for every sixteen growing cotton, whereas by 1964 there were two black farmers producing cotton for every one growing tobacco.

In general, the black-operated farms growing tobacco (1) have been more likely to produce on a commercial scale than farms producing cotton; (2) have tended to yield a higher value of products sold; and (3) are more likely to be operated by owners themselves than the cotton farms. Negroes have achieved a more important role in cigarette-tobacco production than in any other commodity. In 1964 they grew one-seventh of all cigarette tobacco, compared with one-twelfth of cotton (1964). As for the principal cigarette-type flue-cured tobacco—black farmers account for one-fifth of the crop.

This increasing emphasis on tobacco growing is shifting the principal centers of black farming away from the Deep South over toward the Atlantic Coastal Plain. North Carolina, the leading tobacco state, is now second only to Mississippi in number of black farmers, and the total value of its black-operated farms—both owner and tenant—exceeds that of all other states.


# THE POSITION OF BLACK FARMERS TODAY

## Number of Farms

At their peak in 1920, black farm operators numbered 926,000 (Table II) and comprised one-seventh of all farmers in the nation. This number includes all tenant farmers, even though many of them exercised little or no managerial functions and were essentially laborers paid with a share of the crop. As a result of all the influences that have combined to lower the number of farms, only 87,000 black farmers were counted in the 1969 Census of Agriculture, a drop of 90 percent since 1920 and of 85 percent since 1950.

Currently (figures for 1972) about 1 percent of all employed black men work solely or primarily as farm operators. The comparable percentage for white men is 3 percent.

An additional number of both races do some occasional farming but spend most of their time at other jobs. About 4 percent of black men work as farm laborers. Thus agricultural work is the sole or primary employment of about 5 percent of the employed black male labor force. When figures for working women are taken into account, about 3 percent of all black workers are principally in agriculture, compared with 4 percent of white workers.

**TABLE II—BLACK FARM OPERATORS IN THE UNITED STATES, 1920–1969**

| Area | 1969 | 1959 | 1950 | 1940 | 1930 | 1920 |
|---|---|---|---|---|---|---|
| United States | 87,393 | 272,541 | 559,980 | 681,790 | 882,850 | 925,703 |
| Northeast | NA | 596 | 1,002 | 1,432 | 1,021 | 1,469 |
| North Central | NA | 4,259 | 6,700 | 7,466 | 10,083 | 7,911 |
| South | 85,249 | 267,008 | 551,469 | 672,214 | 870,936 | 915,595 |
| West | NA | 678 | 809 | 678 | 812 | 735 |
| Selected States | | | | | | |
| Missouri | NA | 1,684 | 3,214 | 3,686 | 5,844 | 2,824 |
| Maryland | 692 | 2,132 | 3,595 | 4,049 | 5,264 | 6,208 |
| Virginia | 5,453 | 15,629 | 28,527 | 35,062 | 39,598 | 47,690 |
| North Carolina | 13,111 | 41,023 | 69,029 | 57,428 | 74,636 | 74,849 |
| South Carolina | 9,535 | 30,953 | 61,255 | 61,204 | 77,331 | 109,005 |
| Georgia | 5,571 | 20,163 | 50,352 | 59,127 | 86,787 | 130,176 |
| Florida | 1,365 | 3,664 | 7,473 | 9,731 | 11,010 | 12,954 |
| Kentucky | 1,753 | 3,327 | 4,882 | 5,546 | 9,104 | 12,624 |
| Tennessee | 4,930 | 15,018 | 24,044 | 27,972 | 35,123 | 38,181 |
| Alabama | 9,873 | 29,206 | 57,205 | 73,338 | 93,795 | 95,200 |
| Mississippi | 17,184 | 55,174 | 122,709 | 159,256 | 182,578 | 161,001 |
| Arkansas | 3,775 | 14,654 | 40,810 | 57,011 | 79,556 | 72,275 |
| Louisiana | 5,518 | 17,686 | 40,599 | 59,556 | 73,734 | 62,036 |
| Oklahoma | 1,026 | 2,633 | 5,910 | 8,987 | 15,172 | 13,403 |
| Texas | 5,375 | 15,432 | 34,389 | 52,648 | 85,940 | 78,597 |

NA:  Not available

Source:  Advance reports of 1969 Census of Agriculture and 1959 Census of Agriculture, Volume II.

## Location of Farms

The great majority of black farmers are located in a huge sickle-shaped stretch of land that begins in southern Maryland, sweeps southward through Virginia, the Carolinas, and Georgia east of the Blue Ridge Mountains, curves through Georgia below the southern end of the mountains, crosses central Alabama, moves in a northwesterly direction through Mississippi, and ends in western Tennessee and eastern Arkansas. A handle can be thought of as extending across northern Louisiana and curving down into eastern Texas. There are very few black farmers in the mountain and plateau parts of the South, in the Florida peninsula or in the plains portions of Texas.

The densest concentration of farms is in the tobacco and cotton country of eastern North and South Carolina, and in the Cotton Belt for a distance roughly fifty miles north and seventy-five miles south of Memphis, Tennessee. In these areas, together with central Alabama, there were fifty-eight counties in which black farmers were still in the majority in 1964. Mississippi has had more black farmers than any other state throughout this century—one-fifth of the national total in 1969. However, as a result of the rapid loss of cotton tenants now taking place in Mississippi, this distinction will probably go to North Carolina in the future.

## Black Farmers Outside the South

Little more than 1 percent of all black farmers live outside of the states where slavery existed at the time of the Civil War. It is this remarkable concentration in one region of the nation—the South—that so distinguishes the Negro's role in agriculture from his participation in other industries and that has such great influence on his prospects in farming.

In the postrevolutionary period of our history there was a scattering of black farmers in the Hudson Valley, in New Jersey, and in southeastern Pennsylvania. These settlements were relics of the attempt to use Negroes as slaves in the North or of the attraction of Negroes to Quaker communities, which usually took an active interest in the welfare of former slaves.

As the land north of the Ohio River where slavery was forbidden was settled, free blacks and escaped slaves gradually moved in. Many were persons of mixed ancestry, some so distinctive that they formed communities aloof from the general Negro population. A majority of the black settlers went to the hilly wooded country of southern Ohio and Indiana, where farming was largely small in scale. Others, however, obtained better lands in the Corn Belt parts of these states and of southern Michigan and engaged in more commercial types of agriculture.

Often the free black farmer was resented, and repressive laws in some states forbade further numbers to enter the state. The Civil War forced many refugees North, but after the war the black rural settlements began to decline despite ownership of land and an improved social climate. The farms were usually small and of below-average quality, and developing opportunities in the cities drained off the younger people.

West of the Mississippi, blacks took very little part in the great homesteading movement after the Civil War, except in Kansas, where a number of black farming communities were founded in the so-called "exoduster" movement. But here again, almost no sooner had the settlements been founded than they began to decline. People accustomed to cotton farming with almost no managerial experience or capital found it very difficult to succeed as independent farmers in the plains.

In 1900, the North and West (excluding Missouri) had 9,400 black-operated farms, with more than 1,000 each in Ohio, Indiana, Illinois, and Kansas. By 1969, there were only 2,100 left. When the millions of rural Negroes who left the South in the twentieth century went North, they avoided the farm work they had been used to back home like the plague.

Today the largest number of black farmers in the North and West are in Ohio and Michigan. The largest settlement is in Cass and Berrien Counties, Michigan, not far from South Bend, Indiana. This is perhaps the most persistent of the northern areas developed by free Negroes in the generation before the Civil War. After a period of some decline as a commercial farming area, it has begun to grow again as a part-time farming and residential area. South of Chicago near Kankakee, Illinois, is another much more recent rural settlement. It consists largely of middle-aged and older families who combine a rural residence with off-farm sources of income.

In California, some blacks worked in farming as hired hands many years ago. During the 1930s and early 1940s their number was greatly swelled by migrants fleeing the Depression or, later, seeking defense work. A few have gone into agriculture on their own, so that by 1964 California, with 337 farms operated by Negroes, had become the third largest site of black farmers outside the South. The farm families in California, however, are somewhat scattered and no longer increasing. Black farm communities outside the South have been disintegrating in modern times, with few exceptions. The people who have grown up in them are not staying in agriculture. Their stable northern background and higher-than-average education have made it easier for them to succeed in the cities than for their southern cousins, and it is to the cities that they are going.

## Tenure of Farming

In the twentieth century, the traditional image of the black farmer has been that of the sharecropper. This is not surprising since from World War I until 1950, half or more of all black farmers were landless tenants working for a share of the crops they produced. Others rented for cash, but until the end of World War II not more than one-fourth of black farmers owned their property (mortgaged or unmortgaged). Many white farmers were tenants as well, but not in the same proportions as Negroes. Even during the worst years of the 1930s, more than half of the southern white farmers were owners. This difference has had a far-reaching effect on the ability of blacks to survive and prosper in agriculture. Lacking land, the tenant has no defense against mechanization and may find himself displaced if the landlord decides to operate with more machinery and fewer men. He is usually the loser, too, when crop allotments are cut and there is less acreage to be divided among the tenants.

The number and proportion of black tenants has been greatly reduced in the last twenty years because of these and other reasons. Relatively few have become owners. From 1945 to 1964, an 82 percent loss of black tenants took place. Owners declined by 45 percent—a heavy loss in itself, but much less than that of tenants.

The most viable and progressive element among farmers in the post–World War II

period has been the part owners, those who own some land and rent more. This system
has the advantage of enabling a man to expand his operations without tying up additional
money in land. Instead he may use his capital for machinery and then rent enough extra
land to keep himself and his machines fully and profitably employed. Although· the
traditional view of the hierarchy of farmers has placed the full owner at the top, the part
owners as a class have larger operations and earn more money. Black part owners were
increasing in number as late as 1950, but have declined somewhat since then. Their
relative importance has continued to grow, however, and they now account for a sixth
of all black farmers.

Black owners in the South (full and part) numbered 68,000 and operated 5.8 million
acres of land in 1969. (See Table III.) That is a little more than 11,000 square miles, an
area about the size of Maryland.

TABLE III—NUMBER, ACREAGE, AND VALUE OF FARMS OPERATED BY
NONWHITES IN THE SOUTH, 1969, 1959, AND 1920

| Tenure of operator | Number of farms | | | Land in farms (Thou. acres) | | |
|---|---|---|---|---|---|---|
| | 1969[1] | 1959 | 1920 | 1969 | 1959 | 1920 |
| Total | 85,249 | 265,621 | 922,914 | 6,667 | 13,901 | 41,318 |
| Full owners | 52,593 | 89,749 | 178,558 | 3,841 | 5,577 | 11,950 |
| Part owners | 15,374 | 37,534 | 39,031 | 1,935 | 3,104 | 2,126 |
| Managers | NA | 290 | 1,770 | NA | 351 | 368 |
| All tenants | 17,282 | 138,048 | 703,555 | 891 | 4,869 | 26,874 |

| Tenure of operator | Average acres per farm | | | Average value of farms ($) | | |
|---|---|---|---|---|---|---|
| | 1969[1] | 1959 | 1920 | 1969 | 1959 | 1920 |
| Total | 78.2 | 52.3 | 44.8 | 11,553 | 6,240 | 2,414 |
| Full owners | 73.0 | 62.1 | 66.9 | 10,949 | 6,255 | 2,561 |
| Part owners | 125.9 | 82.7 | 54.5 | 18,927 | 9,436 | 2,421 |
| Managers | NA | 1211.0 | 207.9 | NA | 107,072 | 12,166 |
| All tenants | 51.6 | 35.3 | 38.2 | 9,143 | 5,284 | 2,352 |

NA-Not available.

[1]Relates to Negroes only.

Source:   Advance reports of 1969 Census of Agriculture and 1959 Census of Agriculture, Volume II.

There are a few counties (about ten in 1969) in which black farm owners outnumber
white owners. About two-thirds of these counties are located in the Black Belt of
Alabama and the Coastal Plain of South Carolina. In no case, however, do black farmers
own the majority of the farmland in a county. The maximum relative land ownership

occurs in Jefferson Davis County in southern Mississippi, where black owners operate 26 percent of all farmland.

## Type of Farming

The peculiar concentration of black farmers in a few areas can be easily seen from census figures on the types of commercial farms. (See Table IV.) In the fall of 1964, 49 percent of the commercial-size farms run by nonwhite farmers in the South were cotton farms (meaning that over half of their gross income came from the sale of cotton). Considering that Negroes were historically concentrated in the Cotton Belt, this percentage might not seem particularly high were it not for the much lower emphasis on cotton by southern white farmers. The heavier black reliance on cotton was true throughout the South. In its most extreme form (in Mississippi), 87 percent of all nonwhite commercial farmers were cotton specialists in 1964.

TABLE IV—TYPE OF COMMERCIAL FARM BY VALUE OF PRODUCTS SOLD IN 1964, FOR NONWHITE-OPERATED FARMS IN THE SOUTH

| Type of Farm | Value of Products Sold, 1964 | | | | | | |
| --- | --- | --- | --- | --- | --- | --- | --- |
| | Total[1] | $40,000 or more | $20,000 – $40,000 | $10,000 – $20,000 | $5,000 – $10,000 | $2,500 – $5,000 | Under $2,500 |
| All types | 117,707 | 235 | 796 | 5,957 | 21,736 | 34,830 | 54,153 |
| Cash grain[2] | 3,472 | 23 | 47 | 121 | 282 | 514 | 2,405 |
| Tobacco[2] | 31,409 | 7 | 146 | 3,124 | 10,941 | 10,424 | 6,765 |
| Cotton[2] | 58,159 | 83 | 261 | 1,230 | 6,810 | 18,875 | 30,770 |
| Other field crops[2] | 3,596 | 14 | 58 | 335 | 847 | 1,017 | 1,151 |
| Poultry | 426 | 39 | 73 | 84 | 71 | 46 | 113 |
| Dairy | 1,140 | 8 | 34 | 129 | 240 | 365 | 364 |
| Livestock | 4,667 | 8 | 16 | 48 | 184 | 579 | 3,832 |
| General | 8,380 | 28 | 130 | 816 | 2,179 | 2,526 | 2,701 |
| Vegetable, fruit, nut, and miscellaneous[3] | 6,458 | 25 | 31 | 70 | 182 | 484 | 6,052 |

[1]Excludes 107 farms managed by nonwhites.

[2]Value of products sold not known for some farms.

[3]Distribution includes value of products sold for 386 grain, tobacco, cotton, and other field crop farms.

Source:  1964 Census of Agriculture, Volume I.

After cotton, tobacco culture is by far the most common type of farming for blacks, being the principal product of 27 percent of nonwhite southern commercial enterprises. More than half the nonwhite tobacco specialists operate in North Carolina.

The third most common commercial operation for Negroes (7 percent of the total) is the general farm, where no one product accounts for half of the total sales. Such an operation sounds like the acme of stability and diversification—and often is larger than the cotton or tobacco specialty farm. In many cases, however, this category simply represents farms on which small amounts of the traditional crops—cotton and tobacco— are of about equal importance or on which one or the other is supplemented with peanuts. A final grouping which in the official statistics is called "other field crop" farms accounts for an additional 3 percent of the commercial farms and consists principally of peanut specialty farms in North Carolina and Georgia.

The four types of commercial farms cited—cotton, tobacco, general, and other field crops—account for 86 percent of all southern nonwhite farms operated at the commercial level, as compared with 45 percent for southern white farmers. The major significance of this fact is that the crops involved are allotted crops for which the acreage is restricted by law, that more often than not they are in surplus supply, and that they are either stationary or contracting in acreage.

In contrast, the nonwhite farmer has only minor representation in the sectors of agriculture that have been expanding in the South, such as livestock, dairy, or poultry farming and truck crops. Throughout the South the agricultural colleges and other shapers of farming trends have long been preaching the theme of a "green revolution" to southern farmers—that is, a conversion of lands to hay crops and improved pastures and the raising of more livestock. This movement clearly came of age in the 1950s, for the 1959 census revealed that the South as a region for the first time had more livestock farms than cotton farms. But for the black farmer it is almost as though such a change had never occurred. Only 4 percent of the nonwhite southern farmers are livestock specialists (cattle, hogs, and sheep), and only an additional 1 percent are dairymen or poultrymen.

Nothing more sharply distinguishes white from nonwhite farmers in the South than the different degree of reliance on livestock. Ninety percent of the total value of products sold by nonwhite farmers in 1959 consisted of crops and only 10 percent of livestock and livestock products. On southern white-operated farms, 52 percent of the total product value was from crops and 48 percent from livestock—an almost even balance.

## Size of Farms

Perhaps the most widespread trend in American agriculture since the end of the Depression has been the increase in the physical size of farms. The acreage needed to farm successfully differs widely from one part of the country to another—depending on the climate and the quality of land—and from one type of farming to another. In general, the greater the amount of labor per acre required to produce a commodity, the smaller the average amount of land in a family farm will be or need be. And the labor used per acre is roughly proportional to the money yielded. For example, tobacco requires heavy inputs of labor per acre and the average amount of land planted in tobacco per farm is small—only about three acres per farm in the South. However, the value of the crop usually exceeds a thousand dollars per acre. With cotton or peanuts, typical production per acre might be worth one to two hundred dollars, depending on the region. But with soybeans the best areas of the South would yield less than sixty dollars per acre on the average. In livestock production, the acreage needed for pasture and to raise feeds is usually much larger for each dollar of product yielded than is true for cash crop farming.

The farms operated by blacks have historically been small. With their limited capital, Negroes were lucky to acquire land at all. If they were tenants, the usual rental included only as much cotton land as a family could work by hand and mule, plus a few acres to grow corn for the mule.

In 1935, at the time the modern trend toward larger farms was beginning, the average size of a black-operated farm in the South was 44 acres; white farmers averaged 131 acres. As the ability and necessity to have larger units grew, the size of white farms grew. This was not simply the result of landlords displacing tenants and operating their land in fewer units without an overall increase in land holdings. All classes of white-operated farms became steadily larger, including tenant farms, and by 1969 the white average had doubled, rising to 283 acres.

Among black farmers evidences of this trend are slight. Although hundreds of thousands of small tenant units have disappeared, the average size of all farms has gone up to only 78 acres, an increase of 34 acres since 1935. Nonwhite full owners average 73 acres and part owners 126 (See Table III.)

The limited size of land resources has been one of the factors retarding the ability or willingness of black farmers to diversify into more extensive types of farming such as grain and livestock. Typically the pasture land alone on a white livestock farm is larger than the entire acreage of a black-operated farm.

## Economic Scale of Farming

Farms vary widely in the amount of business they do. The best available way to rank them is by the value of products sold from the farm. The Bureau of the Census classes as "commercial" farms those selling over $2,500 worth of products in a year, plus those selling a lower amount whose operators are not elderly and have little off-farm work. Under these rules 117,707 farms in the South operated by nonwhite farmers were termed commercial in 1964, amounting to about five-eighths of all nonwhite-operated farms. Of the others, 33,492 were classed as part-time, and 33,020 as part-retirement farms whose operators were 65 years old or over (Table V).

The Department of Agriculture figures as a rule of thumb that a farmer must sell at least $10,000 of products annually if he expects to make a minimum net income of $2,500. The gross sales needed for a net of $2,500 vary from one type of farming to another. For example, dairy and poultry farms typically have a high volume of sales and a low profit margin, whereas crop farms that do not turn over their capital as often

usually have a higher profit margin. Because profit margins in agriculture have narrowed in recent years, the value of sales needed to return a given net income has risen
steadily and will probably continue to do so. If $10,000 of sales is accepted as a minimum
scale of farming, then only 3.8 percent of all nonwhite farms in the South met even this
standard in 1964. (See Table V.) By contrast, 18.3 percent of southern white farmers had
returns of this size. If because of their concentration in annual cash crops it is suggested
that nonwhite farmers might get by if they sell a minimum of $5,000, the proportion
with adequate-sized units is still only 15.6 percent, compared with 30.2 for white
farmers. It must be remembered that the landlord's share of the crop has to come out of
the value sold by tenant farmers.

TABLE V—ECONOMIC CLASS OF NONWHITE-OPERATED FARMS IN THE SOUTH,
BY TENURE, 1964

| Economic class[1] | Number of Farms | | | | Percentage Distribution | | | |
|---|---|---|---|---|---|---|---|---|
| | Total[2] | Full owners | Part owners | All tenants | Total | Full owners | Part owners | All tenants |
| TOTAL | 184,219 | 70,663 | 31,215 | 82,341 | 100.0 | 100.0 | 100.0 | 100.0 |
| Commercial | 117,707 | 29,814 | 21,359 | 66,534 | 63.9 | 42.2 | 68.4 | 80.8 |
| $40,000 or more | 235 | 39 | 148 | 48 | .1 | .1 | .5 | .1 |
| $20,000– $40,000 | 796 | 106 | 422 | 268 | .4 | .2 | 1.4 | .3 |
| $10,000– $20,000 | 5,957 | 452 | 1,707 | 3,798 | 3.2 | .6 | 5.5 | 4.6 |
| $ 5,000– $10,000 | 21,736 | 2,192 | 4,529 | 15,015 | 11.8 | 3.1 | 14.5 | 18.2 |
| $ 2,500– $ 5,000 | 34,830 | 6,534 | 6,534 | 21,762 | 18.9 | 9.2 | 20.9 | 26.4 |
| Less than $ 2,500 | 54,153 | 20,491 | 8,019 | 25,643 | 29.4 | 29.0 | 25.7 | 31.1 |
| Noncommercial | 66,512 | 40,849 | 9,856 | 15,807 | 36.1 | 57.8 | 31.6 | 19.2 |
| Part-time | 33,492 | 17,439 | 6,065 | 9,988 | 18.2 | 24.7 | 19.4 | 12.1 |
| Part retirement | 33,020 | 23,410 | 3,791 | 5,819 | 17.9 | 33.1 | 12.1 | 7.1 |

[1]Dollar values refer to value of farm products sold from the farm in 1964. Part-time farms are those
selling less than $2,500 of products a year whose operators are under age 65 and depend heavily on off-
farm jobs or income. Part-retirement farms are those selling less than $2,500 of products a year whose
operators are 65 years old or over.
[2]Excludes 109 managers.
Source:   1964 Census of Agriculture, Volume I.

The number of nonwhite farmers in the South who sold $10,000 or more of prod-
ucts in 1969 was 6,988. An additional 21,736 sold between $5,000 and $10,000 worth.
At the lower extreme there were 88,983 commercial farmers whose gross receipts were
less than $5,000. These figures indicate more clearly than any others how very small is
the number of blacks who have a real toehold in agriculture, and how large is the
proportion who have little chance of making a decent living from farming alone without
a radical change in their scale of operation. Among commercial farmers, the average
value of products sold by all southern nonwhite farmers was $3,845; the average for
white commercial farmers was $13,816 (See Table VI.)

**TABLE VI—SELECTED CHARACTERISTICS OF SOUTHERN FARMS AND FARMERS, 1964**

| Characteristic | Grand Total | Nonwhite Operators | | | | | | White Operators | | |
| --- | --- | --- | --- | --- | --- | --- | --- | --- | --- | --- |
| | | Commercial | | | | | | Noncommercial | Grand Total | Commercial Total |
| | | Total | Full Owners | Part Owners | Tenants | | | | | |
| | | | | | Total | Cash | Crop share | | | |
| Average farm size (acres) | 57 | 60 | 75 | 104 | 39 | 63 | 32 | 50 | 283 | 406 |
| Value of farm ($) | 10,064 | 11,553 | 10,949 | 18,927 | 9,143 | 8,982 | 8,954 | 7,431 | 42,253 | 59,526 |
| Value per acre ($) | 176 | 189 | 145 | 180 | 238 | 143 | 279 | 149 | 150 | 147 |
| Cropland harvested (acres) | 19 | 25 | 18 | 42 | 23 | 27 | 21 | 8 | 55 | 86 |
| Pasture, excl. woods (acres) | 11 | 10 | 17 | 19 | 4 | 9 | 2 | 13 | 140 | 205 |
| Have tractor (%) | 32 | 35 | 39 | 63 | 25 | 33 | 23 | 25 | 71 | 80 |
| Have hogs (%) | 64 | 66 | 68 | 79 | 61 | 75 | 60 | 60 | 30 | 35 |
| Have cattle (%) | 50 | 44 | 63 | 62 | 30 | 57 | 26 | 60 | 76 | 74 |
| Sold hogs (%) | 18 | 19 | 23 | 32 | 12 | 21 | 10 | 17 | 17 | 21 |
| Sold cattle (%) | 22 | 19 | 31 | 33 | 10 | 22 | 7 | 27 | 63 | 65 |
| Plant cotton (%) | 59 | 70 | 57 | 67 | 78 | 87 | 79 | 40 | 16 | 26 |
| Plant tobacco (%) | 25 | 32 | 24 | 35 | 35 | 13 | 40 | 12 | 22 | 28 |
| Corn per acre (bu.) | 32 | 34 | 30 | 33 | 36 | 23 | 40 | 23 | 46 | 47 |
| Value of products sold per farm ($): | | | | | | | | | | |
|   All products | 2,705 | 3,845 | 2,203 | 5,108 | 4,130 | 2,844 | 4,413 | 687 | 8,489 | 13,816 |
|   Crops | 2,474 | 3,559 | 1,086 | 4,543 | 4,018 | 2,651 | 4,358 | 555 | 4,731 | 7,776 |
|   Livestock (including dairy and poultry) | 229 | 284 | 443 | 562 | 112 | 193 | 55 | 131 | 3,747 | 6,023 |
| Average value sales per acre ($) | 48 | 64 | 29 | 49 | 107 | 45 | 137 | 14 | 30 | 34 |
| Operators having 100 + days off farm work (%) | 22 | 5 | 4 | 8 | 5 | 5 | 5 | 52 | 38 | 17 |

Source: 1964 Census of Agriculture, Vols. I and II.

One of the most serious ultimate problems for the future of the Negro in agriculture is the low state of production by black farmers who own all or part of their land. With the steady decline of the tenant system of farming, the future of black farmers is increasingly determined by the level of activity of the owner-operator. At present 37 percent of black owners (full and part owners combined) are not even producing enough to be classed as commercial farmers. The part owners, who are the less numerous of the two owner groups, are usually commercial, but more than half of the full owners are not. In part the low production of the full owners is the result of age; many of them are too old to be active. But even among those under 55 years old, a majority fail to sell $2,500 worth of products.

In light of the small size of most farms run by Negroes, one might logically expect that the farms would be fully utilized. However, the proportion of crop land that is idle or had crop failure is high. In 1964 nearly one-fourth of all the crop land on the farms of black owners was idle or had crop failure, compared with one-ninth on farms of white owners.

In addition, the proportion of land remaining in woods is high, amounting to about three-eighths of the total land acreage of commercial black owners. These woodlands are usually of low economic value in their present state, except for hunting and as a source of firewood to feed the archaic stoves that still serve as the means of cooking or heating on many farms.

In short, it is not surprising that with such small farms the black farmers remained concentrated in the production of intensive crops in which labor can be substituted for land. It is contrary to expectation, however, that their limited land resources are not used more fully. Generally the black farmer comes closer to operating his place in the old-time manner, using older methods and equipment and producing much for home use.

A generation ago this emphasis on food for home use would have gladdened the hearts of extension agents and others concerned for the rural Negro's welfare, for it was commonly observed that much of the debt of black tenants was for purchase of food that they would not or were not permitted to raise on their farms. Today the general trend in agriculture is for farmers not to produce their own meat or milk or eggs, although the vegetable garden shows no sign of demise. Specialized production and marketing have commonly made it cheaper or safer or more convenient for the farmer to purchase most foods. The following figures clearly show, however, that even commercial black farmers put much more emphasis on subsistence than do their white neighbors.

|  | Nonwhite | White |
|---|---|---|
| Percent of southern commercial farmers who sold cattle, 1964 | 19 | 65 |
| Percent who kept cattle but sold none | 25 | 9 |
| Percent who sold hogs, 1964 | 19 | 21 |
| Percent who kept hogs but sold none | 47 | 14 |

The majority of white southern commercial farmers who keep cattle or hogs keep them for sale; the majority of black commercial farmers who have them keep them for home-produced meat. A similar although less pronounced pattern shows up for chickens and milk. The additional emphasis that the black farmer puts on subsistence farming certainly offsets to some extent the money-income difference between himself and white farmers, but it is unmistakably associated with less complete commitment to farming as a business.

## Productivity

In the last fifteen years, as profit margins have narrowed, farmers have attempted to maintain their income level by increasing the size of operations and raising yields per acre. Production has been the key to survival.

The patterns of productivity per acre in the three crops that form the backbone of black agriculture—cotton, tobacco, and peanuts—give some interesting insights into the competitive position of black farmers. The table below was compiled for North Carolina, where black farmers have been most successful, on the average, and where all three crops are important. It shows the yields per acre for white and nonwhite commercial farmers in 1964—the latest year for which all data are available (Table VII).

**TABLE VII**—YIELDS PER ACRE OF SPECIFIED CROPS ON COMMERCIAL FARMS IN NORTH CAROLINA, BY COLOR AND TENURE OF THE OPERATOR, 1964

| Crop and color of operator | Tenure | | | | | |
|---|---|---|---|---|---|---|
| | Total commercial | Full owners | Part owners | Tenants | | |
| | | | | Total | Cash tenants | Croppers |
| Cotton (lbs.) | | | | | | |
| White | 523 | 520 | 536 | 488 | 517 | 478 |
| Nonwhite | 473 | 434 | 456 | 483 | 456 | 488 |
| Peanuts (lbs.) | | | | | | |
| White | 2,048 | 2,039 | 2,102 | 1,985 | 2,006 | 1,958 |
| Nonwhite | 1,829 | 1,589 | 1,643 | 1,917 | 1,610 | 1,949 |
| Tobacco (lbs.) | | | | | | |
| White | 2,219 | 2,216 | 2,226 | 2,215 | 2,198 | 2,247 |
| Nonwhite | 1,975 | 1,787 | 1,800 | 2,046 | 1,945 | 2,246 |
| Soybeans (bu.) | | | | | | |
| White | 23.1 | 23.5 | 22.9 | 23.2 | 22.7 | 23.9 |
| Nonwhite | 22.4 | 21.4 | 22.0 | 22.9 | 22.6 | 24.3 |

Source:   1964 Census of Agriculture, Volume I.

Note that the yields obtained by white full and part owners are substantially superior to those of nonwhite farmers for tobacco and peanuts and moderately so for cotton. On the other hand, among tenant farmers the yields of white farmers are only slightly higher than are those of nonwhites. The reasons for these differences are discussed below.

Among the white farmers, owners (full or part) generally obtain somewhat better yields than do tenants. Applying coventional logic, this seems fitting, considering the higher ability and greater experience that one associates with those who have acquired farms, as compared with those who are landless.

But this conventional relationship between the tenure classes does not apply to nonwhite farmers. Among black men it is the tenants who show considerably greater yields of all three crops than do the owners. Furthermore, within the tenant class, the croppers—who have been least successful in advancing toward farming independence, who have the least managerial ability, and bring nothing to their work except their labor—produce higher yields than the tenant groups who operate their own equipment.

The reasons for this are at least threefold. First, black croppers typically occupy high-quality land to which white landlords have access, rather than the poorer average-quality land that Negroes have been able to buy or to rent. Second, the croppers' land is managed by the landlord, who has had broader opportunities to acquire managerial know-how, and who enjoys better credit and cooperation from local business associates. Third, economies of scale may operate; the black farm with its typically small size may be analogous to small family-run businesses in other industries competing with larger firms.

A black county-extension agent in North Carolina attributed many of the difficulties that face black owners to a fear of going into debt and a lack of understanding on their part of the role of credit in modern farming, after years of poor access to credit and little encouragement to learn at first hand.

As indicated under the discussion of diversification, many southern farmers have added soybeans to their cash crops. However, in North Carolina, a leading producer, the proportion of farmers harvesting soybeans was less for nonwhite commercial owners (21 percent) than for white (32 percent) in 1964. Furthermore, the white owner-operators harvested twice as many acres of beans per farm. Thus in newer crops as with the old, Negro farmers have been handicapped by their smaller farms, lagging propensity to change, and such other factors as age, education, and equipment which will be examined later.

## Facilities

Black farmers, like all others, have moved into a completely different era from the days before the first world war when most power was supplied by hand or by animals, when it took all day to get to the county seat and back, and when electrical or engine-driven equipment was unknown. The extension of electricity to farms is now so nearly complete that the census of agriculture no longer bothers to inquire about it. Black farmers were typically the last to obtain it, but today it is standard even in substandard houses.

The great majority of black farmers have also acquired either an automobile or a truck, giving them much greater freedom of movement and choice in purchasing or selling. But there are other facilities now conventional elsewhere that most black farmers do without.

For instance, only one out of every four nonwhite-operated farms has a telephone, compared with two-thirds of the white farms. This is not just the result of so many black farmers being tenants. Even among commercial nonwhite farmers who own their places, just one-third have installed phones. Lack of access to the telephone lines, lack of steady income to afford a phone, and perhaps lack of experience with the advantages of having one have held down telephone usage. Nevertheless the proportion of black farmers with a telephone is double what it was a decade ago.

Another facility of importance to a farmer is the paved or improved road. It defines his marketing ability and reduces his degree of isolation. But here, as with other facilities, the black farmer is likely to find himself at a comparative disadvantage. In the South as a whole, 43 percent of all commercial-scale nonwhite farmers were still located on a dirt or unimproved road in 1959, compared with 28 percent for commercial white farmers. The disparity was even greater for the noncommercial group.

Ironically enough, it is the least independent of the black farmers who are most likely to be on a good road. The croppers, with minor exceptions, work the farms of white landlords. Three-fifths of their farms are on improved roads, whereas only half of the full or part owners are so located. The least fortunate group in this respect are cash tenants, nearly three-fifths of whom have to contend with dirt roads.

As the last claimants to land, black owners more often obtained poorer land away from the main traveled roads. In the case of rented land, a landlord is more likely to rent poorer farms for a fixed rent (cash) than on a share basis. Moreover, black districts in the South have seldom received standard levels of public roads from the governing authorities. In a majority of instances the farmer whose place fronts on a dirt road is more than one mile from an improved road.

With few exceptions, modern types of farming require the use of a tractor for efficient operations. Particularly for farmers as heavily committed to field crops as are black farmers, the lack of a tractor connotes either a lack of capital or lack of incentive to advance beyond a low-income operation.

In examining the extent to which black farmers have acquired tractors, it would be somewhat misleading to focus on the overall frequency of tractors, since so many of the farmers are croppers. Although croppers by definition do not have their own machinery, they usually have the use of a tractor through the landlord. Limiting the comparison to commercial owners shows unmistakably that even the elite group of black farmers is far behind the white in possession of tractors. Among full owners 39 percent of nonwhites had one or more tractors compared with 70 percent of the white farmers, and among part owners the percentages were 63 for nonwhites and 87 for white. Noncommercial southern white farmers are more likely to have tractors than are commercial black full owners.

# CHARACTERISTICS OF FARMERS

## Age

In each of the major tenure classes—full owner, part owner, and tenant—the average age of a nonwhite southern farmer is higher than that of a white farmer. The overall difference is not large, however; white farmers averaged 53 years old as against 54 years for blacks. But among noncommercial farmers, the average black owner or tenant is four to five years older than his white counterpart. With many tenant farmers now being displaced or converted to hired workers, the average age of black operators is rising rapidly.

The most numerous group of farmers is that between the ages of 55 and 64. But among full owners the largest group consists of those 65 years old and over—more than one-third of all full owners. This high age level of owners explains in part the comparatively low level of productivity of black-owned farms in general.

## Education

The position and prospects of the Negro as a farmer cannot be discussed without reference to educational opportunities available to the farm population. Even in the most progressive agricultural areas of the country the notion that a grade-school training was sufficient for a farmer lingered for many years after it ceased to be valid.

For the southern black farmer, several factors, added to the traditionally conservative rural view of education, have produced the lowest levels of schooling in the United States outside of certain Indian tribes. These factors include the extended neglect of rural black school facilities, the closing of schools during peak farm-work seasons for use of child labor, and the lack of educational incentive inherent in the sharecropper mode of life.

In 1971 the average years of schooling completed by the black farm population 25 years old and over was 6.1 years, compared with 11.2 years for the white farm population and 12.3 years for the total urban population. Only 8 percent of adult black farm residents have completed high school. Some gradual improvement is taking place, but the pace is extremely slow. The increase in high-school graduates has gone only from 2 percent to 8 percent in 30 years. In this respect the black farm population is more than a generation behind white farm people, 14 percent of whom had a high school diploma in 1940.

Forty percent of black farm people 25 years old and over did not complete as many as five years of school (compared with 5 percent of the white farm population). The situation is not much better for nonwhites among the rural nonfarm population, but is far better in the cities. Some of the problem in the black farm population is due to the siphoning off to the cities of those young people who do go through high school. Black county extension agents are almost unanimous in saying that it is very difficult to interest rural high-school students in farming. The good student usually associates the widespread poverty of the population from which he comes with agriculture, and sees the city as the avenue of opportunity.

Even among the young, the academic performance of children from black farm families is behind that of the general population. There has not yet been a solution to the 1960 problem that more than half (57 percent) of all southern nonwhite farm boys aged 14 and 15 years old had not reached the grades that are normal for persons of their age. The corresponding proportion for white farm boys that age was 26 percent in the South and only 11 percent in the North and West. Even more astonishing is the fact that of the nonwhite farm boys who were behind in school a substantial majority had fallen two or more years behind. In most instances such retardation becomes a prelude to quitting school altogether—and three-fourths of all black farm boys do drop out before completing high school.

With such a small fraction of the black farm people having received a modern education, it is easy to understand how difficult it is to develop group leadership in that population, and how frequently it is possible for a semiliterate farmer to fail to understand the complexities of government programs that affect his heavily controlled crops or to take full advantage of the services that the government and the experiment stations can provide him.

## Hired Farm Workers

In one aspect of American agriculture the role of the Negro has increased rather than diminished. That aspect is the performance of farm work for cash wages. In many respects the sharecropper has been little different from a hired worker, because he usually contributes nothing to his operation except his labor. But technically the cropper has been an operator, for he is paid with a share of the crop rather than with money and is clearly attached to a particular farm for the season.

The hired farm wage laborer—black or white—is usually society's low man on the totem pole in income and in the respect accorded to him. Some of the reasons for the low standing of the occupation are not hard to find. The average wages paid to farm workers in the South were only $1.45 an hour in 1971 without room and board. The frequency of unemployment is high, the average education of hired farm workers is lower than that of any other major occupation group, and except for inclusion in the Social Security system and partial coverage by minimum wage laws, they are excluded from the basic protections that people in most other jobs take for granted. With few exceptions, farm workers are not included in unemployment compensation insurance, not protected by workmen's disability compensation, and not guaranteed the right to bargain collectively with their employers. As a group they are the closest approximation that the United States has to a pariah occupational caste. Under these conditions it is extremely difficult to develop a career attitude toward hired farm work and to raise the status of the work.

Where does the black worker fit into this picture? Because of the low status of the job and the low degree of education required, Negroes have always been heavily used in hired farm work wherever they have lived and have been a logical group to supply migratory workers to other parts of the nation for seasonal farm work.

In 1971 one-fourth of all days of farm wage work in the United States was performed by Negroes. Today the hired black farm worker makes a greater labor contribution to supplying the nation's agricultural needs than does the black farmer. In the South, where black farmers comprise one-sixth of all farmers, black workers do two-fifths of all farm wage work.

TABLE VIII—DAYS WORKED AND WAGES EARNED BY PERSONS DOING 25 OR MORE DAYS OF FARM WAGE WORK IN 1971, BY COLOR

| Area, color, and sex of worker | Number of workers | Farm work | | |
|---|---|---|---|---|
| | | Days worked | Wages earned | |
| | | | Per year | Per day |
| | Thou. | No. | Dol. | Dol. |
| United States | | | | |
| Total | 1,359 | 135 | 1,576 | 11.65 |
| White | 1,029 | 141 | 1,706 | 12.10 |
| Male | 893 | 128 | 1,829 | 12.35 |
| Female | 135 | 96 | 897 | 9.35 |
| Nonwhite | 331 | 115 | 1,172 | 10.20 |
| Male | 228 | 143 | 1,510 | 10.55 |
| Female | 103 | 54 | 422 | 7.80 |
| South | | | | |
| Total | 608 | 131 | 1,443 | 11.00 |
| White | 312 | 150 | 1,818 | 12.10 |
| Nonwhite | 297 | 111 | 1,049 | 9.45 |

Source:   Hired Farm Working Force of 1971, U. S. Department of Agriculture, Table 9.

The South, like the rest of the nation, has had mechanization, but landowners have often adjusted to it by abandoning the tenant method of working their land and substituting hired workers for tenants. The switch from tenants to hired hands is nowhere more evident than in the Mississippi Delta country. Here in fifteen years' time, from 1954 to 1969, the number of tenant farmers (white and nonwhite) dropped by over 96 percent (from 83,000 to 7,000). The Delta is mostly cotton country. As the farm owners switched from hand cropping and hand picking by tenants to machine methods by wage hands, they initially had to hire about three new regular hands for each ten tenants displaced. Many of the new wage hands were selected from former tenants. But by the mid-1960s, the hired workers were decreasing, too, as cotton acreage dropped and labor-saving techniques continued to be adopted. By 1969 the Delta had no more regular hired workers than in 1964, before the heavy loss of tenants occurred. The same trend has characterized other cotton areas and the tobacco and peanut belts.

In the traditional "tenure ladder" the landless laborer was regarded as a more pitiable creature than the sharecropper. But interestingly enough this does not usually seem to be the case with the new black wage hand. Generally these former tenants who have survived the changeover seem to feel that they are better off. For one thing, there is a regular payday and less likelihood that a man will find himself badly in debt at season's end as tenants often do. Regular wage work is covered by Social Security, which gives some assurance for the future. And if a man can save some money and find off-farm work in slack farm seasons, he may even aspire to buy a house of his own, which as a furnished tenant he would not have done. To an increasing extent the hired workers are living away from the farm on which they work. (See Table VIII for selected statistics on farm workers.)

## THE PROSPECT

### Land—a Key Factor

In a preceding section the anomaly was mentioned that the black farmers who are landowners have poorer land on the average and work it less intensively than the black tenant farmers who do not control the land they work. Despite the apparent underuse of farms by many Negroes who have become owners, the possession of land is nevertheless a key to future participation by Negroes in American agriculture as operators.

Outright tenancy as a form of land occupancy is in full retreat, especially in the South. Until the end of World War II, southern farmers who rented all the land they worked outnumbered the part owners by more than six to one. Since the war, full tenancy has declined so rapidly and part ownership has become so attractive and necessary that in the 1964 census part owners outnumbered full tenants in the South for the first time, as they have in the North and West since 1954.

Some instances of full tenancy will always exist, but the practice is becoming a minor factor in southern farming. The principal use of tenancy in the South was for cotton farming. With the near total elimination of hand and animal labor in this crop, it became logical for landlords to operate their places as complete units, using hired labor if necessary. Although the end result in tobacco is less clear at the moment, the tendency is the same. The majority of black tenant farmers have already vacated, been displaced, or converted to hired work, and a majority of those tenants remaining will follow the same path.

The farmer who does not control the land he works does not control his own destiny in the far-reaching changes now affecting agriculture. This puts the typical black farmer with his limited capital and lack of ownership experience at a disadvantage.

The legacy of racial discrimination and distrust has left most land in the hands of white owners, who have been reluctant to sell good land to black buyers, unless the market is poor. For example, in the heart of the tobacco country in eastern North Carolina it was not uncommon in the 1950s for auctions of farmland to begin with a statement that bids would be received from white persons only.

In addition, distrust by blacks of white officials and of the white-controlled credit structures has left all too many Negroes apprehensive of attempting to purchase land or to develop the land they may already have.

Since 1910 the amount of land owned by black farmers has gone steadily downward, with the exception of the period from 1940 to 1950. During that one decade, under the prosperous conditions of the war and immediate postwar period, there was growth in both the number of black farmers who owned land and in the amount of land owned. Since that time, however, the gains of the 1940s have disappeared so far as agriculture is concerned. Some of the families who obtained land may continue to own it but no longer use it for farming.

## Technological Changes Affecting Black Farmers

Technological innovations are man-made, but the effects of technological change operate on most men in a very impersonal and neutral way. The impact of the rapid and continuing technological advance in agriculture has not been basically different for black farmers than for others. But Negroes often are concentrated in those classes and types of farming that are most affected by technology.

The case of cotton, discussed earlier, is a prime example. The successful mechanization of this crop probably has had a more fundamental effect on the black farm population than any other event. Within the southern states, where most black farmers live (excluding Texas and Oklahoma), the percentage of cotton mechanically harvested accelerated from 11 percent in 1957 to 96 percent in 1970. As a result, very few cotton-tenant farms have been retained, although some blacks continue to work in cotton as machinery operators, mechanics, etc.

The changes in tobacco farming have been much less than those affecting cotton. In the complicated process of harvesting, curing, and marketing cigarette tobacco, a variety of time-consuming hand operations have been necessary. Tobacco requires 491 man-hours of labor per acre, compared with 6 for corn and 27 for all cotton (1966–70 averages). Naturally this tremendous labor requirement in tobacco farming stands as a challenge to agricultural engineers, and they are succeeding in ways to reduce it.

In the last twenty years machines which permit workers to ride through the fields while priming and preparing the leaves for the curing barn have come into use; in addition, new types of curing barns which reduce the handling of the crop have been invented. The major breakthrough, however, is the invention of a machine that will mechanically sever the ripe leaves from the plant and prepare them for curing—a so-called combine. Some such machines are now in operation, and it appears to be only a matter of time before they are more widely adopted.

The mechanization of tobacco will not come overnight. The crop is geared more to family-sized farms and less to plantations than cotton was. But the initial effects of mechanical progress have been evident since the mid-1950s, and the incentive for the larger operatives to procure reliable mechanical methods and free themselves from dependence on a labor pool is great. It seems inevitable that the direct and indirect pressures on black tobacco farmers to get larger or give up will become greater as this decade progresses.

In addition to the technological changes in their production, both cotton and tobacco are affected by recurring surplus supplies. Cotton is under pressure from the competition of synthetic fibers. The prices of such synthetics as rayon and nylon have been greatly reduced, and there are many uses for which manufacturers can switch between cotton and synthetics, depending on prices. If the government's price support should be cut further, many of the higher-cost farmers concentrated in the Southeast could not grow cotton at a profit. There is almost no prospect of an increase in acreage allotments—most of which are now very small among blacks—and the loss of government support threatens whenever the public and the Congress become impatient with the subsidy burden.

The finding by the Public Health Service that cigarette smoking is a health hazard has raised questions about the long-term future of tobacco production. In addition, American cigarette tobacco has had quality problems in recent years, thus endangering the vital export market.

Such are the effects of technological and related changes on the two crops upon which black farmers rely most. Similar comments could be made about peanut farming.

## The Effect of Rural Traditionalism in Racial Matters

The position and prospects of the black farmer cannot be divorced from the fact that he is located almost entirely in the South—and the inner South at that, where the rural areas are for the most part more conservative in race relations than are the medium and large cities. The progress of the Negro in the exercise of his civil rights, in desegregation or equalization of education, in the extension of social courtesies (the handshake, forms of address), in occupational opportunities, in interracial participation in civic life, and in public accommodations in rural areas has lagged far behind advances in the metropolitan areas. James D. Cowhig and Calvin L. Beale of the Department of Agriculture have shown that by most available measures of socioeconomic status the already wide gaps between the white and nonwhite rural populations in the South widened in the

1950s. This was true of income, proportion of young adults without a high-school diploma, unemployment rate, proportion of workers in blue-collar jobs, number of children born per women, proportion of young children living in households where the head is not their parent, proportion of people living in crowded housing, and proportion living without hot and cold running water in the home. By contrast, in urban areas of the South there was some narrowing of the white-nonwhite gap in five of the categories mentioned.[3] Comparative data for the 1960s are not fully available. Existing figures indicate considerable absolute improvement in most categories, but the relative gap between whites and blacks has widened in as many areas as it has narrowed.

In rural communities it is easier for the white population to exercise informal and personal controls over the black population. The anonymity of large city populations is missing, as is the ease of organizing effective protest movements in the settled urban community. The low level of education and income in most rural areas is also a handicap. In addition, it is in rural counties that blacks most often constitute a large segment of the population and thus pose a greater ultimate threat to the traditional structure of southern society. In such situations the white community feels less leeway in granting concessions and promoting change than is true in areas where Negroes are a smaller minority. The general racial conservatism of rural areas makes it difficult for federal authorities—or even state authorities, if so inclined—to secure the impartial operation of government-financed agricultural programs or economic development projects. By the nature of his occupation the farmer must carry on his business in the rural countryside, and in most instances live there as well. This is a basic handicap that the southern black farmer seems destined to suffer in comparison with his industrial or professionally employed brother who can readily perform his occupation in the cities or in the North if he chooses.

## The Status of Farming and Rural Life Among Young People

Is it an exaggeration to suggest that the young black who goes into farming or farm work today is either a person with a great interest in agriculture and some resources to give promise of success, or else a person who is essentially lacking in enterprise or the desire for social acceptance? Undoubtedly such characterizations are oversimplified, but they would seem to have some truth. Observers in the South, both white and black, express the opinion that the prospect of farming in the rural South has become emotionally unattractive to most rural black youth. It is urban and particularly metropolitan life that has status. This attitude is not confined to Negroes. It is common among rural white youth as well. The image of agrarian life as the ideal and inherently best form of society, inherited from the Jeffersonian period, died a slow death, but research indicates that a large proportion of rural youth prefer to seek an urban life even without economic motivation. In the case of rural black youth in the South both the economic and social disadvantages of rural life are magnified, and the majority have been migrating before they are 25 years old. This pattern has helped raise the average age of black farmers until the presently oncoming youth may, in turn, think of farm operation as an old man's job and a relic of an unpleasant past.

## The Future Role of Black Americans in Agriculture

To be optimistic about the future of black farmers would be to disregard almost every facet of their past and present status and handicaps. But then the odds have always been against them, even in the period when they reached their greatest number. The dissolution of their former concentration in farming was probably a precondition to general progress, so limiting were the semifeudal conditions of the rural South under which black farmers lived.

The loss of one-half of all black farm operators in the fifties raised the question of whether there was any future at all for them, and the experience of the 1960s was not reassuring. To an extent—to a great extent—this chapter is really an epilogue to an occupation that in fact has nearly vanished.

Of the 184,000 nonwhite farmers in the South in 1964, 33,000 (one-sixth) were 65 years old and over and producing less than $2,500 of products for sale. They are essentially in retirement. Most of their farms have less than twenty acres of crop land and thus are not suitable as complete farms, although they might be useful as additions to other farms.

Another 89,000 farmers were classed as commercial but selling less than $5,000 of products a year. Few economists would give many of these much hope of becoming capable of providing a decent income from farming alone, especially since half of them are tenant farms. About 4,000 farmers had 150 or more days of off-farm work.

One-sixth of southern nonwhite farmers that same year (33,000) were qualified as small-scale operators who depend primarily on off-farm work (the "part-time" census class). About 23,000 of them had 200 or more days of off-farm work per year and were thus employed on a relatively full-time basis.

Finally, there were about 29,000 nonwhite southern farmers who produced and sold more than $5,000 of products. These men and their families would seem to provide the means for future black farmers in commercial agriculture. But here again, only one-third (10,000) owned their land, and many of those who were tenants have undoubtedly lost their lease or share arrangements since 1964.

In sum, there were in 1964 about 10,000 nonwhite owner-operators with an adequate or marginally adequate level of production; 4,000 owners with inadequate commercial production, but a fair amount of off-farm work; and 23,000 owners and renters who did not produce very much but had relatively steady farm work. The sum of these groups (37,000) appears to be the total number of the black farmers with a tangible expectation of obtaining a minimum adequate income from farming or a combination of farm and nonfarm work. They represent only 20 percent of the total number of black operators in 1964.

Perhaps others could successfully remain in farming or part-time farming if the land in the hands of small-scale owners could be combined through lease or purchase into larger units, or if federal programs of assistance in land purchase could be made effective on a widespread basis for low-income landless farmers, or if additional nonfarm employment opportunities became available for rural Negroes.

Black farm owners have about 7.2 million acres of land, but 3.3 million acres of it is in the hands of elderly and part-time noncommercial farmers, who are cultivating only half of their crop land. If more of this decidedly underused 3.3 million acres were channeled into the hands of aspiring tenants or commercial owners, as many as 10,000 additional commercial black farmers might have a reasonable chance for survival. But the trend has been for a decline in black-owned farmland, while the total of land in white-owned farms has been stable.

In addition to the groups mentioned, who in our judgment probably represent the maximum future potential number of black farm operators earning an acceptable income from all sources, there are other families who will remain in farming at the poverty level. Their numbers are diminishing rapidly, however.

A major effort by the Department of Agriculture to provide impartial access to its programs to all is basic to any successful future for black farmers as a class. It is also essential to focus particular attention on the plight of black farmers to help offset the obvious effects of years of indifference to their problems.

Fortunately the passage of the Civil Rights Act of 1961 gave the government the leverage as well as the obligation to act to remedy many of the conditions that barred the black farmer from proper access to federal programs.

Simultaneously, the U.S. Commission on Civil Rights engaged in a long investigation of discrimination in the programs of the Department of Agriculture. Its report, issued in February 1965, was very critical of many conditions. The commission concluded that ". . . the department has generally failed to assume responsibility for assuring equal opportunity and equal treatment to all those entitled to benefit from its programs. Instead, the prevailing practice has been to follow local patterns of racial segregation and discrimination in providing assistance paid for by federal funds."[4] The commission recommended to the President to end discriminatory practices, encourage full participation by Negroes in agricultural programs, and provide for equal employment opportunities in programs.

The potential benefits that black farmers can derive from the Civil Rights Act and the investigative report of the Commission on Civil Rights are tremendous. But if the widespread and long-entrenched disadvantages under which black farmers operate are not very soon corrected, black farmers may well disappear as a significant group in American agriculture before the end of the twentieth century.

Paradoxically, the prospects for the future continuance of blacks in hired farm work are high. Whereas in operation of a farm the race is being won by the strong who have the capital and organization to survive in modern agriculture, in hired farm work the race is being left to the weak. Because of the relatively unattractive conditions of much farm work, hired farm workers are being drawn from an increasingly atypical section of society. Except for a minority of well-paid supervisory or technical jobs, regular farm wage work has largely become a residual occupation staffed by those who from poor education, lack of vocational training, or other limitations cannot succeed as farmers or do better in nonagricultural jobs. In the South and in migratory farm work the black worker best fits this description.

Although the chances for the continued existence of a large number of black farm operators in the United States are problematical, the persistence of several million Negroes in rural areas seems certain in the foreseeable future, in part because of their continuance in farm wage work. The rural nonfarm black population has increased in every decade since 1920 when first counted. In 1970 there were an estimated 3,328,000 rural nonfarm blacks—up 25 percent from 1960 (Table IX). Over 90 percent are in the South. In addition to those who are in agriculture as hired workers, many work in agriculturally related industries such as food processing, woodcutting, and the making of lumber and other wood products. Other thousands engage in a variety of manufacturing, construction, or service jobs.

TABLE IX—RURAL BLACK POPULATION IN THE UNITED STATES, BY FARM–NONFARM RESIDENCE, 1920–1970

| Year | Population | | |
|------|-------------|----------------|------------|
|      | Total rural | Rural nonfarm | Rural farm |
|      | Thou.       | Thou.          | Thou.      |
| 1920 | 6,903.7     | 1,803.7        | 5,100.0    |
| 1930 | 6,697.2     | 2,016.7        | 4,680.5    |
| 1940 | 6,611.9     | 2,109.6        | 4,502.3    |
| 1950* | 5,649.7    | 2,491.4        | 3,158.3    |
| 1960** |           |                |            |
| Census | 5,056.7   | 3,574.7        | 1,482.0    |
| Revised | 5,056.7  | 2,666.7        | 2,390.0    |
| 1970*** | 4,213.0 | 3,328.0        | 885.0      |

*The definition of rural was made more restrictive in 1950 than formerly, accounting for about 500,000 of the total rural decline from 1940–50.

**The definition of farm residence was made more restrictive in 1960, and the 1960 census obtained a distinct under-identification of the Negro farm population. The revised figure shown is a more accurate estimate based on the Current Population Survey of the Bureau of the Census.

***Farm and nonfarm components estimated.

Source:   U. S. Censuses of Population and estimates of the Economic Research Service.

The total black rural population—farm and nonfarm—declined from 1960 to 1970 by 800,000 primarily because of the heavy loss of farm people. But because the declining farm population is now smaller than the rural nonfarm population, farm losses may no longer be large enough to offset rural nonfarm gains. It is quite possible that the black rural population will not drop much below 4,000,000.

Thus, whatever the fate of black farm operators, the total rural black population is expected to remain numerically significant. Its current rate of social and economic progress is far behind that of the urban black population or of the white rural population. Its problems are somewhat peculiar to their setting, as many rural problems are. They merit the continued attention not only of the Federal Government but also of the predominantly urban Negro leadership.

### Notes

1. See Chapter 4, "The Black Population in the United States," by Karl E. amd Alma F. Taeuber, and Chapter 6, "The Black American Worker," by Dorothy K. Newman.
2. Morton Rubin, *Plantation County* (Chapel Hill, University of North Carolina Press, 1951), p. 64.
3. James D. Cowhig and Calvin L. Beale, "Relative Socioeconomic Status of Southern Whites and Nonwhites, 1950 and 1960," *Southwestern Social Science Quarterly*, 45, September 1964, p. 113–24.
4. *Equal Opportunity in Farm Programs—An Appraisal of Services Rendered by Agencies of the United States Department of Agriculture*, United States Commission on Civil Rights, Washington, 1965, p. 100.

## BIBLIOGRAPHY

Banks, Vera J., and Beale, Calvin L., *Farm Population by Race, Tenure, and Economic Scale of Farming*. Washington, Economic Research Service, AER-228, U. S. Department of Agriculture, 1972.

Beale, Calvin L., "Rural–Urban Migration of Blacks: Past and Future." *American Journal of Agricultural Economics*, 53, May 1971, pp. 302–307.

Boxley, Robert F., Jr., *White and Nonwhite Owners of Rural Land in the Southeast*. Washington, Economic Research Service, ERS-238, U. S. Department of Agriculture, 1965.

"Color, Race and Tenure of Farm Operator," *U. S. Census of Agriculture: 1964*. Washington, U. S. Bureau of the Census, 1968, Vol. II, Chap. 8.

Cowhig, James D., and Beale, Calvin L., "Socioeconomic Differences Between White and Nonwhite Farm Populations in the South." *Social Forces*, 42, March 1964, pp. 354–62.

———, "Relative Socioeconomic Status of Southern Whites and Nonwhites, 1950 and 1960." *The Southwestern Social Science Quarterly*, 45, September 1964, pp. 113–24.

*Equal Opportunity in Farm Programs— An Appraisal of Services Rendered by Agencies of the United States Department of Agriculture*, Washington, United States Commission on Civil Rights, 1965.

Jones, Lewis W., ed., *The Changing Status of the Negro in Southern Agriculture*. Rural Life Information Series, Bulletin No. 3, Alabama, Tuskegee Institute, 1950.

*Land Tenure in the Southern Region—Proceedings of Professional Agricultural Workers Tenth Annual Conference.* Alabama, Tuskegee Institute, 1951.

McElroy, Robert C., *The Hired Farm Working Force of 1971.* Washington, Economic Research Service, AER-222, U. S. Department of Agriculture, 1972.

*Participation in USDA Programs by Ethnic Groups.* Washington, Civil Rights Staff, U. S. Department of Agriculture, 1971.

Ponder, Henry, "Prospects for Black Farmers in the Years Ahead." *American Journal of Agricultural Economics,* 53, May 1971, pp. 297–301.

Rubin, Morton, *Plantation County.* Chapel Hill, University of North Carolina Press, 1951.

Woodson, Carter G., *The Rural Negro.* Washington, The Association for the Study of Negro Life, 1930.

# 8

## The Black Family

### Joseph H. Douglass and Mabel M. Smythe

As black Americans have become increasingly urbanized, the former rural pattern of the large family with close ties to collateral relatives in other households has been modified. This trend approximates the evolution of the American family in general, which has become more and more city-oriented and less and less concerned with agricultural pursuits, service work, and the like. The black family today resembles other American families in its aspirations, values, size, and income, with certain exceptions which will be examined shortly.

Fifty years ago, approximately three-fourths of the black population lived in southern rural areas. Today the proportion is reversed; three out of four live in the city[1] (as compared to 67 percent of whites) and only 52 percent of black Americans remain in the South.[2] These figures show an exodus not only from the farms but from the South as well, with 40 percent of the black population currently living in the North as compared to 22 percent in 1940. Although the movement from the Deep South and toward the cities has continued into the 1970s, the regional distribution of the black population has been relatively stable since 1965.[3]

In emigrating, black families, like other families, have had to relinquish old behavior patterns, leave old associations behind, and learn new ways of doing things. Elderly and unproductive family members often have been a burden in the cramped tenements of the city, in contrast with their greater acceptance in the kinship-oriented environment of smaller towns. Vice, crime, and asocial behavior are much more in evidence in the large cities.

As black families have tried to adjust to a more urbanized and industrialized orientation and life style they have had experiences typical of a folk or peasant people conforming to city living. Historically, urban areas have served as melting pots for the integration of immigrants into the American culture and with time each immigrant group has gradually improved its relative position. In spite of this general trend, however, a proportionate rise in the relative social and economic status of the majority of black families has not occurred. This is true also of other nonwhite urban minority groups in the United States.[4]

## Evolution and Adaptation

The overall urban experience of black families has not been uniform and is marked by definite social gradations. At one end of the ladder are the families who are third- and fourth-generation urban residents and who have developed skills in coping with city life. At the other extreme are the less educated of the more recent migrants, who have found city problems and pressures overwhelming. The success achieved by black families in the cities is dependent on a number of factors: (1) length of urban residence, (2) their social class origins, (3) their economic status, (4) their educational levels, skills, or other "equipment" for competition, (5) their particular experience with racial discrimination, and (6) the particular urban areas to which they migrated.

For some black families, migration and adaptation to urban living has been markedly successful. In 1973, 16 percent of nonwhite families reported annual incomes in excess of $15,000[5] and there are a few black millionaires. Along with a relatively elevated income status, some black city-dwellers have achieved high levels of education and economic security, and have maintained family integrity and solidarity. For these families, an urban setting has provided opportunities leading to middle- and upper-class status. Some of them had been urbanized for fifty or more years preceding the World War I exodus of rural migrants to urban areas. In New York, Washington, Atlanta, Chicago, Houston, Philadelphia, and Detroit, for example, many of these older black residents, along with other successful blacks, live in well-established neighborhoods, travel abroad, enjoy vacation homes and hobbies, and send their children to prestigious colleges. Children of these prosperous business executives, professionals, and successful investors expect to succeed as a matter of course.

In fact, members of young black families from all socioeconomic levels are gradually narrowing the gap between blacks and whites in educational attainment. The majority of Negro youths—apparently irrespective of family income level—are now completing high school, as is the case with whites.

In the 1960s and 1970s, the migration to the cities has been accompanied by increased participation in the labor force and a higher income level. There has been a resulting socioeconomic movement upward toward middle-level clerical and technical occupations, a growing trickle of blacks into managerial and professional areas, and a decline in low-income jobs. The number of black men and women in professional and technical jobs rose more than 50 percent from 1963 to 1973, compared with a gain of 13 percent for white men and 10 percent for white women; and while there was a slight decline in white managers and administrators, except farm, during this period, the number of blacks employed in these fields went up by 50 percent. Even with the apparently dramatic increase in participation in higher status employment, a black man's chance of being in those favored categories was less than half that of his white counterparts; a black woman was about two-thirds as likely as a white woman to be as fortunate. In the same decade, there was a significant decline in the proportions who were self-employed, working as nonfarm laborers, or in domestic service.[6] It should also be noted that while the overall quality of housing occupied by black families has improved, the black population continues to be heavily concentrated in urban core areas of obsolescence and decay.[7]

Migration to the cities today is occurring at a slower rate than in the last decade. This is accompanied by an accelerated but still modest movement of black families to the suburbs, along with some instances of a more rapid redistribution. The National Advisory Commission on Civil Disorders estimated in 1968 that the black population of cities was growing at least eight times as fast as that of the suburbs. Now studies indicate that the multiple has declined to three. A gradual decline of the younger black generation in the central city, its emergence in the inner suburbs, and (as black income increases further) its entry in today's outer, wealthier suburbs can be anticipated. On the other hand, there continues to be an imbalance of the black population in cities, as opposed to suburbs. While approximately 11 percent of the American population is black, this sector comprises about 28 percent of the central cities and only about 5 percent of the suburbs.

Despite the recent widespread trend of black families toward higher socioeconomic levels, many major difficulties persist, particularly for families below the median income. At a time when sociologists assert that the American population in general faces increasing family disorganization and breakdown through separation, divorce, or desertion and authorities recognize a growing proportion afflicted with strain and discord, much attention has been focused on the incidence of these problems in black families.[8]

The most persistent problems of black families, with all their attendant difficulties, are those of continuing low family income and disproportionately high rates of poverty in terms of the total population. Thus, despite the general upward socioeconomic trend of the group, there is, as compared to whites, a higher degree of insecurity in the labor force and a disproportionate number of black families whose breadwinners work in marginal jobs. The black rate of poverty is approximately double the percentage of blacks in the total population. As one result, urban black families continue to show disproportionate percentages of dependence upon various forms of public assistance.[9]

The pressures under which minority families live include discrimination and all of its related manifestations which have severe adverse effects on children in all families throughout our society, especially on those children who identify with the victims.[10] Discrimination thwarts the personality development of children and can impair their characterological development. It adds still another burden to those critically stressful circumstances with which every young child must cope—a burden which, when added to the problems of poverty, results in disastrously lowered self-esteem.[11] Members of heavily burdened families have the most critical and urgent need for community-sponsored services.

It is not surprising that those families which stand at the bottom of the black socioeconomic scale continue to suffer high rates of morbidity and mortality, especially among their infants and young children. They have relatively high rates of family breakup, decay, households headed by females, and births out of wedlock. The occurrence of overly large families, while dwindling, intensifies the effects of poverty for their members. Note that female-headed families are associated with low incomes. (See Table I.)

### TABLE I—FAMILIES BY SEX OF HEAD AND BY INCOME: 1971

| Family Income in 1970 | Black | | | White | | |
|---|---|---|---|---|---|---|
| | All Families (thousands) | Percent of All Families | | All Families (thousands) | Percent of All Families | |
| | | Male Head | Female Head | | Male Head | Female Head |
| Total .............. | 4,928 | 69 | 31 | 46,540 | 91 | 9 |
| Under $3,000 ........ | 1,046 | 40 | 60 | 3,507 | 72 | 28 |
| $3,000 to $4,999 ...... | 857 | 54 | 46 | 4,424 | 80 | 20 |
| $5,000 to $6,999 ...... | 833 | 72 | 28 | 5,259 | 85 | 15 |
| $7,000 to $9,999 ...... | 890 | 84 | 16 | 9,361 | 91 | 9 |
| $10,000 to $14,999.... | 834 | 89 | 11 | 12,993 | 95 | 5 |
| $15,000 and over .... | 468 | 94 | 6 | 10,998 | 97 | 3 |

Source: U. S. Department of Commerce, Social and Economic Statistics Administration, Bureau of the Census, Series P-23, No. 42, p. 103.

In view of the economic and social strains on black families, they have survived remarkably well. One reason for this may be that they have been forced to adapt continually throughout their history in America. The separation of families during slavery, which disrupted marriages and thwarted stability, stimulated emphasis on the more enduring role of the mother. It also encouraged a sense of responsibility for youngsters not one's own on the part of black adults in general. The black family has acquired under such pressures the flexibility necessary for adjusting to the exigencies of circumstances.

Although the black family has frequently been considered as in "error" or "inferior" when its patterns and functioning have deviated from "white" norms, a careful scrutiny of its history indicates that it has been both adaptive and functional in building up the necessary framework and supports to meet the needs of its members and of the black community in general. It is only logical that a community whose family stresses and problems differ significantly in degree, if not in kind, from those of the mainstream should develop specialized forms and structure to cope with those divergencies.

### Strengths of the Black Family

A close examination of the black family shows certain strengths which help to explain why black youths of the current generation are sometimes characterized by higher morale and a greater sense of control of their destiny than are many alienated white youngsters.

A listing of these strengths[12] includes:

1. Strong bonds of kinship which provide a greater sense of responsibility toward relatives beyond the nuclear family.
2. Strong orientation toward work, with a high value placed on keeping a job and upward occupational mobility.
3. Flexibility in assuming family roles, with emphasis on the importance of the role itself, rather than upon who performs it; thus the black community supports and applauds the man who can prepare dinner for his children, the older children who care for younger ones, and the mother who contributes to family income by working.
4. Achievement orientation, which amounts to an expectation that children will do better than their parents. Black families set goals for their members, often undergoing tremendous personal sacrifices to enable their children or younger siblings to obtain the education they see as a passport to greater income, security, and a comfortable life style.
5. Strong religious orientation, which makes use of church or other religious institutions in the upbringing of children, and provides a sense of alliance with other stable and organized sectors of the community.
6. High value placed on family stability, even by individuals who fail to achieve or maintain it.

In addition to the above, the black family fosters a sense of duty and responsibility in attitudes toward marriage, offers substantial person-oriented support to its members, and provides a basis for unity and commitment for the whole family, which strengthens a sense of self in each member.

## Socioeconomic Class and the Black Family

It is important to underscore the complex social situation created by the effect of class differences on black family structure, values, status, and adaptive mechanisms. The family structure of the more highly educated blacks has historically tended to reflect white middle-class family patterns; as rapid advancement in education, employment, and income expanded the black middle class, the newcomers, too, tended to assimilate the values associated with that socioeconomic status. At the same time, poorer black families tended, like poorer white families, to reflect a common poverty as well as the effects of racism, which customarily fall most heavily on the poor. Thus poorer black and white families alike showed a higher percentage of female family heads and births out of wedlock, as well as a smaller percentage of children living with both parents.

The advances in educational opportunity, in open housing and in civil rights tended to further favor the better-informed and more-sophisticated blacks. Before recession became a major concern of the 1970s, sociologists predicted that the 1970s would see the end of a median income lower for blacks than for whites. They found blacks approaching equality with whites in such measures of relative advantage as percent completing high school, percent in clerical occupations and percent with incomes over $8,000. No such equality, however, was or is predicted for those at the bottom of the scale; and it is cold comfort that whites in the poorer category also have a substantial minority unequipped to function successfully in American society.[13] Poverty is clearly the culprit; in the shadow of recession, it will almost certainly equal or even outrank racism as the primary enemy in the decade of the 1970s.

A study of the evolution of the black family since 1960 thus indicates that there has been uneven but generally forward or upward overall socioeconomic progress for families with educational advantages, accompanied by continuing severe and little-improved social, psychological, and intrafamilial and extrafamilial stresses for families submerged in the so-called "culture of poverty."

The average black family today earns less than two-thirds (61 percent) of the average white family's income, the disparity throughout the nation ranging in 1973 from 56 percent in the South to 81 percent in the West. It should be stressed that in 1973, in comparison with whites, blacks were four times as likely to be poor by official standards, only two-thirds as likely to be in college, and more than twice as likely to be unemployed.[14]

## Central City Concentration of Black Families

Census Bureau studies show a difference in migratory patterns between the white and black populations. In 1973, for example, about 60 percent of the black population lived in "central cities," and about 16 percent in fringe and suburban areas, a total of 76 percent metropolitan in location.[15] The census materials show that the white "escape rate" from the central cities has been nearly 500,000 per year.[16] Meanwhile, the black influx to the cities, although continuing, has slowed substantially.[17] The demographer Conrad Taeuber indicates that "the central city represented a kind of mecca in the 1960s for the growing black middle class in the sense that suburbia has become a mecca for the white middle class."[18] Today, however, as was noted earlier, black families increasingly follow the general population trend toward the suburbs. Just as white families, as they have become affluent, have looked to the suburbs as an area where they can achieve what to them represents the highest living standards America offers, black families with growing means and aspirations are finding a place there as well.[19]

Due primarily to suburban expansion, metropolitan areas have increased in population more rapidly than the rest of the nation.[20] "Core" or "inner" city residency nevertheless continues to be characteristic of black families. As has been observed, "Blacks finally appear to be moving throughout the metropolitan region in something like the way that other immigrants did before them. . . ."[21]

## Family Characteristics

In making the transition from rural to urban life, many city-dwelling families have gradually relinquished such rural characteristics as extended or large families, relatively large numbers of children per household, and consensual relationships. From 1965 to 1973 the average number of children ever born declined markedly for younger black women; in 1965 an average of 2.6 children had been born to those aged 25 to 29, whereas in 1973 the comparable figure was 1.7—a drop of more than 34 percent. The number of children black women aged 18 to 39 expect to have declined from 3.7 to 3.0 between 1967 and 1973 (comparable figures for white women were 3.1 in 1967 and 2.6 in 1973).[22] In all the years reported, the fertility of nonwhite women has been higher than for their white counterparts.[23]

While under 10 percent of white families in 1974 were headed by a female, the proportion of female-headed nonwhite families had increased from 17.6 in 1950 to 34 percent in 1974.[24]

In 1974, 49 percent of black female heads of families were separated or divorced, as compared with 45 percent of white female heads. The percentage of black female heads separated from their husbands (33) was more than twice as great as that for whites.[25] The 16 percent of black female divorced heads, however, is only slightly more than half the 30 percent of white divorced female heads. Since divorce is more expensive than separation, economic forces might be expected to discourage it in those at or near the poverty level, even if legal complications did not also exert pressure in the same direction. (See Table II.)

A relatively high percentage of both white and black families continue to be broken by death. Among whites in 1970, 47 percent of the women family heads were widowed, as compared with 30 percent for black women heads.[26]

TABLE II—MARITAL STATUS OF FEMALE HEADS OF FAMILIES: 1973

| Marital Status | Heads, All Ages | | Heads Under 45 Years Old | | Heads Over 45 Years Old | |
|---|---|---|---|---|---|---|
| | Black | White | Black | White | Black | White |
| Total, female heads thousands ........ | 1,822 | 4,672 | 1,163 | 2,062 | 659 | 2,610 |
| Percent ....................... | 100 | 100 | 100 | 100 | 100 | 100 |
| With disrupted marriage ............... | 49 | 45 | 57 | 72 | 34 | 23 |
| Separated ......................... | 33 | 15 | 39 | 25 | 22 | 6 |
| Divorced.......................... | 16 | 30 | 18 | 47 | 12 | 17 |
| Other ............................ | 51 | 55 | 43 | 28 | 66 | 77 |
| Single (never married) ............. | 20 | 10 | 27 | 10 | 6 | 10 |
| Widowed ........................ | 28 | 41 | 11 | 11 | 59 | 65 |
| Husband temporarily absent ......................... | 4 | 4 | 5 | 7 | 2 | 2 |
| Armed Forces ................ | 1 | 1 | 1 | 3 | — | — |
| Other reasons ................ | 3 | 3 | 3 | 5 | 2 | 2 |

Note: Categories refer to marital status at time of enumeration.
— Rounds to zero.
Source: U. S. Department of Commerce, Social and Economic Statistics Administration, Bureau of the Census, Series P-23, No. 48, p. 14 (1973).

## Births out of Wedlock

Currently the rate of births out of wedlock per thousand women aged 15 to 44 continues to be higher for "Negro and other races" than for whites—89.9 per thousand in 1970 for the former as compared with 13.8 for the latter. Since the nonwhite rate has tended to decline in recent years, while the white rate has increased,[27] the two appear to be converging, although the gap is still wide. In 1971, 31.5 percent of black women married between 1965 and 1969 had borne a child before marriage.[28] Obviously, this figure does not take into account unwed mothers who did not subsequently marry. In view of the economic and social pressures on such women, the solution to the problem of providing adequately for the children born out of wedlock depends heavily on the support of relatives and friends as well as upon community social services and, frequently, public assistance.

Because the percentage of broken homes is significantly greater among black families than among white ones, the erroneous idea that broken black families are typical has gained currency. On the contrary, in 1974, 61.8 percent of all black families were husband-wife families.[29] Similarly it should be noted that at family income levels of $7,000 and above, roughly 90 percent of black children are living with both parents. At the other end of the economic scale, only about one-fourth of Negro children in families with incomes below $3,000 are living with both parents.[30] Clearly the broken family is related to poverty rather than to race.

## Education

Recent data also indicate that the approximately 31 percent of black 18-to-24-year-olds who have not completed high school report family incomes of under $3,000, although only 12 percent of all 18-to-24-year-olds are members of such families.[31] Thus while it appears that the school dropout rate is being drastically reduced, particularly in the instance of black youth, the relatively higher dropout rate among blacks as compared with whites is correlated with low family income.

It should be emphasized, however, that the proportion of black young men and women having at least a high-school education is considerably greater today than it was at the beginning of the sixties. Among black men 20 to 24 years of age in 1973, about 70 percent had completed four years of high school work. In 1965 the comparable figure was 50 percent.[32]

The increasing emphasis on higher education in the families of young blacks again is reflected in the fact that in 1973 approximately 684,000 black students were enrolled in college.[33]

The role of the black family in the formal and community education of their children has traditionally been hampered by limited black involvement in policy decisions affecting the kind and quality of education to be made available. The tradition of an educational system developed by and for the white population and extended, often without enthusiasm or adaptation, to black youngsters has tended to inhibit black family participation.

In the past, black parents with little education of their own showed touching faith in the efficacy of education to improve their children's lot. This attitude was accompanied by humility before educational authorities, who sometimes went unchallenged when their understanding of black children and concern for the welfare of the poor and powerless were obviously questionable. Both white and black teachers in numberless communities identified education with rejection of the black child's background—his parents' speech, manners, taste, and judgment—in favor of that of the mainstream. Textbooks failed to recognize even the existence of this black cultural resource.

With the recent growth in black understanding, education, and civil rights, along with more sophisticated insight into the dynamics of black-white interaction in education, the role of the black family has become less passive. The move toward community control of schools has fostered active participation in parent-teacher organizations, closer examination of school policy, and concern as to its suitability for black pupils. No longer are black parents satisfied to leave education to the educators; they are beginning to check results and demand quality and accountability.

Despite the enormous difficulties faced by the schools in the central cities, where the majority of black families reside, and the dilemmas yet to be resolved by school boards, administrators, and community groups, black parents play an increasing part in discussing the problems and taking sides. Family members are included in the operation of some programs; Head Start is an example. In addition, some parents serve as paraprofessionals in the public schools.

The old concept of educational deprivation as a failure of the family to provide for the young child's needs is giving way to a less simplistic view, which nevertheless identifies as crucial to school performance the overall family background of the child.[34] Family status is of great importance to the education of the child, just as education in turn will be a vital determinant of the status of his or her own family in the future.

## Work and Income

The nature of the work done by black family members of the labor force has a direct bearing on their income. With less than three-fifths of the income of white families, the black family continues to be placed in a severely disadvantaged competitive position for the attainment of many of the so-called good things of life.[35]

March 1973 data indicate a higher labor-force participation rate by black than by white wives, 54 percent as compared with 41 percent.[36] Also in 1973 about 49 percent of black mothers of young children worked, as compared with roughly 32 percent of white mothers.[37] Of women between the ages of 15 and 49 who are or have been married but who have no children under 5 years, 66 percent of the blacks and 58 percent of the the whites are in the labor force.[38]

It is often necessary in black families for younger members to work for the economic survival of the family unit, particularly in view of the higher rate of unemployment for black workers. Moreover, the income position of the black family is precarious even when younger members seek jobs, because of the problems black youth encounters in obtaining suitable positions. In the first quarter of 1974, the unemployment rate of nonwhites aged 16–19 was 30.7, well over twice the 13.3 jobless rate for white teenagers. (See Table III.)

**TABLE III—UNEMPLOYMENT RATES BY SEX AND AGE: 1960, 1970, AND 1974 (first quarter)**
(Annual averages)

| Subject | Nonwhite | | | White | | |
|---|---|---|---|---|---|---|
| | 1960 | 1970 | 1974 | 1960 | 1970 | 1974 |
| Total .......... | 10.2 | .8.2 | 9.3 | 4.9 | 4.5 | 4.7 |
| Adult men........ | 9.6 | 5.6 | 6.4 | 4.2 | 3.2 | 3.1 |
| Adult women .... | 8.3 | 6.9 | 8.0 | 4.6 | 4.4 | 4.7 |
| Teenagers[1] ...... | 24.4 | 29.1 | 30.7 | 13.4 | 13.5 | 13.3 |

[1]"Teenagers" include persons 16 to 19 years old.
Sources:  U. S. Department of Labor, Bureau of Labor Statistics.
U. S. Department of Commerce, Bureau of the Census.

In addition, the level of educational attainment of black families is highly correlated with their occupational distribution and income levels. While today black families have not yet achieved incomes comparable to those of whites with similar educational attainment, there now appears to be a trend toward a narrowing of the gap in income levels between the two groups in this context. In 1974 over 71 percent of black men between 25 and 64 with at least some college education earned $10,000 or more; over 61 percent of those with less than 8 years of education earned under $6,000. (See Table IV.)

**TABLE IV—MARCH 1974 INCOME AND EDUCATION OF EMPLOYED MALES 25 TO 64, BY RACE**
Percent of educational category, by race, earning indicated income

| Years of School Completed | Under $3,000 | | $3,000– $5,999 | | $6,000– $9,999 | | $10,000– $14,999 | | $15,000 and Over | |
|---|---|---|---|---|---|---|---|---|---|---|
| Elementary school | White | Black | White | Black | White | Black | White | Black | White | Black |
| 0–4 years | 16.6 | 25.9 | 35.9 | 35.2 | 32.4 | 24.8 | 12.4 | 11.0 | 2.8 | 3.1 |
| 5–7 years | 10.1 | 15.2 | 18.6 | 42.3 | 38.9 | 27.3 | 24.6 | 12.6 | 7.8 | 2.6 |
| 8 years | 6.5 | 12.4 | 15.1 | 34.0 | 34.3 | 37.1 | 30.3 | 11.0 | 13.8 | 5.5 |
| High school | | | | | | | | | | |
| 1–3 years | 4.9 | 10.0 | 11.8 | 26.5 | 31.2 | 38.3 | 36.0 | 20.5 | 16.2 | 4.7 |
| 4 years | 3.0 | 7.9 | 7.0 | 15.2 | 24.9 | 38.2 | 40.7 | 32.5 | 24.4 | 6.2 |
| College | | | | | | | | | | |
| 1–3 years | 3.6 | 6.7 | 6.3 | 12.3 | 20.6 | 33.4 | 35.1 | 31.9 | 34.3 | 15.6 |
| 4 years | 2.7 | 2.9 | 4.7 | 6.4 | 15.1 | 34.3 | 28.7 | 30.0 | 48.8 | 26.4 |
| 5 years or more | 2.6 | 2.4 | 5.2 | 4.8 | 9.8 | 21.4 | 25.2 | 39.3 | 57.3 | 32.1 |

Source:  U. S. Department of Commerce, Bureau of the Census. *Current Population Reports: Population Characteristics,* Series P-20, No. 274, December, 1974, pp. 62–63.

**TABLE V**—MEDIAN INCOME OF FAMILIES OF BLACK AND OTHER
RACES AS A PERCENT OF WHITE MEDIAN
FAMILY INCOME: 1950 TO 1973

| Year | Negro and Other Races | Black Only |
|------|------|------|
| 1950......... | 54 | (NA) |
| 1951......... | 53 | (NA) |
| 1952......... | 57 | (NA) |
| 1953......... | 56 | (NA) |
| 1954......... | 56 | (NA) |
| 1955......... | 55 | (NA) |
| 1956......... | 53 | (NA) |
| 1957......... | 54 | (NA) |
| 1958......... | 51 | (NA) |
| 1959......... | 52 | 51 |
| 1960......... | 55 | (NA) |
| 1961......... | 53 | (NA) |
| 1962......... | 53 | (NA) |
| 1963......... | 53 | (NA) |
| 1964......... | 56 | 54 |
| 1965......... | 55 | 54 |
| 1966......... | 60 | 58 |
| 1967......... | 62 | 59 |
| 1968......... | 63 | 60 |
| 1969......... | 63 | 61 |
| 1970......... | 64 | 61 |
| 1971......... | 63 | 60 |
| 1972......... | 62 | 59 |
| 1973......... | 60 | 58 |

(NA) Not available.

Source:  U. S. Department of Commerce, Social and Economic Statistics
Administration, Bureau of the Census.

Black family income reached 61 percent of white family income in 1969 and 1970, then declined to 58 percent in 1973. (See Table V.) The existence of variables other than educational attainment is reflected in the fact that 44 percent of white men who had completed only 8 years of elementary school had incomes exceeding $10,000, whereas only 38.7 percent of black men with four years of high school had incomes at this level. A comparison between the two groups nevertheless shows that while in the 1960s the percentage gains in income for blacks were higher than for whites, the deepening recession of the 1970s reversed the trend. Even before that, however, the gap in absolute dollars had continued to widen. In 1973 the median family income for whites was $12,595, and for blacks $7,269. (See Table VI.)

Overall, the median nonwhite family incomes in current dollars over the twenty years between 1950 and 1970 increased at a faster rate than the incomes of white families. (See Table V.) Nevertheless, in 1973 only one out of four black families (26 percent) earned at least $12,000 per year, as compared with more than half of all white families—53 percent—in this category.

**TABLE VI**—DISTRIBUTION OF FAMILIES BY INCOME IN 1965, 1969, AND 1973

(Adjusted for price changes in 1973 dollars. Families as of the following year)

| Income | Black | | | White | | |
|---|---|---|---|---|---|---|
| | 1965 | 1969 | 1973 | 1965 | 1969 | 1973 |
| Number of families....thousands .. | 4,424 | 4,774 | 5,440 | 43,500 | 46,023 | 48,919 |
| Percent ...................... | 100 | 100 | 100 | 100 | 100 | 100 |
| Under $3,000..................... | 24 | 16 | 16 | 8 | 6 | 5 |
| $3,000 to $4,999 ................. | 22 | 16 | 18 | 9 | 8 | 8 |
| $5,000 to $6,999 ................. | 17 | 15 | 14 | 10 | 9 | 9 |
| $7,000 to $9,999 ................. | 18 | 20 | 17 | 20 | 17 | 15 |
| $10,000 to $11,999 ............... | 8 | 10 | 9 | 14 | 12 | 11 |
| $12,000 to $14,999 ............... | 6 | 10 | 10 | 15 | 17 | 15 |
| $15,000 and over ................. | 6 | 13 | 16 | 23 | 33 | 38 |
| Median income  ................. | $5,510 | $7,280 | $7,269 | $10,210 | $11,869 | $12,595 |
| Net change over preceding date: | | | | | | |
| Amount ...................... | (X) | $1,770 | $−11 | (X) | $1,659 | $726 |
| Percent ...................... | (X) | 32.1 | −0.2 | (X) | 16.2 | 6.1 |

(X) Not applicable.

Source: U. S. Department of Commerce, Social and Economic Statistics Administration, Bureau of the Census, Series P-23, No. 48, p. 19 (1973).

During the past decade, income gains of the black group have been associated with their changing employment patterns, particularly in the significantly greater employment in clerical, managerial, and professional occupations in the 1960s and 1970s. Overall black employment amounted to 8.1 million jobs in 1973 and the number employed in white-collar and skilled jobs increased for nonwhite workers from 1968 to 1973, while those in lower-paid categories tended to decline.[39]

Some willing to speculate have predicted that by 1985, when black employment is expected to comprise 12 percent of the total, blacks will hold:

—10.6 percent of all professional and technical jobs.
— 8.4 percent of all clerical jobs.
— 6.0 percent of all sales jobs.
— 8.8 percent of all skilled crafts jobs.

But they will still comprise:

—24.0 percent of all laborers.
—38.4 precent of all private household workers.
—24.6 percent of all farm workers.[40]

There is no question that the decade 1960 to 1970 led the black family to a greatly improved position in income levels and occupational distribution. Increasing opportunities for education, lessening of discriminatory barriers in the work force, continuing high levels of national prosperity, and expanding gross national product are some of the variables which doubtless accounted for this developing trend. However, with a contracting economy and a more conservative Federal Government in the 1970s, black families have already experienced a slowing-down of progress; and in 1973 those with low-income status constituted more than four times their proportion of the population.[41]

## Poverty and Dependency

The poverty status of over 28 percent of black families is related to the high dependence of this group upon public assistance programs, disproportionate incidence of family instability, limited educational attainment and employment skills of parents, crowded and depressed housing, and racial discrimination, all of which are associated with high exposure to detrimental influences in the surrounding neighborhoods and communities.

Often Aid to Families with Dependent Children (AFDC) payments make up the largest part of the income of dependent families. Separation, divorce, desertion, unemployment, and death are highly correlated circumstances in these families; and the double burden on a single parent who must both work and act for an absent father or mother is a very heavy one.

Between 1958 and March of 1972, Aid to Families with Dependent Children was the largest and fastest-growing of the four major welfare categories* in terms of number of persons served, rising from about 6,250,000 to nearly 11,000,000 recipients. At the same time it ranked lowest by a considerable margin in monthly benefits paid per person, averaging about $55 in March 1972, as compared with about $78 for Old Age Assistance (OAA), the next lowest category.[42]

This modesty in benefits level reflects the tendency of dependent children to be in multichild families and at the very minimum to live with an adult, whereas the elderly on the OAA program typically live alone or with a spouse only. In 1971, 54 percent of all AFDC families headed by one adult had one or two children; over 31 percent had three or four; and 15 percent had five or more. The average number (arithmetic mean) of child recipients per family was 2.7; in a substantial number of cases, no benefits were given to the adult members of such families.[43]

A 1972 report on the employment of AFDC mothers (using 1969 statistics, however; no later survey was available) revealed that black mothers (55 percent of those employed) are more likely than their white opposite numbers (41 percent of those employed) to have a job—despite a national unemployment rate for black women nearly twice as high (6.4 percent) as that for whites (3.3 percent).[44] The greater tendency of black women to work for a living, plus the likelihood that more pressure may be exerted to make black mothers work as authorities view with greater compassion a white mother's need to be with her young children, together may account for much of the discrepancy.

Between 1965 and 1973 the proportion of blacks as well as whites below the poverty level declined significantly (Table VI), although black families were more than three times as likely to fall in the under-$3,000 income category. At the same time, greater information on welfare benefits, a lessening of employment opportunities for the unskilled, and an increase in community acceptance of the concept of public assistance accompanied a substantial increase in the number of Americans on welfare. Still, less

*Aid to the Blind, Aid to Partially and Totally Disabled, Old Age Assistance, Aid to Families with Dependent Children.

than half (48 percent) of the black families below the low-income level in 1970 were receiving public assistance.[45]

A 1970 study by the Committee for Economic Development reported that the largest category of poor persons consists of children under the age of 18. Approximately 15 percent of all children under 18—10.7 million—are poor. There is a high correlation between poverty among children and the size of families; approximately 44 percent of all poor children are in families with five or more children. In addition, approximately 1.5 million nonwhite children are in households where family income is beneath the poverty level,[46] despite the frequency with which other family members work in addition to the family head. About one-sixth of all black families with two or more wage earners are poor.[47]

Black and white comparisons of household heads by marital status and sex can be seen in Table VII. For both black and white families, women heads of households are well in the minority, with 29.4 percent of black families in this category, as compared to 17.3 percent of whites. Black families are thus more likely than white ones to have female heads, as a result of such influences on black men as shorter life expectancy, greater difficulty getting and holding a job, and other socioeconomic and psychological stresses which sunder the family tie.

TABLE VII—MARITAL STATUS, SEX, AND RACE OF HOUSEHOLD HEADS: MARCH 1972

| Marital Status | Percent Male | | Percent Female | |
|---|---|---|---|---|
| | White | Black | White | Black |
| Head of Household | 73.2 | 58.2 | 17.3 | 29.4 |
| Single | 3.6 | 3.5 | 3.0 | 5.3 |
| Married, spouse present | 65.0 | 46.7 | (X) | (X) |
| Other marital status | 4.6 | 8.0 | 14.4 | 24.2 |
| Not Head of Household | 26.8 | 41.8 | 82.7 | 70.6 |
| Single | 23.9 | 34.4 | 18.3 | 24.1 |
| Married, spouse present | 0.9 | 1.3 | 60.6 | 39.6 |
| Other marital status | 2.0 | 6.1 | 3.8 | 6.9 |

(X) Not applicable

Source: U. S. Department of Commerce, Bureau of the Census, Series P-20, No. 242, November, 1972, p. 30.

Families headed by women are economically handicapped, since a black woman working full-time all year earns only about three-quarters as much as her male counterpart.[48] More than half of the nation's lowest-income blacks now live in fatherless families,[49] and the trend toward a larger proportion of female-headed families below the poverty level is increasing among both blacks and whites. Among such families, the incidence of poverty is especially high; 52.7 percent were below the poverty level in 1973.[50] As can be seen from Table VIII, 15.4 percent of black families headed by men were below the low-income level in 1973, as compared with 52.7 percent headed by women. Although the percentage of families afflicted with poverty has declined, the decline for those headed by men, both white and black, has been far more dramatic than for families headed by women.

TABLE VIII—FAMILIES BELOW THE LOW-INCOME LEVEL, BY SEX OF HEAD: 1959, AND 1967 TO 1973

(Families as of the following year)

| Year | All Families | | Families with Male Head | | Families with Female Head | |
|---|---|---|---|---|---|---|
| | Black | White | Black | White | Black | White |
| | Number (thousands) | | | | | |
| 1959...... | 1,860 | 6,027 | 1,309 | 5,037 | 551 | 990 |
| 1967...... | 1,555 | 4,056 | 839 | 3,019 | 716 | 1,037 |
| 1968...... | 1,366 | 3,616 | 660 | 2,595 | 706 | 1,021 |
| 1969[1] .... | 1,366 | 3,575 | 629 | 2,506 | 737 | 1,069 |
| 1970[1] .... | 1,481 | 3,708 | 648 | 2,606 | 834 | 1,102 |
| 1971[1] .... | 1,484 | 3,751 | 605 | 2,560 | 879 | 1,191 |
| 1972[1] .... | 1,529 | 3,441 | 558 | 2,306 | 972 | 1,135 |
| 1973[1] .... | 1,527 | 3,219 | 553 | 2,029 | 974 | 1,190 |
| | Percent below the low-income level | | | | | |
| 1959...... | 48.1 | 14.8 | 43.3 | 13.4 | 65.4 | 30.0 |
| 1967...... | 33.9 | 9.0 | 25.3 | 7.4 | 56.3 | 25.9 |
| 1968...... | 29.4 | 8.0 | 19.9 | 6.3 | 53.2 | 25.2 |
| 1969[1] .... | 27.9 | 7.7 | 17.9 | 6.0 | 53.3 | 25.7 |
| 1970[1] .... | 29.5 | 8.0 | 18.6 | 6.2 | 54.3 | 25.0 |
| 1971[1] .... | 28.8 | 7.9 | 17.2 | 5.9 | 53.5 | 26.5 |
| 1972[1] .... | 29.0 | 7.1 | 16.2 | 5.3 | 53.3 | 24.3 |
| 1973[1] .... | 28.1 | 6.6 | 15.4 | 4.6 | 52.7 | 24.5 |

[1] Based on 1970 census population controls; therefore, not strictly comparable to data for earlier years.

Source:   U. S. Department of Commerce, Social and Economic Statistics Administration, Bureau of the Census, Special Studies Series P-23, No. 48, p. 30 (1973).

## Housing Conditions

Housing is one of the most critical aspects of the socioeconomic status of urban Negro families and for many of them it symbolizes their "have-not" status. "Black districts" commonly are in the slum areas adjacent to the central business and older sections of the city abandoned by whites. This concentration of black families reflects both economic necessity and the continuing exclusion of blacks from more desirable housing in relatively affluent areas of the city and suburbs.

As Table IX indicates, however, there has been a major trend during this decade toward improved housing conditions among black families.

It may be noted that while both whites and Negroes experienced significant reductions in inadequate housing from 1960 to 1970, nearly a fifth of black housing, as compared to 5 percent of white, remained substandard in 1970. Part of this trend doubtless reflects the substantial black movement to the suburbs, and the acquisition of more adequate dwellings as they have been built or vacated by whites. Federal and state government and private programs in recent years have greatly improved the amount of housing available to the general population, and have substantially reduced the number of substandard dwellings.

### TABLE IX—QUALITY OF HOUSING, BY UNITS
#### (in thousands)

|  | Not meeting specific criteria | | Meeting specific criteria | |
|---|---|---|---|---|
|  | Black | White | Black | White |
| 1960 | 2,096 | 5,689 | 3,048 | 42,190 |
| 1970 | 1,050 | 2,733 | 5,155 | 54,479 |

Source: U. S. Department of Commerce, Bureau of the Census, *The Social and Economic Status of Negroes in the United States,* 1970, Current Population Report Series, P-23, No. 38, p. 89.

## Mortality

While infant and maternal mortality rates have dropped sharply during the past thirty years, recent data show that the infant mortality rate for nonwhites remains considerably higher than for whites. Since 1965 the mortality rate for both white and black mothers has been below 1.0 per 1,000 live births. Both maternal and infant mortality are, however, significantly and consistently higher for blacks (Table X).

### TABLE X—MATERNAL AND INFANT MORTALITY RATES: 1940, 1950, 1960, AND 1965 TO 1972
#### (Per 1,000 live births)

| Year | Black and other races | | | | White | | | |
|---|---|---|---|---|---|---|---|---|
|  |  | Infant | | |  | Infant | | |
|  | Maternal | Under 1 Year | Under 28 Days | 28 Days to 11 Months | Maternal | Under 1 Year | Under 28 Days | 28 Days to 11 Months |
| 1940 .... | 7.6 | 73.8 | 39.7 | 34.1 | 3.2 | 43.2 | 27.2 | 16.0 |
| 1950 .... | 2.2 | 44.5 | 27.5 | 16.9 | 0.6 | 26.8 | 19.4 | 7.4 |
| 1960 .... | 1.0 | 43.2 | 26.9 | 16.4 | 0.3 | 22.9 | 17.2 | 5.7 |
| 1965 .... | 0.8 | 40.3 | 25.4 | 14.9 | 0.2 | 21.5 | 16.1 | 5.4 |
| 1966 .... | 0.7 | 38.8 | 24.8 | 14.0 | 0.2 | 20.6 | 15.6 | 5.0 |
| 1967 .... | 0.7 | 35.9 | 23.8 | 12.1 | 0.2 | 19.7 | 15.0 | 4.7 |
| 1968 .... | 0.6 | 34.5 | 23.0 | 11.6 | 0.2 | 19.2 | 14.7 | 4.5 |
| 1969 .... | 0.6 | 32.9 | 22.5 | 10.4 | 0.2 | 18.4 | 14.2 | 4.2 |
| 1970 .... | 0.6 | 30.9 | 21.4 | 9.5 | 0.1 | 17.8 | 13.8 | 4.0 |
| 1971 .... | 0.5 | 28.5 | 19.6 | 8.9 | 0.1 | 17.1 | 13.0 | 4.0 |
| 1972 .... | (NA) | 29.0 | 20.6 | 8.5 | (NA) | 16.3 | 12.3 | 4.0 |

Note: Date for 1970, 1971, and 1972 are provisional.
(NA) Not available.

Source: U. S. Department of Health, Education, and Welfare, National Center for Health Statistics.

## How the Poor Black Family Sees Itself

The tendency of students of social pathology to view the impoverished black family as the epitome of all that can go wrong has left members of such families defensive and discouraged; constant emphasis on "problems" gives them little opportunity for developing an understanding of avenues to a better life.

The black families on the poverty end of the income scale are undeniably plagued by the social conditions which accompany poverty. One central problem, to which all others are related, is that of low self-esteem from childhood, as members of the family constantly confront the judgment that they are inadequate; the Puritan ethic which makes the individual responsible for working through his problems and those of his family tends to leave the burden of rehabilitation in the lap of the family head.

Yet if one examines the problems, solution within the family is an unpromising strategy since the causes so often lie beyond the family circle, and the family is usually unable to muster the resources to effect corrective action. The poor family suffers more acutely than do better-off black families from early death, abandonment, divorce, and discrimination. Youngsters may be "farmed out" to relatives for custody when the home is broken. The male child may be left without a father model, or he may see this model condemned or demeaned. Sibling rivalry tends to mount when material comforts are scarce. The child often cannot identify comfortably with parents who are discriminated against, because such identification carries with it a guarantee of external and reflected hatred.

Lacking status in the social community, the black parent beset by poverty may resort to overwhelming dominance within the family. If the mother heads the family, her need to make a living may leave her little time to indulge the children; in the eyes of her children she frequently becomes someone ambivalently to fear and to rely upon. The family in these circumstances cannot therefore be as close and protective as can black families with higher socioeconomic status and fewer pressures and problems. The tough competitive and segregated world may provide the main source of satisfactions and values. The mores of the street may make school attendance seem irrelevant and crime the nearest path to success for black youth.

Yet even the poorer families adapt and survive. The substantial reduction in the number and proportion of black families below the low-income level in the past quarter-century attests to their determination to grasp opportunities to escape poverty. At the same time, those who are left in misery have reason to feel even more desolate and incompetent when others improve in income and leave them behind.

## The Role of the Family

The socialization of the black child, a basic function of the black family, is complicated by the traditional role allocated to blacks, particularly the stringent circumscription of black males by white society. It has been necessary for black family patterns to adapt to the special demands put upon them, which force more wives and mothers to work in order to compensate for the low earnings of black men. Poor black mothers work 3 times as often as their white counterparts (see Table XI). Black children have to learn to look out for themselves earlier in life than is customary. Also, dependent relatives often are added to the nuclear family to share the limited family income; thus outsiders—neighbors and other community members or functionaries—assume a more active role than is usual in white family patterns. All of these demands coincide with a shortage of resources in health, housing, income, education, and power, and accompany being black in a white-dominated world.

**TABLE XI**—WORK EXPERIENCE OF WOMEN WITH OWN CHILDREN UNDER 18 YEARS OLD BELOW THE LOW-INCOME LEVEL IN 1972
(Numbers in thousands. Persons as of the following year)

| Work Experience of Mother | Below Low-Income Level | | Percent Below Low-Income Level | |
|---|---|---|---|---|
| | Black | White | Black | White |
| Total, mothers ............ | 1,176 | 2,211 | 35 | 8 |
| Wives ................. | 345 | 1,237 | 18 | 5 |
| Female heads ............ | 832 | 974 | 57 | 34 |
| Worked ..................... | 459 | 885 | 22 | 7 |
| Percent worked year-round | | | | |
| full-time ................ | 19 | 15 | 9 | 3 |
| Did not work ................. | 717 | 1,326 | 54 | 10 |
| Main reason for not working: | | | | |
| Percent ............... | 100 | 100 | (X) | (X) |
| Keeping house ............ | 77 | 89 | 53 | 10 |
| Other .................... | 23 | 11 | 60 | 23 |

(X) Not applicable.
Source: U. S. Department of Commerce, Social and Economic Statistics Administration, Bureau of the Census. *Current Population Reports,* Series P-23, No. 48 (1974), p. 33.

Yet black families have met the challenge with a stubborn determination to survive, to support family members, to cling tenaciously to viability. Despite the great emphasis social researchers have placed upon the minority of families most troubled with socio-economic and health problems, the majority of black families are not only enduring; they are growing in hope, in ego strength, in expectations, and in ability to build and enlarge upon the inner resources they have always had. They continue to be generous in response to the needs of dependent relatives and to place high value on family stability, occupational responsibility, and individual and group achievement.

Black families increasingly participate in major trends affecting American families in general as they develop toward a middle-class and an urban orientation. Their predominantly metropolitan existence has produced an increasing dependence upon money income in patterns very similar to those of the general labor force. Changing also is the older familial model of three-generation groups (that is, grandparents, parents, "other relatives," and children living in a household) toward two- and one-generation groups. As a consequence, numerous individual and intrafamilial expectations are changing along with those of family members toward the larger society.

Parents and youth alike in more fortunate black families increasingly expect that high-school graduation and a college education (often with added professional education, as in teaching, medicine or law) will be achieved, with steady employment and high-income status to follow. The trend away from domestic service and unskilled work especially gives evidence of the determination on the part of the less-favored black family to escape its previous low-skilled and menial identification in the labor force and its subordinate role in the larger society. In terms of recent developments, the managerial and professional levels have been increasing, and more black families are moving to the suburbs, where greatly improved housing is available.

Urban living, nevertheless, has continued to produce more and denser racial ghettos. Many black families have moved from one disadvantaged environment to another in the search for higher status over the past two decades. Since the central portions of the larger metropolitan area are most often the loci of spreading obsolescence and social and economic deterioration, there is a concomitant movement of the white population away from these inner parts of the city to suburban areas. Black families left behind sense rejection and psychological discrimination, even when there are community efforts to desegregate schools, undertake urban renewal programs, and improve the availability of services and facilities.

In this context, the increased movement of black families to the suburbs is of great significance to growing protest movements. While the urban life of metropolitan areas and programs aimed against poverty appear to promise greater freedom, the continuance of varying degrees of racial discrimination produces increased tension between blacks and whites. Black families point to housing restrictions, segregated education, discriminatory policies in trade union membership and apprenticeship opportunities, and other circumstances as prohibitive of their achievement of equal status. (A trend to watch closely is "inner" suburbs which rapidly become predominantly black.)

Like the white family, the black family is faced with a rapidly changing world for which it is difficult to make adequate psychosocial preparation. Such major social forces as rapid communications, the knowledge explosion, the impact of automation on the labor force, the increasing reliance of society upon technically or professionally trained personnel, and continuing high levels of unemployment make it difficult for many families to prepare their members adequately for the future, and there is no assurance that the accelerating forces of change will not rearrange issues before they can be confronted and settled. The sexual revolution, sentiment in favor of zero population growth, the reassessment of prevalent middle-class values, new techniques of birth control, changed attitudes toward births out of wedlock, egalitarianism of the sexes, and widespread experimentation with new social patterns for transmitting cultural values, among other changes, are beginning to raise the question of the survival of the family as we have known it in the total society. The tendency toward newer substitutes for the family, such as the flexible commune or living in couples without a formal ceremony, has already made inroads on older forms of marriage.

While these changes are in process, it is difficult to assess the full impact upon the family, white or black. There is reason to suspect, however, that the black family is undergoing less upheaval than is its white counterpart. The tendency among blacks is to reach toward education and achievement, not to reject them; and the difficulty the black family has had in attaining the level of comfort and stability it covets has often spurred on the young not to reject, but to strive toward these goals. Few blacks today, whatever their political or social views and status, are vocally opposed to the father's conventional role in the family or antagonistic to the ideal of the warm, nurturing mother. There are restless and rebellious young blacks who are disillusioned and critical of the older generation; some of them feel betrayed by old family failings. Yet the way in which black rebellion has dealt with the family is overwhelmingly to want it better managed and more functional and to shore it up with supplementary institutions like breakfast programs, community-run schools, day care centers, well-baby clinics, and similar efforts.

The overall environment in which many black families live contains numerous influences and circumstances which result in substantial differences in cultural values between blacks and whites, and which account for much of the difficulty in communication between them. White society sees black children and youth as "disadvantaged"; e.g., not measuring up to white standards; the very term devalues their human worth. Since it is family influences which socialize the individual and establish his values, this negative judgment attaches to the family as well. Today's black family increasingly rejects the negative identification and works to build support for its members with the help of an increasingly positive black community.

There is no question but that economic deprivation handicaps the family in its task of providing a training ground for good citizenship, education, health, recreation, reading, travel, and involvement in community affairs. That the black family nevertheless places a premium on educational attainment and is strongly work-oriented reflects its often unrecognized strength and validity as a socializing institution, despite energy-eroding hardships.

In attempting to present a "balanced" view of the black family, the current trend is to look to the positive, to recognize the 70 percent of families which are intact and an equivalent percentage in which incomes lie above the poverty level. Yet in a very real sense, the searchlight should seek out the failures and wrongs of society as well as its successes. There is no comfort in the majority when so large a minority suffers the burdens of poverty, unemployment, inadequate education, deficient health, and other consequences of discrimination and disadvantage. The black family per se is a viable institution; but the number of such families which must continue to struggle against the assaults of social, economic, psychological, and political forces beyond their control can be described only as a national disgrace.

Even as regards more prosperous families, there is a danger of extracting too much optimism from developments which merely have *potential* for progress. Professor Karl Taeuber (see Chapter 4) cautions us, for example, that much of the black movement to the suburbs has *not* involved new and integrated housing, but is an enlargement of suburban segregated neighborhoods through taking over old housing being vacated by whites. Greater opportunities for higher education mean little if students drop out before graduation. Access to better jobs has limited effect in a time of growing unemployment, with seniority in the hands of others.

A discerning eye can see in today's mélange of expanded symbolic opportunity at the top and excessive unemployment and frustration at the bottom, of wider public discussion of problems arising from inequality of opportunity, of accelerated change and disillusionment with old procedures, a growing confidence in black families that they are working to help the next generation expand its prospects of achievement. Black institutions today, from the Panthers to the Nation of Islam, are putting emphasis on the welfare of children and their upbringing. Increasing evidence and models of success can be found in the pages of black publications and in black neighborhoods, and are suggested in the general concern over issues which are germane primarily to the black community.

The rising level of health, increasing levels of educational attainment, wider occupational distribution, improved housing conditions, and increased security through participation in public programs, all benefit the black family, as they do American families in general.

## Prognosis

Due in part to a determination to eliminate racial discrimination and achieve equality on all fronts, and in part to the broadened opportunities for personal development and greater public regard for civil rights, it is likely that in the future fewer and fewer distinctions will be drawn between the great mass of black families and those of the general population. The majority of differences which exist today between white and black families already are more closely linked with social class than with racial identity; as black Americans become more widely dispersed along the socioeconomic scale, most of these differences should tend to disappear. It is to this end that the battle against inequality must address itself vigorously until discrimination assumes its rightful place as a dusty relic of the past.

# Notes

1. Jack Rosenthal, "One Third of Blacks Found in 15 Cities," *The New York Times*, May 19, 1971; Tobia Bressler, "Some Population Trends Involving and Affecting the Negro Implication," Address, Association of Social Science Teachers, Nashville, Tennessee, March 22, 1962.

2. U. S. Department of Commerce, Bureau of the Census, *The Social and Economic Status of the Black Population in the United States*, 1973, Special Studies Series P-23, No. 48, pp. 10–11.

3. *Ibid.*

4. For an extended discussion of racial comparisons between white and nonwhites, of income, economic status, working wives, etc., *see* Herman P. Miller, *Rich Man, Poor Man*, Thomas Y. Crowell Company, New York, 1964.

5. U. S. Department of Commerce, *op. cit.*, p. 19.

6. *Ibid.* p. 55.

7. *Ibid.*, pp. 107–109.

8. *Ibid.*, pp. 72–76; Frank Hertel, "Strengthening the Family: Community Strategy Alternatives" (Institute of Community Studies, United Community Funds and Councils of America, New York, 1970.)

9. U. S. Department of Commerce, Bureau of the Census, *The Social and Economic Status of Negroes*, pp. 42–43.

10. Hertel, *op. cit.*

11. *See* Joseph H. Douglass, "Mental Health Aspects of the Effects of Discrimination Upon Children," *Young Children*, Journal of the National Association for the Education of Young Children, Vol. XXII, No. 5, May 1967.

12. Robert B. Hill, *The Strengths of Black Families* (New York: Emerson Hall, 1971, 1972); Elizabeth Herzog and Hylan Lewis, "Children in Poor Families: Myths and Realities," *American Journal of Orthopsychiatry*, April 1971, Vol. 40, No. 3; Hylan Lewis, "Child Rearing Among Low-Income Families," in Louis A. Ferman, Joyce L. Kornbluh and Alan Haber, *Poverty In America* (Ann Arbor: University of Michigan Press, 1965), pp. 342–53; John H. Scanzoni, *The Black Family in Modern Society* (Boston: Allyn and Bacon, 1971), esp. pp. 63–97.

13. Michael J. Flax (Urban Institute) as quoted in Daniel P. Moynihan, "The Schism in Black America," *The Public Interest*, Spring 1972, pp. 3–24.

14. U. S. Department of Commerce, *op. cit.*, pp. 17, 21, 34, 45.

15. *Ibid.*, p. 13.

16. Richard M. Scammon, "The Demographic Profile—And Where It Points," *Newsweek*, June 30, 1969, p. 18.

17. *Ibid.*

18. *Washington Post*, July 20, 1970.

19. *Ibid.*

20. *Ibid.*, p. 6.

21. *The New York Times*, July 12, 1970.

22. U. S. Department of Commerce, *op. cit.*, p. 80.

23. *Ibid.*, 1970 edition, p. 113.

24. *Ibid.*, 1973, p. 73; 1971 edition, p. 107.

25. *Ibid.*, 1973, p. 74.

26. *Ibid.*, 1970, p. 130.

27. *Statistical Abstract of the United States*, 1974, p. 56.

28. U. S. Department of Commerce, *op. cit.* (1973), p. 85.

29. *Ibid.*, p. 73.

30. *Ibid.* (1970), p. 111.

31. U. S. Department of Commerce, *op. cit.* (1971), p. 87.
32. U. S. Department of Commerce, *op. cit.* (1973), p. 68.
33. *Ibid.,* p. 66.
34. David L. Kirp, "Race, Class, and the Limits of Schooling," *The Urban Review,* Vol. 4, No. 3, May 1970, p. 10.
35. U. S. Department of Commerce, *op. cit.,* 1973, p. 17.
36. *Ibid.,* p. 95; *see also* E. Waldman, "Marital and Family Characteristics of the U. S. Labor Force," *Monthly Labor Review,* May 1970, p. 19.
37. U. S. Department of Commerce, Bureau of the Census, *op. cit.,* 1973, p. 95.
38. *Ibid.,* p. 46.
39. *Ibid.,* pp. 54–56.
40. Otto Eckstein, "Education, Employment, and Negro Equality," Seminar on Manpower and Program, U. S. Department of Labor, April 18, 1968, p. 5.
41. U. S. Department of Commerce, Bureau of the Census, *op. cit.* (1973), p. 30.
42. "Recipients of Public Assistance Money Payments," *Welfare in Review,* May-June 1972, pp. 77–78.
43. Leon D. Platky, "Measures of AFDC Family Size," *Welfare in Review,* May-June 1972, pp. 61–65.
44. Howard Oberheu, "AFDC Mothers: Employed and [sic] Not Employed," *Welfare in Review, op. cit.,* pp. 58–61.
45. U. S. Department of Commerce, Bureau of the Census, Series P-23, No. 42, 1971, p. 47.
46. *Ibid.*
47. *Ibid.*
48. U. S. Department of Commerce, Bureau of the Census, *op. cit.,* 1971, p. 33.
49. In New York City, for example, there are more than 150,000 fatherless families on relief rolls, which overall are 50 percent black and 40 percent Puerto Rican. These families have 500,000 children. *See* "Will Work Work?" John A. Hamilton, *Saturday Review,* May 23, 1970, p. 26.
50. U. S. Department of Commerce, Bureau of the Census, *op. cit.* (1973), p. 30.

# BIBLIOGRAPHY

Aptheker, Herbert, "Afro-American Superiority: A Neglected Theme in the Literature." In Goldstein, 1971, pp. 165–179.

Bell, Robert B., "The One-Parent Mother in the Negro Lower Class." Presented at Eastern Sociological Society, New York City, 1965.

Bernard, Jessie, *Marriage and Family Among Negroes.* Prentice-Hall, Englewood Cliffs, N.J., 1966.

Bernard, Sydney E., *Fatherless Families: Their Economic and Social Adjustment.* Florence Heller Graduate School for Advanced Studies in Social Welfare, Brandeis University, Waltham, Massachusetts. A condensation of *The Economic and Social Adjustment of Low-Income Female-Headed Families.* Unpublished Ph.D. dissertation, Brandeis University, 1964.

Billingsley, Andrew, *Black Families in White America.* Prentice-Hall, Englewood Cliffs, N.J., 1968.

Bond, Jean Carey and Pat Perry, 1970, "Is the Black Male Castrated?" In Cade (below), 1970, pp. 113–118.

Cade, Toni, ed., *The Black Woman: An Anthology.* Signet, New York, 1970.

Comer, J. P., "The Black Family: An Adaptive Perspective." Mimeo, Child Study Center, Yale University. New Haven, 1970.

Deasy, Leila Calhoun and Olive Westbrooke Quinn, "The Urban Negro and Adoption of Children." *Child Welfare*, Journal of the Child Welfare League of America, Inc., 1962.

Douglass, Joseph H., "Mental Health Aspects of the Effects of Discrimination Upon Children." *Young Children*, Journal of the National Association for the Education of Young Children, Vol. XXII, No. 5, May 1967.

Duncan, Otis D. and Beverly Duncan, "Family Stability and Occupational Success." *Social Problems*, 16, Winter 1969, pp. 273–285.

Eckstein, Otto, *Education, Employment, and Negro Equality*. Seminar on Manpower and Program, U. S. Department of Labor, April 18, 1968.

Farley, Reynolds and Albert I. Hermalin, "Family Stability: A Comparison of Trends Between Blacks and Whites." *American Sociological Review*, 36, February 1971, pp. 1–17.

Frazier, E. Franklin, *The Negro Family in the United States*. University of Chicago Press, Chicago, 1939, 1966.

Goldstein, Rhoda L., ed., *Black Life and Culture in the United States*. Thomas Y. Crowell, New York, 1971.

Harwood, Edwin and Claire Hodge. 1971, "Jobs and the Negro Family." *Public Interest*, 23, Spring 1971, pp. 125–131.

Hertel, Frank, *Strengthening the Family: Community Strategy Alternatives*. Institute of Community Studies, United Community Funds and Councils of America, New York, 1970.

Herzog, Elizabeth, "Is There a 'Breakdown' of the Negro Family?" *Social Work*, January 1966. Reprinted in Rainwater and Yancey, 1967.

Herzog, Elizabeth and Rose Bernstein, "Why So Few Negro Adoptions?" *Children*, U. S. Department of Health, Education, and Welfare, January-February 1965.

Herzog, Elizabeth and Hylan Lewis, "Children in Poor Families: Myths and Realities." *American Journal of Orthopsychiatry*, 40, 3, April 1970, pp. 375–387.

Herzog, Elizabeth and Cecelia E. Sudia, "Family Structure and Composition." *Race, Research, and Reason: Social Work Perspective*. National Association of Social Workers, New York, 1967, pp. 145–164.

Herzog, Elizabeth, et al., *Families for Black Children: The Search for Adoptive Parents*. A report of the Division of Research and Evaluation, Children's Bureau, Office of Child Development and the Social Research Group, The George Washington University, Washington, D.C., 1971.

Hill, Robert B., *The Strengths of Black Families*. New York, Emerson Hall, 1971, 1972.

Hindelang, Michael James, "Educational and Occupational Aspirations Among Working Class Negro, Mexican-American and White Elementary School Children." *Journal of Negro Education*, 39, Fall 1970, pp. 351–353.

Hyman, Herbert H. and John Shelton Reed, "Black Matriarchy Reconsidered: Evidence from Secondary Analysis of Sample Surveys." Public Opinion Quarterly, 33, Fall 1969, pp. 346–354.

Jackson, Jacquelyn, "Marital Life Among Aging Blacks." Mimeo, Department of Psychiatry, Duke University Medical Center, Durham, North Carolina, 1971.

Ladner, Joyce A., *Tomorrow's Tomorrow: The Black Woman*. Garden City, N.Y., Doubleday, 1971.

Lewis, Hylan, "The Family: Resources for Change." Agenda Paper No. 5, Planning Session, White House Conference "To Fulfill These Rights," November 1965. Reprinted in Rainwater and Yancey, 1967.

Lewis, Hylan, "Family Life Among an Urban Low-Income Population Under a Federally Guaranteed Minimum Income Plan, 1991–1996." A draft prepared for discussion at Conference on Guaranteed Minimum Income, University of Chicago, January 14–15, 1966.

Liebow, Elliot, *Tally's Corner: A Study of Negro Streetcorner Men*. Boston, Little, Brown, 1967.

Madison, Lettie C., "The Black Family." *The Baptist Herald*, Vol. XXIX, No. 5, May 1972, pp. 7–10.

Moynihan, Daniel P., *The Negro Family: The Case For National Action*. Washington, D.C., Government Printing Office, March 1965.

Moynihan, Daniel P., "The Schism in Black America." *The Public Interest*, Spring 1972, pp. 3–24.

Murray, Pauli, "The Liberation of Black Women." In Mary Lou Thompson, ed., *Voices of the New Feminism*. Boston, Beacon Press, 1970, pp. 87–102.

Olson, David H., "The Measurement of Family Power by Self-Report and Behavioral Methods." *Journal of Marriage and the Family*, 31, August 1969, pp. 545–550.

Otto, Herbert A., "What Is a Strong Family?" *Marriage and Family Living*, 24, February 1962, pp. 72–80.

Parker, Seymour and Robert J. Kleiner, "Characteristics of Negro Mothers in Single-Headed Households." *Journal of Marriage and the Family*, 28, November 1966, pp. 507–513.

Phillips, W. M. Jr., "Survival Techniques of Black Americans." In Goldstein 1971, pp. 153–164.

Rainwater, Lee and William L. Yancey. *The Moynihan Report and the Politics of Controversy*. Cambridge, M.I.T. Press, 1967.

Reissman, Frank, "In Defense of the Negro Family." *Dissent*, March-April 1966, pp. 141–155.

Staples, Robert, "The Myth of the Black Matriarchy." *The Black Scholar*, February 1970, pp. 9–16.

Staples, Robert, "The Myth of the Impotent Black Male." *The Black Scholar*, 2, June 1971, pp. 2–9.

Staples, Robert, *The Black Family: Essays and Studies*. Belmont, California, Wadsworth, 1971.

Vontress, Clemmont E., "The Black Male Personality." *The Black Scholar*, 2, June 1971, pp. 10–16.

Waldman, E., "Marital and Family Characteristics of the U. S. Labor Force." *Monthly Labor Review*, May 1970.

Willie, Charles V., *The Family Life of Black People*. Columbus, Ohio, Charles E. Merrill, 1970.

## Periodical:

*Welfare in Review*

# 9

## *The Black Woman**

### *Ernestein Walker*

**"Life for me ain't been no crystal stair."**

**Langston Hughes**

## Historical Background

The astonishing perseverance, the ability to adapt and rise to every occasion that continues to mark the black woman in America today, is grounded in a bitter history. Only in the light of her special past, so full of unusual difficulties, can she be fully understood. It is a long past, beginning in 1619, a year before the arrival of the Pilgrims, when a Dutch frigate landed a cargo of twenty blacks at Jamestown, Virginia. Among them were at least three women.[1]

In her native Africa the black woman, whatever her cultural background, had enjoyed an orderly existence in a social structure with established legal systems and strong family ties. She had filled every position from queen to prostitute.[2] In America, as a slave, she was dropped suddenly and completely to the bottom of the social scale, where her position was totally vulnerable. Lacking status or rights, she became easy prey to men, both black and white, as well as to the vindictiveness of white women. Her personal relationships with the black man encountered peculiar difficulties. For the first two centuries of slavery, black males outnumbered females, and "the casualness of the contacts, when the slaves succeeded in finding women, prevented the development of strong attachments which result from prolonged association between the sexes."[3] Even where there was genuine warmth between slave wife and husband, there was always the shadow of a permanent separation. If the two were ill-matched, and the husband tyrannical, the slave wife suffered without recourse unless a sympathetic owner chose to intervene in her behalf. Charles Ball remembered one such unfortunate black woman whose husband "was very irritable, and often beat and otherwise maltreated his wife, on the slightest provocation, and the overseer refused to protect her, on the ground that he never interfered in the family quarrels of black people."[4] In some cases white owners did take emotional and marriage ties into consideration, but more often they were motivated by the pressure of economics or sheer personal appetite.

Though many apologists for slavery have denied it, slaves were often used for breed-

*For a Selected List of Black Women of Achievement see end of chapter.

ing. The Charleston (S.C.) *City Gazette* provides a typical reference to slaves being sold for this purpose. An advertisement citing the owner's declining planting business as his reason for selling off his blacks, specifies: "They were purchased for stock breeding Negroes, and to any Planter who particularly wanted them for that purpose, they are a very choice and desirable gang."[5] A former slave told how his master bluntly ordered his slaves to enrich his plantation—produce children or be sold. Many white slave owners directly contributed to the increase by fathering mulatto children, who soon abounded.

Sexual intercourse between blacks and whites seems to have begun as soon as the former were introduced into America. Indeed, many white men and women came to think of black women as basically immoral—"loose and easy," deliberate enticers of white men. (Some whites still believe this.) E. Franklin Frazier cites four categories in which sex relations between black women and white men may be grouped. First there was rape, brutal assaults in which any show of resistance often brought on sadistic revenge. One slave wrote that he and two others were once ordered to strip a slave girl naked, then hold her while the master's son, whose advances she had repulsed, flogged her with a bullwhip. At the finish she was near death. Like this unfortunate, many other black women carried scars to their graves for similar resistance. A second category was submission. Here the female did not resist, preferring to avoid the wrath of a displeased master, or to gain the concrete advantages submission would bring, freedom from the drudgery of field labor as well as better food and clothing. A third category was active compliance. Some slave women considered such relationships prestigious—an admixture of blood, they believed, would raise their children in the scale of humanity. There was also the prospect that the half-white child would be allowed certain privileges and perhaps in time be emancipated. Lastly, genuine feeling played a part in securing the compliance of slave women. The fact that slave owners often kept their black mistresses openly, acknowledged and provided for their mulatto children, kept them together as a unit, and sometimes emancipated them and made provision for them in their wills, shows more than a fleeting passion on their part.[6] But even when there was affection and loyalty, the slave was still a property subject to the decisions of an owner.

The case of Phillis Wheatley, purchased in Boston by Mr. and Mrs. Wheatley in 1761 to be trained as a personal servant for Mrs. Wheatley, illustrates the limitations of a black woman in the confines of slavery, even where there was kindness. By all accounts she was well treated and given educational and social advantages not open even to free Negroes. Her poetic ability and "family" connections moved her into social circles in Boston and England that were beyond the reach of most white women of her day. Before his death, John Wheatley emancipated her. Yet the paternalistic treatment of her owner-benefactor had denied her the development that would have enabled her to succeed as a free agent, even had she been in robust health. Her life afterward, following the deaths of several members of the Wheatley family, was one of pain and suffering.

The relationship of the black slave women and the white woman was almost always difficult—sometimes volatile. If the black woman was the mistress of her owner there was understandable resentment on the part of the white wife. Sometimes it manifested itself in particular toward the hapless offspring—a constant reminder of the liaison. Frederick Douglass found that such children often encountered hostility from their own white fathers as well: "Men do not love those who remind them of their sins, unless they have a mind to repent—and the mulatto child's face is a standing accusation against him who is master and father to the child. What is still worse, perhaps, such a child is a constant offense to the wife. She hates its very presence, and when a slaveholding woman hates, she wants not means to give that hate telling effect."[7]

Even when there was no child, the black woman, especially the household slave, was still a convenient object on which the white woman could vent her frustrations. She might well have identified to some extent with the black woman, since she too was oppressed and forced to conform to the narrow role designed for her by the white man. Instead, she took the psychological route of many poor whites in the South, cherishing the idea that she was much superior to all blacks. Shielded by her remote position on the pedestal where her men placed her, she settled for an existence that was in many ways hollow, and was as skillfully manipulated as were many other groups in society.[8] Since her authority was limited, many a white woman wielded it with a vengeance in the sphere where it was unlimited: running her house. Jenny Proctor tells in her autobiography of a severe beating she received as a hungry slave girl because her mistress discovered she had eaten a biscuit she found while cleaning.[9]

No concessions were made to the black woman because of sex, as was routinely the case of the white woman. She was expected to do as much work in the fields as a man, the only exception being the brief respite, about three weeks, for the birth of a child. But not even in pregnancy did she escape physical brutality. There are recorded cases of special contraptions being devised so that she might be beaten even while in advanced stages of pregnancy, without harming the unborn slave. If she were a household slave, a position considered the upper echelon of slave status, she was expected to work from before dawn until late at night, seeing to the comforts of the white household and preparing delicacies she was never to taste. She was not allowed to be literate, yet she was expected to take mental shorthand in a flash. Added to her roles of cook, washerwoman, housecleaner, gatherer and preparer of foods, and runner of errands, was the function of "mammy" to the white children, and sometimes that of confidante to their indolent mothers. In spite of the circumstances, genuine affection often developed between these black mammies and their white charges. The solicitous, devoted care of Charlie Cotchipie by Idella Landy, depicted in the play *Purlie Victorious*, has its roots in reality.[10]

In general, in the slave family the mother or another black woman, rather than the father, was the dominant and important figure. Frequently the slave father was sold away from his family, and even if he were present his decisions could be vetoed by his white owner. A typical case was that of a slave brought to Southampton County, Virginia, who recalled the only time he ever saw his Northampton father: "I remember seeing him once, when he came to visit my mother. . . . He and my mother were separated, in the consequence of his master's going farther off, and then my mother was forced to take another husband."[11] Children, even the sons and daughters of slave owners by black mothers, were often sold away. The most a slave mother might expect was to have her child with her for a few years, though some would and did go to any length to prevent separation.

After a long day in the fields or house, the black mother had to prepare the meals for her own family, in a squalid shack, and provide all the affection her weary mind and body could muster. The accomplishments of these black women between midnight and dawn are little short of miraculous. Frederick Douglass has recorded a personal instance of the endurance and love for their children of which they were capable. "My mother had walked twelve miles to see me," he recalled of the last time he saw his mother before her death, "and had the same distance to travel over again before morning sunrise."[12] Booker T. Washington wrote in his autobiography: "One of my earliest recollections is that of my mother cooking a chicken late at night after the day's work was done," a forbidden morsel which had probably been procured at great risk. These precious night hours were also used in an effort to acquire the forbidden ability to read and write. Jenny Proctor, remembering how whites thought blacks would get too smart if they were allowed to learn, explained: "We slips around and gits hold of that Webster's old blue-back speller and we hides it till way in the night and then we light a little pine torch, and studies that spelling book. We learn it, too."[13]

A good example of the tenacity and strength of black women in the cause of education under the most difficult conditions is cited by Sylvia Dannet:

> On a plantation in Mississippi, Milla Granson, a slave, conducted a midnight school for several years. She had been taught to read and write by the children of her former master in Kentucky, an indulgent man, and in her little school hundreds of slaves benefited from her learning. . . . School started between eleven and twelve at night and lasted until two o'clock in the morning. After laboring all day for their master, the slaves would creep stealthily to Milla's "schoolroom" (a little cabin in a back alley) carrying a bundle of pitch-pine splinters for light, as the door and windows of the cabin had to be kept tightly sealed to avoid discovery. Each class was composed of twelve pupils and when Milla had brought them up to the extent of her ability, she "graduated" them and took in a dozen more. Through this means she graduated hundreds of slaves. Many whom she taught to write a legible hand wrote their own passes and set out for Canada.[14]

Generations before sensitivity sessions, before "relating to others" came into fashion, the black woman had mastered this skill. Slavery forced her to adjust simultaneously to two contradictory worlds—one white, privileged and oppressive, the other black, exploited and oppressed.[15] Not only were her time and energy expended in long hours of toil on the plantation, in the fields or households, but often the few moments she had for her own family were shared with orphans or young children whose parents had been sold away from them, or they from their parents. The willingness to take another's offspring and "do the best you can" for them has traditionally been one of the outstanding attributes of black women.

In spite of her life of constant drudgery and her responsibilities as the head of the slave family, the black woman still found the strength to protest slavery. In the numerous insurrections and frequent harrassment of slave owners, involving everything from hunger strikes to arson, black women played their part. (As early as 1766 a Maryland slave woman was executed for burning down "her master's home, tobacco house, and outhouses.")[16] Most, of course, did not do so on such a heroic scale as Harriet Tubman, who not only escaped but made nineteen successful trips into slave territory to lead 300 others to freedom via the Underground Railroad. This black woman, who could neither read nor write, displayed amazing ingenuity and excellent managerial skills as she poured her time and energy into freeing others. Nothing stopped her. She "would take several months off whenever she was running low in funds and hire herself out as a domestic servant in order to raise money for conveying slaves to freedom."[17]

The capacity for ingenuity in the quest for freedom is well-demonstrated by the escape of the light-skinned quadroon Ellen Craft of Macon, Georgia, and her husband William. Dressed as a man, she posed as a hard-of-hearing, ailing planter going North for medical treatment accompanied by a slave, her husband. Though unable to read or write, and unfamiliar with the white man's world away from the plantation, "for five days the couple traveled through the slave states, always in first-class style, as befitted a planter."[18] The daring scheme demanded consummate skill, particularly of Ellen, but the performance resulted in a successful escape. Later she and her husband lectured abroad in the abolition movement.

Black women participated in all of the many groups and movements that from the early nineteenth century loudly protested slavery and worked for abolition. One of the most notable was Isabella, better known as Sojourner Truth. She traveled through New England and the West denouncing slavery and unerringly pointing out its peculiar evils. Sarah Parker Redmond, as well as Ellen Craft, joined black male abolitionists in decrying slavery from platforms in England, Scotland, France, and Germany.

Black women shared all the high hopes and enthusiasm for the prospects of freedom that arose during the Civil War, taking part in whatever activity was open to them:

> Some Negro women worked in hospitals or camps. Others formed groups designed to raise money for the families of the men at the front, to purchase flags and banners for the regiments, or to buy delicacies for the sick and convalescent soldiers. A number of Negro women's organizations had as their primary goal the assistance of the newly arrived slaves, distributing food and clothing to them. . . . Some women's organizations sent money to assist former slaves still in the South, the Colored Ladies' Sanitary Commission of Boston on one occasion sending $500 for the suffering Freedmen of Savannah. Under the auspices of the Freedmen's aid societies, some Negro women volunteered to teach the three R's in those regions which had come under the Union flag. The best-known of these was young Charlotte Forten, who had been educated in Massachusetts and was personally acquainted with many of its most notable reformers.[19]

News of the Emancipation Proclamation traveled through slave country like wildfire, and Booker T. Washington, in describing his own mother's reaction to this development, has immortalized the response of most black mothers: "My mother, who was standing by my side, leaned over and kissed her children, while tears of joy ran down her cheeks. She explained to us what it meant, that this was the day for which she had been praying, but fearing she would never live to see."[20] Few black people, of course, fully understood or wished to analyze the tangle of political expediencies behind the Proclamation; the glimmer of hope it provided was enough. Soon, however, as the peonage system replaced chattel slavery, it became painfully evident that the dream of freedom had not yet been realized. For the black woman this condition kept old problems alive and created new ones.

## The Mother-Centered Family

The mother-orientation of the black family, fostered by the conditions of slavery, continued after emancipation, although the general disintegration produced by the war further undermined its shaky structure. The black mother—perhaps widowed or deserted, perhaps never married—often was the sole support of her children. And black women, even when a husband was present, often displayed an outspokenness and lack of timidity quite remarkable in view of their recent past. Frazier maintains that only women accustomed to playing the dominant role in family and marriage relations could have exhibited such audacity, and he cites an example of this boldness. It occurred in Mississippi during the 1868 election:

> If a freedman, having obtained [a picture of Grant] lacked the courage to wear it at home on the plantation in the presence of "ole marsa or missus" or of "the overseer," his wife would often take it from him and bravely wear it upon her own breast. If in such cases the husband refused to surrender it, as was sometimes the case, and hid it from her or locked it up, she would walk all the way to town, as many as twenty or thirty miles sometimes, and buy, beg, or borrow one, and thus equipped return and wear it openly, in defiance of husband, master, mistress, or overseer.[21]

This assertiveness of the black woman, of course, was not always welcomed by the emancipated black male. Many men were exceedingly jealous of their newly acquired authority in family relations and insisted upon the recognition of their "superiority" over women. It was this changing attitude, supported by the new economic structure, according to Frazier, which placed the black man in a position of authority in relation to his family and brought about what he considers "the downfall of the matriarchate."[22] But others note that the mother-centered family has still not entirely disappeared from Negro life.*

Too many sweeping generalizations have been made about the black matriarchy. Today, as in the past, proportionate to white women, a higher ratio of black women head families. Indeed the trend is upward rather than downward, reflecting the fact

*See Chapter 8, "The Black Family."

that a larger percentage of black women are deserted, separated, or divorced.[23] But mere statistical data, drawn in relation to white society, leaves much unsaid about the so-called black matriarchy, and how the black woman came to fill that role. The signs, all too familiar until quite recently in the South, reading "White Men," "White Ladies," and "Colored," indicated the manner in which much of white America regarded black people—not only as inferior, classless, and monolithic, but as sexless besides. This lack of distinction between the black sexes tended to permeate every walk of life, from field work even to lynchings, where black women were not spared, though they were less vulnerable to mob violence than were their men.[24]

The black woman was expected at all times to be gainfully occupied. Indeed her employability is one of the reasons she has been termed a matriarch, a fact which must be viewed in context with the difficulties facing many black men, including the semi-skilled, in finding regular employment. The well-known practice of "last hired, first fired," has undermined the economic stability needed to strengthen and steady many a black family.

Increasingly, social investigators are looking behind the labels of matriarchy to seek the reality. Doctors William H. Grier and Price M. Cobbs, for example, suggest that "the black woman has been beset by cruelty on all sides . . . but has stood by her mate or in his stead when he was crippled or crushed by the oppressor," as well as nurturing and protecting her children. "In such a role the black woman has been the salvation of many a family."[25] Sociologist Staples points out that the designation is frequently applied because the black woman participates freely in making decisions. "A closer inspection often reveals that she does not make decisions counter to her husband's wishes but renders them because he fails to do so. The reason he defers to her in certain decisions is simply because she is better equipped to make them. . . . the chances are good that no decisions are made which he actively opposes. The power of black women is much like American democracy—it is more apparent than real."[26] These authorities see the emphasis upon black matriarchy, in spite of the fact that most black families are headed by men, as a general misinterpretation afloat in a racist society. Former ambassador Patricia R. Harris, speaking of middle-class black women, has said, "We were programmed [to work] because our parents were not wealthy and our chances of finding a wealthy black man to take care of us were . . . limited. Therefore, the more secure the parents of a black girl, the more likely she was to have a profession; and the brighter she was, the more likely she was to be encouraged to maximize her employment opportunities." She maintains that:

> White and black male supremacists have interpreted this as the "black matriarchal" attempt to castrate the black male. The truth of the matter is that as the result of her training, the middle-class black woman protected the dignity of the black male professional by aiding him through her employment in maintaining his professional status and by increasing the economic security of the family, including the children.[27]

Staples considers the historic role of the black woman in no way demeaning to black men: "If [black women] had been content to accept the passive role ascribed to the female gender, then the travail of the past four centuries might have found the black race just as extinct as the dinosaur." Staples believes "the myth of [the black female's] matriarchal nature will soon join the death agony" of other myths.[28]

## The Black Woman After the Civil War

As the post-Civil War unreconstructed South gradually found "legal" and extralegal means to reenslave those who had been recently emancipated, black women never lost faith that they could help realize a better day, that much could be accomplished by hard work and education.

From the outset, the education of the black woman differed from that of the white woman in that it was never meant to be ornamental, but was intended to fit her for a profession, a life of service, or both. Mary Jane Patterson, who received an A.B. degree from Oberlin in 1862—perhaps the first Negro woman to gain such a distinction—set a pattern for college-trained black women by seeking a career in education.[29] By the turn of the century, many other black women were at work in this field: Lucy Laney, founder of Haines Normal Institute in Augusta, Georgia; Mary Church Terrell, the first black woman in the world to serve on a board of education; Mary McLeod Bethune, founder-president of Bethune-Cookman College; Nannie Helen Burroughs, founder of the National Trade and Professional School for Women and Girls in Washington, D. C. The full impact of their efforts in education, however, was not to be realized until well into the twentieth century.

Black women were equally active in "uplift" organizations dating from the early postwar period. In this regard a milestone was reached with the organization of the National Association of Colored Women in Washington, D.C., in 1896, at a time when lynchings were on the increase. A. W. Hunton has recorded how black women from every sector came pouring into the organization:

> With such a flocking into camp of its forces, the Association soon realized the necessity of working in groups, so various departments were formed, as the occasion demanded, and placed under the direction of women either experienced or peculiarly fitted for the work assigned them. Of the many departments that now constitute the Association, may be mentioned Kindergarten, Mother's meetings, Day Nurseries, Humane and Rescue, Temperance, Religion, Literature, Domestic Science, Music, Art, Forestry, and Statistics.[30]

The mere coverage and variety of the various departments is impressive, but the organization's accomplishments are even more striking. These black women not only founded and maintained agencies that are now part of regular social or educational services, but they exerted pressure on foot-dragging legislators to get remedial measures passed. Their efforts, for example, led to the creation of probation officers in Denver, Pittsburgh, Atlanta, and other cities. In 1900 the association became affiliated with the National Council of Women.

Black women, furthermore, worked actively for the right to vote. Even before emancipation, some fought for both abolition and suffrage as twin causes. "Negro women, like their white counterparts, wanted to exercise political power directly, not through their presumed influence on their husbands, fathers, and brothers," writes the eminent historian Benjamin Quarles. "Hence the Negro women abolitionists believed in equal suffrage not only between the races but between the sexes. Sojourner Truth was as much at home at a women's rights meeting as at any other kind."[31] Sarah J. S. Garnett, the first black school principal in New York City, was also an active campaigner for the full emancipation of black women. She founded the Equal Suffrage League and was superintendent of the Suffrage Department of the National Association of Colored Women. At the age of 79 her lifelong interest in the suffrage movement took her to London for further work.[32]

By the end of the first decade of the twentieth century a black Greek-letter sorority had been formed and others followed, all of them calling for acts of service. On a national level, by 1911 there were 45,000 black women affiliated with the National Council of Women. The black woman's presence in the labor force was also impressive. In 1910, according to Dr. Sadie T. M. Alexander, more than half of the nearly 3,700,000 black females in the United States, 10 years of age and older, were gainfully employed, compared with less than 20 percent of the nearly 31,000,000 white women. Most of these black women, however, were in agricultural and domestic jobs and it was not until World War I withdrew the men from industry that black women entered manufacturing and the mechanical industries in large numbers. Then, as later, they received lower wages than their white counterparts.

Dr. Alexander reached certain conclusions concerning the effect of black women on the economic life of the country:

> Survey[ing] the field as a whole, we find over 100,000 Negro women employed in the manufacturing and mechanical industries of the United States in 1920, an increase of nearly 100 percent in the number so employed in 1910. . . . Within the two decades during which Negro women have entered industry in large numbers, production has increased at such a rapid rate that economists have been forced to change their theory of a deficit economy . . . to a theory of surplus economy.[33]

Dr. Alexander concluded that in many industries mass production would not have been undertaken if it had not been for the available, low-priced labor supply of black women. Given the opportunity, they participated fully not only in industry but in growing unionism as well. One 1933 report reflects their efforts in behalf of the labor movement:

> Negro women in industry have shown themselves to be quite as active as white women in union organization. In unions of the American Federation of Labor where no color

bar is drawn, Negro women have a high proportionate membership. In New York, and Birmingham, Alabama, Negro women joined in picket lines with their white sister workers in a fight for better wages. A Negro—Lilian Gaskins of New York City—holds an important post in one of the largest locals of the International Ladies' Garment Workers Union. In North Carolina, Negro women are more active than white women in the Tobacco Workers' International Union.[34]

The Depression of the 1930s hit black Americans particularly hard. The great exodus from the rural South already underway—accelerated by the drought, boll weevil plagues, and other vicissitudes of the mid-twenties—continued unabated into the thirties. Since domestic work was all too often the only employment available to blacks, the woman frequently became the sole breadwinner of the family.

But the black woman, whose ancestors had survived generations of psychological depression, did not succumb to the grinding economic difficulties of the twenties and thirties. To mention a few outstanding examples of unslackening effort, there was Jane Bolin, who in 1939 was appointed a judge in the Court of Domestic Relations by New York's Mayor LaGuardia, making her the first black American woman judge.[35] In the arts, N. Elizabeth Prophet, the American-born sculptress, won much critical acclaim in Paris, and Marian Anderson gained renown singing in the major cities of Europe and the United States (though not without a well-remembered snub from the Daughters of the American Revolution). Others, as well, won prominence in a wide variety of fields.

World War II brought tremendous changes to the country, and expanded horizons for black Americans in particular. According to Professor Andrew Hacker, the "Black Revolution," Revolution in the Family, and Women's Liberation can all trace their origins back to 1942.[36] Certainly for the black woman, as for blacks in general, the most visible gains in terms of variety of opportunity and status have been achieved since that time.

Any study of the black woman's past in America, however cursory, can lead only to one conclusion: the strides she has made toward the realization of yesterday's "impossible dream" are the result of an overwhelming dedication and unending hard work.

## The Black Woman in Contemporary Society

Most blacks, male and female alike, find the struggle to survive and advance in a racist society a never-ending burden and challenge. No wonder a little black boy on Art Linkletter's television show, *House Party*, when asked what he wanted to be when he grew up, could respond, "I want to be white." Being white in the United States has often been the chief qualification required for jobs, housing, protection, and privileges of all kinds. This can be quickly illustrated, if illustration is needed, by the following recent examples, which could be multiplied by thousands. They vividly depict the trials and pitfalls facing the black woman, and suggest the skill and finesse required for her survival and the survival of her loved ones.

In Baltimore a black rape victim hailed a white police officer for assistance. He responded, "Another police car will be along later; report it to them." In other words an atrocious crime, for which a black man could get the death penalty in many states, was considered of little moment when the victim was black.

Another black woman, declaring that she had been forced to endure more insults as a married woman than she ever had when single, explained: "My husband is no good to me dead. I would restrain him because I didn't want him hurt, jailed, or possibly killed because he spoke up when I was insulted."

The plight of the black woman is not only confined to racial oppression. She is also exposed to the "double jeopardy" of racial and sex discrimination. Congresswoman Shirley Chisholm of New York has said that in politics she has encountered more sex prejudice than race bias:

> The major thing I have learned is that women are the backbone of America's political organizations. They are the letter writers, envelope stuffers, and the telephone answerers; they are the campaign workers and organizers. They are the speech writers, workers, and the largest number of potential voters. Yet they are but rarely the standard bearers or elected officials.[37]

The same situation applies to churches and other organizations. And ironically, at a time when so much is heard about Women's Liberation, and when so many women are successfully entering previous male strongholds, the presence of women in the professions is decreasing. "Occupationally women are more disadvantaged, compared with men, than they were thirty years ago," writes Elizabeth Duncan Koontz, the first black Director of the Women's Bureau of the U. S. Department of Labor. "In 1940 they held 45 percent of all professional and technical positions. In 1969 they held only 37 percent of such jobs. This deterioration of their role in career fields relative to men has occurred despite the increase in women's share of total employment over the same period. On the other hand, the proportion of women among all service workers (except private household) has increased since 1940—rising from 40 to 59 percent."[38]

Unfortunately, sex discrimination comes from not only white males but blacks as well, who seem as ready as their white counterparts to prevent black women from receiving equal pay for equal work, or advancing to positions of responsibility.

## Color Prejudice

The black woman has been subject to yet another form of discrimination, color prejudice from fellow blacks. The preference for Caucasian features and light skin can be traced to slave days when mulattoes frequently received preferential treatment, and when many blacks learned to identify with their white oppressors.[39] A saying that sums up this type of prejudice became prevalent around the turn of the century: "If you're white, you're right; if you're brown, hang around; if you're black, get back." Brainwashing, do-it-yourself style, was underway. This concern for white standards of beauty applied more to black women than to black men.

Today there is reported to be a big business in the Union of South Africa in lightening the skin and straightening the hair in an effort to qualify for the classification of "colored," since those so classified enjoy a little more freedom than the black-skinned Bantu. But in the United States, where no such classification exists, an unofficial category of "light-skinned" developed which until recently was highly important among blacks, although less so among many whites, who saw all blacks as the same. A decade ago it was next to impossible for a dark-skinned girl at a black college to be elected campus queen. Black male undergraduates at a well-known southern college gave preference to light-skinned dates. In the not-very-distant past, calling a person black, even if the speaker was black, was considered the number-one insult. The following remark of one light-skinned woman about a beautiful black bride was common a few years ago: "I think she is attractive even though she *is* dark."

It is revealing that the country's first acknowledged black millionaire, Madame C. J. Walker, made her name and fortune in products intended to help the black woman look as "white" as possible.

The problems generated by shades of skin color sometimes took strange twists. In his autobiography, Walter White relates the difficulties met by his ivory-colored daughter, Jane, in attempts to get roles in the theater. Broadway considered her skin too light for "Negro" roles, then rejected her for the part of a young Indian woman since "it was 'unthinkable' to cast a Negro girl in an Indian part."[40] Today, ironically, some companies eager to let their black clientele know that "we've hired blacks," insist that their light-skinned display models wear Afro wigs to establish their "identity."

Among many blacks, the new awareness that "black is beautiful" has not yet dispelled the prestige accorded whiteness. Indeed a number of recent articles in national publications deal with intermarriage, particularly between black men and white women. According to Fletcher Knebel, the "white woman-black man pairing has become a smoldering issue at many universities where the black population is on the rise." Whether or not there is an "angry rebellion of black women against black men who prefer white women," as he states, there is certainly current interest and discussion. "What pains the black woman," says Knebel, "is that her newly awakened man thinks, talks, and exhorts black, but, too often for her taste, he mates white."[41] However, such a description applies to only a minority of black men; many make it an article of faith to have nothing to do with white women, while others simply do not find them attractive or do not come in contact with them. The matter is still primarily an emotional one.

The above issue, of course, is not one of the major problems of black women. Their fundamental concerns are still with their families, employment opportunities, education, involvement in politics, and advancement in careers, and this leaves little time for personal rancor.

## Education and Employment

Nonwhite women have traditionally worked in larger percentages than their white sisters. Although the trend in employment between 1959 and 1973 was away from service and farm work and toward white-collar employment, in 1973 nearly two-fifths (39.5 percent) remained in service occupations, while little more than two-fifths (41.9 percent) had achieved white-collar status (see Table I). Over the same period, the employment of white women in service and white-collar categories was relatively stable; in both years, over three-fifths of all white women workers had white-collar jobs; only about 18 percent were in service occupations. (Their role as farm workers declined from 3.2 to 1.3 percent over the same period, while the nonwhite figures fell from 3.4 to 0.8 percent.)

TABLE I—YEARS OF SCHOOL COMPLETED BY MAJOR OCCUPATION GROUP
OF EMPLOYED PERSONS, BY SEX AND RACE: 1959 AND 1973

[Relates to civilian noninstitutional population 18 years old and over as of March of years indicated. Service includes private household workers. Based on Current Population Survey.]

| Year, Race, and Education | Male Total (millions) | Male Percent— White Collar | Blue Collar | Service | Farm | Female Total (millions) | Female Percent— White Collar | Blue Collar | Service | Farm |
|---|---|---|---|---|---|---|---|---|---|---|
| **1959** | | | | | | | | | | |
| White persons, total | 37.8 | 39.7 | 45.5 | 5.6 | 9.2 | 17.8 | 61.1 | 17.2 | 18.5 | 3.2 |
| Completed less than 4 years of high school | 18.7 | 20.3 | 58.9 | 7.2 | 13.7 | 7.0 | 31.5 | 31.4 | 31.6 | 5.5 |
| Completed 4 years of high school or more | 19.0 | 58.8 | 32.3 | 4.0 | 4.9 | 10.8 | 80.3 | 8.0 | 10.0 | 1.6 |
| Black and other, total | 3.7 | 12.6 | 59.3 | 14.3 | 13.9 | 2.5 | 17.6 | 14.7 | 64.3 | 3.4 |
| Completed less than 4 years of high school | 2.9 | 5.3 | 65.4 | 12.6 | 16.7 | 1.7 | 5.8 | 15.7 | 73.8 | 4.7 |
| Completed 4 years of high school or more | 0.8 | 33.8 | 37.3 | 20.2 | 3.7 | 0.8 | 44.5 | 12.4 | 42.6 | 6.5 |
| **1973** | | | | | | | | | | |
| White persons, total | 44.5 | 42.8 | 45.8 | 6.8 | 4.6 | 26.9 | 64.6 | 16.0 | 18.1 | 1.3 |
| Completed less than 4 years of high school | 13.1 | 16.0 | 66.8 | 8.8 | 8.4 | 6.4 | 29.5 | 35.9 | 31.8 | 2.8 |
| Completed 4 years of high school or more | 31.4 | 54.0 | 37.1 | 5.9 | 3.0 | 20.5 | 75.5 | 9.9 | 13.8 | 0.9 |
| Black and other, total | 4.9 | 23.9 | 57.3 | 15.5 | 3.4 | 3.9 | 41.9 | 17.8 | 39.5 | 0.8 |
| Completed less than 4 years of high school | 2.4 | 7.2 | 68.7 | 18.4 | 5.7 | 1.5 | 12.8 | 24.1 | 61.1 | 2.0 |
| Completed 4 years of high school or more | 2.5 | 39.7 | 46.4 | 12.8 | 1.1 | 2.4 | 60.7 | 13.8 | 25.5 | (Z) |

(Z) Less than 0.05 percent.

Source: U. S. Bureau of Labor Statistics, *Special Labor Force Report,* Nos. 1 and 161. U. S. Bureau of the Census, *Statistical Abstract of the United States,* 1974, p. 118.

TABLE II—YEARS OF SCHOOL COMPLETED, BY RACE AND SEX: 1960 AND 1973

[Persons 25 years old and over. 1960 data as of April 1, based on 25 percent sample; 1970–73 data as of March, based on Current Population Survey; see text, p. 1. For definition of median, see preface]

| Year, Race, and Sex | Persons 25 Years Old and Over (1,000) | Percent of Population Completing— | | | | | | | Median School Years Completed |
|---|---|---|---|---|---|---|---|---|---|
| | | Elementary School | | | High School | | College | | |
| | | 0–4 Years | 5–7 Years | 8 Years | 1–3 Years | 4 Years | 1–3 Years | 4 Years or More | |
| **1960, all races** .......... | **99,438** | **8.3** | **13.8** | **17.5** | **19.2** | **24.6** | **8.8** | **7.7** | **10.6** |
| White ...................... | 89,581 | 6.7 | 12.8 | 18.1 | 19.3 | 25.8 | 9.3 | 8.1 | 10.9 |
| Male .................... | 43,259 | 7.4 | 13.7 | 18.4 | 18.9 | 22.2 | 9.1 | 10.3 | 10.7 |
| Female .................. | 46,322 | 6.0 | 11.9 | 17.8 | 19.6 | 29.2 | 9.5 | 6.0 | 11.2 |
| Black ...................... | 9,054 | 23.8 | 24.2 | 12.9 | 19.0 | 12.9 | 4.1 | 3.1 | 8.2 |
| Male .................... | 4,240 | 28.3 | 23.9 | 12.3 | 17.3 | 11.3 | 4.1 | 2.8 | 7.7 |
| Female .................. | 4,814 | 19.8 | 24.5 | 13.4 | 20.5 | 14.3 | 4.1 | 3.3 | 8.6 |
| **1970, all races** .......... | **109,310** | **5.3** | **9.1** | **13.4** | **17.1** | **34.0** | **10.2** | **11.0** | **12.2** |
| White ...................... | 98,112 | 4.2 | 8.3 | 13.6 | 16.5 | 35.2 | 10.7 | 11.6 | 12.2 |
| Male .................... | 46,606 | 4.5 | 8.8 | 13.9 | 15.6 | 30.9 | 11.3 | 15.0 | 12.2 |
| Female .................. | 51,506 | 3.9 | 7.8 | 13.4 | 17.3 | 39.0 | 10.1 | 8.6 | 12.2 |
| Black ...................... | 10,089 | 15.1 | 16.7 | 11.2 | 23.3 | 23.4 | 5.9 | 4.5 | 9.9 |
| Male .................... | 4,619 | 18.6 | 16.0 | 11.1 | 21.9 | 22.2 | 5.7 | 4.6 | 9.6 |
| Female .................. | 5,470 | 12.1 | 17.3 | 11.3 | 24.5 | 24.4 | 6.0 | 4.4 | 10.2 |
| **1973, all races** .......... | **112,866** | **4.5** | **8.0** | **11.4** | **16.3** | **35.8** | **11.4** | **12.6** | **12.3** |
| White ...................... | 100,818 | 3.6 | 7.2 | 11.6 | 15.7 | 37.0 | 11.8 | 13.1 | 12.3 |
| Male .................... | 47,645 | 3.9 | 7.5 | 11.7 | 14.8 | 32.8 | 12.5 | 16.8 | 12.4 |
| Female .................. | 53,173 | 3.4 | 6.9 | 11.5 | 16.5 | 40.7 | 11.1 | 9.9 | 12.3 |
| Black ...................... | 10,585 | 12.6 | 14.8 | 10.1 | 23.2 | 25.8 | 7.5 | 6.0 | 10.6 |
| Male .................... | 4,711 | 14.9 | 15.3 | 10.8 | 20.9 | 25.2 | 7.1 | 5.9 | 10.3 |
| Female .................. | 5,874 | 10.7 | 14.5 | 9.6 | 25.1 | 26.3 | 7.8 | 6.0 | 10.8 |

Source: U. S. Bureau of the Census, *Statistical Abstract of the United States*, 1974, p. 116.

Education was clearly important in determining job categories in 1973. Over 60 percent of nonwhite women with four years or more of high school were in the white-collar category, as compared with 12.8 percent of those with less than a high-school education. A quarter of the more educated nonwhite group still worked in service occupations; but 61.1 percent of their less-educated sisters were in this category.

Census figures for 1973 showed 11 percent of the population to be black and just over half of this number was female.[42] Although the decade of the sixties failed to close the educational gap between black and white women (in 1960, 6.0 percent of white women and only 3.3 percent of black women had completed four or more years of college), by 1973 corresponding percentages of 9.9 for white and 6.0 for black women attaining a college education suggests a trend toward greater equality, although without all the speed one might wish. (See Table II.) The working women of the minority races have added nearly three years to their educational attainment during this period, and increasingly are high-school graduates. (See Table III.)

TABLE III—MEDIAN YEARS OF SCHOOL COMPLETED

|  | Male | | Female | |
|---|---|---|---|---|
|  | Minority Races | White | Minority Races | White |
| March 1959 | 8.3 | 11.9 | 9.4 | 12.2 |
| March 1970 | 11.1 | 12.4 | 12.1 | 12.5 |

Source:   U. S. Department of Labor, Women's Bureau.[43]

In terms of occupations, wages, and employment, however, statistics remain discouraging. Black women continue to heavily outnumber white women in the lower-paid occupations in ratio to the total population. As Table III shows, even the encouraging rise in percentages of black women in professional, technical, clerical, and sales jobs leaves them pitifully far behind their white sisters, whose job potential has been improving. The gap is narrowing, however, with the greatest gain for black women in clerical work, and the smallest in managerial and official positions.

TABLE IV—OCCUPATIONAL GROUPS OF EMPLOYED WOMEN*
(Percentage distribution)

| Selected Major Occupational Groups | 1970 | | 1960 | |
|---|---|---|---|---|
|  | White | Minority Races | White | Minority Races |
| Number | 26,025,000 | 3,642,000 | 19,376,000 | 2,821,000 |
| Percent | 100.0 | 100.0 | 100.0 | 100.0 |
| Professional and technical | 15.0 | 10.8 | 13.1 | 6.0 |
| Managers, officials | 4.8 | 1.9 | 5.4 | 1.8 |
| Clerical | 36.4 | 20.8 | 32.9 | 9.3 |
| Sales | 7.7 | 2.5 | 8.5 | 1.5 |
| Operatives | 14.1 | 17.6 | 15.1 | 14.1 |
| Private household | 3.4 | 17.5 | 6.1 | 35.1 |
| Service workers (except private household) | 15.3 | 25.6 | 13.7 | 21.4 |
| Other occupations | 3.3 | 3.3 | 5.2 | 10.8 |

*Women 16 years and over in 1970, but 14 years and over in 1960.
Source:   U. S. Department of Labor, Bureau of Labor Statistics, *Employment and Earnings*, November 1961 and January 1971.

Table V demonstrates that unemployment among minority women dropouts was alarmingly high. The employment rate for minority high-school graduates, although lower than among whites, was significantly better than for those who failed to complete their schooling. It is not encouraging to note that overall unemployment rates for minority women increased sharply in 1970, according to a release from the U. S. Department of Labor.[44]

TABLE V—HIGH SCHOOL GRADUATES AND SCHOOL DROPOUTS, 16 TO 21 YEARS OLD—EMPLOYMENT STATUS, BY SEX AND RACE: 1965 TO 1971

[In thousands, except percent. As of October. Data for high school graduates relate to those not enrolled in college and include those who attended college prior to survey date ; data for dropouts relate to persons not in regular school and not high school graduates. Based on samples and subject to sampling variability]

| Employment Status, Sex, and Race | Graduates | | | | Dropouts | | | |
|---|---|---|---|---|---|---|---|---|
| | 1965 | 1969 | 1970 | 1971 | 1965 | 1969 | 1970 | 1971 |
| **Civilian noninstitutional population** | **4,898** | **5,339** | **5,823** | **5,973** | **2,986** | **2,683** | **2,757** | **2,812** |
| Not in labor force | 1,129 | 1,115 | 1,257 | 1,257 | 1,123 | 1,096 | 1,146 | 1,097 |
| In labor force | 3,769 | 4,223 | 4,566 | 4,716 | 1,863 | 1,588 | 1,611 | 1,715 |
| Percent of population | 76.9 | 79.1 | 78.4 | 79.0 | 62.4 | 59.2 | 58.4 | 61.0 |
| Male | 1,617 | 1,650 | 1,966 | 2,105 | 1,265 | 977 | 1,024 | 1,111 |
| Female | 2,152 | 2,573 | 2,600 | 2,566 | 598 | 611 | 587 | 604 |
| White | 3,375 | 3,742 | 4,065 | 4,233 | 1,469 | 1,223 | 1,243 | 1,355 |
| Black and other | 394 | 481 | 501 | 483 | 394 | 365 | 368 | 360 |
| Employed | 3,451 | 3,897 | 4,038 | 4,182 | 1,585 | 1,358 | 1,264 | 1,355 |
| Percent of labor force | 91.6 | 92.3 | 88.4 | 88.7 | 85.1 | 85.5 | 78.5 | 79.0 |
| Male | 1,512 | 1,540 | 1,730 | 1,901 | 1,105 | 868 | 805 | 894 |
| Female | 1,939 | 2,357 | 2,308 | 2,281 | 480 | 490 | 459 | 461 |
| White | 3,116 | 3,490 | 3,636 | 3,804 | 1,266 | 1,058 | 1,011 | 1,091 |
| Black and other | 335 | 406 | 402 | 378 | 319 | 301 | 253 | 264 |
| Unemployed | 318 | 326 | 528 | 534 | 278 | 230 | 347 | 360 |
| Percent of labor force | 8.4 | 7.7 | 11.6 | 11.3 | 14.9 | 14.5 | 21.5 | 21.0 |
| Male | 105 | 110 | 236 | 249 | 160 | 109 | 219 | 217 |
| Female | 213 | 216 | 292 | 285 | 118 | 121 | 128 | 143 |
| White | 259 | 250 | 429 | 429 | 203 | 165 | 232 | 264 |
| Black and other | 59 | 76 | 99 | 105 | 75 | 65 | 115 | 96 |

Source : U. S. Bureau of Labor Statistics, *Special Labor Force Report,* Nos. 66, 121, and forthcoming report. *Statistical Abstract,* 1972, p. 113.

Large numbers of minority women carry a heavy economic load by working outside the home in addition, frequently, to heading the household; this is particularly true of families living in poverty. In 1974, 34 percent of minority families were headed by women, as contrasted with less than one tenth of white families. Among minority families headed by women, 53 percent were poor; only a quarter of white families headed by women fell in this category.[45]

If court records are any guide, not only are more black women deserted by their husbands than are their white counterparts; they also suffer more abuse, both financial and physical, than do white women. Far more black women bring delinquent mates or former mates into court for nonsupport of children, and the ratio of black men arrested for assault on black women far exceeds that among whites. It is not known, of course, how many black women endure both financial deprivation and physical abuse silently, but it is well known that many long-suffering black women take pride in saying, "I don't ask him for anything." Many black adults have been heard to comment, "My father never did anything for us," and it is no wonder Abbey Lincoln could write about the black woman: "Her head is more regularly beaten than any other woman's, and by her own man; she's the scapegoat for Mr. Charlie; she is forced to stark realism and chided if caught dreaming; her aspirations for her and hers are, for sanity's sake, stunted; her physical image has been criminally maligned, assaulted, and negated; she's the first to be called ugly, and never yet beautiful. . . ."[46]

Yet despite the harsh historical realities and the continuing adversities faced by black women, collectively and individually their achievements have been remarkable. They have not only held families together against overwhelming odds, but have gone into exciting professional endeavors. There is now scarcely a professional or business area in which black women may not be found, from artists, ambassadors, chemists, and dentists to wireless operators, X-ray technicians, xylophonists, and zoo keepers.

## At the Crossroads

Though her achievements are often taken for granted, the question well might be asked how the black woman has accomplished so much so quickly in view of her unpromising past. The answer seems to be twofold: strength of will plus the encouragement of generations of mothers who have never ceased to dream and exhort.

The long struggle to survive forged a woman with astonishing tenacity, a woman who has learned to use stumbling blocks as stepping-stones, building a self-confidence that no amount of abuse could wholly destroy. Examples of black women literally spurred on by rebuff could be cited by the thousands. Juanita Kidd became the first black woman elected to a judgeship* in the United States because, in the years before, she had unjustly been passed over for a promotion with the National Housing Authority. In answer to her request for an explanation she was admonished, "That's a lot of money for a colored girl," and advised to be grateful for the job she had and its $1,800 a year salary.[47] "If I've made it," wrote tennis star Althea Gibson, "it's half because I was game to take a wicked amount of punishment along the way and half because there were an awful lot of people who cared enough to help me."[48]

In many respects the black woman today stands at the crossroads. Will she continue her historic role as family supporter and guider—meeting every situation with resolve while often remaining in the background? Will she follow the current trend among women and attempt to gain increasing control over her own destiny, rather than reacting

*Jane Bolin was appointed, not elected, in 1939.

to those patterns designed for her? Will she perhaps fling herself into the Women's Liberation movement?

These are large questions, which are not readily answerable. But in order to gain some perspective on what the future may bring, an informal survey was made of a number of black women in various occupations. Three questions were asked: (1) What do you consider the greatest achievements of the black woman? (2) What do you see as the greatest problems facing the black woman today? (3) What do you envision as the future role of the black woman, say a quarter-century from now?[49]

The answers were extremely revealing. Very few gave priority to the black woman's acquisition of material goods. By far the largest number (about three times as many as in any other category) considered holding families together and inspiring children as the greatest achievement. One public-school teacher in Ohio considered this the "transfusive quality" which enabled black women to face inequities and work for her family while maintaining faith in a brighter day. Another described it as the "sustaining of a caring, loving family against all odds in a racist America." Less numerous were those who felt that the greatest achievements were to be found in the spheres of politics, education, and the gaining of higher salaries and positions. One interviewee in Texas considered attaining political office the most impressive achievement, and she pointed to the example of Barbara Jordan, member of Congress from Texas; others of like mind singled out Representative Shirley Chisholm of New York. Another group of answers could be classed as referring to psychic gains—self-pride, identity, a woman's being recognized as an entity in her own right. A few thought giving moral support to the black man the most worthy achievement.

Remarkable consistency was also shown in what black women considered to be the greatest problem facing them today. By far the largest number (twice that in any other category) felt it revolved around their relationships with black men.[50] There were variations on the theme, but it was obvious black women felt more strongly on this point than on any other. "The greatest problem facing the black woman today," stated one interviewee, "is to help her man become a decision maker, not a puppet." Another identified the same difficulty in reverse: "Not being able to defer more to the black male now that he is becoming more confident and manly." Others talked of "gaining unity with, building the image of, getting the moral support of, liberation of, and the respect of the black male." Others spoke of gaining a satisfactory relationship with, and the cooperation of, male members of the family. Practically none of these women complained of the economic responsibilities they shouldered. One beauty-shop operator voiced the opinions of many of her sisters when she sighed that it was not the long working hours away from home that were the most enervating, but the lack of appreciation on the part of her husband.

The survey showed the second greatest problem facing the black woman is in the area of personal identity. This was expressed in such words and phrases as "recognition," "survival," "identity," "determining goals," and "being myself." Racial discrimination ranked third in the order of problems. The concept of "equality," referring generally to both racial bias and parity with white women, as well as the difficulties of black women heading households, ranked fourth.

The responses to question three show the boundless optimism that has always characterized the black woman. A junior high school teacher saw the black woman succeeding in many more of the occupations that once were exclusively white or male, and she felt there would be more activity outside the home, but also saw the woman as "still the glue" in the family. A number of responses envisioned an equal role with white women, "whatever that may be." In general, a full or much greater participation in the economic and political life of the country was predicted, along with increasing assumption of leadership roles (one optimistic interviewee said a black woman would be President of the United States in twenty-five years).

Only one woman replied that she thought the role of the black woman a quarter-century from now would be "the same" as today; another predicted a state of simple and unchanging "motherhood." The haunting theme of the black male appeared again from time to time in this category: "The black woman's future and success are dependent on the black male," or she will be "wherever the black male is," a recognition of the fact that, for weal or woe, black men and women are linked together in their destiny. Both Abbey Lincoln and Eldridge Cleaver acknowledge this interdependence, but move from different directions to reach their conclusions. The former sees the black male as "an exact copy" of the female "emotionally and physically." Cleaver, in his book *Soul on Ice*, appeals to "all black women for all black men," pointedly declaring, "Only, only, only you can condemn or set me free."

A few saw the black woman's role on an even more sweeping scale. One sociology professor in a southern college wrote: "A quarter of a century from now I think the role of the black woman will be to be a *woman* in her own right—not black American, not one of the colored peoples of the world, and not one to be talking 'black, black, black,' but 'woman, woman, woman.' " A public-school teacher in Cleveland considered the future role would be "one of radical action both in the home and abroad." This role, she predicts, "will involve the greater alliance of divergent groups into a cohesive force for the good of all people. The black woman will continue to work until woman is universally accepted on the basis of her qualifications, proficiency, and ability to get the job done." This interviewee wrote of the black woman's fight as "not for herself alone but for justice and liberation of all men." A professor of home economics felt that in addition to community service and a professional "job well done," the black woman "well might serve as a model to women of other races—thereby providing strength and the solution necessary to halt the disintegrating trend so evident in all aspects of our present society."

When it comes to the Women's Liberation movement, black women in general have shown little enthusiasm. When one was asked why she thought more black women did not participate in the Women's March on Washington, she replied, expressing the sentiments of many others, "We've got to liberate black men first." Some have considered the feminist movement a kind of leisure activity, an emotional venting for which black women have little or no time. Still others decline to get involved because they consider it a "white fight." According to Ida Lewis, editor of *Encore*, "The women's liberation movement is basically a family quarrel between white women and white men, and on general principles it's not good to get involved in family disputes. Outsiders always get shafted when the dust settles."[51]

Novelist Toni Morrison sees the manner in which black men and women feel about themselves as reasons for the coolness of black women toward the liberation movement:

> This feeling of superiority contributes to the reluctance of black women to embrace Women's Lib. That and the very important fact that black men are formidably opposed to their involvement in it—and for the most part the woman understands their fears. . . . The consensus among blacks is that their first liberation has not been realized; unspoken is the conviction of black men that any more aggressiveness and "freedom" for black women would be intolerable, not to say counterrevolutionary.[52]

One black woman made the additional point that it was ridiculous for her to fight for the right to take a job outside the home when she wished far more strongly to give up the job she had in order to remain with her family.

Some black women go even further, saying that patient acceptance of discrimination against black women will help black men in their own revolution.[53] Many others, however, feel that this lack of interest in women's rights suggests that for one of the few times in her history, the black woman is ignoring the dictates of reality. They feel that the black woman who neglects her own liberation can expect no more, and possibly less, from the average black man. "Despite the present pattern of equality in black professional families," warns Patricia R. Harris, "large numbers of black men have joined the Mailer-*machismo* troupe and would achieve their black emancipation by reducing black women to subordinate roles new to the black community."

That the spiritual daughters of Sojourner Truth could suddenly conclude that only one thing can be attempted at a time, only one fight fought, strikes many observers as a sad portent. Black women, they say, have always had to carry on more than one struggle simultaneously. Quarles has put this in perspective:

> America has sometimes been defined as the land of permanent revolution. Black women have always been in the forefront of this permanent revolution, particularly of that aspect which aims to make this country a land of liberty and justice for all. Throughout long years black women have sought two forms of revolution—racial liberation and women's liberation. . . . in her day [Sojourner Truth's] women could not sue in the courts and could not vote and hold public office. For over a third of a century Sojourner Truth sought to put an end to all discrimination based on sex or color. If women today have come a long way they owe much to their earlier sisters who, like Sojourner Truth, challenged long-standing abuses.[54]

Ms. Harris sums up the feminist view of the question succinctly:

> My position is that black men and black women were equal in disadvantage and discrimination and that black men and women must emerge from the battle for racial and sexual equality as equals. . . . our individuality is every bit as much at stake as is that of our white sisters, as black men move into positions of leadership and seek to impose sex-role limitations upon women.[55]

On the whole, neither the strident carping of some women's liberationists about the "male chauvinist pig" nor the kind of sloganeering that urges women to "put down the mop and pick up the gun" have had much appeal for black women. Yet it was a black woman at the close of the nineteenth century who perhaps saw most clearly what the total struggle must involve, and her words are just as timely today. Fannie M. Jackson Coppin, an Oberlin honor graduate, was known primarily as a teacher and social worker but was also a noted lecturer. In an address before the Woman's Congress of 1894 she said:

> Not till race, color, sex, and condition are seen as the accidents and not the substance of life; not till the universal title of humanity to life, liberty, and the pursuit of happiness is conceded to be inalienable to all; not till then is woman's lesson taught, and woman's cause won—not the white woman's nor the black woman's nor the red woman's but the cause of every man and every woman who has writhed silently under a mighty wrong.[56]

Who can disagree that what is desperately needed today is a unity of black men and women? Only through mutual assistance and support in all areas of endeavor can each help the other to achieve his or her highest potential.

## Notes

1. The designation "black" is used in a generic sense. It refers to American women who have been called "colored" in the past and "Negro" more recently. Throughout this chapter, black and Negro are used interchangeably and apply to the same women.
2. For the role of black women in the ancient kingdom of Bight, for example, see Sylvia G. L. Dannett, *Profiles in Negro Womanhood*. (Yonkers, Educational Heritage Inc., 1964), I, p. 15.
3. E. Franklin Frazier, *The Negro Family in the United States* (Chicago, University of Chicago Press, 1939), p. 24.
4. Charles Ball, *Slavery in the United States: A Narrative of the Life and Adventures of Charles Ball, a Black Man* (Lewiston, John W. Shugert, 1836), p. 204.
5. Frazier, *op. cit.*, p. 46.
6. *Ibid.*, Chap. IV, *passim*.
7. Frederick Douglass, *My Bondage and My Freedom* (New York, Arno Press and *The New York Times*, 1969), p. 59.
8. For an excellent account of how mill workers were skillfully manipulated by the white mill owners, see W. J. Cash, *Mind of the South* (New York, Alfred A. Knopf, 1941), Chap. 11.
9. Mel Watkins and Jay David, eds., *To Be a Black Woman: Portraits in Fact and Fiction* (New York, William Morrow Inc., 1970), p. 16.

10. For a study of this relationship see Ossie Davis' three-act comedy *Purlie Victorious* (New York, Samuel French, Inc., 1961).

11. Frazier, *op. cit.*, p. 13.

12. Frederick Douglass, *Life and Times of Frederick Douglass* (Boston, De Wolfe, Fiske & Co., 1893), p. 37.

13. Watkins and David, *op. cit.*, p. 18.

14. Dannett, *op. cit.*, p. 74.

15. This is not to imply that every white person was oppressive or "privileged." There were poor whites who were not economically much better off than blacks. But even these were not chattel, and they felt their positions definitely superior to that of a black. There were free blacks—some comparatively well off. Yet these were by no means free to participate fully in the mainstream. For example, at one time free black sailors were placed in jail on arrival in Charleston, South Carolina, and kept there until their ships sailed. The mere presence of a free black was considered inconsistent with the city's well-being.

16. Herbert Aptheker, *American Negro Slave Revolts* (New York, Columbia University Press, 1945), pp. 144–145.

17. John Hope Franklin, *From Slavery to Freedom* (New York, Alfred A. Knopf, 1956), p. 253.

18. Benjamin Quarles, *The Negro in the Making of America* (New York, Macmillan, 1964), p. 78.

19. *Ibid.*, pp. 121–122.

20. Booker T. Washington, *Up From Slavery* (New York, Doubleday and Company, Inc., 1963), p. 15.

21. Frazier, *op. cit.*, p. 125.

22. *Ibid.*, Chap. IX.

23. A recent Community Council of Greater New York release shows an 87 percent increase in "Negro families with female heads" from 1960 to 1970 and about a third (33 percent) of black families headed by females. See Council 1970 Census Bulletin No. 10, August 26, 1971, p. 1.

24. For an example of the savagery that mob violence could direct against black women see Langston Hughes, *Fight for Freedom* (New York, Berkley Publishing Corporation, 1962), p. 37.

25. William H. Grier and Price M. Cobbs, *Black Rage* (New York, Basic Books, Inc., 1968), p. 54.

26. Robert Staples, "The Myth of the Black Matriarchy," *The Black Scholar*, January-February 1970. Vol. I, 14.

27. Patricia Roberts Harris, "New Life Styles for Women," an address by the former U. S. Ambassador to Luxembourg during Commemoration Day ceremonies, February 22, 1971, marking the 95th anniversary of the founding of the Johns Hopkins University (unpublished manuscript), pp. 21–22.

28. Staples, *op. cit.*, pp. 8, 16.

29. Jeanne L. Noble, *The Negro Woman's College Education* (New York, Bureau of Publications, Columbia University, 1956), p. 20.

30. A. W. Hunton, "Women's Clubs," *The Crisis*, May 1911, p. 17.

31. Benjamin Quarles, *Black Abolitionists* (New York, Oxford University Press, 1969), pp. 178–179.

32. Dannett, *op. cit.*, p. 257.

33. Sadie T. M. Alexander, "Negro Women in Our Economic Life," *Opportunity: Journal of Negro Life*, VIII, June 1930, p. 202.

34. "Negro Women in Industry," *Opportunity*, XII, September 1935, p. 286.

35. For biographical sketches of Judge Bolin and nine other black women judges see Alpha Kappa Alpha Society's "Negro Women in the Judiciary," *Heritage Series* No. 1, Chicago, 1968.

36. Andrew Hacker, *The End of the America Era* (New York, Atheneum Publishers, 1970), Chap. II.

37. Shirley Chisholm, "Racism and Anti-Feminism," *The Black Scholar*, January-February 1970, p. 43.

38. *Underutilization of Women Workers* (U. S. Department of Labor Publication, 1971, rev.), p. iv.

39. See Chapter 3, "Black Personality in American Society." For a provocative analysis of the manner in which the oppressed identifies with and often emulates the oppressor see Stanley M. Elkins,

*Slavery: A Problem in American Institutional and Intellectual Life* (Chicago, The University of Chicago Press, 1959), Chap. IV and V.

40. Walter White, *A Man Called White* (Bloomington, Indiana University Press, 1948), p. 338.
41. Fletcher Knebel, "The Black Woman's Burden," *Look*, September 23, 1969, pp. 77–79.
42. *The Social and Economic Status of Negroes in the United States, 1973*, U. S. Department of Commerce, Bureau of the Census, p. 11–12.
43. "Fact Sheet on Women of Minority Races," prepared by the Women's Bureau of the U. S. Department of Labor for this study. See p. 7. Information from the Department of Labor currently is mainly designated "Minority Races" rather than "Negro" as in the past. Information cited in the fact sheet used in this chapter and identified as "Minority Races" is based on 92 percent black men and women.
44. *Ibid.*, p. 3.
45. *Ibid.*, p. 5.
46. Abbey Lincoln, "Who Will Revere the Black Woman?" *Negro Digest*, September 1966, p. 18.
47. Alpha Kappa Alpha Society, "Negro Women in the Judiciary," Heritage Series, No. 1, Chicago, 1968.
48. Althea Gibson, *I Always Wanted to Be Somebody* (New York, Harper & Brothers, 1958), p. 2.
49. This was not a scientific random sampling, for which there was neither time, funds, nor staff. Professional women, students (both graduate and undergraduate), and women in general were queried. Far more of the former, i.e., professional women and students, are included for the simple reason that they were more accessible. No women are included west of the Rockies. Amazing consistency was found in responses to some questions despite the fact there was no possibility of collaboration and replies came from as far apart as Pennsylvania and Texas. In the text the results of the poll are referred to as "the survey."
50. It would be interesting and revealing if white women and black men could respond to the same three questions. Three white women who were graduate students in a class that answered the questionnaire did reply. One said "for the black, white, or any woman the greatest problem is men." The other two thought prejudice and racial discrimination greater problems facing black women than sex discrimination. Their answers were right in line with those of black women on question three.
51. Ida Lewis, in "Conversation" with Nikki Giovanni, *Essence*, May 1971, pp. 32–33.
52. Toni Morrison, "What the Black Woman Thinks About Women's Lib," *The New York Times Magazine*, August 22, 1971, p. 64.
53. Yvonne R. Chapelle, "The Black Woman on the Negro College Campus," *The Black Scholar*, January-February 1970, pp. 36–38.
54. Interview with Dr. Benjamin Quarles at Morgan State College on the historic role of the black woman, September 1971.
55. Harris, *op. cit.*, pp. 22–23.
56. Dannett, *op. cit.*, p. 247.

# BIBLIOGRAPHY

## Books

Anderson, Marian, *My Lord, What a Morning.* New York, The Viking Press, 1958.

Aptheker, Herbert, *American Negro Slave Revolts.* New York, Columbia University Press, 1945.

Ball, Charles, *Slavery in the United States.* Lewistown, John W. Shugert, 1836.

Cade, Toni, ed., *The Black Woman—An Anthology.* New York, New American Library, 1970.

Cash, Wilbur Joseph, *Mind of the South.* New York, A. A. Knopf, 1941.

Christmas, Walter, ed., *Negroes in Public Affairs and Government.* Yonkers, Educational Heritage, Inc., 1966.

Cleaver, Eldridge, *Soul On Ice.* New York, McGraw-Hill, 1968.

Cromwell, Otelia, et al., *Readings From Negro Authors.* New York, Harcourt, Brace, and Co., 1931.

Dannett, Sylvia G. L., *Profiles in Negro Womanhood.* Yonkers, Educational Heritage Inc., 1964.

Davis, Ossie, *Purlie Victorious.* New York, Samuel French, Inc., 1961.

Douglass, Frederick, *Life and Times of Frederick Douglass.* Boston, De Wolfe, Fiske & Co., 1893.

———— *My Bondage and My Freedom.* New York, Arno Press and *The New York Times*, 1969.

DuBois, W. E. Burghardt, *Darkwater.* New York, Harcourt, Brace and Howe, 1920.

Dunbar, Alice, *The Goodness of St. Rocque.* Dodd, Mead & Co., 1899.

Elkins, Stanley M., *Slavery: A Problem in American Institutional and Intellectual Life.* Chicago, The University of Chicago Press, 1959.

Fishel, Leslie H., Jr. and Quarles, Benjamin, *The Negro American: A Documentary History.* Glenview, Scott, Foresman and Company, 1967.

Franklin, John Hope, *From Slavery to Freedom.* New York, Alfred A. Knopf, 1956.

Frazier, E. Franklin, *The Negro Family in the United States.* Chicago, The University of Chicago Press, 1939.

Gayle, Addison, *The Black Aesthetic.* Garden City, Doubleday, 1971.

Gibson, Althea, *I Always Wanted to Be Somebody.* New York, Harper & Brothers, 1958.

Grier, William H. and Cobbs, Price M., *Black Rage.* New York, Basic Books, Inc., 1968.

Hacker, Andrew, *The End of the American Era.* New York, Atheneum Publishers, 1970.

Henderson, Edwin B. and the Editors of Sports Magazine, *The Black Athlete.* New York, Publishers Company, Inc., 1968.

Higgins, Chester, *Black Women.* New York, McCall Publishing Company, 1970.

Horne, Lena and Schickel, Richard, *Lena.* Garden City, Doubleday and Company, Inc., 1965.

Hughes, Langston, *Fight For Freedom.* New York, Berkley Publishing Corporation, 1962.

Lerner, Gerda, *Black Women in White America: A Documentary History.* New York, Pantheon Books, 1972.

Lyle, Jack, ed., *The Black American and the Press.* Los Angeles, The Ward Ritchie Press, 1968.

Mays, Benjamin Elijah, *Born to Rebel.* New York, Scribner, 1971.

Miller, Elizabeth W., ed., *The Negro in America: a Bibliography.* Cambridge, Harvard University Press, 1970.

Noble, Jeanne L., *The Negro Woman's College Education.* New York, Bureau of Publications, Columbia University, 1956.

Patterson, Lindsay, comp., *The Negro in Music and Art*. New York, Publishers Co., Inc., 1967.

Pauli, Hertha, *Her Name Was Sojourner Truth*. New York, Avon Books, 1962.

Quarles, Benjamin, *Black Abolitionists*. New York, Oxford University Press, 1969.

———— *The Negro in the Making of America*. New York, The Macmillan Company, 1964.

Randall, Dudley, ed., *The Black Poets*. New York, Bantam Books, 1971.

Romero, Patricia W., ed., *In Black America 1968: The Year of Awakening*. Washington, United Publishing Corporation, 1969.

Rublowsky, John, *Black Music in America*. New York, Basic Books, Inc., 1971.

Schulz, David A., *Coming Up Black*. Englewood Cliffs, Prentice-Hall, 1969.

Silberman, Charles E., *Crisis in Black and White*. New York, Vintage Books, 1964.

Sinkler, George, *The Racial Attitudes of American Presidents—From Abraham Lincoln to Theodore Roosevelt*. Garden City, Doubleday and Company, 1971.

Southern, Eileen, *The Music of Black Americans: A History*. New York, W. W. Norton and Company, 1971.

Washington, Booker T., *Up From Slavery*. New York, Doubleday and Company, 1963.

Watkins, Mel and David, Jay, eds., *To Be a Black Woman: Portraits in Fact and Fiction*. New York, William Morrow and Company, Inc., 1970.

Wesley, Charles H., *In Freedom's Footsteps: From the African Background to the Civil War*. New York, Publishers Company, Inc. 1968.

———— *The Quest for Equality: From Civil War to Civil Rights*. New York, Publishers Company, Inc. 1968.

White, Walter, *A Man Called White*. Bloomington, Indiana University Press, 1948.

Wish, Harvey, *The Negro Since Emancipation*. Englewood Cliffs, Prentice-Hall, 1964.

Woodson, Carter Godwin, *The Negro in Our History*. Washington, The Associated Publishers, Inc., 1945.

Wright, Sarah E., *The American Negro Writer and His Roots*. New York, American Society of African Culture, 1948.

## Magazines, Monographs, Papers, and Reference Works

*Afro-American*

Alpha Kappa Alpha's Heritage Series Nos. 1, 2, and 3.

*The Black Scholar*

Community Council of Greater New York Census Release, 1970.

*Crisis*

*Current Biography*

Department of Labor Publications, 1970–1971.

*Ebony*

*Essence*

Harris, Patricia, "New Life Styles for Women," (unpublished manuscript), 1971.

*Look*

*The New York Times Magazine*

*Opportunity*

*Who's Who of American Women*

# BLACK WOMEN OF ACHIEVEMENT

The names included in the following listing are not necessarily the most distinguished black American women, nor are they all the first to achieve recognition; nor do all have national reputations. The achievements described, however, suggest a broad range and variety of talents and abilities; where, as in the fields of entertainment or education, there are many whose claim to distinction is incontrovertible, it has been impossible to include more than a fraction of those who are clearly eligible. Women in fields less in the public eye—scientists, university administrators, business executives— have been sought out; again, however, a complete listing of all equally able or distinguished achievers has not been attempted.

## SELECTED LIST*

**Addison, Adele**

Mezzo-soprano. Leading roles with New York City Opera, New England Opera; soloist with New York Philharmonic, and Boston, Chicago, and Cleveland Symphony orchestras.

**Alexander, Sadie T. M.**

First black woman admitted to the bar in the state of Pennsylvania (1927). Chairman of the Philadelphia Commission on Human Relations. Former Secretary of the New York Urban League. Appointed by President Truman to the U. S. Commission on Civil Rights.

**Anderson, Marian**

World-renowned contralto. Recipient of decorations and awards throughout the world. First black star of the Metropolitan Opera at end of distinguished concert career.

**Angelou, Maya**

Actress, dancer, scenarist. Author of *I Know Why the Caged Bird Sings* (nominated for 1971 National Book Award). Formerly Northern Coordinator for the Southern Christian Leadership Conference.

**Arroyo, Martina**

Soprano. Made Metropolitan Opera debut in 1965 in title role in *Aida*. Has sung in Berlin, Buenos Aires, London, and Hamburg opera houses.

**Ayer, Gertrude Elise (1884–1971)**

First black principal in New York City, appointed by Board of Education to her post at P. S. 24 in 1935.

**Bailey, Pearl**

Singer, actress, television performer, nightclub entertainer. Stage debut in *St. Louis Woman*; won the 1946 Donaldson Award as the year's most promising new performer. Starred in the Broadway production of *Hello, Dolly*.

*Compiled by Dr. Ernestein Walker and Judith Miles of the staff of the Phelps-Stokes Fund.

## Baker, Ella

Civil rights leader. Former Executive Director of the Southern Christian Leadership Conference and a founder of SNCC (Student Nonviolent Coordinating Committee).

## Baker, Josephine (1906–1975)

Film and stage actress, exotic dancer, American-born "toast of Paris." Decorated Chevalier of the Legion of Honor, Croix de Guerre, Rosette de la Resistance (World War II).

## Barnett, Ida B. Wells (1862–1931)

Militant civil rights fighter and crusading journalist; fought against lynching; speaker at home and abroad on behalf of Negro rights. A co-founder of the National Association for the Advancement of Colored People.

## Bates, Daisy

Heroine of early public-school desegregation. NAACP leader, Little Rock, Arkansas.

## Bethune, Mary McLeod (1875–1955)

Founder-President of Bethune-Cookman College; adviser to President Franklin D. Roosevelt; President, National Council of Negro Women. Generally conceded to be the most influential black woman in American history.

## Bolin, Jane Matilda

First black woman judge, Court of Domestic Relations, New York City.

## Bonds, Margaret

Composer and pianist. Won Rodman Wanamaker Award. Composed background scores for *Shakespeare in Harlem* and *U. S. A.*, as well as other works.

## Brooks, Gwendolyn

Poet Laureate of Illinois. First black writer to win a Pulitzer Prize (for *Annie Allen*, 1949). Recipient of two Guggenheim Fellowships and the Eunice Tietjeans Award from *Poetry* magazine. Author of *A Street in Bronzeville* (1945), *Poetry in the Mecca* (1968), *Report from Part One* (autobiography), and other writings.

## Brown, Charlotte Hawkins (1882–1961)

Founder and principal, Palmer Memorial Institute, a private coeducational college-preparatory boarding school.

## Brown, Dorothy Lavinia, M.D.

Chief of Surgery, Riverside Hospital, Nashville, Tennessee. Clinical Professor of Surgery, Meharry Medical College. Once performed operation before national television cameras. Former member, Tennessee House of Representatives.

## Brown, Hollis Quinn (1849–1949)

College teacher; elocutionist; lecturer and dramatic reader; participated in national and international movements. Active in Ohio politics. Author of several books.

## Bumbry, Grace

Mezzo-soprano with the Metropolitan Opera; first black soloist invited to sing at Bayreuth; sang by invitation at the White House.

## Burke, Yvonne Braithwaite

Co-chairman, Democratic National Convention, 1972. Member of Congress; former member, California State Assembly. Lawyer.

## Burroughs, Margaret Taylor Goss

Founder and director of The DuSable Museum of African-American History in Chicago.

### Burroughs, Nannie Helen (1883–1961)

Founding President of National Training School for Women and Girls in Washington, D. C. (1909), renamed in 1964 the Nannie Helen Burroughs School. Writer, editor, religious worker. Activist in black social and economic causes.

### Carroll, Diahann

Actress, singer. First black woman to have own successful TV show (*Julia*). Starred in Broadway musicals, *House of Flowers* and *No Strings*.

### Carroll, Vinnette J.

Director, actress. Artistic Director, Urban Arts Corps. Won Outer Critics Circle Award for her direction of *Don't Bother Me, I Can't Cope*. Won Obie award for her performance in the New York production of *Moon on a Rainbow Shawl*. Directed films: *One Potato, Two Potato, Up the Down Staircase*, and *Alice's Restaurant*. Won Emmy award for directing CBS-TV's *Beyond the Blues* (1964).

### Cary, Mary Ann Shadd (1832–1893)

Publisher of *The Provincial Freeman*, Canadian antislavery weekly. Lecturer; active in fight for woman suffrage.

### Catlett, Elizabeth Alice

Award-winning sculptor. Exhibited widely.

### Childress, Alice

Playwright; author of *Trouble in Mind, Wedding Band, Wine in the Wilderness*, and other plays.

### Chisholm, Shirley

Lawyer. Candidate (1972) for Democratic nomination for President of the United States; first black woman ever elected to Congress, 1968. Member, New York State Assembly, 1964–68.

### Clark, Mamie Phipps

Psychologist. Co-founder and director, Northside Center for Child Development. Member, Board of Directors, American Broadcasting System. Numerous awards for outstanding achievement.

### Cobb, Jewel Plummer

Research scientist. Dean of Connecticut College. Cell physiologist concerned with effect of chemicals on cancer.

### Coppin, Fannie M. Jackson (1835–1912)

Noted lecturer; teacher; social worker. Early honor graduate of Oberlin College.

### Dandridge, Dorothy (1924–1965)

Singer, actress, nightclub entertainer. Starred in motion picture version of *Carmen Jones, Island in the Sun, Porgy and Bess*.

### Davis, Angela

Revolutionary heroine. Formerly Assistant Professor of Philosophy, University of California (Los Angeles).

### Dee, Ruby

Stage, film, and television actress. Starred in stage and screen versions of *A Raisin in the Sun*. Obie and Drama Desk awards for best actress, 1971, for lead in *Boesman and Lena*. Emmy award, 1968, for role in television documentary, *Now Is the Time*. Often co-starred with husband, Ossie Davis. Regular appearances on television.

### de Lavallade, Carmen

Dancer. First black woman dance star with the Metropolitan Opera. Numerous stage, concert, and television appearances. In Broadway's *House of Flowers* (1955). Toured Southeast Asia with de Lavallade/Ailey Dance Company in 1963 for U. S. Department of State.

## Dobbs, Mattiwilda

Lyric coloratura soprano. Former member, Metropolitan Opera; first black to sing at La Scala. Broad following in Europe, America, and elsewhere.

## Dunham, Katherine

Dancer, director, producer, author, choreographer. International performer and expert in primitive dance. Director, Performing Arts Training Center, Southern Illinois University. Headed the well-known Katherine Dunham School of Cultural Arts in New York City. Choreographed *Aida* for the New York Metropolitan Opera in 1963. Author: *Journey to Accompong* (1946), and an autobiography, *Touch of Innocence* (1959).

## Dunnigan, Alice

Award-winning Washington journalist. First woman honored by the National Press Club. First black woman White House Correspondent (1948), member of Senate and House of Representatives Press galleries (1947), member of State Department's Correspondents Association (1947), member of the First Lady's Press Association.

## Edelman, Marian Wright

Director, Center for Law and Education, Harvard University. First black woman admitted to the Mississippi bar (1966). Trustee of Yale University and other institutions and agencies.

## Edwards, Esther Gordy

Senior Vice-President, Motown Record Corporation; active in civic and political affairs. Director of the Gordy Foundation.

## Ellis, Effie O'Neal, M.D.

Physician; special assistant for health services to Executive Vice-President of American Medical Association. Lecturer on maternal and child health, child growth and development, and delivery of comprehensive health services.

## Fauset, Crystal Bird (1894–1965)

Politician. First black woman state legislator; elected to Pennsylvannia State Legislature in 1938. Prominent in Democratic Party; advisor to Mayor Fiorello La Guardia of New York and President Franklin D. Roosevelt.

## Fauset, Jessie Redmon (1886–1961)

Novelist. Wrote of the feelings and concerns of able middle-class blacks in a hostile world in *Comedy, American Style*; *Plum Bun*; *The Chinaberry Tree*; and other works.

## Ferguson, Catherine (1774–1854)

Pioneer welfare worker in New York City. Founded the first Sabbath school for destitute children in 1793. The Katy Ferguson Home for unwed mothers in New York commemorates her years of service.

## Fitzgerald, Ella

Jazz stylist and recording artist. Widely acclaimed in United States and abroad. Holds unique place in annals of popular vocal music.

## Franklin, Aretha

Singer, recording artist. Called the "Queen of Soul." Recorded four golden singles in 1967 and was the first female singer to earn five gold records; several of her long-playing albums have sold over a million copies.

## Freeman, Frankie Muse

Lawyer. Member, U. S. Commission on Civil Rights since 1964. Past President, Delta Sigma Theta sorority. Numerous awards for outstanding achievement in community and public service.

### Fuller, Meta Vaux Warrick (1877–1968)

Sculptor. Studied with Rodin in Paris. Work exhibited in Cleveland Museum of Art and Schomburg Collection in New York City.

### Gault, Charlayne Hunter

Journalist; Harlem Bureau chief, *The New York Times*. One of first two black students admitted to the University of Georgia. Adjunct Professor, Graduate School of Journalism, Columbia University.

### Gaynor, Florence S.

Former Executive Director of Sydenham Hospital in Harlem. Named chief administrator of the largest hospital in New Jersey, Newark's Martland Hospital Center of the New Jersey College of Medicine and Dentistry. First woman in the United States to head a major teaching hospital.

### George, Zelma

Actress, singer, lecturer. U. S. Alternate Delegate to the United Nations, 1960. Civic and community leader. Had title role in *The Medium*.

### Gibson, Althea

Wimbledon and Forest Hills tennis star. First black player at Forest Hills. Top-ranked woman playing in the United States in 1957 and 1958. Won Wimbledon singles championship in 1957 and 1958.

### Giovanni, Nikki

Poet. Editorial consultant, *Encore* magazine. Named a Black Heroine for P. U. S. H., 1972. Author of: *Black Feeling Black Talk, RE: Creation, Night Comes Softly, Angela Yvonne Davis, Spin a Soft Black Song* (poems for children), *Gemini* (autobiographical essays), *My House*, and *A Dialogue: James Baldwin and Nikki Giovanni*.

### Goff, Regina

Educator. Formerly Assistant U. S. Commissioner of Education. Professor of Education, University of Maryland.

### Goodwin, Norma, M.D.

Vice-President for community health and ambulatory care, New York City Health and Hospitals Corporation. President, Provident Clinical Society of Brooklyn. Second Vice-President, National Medical Association.

### Gordon, Nora (1866–1901)

Pioneer missionary to Africa. Protested against atrocities committed in the Congo by the Belgians.

### Grant, Micki

Composer-lyricist, actress, singer, television performer. Received Obie award (1972) for the music and lyrics of *Don't Bother Me, I Can't Cope*; Outer Critics Circle Award (1972) for her music, lyrics, and performance in the same show. Other awards. Appears regularly on television in *Another World* and has acted in *The Blacks*; *To Be Young, Gifted and Black*; and *Brecht on Brecht*.

### Greenfield, Elizabeth Taylor (1809–1876)

World-renowned "Black Swan," nineteenth-century soprano acclaimed in leading European and American cities.

### Hamer, Fannie Lou

Grass roots civil rights leader. A founder, Mississippi Freedom Democratic Party.

### Hamilton, Virginia

Leading novelist for children and young people. Author, *Zeely, The House of Dies Drear, Time-Age Tales of Jahdu*.

## Hansberry, Lorraine (1930–1965)

Her play, *A Raisin in the Sun*, was the first by a black playwright to win the New York Drama Critics Award as Best Play (1959 season). Also wrote *The Sign in Sidney Brustein's Window* (1964); *To Be Young, Gifted and Black* (1968), a dramatic representation of her selected writings; and *Les Blancs*, staged in 1970.

## Harper, Frances Ellen Watkins (1825–1911)

Abolitionist and poet. Her first book, *Poems on Miscellaneous Subjects*, was published in 1854.

## Harris, Patricia Roberts

Lawyer; former United States Ambassador to Luxembourg. Chairman, Credentials Committee, 1972 Democratic National Convention. Former Dean, Howard University School of Law. Director, International Business Machines, Scott Paper Company, and other corporations.

## Harrison, Hazel (1881–1969)

Concert pianist; played with Berlin, Chicago, Minneapolis, and Los Angeles Symphony orchestras.

## Harvey, Clarie Collins

Business woman; civil rights and peace leader. Founder and director, State Mutual Savings and Loan Association, Jackson, Mississippi; founder of Woman Power Unlimited, an interracial human-relations group of Protestant, Jewish, and Catholic women; national president of Church Women United.

## Hedgeman, Anna Arnold

As Executive Director of the National Council for a Permanent Fair Employment Practices Commission in the 1940s, one of the most active black women in national politics. Liaison between H.E.W. and Children's Bureau, White House Conference on Children, 1948–50. Assistant to Mayor Robert Wagner of New York City, 1954–58. Author, *The Trumpet Sounds*.

## Height, Dorothy I.

President, National Council of Negro Women; social worker, National YWCA. Presidential appointee to Commission for Employment of the Handicapped, Commission on the Status of Women, and Equal Employment Opportunity Board.

## Henderson, Freddye S.

Co-founder and Executive Vice-president, Henderson Travel Service (Atlanta), largest black travel agency. Certified Travel Counselor; world traveler. Former president, National Association of Fashion Designers.

## Hicks, Eleanor

U. S. Consul to Nice. Past diplomatic assignment in Thailand.

## Hinderas, Natalie

Concert pianist.

## Holliday, Billie (1915–1959)

Jazz stylist, nightclub and Broadway performer. Known as "Lady Day." Subject of books and films, notably *Lady Sings the Blues*.

## Horne, Lena

Stage and screen personality. First black singer to be featured by a white band; Hollywood's first glamorous black star to be put under long-term contract.

## Hotton, Julia

Assistant Director for Interpretation, Brooklyn Museum of Art. First black woman to assume high museum position in the United States. Former Assistant Director, coordinator for higher education programs, National Educational Television (NET).

### Hubbard, Charlotte Moton

Government official (retired). Deputy Assistant Secretary of State for Public Affairs, 1964–70. Member, Advisory Committee of American Friends Service Committee. Community Service Director, WTOP-TV, 1953–58. Coordinator, Women's Activities, Office of Community Services, 1963.

### Hurley, Ruby

Southeast Regional Director, NAACP. Formerly National Youth Secretary, NAACP. Numerous awards and honors for community service.

### Jackson, Mahalia (1911–1972)

World-famous gospel singer. Her recording of "Move On Up a Little Higher" in 1945 sold over a million copies. Appeared on television, radio, and in concerts throughout the world.

### Jamison, Judith

Dancer. Alvin Ailey American Dance Theater.

### Jarboro, Caterina

First black woman to star in American "white" opera company. Widely acclaimed in Europe and America. New York Opera Association once refused her membership on grounds of race.

### Jones, Clara Stanton

Director, Detroit Public Library. Lecturer and consultant, Detroit Commission on Human Relations. Highly acclaimed for distinguished service in library and community affairs.

### Jordan, Barbara

Lawyer. Member of Congress (Democrat), Texas. Former Texas State Senator.

### Kennedy, Adrienne

Actress. Praised for performance in drama, *In White America* (1964). Playwright: *Funnyhouse of a Negro* (1964).

### King, Coretta Scott

President, Martin Luther King, Jr. Memorial Center. Lecturer, writer, concert singer, civil rights activist. Widow of Martin Luther King, Jr. Member, Board of Directors, Southern Christian Leadership Conference.

### King, Helen

Writer of children's literature. Heads Let's Save the Children, Inc., a Chicago publishing house, geared for the black children's market. Author, *Willy* and *The Soul of Christmas*.

### Kitt, Eartha

Actress, singer, dancer, television and film entertainer. International performer; has appeared in London, Stockholm, Turkey, Greece, and Paris. Began as soloist with the Katherine Dunham Dance Company.

### Koontz, Elizabeth Duncan

Deputy Assistant Secretary of Labor for Employment Standards; Director, Women's Bureau, U. S. Department of Labor, 1969–74. First black president of the National Education Association, 1965–66.

### Lafontant, Jewel Stradford

Third-generation lawyer. Deputy Solicitor-General of the United States, 1972–75 (appointed by Richard M. Nixon). Director, Trans World Airlines; Jewel Companies, Inc. U. S. Delegate to the United Nations, 1972. Vice-chairman, U. S. Advisory Commission on International Educational and Cultural Affairs, 1969–72. First black woman Assistant U. S. Attorney (1955).

## Lewis, Edmonia (1845–1890)

First Afro-American woman sculptor. Exhibited at Philadelphia Centennial; held many shows in the United States and Europe; received commissions from Harvard College and from many prominent citizens.

## Lewis, Ida

Editor and publisher, *Encore*. Former Editor-in-Chief, *Essence*. Was U. S. correspondent for *Jeune Afrique*.

## Lewis, Samella

Artist. Associate Professor of Art, California State University (Long Beach). Coordinator of Education, Los Angeles County Museum of Art (1969–71). Co-editor, *Black Artists on Art*, Vols. I & II. Author, *Art: African American*. Works in Baltimore Museum of Fine Arts, Virginia Museum of Fine Arts, High Museum of Atlanta, Palm Springs Museum, and the Oakland Museum of Art.

## Mahoney, Mary Eliza (1845–1923)

First black graduate nurse in the United States. Helped to found the National Association of Colored Graduate Nurses.

## Marr, Carmel Carrington

Lawyer. Member Public Service Commission, State of New York. Former advisor on legal affairs, U. S. Mission to the United Nations. Former member, Human Rights Appeal Board, State of New York.

## Maynor, Dorothy

Concert soprano. Appeared in the United States and abroad with the New York Philharmonic and Boston, Philadelphia, Chicago, Cleveland, San Francisco, and Los Angeles Symphony orchestras. Founded the Harlem School of the Arts.

## McCullogh, Geraldine

Sculptor. Teacher, Wendell Phillips High School (Chicago). Won the George D. Widener Gold Medal, Pennsylvania Academy of Fine Arts (1964).

## McDaniel, Hattie (1898–1952)

Radio and film actress. First black woman to win Academy Award (for supporting role in *Gone With the Wind*), 1939. Played the title role in the *Beulah* television series.

## Mercer, Mabel

Singer celebrated for subtlety of technique, especially in intimate settings. Born in England, she attained international renown, particularly in Paris. Currently a recording artist for Atlantic Records.

## Michel, Harriet P.

President, New York Foundation.

## Mills, Florence (1895–1927)

Singer, dancer, comedienne. Acclaimed as the leading black entertainer of her time. Roles in *Shuffle Along* and *From Dixie to Broadway*.

## Moore, Melba

Singer, television and nightclub entertainer. Principal role in Broadway production of *Hair*. Won Antoinette Perry award for her performance in *Purlie*.

## Morgan, Norma

Award-winning artist (watercolors, engravings, etchings). Solo exhibitions. Represented in Victoria and Albert Museum, London; Museum of Modern Art, New York; National Gallery and Library of Congress, Washington, D. C.; and other permanent collections.

## Morgan, Rose

Businesswoman. Supervisor of chain of beauty salons; television personality and speaker; executive in mail-order business. Former partner in Rose Meta cosmetics business.

### Motley, Constance Baker

United States District Judge, Southern District of New York. Former Associate Counsel, NAACP Legal Defense Fund. First black woman to serve in New York State Senate and first woman Borough President of Manhattan. Numerous honors and appointments.

### Murray, Pauli

Stulberg Professor of Law and Politics, Brandeis University. Author, *Proud Shoes* (1956); *Dark Testament and Other Poems* (1970); "Jane Crow and the Law: Sex Discrimination and Title VII," *George Washington University Law Review* (1965), the first modern legal article to argue for equal employment rights for women.

### Noble, Jeanne L.

Professor of Education, New York University. Past president, Delta Sigma Theta sorority. Executive Vice-president, National Council of Negro Women. Author, *The Negro Woman's College Education.*

### Norton, Eleanor Holmes

Lawyer. Chairman, New York City Commission on Human Rights. Member, National Staff, March on Washington, 1963. Vice-president, Studio Museum in Harlem. Assistant Legal Director, American Civil Liberties Union, New York City.

### Parks, Rosa

Precipitated Montgomery, Alabama, boycott to end segregation on buses, 1955. Now on staff of Hampton Institute, Hampton, Virginia.

### Perry, Julia

Composer of vocal and orchestra music, including operas. Awards include a Fontainebleau and Boulanger Grand Prix for her Violin Sonata.

### Petry, Ann

Novelist, short-story writer, critic. Early short stories appeared in *Crisis* and *Phylon*. Received Houghton-Mifflin Fellowship 1946. Author, *The Street* (1946), *A Country Place* (1947), other works.

### Pierre-Noel, Lois Mailou Jones

Award-winning landscape painter. Professor of Design and Watercolor Painting, College of Fine Arts, Howard University. Her works hang in the Brooklyn Museum, Corcoran Art Gallery, and other public and private collections around the world. Numerous awards and prizes; decorated by the government of Haiti. Fellow, Royal Society of Arts, London.

### Player, Willa B.

Director, Division of College Support, U. S. Office of Education. Former President, Bennett College. President, National Association of Schools and Colleges of the Methodist Church (1962). Trustee, Ohio Wesleyan University. Distinguished Service Award, Department of Health, Education, and Welfare (1972).

### Price, Florence B. (1888–1953)

First black woman composer to achieve recognition. Won Wanamaker Foundation Award for *Symphony in E Minor* (1925).

### Price, Leontyne

Soprano. Prima donna, Metropolitan Opera. Debut as Leonora in *Il Trovatore* (1961) won a forty-two-minute ovation. Made history in title role in the NBC-TV production of *Tosca*, 1955.

### Primus, Pearl

African dance specialist. Led celebrated dance troupe in performances of African tribal dances. Once called "the greatest Negro dancer of them all" by John Martin, dean of American dance critics.

## Ray, Charlotte E.

First black woman to be graduated from law school (Howard University, 1872).

## Ross, Diana

Singer; recording artist; nightclub entertainer. Led Motown's "Supremes" to international fame. Widely acclaimed for film performance as star of *Lady Sings the Blues* (nominated for Academy Award, 1973). Named female Entertainer of the Year by NAACP (1970). Grammy Award as outstanding female vocalist. Won London *Express* poll as Top Female Singer in the World.

## Sampson, Edith Spurlock

Judge, Circuit Court of Cook County. First black American to represent the United States at the United Nations, 1950, 1952. Trustee, Roosevelt University. Numerous awards and honors, including five honorary degrees.

## Sands, Diana (1934–1975)

Actress. Played the title role in Shaw's *Saint Joan* at New York's Lincoln Center Repertory Theatre. Starred in the Broadway productions of *We Bombed in New Haven*, *The Owl and the Pussycat*, *Blues for Mr. Charlie*. In original cast of *A Raisin in the Sun*.

## Saunders, Doris Evans

Director, Book Division, Johnson Publishing Co., Inc. Secretary, Black Academy of Arts and Letters. Columnist, Chicago *Daily Defender* (1966–70) and Chicago *Courier* (1970–72). Writer, producer of TV show, *Our People* (1968–70). Associate Editor, *Negro Digest* (1962–66). Editor, *The Day They Marched* (1963); *The Kennedy Years and the Negro* (1964).

## Savage, Augusta (1900–1962)

Sculptor, teacher, organizer; studied in New York, Paris, and Rome; exhibited widely in the United States and Europe during the 1920s and 1930s. First director, Harlem Community Arts Center.

## Schuyler, Philippa Duke (1932–1969)

Concert pianist and composer. Child prodigy; first composition, *Manhattan Nocturne*, a symphony for orchestra, written when she was 12, performed at Carnegie Hall. Soloist with the New York Philharmonic Orchestra. Author, *Adventures in Black and White* (1966), *Who Killed the Congo?* (1962).

## Simone, Nina

Pianist-singer. National Association of Television and Radio Announcers named her Female Jazz Singer of the Year (1967). Considered by many to be the top woman jazz performer in the United States.

## Smith, Bessie (1894–1937)

"Queen" and "Empress" of blues. Influenced all contemporary blues singers. Made several "formal city blues" regarded as landmarks ("A Young Woman's Blues," "Lost Your Head Blues"). In 1923 her recording of "Down-Hearted Blues" sold over two million copies in a single year. Appeared in film production of *St. Louis Blues* (1929).

## Spurlock, Jeanne

Professor and Chairman, Department of Psychiatry, Meharry Medical College. First black and first woman to receive the coveted Strecker Award of the Institute of Pennsylvania for outstanding contributions in psychiatric care and treatment (1971).

## Talbert, Mary Burnett (1886–1923)

Patriotic worker during World War I; Red Cross nurse with the American Expeditionary Forces in France. Vice-president and a director of NAACP; chairman of Anti-Lynching Committee. Lectured throughout Europe on race relations and women's rights. Delegate to International Council of Women; fighter for first-class citizenship.

## Terrell, Mary Church (1863–1954)

Co-founder and first president, National Association of Colored Women. Represented black women of America at three international conferences; active in civil rights and in desegregation of Washington, D. C.

## Thompson, Era Bell

International Editor, Johnson Publishing Co., Inc. Author, *American Daughter* (1946, 1967); *Africa, Land of My Father* (1954); *White on Black* (1963). Two honorary degrees; Patron Saints Award (1968) for *American Daughter*; Iota Phi Lambda's Outstanding Woman of the Year (1965).

## Tolliver, Melba

Featured ABC-TV news commentator. Co-host of New York City daytime news/talk show. Anchor person, news program.

## Truth, Sojourner (Isabella Bainfier) (1797–1883)

Civil rights activist, emancipator, fighter for rights of women.

## Tubman, Harriett Rose (1823–1913)

"Conductor" on the Underground Railroad; nurse; spy for Union troops in the Civil War.

## Tucker, C. Delores

Secretary of State, Pennsylvania.

## Turner, Doris

Executive Vice-president, New York's District 1199 Drug and Hospital Workers' Union. Highest ranking woman within the American labor movement.

## Tyson, Cicely

Actress. Two Emmy awards for title role in *The Autobiography of Miss Jane Pittman* (1974). Academy award nomination for Best Actress (*Sounder*, 1972). Other awards. One of first blacks in a television series (*East Side, West Side*).

## Vaughan, Sarah

Vocalist with Earl (Fatha) Hines and Billy Eckstine bands in the forties. Her first record, "It's Magic" sold over two million copies. Selected in 1947 by *Esquire* magazine as the new star of the year. Won the top award in the *Down Beat* polls from 1947 through 1952 and from *Metronome* from 1948 through 1953.

## Verrett, Shirley

Mezzo-soprano. Performed title role in Bizet's *Carmen* at the Spoleto Festival in Italy in 1962 and in the Soviet Union in 1963. Performed with the New York City Opera on the opening program of Lincoln Center, 1964. Soloist with Metropolitan Opera.

## Walker, Maggie L. Mitchell (1867–1934)

Virginia founder of one of the first black banks. Started a fraternal newspaper. First woman bank president.

## Walker, Sarah McWilliam (Madame C. J.) (1867–1919)

Developed a system of beauty culture and hair preparations and products. Reputed to have been the first black American millionaire.

## Washington, Bennetta Bullock

Director, Women's Centers, Job Corps (Department of Labor). Formerly program director of young adults, Phillis Wheatley YWCA in Washington, D. C. Speaker, lecturer. Author, *Youth in Conflict* (1963), *Colored by Prejudice* (1964), other works.

**Waters, Ethel**

Stage and film actress; singer. Starred in *Mamba's Daughters* (1939); *Cabin in the Sky* (1940–44); won New York Drama Critics Award for appearance in *A Member of the Wedding* (1950–51).

**Watson, Barbara**

Lawyer. Assistant Secretary of State; Administrator for Security and Consular Affairs. Former Executive Director, New York City Commission to the United Nations. Trustee, Barnard College.

**Williams, Lorraine A.,**

Vice-president for Academic Affairs, Howard University; historian; author. Editor, *The Journal of Negro History, The Second Series of Historical Publications* (1970–1973), *Africa and the Afro-American Experience* (1973).

**Williams, Maria "Selika" (1860–c.1920)**

A prima donna of the nineteenth-century opera. Gained international fame as a coloratura soprano.

**Williams, Mary Lou**

Composer, pianist, arranger for Duke Ellington, Benny Goodman, and Louis Armstrong. One of the great jazz figures. Recently composed a jazz "Mass" for the Alvin Ailey Dance Company.

**Wilson, Margaret Bush**

Chairman of the Board, National Association for the Advancement of Colored People (NAACP).

**Wright, Jane C., M.D.**

Physician. Internationally known for chemical therapy of cancer. Professor of Surgery and Associate Dean, New York Medical College. Numerous awards and board memberships.

# 10

## *Young Black Americans*

### *Christine Philpot Clark*

## INTRODUCTION

Current concern with both the "generation gap" and racial problems prompts focusing special attention on the young people of America's largest minority group. All societies are committed to the encouragement and channeling of adolescent abilities and energies, but the double challenge of youth and minority membership makes the condition of young blacks a matter of particular importance to the nation.

What *is* the status of black youth today? In what ways can they hope to contribute to and profit from the years to come? Whether working, in the military, unemployed, studying, imprisoned, starting families, or in experimental programs of apprenticeship or learning, are they undergoing an effective and realistic period of preparation? Preparation for what? The kind of adulthood their parents faced, or a life style as yet unknown and hopefully improved as a result of national insights gained during the sixties and seventies?

Blacks presently constitute 11 percent of the American population,[1] but at the lower age levels they account for an increasingly greater proportion of the total citizenry within their respective age groups. Those blacks between 15 and 25 years of age, for example, represent almost 12 percent of that age group; those between 5 and 15, 13 percent; those below 5 years of age, almost 15 percent.[2] Furthermore, with their shorter life expectancy and higher birth rate the median age of blacks is significantly lower than is that of whites: 21.2 years as compared to 29.3 years.[3]

Young black Americans are becoming an increasingly powerful force in the American political consciousness. Speculation about the effect this will have on American public policy includes the possibility of an increase in public employment for blacks, if the private sector continues its reluctance to hire them. It might also lead to a diminution of the importance of the military in national decision-making, given larger proportions of blacks in the armed forces. Possible erosion of basic constitutional guarantees through the use of such measures as preventive detention could also increase, along with a public sense of physical threat from young blacks and fear of their effect on young whites. But whatever the consequences, it is clear that there is a new influence emerging from that growing proportion of American minority youth which is actively if warily testing some treasured American premises.

The notion of leadership as interpreted by young blacks can also be expected to change. The tendency of whites to recognize and expect certain traditional styles and goals in black leadership overlooks the cogent statistic that blacks under 18 years of age represent almost half (44.3 percent) of all blacks. Fifty-five per cent of all black Americans are under 24, two-thirds (67.1 percent) under 35. Among whites, where the phrase "generation gap" is so popular, about a third of all whites (34.2 percent) are under 18; 44.9 percent are under 24.[4]

## YOUNG BLACKS AS STUDENTS

As the major determinant in insuring financial, cultural, and personal advancement in America, education is prized as the *sine qua non* for the better life.

Consequently, those young blacks who seek education are worthy of special note. It is they who are most likely to occupy those positions long closed to their forebears; it is they who will test the old American adage that achievement, rather than birth, is what matters; it is they who within the educational framework have experienced what is probably the first mass attempt at interracial contact on an "equal" basis in America and can thus provide the country with some knowledge of the realities of such contact; it is they who will shape and voice the future ideologies of their people.

### Public School Integration

Throughout the early 1970s, the educational issue of dominant social concern nation-wide has been racial integration in the schools. This has led in turn to widespread political conflict over busing. The census of 1970 showed that the 6,724,000 black youngsters in American public elementary and secondary schools that year constituted 15 percent of all such students nationally.[5] By area, they represented 9.8 percent of that school population in the thirty-two northern and western states; 17.3 percent of that group in the border states (Delaware, Kentucky, Maryland, Missouri, Oklahoma, and West Virginia) and in the District of Columbia; and 27.2 percent of the total public elementary and secondary school enrollment in the eleven southern states.[6]

As to the extent of actual integration nationally, aside from any examination of the qualitative contact within the schools themselves (intraschool and intraclassroom segregation continues even where the school itself is officially characterized as "integrated"), almost two-thirds of all black pupils (66.2 percent) in 1970 were in schools where they constituted from 50 to 100 percent of the enrollment.[7] Given the "tipping point," beyond which whites flee integrated situations in which they are not likely to constitute the majority, future shifts in these figures will probably be substantial. Public school enrollment statistics in the 1970s revealed that only twenty-three of the fifty states had one-half or more of its black youngsters in integrated schools (defined as those attended by minority groups in which white enrollment comprises at least 50 percent).

### Educational Ventures; The Private–Public Mix

Not surprisingly, the early attempts to reduce the statistical gaps for young blacks focused on educational programs that would provide motivation, cultural experiences, and exposure traditionally unavailable to them.

A wholly new vocabulary developed to describe the young whose abilities were not directed toward developing skills required for full functioning in American society. Terms like "disadvantaged" or "culturally deprived" focused on insufficiencies and irrelevancies of the education assigned to black children in terms of mainstream values.

Frequently ventures to reduce these "deprivations" were privately initiated, with eventual resort to governmental aid. Often they were demonstration projects within given school systems that either supplemented or substituted for the standard curriculum. Nevertheless, the need for a national focus on solving the educational problems of black youngsters was so strong that the Federal Government established a Division of Compensatory Education within its Department of Health, Education, and Welfare under Title I of the Elementary and Secondary Education Act of 1965. The Division was eliminated by the Nixon Administration in 1973.

Some of the better known programs have been Higher Horizons, Upward Bound, and the Great Cities School Improvement Program. Each of these represents a different approach toward the same goal: assuring some potentially able young people a broader range of life choices than are offered by the usual sources of education.

Traditionally white private institutions have responded to the need for better education by offering scholarships to black candidates, then adapting curriculum and recruiting black faculty members as they have come to perceive that integrated education involves more than the mere presence of black students. By and large, however, private schools, particularly boarding schools, have not achieved dramatic success in educating black students or even in attracting black faculty and students in a steady stream. It is possible that the changes necessary to reach such objectives are so extensive as to severely strain the commitment and resources of the institutions involved. Nevertheless, considerable efforts have been devoted to furthering such projects as special tutoring, scholarships, and summer and winter enrichment programs by clusters of private schools or individual institutions.

On the whole, neither private nor public education has achieved the easy racial blending once anticipated. Perhaps the history of race conflict has set too controlling a pattern. Yet although tensions have abounded, they have given birth to insights and accompanied educational integration; and as painful as the present transition appears, it may portend fewer and less massive social misunderstandings in the future.

## A New Private Approach to Education

One of the best-known of many private attempts to educate ghetto youth in non-traditional ways has been the Harlem Preparatory School ("Harlem Prep") which grew out of the Street Academy Program of the New York Urban League.

The policies of the Street Academies and of Harlem Prep recognize that rigidities and irrelevancies in curriculum and in teachers' attitudes have blunted the interest of many young blacks in standard approaches to education, especially in large urban areas. (Young whites, of course, level the same criticism against the educational system as it affects them; nevertheless, in the case of black youth, racial and social factors combine to make this a problem of a totally different dimension and character.)

With careful concern for semantics, state-chartered Harlem Prep declares itself an "alternative system" for "early school-leavers."[8] Established in 1967, largely thanks to a two-year $350,000 grant from the Carnegie Corporation, its success has been attributed by its director to a meaningful curriculum with adult interests, honesty of approach, and the aura of acceptance it offers.

Its immediate index of success, in addition to the sense of options it has established, is its 551 graduates, originally dropouts, who have gone on to such colleges as Colgate, Vassar, Berkeley, the University of Buffalo, Harvard, Fordham, and Brown.

In the fall of 1974, Harlem Prep became a part of the public school system. Many of its innovative techniques have been adopted by other high schools throughout the New York City school system.

The Street Academies, of which there are six in New York, are "designed to meet the needs of students who have given up on public school."[9] Their enrollment in 1972 was approximately 500; 50 percent of their graduates go on to college, 20 percent attend professional school, 15 percent go on to work; and the others succumb to social pressures which lead notably to delinquency and the drug culture. The director of the program, Kwami A. Taha, notes that one special "plus" about the academies is that they are not faced with the burden of motivating students. The program is voluntary and young people come because they want to be there.

The innovations in presentation, subject matter, and approach to learning offered by Harlem Prep and the Street Academies have made them models for comparable ventures. The Labor Department's recent $800,000 funding of a similar experimental program aimed at creating a "positive, noninstitutionalized and nontraditional learning climate"[10] indicates a beginning commitment to fresh ways of granting young blacks other options.

## The Evolution of Higher Education

The desire for higher education has increased among blacks, and the 1960s brought revolutionary changes in the kinds of opportunities available to them for college and graduate work. During this period, the thinking about who is "entitled" to higher learning and on what terms shifted quickly and drastically. This was in part the result of some cogent analyses which emphasized the necessity of undergraduate and graduate degrees for even a chance at success in the America of the cybernetics era, pointed up the casual or deliberate exclusion of blacks from access to education in the past, and stressed the implications to America if it failed to respond to the claims of these descendants of slaves, deprived of profit from their labors, while newer immigrants found opportunities awaiting them on these shores.

The nation has responded to this new climate of thought. The greater flexibility of admissions standards in private institutions, open admission in public ones, and increased financial aid and compensatory programs in both types spurred a substantial increase in black college enrollment in the late sixties and early seventies. Incidentally, the granting of some of the demands of young blacks has been beneficial to all American youths. Despite some negative public reactions[11] to the Open Admissions Program in the City University system of New York, for example, 75 percent of those entering under the new admissions policies are white and not black or Puerto Rican, as had been predicted.[12]

Within a five-year period, total black enrollment in American institutions of higher learning more than doubled. The 1964 figure of 234,000 became 434,000 in 1968 and 492,000 in 1969.[13] This rate of increase, impressive as it is, would have to immediately redouble, however, were proportional representation to be achieved with the same percentage of the black population as of the white enrolled in colleges.[14] Since the last two years of the 1960s saw greater commitment to the principle of increasing the numbers of black college students, freshmen enrollment estimates are informative.

In a study by Alexander W. Astin for the American Council of Education and the University of California in the fall of 1974, he noted that while black freshmen had constituted 8.7 percent in 1972, the proportion had declined to 7.4 percent in 1974, although it remained above 6.6 percent in 1970.[15]

The all-black colleges that began to develop after Emancipation, located primarily in the South, have had a legendary influence on black thought and goals in this country.[16] Justice Thurgood Marshall, the only Negro on the Supreme Court, like numerous black leaders, received all his formal education, undergraduate and legal, in black institutions.

By the end of the 1960s there was a decrease in the *proportion* of black students educated at all-black institutions, chiefly due to the expanded efforts of predominantly white institutions to enroll blacks. In 1960 about two-thirds of all black undergraduates were enrolled in black colleges. By 1964 the proportion was just about half (51 percent); and by 1968 it was down to about a third (36 percent).[17]

Thus, "83 percent of the national increase in black American enrollment took place in other than traditionally black institutions,"[18] for although enrollment increased from 120,000 to 160,000 (a 33 percent gain) in the black colleges, with more and more blacks seeking a college education, the proportion of black students attending these institutions diminished, as their enrollment in all other or predominantly white institutions increased by 172 percent, from 114,000 to 310,000.[19] Nevertheless, the majority of black *graduates* still came from black colleges in 1971.[20]

## Black Separation on the Campus

As integration in classrooms increased throughout the nation, youthful cries of "Black Power" abounded, and black students gravitated toward all-black social and political groupings on campus. Was this an answer to the brand of racism practiced by whites? What did it all mean?

Several factors were involved here. Young blacks described the stance of black integrationist leaders as one of begging; they noted with pride the revolutions and new independence of African people; they were all too familiar with the statistical disparities between America's blacks and whites, especially those where "qualifications" were not at issue; and they also knew that their inclusion at white colleges and universities was the result of the pressures exerted and the issues raised, frequently in the streets, by their sisters and brothers during the sixties. Thus this new generation was quick to take advantage of these admittedly superior opportunities for learning; at the same time, it sought the admission of greater numbers of blacks, preached minimal contact with whites, and urged broader curricula to include specific black studies as well as greater academic attention to black roles in history, literature, and science. In so doing, these young people directly countered the behavior of the few Negroes who had preceded them at such institutions, whose small number and often more-favored family background had fostered a belief in their own specialness, thus isolating them from the interests of Negroes as a whole. The lifestyle and values of these earlier black students merged with those of whites, allowing the former to achieve a "success" generally unknown to the masses of Negroes. Also, this earlier group had resisted attracting any special attention for fear that such attention might be negative. Thus there was a substantial shift in stance and attitude in less than half a decade.[21]

Although black students were now *in* "white" institutions, attempting to absorb the great educational resources these institutions had to offer, they were not quite *of* them. In association with whites, as well as other blacks, they remained constantly on the alert for discriminatory attitudes. Young black students today regard relationships with white peers, at a time when they are more possible than ever before, as suspect, feeling that such familiarity could be construed as part of a traditional eagerness among blacks for white regard or favor. There is also another more subtle reason for black resistance to interracial socializing; black Americans resent what they perceive as a tendency among whites to appear to compensate for their past delinquencies by "pumping" blacks for racial insights and information.

Furthermore, the need to keep America on its racial toes dictates the training of a permanent young black eye on racist premises and possibilities in white institutions. Even the selection of major fields of study has its racial implications for young blacks. The heavy concentration of black American youth in such fields as sociology and psychology reflects respectively the assumed availability of related jobs for blacks in the public sector and a need to comprehend the nature of racism and its effect on social structures and personality.[22] The interest in and demand for black history evidenced by young blacks has helped them to note parallels between present events and past experience. Where black students have seemed something less than open to learning, their attitudes have usually derived from the knowledge that if they are too open, they may all too readily become infected with an attitude of racism or class superiority toward other blacks that would prevent the unity essential to the advancement of their people. As young blacks see it, white colleges and universities by their very nature and their previous exclusion of blacks have proved themselves antiblack. Therefore they are automatically suspect.

This need for black solidarity within the white college environment, as well as the political implications of such solidarity, has had a dual effect on black students. Group allegiance is sustaining and psychologically supportive; yet it can be time-consuming, thus leaving less opportunity to study. Since constant or at least regular availability to one another is important and often assumed on campus, if denied it is often interpreted as a lack of commitment to the group (i.e., blacks, fellow black students, or black people in general) and "going for self." This creates a situation in which the concern for academic achievement is secondary to solidarity in the lineup of priorities. This attitude is reinforced by the fact that a major white technique in oppressing blacks has been to measure and set black against black, making any competitive concern for individual excellence appear a sort of betrayal for many black students. After all, it is argued, the best-educated blacks in the nation found their learning little protection against white racism. First things must therefore be first. The group concern for black studies programs, black dormitories, and black cultural centers serve as an important "survival" technique. The following appraisal of black motivation, made in 1940, still applies today. "Consciousness of their status as Negroes and the discrimination which they suffer because of their racial identity not only influences their attitudes toward white people and toward themselves but also affects their attitudes toward broader issues facing mankind generally."[23]

Another phenomenon among young black students is their strong identification with ghetto interests and life styles. There are several obvious reasons for this; for again, these young people do not want to be guilty of the attitudes of superiority which older educated blacks evidenced; further, this ghetto focus is one which whites cannot validly duplicate—giving blacks access to a domain free of possible white intrusion or expertise;

and finally, such expressed commitment to the ghetto excuses their perhaps temporary departure from it. The fact that more black students come from truly poor families instead of "striving" ones that are actually or almost middle-class is another reason for a greater general cynicism about the probabilities and meaning of success. The few early black beneficiaries of education in white schools, coming as they did from relatively affluent backgrounds, moved toward integration largely because their own life styles and those of whites appeared more or less comparable. Increasing economic lags and psychosocial barriers between blacks and whites have caused a greater proportion of young blacks to feel deprived than in earlier years and the stronger thrusts of black leadership will probably emerge from their ranks.

Though dominant, these are not the only forces that motivate black students today. One analysis breaks them down into five basic types: radical activist, militant, revolutionary, anomic activist, and conforming Negro ("Negro" defined as a middle-class-oriented black)—with each category moving toward greater passivity and acceptance of "white" values and goals. The study notes:

> . . . the majority of students involved in the Black student revolt today (mostly militants, radical activists and conforming Negroes) are by no means dead set on destroying America and its institutions. They are, basically, reformers. . . . it is . . . not (Stokely) Carmichael or people like him who will determine if reform or revolution will be the prevailing mode of operation. Under the present circumstances, the chief determiners of this all-important choice will be America itself and those who control this nation. And as far as the Black student revolt is concerned, the sincerity and speed with which this nation's institutions of formal education solve their racial problems will influence strongly the character and the future directions of Black student activities, both in the society at large and on campus.[24]

Students attending all-black institutions are faced with entirely different problems. Although they engineered and realized the dramatic sit-ins in the late fifties and early sixties, their relative decline—both in proportion of all blacks in colleges and ideological influence—stems from the facts of financing faced by those institutions. Their southern locations and dependence on white donors or on conservative state legislatures affect several criteria by which colleges are usually assessed: presidential leadership, attraction of faculty with advanced degrees, and recruitment of upper-level high-school students.

Those black students for whom functioning within the white college has posed conflicts may nevertheless seek haven in the totally black institution, especially now that the recent promise of increased financing raises hopes for the provision of better faculties, plants, libraries, and programs they also seek.[25] Toward the end of the 1960s Vincent Harding, head of the Institute of the Black World in Atlanta, wrote in an open letter to black students in the North entitled "New Creation or Familiar Death," that the sudden, fright-inspired, and probably ephemeral interest of white colleges in black youth should not diminish a necessary commitment to building black ones as well. Suggesting fund-raising as a primary means, he said: "the schools you attend . . . will need our products (both human and informational) if they are to be transformed into viable situations."[26]

The guilt and confusion felt by black students in white colleges has been described by a number of students whose families remain in the black ghettos.[27] At the same time, the dramatic improvement in the economic viability of such families when young members acquire a first-class education is one of the influences which motivates them to continue. How inevitable is a psychological separation, real or imagined, after an academic degree had been earned?

The decision of young blacks to study at white colleges and universities is consistent with their determination to be technically better prepared for responsibilities which only they can assume. At the same time, the demands they make and the attitudes they evidence, although sometimes similar to white ones, have the key distinctions of being voluntary, tactical, and probably temporary, pending their achievement of a firm basic commitment to black people and purposes.

Black students argue the necessity of such an approach for the psychic integrity they need in structuring a functioning and healthy world for their people. Who can but expect that they will do a better job at this than any yet attempted in the American context?

## YOUNG BLACKS AND EMPLOYMENT

Since color has a significance in America that goes beyond the merely visual, we can learn much about its impact by studying comparative rates of unemployment for whites and blacks.[28] The following statistics (Table I) show that the rate of unemployment for teenaged minority members was almost consistently more than double that for whites.

Statistics for the first quarter of 1974 indicate that for the United States as a whole, young whites between 16 and 19 years of age had an unemployment rate of 13.3 percent as compared with 30.7 for nonwhites. White men 20 years and older had an unemployment rate of 3.1 percent as against 6.4 percent for nonwhite men. Again, the unemployment rates for white women 20 years old or more was 4.7, not much more than half the rate for nonwhites (8.0 percent). The pattern conforms with comparative unemployment figures over the past decade at least;[29] and the figures have been relatively stable since early 1973. In short, for all ages, non-white unemployment was much higher—more than double the white rate—in all comparisons except that for women.

According to James Reston, writing in *The New York Times* in March 1975, the recession was an important part of the reason why 41.1 percent of all black teenagers in the country were unemployed.

TABLE I—UNEMPLOYMENT RATES, BY SEX AND AGE: 1973 AND 1974
(Seasonally adjusted. Quarterly averages)

| Sex, Age, and Race | 1973 | | | | 1974 |
| --- | --- | --- | --- | --- | --- |
| | 1st Quarter | 2nd Quarter | 3rd Quarter | 4th Quarter | 1st Quarter |
| BLACK AND OTHER RACES | | | | | |
| Total ...................... | 9.0 | 9.0 | 9.0 | 8.6 | 9.3 |
| Men, 20 years and over ........ | 5.6 | 6.1 | 5.7 | 5.3 | 6.4 |
| Women, 20 years and over ...... | 8.4 | 7.8 | 8.1 | 8.4 | 8.0 |
| Both sexes, 16–19 years ........ | 30.1 | 30.7 | 31.6 | 28.4 | 30.7 |
| WHITE | | | | | |
| Total ...................... | 4.5 | 4.4 | 4.2 | 4.2 | 4.7 |
| Men, 20 years and over ........ | 3.1 | 3.0 | 2.8 | 2.8 | 3.1 |
| Women, 20 years and over ...... | 4.5 | 4.3 | 4.3 | 4.2 | 4.7 |
| Both sexes, 16–19 years ........ | 12.8 | 12.9 | 12.3 | 12.7 | 13.3 |

Source: *The Social and Economic Status of the Black Population in the United States, 1973, 1974,* U. S. Department of Commerce, Bureau of the Census.

The above statistics clearly indicate that the crucial years of disparity are the teens, an age when options are psychologically important and the necessity for realistic hopes is vital. The adage, "As the twig is bent, so grows the tree," still holds. How then will young blacks react to these continued disparities? What do such social failings as these unemployment rates imply about a nation that boasts of its achievements and potential?

## Income

Participation and unemployment rates alone, however, throw little light on the respective gains that blacks and whites reap for their labors. With nearly a third of blacks and less than a tenth of whites below the poverty level (see Chapter 5, "The Black Role in the Economy") data about earnings present few surprises. Those statistics available for the earnings of youth by race indicate generalized racial disparities among males.

TABLE II—HOURLY WAGE EARNINGS OF YOUNG MEN, 1970

| Age | White | Nonwhite |
| --- | --- | --- |
| 15–17 | $1.59 | $1.53 |
| 18–19 | 1.93 | 1.75 |
| 20–25 | 2.78 | 2.14 |

Source: *The Job Crisis for Black Youth,* Report of the Twentieth Century Fund Task Force on Employment Problems of Black Youth (New York, Praeger, 1971), p. 43.

For females, 28 percent of black, as compared to 18 percent of white, out-of-school females in 1970 aged 18 to 24 earned less than $1.50 an hour.[30]

When it comes to who does and does not get jobs, race is more important than education. Even when young blacks manage to acquire levels of schooling comparable to those of their white peers, equivalent benefits do not follow. The 6 percent unemployment rate of white high-school graduates between 16 and 21 years of age is more than doubled (to 12.5 percent) for nonwhite high-school graduates.[31]

And the disparities continue beyond outright joblessness, since once young blacks *do* get jobs, "[t]heir wages are lower; they work fewer hours; their jobs are less attractive; and their advancement is more limited."[32]

It is ironic that it is in the *younger* years, when wage-earners can hold several and varied kinds of jobs, that black earnings are highest in relation to those of whites. Even then, however, black family income is less than three fifths (58 percent) that of whites for all families, although it comes closer (85 percent) for husband-wife families where the age of the family head is under 35 years old. It is not to be forgotten that the black wife is more likely to work than is her white counterpart.[33]

The recession of the 1970s caused nonwhite teen-aged unemployment (16 to 19 years) to rise in metropolitan areas with population of more than 250,000, going from 41,000 in 1969 to 75,000 by the end of 1970. "In addition, perhaps 10,000 more dropped out of the labor force because they could not find jobs."[34]

The diminution in the military draft will also affect the employment possibilities of young blacks.[35] Despite popular beliefs about the advantages of military service for subsequent black male employment, however, closer analyses show racial differentials here as well. "During 1969, 19 percent of the nonwhite males aged from 20 to 24 in the civilian noninstitutional population were veterans (compared with 25 percent of the whites of this age). The unemployment rate for nonwhite veterans was 10.0 percent, compared with 8.1 percent among nonveterans of the same age and race; for white veterans the rate was 5.1 percent compared with 4.5 percent for nonveterans."[36] Thus rates for blacks nearly doubled the corresponding white rates. Furthermore, wages, opportunities for promotion, and use of skills gained in the military depended on the race of the veteran, with the white one benefiting disproportionally.

## Beyond Facts and Figures

In our work-oriented society, a man's employment is the primary measure of his worth. Thus the presence or lack of job opportunities colors every aspect of the social fabric, and recessions and unemployment become focal points of public attention and planning. Furthermore, since the work ethic is so highly valued in the American milieu, employment possibilities frequently determine the absence or presence of family and personal pathologies, because nutrition, education, health, and recreation are all variations of an American's income.

A moving study of street-corner Negroes[37] has portrayed how jobs, more than any other single factor, determine the tone and quality of marriages, friendships, and commitments to children and communities within this group. Given the public concern for possible deterioration of the society, the question of work opportunities for young blacks becomes central. It is yet to be seen whether the stirrings and promises of the sixties and early seventies will make the black American's formative years more profitable in possibility of employment and in level of earnings, but there is hope that the Federal public employment programs being discussed early in 1975 may be advantageous to black youth if administered equitably.

## Government Job-Training Programs

A key effort to reduce personal and psychic losses of all underemployed or unemployed Americans was made under the program authorized by the Manpower Development and Training Act of 1962, since amended. In recognition of the disproportionate burden of social disadvantages that nonwhites bear, the Government, in five out of its eleven work and training programs, had a majority (i.e., more than 50 percent) of nonwhite enrollees. (See Table III.)

**TABLE III**—WORK AND TRAINING PROGRAMS—SELECTED CHARACTERISTICS OF ENROLLEES: 1970

| Year and Program | Total Enrollees (1,000) | Percent | | |
|---|---|---|---|---|
| | | Black and Other Races | Age in Years | |
| | | | Under 22 | Over 22 |
| 1970 | | | | |
| Manpower Development and Training Program (MDTA) | | | | |
| Institutional | 130 | 41 | 37 | 63 |
| On-the-job | 91 | 33 | 35 | 65 |
| Neighborhood Youth Corps | | | | |
| In school (enrolled Sept.-May) | 74 | 46 | 100 | — |
| Out of school (enrolled Sept.-Aug.) | 46 | 50 | 98 | 2 |
| Summer (enrolled June-Aug.) | 362 | 56 | 100 | — |
| Operation Mainstream | 12 | 38 | 4 | 96 |
| Public Service Careers | 4 | 68 | 21 | 79 |
| Concentrated Employment Program | 110 | 74 | 41 | 59 |
| JOBS Program | 87 | 78 | 47 | 53 |
| Work Incentive Program | 93 | 48 | 23 | 77 |
| Job Corps | 43 | 74 | 100 | — |

Source: U. S. Bureau of the Census, *Statistical Abstract of the United States, 1971* (92nd edition.) Washington, D.C., 1971, Table No. 211, p. 133.

Although the data given in Table III includes both the percentages of nonwhites in each of the programs and the percentage breakdown by age for *all* enrollees, it fails to indicate the percentages by age *within* the respective racial groups. It is therefore an assumption that the nonwhite percentage in a given work and training program holds true for any age group therein. Proceeding thus, the number of young blacks—those under 22—reached by these federal work and training programs probably approximates 185,000. But the 368,000 minority group dropouts from high school[38] and the 235,000 still unemployed and seeking work in 1970[39] are living testimony that work and training programs for those under 22 still leave too many unreached. The scope of what remains to be done in providing options for those thousands of young blacks within these groups indicates that governmental programs alone, as massive and expensive as they may be, simply do not yet meet the need.

In addition to work and training programs, other efforts under governmental sponsorship are reaching some young blacks. The Peace Corps, for example, founded in 1961 by President John F. Kennedy as a means of aiding developing nations in need of key skills like teaching, agricultural development, or economic planning has attracted many idealistic people, especially among the young, interested in going forth to other lands and cultures for a two-year period. The ability to participate in this program, however, is limited to those fortunate enough to have gained the necessary skills, to be economically unpressured enough to spare two earning years at subsistence pay, and to have the sophistication required to appreciate and tolerate the long period of alien living. Thus there is an obvious class bias, limiting the number of blacks who can commit themselves to the Peace Corps experience.

One special recruiter of minorities estimates that there are only 1500 nonwhites out of the 50,000 who have volunteered for Peace Corps service;[40] the 1500 figure includes all American minorities, not just blacks, and constitutes under 3 percent.[41] The limited involvement of blacks in the Peace Corps and other such programs emphasizes that only a certain level of educational and economic security allows people "the luxury of giving unto others—without worry."[42]

## Programs Sponsored by Industry

Corporations have made some attempts to alleviate the plight of young blacks whose general welfare ultimately affects business interests.

Some companies have involved themselves directly in local education, providing instruction and promising to employ graduates. General Electric's Corning Lamp Division in Cleveland equipped and staffed a special school for the disadvantaged. Michigan Bell Telephone and Chrysler "adopted" ghetto-based schools in Detroit.[43]

In Huntsville, Alabama, a center for the aerospace industry, several contractors organized the Association of Huntsville Area Contractors, which sought to supplement the science curriculum in local schools by providing their own personnel to teach aerospace courses.[44]

The Mobil Corporation sponsors a "work co-op" program at a New York City high school, whose success leads to the hope that similar efforts will be put into effect around the nation. Called the "High School Service Station Training Program," its students attend school full-time during the first semester and alternate weeks in the second semester, one week working in a Mobil service station and the other in the classroom. Initiated in 1971, the program is now being extended because the weekly attendance rate of those participating in the program is 95 percent, compared to 30 percent for the rest of the school.[45]

Corporations recognize, however, that with the best of intentions and efforts they can do little to lessen the magnitude of problems affecting young blacks. The Director of Urban Affairs for Standard Oil of Indiana noted that during the period that the company had committed itself to training 15,000 Chicago high-school dropouts considered "hard-core unemployed," 45,000 more students dropped out.[46]

The traditional American focus on the role of the private sector continues. When the Committee for Economic Development issued a 1971 report on "Social Responsibilities of Business Corporations," it acknowledged that "in national problems such as racial discrimination, a company's concern usually is focused on the local community."[47] Thus a nationwide compilation of such efforts is not readily available, but the dollar amounts from the corporate coffers to such social causes do indicate that voluntary corporate contributions will hardly provide final solutions.

Federal tax law allows corporations to deduct donations of up to 5 percent of their profits from their taxable income. But corporate contributions in this area average only 1 percent of profits annually.[48] Young companies like Xerox and IBM have established progressive records, but according to the *Wall Street Journal* the "richest companies are skinflints,"[49] with banks appearing the most generous because they give 2.1 percent of their pretax income to charities. The fact that companies also write off these financial contributions[50] suggests the light in which corporations view their support for the solution of social problems.

An examination of how private philanthropy is directed demonstrates that the social problems of young blacks are hardly a priority item (see Chapter 13); religious institutions received 44.8 percent ($8.2 billion) of these contributions in 1970. Education and health or hospitals were the runners-up, with respective gifts to them of $3.05 and $3.02 billion, or about 16 percent in each case. With 77 percent of all private giving allotted to the above causes, $1.26 billion was assigned to the "human resources" category and corporations gave only a small part of this to programs of interest to young blacks. The arts, civic causes, and foreign aid brought up the rear of American philanthropic recipients.[51]

This 1970 *total* expenditure of $1.26 billion in private philanthropy for "human resources," only part of which went to the cause of young blacks, is less than the $1.34 billion which the Federal Government granted to *compensatory education programs*[52] alone or the $1.36 billion it gave to work and training programs in that same year.[53] Such comparisons give a sense of the minuscule proportion of private, and especially corporate, assumption of responsibility toward the predicament of young black Americans.

Total corporate contributions have diminished with the economic recession. Also, according to one authoritative assessment, "Much has been made of these limited activities. . . . There is no reason to expect that employers will be any more willing to involve themselves in education than they have in the federally subsidized training programs, where their voluntary contributions frequently dried up when the publicity value waned."[54]

Surprisingly, corporate sources themselves do not disagree. *Fortune* devoted a special issue to "Business and the Urban Crisis," in which it editorialized that it would not "do to pretend that corporations can make major investments in the cities on a nonprofit basis."[55]

# THE BLACK SOLDIER

The draft laws, with their network of allowances for the pursuit of higher education and for religious objections, combine with everyday social forces in determining that people with fewer civilian options are more likely to choose the military for employment, education, or other advancement. Thus young blacks, pressed as they are by racial limitations on school and work opportunities, frequently resort to the military as a means of circumventing such limitations.

The data indicating the proportions of blacks who are drafted or who attempt enlistment are less useful than reenlistment figures, since the initial disqualification rates for blacks, based on medical, mental, or administrative criteria, are higher.[56] A study of first-term reenlistments suggests the awareness that young blacks have about their relatively limited chances in the civilian world.

TABLE IV—REENLISTMENT RATES OF SERVICEMEN: 1968 TO 1970

| Year | Inductees | | Enlistees | |
|---|---|---|---|---|
| | Black | White | Black | White |
| 1968 | 15 | 9 | (NA) | (NA) |
| 1969 | 14 | 11 | 21 | 14 |
| 1970 | 14 | 9 | 18 | 11 |

Note: Figures are for servicemen who have earned honorable status and otherwise demonstrated the qualities necessary for career service in the Armed Forces. Only first-term servicemen are included.
(NA) Not available.

Source: *The Social and Economic Status of Negroes in the U. S., 1970*, p. 137.

On the whole, the proportion of blacks in the armed services is consistent with their ratio in the total American population. On March 31, 1970, blacks comprised 10 percent of the armed forces. They constituted a tenth of those serving in Southeast Asia, and accounted for 13 percent of service-connected deaths in Vietnam.[57]

In 1965, blacks constituted 14.6 percent of those killed in Vietnam; by 1966 the percentage was up to 16 but this figure declined in each succeeding year to 12.5 percent in 1970.[58] This steady decrease was not a result of the winding down of the Vietnam War, because in 1968 when the total number of deaths for all American forces was at its peak of 14,592[59] the black percentage of these deaths had declined to 13.5 percent. Still, civil rights activists focused on this disproportionate number of deaths among blacks as additional evidence of both racist military assignments and the attraction of higher combat pay to black soldiers, fostered by the same social and economic pressures they endure at home.

## Beyond the Facts and Figures

The young black soldier has gradually gained attention for several reasons. His demands for equality have focused international attention on its absence, thus making the concept of American protection of democracy on foreign territory suspect. His exposures to other cultures, values, and political systems have made him more sophisticated and less amenable to the kinds of explanations and techniques used in the past to pacify his people. And there is yet another aspect to the matter that is revealed by two widely distributed public-service posters. One reads, "He's home—with maturity, ambition, and skills." The other has in the foreground a large picture of a black soldier in combat gear and with rifle in hand; it urges, "Don't forget, hire the vet." These messages have a particular implication for the returning black soldier: will his youth and much-publicized anger against the injustices perpetrated upon him in civilian and military life prompt him to use his combat training when he inevitably encounters discrimination on the home front?

Mark Essex, the 23-year-old black Navy veteran whose sniping and suicidal shoot-out with New Orleans police in January 1973 resulted in the deaths of six whites, is a case in point. Psychological postmortems attribute his shift from an easy-going, good-natured youth to a defiant and determined killer to his "treatment by white enlisted men and petty officers in the Navy."[60]

A *New York Times* survey[61] noted the new trends in thinking among black veterans returning to American civilian life; it observed that the military has "outstripped civilian moves towards racial cooperation" but was "particularly inept at dealing with an aroused black consciousness in Negroes." Concluding that the "situation of the Negro veteran cannot be separated from the situation of the Negro community," the *Times* quoted a range of opinions that black GI's have about their service and status in America:

> We shouldn't fight for this country until it's worth fighting for. . . . we're questioning everything now.

> I'm ashamed of what I did in Vietnam. We did to yellow people what whites do to us.

> The rights we fought for for someone else just don't exist for us.

> . . . we've come back to SOS—the same old stuff. It's business as usual in America, and business as usual means black people are going to catch hell.

> The brother in Vietnam closed his eyes to the prejudice he knew existed [hoping] America would change because he fought for her. It didn't make a bit of difference.

The views of older black veterans, one an octogenarian who fought in World War I and the other a survivor of World War II, lend some historical perspective:[62]

> These young people know what they want and they know what's going on in this country. When I was in the war I believed everything they told us. I had no education. They told us to "go catch the Kaiser and everything'll be all right." We went over there and fought and the first thing I heard when I got back to Waco, Texas, was a white man telling me to move out of the train station. He said, "Nigger, you ain't in France any more, you're in America." He didn't even give me time to take off the uniform.

And from the World War II vet:

> No more of that . . . stuff about it takes time. It didn't take time to get a whole lot of colored boys killed in Vietnam, did it?

Finally, because the routines and regimen of military life make it possible to impose order upon racist and disruptive behavior in a way that seems less feasible in American civilian life, the military appears better to control and respond to its racial problems. For example, after an investigation of internal racial troubles among servicemen stationed in Germany, the Defense Department established courses in race relations and ordered post commanders to set numerical goals and timetables aimed at ending off-base discrimination, not an impossible task in light of the fact that numerous private facilities could survive only through the expenditures made by military personnel. To assure decisive action, the department threatened the removal or reassignment of officers, failing to produce satisfactory results.[63]

The government has indeed been concerned about the problems of returning servicemen—their cynicism about the Vietnam War, their reactions to unemployment, and their drug problems which several programs have been designed to alleviate. The Department of Defense has established the Jobs for Veterans program that urges employers to hire returning GI's, and Project Transition, which trains those veterans with marginal skills to upgrade them for civilian employment.[64] The Department of Health, Education, and Welfare has established a Servicemen's Early Educational Counseling program under which specialists are dispatched to military billets around the world to inform soldiers soon to be discharged about the opportunities and federally financed benefits available for further education.[65] Thus it is hoped that the disappointments of idleness and the frustration of fruitless searching for employment can be forestalled. Naturally, black servicemen will reap some benefits from such efforts.

Recognizing the fact that the difficulties of black veterans require special attention, private agencies have acted to supplement governmental programs. One such instance has been a Rockefeller grant to the Urban League "to establish an independent veterans' affairs center in eleven different cities to aid returning black GI's in their transition to civilian life." The League in turn hopes to expand its efforts to forty cities; to do so it needs a $2.2 million budget. Some indication of the gap between the need and the reality, however, is the fact that this effort reached only 5 percent of the 100,000 black GI's mustered out of the armed forces in 1970.[66]

As of January 1973, the total unemployment rate for veterans was 5.2 percent; for black veterans, however, it was 14.5 percent.[67]

In spite of the difficulties involved, it is glaringly obvious that only changes in the racial climate on the domestic front can make civilian life comfortable for the black soldier both before and after he has served his country.


## THE YOUNG BLACK PRISONER: NEW FACTORS AND OLD FIGURES


An assessment of a people's progress might normally exclude an examination of its prisoners. In the inverted experience that is black American life, however, it is essential to look to this area to comprehend the black expectations of today and tomorrow.

The many contemporary heroes of young blacks have spent considerable time in prison; and most of these have written of their views while there. Among them are Malcolm X, Rap Brown, Martin Luther King, Eldridge Cleaver, Angela Davis, and George Jackson[68]—all people who in their individual ways challenged the American exclusion of black people from seeking or achieving such essentials to the good life as decent jobs, housing, and education. All but the first two named wrote major works while imprisoned.

The civil rights movement of the early 1960s saw masses of young blacks beaten by policemen, bitten by dogs, knocked down by the force of fire hoses, and herded into huge prison camps all too reminiscent of World War II Germany. Their crime: sitting-in at restaurants to establish their legal right to the same type of service in public accommodations that whites took for granted.

Television made vivid to all American youth the inappropriateness of the punishment for the crime. The eventual reversals by the Supreme Court of the lower court convictions of those idealistic young people who had put their bodies on the line could not, therefore, erase the memory of injustice. The riots throughout the last half of the sixties, while offensive to whites, seemed understandable and anything but wrong to blacks.

At the same time, the inequities of the American legal system received public attention. Not everyone could get a lawyer; no rich man suffered execution; the wealthy were given shorter sentences. All of these circumstances were common knowledge; but since widespread poverty within the black community was almost considered routine, it was the racism in the workings of American law rather than the economic aspects of the problem that glared most harshly in the public eye.

Whereas at one time preceding the sixties, blacks might have thought with some shame about their greater presence in prisons, imperceptibly this attitude began to change. The civil rights movement had "proven" to young blacks that whites will themselves go so far as to commit the illegal in order to keep blacks in line. Furthermore, to young blacks the message of police shootings during the riots was that a black life was not worth a television set. Given the fact that the unemployed black worker could not get a job when he sought one, and his employed brother was among the lowest paid and the first fired if times were hard, stealing could be readily justified. The tenor of young black thought has seemed to follow along such lines.

Some young black prisoners have done in jail what whites do at college. They have sought new ways of looking at themselves in relation to their environment and past values. They have read, thought, and learned by testing their ideas against those held by others, whether fellow prisoners, guards, prison administrators, or newly discovered writers. Prison is frequently the first place in a poor black's life where he does not have to worry about eating and has access to a decent library.

Malcolm X writes:

> ... feeling I had time on my hands, I did begin a correspondence course in English. When the mimeographed listings of available books passed from cell to cell, I would put my number next to titles that appealed to me. ... After about a year, I guess, I could write a decent and legible letter. About then, too, influenced by having heard Bimbi [another inmate] often explain word derivations, I quietly started another correspondence course—in Latin.[69]

And more:

> Norfolk Prison Colony's library was one of its outstanding features. A millionaire named Parkhurst had willed his library there; he had probably been interested in the rehabilitation program.

> History and religions were his special interests. Thousands of his books were on the shelves, and in the back were boxes and crates full, for which there wasn't space on the shelves. At Norfolk, we could actually go into the library ... walk up and down

the shelves, pick books. There were hundreds of old volumes, some of them probably quite rare. I read aimlessly, until I learned to read selectively, with a purpose.[70]

Eldridge Cleaver has devoted a whole essay[71] to his daily prison routines, focusing on the prison library and the unavailability of contemporary reading matter that the state authorities believe might incite inmates to the kinds of thoughts and actions pertinent to their political predicament. Apart from that objection, Cleaver noted that the library "does have a selection of very solid material, things done from ten years ago all the way back to the Bible."[72]

Claude Brown found his reformatory experience neither so harsh and strange as prison is for adults nor as Harlem had become for him. He writes in his autobiography *Manchild in the Promised Land:*

> The Harlem that I had dreamed of and wanted to get back to seemed gone. . . . I was like a stranger. . . . But I knew that more than anything in the world, I wanted to get back to Wiltwyck. Wiltwyck had become home, and I felt like a butterfly trying to go back into the cocoon.[73]

Increasingly popular in the repeated litany of racial injustices is the "revolutionary" young black notion that since American politics structure the societal conditions causing the crimes of which blacks are accused, black inmates are in fact political prisoners. Consequently, their plight resembles that of those dissidents in foreign countries who find themselves incarcerated because of their opposition to the regime in power.

George Jackson, another author-hero of young blacks, presents this analysis:

> Very few men imprisoned for economic crimes or even crimes of passion against the oppressor feel that they are really guilty. Most of today's black convicts have come to understand that they are the most abused victims of an unrighteous order.[74]

> These prisons have always borne a certain resemblance to Dachau and Buchenwald, places for the bad niggers, Mexicans, and poor whites. But the last ten years have brought an increase in the percentage of blacks for crimes that can *clearly* be traced to political-economic causes. There are still some blacks here who consider themselves criminals—but not many. Believe me, my friend, with the time and incentive that these brothers have to read, study, and think, you will find no class or category more aware, more embittered, desperate, or dedicated to the ultimate remedy—revolution.[75]

And Angela Davis writes similarly:

> Even in all Martin Luther King's numerous arrests, he was not so much charged with the nominal crimes of trespassing, disturbance of the peace, etc., but rather with being an enemy of southern society, an inveterate foe of racism. When Robert Williams was accused of a kidnapping, this charge never managed to conceal his real offense—the advocacy of Black people's incontestable right to bear arms in their own defense.[76]

The September 1971, tragedy of Attica, in which forty-three prisoners and hostages were killed by state authorities who sought to retake the captured New York prison in the belief that the lives of the hostages were in the balance, heightened the presence and strength of blacks in articulating such sophisticated ideas. Although whites, other than a liberal minority concerned with the profound racial implications involved, were generally reported as unsympathetic, young blacks voiced pride in the effective and well-reasoned arguments of the black leaders at Attica, themselves young people. Here, then, is further evidence that their awareness of the discrimination they suffer has caused young blacks to view broader issues in a light totally different from that of whites.

The figures for black prisoners[77] in New York State are of special interest in light of the Attica riots of 1971. At the end of 1970 blacks constituted 51 percent of the 12,579 inmate population under custody in the state's correctional institutions; whites comprised 32 percent. (See Table V.) Young people under 30 constituted 66 percent of the total state inmate population. Within each age category, blacks were consistently greater than one-half: specifically, between the ages of 16 and 18, the black and white percentages were 51 and 39 respectively; between 19 and 20 years of age the percentages were 55 and 31; and the 21 to 29 age group found the black percentage at 54 and the white at 29 percent.

TABLE V—INMATES UNDER CUSTODY IN NEW YORK STATE CORRECTIONAL INSTITUTIONS, BY AGE AND RACE OR NATIONALITY; DECEMBER 31, 1970

| Race or Nationality | Total | Age on Commitment | | | | | | |
|---|---|---|---|---|---|---|---|---|
| | Number | Age Not Available | 16–18 Years | 19–20 Years | 21–29 Years | 30–39 Years | 40–49 Years | 50 Years and Over |
| Total Inmates | 12,579 | 72 | 1,784 | 1,452 | 5,323 | 2,658 | 904 | 386 |
| White | 4,146 | 42 | 695 | 463 | 1,594 | 831 | 340 | 181 |
| Black | 6,735 | 26 | 921 | 807 | 2,918 | 1,408 | 476 | 179 |
| Puerto Rican | 1,639 | 1 | 155 | 171 | 791 | 411 | 85 | 25 |
| Other | 56 | — | 13 | 11 | 20 | 8 | 3 | 1 |
| Not Available | 3 | 3 | — | — | — | — | — | — |

Source: New York State Special Commission on Attica, Robert McKay, Chairman, December 31, 1970 (Internal Document).

National figures for 1972 indicate a similar pattern for the United States as a whole. Blacks that year constituted 33 percent of the total number of persons arrested for serious offenses, according to the Federal Bureau of Investigation *Uniform Crime Reports* (1970). (See also Table VI.)

These statistics have been open to a variety of interpretations. Young blacks reject the contention of some whites that incidence of criminal activity reflects something other than the debilitating social conditions which blacks experience almost routinely but which whites have not been forced to endure.

TABLE VI—PERSONS ARRESTED—RACE, SEX, AND AGE: 1960 TO 1972
[Population represented and persons arrested in thousands]

| Item | 1960 | 1965 | 1967 | 1968 | 1969 | 1970 | 1971 | 1972 |
|---|---|---|---|---|---|---|---|---|
| RACE | | | | | | | | |
| Agencies reporting, number .............. | (1) | 4,043 | 4,508 | 4,758 | 4,627 | 5,208 | 5,610 | 6,114 |
| Population represented.. | 73,474 | 125,139 | 135,203 | 135,545 | 133,028 | 142,474 | 146,564 | 150,922 |
| Persons arrested[2] ........ | 3,499 | 4,743 | 5,265 | 5,349 | 5,577 | 6,257 | 6,626 | 6,707 |
| White ............... | 2,321 | 3,235 | 3,631 | 3,700 | 3,843 | 4,373 | 4,624 | 4,664 |
| Black................. | 1,065 | 1,348 | 1,463 | 1,472 | 1,559 | 1,688 | 1,791 | 1,848 |
| Other................. | 113 | 160 | 172 | 178 | 175 | 196 | 211 | 195 |
| SEX AND AGE | | | | | | | | |
| Agencies reporting, number .............. | (3) | 4,062 | 4,566 | 4,812 | 4,759 | 5,270 | 5,649 | 6,195 |
| Population represented.. | 81,661 | 134,095 | 145,927 | 145,306 | 143,815 | 151,604 | 155,446 | 160,416 |
| Persons arrested[2] ........ | 3,679 | 5,031 | 5,518 | 5,617 | 5,862 | 6,570 | 6,967 | 7,013 |
| Male .................. | 3,272 | 4,432 | 4,830 | 4,891 | 5,058 | 5,624 | 5,923 | 5,956 |
| Female ............... | 406 | 600 | 689 | 725 | 804 | 947 | 1,044 | 1,057 |
| Under 18 years ........ | 527 | 1,074 | 1,340 | 1,457 | 1,500 | 1,661 | 1,797 | 1,794 |
| 18–24 years .......... | 654 | 1,050 | 1,274 | 1,372 | 1,514 | 1,785 | 1,935 | 1,958 |
| 25–34 years .......... | 787 | 891 | 928 | 931 | 990 | 1,128 | 1,203 | 1,270 |
| 35–44 years .......... | 793 | 917 | 882 | 828 | 823 | 887 | 900 | 884 |
| 45–54 years .......... } | 916 { | 670 | 667 | 627 | 635 | 685 | 697 | 681 |
| 55 and over ........... } | { | 421 | 426 | 401 | 398 | 425 | 430 | 413 |

[1]For 2,446 cities with population over 2,500.

[2]Each person arrested is counted rather than the number of charges filed against one person. Includes persons for whom age was not known, not shown separately in breakdown by age.

[3]For 2,460 cities with population over 2,500.

Source: *Statistical Abstract of the United States*, 1974, U. S. Department of Commerce, Bureau of the Census, p. 152.

Execution figures are even more stark. Although representing only 10 to 12 percent of the population, blacks have suffered 54 percent of the executions between 1930 and 1973. Young blacks believe that America values black life much less than impartial justice would have it. Also the figure indicating that blacks have accounted for 89 percent of all executions for rape appears to them more revealing of white fantasies and fears than true criminal behavior on the part of Negro Americans. (See Table VII.)

Both white perceptions and reactions to young black criminality and the relative absence of positive options to young blacks for alternative kinds of behavior accounts for their disproportionate executions and presence in the nation's correctional institutions. As we have seen, young blacks, in and out of prisons, believe this to be so and they go on to point out the inadequacy of recreational opportunities as almost demanding youthful black activity to take the form of criminal outbursts.

**TABLE VII—PRISONERS EXECUTED UNDER CIVIL AUTHORITY, BY RACE: 1930 TO 1973**
[Includes 3 Federal executions in Alaska, 1 each in 1918, 1939, and 1950. Excludes executions by military authorities. The Army (including the Air Force) carried out 160 (148 between 1942 and 1950, 3 each in 1954, 1955, and 1957, and 1 each in 1958, 1959, and 1961). Of the total, 106 were executed for murder (including 21 involving rape), 53 for rape and 1 for desertion. The Navy carried out no executions during the period. See also *Historical Statistics, Colonial Times to 1957*, series II, 432–444]

| Type of Offense and Race | All Years | 1930– 1939 | 1940– 1949 | 1950– 1959 | 1960– 1961 | 1965 | 1966 | 1967 | 1968– 1973[4] |
|---|---|---|---|---|---|---|---|---|---|
| Total ............. | 3,859 | 1,667 | 1,281 | 717 | 181 | 7 | 1 | 2 | – |
| White ........... | 1,751 | 827 | 490 | 336 | 90 | 6 | 1 | 1 | – |
| Black ........... | 2,066 | 816 | 781 | 376 | 91 | 1 | – | 1 | – |
| Other ........... | 42 | 21 | 13 | 5 | – | – | – | – | – |
| Murder ............. | 3,334 | 1,514 | 1,064 | 601 | 145 | 7 | 1 | 2 | – |
| White[1] ........... | 1,664 | 803 | 458 | 316 | 79 | 6 | 1 | 1 | – |
| Black[1] ........... | 1,630 | 687 | 595 | 280 | 66 | 1 | – | 1 | – |
| Other ........... | 40 | 24 | 11 | 5 | – | – | – | – | – |
| Rape .............. | 455 | 125 | 200 | 102 | 28 | – | – | – | – |
| White ........... | 48 | 10 | 19 | 13 | 6 | – | – | – | – |
| Black ........... | 405 | 115 | 179 | 89 | 22 | – | – | – | – |
| Other ........... | 2 | – | 2 | – | – | – | – | – | – |
| Other offenses[2] ...... | 70 | 28 | 20 | 14 | 8 | – | – | – | – |
| White[3] ........... | 39 | 14 | 13 | 7 | 5 | – | – | – | – |
| Black ........... | 31 | 14 | 7 | 7 | 3 | – | – | – | – |

– Represents zero
[1]White includes 18 females; black, 12 females
[2]25 armed robbery, 20 kidnaping, 11 burglary, 8 espionage (6 in 1942 and 2 in 1953), and 6 aggravated assault.
[3]Includes 2 females, both executed in 1953, 1 for kidnaping and 1 for espionage.
[4]There have been no executions since 1967, and the legal basis for capital punishment was undermined by the Supreme Court on June 29, 1972. (*The New York Times,* June 30, 1972, p. 1.)
Source: *Statistical Abstract of the United States,* 1972, p. 164.

Since prisons contain those blacks who either dared or are considered to have dared the criminal conventions, it is there that the nation's most intensive concentration per square yard of young and angry blacks can be found. It is a truism that prisoners feel the need to allege their innocence. The racial twist here is the fact that those who are not white can now "justify" many of their actions in the light of the never-ending list of social, economic, and legal disparities they have met. Though the outside world rarely makes or accepts the connection between something so apparently vague as "social climate" and individual criminal behavior, young black, Mexican-American, and Puerto Rican prisoners now do. Their belief in their own victimization eliminates the guilt and sense of wrongdoing on which notions of rehabilitation rely.

Prison as a base for learning the refinements of criminal techniques is no new topic.

> We all came out of Warwick better criminals. Other guys were better for the things that
> I could teach them, and I was better for the things that they could teach me. Before I

went to Warwick, I used to be real slow at rolling reefers and at dummying reefers, but when I came back from Warwick, I was a real pro at that, and I knew how to boost weak pot with embalming fluid. I even knew how to cut drugs. . . . I learned a lot of things at Warwick.[78]

The fact that inmates gain greater direction toward the very activities and attitudes that the prisons theoretically aim to correct means that drug pushing and use, homosexuality, and other such socially-disapproved behavior can only spiral. To the young black eye, the irony implicit here is evident.

If anything, the new breed of blacks regards iron bars and mere physical confinement as little contrast to their daily imprisonments of poor education, employment problems, low housing or health standards, and limited income. The possibility that a jail record could make much difference in a future already guaranteed to be clouded by the distortions of racism is comparatively unalarming. Thus many articulate young blacks feel that they must at all costs reject the values and premises of a society that denied them reasonable chances in the first place. Consequently, their participation and investment in society may not resemble what America would wish of them.

## ORGANIZED MOVEMENTS OF YOUNG BLACKS

In view of what they feel to be the gulf between the immensity of their problems and any solutions so far attempted, young blacks have decided to move toward their own relief. The various church groups, scout troops, neighborhood youth efforts, social clubs, and basement gatherings that have sprung up toward this end are too numerous to be mentioned here but special attention must be given to the impressive role played by the student movement. It is the students who have demanded black studies and the spotlighting of black heroes, who have promoted black art and insisted on black participation at top levels of decision-making, who have detected and publicized premises damaging to the black psyche. They have not limited themselves to any single aspect of racism nor focused on a single target. In the sense of the term that for blacks indicates constant motion directed against racial onslaughts, black students have been *the* national movement. Any successful and sustaining thrust to promote the interests of black people is likely to number students among its most important members.

The student movement's rallying point has been the university, a microcosm of the nation at large, reflecting all the issues hurting black people. Academic life not only provides the time to study, probe, peruse, and finally document, but to strengthen determination as well. The Afro-American Societies and Black Student Unions, although not formally organized into a single national movement, have served as focal points for activity on the local level as well as providing a basis for intercampus contacts.

Three additional major movements of young blacks have particularly impressed the American consciousness. These are the Southern Christian Leadership Conference (SCLC), the Student Nonviolent Coordinating Committee (SNCC), and the Black Panther Party. The SCLC gained national attention thanks to the forthrightness and determination of a young man still in his 20's who organized a boycott against the segregated bus system of Montgomery, Alabama, in 1956. Attracting other youths of like spirit who were mostly ministers like himself, Martin Luther King, Jr., dedicated SCLC to the elimination of those symbols and realities that denied black dignity.

By 1964 SNCC was using the talents and energies of 150 young people,[79] the majority of them black, to defy segregation. Their sit-ins, boycotts, protest marches, and voter registration efforts spawned workers like James Forman, Diane Nash, Stokely Carmichael, Bob Moses, Gloria Richardson, John Lewis, and Julian Bond. Averaging 19 years of age,[80] SNCC members like these had their lives and perspectives stamped by the brutalities suffered while seeking a hamburger and the vote.

The experiences of SCLC and SNCC members undoubtedly shaped the thinking and tactics of the Black Panther Party. This group, given widespread exposure in the mass media, has incurred white fear, attention, and attempts at statistical, social, and political assessment.

Voicing the litany of inequities and abuses not only attested to by private and governmental data but confirmed by their personal daily experiences, members of this black revolutionary group have expressed an unusually fiery and determined commitment to the extrication of black people from what they regard as the American system of injustice. Publicity has focused on the Panthers' adoption of Marxist-Leninist principles, on their program for feeding poor black children breakfast and "propaganda," on their shoot-outs with policemen throughout the United States, on the lives, thoughts, or actions of Panther leaders like Huey Newton and Eldridge Cleaver and his wife, Kathleen, and on the extended trials of Panther members.[81]

Consequently, popularly identified with the Panthers are such expressions as "Power to the People," "pig," and "by any means necessary." Of special white concern is the Panther involvement with violence, which they themselves explain as follows:

> Let us make one thing crystal clear: We do not claim the right to indiscriminate violence. We seek no bloodbath. We are not out to kill up white people. On the contrary, it is the cops who claim the right to indiscriminate violence and practice it every day. It is the cops who have been bathing black people in blood and who seem bent on killing off black people. But black people, this day, this time, say HALT IN THE NAME OF HUMANITY! YOU SHALL MAKE NO MORE WAR ON UNARMED PEOPLE. YOU WILL NOT KILL ANOTHER BLACK PERSON AND WALK THE STREETS OF THE BLACK COMMUNITY TO GLOAT ABOUT IT AND SNEER AT THE DEFENSELESS RELATIVES OF YOUR VICTIMS. FROM NOW ON, WHEN YOU MURDER A BLACK PERSON IN THIS BABYLON OF BABYLONS, YOU MAY AS WELL GIVE IT UP BECAUSE WE WILL GET YOU ... AND GOD CAN'T HIDE YOU.[82]

Despite the controversy and apprehension caused by the Panthers, they have achieved concrete and affirmative results. Because of the Panthers and their challenges, the original American vision of the jury as offsetting state abuse of the power to prosecute has been revived, for twelve citizens sitting in judgment have several times in Panther trials refused to convict. Thus the revolutionary American system of justice has been ironically vindicated. Further, thanks to the publicity regarding the nutritional inadequacies of poor children, the United States Congress and the Department of Agriculture have instituted a program for Government payment of a part of the expenses for providing breakfast.[83] At the end of February 1972, however, the department made the decision to "pay all costs of operating breakfast programs in schools with high concentrations of poor children starting in the 1972–73 school year."[84]

It should be remembered that all three groups, SCLC, SNCC, and the Black Panther Party, were organized solely because all was not racially right in this land. Consequently, they could hardly be expected to take a business-as-usual approach in marshalling young blacks.

In that each of them set out to meet certain American traditions and practices head-on and in particular to counter them, they have shown little resemblance to the Boy Scouts. Yet, discomfiting as their tactics have been, strident as their voices have sounded, any account of a black youth movement begins with these three groups and would have trouble moving elsewhere. Controversial as their strategies have been, the Black Panther Party has nevertheless provoked action and thought that might never have occurred otherwise, especially among other young blacks still pondering their predicament. The Panthers purposefully brought change to the American scene; their national impact may henceforth be the very factor responsible for a broader black participation in American life. They are now working increasingly within the system to bring about change.

The much-publicized Black Liberation Army is said to consist of former Black Panthers who favor more vigorous revolutionary action. Inquiries about its existence, purposes, methods, and alleged involvement with attacks on policemen across the nation prompt a more basic question: Why?

Revolutions are concerned with realignment of the position of the dispossessed, who become the "haves" of a new era. The revolutionary movement among these young black Americans replicates the concern of other groups in history who have sought to right old wrongs and to share in societal benefits. The deep, unspoken recognition (by the haves as well as the have-nots) that real injustice has been done makes particularly threatening the prospect of black revolution: What if the action taken is as severe as the injustices endured over the past two centuries?

These profiles of young blacks as students, workers, soldiers, and prisoners clearly indicate that the American emphasis on skin color influences the assignment of black Americans to certain roles and the manner in which the latter react to them.

The tendency to rebel against those restrictions they know young whites do not face is strong among black students, soldiers, and prisoners. The young black worker, although not as highly publicized in the mass media, is also prone to react in this fashion, as the following shows:

> These black workers represent the new street force whose allegiance is to the black community, not to labor. Unlike the older black workers who were grateful for any job, the younger man believes that their confinement to the old back-breaking jobs on the production lines is strictly a manifestation of the racism in American society.[85]

It cannot be denied that young blacks have statistical and social specifics beyond those common to all young people, upon which to focus their expressions of grievances. The peculiar pull of forces within and among young blacks differs from anything experienced by whites. A 1940 study of young blacks by an eminent black sociologist noted that their interests in sports, sex, possible careers, and parental pressure are quite similar to those of young whites. The sole and striking difference, he observed, was "that an ever-recurring subject in their conversation is the fact that they are Negroes."[86] This necessary obsession, as strong today as ever, is based on the many and likely limitations that their color will impose upon them as they pursue marriage, jobs, friendships, homes, choices in old age, and finally even burial sites. They are constantly concerned therefore with the question of how race will affect these pursuits. ("Race" both as whites *make* meaning of it, and as young blacks must *give* meaning to it in the light of their commitment to their own people.) A goodly proportion of black psychic energy, then, is consumed in evaluating the racial implications of any move they might make.

Some optimistic glimpses suggest progress toward the ultimate goal, but young blacks take small comfort in improvements which they see as overshadowed by remaining restrictions.

At one time, athletics and entertainment were the only American areas of endeavor in which blacks could achieve "stardom." Now not only are there new athletic areas in which blacks can compete, such as tennis and golf, but entertainment is no longer limited to "singing and dancing." The perception-expanding concepts of Alvin Ailey and his dance troupe and the theatrical advances seen in the work of the Negro Ensemble Company and the New Lafayette Theatre in New York City (many have noted that the major theatrical contributions to American theater in the last decade have emerged largely from blacks) bear witness to the fact that blacks today are creating and promoting their own cultural visions, not simply acting out those of others. (See Chapter 22, "Black Influences in the American Theater: 1960 and After.") This is in part due to the insistence, springing from the streets, on power at all levels, and has given rise to an artistic expression equaling jazz in uniqueness and reflecting the challenges of the black experience. The popularity of "black" films in the early 1970s, while giving employment to some black talents and promoting black "heroes," is seen by many young persons as another focus on negative and even criminal stereotypes for the profit of white financiers and producers.[87]

Other areas in which response to the thrust of young blacks can be seen is in governmental and private consideration of their claims and needs. The increased rates of college enrollments, special counseling and hiring programs for veterans, new ways of viewing the social factors that virtually route young blacks to prisons, and nationwide efforts—fragmented as they are—to establish substitute channels to better opportunities can all be attributed to a pervasive concern about past injustices and inadequacies that young blacks have faced.

In the political sphere, the implications of the 18-year-old vote are clearly substantial for young blacks. Remedies for their alienation and numerous grievances should now be possible of attainment through the political process, making the tactics of sitting-in and demonstrations things of the past.

A recent study shows, however, that young black New Yorkers showed greater apathy toward voter registration than their white counterparts. Efforts at neighborhood enrollment were labeled an "expensive flop." Since Brooklyn's black Bedford-Stuyvesant contains the largest number of 18- to 20-year-olds in New York City,[88] their impact on the vote could be substantial.

The Democratic party, a reasonable bellwether because of its traditional attraction to black people (only 12 percent of the black vote is Republican),[89] seems prepared to foster the cause of young blacks, judging by their widespread participation at the Democratic National Convention in July of 1972.

Blacks between the ages of 18 and 25 represent 13.6 percent of the total population aged 18 and over. In the light of the energies and concerns of these young voters, their political participation could reduce their own cynicism and despair, increase the relatively low registration of all blacks, and expand young black influence with whites beyond the cultural sphere. Such developments would bring obvious changes to the complexion of the nation. But are they likely? Budget changes in the 1970s have repeatedly curtailed or eliminated social programs considered vital to the interests of young black Americans.

One of our basic American tenets is that change is possible. Young blacks, both by the enormity of the inequities assigned to them and by their sense of having relatively little investment in the future of the country, have tried to set the necessary machinery in motion. How quickly things can be altered and to what degree only the future can tell.

### Notes

1. U. S. Bureau of the Census, *Statistical Abstract of the United States*, 1971 (92nd edition), Washington, D.C., 1971, Table No. 22, "Population by Sex, Race, Residence, and Median Age: 1790 to 1970," p. 24.
2. Total figures given by Ms. Clauson of the Population Division of the Bureau of the Census, on October 4, 1971. Percentages figured by author. *See also* Fred E. Crossland, *Minority Access to College*, a Ford Foundation Report (Schocken Press, New York, 1971), p. 11.

3. *Statistical Abstract of the U. S., 1971*, Table No. 26, "Population, by Race: 1960 and 1970," p. 26.

4. See Footnote #2; extrapolations from Ms. Clauson's figures again. Also, *Statistical Abstract, 1971*, Table No. 26, "Population, by Age, 1940 to 1970, and by Race, 1960 and 1970," p. 26.

5. *Statistical Abstract, 1971*, Table No. 177, "Negro and Nonminority Group Enrollment in Public Elementary and Secondary Schools, by Specified Areas: 1968 and 1970," p. 117.

6. *Ibid.*

7. *Ibid.*

8. Interview with Edward Carpenter, Headmaster, October 13, 1971.

9. Interview with Kwami A. Taha, Director, October 14, 1971.

10. *The New York Times*, August 15, 1971, p. 47.

11. For example, that such "mass" admissions would lower standards and devalue degrees and that the university would be required to undertake remedial education.

12. Interview with Mrs. Bonnie Dill, Counselor, SEEK Program (Search for Education, Elevation, and Knowledge), Bernard M. Baruch School, City University of New York, September 30, 1971.

13. Fred E. Crossland, *Minority Access to College*, a Ford Foundation Report. (Schocken Press, New York, 1971), p. 13.

14. *Ibid.*, pp. 15–16.

15. Malcolm G. Scully, "A Decline in Black Enrollment," *The E.P.E. 15-Minute Report for College and University Trustees* (published by Editorial Projects for Education, Inc.), Vol. XI, No. 7, January 10, 1975, p. 2.

16. Christopher Jencks and David Riesman, "The American Negro College," *Harvard Educational Review*, Vol. 37, No. 1, 1967, pp. 14–15.

17. Crossland, *op. cit.*, p. 38.

18. *Ibid.*, p. 39.

19. *Ibid.*

20. The supportive environment of the black college has been credited with forestalling dropouts and helping marginal students to succeed.

21. See, for example, "Right On!... Where? Historical Contradictions of the Black Student Movement," by Yusuf Kauroma in *The Minority Student on the Campus: Expectations and Possibilities*, edited by Robert A. Altman and Patricia O. Snyder, Center for Research and Development in Higher Education, University of California, Berkeley, and Western Interstate Commission for Higher Education, P. O. Drawer P, Boulder, Colorado 80302, November 1970.

22. The same is true of all graduates; the motivating forces differ, however. *Statistical Abstract of the U. S.: 1971*, Table No. 204, "Earned Degrees Conferred, by Field of Study, Level of Degree and Sex: 1969," p. 130.

23. E. Franklin Frazier, *Negro Youth at the Crossways*. Copyright 1940 by the American Council on Education, Schocken Books, New York, 1967), p. xxxiv.

24. Harry Edwards, *Black Students* (The Free Press, New York, 1970), pp. 97–119.

25. *The New York Times*, October 10, 1971, p. 1.

26. *Negro Digest*, March 1969.

27. Sylvester Monroe, "Guest in a Strange House," *Saturday Review of Education*, February 1973, pp. 45–48.

28. Sar A. Levitan & Robert Taggart, *The Job Crisis and Black Youth*, Twentieth Century Fund, 1971; A Report of the Twentieth Century Fund Task Force on Employment Problems of Black Youth (Praeger Publishers, New York, 1971).

29. *Ibid.*, Table No. 1, "Employment Status of Civilian Noninstitutional Population by Area, Race, and Age, 1970 Annual Average," p. 28.

30. *The Job Crisis and Black Youth*, *op. cit.*, p. 43.

31. *Ibid.*, p. 70 (Chart 4B, "Education and Unemployment, 1969, for 16- to 21-year-old Males").

32. *Ibid.*, p. 26.

33. *The Social and Economic Status of Negroes in the United States, 1973*, p. 25. See also Chapter 5, "The Black Role in the Economy."

34. *The Job Crisis, op. cit.*, p. 122.

35. *Ibid.*, p. 59.
36. *Ibid.*, p. 58.
37. Elliot Liebow, *Tally's Corner* (Little, Brown and Co., Boston, 1967).
38. *Statistical Abstract, 1971*, Table No. 169, "High School Graduates and School Dropouts, 16 to 21 Years Old—Employment Status, by Sex and Race: 1965 to 1970," p. 112.
39. *The Social and Economic Status of Negroes in the U. S., 1970*, Table No. 39, "Work and School Status and Unemployment Rate of Teenagers of Negro and Other Races: 1970," p. 51. The author has totaled the figures for unemployed, in school and out.
40. "Volunteer Corps Seek Minorities," San Francisco *Chronicle*, February 21, 1972, p. 8.
41. Author's extrapolation.
42. Chris Clark and Sheila Rush, *How to Get Along with Black People* (Third World Press, New York, 1971), p. 67.
43. The *Job Crisis, op. cit.*, p. 110.
44. Mario D. Fantini and Gerald Weinstein, *Disadvantaged: Challenge to Education* (Harper & Row, New York, 1968), p. 240.
45. *The New York Times*, February 3, 1972, p. 33.
46. *The New York Times*, October 26, 1971, pp. 1, 22.
47. *Social Responsibilities of Business Corporations*, A Statement on National Policy by the Research and Policy Committee of the Committee for Economic Development, June 1971 (477 Madison Ave., NYC 10022), p. 42.
48. *Wall Street Journal*, January 11, 1971, p. 2.
49. *Wall Street Journal*, November 16, 1971, p. 20.
50. *Ibid.*
51. *The New York Times*, April 13, 1971.
52. Supra, p. 48.
53. *Statistical Abstract, 1971*, Table No. 209, "Work and Training Programs—Enrollment Opportunities and Federal Obligations, by Program: 1963 to 1970," p. 132.
54. *The Job Crisis, op. cit.*, p. 110.
55. *Fortune*, January 1968 (Vol. LXXVII, No. 1), p. 128; *see also* "A 'Social Audit'" by David Rockefeller, *The New York Times*, May 1, 1972, p. 33, in which the chairman and chief executive officer of the Chase Manhattan Bank warns businessmen to take the initiative in meeting the growing criticism of industry and the private sector's shunning of solutions to social problems.
56. *Statistical Abstract, 1971*, Table No. 414, "Status of Selective Service Draftees Examined for Military Service, 1950 to 1970, and by Race, 1970," p. 259. The disqualification percentage for "Negro and other" is 54.3 percent; for whites, it is 45 percent.
57. *Black Americans: A Chartbook*. U. S. Department of Labor, Bureau of Labor Statistics, Bulletin 1699, 1971, p. 106.
58. *Statistical Abstract, 1971*, Table No. 403, "Negro Men in the Armed Forces: 1965 to 1970," p. 253.
59. *Statistical Abstract, 1971*, Table No. 402, "Vietnam Conflict—U. S. Military Forces in Vietnam and Casualties Incurred: 1961 to 1971," p. 253.
60. *The New York Times*, January 20, 1973, p. 62.
61. *Ibid.*, July 29, 1968, pp. 1, 14.
62. "The Returning GI: What Does He Do Now?" *Black Enterprise*, February 1971, p. 25.
63. *Ibid.*
64. *Ibid.*, p. 23.
65. Operation MEDIHC (Military Experience Directed into Health Careers), October 1971, Vol. 2, No. 1. Newsletter Published by the National Health Council, 1740 Broadway, NYC 10019.
66. "The Returning GI: What Does He Do Now?" *op. cit.*, pp. 23, 26.
67. Respectively: *Autobiography of Malcolm X, Die; Nigger, Die;* "Letter from a Birmingham Jail"; *Soul on Ice*, (McGraw-Hill, New York, 1968); *If They Come in the Morning* (Signet, New York, 1971); and *Soledad Brother: The Prison Letters of George Jackson* (Bantam, New York, 1970).
68. See Malcolm X and Alex Haley, *Autobiography of Malcolm X* (Grove Press, New York, 1964), pp. 153–6.
69. *Ibid.*, pp. 158–9.

70. Eldridge Cleaver, "A Day in Folsom Prison," *op. cit.*, pp. 40–49.

71. *Ibid.*, p. 48.

72. Claude Brown, *Manchild in the Promised Land* (N.Y., The Macmillan Co: 1965), pp. 119–20.

73. *Wall Street Journal*, January 15, 1973, pp. 1, 13.

74. George Jackson, *op. cit.*, p. 30.

75. *Ibid.*, p. 31.

76. Angela Davis, *op. cit.*, p. 31.

77. Attica Commission, Robert McKay, Chairman, December 31, 1970 (Internal Document).

78. Claude Brown, *op. cit.*, p. 141.

79. Howard Zinn, *SNCC: The New Abolitionists* (Boston: Beacon Press, 1964), p. 3.

80. *Ibid.*, p. 10.

81. Robert Chrisman, "The Black Panther Thrust in American Revolution." *Saturday Review*, July 24, 1971, p. 36.

82. Philip S. Foner, ed., *The Black Panthers Speak* (J. B. Lippincott Co., Philadelphia, 1970), p. 19 (essay is entitled "On Violence").

83. *The New York Times*, February 17, 1972, p. 40.

84. *Ibid.*, February 26, 1972, p. 32.

85. James Boggs, "A Black View of the White Worker," in *The White Majority: Between Poverty and Affluence,* edited by Louise Kapp Howe (Random House, Vintage Books, New York, 1970), p. 109.

86. Ira D. Reid, *In a Minor Key* (American Council on Education, Washington, 1940).

87. "The New Films: Culture or Con Game?" *Ebony*, December 1972, pp. 60–68.

88. *The New York Times*, August 13, 1972, p. 37.

89. Statement by Senator Dole, Chairman, Republican National Convention, on "Meet the Press," NBC-TV, seen July 16, 1972.

# BIBLIOGRAPHY

Allen, Robert L., *Black Awakening in Capitalist America.* Garden City, Doubleday, 1969.

Baughman, Emmett Earl, *Black Americans.* New York, Academic Press, 1971.

Boggs, James, *Racism and the Class Struggle.* New York, Monthly Review Press, 1970.

Corson, William R., *Promise or Peril: The Black College Student in America.* New York, Norton, 1970.

Ferman, Louis A., *The Negro and Equal Employment Opportunities.* New York, Praeger, 1968.

Goff, Regina Mary, "Problems and Emotional Difficulties of Negro Children as Studied in Selected Communities and Attributed By Parents and Children to the Fact that They Are Negro." New York, Columbia University, Bureau of Publications, Teachers College, 1949.

Hauser, Stuart T., *Black and White Identity Formation.* New York, Wiley Inter-science, 1971.

Heywood, Chester Dodd, *Negro Combat Troops in the World War.* New York, AMS Press, 1969.

Jacobson, Julius, ed., *The Negro and the American Labor Movement.* Garden City, Anchor Books, 1968.

Jaffe, Abram J., Adams, Walter, and Meyer, Sandra G., *Negro Higher Education in the 1960s.* New York, Praeger, 1968.

Johnson, Charles Spurgeon, *The Negro College Graduate*. Chapel Hill, University of North Carolina Press, 1938.

Knight, Etheridge and other inmates of Indiana State Prison, *Black Voices from Prison*. New York, Pathfinder Press, 1970.

Ladner, Joyce, *Tomorrow's Tomorrow*. Garden City, Doubleday, 1970.

LeMelle, Tilden J. and LeMelle, Wilbert J., *The Black College: Achieving Relevance*. New York, Praeger, 1969.

Lott, Albert J. and Lott, Bernice E., *Negro and White Youth*. New York, Holt, Rinehart and Winston, 1963.

Marshall, F. Ray and Briggs, Vernon M. Jr., *The Negro and Apprenticeship*. Baltimore, Johns Hopkins Press, 1967.

McEvoy, James and Miller, Abraham, *Black Power and Student Rebellion*. Belmont, California, Wadsworth, 1969.

*The Negro and the City*, New York, Time-Life Books, 1968.

Parsons, Talcott and Clark, Kenneth B., eds., *The Negro American*. Boston, Houghton-Mifflin, 1968.

Porter, Judith D., *Black Child, White Child*. Cambridge, Harvard University Press, 1971.

Reid, Ira De Augustine, *In a Minor Key: Negro Youth in Story and Fact*. Washington, D.C., American Council on Education, 1940.

Robinson, Armstead L., Foster, Craig C., and Ogilvie, Donald H., eds., *Black Studies in the University*, a symposium sponsored by the Black Student Alliance at Yale. New Haven, Yale University Press, 1969.

Schulz, David A., *Coming Up Black*. Englewood Cliffs, New Jersey, Prentice-Hall, 1969.

# 11

## *Educating Black Americans*

### *Regina Goff*

The education of the black American has become an increasingly important national issue. It is in this area perhaps more than any other that white America has had to come face to face with its conscience. For the black population full access to education is essential to an equitable reshaping of its national fortunes, yet attempts to secure such access have met with uneasy and often hostile reactions.

## HISTORICAL BACKGROUND

### Education in Slave Days

During slavery, the southern states forbade any practice which might contribute to the literacy of slaves, regarding education as a potentially dangerous tool in the hands of those who were to be kept in subordination.

Nevertheless, informal elementary schooling was sometimes available, particularly to house servants.[1] Such opportunity was usually a function of the planter's self-interest since protection of his family necessitated the training of his entourage in basic cleanliness and hygiene. Slaves were also instructed in the care of the ill, the aged, and children. In addition, the physical proximity inherent in plantation living narrowed the sense of social distance between the gentry and house servants and encouraged some intermingling of white and black children. White children sometimes taught black children to read and write, and they in turn might tutor their younger white playmates. In some instances where masters defied custom and made their slaves literate, the latter were equipped to help the children of the "big house" with their school assignments.

From the first, black Americans regarded education as a means for escape from personal degradation. Clandestine learning sessions, sometimes with the cooperation of sympathetic whites, were not uncommon. Many who fled North to freedom immediately applied themselves to mastery of the printed page.

Early official attempts to educate blacks went hand in hand with their "Christianization." From the first, those whose Puritan religious tenets rejected the notion of enslavement had called for at least minimal education for slaves. Richard Baxter, in a tract published in England as early as 1673, supported the conversion and training of slaves. The troubled conscience of the Quakers, traditional opponents of slavery, found expression in open protest in 1688, 1693, and 1696, when the Society of Friends denounced the prohibition against education as unchristian and opposed to the nature of man.[2]

The question of the Christianization of slaves soon became a major issue in the colonies. Royal governors to the New World were directed to aid in the conversion of black people, and the Church of England conducted instruction in New York in 1704 in a school under the direction of Elias Neau.[3] The school was forced to close in 1712, however, when Neau was accused of abetting slave uprisings.

Reverend Thomas Bray and his associates supported conversion and instruction efforts in Maryland, Philadelphia, and North Carolina until 1760. New Orleans, with its unique social and cultural background, went so far as to tolerate the establishment of a school for Negroes in 1734 under the direction of the Ursuline nuns.

In spite of such occasional attempts to help black people improve their lot, it should be remembered that the rationalizations for slavery included assertions that blacks had inferior intellectual endowment. Hence even those who opposed slavery were reluctant to attribute to blacks the mental capacity which they considered natural in themselves. Thus blacks were forced to turn to each other for the leadership essential to their development. Free individuals highlighted education as the most powerful determinant of advancement and by the late 1700s blacks could look to several outstanding models to be emulated.

One of the most successful black men of his time was Benjamin Banneker, who by 1789 had proved himself intellectually competent in mathematics, astronomy, and the engineering sciences. President George Washington appointed him to the commission to survey and plan the city of Washington.

Paul Cuffee, a New England shipowner by the age of 16, was another notable figure of his day. Cuffee purchased his first vessel in 1780 and in time set up shipping routes to Europe and Africa. Although he accumulated great wealth, he remained concerned to the end with the plight of his fellow blacks, and organized a "back to Africa" movement among them. He built a school for his community.

Phillis Wheatley, eighteenth century poet and literary scholar, was a living negation of the argument that blacks were inherently intellectually inferior. Taken directly from a Senegalese ship and reared in the exemplary family of the John Wheatleys of Boston, she learned to read the Bible and was a student of Latin, history, and geography. At the age of 20, when she was sent to England for her health, she published her first book of poems. Great praise was accorded to her talents, including a tribute to her poetic gifts from George Washington.

The first American-born black to receive what has been referred to as a "thorough" education was John Chavis. Chavis was born and reared in North Carolina and sent to Princeton where, according to report, he was taught by the president, Dr. John Witherspoon. For thirty years he taught in a school in Wake County, North Carolina, which was attended by white boys in the day and black boys at night. In 1831, when education for Negroes was prohibited, he was forced to abandon his work. Between 1787 and 1820, another successful school of the period, the African Free School in New York, had enrolled hundreds of students; one of its most illustrious products was Ira Aldridge, who won international fame as a Shakespearean actor. In 1826, Edward Jones and John Russwurm became the first black graduates of American colleges (Amherst and Bowdoin, respectively). By this time, ex-slaves were practicing medicine, teaching school, and preaching sermons before attentive white audiences.[4]

Throughout the period of colonial history, the Quakers assiduously worked for the education of blacks and were perhaps as distressed as blacks themselves when the invention of the power loom and the rise of industrialism in England in 1794 enthroned cotton and reinforced the demand for illiterate slave labor.

## Emancipation and Education

With emancipation, public attention and political leadership focused on ways and means of controlling the large, newly freed, black population. Education was to play an important role.

During the Civil War, with the endorsement of the War Department, freedmen's aid societies had established schools for blacks in the wake of the Union army. As the army advanced, these schools sprang up behind them. The societies' efforts were reinforced by the work of the Freedmen's Bureau, established in 1865 to deal with the grave social problems of the time. The Freedmen's Bureau, which was to have a tremendous impact on education, expanded the earlier efforts of missionary organizations and the War Department, establishing many kinds of schools. The work already done in this field by private organizations was impressive. The American Missionary Association had set up schools in Virginia in the towns of Newport News, Portsmouth, Suffolk, and Yorktown; in Washington, D.C.; and in Columbus, Ohio, as early as 1863. The Friends Association for Aid to Freedmen and the Board of Freedmen's Missions of the United Presbyterian Church were also significant supporters of educational activities. The American Baptist Home Society, the American Church Institute of the Episcopal Church, and the African Methodist Episcopal Church too made important contributions to the movement.

The Freedmen's Bureau went on to establish and finance Howard University and helped to found Atlanta University, Fisk University, Talladega College, Tougaloo College, and Hampton Institute. By 1872, when the bureau closed down, it had spent more than five million dollars on educational pursuits and enrolled more than a million blacks in 4300 schools.[5] There was real substance behind the comment of Booker T. Washington, who saw "a whole race trying to go to school." Such efforts were a repudiation of white beliefs that black Americans were slothful, uninterested, and unable to learn.

In Congress, such black voices as Joseph Rainey of South Carolina and Josiah Well of Florida strongly advocated federal aid to education. But the momentum they generated waned in the battle to contain black voting strength. By 1896 when the Supreme Court, in *Plessy v. Ferguson*, sanctioned a state segregation law involving transportation and enunciated its "separate but equal" doctrine, black citizens were faced with the prospect of separate schools wherever these were decreed by state law.

The black schools in the postwar South were not only separate but also clearly inferior in every respect: budget, program, equipment, facilities, and construction. Although the Morrill Act of 1890 provided that federal funds should be equitably distributed between white and black land-grant colleges, as late as 1916 none of the black institutions in this category were offering college degree programs and none received equal funding. However, thirty-four institutions of higher learning were being supported by the black church.[6]

Black institutes of learning received the majority of their financial aid from northern white philanthropists, who provided funds for construction, endowments, scholarships, teacher education, and industrial education. Two extremely important sources of such moneys were the Peabody Fund, set up in 1867 in the amount of $3,500,000, and the John F. Slater Fund, established in 1882 with $1,000,000. Schools receiving grants were located in Virginia, North and South Carolina, Georgia, and Alabama. Shaw University and Hampton and Tuskegee Institutes were among the recipients. In the early 1900s fund trustees set up industrial-training programs which led to the development of the first black high schools in southern communities.

In 1902, wealthy industrialist and philanthropist Andrew Carnegie contributed $10,000,000 to establish libraries on the campuses of black schools and colleges. Julius Rosenwald also contributed many millions for schools and fellowships for advanced study, as did John D. Rockefeller and Caroline Phelps Stokes, both of whom helped further the development of black education. The Anna T. Jeanes Fund, established in 1905 specifically to construct and supervise rural schools for Negroes, was another important source of badly needed revenue. (For a more detailed discussion of the role of philanthropy in black education, see Chapter 13, "Blacks and American Foundations: Two Views.")

State support of black public education was almost nonexistent in the latter 1800s, although feeble efforts were made to comply with congressional rulings between 1864 and 1877 which required the provision of education for blacks. In 1864 and 1867 Maryland created a public-school system within the framework of school districts and under the direction of a State Board of Education. North Carolina, Arkansas, and Virginia soon followed and South Carolina complied with the rulings in 1877.[7] By 1900, more than 1,500,000 black children were in schools taught by 28,500 black teachers, and more than 2,000 blacks had been graduated from institutions of higher learning.[8] Despite persisting inadequacies in educational opportunities, the number of high-school graduates rose from 4,056 in 1900 to 30,009 in 1920.[9]

## Industrial Training Versus the "Talented Tenth"

The persistence of blacks in seeking equal opportunities in education and employment played a major part in the exodus of blacks from the South, the outbreak of riots in the unwelcoming North, and continuing mutual racial distrust. In this time of division, the conciliatory philosophy of Booker T. Washington, founder of Tuskegee Institute, was avidly seized upon by national white leadership. Washington, in a speech at the Atlanta Cotton States and International Exposition in 1895, urged Negroes to "Cast down your buckets where you are." Skilled hands were needed in the fields and shops of the South, and the economic well-being of the nation depended upon such trained and thrifty workers.

Washington, thoroughly in tune with the times, no doubt sincerely felt that manual work was all that the majority of blacks could realistically expect; social rejection was a reality, and the only common-sense approach to mass education was to gear it to training for excellence in the industrial arts and domestic science. The black man would have to settle for a success limited by the confines of an imposed caste structure. Under Washington's direction, therefore, Tuskegee Institute emphasized self-help and offered farming, animal husbandry, and training in the crafts. Washington also worked to encourage the formation and development of black business enterprise. In accordance with his general philosophy, he deemphasized the issue of political rights, feeling that a firm economic base must be established before black citizens could hope to attain real political power. In his eyes, white cooperation and support were essential to the attainment of this basic objective. No doubt he also saw a strategic advantage in first attacking the barriers to economic rights, since they seemed the most vulnerable.

Whatever Washington's motives, the white power structure, persuaded that he would work within the boundaries they set, called him "the Moses of his people." Andrew Carnegie gave Tuskegee Institute $600,000, with $150,000 earmarked for personal use by Washington to relieve him of "pecuniary cares that he may devote himself wholly to his great mission."[10]

Washington's "conciliatory" strategy was less popular in black circles, however, especially in the North where W. E. B. DuBois, a scholarly, Harvard-trained Ph. D., educator, and sociologist advocated the education of an intellectual elite ("the talented tenth"). DuBois, who refused several offers from Washington to join him at Tuskegee, believed that the most able should receive thorough professional training, engage in scholarly research, contribute to the arts and furnish leadership to the black masses. In 1905 he launched an organization composed of trained blacks and liberal whites, known as the Niagara Movement. The movement's platform constituted an unequivocal refutation of Washington's philosophy and an uncompromising demand by DuBois for " . . . full manhood rights . . . every single right that belongs to a free-born American, political, civil, and social. . . . "[11] Out of this early movement grew the National Association for the Advancement of Colored People.

Although neither Washington nor DuBois would yield his respective position, each nevertheless complemented and respected the other. Upon the death of Washington, DuBois hailed him as the greatest black leader since Frederick Douglass.

## Urbanization and the Movement Toward Equality

By the 1930s and 1940s, white educators were troubled by the "cultural lag" occasioned by the attempt to cope with the demands of a machine age through schooling geared to an agrarian economy. The black man needed a more sophisticated education than was afforded by industrial training. The problem was further compounded by the accelerating flight of blacks from the southern fields to the cities of the North. By now, more than two million blacks had settled in the large metropolitan areas[12] and the North faced acute problems of overcrowding, in both the schools and housing in the teeming black neighborhoods. New trends in education were discernible, however, and at the same time that curricular offerings were improving, the number of schools open to blacks increased, both North and South. There were also signs of progress in the field of higher education. Black colleges ceased to offer high-school subjects, and a growing number received accreditation.

As he began to adjust to his new, increasingly complex social situation, the black man became more vocal and aggressive in demanding equal rights. Finding that attempts to gain his ends through reason and persuasion were not meeting with any notable success, he turned to the courts to attack segregation in tax-supported schools. In 1935 Donald Gaines Murray, a graduate of Amherst College, was refused admission to the University of Maryland School of Law. An injunction was sought in the local courts under the counsel of Charles Houston, the first black editor of the Harvard Law Review, and Thurgood Marshall, later to become the first black justice of the Supreme Court. Both the lower court and the Court of Appeals of the State of Maryland ordered his admission. Shortly thereafter Lloyd Gaines, a graduate of Missouri's Lincoln University, filed suit for admission to the University of Missouri Law School. The case reached the Supreme Court in 1938, and a decision handed down by Chief Justice Charles Evans Hughes stated that the state must furnish legal education equal in quality to that afforded for white persons. A law school was subsequently set up at Lincoln University.

In May 1950, sixty-seven blacks in Charleston, South Carolina, petitioned for admission to public schools without regard to race. This case went to the Supreme Court with *Brown v. Board of Education of Topeka* and three others; they were known collectively as the School Segregation Cases. In May 1954, Chief Justice Earl Warren handed down the court's unanimous and historic decision in the case, which stated: "We conclude that in the field of public education the doctrine of 'separate but equal' has no place. Separate facilities are inherently unequal."[13]

Initial reaction to the decision was favorable both in the United States and abroad. However, implementation of the new ruling was slow; resistance quickly developed in the South, and with it renewed activity on the part of the Ku Klux Klan and similar bitterly opposed groups. In 1956, 101 southern members of the House and Senate signed a Southern Manifesto declaring that they would use every means available to resist desegregation. Senators Estes Kefauver of Tennessee and Lyndon Johnson of Texas were the only southern senators to refuse to sign it. Senator Harry Byrd of Virginia presented a plan which made provisions for the issuance of tuition grants to students for attendance at private or public schools. Hastily established private schools were readily filled by white students who deserted the public system. In some states, funds were denied any district which attempted integration.[14] Many public schools were closed, and Prince Edward County, Virginia, offered no formal public education for seven years.

In September 1957, on the eve of the opening of school, Governor Orval Faubus of Arkansas announced the impending arrival of 270 National Guardsmen in the city of Little Rock to maintain order, although no disorder was apparent. Arkansas had experienced no prior difficulty in its integration at the college level. A plan for gradual desegregation at the high-school level was to have been implemented that fall. In the absence of trouble or of any requests for state police aid, it became evident that the National Guard was to be used to prevent implementation of the federal court order. And indead, the military force remained in Little Rock for eighteen days, denying black children access to school. When frustration exploded into violence, President Eisenhower sent in federal troops to establish and maintain order while black children went to school with whites. The high schools of Little Rock were closed for the school year 1958–59, reopening on a token basis in 1959.

By that year there had been 530 cases of violence associated with school integration, including bombings of houses, churches, and synagogues in addition to riots and murder.[15] In 1962 when James Meredith attempted to enroll at the University of Mississippi, rioting followed. In this instance, as when Governor George Wallace stood in the doorway of the University of Alabama to bar the entrance of black students, the Federal Government provided protective authority for the latter.

Such events led President John F. Kennedy to declare: "This nation, for all its hopes and all its boasts, will not be fully free until all its citizens are free. We face, therefore, a moral crisis as a country and a people. . . . It is time to act in the Congress, in our state and local legislative bodies and, above all, in our daily lives."[16]

# EDUCATION TODAY

## School Enrollment and Teacher Distribution

In 1972 the United States had a total public-school population of approximately 46,668,000 young people. Blacks numbered 6,796,000, or 14.6 percent of the total.[17] In 1974, between 60 and 70 percent of blacks aged 25 to 34 had completed high school, as against only about 40 percent in 1960. (See Figure 1.) Despite this gratifying improvement, black high school completion falls far short of the comparable levels for whites, which rose from about 65 percent in 1960 to over 80 percent in 1974. Thus a significant discrepancy in attainment remains.

Comparative figures for educational attainment by family heads reflect a consistent but narrowing gap between blacks and whites up to the college level. Both groups show higher levels of educational attainment among younger people.

Recent evidence points to the power of early environmental intervention, particularly among "deprived" children, to strengthen intellectual development, thus the current emphasis on pre-school training and the emergence of day-care centers and nursery schools for the less affluent. By 1973, 713,000 or 43.3 percent of black children were in nursery schools or Head Start programs.[18] It is interesting that a much larger proportion of black (45 percent) than white (18 percent) children attended full-day pre-primary programs in 1973.[19] This is probably due to the fact that such public programs were concentrated in the central cities.

Black children in 1973 comprised 18.5 percent of the total enrollment of 3- to 5-year-olds in public nursery schools and kindergartens, a figure significantly higher than their proportion of the population. (See Table I.)

In 1971 the total teaching force in American elementary and secondary schools numbered 1,780,000 teachers, of which 170,000, or 9.6 percent, were black. The largest percentages of black educators in terms of national totals were found in Mississippi (44.1), Louisiana (35.6), and South Carolina (34.3). The District of Columbia had a black teaching force of 77.6 percent which comprises 2.8 percent of the national total. New Hampshire, Utah, and Montana report 0.1 percent black teachers, while Wyoming reports less than half of 1 percent.[20]

The geographic distribution of black teachers parallels population densities and reveals the tendency for minority teachers to serve minority children, since social pressures have discouraged black teachers from taking initiative in seeking positions in white communities. It is clear that much of the responsibility for developing latent potential and encouraging perseverance in school tasks in black children remains with black teachers.

**FIGURE 1**—PERCENT OF PERSONS 25 TO 34 YEARS OLD WHO HAVE COMPLETED
HIGH SCHOOL, BY RACE AND SEX: 1940–1974

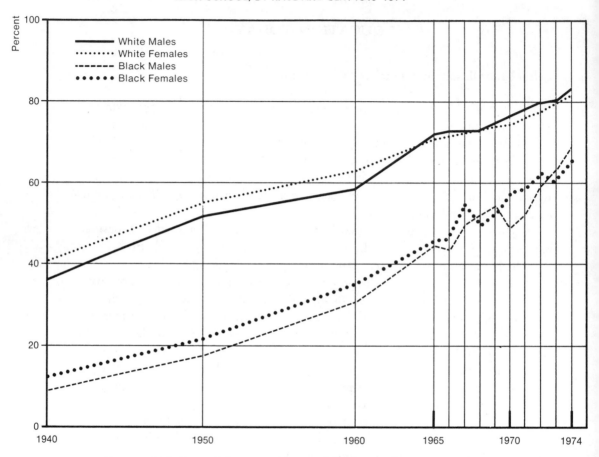

Source:   U. S. Dept. of Commerce, Bureau of the Census, *Current Population Reports*, Series
P-20, No. 274, December 1974, "Educational Attainment in the U.S."

FIGURE 2—YEARS OF SCHOOL COMPLETED FOR WHITE AND BLACK FAMILY
HEADS, BY AGE: MARCH 1973

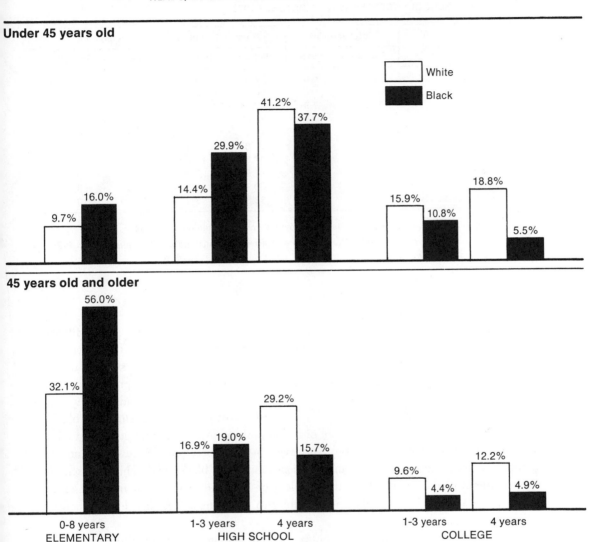

Source: U.S. Dept of Commerce, Bureau of the Census, *Current Population Reports,* Series P-20, No. 238. "Household and Family Characteristics," March 1973–December 1973.

TABLE I—BLACK CHILDREN AS PERCENT OF TOTAL 3- TO 5-YEAR-OLD ENROLLMENT IN NURSERY SCHOOL AND KINDERGARTEN BY CONTROL AND TYPE OF SCHOOL: OCTOBER 1964 TO OCTOBER 1973

| Year | Total Enrolled | | Nursery School | | Kindergarten | |
|------|--------|---------|--------|---------|--------|---------|
|      | Public | Private | Public | Private | Public | Private |
| 1973 ............. | 18.5 | 6.8 | 36.5 | 6.9 | 15.5 | 6.7 |
| 1972 ............. | 17.5 | 8.6 | 28.5 | 8.2 | 15.7 | 9.4 |
| 1971 ............. | 17.2 | 7.9 | 28.3 | 8.2 | 15.8 | 7.6 |
| 1970 ............. | 17.2 | 7.7 | 38.9 | 6.4 | 14.4 | 9.6 |
| 1969 ............. | 16.2 | 10.7 | 42.1 | 11.1 | 13.7 | 10.4 |
| 1968[1] ........... | 18.1 | 9.8 | 37.8 | 9.6 | 16.0 | 10.1 |
| 1967[1] ........... | 18.1 | 9.0 | 41.5 | 11.2 | 16.0 | 7.4 |
| 1966[1] ........... | 16.8 | 8.8 | 41.3 | 7.8 | 14.6 | 9.6 |
| 1965[1] ........... | 15.1 | 8.8 | 29.1 | 8.9 | 14.3 | 8.7 |
| 1964[1] ........... | 14.6 | 11.5 | 38.5 | 8.9 | 13.7 | 13.6 |

[1] Negro and other races. Data for Negroes separately not available prior to 1969.

Source:  U. S. Dept. of Commerce, Bureau of the Census, Current Population Reports, Series P-20, No. 268, *Nursery School "Kindergarten" Enrollment*, August 1974, p. 1.

## Dropouts

In 1965 President Johnson in his Message to Congress noted that in our fifteen largest cities, 60 percent of the tenth-grade students from poverty areas dropped out before finishing high school. The Research Council of the Great Cities Program for School Improvement in 1968 estimated that one-third of their school population was "culturally deprived" and that one out of every three then at the fifth-grade level would drop out before reaching high school. In the fall of 1970 only 53 percent of all blacks aged 14 to 24 were enrolled in school or had completed high school (as compared with 75 percent of the white population). However, in 1973, between the ages of 7 and 17, there is no statistically significant difference between blacks and whites in school enrollment. (See Table II.) Thus the problem of dropouts, acute both in inner cities and in rural areas, is primarily one of failing to graduate, rather than leaving before age 16 or 17.

A factor which encourages school leave-taking among black high school students is grade retardation. In 1971, of black American boys aged 14 to 17, 14.3 percent were two or more years below the modal or expected grade for their age; 9.7 percent of black girls of the same age group were similarly behind their age group. Among white youth of the same age, 5.4 percent of males and 3.1 percent of females were two or more years below the mode.[21]

The limited education of blacks has been reflected in the job market. In early 1974 the rate of unemployment among black youth was 30.7, as against 13.3 percent among

**TABLE II—PERCENT ENROLLED IN SCHOOL, BY AGE AND RACE: 1955 TO 1973**

(As of October.)

| AGE (in years) | 1955 White | 1955 Black and other | 1960 White | 1960 Black and other | 1965 White | 1965 Black and other | 1970 White | 1970 Black and other | 1972 White | 1972 Black and other | 1973 White | 1973 Black and other |
|---|---|---|---|---|---|---|---|---|---|---|---|---|
| Total, 3–34 | ¹50.8 | ¹50.7 | ¹56.4 | ¹55.9 | 55.6 | 55.3 | 56.2 | 57.7 | 54.4 | 58.0 | 53.1 | 55.8 |
| 3 and 4 | (NA) | (NA) | (NA) | (NA) | 10.3 | 11.8 | 19.9 | 23.1 | 23.8 | 27.7 | 23.2 | 28.9 |
| 5 and 6 | 79.2 | 71.1 | 82.0 | 73.3 | 85.8 | 79.9 | 90.3 | 85.4 | 92.2 | 90.6 | 93.0 | 89.9 |
| 7–9 | 99.3 | 98.2 | 99.7 | 99.3 | 99.4 | 99.0 | 99.3 | 99.4 | 99.1 | 98.7 | 99.1 | 99.2 |
| 10–13 | 99.3 | 98.2 | 99.5 | 99.0 | 99.4 | 99.3 | 99.1 | 99.4 | 99.3 | 99.4 | 99.3 | 99.0 |
| 14 and 15 | 87.5 | 82.8 | 98.1 | 95.9 | 99.0 | 98.2 | 98.2 | 97.6 | 97.6 | 97.7 | 97.6 | 96.7 |
| 16 and 17 | 87.5 | 82.8 | 83.3 | 76.9 | 87.8 | 84.6 | 90.6 | 86.2 | 88.9 | 89.1 | 88.3 | 87.7 |
| 18 and 19 | 32.1 | 27.6 | 38.9 | 34.6 | 47.1 | 40.1 | 48.7 | 41.9 | 46.6 | 44.8 | 43.4 | 37.8 |
| 20–24 | 11.6 | 7.2 | 13.9 | 7.5 | 20.2 | 10.2 | 22.5 | 15.2 | 22.1 | 17.8 | 21.3 | 15.7 |
| 25–34 | 2.8 | 3.3 | 3.8 | 1.9 | 4.9 | 3.1 | 6.1 | 5.2 | 6.8 | 6.6 | 6.8 | 5.6 |

(NA) Not available.  ¹ Data are for persons 5 to 34 years of age.

Source: U. S. Department of Commerce, Bureau of the Census, *Statistical Abstract*, 1974, p. 113, Table 179.

white youth. Educational deficiencies and lack of skills were held as prime reasons for unemployment or employment in unskilled, low-paying labor and service jobs. On the other hand, it is clear that racial discrimination in employment has also withheld rewards from many blacks who were fully prepared to earn them. Adequate counseling services to inform youth of available training and job opportunities have traditionally been missing from black schools; and in integrated institutions, counselors have often been reluctant to encourage black students to venture beyond the traditional occupations. By early 1975 a general slump in the economy had pushed the unemployment figures for black youth over the 40 percent mark. This led many to sporadic employment in illicit jobs, petty thievery, narcotics, and finally serious crime.

## Illiteracy

In 1870, 80 percent of the nonwhite population (compared with 12 percent of the white population) was illiterate. One hundred years later, approximately 4 percent of all (slightly over 500,000) nonwhites aged 14 years and over, and 0.7 percent of whites were in that category.[22] Studies show that illiteracy is correlated with educational attainment, sex, and race. Six or more years of schooling is a traditional standard of minimum literacy, since it is easy for skills only partly mastered to be lost after school-leaving. It is interesting to note that illiterate white men and women are likely not to have completed any schooling whatsoever. In 1969, 60 percent of illiterate white men had completed no years of schooling, while 39 percent of illiterate black men were in this category. Among illiterate white women, 70 percent had completed no years of schooling, compared with 53 percent of illiterate black women. Blacks replying to census questions may have been reluctant to admit that they had not attended school. On the other hand, the poor quality of black schools may have rendered meager exposures ineffective.

In terms of sex differentials, in 1969 4 percent of black men and 3 percent of black women were illiterate. A decade earlier the percentages were 10 percent and 5 percent, respectively.

The decrease in illiteracy among males may have reflected such differential mortality as existed in the white population, that is, older illiterate men were replaced by young men with some training at a faster rate than were illiterate older women. Differential mortality favored older women. A larger number of older women survived to 1969 with the result that there were as many illiterate women as men in the 1969 population, although this was not the case in 1959.

There is an increasing concern about the problem of functional illiteracy among young people who have spent several years in school, but never learned to read adequately. Among reasons for this are poor instruction, lack of motivation, poor physical or mental health, lack of reinforcement by family or peers, lack of rapport with teachers, and the physical hardships of substandard housing. In addition, skills may fade away from disuse as time passes.

**FIGURE 3**—COMPARATIVE DATA ON ILLITERACY IN THE UNITED STATES

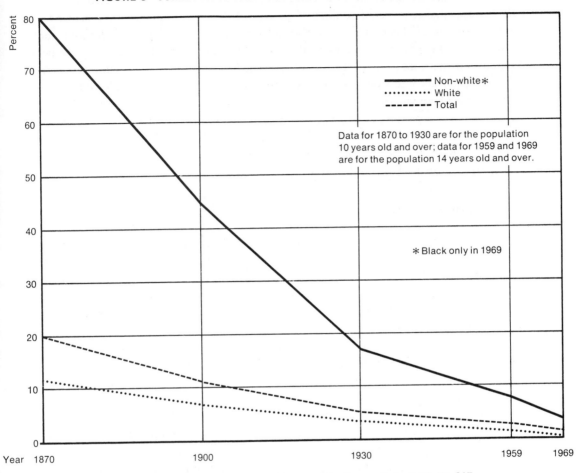

Data for 1870 to 1930 are for the population 10 years old and over; data for 1959 and 1969 are for the population 14 years old and over.

──────── Non-white*
············· White
── ── ── Total

* Black only in 1969

Source:   U. S. Department of Commerce, Bureau of the Census, Series P-20, No. 217.

The significance of the level of educational attainment is clearly reflected in Table III. In 1973, 7,400,000 blacks or about 31 percent of the black population fell below the low income level.[23] There is an obvious correlation between low levels of education and low income. In 1972, 16.4 percent of all nonwhite families earned less than $3,000 per annum. Of these, 44 percent of these were headed by men or women who had completed eight years of schooling, or less. An additional 17 percent had completed less than four years of high school. On the other hand, of those families with incomes of $15,000 and over, only 8 percent were headed by persons with under eight years of schooling. The median income for these minimally-educated nonwhite families was $4,958, while that for families headed by college graduates was $14,158, well below the median for similarly-educated white families, which was $18,479.

## Compensatory Education

Even when black youth remained in school, evidence of a lower level of achievement in basic skills, particularly in reading and arithmetic, than was attained by white children of equal age stood as an indictment of his schooling. Poverty, and its concomitants of malnutrition and limitations on experiences and learning materials which tend to foster both intellectual growth and affirmative racial attitudes and expectations, were primary handicaps. The legislative intent of Title I of the Elementary-Secondary Education Act, passed in 1965, was to provide funds for programs specifically addressed to these deficient areas. It was hoped that remedial action in the form of specially planned curricula and new teaching techniques could make up for, or at least partially compensate for, earlier lacks.

The National Advisory Council on the Education of Disadvantaged Children, in its first report to the President in 1966, noted that out of 8.1 million children from families with incomes of less than $3,000, then the established poverty level, 7 million were participating in Title I programs. The major classroom emphasis was on the language arts, reading, and writing, with particular concentration on speech in the primary grades. In some areas black parents were trained as auxiliary personnel aiding in classrooms and on playgrounds. In the poorest neighborhoods school libraries included audiovisual and other equipment which scanty budgets had formerly precluded. Food and health services were available for the first time in many urban slum and rural schools. To increase productive teaching, institutes for the training of teachers for disadvantaged youth appeared in college and university programs supported by federal funds provided under the Higher Education Act. Another important development was the creation, by the U. S. Department of Labor in cooperation with the U. S. Office of Education, of manpower training, work-study, and literacy programs for dropouts.

The most popular and widely accepted national program of this nature was Head Start, the preschool program directed by the Office of Economic Opportunity (since incorporated into the Office of Child Development). Although the poor of all races and

**TABLE III—MONEY INCOME—FAMILIES WITH HEADS 25 YEARS OLD AND OVER, BY INCOME LEVEL, BY RACE OF HEAD, AND YEARS OF SCHOOL COMPLETED: 1972**

| Race of Head and Years of School Completed | Number of families (1,000) | Percent Distribution by Income Level | | | | | | Median income |
|---|---|---|---|---|---|---|---|---|
| | | Under $3,000 | $3,000–$4,999 | $5,000–$6,999 | $7,000–$9,999 | $10,000–$14,999 | $15,000 and over | |
| **White families** .............. | 44,883 | 5.4 | 8.1 | 9.1 | 15.9 | 27.4 | 34.1 | 11,943 |
| Elementary school, less than 8 years ...... | 4,926 | 15.8 | 20.8 | 15.7 | 18.1 | 17.5 | 12.1 | 6,689 |
| 8 years ..................... | 5,183 | 8.6 | 15.5 | 15.9 | 18.9 | 23.4 | 17.8 | 8,595 |
| High school, 1–3 years ........... | 6,967 | 6.1 | 9.8 | 10.8 | 19.4 | 29.1 | 24.7 | 10,587 |
| 4 years ..................... | 15,272 | 3.5 | 5.1 | 7.7 | 17.2 | 32.7 | 33.8 | 12,426 |
| College, 1–3 years .......... | 5,435 | 2.7 | 3.8 | 6.4 | 13.2 | 30.1 | 43.9 | 13,987 |
| 4 years or more ............. | 7,099 | 1.7 | 1.9 | 2.8 | 8.2 | 21.8 | 63.5 | 18,479 |
| **Nonwhite and other families** ...... | 5,297 | 16.4 | 17.0 | 14.3 | 17.3 | 18.5 | 16.6 | 7,352 |
| Elementary school, less than 8 years ...... | 1,285 | 25.8 | 24.8 | 14.8 | 14.6 | 11.9 | 8.3 | 4,958 |
| 8 years ..................... | 546 | 18.2 | 17.5 | 19.1 | 18.7 | 15.3 | 11.2 | 6,419 |
| High school, 1–3 years ........... | 1,248 | 17.4 | 20.4 | 15.3 | 18.6 | 16.8 | 11.6 | 6,612 |
| 4 years ..................... | 1,372 | 11.5 | 12.8 | 13.1 | 20.3 | 22.5 | 19.7 | 8,893 |
| College, 1–3 years .......... | 420 | 10.2 | 9.2 | 15.1 | 13.5 | 27.6 | 24.7 | 10,379 |
| 4 years or more ............. | 425 | 3.4 | 4.0 | 6.6 | 14.3 | 25.8 | 46.0 | 14,158 |

Source: . U. S. Department of Commerce, Bureau of the Census, *Statistical Abstracts*. 1974, p. 386, Table 626.

ethnic groups participated in the programs, the term "disadvantaged" quickly became synonymous with "black," because of the disproportionate visibility of black persons in the poor population. That this general intellectual awakening was reaching the higher educational level as well was evidenced by an increase in black-studies programs and mounting protests over the use of textbooks which ignored the plural character of American society and omitted mention of the contributions of a variety of ethnic groups to the development of society. During the 1960s, emerging federal leadership and funding led blacks and other groups to anticipate a new era in education which could conceivably improve their economic status and pave the way to achievement and self-esteem.

In spite of these encouraging signs, assessment of the aforementioned programs through cost effectiveness and cost-benefit analyses, devised and conducted by economists, led to misgivings as to the actual intellectual gains resulting from the vast expenditures involved. Some critics declared that there was overexpenditure with minimum returns. Test results showed that after program exposure children still could not read and write at an "acceptable" level, as measured against standard norms. Others, however, considered the evaluation of the performance of black and poor youth against norms established for middle-class whites inappropriate; the intangibles not measured by conventional tests—morale, enjoyment of school, a sense of identity—were of enormous importance, they said.

Whatever the statistics might show, the new awareness provided educators with much more understanding of how low-income black children learn. This research was later to be applied to develop school practices more in keeping with the students' real needs. Other intangible gains included those stemming from improved nutrition and health care as well as improved teacher-pupil interaction, which undoubtedly contributed to mental alertness and greater responsiveness to academic subjects.

In 1974, a 25.2 billion dollar amended Elementary and Secondary Education Act (ESEA) was enacted by Congress and signed by President Ford. In general, the programs were extended through 1978, and no state would receive less funding than in 1974. Special incentive grants, programs in reading, and ethnic studies were extended until 1978, 1976, and 1978 respectively. Grants to school districts with high percentages of children from low-income families were continued through 1975. Title I funds were expanded to include the training of teachers and grants of $100,000 to one million dollars for states to equalize school finances.[24] The major deviation from the provisions of the Act of 1965 lay in a curtailed list of guidelines for busing, which is discussed below.

## School Integration

Although the mandate for integrated schools has been publicly acknowledged for two decades, attempts to move from verbalization to action have been characterized in many quarters as too sudden a change to impose upon stabilized dual systems. While many white administrators in the South openly declared their disapproval of desegregation mandates from the U. S. Office of Education, they were nevertheless forced to accept the reality of the law and the probability of government intervention in its enforcement, and used federal funds to plan their approaches to desegregation. Attitudes of white parents were less amenable to the proposed change and in many areas, as we have seen, the Ku Klux Klan encouraged incipient unrest. Political leaders in the highest state offices warned of impending violence, adding to the general tension.

School segregation, the embodiment of the commitment to different treatment of the two major races in the South, had become an anomaly in a society whose central creed now proclaimed equality of opportunity as the way to assure fair treatment, with each citizen equally prepared to contribute and achieve. Declaring segregation no longer the law of the land, however, did not assure equality of opportunity. A whole system of inequities had grown out of the initial evil of segregation; and the unequal education dispensed by the underfinanced, poorly constructed, poorly equipped and poorly staffed "Jim Crow" schools had already handicapped successive generations of black parents who, as a result of this and other discriminations, were unable to offer their children intellectual involvement and support in the home.

These segregated schools, which emulated the more favored white schools, had few curricular or other resources designed to invest their pupils with a sense of identity, pride, and the will to succeed and conquer. One might almost say that they conditioned black children to languish at the bottom of the social and economic scale, admiring but not expecting to join the more fortunate whites higher up the ladder.

The ending of segregation did not insure instant access to equal opportunity, nor did it put an end to deeply engrained racial attitudes. At first it was widely assumed that desegregation would mean simply removing racial designations from the buildings and letting the population of each school reflect the population of the whole community. It soon became obvious, however, that true integration of the schools would require the creation of a curriculum for all the community, with textbooks and heroes and villains representing all racial and ethnic backgrounds, thus generating a universal feeling of pride and ambition. First, however, it would be necessary for the mixture of pupils, teachers, and other personnel to reflect the total community; and this had been made exceedingly difficult by the extent to which racial barriers had permeated American life. When desegregation became official policy the physical separation of blacks and whites in residential neighborhoods appeared to be so extensive that automatic integration would *not* result from the simple removal of former barriers. Ironically, thousands of white and black children who for generations had been bused past each other's schools to get to the appropriate segregated one, now found no school within easy reach not already assigned overwhelmingly to pupils of their own race.

Confronted by this circumstance, school boards did what they had done in the past when they wished to consolidate rural schools: they resorted to mass transportation of children by school bus. In the past no damage, either physical nor psychological, had been claimed as a result of busing. However, when this was proposed as a means of achieving racial balance, the reaction was entirely different. In some cases white parents challenged the entrance of black children at the school door; pickets flaunted the message, "Go back to your neighborhood"; buses were overturned; and verbal abuse was directed at the children. It should be pointed out that although white parents have objected to having their children bused into slum areas, black parents have not subjected white children to this kind of hostile treatment. Black children who have physically survived such crisis situations have had ample reason to develop new self-doubts; however, Dr. Robert Coles discovered surprising strength and determination to survive in these youngsters.[25]

Some whites protest the use of the schoolhouse as a vehicle for the resolution of social issues, while many black parents refuse to expose their children to the psychological damage which they consider inherent in a classroom atmosphere of rejection. Militant parents spurn integration on the basis of a separatist philosophy and opt for the use of private, black-sponsored institutions.

The achievement of the goal of integration requires greater creative thought and involvement than has thus far been evident. The school years of the immediate future hold little promise of consistent progress in the area of desegregation unless there are dramatic changes in political thinking as well.

## The Issue of Busing

Increasingly the most visible instrument, and certainly the most discussed technique to promote racial balance in schools when neighborhoods are segregated, has been busing. The busing issue quickly acquired an exaggerated symbolic importance and was associated in the public mind with every school problem. Negative attitudes toward the issue were not confined to the South, nor were they limited to whites. Some black parents charged that the busing of black children in a one-way plan placed all the burden on blacks; they favored local school improvement and reciprocal busing of white children to black neighborhoods. Others, eager to get their children out of inadequate slum schools, raised funds to cover the transportation costs not available from public sources. White parents on their part resisted the transporting of their children to unfamiliar neighborhoods, and the neighborhood school was enshrined in white oratory as speakers forgot the advantages that had come with consolidated and, later, comprehensive schools.

Busing rapidly grew into a political issue as well. School board candidates campaigned on pro- and antibusing platforms and contenders for high political offices found it expedient to declare where they stood. Reports showing examples of successful use of busing in cities in Massachusetts, New York, New Jersey, and Connecticut indicated that the parents involved had shown greater concern for the quality of education available to their children than for the color composition of the classroom. However, such positive experiences as these tended to be drowned in the flood of negative rhetoric indulged in by political candidates more eager for popularity than for the task of debunking a widespread delusion.

During the summer of 1971 President Richard Nixon declared that busing should be used only to the minimum required under law. This threw school officials who had worked for years to develop acceptance of school integration into a state of confusion concerning the extent of their obligations under the law.

For a time, the presumption in some cities seemed to be that black children from crowded slum schools would have to be taken by bus into white communities where schools were less crowded. At the same time, many cities built new and more attractive schools in black neighborhoods, as if to persuade black parents to keep their children at home; others built new schools on the fringes of neighborhoods committed to one or the other race so that a mixed population would be a natural consequence.

Although the U. S. Commission on Civil Rights reaffirmed its view that it remained the responsibility of the Congress to establish a uniform standard to provide for the elimination of racial isolation, an undisputable movement away from desegregation began to emerge. In 1971 President Nixon seized upon latent fears by using the busing issue in his political campaign. The then President said, "I have consistently opposed the busing of our nation's school children to achieve racial balance, and I am opposed to the busing of our children simply for the sake of busing."[26] During that same year the Supreme Court stated that "busing is a proper method by which to achieve desegregation."[27]

Signals from different elements of government have thus been highly contradictory. In 1972 Nixon signed a bill which would delay the implementation of busing orders until all court appeals had been exhausted.

In 1973, in a further reversal of the twenty-year-old trend toward desegregation, the Supreme Court voted 4 to 4 to uphold a decision against a plan to integrate inner city and suburban school districts in Richmond, Virginia.

The issue of busing became more and more explosive. A historic Supreme Court decision rendered in 1974 rejected inter-district busing in the case of Detroit's 70 percent black schools. The NAACP had sued to equalize racial balance, and a federal judge ruled in favor of the plaintiff. He went even further to order the integration of black inner city children into 53 outlying school districts. The children were to be transported in buses.

Two suburbs and the state appealed to the Supreme Court, which overruled the decision of the Appellate Court by a vote of 5-4. The four Nixon appointees, Justices Warren Burger, Lewis Powell, Harry Blackman, and William Rehnquist voted with Potter Stewart against the order, while Justices Thurgood Marshall, William Brennan, William Douglas, and Byron White dissented. In a dissenting opinion, Justice Marshall accused the Court of "taking a giant step backward."[28] The Court held that children could not be required to be bused across city lines, and that busing to achieve integration could not extend beyond the second nearest school. The Court maintained, however, that desegregation, within established boundaries, should be pursued.

In almost the same language as that of the Supreme Court, the 1974 amended Elementary and Secondary Education Act (ESEA) prohibits busing beyond district boundaries. The policy embodied in the Court decision and in ESEA could have several adverse effects. In cities like Louisville and Indianapolis, plans to integrate city and suburban school districts could be overturned by courts using the Supreme Court decision as a precedent, and endless lawsuits could occur in district after district.

In 1974–75 a particularly explosive busing controversy developed in Boston when Federal Judge W. Arthur Garrity ordered the desegregation of several districts in Boston's 70 percent black schools.[29] Children were to be bused from Roxbury and Mattapan, both black, to South Boston and Hyde Park, both white. Violence flared as white parents organized to keep the busloads of black children from entering their neighborhoods. President Ford did little to help matters when, on October 9, 1974, he said on nationwide television, "The court decision in that case . . . was not the best solution to quality education in Boston. I have consistently opposed forced busing to achieve racial balance as a solution to quality education"[30]—a slightly less grammatical repetition of Mr. Nixon.

Judge Garrity ordered a more extended desegregation plan for September 1975, and some two thousand National Guardsmen underwent training to cope with possible violence.[31]

Further evidence of the confusing and contradictory handling of busing appeared in Los Angeles when the state Court of Appeals overturned an order by a lower court to desegregate the schools by busing.[32] A Federal district court judge "ordered the government to move quickly to enforce school desegregation requirements in 125 school districts in southern and border states."[33] Both occurred in March of 1975. It is likely that for some time opposition to busing will prevent its widespread use, and inner city school systems will become more black.

### The Dilemma of Black School Personnel

In some southern areas, in efforts to achieve integration, school districts were redrawn to encompass a more diverse population. Some black schools were closed and black teachers and administrators were released or redistributed. Within a five-year period, 1965–70, 1200 black principals were said to have been fired or demoted.[34] In the state of Virginia, for example, in 1964 there were 107 black principals; in 1971, there were 17.[35] A frequent complaint was that principals who escaped outright firing were reassigned to lower prestige roles in "white" schools. Some teachers were released without recourse. A few received scholarship aid for advanced study from private foundations, presumably to increase their adequacy for reemployment to positions in which opportunities were greater. Systematic study of the problem with particular attention to wasted black talent remained an urgent necessity.

## Quality Education and Quality Integrated Education

Experience had taught black parents that separate schools were inferior: less money was spent on them; their curricular choices were limited; and in every area, from the physical plant and equipment to the quality of maintenance, the white school had the advantage.

Integration promised a way to share in the benefits of better schools and facilities, special programs, and broader opportunities. In the past, those black children fortunate enough to attend integrated schools had been exposed to richer educational experiences than those offered in the slum schools.

But white resistance to the sharing of such opportunities made the reality of integration less attractive than blacks had anticipated. The slow pace of desegregation and the large number of neighborhood schools entrenched in solidly segregated communities led to a more immediate concern for the quality of education available in these settings as well as a search for realistic means by which to offset glaring deficiencies. The term "quality education," heralded in the late 1960s as a new concept, simply denoted long-known basic principles for promoting intellectual growth, academic success, and subsequent feelings of personal worth. One of its basic premises was that, barring genetic impairment, children *could* learn. However, to realize their fullest potential they needed rich experiences from the earliest years, thoughtfully designed academic approaches, scholastic materials commensurate with their stage of growth, and sensitivity to their affective needs.

The notion of "quality education" was given a public dimension when a bill was introduced in the Senate to be known as the Quality Integrated Education Act of 1971. The intent was to refocus on school integration as a means of meeting the educational needs of all children and as a means of offsetting further polarization between blacks and whites which carried with it the threat of a divided nation. Support for drafting the bill grew out of documented misuse and abuse of federal funds which had been appropriated for integration but used instead to support segregated schools, faculty, and staff, and in clear violation of the law had been given to local educational agencies which systematically demoted and fired black teachers, principals, and athletic coaches. Funds were also used by agencies to supplant state funds instead of supplementing them.

Drafters of the 1971 bill took into account findings of a 1966 study entitled *Equality in Educational Opportunity*[36] and the testimony of Dr. Thomas Pettigrew, Chairman of the Advisory Committee on Race and Education of the Civil Rights Commission, before the Select Senate Committee on Equal Educational Opportunity. Both of these sources emphasized that the single most influential factor affecting improved learning of the disadvantaged child was interaction in the classroom with children from educationally advantaged backgrounds. Among other things, the bill provided for the development of educational parks, large campus-like settings for elementary and secondary schools envisioned as developing on fringe areas of cities, thereby crossing political boundaries, breaking down the neighborhood concept, and integrating suburban and city children. There would be practical benefits as well in the clustering of schools in a park arrangement. Such facilities as swimming pools, libraries, and health units, too costly for individual schools and notably absent in low-income areas, would now be feasible.

## The Politics of Education

Federal aid to education is not new. The Morrill Act of 1862 granted land for state-supported institutions of higher education. However, passage of the Elementary and Secondary Education Act and the Higher Education Act of 1965, with their overtones of equality in educational experience and their direct aim at children and youth in impoverished areas, was of special significance to the black population. Politically, these acts represented the culmination of a larger, long-standing struggle to obtain general aid to education. Achievement of this aim had been repeatedly thwarted both by conservative elements who espoused completely local control of education, and parochial school advocates who insisted on comparable aid to nonpublic schools.

In 1955, under the Eisenhower Administration, an attempt was made to draw up a bill providing federal funds for school construction. Projections in support of such a bill skirted the religious issue and attempted to minimize pressure for compliance with the Supreme Court decision of 1954 which outlawed segregation in public schools. The proposed bill, considered a weak one from the outset, was unable to survive Republican opposition and the adoption of the Powell Amendment which denied funds to states which failed to comply with the desegregation decision. Southern Democrats who had voted for the amendment had done so with the certainty that such a rider would defeat the entire measure through a coalition vote of the Republican opposition and themselves. The collapse of the measure attested to the success of their strategy.

Hope was rekindled in 1961, however, when President John F. Kennedy, deeply committed to education, took office. Unfortunately, the immediate reopening of the issue of aid to religious schools again prevented passage of effective legislation. However, passage of the Civil Rights Act of 1964 became a powerful influence in behalf of federal funds for education. Under Titles IV and VI of the Act, the Attorney General of the United States was empowered to enforce desegregation of schools and colleges, and the United States Office of Education was authorized to provide technical and financial assistance to school districts which were in the process of desegregating. Those practicing segregation were to be considered ineligible to receive federal funds. With the passage of the Civil Rights Act the Powell Amendment was no longer necessary.

A combination of factors accounted for final passage of the above bills. The assassination of President Kennedy in 1963 had not only stunned the nation; it had engendered sympathy for his programs. In addition, the bills were presented to Congress simultaneously as a poverty measure, a just means of helping deprived children and youth, and as an antidote to the civil disorders in the nation's ghettos. In 1965, under the leadership of President Johnson, the bills were passed by the Congress and signed into law.

## Civil Rights and Education

As we have seen, there was a direct correlation between the new thrust in school desegregation and the civil rights movement. Black insistence on recognition of the 1954 Supreme Court Decision in the School Segregation Cases led to court suits for withholding state and federal funds from school districts not in compliance with the law. The threat of withdrawal of funds led to a variety of patterns of token integration, in-school segregation, and discrimination in new unitary systems. Politically, attention turned to the discriminatory patterns of the North. Black ghetto schools of central cities were charged with perpetuating the segregated patterns of the South with the added dimension of turbulence created by crowded slums and urban unrest.

Through enforcement of the guideline regulations developed under Title VI of the Civil Rights Act, by 1968, 20 percent of black children in the South were in desegregated schools. Since that time various reports have revealed a slackening of progress due to weakening of guidelines, failure to follow through on court orders, failure to cut off funds for noncompliance and toleration of new strategies for perpetuating segregation. Examples of the latter type of abuse were tax-free, private, all-white southern academies with the Justice Department sustaining tax exemption on the grounds that such action did not constitute unlawful support.

In June 1971 a report issued by the Department of Health, Education, and Welfare noted that the percentage of black students attending predominantly white schools increased from 23 percent to 33 percent between the fall of 1968 and the fall of 1970. The increase was attributed almost wholly to the rapid rise of integrated schools in the South. In seventeen southern states the percentage of black students enrolled in schools with white students increased from 6.4 percent in 1960 to 84.3 percent in 1970.* The number increased from 19,500 to 3,220,000 respectively.[37]

*Integration gains (in precentages) noted for 1971 were:

| | |
|---|---|
| Alabama 8.3 to 36.5 | North Carolina 28.3 to 54.1 |
| Arkansas 22.6 to 43 | South Carolina 14.2 to 44.8 |
| Florida 23.2 to 48.4 | Tennessee 21.2 to 32.3 |
| Georgia 14. to 35.9 | Texas 25.3 to 34.9 |
| Louisiana 8.9 to 31.2 | Virginia 26.9 to 41.4 |

Southern Congressmen claimed that desegregation efforts by the Government had been directed in the main against the South, and that more integration was being required of their schools than of those in the rest of the nation. In June 1972 the Congress enacted the Equal Education Opportunity Amendment to the Higher Education Act which provided funds for support of integration efforts in the North as well as the South.[38]

It should also be noted that despite the trend toward integration in the South, integration in the big cities of the North and South generally declined. In New York, where blacks comprised 34 percent of the school population, the percentage of blacks in "white" schools during 1968 to 1970 dropped from 19.7 to 16.3. In Minneapolis the percentage fell from 70.8 to 57.6; Boston from 23.8 to 18; St. Louis, 7.1 to 2.5; Detroit, 9 to 5.8; and Philadelphia, 9.6 to 7.4. In 1970, seventeen large cities had a majority of black pupils: Washington, D. C, 94.6; Compton, California, 83; Newark, 72.2; New Orleans, 69.5; Atlanta, 68.7; Baltimore, 67.1; St. Louis, 65.6; Gary, Indiana, 64.7; Richmond, 64.2; Detroit, 63.8; Philadelphia, 60.5; Cleveland, 57.6; Oakland, 56.9; Chicago, 54.8; Birmingham, 54.6; Memphis, 51.6; and Kansas City, 50.2.[39] The rush of whites to the suburbs was clearly reflected in the increasingly black composition of metropolitan classrooms.

## BLACK YOUTH IN COLLEGE

Nationally, college attendance among blacks increased significantly from 1964 to 1974. In 1964, only 306,000 out of a total college enrollment of 4,338,000 were nonwhite students (see Table IV) and 5 in 100 students were black.[40] By 1974 the number had increased to 814,000 or approximately 10.5 percent of a total enrollment of 7,781,000.

In 1974 there were nearly 300,000 more black college students than there were in 1970, an increase of 56 percent in four years. However, since 12 percent of all 18-to-21-year-olds are black, blacks continue to be underrepresented among college students.

Table IV compares enrollment over a ten-year period.

In the past, the vast majority of black students were enrolled in black colleges. However, with the lowering of economic, racial, and even academic barriers, the picture has changed dramatically. As will be seen from Table V, 73 percent of black college students are now enrolled in predominantly white institutions.

The redistribution of black students reflects a wide spectrum of social and political changes in the nation. No longer are most of the brightest black students and finest black professors concentrated on southern black campuses. Promising black high school graduates have wider options. However, the black college still fulfills its traditional function of offering education and professional training to students of limited means on the way up the social and economic ladder.

**TABLE IV—SCHOOL ENROLLMENT OF THE POPULATION 3 TO 34 YEARS OLD BY LEVEL AND CONTROL OF SCHOOL AND RACE: OCTOBER 1964 TO OCTOBER 1974**

(Numbers in thousands. Civilian noninstitutional population)

| Level and Control of School | 1974 | 1973 | 1972 | 1971 | 1970 | 1969 | 1968 | 1967 | 1966 | 1965 | 1964 |
|---|---|---|---|---|---|---|---|---|---|---|---|
| **WHITE** | | | | | | | | | | | |
| Total enrolled | 50,992 | 50,617 | 51,314 | 52,081 | 51,719 | 51,465 | 50,608 | 49,721 | 48,620 | 47,451 | 45,541 |
| Nursery school | 1,340 | 1,087 | 1,079 | 888 | 893 | 676 | 664 | 564 | 564 | 451 | 399 |
| Public | 293 | 242 | 285 | 225 | 198 | 136 | 163 | 134 | 127 | 93 | 55 |
| Private | 1,048 | 845 | 794 | 664 | 695 | 539 | 501 | 429 | 437 | 358 | 344 |
| Kindergarten | 2,745 | 2,584 | 2,633 | 2,735 | 2,706 | 2,803 | 2,775 | 2,840 | 2,693 | 2,648 | 2,450 |
| Public | 2,268 | 2,139 | 2,185 | 2,207 | 2,233 | 2,289 | 2,272 | 2,254 | 2,163 | 2,086 | 2,031 |
| Private | 477 | 445 | 448 | 527 | 473 | 515 | 504 | 587 | 530 | 562 | 419 |
| Elementary school | 26,051 | 26,531 | 27,185 | 28,187 | 28,638 | 28,572 | 28,634 | 28,415 | 28,012 | 27,679 | 27,097 |
| Public | 23,063 | 23,506 | 23,869 | 24,720 | 24,923 | 24,803 | 24,580 | 24,044 | 23,469 | 22,976 | 22,381 |
| Private | 2,990 | 3,025 | 3,316 | 3,466 | 3,715 | 3,768 | 4,054 | 4,371 | 4,542 | 4,703 | 4,716 |
| High school | 13,073 | 13,091 | 12,959 | 12,998 | 12,723 | 12,588 | 12,280 | 11,997 | 11,643 | 11,356 | 11,257 |
| Public | 11,966 | 11,967 | 11,876 | 11,937 | 11,599 | 11,502 | 11,007 | 10,769 | 10,312 | 9,961 | 9,898 |
| Private | 1,107 | 1,124 | 1,083 | 1,061 | 1,124 | 1,085 | 1,272 | 1,228 | 1,329 | 1,395 | 1,359 |
| College | 7,781 | 7,324 | 7,458 | 7,273 | 6,759 | 6,827 | 6,255 | 5,905 | 5,708 | 5,317 | 4,338 |
| Public | 6,049 | 5,550 | 5,644 | 5,624 | 5,168 | 4,967 | 4,501 | 4,155 | 3,914 | 3,568 | 2,798 |
| Private | 1,732 | 1,773 | 1,814 | 1,650 | 1,591 | 1,860 | 1,753 | 1,750 | 1,795 | 1,749 | 1,540 |
| **BLACK[1]** | | | | | | | | | | | |
| Total enrolled | 8,215 | 7,834 | 7,959 | 8,178 | 7,829 | 7,680 | 7,448 | 7,196 | 7,547 | 7,252 | 6,946 |
| Nursery school | 227 | 210 | 185 | 151 | 178 | 170 | 132 | 140 | 125 | 72 | 69 |
| Public | 121 | 146 | 113 | 90 | 129 | 102 | 89 | 92 | 88 | 37 | 35 |
| Private | 106 | 64 | 72 | 61 | 49 | 68 | 43 | 47 | 37 | 35 | 34 |
| Kindergarten | 463 | 423 | 448 | 464 | 426 | 425 | 448 | 418 | 420 | 407 | 381 |
| Public | 416 | 391 | 402 | 422 | 374 | 361 | 397 | 375 | 364 | 353 | 318 |
| Private | 47 | 32 | 46 | 42 | 53 | 64 | 51 | 44 | 56 | 54 | 63 |
| Elementary school | 4,585 | 4,473 | 4,573 | 4,877 | 4,868 | 4,785 | 4,716 | 4,618 | 4,904 | 4,796 | 4,634 |
| Public | 4,455 | 4,277 | 4,382 | 4,712 | 4,668 | 4,633 | 4,569 | 4,444 | 4,739 | 4,620 | 4,430 |
| Private | 131 | 196 | 191 | 165 | 200 | 151 | 146 | 173 | 165 | 176 | 205 |
| High school | 2,125 | 2,044 | 2,025 | 2,006 | 1,834 | 1,808 | 1,718 | 1,651 | 1,721 | 1,619 | 1,556 |
| Public | 2,072 | 1,988 | 1,971 | 1,951 | 1,794 | 1,751 | 1,656 | 1,605 | 1,673 | 1,556 | 1,505 |
| Private | 54 | 56 | 54 | 55 | 41 | 57 | 62 | 46 | 48 | 62 | 51 |
| College | 814 | 684 | 727 | 680 | 522 | 492 | 434 | 370 | 377 | 358 | 306 |
| Public | 659 | 537 | 582 | 532 | 422 | 372 | 359 | 280 | 264 | 272 | 227 |
| Private | 155 | 147 | 145 | 148 | 100 | 120 | 75 | 90 | 113 | 86 | 78 |

[1]Data for 1964 to 1966 are for Negro and other races.

Source: U. S. Department of Commerce, Bureau of the Census, *Population Characteristics, School Enrollment . . . October, 1974*, Series P-20, No. 278, p. 3.

TABLE V—BLACK ENROLLMENT IN INSTITUTIONS OF HIGHER EDUCATION: 1973

|  | Predominantly White | | Predominantly Black | | Total |
|---|---|---|---|---|---|
|  | Number | % | Number | % |  |
| All colleges | 500,000 | 73.1 | 183,419 | 26.8 | 684,000 |
| Public | 402,000 | 74.9 | 135,000 | 25.1 | 537,000 |
| Private | 98,000 | 71.0 | 40,000 | 29.0 | 138,000 |

Sources: Elias Blake, Jr., et al., Comps., *Degrees Granted and Enrollment Trends in Historically Black Colleges: An Eight-Year Study,* Institute for Services to Education, Inc., Washington, D. C., 1974; and Jack Magarrell, "Black Enrollment Rising Again," *The Chronicle of Higher Education,* March 17, 1975, p. 1.

## Black Colleges

Astute observers of human growth note that a hazard accompanies every hurdle. As the infant progresses toward adulthood, each stage of his growth requires new abilities and increased competencies. He must exercise his fledgling talents and seek to make his presence known and respected in an environment which cannot be completely protective against injuries, threats, and dangers. Similarly, hazards have been encountered by blacks as they have pressed forward toward higher educational attainment. For example, the invoking of court procedures to cut off funds from school districts not in compliance with civil rights regulations can work to the detriment of blacks as well as whites, and efforts to eliminate or at least reduce racism in white institutions of higher learning have stripped many black institutions of some of their brightest students and best faculty members. The problems of black colleges have been further complicated by overwhelming financial pressures. Historically, black institutions of higher learning have received less federal support than white institutions. This led the presidents of these institutions to organize formally and in 1969 to petition President Nixon to examine their plight in the context of their special needs, functions, and commitments. In 1970 the National Association for Equal Opportunity in Higher Education was formally organized.

In 1972 there were 111 black colleges in existence, 68 private and 43 public, serving 160,000 students. Fifteen had graduate programs leading to the master of arts degree in disciplines other than education. Two, Howard and Atlanta Universities, offered a program leading to the degree of doctor of philosophy. In 1968, 80 percent of all black college graduates received degrees from black institutions.[41] Yet these institutions have had to fight for survival in a world which has assumed that a system of integrated education has rendered them unnecessary. In reality, in our credential-oriented society in which higher education is the core of upward social and economic mobility, the black college is uniquely prepared to deal with the special problems, concerns, and handicaps of the black student and to instill in him the clear expectation that he and his classmates will succeed. The black college also serves as a repository for creative productions in art and literature as well as a keeper of the archives of research on problems unique to the population it serves. It claims the competence for setting guidelines for scholarly research, aiding in honest social inquiry and securing access to minority populations who are becoming increasingly hostile to "alien" researchers. It is precisely in an examination of such populations that the roots for achievement lie. In addition to providing information and intellectual stimulation, such studies have interest as psychological interpretations of the black experience.

Black colleges can also make an important contribution to occupational retraining and continuing education, which can be decisive factors in achieving upward economic mobility. As the college serves the basic educational and social needs of the community, it becomes a center of influence and a focus for the training of young people in intelligent leadership. The black institution sees as one of its many roles the creation of a pleasant, nonthreatening atmosphere in which latent talent will find fruition under the guidance of empathetic individuals. Techniques for offsetting educational handicaps as well as stimulation of continuing interest in higher education are also among its primary goals.

A report by the Federal Interagency Commission on Education revealed that out of $4 billion appropriated to institutions of higher learning in 1969, only $122 million, or 3 percent, was received by black colleges. The majority of black colleges were invariably precluded from greater financial assistance because of legislative funding criteria which required the presence of established graduate programs in the areas to be funded. Funds earmarked for aid to developing colleges or for training for disadvantaged youth were far from adequate and not to be compared with the lavish grants available, for example, in the sciences. Historically, black colleges have struggled for aid in the maelstrom of legislative proceedings which have rendered their efforts practically hopeless. Today, however, the picture is beginning to change thanks to the increasing political sophistication of black administrators, the growth in black congressional representation, and the increasing general demand for more realistic levels of support for black colleges. Nevertheless, despite the efforts of private foundations to identify and aid those black institutions which appear most viable (according to criteria of their selection), some have found their financial problems insoluble and are closing or being absorbed by other colleges.

The number of public-supported black-oriented colleges was, for a time, on the increase in large cities as inner-city community colleges grew. At the same time, the integration of colleges like West Virginia State College and Lincoln University in Missouri altered the totally black orientation of these campuses. The legal complications entailed in dual educational systems have created pressures to merge black and white state colleges. For a while there were instances of attempts to found new white units of state universities in the same towns where black ones already existed. But black educational communities, concerned over the prospect that many black college administrators and faculty would be replaced by whites, came to interpret such unification policies as the death knell of black self-determination in public higher education.

TABLE VI—PERCENTAGE OF BACHELOR DEGREES AWARDED BY SELECTED FIELDS IN HISTORICALLY BLACK[1] AND OTHER COLLEGES[2]

| | | 1965–66 | 1966–67 | 1967–68 | 1968–69 | 1969–70 | 1970–71 | 1971–72[2] | 1972–73[2] |
|---|---|---|---|---|---|---|---|---|---|
| Biological Sciences | Black Colleges | 6.7 | 6.0 | 6.1 | 5.7 | 4.9 | 4.9 | 4.2 | 3.5 |
| | Other Colleges | 5.2 | 5.1 | 5.0 | 4.8 | 4.7 | 4.3 | 4.4 | 4.4 |
| Business & Management | Black Colleges | 4.9 | 5.9 | 7.3 | 8.9 | 11.0 | 13.7 | 14.0 | 15.1 |
| | Other Colleges | 12.1 | 12.4 | 12.6 | 12.9 | 13.3 | 13.8 | 13.4 | 13.1 |
| Education | Black Colleges | 44.9 | 43.3 | 40.2 | 37.6 | 36.1 | 35.1 | 34.6 | 33.4 |
| | Other Colleges | 22.6 | 21.5 | 21.3 | 20.9 | 20.9 | 21.0 | 15.5 | 15.4 |
| Physical Sciences | Black Colleges | 2.6 | 2.4 | 2.2 | 1.9 | 2.0 | 1.6 | 1.7 | 1.6 |
| | Other Colleges | 3.3 | 3.2 | 3.1 | 2.9 | 2.7 | 2.5 | 2.5 | 2.4 |
| Social Sciences | Black Colleges | 17.2 | 18.5 | 19.4 | 20.8 | 22.3 | 22.6 | 21.9 | 19.6 |
| | Other Colleges | 17.9 | 18.6 | 19.1 | 19.3 | 19.4 | 19.9 | 19.7 | 20.2 |
| Other | Black Colleges | 23.7 | 23.9 | 24.8 | 25.1 | 23.8 | 22.1 | 23.6 | 26.8 |
| | Other Colleges | 38.9 | 39.2 | 38.9 | 39.2 | 38.9 | 38.5 | 44.5 | 44.5 |
| Total Bachelors | Black Colleges | 100.0 | 100.0 | 100.0 | 100.0 | 100.0 | 100.0 | 100.0 | 100.0 |
| | Other Colleges | 100.0 | 100.0 | 100.0 | 100.0 | 100.0 | 100.0 | 100.0 | 100.0 |

[1]Historically black colleges are defined as those 1) founded primarily for black Americans and 2) identified with service to this group for at least two decades. The term does not include those predominantly black institutions which fail to satisfy both criteria.

[2]Projected national figures. (Actual figures not available)

Source: Elias Blake, Jr., et al., Comps. *Degrees Granted and Enrollment Trends in Historically Black Colleges*, Institute for Services to Education, Washington, D.C., 1974, p. 38.

## Trends in Black Colleges

An analysis of the academic disciplines selected by students in black colleges reveals certain clearly identifiable directions of change. Those changes generally parallel those in the predominantly white colleges, but are greater in degree, and have special significance for the black population. There is a decline in the proportion of degrees awarded in the field of education from 44.9 percent in 1965 to 33.4 percent in 1973. (See Table VI.) While education is still an important choice for black students, they are venturing into other fields as opportunities broaden, and they are less limited by the traditional choices—teaching, the ministry, and social work.

As a logical concomitant of this trend, the number of students studying business administration has tripled from 5 to 15 percent between 1966 and 1973.[42] Interest follows opportunity, and young blacks tend to study in fields which offer potential for earning a living. Thus the old, vicious circle—being untrained for the job, and unable to get the job because one is untrained—is being slowly broken. More corporations are interested in blacks beyond mere window dressing. More are beginning to recruit young blacks for executive training programs and policy-making positions.

The broader intellectual spectrum of students in black colleges may also reflect richer curricula, better libraries, reciprocal relationships with other colleges, increased federal funding, and other advances.

Between 1966 and 1973, there was a decrease in the proportion of degrees awarded in the biological sciences (from 6.7 percent to 3.5 percent) and in the physical sciences (from 2.6 to 1.6 percent). In the social sciences there was a slight increase.

While the percentage of black college students enrolled in historically black colleges has declined, their actual numbers have not. There are, in fact, more students in these colleges than ever before. A few, like Howard and Tennessee State Universities, have grown into sizeable institutions with student bodies of 10,000 to 15,000. Table VII shows that from 1970 to 1971 black college enrollment increased at a higher rate than did enrollment in all colleges and universities.

**TABLE VII—BLACK ENROLLMENT IN COLLEGES AND UNIVERSITIES: 1970 AND 1971**

| Enrollment | Fall 1970 | % Change | Fall 1971 |
|---|---|---|---|
| Total Black Undergraduate | 154,602 | 5.2% | 162,638 |
| Total National Undergraduate | 7,432,963 | 5.1% | 7,815,718 |
| Total Black Graduate | 13,726 | 13.0% | 15,505 |
| Total National Graduate | 1,216,405 | −0.6% | 1,209,313 |
| Grand Total Black Enrollment | 168,328 | 5.8% | 178,143 |
| Grand Total National Enrollment | 8,649,368 | 4.3% | 9,025,031 |

Source:  Elias Blake, Jr., et al., Comps., *Degrees Granted and Enrollment Trends in Historically Black Colleges,* Institute for Services to Education, Washington, D. C., 1974, p. 22.

Total enrollment in these colleges (see Table VIII) has increased from roughly 139,000 in 1966 to 183,000 in 1973, an increase of 32 percent.

Although only 30 to 40 percent of the blacks enrolled nationally were in historically black colleges, it is these colleges which have in the past produced the largest number of actual graduates. (See Table VIII.) About 80 percent of the baccalaureate degrees awarded to black students in 1968 were conferred by black institutions. It is likely that the latter still confer upon black students a considerably higher proportion of baccalaureate degrees than their enrollment would suggest. A major reason for this is the expectation of routine success in a black college, as compared with fear of failure for many black students in what seems to be an alien environment. A second is that a much larger percentage of freshmen (93 percent) in black colleges are enrolled in four-year, full-time programs, thus avoiding the automatically high rate of student loss after completion of the two-year college program.

**TABLE VIII—**_HISTORICALLY BLACK COLLEGES*:_ PERCENTAGE OF THEIR TOTAL FALL ENROLLMENT AND FIRST-TIME FRESHMEN IN FOUR-YEAR AND TWO-YEAR COLLEGES FROM 1966 TO 1973

|  | 1966 | 1967 | 1968 | 1969 | 1970 | 1971 | 1972 | 1973 |
|---|---|---|---|---|---|---|---|---|
| Four-year Total | 134,099 | 142,851 | 149,847 | 155,960 | 162,134 | 171,757 | 174,691 | 177,022 |
| % Total Enrollment | 96.2 | 96.3 | 96.7 | 96.4 | 96.3 | 96.4 | 96.4 | 96.5 |
| Two-year Total | 5,345 | 5,450 | 5,130 | 5,749 | 6,194 | 6,386 | 6,598 | 6,397 |
| % Total Enrollment | 3.8 | 3.7 | 3.3 | 3.6 | 3.7 | 3.6 | 3.6 | 3.5 |
| Grand Total Enrollment | 139,444 | 148,301 | 154,977 | 161,709 | 168,328 | 178,143 | 181,289 | 183,419 |
| Four-year First-time | 39,432 | 37,155 | 37,897 | 37,160 | 39,566 | 39,644 | 38,393 | 36,924 |
| % Total First-time | 92.5 | 92.9 | 92.8 | 92.8 | 92.7 | 92.6 | 92.8 | 92.8 |
| Two-year First-time | 3,183 | 2.852 | 2,928 | 2,864 | 3,108 | 3,170 | 2,985 | 2,448 |
| % Total First-time | 7.5 | 7.1 | 7.2 | 7.2 | 7.3 | 7.4 | 7.2 | 7.2 |
| Grand Total First-time Freshmen | 42.615 | 40,007 | 40,825 | 40,024 | 42,674 | 42,814 | 41,378 | 39,372 |

*See Note [1], Table VI.
Source: Elias Blake, Jr., et al., Comps., _Degrees Granted and Enrollment Trends in Historically Black Colleges,_ Institute for Services to Education, Washington, D. C., 1974, p. 29.

There are several other trends of interest. In 1973, 6,231 graduate degrees were conferred by black colleges; 5,545 of these were master's degrees, 43 were doctorates and 643, professional degrees. Of the 118 doctoral degrees conferred between 1971 and 1973, 27 percent were in the physical sciences and 35.6 percent in the biological sciences.

The proportion of male students, historically less numerous than females, increased 46.3 percent in 1966 to 48.2 percent in 1973, slightly more than their proportion in the black population (47 percent). Historically, black families have encouraged their daughters to get an education as protection against the sexual exploitation of black women domestic servants, while there was greater pressure on boys to enter the labor force. (See Table IX.)

**TABLE IX—HISTORICALLY BLACK\* AND ALL COLLEGES AND UNIVERSITIES: TOTAL FALL ENROLLMENT AND FIRST-TIME FRESHMEN BY SEX AND BY CONTROL FOR SELECTED YEARS FROM 1966 TO 1973**

| | | 1966 | | 1969 | | 1971 | | 1973 | |
|---|---|---|---|---|---|---|---|---|---|
| | | Black | National | Black | National | Black | National | Black | National[1] |
| **Public** | | | | | | | | | |
| Total Enrollment | % Male | 46.3 | 59.6 | 48.0 | 58.5 | 48.4 | 57.5 | 48.2 | 55.2 |
| | % Female | 53.7 | 40.4 | 52.0 | 41.5 | 51.6 | 42.5 | 51.8 | 44.8 |
| | Total | 100.0 | 100.0 | 100.0 | 100.0 | 100.0 | 100.0 | 100.0 | 100.0 |
| First-Time Enrollment | % Male | 47.0 | 57.6 | 50.0 | 57.4 | 48.0 | 55.8 | 48.7 | NA |
| | % Female | 53.0 | 42.4 | 50.0 | 42.6 | 52.0 | 44.2 | 51.3 | NA |
| | Total | 100.0 | 100.0 | 100.0 | 100.0 | 100.0 | 100.0 | 100.0 | 100.0 |
| **Private** | | | | | | | | | |
| Total Enrollment | % Male | 43.0 | 61.6 | 44.2 | 61.2 | 45.5 | 59.9 | 46.7 | 57.8 |
| | % Female | 57.0 | 38.4 | 55.8 | 38.8 | 54.5 | 40.1 | 53.3 | 42.2 |
| | Total | 100.0 | 100.0 | 100.0 | 100.0 | 100.0 | 100.0 | 100.0 | 100.0 |
| First-Time Enrollment | % Male | 42.7 | 55.9 | 44.2 | 54.8 | 46.5 | 52.9 | 45.8 | NA |
| | % Female | 57.3 | 44.1 | 55.8 | 45.2 | 53.5 | 47.1 | 54.2 | NA |
| | Total | 100.0 | 100.0 | 100.0 | 100.0 | 100.0 | 100.0 | 100.0 | 100.0 |
| **Grand Total** | | | | | | | | | |
| Total Enrollment | % Male | 45.3 | 60.2 | 46.9 | 59.2 | 47.6 | 58.0 | 47.8 | 55.8 |
| | % Female | 54.7 | 39.8 | 53.1 | 40.8 | 52.4 | 42.0 | 52.2 | 44.2 |
| | Total | 100.0 | 100.0 | 100.0 | 100.0 | 100.0 | 100.0 | 100.0 | 100.0 |
| First-Time Enrollment | % Male | 45.5 | 57.2 | 48.1 | 56.8 | 47.5 | 55.2 | 47.8 | NA |
| | % Female | 54.5 | 42.8 | 51.9 | 43.2 | 52.5 | 44.8 | 52.2 | NA |
| | Total | 100.0 | 100.0 | 100.0 | 100.0 | 100.0 | 100.0 | 100.0 | 100.0 |

\*See Note [1], Table VI.
[1] Preliminary National Data

Source: Elias Blake, Jr., et al., Comps., *Degrees Granted and Enrollment Trends in Historically Black Colleges*, Institute for Services to Education, Washington, D. C., 1974, p. 30.

Since about 60 percent of black students come from families with an income of between $3,000 and $9,999, the availability of financial aid is a major determinant of black students' ability to enter college after they have been admitted. It is also an important factor in enabling students from the two-year colleges to continue their education and will be a factor in keeping them in attendance until they graduate.

## Blacks in White Colleges

Black students in the major state-supported universities comprised less than two percent of the college population in 1968 and were exceeded in number by foreign students.[43]

Region is not a significant factor in accounting for the presence of black students, although there are slightly more in the Midwest. In the West they account for 1.3 percent of the total; the South, 1.8 percent; the East 1.8 percent; and the Midwest 2.9 percent. The fact that the proportion in college is far smaller than the 11 percent which is the black percentage of the total population has caused some institutions to extend special services to students who because of economic and educational deficits would otherwise have no access to their offerings. Further, the urgent need for the economic competence that is provided by an educated citizenry has led some educators to reconsider the consequences of large scale manpower wastage.

Traditionally, blacks have been present in token numbers in universities of the North, West and Midwest and have performed on a scholastic level equal to that of other students. They have usually come from backgrounds which valued education as the key to opportunity. This changed, however, with the inauguration of deliberate efforts to enroll disadvantaged youth. Along with such programs arose the need for parallel efforts to modify admission policies, to design special programs to supplement educational deficiencies, and to provide guidance in social adjustment.

The problem of selection of suitable candidates for admission became a difficult and controversial area. Traditional grades and test scores were admittedly imperfect indicators of future success; so were interviews, which might be judged heavily on conventional manners, dress, or familiarity with the trappings of higher education. Between the cultural biases of the tests and interviews and the absence of financial and psychological supports, black candidates could not easily compete; yet experimental admissions on less conventional bases had proved capable of producing able students. In the mid-70s there was still controversy over what criteria were appropriate and reliable, and a court case, *DeFunis v. Odegaard*, — U. S. —, 94 S. Ct. 1704 (1974), leaned heavily on the presumption that grades and test scores were valid criteria, not to be outweighed by other considerations. The Supreme Court declared the case moot, and the issue remained unresolved; but a growing number of publicly supported institutions of higher education had already adopted a policy of open admissions which gave all high school graduates a chance for higher education. More white than black candidates took advantage of the opportunity; and where there was a serious commitment to give the necessary support to students who were overcoming weaknesses in their high school preparation, a record of successful students from unconventional beginnings began to take shape. Such commitment was not always in evidence, however, and opponents of the program were sometimes accused of making certain that it would not function effectively, while proponents pointed to gratifying successes in developing greater black participation in higher education. Some students found it a great hardship to maintain the "B" average required for scholarships and also maintain their work responsibilities. Financial problems were added to the black students' social and emotional concerns regarding dormitory housing, dating, and acceptance on the campus.

Studies by Lawrence Clark and Kenneth P. Plotkin (1963) and Morris Meister (1965) showed that the dropout rate for black students, despite their problems, was lower than the national rate for white students as well as for those attending predominantly black colleges. Furthermore, grade point averages required for the baccalaureate were generally maintained, although few of the initially disadvantaged were among the top-ranking students.

Things did not always move smoothly, however, in the aftermath of admittance of blacks to universities. There were confrontations at Cornell, Illinois, San Francisco State and the University of Florida. Black students raised such issues as the stepping up of black-student recruitment to allow a sense of valid participation in an in-group, the increasing of the number of black faculty members and administrators, the inclusion of black studies in the curriculum, and in some instances, provisions for separate living facilities in which blacks could escape from the constant reminder of their difference. Students claimed that white institutions were insensitive to their feelings and needs and made little effort either to reorient practices to accommodate less-affluent students or to eliminate traces of racism. Universities were challenged to self-examination in areas hitherto ignored.

Some private white institutions, however, were committed to expanding their services to black students and engaged in considerable activity on their behalf. In the summer of 1964, Oberlin, Dartmouth, and Princeton began to experiment with strengthening the academic background of potentially talented high-school students with severely deprived backgrounds in the hope of their eventual acceptance in the nation's universities and a subsequent achievement of productive life. The program was financed by the Rockefeller Foundation; curriculum content was determined by each institution. Oberlin, interested in the downward extension of age level accepted both girls and boys at the seventh- and eighth-grade levels. Princeton, working with boys, centered on skills requirements for mathematics and science. Dartmouth, with the most formalized procedures, revealed in an evaluation that of the fifty-five initial students, thirty-five were advanced enough to be recommended for preparatory-school admission, twelve were recommended with reservation, and eight were not recommended. Two of the latter, however, were admitted to private academies, resulting in total admissions of forty-nine out of the original fifty-five.

After the passage of the 1965 Higher Education Act and the establishment of the Office of Economic Opportunity during the same period, Mount Holyoke and Connecticut colleges inaugurated A Better Chance programs for girls, and a number of other institutions across the country developed and adapted the concept of working to strengthen college preparation.

Public as well as private institutions sponsored Upward Bound and Early Identification programs; some, like the Search for Elevation, Education, and Knowledge (SEEK) program of the City University of New York, were local in origin.

The traditional role of the black professional school has been to produce graduates rooted in the black experience and committed to service in the black community. These are generally located and trained among black populations. The vast majority of black doctors and lawyers practicing today were produced by black institutions, because of exclusion from other schools, less sophisticated undergraduate preparation, more moderate tuitions, and the southern background of most of the students. For a summary of professional degrees awarded by black colleges, consult Table X.

**TABLE X—PROFESSIONAL DEGREES AWARDED IN HISTORICALLY BLACK COLLEGES***
IN SELECTED FIELDS: 1971 TO 1973

|  | 1970–71 | 1971–72 | 1972–73 |
|---|---|---|---|
| Law | 164 | 195 | 259 |
| Theology | 59 | 47 | 67 |
| Dentistry (D.D.S. or D.M.D.) | 95 | 106 | 128 |
| Medicine (M.D.) | 160 | 176 | 173 |
| Veterinary Medicine (D.V.M.) | 25 | 27 | 16 |
| Total Professional Degrees | 503 | 551 | 643 |

*See Note [1], Table VI.

Source: Elias Blake, Jr., et al., Comps., *Degrees Granted and Enrollment Trends in Historically Black Colleges.* Institute for Services to Education, Washington, D. C., 1974, p. 48.

In 1974, 6.8 percent of the medical students in the United States were black. The black National Medical Association (N.M.A.), considers this small percentage inadequate to the health needs of the black population, as well as underrepresenting the 11 percent of the population which is black. The N.M.A. is concerned not only with the number of black medical students but with the ability of those entering medical schools to complete their training and, once trained, to serve in black communities.

In 1974 there were two traditionally black medical schools, Meharry Medical College in Nashville and Howard University School of Medicine in Washington, D.C. Both Howard and Meharry also have departments of dentistry. In 1974 Morehouse College in Atlanta received a grant of $800,000.00 from the Human Resources Administration of the Department of Health, Education and Welfare to study the feasibility of establishing a two year graduate medical training program. After the projected medical course at Morehouse, students would be able to complete the remaining two years at other medical schools. The prospective date for the first admissions is 1977.

Tables XI and XII based upon 1970 statistics give some indication of the distribution of students in the field of dentistry and medicine.

**TABLE XI—MEDICAL SCHOOL ENROLLMENT: 1970**
(Region and U. S. Summaries)

| | American Indian | | Black | | Oriental | | Spanish Surname | | Total Minority | | Other | | Total | |
|---|---|---|---|---|---|---|---|---|---|---|---|---|---|---|
| | Number | Percent | Number | Percent | Number | Percent | Number | Percent | Number | Percent | Number | Percent | Number | Percent |
| I. Northern and Western States Region Totals | 33 | .1 | 949 | 3.2 | 709 | 2.4 | 236 | .8 | 1,927 | 6.5 | 27,615 | 93.5 | 29,542 | 100.0 |
| II. Southern States Total | 6 | .1 | 397 | 4.5 | 30 | .3 | 90 | 1.0 | 523 | 6.0 | 8,265 | 94.0 | 8,788 | 100.0 |
| III. Border States + D.C. Region Totals | 10 | .1 | 803 | 6.2 | 59 | .5 | 104 | .8 | 976 | 7.5 | 11,983 | 92.5 | 12,959 | 100.0 |
| United States Summary Total | 43 | .1 | 1,752 | 4.1 | 768 | 1.8 | 340 | .8 | 2,903 | 6.8 | 39,598 | 93.2 | 42,501 | 100.0 |

Source: DHEW, Office of Civil Rights, OCR-72-8. Fall, 1970, p. 185.

**TABLE XII—DENTAL SCHOOL ENROLLMENT: 1970**

(Region and U.S. Summaries)

| | American Indian | | Black | | Oriental | | Spanish Surname | | Total Minority | | Other | | Total | |
|---|---|---|---|---|---|---|---|---|---|---|---|---|---|---|
| | Number | Percent | Number | Percent | Number | Percent | Number | Percent | Number | Percent | Number | Percent | Number | Percent |
| I. Northern and Western States Region Totals | 11 | .1 | 138 | 1.3 | 217 | 2.0 | 63 | .6 | 429 | 4.0 | 10,342 | 96.0 | 10,771 | 100.0 |
| II. Southern States Total | 5 | .2 | 125 | 5.1 | 12 | .5 | 19 | .8 | 161 | 6.6 | 2,276 | 93.4 | 2,437 | 100.0 |
| III. Border States + D.C. Total | 1 | .1 | 307 | 17.3 | 13 | .7 | 18 | 1.0 | 339 | 19.1 | 1,435 | 80.9 | 1,774 | 100.0 |
| United States Summary Total | 17 | .1 | 570 | 3.8 | 242 | 1.6 | 100 | .7 | 929 | 6.2 | 14,053 | 93.8 | 14,982 | 100.0 |

Source: DHEW, Office of Civil Rights, OCR-72-8. Fall 1970, p. 186.

Black dental school enrollment accounted for 3.8 percent of the national total, with the largest proportion of students in terms of regional totals found in the border states and Washington, D. C. and the least in the northern and western states.

Some 4,400 black students were enrolled in law schools across the nation in 1974; 1,200 of these were in black law schools.[44] Of some 13 black law schools located on black campuses at various times, only 4 remain: at Howard, Texas Southern, North Carolina Central and Southern Universities. Black law schools have trained most of the black lawyers in the past and continue to train the majority of those who practice in the South. Black students are now in law schools all over the country, although many schools admitted few or excluded them altogether until recently. Table XIII shows the distribution of black law students in 1970.

For historical reasons the black law school serves two purposes; it trains experts in civil rights and other areas of special concern to blacks, and it provides legal education to college graduates who would otherwise be unable to acquire it. The high-prestige law schools have been accepting a declining number of graduates of black universities; e.g., at Harvard University Law School in 1967, 21 out of 25 black students came from black undergraduate colleges; in 1970, less than 10 percent; and in 1972, only about 6 percent.[45]

Black communities demand the services of professionals. There is a demonstrable tendency for the graduates of white professional schools to be employed outside the black community, especially if they are outstanding. In contrast, Howard University Law School offers close contact with the preparation of briefs and arguments for actual civil rights cases in the appellate courts or the Supreme Court, using moot courts and the participation of experienced black lawyers and judges. The student is likely to emerge with a sense of commitment which is particularly germane to legal work in the black community.

On the other hand the broader opportunities for professional training offer the black student more options and a broader spectrum of professional opportunities. However if the "affirmative action" recruitment of black students by white colleges is interpreted as tokenism or "racism in reverse," the black institution may regain its leadership in producing the black professional.

## The Emergence of the New Black University

One of the consequences of the Black Revolution has been the extension of black protest to the campus. Black universities expounding a philosophy of Pan-African nationalism have emerged in the Midwest, East, and South. These institutions generally spurn financial aid from established sources, consider traditional accreditation and administrative practices irrelevant, reject "white," western values, and pursue a goal of liberation and self-knowledge.[46] The traditional black college is rejected on the grounds that its programs train students to fit into a racist society and serve the needs of a white-

**TABLE XIII—LAW SCHOOL ENROLLMENT: 1970**
(Region and U. S. Summaries)

| | American Indian | | Black | | Oriental | | Spanish Surname | | Total Minority | | Other | | Total | |
|---|---|---|---|---|---|---|---|---|---|---|---|---|---|---|
| | Number | Per-cent | Number | Per-cent | Number | Per-cent | Number | Per-cent | Number | Per-cent | Number | Per-cent | Nnmber | Per-cent |
| I. Northern and Western States Region Totals | 136 | .3 | 1,498 | 3.5 | 243 | .6 | 459 | 1.1 | 2,336 | 5.5 | 40,407 | 94.5 | 42,743 | 100.0 |
| II. Southern States Total | 38 | .3 | 443 | 3.4 | 16 | .1 | 195 | 1.5 | 692 | 5.3 | 12,475 | 94.7 | 13,167 | 100.0 |
| III. Border States + D.C. Total | 18 | .3 | 513 | 8.2 | 18 | .3 | 32 | .5 | 581 | 9.3 | 5,668 | 90.7 | 6,249 | 100.0 |
| United States Total | 192 | .3 | 2,454 | 3.9 | 277 | .4 | 686 | 1.1 | 3,609 | 5.8 | 58,550 | 94.2 | 62,159 | 100.0 |

Source: DHEW, Office of Civil Rights, OCR-72-8. Fall, 1970, p. 200.

oriented, white supremacist nation. One example of these new seats of learning, the Black Communiversity in Chicago, emphasizes the relationship implied in its name: community and university. In addition to courses in Pan-African subjects, history, and literature, it offers instruction in nutrition and child care, "Father-Son" and "Mother-Daughter" interactions, and presumably such subject matter as would contribute to the strengthening of individual and family life. Though the impact of this new movement in black education cannot be assessed at the present time, it reflects an upsurge of creative thinking and a firm commitment to the goal of unity and advancement in the black population.

## TRENDS IN THE 1970s

An examination of the current status of blacks in education reveals substantial disparities between America's declared beliefs and her actual practices. These are reflected in discrepancies in educational attainment between blacks and whites, the integration controversy highlighted by the busing issue, the dismissal of black professional personnel at a time when black students need models to follow, and negative attitudes toward young people who criticize traditional education.

Statistics alone fail to convey the strength and durability of spirit which has made survival possible for the black American in spite of the frustrations and heartbreak of the past, and the ferment and upheaval of the present. As black Americans continue to press forward, black parents in the most humble circumstances have declared their determination to insure an adequate education for their children. Their quest for greater control of schools has been rewarded by the appointment of black school-board members in the South as well as the North. The rise of Freedom schools, Muslim schools, and other private educational institutions illustrates the intent to emphasize basic education along with group identity. Black youth increasingly recognizes the vital importance of education as a means to achieve its goals and gradually the white establishment is awakening to these needs. Congress, particularly in the mid-1960s, provided a legislative basis for several programs to strengthen education; Francis Keppel, U. S. Commissioner of Education, resigned his position rather than compromise his pro-integration stand; and Commissioner Harold Howe II suffered verbal invectives from some members of Congress because of his outspoken support of educational equality. Private foundations have supported research and innovative programs on behalf of black students.

Today black citizens and their white supporters alike are hard at work planning the ways and means to improve the quantity and quality of black education on all levels.

# PROJECTIONS

As this study shows, the black man's struggle for education has been a consistent thread in his history. In spite of the significant changes incurred by the passage of time, he has remained steadfast in his faith in learning as a way to a better life.

But in spite of his hopes, the end of the assignment of blacks to lower status and unequal treatment is not yet in sight and the black American remains faced with the prospect of continued shortages of money and a consequent denial of enriching educational experiences. This is borne out by the following statement by the President's Commission on School Finance (1971): "The combined present local, state and federal mechanisms for financing education seem outdated, insufficient, or inadequate to overcome the great differences in taxing ability between states and communities within the nation." Presumably, greater attention will be given in the future to leveling the disparities in tax resources between rich and poor localities with greater emphasis on the educational needs of the urban poor.

The glimmer of hope which accompanied the first great wave of concern for the disadvantaged minorities in the mid-sixties has receded with the growth of separatism. Frustration classically leads to hostility and with the intensification of social problems in school settings and the actions of those politicians who have shown less concern for the humanitarian ends of education than for appeasements which assure retention in political office, the problems of education can only worsen and black hostility increase.

Intermittent attempts to revive the notion of intellectual inferiority of blacks have not won professional support. However, when evaluation of programs funded under Title I of the Elementary-Secondary Education Act revealed little change in academic progress of disadvantaged black children after program exposure, some Congressmen and others interpreted the findings as evidence of inherent inabilities and as reason for the discontinuation of federal funding in support of the programs. It is not improbable that the question of inherent inability will again arise during the seventies as blacks continue to press for equality in the classroom. However, such thinking will hopefully be offset by the growing realization that there is overlap in the ability of various groups and a growing recognition of the pluralism of American society.

A unified, well-conceived educational system requires the development of mutual trust. The general aura of skepticism which currently pervades intergroup relationships can be dispelled only through honest efforts to reshape tradition. It is possible that at the end of the seventies classrooms will differ drastically from what they are today, and that there will be serious pursuit of the ideals of democratic education. However, it would appear that any radical changes in ghetto schools are likely to stem from the efforts of blacks themselves.

# Notes

1. Henry Allen Bullock, "A Hidden Passage in the Slave Regime," in *The Black Experience* (University of Texas Press, Austin, 1970), pp. 10–32.

2. Saunders Redding, *They Came in Chains* (J. B. Lippincott, New York, 1950), p. 25.

3. W. A. Low, "The Education of Negroes Viewed Historically," in *Negro Education in America* (Harper and Brothers, New York, 1962), p. 34.

4. Redding, *op. cit.* pp. 57–61.

5. N. S. Aplin, S. Seaton and J. Storey, *The Negro American: His Role, His Quest* (Cleveland Public Schools, Cleveland, 1968), pp. 68, 98–99.

6. Benjamin Quarles, *The Negro in the Making of America* (Collier Books, New York, 1966), pp. 162–164.

7. Edgar W. Knight, *Public Education in the South* (Ginn and Co., Boston, 1922), p. 422.

8. John Hope Franklin, *From Slavery to Freedom* (Alfred Knopf, New York, revised ed. 1967), p. 389.

9. Aplin, et al., *op. cit.*, p. 164.

10. *Ibid.*, p. 129.

11. Redding, *op. cit.* p. 201.

12. Aplin, *op. cit.* p. 58.

13. United States Supreme Court, 347 U. S. 483, 74 S. Ct. 686, 98 L Ed. 873, May 17, 1954.

14. Quarles, *op. cit.*, p. 204.

15. Guy H. Wells and J. Constable, "The Supreme Court Decision and Its Aftermath in Negro Education," in *Negro Education in America* (Harper and Brothers, New York, 1962) p. 201.

16. Harry Golden, *Mr. Kennedy and the Negroes* (The World Publishing Co., Cleveland, 1964), pp. 285–89.

17. Department of Commerce, Bureau of the Census, *Statistical Abstract of the United States*, 1974, pp. 123, 124.

18. *Ibid.,* p. 115.

19. Department of Commerce, Bureau of the Census, *Current Population Reports*, Series P-20, No. 268, August 1974, p. 1.

20. Department of Health, Education, and Welfare. *Directory of Public Elementary and Secondary Schools in Selected Districts.* Office of Civil Rights, June 1971, pp. 34, 35, 68, 69.

21. Department of Commerce, Bureau of the Census, 1917, Series P-23, No. 42, pp. 80, 81.

22. *Ibid.*, *Statistical Abstract*, 1974, p. 115, Table 185.

23. Department of Commerce, Bureau of the Census, *Current Population Reports, The Economic and Social Status of the Black Population*, Special Studies Series P-23, No. 48, July 1974, p. 28.

24. Mathews, John, "Congress Extends ESEA Compromises on Busing," *Compact*, September–October 1974, pp. 16–18.

25. Robert Coles, *Children of Crisis; A Study of Courage and Fear* (Boston: Little, Brown, 1967).

26. *The Ebony Handbook*, Johnson Publications, Chicago, 1974, p. 131.

27. Mathews, John, "Busing Stops at the City Line," *Compact, op. cit.*, p. 14.

28. "Desegregation, a Historic Reversal," *Time*, August 5, 1974, p. 55.

29. "Backdrop to Boston," *Crisis*, January 1975, p. 9.

30. *Ibid.*, p. 10.

31. "Troops Training for a Role in Boston Schools Battle," *The New York Times*, March 11, 1975, p. 21.

32. "Court Overturns Ruling on Busing in Los Angeles," *The New York Times*, March 15, 1975, p. 13.

33. "Court Tells HEW to Enforce Integration in 16 States," *The New York Times*, March 15, 1975, p. 13.

34. Robert W. Hooker, *Displacement of Black Teachers in Eleven Southern States* (Race Relations Information Center, Nashville, 1970), p. 186.

35. John F. Banks, *Survey for Senate Select Committee on Equal Educational Opportunity* (State Department of Education, Richmond, Virginia, 1971).

36. James S. Coleman, *Equality of Educational Opportunity* (Department of Health, Education, and Welfare, Washington, D.C., 1966), pp. 3, 20, 29.

37. Department of Commerce, Bureau of the Census, *Statistical Abstract of the United States, 1974,* p. 124, table 200.

38. Equal Education Opportunity Amendment of the Higher Education Act of 1972, Congressional Hearings, P. L. 92–318, 659, 92nd Congress, June 23, 1972.

39. John Herbers, "South Integrates as North Lags," accompanied by Statistical Tables on Levels of Racial Isolation, Office of Civil Rights, Department of Health, Education, and Welfare, Congressional Record, June 18, 1971, pp. S9429–S9431.

40. Department of Commerce, Bureau of the Census, Population Characteristics, *School Enrollment* . . . October 1974, Series P-20, No. 278, p. 2.

41. Elias Blake, "Background Paper on the Traditionally Negro College" (Institute for Services to Education, Washington, D. C., 1970).

42. Elias Blake, Jr., and others, Comps. *Degrees Granted and Enrollment Trends in Historically Black Colleges: An Eight-Year Study* (Institute for Services to Education, Washington, D. C., 1974), p. 2.

43. *Ibid.,* p. 2.

44. *Howard Law Journal,* Volume 18, No. 2, 1974, page 385.

45. *Ibid.,* page 387.

46. National Association of State Universities and Land Grant Colleges, "State Universities and Black Americans," (Southern Education Foundation, Atlanta, Georgia, 1968).

# 12

## The Black Professional

### Hugh H. Smythe

**Historical Background**[1]

In studying the emergence of the black professional on the American scene, his long history of bondage must be kept in mind. For the nearly 250 years that slavery reigned, every effort was made to keep blacks illiterate, thus making it impossible for them to secure the training and experience necessary to qualify for the professions.

With emancipation came only the most limited access to institutions where skills and knowledge could be acquired. Even if blacks did manage to obtain the necessary training, they found themselves faced with barriers that excluded or limited opportunities for them to practice what they had learned.

There is no existing record of the first black professional in what is now the continental United States, but as early as the seventeenth century at least one black, Dr. Lucas Santomee, who had been trained in Holland, was practicing medicine in New York (then the colony of New Amsterdam). By the middle of the eighteenth century, a handful of other professionals had appeared on the scene, including Benjamin Banneker, the mathematician, astronomer, and surveyor who helped plan the national capital of Washington, D. C., and Norbert Rillieu, inventor of an evaporation instrument that transformed the sugar industry.

Although even before the American Revolution a few blacks had secured secondary and higher education, by 1830 existing records show only four black Americans with college degrees. Edward A. Jones was the first among them, graduating from Amherst in 1826 a few days before John B. Russwurm received his own degree from Bowdoin. Then in 1828 Theodore S. Wright matriculated at the Princeton Theological Seminary, followed in 1829 by Edward A. Mitchell of Dartmouth.

A few other black Americans managed to secure professional training either at home or abroad before the Civil War in the fields of medicine, the ministry, and teaching. Members of this last group were responsible, in turn, for the education of a student body which after Appomattox went on to produce renowned poets, preachers, journalists, professors, and educators. Their number included Alexander Crummel, founder of the American Negro Academy; the scholar-sociologist-civil rights leader W. E. B.

DuBois; the educator and founder of Tuskegee Institute in Alabama, Booker T. Washington; the bibliographer Monroe Work; philologist William S. Scarborough; and historian Kelly Miller.

On the whole, however, the ranks of black professionals remained small, both numerically and in proportion to the total black American population. No black received a Ph.D. in this country until 1876 when Edward S. Bouchet earned one in physics from Yale, although the first American black Catholic bishop, Patrick Francis Healy, S. J., had already acquired the degree in 1865 from the University of Louvain in Belgium. Black holders of the doctorate and members of the black professional body were slow to increase in number until well into the fourth decade of the present century, since barriers to training and a dearth of opportunities for gaining the necessary experience remained widespread.

It is a well-known fact that professional groups tend to proliferate in urban areas and the 1970 United States Census (special studies) shows that among blacks, in an even larger proportion than among white Americans, the majority live in urban communties. As urbanization spread after World War I, the black professional group expanded with it, taking on a different basic character. The original black professional group, on the whole, sprang from families emphasizing family background, education, and a conventional upbringing. All this began to change as the black experience evolved and today black American professionals come from homes stressing occupation and income, and in increasing numbers from families with extremely modest means.

### Education[2]

Since higher education is basic to the attainment of professionalism, it is encouraging to see that blacks have made measurable gains in this area since 1960. In that year, 4.3 percent of the black population in the 25- to 34-year-old group had completed four years or more of college (3.9 percent of the men and 4.6 percent of the women). By 1970, these figures had increased to an overall 6.1 percent, 5.8 percent of the males and 6.4 percent of the females. Corresponding figures for whites were an overall 11.7 percent (15.7 percent of the men and 7.8 percent of the women) in 1960 and an overall 16.6 percent broken down into 20.9 percent and 12.3 percent respectively in 1970.

There was no appreciable difference between the sexes in the number of 18- to 24-year old blacks enrolled in college in 1970. Figures show 16 percent of the males and 15 percent of the females enrolled (in 1965 the corresponding figures were 11 percent for males and 12 percent for females). Of the total 1,220,000 black American males in this age group, 192,000 were attending college while corresponding figures for black women showed a college enrollment of 225,000 out of a possible 1,471,000. Among white males in this category, 3,096,000 out of a total 9,053,000 (34 percent) were in higher institutions of learning compared to 2,209,000 out of 10,555,000 (21 percent) for females.

Although most blacks had historically secured education in predominantly black colleges and universities, a change in this pattern occurred in the 1960s. In 1964 the total of 234,000 blacks were enrolled in colleges, 120,000 or 51.3 percent were in predominantly black institutions. By 1970, with black enrollment increased to 522,000, some 378,000, or 72.4 percent were attending institutions that were not predominantly black.

The most current data show that the 34 historically black public colleges and universities reported a total (spring and summer) graduating class for 1974 of over 20,000, bringing the number of degrees awarded by these institutions since their founding to more than 300,000. Forty percent of all degrees granted were in the field of education. Professional degrees in engineering, law, and pharmacy totalled 367. It should be noted that the proportion of nonblack students continued to rise in these black schools, reaching a figure close to 12 percent. The most recently available data on black-white college attendance and school enrollment, as of October 1973 are given in Tables I and II.

TABLE I—FALL COLLEGE ENROLLMENT OF THE POPULATION 16 TO 34 YEARS OLD, BY WHETHER ATTENDING FULL-TIME, YEAR AND CONTROL OF COLLEGE, AGE, RACE, SEX, AND METROPOLITAN-NONMETROPOLITAN RESIDENCE: OCTOBER 1973

(Numbers in thousands. Civilian noninstitutional population. Metropolitan areas based on 1970 definition)

| Year and Race | Both Sexes | | | | Male | | | | Female | | |
|---|---|---|---|---|---|---|---|---|---|---|---|
| | Total Enrolled | Attending Full Time | | | Total Enrolled | Attending Full Time | | | Total Enrolled | Attending Full Time | |
| | | Number | Percent | | | Number | Percent | | | Number | Percent |
| BLACK | | | | | | | | | | | |
| Total, 16 to 34 years | 684 | 536 | 78.3 | | 358 | 282 | 78.8 | | 326 | 253 | 77.7 |
| College Year: | | | | | | | | | | | |
| 1 through 4 | 624 | 497 | 79.6 | | 321 | 255 | 79.1 | | 316 | 250 | 80.0 |
| Graduate | 61 | 39 | 63.9 | | 37 | 27 | 73.0 | | 10 | 3 | 33.3 |
| WHITE | | | | | | | | | | | |
| Total, 16 to 34 years | 7,317 | 5,402 | 73.8 | | 4,218 | 3,140 | 74.4 | | 3,099 | 2,262 | 73.0 |
| College Year: | | | | | | | | | | | |
| 1 through 4 | 6,027 | 4,834 | 80.2 | | 3,391 | 2,714 | 80.0 | | 2,635 | 2,120 | 80.5 |
| Graduate | 1,290 | 568 | 44.0 | | 827 | 426 | 51.5 | | 464 | 142 | 30.6 |

Source: Compiled from tables on "Social and Economic Characteristics of Students: October 1973," *Current Population Reports: Population Characteristics*, Series P-20, No. 272, issued November 1974, Washington, D.C.: U.S. Department of Commerce, Social and Economic Statistics Administration, Bureau of the Census.

TABLE II—ENROLLMENT STATUS OF THE POPULATION 3 TO 34 YEARS OLD, BY REGION OF RESIDENCE, AGE, AND RACE: OCTOBER 1973

(Numbers in thousands. Civilian noninstitutional population)

| Age and Race | United States | | Northeast | | North Central | | South | | West | |
|---|---|---|---|---|---|---|---|---|---|---|
| | Total Enrolled | Percent Enrolled | Total Enrolled | Percent Enrolled | Total Enrolled | Percent Enrolled | Total Enrolled | Percent Enrolled | Total Enrolled | Percent Enrolled |
| **BLACK** | | | | | | | | | | |
| Total, 3 to 34 years .. | 7,834 | 55.8 | 1,461 | 56.4 | 1,616 | 56.0 | 4,054 | 56.0 | 702 | 56.2 |
| 3 and 4 years ......... | 292 | 28.9 | 45 | 27.2 | 66 | (B) | 141 | 26.5 | 41 | (B) |
| 5 and 6 years ......... | 835 | 89.9 | 162 | 97.5 | 192 | 84.0 | 403 | 84.0 | 78 | 97.3 |
| 7 to 13 years ......... | 3,797 | 99.1 | 713 | 99.1 | 751 | 99.3 | 2,032 | 99.3 | 300 | 98.2 |
| 14 to 17 years ........ | 2,037 | 92.2 | 370 | 92.4 | 432 | 91.7 | 1,077 | 91.7 | 158 | 93.8 |
| 18 to 24 years ........ | 709 | 22.7 | 147 | 25.7 | 141 | 20.8 | 330 | 20.8 | 91 | 30.4 |
| 25 to 34 years ........ | 164 | 5.6 | 24 | (B) | 34 | (B) | 71 | (B) | 34 | (B) |
| **WHITE** | | | | | | | | | | |
| Total, 3 to 34 years .. | 50,617 | 53.1 | 11,906 | 53.8 | 15,008 | 54.4 | 14,069 | 51.0 | 9,634 | 53.4 |
| 3 and 4 years ......... | 1,364 | 23.2 | 314 | 24.1 | 315 | 18.9 | 442 | 25.3 | 294 | 25.1 |
| 5 and 6 years ......... | 5,270 | 93.0 | 1,248 | 95.8 | 1,552 | 95.0 | 1,506 | 87.4 | 963 | 95.4 |
| 7 to 13 years ......... | 23,103 | 99.2 | 5,375 | 98.9 | 6,972 | 99.3 | 6,553 | 99.3 | 4,202 | 99.4 |
| 14 to 17 years ........ | 13,108 | 93.0 | 3,034 | 93.4 | 4,047 | 94.2 | 3,591 | 90.9 | 2,436 | 93.8 |
| 18 to 24 years ........ | 6,096 | 28.0 | 1,547 | 30.0 | 1,736 | 28.0 | 1,571 | 25.2 | 1,241 | 29.7 |
| 25 to 34 years ........ | 1,676 | 6.8 | 389 | 6.8 | 385 | 5.7 | 405 | 5.5 | 497 | 10.2 |

(B) Base less than 75,000.

Source: Compiled from tables on "Social and Economic Characteristics of Students: October 1973," *Current Population Reports: Population Characteristics*, Series P-20, No. 272, issued November 1974, Washington, D.C.: U. S. Department of Commerce, Social and Economic Statistics Administration, Bureau of the Census.

## Career Planning[3]

In the mid-1960s a study of students in predominantly black colleges revealed that they tended to choose life careers at a slightly earlier age than their white counterparts, and more of them (65 percent compared to 53 percent for whites) said it was not a difficult choice to make. No doubt this is due to the fact that career choices traditionally have been more limited for blacks than for whites and where fewer opportunities are open there is less cause to explore other possibilities. It is worth noting here that the women of both races tended to make their choice at an earlier age than the males.

The above study also showed (and it still reflects a partially valid projection in the early years of the 1970s) that the largest group of male blacks choose careers in education fields above the primary and secondary levels, specializing in the following major areas: physical education, music, art, agriculture, business, trade, industrial arts, and administration. (For male whites the largest group enters business fields that include sales, advertising, financing, marketing, purchasing, management, and accounting. Among women, black and white alike, teaching is the most attractive field with two-thirds of them opting for this profession.

The 1967 Fichter report revealed that the career spread for black males by their senior year in college was as follows: education 27 percent; business 12 percent; the physical sciences 9 percent; the social sciences and humanities 7 percent each; medicine 6 percent, and an equal percentage in other health fields; 5 percent each in biological sciences and social work. Law attracts 4 percent, and another 4 percent choose elementary and secondary education. It should be noted, however, that two surveys made in 1971 revealed that the academic career goals of college-bound black students were found to be similar to those of the student population as a whole. These studies also showed that while young black people often showed markedly different backgrounds from those of white students, their plans for earning college degrees and majoring in particular fields showed comparable patterns.

Although the results of the 1971 surveys mentioned above caused the head of the agency making the studies to feel that the results indicated that "black students are just students, like everybody else," the employment preparations and plans of nonwhite college graduates do differ in some ways from those of whites. Blacks, male and female alike, are particularly influenced by the fact that they are less likely than whites to be assured of a definite job upon graduation. As we have seen, blacks tend to plan earlier and decide sooner. They are also more strongly committed to their initial career choice. Although they switch career fields between their freshman and senior years in approximately the same proportion as whites, they do not shift so strongly into the business fields. Until very recently, due to changes in the educational demands for teachers during the first years of the 1970s, more blacks moved into teaching at the elementary and secondary levels, while whites continued to opt for careers in business and industry, areas which promised little advancement for blacks. As a general pattern more black women go into teaching than into all of the other professional fields combined, but for black college graduates in general the kind of job activity and the kind of employer they anticipate are in accord with the demands of the occupation they choose and the availability of jobs in the field.

## Professional Opportunities[4]

Blacks are greatly underrepresented in all the professions due to the barriers that have been raised against them. In the 1960s, the Federal Government made a noticeable effort to open up the job market to blacks as a matter of policy and to set a positive example in hiring. This experience proved once again, however, that even when opportunities expand, blacks remain hampered by poor educational preparation and standardized examinations which do not take into account those of their experiences which diverge from the white norm.

Job discrimination continues to be a major handicap to the enlargement of the black professional category, and qualified blacks suffer from this fact. In the 1960s, a group of black college graduates were asked when they thought they would have job opportunities equal to those of whites of the same educational level. Of those queried, 80 percent thought it would take at least a decade to achieve equality in the large northern cities; 75 percent of the graduates polled thought that it would take at least twenty years for equality to come about in the nation as a whole.

In the South, where most of the black college students live, they believed it would be almost a third of a century before they could expect employment opportunities commensurate with their education.

The same group was then asked to rate opportunities in seventeen selected career fields. They estimated possibilities of employment as good for those who planned to become elementary and high-school teachers, social workers, college instructors, or career personnel in the armed services. Opportunities were seen as average in the fields of medicine, law, social and physical science research, engineering, the creative arts, and writing. The respondents felt that their chances were poor in the areas of accounting, selling in business or industry, advertising, marketing, general business, and as state- and Federal-Government service executives. Few anticipated careers in administration or management.

The above study reflects the fact that most black professionals still function within a system of segregated employment comparable to the still existing dual school system. They feel that for consideration in executive civilian government positions blacks are required to be superior to their white counterparts. Although they believe they have what it takes to succeed in business careers, they cite racial discrimination here more than in any other occupational category as a reason for turning away from these areas of endeavor.

Substance for this position is found in the fifth report of the U. S. Commission on Civil Rights issued in November 1974. It revealed that the Interstate Commerce Commission, Federal Power Commission, Civil Aeronautics Board, Securities and Exchange Commission, and the Federal Communications Commission had all failed to carry out their responsibility to erase employment discrimination in the industries they regulate, and that the nondiscrimination efforts of the industries regulated were still complaint-oriented and not effective. Further, another survey by Marilyn Bender indicated that while Title VII of the federal civil rights law bars job discrimination by race, sex, color, religion, or national origin where more than fifteen persons are employed, in both the private and public sector, the severe economic downturn in 1974 makes the matter of job discrimination a decade after the law was passed still a serious problem that created conflicts between seniority systems and equality objectives.

Like others in the society, however, and in spite of the still prevailing difficulties blacks faced in the job market, they still subscribe to the need for intelligence, hard work, the right connections, talent, and natural leadership, plus the ability to mix easily with whites and stick up for one's rights as of major importance in succeeding as a career professional. They also feel it is helpful to go to the right schools and to have a powerful white sponsor. As far as professional advancement in the strictly black world is concerned, they feel that skin color is insignificant, whereas being an Uncle Tom can be harmful. Like their white compatriots they regard the exhibiting of high moral standards as having almost nothing to do with attaining success as a professional.

## Health Professions[5]

Although the occupational range of blacks has broadened in recent years, professionals remain concentrated in medicine, teaching, the ministry, law, and social work. Of these, medicine early became the most prestigious among blacks, since the inadequacy of medical care and the protection from competition afforded by a usually segregated practice almost guaranteed success to the black American physician.

The first recorded black physician trained in America was Dr. James Derham of New Orleans, who began practice in the latter part of the eighteenth century. In the early nineteenth century a small group of blacks were trained as doctors under the auspices of the American Colonization Society for practice in Liberia.

Although there were at one time eight black medical schools in the United States, only the original two survive today. Howard, founded in Washington, opened in 1868, and Meharry, established in Nashville in 1876, have together turned out the bulk of black American physicians. It is estimated that the persistent dearth of black physicians arises in part from the fact that only about 180 students graduate annually from all medical schools. As of 1970, there were estimated to be 6,840 black physicians in the United States (see Table III). It should be noted that at the two existing predominantly black medical schools a significant proportion of the students are white.

TABLE III—ESTIMATES OF NUMBER AND PROPORTION OF BLACKS
IN SELECTED HEALTH OCCUPATIONS: 1970

| Health Occupation | Total Active in Profession | Estimated No. of Blacks | Percent Blacks Are of Total |
|---|---|---|---|
| Physicians | 311,200 | 6,840[1] | 2.2 |
| Dentists | 102,220 | 2,800[2] | 2.7 |
| Registered nurses | 700,000 | 40,000[3] | 5.7 |
| Optometrists | 18,300 | 200[4] | 1.1 |
| Pharmacists | 129,000 | 3,500[5] | 2.7 |
| Podiatrists | 7,100 | 125[6] | 1.8 |
| Veterinarians | 25,600 | 460[7] | 1.8 |

[1] American Medical Association, *A Report on Physician Manpower and Medical Education*, June 1971.

[2] Haynes and Dates, "Educational Opportunities in the Health Professions for Negroes in the State of Maryland." *Journal of Medical Education*, 43, October 1968.

[3] The estimate provided here is for Negro and other nonwhite groups. Based upon estimates from 1971 Census Bureau Current Population Survey.

[4] Based upon estimate of President of National Optometric Association.

[5] Based upon estimates from 1971 Census Bureau Current Population survey and trends in enrollment in schools of pharmacy.

[6] Based upon enrollment trends in schools of podiatry.

[7] Based upon estimates from 1960 Census of Population.

Source:    Department of Health, Education, and Welfare, Bureau of Health Manpower Education, Report No. 73-27, September 8, 1972.

In 1974 the Journal of the American Medical Association published an estimate that there were 500 black women doctors in the United States in 1967, the latest year for which detailed figures were available. A third of these were in general practice while the remainder, in decreasing numerical order, specialized in pediatrics, internal medicine, psychiatry-neurology, obstetrics-gynecology, public health, surgery, and anesthesiology, with one to four in each of the fields of dermatology, geriatrics, occupational medicine, ophthalmology, pathology, pulmonary diseases, and radiology.

As for dentists in training, in 1965, 306 or 2.2 percent of the 13,876 dental students in the United States were black. By 1972 this number had increased to 597, or 3.5 percent of the 17,305 American dental students.

## Occupational Spread[6]

Although there was a scattering of black professionals prior to 1865, they began to appear in substantial numbers only after the Civil War, since the higher institutions of learning essential to the formal training of blacks were few and insignificant before the Reconstruction era. Growth in this area was slow. In 1876 there were only 314 black college graduates and only 96 of these held professional degrees. No college graduated as many as 1,000 blacks annually until the 1920s, and as would be expected these alumni gravitated into professions where openings were most likely to exist.

Before 1880 teachers and clergymen emerged as the only black professional groups. Thereafter, medical doctors and dentists began to appear on the scene in noticeable numbers, although they have since become proportionately small in number. Lawyers have also remained a limited group, with only 3,500 practicing black attorneys in 1972. Social workers, on the other hand, who began to appear in the census reports about the turn of the century, have continued to increase in number since that time. Development in the other professions has been slow, so that in terms of the overall picture blacks have continued to focus on and concentrate in the old-line fields of teaching, the ministry, medicine, and law.

This situation is beginning to change, however, as blacks branch out into new fields. The "Speaking of People" section in the monthly *Ebony* magazine is built around the interest among its readership in unaccustomed occupations and a quick survey of a few issues reveals black activity in a variety of spheres in which black Americans were practically unknown as late as the early 1950s. These include, although often in minimal numbers, television producers and directors, maritime union contract officers, Red Cross Directors, museum exhibit curators, district sales supervisors and managers, Federal Government legal advisors, construction superintendents, purchasing managers, personnel directors, recipe test supervisors, stars in movies and the theater, education board managers, television legal counselors, hospital biochemists, corrections department chiefs, cooperative education administrators, auto dealership recruiters, Boy Scout executives, charity fund executives, utility firm employment managers, tobacco company product managers, radiation lab researchers, office executives, transit system engineering heads, air recovery system designers, bank managers, space scientists, and others. Between 1950 and 1960 the number of black engineers tripled, and in the same period blacks in the field of the natural sciences rose 77 percent and architects increased by 72 percent. Since 1969 there has also been a sharp increase in blacks in the physical sciences. The American Institute of Architects in 1972 listed some 320 blacks in the professions. Furthermore the armed services have several black generals and the Navy has elevated one to the rank of rear admiral. (See Chapter 29.)

These specialties are not newsworthy for whites. However, for blacks who have traditionally been bunched in the "learned" professions of medicine, law, theology, and teaching such diversification is very recent and leads blacks today to feel that it is worthwhile to prepare themselves for a wider variety of professions.

As for the Federal Government, for years it has been an avenue into the professional ranks with appointments or promotions in civil service to the higher ranks. Under Presidents John F. Kennedy and Lyndon B. Johnson a determined effort was made to upgrade blacks in civil service government posts and to place blacks by appointment in higher government positions. Thus Thurgood Marshall was elevated to the Supreme Court; Robert C. Weaver became the first black Cabinet member as Secretary of the

Department of Housing and Urban Development; Andrew Brimmer was made a governor of the Federal Reserve System; Clifton Wharton, Carl T. Rowan, Patricia Roberts Harris and Hugh H.Smythe were appointed as ambassadors to countries outside Africa (see Table V), and Franklin H. Williams was named to the Economic and Social Council of the United Nations, and later to Ghana. The bureaucratic hierarchy also saw an increase in middle- or upper-level government executives: assistant secretaries, deputy assistant secretaries, desk directors, and the like. Highly educated and politically oriented, this group comprises what may well be the most sophisticated black professional group in the country, forming an intellectual elite drawn from the nation at large, which has moved from professional jobs in the private sector to those in the public domain.

Several years ago a National Opinion Research Center study revealed that there were some occupations enjoying high-prestige value which were seldom mentioned by young blacks as career choices, such as Supreme Court Justice, Cabinet officers, diplomat, positions in the foreign service, Congressmen, and mayors and other high elective officers of large cities. The modern generation knows that these types of positions are not easy to attain, and that extremely few black Americans have managed to achieve them; yet the concrete evidence of what is possible cannot help but influence black students toward new and broader horizons.

## Business[7]

The early experience of the American Negro affected his position in the business world today. Due to his downtrodden role in society he was prevented from learning how to penetrate the free-enterprise world of the American marketplace. The present black business executive group is small, indicating that successful business careers are still unusual.

The first recorded study of blacks in business, made in 1898, found that the average capital investment was less than $5,000, and then, as now, the majority of the enterprises were small retail stores and service establishments operated primarily for blacks in black communities.

Just before the turn of the century the stringent application of Jim Crow laws and practices to practically every aspect of American life forced a separate existence for blacks. Unable to secure acceptance on an integrated basis, black leadership urged the masses in 1898 to place their faith in business property as a way to escape poverty and achieve economic independence. Two years later Booker T. Washington organized the National Negro Business League and predicted a bright future for the black man in business. But the realities of the black business experience even today incontestably prove that the shining hopes of the past have not yet come to fruition. Up to the present, blacks have had little access to the corporate business structure which dominates the wealth and life of the United States.

Thus black business has never been able to develop a substantial community of truly professional people. Two major reasons for this are a lack of large-scale business development, part of which can be traced to the limitations on the kinds of enterprises open to minorities with poor access to capital, and the fact that there is no entrepreneurial tradition among blacks. This condition could not anticipate early improvement as 1974 drew to a close with a worsening of inflation and the specter of a recession moving toward a real economic depression. This led economist Andrew F. Brimmer, first and only black to serve as a governor of the Federal Reserve System (he resigned in 1974 to accept a faculty post at Harvard University) to say that, while the long-term prospects might appear to be promising, "the current year will undoubtedly be a difficult one for black businessmen."

Consequently, the number of business-management professionals increases slowly. From 1950 to 1960 there was actually a 20 percent decline in black ownership and operation of business enterprises. And between 1962 and 1965, while black professional and technical occupations were increasing by 41 percent, blacks in managerial jobs showed a rise of only 9 percent. Black Americans make up approximately 11 percent of the civilian labor force, but have only 3 percent of managerial posts, partly because they have systematically been excluded from many companies. Top white executives still as a rule do their best to keep nonwhites out of positions of authority, and many firms simply avoid placing blacks in jobs which could lead to such positions. The situation is further aggravated by the difficulty of locating qualified candidates since past patterns of exclusion have made blacks feel that there is no use in seeking managerial posts. Furthermore, most white businesses simply do not search for blacks when they recruit large numbers of young college graduates for management jobs.

An effort is being made, however, to increase the number of black professional managers. PACT (Plan of Action for Challenging Times) and the Merit Employment Committee of the Chicago Association of Commerce and Industry are examples of those pledging equal opportunity in promotion and hiring practices. But even while blacks may benefit in a limited way from belated offers of greater opportunity from American business, some black professionals assail companies for continuing mere "tokenism." Others are aware that while new categories have been opened to them, they are concentrated in the less prestigious and lower-paying posts within each classification in a company. Even on the secretarial level few are really secretaries or stenographers; and as for sales positions, blacks usually remain confined behind the counters of retail stores rather than being developed for higher levels as buyers or prepared to enter the executive suite.

Usually in business black professionals are concentrated in such fields as personnel relations or the development of special—meaning black or broader minority group—markets. In discussing the advances made so far, the majority qualify their satisfaction with strong reservations. Black professionals find themselves caught between the pressure of an overall cultural syndrome lauding individual success and the need for personal sacrifice in order to help blacks as a group to move into the economic mainstream. The situation has not been helped by the general resurgence of conservatism in the 1970s although, as we shall later see, black professionals today are seriously questioning their traditional roles and attitudes.

### Communications Media[8]

While blacks as professionals in the communications media field might be said to have begun with John Russwurm and Samuel Cornish, who published in 1827 the first black newspaper, *Freedom's Journal*, it is only since the 1960s that some have gained limited entree to the mainstream of the U. S. communications field of television, radio, and the various printed publications. Prior to the 1960s the black presence in the mass media was projected almost exclusively and sporadically by a few big-name entertainers. However, the civil rights movement of the sixties exerted some pressure here, too, and the almost total exclusionary practices abated somewhat as a few black professionals were hired as journalists, reporters, writers, and producers. While the three major networks, ABC (American Broadcasting Company), NBC (National Broadcasting Company), and CBS (Columbia Broadcasting System), as well as PBS (Public Broadcasting Service), all now have black professionals, blacks continue to be systematically excluded from employment at most levels in newspapers, radio, and television stations.

As Edith Efron pointed out, the figures in Table IV suggest that little has been done to break the virtually lily-white stranglehold by the unions on technical jobs; that in the professional area, "hiring is moving toward a uniform but unavowed 10 percent quota system—a tacit cut-off line which is approximately the abstract national black population percentage." They also tell us that "black managers are as rare as hen's teeth," and portray a picture of tight control by whites over the media's intellectual, political and technological operations, with a limited number of blacks being filtered into staff jobs.

Thus while blacks finally established the nation's first major black radio chain, the National Black Network which began in 1973 with 38 affiliated stations, the communications field in general continues to be occupied with reflecting the interests of their white constituencies and blacks hold no positions of significance, authority, or power. Consequently, Benjamin Hooks, the first and only black member of the Federal Communications Commission, who was appointed in 1973, is quite vocal about the discriminatory state of affairs in the media as thoroughly unfair to blacks and other minorities. As 1974 neared its end he did not foresee any improvement for the black professional in the communications media until they are permitted to have more input at the decision-making level of broadcast operations where they are still totally excluded.

**TABLE IV—BLACKS IN BROADCASTING: MAY 1972**

| Station | Officials and Managers | | *Professional Staff | | **Technical Staff | |
|---|---|---|---|---|---|---|
| | Total | Blacks | Total | Blacks | Total | Blacks |
| WABC-TV, New York | 26 | 1 | 51 | 4 | 32 | 2 |
| KABC-TV, Los Angeles | 29 | 1 | 79 | 8 | 25 | 3 |
| WLS-TV, Chicago | 45 | 4 | 68 | 8 | 92 | 4 |
| WXYZ-TV, Detroit | 38 | 2 | 40 | 5 | 94 | 5 |
| KGO-TV, San Francisco | 26 | 0 | 74 | 10 | 70 | 5 |
| WCBS-TV, New York | 37 | 3 | 72 | 10 | 52 | 5 |
| WCAU-TV, Philadelphia | 37 | 1 | 52 | 3 | 88 | 5 |
| WBBM-TV, Chicago | 35 | 1 | 58 | 5 | 94 | 6 |
| KMOX-TV, St. Louis | 22 | 1 | 26 | 2 | 53 | 1 |
| KNXT-TV, Los Angeles | 39 | 2 | 83 | 3 | 105 | 8 |
| WNBC-TV, New York | 42 | 3 | 52 | 9 | 80 | 4 |
| WRC-TV, Washington | 38 | 1 | 40 | 14 | 83 | 11 |
| WMAQ-TV, Chicago | 41 | 2 | 79 | 10 | 106 | 9 |
| KNBC-TV, Burbank | 36 | 1 | 51 | 6 | 70 | 5 |
| WKYC-TV, Cleveland | 32 | 4 | 42 | 3 | 71 | 6 |

*This category includes trainees, production staff, researchers, writers, reporters plus entertainment staffers
**This category includes cameramen, sound men, and all technological workers
Source:   Employment figures filed with the FCC in May, 1972, for the TV stations and operated by the networks. (Do not include clerks and the unskilled.) (*TV Guide*, August 19, 1972, p. 22)

## Federal Service[9]

Blacks employed in professional, technical, and managerial positions in the Federal Government were rare until the 1960s. During that decade the Administrations of Presidents John F. Kennedy and Lyndon B. Johnson took some positive steps toward equal employment practices. As a result, black positions tended to rise in level. Between 1960 and 1970, in the higher General Service grades (the professional ranks can be said to begin in grades nine through eleven, where salaries move beyond $10,000), black Americans experienced a 29 percent upward movement. Grades twelve through thirteen witnessed a 38 percent jump, while an even more impressive gain was made in grades fourteen and fifteen, where improvement was almost 55 percent. But the general condition of blacks in higher professional grades, as of 1970, reveals that although they were 15 percent of all Federal Government employees, they held only 3 percent of grades twelve through eighteen, only 4 percent of the higher Postal Field Service positions, and 9 percent of the upper Wage Systems (blue-collar type) jobs. At the very top, grades sixteen through eighteen, there were only sixty-three blacks serving out of a total of 5,300 jobs in this category as 1970 began.

It is worth noting that since the Department of State was created in 1787, of the thousands of persons who have served in all types of foreign service and diplomatic work, fewer than twenty blacks have ever reached the ambassadorial level. Although a number of blacks were sent as official envoys and ministers to both Haiti and Liberia (beginning in 1871 with J. Milton Turner, who helped establish closer commercial relations with the latter country), none attained the status of ambassador until 1948 when Liberia was raised to embassy level and the incumbent minister, Edward Dudley, was elevated to this rank. Since then about twenty blacks have served as Ambassador Extraordinary and Plenipotentiary, mostly to African nations, as Table V shows.

### TABLE V—BLACK AMBASSADORS

| | |
|---|---|
| Edward Dudley | Liberia, 1948–53 |
| Richard Jones | Liberia, 1955–60 |
| Clifton Wharton | Norway, 1961–64 |
| Carl Rowan | Finland, 1963–64 |
| Mercer Cook | Niger, 1961–64 |
| | Senegal and Gambia concurrently, 1964–66 |
| Patricia Roberts Harris | Luxembourg, 1965–67 |
| Hugh H. Smythe | Syria, 1965–67 and Malta, 1967–69 |
| Elliott P. Skinner | Upper Volta, 1966–68 |
| Franklin H. Williams | United Nations Economic and Social Council, 1964–65 and Ghana, 1965–68 |
| Samuel Adams, Jr. | Niger, 1968–69 |
| Clinton Knox | Dahomey, 1964–68 and Haiti, 1972–74 |
| Samuel Z. Westerfield | Liberia, 1968–72 |
| *Terence Todman | Chad, 1969–1972, Guinea, 1972–January 1975 and Costa Rica, January 1975– |
| Jerome Holland | Sweden, 1970–72 |
| Clyde Ferguson | Uganda, 1971–72 |
| *John Reinhardt | Nigeria, 1972– |
| Charles Nelson | Botswana, Lesotho, and Swaziland concurrently, 1972–74 |
| *Beverly Carter | Tanzania, 1972– |
| *Rudolph Aggrey | Senegal and Gambia 1973– |
| *Theodore Britton | Barbados-Grenada, 1974– |

*Incumbents as of February 1975

In addition to ambassadorial posts, as of May 1972 blacks also held such high-ranking positions as Assistant Secretary in the Departments of Agriculture; Housing and Urban Development; and Health, Education, and Welfare; Assistant Administrator in the Small Business Administration and the Agency for International Dvelopment; and Administrator in the Department of the Interior and in the Bureau of Security and Consular Affairs of the Department of State. The last, Barbara Watson, served until December, 1974. Others held positions of ministerial rank in the ECOSOC section of the United States Mission to the United Nations, and as General Counsel of the Treasury and of the Department of Transportation. One black American had been appointed to the Federal Communications Commission and several occupied positions as Deputy Assistant or its equivalent in the State, Defense, Labor, HEW, and Transportation Departments and with the Equal Employment Opportunity Commission. Others have served as Directors or Deputy Directors for A. I. D. missions overseas, or on regional desks in such agencies as the Peace Corps and the Department of Justice. In 1972 there was a black advisor on the White House Staff, a black American held office as Governor of the Virgin Islands, and the President had named three blacks as judges on the District Courts of California, Washington, D. C., and New York. Supreme Court Associate Justice Thurgood Marshall and Secretary of Transportation William T. Coleman were the highest-ranking blacks in the federal structure.

Salaries for all the above-named positions range from $27,000 for those in the assistant category to $60,000 for Justice Marshall and Secretary Coleman.

## Women Professionals[10]

The thrust forward of women in general in conjunction with the Women's Liberation movement in the sixties and seventies included the participation of black women. Significantly, more black women than men have received the first college degree, although like whites, more black men than women go on to postgraduate and professional training. It is worth noting that neither black nor white women professionals or potential professionals seek careers to the total exclusion of marriage and children. About half of the black women in the professions in this category combine their working lives with matrimony and child rearing, while only a fifth of the white women follow this pattern, preferring to work before having children or after the latter have matured.

Educational careers claim more than half of all black professional women; the rest enter social work, the humanities, medicine, and other health fields in near-equal proportions. Smaller numbers follow careers in the social sciences and business, while only a few become professionals in the physical sciences. They share the attitude of black males in expecting almost no opportunity in such business professions as accounting or finance, and only a handful are found in engineering. It is interesting to note that black career women tend to have more confidence in their professional abilities than do white women, and they believe more strongly than whites that they have the talent to make good in a variety of occupations.

## Overall Employment Trends: 1960–1970[11]

The status of blacks in the professions has shown definite changes in recent years. Between 1960 and 1970, the total employment of nonwhites increased by 22 percent while their employment in professional, technical, and clerical occupations doubled. Substantial gains were also made in sales, craft, and managerial jobs. Yet in spite of these positive developments, reports from the largest companies in the nine industries in which workers' earnings are relatively the highest, revealed in 1970 that the proportion of nonwhites in the highest-paid positions as professional, technical, and managerial workers is still far below their proportion in the total labor force of 81 million plus, of whom nonwhites represent about 11 percent, or about 9,200,000 in 1970. Table VI shows the number of nonwhites employed in professional and other upper-level occupations for 1960 and 1970.

TABLE VI—TOTAL EMPLOYMENT OF WHITES AND NONWHITES IN SELECTED WHITE-COLLAR OCCUPATIONS: 1960 AND 1970

| Occupation | Total Employment of Nonwhites and Whites in White-Collar Occupations | | Occupational Distribution | | White Occupational Distribution No. and Percent | | Nonwhites: Percent of Total in Major White-Collar Occupations | |
|---|---|---|---|---|---|---|---|---|
| | 1970 | 1960 | 1970 | 1960 | 1970 | 1960 | 1970 | 1960 |
| | Number in Thousands | | Percent | | Percent | | Percent | |
| Professional and Technical | 766 | 331 | 9.1 | 4.8 | 14.8 | 12.1 | 6.9 | 4.4 |
| Managers, Officials, and Proprietors | 297 | 178 | 3.5 | 2.6 | 11.4 | 11.7 | 3.6 | 2.5 |

Source:  From figures in Tables 4, 5, and 6, *Employment in Perspective: The Negro Employment Situation,* Report 391, U. S. Department of Labor, Bureau of Labor Statistics, 1971, pp. 8–9.

## Geographical Distribution[12]

The distribution of the black professional has not been uniform throughout the country. The South contains the largest concentration of teachers and members of the clergy as has traditionally been the case; but it has less than its proportionate share of doctors, dentists, social workers, and lawyers. As blacks migrated to the North and West, especially after the first and second world wars, they formed large ethnic communities which supported a sizable professional body. Since the racial attitudes of the nation still confine or at least encourage black professionals to practices and positions in the black community, they tend to be concentrated in the large urban areas where blacks comprise upwards of 25 percent of the population. Consequently, most black professionals are found in selected cities of the North, the Southeast, and California.

According to the 1970 census the majority of black professionals are to be found in the thirty cities with the largest black populations: New York with nearly 2,000,000; Chicago with more than 1,000,000; Detroit, Los Angeles, and Philadelphia with nearly 700,000 each; Washington, D. C. with approximately 600,000; Baltimore with more than 400,000; Houston and Cleveland with over 300,000; Atlanta, Memphis, New Orleans, and St. Louis with more than 250,000 each; Dallas, Newark, and San Francisco having more than 200,000 each; and from 100,000 to more than 150,000 in such cities (in order of rank) as Oakland, Indianapolis, Birmingham, Cincinnati, Jacksonville, Kansas City, Milwaukee, Pittsburgh, Richmond, Boston, Columbus, Buffalo, Gary, and Nashville.

Black professionals also tend to gravitate to those smaller black communities where the proportion of blacks to the overall population is high. These include such smaller urban locales as Willowbrook and Westmont, California, where black Americans account for more than 80 percent of the inhabitants, and Prichard, Alabama; Goldsboro, North Carolina; Chester, Pennsylvania; Inkster, Michigan; Atlantic City, New Jersey; and Wilmington, Delaware, where blacks make up about fifty percent or more of the population.

## Black Professional Organizations[13]

The foundations for black professional organizations were laid after the Civil War when a separate black world began to emerge. Before that time, although a number of free blacks and a few slaves had managed to move out of the laborer and agricultural-worker category and pursue careers in the ministry, law, teaching, dentistry, and architecture, sometimes practicing in violation of the law, they were too few in number, labored under too many restraints, and were geographically too thinly distributed to permit the forming of professional groups.

With the evolution of the black community, however, whether in the North or South, East or West, mores and housing patterns have consistently fostered a segregated existence for the majority of whites and nonwhites, laying the groundwork for the formation of separate professional organizations. The isolated black community has needed its own preachers, teachers, pharmacists, physicians, dentists, lawyers, social workers, and others to perform a variety of professional services. The first to form associations may have been teachers and social workers in the late nineteenth century when black physicians also organized the National Medical Association, but more significant growth among black professional groups occurred after World War I. Long barred from membership in white organizations, blacks in almost every profession formed their own associations for protection and mutual assistance, since in spite of some modification in recent years, professional activities among blacks for the most part have depended upon a black clientele.

The 1960s saw the creation of national membership bodies in new fields of endeavor. These included the Association of Black Sociologists, National Association of Black Psychologists, National Association of Black Political Scientists, National Association of Black Social Workers, National Association of African-American Education, National Committee of Black Churchmen, National Black Nuns, Caucus of Black Economists, African Heritage Studies Association, Society of Black Music Composers, Black Academy of Arts and Letters, National Conference of Black Lawyers, National Association of Minority Consultants and Urbanologists, and the National Black Planning

Network. While the exact membership total of these and other associations is not known, it is estimated that there are more than 100,000 members affiliated with the various black professional groups.

Although no master list of current professional organizations exists, there are organizations on some level for almost every major occupation considered to be professional. Some idea of their variety may be gleaned from the above-mentioned groups to which can be added such older established entities as the National Bar Association, National Medical Association, National Dental Association, National Pharmaceutical Association, Association of Social Scientists, American Teachers Association and the newer Association of Black Foundation Executives.

## Life Style[14]

Black professionals share with white fellow Americans the traditional values of the nation and thus represent an element of strength in the attempt to develop a truly interracial society. Their consumption patterns duplicate those of their white counterparts, and despite stereotypes and myths, their discretionary expenditures are made typically to educate their children and enhance family comfort, rather than to achieve status through conspicuous consumption. The majority tend to spend their leisure time in conventional middle-class pursuits.

As a group, black professionals are basically oriented toward the larger society of America in general and do not seek racial separation. Like other blacks, however, they are discontented and frustrated with the failure of the white community to accept their full participation. Although they have escaped the blight and poverty of the ghetto, they retain strong ties to the black poor and identify with their less-privileged brethren. But they have not as yet developed a strong philanthropic attitude toward those in need, whether individuals, organizations, or institutions. Successful professionals are not as strong financial supporters of alumni associations, for example, as might be expected, partly because few of them have had enough years of real prosperity to have accumulated substantial wealth and a sense of security.

They are disappointed with the white community for continuing to reject them in spite of their personal success, and they impatiently await genuine equality. En masse they are more aware than ever of the daily limitations they suffer, and few truly believe that their professionalism will make them acceptable as first-class citizens. Yet access to the white world is important for a doctor who needs the best medical facilities for his patients, the lawyer who needs the contact with the judiciary and with a wide variety of legal specialists if he is to serve his clients well, and the academician whose isolation in the smaller black professional community deprives him of the opportunity to test his analyses against those of others of equal standing in his specialty. Black professionals also object on principle to exclusion, feeling that they have earned the right to live as equals. At the same time, they tend to enjoy more acceptance in the white world than their brothers because of their professional competence and can thus sometimes serve as constructive links between the black and white communities.

Some professional people express their blackness by affecting "Afro" hair styles and wearing African prints; on the whole, however, the majority does not seem to identify any more strongly with revolutionary life styles than do white professionals despite the black American's greater sympathy for and identification with the Black Revolution. After the new crop of college students from the 1960s become established professionals, however, there may well be a more significant departure from present norms of appearance and manners.

## New Era: New Image[15]

As we have seen, limitation and exclusion from the larger white community led to the development among blacks of vested interests in such areas as separate hospitals, schools, libraries, churches and welfare organizations servicing a strictly black clientele. Those at the top have tended to form a sort of racial aristocracy that because of its privileged position and economic aspects has become very concerned with self-perpetuation. Some members of this group, however, became conscious of the disadvantages from the professional standpoint of having to work in a segregated atmosphere and as far back as 1908 began working to overcome their forced separate existence by fighting discriminatory practices. That year, the National Association of Colored Graduate Nurses (now merged with the American Nurses Association), came into being and devoted itself to the elimination of professional restrictions in an attempt to expand opportunities for its members. Then, starting in the 1930s, black organizations began to initiate lawsuits to equalize opportunities and remove restrictions. Such activity involved a calculated risk, however, for the abolition of segregation could create unemployment for many who have been insured a good living free from the competition of whites, and the elimination of barriers could threaten the status and nominal leadership positions of others.

Compared to black counterparts of a generation ago, the black professional today is, in general, better off but perhaps less content. He represents a manifestation of the revolution of rising expectations. He would like to see the race problem ameliorated and hoped at one time that his climb up the socioeconomic ladder might help to speed the process. Disillusionment with the slowness of the larger community to open its doors has caused some, especially the younger, professionals to turn from thinking that a concrete demonstration of success within the system can lead to acceptance in the mainstream. They have thus assumed varying degrees of militancy and assertiveness within the context of what might be called a national black professional movement. In the past, as the group among blacks with the required education and relatively greater freedom of movement, they historically have supplied most of the leadership. Today, however, elements from other segments of the black community serve as spokesmen.

Some black professionals even talk about rejecting all the values of the "sick" white capitalist society and discuss the possibility of leading a "humanist" revolution.

Today's black professional knows that segregation is harmful, fostering discrimination and limiting professional development. Although radical professionalism is an anomalous position, members of this group are in sympathy with the less privileged blacks who seek equal opportunity. They are keenly aware of the problems faced by the black poor. Many, perhaps most, were born into poverty-ridden families, and a hard-won college education moved them upward. Thus their poverty origins have given some of them a concerned social outlook. Although glad themselves to have escaped the poverty and suffering of their parents, they retain strong emotional ties to the background from which they evolved, and some still have close relatives who have not yet acquired middle-class status. Such tendencies are reinforced by the fact that a lack of social consciousness is no longer tolerated in black communities.

Yet the problem of relationship between the middle-class professional and the larger black masses remains unique. Black professionals are aware that in the past less privileged blacks took pride in the achievement of a fellow individual, despite some natural envy, suspicion that one who did well must have sold out to the whites, and a too-often-justified conviction that he who escaped the slums would soon forget those left behind. Some in the ghettos have seen black professionals as "outsiders," much like white professionals, an attitude which has made some black professionals uncomfortable and defensive. What they want is for their less privileged black fellows to realize that whites created the problem, that black professionals are not superhuman, and that they, like all blacks, are burdened by racism and social responsibility.

More black professionals are now becoming involved in the general problems of blacks and making concrete gestures of solidarity. Like many blacks, they have been caught up in the identity question, especially since their position may cause them at times to experience a sense of alienation from both white and black communities. Many of them are faced with a special dilemma, for while personal ambition pulls them toward the larger overall society, they are apprehensive that racism will deny them any real identity in the nonblack world. This accounts in part for the tendency of some black professionals to pay more attention to their "African heritage" and support more black movements, organizations, individuals, and events than they did in the past. This they translate into practical action and suffer a feeling of guilt that they may not be doing enough.

Others feel that simply "proving" themselves in white society is a contribution and helps the cause of general improvement among blacks.

Today's black professionals see their role as larger than the achievement of personal success, tending to view themselves as models for black Americans as a whole and their children in particular. They tend to engage in self-help projects of various kinds, employing as many blacks on their staffs as possible when they must hire employees, and harboring a feeling that they must help other blacks in order to survive. Some take leading roles in militant protests and highlight the lack of help and cooperation from public officials. Although they generally favor full integration, they are usually tolerant of others who propose developing separate economic and political power for blacks so as to be able to bargain with whites on more equal terms. Basically the black professionals tend to seek a formula leading to their acceptance in a larger pluralistic society while allowing them to retain unique positive values or traits they possess as a group. They know white America is not homogeneous and that ethnic, religious, or cultural bonds among whites are encouraged, even as they enjoy free movement in the total society. This is the sort of integration that black professionals want for blacks.

Black professionals recognize that institutional and individual racism has no boundaries; they are aware that self-determination is necessary to combat alienation, ineffectuality, and apprehension, and that there is a real need for shared power in the pluralistic society of the United States. There is a serious effort underway to confront and resist institutional racist practices and policies. Although in general, established white professional organizations now admit blacks to membership, the contemporary black professional sees his strength as stemming from effective coalition with his fellow black Americans.

## Notes

1. John Hope Franklin, *From Slavery to Freedom: A History of American Negroes* (A. A. Knopf, New York, 1947).

   W. Montague Cobb, "The Black Physician in America," *The New Physician*, vol. 19, November 1970.

   Langston Hughes and Milton Meltzer, *A Pictorial History of the Negro in America* (Crown Publishers, New York, 1956).

   Charles S. Johnson, *The Negro College Graduate* (The University of North Carolina Press, Chapel Hill, 1938).

   Carter G. Woodson, *The Negro Professional Man and the Community, with Special Emphasis on the Physician and Lawyer* (The Associated Publishers, Washington, D. C., 1934).

   William T. Alexander, *History of the Colored Race in America* (Palmetto Publishing Co., New Orleans, 1888), 3rd revised edition.

   Horace Mann Bond, "The Negro Scholar and Professional in America," in *The American Negro Reference Book*, John P. Davis, ed. (Prentice-Hall, Englewood Cliffs, 1966).

   George W. Williams, *History of the Negro Race in America: From 1619 to 1880* (G. P. Putnam's Sons, New York, 1882).

   William J. Simmons, *Men of Mark: Eminent, Progressive, and Rising* (G. M. Rowell & Co., Cleveland, 1887).

   Frank Lincoln Mather, *Who's Who in the Colored Race: A General Biographical Dictionary* (Published by the author, Chicago, 1912).

2. Joseph H. Fichter, *Graduates of Predominantly Negro Colleges: Class of 1964*, U. S. Department of Health, Education, and Welfare, Public Health Service Publication No. 1571 (U. S. Government Printing Office, Washington, D. C., 1967).

*The Social and Economic Status of Negroes in the United States, 1970*, Special Studies, BLS Report No. 394, Current Population Reports, Series P-23, No. 38. Washington, D. C., U. S. Department of Commerce, Bureau of the Census, U. S. Department of Labor, Bureau of Labor Statistics, July 1971.

*Black Americans: A Chartbook*, U. S. Department of Labor, Bureau of Labor Statistics, Bulletin No. 1699 U. S. Government Printing Office, Superintendent of Documents, Washington, D. C., 1971.

James A. Davis, *Great Aspirations* (Aldine, Chicago, 1964).

———, *Undergraduate Career Decisions* (Aldine, Chicago, 1965).

Thomas F. Pettigrew, *A Profile of the American Negro* (D. Van Nostrand, Princeton, 1964).

Meyer Weinberg, *The Education of the Minority Child: A Comprehensive Bibliography* (Integrated Education Associates, Chicago, 1970).

3. Robert L. Jackson, ed., *The E-P-E 15-Minute Report for College and University Trustees* (Editorial Projects for Education, 1717 Massachusetts Ave. N.W., 1972).

James A. Davis, *Undergraduate Career Decisions* (Aldine, Chicago, 1965).

D. Beardslee and D. O'Dowd, "Students and the Occupational World," in *The American College*, Nevitt Sanford, ed. (Wiley, New York, 1962).

Laure M. Sharp, *Two Years After the College Degree*, Bureau of Social Science Research, National Science Foundation, NSF 63-23 (U. S. Government Printing Office, Washington, D. C., 1963).

Paul H. Norgren, et al., *Employing the Negro in American Industry* (Industrial Relations Counselors, Inc., New York, 1959).

Maxine G. Stewart, "A New Look at Manpower Needs in Teaching," *Occupational Outlook Quarterly*, May 1964.

James Tobin, "On Improving the Economic Status of the Negro," *Daedalus*, Fall 1965.

Richard McKinley, Peter Rossi, and James A. Davis, *Students at the Midway* (National Opinion Research Center, Chicago, 1962).

A. J. Lott and B. E. Lott, *Negro and White Youth* (Holt, Rinehart and Winston, New York, 1963).

Robert Reinhold, "Black Scholars Confer in Texas: National Congress Strives for Educational Change," *The New York Times*, April 9, 1972, p. 26.

James A. Davis, *Undergraduate Career Choices* (Aldine, Chicago, 1965).

W. F. Brazziel, "Occupational Choices in the Negro College," *Personnel and Guidance Journal*, vol. 39, 1961.

Fred M. Hechinger, "Job Recruiters Hunt for Negroes in Stepped-up Drive at Colleges," *The New York Times*, May 30, 1965, section 1.

4. Gloria P. Green, *Employment in Perspective: The Negro Employment Situation*, Report 391, (U. S. Department of Labor, Bureau of Labor Statistics, Washington, D. C., 1971).

*The Social and Economic Status of Negroes in the United States, 1970, op. cit.*

Claire Hodge, "The Negro Job Situation: Has it Improved?" *Monthly Labor Review*, January 1969.

James G. Perry, "The Job Outlook for Negro Youth," *Journal of Negro Education*, Vol. 33, Spring 1964.

Joseph H. Fichter, *op. cit.*, ch. 8.

John Hope II, "The Problem of Employment as it Relates to Negroes," *Studies in Unemployment*, Special Committee on Unemployment Problems, (U. S. Government Printing Office, Washington, D. C., 1961).

William Brink and Louis Harris, *The Negro Revolution in America* (Simon & Schuster, New York, 1964.)

"Negroes in Federal Jobs: Moving Upward," *U. S. News & World Report*, May 25, 1970 and August 3, 1970.

"Negro Americans in the Foreign Service in Africa," Communication to Mabel M. Smythe, Director of Publications and Research, the Phelps-Stokes Fund, New York, N. Y., of October

14, 1970, from Frederick D. Pollard, Jr., Director, Equal Employment Opportunity Program, Department of State, Washington, D. C.

"Negro Americans in Government Service in Africa," communication to Mabel M. Smythe, October 14, 1970, from Frederick W. Hahne, Director, Office of Management, Department of State, Agency for International Development.

Shawn G. Kennedy, "Civil Rights Commission Charges 5 U. S. Agencies Fail to Act Againt Job Discrimination," *The New York Times*, November 12, 1974; Marilyn Bender, "Job Discrimination, 10 Years Later," *The New York Times*, Sunday, November 10, 1974, Section 3, p. 7.

5. Gloria P. Green, *op. cit.*

Dan Cordtz, "The Negro Middle Class is Right in the Middle," *Fortune*, November 1966.

Percy Young, "The Black Middle Class," New York *Post*, August 10 to 14 inclusive, 1970 (5-part series).

James A. Michener, "The Revolution in Middle-Class Values," *The New York Times Magazine*, August 18, 1970.

Cecil C. North and Paul K. Hatt, "Jobs and Occupations: A Popular Evaluation," *Opinion News*, September 1, 1947.

W. Montague Cobb, *op. cit.*

Forrester B. Washington, "The Need and Education of Negroes in Social Work," *The Journal of Negro Education*, vol. 4, January 1935.

Ira DeA. Reid, "Fifty Years of Progress in the Professions," The Pittsburgh *Courier*, July 1, 1950.

E. Franklin Frazier, "Occupational Classes Among Negroes in Cities," *The American Journal of Sociology*, vol. 35, March 1930.

*The Social and Economic Status of Negroes in the United States, 1970, op. cit.*

Ramon J. Rivera, "A Dilemma; The Educational Goals of American Negroes," NORC (National Opinion Research Center), 1965.

Norval D. Glen, "Some Changes in the Relative Status of American Non-Whites," *Phylon*, vol. 24, Winter 1963.

Richard D. Lyons, "New Doctors at Peak; Shortages are Seen," *The New York Times*, November 21, 1972, p. 26.

The *Journal of the American Medical Association*, September 23, 1974, Vol. 229, No. 13, p. 1758.

6. S. L. Wormley and L. Fenderson, eds., *Many Shades of Black* (William Morrow, New York, 1968).

Joseph H. Fichter, *op. cit.*

*Ebony*, April and May 1972; December 1971; March 1971; September 1970; and December 1969.

G. Franklin Edwards, *The Negro Professional Class* (The Free Press, Glencoe, Illinois, 1959).

*National Survey of Higher Education*, Federal Security Agency; U. S. Office of Education, Division of Higher Education, 4 Vols. (U. S. Government Printing Office, Washington, D. C., 1942).

*U. S. News & World Report*, May 25 and August 3, 1970.

James T. Wooten, "Few Blacks Study Law in the South," *The New York Times*, November 12, 1970.

"More Negroes Hold Better-Paying Jobs," *The New York Times*, September 27, 1971.

Eli Ginzberg, *The Negro Potential* (Columbia University Press, New York, 1956).

Jack Rosenthal, "Progress Yes, But There Is Still Much Poverty," *The New York Times*, March 7, 1971.

M. L. Stein, "The Black Reporter and His Problems," *Saturday Review*, February 13, 1971.

*Measures of Overlap of Income Distribution of White and Negro Families in the United States*, Technical Paper 22, U. S. Department of Commerce, Bureau of the Census (U. S. Government Printing Office, Washington, D. C., 1970).

Robert D. Hershey, Jr., "Black Firm Applies to Exchange," *The New York Times*, June 27, 1970.

*We The Black People of the United States*, U. S. Department of Commerce, Bureau of the Census, 338–305 (U. S. Government Printing Office, Washington, D. C., 1969).

Richard Halloran, "Trail Blazer in the Navy: Samuel Lee Gravely, Jr.," *The New York Times,* April 28, 1971.

"Air Force Names a Black General," *The New York Times,* January 28, 1972.

"U. S. Names First Black to Lead Army Division," *The New York Times,* April 20, 1972.

George Gent, "Black Women Take Roles as Directors," *The New York Times,* November 17, 1971.

7. John Seder and Berkeley G. Burrell, *Getting It Together: Black Businessmen in America* (Harcourt, Brace and Jovanovich, New York, 1971).

Herman D. Bloch, *The Circle of Discrimination: An Economic and Social Study of the Black Man in New York* (New York University Press, New York, 1969).

Nan Robertson, "Blacks Attack Media as Racist in Programs and Hiring Policies," *The New York Times,* March 7, 1972.

Charles E. Silberman, "The Businessman and the Negro," *Fortune,* Vol. 68, September 1963.

Jane Greverus Perry, "Business: Next Target for Integration?" *Harvard Business Review,* vol. 41, March 1963.

"More Room at the Top: Company Experiences in Employing Negroes in Professional and Management Jobs," *Management Review,* Vol. 52, March 1963.

Harding P. Young, "Negro Participation in American Business," *Journal of Negro Education,* Vol. 32, Fall 1963.

Joseph A. Pierce, *Negro Business and Business Education* (Harper, New York, 1947).

Abram L. Harris, *The Negro As Capitalist* (American Academy of Political and Social Science, Philadelphia, 1936).

*Proceedings of the National Negro Business League.* First meeting, held in Boston, Massachusetts, August 23–24, 1900 (Copyright 1901).

W. E. B. DuBois, ed., *The Negro in Business* (Atlanta University Press, Atlanta, 1899).

Booker T. Washington, *The Negro in Business* (Hertel, Boston, 1907).

E. Franklin Frazier, *The Negro in the United States* (Macmillan, New York, 1949).

Douglas W. Cray, "Enterprise Gains of Minorities Lag," *The New York Times,* May 24, 1971.

James K. Brown and Seymour Lusterman, *Business and the Development of Ghetto Enterprise* (The Conference Board, New York, 1971).

*Review of Black Political Economy,* various issues beginning with Vol. 1 1970 and continuing through Summer 1972 (Black Economic Research Center, 112 West 120th Street, New York).

Earl Ofari, *The Myth of Black Capitalism* (Monthly Review Press, New York, 1970).

Prakesh S. Sethi, *Business Corporations and the Black Man* (Chandler Publishing Co., New York, 1970).

Frederick D. Sturdevant, *The Ghetto Marketplace* (The Free Press, New York, 1970).

*Black Enterprise,* various issues, 1971 ff.

Andrew F. Brimmer, "The Future of Black Business," *Black Enterprise,* Vol. 4, No. 11, June 1974, pp. 27–30.

8. "Blacks in the Communications Media," *Black Enterprise,* Vol. 5, No. 2, September 1974.

Louis Calta, "Minorities' Lag in Public TV Seen," *The New York Times,* November 2, 1973, p. 83.

Paul Delaney, "Blacks Complain of Media to FCC," *The New York Times,* March 19, 1973, p. 13.

"Public TV Reported Lagging in Minority Hirings," *The New York Times,* January 31, 1973, p. 82.

George Dugan, "Minority Gap is Found in Top TV Jobs," *The New York Times,* November 22, 1972.

Les Brown, "Ethnic Pressures Are Effective in Barring 'Offensive' TV Films," *The New York Times,* November 28, 1973. p. 1.

Eugenia Collier, "TV Still Evades the Nitty-Gritty Truth!" *TV Guide,* January 12, 1974, pp. 6–10.

Martin Mayer, "Local Broadcasters Under Siege," A three-part series, *TV Guide,* February 3, 10, and 17, 1974.

Edith Efron, "What is Happening to Blacks in Broadcasting?" *TV Guide*, August 19, 26, and September 2, 1972.

John J. O'Connor, "Television: If You're White and a Male, O.K.," *The New York Times*, Sunday, December 3, 1972.

"Minority Groups Score Rules Easing Renewal of TV Licenses," *The New York Times*, March 30, 1973, p. 78.

Michael Knight, "Black Radio Chain Will Open July 1," *The New York Times*, May 13, 1973, p. 23.

9. "Negroes in Federal Jobs: Moving Upward," *U. S. News & World Report*, May 25, 1970.

"Blacks in Top Federal Jobs—The Nixon Record," *U. S. News & World Report*, August 3, 1970.

*Black Americans: A Chartbook, op. cit.*

Frederick Quinn, "Black Students and the Foreign Service," *Foreign Service Journal*, Vol. 47, October 1970.

Philip Shabecoff, "U. S. Employment Service Called Insensitive to Poor," *The New York Times*, April 22, 1971.

Saul Friedman, "Race Relations Is Their Business," *The New York Times Magazine*, October 25, 1970.

Milton Viorst, "The Blacks Who Work For Nixon," *The New York Times*, November 29, 1970.

"Negro Appointed to F.C.C. by Nixon," *The New York Times*, April 13, 1972.

10. D. Wolfe, "Women in Science and Engineering," *Science*, Vol. 145, September 1964.

Joseph H. Fichter, *op. cit.*

Otis D. Froe, "Educational Planning for Disadvantaged College Youth," *Journal of Negro Education*. Vol. 33, Summer 1964.

*United States Manpower in the Nineteen Seventies* (U. S. Department of Labor, Washington, D. C., 1970).

Charlayne Hunter, "200 Black Women 'Have Dialogue,'" *The New York Times*, January 10, 1972.

Inez Smith Reid, *The Black Woman* (Third Press, New York, 1972).

11. Gloria P. Green, *op. cit.*

*The Social and Economic Status of Negroes in the United States, 1970, op. cit.*

*Black Americans: A Chartbook, op. cit.*

"Black Pilots Are Laid Off," *The New York Times*, March 26, 1972.

"CBS Is Accused on Minority Jobs," *The New York Times*, November 20, 1971.

Raymond W. Mack, *Transforming America: Patterns of Social Change* (Random House, New York, 1967).

Edwin L. Dale, Jr., "Rate of Jobless Down in October," *The New York Times*, November 6, 1971.

Sar A. Levitan, Garth L. Mangum, and Ray Marshall, Human Resources and Labor Markets: *Labor and Manpower in the American Economy* (Harper & Row, New York, 1972).

Jack Rosenthal, "Doubt Is Cast on Heralded Sign of Negroes' Economic Progress," *The New York Times*, December 20, 1971.

Whitney M. Young, Jr., "The Ghetto Investment," *The New York Times*, March 13, 1971.

"Moral Issues in Hiring," Letter to the editor by L. Pearce Williams, Alvin H. Bernstein, John T. Marrone, and Charles A. Zuckerman, *The New York Times*, January 6, 1972.

Philip Shabecoff, *op. cit.*

"Joblessness Up in Poor Urban Areas," *The New York Times*, October 19, 1971.

"Phase Two Benefits Outlined to Blacks," *The New York Times*, February 16, 1972.

"Slow Pace Toward Equality," Editorial in *The New York Times*, May 14, 1971.

James T. Wooten, *op. cit.*

12. Jack Rosenthal, "One-Third of Blacks Found in 15 Cities," *The New York Times*, May 19, 1971.

*The Social and Economic Status of Negroes in the United States, op. cit.*

*Black Americans: A Chartbook, op. cit.*

Claire Hodge, *op. cit.*

*Current Population Reports: Population Estimates and Projections*, "Projections of the Population of Voting Age for States: November 1972," Series P-25, No. 479, Washington, D. C., March 1972.

13. Charles L. Sanders, "Black Assertion Among Black Professionals," *Journal of the National Medical Association*, Vol. 63, No. 6, November 1971.

Charles L. Sanders, *A Comparative Study of Black Professional Organizations*, research in progress under auspices of Afram Associates, 103 East 125th Street, New York, N. Y. 10035, May 1972.

Charles L. Sanders, *Comparative Study of Black Professional Leaders*, Doctoral Dissertation, Graduate School of Public Administration, New York University, February 1972.

Maurice R. Davie, *Negroes in American Society*, ch. 14 (McGraw-Hill, New York, 1949).

Charles L. Sanders, "Growth of the Association of Black Social Workers," *Social Casework*, May 1970.

M. P. Dumont, "The Changing Face of Professionalism," *Social Policy*, May-June 1970.

W. Montague Cobb, *op. cit.*

14. Dan Cordtz, *op. cit.*

Percy Young, *op. cit.*

James A. Michener, *op. cit.*

E. Franklin Frazier, *Black Bourgeoisie: Rise of a New Middle Class in the United States* (The Free Press, Glencoe, Illinois, 1957).

Judy Harkison, "Washington's Black Society: New Leaders," *The New York Times*, January 30, 1972.

15. Charles L. Sanders, "Black Assertion Among Black Professionals," *op. cit.*

C. Gerald Fraser, "Decades Change in Blacks Studied," *The New York Times*, April 16, 1972.

Charles V. Hamilton, "Black Americans and the Modern Political Struggle," *Black World*, May 1970.

Dan Cordtz, *op. cit.*

Percy Young, *op. cit.*

C. Gerald Fraser, "Black Social Workers Assail Agencies," *The New York Times*, November 7, 1971.

Paul Delaney, "Heads of Black Colleges Discuss Possibility of Merging Some of their Schools," *The New York Times*, April 7, 1972.

Linda Charlton, "Blacks Ask Media for Larger Role," *The New York Times*, April 7, 1972.

# BIBLIOGRAPHY

Cobb, W. Montague, "The Black Physician in America." *The New Physician*, Vol. 19, November 1970.

Cordtz, Dan, "The Negro Middle Class is Right in the Middle." *Fortune*, November 1966, pp. 174-80.

Davis, James, *Great Aspirations*. Chicago, Aldine, 1964.

———, *Undergraduate Career Decisions.* Chicago, Aldine, 1965.

Edwards, G. Franklin, *The Negro Professional Class*. Glencoe, Illinois, The Free Press, 1959.

Friedman, Saul, "Race Relations is Their Business." *The New York Times Magazine*, October 25, 1970, pp. 44-52.

Green, Gloria P., *Employment in Perspective: The Negro Employment Situation*. U. S. Department of Labor, Bureau of Labor Statistics, Washington, D.C., Government Printing Office, 1971.

Hodge, Claire, "The Negro Job Situation: Has It Improved?" *Monthly Labor Review*, January 1969.

Levithan, Sar A.; Mangum, Garth L.; and Marshall, Ray; *Human Resources and Labor Markets: Labor and Manpower in the American Economy*. New York, Harper and Row, 1972.

"Negroes in Federal Jobs: Moving Upward." *U. S. News & World Report*, May 25 and August 3, 1970.

"The Negro Businessman in Search of a Tradition." *Daedalus*, Winter 1966.

Quinn, Frederick, "Black Students and the Foreign Service." *Foreign Service Journal*, Vol. 47, October 1970.

Rivera, Ramon J., "A Dilemma: The Educational Goals of American Negroes." Chicago, A Report of the National Opinion Research Center, 1965.

Sanders, Charles L., "Black Assertion Among Black Professionals." *Journal of the National Medical Association*, Vol. 63, No. 6, November 1971.

—— *A Comparative Study of Black Professional Organizations*. New York, Afram Associates, 1972.

—— *A Comparative Study of Black Professional Leaders*, New York, Doctoral Dissertation, Graduate School of Public Administration, New York University, February 1972.

—— "Growth of the Association of Black Social Workers," *Social Casework*, May 1970.

Seder, John and Burrell, Berkeley G., *Getting It Together: Black Businessmen in America*. New York, Harcourt, Brace and Jovanovich, 1971.

Sethi, Prakash S., *Business Corporations and the Black Man*. New York, Chandler Publishing Co., 1970.

Stein, M. L., "The Black Reporter and His Problems." *Saturday Review*, February 13, 1971.

Straus, R. Peter, "Is The State Department Color-blind?" *Saturday Review*, January 2, 1971.

Tobin, James, "On Improving the Economic Status of the Negro." *Daedalus*, Fall 1965.

U. S. Department of Labor, Bureau of Labor Statistics, *The Social and Economic Status of Negroes in the United States, 1970*. Special Studies, Report No. 394, Current Population Reports, Series P-23, No. 38. Washington, D.C., U. S. Government Printing Office, July 1971.

Woodson, Carter G., *The Negro Professional Man and the Community With Special Emphasis on the Physician and Lawyer*. Washington, D.C., The Associated Publishers, 1934.

Wormley, S. L., and Fenderson, L., editors, *Many Shades of Black*. New York, William Morrow, 1968.

# 13

## Blacks and American Foundations: Two Views

### Vernon E. Jordan, Jr. and Ernest Kaiser

## I. A HISTORICAL SURVEY *by Ernest Kaiser*

At the end of the Civil War, the defeated South was in terrible social and economic shape. The four million liberated black slaves needed help in many areas. Dedicated northern white teachers went South to help educate the freed slaves. The Freedmen's Bureau, set up by the Federal Government in 1865, did a creditable relief and rehabilitation job against bitter southern opposition. It provided badly needed medical services, employment supervision, a bank, and lands and resettlement management for the freedmen. The Bureau contributed to the grounds and buildings for many schools of all kinds, while church associations and private philanthropy paid the teachers' salaries. The Bureau aided some of the black colleges founded at this time: Atlanta University, Fisk University, Howard University, Biddle Memorial Institute, Hampton Institute, Storer College, and St. Augustine's College.

The major religious denominations (including the American Missionary Association with its Daniel Hand Fund) established many schools such as Fisk University, Hampton Institute, Talladega College, Walden College, Claflin University, Howard University, Richmond Theological Seminary, Morehouse College, Shaw University, and others.[1] The black denominations such as the Baptists, the African Methodist Episcopal Church, the African Methodist Episcopal Zion Church, and the Colored Methodist Episcopal Church also set up many schools and colleges in the South at this time. Some of these were Zion Wesley Institute, Lane College, Allen University, Paul Quinn College, Paine College, and others.

Then came the reaction leading to the complete overthrow of Reconstruction. The Freedmen's Bureau was ended in 1872 leaving only the philanthropy of the church denominations to aid the black academies and colleges. Much of this help slowly dried up.[2] But the Civil War prepared the way for the opening of the vast western region of the continent and for a booming period of tremendous industrial expansion and growth.[3] These newly rich industrial tycoons, or robber barons, as Matthew Josephson called them, became philanthropists who founded 260 mostly white institutions of higher learning between 1860 and 1900.[4] But black education was also aided. From 1865 to 1914, many educational foundations were set up which worked either generally or specifically in behalf of black education, both elementary and college.[5]

The Peabody Education Fund, established by George F. Peabody in 1867, was the first set up for general aid to education in the southern and southwestern states.[6] The fund gave more than $3.5 million for southern education from 1867 to 1914.[7] Black schools and colleges benefited, but indirectly. A school for blacks was allotted by the Peabody Fund only two-thirds as much money as a school of the same size built for whites. The trustees of the Peabody Fund also used their influence to defeat the Civil Rights Bill in Congress in 1873. In 1880 these trustees asked Congress for special federal funds for black education in the South. At this time the fund made its main focus the training of teachers, black and white. When the fund was terminated in 1914, $350,000 went to the John F. Slater Fund, a specific black education fund.[8]

Next came the John F. Slater Fund, a permanent fund set up by John F. Slater with $1 million in 1882 specifically to aid black education in the South, elementary and collegiate.[9] The Slater Fund's emphasis upon industrial or vocational education was due to Booker T. Washington's influence. Over the fifty-year period from 1882 to 1932 nearly $2 million were given mostly to forty-eight black colleges and other institutions with almost $2 million more already appropriated for future use. This fund money was not spent for land or buildings but for improving black teaching by raising salaries or by helping black teachers get good training.[10] It was a Slater Fund Fellowship for Graduate Study Abroad that W. E. B. DuBois obtained in 1892, which enabled him to go to Europe for two years (1892–94) of doctoral study at the University of Berlin.

The Daniel Hand Educational Fund for Colored People, established by Daniel Hand in 1888, was the second of the permanent funds set up solely for black education. This fund of over $1 million was placed under the administration of the American Missionary Association. The fund was to be used generally to help the work of the association in the field of black education. This principally meant aid to black colleges.[11]

In 1902 John D. Rockefeller, whose family had already aided some black colleges and black education in general, offered $1 million to an organization to be set up to aid education without regard for sex, race, or religion. The General Education Board was thus established in 1903. Among its many objectives were the building and equipping of all sorts of elementary schools, teacher training schools, colleges and universities, libraries, etc.; also to aid teacher employment, lecturers, and to endow educational associations; to collect educational information and to publish and distribute documents and reports of educational data and information. From 1902 to 1914, black schools were granted about $700,000 out of almost $16 million spent. Rockefeller gave $53 million to the General Education Board between 1902 and 1909.[12] The General Education Board's aid has many ramifications in black education: aid to state-supported black colleges, teacher-training programs, state agents for black schools, elementary schools, the setting up of several private black university centers through mergers in Atlanta, Nashville, New Orleans, and Washington, D. C.; the building of libraries and underwriting of teachers' salaries at private black colleges; aid to Meharry Medical College and the Howard University School of Medicine to improve medical education for blacks; and scholarship grants to members of faculties of black colleges for advanced study. From 1902 to 1932, a thirty-year period, blacks received more than $32.5 million, black colleges and schools over $23 million, and whites were granted over $193 million.[13]

Booker T. Washington was able to get the wealthiest men of his time to support Tuskegee Institute and Hampton Institute, both emphasizing industrial education for blacks. John D. Rockefeller, Andrew Carnegie, Collis P. Huntington, Seth Low, Julius Rosenwald, and George Eastman gave money and time to these two schools.[14]

Anna T. Jeanes, the daughter of a wealthy Quaker, at the urging of Hollis Frissell and Booker T. Washington, gave $200,000 to the General Education Board in 1905 for aid to black rural schools in the South, almost nonexistent at the time. This gift set up the Anna T. Jeanes Fund for the Assistance of Negro Rural Schools in the South. In 1907 Miss Jeanes gave $1 million to build up the work with Dr. James H. Dillard as president of the fund. The fund sought industrial-work teachers for black rural schools, special teachers for extension work, and county agents to improve rural homes and schools and to create a climate for improved black schools. The Jeanes Fund initiative in paying these teachers resulted in counties paying for some of this work, and also attracted other money gifts.[15]

The will of Caroline Phelps Stokes set up the Phelps-Stokes Fund with $900,000 in 1911 for several purposes, among them the improvement of the education of blacks in America and in Africa. It is the oldest existing foundation to have emphasized service to black Americans and to Africans from its inception. Among its earlier contributions were two landmark reports on education in Africa, with some highly regarded recommendations, and a survey and two-volume report entitled *Negro Education: A History of the Private and Higher Schools for Colored People in the United States* (1916), directed by Thomas Jesse Jones of the fund and sponsored also by the U. S. Bureau of Education. Jones was accused with some validity of favoring industrial education for blacks and white determination of black educational policy, with white leadership of black colleges; nevertheless, the survey is said to have stimulated higher standards in black colleges. As the fund acquired black leadership and influence, its paternalistic image changed. It gave $10,000 to the Southern Christian Leadership Conference in 1968[16] and has developed a substantial program of services to developing colleges. It no longer makes grants; it is now an operating foundation whose projects are supported by outside funding.

The Phelps-Stokes Fund aided Monroe N. Work's *Bibliography of the Negro* (1928). In 1931 an *Encyclopedia of the Negro* project, initiated by the fund, brought together black and white scholars under the leadership of W. E. B. DuBois. After considerable work in the 1930s and early 1940s, a preparatory volume edited by DuBois and Guy B. Johnson—the only publication to result from the project—appeared in 1945 and was reprinted in 1946. Later, aided by a grant from the fund for the Advancement of Education, the Phelps-Stokes Fund surveyed the demand and brought out *The American Negro Reference Book* (1966), edited by John P. Davis.[17] This article appears in a second, new edition, *The Black American Reference Book*, edited by Mabel M. Smythe.

Among other contributions of the fund have been the development of the African Student Aid Fund (for emergency assistance to academically successful African students), and the Moton Conference Center in Capahosic, Virginia.

Julius Rosenwald wanted to improve black conditions of life as early as 1910. He went to Tuskegee Institute in Alabama in 1911 and became a member of its Board of Trustees in 1912. Then he began helping black rural schools at Booker T. Washington's suggestion, going from $5,000 gifts to large amounts to help improve black southern schools. From 1913 to 1932, Rosenwald helped to build over 5,000 black schools in fifteen southern states; he gave 15 percent of $28 million or $4,200,000 for this program. Over 30 percent of the blacks in southern schools when the building program was finished were in buildings put up with the help of Rosenwald's money.[18] Rosenwald also helped construct seventeen YMCA-YWCA buildings and a big housing project for blacks in Chicago.

The Julius Rosenwald Fund was founded formally in 1917 (reorganized in 1928) with about $40 million. It aided the aforementioned rural schools and high schools, including libraries. It also helped selected black colleges and professional schools in terms of buildings, equipment, books for libraries, and current expenses. The fund also assisted black college faculty members engaged in advanced study toward the master's and doctoral degrees and gave fellowships to young blacks and whites who showed great promise, mostly in the creative or artistic fields, and who wanted to develop in their careers.[19] This fund had a great impact on black education in the South. It also had an active race-relations program. It combined with the General Education Board in assisting the construction of the black Flint-Goodridge Hospital in New Orleans. The fund's principal was to be completely spent within twenty or twenty-five years after Rosenwald's death, which occurred in 1932, so the fund closed its work and went out of business in 1948.

Andrew Carnegie, the millionaire steel magnate, was a member of the first board of trustees of the Anna T. Jeanes Fund in 1908 and 1909. He was a good friend of Booker T. Washington, who influenced Carnegie's philanthropic gifts. The Carnegie Corporation of New York, set up by Carnegie in 1911, built libraries for many black colleges in the South and some in northern communities. It was persuaded by a Harlem citizens' committee to buy Arthur A. Schomburg's large private library on the Negro for the New York Public Library in 1926, at a cost of $10,000, and to place it in a branch in the heart of Harlem. The Carnegie Corporation also gave money for special research work over the years. It subsidized Lord Hailey's multivolume *An African Survey* in the 1930s. Between 1911 and 1937, the corporation made grants to blacks of over $2.5 million. It also financed the big Gunnar Myrdal study, *An American Dilemma* (1944), including the eighty-one manuscripts and research memoranda prepared by black and white scholars for Myrdal. The grant for the Myrdal study was almost $300,000. Recently the Carnegie Corporation gave initial financial support to the Upward Bound program, a pilot project for seventeen colleges which helps inadequately prepared black and white high school students,[20] and $500,000 to a black genealogical project.

The John Simon Guggenheim Memorial Foundation, established in 1925, provides research fellowships to scholars and subsidy grants to creative writers, artists, photographers, etc. Between thirty and forty blacks have received these fellowships in the various categories.[21]

The John Hay Whitney Foundation, set up in 1949 with $10 million in New York City, began its Opportunity Fellowship Program in 1950 with $100,000 allocated annually to the program, which continues to operate today. The program was directed by Dr. Robert C. Weaver from 1950 to 1955. Fellowships are granted annually to forty or fifty college-trained blacks, American Indians, the Spanish-speaking, and others between 22 and 35 years of age for graduate study in the creative arts and for other specialized training or advanced study. Most of the recipients are blacks.

The Ford Foundation, early in the presidency of McGeorge Bundy, in the late sixties gave grants to three experimental projects in school decentralization in New York City in its efforts to eliminate racial prejudice. The Ford Foundation also contributed to the endowment of Claflin University in South Carolina. In October 1971 the foundation announced a plan to distribute $100 million between 1972 and 1977 to improve higher educational opportunities for black, Mexican-American, Puerto Rican, and American Indian students. Awards are made as scholarships and fellowships to individuals and as funds to twenty-five (originally ten) private, predominantly black colleges to help these colleges improve their academic standards. This project stimulated the U. S. Department of Health, Education, and Welfare to grant $1.6 million for upgrading social services and educational programs at twenty-two predominantly black colleges. Since 1961 the Ford Foundation has aided organizations (and publications sponsored by them) concerned with equal opportunity in the fields of legal rights, voting rights, housing, public schools, and economic well-being. The Association for the Study of Negro Life and History got a $40,000 Ford Foundation grant in 1972.[22]

The Harmon Foundation, from the 1920s until its demise in the 1960s, gave many awards of financial support to blacks for outstanding creative achievements in various fields and sponsored fine arts exhibits by blacks.[23]

The Spingarn Medal, established by Joel E. Spingarn for the NAACP, is a gold medal awarded annually for the highest or noblest achievement of an American black during the preceding year or years, thus calling attention to and rewarding the achievement and also stimulating the ambition of black youth. The first medal went to biologist Ernest E. Just in 1915, and the award has continued up to today. Those honored have been in the arts and sciences, education, civil rights, law, leadership, and other fields.[24]

The Duke (family) Endowment Fund in North Carolina has made gifts to black colleges in North Carolina. The fund has also helped in the construction of hospitals for blacks in North Carolina and South Carolina.[25]

The Du Pont family in Delaware has given much money for black education in that state. In 1928 enough money was given by the family to construct and equip a school in every district in the state where black children were enrolled.[26]

Foundation money, used to aid black education and other fields, has been a great aid to blacks in their impoverished state. Outspoken and independent intellectuals and leaders such as W. E. B. DuBois and Carter G. Woodson, however, never received any significant foundation funding for their many projects. Although DuBois did receive small foundation grants for his projects on three occasions after his graduate-study fellowship, these men had to struggle along without the real financial help which would have made their work infinitely easier to carry through. With the economic improvement of blacks, many wealthy black individuals or organizations are setting up endowments of various sorts in the black colleges, and constructing buildings as memorials in the black communities. The foundations' largesse stimulated federal, state, and local governments to use their moneys for the public good. This was true especially in the South, where blacks were usually neglected. But in many poor areas philanthropy provided the money for projects that the government had no real money for. Certainly black education, especially higher education, is deeply indebted to philanthropists. And these wealthy men and women were only showing a decent public spirit in giving some of their riches back to the black and white communities which were the sources of their great wealth.

## II. ATTITUDES AND OUTLOOK *by Vernon E. Jordan, Jr.*

The response of American foundations to the black man in America has been consistent with the nation's general attitude toward his plight. Just as black people have remained "invisible men" in the eyes of their fellow citizens, so too have the foundations passed them by unseen. With notable exceptions this has resulted in ignorance on the part of the bulk of American foundations of black needs and aspirations, causing their philanthropic activities to be marked by insensitivity in these areas.

To be sure, the number of foundations that have exhibited concern for the welfare of the black community has increased over the years. Gradually the hardy few that pioneered in the support of struggling black institutions in the first half of this century have been joined by others, including some of the largest and most prestigious foundations.

The main impetus toward greater involvement in black affairs sprang from the civil rights movement. The 1954 Supreme Court decision in *Brown v. the Board of Education*, ruling segregated school systems unconstitutional, heralded a new national awareness of the need for racial progress.

It should be noted, however, that the early civil rights victories came about without significant foundation support. Too few foundations contributed to the NAACP Legal Defense and Educational Fund, which successfully challenged school segregation and initiated the cases that resulted in the Supreme Court's action. The drive to win the right to vote in the South was also accomplished virtually without foundation aid. It was not until 1962 that three relatively small foundations, the Taconic Foundation, the Field Foundation, and the Edgar Stern Family Fund, made grants to the tax-exempt Voter Education Project of the Southern Regional Council to make available voter-registration funds for the major civil rights organizations and community groups to implement these fundamental programs.

It would appear either that established American philanthropy viewed voter-registration grants to blacks as overly controversial or irrelevant, or that it totally lacked interest in and understanding of the American scene at that time. It was left to the smaller foundations with less money, less bureaucracy, and less influence to explore the area of race relations and fund minority causes, giving them both credibility and visibility, at a time when the larger foundations could find no funds to do so. This was clearly shown in the case of voter registration in the South.

The 1960s were marked by an upsurge in foundation support for black causes. The most significant factors in bringing this about were the aforementioned increase in civil rights activity, the national Government's emphasis on social reforms and broadened opportunity for all, and the urban crisis which led society's leaders, including corporate leaders and foundation heads, to the realization that it was essential to deal constructively with the problems of poverty and racism.

During this period, such black-led organizations as the Urban League, NAACP, the NAACP Legal Defense and Educational Fund, SCLC, CORE, and others found a greater willingness on the part of foundations to fund key projects. The Urban League's "New Thrust" program of heightened ghetto involvement was supported by several foundations; and other agencies, too, found that programs heretofore labeled "controversial" were becoming more acceptable to vested interests.

Although such support was on the rise, it was still limited to relatively few foundations. Among the majority, black causes and black needs continued to remain "invisible." And despite the publicity attached to those grants awarded for black activities, the sums actually expended were small, both in absolute dollars and in percentages of total grants.

Despite this fiscal caution, there was a "backlash" against foundation influence in the social arena. The 1969 Tax Reform Act, which included provisions limiting foundation activity, was interpreted by many as a federal signal to foundations to "go slow" in the social sphere. The Act provided for extensive regulation of foundation activities and a tax on investment income, as well as calling for a mandatory "payout" of an amount equal to a percentage of a foundation's total assets. Although the ruling has hampered many foundations by increasing their administrative burdens, it has not, in fact, significantly affected their activities. Rather the result of the provisions seems to have been to close off legal loopholes that allowed creation of privately held or family foundations that had as their reason for being escape from taxation rather than bona fide philanthropic activities.

Nevertheless, the act has been invoked as a reason for foundations to stay out of the social arena, thus tending to reduce the flow of grants to blacks and black-led programs. Some anti-reform elements have even suggested that in encouraging social change, foundations are harming their own interests as guardians of private wealth, and are undermining the existing economic and power relationships in the society.

Such thinking is a reflection of the society in which foundations operate. As the seventies began, the reforming spirit evident in the 1960s seemed spent, and the nation appeared morally exhausted by the burdens of an unpopular war and the difficulties of enacting egalitarian social programs. Thus attitudes toward the role of the foundations can be seen as part of a general withdrawal from tackling domestic problems, a withdrawal that was being felt at all levels of society. This attitude also accounts for the willingness of many foundations to shy away from programs in the ghetto and refrain from breaking with past tradition by initiating funding for black-led agencies.

A 1972 study by the Research Department of the National Urban League clearly demonstrates that there has been little foundation support for programs affecting black people and that the funds expended on such programs are less than might be expected. An examination of grants made in 1970 and 1971, as compiled in the *Foundations Grant Index*, reveals that black agencies and issues of black concern received relatively small support from the so-called activist foundation community. The following analysis of grants made in several key areas of welfare points up this generally lukewarm national attitude toward social change:

> *Less than a fifth of all grant moneys were expended on social welfare programs, and only about a fifth of those funds found their way into the black community.*
>
> Less than one-fourth of the money in the welfare category went to programs serving the black and Spanish-speaking communities.
>
> Over 40 percent of it went to all-white community programs.
>
> Less than 5 percent of the dollars granted for child welfare went to the black communities, and only one-half of 1 percent to black agencies.
>
> Less than 10 percent of grants for youth programs went to the black community, including funds allocated to the programs of the Ys. Only 1 percent was granted to black agencies.
>
> Of the money granted for assisting the aged, only 3 percent found its way into the black community.

In the area of race relations, which includes such crucial social-change programs as legal aid, voter education, and civil rights agencies, instead of the enormous support one would expect to find for black agencies serving the black community, only a third of these funds went to national black-led organizations, while two-thirds were distributed to hundreds of small, local race relations councils and discussion groups. Overall, grants for race relations amounted to only $24 million, or about 10 percent of the total spent in the welfare category. While 19 percent of the total spent on welfare went to community development, and half of that went to programs in the black community, less than a fifth of the community development funds were granted to black agencies.

Grant-giving in education was even more one-sided during the 1970–71 period. Of all grants made to colleges and universities at that time, black colleges received only 6 percent of the total. It should be pointed out here that there is considerable confusion about categories relating to black people. The latter are set apart not only by a general neglect of their interests and the inadequacy of the funds made available to them but also by a definite tendency among white philanthropists to lump every dollar that goes to blacks as money for social change or for equal opportunity. Thus a grant to a black school of veterinary medicine is considered an equal opportunity grant.

In spite of individual instances of great generosity, an honest appraisal of foundation activities leads to the conclusion that foundations have placed black people and black agencies in the same ghettoized category that typifies their living arrangements in the cities. One need only look at the disproportionately small funding made available to black causes to know that these areas represent the slum sector of foundation giving. Here, as elsewhere, black folk get the leftovers. And ironically, while still hungry from a supper of crumbs, black Americans find themselves accused of being gluttons, while the foundations in turn are accused of heaping their plates too full.

It is due to the failure of private philanthropy and foundation giving to realize existing imperatives that some of the most important black agencies, in order to provide basic services and fulfill crucial needs, have been forced to turn to the Federal Government for funds. Half the budget of the Urban League consists of federally financed projects. Two-thirds of Opportunities Industrialization Center Institute, Inc.'s budget is in federal contracts. Other black-led agencies on state and local levels are turning to Washington for financial assistance that should be forthcoming from the private sector.

In my opinion this is taking place not because of an overly activist federal sector, but because Washington recognizes that there are important programs that must be run and that the black-led civil rights and social service agencies are best equipped to run them. I believe that increased governmental participation reflects an indifference or a failure of imagination on the part of many foundations, whose refusal to support programs of social change and programs for the powerless has created a vacuum which Washington feels obligated to fill.

History has shown that dangerous or, at best, relatively unhealthy situations can be created when governments assume roles previously filled by the private sector. It should also be stressed that among the recipients of foundation moneys there is a preference for funding from a variety of sources, which decreases dependence upon any single source. If private and foundation giving does not increase to a reasonable level, black agencies are likely to find themselves seriously restricted in their movement potential and open to buffeting by political winds.

As we move further into the seventies, there are definite reasons to hope that foundations will at worst hold the line and, at best, increase their involvement in the black sector. Some foundations, including the major ones to enter the field in the 1960s, show every indication of continuing such activities. Another cause for optimism is the fact that the black-led agencies are themselves adapting to the new stage of the civil rights movement, replacing marches and demonstrations with more sophisticated programs and techniques that, in addition to being more effective, are also more conducive to attracting support. Finally, the composition of foundation staffs is changing. Blacks have been hired to fill numerous posts and foundations have become equal opportunity employers. This has led to the creation of the Association of Black Foundation Executives, which has called for sharply increased foundation activity in helping to resolve problems afflicting blacks and the cities.

However cautiously and hesitantly foundations may have stepped into the periphery of important social concerns, there is no denying that they are now involved to varying degrees in urban problems and that the public and especially black people expect them to fulfill the obligations their wealth and leadership roles place on them. Despite their disappointing record of the past and their indifferent record of the present, there is decided reason to hope that foundations will become more responsible in using their resources on behalf of black Americans.

## Notes

1. J. H. Franklin, *From Slavery to Freedom* (New York, A. A. Knopf, 1963), pp. 302–305; Henry Allen Bullock, *A History of Negro Education in the South* (Cambridge, Harvard University Press, 1967), pp. 31–35.
2. Horace Mann Bond, *The Education of the Negro in the American Social Order* (New York, Prentice-Hall, 1934; Octagon Books, New York, 1966), p. 128.
3. Louis M. Hacker, *The Triumph of American Capitalism* (New York, Columbia University Press, 1940).
4. Franklin, *op. cit.*, p. 378.
5. *Ibid.*
6. D. O. W. Holmes, *The Evolution of the Negro College* (Teachers College, Columbia University, 1934), p. 164.
7. Franklin, *op. cit.*, p. 379.
8. Holmes, *op. cit.*, pp. 164–65; Bond, *op. cit.*, pp. 131–32.
9. Holmes, *op. cit.*, p. 165; Bond, *op. cit.*, p. 133.
10. Holmes, *op. cit.*, pp. 168–72.
11. *Ibid.*, pp. 100, 163–64.

12. Franklin, *op. cit.*, pp. 379–80; Holmes, *op. cit.*, p. 172.
13. Holmes, *op. cit.*, pp. 173–76.
14. Bond, *op. cit.*, pp. 129–30.
15. Franklin, *op. cit.*, p. 380.
16. Holmes, *op. cit.*, pp. 177–78; Franklin, *op. cit.*, pp. 538–39; Bond, *op. cit.*, pp. 143–44.
17. John P. Davis, ed., *The American Negro Reference Book* (Englewood Cliffs, Prentice-Hall, Inc., 1966), p. vii.
18. Franklin, *op. cit.*, p. 380, 535–36.
19. Bullock, *op. cit.*, pp. 127, 138–43.
20. Gunnar Myrdal, *An American Dilemma* (New York, Harper and Row, 1944, 1962; New York, McGraw-Hill, 1964), pp. xlvii–l.; Bullock, *op. cit.*, pp. 118, 133, 286.
21. Myrdal, *op. cit.*, p. 892.
22. *Crisis*, December 1971, pp. 312, 317–18; *Negro History Bulletin*, Vol. 35, No. 8, December 1972, p. 189.
23. Myrdal, *op. cit.*, p. 892.
24. Langston Hughes, *Fight for Freedom: The Story of the NAACP* (New York, W. W. Norton, 1962; New York, Berkley Publishing Co., 1962), pp. 67–70.
25. Myrdal, *op. cit.*, pp. 891, 893.
26. Bond, *op. cit.*, p. 144.

## BIBLIOGRAPHY

Bond, Horace Mann, *The Education of the Negro in the American Social Order.* New York, Prentice-Hall, 1934; New York, Octagon Books, Inc., 1966. Chapter VII, "The Awakening of Private Conscience," pp. 127–150.

Brawley, Benjamin, *Dr. Dillard of the Jeanes Fund.* New York, Fleming H. Revell Co., 1930.

Bullock, Henry Allen, *A History of Negro Education in the South: From 1619 to the Present.* Cambridge, Harvard University Press, 1967. Chapter V, "Deeds of Philanthropy," pp. 117–146.

Dykeman, Wilma and Stokely, James, *Seeds of Southern Change: The Life of Will Alexander.* Chicago, University of Chicago Press, 1962. (Alexander gave Julius Rosenwald the idea of the Rosenwald fellowships, was a member of the board of trustees of the Julius Rosenwald Fund from 1930 on and a vice-president of the fund from 1940 to 1948.)

Embree, Edwin R. and Waxman, Julia, *Investment in People: The Story of the Julius Rosenwald Fund.* New York, Harper, 1949.

Fosdick, Raymond B., *Adventure in Giving: The Story of the General Education Board.* New York, Harper and Row, 1962.

———, *The Story of the Rockefeller Foundation.* New York, Harper and Brothers, 1952. (Raymond B. Fosdick, who died in 1972, was president of the Rockefeller Foundation.)

Franklin, John Hope, *From Slavery to Freedom: A History of American Negroes.* New York, A. A. Knopf, 1963. Chapter XXI, "Philanthropy and Self-Help," pp. 377–390.

Goulden, Joseph C., *The Money Givers.* New York, Random House, 1971.

Holmes, D. O. W., *The Evolution of the Negro College.* New York, Teachers College, Columbia University, 1934.

Chapter XIII, "Organized Philanthropy,"
pp. 163–178.

Jones, Lance G. E., *The Jeanes Teacher in
the United States, 1908–1933*. Chapel Hill,
University of North Carolina Press, 1937.

Josephson, Matthew, *The Robber Barons:
The Great American Capitalists, 1861–1901*.
New York, Harcourt, Brace, 1934.
(Also paperback.)

King, Kenneth James, *Pan-Africanism and
Education: A Study of Race Philanthropy
and Education in the Southern States of
America and East Africa*. New York,
Oxford University Press, 1971. (About
the Phelps-Stokes Fund's educational
activities in Kenya [East Africa] and the
industrial-education-for-blacks orientation
of the fund's early director, Thomas
Jesse Jones.)

Leavell, Ullin W., *Philanthropy in Negro
Education*. Nashville, George Peabody
College for Teachers, 1930.

Myrdal, Gunnar, *An American Dilemma:
The Negro Problem and Modern Democracy*.
New York, Harper, 1944, 1962; New
York, McGraw-Hill, 1964 (2 vols.)

Nielsen, Waldemar A., *The Big Foundations*.
New York, Columbia University Press,
1972.

Rubin, Louis D., Jr., ed., *Teach the Freeman:
The Correspondence of Rutherford B. Hayes
and the Slater Fund for Negro Education,
1881–1887* (2 vols.). Baton Rouge,
Louisiana State University Press, 1959.

Smith, S. L., *Builders of Goodwill: The
Story of the State Agents of Negro Education
in the South, 1910 to 1950*. Nashville,
Tennessee Book Co., 1950. (The state
agents of black schools in the South were
subsidized by grants from the General
Education Board. There is also a chapter
on the Julius Rosenwald Fund school
building program in the South.)

Werner, M. R., *Julius Rosenwald: The Life
of a Practical Humanitarian*. New York,
Harper & Brothers, 1939. Chapter V,
"The Negroes," pp. 107–136; Chapter
XII, "A Philanthropist and His Money,"
pp. 320–355.

# 14

## Afro-American Religion

### Harry V. Richardson and Nathan Wright, Jr.

## I. THE ORIGIN AND DEVELOPMENT OF THE ESTABLISHED CHURCHES *by Harry V. Richardson*

### THE SLAVE ERA

The great majority of black slaves imported into the Western Hemisphere came from the west coast of Central Africa. The region that is now the nation of Ghana was one of the focal points of the trade.

The natives of this region who were caught and sold into slavery came from tribes that had well-developed religions. As with most tribal peoples, religion played a large and deeply important part in their lives. They were animistic, believing in spirits, good and bad, and they practiced fetishism. In religions with a multiplicity of spirits, there is usually one dominant or father spirit who is creator, ruler, and protector. References to this dominant spirit, sometimes called Anyambe or Onyambe, are found in the language and practices of African people today, both westernized and indigenous.

The fact that the African slaves already had a highly developed religious life when they arrived in America probably explains why many slaves, as they had the opportunity, took so readily to the Christian religion, and had so little trouble making the spiritual transition despite language and cultural barriers.

From the beginning, there was a serious effort to convert the slaves to Christianity. Indeed, this was one of the justifications for the slave trade. But for the first hundred years the question of converting slaves was highly controversial, and therefore efforts of conversion were not as widespread or as effective as they might have been.

For example, at the time when the importation of black slaves began, it was commonly believed that one Christian should not hold another Christian in bondage. This meant that when a slave became a Christian he also should have been freed. This would have been ruinous to those who had invested in slaves, and it led to much of the opposition that missionaries faced in their efforts to convert the slaves.

To settle the issue in Virginia the legislature of that colony declared in 1667 that baptism did not alter the condition of a person as to his bondage or freedom. This started a process of enactments and rulings that removed the Christian religion as a legal barrier to slavery in the colonies. In 1729 the Crown Attorney and Solicitor General ruled that baptism in no way changed a slave's legal status. Two years previously the Bishop of London had declared:

> . . . Christianity does not make the least alteration in civil property; . . . the freedom which Christianity gives, is a freedom from the bondage of sin and Satan, and from the dominion of their lusts and passions and inordinate desires; but as to their outward condition they remained as before, even after baptism.[1]

As the principle became established that conversion did not alter slave status, ministers and missionaries were freer to work among the slaves. The religious body that most actively undertook this work in the seventeenth and early eighteenth centuries was the Church of England through its Society for the Propagation of the Gospel in Foreign Parts. Since the Anglican Church was the major religious body in the colonies, the responsibility of winning converts to Christianity fell mainly upon the ministers of this church. However, for many reasons they were not able to devote adequate effort to the task. To assist in evangelizing the growing colonial population the Society for the Propagation of the Gospel was organized in 1701. Its specific duties were "the care and instruction of our people settled in the colonies; the conversion of the Indian savages, and the conversion of the Negroes."

Other bodies were active as well in the colonial period, but on a much smaller scale. Chief among them were the Moravian Brethren, the Presbyterians, and the Society of Friends. The Friends took the most positive stand against slavery of any of the religious bodies during this period. They alone made the possession of slaves a cause for expulsion from the Society.

It is the opinion of Marcus W. Jernigan, a student of colonial history, that prior to the American Revolution comparatively few slaves were converted to Christianity. His reasons, as summarized from a published discussion of the subject, are:

1.  Masters feared that conversion would interfere with slave labor. Slaves were required to work on Sundays, which conflicted with Christian teaching, and further, when converted, slaves would be equal in one respect to their masters, which would make them harder to control.

2.  The general interest in religion was low in colonial times. Masters were not much interested in their own spiritual welfare, and consequently were not deeply concerned about the welfare of their slaves.

3.  Many slaves were unable to understand religious teachings, due in large part to their lack of knowledge of the English language.

4.  The slave's environment was not conducive to the Christian life.

5.  The sparsely settled country and the difficulties of travel made it hard for ministers to serve their members, to say nothing of evangelizing the unchurched.[2]

It was not until the latter half of the eighteenth century, around the time of the American Revolution, that a number of significant developments took place that did much to spread Christianity among the slaves and to shape the course of black religion in America.

## The Influence of Cotton

The first of these developments was the increased production of cotton in response to a rapidly rising world demand. A series of remarkable inventions, beginning with the spinning and weaving machines in England and culminating in Whitney's cotton gin in America, greatly increased the output of cotton goods. The soil of the southern colonies was admirably suited to grow the necessary cotton if an adequate supply of labor could be obtained. This labor was found in African Negro slaves, who first were legally imported into the country, then illegally smuggled, and all the while bred to meet the great demand. In 1790 there were approximately 700,000 slaves in the United States. In 1860 there were 4 million. Over 3 million were in twelve southern states, engaged for the most part in producing the cotton and other crops that were rapidly building up the fortunes of the wealthier southern planters.

This concentration of blacks on the farms and plantations of the South gave the busy evangelists of the time excellent opportunities to reach the black population and to win large numbers of them to Christianity.

## The Evangelicals and the Slave

The second great development in the evolution of black religion was the coming of the evangelical Christian bodies, particularly the Methodists, Baptists, and Presbyterians. These groups, in their zeal to evangelize young America, gave much attention to the growing body of slaves. At first they were strongly abolitionist. Not only did they feel that slavery was wrong, they openly preached against it. Freeborn Garretson said in 1776:

> It was God, not man, that taught me the impropriety of holding slaves; and I shall never be able to praise him enough for it. My very heart has bled since that for slaveholders, especially those who make a profession of religion; for I believe it to be a crying sin.[3]

Bishop Asbury records in his Journal in 1780: "This I know. God will plead the cause of the oppressed though it gives offense to say so here. . . . I am grieved for slavery and the manner of keeping these poor people."[4]

Many preachers backed up their words by freeing slaves they already held or by refusing to become slaveholders. In 1780 the Methodists required all traveling preachers to set their slaves free. The Baptists, because of their policy of local church government, were not as uniform or effective in their attack on slavery as were the Methodists. Yet in 1789 a Baptist Convention declared:

> Slavery is a violent depredation of the rights of nature and inconsistent with a republican government, and therefore, [we] recommend it to our brethren, to make use of their local missions to extirpate this horrid evil from the land; and pray Almighty God that our honorable legislature may have in their power to proclaim the great jubilee consistent with the principles of good policy.[5]

Although the evangelicals found it necessary to retreat considerably from the moral stand they first had taken against slavery, they continued their efforts to convert the slaves and to plead in the name of Christianity for amelioration of the more brutal aspects of slavery.

In seeking converts, the evangelicals had one great advantage over the Anglicans and other early missionaries. The evangelical religion was simple, personal, and only slightly ritualistic. It was ideally suited to the unlettered masses of the colonial frontier, both white and black. In order to become an Anglican it was necessary to know the creed, the catechism, and other articles of faith, as well as to be able to follow the ritual of the service. To become a Methodist or Baptist it was only necessary to repent and accept Christ as personal Savior. This was a religion even the fieldhand slave could understand. In the early evangelistic drives such as the Great Awakening and the Great Revival, large numbers of blacks were converted. But if the simplicity of the evangelical faith did much to determine the number of Negroes who became Christians, the emotionalism of the early evangelical faith did much to determine the nature of black worship. The religion that the black masses first received was characterized by such phenomena as laughing, weeping, shouting, dancing, barking, jerking, prostration, and speaking in tongues. These were regarded as evidence of the Spirit at work in the heart of man, and they were also taken as evidence of the depth and sincerity of the conversion. It was inevitable, therefore, that early black worship should be filled with these emotional elements.

Although there is some tendency to regard high emotionalism as a phenomenon peculiar to the black church, in reality it is a hangover from the days of frontier religion. It should also be said that emotionalism of this type is to be found today chiefly among the less sophisticated rural and urban churches.[6]

## The Black Preacher

The third development that did much to shape the course of black religion was the rise of black preachers. These leaders began to appear in the latter part of the eighteenth century, the time when large numbers of Negroes were being converted to Christianity. Prominent among them were Black Harry (c. 1782), who traveled with Bishop Asbury and was a great attraction; David George (c. 1775), preacher of the first Negro Baptist Church at Silver Bluff, South Carolina; George Liele, of Burke County, Georgia, an eloquent preacher to blacks and whites; Andrew Bryan of Georgia (1737–1812), founder of the First African Baptist Church of Savannah; John Chavis (c. 1801), who was made a missionary to the slaves by the Presbyterians; and Henry Evans, organizer of the white Methodist Church at Fayetteville, North Carolina, in 1790.[7] Most unusual among these early preachers was Lemuel Haynes, 1753–1833, a mulatto of learning and eloquence who through all of his ministry pastored only white Congregational churches in New England. He was an accomplished theologian, and debated with power the theological issues of his time.

The black preacher played a significant part in the social and religious development of Negro life. First, preaching was an outlet for leadership ability. It was the one position of leadership permitted Negroes, and the office carried considerable prestige. It did much to keep aspiration alive among gifted black men. Secondly, the black preacher was able to communicate religion to the slave in a useful and intimate form. Being one of the people and suffering with them, he could make religion not only a discipline, but also a living ground of hope.

The preachers' task was a difficult one, however. While preaching to slaves, they could not attack slavery, at least not openly. The preacher himself was always suspect and closely watched as a potential source of rebellion. The controls over slave meetings even for worship were so rigid and severe that an attack on the slave system would have readily brought down terrible penalties upon both preacher and people.

Yet from the beginning the church served as the main outlet through which the slaves could express their sufferings and dissatisfaction. Although it did so covertly, the church rendered two greatly needed services to the slaves: first, it kept alive the consciousness that the slave system was wicked; and second, it kept alive the hope that in the plan of a good, just God, the wicked, brutal system under which they lived would in time pass away.

It should be said, however, that not all preachers were patient or unresisting. Nat Turner, for instance, who led the bloody revolt of 1831, was a Baptist exhorter.

In the time of slavery there were three distinct types of slave churches: the "mixed" church with slaves as members of the congregation; the separate church under white leadership; and the separate church under black leadership. All three types existed simultaneously, but there was a gradual evolution toward the separate, all-black church.


## THE EMANCIPATION AND AFTER


On September 22, 1862, President Lincoln issued the Emancipation Proclamation that was to become effective January 1, 1863. Although it was not immediately enforceable in many parts of the South, since unoccupied sections were outside the control of the national Government, freedom became a reality for all Negroes with the close of the Civil War. Thenceforth they were free to move and to organize as they wished.

The great mass of undeveloped, unchristianized freedmen in the South presented opportunity for many kinds of humanitarian service. Along with philanthropic whites who came into the South to render educational as well as religious aid to the freedmen, black missionaries also came as representatives of independent black denominations, seeking to win members for their particular churches from among the former slaves.

Partly because of their racial appeal and partly because of their greater activity, the black workers won far more members than the representatives of the white church bodies. In fact, the early days of the Reconstruction were marked by a strong tendency toward independent, all-Negro religious organizations. In the decade between 1860 and 1870 the African Methodist Episcopal Zion (AMEZ) Church, one of the two principal black Methodist bodies, grew from 26,746 members to 200,000. The African Methodist Episcopal (AME) Church, the leading black Methodist group, in 1880 claimed a membership of 400,000. For both churches most of their members were freedmen in the rural South.

Baptists quickly became the most numerous group among blacks in the South. In this church, as in the Methodist, the tendency was toward independent, all-black units. Even in cases where Negroes had been members of white churches on amicable terms, there still was a desire for the separate all-black church.

### TABLE I—THE PRESENT CHURCH
Major Black Denominations*

| Denomination | Number of Members | Number of Churches | Number of Pastors | Sunday School Members |
|---|---|---|---|---|
| National Baptist Convention, U. S. A. | 5,600,000 | 26,000 | 27,500 | 2,407,000 |
| National Baptist Convention of America | 2,750,000 | 11,398 | 7,598 | 500,000 |
| Progressive National Baptist Convention | 521,692 | 655 | 863 | N.A. |
| AME Church | 1,166,000 | 5,878 | 5,878 | 363,432 |
| AMEZ Church | 940,000 | 4,500 | 5,500 | 162,000 |
| Christian Methodist Episcopal Church | 466,718 | 2,598 | 2,259 | 115,424 |
| Church of God in Christ | 600,000 | 5,000 | 6,000 | |

N.A.  Not Available.

*Based on reported figures in the *Yearbook of American Churches, 1972,* published by the National Council of the Churches of Christ in the U. S. A., New York, N. Y., plus conferences with responsible church officials.

## The Baptists

Prior to the Civil War, the Baptist Church among Negroes consisted almost entirely of local congregations. Organization into district, state, or national bodies was difficult for both slaves and free blacks. With the coming of freedom, the organization of larger bodies rapidly took place. The first state convention was organized in North Carolina in 1866, just one year after the close of the war. Alabama and Virginia followed in 1867, and by 1870 all the southern states had state conventions.

On the national level, these black groups were at first affiliated with white national bodies. In 1867, however, the Consolidated American Baptist Convention was organized and continued until 1880, when the National Baptist Convention was established at Montgomery, Alabama. Three smaller conventions grew out of this body: the Foreign Mission Baptist Convention of the U.S.A., 1880; the American National Baptist Convention, 1880; and the American National Educational Baptist Convention, 1893. All of these were united in 1895 at Atlanta, Georgia, into the National Baptist Convention of the U.S.A., which was incorporated in 1915. This convention when formed had three million members, and thereby became the largest single denomination of black Christians in the world. Such tremendous growth in the fifty years from 1865 to 1915 reveals the rapidity with which the church grew among blacks after emancipation.

With the passing years the National Baptist Convention of the U.S.A. [Incorporated] has suffered a number of splits. The largest of these separating groups is the National Baptist Convention of America.

The tendency toward division, so characteristic of Baptists, continues to the present time. Today there are three national conventions: the National Baptist Convention of the U.S.A., the National Baptist Convention of America and the Progressive National Baptist Convention.

Although divided, Baptists are by far the largest single group of black Christians in the world. They have approximately 9,000,000 members, 38,000 churches, and 4,900,000 children in church schools. There are over 35,000 preachers in the Baptist ministry.

There are no distinctive doctrines or patterns of policy in the black Baptist Churches. They adhere in all basic essentials to the beliefs and practices of the major Baptist bodies of the nation. The Baptists have played an important part in the progress of the black population in education, in civic leadership, and in other areas. They also have an extensive foreign mission program.

## The Methodist Churches

Methodists were early active among blacks in both Colonial and post-Revolutionary times. They won large numbers to Methodism and took them readily into church membership. They organized a number of black congregations, usually presided over by white preachers, and took a number of Negroes into the ministry.

The black members, both slave and free, were usually restricted, however, in their participation in church life. They sat in segregated seats during services, and communed after the others or in special services. Dissatisfaction with such arrangements steadily increased, so that by 1785 in several northern cities black members had organized themselves into separate congregations. In 1787 a company of blacks in Philadelphia withdrew from the white church, and under the leadership of Richard Allen, a free and well-to-do Negro, built a chapel where they held separate services under an ordained black Episcopal priest.

Despite opposition from the white Methodists in Philadelphia, in 1793 Bishop Asbury dedicated the chapel as Bethel Church, and in 1799 he ordained Richard Allen a deacon.

In 1814, out of litigation brought by the white Methodists, the Supreme Court of Pennsylvania ruled that Bethel Church was an independent body. In 1816 Richard Allen and others called together representatives of separate churches similar to Bethel that had been organized in Delaware, Maryland, and New Jersey. This meeting resulted in the formation of the AME Church, the second separate black Methodist denomination. The first was the Union Church of Africans which had been incorporated in Wilmington, Delaware, in 1813. This church, however, has grown very little. About the same time a third separatist movement, much like the first, resulted in the formation of the AMEZ Church in 1820.

Prior to the Civil War, the Negro Methodist Churches were not able to expand widely. The national pattern of church life characteristic of Methodism, with its itinerant ministry and traveling officers, was not possible for blacks, either slave or free. With the coming of freedom, permitting the movement and evangelism necessary for expansion, the black Methodist bodies grew very rapidly, although not as much as the Baptists. The Christian Methodist Episcopal (CME) Church, discussed below, illustrates the rise and growth of a church after the emancipation.

## The AME Church

The AME Church today is truly international in scope. It has churches in Africa, Canada, and the Caribbean area. When the Sunday school enrollment is added to the adult membership, the total is more than a million and a half members. These are in 5,878 churches and 6,472 Sunday schools.

The AME Church is divided into eighteen episcopal districts. The governing bodies of the church are the General Conference, which meets quadrennially, the Council of Bishops, and the General Board. The work of the church is under the supervision of ten boards or departments, including the Board of Missions, the Board of Church Extension, the Department of Education, and the Department of Evangelism. There are five church publications, the *Christian Recorder*, *The AME Review*, the *Voice of Missions*, the *Southwestern Christian Recorder*, and the *Woman's Missionary Recorder*. The church maintains a publishing house in Nashville, Tennessee.

## The AMEZ Church

The orgin of the AMEZ Church is much like that of the AME. In 1796 a group of black members, led by James Varick and others, withdrew from the John Street Methodist Church in New York City to escape the problems of segregation in church life. In 1800 they built a church which they named Zion. They at first maintained cooperative relationships with the white Methodist Church, but in 1820 this cooperation failed.

Joining with separate black congregations in other cities, in 1821 they held an annual conference and elected James Varick their first bishop. Several elders had been ordained by sympathetic white Methodist ministers. This gave them a ministry.

This church, like the others, experienced its great growth after the Civil War. By 1880 fifteen annual conferences had been organized in the South. Today the AMEZ Church performs missionary work in West Africa, South America, and the West Indies.

## The CME Church

The third major black Methodist body is the aforementioned CME Church. Originally it was called the Colored ME Church, but in 1956 the word *Colored* was changed to *Christian*.

At the close of the Civil War there were over 250,000 black members in the Methodist Episcopal Church, South. They had long been dissatisfied with the segregation and restrictions imposed upon them. Immediately after the war, in 1866, they appealed to the General Conference of the ME Church, South, to be set apart in a church of their own. The conference ruled that wherever there were sufficient numbers, they would set up separate annual conferences. It further appointed a commission to study the request for a separate church and to report to the next general conference. In 1870 the commission recommended that the Negro members be organized into a church of their own. Later that year, in December, the first General Conference of the CME Church was held at Jackson, Tennessee. Two black bishops were elected, Henry Miles and Richard H. Vanderhorst.

In the years since the separation the ME Church, South, has kept its interest in the CME Church, and has assisted it in many ways, especially in organizing and operating the educational program.

This church, like the others, has had substantial growth. It now has 466,718 members and 2,598 churches.

## Black Membership in White Churches

The great majority of black Christians are in seven separate and predominantly black denominations. All major church bodies, however, have some black members, and sometimes this membership is large. When these memberships are added together they constitute a significant segment of black Christendom.

The United Methodist Church has the largest number of Negro members, more than 370,000. This membership formerly constituted a separate, nationwide "Central Jurisdiction," organized on racial grounds, but this separate jurisdiction was dissolved in 1972. Other churches with sizable Negro memberships include the Protestant Episcopal Church, the United Church of Christ, the Seventh Day Adventist Church, the Presbyterian Churches, the American Baptist Convention, and the Churches of God. Some churches keep figures on members by race and some do not. This makes it difficult if not impossible to get an accurate total. A reasonable estimate would seem to be about 800,000.

In all of these bodies black membership varies from a few individuals in white congregations to separate local churches composed wholly or almost wholly of Negroes. Some of these black congregations may be quite large, such as St. Mark's Methodist Church in New York City, one of the largest churches in the denomination, or the First Congregational Church in Atlanta, the largest such church in the region.

In these denominations, blacks often enjoy full participation in the life of the church, both as members and as officials. This is especially true of local congregations in northern and western regions, and in the regional and national boards of the churches. In the Methodist Church, for instance, the five black bishops in America all preside over predominantly white areas. A Negro has served on the Judicial Council, one of the highest bodies in the church, and a black bishop has served as president of the Bishops' Council. Also, a Negro has recently been elected president of the National Council of the Churches of Christ in America.

In addition to the established churches that have black members, there are also 200 or more sects, or smaller religious groups, nearly all of which have black members. Examples of such sects are various Churches of God, Holiness Churches, and Spiritualist Churches.

In the sects, as in the denominations, blacks may be in separate congregations, or they may be full members of white congregations. Likewise, they hold offices in the ministries and official life of these bodies. An estimate of this black membership is not possible.

## Store-Front Churches

For the past half-century an accelerating movement has been going on in America which is having a profound influence on black church life. That movement began with the migration of blacks from the rural areas of the South into the urban centers of the South, North, and West. The movement began during the first world war, and it has grown continually ever since. It was especially heavy in the 1950s and 1960s because of the agricultural and technological changes in the South.

The present result of this migration is that large numbers of blacks are crowded together in the decaying older sections of cities, living in poverty, without adequate employment or living necessities or hope. The more financially secure citizens, white and black, have fled to the suburbs, leaving the poorer masses piled in the inner city. The established church in many cases has followed its members, thus depriving the newly migrant masses in the city of effective service from the established church.

There are, however, certain churches that serve the inner city. These are the "store-front" or "house-front" churches. In depressed neighborhoods there are usually numerous vacant stores which can easily be converted into meeting places. Or, where a store is not available, a residence may serve this purpose.

These churches are usually of the cult or sect type. Sometimes they are affiliated with national bodies, such as Holiness or Pentecostal groups. Sometimes they are single, separate churches arising out of the zeal of an interested evangelist. In most cases, these churches are marked by their emotionalism, by strict adherence to a biblical way of life, and by severe injunctions to moral living. Their ministers are often poorly trained and have little concern with or ability to handle the social and economic conditions that depress the people.

There are four main reasons for the existence of the store-front churches: (1) the lack of adequate follow-up by the established churches from which the migrants come; (2) lack of concern or programs by the established churches in the areas; (3) the evangelistic zeal of preachers and Christian workers who want to save the people from the sins of their environment; and (4) the continuing and genuine interest of the depressed people in religion as a source of help in their troubles.

A more detailed discussion of the above points is not possible here. It is known, however, that many of the migrants were church members in their home towns, but because their churches have been derelict in keeping membership records, or in following members who move, there is no continuity of church life for the migrant. Also, studies have shown that membership in the established church is too often a matter of status; that is, membership declines as the people lose economic and social standing.

Despite its obvious faults, the store-front church does serve an important function among the depressed people who have urgent religious needs: ". . . it provides a reason for existence, a feeling of belonging, and a temporary escape from the dreariness of their lot. It also provides for the large number of rural southern migrants a means of facilitating urbanization by becoming part of a closely knit 'we group' with which they can identify and emulate."[8]

## The Church and Education

The Emancipation Proclamation of 1863 gave the black man freedom, but it offered the freedmen few means with which to secure their education and cultural development. To provide these essentials, men and women from the established churches rushed into the South—often at great personal sacrifice—to establish schools, to teach, and to render other needed services to the freedmen. In doing this they wrote one of the brightest pages in the history of Christian missions. Among the most active of these churches were the Methodists, Congregationalists, Presbyterians, and Baptists. They opened schools, sometimes called "colleges" or "universities," which in the beginning were little more than high schools or academies. However, as educational levels have risen, many of these schools have developed into first-rate, fully accredited institutions of higher learning. These schools taught not only academic subjects, but also the basic elements of American culture. They helped the Negro to bridge the gap between slavery and citizenship, and they have provided much of the black leadership of the past century.

## The Black Church and Education

The coming of freedom made it possible for the black church to work freely across the nation, but especially in the South where most blacks lived. The Negro churches were interested in gaining members, but they were also interested in the educational development of their people. They devoted a large share of their meager resources to setting up schools, colleges, and seminaries. The AME Church, for instance, has seven colleges; the CME Church has three colleges plus several secondary schools and a seminary.

The schools of the white and black denominations constitute the main source of private education among Negroes. At present these church schools have about 40,000 black students.

## The Church and Civil Rights

It has already been seen that in the days of slavery the Negro's church was the main instrument for the expression of his sufferings on the one hand and his hopes on the other. Similarly, in the contemporary struggle for civil rights the church is the main institution through which social dissatisfactions and civil aspirations can be expressed. In many communities, especially in the South, the black church is the only institution capable of working for civil rights. Because of its independent support and its relative freedom from governmental intimidation, the black church is often the center of protest meetings, voter registration projects, and other mass efforts.

What is true of the church is also true of the black minister, who has played a leading part in the struggle for equality. In this social role he is perhaps best symbolized by Dr. Martin Luther King, Jr., a well-trained black pastor who started with a revolt against segregated bus transportation in Montgomery, Alabama, and led that revolt into a great national demand for complete integration in the whole of American life. The black pastor and his church are still powerful influences in the social life and aspirations of blacks in America.

In religion the push for rights has resulted in the "black caucus" movement. Groups of blacks in predominantly white bodies, usually the younger and more vocal blacks, join in protesting discrimination and in demanding full participation in all levels of denominational activities. On a national scale they have joined to form the National Council of Black Churchmen.

In addition to the push for participation, there has come in recent years the demand upon predominantly white churches for economic assistance or "reparations" in return for opportunities denied black people through the years. In response, many of the major denominations have appropriated sums, sometimes running into the millions, to be used to assist minority businesses, to establish scholarship funds, to provide day-care centers, and to set up such social improvement projects as vocational training programs. Among the leading churches in these efforts are the United Methodist Church, the Roman Catholic Church, the Unitarian Universalist Church, the Presbyterian Church, the Protestant Episcopal Church, and the American Baptist Convention.

### The Catholic Church and the Black American

The Catholic Church has always been interested in the conversion of Negroes to that faith. In comparatively recent years, however, the work among blacks has grown remarkably in scope and intensity. Black membership has practically tripled in the past twenty-five years.

In 1972 the Roman Catholic Church in America had 863,616 black members, 138 black priests, and 692 black nuns. There are now three black bishops. In Catholic elementary and secondary schools there were 183,778 black students, Catholic and non-Catholic. There were 616 predominantly black churches or missions.[9]

It thus can be seen that within a quarter-century the Catholic Church has grown to be one of the leading religious groups among black Americans, surpassing three of the major black denominations.

## CHARACTERISTICS AND CONTRIBUTIONS

The question is often raised as to whether or not the black church possesses any distinct or unique features that would differentiate it from other church bodies. Does it differ significantly from other churches in theology or in polity or in patterns of church life?

The general conclusion is that the black church does not possess any significantly different features. In faith, in polity, and in practice the black denominations all follow closely the parent white bodies from which they came. The black church was not born out of differences over theology or polity. It is simply a black division of the general church.

Indeed, there is widespread objection to the very term "black church" on the ground that this is in itself a misnomer, and that there is no such thing as a "black" church. A more accurate term would seem to be the "blacks' church," or better still, "the church among blacks."

But despite the lack of distinctive features, what we call the black church is well established as a separate institution or group of institutions, and bids well to remain so for a long time. The black church does participate fully, however, in cooperative activities with other churches. All major black denominations are members of the

National Council of the Churches of Christ. They also share fully in state and local councils of churches. In a number of instances black churchmen hold prominent places in these bodies, even in the South. A black man was elected President of the Georgia Council of Churches, and a Mississippi black woman as President of Church Women United.

The beginnings of interchurch cooperation among the black denominations themselves may be seen in the Fraternal Council of Churches, an organization that embraces all of the major groups. It is perhaps best seen in the Interdenominational Theological Center in Atlanta, Georgia, a new, well-equipped, fully accredited seminary, formed through the cooperation of the Methodist, AME, CME, and Baptist Churches.

Perhaps the most distinguished contribution the black church has made to general Christendom has not been in theology but in music—the Negro "spirituals." These simple, rhythmic, harmonious songs, born in the hearts of slaves and freedmen, have spoken to the hearts of people everywhere. They have been accepted in established church music.

In their messages the spirituals reveal: (1) faith in God and in His ultimate justice ("My Lord Is A-writin' All the Time"); (2) patience and suffering ("Nobody Knows the Trouble I've Seen"); (3) the desire for freedom ("Go Down, Moses—Tell Ol' Pharaoh to Let My People Go"); (4) the passion for progress ("We Are Climbin' Jacob's Ladder"); and (5) the deep reverence of the black Christian ("Steal Away to Jesus" and "Were You There When They Crucified My Lord?").

## THE CHURCH: PRESENT AND FUTURE

The church has traditionally been a formative and controlling influence in the life of the black American, not only in spiritual matters, but in other areas as well. It is by far the largest institution the group has had, having today better than thirteen million members. It has served as an instrument of expression and action in civic, cultural, and educational concerns. It has provided inspired leadership for the group in the struggle for fuller life. Will this position of preeminence continue? The answer will depend upon several factors.

First of all, life among blacks is changing. From a predominantly rural people, they have become a predominantly urban people. At present most blacks are a disadvantaged people, constituting pockets of poverty in inner cities, suffering serious social and economic privations in the midst of an affluent society. These conditions call for spiritual and cultural services of the most intensive kind. Can the church render these services?

Studies conducted in a number of major cities show that the established church is not serving the depressed urban masses as it should and as the people need. In the first place, as we have seen, the church tends to follow its members to the suburbs. It has not yet developed an effective program of serving the indigent masses in inner cities. Unfortunately, church service declines as economic status declines.

Secondly, the black church is handicapped by an inadequately trained ministry. Recent figures show that only one out of fifteen men entering the ministry has had seminary training. In other words, 92 percent of the men entering the black ministry each year are professionally unprepared. Can untrained leaders develop the intensive service programs necessary for the development of a handicapped people?

The answer, obviously, is that they cannot. As studies show, in black communities there are few church-sponsored programs for guidance of the young, for adult education, for health and cultural improvement, or for help in occupational skills and placement. These are the kinds of services that will lead the people into a more abundant life.

At present the black church is a vast, influential, respected institution with between fifty and sixty thousand churches and more than fifty thousand pastors. If this great body can develop the services that a growing and changing population needs, it will continue to grow and to hold its place in the life and esteem of the group. On the other hand, it is certain that people will not long respect or support an agency that plays no needed part in their lives.

## II. NON-ESTABLISHMENT BLACK RELIGION
*by Nathan Wright, Jr.*

The most striking phenomenon in black religion today is the attempt on a number of parallel fronts to rediscover African religious roots. A number of Christian, Muslim, and secular groups have cooperated toward this end. Much of the coordination has been provided by the National Committee of Black Churchmen.

Organized in July of 1966, the then National Committee of Negro Churchmen was comprised originally of distinguished representatives of the traditional white and black churches. These churchmen had responded quickly to the call for Black Power and they sought to work together to emphasize the religious foundations of and tradition for Black Power in the historical black religious experience. The group later changed its name to the National Committee of Black Churchmen (NCBC) as an expression of the new mood of emancipation from an outwardly imposed racial definition, and further interpreted the meaning of the church itself to include all forms of religious expression within the life of the black community. Orientals and Muslims have been welcomed into its fellowship.

The NCBC cooperated actively with the 1967 National Conference on Black Power. Its members gave leadership to the conference's religious workshop, which defined black religion as that which gives expression on both an immediate and ultimate level to human liberation and the fulfillment of needs of the oppressed or darker peoples of the world. The conference urged the study of black religious roots as a means of religious renewal for the white western world. The underlying conviction here was that the basic plan of divine or religious salvation in every age is expressed best through the meeting of the total immediate human needs of those who are the most benighted or oppressed. This viewpoint was said to be in line with the scriptural declaration that "Inasmuch as you have done it to the most needful of my brothers, you have done it to me."

What was begun or encouraged largely by these initial endeavors quickly took root in widely diverse areas. In the field of scholarship a new interest was quickened. Dr. Joseph Washington, speaking to a new consensus, declared that "native African beliefs, practices, and institutions conditioned the response of Afro-Americans to the New World Christianity. We can be certain today that indigenous African religions were far more influential than historical interpretations allowed."[10] Dr. Washington isolated eight characteristics of the black African religious experience which, incidentally, are finding renewed expression among black churchmen today.

Washington notes that a white culture-conditioned scholarship had earlier discovered that African religions were without creed or texts. From this the inference was drawn that African religion was "primitive, non-normal, devoid of function" and possessed of nothing of abiding worth. Washington concludes that what had really been discovered by white European scholars was the simple fact that African religions were preliterate. The nonverbal expressions of the religious experience—more common to popular Asian, native American, and African religions—play little part in the popular aspects of contemporary western Christianity. "The present-day meaning of religious life to the average, or even thoughtful, white American or European churchman is mainly an exercise of the mind, a system of intellectual propositions supported by formal fellowship at a stated time and place on one day of the week." So explains Metz Rollins, Director of the NCBC. He adds: "The most unfortunate aspect of this sad state of affairs is that whites who have been led to think of themselves as right, miss out on what may be the best elements in the world's religious inheritance. We as blacks must break out of the shackles imposed by western Christianity and, in freeing ourselves, also free those who have made us temporarily captive." "The theology of black religion," says Saul Williams, vice-president of the Empire State Baptist Convention, "is our relationship with each other and with the earth which symbolizes both our origin and our end. Our brother Martin spoke of man's purpose or gospel imperative in the context of creation when he said: 'We are witnesses of the resurrection. I just want to be there in love, in justice, in truth, and in commitment to others so we can make of this old world a new world.'"

Washington observes that traditional African religions were open to all avenues that might fulfill the divine purpose of the union of God and man. The creed of the Black Christian Nationalist Movement under the leadership of the Reverend Albert Cleage of Detroit asserts:

> I believe that human society stands under the judgment of one God, revealed to all, and known by many names. His creative power is visible in the mysteries of the universe, in the revolutionary Holy Spirit which will not long permit men to endure injustice nor to wear the shackles of bondage, in the rage of the powerless when they struggle to be free, and in the violence and conflict which even now threaten to level the fields and the mountains.[11]

The catholicity of the Black Christian Nationalist Movement is evident in its cooperation with Islamic groups, in its acceptance of the non-Christian humanistic religious teachings of Imamu Amiri Baraka (Leroi Jones), and in its official affiliation with the predominantly white United Church of Christ. Man's immediately becoming one with the God who reigns over the earth in perpetual glory is the imperative under which the Black Christian Nationalist Movement operates. Dr. Cleage writes:

> The Black Liberation Struggle is the black man's key to the universe in which he lives. Everything is evaluated in terms of that struggle. We understand God in terms of the Liberation Struggle. We interpret Jesus in terms of the Liberation Struggle. We define the role of the Church in terms of the Liberation Struggle. We seek Christian Commitment in terms of the Liberation Struggle. Morality and ethics are meaningless except in terms of the demands of the Liberation Struggle.[12]

The African religious experience included the worship, affirmation, and appropriation of power wherever it might be found. Joseph Washington states: "Basic to the religions of Africa was the belief that everything is filled with soul or power which can be released for good (religion) or evil (witchcraft) objectives by priests or other mediums rightly attuned to the power. . . . All power gains its dynamic nature from God, the supreme power." The National Black Sisters' Conference of the Roman Catholic Church in 1970 reflected upon the nature of Soul Power. Sister Teresita Weind, SMP, in the conference's opening statement, declared:

> Hosea says, 'I will betroth you to myself forever, betroth with integrity and justice, with tenderness and love.' And it did seem that if *soul* meant anything to any one of us, one of its most profound dimensions is that which is centered around and rooted in integrity. That which is the integration of our physical, our spiritual, our emotional, our psychological being . . . the truly integrated men and women, out of whom the vibrations of integrity resound loud as the rolling sea . . . And so, with *soul* . . . with integrity and justice, tenderness and love . . . we come to know Yahweh.[13]

Soul Power, the integration of man's spirit with and into God's Spirit, is what the Reverend William A. Jones, Director of New York's Operation Breadbasket, claims is behind the economic demands for black people spearheaded by leadership in the black churches. Soul Power became, under the banner of the Reverend Jesse Jackson, then

National Director of Operation Breadbasket, the antiphonal declaration and response which sums up the social, political, economic, psychological, and religious needs of black people. "Black people are reaching out to touch the hem of Christ's garment," says the Reverend Otis Saunders, the community organizer-pastor of Detroit's Trinity African Methodist Episcopal Zion Church. "Indeed," he adds, "it is our firm intention to put on Christ's robes and to wear them in this present world in majesty, even as we have endured with Christ in the present world His sorrows and afflictions."[14]

Closely related to the belief in the appropriation of Soul Power as a concrete revelation of the eternal in the midst of the contemporary life of man is the African religious conviction that the sacred and the secular are one. With this in mind, the NCBC agreed to serve as the official institutional church vehicle for financing the demands of James Forman's Black Economic Manifesto. The Reverend Calvin Marshall, of NCBC's board of directors, serves as the church executive for the secular-oriented work of the Manifesto.[15] Other notable expressions of the emerging secular dimension to black religious life are evident in the functioning of the Blue Hill Christian Center in Boston under the leadership of the Reverend Virgil Wood, and the Glide Memorial United Methodist Church in San Francisco under the leadership of the Reverend A. Cecil Williams.

The Blue Hill Christian Center was opened in the early 1960s, under United Church of Christ auspices, largely to promote interracial harmony and to engage in social group work. By the mid-1960s it had become evident that blacks in the community sought to promote interracial harmony from a strong base of black ethnic solidarity. With the thrust toward Black Power in 1966, the center quickly became the focus for most of the organized efforts for black group power in the greater Boston area. The center has opened its doors to all people, but contemporary black expressions of worship are the normal practice of the center, attracting a large established congregation of predominantly young blacks. The center's economic thrust is B.R.E.A.D., Incorporated (Bluehill's Redistribution of Economic Assets and Dividends, Incorporated) which marks a shift, according to the center's report, "from piety to politics." The center cooperates actively with the Black Economic Development Union, which claims nearly a million dollars in assets for skill training, manufacturing, and marketing development for blacks in the Roxbury-Dorchester area of Boston. "From Christian paupers," says Virgil Wood, "we as blacks are to become participants and pioneers in the reordering of the economic and political priorities of our community."[16]

The Glide Memorial Church holds what its pastor calls the sacred celebration of the secular. This begins with a period of formal worship which is followed by a congregational family festival where, at nearly fifty booths, participants are advised on the draft or given drug counseling, and invited to become involved in a wide range of community, educational, social, political, economic, and religious endeavors. Formerly a white church with a white pastor, Glide now has a congregation of many races and many creeds. The basic theology is that of human liberation in active present-day terms. The invitation to Christmas Day worship in 1970 read: "Come! Let all the People Participate in the Celebration of Liberation. 'Christmas! Right On!' By Reverend A. Cecil Williams, with the Meridian West Jazz Folk Group, the Soulful Glide Ensemble, the Glide Theatre Group, the Glide Dance Group; Dancers, Singers, Musicians, Poets, Dramatists from all over the Bay Area, in a *Righteous Christmas Jam Session.*"

The African religious value of social solidarity is being emphasized in the work of the National Black Theatre under the leadership of its noted director Barbara Ann Teer. She writes: "The very foundation of NBT's ideology is based on the spiritual essence of black people, for we are an African people, and African people are a spirit-faced people."[17] Miss Teer holds that white European-American Christianity has spawned the twin evils of racism and oppression: "We see that we are surrounded by cold, calculating, inhuman beings driven by their lust and greed for the possession of things."[18] The black theater in Miss Teer's view must serve as a liberating and redemptive instrument whereby a spirit-possessed people may renew or revolutionize a largely inhumane world. The entire artistic thrust of the National Black Theatre is toward generating a spirit-filled and redemptive revolution by blacks not only for blacks but also for mankind as a whole. Miss Teer explains: "We must destroy the western civilization's value of the individualistic me/my/I reality and replace it with the black value of the collective we/us/our necessity. We now concentrate on developing our spiritual powers so we can create and perpetuate healthy positive images of blackness in our community. We refer to ourselves in the National Black Theatre as Liberators/Healers. This means that we are each evolving instruments of righteousness, charged with a magnetic force and filled with a power to heal."[19]

Miss Teer serves as a kind of high priestess by the common assent of those to whom the theater ministers. She explains what is seen as another African religious value—that of emotional fervor—which is underscored in her work through her definition of ritual. "A ritual," she notes, "is a spiritual ceremony of celebration which does not involve an audience per se, but rather a congregation of people participating as one big family, greeting and meeting, sharing and caring."[20] She adds:

> We remove the western psyche distance that keeps us apart and grow into one group spirit/one group force. In our community revivals we make sure the content is political, the story line has a beginning, middle, and end, that it is entertaining, has music and movement, that it be conscious- and value-raising, and that it in some way involves the use of our spirit powers.
> "We . . . are a spirit people, magical, mystical entities, remnants of a great race. You can see our divinity in motion when we dance."[21]

In the African religious experience, as Joseph Washington notes, there were traditionally no temples—only the home and the tribe. One's religion—as with the Jews—was one's nationality. Order prevailed under the leadership of a priest or priestess.

In the African religious tradition, the Creator was seen to permeate the whole of creation. This aspect of African religion gave rise to the belief that Africans were fetish worshippers. Rather, they saw the Creator in all aspects of creation. This was especially true of human life; thus the aged and the deceased, who had reflected the Creator's power over long periods of time, were held in particular veneration. Implicit in the reverence for human beings was a respect for the specific manifestations of personal power which each individual or group might uniquely represent. Dr. Preston Williams, of the Boston University School of Theology, remarks that black men in America today are emphasizing the need to appreciate men's differences which reflect the diversity of ongoing creation. He says: "The very springs of action and motivation in the black man are conditioned in a manner different from that of the white man. The difference in the final analysis is not asserted to be racial but cultural and historical. . . . Christianity cannot rob the black man of his blackness unless it desires him to be something less than a man. The black church and black theology thus seek to permit the black man to be both black and Christian."[22]

The social emphasis implicit in the religious life of black Africans is being renewed among black American religious leaders today. In the Muslim community, the Nation of Islam, so Dr. C. Eric Lincoln reports, there has long been a concern with the "whole man," that is, with the educational, economic, social, political, and health needs of black men.[23] All of these the late Messenger, the Honorable Elijah Muhammad, saw as essentially religious in nature. The Nation of Islam operates what is now the largest chain of black-owned restaurants in the country. It operates schools and community centers and has given perhaps the country's most sustained encouragement to black entrepreneurship. Mr. Muhammad said that all black men must build the black nation and own their own soil, beginning with their own homes.[24] New York's minister Louis X. Farrakhan symbolizes the Muslim's present thrust toward extensive cooperation with other black religious bodies in "nation building" on the local scene. Churches in Harlem, Brooklyn, and the Bronx are reported by the officers of the NCBC to rely heavily upon continuing leadership and support from the Muslim mosques in all of their community concerns.

Perhaps even more striking than the Muslim cooperative involvements with black churchmen has been the recent participation of the Pentecostal, "spirit-filled" or store-front-type churches in social, political, and economic programs for the largely impoverished black communities which these churches serve. The largest black Pentecostal group in America is the Church of God in Christ, with an estimated membership as high as three million.[25] Other black Pentecostal groups claim an additional million. Hence possibly as many as one out of every three blacks in America may be in some way associated with the Pentecostal tradition. James Baldwin, in Go Tell It On the Mountain (New York, Dell Publishing Co., 1953, pp. 14–16), tells of his early experiences in a Pentecostal church and suggests that his experience is representative of large numbers of urban blacks.

Typical of the new social concerns of these spirit-filled churches is the current record of Pentecostal involvement in the renewal program of the Bedford-Stuyvesant section of Brooklyn, New York. A block-by-block study in 1969 by community aides identified approximately 325 mission store-front churches.[26] One Pentecostal minister, Elder Herbert Daughtry, is vice chairman of both Operation Breadbasket of Greater New York and the Brooklyn/Bedford-Stuyvesant Youth in Action. The Reverend Mr. Daughtry's leadership symbolizes the spirit of black identification and determination which is abroad not only in the Pentecostal sects but also in the traditional or main-line churches of the black community. The familiar fervor of the Pentecostal churches has moved, in Elder Daughtry's words, "from the pulpit to the picket line." His House of the Lord Pentecostal has not only groups for prayer, a choir, and Bible study classes but also groups for demonstrations and marches, thus testifying that even these latter activities are spiritual aspects of the church. In the Bedford-Stuyvesant community, a Youth in Action report for 1970 recognized that without Pentecostal support and, indeed, leadership, the masses of the needy could not be mobilized, nor could there be hope of meeting their basic needs.[27]

Cell groups for prayer and meditation are now being used throughout the Bedford-Stuyvesant area for community-action mobilization. Pastors are proclaiming what they call an eschatological gospel (or a gospel of heaven now on earth) where the black poor no longer wait as beggars at the gate of the whites who are in power but participate with power in the present realization of eternal benefits and rewards. The matriarchal/patriarchal aspects of Pentecostal religion are being utilized toward charismatic leadership aimed at combating the cynicism and inertia born of ingrained poverty. The 1970 Bedford-Stuyvesant Youth in Action report notes: "There is still a good deal of genuine feeling of need for religious and social isolation. Some store-front ministers resent the prospect that their ideologies will become diffused or buried in politics, economics, and secular rather than purely evangelistic activities. The homogenizing of religious beliefs is the major source of criticism of the church and the community by store-front leaders."[28]

While store-front and Pentecostal have often been seen to be synonymous, large abandoned edifices of Jewish and Protestant congregations have also been purchased by the presently fast-growing Pentecostal sects. Some Pentecostals pride themselves on the fact that it was in the big Masonic Temple of the Church of God in Christ in Memphis that the sanitation workers' strike to which Dr. Martin Luther King gave his last days was headquartered.[29]

Black religion today is undergoing dramatic changes—perhaps the most dramatic in its history in America—as the direct result of the new impetus toward Black Power. Ethnocentrism, or group aspiration toward the realization of its past ideals, is a natural phenomenon for American blacks. That religion should play a leading role is logical since, as Joseph Washington has noted, religion has been the major integrating factor in the black African experience.

A. Cecil Williams, black poet-theologian of San Francisco, sums up much of the new black mood in the churches in this regard when he writes:

When i say jesus christ
I ain't goin' to say it like I used/to.
  I was taught one way to say it
    but
from now on,
  goin' to say it like the way the brothers
    and sisters
say it
standin' on the street
  getting it on
  rappin'
  clappin'
  and checkin' it out
  and gettin' it on
  and gettin' caught up with each other
start caring for each other
feeling blood
and soul
and struggle
come together
the same.
There's power in coming together, man.[30]

# Notes

1. W. E. B. DuBois, *The Negro Church* (Atlanta, The Atlanta University Press, 1903), p. 10.
2. Summary of statement from "Slavery and Conversion in the American Colonies," by Marcus W. Jernigan, in *American Historical Review*, XXI, No. 3 (April 1916), pp. 504–527. Used by permission.
3. Carter G. Woodson, *History of the Negro Church* (Washington, D.C., The Associated Publishers, 1921), p. 28. Used by permission.
4. *Journal of Reverend Francis Asbury*, I (New York, Lane and Scott, 1852), p. 306.
5. Woodson, *op. cit.*, p. 32.
6. Gunnar Myrdal, *An American Dilemma*, II (New York, Harper and Brothers, 1944), pp. 937–38.
7. Woodson, *op. cit.*, Chapter III.
8. Patricia M. Pettiford, "Harlem's Ministry," unpublished master's thesis, College of the City of New York, 1963.
9. *Yearbook of American Churches, 1972*, published by the National Council of the Churches of Christ in the U.S.A., New York, N. Y.
10. Joseph Washington, lecture notes, used by permission; all quotations from Dr. Washington are from notes used for his book, *Black Sects and Cults* (New York, Doubleday, 1972).
11. Church Bulletin Series, Shrine of the Black Madonna, Detroit, April 4, 1971.
12. Albert Cleage, *Handbook for the Second Annual Spring Forum Series*, Shrine of the Black Madonna, Detroit, April 1970, p. 5.
13. From Sister Martin De Porres Grey's Report of the Third Annual National Black Sisters' Conference, University of Notre Dame, Notre Dame, Indiana, August 9–15, 1970, p. 15.
14. Reverend Otis Saunders, sermon notes, May 2, 1970.

15. Annual Report, National Committee of Black Churchmen, 103 E. 125th Street, New York City, 1970. See also *Time*, Vol. 95, No. 14, April 1970.
16. Blue Hill Center Report, December 1968.
17. Barbara Ann Teer, "The National Black Theatre As It Relates to Western Theatre," an unpublished paper for the National Black Theatre, 9 E. 125th Street, Harlem, New York, 10035, p. 1.
18. *Ibid.*, p. 2.
19. *Ibid.*, p. 8.
20. *Ibid.*, p. 15.
21. *Ibid.*, pp. 15–16.
22. Preston Williams, "The Ethical Aspects of the 'Black Church/Black Theology' Phenomenon," an unpublished paper, Boston University School of Theology, January 1969, p. 3.
23. C. Eric Lincoln, *Black Muslims in America* (Boston, Beacon Press, 1961), Chapter I.
24. Nathan Wright, *Let's Work Together* (New York, Hawthorn, 1968), pp. 131–132.
25. Walter J. Hallenweger, "The Black Pentecostal Concept," in *Concept*, Special Issue No. 30, June 1970, World Council of Churches, Geneva, Switzerland.
26. "Operation Impact: Leadership Training Institute for Mission Ministers," Bedford-Stuyvesant Youth in Action, 1970, p. 2.
27. *Ibid.*
28. *Ibid.*, p. 14.
29. Hallenweger, *op. cit.*, p. 19.
30. A. Cecil Williams, "Black Folks Are Not For Sale," *The Black Scholar, Journal of Black Studies*, Vol. 2, No. 4, December 1970.

# 15

## Prejudice: A Symposium*

### Gordon W. Allport, Thomas F. Pettigrew, and Robin M. Williams, Jr.

In the following study, prejudice is considered first as a psychological condition existing within an individual mind, second in terms of its psychosocial impact in varying situations, and third as it functions in society.

## I. PREJUDICE AND THE INDIVIDUAL by Gordon W. Allport[1]

### DEFINITION AND EXTENT OF PREJUDICE

There are two ingredients implicit in any prejudiced state of mind: (a) a feeling of favorableness or unfavorableness which in turn is (b) based on unsupported judgment. While some prejudice can be *pro*, or "love prejudice" (as when we think too well of our own group), the ethnic attitudes that cause most social concern are *con*, or "hate prejudice."

A scholastic definition states that hate prejudice is "thinking ill of others without sufficient warrant." An equivalent slang definition says "prejudice is being down on something you are not up on." Whatever wording we prefer, there is always an element of inadequate knowledge or false judgment in prejudice; if not, then we are dealing with a well-grounded dislike, not with prejudice. If a criminal gang threatens my safety, my fear and hatred of it are not prejudice; but if I say that no ex-convict can be trusted, I am overgeneralizing and am therefore prejudiced. Examples are legion. "Every Jew will cheat you if he gets a chance." "Negroes are a violent lot; they carry razors." "Puerto Ricans are ignorant." "I couldn't trust any white man."

It should be added that overgeneralized prejudgments of this sort are prejudices only if they are not reversible when exposed to new knowledge. A person (e.g., a child) can start with a misconception about Jews, Negroes, or Puerto Ricans; but if he changes

*For additional insights into prejudice, see Chapter 3.

his mind when new evidence comes along he was not really prejudiced, only misinformed. Prejudices are inflexible, rigid, and erroneous generalizations about groups of people.

# DISCRIMINATION AND PREJUDICE

While discrimination ultimately rests on prejudice, the two processes are not identical. Discrimination denies people their natural or legal rights because of their membership in some unfavored group. Many people discriminate automatically[2] without being prejudiced; and others, the "gentle people of prejudice," feel irrational aversion, but are careful not to show it in discriminatory behavior. Yet in general, discrimination reinforces prejudices, and prejudices provide rationalizations for discrimination. The two concepts are most distinct when it comes to seeking remedies. The corrections for discrimination are legal, or lie in a direct change of social practices; whereas the remedy for prejudice lies in education and the conversion of attitudes. The best opinion today says that if we eliminate discrimination, then—as people become acquainted with one another on equal terms—attitudes are likely to change, perhaps more rapidly than through the continued preaching or teaching of tolerance.

### Generality of Prejudice

While some people are prejudiced against one group only, it is more common to find that if a person is bigoted in regard to one nationality, race, or religion, he is likely to be bigoted regarding all "out-groups." He feels safe only within the narrow confines of his own familiar circle. It is this finding that argues most cogently for regarding prejudice as rooted in personal character structure.

How widespread is prejudice? Research suggests that perhaps 80 percent of the American people harbor ethnic prejudice of some type and in some appreciable degree. Only 20 percent of the people are, in Gandhi's terms, "equiminded" or completely democratic in all their attitudes.[3] Widespread though ethnic prejudice is, there is good reason to believe that in the United States it is declining year by year.

# ORIGINS OF PREJUDICE

While some animals have an instinctive aversion to others, this is not true among species that are cross-fertile. Human beings of all races can, and do, mate and procreate. There is therefore no reason to assume that instinctive aversion exists between ethnic and racial groups. A young child may be frightened by a person of unfamiliar color or appearance, but ordinarily this fear lasts only a few moments. It is well-known that young children will play contentedly together whatever their race or national origin. Thus since prejudice is not inborn but acquired, the question is: What are the chief factors in the complex process of learning?

Some prejudice is deliberately taught by parents. Children obediently learn the lesson, as in the case of the little girl who asked her mother, "What's the name of those children I am supposed to hate?" The parent may pass on prejudice by punishing a child for his friendliness to minority groups. A child thus punished may acquire a conditioned aversion to members of the out-group. Sometimes the teaching is subtler. Even to a four-year-old, dark skin may suggest dirt; and since he is repeatedly warned to keep clean, he may develop an avoidance for dark-skinned people.

Tags are powerful factors in learning. Most children learn the emotional force of words long before they know the meanings of the words. An angry first-grader once called his white teacher a "nigger." She asked him what "nigger" meant. He replied, "I don't know, but you're supposed to say it when you're mad." Before the child has knowledge of the meaning of Jap, Jew, nigger, Polack and similar labels, he senses the potency of the negative feeling-tone behind these labels. Derogatory chatter in the home may thus dispose a child of six or eight to "think ill of others without sufficient warrant."

Much prejudice is *caught* rather than directly *taught*. The whole atmosphere of child-training may be subtly decisive. Thus a child who is sometimes rejected, sometimes loved, who is punished harshly or capriciously, who does not know unconditional trust at home—such a child grows up "on guard." Unable to depend emotionally upon his parents, he enters school with a suspicious, fearful attitude toward people in general, and especially toward those who have an unfamiliar appearance and (to him) odd and threatening ways of talking, or worshiping, or behaving. Although we cannot make the assertion with finality, it seems likely that the major factor in predisposing a child toward a lifetime of prejudice is this rejective, neglectful, harsh, or inconsistent style of preschool training.[4]

As the child grows older additional factors may create or intensify prejudice. Around the age of eight or ten he goes through a period of fierce identification with his family. Whatever the family is, is "right" (whether it be Catholic, Jewish, white, black, Scotch-Irish, or Hottentot). By comparison all other groups are of doubtful status and merit. At this point the church and the school have the opportunity of teaching the child the concept of reciprocity and basic equality among human groups. The lesson is difficult to learn, because as adolescence approaches, the child seeks personal security and a new identity in his peer groups, which usually are of his own color, class, and neighborhood. If adolescents are friendly with out-groups they risk a diffusion and loss of their own precarious identity.[5] To build up a sense of personal importance they often persecute out-groups. *West Side Story* is an epic of this gang-age phenomenon.

Occasionally prejudice is formed on the basis of a single emotional trauma. A certain youngster who was chased by a Chinese laundryman felt ever after a terror of

Orientals (a clear case of overgeneralizing from a single experience). Such traumatic origins are relatively rare. But we see that throughout childhood and youth there are many opportunities for irreversible and unfavorable belief-systems to become set.


# THE PSYCHODYNAMICS OF PREJUDICE


However prejudice is learned it takes root in a personality because it meets certain basic needs or cravings. It works for the person and may be a pivotal factor in the economy of his life.

## Need for Categorization

All mortals require simplified rubrics to live by. We think of school teachers, of physicians, of blind people, of Russians, or of ex-convicts in homogeneous groups. All Orientals we perceive as mysterious (though many are not); we regard all weeds as inedible (though some are nutritious). Thus our thinking seems to be guided by a law of least effort. If I reject all foreigners (including the United Nations), I simplify my existence by ruling out the troublesome issues of international relations. If I say "all blacks are ignorant," I dispose of twenty million more people. If I add "Catholics know only what the priest tells them," I eliminate forty million more. With the conviction that Jews will cheat me, I discard another five million. Labor unions I exclude by calling them "pirates." Intellectuals are simply "long-haired communists." And so it goes. My life is simplified when I invoke these stereotyped rejections. With the aid of aversive categories I avoid the painful task of dealing with individuals as individuals. Prejudice is thus an economical mode of thought, and is widely embraced for this very reason.

## Anxiety and the Need for Security

A major source of prejudice is the sense that one's security and status are threatened. One fears for one's job, for one's home, especially for one's prestige. American culture is enormously competitive, and so we find ourselves keenly fearful of our rivals. Downwardly mobile people on the whole are more prejudiced than people who hold a stable social position.[6] Now in cold logic it is very seldom that any minority group actually threatens the well-being, safety, or equity of our lives, but we nonetheless perceive them as the cause of our distress. Racist agitators play upon this anxiety. The easiest idea to sell anyone is that he is better than someone else, and that this someone else must be kept "in his place" so that we may enjoy our own position of superiority.

## Scapegoating

When things go wrong we find it convenient to blame others. Since biblical times it has been known that a scapegoat relieves our own sense of failure or guilt. We say it is the Jews who are keeping us from a promotion or the migration of blacks that takes away available jobs. Or we may vaguely blame our failures or discomforts upon "the politicians." Few people take blame upon themselves. They are quick to adopt an extrapunitive ego-defense.

## Sexual Conflict

A peculiarly deep complex is found in accusations that out-groups (especially Negroes) are immoral. Simply because they are "forbidden fruit," many white people find blacks sexually attractive; much miscegenation has been the result. Since looseness of morals is condemned, the white person may exonerate himself from his web of desire, fantasy, and guilt by projecting it upon the black male, who, he says, is sexually aggressive—at heart a rapist. In Germany, Hitler accused the Jews of all manner of sexual irregularities; in the United States it is the black who is the projection screen (the "living inkblot") for one's own frightening id-impulses.

## The Authoritarian Pattern

To summarize these and other similar emotional needs, trends, and twists that enter into the psychodynamics of prejudice, psychologists have formulated the concept of "authoritarianism."[7] It says that a person who is basically insecure, anxious, sexually repressed, suffering from unresolved Oedipal conflicts with his own parents, given to projection—such a person will develop a rigid, conventional, hostile style of life. Ethnic prejudice fits into this character syndrome. This formulation has been widely studied and debated. Just how to define it in detail is a matter of dispute, but most scholars believe that it contains an important truth. People having this syndrome are "functional bigots" whose whole style of life is hostile, fearful, rejective of out-groups. Such people need prejudice and are ready to follow a demagogue who focuses all this latent hate upon some ethnic target.

# CONFORMITY

Although the authoritarian pattern clearly exists, we must not assume that it accounts for all prejudice. What we call "conformity prejudice" springs from the tendency of people to yield to local custom and to the legends and ideology of their own class.[8]

If bigotry is in the air, they are bigots; if tolerance is customary, they are tolerant. Perhaps half of our population can be considered to be in this middle range. Since prejudice is to some degree prevalent, especially in the southern regions of the United States, this half of the population can be expected to go along with the existing biases.

What we have called the authoritarian syndrome accounts for about the same amount of prejudice in both northern and southern states, but there is much more conformity prejudice in the South.[9]

## VICTIMIZATION

Those who are victims of prejudice cannot be indifferent to their plight; they must constantly defend themselves from discomfort or insult. One study states that 50 percent of blacks say that when they are with a white person they expect him "to make a slip and say something wrong about Negroes."[10] Even when not expecting an insult, a minority group member must ordinarily plan his life within a racial or ethnic frame of reference.

Besides this chronic sensitization to the problem, additional psychological reactions to victimization may be noted; among them, withdrawal and apathy, slyness and cunning, clowning, rejection of one's own group—or quite the reverse, forming closer in-group ties, resignation, neuroticism, sympathy with other minorities, and enhanced striving and militancy.[11] Of course not all members of a minority group will show all of these types of response.

## REDUCING PREJUDICE

Someone has said that it is easier to smash an atom than a prejudice. In the case of deep-dyed functional bigots this verdict may be true. And yet change in prejudice does occur, and has clearly happened since World War II in America. Prejudiced attitudes change when it makes sociological, economic, and personal sense to change them. Not all people are incurably blind to their own illogical and harmful ways of thinking. Education combats easy overgeneralizations, and as the educational level rises we find a reduction in stereotyped thinking.[12] Also we know that increased self-knowledge and personal insight reduce prejudice.[13] Education for mental health works in this direction. Furthermore, militant protests call attention to needed reforms and win the sympathy of potentially democratic citizens. Various measures of prejudice have been invented to help follow these trends, even the subtle factor of human-heartedness within the population.[14]*

All progress toward the reduction of prejudice will be met by vociferous resistance from the functional bigots. And yet even when violence flares up the trend is unmistakable. Antidiscrimination laws, revised school curricula and effective desegregation, raising of educational levels, open discussion and enlightenment, nonviolent protests that focus attention and win sympathy—all these, and other forces, are working in a single direction. Let the reader also keep in mind the fact that the problem we are here discussing has had in the past quarter-century more attention and intelligent study among people of goodwill than in all the millennia of human history previously. Recent research on ethnic prejudice has been remarkably rich and informative,[15] and shows clearly that the forces of social science are strongly arrayed in the battle against bigotry.

## II. PREJUDICE AND THE SITUATION *by Thomas F. Pettigrew*

A white Little Rock garage mechanic stood patiently in line waiting to cast his ballot at his local voting precinct. Most of the other citizens standing with him were black. A few months before he had enthusiastically participated in the white mobs protesting the city's school desegregation, yet the mechanic was not in the least disturbed over the interracial character of his surroundings. "It would be un-American," he later explained, "not to let'em vote."

"'Round here I support segregation," firmly announced a white veteran in south Georgia, "'cause most folks want it and it's right. Of course, in the Army things were a little different. In fact my best friend in Korea was a colored guy from Alabama. You see, we were the only southern boys in the whole platoon."

A white mother in New Orleans turned livid with anger over the prospect of educational desegregation. She joined the screaming, shouting women rallying near an embattled school. "I'll demonstrate as long as I have to," she asserted. And she was prepared for a long siege, for she had arranged with her black neighbor to look after her children each morning while she protested.

Such contradictions are the rule in American race relations today. Social change does not come in logical, even paces. Nor do people caught in a changing society necessarily alter their behavior and attitudes in rationally consistent ways. Racial prejudice

*Rejection of the closed life style of the conservative middle-class on the part of young Americans would appear to be a measurable aspect of conscious human-heartedness. One might also measure the extent to which the so-called flower children have reduced black-white prejudice; the black movement also emphasizes intra-group humanity and compassion.—*Editor*

may be elicited in one situation, tolerance in a related situation. Thus the structure of the situation in which the two races meet face to face assumes critical importance; indeed, the *situation* provides the vital link between the *individual* and *societal* factors which determine racial prejudice and discrimination.

Social psychology has focused considerable attention upon the role of the situation in shaping intergroup attitudes and behavior. Answers can now be offered to the recurring questions: Will more contact between the races lead to improved relations? Can law change "the hearts and minds of men"?

## CONTACT AND CHANGE

Many well-meaning Americans have expressed the opinion that if only blacks and whites could experience more contact with each other the nation's racial difficulties would solve themselves. Unfortunately, the case is not so simple. Africans and Europeans have more contact in the Republic of South Africa than anywhere else on the African continent and black and white Americans have more contact in the South than in any other region of the nation, yet neither of these areas has been conspicuous for its interracial harmony. It almost appears as if contact between two peoples exacerbates, rather than relieves, intergroup hostility; yet this conclusion would be just as hasty and fallacious as the naïve assumption that contact invariably lessens prejudice.

Increasing interaction, whether it be of groups or individuals, intensifies and magnifies the processes already underway. Hence more interracial contact can lead either to greater prejudice and rejection or to greater respect and acceptance, depending upon the situation in which it occurs. The basic issue, then, is to differentiate between the types of situations in which contact leads to distrust and those in which it leads to trust.

Gordon Allport, in his study of this question concludes that four characteristics of the contact situation are of utmost importance in determining its outcome.[16] Prejudice is lessened when the two groups (1) possess equal status, (2) seek common goals, (3) are cooperatively dependent upon each other, and (4) interact with the positive support of authorities, law, or custom.

### Equal Status Between Groups

If groups are of widely different social status, contact between them may do little more than reinforce old and hostile stereotypes. In the typical southern situation of interracial contact, the majority of blacks encountered by white southerners are servants and other low-status service workers. Many whites eventually conclude that these are the types of jobs best suited for blacks, that somehow this is their "proper place." To be sure, there are professional black southerners—doctors, ministers, teachers—but segregation forces them to stay deep within the black ghetto, where whites rarely meet them. The segregationist who boasts that he "really knows Negroes" is usually referring to his casual encounters with blacks of lower status. This is a principal reason why the plentiful black-white contact in the South has not led to interracial understanding.

The psychologically crucial aspects of equal-status situations are pointed up by recent research on the similarity of backgrounds, interests, and values. This work suggests that such similarities are especially significant in prejudice. One study investigated the attitudes of a group of white teenagers in California toward four different types of peers: black and white youths with the same values as the respondents, and black and white youths with contrasting values.[17] The results were unequivocal. While race did affect "friendliness" and social-distance ratings, similarity of values was by far the most important variable. Thus, the black teenager with consonant values was liked far better than the white teenager with different values.

The practical problem, however, is that many whites believe that blacks do not share their interests and values; consequently, racial prejudice and assumed value conflict are often compounded. Equal-status contact attacks this problem in two ways. First, people of equal status are more likely than others to possess congruent outlooks and beliefs simply by virtue of their common positions in society. Second, equal-status situations provide the setting where this congruence can best be mutually perceived.

## Common Goals of the Groups

When groups work together toward common goals, further opportunities are presented for developing and discovering similarities of interests and values. The reduction of prejudice through contact generally requires an active, focused effort, not simply a gathering together for the sheer sake of intermingling. Athletic teams furnish a pertinent example. In striving to win, interracial teams create a contact situation not only of equal status but also of shared dependence. Black and white team members cannot achieve their common goal of winning without the assistance of each other. Under such conditions, race becomes irrelevant. Indeed, this process is enhanced further if the interracial group actually attains the common goal.

## Cooperative Interdependence of the Groups

The shared dependence of athletic teams suggests a third condition. Not only must the groups seek common goals, but the attainment of these goals must be a mutually dependent effort involving no competition along strictly racial lines. For instance, if the San Francisco Giants were all white and the Los Angeles Dodgers were all black, they could probably play indefinitely and not become more racially tolerant. Though equal-status and common-goal conditions would prevail, the lines of competition would make race relevant. Fortunately, professional athletic teams are interracial and provide a notable case of successful desegregation. But the lesson is clear. The contact situations which lead to interracial harmony must involve cooperative interdependence.

## Positive Social Support by Authorities, Law, or Custom

The final factor concerns the auspices of the contact. If the situation has explicit social sanction, interracial contact is more readily accepted and has more positive effects. Though the situation may be a bit awkward at first, recognized authority support helps make it "right." Failure of authorities, law, and custom to bolster even minimal desegregation in much of the South is a chief reason why many white southerners have failed to support federal court orders. Indeed, recent resistance to desegregation throughout the nation can be directly traced in part to the failure of President Ford or former President Nixon to provide the moral authority of their high office to the process.

An interesting application of this social-support principle occurs in situations where there are no established norms for interracial behavior. An ingenious project at Cornell University studied New York State facilities unaccustomed to black patronage.[18] Black researchers would enter a tavern, seek service, and later record their experiences, while white researchers would observe the same situation and record their impressions for comparison. Typically, the first reaction of waitresses and bartenders was to turn to the owner or others in authority for guidance. When this was not possible, the slightest behavioral cue from anyone in the situation was utilized as a gauge of what was expected of them. And if there were not such cues, confusion often continued until somehow the threatening new situation was structured. Depending upon which way the delicate scales tipped, these interracial confrontations could either lead to increased animosity or increased acceptance.

## Examples of Contact and Change

The research literature abounds with examples of these contact principles in operation. One study found that white merchant seamen tended to hold racial attitudes in direct relation to how many voyages they had taken with equal-status black seamen—the more desegregated voyages, the more positive their attitudes.[19] Another investigation noted that white Philadelphia policemen who had personally worked with black colleagues were far more favorable toward the desegregation of their force than other white policemen.[20] A third study of white government workers, veterans, and students found that those who had known black professionals were far less prejudiced toward blacks than those who had known only unskilled blacks.[21]

Evidence comes even during times of crisis. While black and white mobs raged during the Detroit race riot of 1943, integrated co-workers, university students, and neighbors of long standing peacefully carried on their lives side by side.[22] Mention of neighborhood integration introduces the integrated living in public housing developments that meet all four of Allport's contact criteria sharply reduces racial prejudice among both black and white neighbors.[23] And these same studies demonstrate that living in segregated but otherwise identical housing developments structures interracial contact in such a way that, if anything, racial bitterness is enhanced. Additional data derived from the desegregation of the armed forces.[24] Once again, conditions involving equal status, cooperative striving toward common goals, and social support lead directly to the reduction of racial prejudice among both black and white servicemen. As a black officer in Vietnam candidly phrased it: "After a while you start thinking of whites as people."

## One Qualification

One important qualification attends attitude change through interracial contact: at least in the early stages, the change is often limited to the specific situation involved. Recall the previously mentioned Little Rock garage mechanic, the Georgia veteran, and the New Orleans mother; each of them had learned to accept blacks fully in one context but not in another. This phenomenon is not peculiar to the South. Research on white northern steel workers found that they often approved of the desegregation of their unions to the point of sharing all union facilities with blacks and electing blacks to high office, yet they sternly opposed the desegregation of their all-white neighborhoods.[25] Factors underlying this situational inconsistency are considered more fully in the next section by Professor Williams.

## Two Summary Principles

These studies illustrate two related principles. First, attitudes and behavior need not always be congruent; particular situations can structure how most people behave in spite of what attitudes they may hold.[26] Second, prejudice and discrimination do not always coincide.[27] Many antiblack people do not racially discriminate, because they find themselves in situations where discriminatory behavior is not sanctioned (e.g., professional baseball games). And many unprejudiced people discriminate every day of their lives, because they find themselves in situations which demand it e.g., certain public facilities in Durban, South Africa).

## LAW AND CHANGE

Within this situational perspective, a reappraisal can be made of the old saw—"laws cannot change the hearts and minds of men." A case in point is the 1945 antidiscrimination employment legislation enacted by New York State. This law led to the hiring of blacks as salesclerks in New York City department stores for the first time. Two investigations conducted separate tests of the effects of this law-induced desegregation. One study of white sales personnel revealed that those who had experienced the new equal-status job contact with blacks held more favorable attitudes toward interracial interaction in the work situation.[28] Once again, however, the initial effects of this contact did not extend beyond the immediate situation; equal-status clerks were not more accepting of blacks in eating and residential situations.

The other investigation questioned customers.[29] Though reactions to later questioning varied, there was a widespread acceptance of this legally required racial change. Customers were largely concerned with shopping conveniently and efficiently; many hesitated to challenge the firm *fait accompli* established by the law; and for many the new situation was consistent with their belief in the American creed of equal opportunity for all.[30]

## Law versus Exhortation

Law, then, *can* change the hearts and minds of men. It does so through a vital intermediate step. Law first acts to modify behavior, and this modified behavior in turn changes men's hearts and minds. Notice that this is precisely the opposite sequence commonly believed to be the most effective method of social change. Persuade people to be less prejudiced through informational and goodwill campaigns, goes the reasoning, and then they will discriminate less. To be sure, this sequence is sometimes effective, but the preponderance of social psychological evidence attests to the greater efficacy of the opposite approach. Behaving differently is more often the precursor to thinking differently.

The celebrated annual rituals of brotherhood week, brotherhood dinners, and brotherhood awards illustrate the point. While they remind participants of their religious and national ideals and strengthen the already convinced, these events appear of limited value in convincing the unconvinced. The basic problem with such observances is that they do not *require* participants to change their behavior. The interracial contact is brief and artificial, and the emphasis is placed on exhortation and directly influencing attitudes. A vast body of psychological data indicates that prejudiced individuals in such situations will avoid the message altogether, deny the relevance of the message for themselves, or find ways of twisting the meaning of the message.[31] In addition, ritualistic exhortations for brotherhood may often serve an unanticipated negative function. By attending the annual dinner and paying the tax-deductible fifty or one hundred dollars per plate, many individuals of considerable influence regularly relieve their guilt. Having gone through the motions of supporting "equality for all," participants are psychologically released to go on discriminating as before.

Antidiscrimination laws can also be tuned out by prejudiced individuals and used as conscience salves by the guilty. But if properly enforced, such legislation has the potential for achieving behavioral change not possessed by exhortation. Several reasons for this are apparent. There is, of course, the threat of punishment and unfavorable publicity for recalcitrants. But more important is the "off-the-hook" function such laws provide. Thus Macy's and Gimbel's stores in New York City may each have been afraid to hire black sales personnel as long as there were no assurances that their competitors would follow suit—but the law furnished this assurance. Finally, as noted in many of the studies cited, the legally established *fait accompli*, unlike exhortations for tolerance, generates its own acceptance.[32] The situational face-lifting it achieves is a fifty-two-weeks-a-year process, not just a single week in celebration of brotherhood.

## A FINAL STUDY

The fundamental principles underlying situational factors in prejudice are dramatically highlighted by an ingenious field experiment conducted in Oklahoma.[33] Twenty young boys, of homogeneous backgrounds but previously unacquainted with one another, attended a summer camp set up for the investigation. From the start, the boys were divided into two groups—the Rattlers and the Eagles. The first stage of the experiment was designed to develop high *esprit de corps* within each of the groups. Totally separated from each other, the Rattlers and Eagles engaged in a variety of satisfying experiences, and each group soon developed the pride and sense of "we-ness" characteristic of strong in-group solidarity.

The second stage brought the groups face to face in a series of grimly competitive tasks—tugs-of-war, baseball and football games, and tent pitching. In all of these contact situations, only one group could win and the other had to lose. The inevitable intergroup animosity soon appeared. Derogatory songs and slogans were composed; destructive raids on "the enemy's cabin" began; negative stereotypes developed; and even preferences for group segregation were voiced. Competitive contact had wreaked its usual havoc.

The experiment's third stage tried to mend the damage. "The brotherhood dinner" approach came first. The boys met in such noncompetitive situations as eating good food in the same room, shooting off fireworks, and attending a movie together. Note that all of these involve passive conduct without common goals or group interdependence. And, understandably, intergroup friction did not abate; in fact, the boys employed these unfocused events as opportunities for further vilification of their hated rivals. Next the investigators introduced carefully contrived problems that required the cooperation of both groups for their solution. Fixing together the damaged water tank that supplied the entire camp, raising jointly the funds to show a favorite movie, and other functionally dependent behavior achieved a striking decrement in intergroup hostility.

While at the close of the competitive second stage over half of the characteristics assigned by the boys to their group rivals were sharply unfavorable, over two-thirds of such judgments were favorable at the close of the interdependent third stage. Moreover, the percentage of friendship choices across group lines multiplied fourfold.

One final result of this intriguing investigation replicates the limited nature of the attitude change initially induced even under optimal contact conditions. The first interdependent encounters of the two camp groups by no means removed all of the bad feeling between the Rattlers and the Eagles. But as these socially sanctioned confrontations continued, the prejudice-reducing power of this type of contact accumulated. This suggests that as the desegregation process proceeds, it may well receive increasingly greater support and have increasingly greater effects upon the participants, both black and white.

## III. PREJUDICE AND SOCIETY *by Robin M. Williams, Jr.*

Intergroup relations cannot be understood merely in terms of the "attitudes" of undifferentiated masses of individuals. Real societies and communities are highly differentiated systems, made up of networks of social relationships within and among subsystems. Groups, associations, and other collectivities exist side by side; they overlap, interpenetrate, and form complex sets of interrelations. In complex urban societies, intergroup relations necessarily transcend small groups and diffuse interpersonal relations; they necessarily come to be regulated in part by law and organized political and administrative action. Intergroup relations often are extensive, complex, persistent, and highly structured. Their nature is often strongly influenced by organized intergroupings. Much discrimination is not primarily an expression of prejudice but rather a by-product of purposeful striving to attain or hold economic, social, and political advantages or privileges. And, indeed, research often shows that an individual's prejudiced or nonprejudiced initial attitudes are not closely related to intergroup behavior in the marketplace or in the political arena.

The sheer fact of social differentiation means that there are individuals and collectivities that may differ in their interests and in their control of (and aspirations for), power, wealth, prestige, and other scarce values. Whenever members of collectivities or social categories of persons engage in competition or rivalry for such values, the possibility arises for intergroup tension and conflict. This possibility would remain even in a world of psychologically stable and mature adults who always sought their goals in a rational manner.

Furthermore, conflicts often are not simply expressions of "prejudice" but arise from genuine injuries or threats. Real differences in values often lie back of the fears that so often lead to aggressive behavior and thence to conflict. Also, persons of similar interests and values tend to associate together and to distinguish themselves from others who differ. Besides, some preferential association would continue even in a homogeneous society. Time and effort are involved in social interaction. Functional proximity alone, in the absence of any other factors, would result in selective interaction. Group relations are embedded in an environing social structure.

Prejudice is a psychological condition lodged in specific individuals. Discrimination is a particular quality of overt social behavior. As Professor Allport has pointed out, the two sets of phenomena are interrelated, but neither one is a mere reflection or expression of the other. There may be prejudice without grossly detectible discrimination; there may be much clear discrimination with little or no prejudice. We cannot simply assume that the one always leads to or accompanies the other. A white Realtor may refuse to sell a listed house to a black buyer, not because he personally dislikes blacks or accepts stereotypes about them, but because he will be expelled from the local real estate association if he does sell in violation of the enforced policy of the association. A prejudiced white person may accept black customers because of antidiscriminatory legal provisions, or because his desire for profits outweighs his desires to express prejudice in overt acts.

It therefore follows that social patterns of exclusion, segregation, and differential treatment of whole social categories of persons can not be fully or adequately "explained" solely by invoking the prejudiced attitudes of individuals. Nor can we precisely infer from the sheer fact of conformity to discriminatory patterns how widespread, salient, or intense prejudice may be. Prejudices are learned; they grow out of social experiences. The institutional structures and organization of a community or society shape and restrict the experiences particular individuals will have. Knowing that certain individuals have prejudices, we want to go on to ask what social conditions favored the establishment of such attitudes, and what shared social and cultural circumstances facilitate or hinder various modes of expressing prejudices in behavior.

By discrimination in the most general sense we mean, simply, any behavior that represents differential treatment of persons solely because of their membership in a certain social category or collectivity, regardless of their personal qualities and achievements. Discrimination in this broad sense exists when there are systematic differences in conduct toward officers versus enlisted men, local residents and outsiders, Democrats or Republicans, Protestants and Catholics, blacks and whites, southerners and northerners, farmers and bankers. Discrimination may be favorable or unfavorable toward the objects of discrimination. For our present purposes we are interested in the kind of discrimination that is disadvantageous to those discriminated against. The major kinds of negative discrimination in our society are so widespread and conspicuous as to be easy to identify:

exclusion or inferior opportunity with regard to education, employment and promotion, housing, public accommodations and services, political rights, and civil liberties and protections.

Of course it is apparent that we all act toward other people partly in terms of the statuses or social positions they occupy. How we will behave differs as between men and women, young people and older people, between a policeman and a storekeeper, a judge and a longshoreman. Such differentiated behavior is found in every social system, and to some extent has a *functional* basis. That is, children are not adults and cannot be treated entirely as if they were; men and women do differ; different occupations serve different social functions. Ordinarily we would speak of discrimination in cases of this kind only if a person is denied rights otherwise available to all equally qualified persons. In American society all adult citizens, with only a few stated exceptions, are supposed to have the right to vote and hold public office, but in some parts of our nation millions of black Americans have been denied the exercise of these nominally universal rights. For the most part we are said to believe that "everyone" has the right to an education to the limits of his desires and abilities, to work in an occupation of his own choosing, to reside wherever he wishes within the limits of his economic resources, and in general to have access to all public facilities and services on equal terms with others. Very clearly, however, deep-seated and widespread patterns of discrimination often nullify these so-called rights for many members of minority groups—blacks, Catholics, Jews, Mexican-, Japanese-, or Chinese-Americans, and many others.

It is sometimes possible to reduce or eliminate discrimination in advance of any very great reduction in prejudice, as we have seen in the case of the elimination of official segregation in the armed services and in certain public housing developments. In general, however, prejudice and discrimination (including enforced segregation) mutually support one another. Discrimination reinforces people in the prejudices; prejudice furnishes the basis for and rationalizations of discriminatory conduct.

In any study of prejudice it should be kept in mind that many people hold stereotypes and express prejudices without having any strong or active hostility toward the objects of their prejudicial attitudes. Those persons who have such attitudes and beliefs are the "gentle people of prejudice" referred to earlier by Professor Allport. They have learned their prejudices from their social environment in much the same way they learned table manners, how to speak English, or tastes in music. They conform to the opinions of their associates, follow the local customs, and voice the accepted stereotypes without much reflection, self-consciousness, or emotional involvement. For many such people their prejudices are peripheral aspects of their personalities, not central to their self-conception or their basic emotional organization. On the other hand, we find people whose out-group stereotypes are saturated with active *hostility*. They feel and express attitudes of dislike, repugnance, or hate; they actively want to exclude, insult, deprive, or hurt members of the groups toward which they are prejudiced. A basic question, accordingly, is: What are the social conditions most likely to lead to active hostility, to turn the mild prejudice of conformity into the hostility that leads to acts of aggression?

Back of prejudiced attitudes are massive economic and political arrangements and forces. Minority groups are formed, in the first instance, in these ways: by conquest, as with the American Indians; by shifts in national boundaries, as in Europe after World War I; by forced importation, as of Negro slaves into the United States; by forced transfers of populations, as in Europe and the Soviet Union; and by voluntary migration, as of the Chinese in Southeast Asia or the mass immigration of Europeans to America. Considerations of economic and political advantage—of group superordination and subordination—obviously loom large in these massive historical events.

In every society, men are interested in and strive for the scarce values represented by power, wealth or income, and social prestige and deference. Whenever groups or categories of men who differ in visible physical and cultural characteristics are thrown into situations of competition or rivalry for these values, the likelihood of prejudice and discrimination is increased. When the Chinese first came to the West Coast as laborers, they were welcomed; although they were regarded as "exotic," they were received, for the most part, with friendly curiosity and were held to be industrious, sober, reliable, and law-abiding. When the railroads were built and economic depression struck, the Chinese abruptly became the object of negative stereotypes and marked discrimination. Throughout our history, the waves of anti-immigrant agitation have been highest in periods of difficulty. For centuries in Europe, Jews were often welcomed when their economic services were wanted; often persecuted when it was to the economic or political advantage of ruling groups to do so. In the United States, the southern defense of slavery became entrenched only after inventions and commercial developments made the system highly profitable. The disfranchisement of Negroes and the growth of legalized segregation a generation after the end of Reconstruction was partly a result of political struggles within the dominant white groupings.

In a very basic sense, "race relations" are the direct outgrowth of the long wave of European expansion, beginning with the discovery of America. Because of their more highly developed technology and economic and political organization, the Europeans were able by military force or by economic and political penetration to secure control over colonies, territories, protectorates, and other possessions and spheres of influence around the world. In a way, the resulting so-called race relations had very little to do with "race"—initially it was a historical accident that the peoples encountered in the European expansion differed in shared physical characteristics of an obvious kind. But once the racial ideologies had been formed and widely disseminated, they constituted a powerful means of justifying political hegemony and economic control.

In much the same way, present-day vested political, economic, and social privileges and rights tend to be rationalized and defended by persons and groups who hold such prerogatives. Whenever a number of persons within a society have enjoyed for a considerable period of time certain opportunities for getting wealth, for exercising power and authority, and for successfully claiming prestige and social deference, there is a strong tendency for these people to feel that these "vested interests" are theirs "by right." The advantages come to be thought of as normal, proper, customary, as sanctioned by time, precedent, and social consensus. Proposals to change the existing situation arouse reactions of "moral indignation." Elaborate doctrines are developed to show the inevitability and rightness of the existing scheme of things.

An established system of vested interests is a powerful thing, especially when differences in power, wealth, and prestige coincide with relatively indelible symbols of collective membership, such as shared hereditary physical traits, a distinctive religion, or a persistently held culture. The holders of an advantaged position see themselves as a group and reinforce one another in their attitudes; any qualms about the justice of the status quo seem to be diminished by the group character of the arrangements.

Economic competition tends to arouse prejudice, given a visible group and a definition of its members as "different." Such prejudice is especially likely to appear when a racially or culturally recognized grouping is concentrated in highly visible occupations which involve direct contact with the public and in which economic conflicts of interest are already close to the surface—as for example in money-lending and retail trade. Such vulnerable occupations are particularly likely to be entered into by persons with little capital who risk a venture into marginal positions not already preempted by established groups. Prejudice is reinforced also by a concentration of members of a highly visible grouping in occupations of low prestige—the poorly paid, hot, heavy, dirty, and otherwise disagreeable jobs as well as morally questionable types of work.

Diffuse prejudices often are focused, intensified, and sharpened by the struggle for political power. There is a notable and well-documented tendency for political candidates in some parts of the United States to appeal to the group prejudices of their constituents in the course of gaining and holding power. Once a tradition of prejudice has become well established, an appeal to voters on ethnic, religious, or racial grounds constitutes a weapon that comes readily to hand in political maneuvers. It is, of course, a double-edged sword. It is of maximum effectiveness only when one element of the population is a definite political minority, as is the case with Negroes in many parts of the country. The larger the number of minority groups in the electorate and the more nearly equal they are in numbers of effective voters, the less likely it is that what we might call "ethnic politics" will be either effective or safe. In the United States the possibilities of serious social disruption from ethnic or racist politics are too obvious to require elaboration here.

Any careful study of the role of economic and political factors in intergroup relations quickly shows the importance of understanding the particular total situation in which they operate. Studies in Chicago showed that white union members who cooperated with blacks in their labor union, even electing blacks to leadership positions, nevertheless could be brought, partly by the agitation of an organized neighborhood association, to intense opposition against Negroes moving into their residential area. A common device in real estate dealings is that of "block-busting"—in which blacks (or other discriminated-against minority people) are induced or permitted to move into an area. The real estate dealers then seek to encourage "panic selling" by persuading the white residents that property values will drop. If the tactic is successful, the dealer acquires the properties at bargain-basement prices, and then proceeds to raise the values above the original level by renting and selling at high prices to home-hungry members of minority groups. Thus, by reason of economic exploitation, preexisting prejudice is used in such a way as to reinforce and intensify prejudice.

Examples of such situational variation can be multiplied almost endlessly. The self-same employer may on one occasion actively recruit black persons to fill sales positions and on another occasion subtly contrive to hire as few blacks as possible, depending upon such factors as the anticipated reactions of black and white customers and the possibility of a court suit or administrative ruling involving penalties. The managers of business establishments, governmental agencies, or educational organizations may act in either a nondiscriminatory or discriminatory manner, relatively apart from their personal attitudes, when confronted with strong situational constraints and inducements. Important in determining their public behavior are their expectations concerning probable responses of customers, clients, voters, legislators, donors, and other significant "third parties." Thus the perceived prejudices of significant others often are more crucial than the immediate personal views of individual decision-makers.

Once prejudices are formed as a part of the basic social outlook of large numbers of like-minded persons within a society, the whole complex of beliefs, values, and sentiments becomes a part of the social processes of socialization and conformity. The stereotypic images of ethnic, religious, and racial groupings come to be embodied in literature, song, and story. They impinge on us through newspapers and popular magazines, through movies, radio, and television. They reach us through the nearly irresistible medium of jokes. And, perhaps above all, they may be so pervasive as to become almost a test of belonging to the in-group. In the family, the congeniality group, the local community lie the individual's most essential ties of social belonging. If these in-groups share stereotypes and prejudices, the lone individual finds that to question the assumptions of neighbors, friends, and kinsmen is to risk ridicule, displeasure, or even social rejection. In such circumstances, the forces of conformity are strong. It is through a process of interlocking demands and expectations of conformity that a cultural tradition of prejudice and discrimination gains much of its tenacity in influencing behavior. Under conditions of tight social conformity there often appears the phenomenon of *pluralistic ignorance*. Each person believes that the publicly accepted beliefs and attitudes are, in fact, the private attitudes of each of his fellows. No one dares to expose his own privately deviant attitudes to others, and hence remains in ignorance of the similarly deviant views of some of his associates.

## Notes

1. The late Gordon Allport wrote this statement for *The American Negro Reference Book*. It has been retained as a background statement with relevance for the 1970s.

2. An example of this in the past might have been the use of a waiting room labeled "White" or "Colored." A contemporary example could involve the choice between rest rooms marked "Ladies" and "Gentlemen."

3. Gordon W. Allport, *The Nature of Prejudice* (New York, Doubleday Anchor Books, 1958), p. 77.

4. Dale B. Harrison, G. Gough, and William E. Martin, "Children's Ethnic Attitudes: II, Relationship to Parental Beliefs Concerning Child Training," *Child Development* 21, 1950, pp. 169–81. Also David P. Ausubel, *Ego Development and the Personality Disorders* (New York, Grune and Stratton, 1962).

5. Bettelheim and Janowitz, *Social Change and Prejudice* (New York: The Free Press of Glencoe, 1964), p. 57.

6. *Ibid.*, pp. 29–34.

7. T. G. W. Adorno, E. Frenkel-Brunswik, D. J. Levinson, and R. N. Sanford, *The Authoritarian Personality* (New York, Harper & Brothers, 1952).

8. Gordon W. Allport, "Prejudice: Is It Societal or Personal?" *Journal of Social Issues*, 18, 1961, pp. 120–34.

9. Thomas F. Pettigrew, "Regional Differences in Anti-Negro Prejudice," *Journal of Abnormal and Social Psychology*, 29, 1959, pp. 28–36.

10. Robin M. Williams, Jr., *Strangers Next Door* (Englewood Cliffs, Prentice-Hall, Inc., 1964), p. 47.

11. Gordon W. Allport, *The Nature of Prejudice* (New York, Doubleday Anchor Books, 1958), Chapter 9.

12. Charles H. Stember, *Education and Attitude Change* (New York, Institute of Human Relations Press, 1961). Also, Henry G. Stetler, *Attitudes toward Racial Integration in Connecticut* (Hartford, Commission on Civil Rights, 1961).

13. Richard M. Jones, *An Application of Psychoanalysis to Education* (Springfield, Ill., Charles C. Thomas, 1960).

14. Howard Schuman and John Harding, "Sympathetic Identification with the Underdog," *Public Opinion Quarterly*, 27, 1963, pp. 230–41.

15. Bernard Berelson and Gary A. Steiner, *Human Behavior: An Inventory of Scientific Findings* (New York, Harcourt, Brace & World, 1964).

16. Gordon W. Allport, *The Nature of Prejudice* (Cambridge, Addison-Wesley, 1954), Chapter 16.

17. D. D. Stein, Jane A. Hardyck, and M. B. Smith, "Race and Belief: An Open and Shut Case" (Unpublished paper, University of California at Berkeley.)

18. Melvin L. Kohn and Robin M. Williams, Jr., "Situational Patterning in Intergroup Relations," *American Sociological Review*, 21, 1956, pp. 164–174.

19. I. N. Brophy, "The Luxury of Anti-Negro Prejudice," *Public Opinion Quarterly*, 9, 1946, pp. 456–66. One possible explanation for the results of this study and others cited below is that the people who were the least prejudiced to begin with sought out interracial contact. Most of these studies, however, rule out the operation of this self-selection factor.

20. William M. Kephart, *Racial Factors and Urban Law Enforcement* (Philadelphia, University of Pennsylvania Press, 1957), pp. 188–89.

21. Barbara MacKenzie, "The Importance of Contact in Determining Attitudes Toward Negroes," *Journal of Abnormal and Social Psychology*, 43, 1948, pp. 417–41.

22. Alfred M. Lee and Norman D. Humphrey, *Race Riot* (New York, Dryden Press, 1943), pp. 97, 130, 140.

23. Morton Deutsch and Mary Collins, *Interracial Housing: A Psychological Evaluation of a Social Experiment* (Minneapolis, University of Minnesota Press, 1951); Marie Jahoda and Patricia West,

"Race Relations in Public Housing," *Journal of Social Issues*, 7, 1951, pp. 132–39; Daniel M. Wilner, Rosabelle Walkley, and Stuart W. Cook, *Human Relations in Interracial Housing: A Study of the Contact Hypothesis* (Minneapolis, University of Minnesota Press, 1955); and Ernest Works, "The Prejudice-Interaction Hypothesis from the Point of View of the Negro Minority Group," *American Journal of Sociology*, 67, 1961, pp. 47–52.

24. Samuel A. Stouffer, Edward A. Suchman, Leland C. DeVinney, Shirley A. Star, and Robin M. Williams, Jr., *Studies in Social Psychology in World War II*, Vol. 1, *The American Soldier: Adjustment During Army Life* (Princeton, Princeton University Press, 1949), Chapter X.

25. Joseph D. Lohman and Dietrich C. Reitzes, "Note on Race Relations in Mass Society," *American Journal of Sociology*, 58, 1952, pp. 340–46; J. D. Lohman and D. C. Reitzes, "Deliberately Organized Groups and Racial Behavior," *American Sociological Review*, 19, 1954, pp. 342–44; and D. C. Reitzes, "The Role of Organizational Structures: Union Versus Neighborhood in a Tension Situation," *Journal of Social Issues*, 9 (1), 1953, pp. 37–44.

26. For research demonstration of this principle, see: Richard T. LaPiere, "Attitudes Versus Actions," *Social Forces*, 13 (1934), pp. 230–37; and Bernard Kutner, Caroll Wilkins, and Penny R. Yarrow, "Verbal Attitudes and Overt Behavior Involving Racial Prejudice," *Journal of Abnormal and Social Psychology*, 47, 1952, pp. 649–52.

27. For research demonstrations of this principle, see: Henry A. Bullock, "Racial Attitudes and the Employment of Negroes," *American Journal of Sociology*, 56, 1951, pp. 448–57; and A. Kapos, *Some Individual and Group Determinants of Fraternity Attitudes Toward the Admission of Members of Certain Minority Groups*. Unpublished doctoral dissertation, University of Michigan, 1953.

28. John Harding and Russell Hogrefe, "Attitudes of White Department Store Employees Toward Negro Co-workers," *Journal of Social Issues*, 8, 1952, pp. 18–28.

29. Gerhart Saenger and Emily Gilbert, "Customer Reactions to the Integration of Negro Sales Personnel," *International Journal of Opinion and Attitude Research*, 4, 1950, pp. 57–76.

30. Prohibition provides an interesting contrast at this point. Prohibition apparently failed largely because it was neither rigorously enforced nor, despite its moral overtones for some Protestants, did it articulate with national traditions or ease the consciences of many Americans.

31. Eunice Cooper and Marie Jahoda, "The Evasion of Propaganda: How Prejudiced People Respond to Anti-Prejudice Propaganda," *Journal of Psychology*, 23, 1947, pp. 15–25; and Herbert H. Hyman and Paul B. Sheatsley, "Some Reasons Why Information Campaigns Fail," *Public Opinion Quarterly*, 11, 1947, pp. 413–23.

32. For an interesting political example of this phenomenon, *see* Hadley Cantril, ed., *Gauging Public Opinion* (Princeton, Princeton University Press, 1944), pp. 226–30.

33. Muzafer Sherif, and others, *Intergroup Conflict and Cooperation: The Robbers Cave Experiment* (Norman, Oklahoma, Institute of Group Relations, 1961).

# BIBLIOGRAPHY

Allport, Gordon W., *The Nature of Prejudice*. Cambridge, Mass., Addison-Wesley, 1954, Chapter 13.

Cox, Oliver C., *Caste, Class and Race*. Garden City, New York, Doubleday, 1948.

Glazer, Nathan and Moynihan, Daniel Patrick, *Beyond the Melting Pot*. Cambridge, Mass., The MIT Press and Harvard University Press, 1963, pp. 1–85, 288–315.

Higham, John, *Strangers in the Land: Patterns of American Nativism, 1860–1925*. New Brunswick, N. J., Rutgers University Press, 1955.

Marden, Charles F., and Meyer, Gladys, *Minorities in American Society*. 3rd edition. New York, American Book Company, 1968, Chapters 11–15.

Pettigrew, Thomas F., *Racially Separate or Together*? New York, McGraw-Hill Book Company, 1971.

Rose, Peter I., *The Subject is Race*. New York, Oxford University Press, 1968, Chapters 2–4.

Simpson, George Eaton and Yinger, J. Milton, *Racial and Cultural Minorities*. 3rd edition. New York, Harper & Row, 1965, Chapters 4–5, 8, 22–23.

Van den Berghe, Pierre, *Race and Racism*. New York, John Wiley & Sons, Inc., 1967; Chapters 1, 4–7.

Williams, Robin M., Jr., *Strangers Next Door*. Englewood Cliffs, N. J., Prentice-Hall, Inc., 1964; Chapters 4–5, 9–10.

# 16

## Black Protest
## in America

### Robert H. Brisbane

The historian Arnold J. Toynbee put forth an interesting and workable designation for such national ethnic minorities as the black Americans. He dubbed them the "internal proletariat"—which he defined as "any social element or group which, in some way, is *in* but not *of* any given society at any period of that society's history." The applicability of this categorization to Negroes in America is obvious. Indeed, there has been no ethnic group in American history that has suffered ostracism and exclusion as rigid and lasting as that imposed by the dominant white majority on the blacks. While other ethnic groups such as the Poles, Italians, and Irish have been encouraged to give up their national identities, the black American, to the contrary, has had consciously to develop a spirit of nationalism to cope with his extraordinary condition.

This does not mean that for the entire 350 years of their existence in America Negroes have failed to attempt to bridge the gap between the *in* and *of*, of American society. Indeed, such a rapprochement has been the basic objective of all black protest movements, whether expressed in low-keyed petitions or in the invective of militant black nationalists. The majority of black Americans have not proposed to leave the country, and only once has there been a serious threat of migration en masse (discussed later in this chapter). As Frederick Douglass averred of his black brethren, "We are *here* and here we are likely to remain." And so the black protest will continue. It will vary in intensity with the fluctuations of white racism—but it will continue until black Americans are accepted into the body politic as equals, or until some other "definitive" solution is reached.

### Early Forms of Protest

There were very few aspects of life and history in the slave South that were not in some way affected by the fear or actuality of concerted slave rebellion. Indeed, the basic problem in the formulation of the social, legal, theological, and even philosophical aspects of antebellum southern life was how best to prevent or how most effectively to put down individual and mass black rebelliousness. To this end the slave codes forbade slaves to learn to read or write, to testify against white men, to possess weapons, or to resist the demands and commands of their masters. Overseers, patrolmen, volunteer vigilantes, militiamen, and federal troops were marshalled to quell possible uprisings but none of these measures was ever sufficient to destroy the Africans' urge toward freedom. The blacks resisted in the barracoons (slave pens), mutinied aboard the slavers, drowned themselves upon debarkation and, finally, plotted escape and rebellion against the system on the plantations. In the final analysis, things could not have been otherwise, for as one eminent observer asserted: "Slavery is a state of war."[1]

In the 350 years between the beginning of the sixteenth and the middle of the nineteenth centuries, more than fifteen million blacks were shipped into slavery across the Atlantic. The brutal and unspeakable conditions aboard the slavers during the so-called "middle passage" brought about the deaths of approximately half as many more en route. Self-imposed starvation was common. In 1807, a few days before Christmas, two boatloads of newly arrived slaves starved themselves to death in the port of Charleston, South Carolina.[2]

Harvey Wish, the historian, has cataloged fifty-five revolts aboard slave ships during the period from 1699 to 1845.[3] In general, these revolts were abortive; nevertheless, the unsuccessful ones were numerous enough to impel insurance companies to write a special form of coverage against insurrections aboard slave ships. Undoubtedly, the best known of these mutinies occurred in July 1839 aboard the *Amistad*,[4] a low-slung American clipper built especially for the slave trade. After having spent three months crossing the Atlantic from Africa to Cuba, the *Amistad*, with its forty-nine slaves, sailed on June 28, 1838, for Puerto Principe.

On the fifth day out of Havana the captives, under the leadership of a young slave named Singbe, mutinied, killing the captain and taking control of the ship. Singbe, a member of the Mendi tribe of West Africa, was 25 years of age, intelligent, and courageous. Under his captaincy, the *Amistad* began a six weeks' odyssey along the coast of the United States, ending finally on August 24 off the port of New London, Connecticut. Under the custody of American officials, Singbe and his fellow captives sat through two trials in federal courts while their status was determined under American and international law. Abolitionist lawyers, aided by ex-president John Quincy Adams, secured their freedom in January 1840, and on November 25, 1841, Singbe and his African brothers sailed for Sierra Leone.

In less than two generations after slavery was introduced into the American colonies, it became obvious that the establishment and maintenance of this institution in the New World would encounter serious difficulties. The first slave revolt on record occurred in Virginia in 1663 and for the next 200 years the history of slavery in America abounds with instances of violence, terror, and bloodshed. Slave revolts ran the gamut from individual resistance to group conspiracies and rebellions. Concerning the matter of individual resistance, Aptheker writes:

> Individual attempts of assassination or property damage by gun, knife, club, axe, poison, and fire were so numerous that undertaking an enumeration would be a well-nigh impossible task.[5]

The slaves also resorted to sabotage, suicide, and self-mutilation; but most costly to their master were the runaways. Between 1830 and 1860 no fewer than 2,000 slaves per year escaped to freedom. Slaves, however, did not rely solely upon violence or escape to achieve release from bondage. They carried their fight for freedom into the courts of the land. Between 1640 and 1860, some 670 slaves sued for their personal freedom in state and federal courts; out of this number 327 were successful, 248 lost their bids, and the cases of 95 remained undecided.[6]

The successful revolutionary activity of the slaves in the islands of the French West Indies caused near panic among the slaveholders of the Deep South, who feared that the news of these black revolutions would spread to the American states. The governors of several of the Deep South states called for increased vigilance, and placed their national guards on military alert. The menacing figure of the Haitian leader Toussaint L'Ouverture, however, cast a shadow as far north as the American capital. Such outstanding personalities as George Washington, Charles C. Pinckney, and Albert Gallatin publicly expressed concern over the impact of the events in the Caribbean. Thomas Jefferson warned:

> I become daily more [and] more convinced that all the West India Islands will remain in the hands of the people of color, and a total expulsion of the whites sooner or later will take place. It is high time we should foresee the bloody scenes which our children certainly and possibly ourselves (South of Potomac) have to wade through, and try to avert them.[7]

While it would be impossible to find documented evidence of every revolt or conspiracy to revolt by slaves during the history of slavery in America, records and other data do exist on approximately 250 of them. Of this number, the following four warrant special mention:

1. The New York City Slave Troubles, 1741.
2. The Gabriel Prosser-Jack Bowler Plot, Henrico County, Virginia, 1800.
3. The Denmark Vesey Conspiracy, Charleston, South Carolina, 1822.
4. The Nat Turner Revolt, Southampton County, Virginia, 1831.

In 1741, New York City became the scene of the first mass execution of Negroes in the nation's history. Ironically, the killings were not occasioned by an actual slave revolt nor was any conspiracy to revolt ever proved. Like all slave communities, the city lived in perennial fear of a slave uprising and the mere rumor of a slave plot was enough to cause panic which quickly led to hysteria. The result was the prosecution and conviction for conspiracy of 154 blacks and 25 whites solely on the basis of hearsay evidence and obvious falsifications. Thirty-one blacks were executed, eighteen being hanged and thirteen being burned alive; four whites, two of whom were women, were hanged.

Gabriel Prosser and Jack Bowler were something more than mere local insurrectionists; they were among the nation's first authentic black militant leaders. Intelligent, courageous, and resourceful, they conceived the idea of and planned for a general uprising against slavery in Virginia. It is quite possible that they had heard of and been inspired by the successful slave revolts in the Caribbean. For several months in 1800 they trained secretly and managed to arm more than 1,000 slaves. On the eve of the attack they marched their army virtually to the gates of Richmond, but because of a violent rainstorm the attack was postponed. Meanwhile, Governor James Monroe, who had received news of the impending revolt, placed the state under military alert. Prosser's army voluntarily dispersed but he and some thirty-five of his followers were caught and hanged.

Perhaps no black man of his time regarded slavery with as much hatred, loathing, and repugnance as did Denmark Vesey. In his youth, Vesey had served aboard a slaver as the chattel of its master. He acquired a good informal education plus the mastery of several languages. In his early twenties, he purchased his freedom and from then on, for more than two decades while in South Carolina, he looked toward the day when he could deliver a crippling blow to slavery in the South. By 1820, he was training lieutenants and methodically recruiting a slave army of some 6,000 men. His plan of attack called for assaulting Charleston simultaneously from five points, with a sixth force on horseback to patrol the city. The date selected was the second Sunday in July 1822, but when news of the plot leaked out (as was commonly the case), the date was moved forward one month. During the interim defections mounted, and before the appointed day the authorities moved in and arrested Vesey and 139 others. Forty-seven of the black conspirators, including Vesey, were hanged.

Of the handful of great slave leaders of the nineteenth century, Nat Turner emerges as the most controversial and fascinating.[8] Turner was a lay preacher and devoutly religious. He was also a mystic. While perhaps too much has been made of this phenomenon, Turner undoubtedly did have visions and hear voices which he considered to be representations of the Almighty. This led him to conclude that he had been ordained by God to strike the chains of bondage from his brethren. The sign he was waiting for came in the form of a solar eclipse in February 1831; and he immediately set the date of the revolt for August 21. At the appointed hour, Turner and his followers calmly killed Turner's master, Joseph Travis, and his entire family. They proceeded to kill sixty-four more whites before they were met and overpowered by state and federal troops. In the encounter more than one hundred slaves were killed. Turner was captured on October 30 and hanged on November 11, 1831.

In July 1831, The Reverend Samuel J. May observed:

> The slaves are men. They have within them that unextinguishable thirst for freedom which is born in man. They are already writhing in their shackles. They will one day throw them off with vindictive violence, if we do not loose them.[9]

The tempo of slave insurgency quickened during the years preceding 1865. Even if emancipation had not been granted, it is doubtful that slavery could have continued to survive much longer.

### The Origins of Self-Determination

In 1790, the first decennial Census of the United States reported a total of 59,000 free Negroes in the country, of whom 27,000 lived in the North and 32,000 in the states to the South. The free black population accounted for a mere 2 percent of that of the United States taken as a whole, but it was beginning to develop a group consciousness. In 1787 the Free African Societies began to organize the free blacks of Pennsylvania, New York, Rhode Island, and other regions. Black leaders were emerging and beginning to speak out on behalf of the general welfare of all blacks, whether slave or free. This was the Age of Revolution and of the Lockian creed of the inalienable rights of man, and blacks as well as whites were inspired and aroused by the egalitarian ideology of the revolutionists and by the antislavery activities in the northern colonies. At the first call to arms, therefore, blacks by the thousands sought to enlist. Despite colonial laws excluding them from the militia and an early hesitancy on the part of the Continental Army to enlist them, between 1775 and 1781 blacks fought in every major engagement of the war.

For a time it appeared that the new nation would respond favorably to the hopes of the black people. Two months after the enactment of the Declaration of Independence, the Massachusetts General Assembly resolved that:

> . . . Human bondage violated the natural rights of man and was utterly inconsistent with the avowed principle in which this and other states have carried on their struggle for liberty.[10]

Between 1777 and 1800 seven other northern states abolished slavery, and in the upper South the Virginia and North Carolina legislatures encouraged owners to emancipate their slaves.

Toward the end of the eighteenth century, however, the fervor for liberty, equality, and natural rights began to wane. Negroes began to discover that much of this egalitarian thinking was a veneer and that beneath it, the racism of northern as well as southern whites remained as formidable as ever. Emancipation was one thing; political, civil, and social equality was, for most whites, an entirely different matter.

Shortly after Massachusetts abolished slavery, its legislature voted to bar interracial marriages and to expel from within its boundaries all blacks who were not citizens of one of the states. In 1780, Paul Cuffee, a wealthy black New England ship owner, and eight other blacks refused to pay taxes to the state on the grounds that as citizens they were being denied the right to vote.[11] In 1800 Boston authorities ordered 240 blacks to leave Massachusetts. Crying out in protest, a black leader, Prince Hall, called upon Negroes to have patience and "bear up under the daily insults we meet with in the streets of Boston," in spite of the fact that "we may truly be said to carry our lives in our hands and the arrows of death are flying about our heads."[12]

By 1815 the legal status of free blacks had little to recommend it. No state, whether in the North or the South, regarded them as suitable members of the political community. Almost every state barred them from voting, giving evidence in court, and marrying whites. No state would have them in the militia or make them citizens by legislative act. By its so-called "Black Laws" of 1804 and 1807, the state of Ohio compelled blacks entering the state to post a $500 bond guaranteeing their good behavior. The Federal Government excluded them from the postal service, and in 1820 authorized the citizens of Washington, D. C. to elect "white" city officials and to adopt a code governing free Negroes and slaves.

In the face of what appeared to be almost universal rejection, blacks, partly in protest but largely from necessity, began to lay the foundations for black parallel institutions, institutions which still exist today. Chief among these was the black church.

Since early Colonial times free blacks had been welcomed in the local churches to worship together with whites. With the advent of such legislation as the Black Laws, however, even this acceptance was withdrawn. Thus, late in 1787 Richard Allen and Absolom Jones were pulled from their knees and ejected from the white St. George Methodist Episcopal Church in Philadelphia. Shortly thereafter, Allen and other blacks established the first black Methodist Church in the nation. Jones and his friends went even further and established the black St. Thomas Protestant Episcopal Church of Philadelphia. As early as 1776, however, blacks in the South had established their own Baptist Churches.

Blacks began to protest against the denial of equal education as early as 1787. In that year, Boston Negroes petitioned the legislature to grant them educational facilities, for, as they said, they "now receive no benefit from the free schools."[13] Indeed, at the turn of the century, almost every northern state either segregated black children in the existing schools or provided them with separate facilities. Some of the more recently formed states made no provisions for black children at all. The numerous petitions by blacks protesting the denial of adequate educational facilities have traditionally fallen on deaf ears. Some assistance to provide schools for black children came from white groups such as the Quakers but, by and large, Negroes used their own meager funds to provide an education for their offspring.

## Emigration and the American Colonization Society

As it became increasingly evident that racism was deeply rooted in the American consciousness, blacks began to experience a profound sense of alienation, and nationalistic and emigrationist sentiments began to crop up among black leaders. Since the earliest days of the Colonial period, various proposals to colonize emancipated blacks had been put forward and discussed. In 1789, the Free African Society of Newport, Rhode Island, proposed to its sister organization, the Free African Society of Philadelphia, that they jointly urge Negroes to return to Africa to escape the humiliating conditions in the United States. With the steady rise in the number of free blacks after 1800, there was an added impetus for more positive action. Paul Cuffee was instrumental in promoting the

idea of colonization for American Negroes during this period. Cuffee made an explora-
tory trip to Sierra Leone in 1811 and became so enamored of the idea of settlement there
that in 1815, mostly at his own expense, he transported thirty-eight blacks to the African
West Coast colony. Cuffee stated later that he had received so many applications for the
trip that he could have colonized the greater part of Boston.[14]

In December 1816, delegates from several states, North and South, gathered in the
Chamber of the House of Representatives in Washington, D.C. to establish the American
Colonization Society (ACS). The avowed purpose of the organization was to colonize
Negroes on a voluntary basis in Africa or any other foreign territory that Congress
might deem expedient. Henry Clay, one of the distinguished delegates, asked:

> Can there be a nobler cause than that which, while it proposes to rid our own
> country of a useless and pernicious, if not dangerous portion of its population, contem-
> plates the spreading of the arts of civilized life and the possible redemption from igno-
> rance and barbarism of a benighted quarter of the globe?[15]

The reaction of free Negroes to the new movement was immediate. With few
exceptions, leading blacks had long opposed any scheme to repatriate blacks to Africa,
or to colonize them in any place outside of the United States. In little more than one
month after the appearance of the new society, the free blacks of Richmond, Virginia,
staged a demonstration of about 3,000 people, who voiced their opposition to the organization. Speakers denounced what they considered to be the true motive of the ACS.
Particular exception was taken to Henry Clay's characterization of free Negroes as
"useless and pernicious." "Let us alone," they said. "But if the whites are determined to
be rid of free Negroes, let it be in some part of the United States. We prefer being colonized in the most remote corner of the land of our nativity than being exiled to a foreign
country."[16] Printed resolutions were sent to agencies of the Federal Government, churches,
black organizations, and antislavery societies.

Agitation continued to mount in black circles throughout the seaboard cities over
the back-to-Africa scheme, which was considered to be destructive to the black American identity. Black leaders, including Richard Allen, Absolom Jones, and James Forten,
called for a national meeting to consider the problem. The resulting conclave that met
in Philadelphia on August 10, 1817, proved to be a milestone in black history; it was
the first of the great national conventions that blacks were to hold in order to air their
grievances. With James Forten as chairman, the convention adopted a basic resolution:

> We will never separate ourselves voluntarily from the slave population of this coun-
> try; they are our brethren by the ties of consanguinity, suffering and wrong; we feel
> there is more virtue in suffering privation with them, than fancied advantage for a
> reason.[17]

Speakers pilloried the ACS. Its leaders were declared to be agents of the largest slave
owners and dealers in the country whose design was nothing less than the suppression
and expulsion of the free black population of the United States. Delegates to the convention went home to continue the agitation in the local black communities.

In spite of such resistance, the ACS went ahead with its plans. After investigating several available areas on the west coast of Africa, the society decided in 1821 to establish a settlement at Cap Mesurado, located just southeast of the British colony of Sierra Leone. A few years later, the settlement adopted the name "Liberia." For almost a quarter of a century, the colony was not much more than a dependency of the ACS. However in 1847 a national constitution was adopted and Liberia declared itself to be a sovereign independent republic. There were fewer than 3,000 repatriated American slaves or their descendants in the land in 1847, but American settlers numbered about 12,000 a half-century later.

## The Emergence of Black Nationalism

If the protest activities of free Negroes during the postrevolutionary period were mostly tentative in nature and confined more or less to prayerful petitions, the period after 1820 presents a startlingly new picture. For one thing, there were now some 200,000 free blacks in the cities of the Atlantic seaboard. Group consciousness among them was gaining in strength. The new vehicle of protest was to be the mass demonstrations and conventions which were to be marked by a rising feeling of black nationalism and a new militancy. For the first time in the nation's history, the activities of free blacks were to become of national interest. While slavery remained the dominant issue, in the period between 1817 and 1857 three successive but distinct developments occurred. They were: (1) anticolonization agitation, 1817–1830; (2) the Negro national convention movement, 1830–1840; and (3) the rise of militant black abolitionism, 1843–1859.

In 1827 the anticolonization movement hailed the appearance of *Freedom's Journal*, the nation's first black newspaper. The publication was founded by John Russwurm, the nation's first black college graduate, and Samuel E. Cornish, a Presbyterian minister who opposed colonization. During the first two years of its existence, the paper featured articles on the evils of slavery, the importance of education to Negroes, and news of the activities of blacks throughout the country. By 1829, however, it appeared that agents of the ACS had been able to subvert at least one of the editors. Russwurm broke with his partner to become a representative of the society, and was bitterly denounced by many of his associates. Carter G. Woodson states:

> At first, [Russwurm] refused to connect himself with the colonizationists but finding their later proposals more flattering he joined their ranks, going to Liberia where he served as editor and public functionary.[18]

Cornish subsequently established a short-lived newspaper, *The Rights of Man*.

Toward the end of the 1820s, fiery David Walker from Boston added his voice to the anticolonization agitation.[19] Apart from Henry Highland Garnet, about whom we shall hear more later, Walker was the most militant free Negro in the antebellum period.

In his famous *Appeal in Four Articles,* Walker denounced Henry Clay and his "slave-holding party" as "murderers and oppressors" who advocated the colonization of blacks more out of apprehension than humanitarianism.

> Let no man of us budge one step and let the slave holders come and beat us from our country. America is more ours than it is the whites'—we have enriched it with our *blood and tears.*[20]

Walker considered the liberty and freedom of all blacks to be in imminent peril and advised them to strike out directly and violently. And once their thrust had been made, Walker warned:

> Make sure you work—do not trifle, for they will not trifle with you—they want us for their slaves and think nothing of murdering us in order to subject us to that wretched condition—therefore if there is *attempt* made by us—kill or be killed.[21]

The *Appeal* was printed and distributed by the thousands. It caused alarm and consternation in the slave states. Undoubtedly it accounted for some of the militancy displayed during the black conventions of the 1830s.

By 1830 the feeling of unity and militancy born of the anticolonization struggle had taken deep root among the free blacks. Leaders with national status had emerged and with them had arisen their forums—the national conventions. The issues would not be confined to colonization. A whole new era in the antislavery movement had dawned, one which would ultimately shoulder the colonization problem off the stage. Between 1830 and 1835, six great national conventions were held, all of them except the fifth meeting in Philadelphia.[22] The first convention established the American Society of Free Colored Persons as a parent organization. Auxiliaries were to be established in every black community; they in turn would send five delegates to the annual conventions. At the time of the first convention there were about fifty black antislavery societies in existence. Members of these organizations were represented heavily at the conventions. Many of the members, such as William Whipper of Pennsylvania, favored passive resistance to slavery; however, among the minority there was a growing demand for a more militant stance.

The overall impact of the new movement on the free Negro population was considerable. Blacks were urged to ignore the Fourth of July holiday, and asked to observe the fifth day of July instead as a day of prayer and fasting for their brothers in bondage. Funds were collected throughout black communities in behalf of the 2,000 blacks forced by Ohio's Black Laws to emigrate to Canada. The conventions set up and maintained Free Produce Societies in order to support the boycott by blacks of all products of slave labor and slave plantations. Temperance societies and even African missionary groups were organized. In the last analysis, however, the conventions were folk meetings—occasions where troubled people could empty their hearts and testify to their common trials and tribulations.

Almost from their inception, the Negro conventions were regarded with apprehension by white antislavery leaders. This was an all-black movement—and the whites were troubled by such evidences of what in the twentieth century would be called "black separatism." William Lloyd Garrison was particularly disturbed. His view was that any separatist Negro movement would injure the abolitionist cause; moreover, some of the sentiments expressed by the black leaders were too militant for the pacifist predilictions of the antislavery faction as a whole. He felt a possible solution to the problem might be to quietly take control of the movement's leadership and steer these well-meaning but misguided Negroes along the proper path. A campaign in accordance with this plan appears to have begun in earnest at the 1832 convention when Garrison, who was a guest, took the floor and called upon the black delegates to repudiate Nat Turner's insurrection and denounce all those associated with it. He warned the convention against political action and advised against resorting to organized resistance against slavery. The power of "moral suasion" (which he did not define) should be relied upon exclusively.

Within the next two years, the antislavery forces were able to infiltrate and split the leadership of the convention movement. At the 1834 convention the Garrisonians, led by William Whipper, prevailed upon the delegates to accept the principle of "moral suasion." The body voted to establish two separate organizations: the National Negro Convention and the National Convention of the American Moral Reform Society. This move was the beginning of the end for the Negro convention movement; after 1835 its decline was precipitous. Some of its most esteemed leaders, such as Charles Forten, Sr., had defected to the Reform Society. The Garrisonians had won the day.

Outside of Philadelphia and Boston, however, the Moral Reform Society could count on little support from the black rank and file. Negro leaders generally were bitter over the demise of the convention movement and laid the blame squarely at the feet of the Garrisonians. In New York a new weekly newspaper, *The Colored American*, was launched in 1837. Its editor, the aforementioned Samuel Cornish, characterized the moral suasionists as a group who were vague, wild, indefinite, and confused in their views. He considered Garrison's contention that racial distinctions had no place in American society to be sheer nonsense. To Cornish and other black leaders, there was still a need for independent action. Although the abolitionists had done much for Negroes, "too many of them best loved the colored man at a distance and refused to admit or eradicate their own prejudice."[23]

Perhaps the chief reason for the success of the Moral Reform Society among blacks was their conviction that passive resistance rather than physical violence or political action was the best means for achieving freedom for their brothers in bondage. By 1840, however, free Negroes were becoming restive and impatient. The moral suasionists had stood by, wringing their hands, while free blacks were kidnaped and sold into slavery and while agents of the slaveholders had seized, chained, and dragged runaways off the streets. Many Negroes began to reject white antislavery leadership. Cornish, in the

*Colored American*, declared:

> ... give us facts, show us how and when any people who were groaning under oppression ever succeeded in releasing themselves from the yoke without making a special effort themselves whenever they possessed the power to do so.[24]

Young black militants of New York and Philadelphia began to demand a national meeting to adopt a new policy. Their demands resulted in the Buffalo, New York, Convention of 1843.

More than seventy black leaders, young and old, attended this meeting. Among the younger ones were such rising figures as Frederick Douglass and the 27-year-old Presbyterian minister, Henry Highland Garnet. The delegates were more or less evenly distributed between the moral suasionists and those of a more militant disposition, but the temper of the gathering was definitely militant. Samuel H. Davis, in opening the convention, hinted at using other than peaceful means to obtain rights long overdue, but it was left to the eloquent Garnet to sound the tocsin. His speech was entitled "An Address to the Slaves of the United States of America."

Garnet was a powerful and persuasive speaker. One reporter was so enraptured that, as he later insisted, "for one hour of his life his mind was not his but wholly at the control of the eloquent Negro."[25] Working up slowly but deliberately to the subject of violence, Garnet suggested that slaves should go to their masters and demand their freedom immediately, then refuse to work if that freedom were denied.

> ... If they then commence the work of death, they and not you will be responsible for the consequences. You had better all die, *die*, immediately, than live slaves, and entail your wretchedness on your posterity. ... However much you and all of us may desire it, there is not much hope of Redemption without the shedding of blood. If you must bleed, let it all come at once—rather die freemen than live to be slaves.[26]

The speech was received with tremendous applause, but after it had been printed and presented to the body, it failed adoption by one vote. The delegates were not yet ready to endorse insurrection. In fact, the day was saved for the moral suasionists by a handful of blacks who continued to reject violence. One of these was Frederick Douglass. By the end of the decade, however, Douglass was to break with Garrison and his doctrines. The convention went on to adopt a series of resolutions which denounced the ACS and the proslavery churches, endorsed the Liberty Party, and stressed the value of temperance and education. The militants did not lose all; the moral reformers had won the vote but the militants had won the future. Some six years later, Garnet's address and Walker's *Appeal* appeared together in a pamphlet reportedly published at the expense of none other than John Brown.

The Fugitive Slave Act of 1850 posed an obvious threat to free blacks the length and breadth of the country. At any time they could be "mistakenly" identified as fugitives and carried to the South. Northern Negroes organized and, when necessary, armed themselves to sabotage the operation of the new law. Frederick Douglass, who by this time had broken with Garrison, declared, "Every slave hunter who meets a bloody death in his infernal business is an argument in favor of the manhood of our race."[27] As the decade moved on and the outlook for blacks steadily deteriorated, some of them began to reconsider their objections to colonization, particularly in some parts of the Western Hemisphere. With this in mind, a convention was held in Cleveland, Ohio, in 1854. Dr. Martin Delany and other leaders explored proposals to settle in Central or South America.

It was the *Dred Scott* decision in 1857, however, that pronounced the final proscription of all the nation's blacks, slave or free. The dicta that Negroes were "so far inferior that they had no rights which a white man was bound to respect," and that blacks were not included and were not intended to be included in the meaning of the word "citizen" in the Constitution, reduced all blacks to the status of aliens. On the basis of this decision, the U. S. Department of State refused to grant passports to blacks for foreign travel. The protest from Negroes was instantaneous. Their bitterness reached an intensity that would not be exceeded for well over a hundred years to come. H. Ford Douglass, a black militant abolitionist, spoke for many blacks when he said in 1858:

> I can hate this government without being disloyal, because it has stricken down my manhood and treated me as a saleable commodity. I can join a foreign enemy and fight *against* it, without being a traitor because it treats me as an alien and a stranger, and I am free to avow that should such a contingency arise, I should not hesitate to take any advantage in order to procure such indemnity for the future.[28]

Robert Purvis, a wealthy light-skinned alumnus of Amherst and militant antislavery leader and emigrationist, was to go even further, stating the same year:

> ... to support the government of the United States and the Constitution upon which it was based was to endorse one of the basest, meanest, most atrocious despotisms that ever saw the face of the sun [and] ... any self-respecting man would look upon this piebald and rotten Democracy with contempt, loathing, and unutterable abhorrence.[29]

He would welcome the overthrow of this "atrocious government" and construct a better one in its place. But Frederick Douglass, now the universally recognized leader of blacks in the country, took a calmer view. He said:

> The truth is we are *here* and here we are likely to remain. . . .We have grown up with this republic, and I see nothing in her character or even in the character of the American people, as yet, which compels the belief that we must leave the United States.[30]

The Civil War was soon to put a temporary end to the troubles of black men. But after the war, their tribulations would begin anew and so would their protests.

## Reconstruction and Its Aftermath

On August 20, 1866, President Andrew Johnson declared that the Civil War was at an end and "that peace, order, tranquility, and civil authority now exist in and throughout the whole United States." Indeed, as early as January 1866, civil administrations were functioning in every former southern state except Texas. Johnson had assiduously carried out President Lincoln's 10 percent plan for restoration of the so-called Confederate states to the Union. This plan stipulated that in any state, when a number equal to 10 percent of the people who had voted in 1860 had taken the loyalty oath to support the Union, they could set up a state government. Conditions attached required that whites recognize the "permanent freedom" of blacks—and nothing else. Thus under the first Reconstruction, blacks could not vote, or run for or hold public office. In other words, they were completely bereft of political, civil, and social rights.

This was nothing less than a reentrenchment of the defeated slaveholders as the political and economic overlords of the South; it also meant the subjugation of blacks to a position closely approximating chattel slavery. The northern reaction to this tour de force was decisive and vindictive, but ultimately ineffective. The so-called Radical Reconstruction mounted by Congress in 1867 merely led to counterrevolution on the part of the white South. The eight-year period between 1867 and 1875 was the bloodiest peacetime interval in American history, and after the Hayes-Tilden Compromise in 1877, the question of white rule in the South was no longer moot.

It is generally assumed that with the shattering of the Radical Reconstruction, blacks retreated passively into the shadows of southern life. This impression, similar to that of the docility of blacks during slavery, does not accord with the facts. As early as 1865 Negroes in the South began to battle against what to many must have seemed to be a lost cause. They fought against violence and terrorism and for the right to vote, to serve on juries, and to testify and, above all, to escape from peonage. They petitioned state governors, Congress, and even the President of the United States. The black conventions, which had been used so extensively in the antebellum period, were revived. Scores of local and regional conclaves were convened in order that blacks could air their grievances. The inauguration of Rutherford B. Hayes as President, however, presaged disaster. The last hope of blacks in the South literally departed with the withdrawal of the last federal troops.

The response to the Compromise of 1877 by blacks was threefold: adjustment, escape, and challenge (in the form of nationalism). The majority of blacks chose adjustment, which involved not only bending to the lash (in some cases, not only figuratively) but also the building of parallel institutions which would be necessary for their survival. These organizations included churches as before, as well as a press; professional, social, and economic organizations; and educational institutions. In the South far more than in the North, there to be two societies—one black and the other white. Perhaps the most dramatic Negro reaction to the Compromise of 1877 was the mass exodus of 1878–1879, which saw approximately 50,000 blacks leave the South within a few months. After 1879, the migration continued in spurts, resuming on a large scale to Oklahoma after 1890.

Every period of rampant white racism in the United States has been marked by the appearance of militant black nationalists. Among other things, they invariably advocate that blacks separate themselves from whites within the United States or emigrate to some other land, usually Africa. The post-Reconstruction period produced this ideology and its apostles. Both Arthur A. Anderson, a post-Reconstruction separatist and emigrationist, and the Reverend James Theodore Holly stridently denounced white racism in the United States and advised blacks to get out of the country.[31] It was the voice of Bishop Henry McNeal Turner, however, that was heard above all others. For more than fifty years he directed a passionate and sustained assault on white racism in America, and with equal consistency he advised blacks to emigrate and to establish their own powerful, proud nation in Africa. During the period of "African fever" between 1875 and 1900, he was the prime mover in the emigrationist movement which gripped southern blacks.

## Migration to the American West

On the morning of March 11, 1879, 280 migrant Negroes stopped briefly in cold, wintry St. Louis en route to Kansas. They were the first of the so-called Exodusters.[32] During the ensuing weeks, some 20,000 more blacks, in torn and tattered clothing, with their few belongings on their backs, poured through the St. Louis gateway into the "promised land" of Kansas. As with most social movements of this kind, both push and pull factors were involved. The push was provided by the brutalizing conditions to which blacks were being forced to submit in the South. The pull influences, however, were much more varied and complex.

The person most closely associated with the exodus was Benjamin "Pap" Singleton, a mulatto ex-slave from Tennessee who had fled to Canada and was an avowed separatist. Indeed, Singleton, who called himself the "Moses of the Exodus," took credit for the whole movement. Be that as it may, in 1874 he organized the Tennessee Real Estate and Homestead Association for the purpose of encouraging black Tennesseans to settle on government lands in Kansas. From then until the end of 1878, he assisted some 7,000 Negroes in leaving the Deep South. Second in influence to Singleton in the movement was Henry Adams, originally from Shreveport, Louisiana. In 1874 Adams began to enroll Deep South Negroes into a "colonization council." The members of this council were pledged to migrate to some region in the West where they could have a state of their own. During a four- or five-year period, Adams claimed to have signed up about 98,000 persons for the venture.

In addition to the activities of Singleton and Adams, there were other forces operating to attract black settlers to Kansas. The imagination of some Kansas migrants must certainly have been stimulated by circulars sent out by the railroad and land companies offering cheap lands for low, easy payments. Chromolithograph scenes of Kansas were distributed throughout the South. One such circular, entitled "A Freedman's Home," projected the following:

> The colored father . . . sat on an easy chair reading a newspaper while the children and babies rollicked on the floor of the piazza. Through an open door of the kitchen, the colored wife could be seen directing the servants and cooks who were preparing the evening meal. In the parlor, however, was the most enchanting feature, for, at a grand piano, was poised the belle of the household.[33]

The exodus was short-lived, however, ceasing almost as abruptly as it had begun. The disillusioned who returned from Kansas gave such dismal reports of the barren country, the bleak climate, and the hard work necessary to open new lands for cultivation that their brothers and sisters were deterred from making the move.

Schemes for creating an all-black state out of the western territories had occurred to many Negroes throughout the nineteenth century; however, none ever came as close to realization as that of Edwin P. McCabe's.[34] Originally a Pullman porter, McCabe went to Kansas in 1879 during the period of the exodus. He entered politics there and in 1884 was elected to the post of state auditor. During the next few years he conceived the plan of making the Oklahoma territory an all-Negro state with himself as governor. Launching a high-powered campaign, he sent Oklahoma boosters throughout the South and organized black colonies which were to migrate to Oklahoma and set up Negro communities. His efforts were so successful that when the Oklahoma territory opened in 1889, between seven and ten thousand Negroes crossed the border to get a foothold in the new land.

In 1890 McCabe established a newspaper, the Langston City *Herald*, which he distributed throughout the South. The paper carried full-page maps of projected all-black towns and glowing accounts of newly arrived settlers. Oklahoma "clubs" sprang up across the entire South. Agents of the McCabe Town Company went into the black communities selling contracts for lots. Upon the purchase of a lot, the client received a free ticket to Guthrie, where at the company's office he could make his choice of lots. The title to each lot stipulated that the lot could never pass to any white man nor could any white man ever reside or do business on it. While McCabe's dream of an all-black state never materialized, more than a score of all-black communities did emerge as a result of his efforts. Among them was Langston, which later became best known for the black university located there.[35]

### The Era of "African Fever"

With regard to emigration and colonization, Bishop Henry McNeal Turner and Dr. Martin Delany were the most effective black nationalists of the post-Reconstruction period. Turner also anticipated a good deal of the rhetoric of the midtwentieth-century black militants. He was the first Negro to demand financial indemnity to blacks for services they had rendered during slavery, calling for forty billion dollars, an estimated "one hundred dollars a year for two millions of us for two hundred years."[36] He was also the first to preach that God is black. He insisted that Negroes should be atheists and believe in no God at all rather than "to believe in the personality of God and not to believe that he is a Negro." He also insisted that black Americans should return to Africa more for the redemption of self-respect and national identity than out of a desire to escape. Thus he thundered:

> Till we have black men in the seat of power, respected, feared, hated, and reverenced, our young men will never rise up for the reason that they will never look up.[37]

Dr. Martin Delany had been a fervent nationalist and emigrationist even before the war. His book, *Condition, Elevation, Emigration and Destiny of the Colored People of the United States*, is considered by one observer to be the *"locus classicus* of black nationalism" in America. During the year 1859, Delany traveled throughout Africa signing treaties with eight native kings of Abeokuta for grants of land to establish American Negro colonies in the Yoruba area. The kings later reneged on the grants.

In spite of somewhat bizarre overtones, the so-called African fever was merely one facet of the oftentimes hysterical urge on the part of many blacks to leave the South between 1875 and 1900. Where the movement began specifically is not known, but in January 1877, in South Carolina, a black minister noted "a deep and growing interest" in the possibilities of emigration. Some time later the *Missionary Record* reported that "thousands of Colored people in South Carolina would leave [for Liberia] if the means of transportation were furnished."[38] In view of this interest, Dr. Delany and other Negroes established the Liberian Exodus Joint Stock Steamship Company in 1878. During the spring of that year, the company purchased the bark *Azor* and on April 23, 206 black emigrants sailed aboard her bound for the Wando River plantation in Liberia.

By 1890, African fever had spread to Kansas and Oklahoma. Many of the blacks who had gone West in search of a better way of life had become sadly disillusioned. They began to look toward Africa and especially to the Edenlike forests and fields of Liberia as extolled in the pamphlets of the ACS and Bishop Turner's *Christian Recorder*. The ACS received so many requests for assistance to emigrate that in November 1889 it "warned that thousands of people are applying but we can help only a few." In the summer of 1890 the ACS successfully arranged for the passage of fifty-four blacks to Liberia.

Others were not so fortunate, however. In Kansas and Oklahoma, at the height of the fever, a few promoters established "emigration clubs." These caught on almost immediately. In their haste to get to New York and depart for Africa, many blacks virtually gave away some of their hard-earned possessions. Farms valued at $1,500 were sold for $100 or less. Unfortunately, some of the promoters were swindlers and their emigration "package deals" were frauds. When about 300 members of three of these clubs finally made their way to New York City in the winter of 1891–1892, there was no "bon voyage"—there was no ship. Penniless, hungry, and badly clothed for the rigors of winter, they became public charges. In March 1892 the ACS was able to arrange for the passage of about forty of them to Liberia; the rest of them merged into the black population of New York City.[39]

Perhaps the most unfortunate episode of the entire emigration movement was that involving the so-called African Band of Georgia.[40] During 1890 and 1891, the United States and Congo Emigration Company sent agents into the South to recruit emigrants and promote its grandiose plans for colonizing Liberia. Some of the agents in Georgia offered blacks an opportunity to become "preferred passengers" on future sailings merely for the purchase of one-dollar tickets and a postage stamp. The meaning of a "preferred passenger" was never explained; however, many of the more illiterate and gullible assumed that the dollar ticket would cover their entire fare to Liberia; at least, this was the notion that was spread around southern Georgia. Tickets were sold by the hundreds throughout 1890.

Toward the end of the year the company was pressured into naming a sailing date. It was announced that a ship would depart from Savannah in November 1890. Even after the month of November had come and gone without a sailing, faith in the venture persisted. From all over Georgia and beyond, people had sold their possessions, packed up, and started moving toward Atlanta, where they expected to receive final orders to go to Savannah and thence to Liberia. Some of the prospective emigrants elected local leaders to watch over them on their journey.

And so it was that during the last week of January 1891, some 1,500 blacks from the interior of Georgia joined more than 1,000 already in Atlanta waiting to go to Africa. Dubbing themselves the African Band, the would-be emigrants shrugged off the taunts and derision of the local community and took to singing, praying, and making plans. On January 31 the *Atlanta Constitution* reported:

> There has been a pow wow among the emigrants of the African band every night for the past two or three weeks. They are growing restless and the matter is coming to a head.

Matters did not come to a head, but by the middle of February the African Band began to disperse—some remaining in Atlanta and others going back home.

In 1892, after seventy-five years of encouraging and assisting Negroes to emigrate to Liberia, the ACS withdrew from colonizing activities. It continued to disseminate information about Africa through its *Liberia Bulletin*, but because of a shortage of operating funds, it could no longer provide transportation and the other services necessary to emigrants. Bishop Turner, however, was to step into the breach. In January 1894 the bishop organized the International Migration Society. Mindful of the financial difficulties of other emigration ventures, the new society established a dollar-a-month plan for payment of passage. The prospective emigrants agreed to pay at least one dollar monthly until forty dollars had accumulated; the society then agreed to furnish them steamship passage and provisions.

To advertise and promote its program, the society despatched 138 special agents to the South. In the summer of 1894 it took on the African Steamship Company as a subsidiary; capital for the new company proved difficult to obtain, however, and in March 1895 it collapsed. Nevertheless, the society was determined to live up to its contracted obligations to deliver emigrants to Liberia.[41] On March 8, 1895, therefore, it dispatched 220 emigrants to Liberia aboard the S.S. *Horsa*. One year later, the society chartered the S.S. *Laurada* to take 321 more. The African fever began to subside during the next few years; the war with Spain distracted both the nation and the blacks. By 1900 there were very few Negroes still interested in emigrating to Africa, or anywhere else for that matter.

The African emigration movement was not without its critics and detractors. Frederick Douglass accepted some degree of emigration but he was utterly opposed to colonization. T. Thomas Fortune of the New York *Age* considered the ACS a white man's organization which for more than half a century had "thrived on the gullibility of simple-minded and irresponsible Negroes." Generally, both northern and middle-class blacks had opposed emigration. The African fever was an affliction confined primarily to the southern black peasantry. Nevertheless, had adequate organization, financing, and transportation been provided between 1875 and 1900, it is likely that not fewer than 100,000 blacks would have set out for their ancestral continent.

## Booker T. Washington, the Niagara Movement, and the Birth of the NAACP

The twenty-year period between 1895 and 1915 in the history of blacks in the United States is often referred to as the Age of Booker T. Washington. The controversy, pro and con, over Washington's leadership so dominated the era that what is known as "black political thought in America" originated during this period. By 1900 Washington was wielding more power than any other Negro had done in the history of the nation. He had become the consultant to presidents and his influence in official circles in Washington, D.C., had become so great that he was dubbed the "unofficial Secretary of Negro Affairs." Few whites assayed into the area of race relations without first seeking his advice. If Washington's accomplishments won the full acclaim and admiration of blacks, however, his philosophy was another matter. Both in his celebrated Atlanta speech in 1895, which catapulted him to fame, and thereafter, Washington advised Negroes to work within the system and attempt to improve themselves in accordance with the social and economic rules prescribed by the white majority. This was the meaning of his admonition, "Cast down your buckets where you are."

To a small but hard core of black intellectuals, Washington's advice was both objectionable and insulting. John Hope, the future president of Morehouse College and Atlanta University, cried out: "I regard it as cowardly and dishonest for any of our colored men to tell white people or colored people that we are not struggling for equality." And from the aging Bishop Turner came: "Washington would have to live a long time to undo the harm he has done to our race." It was left to a young alumnus of Harvard University, however, to carry the battle against Washington into the twentieth century and make it a *cause célèbre*. The young man was William Monroe Trotter.

Trotter was reared and educated in the city of Boston. A brilliant student at Harvard, he was elected to membership in Phi Beta Kappa in his junior year. It was during his days at Harvard that he became the fast friend of another outstanding young black student, William E. B. DuBois. Toward the end of the century, both young men became increasingly alarmed at the rising eminence of Washington and his compromise, or accommodation, philosophy. DuBois went on to teach at Atlanta University, but Trotter decided to devote his energies to stopping the "Sage of Tuskegee." In 1901 Trotter established a militant weekly newspaper, the *Guardian*. The main thrust of this journal, indeed the major preoccupation of Trotter himself, was the destruction of Booker T. Washington and all he stood for. In 1905 Dr. Kelly Miller observed:

> Through the influence of the *Guardian*, Mr. Trotter has held together and inspirited the opposition to Mr. Washington. His every utterance leads to the Cato-like refrain—Booker T. Washington must be destroyed.[42]

For several years, Trotter had been seeking a confrontation with Washington; finally, in the summer of 1903, Trotter got his chance when Washington accepted an invitation to speak at a meeting of the Negro Business League in Boston. Trotter and his friends used the occasion to heckle the speaker and to break up the meeting. The event became known as the "Boston Riot." Trotter and one of his companions were fined fifty dollars and sentenced to thirty days in jail.[43] Trotter now became something of a martyr to the Negro radicals. Leading the latter group was Trotter's friend and former schoolmate, W. E. B. DuBois. DuBois was fast becoming the leading black scholar in the nation. He had received both his bachelor's and master's degrees from Harvard, and in 1895 he earned his doctorate with a dissertation that became the first number in the famous *Harvard Historical Series*. His *Souls of Black Folk* (1903) was to become a classic. When news of Trotter's imprisonment reached him, DuBois became incensed. Coming to his friend's defense, he said that Trotter was an "honest, brilliant, unselfish man, and to treat as a crime that which at worst was mistaken judgment was an outrage."[44]

With the time obviously at hand for some effective action to be taken against Washington, in 1905 Trotter and DuBois organized the Niagara Movement. The avowed purpose of the movement was to bring about organized aggressive action on the part of men who believed in the freedom and growth of Negroes. Trotter's real purpose, however, was to assemble the most capable opponents of Washington and to evolve methods of counteracting his influence and power over blacks and in the nation as a whole. The Niagara Movement was the first black protest movement of the twentieth century, but it was a movement in name only. With a membership of under thirty, it never became more than an annual round-table conference of young Negro intellectuals. Without funds or permanent organization, it was a mere paper tiger against Washington's formidable "Tuskegee Machine." In 1910 the movement died almost without a whimper. Most of its members had long since found other interests.

To a very great degree, however, the Niagara Movement paved the way for the National Association for the Advancement of Colored People (NAACP). The small committee which founded this new organization in 1910 included both DuBois and Trotter, and its projected program was hardly more than an enlargement of that of the Niagara Movement. The big difference between the two groups was that the NAACP was sponsored by prestigious, well-heeled white liberals, some of whom, like Oswald Garrison Villard, were lineal descendants of nineteenth-century abolitionists. Within five years of its founding, the NAACP had spread across the country, with fifty-four branches, nine locals, and four college chapters. Its membership had mushroomed to ten thousand.[45] The program, tactics, and strategies of the association were strictly conventional, although it was branded as radical by those who opposed the organization's demands for equality and rights for Negroes. The NAACP strategy was to work within the system using the system's professed ideals and legal institutions to obtain civil rights for blacks, an approach which ruled out violence or crusades.

From its very beginning, the presence of DuBois gave the organization real meaning to most blacks and to many whites. DuBois's greatest efforts were exerted through *The Crisis*, the organization's monthly journal founded in 1910. To DuBois, the magazine offered an opportunity to enter the lists in a desperate fight aimed straight at the real problem: the question of how educated black opinion in the United States could best be channeled for the good of the group. During the next twenty-five years, DuBois was to make *The Crisis* the most powerful medium for black people in the United States. In the meantime, the NAACP had become the major agency for the protection and promotion of the welfare of the black population.

## The "Great Migration"

Perhaps the greatest manifestation of protest by the black rank and file during the first half of the twentieth century was the "great migration." In the decade between 1910 and 1920, about half a million blacks left the South for northern and western destinations. To a large degree the migration was a resumption, on a grander scale, of the exodus of blacks that had occurred thirty years earlier. The basic causes of both migrations were the same, with one exception. The shortage of unskilled labor in the North brought about by the outbreak of World War I was a decisive factor in the later migration. In spite of this, however, the migration was basically a protest movement. The *Christian Recorder* commented in 1917: "If a million Negroes move North and West during the next twelve-month, it will be one of the greatest things for the Negro since the Emancipation Proclamation."

Be that as it may, the relocation of half a million semiliterate and rural-oriented blacks ultimately was to have profound effects on the American social system. One of these was the establishment of large black ghettos in half a dozen northern metropoles.

With the shutdown of defense industries at the conclusion of the war, tens of thousands of black migrants found themselves jobless in the promised land. Economically, at least, they were far worse off than they had ever been in the rural South. In the absence of public welfare, some assistance was given by charitable organizations, but not much. The National Urban League stepped into the breach. Formed in 1911 from two existing groups (the Committee for Improving Industrial Conditions of Negroes in New York City and the League for the Protection of Colored Women), the league was established for the specific purpose of helping black migrants to adjust to their new environment.[46] Its activitities extended to virtually all types of social service for blacks. Branches throughout the country established vocational training and guidance centers, day nurseries, baby clinics, and child-placement centers. Pregnant girls and illiterate mothers were given needed instruction. The league branches even established schools for domestics and janitors in order to improve the earning ability of these groups. By 1929 National Urban League branches had been organized in all of the major cities in the United States. It had taken its place beside the NAACP as one of the two major betterment and protest organizations for blacks in the country.

## The Ascendency of Marcus Garvey

The postwar competition between blacks and lower-class whites for jobs and living space in northern cities led to the first race riots of the twentieth century. The "long, bloody summer" of 1919 saw interracial conflicts flare up in half a dozen metropoles with approximately 400 persons killed and more than 1,000 injured, Although blacks remained on the defensive, the riots converted the black communities into hotbeds of militancy and black nationalism. A new black press had sprung up since 1910 and contributed greatly to the new mood. The *Challenge*, in 1919, warned:

> New Negroes are determined to make their dying a costly investment for all concerned. If they must die, they are determined that they shall not travel through the valley of the shadow of death alone, but some of their aggressors shall be their companions.

During the same year, U. S. Attorney General Mitchell Palmer reported that in all discussions about the riots, there was reflected the "note of pride" that the Negro had "found himself," that he had fought back, and that never again "will he tamely submit to violence and intimidation." A black revolution was in the making—now all it needed was a leader. Among all the great leaders in the area of black nationalism in the twentieth century, Marcus Garvey stands without peer.[47] The fact that Garvey was a product of the British West Indies was of special significance. After the successful black revolts of the early nineteenth century, black nationalism had thrived and spread through every nook and cranny of the Caribbean region. The British West Indies area was particularly affected. In Jamaica, at an early age, Garvey had become a recruit of the new ideology. It was while he was a student in pre-World War I London, however, that Garvey received his real education in militant nationalism. There he met and associated with young, fiery nationalists from the British colonies in Africa, Asia, and the Middle East. They were all plotting the downfall of the "British Raj" and hoping someday to lead their respective peoples out of colonial bondage into nationhood. Garvey was deeply influenced.

When he came to the United States in 1916, therefore, he came with a vision. He would build black nationalism in the United States into a mighty force. He would teach black Americans to take pride in their race, to develop self-esteem, and most of all, to cease their futile beating on the solid bastion of American racism and look homeward to Mother Africa. The watchword would be: "Africa for the Africans, at home and abroad." In 1917 Garvey set up his organization, the Universal Negro Improvement Association (UNIA). Within three years the organization had chapters in thirty-eight states and six foreign countries. Its membership totaled approximately 300,000, and Garvey counted his followers at two million.[48] In addition his weekly, *Negro World*, had become the most widely read black publication in the nation, if not in the world. Garvey had amassed the greatest black following in the history of the nation.

The key to Garvey's success lay in the peculiar social and historical backgrounds of his constituency, a constituency made up of the new blacks—the migrant population of the northern ghettos and the rank and file black peasantry of the Deep South. These people were the descendants of the Exodusters and the emigrationists of the late nineteenth century. They were insecure and rootless and, in a racist-oriented society, race pride and self-esteem were in constant short supply among them. If they were receptive to Garvey's emigrationist notions, it was partly because many of them, as young people, had listened to the back-to-Africa harangues of Bishop Turner. African fever among blacks was not entirely dead.

In the end, however, Garvey was to achieve no more success in black nation-building than had Bishop Turner or Dr. Delany before him. For one thing, Garvey's schemes were too grandiose and impractical to have any chance of success. For another, blacks remained too marginal in economic power to be able to support any high-cost, long-term ventures. Garvey was also hindered by the fact that he aroused the ire of the black middle class as had no other nationalist before him. DuBois averred that:

> Marcus Garvey is without doubt the most dangerous enemy of the Negro race in America and in the world. He is either a lunatic or a traitor.[49]

Finally, from the very beginning Garvey's organization had been infiltrated with interlopers, con men, and outright swindlers who bled the organization dry. When Garvey went to prison in 1925 after conviction in a federal court for "using the mails to defraud," the UNIA collapsed. Garveyism had reigned for a decade. During that time, it constituted the first and greatest black mass movement in American history. In the final analysis, however, Garveyism, like African fever, was more a protest against American racism than an affirmation of elaborate schemes of nation building in Africa.

## Black Protest and the Communist Party

For almost an entire decade after its founding in 1921, the American Communist party conducted a futile campaign to enroll Negroes in its movement. In doing so, the party was following Leon Trotsky's instructions to stir up "revolutionary protests among the black slaves of American capital." Both Trotsky and the American Communist party, however, failed to understand that what blacks really wanted was to overthrow racism, not capitalism, and that they actually wanted to *join* the system. Moreover, except for occasional flirtations with black nationalism, they showed little inclination toward ideology in general. Benjamin Gitlow, one of the founders of the Communist party in the United States, complained in 1930 that "...in spite of our efforts and the large sums of money spent on that sort of propaganda, we made very little headway among the Negro masses."[50]

Seeing that a new approach was clearly necessary to successfully woo the blacks, the party decided to de-emphasize ideology. All previous strategies and tactics were revised. Party workers equipped with at least a rudimentary knowledge of black history, customs, psychology, music, and so on, were sent out among the black population. Infiltration into black organizations and informal social and cultural contacts with blacks were promoted. In addition, the party gradually came to appreciate the importance blacks attached to civil and political rights. The International Labor Defense, created by the party to work in these areas, won black plaudits for the yeomanlike efforts it expended on behalf of the nine Negro youths involved in the world famous Scottsboro case. By 1935 the American Communist party had almost completely reversed the poor showing it had made among blacks during the previous decade. In a few short years it had gained immense prestige in black communities throughout the nation. The Chicago *Defender* declared:

> We may not agree with the entire program of the Communist Party but there is one item with which we do agree wholeheartedly and that is the zealousness with which it guards the rights of the race.[51]

In 1935, the Communist party received a rare opportunity to participate officially in the reorganized leadership of the black people in the United States. It was invited to be a member organization of the new National Negro Congress. The idea for the congress originated with Dr. Ralph J. Bunche and several other leaders attending a meeting at Howard University in 1935. It was their opinion that while a good deal of effort had been expended in the area of black political and civil rights, nothing much had been accomplished with regard to economic and social betterment. The congress was to be called upon to remedy this situation.

The first meeting of the congress was convened in Chicago on February 14, 1936. Present were 817 delegates representing some 585 organizations from twenty-eight states. Labor leader A. Philip Randolph was elected president.[52] Although the delegates representing civic, religious, and educational organizations were in the majority, their lack of sharply defined economic and social views made them little more than spectators at the congress. From the outset, the real management of the congress was in the hands of the communists and other leftist groups. Dr. Bunche himself concluded that the black delegates were terribly "confused and often frustrated" and that the congress was "taking its cue in the major essentials" from the line laid down by the American Communist party. At the last meeting of the congress in 1940, communist influence and control was sufficient to bring about the defeat of A. Philip Randolph and the election of Max Yergan, co-founder of the Council on African Affairs, as president. With the advent of the 1940s and the outbreak of World War II, the appeal of the congress waned and it faded into oblivion.

One of the principal objectives of the National Negro Congress was to find ways and means of softening the impact of the Great Depression on the nation's blacks. The congress, however, was comprised of black leaders of whom the black rank and file had heard little and cared even less. The majority of blacks were more interested in such direct-action programs as the Jobs-for-Negroes campaign than in more theoretical ventures. Beginning in 1933 in Detroit, the Jobs-for-Negroes movement spread quickly to other midwestern cities, finally reaching the metropoles along the Atlantic seaboard. With the boycott as its basic tactic, the movement decreed that not a dollar was to go to any producer or retailer of goods or services who did not pursue what the local black community considered to be a fair policy with respect to the employment of blacks. Before it ended in 1936 the campaign had put Negroes into white-collar jobs for the first time.

In New York City, the movement was directed by the youthful Reverend Adam Clayton Powell. Due largely to his militant and aggressive leadership, blacks for the first time were employed by retail shops and the telephone, gas, and electric companies. They were also taken on as subway motormen and bus drivers. In 1941 Powell was elected as a member of the New York City Council. Three years later he began serving in the United States House of Representatives as the first black member of that body from the East. By 1960 he had become chairman of the powerful Education and Labor Committee of the House, and during the next seven years became famous for his "Powell Amendments" which sought to deny federal funds for the construction of segregated schools.

## The Emergence of the Black Muslims

With the disintegration of the Garvey movement in the middle 1920s, most of its members and sympathizers set aside the banners and colorful uniforms that were part of Garveyism and took to more mundane pursuits. The black ideology advocated by Garvey, however, had its true believers, some of whom began casting about for a new vehicle for their faith. Their search ended fruitfully in the early 1930s in the teeming black Detroit ghetto, when a young black by the name of Wallace Fard proclaimed a new religion.

Fard declared that Africans had been brought to the New World against their will by white men and that all black Americans were really children of Islam with Allah as their God. The Caucasians, of course, ruled the world temporarily, but black men would return to power if they united and worked under what came to be called Black Muslim leadership. The first gatherings of the believers in the new creed were held in the homes of a handful of converts, but soon a large hall was acquired. This hall was consecrated as the first Temple of Islam. Within three years the movement had caught on in the black community of Detroit. Fard then retired from the active leadership of the organization and left it in the capable hands of a group of able young stalwarts.

Chief among these was Elijah Poole, later to be known as Elijah Muhammad, Georgia-born son of a Baptist minister. Under his leadership, the Nation of Islam, as he called his organization, enjoyed its most rapid growth. Fard had recruited some 8,000 members and had established a handful of temples. Through tireless efforts, however, Muhammad expanded the membership to more than 100,000 and set up fifty temples throughout the country.[53] Three main institutions of the religion were developed: the Fruit of Islam, a quasi-military legion of young black men; a University of Islam, which was a combined elementary and secondary school; and the Muslim Girls' Class. All of these were greatly expanded as time progressed.

The Muslims believe that the low status of Negroes in the United States is due primarily to their lack of economic power. Thus they urge the establishment of black businesses and economic ventures. The Muslims, incidentally, follow their own advice; they have established numerous small businesses, shops, and itinerant ventures of many varieties. Chicago has become a showcase of their enterprises. In the Windy City, they operate department stores, restaurants, grocery stores, and a number of service establishments. Because of sound, intelligent leadership and a penchant for economic independence, the Muslims have been one of the longest-lived black protest movements in the nation's history. (Their most illustrious prophet, Malcolm X, will be discussed later in this chapter.) Wallace D. Muhammad has continued his father's economic concern.

### World War II and After

On the eve of America's entry into World War II, the nation's blacks found themselves in a particularly taxing and unfortunate situation. In spite of the acknowledged and widely publicized shortage of labor, defense industries and war contractors adamantly refused to hire either skilled or unskilled blacks or to upgrade the meager number they had already taken on. Negro and white liberal newspapers and black and white organizations throughout the country denounced this discrimination as a practice worthy of a fascist nation. These protestations provoked some sympathetic responses from congressmen, the President, and other federal officials, but there was no effective remedial action forthcoming from Washington.

Finally, out of desperation, in the spring of 1941 Negroes decided to take matters into their own hands. Under the leadership of A. Philip Randolph, blacks began mobilizing throughout the country for a march on Washington. Buses were hired and trains were chartered to take some 50,000 to the nation's capital for a demonstration scheduled for July 1, 1941.[54] In New York City, alternatives to the march were discussed by Mayor Fiorello La Guardia, Mrs. Eleanor Roosevelt, Aubrey Williams of the National Youth Administration, Walter White of the NAACP, and Randolph, but no satisfactory agreement was reached. Just a few days before the critical date, however, Randolph and other leaders were called to Washington; they went, demanding the issuance of an executive order decreeing the end to discrimination in defense industries. President Roosevelt complied almost immediately with his famous Executive Order 8802, establishing the Fair Employment Practices Committee (FEPC).

The reaction of blacks to the FEPC was enthusiastic. Many hailed 8802 as the most significant document affecting Negroes since the Emancipation Proclamation. Some southern whites, on the other hand, were bitter. Mark Etheridge, a southerner and an original member of the committeee, declared:

> No power in the world—not even all the mechanized armies of the earth, Allied and Axis, could force the southern white people to the abandonment of the principle of social segregation.[55]

The committee had no real power to enforce its mandate, but the unfavorable publicity resulting from an enforced appearance before it caused many defense contractors to drop their ban on black employment. The FEPC went out of existence in 1945, but thereafter several of the states created permanent fair employment practices commissions.

In February 1942, James Farmer, then Race Relations Secretary of the Quaker-Pacifist Fellowship of Reconciliation, laid down guidelines for a new organization—the Congress of Racial Equality (CORE). In Farmer's thinking, the new group would pursue "positive and effective alternatives to violence as a technique for resolving conflict." CORE would seek to translate love of God and man, on the one hand, and hatred of injustice on the other, into specific action. The movement would be projected in a Gandhian direction and its techniques would be identified as "nonviolent direct action." Farmer therefore anticipated Martin Luther King, Jr., and the Student Nonviolent Coordinating Committee (SNCC) by more than a dozen years.

In June 1943 CORE staged the first publicized sit-in demonstration in the nation's history. For more than six months, an interracial group from the organization had been attempting to force a Chicago restaurant to serve black people. Finally some sixty-five persons, sixteen of whom were Negroes, entered the establishment, sat down and remained seated until they were served. During the 1950s CORE began to abandon its independent pursuits and joined in cooperative actions with other protest organizations.. In 1958 the organization was instrumental in ending discrimination against blacks in the commercial bakeries in St. Louis. By the early 1960s, however, the rather isolated activities of the organization were eclipsed by the thunder and din of Martin Luther King's triumphs and trials.

### Desegregation in the Postwar Period

In terms of protest activity, the largely postwar years from 1944 to 1954 were almost completely dominated by the successful activities of the legal defense arm of the NAACP. By the end of the decade the association's lawyers had clearly won *de jure* desegregation of tax-supported public facilities and institutions in the United States. As early as 1934 the association, under the new direction of Walter F. White, had dedicated itself to the overthrow of the degrading separate-but-equal doctrine of the *Plessy v. Ferguson* decision.[56] It created a new legal department and staffed it initially with Charles H. Houston and his cousin, William H. Hastie, both honor graduates of Amherst College and Harvard Law School. Some time later the services of the youthful Thurgood Marshall were acquired.

The first important victory of the new legal staff came in 1944 with the *Smith v. Allwright* decision, which struck down southern white primary laws—laws which kept blacks from participating in party primary elections.[57] Back in 1927 and 1932, the association lawyers had won initial actions against these laws in the federal courts, only to have them reversed in 1935. The *Smith v. Allwright* decision virtually reenfranchised Negroes in the southern states. In the matter of segregation and discrimination in institutions of higher education, lawyers for the association won limited actions against Maryland in 1936 and Missouri in 1938. During World War II the association concerned itself primarily with the rights and welfare of the hundreds of thousands of blacks in the nation's armed forces. After the war it resumed the fight against the separate-but-equal doctrine.

The basic objective of the association was to gain unrestricted admission to all tax-supported institutions of higher learning, regardless of where they were located. Beginning in 1946, Thurgood Marshall, then chief counsel for the association, brought actions on behalf of black applicants against southern white state universities on seven successive occasions. Victory was achieved in every instance, so that by 1953 separate-but-equal was a dead issue in institutions of higher learning.[58] The association now turned to segregation in elementary and secondary schools. To this end, it filed suit in five separate cases, hoping to have them decided by one umbrella decision of the U. S. Supreme Court.

The decision in the case of *Brown v. Board of Education* (1954) (popularly called the School Segregation Case) was historic for two reasons. First of all, it brought an end to the separate-but-equal doctrine as a standing principle of American constitutional law. Segregation in the common (public tax-supported primary and secondary) schools might thereafter exist, but it would not have the sanctity of law. Secondly, the decision relied more heavily on sociological and psychological data than it did on conventional legal precedent. In the famous "eleventh footnote" to its decision, the Court honored the black social psychologist, Kenneth B. Clark, by citing directly from the brief material prepared under his supervision. The 1954 decision was modified a year later in the Court's dictum of "all deliberate speed." This phrasing, alas, was to be the major cue to southern reaction—deliberate, slow—in the years ahead.

The 1954 decision in the *Brown* case filled Negroes with immense jubilation. The inevitable comparison with the Emancipation Proclamation was made. Going even further, the Chicago *Defender* declared:

> Neither the atom bomb nor the hydrogen bomb will ever be as meaningful to our democracy as the unanimous decision of the United States Supreme Court that racial segregation violates the spirit and letter of our Constitution.[59]

By the fall of 1955, however, the reaction had set in. Not only had the Court modified its position in the 1955 supplementary decision, but much of the white South remained adamant with regard to the separation of blacks and whites. A mood of depression set in among blacks; the promised land of desegregation seemed further away than ever. The system had failed them again. What could be done now?

The answer to this question was given rather dramatically by Mrs. Rosa Parks on December 1, 1955, in Montgomery, Alabama. When she refused to yield her seat to a white passenger on an intercity bus, she was arrested and charged with violating a city segregation ordinance. Word of Mrs. Parks's arrest spread quickly throughout the black community. Three young and obscure black ministers, two of whom were Martin Luther King, Jr., and Ralph Abernathy, picked up the story and moved immediately to organize Montgomery Negroes in support of Mrs. Parks. The decision was made to stage a twenty-four-hour boycott of all Montgomery buses. What began as a one-day boycott lasted for 382 days; it was to become one of the most effective extralegal campaigns ever waged by American Negroes against social injustice. After the successful conclusion of the boycott, young Martin Luther King, now nationally acclaimed, organized the Montgomery Improvement Association. King, who had been jailed during the course of the boycott, and his followers had given a dramatic demonstration of the value of passive resistance as a medium of social protest. In 1957 King went on to organize the Southern Christian Leadership Conference (SCLC) to broaden and nationalize work along the line of passive resistance.

It should not be forgotten that the road to success traveled by King and his organization had been paved by a decade of successful litigation against segregation and discrimination, as well as by countless individual and group assaults against the bastions of racism in the United States. Sufficient change had taken place in the social milieu so that a white South which might well have lynched King a generation earlier stopped short of it in 1955. The year 1957 was marked by the emergence of other factors directed at easing the social climate. That year the Congress of the United States enacted its first major civil rights legislation since 1883, and a President of the United States, Dwight D. Eisenhower, for the first time in eighty-one years, sent federal troops into the South to defend the constitutional rights of black citizens. Finally, in the summer of 1957, diplomatic representatives from Ghana, the first African former colony to join the United Nations, took up residence in New York City and Washington, D.C. "Black men from the old world had arrived just in time to help redress the racial balance in the new."[60]

Beneath its sometimes lofty rhetoric and emphasis on moral imperatives, the basic hard-nosed objective of the newly founded SCLC was the desegregation of all establishments and facilities catering to the public. Thus Reverend King and some of his followers were jailed again in October 1960, this time for attempting to desegregate a restaurant in Atlanta's leading department store. Desegregation was also the direct objective of the four black students who inaugurated the sit-in movement in Greensboro, North Carolina, in February 1960. Ten days later the sit-in tactic had been adopted by black students in fifteen cities in five southern states. The chief targets of the students were department stores which maintained segregated lunch facilities while welcoming Negro trade in other sections of the store. The black students also concentrated on segregated downtown eating establishments. They were spat upon, jeered at, chased, beaten, and even stomped upon, but their courage did not desert them. On April 15, 1960, the students organized themselves into the Student Nonviolent Coordinating Committee (SNCC) to carry on their work nationally. The high tide of SNCC activity was reached in September 1961 when, as estimated by the Southern Regional Council (SRC), more than 120 cities in 20 states had been involved and one or more establishments in 10 southern and border states had been desegregated. Some 70,000 students, black and white, were arrested during the campaigns.

In May 1961 the desegregation drive spread to carriers in interstate commerce. The directors of CORE sent "Freedom Riders" into the South purposely to violate segregation laws and practices in interstate transportation. After riding through several southern cities and towns, and even doubling back through some of them, a group of interracial riders was set upon and beaten by a mob in Montgomery, Alabama. A very bloody scene was narrowly averted by the timely appearance of approximately 600 deputy marshals and other federal officials dispatched by the U. S. Attorney General, Robert F. Kennedy. With emotions running high, the Freedom Riders were now joined by forces from SCLC and SNCC. A thousand new riders, white ministers and priests, and activist white liberals embarked southward. On September 22, 1961, largely through the intervention of the U. S. Attorney General, the Interstate Commerce Commission ruled that all passengers on interstate carriers were to be seated without regard to race and that all terminals must be operated on a nonsegregated basis. Desegregation had been carried one step further.

By the fall of 1962 the goals of Reverend King and his organization were moving beyond the limited scope of desegregation. SCLC was now looking toward the attainment of full freedom, justice, and dignity for the twenty million black people in the United States. King announced that he would lead racial demonstrations in Birmingham until "Pharaoh lets God's people go." He selected Birmingham because he felt that if that city could be cracked, the direction of the entire nonviolent movement in the South could take a significant turn. He said: "It was our faith that as 'Birmingham goes, so goes the South.' " Therefore on Good Friday, April 12, 1963, the Reverend Dr. King, defying a writ of injunction as well as the K-9 dogs of Police Chief Eugene "Bull" Connor, led a mass march down the main thoroughfare of the city, with the result that King and about fifty demonstrators were arrested. It was while in prison for this incident that King wrote his celebrated *Letter from a Birmingham Jail*, a reply to the charge of eight white Birmingham churchmen that he was an "interloper" who was disrupting the black community with "unwise" and "untimely" demonstrations.

But even as the "unwise" and "untimely" demonstrations in Birmingham began to wane, others of a more explosive and menacing nature were being set into motion, although not by Dr. King. On June 11, 1963, Medgar Evers, Field Secretary of the Mississippi NAACP, was shot dead by whites in front of his home. An immediate outcry throughout the land came from blacks as well as whites. Negro demonstrators went into the streets in every major city in the nation. They staged sit-ins in the offices of Mayor Robert Wagner of New York City and Governor Nelson Rockefeller of New York State. They closed down construction on buildings in Philadelphia and New York in which Negroes could not gain employment. They disrupted the operation of public school systems in protest against racial imbalances. With official Washington becoming increasingly disturbed and apprehensive, President John F. Kennedy delivered a fourteen-minute speech to the nation in which he declared that ". . . the fires of frustration and discord are burning in every city North and South. . . . We face, therefore, a moral crisis as a country and as a people."

Kennedy's speech was hailed by blacks and whites across the land but it did not perceptibly decrease the momentum of black protest. During July and August of 1963, the blacks were joined by a host of white supporters from all walks of life. One prominent white churchman exclaimed, "Some time or other, we are all going to have to stand and be on the receiving end of a fire hose." Black and white leaders worked together to sponsor a gigantic protest rally in the nation's capital. On August 28, 1963, nearly a quarter of a million people, black and white, from the North, South, East, and West, listened to a memorable speech by Dr. King, in which he said: "I have a dream that one day this nation will rise up and live out the true meaning of its creed." In the meantime President Kennedy sent some historic legislation to Congress that was enacted into law only after his death. This was the 1964 Civil Rights Act, which outlawed discrimination and segregation in all public accommodations and public facilities that affected interstate commerce.

## The Rise of Black Nationalist Organizations

By 1964 the black protest movement in the United States had taken on a life of its own. With the achievement of its immediate goals, the movement was fast becoming chaotic, directionless, and unmanageable. The temper of the times leaned toward militant black nationalism.

If Martin Luther King of Nobel Prize fame was out of step with this new trend in black thinking, there was one man who was not—Malcolm X of the Nation of Islam. On May 29, 1964, speaking to an interracial audience in New York City, Malcolm X said:

> Nowadays, as our people begin to wake up, they're going to realize they've been talking about Negro revolt. Negro revolution—you can't talk this stuff to me unless you're really for one. And most of you aren't. When the deal goes down, you back out every time.[61]

On April 8 he spoke on the "Black Revolution" at the Militant Labor Forum in New York City. The term Black Revolution was soon to become familiar in every household in the country.

In 1964 Malcolm X, whose original name was Malcolm Little, had been a member of the Nation of Islam for about sixteen years. He had been converted after his imprisonment for burglary in 1946. Upon his release in 1952, he rose swiftly through the ranks. In 1954 he was installed as Minister of the Temple in Harlem. During the next ten years Malcolm X literally became the nation's number-one Black Muslim. As he achieved this distinction, however, he fell out of step and thus out of favor with the leadership of the movement. In 1964 he made a clean break with the parent group and established the Organization of Afro-American Unity. On February 21, 1965, he died from an assassin's bullet. While Malcolm X achieved considerable renown before his death, his greatest acclaim came to him posthumously. Much of it was due to the image of him projected by Alex Haley, a gifted black writer, in *The Autobiography of Malcolm X*, a book that became almost required reading by young black and white militants alike.

Among the most avid readers of the *Autobiography* and of the Martinican psychiatrist Frantz Fanon's *Wretched of the Earth* were the young and restless members of SNCC. These students had suffered insults and risked their lives and limbs in battle for the rights of members of their race. Many of them had abandoned their own education in order to teach the less fortunate blacks of the South. Now they were beginning to lose faith in the system; they also feared that some blacks might "bargain" with the enemy and settle for less than full equality. It was against this setting that Stokely Carmichael, a young native of Trinidad and a graduate of Howard University, was elected president of SNCC. One of his first moves was to expel all of the white members and make SNCC an all-black movement.

In Chicago on July 28, 1966, Carmichael made a speech in which he said:

> When we form coalitions, we must say on what grounds we are going to form them. We must build pride among ourselves. We must think politically and get power because we are the only people in this country that are powerless. We are the only people who have to protect ourselves against our protectors. . . . We have got to get us some Black Power.[62]

Carmichael had used the term Black Power earlier that summer during a protest march in Mississippi, but after the Chicago speech it caught on among young blacks like wildfire, becoming the rallying cry of black militants and appearing as graffiti on thousands of walls in the land. Finally it was to be heard amidst the din of breaking glass and rifle shots during the long hot summers of 1966, 1967, and 1968.

To a great degree the civil rights gains achieved by black protest groups in the 1960s were by, for, and of the black middle class, even if things had not been intended to come out that way. Except for the suffrage, lower-class blacks did not benefit from their new freedom; they did not have the money to pay the prices in desegregated motels, hotels, and costly downtown restaurants, nor could they afford to send their children to colleges and universities, desegregated or otherwise. Speaking for himself and other black leaders, Bayard Rustin observed: "The answer to this problem is not to give the impoverished masses of the black ghetto sermons about middle-class virtue. It is to give them jobs and decent integrated housing and schools."[63] It was out of sheer desperation, therefore, that lower-class blacks "took to the streets." The violence-ridden summers of 1966, 1967, and 1968 focused national attention on the gut grievances of the black ghettos—malnutrition, substandard housing, poor schools, and unadulterated neglect. The central city was being abandoned to the blacks as whites scrambled frantically to the suburbs. Thus it was that the authors of the government-sponsored *Kerner Report* found that the nation was moving "toward two societies, one black and one white, separate and unequal." The *Report* warned that

> . . . frustrations of powerlessness have led some Negroes to the conclusion that there is no effective alternative to violence as a means of achieving redress of grievances and of moving the system.[64]

It concluded that these frustrations

> . . . are reflected in alienation and hostility toward the institutions of law and government and the white society which controls them and in the reach toward racial consciousness and solidarity reflected in the slogan, "Black Power."[65]

A critical exception to the prevailing hopelessness and despondency among blacks was the activity of Reverend Leon H. Sullivan, Pastor of Zion Baptist Church in Philadelphia. Inspired by the sit-in activities taking place in the Deep South, Sullivan and some 400 black preachers of Philadelphia organized the Selective Patronage Program in 1960. Consisting essentially of a succession of black boycotts of major businesses which gave less opportunity to black workers than to whites, the program met with great success. By 1963 it had opened up some 2,000 skilled jobs to black workers. In 1964 Sullivan went on to establish the Opportunities Industrialization Center (OIC), a job-training program for blacks and other minorities. The idea quickly earned the support of Philadelphia's black community, private industry, and ultimately that of the Federal Government. By 1967 OIC programs had been set up in upwards of eighty cities throughout the nation. It was to continue to grow. Some few years earlier Sullivan had been invited by Dr. Martin Luther King, Jr. to come to Atlanta and talk about his Selective Patronage Program to a group of local ministers. Sometime later King's own group, the SCLC, launched a similar program known as Operation Breadbasket. Under Reverend Jesse Jackson's leadership, the Chicago Operation Breadbasket was to achieve national acclaim. Jackson was a close associate of Dr. King, and after the latter's demise Jackson went on to become one of the top black leaders in the country.

The term Black Revolution, similar to its counterpart, Black Power, has been given so many definitions that by now it is virtually meaningless. In terms of the context in which it is usually employed, however, it is simply a modern nomenclature for a cyclical phenomenon—black nationalism. Viewed in this context, the term Black Revolution is not meant to advocate a revolution geared to the overthrow of an established political, economic, or social system, but one which would occur principally in "the minds and attitudes" of those subject to it. Unlike those of the past, the Black Revolution of the 1960s was both initiated and directed by people under 30 years of age: a group of young people who had absorbed the ideas of such writers and activists as Frantz Fanon, James Baldwin, LeRoi Jones (Imamu Amiri Baraka), Louis Lomax, and Malcolm X; a group who wore the Afro hair styles, the dashikis, and African jewelry. It was the younger blacks who most desperately sought black self-esteem and black identity and who worked so diligently to produce a new black life style.

The Black Revolution was new only in externals and rhetoric, not in basic ideology. As we have seen, debates on the relative merits of separation, integration, and emigration had engaged such black leaders as Paul Cuffee in the early nineteenth century; Dr. Martin Delany and other black militants during the 1840s and 1850s; Bishop Turner's group in the period from 1880 to 1900; and in the twentieth century, the Garveyites. Black Nationalism in the 1960s, however, was distinctive in one respect. It probably produced more black nationalist organizations than had any other comparable period in Negro history. Indeed, in 1964 there were more than two dozen such organizations in Harlem alone. Of all the black nationalist organizations of the period, the Black Panther Party is the most noteworthy.

In October 1966, at Oakland, California, the party was established by two young black militants, Bobby Seale and Huey P. Newton. Its name was a shortened form of Black Panther Party for Self-Defense, a group which had been formed in Lowndes County, Alabama, some six months earlier. The initial thrust of the Black Panther party was the maintenance of armed patrols on the streets of Oakland, California. Early in 1967 the party was able to enlist Eldridge Cleaver, author of *Soul on Ice*, as a supporter. (Cleaver was a former member of the Black Muslims and a friend and supporter of Malcolm X.) Both H. Rap Brown and Stokely Carmichael were party members for short periods. Within three years of its founding, the Panthers had become the best-known and the most formidable of all black nationalist movements in the country. They had established about thirty chapters throughout the country and had a membership of upwards of 5,000.

The party provided much of the leadership and inspiration for Afro-American societies in universities, colleges, and high schools. Very early in its history the party declared an important policy:

> We believe we can end police brutality in our black community by organizing black self-defense groups that are dedicated to defending our black community from racist police oppression and brutality.[66]

This activity was the basis for the party's running conflict with the law-enforcement agencies everywhere. Basically, however, the party rejected the stock rhetoric, jargon, and goals of typical black nationalist organizations. In opposing emigration, Newton declared:

> As far as we are concerned, we believe that it's important for us to recognize our origins and to identify with the revolutionary black people of Africa. . . . But as for us returning per se to the ancient customs, we don't see any necessity in this.[67]

The Black Panthers denounced black studies as "a new trick bag." They felt that although this type of program had initially been a "revolutionary step" in the right direction, " . . . many cultural, nationalist, opportunist bootlicking cowards and freaks have latched on to it."[68] At its convention in Philadelphia in 1970, the Panthers appeared to take a new direction. The antagonism toward the police was still present, but the new approach emphasized voter registration, political involvement, and free breakfast programs instead of shoot-outs and guerrilla warfare with the police. Nevertheless, Hilary Ng'weno, former editor of the *Daily Nation* in Nairobi (Kenya), felt that either way the Panthers faced extinction. He said:

> The Panthers have now been reduced to two alternative courses: annihilation by police gunfire, jail, and forced exile; or "respectable" existence devoid of revolutionary pretensions. The former may be heroic and the latter repugnant; both spell the same fate as far as the Black Panther Party is concerned.[69]

Manifestations of black nationalism have not been limited to the political arena. The outburst of Negro American creativity in the 1920s known as the Harlem Renaissance reflected the aesthetic side of the movement. Polemic was limited essentially to literature, however, with little manifestation of black social protest in the theater and even less in the areas of painting and sculpture.

During the 1960s, however, the impact of black nationalism upon Afro-American culture was to be far more pervasive. The young black poets of the decade were to become almost totally preoccupied with the concept of "black consciousness." Indeed, it was to become the dominant theme of the vibrant new black poetry created by such gifted artists as Don Lee, Nikki Giovanni, LeRoi Jones, Larry Neal, and Gwendolyn Brooks. Among the younger black novelists Richard Wright, who had flowered almost a generation earlier, was a major influence. In fact, no significant black work of the period was entirely to escape the influence of Wright's monumental *Native Son*. Ralph Ellison, John A. Williams, John O. Killens, and James Baldwin were among the leading black novelists. And while Ellison's *Invisible Man* was rated the most important black novel since publication of *Native Son*, James Baldwin was easily the dominant literary figure. His novels *Go Tell It on the Mountain* and *Another Country* and his essays *Fire Next Time* were read by millions of people, black and white alike.

Toward the end of the decade, however, Baldwin began to decline in popularity. He was deemed not "black" enough in point of view by militant critics. His position of preeminence among the new black literati was quickly filled by LeRoi Jones, now known as Imamu Amiri Baraka. Baraka was generally considered to be the most gifted black writer to emerge during the period. A poet as well as an essayist, he was to earn his greatest acclaim as a playwright. His plays included the prize-winning *The Dutchman*, *The Slave*, and *The Toilet*. His impact upon black literature was so pervasive that by the end of the decade he was being dubbed the "high priest of the black aesthetic." In 1965 Baraka set up the Black Arts Theater and School in Harlem. A year later he moved to Newark, New Jersey, where along with his cultural activities he was to become a power in local politics.

The Black Revolution moved into the New York theater chiefly through the productions of the Negro Ensemble Company (NEC). In the areas of painting and sculpture, several exhibitions of black art were held in cities such as Atlanta, New York, and Boston. All of them mirrored the Negro social protest. While the responses to the productions of the NEC and to black art were generally favorable, some serious questions were raised by professional critics. Martin Gottfried of the *The New York Times* complained:

> Professional and artistic standards are being compromised for the sake of black plays, playwrights, and actors; standards of writing, production, performance, and judgment are being lowered for blacks and it is prejudice all over again and this time for blacks.[70]

Picking up the issue a veteran black critic, Clayton Riley, replied:

> Black art will ultimately have to structure its own forms and usable value system. Duplicating the exhausted death-wish energies, the contradictions, and the shattered criteria of the American theatre—"an art form" now populated in exorbitant numbers with its own naked sagging bodies and equally shabby collective consciousness—brings the Black artist into a trap that all people of good will and good sense, Black and White, should avoid.

However, the creation of "new forms" and a "usable value system," that is, a black aesthetic, was to prove to be a formidable task. As the decade ended there was still no commonly accepted critical standard by which to adjudge the work of the black artist.

It was in the motion picture area, however, that the movement had its most dramatic impact. Gone from the scene were such slack-mouthed versions of Uncle Tom as Stepin Fetchit, Mantan Moreland, and Eddie "Rochester" Anderson. The so-called black film had made its debut and it was presenting black audiences with such new characters as Shaft, Nigger Charlie, and Superfly. The new films were popular enough but they did not meet universal approval. They tended to make heroes of black narcotics pushers, pimps, and miscellaneous hustlers. In the view of many observers they were producing new black stereotypes. Many others, however, mostly those connected with the motion picture industry, felt that the films were above all producing unprecedented opportunities for black directors, black producers, black technicians, and black actors. As the controversy continued there was the growing demand for the establishment of a Black Review Board.

## Education and the Black Experience

Perhaps there was no aspect of the Black Revolution of the 1960s that was more controversial or that involved more people directly than the matter of black studies. Actually, the serious study of black cultural and social history had been initiated more than half a century ago. In 1916 the Association for the Study of Negro Life and History began publishing the *Journal of Negro History*, which under the editorship of Carter G. Woodson became one of the major historical journals in the country. The teaching of black history per se dates back to the establishment of black schools in the South after the Civil War. The emphasis on the African background of American Negroes became prominent during the Harlem Renaissance. As a discipline, therefore, black studies have deep roots.

Whenever the black community enters a new cycle of black nationalism—for instance, during the Garvey period of the 1920s—there is a renewed demand for greater study and "celebration" of the "black experience." The current emphasis on black studies was begun by black students on predominantly white campuses after 1966. Black nationalist youths, emphasizing their "separatist" beliefs, established at various institutions organizations such as The United Black Students, The Association of African and Afro-American Students, The Onyx Society, Soul Students Advisory Council, and most frequently, Black Student Unions. The specific demands of these students varied from campus to campus and included the "open admission" of all black students applying for entrance, blanket subsidies for all black students, all-black student halls and dormitories, and moratoriums for failing grades. The one universal demand was for black studies.

In the spring of 1966, San Francisco State College offered a course in the study of black nationalism. The college expanded this offering during the academic year 1967–1968 into a full black-studies curriculum consisting of eleven courses for thirty-three units of credit. Toward the end of 1968 the black students, still not satisfied, demanded an all-black department with the power to grant a bachelor's degree in black studies. They also demanded the sole power to hire and fire the faculty of the department. The success of the black students at San Francisco State College (they were granted 90 percent of their demands) prompted similar efforts on predominantly white campuses throughout the country. When an Afro-American Institute and black dormitory, from which all white faculty and students were rigorously excluded, were established at Antioch College, Dr. Kenneth B. Clark, a black member of the Board of Trustees, resigned. He said: "Such racial distinctions are arbitrary, dangerously ignorant, and cruel. They are destructive and inimical to the goals of serious education."[71] Ultimately the Department of Health, Education, and Welfare ruled such segregration to be in violation of federal law, and they were discontinued.

Perhaps the most widely publicized and widely condemned of all the black student "putsches" was that which occurred at Cornell University, where at one point armed black students gave the university "one hour to live." The troubles at Cornell resulted in the resignation of several outstanding faculty members as well as that of the president.

The concepts and objectives of black studies in the 1960s moved far beyond the rather straightforward and uninvolved treatment of Negro history in previous years. There appear to be in the 1970s at least three distinct approaches to black studies. The first of these is the type adopted at Yale University in December 1968: basically an undergraduate interdisciplinary program in Afro-American Studies. There is no "black hegemony" or separate department, and the direction of the program has to conform to the academic standards of Yale University. The program was structured in line with the area-studies concept. The Yale program has become the model for several hundred colleges and universities which have adopted black studies programs.

The second type of black studies program could more aptly be called "Black Liberation Studies." It is a frank, unadorned, politicalization of black studies. Its basic objectives are to teach black students "new ideologies and philosophies" which will contribute to the development of "the Black Nation." One such program projected a course listed under the name Physical Education, and described as "Theory and practice in the use of small arms and hand-to-hand combat. Discussions in the proper use of force."[72] Under this type of program, the black students have generally demanded virtually complete autonomy, albeit with little success.

Last, there is the idea of the black university. Its advocates think in terms of a black academic institution in which the concept of a "universal black man" replaces the traditional one of "western man." The central focus of the black university is to be on the humanities. And in the development of a "black humanities," comparative studies of black expressions in music, drama, dance, and literature would all be placed in the context of a "universal black" way of life. There would be a reordering of the values, goals, and perspectives of all black students through *saturation*. Ultimately and ideally, the black student would come to understand, accept, utilize, and celebrate his blackness and "become as unself-conscious about it as his brethren on the ancestral continent."[73] The so-called Malcolm X University and the Center for Black Education in Washington, D.C. are ventures in the direction of the black university. The black university, however, is still largely an idea, or as its chief sponsor, Dr. Vincent Harding, describes it: "a concept in search of a concrete expression."[74]

## Trends in the 1970s

With the exception of Martin Luther King, Jr., and Malcolm X, perhaps the most dynamic black leader to emerge during the decade of the 1960s was Whitney M. Young. Young became the Executive Director of the National Urban League in 1961 upon the retirement of Lester Granger. During the nine-year period between 1961 and 1970, Young brought about a tremendous expansion and revitalization in the work, power, and influence of the league. In 1969 the national headquarters and individual chapters expended a total of some thirty-five million dollars. There were autonomous chapters of the league in ninety-seven cities throughout the country. Under Young the National Urban League became one of the most powerful and prestigious private organizations in the country, black or white.

Even apart from his connections with the league, Young was recognized as one of the top black leaders in the nation. In this role, Young, at the sixtieth anniversary meeting of the league, made what several black leaders thought to be a bid to head up a long-heralded coalition of the nation's black leaders. The bid was rejected out of hand. Young's leadership had never set too well with youthful black militants who frequently dubbed him "Whitey Young" or "Uncle Whitney." Nevertheless, Young's prestige at the time of his premature death by drowning in 1971 (while in Lagos, Nigeria, where he had been attending a conference designed to improve communications between Africans and Afro-Americans) was still high among both the black middle class and the black rank and file. As a kind of modern-day "accommodationist," he was a chief spokesman for the black majority that still elects to work within the system.

Young was succeeded as executive director of the league on June 15, 1971, by

Vernon E. Jordan, Executive Director of the United Negro College Fund (UNCF). A lawyer by profession, Jordan served as chief of the Voter Education Project of the Southern Regional Council from 1966 to 1969. During this period he directed voter registration campaigns which helped to add hundreds of thousands of black voters to the rolls in the southern states. He became head of the UNCF in January 1970 and had served there for a year before Young's death.

Another important figure in current black leadership is Roy Wilkins, who became the Executive Director of the NAACP on the death of Walter F. White in 1955. During the ensuing ten years, both Wilkins and his dedicated organization were overshadowed by the activities of Reverend King and the SCLC, by Young and the revitalized National Urban League, and most of all, by the noise and din of the Black Revolution. Nevertheless, the NAACP continued on its traditional path, remaining wedded to the principles of integration and peaceful change rather than violence and separation or emigration. As Wilkins put it:

> Given the position of the Negro American population as a numerical minority of one-tenth and an economic, political, and social minority of far less than one-tenth, the only tactical road for the black minority is integration into the general population.[75]

The NAACP has been shunted aside before; for example, during the Garvey period and during the 1930s by the Communist party successes among blacks. The association has always regarded black flirtations with violence, separation, or emigration as temporary aberrations. With the demise of the Black Revolution of the 1960s clearly apparent on the horizon, the NAACP may find itself once again pointing the direction for the black protest movement.

The atmosphere of the 1970s is calmer, more sober, more conservative, in response to a less sympathetic political climate and greater pressures from inflation, recession, and loss of funds for minority-oriented betterment programs. After a decade of popular support for civil rights and minority economic and political advancement, erosion of hard-won progress became a trend in the 1970s. Even so obvious an issue as the South Boston school integration controversy has been met with relatively low-key responses from black organizations, despite their quiet determination to resist re-segregation.

The mid-seventies, in short, have become a time of trying to hold on to past gains, rather than to win new power. Newly-won minority jobs are endangered by seniority rules as retrenchment occurs. The pace of entry into higher-level positions slows down and the fight for new gains runs out of steam when a loss of existing employment becomes a reality. *The New York Times* in 1975 reported that Reverend Jesse L. Jackson's PUSH was seen by some as a local organization rather than a national one.[76]

With reductions in foundation and government funds, employees of civil rights organizations cannot be maintained at full force.

Still, tension is occasionally high, and the familiarity with protest techniques makes it easy for sporadic protests to take place.

# Notes

1. Frederick Douglass, *Life and Times of Frederick Douglass* (Boston, DeWolfe, Fiske and Co., 1898), p. 341.
2. Winfield Scott, *Memoirs of Lieutenant-General Winfield Scott*, I (New York, Sheldon Co., 1864), pp. 23–24.
3. Harvey Wish, "American Slave Insurrections before 1861," *Journal of Negro History*, XXII (1937), pp. 304–06.
4. For a definitive treatment of this story see: Christopher Martin, *The Amistad Affair* (London, Abelard Schuman, 1970).
5. Herbert Aptheker, *American Negro Slave Revolts* (New York, Columbia University Press, 1943), p. 143.
6. Marion J. Russell, "American Slave Discontent in the High Courts," *Journal of Negro History*, XXXI (1946), p. 392 ff.
7. Aptheker, *op. cit.*, pp. 41–42.
8. See, for example, John Henrik Clarke, ed., *William Styron's Nat Turner: Ten Black Writers Respond* (Boston, Beacon Press, 1968).
9. Aptheker, *op. cit.*, p. 49.
10. Leon F. Litwack, *North of Slavery* (Chicago, University of Chicago, 1961), p. 9.
11. H. N. Sherwood, "Paul Cuffee," *Journal of Negro History*, VIII (1923), pp. 162–66.
12. Litwack, *op. cit.*, p. 191 ff.
13. Herbert Aptheker, *A Documentary History of the Negro People in the United States*, II (New York, The Citadel Press, 1967), p. 19.
14. Sherwood, *op. cit.*, pp. 167–73.
15. Bella Gross, *Clarion Call* (New York, B. Gross, 1947), p. 4.
16. *Ibid.*, p. 5.
17. *Ibid.*, p. 6.
18. Carter G. Woodson, *The Mind of the Negro* (Washington, D.C., The Association for the Study of Negro Life and History, 1926), p. 160.
19. Herbert Aptheker, *One Continual Cry, David Walker's Appeal* (New York, Humanities Press, 1965).
20. *Ibid.*, p. 131.
21. *Ibid.*, p. 89.
22. Gross, *op. cit.*, p. 10 ff.
23. Litwack, *op. cit.*, p. 239.
24. Gross, *op. cit.*, p. 43.
25. Howard W. Bell, "National Negro Conventions of the Middle 1840's: Moral Suasion vs. Political Action," *Journal of Negro History*, XLII (1957), p. 251.
26. *Ibid.*
27. Litwack, *op. cit.*, p. 251.
28. *Ibid.*, p. 266.
29. *Ibid.*, p. 265.
30. Douglass, *op. cit.*, p. 355.
31. John H. Bracy, Jr., August Meier, and Elliott Rudwick, eds., *Black Nationalism in America* (New York, Bobbs Merrill Company, Inc., 1970), pp. 177–81, 110–13.
32. John G. Van Deusen, "The Exodus of 1879," *Journal of Negro History*, XXI (1936), p. 111 ff.
33. *Ibid.*, p. 119.
34. Mozell C. Hill, "The All-Negro Communities of Oklahoma," *Journal of Negro History*, XXXI (1946), pp. 260–63.

35. *Ibid.*, pp. 264–68.
36. Edwin S. Redkey, *Black Exodus* (New Haven, Yale University Press, 1969), pp. 38–39.
37. *Ibid.*, p. 34.
38. George B. Tindall, *South Carolina Negroes: 1877–1900* (Columbia, S.C., University of South Carolina Press, 1952), p. 154.
39. Redkey, *op. cit.*, pp. 102–07.
40. For a good account of this episode, see *ibid.*, pp. 154–60.
41. *Ibid.*, p. 19 ff.
42. Robert H. Brisbane, *The Black Vanguard* (Valley Forge, Judson Press, 1970), p. 37.
43. *Ibid.*
44. William E. B. DuBois, *Dusk of Dawn: Essay Toward an Autobiography of a Race Concept* (New York, Harcourt, Brace and World, Inc., 1940), pp. 87–88.
45. Charles F. Kellogg, *NAACP, A History of the National Association for the Advancement of Colored People* (Baltimore, Johns Hopkins University Press, 1967), p. 44 ff.
46. John Hope Franklin, *From Slavery to Freedom* (New York, Alfred A. Knopf, 1967), p. 441.
47. Brisbane, *op. cit.*, p. 81 ff.
48. *Ibid.*
49. *Ibid.*, p. 96.
50. Benjamin Gitlow, *I Confess* (New York, E. P. Dutton and Co., 1940), p. 480.
51. Brisbane, *op. cit.*, p. 149.
52. Ralph Bunche, "The Programs, Ideologies, Tactics and Achievements of Negro Betterment and Interracial Organizations," *The Negro in America*, II (Unpublished ms. Carnegie-Myrdal Study), pp. 319–30.
53. C. Eric Lincoln, *The Black Muslims in America* (Boston, Beacon Press, 1961), pp. 106–8.
54. Brisbane, *op. cit.*, p. 166.
55. *Ibid.*, p. 171.
56. 163 U.S. 537 (1896).
57. 321 U.S. 649 (1944).
58. Brisbane, *op. cit.*, pp. 238–39.
59. *The Chicago Defender*, May 18, 1954.
60. John Hope Franklin, *op. cit.*, p. 622.
61. George Breitman, *The Last Year of Malcolm X* (New York, Merit Publishers, 1967), p. 31.
62. Bracy, *et al.*, *op. cit.*, pp. 475–76.
63. Benjamin Muse, *The American Negro Revolution, 1963 to 1967* (Bloomington, Indiana University Press, 1969) p. 109.
64. Hugh Davis Graham and Ted Robert Gurr, *The History of Violence in America: A Report to the National Commission on the Causes and Prevention of Violence* (New York, Bantam Books, 1969).
65. *Ibid.*
66. Bracy, *et al.*, *op. cit.*, p. 533.
67. Theodore Draper, *The Rediscovery of Black Nationalism* (New York, The Viking Press, 1970), p. 105.
68. *Ibid.*, p. 106.
69. *The New York Times*, October 2, 1970, p. 35.
70. *Ibid.*, June 7, 1970, Section 2, p. 1.
71. A. Philip Randolph Educational Fund, *Black Studies: Myths and Realities* (New York, Current Educational Fund Publications, 1969), p. 32.
72. Draper, *op. cit.*, p. 153.
73. Stephen Henderson, "Toward the Black University," Part II, *Ebony*, September 1970, p. 112.
74. Vincent Harding, "Toward the Black University," Part I, *ibid.*, August 1970, p. 157.
75. Roy Wilkins, "Integration," *ibid.*, p. 54.
76. *The New York Times*, January 5, 1975, p. 43.

# BIBLIOGRAPHY

## Articles

Bell, Howard W., "National Negro Conventions of the Middle 1840's: Moral Suasion vs. Political Action." *Journal of Negro History*, XLII (1957), p. 251.

Harding, Vincent, "Toward the Black University," Part I. *Ebony*, August 1970, p. 157.

Henderson, Stephen, "Toward the Black University," Part II. *Ebony*, September 1970, p. 112.

Hill, Mozell C. "The All-Negro Communities of Oklahoma." *Journal of Negro History*, XXXI (1946), pp. 260–63.

Russell, Marion J. "American Slave Discontent in the High Courts." *Journal of Negro History*, XXXI (1946), p. 392.

Sherwood, H.N., "Paul Cuffee." *Journal of Negro History*, VIII (1923), 162–66.

Van Deusen, John G., "The Exodus of 1879." *Journal of Negro History*, XXI (1936), p. 111.

Wilkins, Roy, "Integration." *Ebony*, August 1970, p. 54.

Wish, Harvey, "American Slave Insurrections before 1861." *Journal of Negro History*, XXII (1937), pp. 304–06.

## Unpublished Works

Bunche, Ralph V., "The Programs, Ideologies, Tactics and Achievements of Negro Betterment and Interracial Organizations." *The Negro in America*, II (Unpublished ms. Carnegie-Myrdal Study), pp. 319–30.

## Books and Pamphlets

Aptheker, Herbert, *American Negro Slave Revolts*, New York, Columbia University Press, 1943.

———, *A Documentary History of the Negro People in the United States*, I. New York, The Citadel Press, 1967.

———, *One Continual Cry, David Walker's Appeal*. New York, Humanities Press, 1965.

Bracy, John H., Jr.; Meier, August, and Rudwick, Elliott, eds., *Black Nationalism in America*. New York, Bobbs Merrill Company, Inc., 1970.

Breitman, George, *The Last Year of Malcolm X*. New York, Merit Publishers, 1967.

Brisbane, Robert H., *The Black Vanguard*. Valley Forge, Judson Press, 1970.

Clarke, **John** Henrik, *William Styron's Nat Turner: Ten Black Writers Respond*. Boston, Beacon Press, 1968.

Douglass, Frederick, *Life and Times of Frederick Douglass*. Boston, DeWolfe Fiske and Co., 1898.

Draper, Theodore, *The Rediscovery of Black Nationalism*. New York, The Viking Press, 1970.

DuBois, William E. B., *Dusk of Dawn: Essay Toward an Autobiography of a Race Concept.* New York, Harcourt, Brace and World, Inc., 1940.

Franklin, John Hope, *From Slavery to Freedom.* New York, Alfred Knopf, 1967.

Gitlow, Benjamin, *I Confess.* New York, E. P. Dutton and Co., 1940.

Graham, Hugh D., and Gurr, Ted R. *The History of Violence in America: A Report to the National Commission on the Causes and Prevention of Violence.* New York, Bantam Books, 1969.

Gross, Bella, *Clarion Call.* New York, B. Gross, 1947.

Kellogg, Charles F. *NAACP: A History of the National Association for the Advancement of Colored People.* Baltimore, The Johns Hopkins University Press, 1967.

Lincoln, C. Eric, *The Black Muslims in America.* Boston, Beacon Press, 1961.

Litwack, Leon F., *North of Slavery.* Chicago, University of Chicago Press, 1961.

Martin, Christopher, *The Amistad Affair.* London, Abelard Schuman, 1970.

Randolph, A. Philip Educational Fund, *Black Studies: Myths and Realities.* New York, Current Educational Fund Publications, 1969.

Redkey, Edwin S., *Black Exodus.* New Haven, Yale University Press, 1969.

Scott, Winfield, *Memoirs of Lieutenant-General Winfield Scott,* I. New York, Sheldon Co., 1864.

Tindall, George Brown, *South Carolina Negroes, 1877–1900.* Columbia, S.C., University of South Carolina Press, 1952.

Woodson, Carter G. *The Mind of the Negro as Reflected in Letters Written during the Crisis, 1800–1860.* Washington, D.C., The Association for the Study of Negro Life and History, Inc., 1926.

# 17

## The Black Role in American Politics: Part I, The Present

### Hugh H. Smythe and Carl B. Stokes

At a meeting of black political leaders in Chicago in 1971, John Cashin, a black dentist, was congratulated on his remarkable showing in gaining nearly a third of the vote when he ran for Governor of Alabama the year before. But he quickly focused attention on something he considered much more significant. "We have four black coroners in Alabama now,"[1] he pointed out, indicating that victories in the races for lesser offices were a matter blacks should value as much as progress on the higher levels. Cashin went on to explain why blacks have turned their energies, interests, and talents to politics and the search for political office in the United States: that they have learned to recognize political power as useful and valuable, not as an end in itself but as an effective means of obtaining justice, dignity, and respect, and for gaining their long-sought entry into the mainstream of American society.

The interest, effort, and participation of blacks in contemporary politics form a mosaic that defies simple labeling. There is now deeper concern about presidential candidates. New groups have emerged and gained power; old organizations have become more politically active. Efforts in fund raising to finance black candidates and other candidates who are responsive to black needs, have increased. There is a new awareness of the value, significance, and limitations of the black vote. Moves to unify, solidify, and consolidate the divergent groups in the black electorate are prevalent. There is greater understanding of the practical and positive implications of radical elements and black nationalism.

The role of women has come to the fore, along with concern over how the new youth vote which came into being with the lowering of the voting age to eighteen may best be turned to useful ends. Another important issue is how best to utilize and assist the vote of the black elderly. There is wider comprehension of the relation of politics to such government institutions as the Supreme Court; the White House; federal, state, and local agencies; and legislatures. No longer are chances for victory negligible if a black stands for a major political office; and blacks know they can have telling impact in the making of appointments, even in some of the highest offices.

Blacks now tend to use the weapon of protest with greater skill and knowledge, and know more about the intricacies and effect of redistricting and reapportionment of voting districts. They can judge more critically the credibility of candidates and office-holders, and have come to be wary of racial polarization on the political front as well as elsewhere. They now scrutinize with greater care all shades of political opinion, whether conservative, liberal, radical, or otherwise, to see how each can be beneficial or harmful to the cause of obtaining full equality for blacks.

In addition, they are aware of the dynamics of factionalism both among themselves and in the larger political arena, and have better insight into the nature of coalitions. They attentively observe voting trends, giving more heed to issues which affect their individual lives, such as busing to achieve school integration and laws and rulings against discrimination in employment, housing, or public accommodations. They focus on how urban planning and redevelopment will affect them, and keep a wary eye on the enforcement of voting and other civil rights laws. Above all, they have no illusions about the true extent of their power and strength on both the national and local levels. It is against this broad panorama that we shall examine the political scene of the 1970s.

## Political Base[2]

In spite of some unusual victories in a few of our large cities during the late 1960s and early 1970s, blacks still consider a black constituency necessary for the election of nonwhites. In the United States race remains a factor in the voting preferences of the masses of whites. With few exceptions, where blacks have triumphed there is a sizable black base. This is true even for appointment to public office, as in the case of the mayor of Washington, D. C., a city whose nonwhite population of more than 70 percent almost required Republican President Richard M. Nixon to reappoint a black mayor first put in office by a Democratic president.

This position is now elective. The increasingly heavy concentration of blacks in a number of cities has encouraged more and more blacks to stand for election on all levels, with growing success. As of April 1974, only five of the fifty states were without at least one black elected official. (See Table I.)

This success occurred not simply because of numbers, but because blacks had gained more political sophistication. Realizing the need for cooperation, they had formed coalitions and learned to make use of established institutions in the black community. The late Reverend Martin Luther King's Southern Christian Leadership Conference (SCLC) and a more recent organization, People United to Save Humanity (PUSH), are examples of this trend. Old-line organizations, such as the nonpolitical National Association for the Advancement of Colored People (NAACP) and the largely job-oriented National Urban League, began to take a firmer political stance.

The black political base, furthermore, has been strengthened by the awareness churned up by young black militants. Although some disapproved of the militant pursuit of separatism and black nationhood, it can hardly be denied that their "awful roar of struggle," as Frederick Douglass called it, has helped to awaken the black masses to

**TABLE I—BLACK ELECTED OFFICIALS IN THE UNITED STATES AS OF APRIL 1974**

| | Total | Federal | | State | | | County | | Municipal | | | | | Law Enforcement | | | | Education | | |
|---|---|---|---|---|---|---|---|---|---|---|---|---|---|---|---|---|---|---|---|---|
| | | Senator | Representatives | State Executives | Senators | Representatives | Commissioners, Supervisors, Councilmen | Other County Officials | Mayors | Vice Mayors | Mayors Pro Tem | Councilmen, Aldermen, Commissioners | Other Local Officials | Judges, Justices, Magistrates | Chiefs of Police, Constables, Marshals, Sheriffs | Justices of the Peace | Other Law Enforcement Officials | State And College Boards | Local School Boards | Other Education Officials |
| Alabama | 149 | · | · | · | · | 3 | 9 | 8 | 8 | · | 1 | 47 | 1 | 1 | 51 | · | 4 | · | 16 | · |
| Alaska | 6 | · | · | · | · | 2 | · | · | · | · | · | 1 | · | · | · | · | · | · | 3 | · |
| Arizona | 10 | · | · | · | · | 2 | · | · | · | 1 | · | 1 | · | · | 1 | · | · | 1 | 4 | · |
| Arkansas | 150 | · | · | · | 1 | 3 | 19 | 1 | 8 | 1 | · | 54 | 11 | · | · | · | · | · | 52 | · |
| California | 132 | · | 3 | 1 | 1 | 6 | · | · | 6 | 4 | · | 28 | 10 | 15 | · | · | · | 8 | 50 | · |
| Colorado | 13 | · | · | · | 1 | 3 | · | · | 1 | · | · | 4 | · | 3 | · | · | · | · | 1 | · |
| Connecticut | 50 | · | · | · | 1 | 5 | · | · | · | · | · | 27 | 4 | · | 4 | · | · | · | 9 | · |
| Delaware | 8 | · | · | · | 1 | 2 | · | · | · | 1 | · | 4 | · | · | · | · | · | · | · | · |
| District of Columbia | 8 | · | 1 | · | · | · | · | · | · | · | · | · | · | · | · | · | · | · | 7 | · |
| Florida | 73 | · | · | · | · | 3 | 1 | · | 3 | 10 | · | 51 | 1 | 1 | · | · | · | · | 3 | · |
| Georgia | 137 | · | 1 | · | 2 | 14 | 8 | 1 | 2 | 2 | · | 67 | 1 | 1 | · | 5 | 1 | · | 31 | 1 |
| Idaho | 1 | · | · | · | · | · | · | · | · | · | · | 1 | · | · | · | · | · | · | · | · |
| Illinois | 152 | · | 2 | · | 5 | 14 | 3 | · | 7 | · | · | 58 | 8 | 14 | · | · | · | 1 | 40 | · |
| Indiana | 55 | · | · | · | 1 | 6 | 2 | 1 | 1 | · | · | 24 | 2 | 3 | 2 | 2 | · | · | 11 | · |
| Iowa | 9 | · | · | · | · | 1 | · | · | · | · | · | 3 | · | 1 | · | · | · | · | 4 | · |
| Kansas | 25 | · | · | · | 1 | 4 | 1 | · | 2 | · | · | 9 | · | 1 | · | · | · | · | 7 | · |
| Kentucky | 59 | · | · | · | 1 | 2 | 2 | · | 2 | · | · | 41 | · | 2 | 2 | · | · | · | 7 | · |
| Louisiana | 149 | · | · | · | · | 8 | 32 | · | 4 | 2 | · | 36 | · | 2 | 14 | 10 | · | · | 41 | · |
| Maine | 5 | · | · | · | · | 1 | · | · | · | · | · | 2 | 1 | · | · | · | · | · | 1 | · |
| Maryland | 65 | · | 1 | · | 4 | 15 | 1 | · | 4 | 1 | · | 27 | · | 5 | · | · | 2 | · | 5 | · |

| | | Federal | | State | | | County | | Municipal | | | | | Law Enforcement | | | | Education | | |
|---|---|---|---|---|---|---|---|---|---|---|---|---|---|---|---|---|---|---|---|---|
| State | Total | Senator | Representatives | State Executives | Senators | Representatives | Commissioners, Supervisors, Councilmen | Other County Officials | Mayors | Vice Mayors | Mayors Pro Tem | Councilmen, Aldermen, Commissioners | Other Local Officials | Judges, Justices, Magistrates | Chiefs of Police, Constables, Marshals, Sheriffs | Justices of the Peace | Other Law Enforcement Officials | State And College Boards | Local School Boards | Other Education Officials |
| Massachusetts | 23 | 1 | | | | 5 | | | | | | 6 | 4 | | | | | 1 | 6 | |
| Michigan | 194 | | 2 | 1 | 2 | 11 | 24 | 4 | 7 | 6 | | 43 | 17 | 20 | 2 | | | 8 | 47 | |
| Minnesota | 8 | | | | 1 | 1 | | | | | | 1 | | 2 | | | | | 3 | |
| Mississippi | 191 | | | | | 1 | 8 | 18 | 7 | 1 | | 61 | 22 | | 23 | 19 | 1 | | 30 | |
| Missouri | 93 | | 1 | | 2 | 13 | 3 | 1 | 4 | | | 36 | 7 | 10 | 2 | | | | 14 | |
| Nebraska | 2 | | | | 1 | | | | | | | | | | | | | | 1 | |
| Nevada | 6 | | | | 1 | 2 | | | | | | | | 1 | | | | | 1 | 1 |
| New Hampshire | 1 | | | | | | | | | | | | | | | | | | 1 | |
| New Jersey | 152 | | | | 1 | 6 | 4 | | 8 | 2 | 1 | 49 | 2 | | | | | 1 | 78 | |
| New Mexico | 4 | | | | | 1 | | | | 1 | | 2 | | | | | | | | |
| New York | 174 | | 2 | | 3 | 11 | 9 | | 1 | 3 | | 13 | 1 | 26 | | | | | 105 | |
| North Carolina | 159 | | | | | 3 | 7 | | 8 | 10 | | 95 | | 2 | | | | | 34 | |
| Ohio | 139 | | 1 | | 2 | 9 | 2 | 1 | 8 | 1 | | 70 | 6 | 14 | 1 | | | 2 | 22 | |
| Oklahoma | 66 | | | | 1 | 3 | | | 6 | 1 | | 23 | 10 | 1 | | | | | 20 | 1 |
| Oregon | 6 | | | | 1 | 1 | | | | | | 1 | | | | | | | 3 | |
| Pennsylvania | 83 | | 1 | 1 | 2 | 11 | | 2 | | | | 19 | | 25 | 4 | 1 | 1 | | 16 | |
| Rhode Island | 7 | | | | | 1 | | | | | | 2 | | | | | | | 4 | |
| South Carolina | 116 | | | | | 3 | 18 | 2 | 6 | | | 51 | | 12 | | | | | 24 | |
| Tennessee | 87 | | | | 2 | 7 | 28 | 1 | | 1 | | 26 | | 2 | 1 | 5 | | | 14 | |
| Texas | 124 | | 1 | | | 8 | | | 4 | 4 | | 50 | 1 | 2 | 3 | 2 | | 2 | 47 | |
| Vermont | 2 | | | | 1 | | | | | | | 1 | | | | | | | | |
| Virginia | 63 | | | | 1 | 1 | 15 | 2 | 1 | 8 | | 30 | 1 | 3 | 1 | | | | | |
| Washington | 15 | | | | 1 | 1 | | 1 | | 1 | | 6 | 1 | | 1 | | | | 3 | |
| West Virginia | 5 | | | | | | | | | | | | | 1 | | 4 | | | | |
| Wisconsin | 14 | | | | 1 | 2 | 3 | | | | | 6 | 1 | 1 | | | | | | |
| Wyoming | 1 | | | | | | | | | | | | | | | | | | 1 | |
| TOTALS | 2991 | 1 | 16 | 3 | 40 | 196 | 200 | 42 | 108 | 62 | | 1080 | 110 | 172 | 111 | 48 | 9 | 24 | 767 | 2 |

Prepared by Office of Research, Joint Center for Political Studies
1426 H Street, N.W., Washington, D.C. 20005

Reprinted by permission from *National Roster of Black Elected Officials*, 1974 edition. Copyright © 1974 Joint Center for Political Studies. 

their plight and to the need for political power. The larger white world as well has been disconcerted and awakened as blacks have pressed forward toward the mainstream of American society.

As some of the youth groups, like the Congress of Racial Equality (CORE) and the Student Nonviolent Coordinating Committee (SNCC), began to lose their force and fervor, other groups, such as the Law Students Civil Rights Research Council and the black power movement in sports emerged. Young blacks, abetted by the lowering of the voting age to eighteen, began to coalesce with organizations which included other ethnic and religious elements and a variety of shades of political opinion, such as the National Youth Caucus, Frontlash, and the Emergency Conference for New Voters. Some black youths concluded that it was to their advantage to take aid from any legitimate source offering help, such as the Young Socialist Alliance. The black elderly were also recognized as a resource to be drawn upon, and the National Caucus on the Black Aged was created. Women began to make themselves felt in 1968 with the election of the first black woman to the House of Representatives, Democrat Shirley Chisholm of Brooklyn, New York.

### Strategy and Tactics[3]

With the 1960s came a growing awareness among blacks that if they were to move into the mainstream of American life, they must try to get the most possible from the two major political parties which had heretofore offered them only token rewards. Thus the civil rights and black liberation movements decided to develop new political tactics and strategies. Ways and means to implement such strategies were imperative, and one of the first steps taken was to make a survey of the black population.

As of 1970 little more than a million blacks remained on farms; more than half the black population had settled in fifty cities across the nation, and in six—Washington, D. C.; Atlanta, Georgia; Gary, Indiana; Newark, New Jersey; Compton, California; and East St. Louis, Illinois—they were in a majority or approaching it. In an additional twenty they comprised from 30 to 46 percent of the total population. Yet they were realistic enough to know that mere concentration was no guarantee of the election of blacks to office; organizing and getting out the potential vote was essential. Increasingly they recognized that although they had for a generation consistently supported the Democratic party, giving about 90 percent of their vote in national and local elections and providing margins of victory for Democrats in campaigns around the country, they had never had influence in party affairs in any way commensurate with their loyalty.

The survey also revealed that only 211, or 5.5 percent of the 3,049 delegates at the 1968 Chicago Convention had been black, while in 1964 they had constituted only two percent of the constituency. Blacks recalled that their past demands for more reasonable representation on delegations from several southern states had been rejected, and that in reality black Democrats had almost nothing to say on such matters as the selection of the presidential candidate or the formulation of the party platform and program, even though they represented seven million Democratic votes, about 20 percent of the total.

Aware of this disparity, and in light of the forthcoming national elections, a group headed by black Mayor Richard G. Hatcher of Gary, Indiana, early in 1972 caucused with Chairman Lawrence O'Brien of the Democratic National Committee. Demands were presented for fair representation on all staff, convention, and budget committees, and on delegate slates supporting presidential aspirants. The need for financial support for black candidates in 1972 congressional and local elections was specified, along with a greater effort to elect blacks to the Senate in such heavily black states as Ohio and Michigan. National Committee pressure on state parties to redistrict and reapportion, with an eye toward broadening rather than limiting black participation, was also demanded. When it was made plain that Hatcher's group was prepared to consider boycotting the national convention, forming a new party, or sitting out the national convention, agreement was reached. The tactic of sitting out the campaign was de-emphasized throughout, however, as the black spokesmen were conscious that power is exercised only by those holding the cards.

Black politicians advanced several ploys for the 1972 elections. The "single candidate" strategy was advocated by some who felt a black candidate should seek the Democratic presidential nomination, but knew that the weakness of black Republicans precluded a similar strategy in that party. Congresswoman Chisholm announced her candidacy early in 1972, aware that she stood little or no chance but offering a nucleus around which to rally a political movement that could attain power in the 1970s.

Then there was the commitment strategy. Some thought it would be better to use their delegate strength to extract firm pledges from a white presidential candidate for more black judgeships; cabinet posts; chairmanships of such agencies as the Securities and Exchange Commission, Federal Trade Commission, Federal Communications Commission, Federal Reserve Bank; and other traditionally nonblack positions in the nation's power structure. Further, black delegates would seek firm promises on the sixty-one recommendations for administrative action, designed to remedy black deprivation, delivered to President Nixon by the Congressional Black Caucus in March 1971.

Georgia State Representative Julian Bond had a third strategic approach. He proposed running black "favorite-son" candidates in Democratic primaries in states with large black populations. This would commit black voters to the leading black public official in the state who would then hopefully arrive at the Democratic convention with a large number of delegate votes. Knowing, however, that new party rules had virtually outlawed favorite sons, Bond indicated that his tactic was really meant to form a power bloc at the Miami Democratic National Convention later in the summer to secure concessions from the party and its presidential aspirants. He also believed that his strategy would increase local black political involvement, develop a stronger political base, be less expensive then trying to field a single black candidate, allow greater local autonomy for black politicians, and reduce the danger of what he called "personality politics." The Washington, D. C. nonvoting delegate in Congress, Walter Fauntroy, decided to employ the favorite-son plan to manipulate his voting delegates at the National Democratic Convention to select a presidential candidate.

## National Party Politics[4]

A fourth major strategy was to form a black political party that would be ready to declare itself by 1976. This idea was not new; it had been put forward as long ago as 1904 by the then National Liberal Party which ran black George Edwin Taylor unsuccessfully for the presidency, and there have been several other black parties in the past. Playwright LeRoi Jones, now known as Imamu Amiri Baraka, head of the African Nationalist party operating out of New Jersey, has been a leading proponent of this plan. It has had backing as well from some blacks throughout the nation who have sensed that they were not receiving equitable treatment by either Democrats or Republicans. This feeling gave rise in some states to the formation of local political units, especially in the South, which in the 1960s and early 1970s saw the formation, among others, of the United Citizens party led by Mrs. Victoria DeLee in South Carolina, the National Democratic party in Alabama, and the Freedom Democratic party in Mississippi— organized when the white regular Democratic organization refused blacks a voice— which gained recognition in the 1968 Democratic National Convention. On occasion blacks, when caucusing, have not hesitated to inveigh against both major parties.

While wisely letting it be known that their theme for the 1970s would be "No permanent friends, no permanent enemies, just permanent interests," as enunciated by Julian Bond, and broadening their vision to transcend "ghetto politics," the practical-minded politicians remained aware that national third-party movements historically have not fared well in the U. S. Consequently, like their white counterparts, blacks have continued to adhere to the two major parties, while demonstrating independence in both as they become more openly aggressive in pursuit of a fair share of the political pie.

Although the Nixon Administration and the Republican party were criticized by even some black Republicans for their record on aid to blacks and other minorities, some white and black Administration officeholders, especially the President's only black White House aide, Robert J. Brown, defended the President and his party. In May 1971 more than thirty black leaders from around the country, mainly businessmen and black Republican officials, were called to a meeting at the White House to form what some called the Republican Black Caucus as a counterforce to the Congressional Black Caucus of Democrats. In July 1971, with financial help from the party, the group created what they called the National Black Silent Majority Committee, under the leadership of

Clay J. Claiborne of Atlantic City, with the major purpose of increasing the black vote for the Republican candidates. The movement was set back, however, by the resignation of their leading officeholder, Arthur A. Fletcher of Oregon, an Assistant Secretary of Labor, who left to become Executive Director of the United Negro College Fund. It had been expected that Fletcher would be a key leader in efforts to corral at least 20 percent of the black vote in 1972. (The President received, however, approximately the same 10 percent received in 1968.)

In December 1971 the White House called a parley of black and white Nixon aides and began to organize black Republicans holding state offices into a political propaganda network to help sell the President's civil rights record. Blacks present at the meeting included Ersa Poston, president of the New York State Civil Service Commission; Samuel Singleton, Special Assistant to New York's then Governor Nelson Rockefeller; John Silvera, Deputy Commissioner of the New York State Division of Human Rights; and Bud Simmons, aide to New Jersey Governor William Cahill, as well as Robert J. Brown. The main purpose of this group was to develop strategies to attract more than the 10 percent of the black vote Nixon had received in the 1968 election.

## Nixon Administration[5]

Looking back over the past two decades, blacks considered that they had made some progress toward equality. It had begun in 1952 with the Administration of Republican President Dwight D. Eisenhower, and real strides toward an integrated society had been made under Democratic Presidents John F. Kennedy and Lyndon B. Johnson. But the pace of civil rights legislation and ground-breaking black appointments slowed with the election of Republican President Richard M. Nixon. His so-called Southern Strategy and civil rights policies dismayed black political leaders, who began to believe that "He was on the side of the South, the white majority, and the status quo."

Mr. Nixon was not long in office before lowering the level of enforcement of civil rights laws. Blacks considered him less enthusiastic than his predecessors in compelling equal opportunity in employment from those holding federal contracts or in encouraging integration in housing.

Furthermore, his wish to end the liberal control of the Supreme Court and to undo some of its progressive decisions met with black disfavor. Equally unpopular was his unsuccessful attempt to appoint to the Supreme Court two southerners, one of whom, G. Harold Carswell, a judge of the federal Fifth Circuit Court of Appeals, was an active segregationist. He took action as well to limit funding and effectiveness of the Federal Legal Services program for the poor, and offered leadership to opponents of busing for the purpose of desegregating public schools.

In light of the implications of the President's policies and appointments, blacks realized that they must step forward and began hammering away at the issues and working strenuously to win office.

When the 1974 elections were over, more blacks held elective office than ever before. This was due largely to the Voting Rights Act of 1965 which increased black voter enrollment in the South alone by more than 800,000. The first impact was gradual, and as late as 1970 there were only 78 blacks holding elective posts; but by the spring of 1974 there was a total of 2991 black elected officials holding office in all parts of the country. (See Table I.)

## Ford Administration[6]

Mr. Nixon, forced to resign in August 1974, during the continued investigation that linked him directly to the Watergate affair, was succeeded in the Presidency by his hand-picked Vice-President, former Michigan Republican Minority Leader in the House of Representatives, Gerald R. Ford. As Vice-President he had tried to open communications with blacks, delivering his first major civil rights address to the annual convention of the National Urban League that convened in San Francisco in 1974. On August 21, after assuming office, he granted an audience to the Congressional Black Caucus, fifteen of whom had voted against confirmation of him as Vice-President. They exchanged views and presented him with a list of legislative issues of special concern to minorities that included public employment, housing, health, education, transportation, and extension of antipoverty programs. Knowing Mr. Ford's conservative views, the Caucus expected nothing spectacular to be resolved, viewing the meeting as mainly cosmetic and simply "a good symbol." Thus it was understood that black leaders exhibited only cautious optimism, a stance well borne out after another gathering with the President in October of heads of the NAACP, National Urban League, PUSH, National Council of Negro Women, LINKS, and other black organizations. Mr. Ford listened politely and simply told the blacks he understood their position but promised nothing definite to ameliorate the deteriorating position of blacks and other minorities as unemployment rates continued to rise at an accelerating pace among blacks as a consequence of soaring inflation. As the year drew to a close with widespread defeat of Republicans in the November 5 national off-year elections, the outlook among blacks was one of hopeful pragmatic expectations only.

## Internal Problems[7]

In the move to develop political strength, blacks, like other groups, were occasionally plagued with internal difficulties. In late 1971, for example, the Congressional Black Caucus at its Washington conference, which aimed at uniting blacks "around the issues that affect our people," opened on a discordant note. Mrs. Chisholm complained that she had been prevented from leading a political workshop even though she was an elected official and a member of the Democratic National Committee, and she resented being relegated to a committee on early childhood education. This incident grew from a more serious conflict between the congresswoman and her black colleagues who felt that her announced candidacy for the presidency made it difficult for other blacks to bargain within the Democratic party for overall gains for blacks in general.

Another issue involved the late Reverend King's titular successor, the Reverend Ralph David Abernathy, head of the SCLC, and the challenge to his leadership by the rising young head of the SCLC's economic arm, Operation Breadbasket, the Reverend Jesse L. Jackson of Chicago, who resigned in December 1971 and organized PUSH, mentioned earlier.

A schism having wider national import was caused by the election of black lawyer and former ambassador Patricia Roberts Harris as temporary chairman of the Democratic Party Credentials Committee for its 1972 national convention, over the opposition of four or five black members of the Democratic National Committee, including Mrs. Chisholm, all of whom supported the candidacy of white Senator Harold E. Hughes of Iowa. Although pressured by some members of the Congressional Black Caucus to remove herself from the running, Mrs. Harris remained firm and won an overwhelming victory by a vote of 72 to 31 in the showdown in October 1971.

Yet in spite of occasional in-fighting, the black drive for power continued, with such insiders as New York's Manhattan Borough President Percy Sutton working energetically and skillfully to minimize differences and establish a unified front.

## Congressional Black Caucus[8]

A significant instrument in the drive for unity was the Congressional Black Caucus. In 1969 the six black members of the House of Representatives began to meet informally as a group with Charles Diggs, the senior member in years of service, serving as chairman. The group expanded to twelve in 1970 and formally organized in January 1971, setting up an office in Washington with Howard Robinson as director. At this point several younger and more aggressive members questioned Diggs's leadership. The seniority rule was scrapped, and in February of 1972 Congressman Louis Stokes of Cleveland, Ohio, became chairman. The caucus eventually expanded to sixteen, including nonvoting delegate Walter Fauntroy from Washington, who joined the caucus after his election in the fall of 1971. Representative Charles Rangel of New York assumed the chairmanship in 1974.

The Black Caucus came to national attention when its members boycotted President Nixon's 1971 State of the Union address on the ground that he had refused to meet with them to discuss problems of minorities, even though they had been requesting an audience for almost a year. The President scheduled a meeting at the White House in March, during which the caucus presented him with more than sixty recommendations in such areas as employment, welfare, crime, manpower, African affairs, and racial matters. Nixon appointed a group to study the proposals and in May rejected most of them. This failure to respond affirmatively to black needs forced the caucus to focus on the problem of organization and registration of the mass of black voters in order to marshal their immense political potential. The need for campaign financial reform was also stressed. Black politics emerged as a real movement in 1971 with formulation of an articulated plan as the major goal of a series of strategy meetings beginning in May of that year. In July, Jesse Jackson invited prominent political leaders to discuss the possibility of a black political party. In August, the convention of the National Welfare Rights Organization heard Executive Director George Wiley urge all members to try to become delegates to the 1972 Democratic National Convention. Later that month, at an outdoor rally of several thousand supporters of the SCLC in Atlanta, Dr. Abernathy called for greater black participation in the primary and general elections.

Soon afterward several hundred rank-and-file blacks from about a dozen states joined with elected officials in Mobile, Alabama, for the first Southern Black Political Caucus, summoned by Dr. Cashin, Julian Bond, and Fayette, Mississippi's Mayor Charles Evers. Early in September the Congress of African People, convening in Newark, New Jersey, proposed to hold conventions in at least twelve states to draft black tickets to join in a national black political convention. Later the same month fifty black leaders gathered in North Lake, Illinois, as the National Assembly for a Black Political Strategy in '72. In January 1972, elected and appointed officials convened in New York to plan their election role and to make certain that blacks, Chicanos, Puerto Ricans, Indians, poor whites, and younger people were represented in Democratic and Republican policy-making. Further, in April the Congressional Black Caucus, with most of the financing provided by the Boston *Globe*, the Louisville *Courier-Journal*, the Philadelphia *Bulletin*, and the Chicago *Sun-Times* newspapers, met at and in collaboration with the Harvard University Institute of Politics, to establish new domestic priorities for the nation.

## National Black Political Conventions[9]

All of these developments indicated the clear intent to work out a black political posture for the presidential election year and for the period beyond it. The purpose of the various meetings was to create a united front for black participation in the Democratic and Republican conventions and in local, state, and national elections; and to highlight issues of major concern to blacks as well as to the public in general. Clearly blacks in politics had learned much from the past. They finally saw electoral politics as the simplest way to gain power for the powerless. Having almost no access to accumulations of private wealth, no control of any of the nation's largest corporations, no significant part in its military-industrial complex, the crime syndicate, or in organized labor, blacks awakened to the fact that they were powerless in a nation which stresses power. Massive involvement of blacks in electoral politics, they realized, could lead to a proportionate sharing of the nation's powerful federal and state governmental apparatus, and make available significant economic leverage through the control of millions of dollars from the public sector.

New directions were charted, new realignments made, and in March 1972 a National Black Political Convention convened in Gary, Indiana, co-chaired by Diggs, Hatcher, and Baraka. A major purpose of the conclave was to bring black people together to develop a national black agenda that set forth priorities, as well as to develop plans for unified black action at the summer conventions of the Democratic and Republican parties. The more than 8,000 people who attended, of whom slightly less than half were delegates and observers, represented practically the entire spectrum of current black thought, from orthodox political and social integrationists to black nationalist separatists. But the desire for a united front was sufficiently strong to hold them together by what was called "operational unity," and in addition to passing a number of resolutions, the gathering set forth a rather general program in a black agenda.

This document deliberately was not very specific, detailed, or partisan; and it neither set up a black political party nor endorsed anyone as a presidential candidate. It did, however, provide for setting up an independent black political movement with a National Black Assembly and a chairman in each of the states and the District of Columbia—an attempt to unify black voters by cutting through philosophical and political differences. It also declared an intention to bring blacks together in convention every four years prior to the national Democratic and Republican conventions. It called for black participation in elective offices equal to their population percentage, meaning a minimum of sixty-six congressmen and fifteen senators, and proportionate black employment and control at every level of the Federal Government structure. There were recommendations in the areas of economic, human, and rural development. Also, it suggested that blacks should exert influence on American foreign policy in general, but especially with regard to our relations with Africa and the Caribbean nations. It criticized United States relations with the Republic of South Africa, Rhodesia, and Portugal. Additionally, it called for environmental planning and community development, self-determination for the District of Columbia, the establishment and control of black communications media, quality education for all black youth, and massive federal funds to accomplish these objectives.

As might be expected, there were some basic differences in viewpoint among the attending groups. The NAACP, for example, condemned the preamble to the agenda because it called for an independent black political movement which the NAACP regarded as promoting racial separatism. However, there was an underlying realization that the document sought only to set general guidelines, and an awareness that its purpose, which transcended the wide-ranging diversity of views, was keyed to the betterment of all blacks in the social, cultural, economic, and political spheres of American life.

The second national meeting, which convened for three days in Little Rock, Arkansas, beginning March 15, 1974, with about 1700 or only half the delegates present in Gary, was more subdued than that one. Many well known black officials failed to attend, including Congressman Charles Diggs, who had resigned previously as one of the three convention co-chairmen. Ronald Dellums of California and John Conyers of Michigan were the only two congressmen to participate, while few of the black mayors of large cities or widely known state legislators came. Some of the latter failed to show up because they felt the conference simply could not serve as an effective political instrument; others were concerned over the role they would play, were against extreme policy positions that might be adopted, or were cautious about how they would be treated.

Co-chairmen Baraka and Mayor Hatcher of Gary held the factions together and kept the agenda moderate. While more than 200 resolutions were submitted (one of those shelved called for an independent black party) the convention approved only nine. Among these were resolutions calling for an advisory Supreme Court of Appeals to handle the cases of "political prisoners"; African studies in public schools; against psychological testing in public schools and colleges; for home rule in the District of Columbia, the one resolution translated into successful action when Washington, D. C.'s referendum on the matter was passed in 1974, with incumbent appointed Mayor Walter Washington winning in November as the first elected head of the nation's capital.

## Leadership[10]

As the gathering in Gary revealed—unlike the past when the "great man" pattern prevailed and a single black leader or two served as spokesmen for the race—there is now a recognition that the black community is as diverse in viewpoint as is any other community, and that contemporary politics calls for a variety of leaders throughout the nation, since no one black leader today can pretend to speak for all black people. Consequently, current black leadership is in the hands of officials with varying points of view. The nation's one black senator, Edward W. Brooke, and the black members of the House of Representatives, as well as the one nonvoting delegate from Washington, D. C., may be looked upon as the leadership group in national politics. In 1972 State Senator Barbara Jordan from Texas, attorney Andrew Young from Atlanta, Georgia (a former aide to the late Martin Luther King, Jr.), and Yvonne Braithwaite Burke (a member of the California State Assembly and co-chairman of the 1972 Democratic National Convention) were elected to the United States House of Representatives, raising the number of black congressmen in the House to sixteen. (When Cardiss Collins of Chicago was elected in 1974 to the vacancy left by the death of her husband, George, the total of women rose to four.) The election of Barbara Jordan and Andrew Young marked the first time since Reconstruction that blacks representing southern states had been elected to these posts. The state level finds senators and members of legislatures representing their districts (see Tables II and III), while in the city, county, and township, aldermen, council members, selectmen, supervisors, as well as commissioners, school board members, and holders of other important offices, serve as local spokesmen. (See Table IV.)

**TABLE II**—ACTUAL AND PROJECTED BLACK REPRESENTATION BY STATE
FOR UPPER HOUSE (STATE SENATE)

| State | Total Number Senate Seats | Black % of Population | Number Black State Senators | % Black Senators | Projected Black Senators |
|---|---|---|---|---|---|
| Alabama | 35 | 26.4 | — | — | 9 |
| Alaska | 20 | 3.0 | — | — | 1 |
| Arizona | 30 | 3.0 | 1 | 3.3 | 1 |
| Arkansas | 35 | 18.6 | — | — | 7 |
| California | 40 | 7.0 | 1 | 2.5 | 3 |
| Colorado | 35 | 3.0 | 1 | 2.5 | 1 |
| Connecticut | 36 | 6.0 | 1 | 2.7 | 2 |
| Delaware | 19 | 14.3 | 1 | 5.2 | 3 |
| Florida | 48 | 15.5 | — | — | 7 |
| Georgia | 56 | 26.0 | 2 | 3.5 | 15 |
| Hawaii | 25 | 1.0 | — | — | — |
| Idaho | 35 | .3 | — | — | — |
| Illinois | 58 | 12.8 | 5 | 8.6 | 7 |
| Indiana | 50 | 6.9 | — | — | — |
| Iowa | 50 | 1.2 | — | — | 1 |
| Kansas | 40 | 4.8 | — | — | 2 |
| Kentucky | 38 | 7.5 | 1 | 2.6 | 3 |
| Louisiana | 39 | 29.9 | — | — | 12 |
| Maine | 32 | .3 | — | — | — |
| Maryland | 43 | 17.9 | 4 | 9.3 | 8 |
| Massachusetts | 40 | 3.1 | — | — | 1 |
| Michigan | 38 | 11.2 | 3 | 7.8 | 4 |
| Minnesota | 67 | .9 | — | — | 1 |
| Mississippi | 52 | 36.8 | — | — | 19 |
| Missouri | 34 | 10.3 | 2 | 5.8 | 4 |
| Montana | 55 | .3 | — | — | — |
| Nebraska | 49 | 2.7 | 1 | 2.0 | 1 |
| Nevada | 20 | 5.7 | — | — | 1 |
| New Hampshire | 24 | .2 | — | — | — |
| New Jersey | 38 | 10.8 | 1 | — | 4 |
| New Mexico | 42 | 1.9 | — | — | — |
| New York | 57 | 11.9 | 3 | 5.2 | 7 |
| North Carolina | 50 | 22.4 | — | — | 11 |
| North Dakota | 202 | .4 | — | — | — |
| Ohio | 33 | 9.1 | 2 | 6.0 | 3 |
| Oklahoma | 48 | 4.6 | 1 | 2.0 | 2 |
| Oregon | 30 | 1.3 | — | — | — |
| Pennsylvania | 49 | 8.6 | 2 | 4.8 | 4 |
| Rhode Island | 50 | 2.7 | — | — | 1 |
| South Carolina | 50 | 30.5 | — | — | 15 |
| South Dakota | 35 | .2 | — | — | — |
| Tennessee | 33 | 16.1 | 2 | 6.0 | 5 |
| Texas | 31 | 12.7 | 1 | 3.0 | 4 |
| Utah | 28 | .6 | — | — | — |
| Vermont | 30 | .2 | — | — | — |
| Virginia | 40 | 18.6 | 1 | 2.5 | 7 |
| Washington | 49 | 2.1 | 1 | 2.0 | 1 |

**TABLE II**—(Cont.)

| State | Total Number Senate Seats | Black % of Population | Number Black State Senators | % Black Senators | Projected Black Senators |
|---|---|---|---|---|---|
| West Virginia | 34 | 4.2 | – | – | 1 |
| Wisconsin | 33 | 2.9 | – | – | 1 |
| Wyoming | 25 | .8 | – | – | – |
| TOTALS | 2,130 | 11.1 | 37 | 1.7 | 182 |

Sources:   U. S. Census Bureau, *1970 Census of Population and Housing; 1967 Census of Govern-ments;* Joint Center for Political Studies, *National Roster of Black Elected Officials, March 1972.*

Copyright 1972 Joint Center for Political Studies

**TABLE III**—ACTUAL AND PROJECTED BLACK REPRESENTATION BY STATE FOR LOWER HOUSE (STATE HOUSE OF REPRESENTATIVES)

| State | Total Number House Seats | Black % Population | Number Black House Members | % Black House Members | Projected Number Black House Members |
|---|---|---|---|---|---|
| Alabama | 106 | 26.4 | 2 | 1.8 | 28 |
| Alaska | 40 | 3.0 | 2 | 5.0 | 1 |
| Arizona | 60 | 3.0 | 3 | 5.0 | 2 |
| Arkansas | 100 | 18.6 | – | – | 19 |
| California | 80 | 7.0 | 5 | 6.2 | 6 |
| Colorado | 65 | 3.0 | 2 | 3.0 | 2 |
| Connecticut | 177 | 6.0 | 5 | 2.8 | 11 |
| Delaware | 39 | 14.3 | 2 | 5.1 | 6 |
| Florida | 119 | 15.5 | 2 | 1.7 | 19 |
| Georgia | 195 | 26.0 | 13 | 6.6 | 51 |
| Hawaii | 51 | 1.0 | – | – | 1 |
| Idaho | 70 | .3 | – | – | – |
| Illinois | 177 | 12.8 | 14 | 8.0 | 23 |
| Indiana | 99 | 6.9 | 5 | 5.0 | 7 |
| Iowa | 100 | 1.2 | 1 | 1.0 | 1 |
| Kansas | 125 | 4.8 | 3 | 2.0 | 6 |
| Kentucky | 100 | 7.5 | 2 | | 8 |
| Louisiana | 105 | 29.9 | 8 | 8.0 | 31 |
| Maine | 151 | .3 | – | – | 1 |
| Maryland | 142 | 17.9 | 14 | 9.8 | 25 |
| Massachusetts | 240 | 3.1 | 3 | 1.2 | 7 |
| Michigan | 110 | 11.2 | 13 | 11.8 | 12 |
| Minnesota | 135 | .9 | – | – | 1 |
| Mississippi | 122 | 36.8 | 1 | .1 | 45 |
| Missouri | 163 | 10.3 | 13 | 7.9 | 17 |
| Montana | 104 | .3 | – | – | – |
| Nebraska | | | | | |
| Nevada | 40 | 5.7 | 1 | 2.5 | 2 |
| New Hampshire | 400 | .2 | – | – | 12 |
| New Jersey | 80 | 10.8 | 4 | 5 | 9 |
| New Mexico | 70 | 1.9 | 1 | | 1 |

**TABLE III—(Cont.)**

| State | Total Number House Seats | Black % Population | Number Black House Members | % Black House Members | Projected Number Black House Members |
|---|---|---|---|---|---|
| New York | 150 | 11.9 | 9 | 6 | 18 |
| North Carolina | 120 | 22.4 | 2 | 1.6 | 27 |
| North Dakota | 49 | .4 | – | – | – |
| Ohio | 99 | 9.1 | 10 | 10 | 9 |
| Oklahoma | 99 | 4.6 | 5 | 5 | 5 |
| Oregon | 60 | 1.3 | – | – | 1 |
| Pennsylvania | 202 | 8.6 | 9 | 4.1 | 17 |
| Rhode Island | 100 | 2.7 | 1 | 2 | 3 |
| South Carolina | 124 | 30.5 | 3 | 2.4 | 38 |
| South Dakota | 75 | .2 | – | – | – |
| Tennessee | 99 | 16.1 | 6 | 6.0 | 16 |
| Texas | 150 | 12.7 | 2 | 1.4 | 19 |
| Utah | 69 | .6 | – | – | – |
| Vermont | 150 | .2 | – | – | – |
| Virginia | 100 | 18.6 | 2 | 2.0 | 19 |
| Washington | 99 | 2.1 | 2 | 2.0 | 2 |
| W. Virginia | 100 | 4.2 | 1 | 1 | 4 |
| Wisconsin | 100 | 2.9 | 1 | 1 | 3 |
| Wyoming | 61 | .8 | – | – | 1 |
| TOTALS | 5,571 | 11.1 | 169 | 3.0 | 527 |

Sources:   U. S. Census Bureau, *1970 Census of Population and Housing; 1967 Census of Govern-ments,* Joint Center for Political Studies, *National Roster Black Elected Officials, March 1972*

Within this broad spectrum, however, certain groups and individuals serve as focal points around which major activity is concentrated. The Congressional Black Caucus is one of these spearheads. Representing a cross-section of ages, ideologies, and political shadings, it receives strong support from such groups as the National Conference of Black Elected Officials and the California Conference of Black Elected Officials, the Leadership Conference on Civil Rights, and others. But state and local leadership is still in the hands of those blacks close to their constituencies who collaborate with the Congressional Black Caucus. Some forty-three states have black elected public officeholders, who are in the van as spokesmen. Their names are known locally and they are far too numerous to list individually, but some idea of their numbers in specific roles can be gleaned from Table IV.

Besides these elected officials, black leadership is further diffused among a number of persons well known both nationally and locally. They head special groups, hold significant appointive offices, or have gained repute as public speakers forcefully voicing the feelings and conditions and demands of blacks. Although the death of Whitney Young of the National Urban League in March 1971 stilled one such voice, Vernon

Jordan, Jr., who took his place, has proved to be an articulate successor. Septuagenarian Roy Wilkins, longtime head of the NAACP, continues to wield influence on behalf of integration and the cause of civil rights, using constitutional and other legal means to achieve these ends. Economic approaches are stressed by Jesse Jackson (who is in his early thirties), through his work with PUSH. Jackson considers himself an "organizer" of leaders. He attracted national attention with his annual Black Expositions, the first held in 1969, which attracted some 800,000 visitors in 1971 and a similar number in 1972 to view "black life styles," and with the advancement in 1971 of his Domestic Marshall Plan of economic proposals to uplift the black community.

**TABLE IV**—BLACK LEGISLATORS AND BLACKS ELECTED TO OTHER PUBLIC OFFICE: 1964, 1966, 1968, 1970, AND 1972

| Subject | 1964 | 1966 | 1968 | 1970 | 1972 |
|---|---|---|---|---|---|
| U.S. Senate: | | | | | |
| United States.................. | – | 1 | 1 | 1 | 1 |
| South ...................... | – | – | – | – | – |
| U.S. House of Representatives: | | | | | |
| United States.................. | 5 | 6 | 9 | 13 | 13 |
| South ...................... | – | – | – | 2 | 2 |
| State Legislatures: | | | | | |
| United States.................. | 94 | 148 | 172 | 198 | 206 |
| South ...................... | 16 | 37 | 53 | 70 | 78 |
| Mayors: | | | | | |
| United States.................. | (NA) | (NA) | 29 | 81 | 86 |
| South ...................... | (NA) | (NA) | 17 | 47 | 44 |
| Other :[1] | | | | | |
| United States.................. | (NA) | (NA) | 914 | 1,567 | 1,958 |
| South ...................... | (NA) | (NA) | 468 | 763 | 949 |

Note: Figures for the years 1964, 1966, and 1968 represent the total number of elected blacks holding office at that time, not just those elected in those years. Figures for 1970 also include persons elected the first 3 months of 1971. The 1972 numbers represent elected officials holding office as of March 1972.

— Represents zero.    (NA) Not available.

[1]Includes all black elected officials not included in first four categories.

Source: Potomac Institute and Joint Center for Political Studies (Washington, D. C., 1972).

On another level one finds such representative leaders as Aaron Henry of the Freedom Democratic party in Mississippi and Harry Means, a County Supervisor in Alabama's heavily black Greene County, who in 1969 helped snatch political control in the area from the long-dominant whites. Other important figures include the comedian, political analyst, commentator, entertainer, sometime candidate, civil rights advocate, and sharp-tongued satirist Dick Gregory; the Scholarship Education and Defense Fund for Racial Equality's Alabama Representative Stiver W. Gordon; Florida Democratic leader and lawyer Alcee Hasting; Professor of Political Science Inez Smith

Reid, former Executive Director of the Black Women's Community Development Foundation based in Washington; Yvonne Braithwaite Burke, then a member of the California Assembly, who was co-chairperson of the National Democratic Convention in Miami in July 1972; Mrs. Dorothy Bolden, founder and president of the National Domestic Workers Union of America headquartered in Atlanta; John Lewis, Director of the Southern Regional Council-founded Voter Education Project in Georgia; Basil A. Paterson, former New York State Senator and candidate for lieutenant governor, and now president of the Center for Mediation and Conflict Resolution; and Democratic Mayor Reverend Walter S. Taylor of Englewood, New Jersey. George Wiley, who had been Director of the National Welfare Rights Organization, headed the Movement for Economic Justice just before his untimely death in August 1973.

One must also include black members of the judiciary in the leadership group. Because of the unique prestige accorded their offices, black judges command respect and exercise influence; and black citizens expect them to see that equal justice under law is made real. This mandate and responsibility are placed at the top upon the federal judges: U. S. Supreme Court Justice Thurgood Marshall, U. S. District Judges Leon Higginbotham of Pennsylvania and Constance Baker Motley and Robert L. Carter of New York (the former is also the first and only woman ever elected Borough President of Manhattan); and U. S. Customs Court Judges Scovel Richardson and James Watson; all of them are among the more than 270 black judges—mainly serving on the lowest level of local small claims and police courts—in the nation, who are looked to for protection. Blacks are aware that these jurists have become a real force in the legal community, while the judges know that blacks expect them to see that the white-dominated legal system becomes more responsive to blacks, the poor, and to others who have had less than a fair share of wealth and influence.

### Financing Campaigns[11]

Black leadership understands that to function successfully money is necessary, and they know that lack of financial support is a major obstacle to black political action. While whites tend to worry about the corrosive effects on American society of favoring special interests which underwrite campaigns, blacks must worry about how to assemble enough funds. It takes enormous sums to conduct effective campaigns, since political financing is grossly unregulated, despite recent efforts to limit campaign spending. The 1968 elections are estimated to have cost nearly a third of a billion dollars, while in 1972 Common Cause reported that in the presidential and congressional campaigns alone $200,000,000 was spent by politicians in their quest for office.[12]

It is with such staggering sums as these that the black masses must compete fully to realize their increasing political potential. They have learned that they must integrate black power with "green" power and, to this end, like their white counterparts, go about the business of giving fund-raising affairs to help elect blacks across the country. In the South, because of the meagerness of available resources and the hostility of local white politicians, office-seekers rely upon traditional grass-roots efforts, or try to secure small grants from the Southern Election Fund in Atlanta. Better known candidates search for outside aid, some candidates borrow money, and others even sell some of their property holdings. The treasuries of the major Democratic and Republican parties at best make only token contributions to black candidates in the South. More generous "outside" funding arouses suspicions that the candidate may be a "tool" of the givers. Another difficulty arises when black candidates oppose each other and compete for the limited funds available; sometimes the same donor gives funds to both in the hopes of reaping later profit no matter which side wins.

Outside the South, fund-raising events have become fairly common. Such affairs are held regularly for those seeking major offices on the national, state, and local levels. In comparison with white-sponsored events, black fund-raising efforts are usually modest, but they nevertheless serve a valuable function by involving the black middle class more intimately in politics and setting in motion a trend of political giving among people who are not yet accustomed to being donors. They also tend to give black candidates a certain feeling of independence that comes from having a number of modest contributions, rather than a few large ones. There are occasional $100-a-plate dinners, but wealth among blacks is still too limited to support many such efforts. Other techniques range from small, informal fund-raising gatherings in private homes to huge affairs where as many as 2,000 ticketholders assemble in leading hotels to enjoy big-name bands and entertainers.

## Voting Habits[13]

The fund-raising difficulties experienced by black candidates have been matched by lethargy on the part of potential voters. Blacks who run for office have to overcome a definite psychological problem, especially among the poor in the rural hinterlands of the South. This was well summed up by black candidate Robert Vanderson in a Mississippi sheriff's contest:

> I keep pushing because so many black people in Mississippi have been brainwashed for so long that they don't believe a black man can do anything. They think only white is right, no matter what, and—except for the younger people coming up—so many blacks have so little trust in their ability to do, or in the ability of their people to do.[14]

But it is not only with this lack of confidence in black abilities that the present push for political power must contend. Campaigners and political workers in the South have discovered that signs of activism in the new black electorate are often counterbalanced by a general apathy. Spotty registration, erratic or occasional voting, and the fact that political organization is still in the embryonic stage seriously hamper political progress even in areas where blacks have a numerical majority and hence could have the controlling voice. The masses simply have not fully grasped the fact that the ballot is a weapon for constructive change only when it is exercised. (See Tables V, VI, and VII.)

TABLE V—REPORTED VOTER REGISTRATION FOR PERSONS OF VOTING AGE, BY
REGION: 1966, 1968, AND 1970
(Numbers in thousands)

| Subject | Black | | | White | | |
|---|---|---|---|---|---|---|
| | 1966 | 1968 | 1970 | 1966 | 1968 | 1970 |
| All persons of voting age  .. | 10,533 | 10,935 | 11,473 | 101,205 | 104,521 | 107,997 |
| North and West . . . . . . . . . | 4,849 | 4,944 | 5,277 | 72,593 | 75,687 | 77,158 |
| South  . . . . . . . . . . . . . . . | 5,684 | 5,991 | 6,196 | 28,612 | 28,834 | 30,839 |
| Number who reported they had registered: | | | | | | |
| United States . . . . . . . . . . . | 6,345 | 7,238 | 6,971 | 72,517 | 78,835 | 74,672 |
| North and West . . . . . . . . . | 3,337 | 3,548 | 3,406 | 54,125 | 58,419 | 54,591 |
| South  . . . . . . . . . . . . . . . | 3,008 | 3,690 | 3,565 | 18,392 | 20,416 | 20,081 |
| Percent of voting age population: | | | | | | |
| United States . . . . . . . . . . . | 60 | 66 | 61 | 72 | 75 | 69 |
| North and West . . . . . . . . . | 69 | 72 | 65 | 75 | 77 | 71 |
| South  . . . . . . . . . . . . . . . | 53 | 62 | 58 | 64 | 71 | 65 |

Source:  U. S. Department of Commerce, Social and Economic Statistics Administration, Bureau of the Census, Series P-23, No. 42, p. 116.

TABLE VI—REPORTED VOTER PARTICIPATION FOR PERSONS OF VOTING AGE, BY
REGION: 1964, 1966, 1968, AND 1970
(Numbers in millions)

| Subject | Black | | | | White | | | |
|---|---|---|---|---|---|---|---|---|
| | 1964 | 1966 | 1968 | 1970 | 1964 | 1966 | 1968 | 1970 |
| All persons of voting age  .... | 10.3 | 10.5 | 10.9 | 11.5 | 99.4 | 101.2 | 104.5 | 108.0 |
| North and West . . . . . . . . . . . | 5.4 | 4.8 | 4.9 | 5.3 | 72.8 | 72.6 | 75.7 | 77.2 |
| South  . . . . . . . . . . . . . . . . . | 5.8 | 5.7 | 6.0 | 6.2 | 26.6 | 28.6 | 28.8 | 30.8 |
| Number who reported that they voted: | | | | | | | | |
| United States . . . . . . . . . . . . . | 6.0 | 4.4 | 6.3 | 5.0 | 70.2 | 57.8 | 72.2 | 60.4 |
| North and West . . . . . . . . . . . | 3.9 | 2.5 | 3.2 | 2.7 | 54.4 | 44.8 | 54.4 | 46.1 |
| South  . . . . . . . . . . . . . . . . . | 2.6 | 1.9 | 3.1 | 2.3 | 15.8 | 12.9 | 17.9 | 14.3 |
| Percent who reported that they voted: | | | | | | | | |
| United States . . . . . . . . . . . . . | 59 | 42 | 58 | 44 | 71 | 57 | 69 | 56 |
| North and West . . . . . . . . . . . | 72 | 52 | 65 | 51 | 75 | 62 | 72 | 60 |
| South  . . . . . . . . . . . . . . . . . | 44 | 33 | 52 | 37 | 60 | 45 | 62 | 46 |

Source:  U. S. Department of Commerce, Social and Economic Statistics Administration, Bureau of the Census, Series P-23, No. 42, p. 117.

**TABLE VII**—PROJECTED BLACK POPULATION AS A PERCENTAGE OF THE VOTING-AGE
POPULATION IN THE UNITED STATES AND REGIONS, BY AGE: 1972

| Age | United States | North-east | North Central | South | West |
|---|---|---|---|---|---|
| 18 years and over .. | 10.0 | 8.5 | 7.6 | 16.4 | 4.6 |
| Under 25 years ............ | 13.6 | 11.4 | 10.1 | 22.3 | 6.1 |
| 25 to 44 years ............ | 10.6 | 10.5 | 8.4 | 15.9 | 5.1 |
| 45 to 64 years ............ | 8.9 | 7.0 | 6.7 | 15.4 | 4.0 |
| 65 years and over ......... | 7.9 | 5.1 | 5.3 | 15.2 | 2.8 |

Source: U. S. Department of Commerce, Social and Economic Statistics Administration, Bureau of the Census, Series P-23, No. 42, p. 120.

## Women[15]

Another problem stems from the fact that for too long black politicians have failed to consider the potential of the women in their midst. Only when a general thrust by women began to gain momentum throughout the country did black male politicians awaken to this long bypassed source of strength.

Among women, former Ambassador Patricia Harris and Congresswomen Shirley Chisholm, Yvonne Braithwaite Burke, and Barbara Jordan stand out nationally. State and local black women holding public office are exemplified by Alderman Bertha Sanders of Winstonville, Mississippi; Town Marshal Zelma C. Wyche in Tallula, Louisiana; State Representative Peggie Joan Maxie of Washington; City Council member Ruth Charity of Danville, Virginia; school board member Agnes Sherman of Frogmore, South Carolina; Justice of the Peace Patricia McAlpin of Gadsen, Alabama; school board member Mabel Allen of Eudora, Arkansas; and a growing number of others. Nonofficeholders include Fanny Lou Hamer of Mississippi, Victoria DeLee of South Carolina, and many more.

The presidential ambitions of Congresswoman Chisholm helped in fostering this new awareness, although it was gathering strength well before her campaign, with the establishment in some communities of a Black Women's Political Caucus, and more particularly with the formation of the Coalition of 100 Black Women (the title does not indicate a limit to the membership). Convened in New York in January 1972, with Evelyn Payne Davis and Cathy Aldridge Chance as co-chairwomen, its organizing conference was attended by an array of black political figures and officials who addressed the more than 200 women present.

Throughout the country black women have begun holding public offices that range from constable; justice of the peace; school board member; town, city, and court clerk; ordinary; village secretary; town marshall; town supervisor; township and city treasurer; state university and college trustee; election commissioner; tax collector; judge; member of the state education board; alderman; city council member; state representative and senator; to member of the U. S. Congress. With this growth of opportunity has come a new political sophistication as women realize that at this stage in their drive for recognition and political leverage they might focus their energies on issues rather than on candidates.

Much of this progress is due to the efforts of those black women who, long conscious of their significant role behind the political scenes, began to insist upon public recognition of their talents, energies, and abilities. Feeling that they had been exploited in the past by male politicians and cognizant of their true potential, they began to work with women's rights groups and in alliance with the integrated National Women's Political Caucus. Within the latter they began to demand, and get, a more substantial voice.

## Youth[16]

Black politicians have yet to pay much attention to the newly enfranchised 18- to 21-year-old black youths. Even though some states passed laws and courts ruled that youths may vote where their colleges are located, political activity on largely white, integrated, or black college campuses was still far from focused. In 1972 there were expected to be more than 25 million young people eligible to vote within this new age group and it was admitted that they could be a potentially decisive factor in the total electorate. But expectations were that these new young voters, 70 percent of whom were working or looking for a job, would probably count for only about 6 percent of the total vote in the 1972 elections.

An analysis of the 1970 census data revealed that the young new voters were very much like the population as a whole in terms of race, residence, and family income. The data revealed, however, that young voters were not as likely to vote as older persons. In the 1970 elections, about 30 percent of the eligible 18- to 24-year-olds reported that they had voted, as compared with 58 percent of the population 25 years old and over. As for the nearly 11,500,000 black youths under 25 years of age, only 22.5 percent of the 1.5 million youths in the 21 to 24 age bracket voted, while out of nearly a million 18- to 20-year-olds, only 20.4 percent voted. In the 1972 general election only 48 percent of the eligible 18- to 20-year-olds reported that they had voted.

Whether black or white, the youth vote is clearly a distinct group. More pragmatic than ideological, it tends to be cynical about politicians and politics, perhaps due to a lack of confidence in its ability to influence either. It is above all a group which must be cultivated and helped to function usefully.

## Ideologies and Isms[17]

Black political workers have remained unruffled by the problems posed by young people, women, voting habits and so on, just as they have refused to devote precious time to contention over ideologies and isms. As one writer put it, many activists who were once caught up in Martin Luther King's majestic dream now can see no further than Malcolm X's nightmare. The hardheaded, practical politician, witnessing confusion among black ideologists as they change their goals from integration and assimilation to pluralism, and in some cases, separatism, senses a dearth of thoughtful attention to black nationalism and the absence of broad-based strong commitment to it.

As for the black masses, they are well aware of existing intraorganizational conflicts and have watched the Black Panther party challenge the Establishment and make a bid for power. The capture and jailing of H. Rap Brown has taught them the futility of violent posturing and they pay little heed to empty rhetoric. They question the feasibility of the advocacy of black nationalism by CORE's Roy Innis as the road to equality. In spite of the ferment around them, the black population overwhelmingly has continued to concentrate on the day-to-day practical problems of food, jobs, housing, across-the-board discrimination, and denial of equal opportunity.

Yet neither the masses nor the practical leadership write off those black nationalists who seek to use political power realistically within the dominant white power structure. They saw the usefulness of the September 1971 meeting in Newark, New Jersey, of the Congress of African Peoples led by Imamu Baraka that singled out the nationwide organization of black districts as a matter of top priority. While not subscribing to it, they could comprehend the desire of these black nationalists who helped elect Kenneth Gibson as the first black mayor of Newark to create their own all-black "national-international African political party," because Baraka showed realism in not ruling out coalition with those blacks committed to the major political parties, especially to the Democrats. Baraka also played an active role as co-coordinator for the Gary, Indiana, Black Political Convention.

### Racism[18]

The new breed of black politicians has sensed that race no longer plays the overt dominant role it once did, even in the South. They know that racism is still with us; but the practice of appealing to racist sentiments, long a standard white campaign technique in the Deep South, is on the decline. Blacks realize, however, that racism is far from dead and exists in a new and subtler form in both the North and the South. The fact that it remains part of the political repertoire was pointed up when Governor George Wallace, campaigning in the 1972 Florida primaries, told a Jewish audience that he could claim a Jewish cousin and uncle. (Other candidates in that state primary recalled what they had done for Israel, sponsored Purim parties, and took advertising space in Jewish newspapers.)

Racism also surfaced in white opposition to the development of integrated housing and busing as a means of achieving racial balance in the schools. It revealed itself as well in the redrawing of district lines to comply with court reapportionment mandates, an excuse for some white officials to try to weaken heavily black districts, or to gerrymander to prevent the development of new areas where blacks or other nonwhites might come into political ascendancy.

How deep-rooted racism is in some parts of our society was demonstrated, too, in the early efforts of Senator Fred Harris of Oklahoma to seek the Democratic nomination in the 1972 presidential race. Senator Harris spoke of a "new populism," meaning that every citizen should be guaranteed a decent income and higher social security benefits, and that industrial monopolies should be broken up. He planned to form a coalition of poor whites, poor blacks, white blue-collar ethnics, Indians, Spanish-speaking Americans, and other minorities. However, he soon encountered difficulty in trying to convince whites that the black influence is desirable. He learned that white workers had trouble identifying with a white politician who believes that "the best new populist ideas being said today in this country are being said by black folks," and, as another white said, "All he talks about are social and human issues."

Blacks saw use of the racial issue as a basic ingredient in Mr. Nixon's Southern Strategy. To gain support there, he appealed to southern sensitivities by keeping just within the letter of the law on civil rights and doing no more than legally required on school desegregation and the dispersal of low income and black families to the suburbs. His policy carefully balanced every gesture he made to the black community with a comparable one to segregationist opinion, saying for instance that court-ordered school desegregation would be carried out, while at the same time advocating a moratorium on busing to achieve racial integration; or taking action in one case against a private contractor for failing to train and employ blacks in a federally financed construction job, but tolerating similar failures elsewhere or allowing federal agencies to get by without properly implementing and promoting equal employment opportunity in their programs. Racism is also evident today in some of the positions taken by "hard hats," immigrant-stock white ethnics of Irish, Italian, Slavic, and Middle-European descent.

Nowhere was race more clearly a factor than in some of the November 1971 elections. In various sections of the nation voting tended to run along racial, rather than traditional, party lines: this was true in mayoralty contests in such cities as Cleveland, Philadelphia, and Baltimore, in the gubernatorial race of black candidate Charles Evers in Mississippi, as well as in the 1970 race for governor of Alabama by John Cashin, and in the Georgia congressional race of Andrew Young. But nowhere was the racial issue more clearly pointed up than in the furor over Maine Democratic Senator and presidential candidate Edmund Muskie's remark that if he had a black running mate for Vice-President, in his judgment such a ticket would not be electable. Other candidates tried to secure political advantage from the momentary storm that resulted from such candor, but Mr. Muskie's position, while deplored, was considered realistic by some leading black civil rights leaders and prominent southern black political officeholders. Race also was an important factor in the 1972 presidential election, focusing on the school busing issue in particular. However, 1974 saw a real change where racial politics of the South was concerned.

White candidates are now willing to talk to blacks about their need for better schools and jobs, while simultaneously convincing whites they are no advocates of big government spending. They do this, in part, because in more and more places they know the black vote is crucial to victory, but also because the new white candidates are interested and serious about furthering better relationships and improving conditions for everyone in that region. They are following the trail of gubernatorial progressivism blazed in the early 1970s by Dale Bumpers of Arkansas, Reubin Askew of Florida, George Busbee of Georgia, John West of South Carolina, Linwood Holton of Virginia, and Georgia's Jimmy Carter, among others, especially George Wallace of Alabama. (Former Governor and then Lt. Governor Lester Maddox of Georgia reflected the changed racial climate. During the run-off primary he attempted to use race through linking his principal rival, George Busbee, to the well-known black state legislator Julian Bond, while at the same time disavowing Ku Klux Klan endorsement and refusing to renounce his stand on segregation. He was roundly defeated by Mr. Busbee.)

Looking ahead to the presidential election of 1976 as a possible candidate, kingmaker, or decisive third-party threat, and becoming a force of serious proportions with the regular national Democratic party, Wallace began to develop a differing image of the "new Wallace" as he reached out from his wheelchair to the black community in Alabama in the primaries in the spring of 1974. This man, who once made "segregation forever" his war cry, won a standing ovation at a meeting of Alabama black elected officials in recognition for extra state aid he provided their cities. He shook hands with Rev. Ralph Abernathy, the successor to the late Martin Luther King, as they both received honorary degrees at predominantly black Alabama State University in Montgomery in May 1974; closed the racial gap further by appearing unannounced and speaking from the pulpit of the Dexter Avenue Baptist Church in that city from which the late Reverend King first preached nonviolent resistance, and won applause when he told the assembled blacks, "As far as I was concerned, there was never a race question; it was a question of big government." Such behavior won him widespread black votes in both the primaries and general elections in 1974.

That race in politics had changed was made quite clear when the Southern Conference of Black Mayors met in Santee, S.C., in June 1974. "No permanent enemies. No permanent friends. Just permanent needs," became their guiding political philosophy. As Mayor Judge Stringer of Hobson City, Alabama, noted, the 1900 blacks in his town voted overwhelmingly for Governor Wallace because "you go with the man who can help you," and just before elections that year Governor Wallace "saw to it that we got $153,000 in road funds. Everybody in town remembered that, instead of all he had done to us before." The mayors said their constituencies now ask, "What have you done for me?" instead of crying "Freedom, now!" They felt the civil rights movement had gone over to politics and that "It's better to work within the system and get things done than to be standing on some street corner with an upraised clenched fist that is empty and a head that is empty, too."

## Politics Outside the South[19]

Blacks were determined not to let race interfere with their plans to become meaningful participants in the decision-making process. Thus they became increasingly active in politics, both in the South and elsewhere. Real strides forward were made on the Pacific Coast during the 1970 election which marked victories for two black congressmen from California: August Hawkins of Los Angeles and much younger Ronald Dellums from the Oakland area. Elsewhere, the Middle West sent youthful William Clay of Missouri and Louis Stokes from Cleveland, Ohio, to the House of Representatives, while Ralph Metcalfe succeeded the aging Chicago Congressman William L. Dawson, who died not long after his retirement. Charles B. Rangel unseated Adam Clayton Powell of New York's Harlem, and Maryland sent young Parren Mitchell of Baltimore to Congress.

As a result of sharp focusing on the "grass roots" in city, state, and county politics, a number of additional black milestones were achieved in the elections of the early 1970s. Wilson Riles was elected superintendent of public instruction in California. More black mayors were voted into office, including Kenneth Gibson in Newark, Tom Bradley in Los Angeles, and Coleman Young in Detroit. Blacks also won office in increasing numbers in a variety of other areas including city councils, boards of aldermen or similar bodies, state legislatures, school boards, the judiciary, and county government.

These nationwide developments were accompanied by a tightening of political discipline. Black leaders began to advise delegates to beware of blind alignment with those who could not further the interests of their constituency. They also advocated maintaining close contact with the local citizenry and the construction of strong, viable organizational foundations. District, city, county, and state caucuses began to form, and stress was laid on the importance of keeping black officials on the national level informed of the problems of local appointees. Black elected officials were implored to hire key black administrative personnel who could in turn hire blacks for subordinate positions. A start was made in winning over the new labor force, black and white alike, and special emphasis was given to reaching women and the under-35-year-olds, since blacks began to see that coalitions in the seventies would differ sharply from those of the past. Stress was laid on developing instruments to insure voter turnout on election day, on creating ways to attract nation-wide attention, and on convincing the black masses of the need for cooperation with other minorities.

## The South[20]

This spirit of progressive change was also being felt in the South. Today, although only three black members from the South sit in the U.S. House of Representatives (Andrew Young of Georgia, the first black member since Reconstruction; Barbara Jordan of Texas; and Harold Ford of Tennessee—all Democrats), the South has undergone a real transformation in politics. The Southern Black Caucus, composed of a variety of elected public officials ranging from sheriffs and town clerks to councilmen, judges, and mayors, translates black unity into black political strength and exudes an air of optimism. According to a 1974 survey by the Joint Center of Political Studies, 1,383 blacks were in office in eleven southern states: Mississippi leads with 191. Aside from the significance of sheer numbers, the 1974 elections saw a rise in the importance of local offices held and provided channels through which blacks could help to make and implement decisions directly affecting the black community. For example, blacks captured control in Sparta, Georgia; swept the municipal elections in Gretna, Florida, where there had been no black registered voters before September 1971; gained control of local government in two Virginia counties; and elected a black mayor in Atlanta, Maynard Jackson. Table VIII gives details by state for 1972.

**TABLE VIII—BLACK ELECTED OFFICIALS BY STATE: MARCH 1972**

| State | 1970, percent Black | Black elected officials | | | | | |
|---|---|---|---|---|---|---|---|
| | | Total | Congress | State | City | County | Other[1] |
| United States .......... | 11.1 | 2,264 | 14 | 210 | 932 | 176 | 932 |
| Maine ................. | 0.3 | – | – | – | – | – | – |
| New Hampshire ........... | 0.3 | 1 | – | – | – | – | 1 |
| Vermont.................. | 0.2 | 1 | – | – | 1 | – | – |
| Massachusetts............. | 3.1 | 16 | 1 | 3 | 7 | – | 5 |
| Rhode Island ............ | 2.7 | 7 | – | 1 | 2 | – | 4 |
| Connecticut ............... | 6.0 | 51 | – | 6 | 28 | – | 17 |
| New York ................. | 11.9 | 163 | 2 | 12 | 16 | 6 | 127 |
| New Jersey ............... | 10.7 | 121 | – | 5 | 44 | 4 | 68 |
| Pennsylvania ............. | 8.6 | 63 | 1 | 11 | 15 | 1 | 35 |
| Ohio ..................... | 9.1 | 110 | 1 | 13 | 60 | – | 36 |
| Indiana ................... | 6.9 | 52 | – | 2 | 28 | 4 | 18 |
| Illinois ................... | 12.8 | 123 | 2 | 19 | 47 | 3 | 52 |
| Michigan ................. | 11.2 | 179 | 2 | 18 | 55 | 37 | 67 |
| Wisconsin ................. | 2.9 | 9 | – | 1 | 5 | 2 | 1 |
| Minnesota................. | 0.9 | 8 | – | – | 3 | – | 5 |
| Iowa ..................... | 1.2 | 10 | – | 1 | 2 | 1 | 6 |
| Missouri ................. | 10.3 | 77 | 1 | 15 | 30 | 1 | 30 |
| North Dakota ............. | 0.4 | – | – | – | – | – | – |
| South Dakota ............. | 0.2 | – | – | – | – | – | – |
| Nebraska ................. | 2.7 | 3 | – | 1 | 1 | – | 1 |
| Kansas ................... | 4.8 | 18 | – | 3 | 5 | 3 | 7 |
| Delaware ................. | 14.3 | 11 | – | 3 | 6 | 1 | 1 |
| Maryland ................. | 17.8 | 54 | 1 | 18 | 23 | – | 12 |
| District of Columbia ........ | 71.1 | 8 | 1 | – | – | – | 7 |
| Virginia .................. | 18.5 | 54 | – | 3 | 32 | 15 | 4 |
| West Virginia ............. | 3.9 | 5 | – | 1 | 4 | – | – |
| North Carolina ............. | 22.2 | 103 | – | 2 | 68 | 3 | 30 |
| South Carolina ........... | 30.5 | 66 | – | 3 | 41 | 7 | 15 |
| Georgia .................. | 25.9 | 65 | – | 15 | 32 | 7 | 11 |

**TABLE VIII—(Cont.)**

| State | 1970 percent Black | Black elected officials | | | | | |
|---|---|---|---|---|---|---|---|
| | | Total | Congress | State | City | County | Other[1] |
| Florida | 15.3 | 51 | – | 2 | 45 | 1 | 3 |
| Kentucky | 7.2 | 57 | – | 3 | 35 | 1 | 18 |
| Tennessee | 15.8 | 48 | – | 8 | 17 | 4 | 19 |
| Alabama | 26.2 | 83 | – | 2 | 42 | 16 | 23 |
| Mississippi | 36.8 | 129 | – | 1 | 40 | 27 | 61 |
| Arkansas | 18.3 | 97 | – | – | 44 | – | 53 |
| Louisiana | 29.8 | 119 | – | 8 | 28 | 31 | 52 |
| Oklahoma | 6.7 | 62 | – | 6 | 35 | – | 21 |
| Texas | 12.5 | 61 | – | 3 | 37 | – | 21 |
| Montana | 0.3 | – | – | – | – | – | – |
| Idaho | 0.3 | – | – | – | – | – | – |
| Wyoming | 0.8 | 2 | – | – | 1 | – | 1 |
| Colorado | 3.0 | 7 | – | 3 | 3 | – | 1 |
| New Mexico | 1.9 | 4 | – | 1 | 3 | – | – |
| Arizona | 3.0 | 10 | – | 4 | – | – | 6 |
| Utah | 0.6 | – | – | – | – | – | – |
| Nevada | 5.7 | 4 | – | 1 | 1 | – | 2 |
| Washington | 2.1 | 9 | – | 3 | 1 | – | 5 |
| Oregon | 1.3 | 5 | – | – | 1 | – | 4 |
| California | 7.0 | 134 | 2 | 7 | 43 | 1 | 81 |
| Alaska | 3.0 | 3 | – | 2 | – | – | 1 |
| Hawaii | 1.0 | 1 | – | – | 1 | – | – |

Note : Figures shown represent the total number of elected blacks holding office as of March 1972.

– Represents zero.

[1] Includes law enforcement and education.

Source :   Joint Center for Political Studies and U. S. Department of Commerce, Social and Economic Statistics Administration, Bureau of the Census.

A southern state-by-state roundup of black elected officeholders at the beginning of 1975 showed: Alabama, 149; Arkansas, 150; Florida, 73; Georgia, 136; Louisiana, 139; Mississippi, 191; North Carolina, 157; South Carolina, 115; Tennessee, 87; Texas, 123; and Virginia, 63. These figures should be measured against both the political panorama of yesteryear, which saw bloody turmoil in Selma, Alabama, and the fact that at the time of the enactment of the Voting Rights Act of 1965, fewer than 100 blacks held office in the above eleven southern states.

Another point worth noting is that there has been a decline in racial demagoguery and an increased reliance on reason in campaigns conducted by white politicians. This does not mean that racism has disappeared. But southern white politicians in increasing numbers are beginning to realize the importance of the black electorate. More than 300 blacks stood for office in Mississippi alone in the 1971 elections; only a few years ago, not one would have dared aspire to office for fear of reprisals ranging from economic pressure to brutal murder. The fact that so many candidates now step forward is vivid proof of positive change, change that can be directly traced to the efforts of the Voter Education Project.

In spite of such progress, there is still a major task to be done: the mobilization into voters of the 2.5 million blacks still unregistered in the South. Whites still control jobs, welfare checks, housing, social security food stamps, Medicare, and mortgages in the southern states. All of these are very real weapons with which to threaten blacks who take the risk of registering and voting. Southern blacks have had little confidence in recent Republican Administration policy regarding the enforcement of voting rights in the South.

The fact that there is still a long way to go was made clear to southern blacks in the 1974 fall elections. Although breakthroughs were made, thanks to blacks running more candidates than ever before, after the votes were counted they found themselves still victims of traditional racial tactics. The Arkansas Advisory Committee to the United States Civil Rights Commission pinpointed the following: intimidation, election fraud, police indifference to violence against blacks, and discrimination in hiring and in the administration of government programs. Witnesses in predominantly black areas complained of irregularities in recent elections where blacks opposed white officials. Blacks involved in these elections had been "suppressed, brutalized, abused, maimed, beaten, jailed, and intimidated." There were reports that sheriffs' deputies wearing guns looked over the shoulders of blacks when they voted at several precincts, and that black poll watchers had been kept so far from the voting places that they could not observe what was happening.

In Mississippi in 1971, irregularities and harassment, intimidation, and even violence were so widespread that Charles Evers, the defeated black gubernatorial candidate, announced that a group of black candidates would challenge the state-wide elections in the federal courts and ask for federal troops to supervise new elections. In spite of continuing progress, southern blacks were left with serious problems to thrash out in the political arena.

### General Concerns[21]

The foregoing study of the black political kaleidoscope points up several general problems. In the drive to build political strength today, blacks know they must be wary of certain pitfalls, and must strive to face political realities as squarely as possible. Although the 1970s began favorably with some impressive black victories, thoughtful observers realized that these triumphs were nothing more than flotsam on the national electoral tide. Blacks could still win, by and large, only in jurisdictions with black majorities or large nonwhite minorities, and these, although growing, are still limited in number. Since blacks made up little more than 11 percent of the population and cannot count on any substantial support from whites or other segments of society, a major question for blacks is how to consolidate current political gains in order to have the greatest possible national impact—or conversely, how to avoid dissipating vital votes in white-dominated state, trade union, or other organizations.

Also of extreme importance in the development of an effective thrust is the avoidance of splinter politics, which could fragment and retard the contemporary movement toward unity. This pitfall is a grave one given the national trend toward the proliferation of presidential candidates, which indicates that people generally are finding it harder to find acceptable political shelter under the umbrellas of the two major parties. Polls show that there are now about as many people calling themselves political independents as there are claiming to be Republican, and ticket-splitting occurs on more than half the ballots cast in modern elections.

Another consideration, and one that annually poses a problem for blacks as a group, is which black major party candidates to support. If black momentum is to increase, mistakes cannot be made in this area—to keep growing, political power must ride with the winner. The difficulty here, of course, is that no candidate or platform appeals to all the people. The presidential race of 1972, for instance, with its multiplicity of official and unofficial candidates, forced blacks to make a complex series of choices.

The elections of 1970 pointed up further problems facing blacks in the political sphere. To keep moving toward the political mainstream, for example, black candidates had to be of the highest quality, but in this election they were mainly first-time office-seekers, and so lacked the additional advantage that came with simply having been in office. Efforts were also hampered by the fact that since blacks are novices at big-time politics, they have no smoothly functioning ready-made machinery at their disposal. Under such circumstances, the question of who will compose a truly loyal and competent staff and how it is to function and be supported raises grave difficulties. Also, since even the smallest blunders can be disastrous for blacks in public life, they must learn how to cope with the inevitable political pressures for accommodation and compromise; how to coalesce high ideals and principles with pragmatic purpose and interests, without appearing to be acting out of expedience. And hovering over all political activity is the dark cloud of insufficient funds, money so badly needed to make the wheels go round.

## Redistricting Problem[22]

Blacks are faced with other difficulties as well. Among these is the reapportionment and remapping of political districts. As blacks grow in strength and as the courts instruct legislatures to redraw districts to conform to population statistics, as has been done recently, whites who have been given this authority may not always act with equity. Some remappers of political districts have been accused of a "callous, calculated conspiracy" to disenfranchise minorities by reducing their political effectiveness.

Yet other factors may intervene to deter blacks. For example, after the U.S. Justice Department in 1974 ordered a redrawing of lines in New York's 14th Congressional

District in Brooklyn to improve its ethnic balance and it became about 45 percent black and 18 percent Puerto Rican, black city Councilman Samuel D. Wright of Ocean Hill-Brownsville, refused to run for the seat. He said that because of the traditionally low turnout of black voters and the exclusion of his home neighborhood from the new district, he could not expect to win in the area. As a consequence, in November, white Fred Richmond won election as the Democratic Representative to Congress.

A survey made by the Congressional Black Caucus showed that a black candidate for Congress would have had a better chance of being elected in 1968 than in 1972. The findings, covering congressional districts with 10 percent or more black registered voters, showed a reduction of the black voting percentage during the 92nd Congress in those districts that had a substantial number of black voters during the 90th Congress. For example, in the Second District of Mississippi, the percentage of the black population was reduced from 59.1 percent during the 88th Congress, to 43 percent during the 90th, to 35.7 percent during the 92nd Congress. In North Carolina's Fifth District the black population percentage dropped from 26.7 during the 90th to 14.6 during the 92nd Congress. The Congressional Black Caucus, concerned about this development, sought to alert responsible black leaders to these facts.

## Principle and Practice[23]

Another problem blacks must confront and resolve, now that they have settled upon politics as the major way to attain parity in the land, is whom to trust among the whites with whom they must work. They know from past experience that all too often those they looked upon as liberal white allies have failed and ignored them when they have insisted upon a single high standard for blacks and whites alike. Moreover, such whites have tended to welcome mediocrity in black leadership. Such behavior in the past gives blacks reason to wonder how selfless present white dedication is to the cause of black progress.

Furthermore, blacks have seen these same liberals divert the energies of proven, fair, dependable white champions of civil rights to causes with lower priority for blacks, such as Vietnam, Cambodia, and ecology. Because there are many in the white majority who still show an unreadiness to jeopardize personal interests for the sake of ideals, blacks wonder whether they can make real political headway by continuing to support such white leaders—people who seem to prefer to adhere to the status quo rather than risk reform to gain something new.

As regards the extremist fringe, ever present in some form on the American political scene, the small number of blacks who tried this solution have been taught a harsh lesson from the tragic harvest reaped by black militants Eldridge Cleaver, H. Rap Brown, Bobby Seale, Fred Hampton, Stokely Carmichael, and Huey Newton, who came to the fore on the surge of the civil rights movement in the 1960s and were nurtured on the outrage expounded by the late Malcolm X. Today these men are either in exile, in court, forced to live abroad, out on bail, in jail, awaiting possible trial, or dead. Those black radicals who remain have lost their sense of purpose and drifted into disunity and despair. They have learned a harsh lesson: that American society is still essentially conservative.

In the national legislature to which blacks must look for the attainment of equity in public life, blacks have a minimal voice. They have only one voting member in a Senate of 100 and but seventeen voting members out of 435 in the House of Representatives, most of whom are of very recent service. The influence of these eighteen blacks is further limited by the fact that they are the victims of the antiquated seniority system that still governs committee assignments. They are thus unable to move into those key spots where the sentiments of their constituencies can be expressed on such pressing issues as hunger, food stamps, rural and urban poverty, school lunches, race and sex discrimination, legal aid, medical and health support, and improved housing.

In addition, they are hamstrung by the fact that the committee power of the purse in the House of Representatives is largely in the hands of white conservatives, mainly from southern and border states, who are largely unconcerned about the needs of blacks and other underprivileged citizens and thus are generally unresponsive to their depressed social condition. Blacks play no role of any consequence in such powerful bodies as the House Appropriations Committee, the group which determines how much money can be spent, with only one black out of each fifty-five members, or the Rules Committee, which among other things decides which bills can be brought up before the House for action.

## National Elections of 1974[24]

In the November 5, 1974, national elections, more blacks ran for major office than in 1972. James H. Brannen, III, was an unsuccessful Republican candidate for the U. S. Senate from Connecticut. Democrat Mervyn Dymally was elected lieutenant governor of California, an especially noteworthy feat, since he ran as an independent. The other successful candidate for lieutenant governor was George L. Brown, who was on the Democratic slate which elected Richard Lamm as Governor of Colorado. While in the Reconstruction era blacks were appointed as lieutenant governors in South Carolina and Louisiana, Dymally and Brown are the first ever to be elected to that office. Other black candidates for high state offices—governor (Nebraska), state treasurer, secretary of state, and attorney general—were defeated.

Although 50 blacks sought congressional seats, only 29-year-old Democratic state Representative Harold Ford of Tennessee won, raising to 17 the number of black members to serve in the House of Representatives in the 94th Congress, opening in January 1975. The 16 black incumbents (including the nonvoting delegate from Washington, D. C.) were all victorious. In southern states blacks accumulated a total of 35 new seats in state legislatures, where 85 of 118 black candidates were successful: in Alabama, with a 26 percent black population, 13 won in the 108-member House, and two in the Senate; South Carolina, 30 percent black, elected 9 for a total of 13 in its 124-member House; while Georgia, 25 percent black, added six to its 180-member House for a total of 20, plus two seats won in the state Senate.

Increasingly, black candidates have won in predominantly white districts; Mrs. Geraldine Ford, for example, became the first black elected to the state legislature of Montana, winning with 78 percent of the votes cast in a state with a negligible black population. A total of 94 black legislators, 10 of them senators, were serving in state houses from the Mason-Dixon line to the Gulf of Mexico; almost all were Democrats. It should be noted, too, that black registration increased from less than 1.5 million in 1965 to some 3.5 million by November 5, 1974, out of a voting-age population of six million. While some lag can be traced to discriminatory tactics not yet eliminated in the South, there is little doubt that lack of a long tradition of political participation has hampered the achievement of full representation relative to the proportion of blacks in the population; the Georgia-based Voter Education Project continues to work on the problem of motivation among southern blacks. While 1975 recorded a higher level of political activity than in former years, it should be viewed against a background of 79,000 elective offices in the 11 southern states, of which blacks held less than two percent at the beginning of 1975.

A look at the overall picture, however, offers definite reason for hope. The Democratic National Convention in Miami, Florida, in July 1972, pointed up the fact that while black political power is still a long way from attaining its full potential, it continues to move positively toward that goal. Blacks have accelerated their push into the political and economic arenas, having learned that these two are intimately related, and are rapidly learning how best to cope with and use the existing power structure. Present political activity among blacks seems more confident, more pragmatic, more tough-minded, and more sophisticated then ever before.

## Notes

1. Carl B. Stokes, "Inside Black Politics: A Personal View," Manuscript prepared for the Phelps-Stokes Fund, November 1971, p. 1.

2. James Q. Wilson, *Negro Politics: The Search for Leadership* (New York and Glencoe, Ill., The Free Press, 1971).

   "Developing Black Political Power: Meaningful Coalitions Stressed," Congressional Black Caucus Report, December 1971, Statements from First National Conference for Black Elected Officials, Washington, D. C., November 18–20, 1971.

   James T. Wooten, "Few Blacks Study Law in the South," *The New York Times*, November 12, 1970.

   Neil Amdur, "Black Power in Sports: From Protest to Perspective," *The New York Times*, March 12, 1972, sec. 5, p. 1.

"Elderly Negroes Present Demands: Meeting Seeks Recognition at White House Parley," *The New York Times*, November 14, 1971.

Paul Delaney, "Black Legislators' Impact Begins to Grow in Nation," *The New York Times*, March 19, 1972, p. 1.

Robert Reinhold, "Politicians Snapping Up Book That Most Publishers Rejected," *The New York Times*, March 14, 1972.

"The New Black Politics," *Newsweek*, June 7, 1971.

"Black Lawmakers in Congress," *Ebony*, February 1971.

"Vote Mobilization for the 1970s," *Ebony*, July 1971.

Kenneth B. Clark, "The Black Man in American Politics" (New York, Metropolitan Applied Research Center, Inc., December 1969).

"Political Gains by Negroes," *U. S. News & World Report*, July 13, 1970.

Mervyn M. Dymally, ed., *The Black Politician: His Struggle for Power* (Belmont, California, Duxbury Press, 1971).

"Census Shows Dixie Blacks' Immense Political Potential," *The New York Times*, July 6, 1971.

"Black Power: Political Surge," Washington *Post*, May 2, 1971, pp. A-1, A-18.

3. "National Notes: Black Power," *The New York Times*, October 24, 1971.

R. W. Apple, Jr., "Democratic Rules Reform Ending Favorite-Son Bids," *The New York Times*, January 10, 1972.

Paul Delaney, "Julian Bond Says Blacks Plan Favorite-Son Primary Races," *The New York Times*, September 20, 1971.

Robert L. Bartley, "A Black Vice-Presidential Candidate?" *Wall Street Journal*, November 16, 1971.

C. Gerald Fraser, "Mrs. Chisholm Completes 3-Day Campaign in Florida," *The New York Times*, February 28, 1972.

Jack Rosenthal, "One-Third Blacks Found in 15 Cities," *The New York Times*, May 19, 1971.

Michael Barone, Grant Ujifusa, and Douglas Matthews, *Almanac of American Politics* (Boston, Gambit Publishing Co., 1972).

4. James T. Wooten, "New Black Caucus in the South Aloof for Presidential Race," *The New York Times*, August 16, 1971.

Thomas A. Johnson, "Blacks Advised to Transcend Ghetto Politics," *The New York Times*, October 24, 1971.

"Black HUD Aide Critical of Agnew," *The New York Times*, July 21, 1971.

" 'Dismal,' Says Top Black of Nixon Record," New York *Daily News*, October 7, 1971.

"Aide Says Nixon Respects Blacks," *The New York Times*, July 20, 1971.

Paul Delaney, "Negro Aide Says Nixon Concern With Black Problems Is Growing," *The New York Times*, August 9, 1970.

Paul Delaney, "Nixon Defended on Rights Record," *The New York Times*, May 20, 1971.

"Aide Says President Respects Blacks, Domestic and Foreign," *The New York Times*, July 20, 1971.

Thomas A. Johnson, "Blacks Dismayed by Resignation," *The New York Times*, December 5, 1971.

"Silent Majority of Blacks Formed," *The New York Times*, July 12, 1970.

Warren Weaver, Jr., "1972 Black Drive for Nixon Mapped," *The New York Times*, December 17, 1971.

"White House Forms Its Own Black Caucus to Counter 13 Democrats in the House," *The New York Times*, June 2, 1970.

Roy Reed, " 'Loyalists' Accept Talks in Mississippi," *The New York Times*, February 28, 1972.

Tom Wicker, "The Last Word in Charleston," *The New York Times*, April 22, 1971.

"White House Defending Record, Cites Progress on Civil Rights," *The New York Times*, February 16, 1972.

5. Rowland Evans, Jr. and Robert D. Novak, *Nixon in the White House: The Frustration of Power* (Random House, New York, 1971).

Paul Delaney, "Blacks Give Nixon May 17 Deadline," *The New York Times*, March 27, 1971.

"Nixon's Odd View of the Court," editorial, *Life*, November 5, 1971, p. 36.

"Carswell Called Foe of Women's Rights," *The New York Times*, January 30, 1970.

Fred P. Graham, "Senators Are Told Carswell Was 'Insulting' to Negro Lawyers," *The New York Times*, February 3, 1970.

"A Nixon Crisis: Advice But No Consent," *Newsweek*, April 20, 1970.

"Administration Posture on Segregation," Letter to the Editor by James E. Allen, Jr., former U. S. Commissioner of Education, *The New York Times*, August 17, 1971.

James Rhodes, Jr., "The Administration's Vision of the World," Op-Ed page, *The New York Times*, September 22, 1970.

John Herbers, "President Orders a Study to Devise Antibusing Plan," *The New York Times*, February 11, 1972.

"Mr. Nixon on School and Race," editorial, Washington *Post*, March 18, 1972, p. A-14.

Robert B. Sample, Jr., "Nixon Asks Bill Imposing Halt in New Busing Orders: Seeks Education Equality," *The New York Times*, March 17, 1972, p. 1.

John Herbers, "President Seeks Permanent Curb on School Busing," *The New York Times*, March 18, 1972.

"Group to Monitor Civil Rights Laws," *The New York Times*, September 26, 1971.

Jack Rosenthal, "Lawyer for the Poor," *The New York Times*, February 12, 1972.

"For Legal Equality," editorial, *The New York Times*, February 15, 1972.

"Legal Services Program," Letter to the Editor by David Gladfelter, *The New York Times*, February 12, 1972.

"White Magic," editorial, *The New York Times*, August 24, 1970.

Max Frankel, "Is 'Benign Neglect' the Real Nixon Approach?" *The New York Times*, March 8, 1970.

"Neglect—But Not Benign," editorial, *The New York Times*, March 3, 1970.

Peter Kihss, "Benign Neglect on Racial Issues Is Proposed by Moynihan," *The New York Times*, March 1, 1970.

*National Roster of Black Elected Officials*, compiled by the Joint Center for Political Studies, Washington, D. C., March 1972.

"Political Gains by Negroes," *U. S. News & World Report*, July 13, 1970.

"Where Blacks Hold Elected Office," *ibid.*

Steven Morris, "Annual Progress Report: A Term of Trials—Caucuses and Confrontations Continued Trend Toward Political Black Unity," *Ebony*, January 1972.

6. Paul Delaney, "President Meets Blacks in House," *The New York Times*, August 22, 1974, p. 24.

Paul Delaney, "Black Leaders Exhibit Cautious Optimism on Ford," *The New York Times*, September 1, 1974, p. 32.

7. Paul Delaney, "Black Legislators' Impact Begins to Grow in Nation," *The New York Times*, March 19, 1972.

Paul Delaney, "Chisholm Appeal Divides Blacks; Imperils Liberals in Florida Race," *The New York Times*, March 14, 1972.

Thomas A. Johnson, "Mrs. Chisholm Chides Black Caucus," *The New York Times*, November 20, 1971.

"How to Foster Division in Black Ranks," Letter to the Editor by John A. Morsell of the NAACP, *The New York Times*, October 16, 1971.

R. W. Apple, Jr., "Black Democrats Back Hughes Bid," *The New York Times*, October 10, 1971.

R. W. Apple, Jr., "Democrats Back Mrs. Harris, 9-3," *The New York Times*, October 13, 1971.

Thomas A. Johnson, "Head of Operation Breadbasket Says He Opposes Mrs. Chisholm," *The New York Times*, January 27, 1972.

R. W. Apple, Jr., "Mrs. Harris Wins Democratic Post," *The New York Times*, October 14, 1971.

Thomas A. Johnson, "Blacks at Parley Divided on Basic Role in Politics," *The New York Times*, March 12, 1972.

Thomas A. Johnson, "NAACP Aide Opposes Draft of Black Preamble," *The New York Times*, March 10, 1972.

8. Paul Delaney, "Black Caucus Adopts Realistic Goals," *The New York Times*, June 18, 1972.

Thomas A. Johnson, "Black Group Maps Political Action," *The New York Times*, September 6, 1971.

C. Gerald Fraser, "Blacks Meet Here to Plan Election Role," *The New York Times*, January 9, 1972.

"Black Caucus Plans Forum on Priorities," *The New York Times*, February 3, 1972.

"Blacks End Parley on a '72 Convention," *The New York Times*, September 27, 1971.

Alex Poinsett, "Black Political Strategies for '72." *Ebony*, February 1972.

"Black Caucus in House Scores Nixon Reply on Aid to Minorities," *The New York Times*, May 24, 1971.

Paul Delaney, "Blacks Give Nixon May 17 Deadline," *The New York Times*, March 27, 1971.

"Congressional Black Caucus: U. S. House of Representatives," leaflet, Washington D. C. Headquarters, 415 Second Street, N. E., 1971.

*The Congressional Black Caucus Report*, Vol. 1, No. 1, November 1971.

"The New Black Politics," *Newsweek*, June 7, 1971.

Paul Delaney, "Rep. Stokes Heads the Black Caucus," *The New York Times*, February 9, 1972.

9. Paul Delaney, "Hatcher Chosen to Keynote Black Convention," *The New York Times*, March 7, 1972.

"Black Parley Aides Promise Admission of White Newsmen," *The New York Times*, March 9, 1972.

Thomas A. Johnson, "Black Assembly Voted at Parley," *The New York Times*, March 13, 1972.

Hugh Wyatt, "Nationalists Win and Blacks OK Tough Agenda," New York *Daily News*, March 13, 1972.

Thomas A. Johnson, "Parley Shows Complexity and Vitality of Black America," *The New York Times*, March 14, 1972.

"Hatcher Reviews Parley of Blacks," *The New York Times*, March 16, 1972.

Stephen S. Rosenfeld, "Blacks Signal Turn in Foreign Policy," Washington *Post*, March 16, 1972.

Roger Wilkins, "Gary Convention Points to a Black Political Party," Washington *Post*, March 18, 1972.

"Home Rule Charter is Approved by a Margin of 4 to 1," *The New York Times*, May 8, 1974, p. 41.

Paul Delaney, "Low Key Black Meeting," *The New York Times*, March 22, 1974, p. 28.

"Report to Black Parley Scores Avoidance of Minority Needs," *The New York Times*, March 16, 1974, p. 11.

10. Marjorie Hunter, "Democratic Rules Panel Backs Sweeping Changes," *The New York Times*, June 25, 1972.

Thomas A. Johnson, "Power in Harlem Emanates From Many Bases," *The New York Times*, December 6, 1970.

John J. O'Connor, "TV: The White House and Public Programming," *The New York Times*, February 11, 1972.

Maurine Christopher, *America's Black Congressmen* (New York, Crowell, 1971).

Richard Bruner, *Black Politicians* (New York, David McKay, 1971).

"Group to Monitor Civil Rights Laws," *The New York Times*, September 26, 1971.

Dick Gregory, *Dick Gregory's Political Primer* (New York, Harper & Row, 1972.).

Thomas A. Johnson, "Blacks Take Charge, and Changes Follow in Eutaw, Ala.," *The New York Times*, August 4, 1970.

Earl Caldwell, "Separatism Deplored by a Black Jurist," *The New York Times*, July 8, 1971.

Earl Caldwell, "Black Judges Set Goals at Parley," *The New York Times*, August 8, 1971.

Paul Delaney, "Black Exposition Marked by Politics," *The New York Times*, October 1, 1972.

"Platform Formed by State Blacks," *The New York Times*, March 6, 1972.

Paul Delaney, "Operation PUSH Opens a Black Expo in Chicago," *The New York Times*, September 28, 1972.

11. Thomas A. Johnson, "Fish Fries Raise Funds for Mississippi Black," *The New York Times*, November 1, 1971.

"The $400 Million Election Machine," *Newsweek*, December 13, 1971.

Paul Delaney, "Fund Events Aid Black Candidates," *The New York Times*, September 28, 1970.

12. "The $400 Million Election Machine," *Newsweek*, December 13, 1971.

Telephone interview with Common Cause on March 5, 1975.

13. Thomas A. Johnson, "The Mississippi Elections," *The New York Times*, November 15, 1971.

James T. Wooten, "Rights Aides Find Southern Blacks Failing to Use Voting Power," *The New York Times*, August 8, 1971.

"We the Black People of the United States (Our Voting Record)," U. S. Department of Commerce, Bureau of the Census, Washington D. C., 1969.

James Reston, "The Forgotten Battle," *The New York Times*, November 17, 1971.

Paul Delaney, "Apathy Big Problem of Black Candidates," *The New York Times*, July 22, 1972.

14. Thomas A. Johnson, "Negro Candidates in Mississippi Combat 'White Is Right' Feelings," *The New York Times*, October 5, 1971.

15. Laurie Johnston, "Women's Caucus Has New Rallying Cry: 'Make Policy, Not Coffee,'" *The New York Times*, February 6, 1972.

"Candidates' Day: Mrs. Chisholm Asks Help of Students," *The New York Times*, March 4, 1972.

C. Gerald Fraser, "Black Women Form a Group for Political Leverage," *The New York Times*, January 30, 1972.

"Women's Caucus Target of White House Jokes," *The New York Times*, July 15, 1971.

"Plans Revealed by Mrs. Chisholm," *The New York Times*, March 4, 1972.

R. W. Apple, Jr., "Gains in House Foreseen for Blacks and Women," *The New York Times*, October 19, 1970.

Ted Lewis, "Nixon Should Open the Door Wider to Critics," New York *Daily News*, March 24, 1971.

"Women's Caucus May Enlist Men," *The New York Times*, July 22, 1971.

"Caucus to Seek Equal Number of Women Convention Delegates," *The New York Times*, November 10, 1971.

"Two Black Women Head for House," *The New York Times*, October 7, 1972.

16. *Characteristics of American Youth: 1971*, Current Population Reports, Special Studies, Series P-23, No. 40. U. S. Department of Commerce, Bureau of the Census, Washington, D. C., January 1972, Table 18, p. 21.

*Characteristics of New Voters: 1972*, U. S. Census Report, P-20, No. 230, 1972.

Jack Rosenthal, "5 to 7 Percent of Voters May Be 18–20," *The New York Times*, January 2, 1972.

Stephen Hess, "Corrections Please, On the Youth Vote," *The New York Times*, November 29, 1971.

"Kansas Ruling of Youth Vote May Peril Colleges," *The New York Times*, January 10, 1972.

"The Youth Vote Will Count," Letter to the Editor, *The New York Times*, December 14, 1971.

Agis Salpukas, "Youth See Little Effect from Newly Won Rights," *The New York Times*, January 1, 1972.

Steven V. Roberts, "Working Youth: The 17 Million 'Invisible' New Voters," *The New York Times*, March 11, 1972.

"Pro Bono Publico—The New Activism," pamphlet of the Law Students Civil Rights Research Council, New York, 1972.

Jack Rosenthal, "Youth Vote Held of Little Impact," *The New York Times*, January 4, 1973, p. 19.

17. John L. Hess, "Cleaver Sees a Threat to Blacks in U.S.-China Thaw," *The New York Times*, October 7, 1971.

Theodore Draper, *The Rediscovery of Black Nationalism* (New York, Viking, 1970).

John H. Bracey, Jr., August Meier, and Elliott Rudwick, *Black Nationalism in America* (Boston, Bobbs-Merrill, 1970).

"Wrong Road to Equality," editorial, *The New York Times*, October 12, 1971.

Thomas A. Johnson, "Black Nationalists Now Focusing on Politics," *The New York Times*, September 11, 1971.

Floyd B. Barbour, ed., *The Black Seventies* (Extending Horizon Books Published by Porter Sargent, Boston, 1970).

William V. Shannon, "A New Reform Era," *The New York Times*, September 15, 1971.

Karsten Prager, "Right On Toward a New Black Pluralism," Special Issue on the Cooling of America, *Time*, February 22, 1971.

Donald Reeves, "Nothing in Common With Whites," *The New York Times*, March 11, 1972.

18. "Wallace Says He Has Two Jewish Relatives," *The New York Times*, February 10, 1972.

Richard Mathieu, "Puerto Ricans See a Plot to Soften Their Vote Clout," New York *Daily News*, February 9, 1972.

R. W. Apple, Jr., "Conservative Victories in Major Cities Reflect Continuing Racial Polarization," *The New York Times*, November 3, 1971.

Robert B. Semple, Jr., "Nixon's Racial Stance," *The New York Times*, May 21, 1971.

Kevin Phillips, *The Emerging Republican Majority* (New York, Arlington House, 1969).

Reg Murphy and Hal Gulliver, *The Southern Strategy* (New York, Charles Scribner's Sons, 1971).

Leon E. Panetta and Peter Gall, *Bring Us Together: The Nixon Team and Civil Rights Retreat* (New York, J. B. Lippincott Co., 1971).

R. W. Apple, Jr., "Elections in U. S. Tomorrow Focus on Racial Issues," *The New York Times*, November 1, 1971.

Joseph Lelyveld, "Candidates in Florida Enticing Jewish Voters," *The New York Times*, March 10, 1972.

Martin Waldron, "Race Flare-Ups Mar Campaign in Florida," *The New York Times*, March 19, 1972.

"Mississippi Dispute Is Won by Loyalists," *The New York Times*, July 9, 1972.

"F. C. C. Won't Block Racist Ad in South," *The New York Times*, August 4, 1972.

Roy Reed, "New Voter Form Stirs Mississippi," *The New York Times*, August 7, 1972.

Paul Delaney, "All He Talks About Are Social and Human Values," *The New York Times*, September 26, 1971.

Andrew M. Greeley, "A Black for Vice President in 1972," *The New York Times Magazine*, September 19, 1971.

Roy Reed, "Evers Is Defeated in Large Turnout in Mississippi Vote," *The New York Times*, November 3, 1971.

"Dole Asserts G. O. P. Wins Ethnic Groups," *The New York Times*, October 11, 1971.

James T. Wooten, "White Alabama Loser Sues to Upset Victory of Negro," *The New York Times*, December 6, 1970.

James T. Wooten, "Judge Is Found Guilty in Keeping Negroes off the Slate," *The New York Times*, January 8, 1971.

"Lubell Says Study of '69 Voting Here [New York City] Shows Racial Trend," *The New York Times*, July 13, 1970.

James M. Naughton, "Muskie Rules Out a Black Running Mate," *The New York Times*, September 9, 1971.

"Evers Supports Muskie on Blacks; Agrees Negro Could Not Be Elected Vice President," *The New York Times*, October 12, 1971.

Les Ledbetter, "Wilkins Says Muskie is 'Probably Right' in Stand Against a Black Running Mate," *The New York Times*, January 11, 1972.

Martin Waldron, "Busing Held Key Issue to Florida Blacks," *The New York Times*, March 3, 1972.

"Racism and the Reporting of Politics," editorial, Washington *Post*, March 3, 1972.

James M. Naughton, "Muskie Denies an Ethnic Slur," *The New York Times*, February 27, 1972.

"President Scores a Muskie Remark: Says Senator 'Libels' U.S. Public in Barring Negro as a Running Mate," *The New York Times*, September 17, 1971.

Carl Bernstein, "Virginia House Passes Open Housing Bill," Washington *Post*, March 3, 1972.

"Black Picture on Flyer Found To Be That of Ex-Ambassador," *The New York Times*, October 14, 1972.

B. Drummond Ayres, Jr., "The South's Old Racial Politics Is Finished," *The New York Times*, September 8, 1974, section 4, p. 4.

B. Drummond Ayres, Jr., "Racism Shunned by Black Mayors," *The New York Times*, June 3, 1974, p. 3.

Wayne King, "Maddox Links Rival to a Black Leader," *The New York Times*, August 30, 1974, p. 17.

"At the Polls," editorial in *The New York Times*, May 10, 1974, p. 36.

Ray Jenkins, "Black Vote for Wallace Is Put at 20–25% in Alabama Primary," *The New York Times*, May 9, 1974, p. 50.

B. Drummond Ayres, Jr., "Alabama Primary Won By Wallace," *The New York Times*, May 8, 1974, p. 41.

"Notes on People," *The New York Times*, November 8, 1974, p. 45.

"Notes on People: Bury Hatchet in Alabama," *The New York Times*, May 17, 1974, p. 35.

19. "The New Black Politics," *Newsweek*, June 7, 1971.

"Black Lawmakers in Congress," *Ebony*, February 1971.

James Q. Wilson, *op. cit.*

"Vote Mobilization for the 1970s," *Ebony*, July 1971.

Mervyn M. Dymally, *op. cit.*

"Political Gains by Negroes," *U.S. News & World Report*, July 13, 1970.

"5 of New Jersey's 6 Black Mayors Find Money Major Problem," *The New York Times*, February 23, 1972.

"Black Power: Political Surge," Washington *Post*, May 2, 1971.

"Developing Black Political Power: Meaningful Coalitions Stressed," *Congressional Black Caucus Report*, from first national conference for black elected officials, November 18–20, 1971, Washington, D.C.

20. Tom Wicker, "Facing Up in the South," *The New York Times*, May 9, 1971.

"Grassroots Politics in Alabama," special issue of *Imani*, February 1971.

Peter Schrag, "A Hesitant New South: Fragile Promise on the Last Frontier," *Saturday Review*, February 12, 1972.

James T. Wooten, "New Black Caucus in the South Aloof from Presidential Race," *The New York Times*, August 16, 1971.

"Black Voters Win Control of a Town in North Florida," *The New York Times*, December 12, 1971.

Thomas A. Johnson, "Negro Candidates in Mississippi Combat 'White Is Right' Feeling," *The New York Times*, October 5, 1971.

John Herbers, "Nixon Will Move to Offset Rulings for Pupil Busing," *The New York Times*, February 15, 1972.

"Arkansas Blacks Voice Complaints," *The New York Times*, November 8, 1971.

Thomas A. Johnson, "Mississippi Election Results Challenged by Scores of Defeated Black Candidates," *The New York Times*, November 4, 1971.

Thomas A. Johnson, "Mississippi Poll Watchers Say Harrassment Barred Fair Tally," *The New York Times*, November 7, 1971.

Roy Reed, "Waller Sees Harmony in Mississippi," *The New York Times*, November 4, 1971.

R. W. Apple, Jr., "New-South Politics Found to Be Not so New," *The New York Times*, February 24, 1972.

"Democratic Groups in Mississippi Pick Convention Slates," *The New York Times*, February 14, 1972.

Eileen Shanahan, "Democratic Women in South to Challenge Rules on Picking Convention Delegates," *The New York Times*, February 14, 1972.

Nan Robertson, "Tracking Florida Voters Along the Chisholm Trail: The Route is Uphill, Tough but Very Well Defined," *The New York Times*, February 14, 1972.

Bill Kovach, "Politics Is Ho-Hum in Ethnic Baltimore," *The New York Times*, October 16, 1972.

Bill Kovach, "Both Parties Stepping up Campaigns for the Allegiance of Ethnic Voters," *The New York Times*, September 24, 1972.

Tom Wicker, "New Mood in the South," *The New York Times*, April 25, 1971.

Alex Poinsett, "Black Politics at the Crossroads," *Ebony*, October 1972.

Thomas A. Johnson, "Louisiana Negroes Seek Power," *The New York Times*, September 29, 1971.

Paul Delaney, "Blacks Reassess Political Role After Atlanta Loss," *The New York Times*, November 9, 1970.

Jon Nordheimer, "Equal Rights: We're Gonna Do Things Just Like in the Past," *The New York Times*, March 28, 1961.

Paul Delaney, "Black Potential in South Shown," *The New York Times*, July 6, 1971.

Paul Delaney, "Blacks to Decide Mississippi Race," *The New York Times*, August 22, 1971.

"Black Activist Appears Winner Over Representative Friedel in Maryland," *The New York Times*, September 28, 1970.

R. W. Apple, Jr., "New Figures in South's Politics, *The New York Times*, September 11, 1970.

"Blacks Win Posts in North Carolina," *The New York Times*, May 6, 1971.

Thomas A. Johnson, "The Mississippi Election," *The New York Times*, November 15, 1971.

Roy Reed, "Democrats Seek Mississippi Pact," *The New York Times*, February 27, 1972.

Thomas A. Johnson, "Blacks in Georgia Let White Minority Share Power," *The New York Times*, September 8, 1972.

Paul Delaney, "Black Political Power in South Up in '71," *The New York Times*, January 31, 1972.

John Herbers, "Gardner's Common Cause Widens Impact," *The New York Times*, October 11, 1971.

"Black America," special issue of *Time*, April 6, 1970.

James Reston, "Voices of the South," *The New York Times*, January 22, 1971.

Jon Nordheimer, "16 Georgia Blacks Named Delegates," *The New York Times*, March 12, 1972.

Jon Nordheimer, "2 Blacks Returning to Alabama Take Office as Mayors," *The New York Times*, October 5, 1972.

21. R. W. Apple, Jr., "Black Politics: 'How Can We Have a Real National Impact?'" *The New York Times*, September 26, 1971.

Paul Delaney, "Blacks Are Divided on the Convention," *The New York Times*, July 16, 1972.

Tom Wicker, "Splinter Politics," *The New York Times*, January 2, 1972.

Paul Delaney, "Blacks for Nixon Sharply Rebuked," *The New York Times*, August 3, 1972.

Tom Wicker, "Reaching for the Ring," *The New York Times*, November 23, 1971.

Paul Delaney, "Blacks Are Split at Miami Beach," *The New York Times*, July 9, 1972.

Fred Powledge, "The Marketing of Nelson Rockefeller," *New York Magazine*, Vol. 3, No. 48, November 30, 1970.

Paul Delaney, "Black Supporters of President Under Fire," *The New York Times*, October 17, 1972.

22. James F. Clarity, "Remapping May Hurt Democrats Here (New York City)," *The New York Times*, February 13, 1972.

"Blacks Lose Voting Strength in Congressional Redistricting," *The Congressional Black Caucus Report*, Vol. 1, No. 1., November, 1971.

*Ibid.*, "National Parties Silent on Redistricting."

Grace Lichenstein, "Whites Lead in Race in Rooney's Redrawn District," *The New York Times*, August 11, 1974, p. 38.

"Members of the New Congress, Governors and the Winners in Westchester," *The New York Times*, November 7, 1974, p. 41.

23. William V. Shannon, "Ideals vs. Interests," *The New York Times*, October 14, 1971.

"Violent Harvest for Black Militants," *Life*, October 29, 1971.

Donald Reeves, "Nothing in Common With Whites," *The New York Times*, March 11, 1972.

William V. Shannon, "The Money Men," *The New York Times*, September 24, 1971.

William V. Shannon, "The Lopsided House," *The New York Times*, September 22, 1971.

"The Black Mood: More Militant, More Hopeful, More Determined," A Time-Louis Harris Poll, *Time*, April 6, 1970, pp. 28–29.

Stephan Lesher, "The Short, Unhappy Life of Black Presidential Politics, 1972," *The New York Times Magazine*, June 25, 1972.

Paul Delaney, "Black Caucus Adopts Realistic Goals," *The New York Times*, June 18, 1972.

24. S. G. Kennedy, "California and Colorado Name Blacks as Lieutenant Governors," *The New York Times*, November 7, 1974, p. 30.

"Center Finds a Rise in Black Candidates, But Not in Hopes," *The New York Times*, October 22, 1974, p. 3.

Paul Delaney, "Big Rise Noted in Total of Black Elected Officials," *The New York Times*, April 23, 1974, p. 20.

B. Drummond Ayres, Jr., "Southern Blacks Make Major Gains," *The New York Times*, November 11, 1974, p. 30.

# BIBLIOGRAPHY

Barone, Michael; Ujifusa, Grant; and Matthews, Douglas, *Almanac of American Politics*. Boston, Gambit Publishing Co., 1972.

"Black America," special issue of *Time*. April 6, 1970.

Bruner, Richard, *Black Politicians*. New York, David McKay, 1971.

Christopher, Maurine, *America's Black Congressmen*. New York, Crowell, 1971.

Davidson, Chandler, *Bi-racial Politics: Conflict and Coalition in the Metropolitan South*. Baton Rouge, Louisiana State University Press, 1972.

Draper, Theodore, *The Rediscovery of Black Nationalism*. New York, Viking, 1970.

Dutton, Frederick G., *Changing Sources of Power*. New York, McGraw-Hill Book Co., 1971.

Dymally, Mervyn, ed., *The Black Politician: His Struggle for Power*. Los Angeles, Duxberry Press, 1971.

Evans, Rowland and Novak, Robert D., *Nixon in the White House: The Frustration of Power*. New York, Random House, 1971.

Gregory, Dick, *Dick Gregory's Political Primer*. New York, Harper & Row, 1972.

Lesher, Stephan, "The Short, Unhappy Life of Black Presidential Politics." *The New York Times Magazine*, June 25, 1972.

Meier, August and Rudwick, Elliott, *Black Nationalism in America*. Boston, Bobbs-Merrill, 1970.

Murphy, Reg and Gulliver, Hal, *The Southern Strategy*. New York, Charles Scribner's Sons, 1971.

Panetta, Leon E. and Gall, Peter, *Bring Us Together: The Nixon Team and Civil Rights Retreat*. New York, J. B. Lippincott Co., 1971.

Schrag, Peter, "A Hesitant New South: Fragile Promise on the Last Frontier." *Saturday Review*, February 12, 1972.

The Joint Center for Political Studies, *National Roster of Black Elected Officials*. Washington, D. C., 1426 H Street, N. W., March 1972.

"The New Black Politics," *Newsweek*, June 7, 1971.

Wilson, James Q., *Negro Politics: The Search for Leadership*. New York, The Free Press, 1971.

Walton, Hanes, Jr., *Black Political Parties: An Historical and Political Analysis*. New York, The Free Press, 1972.

Wright, Nathan, Jr., ed., *What Black Politicians Are Saying*. New York, Hawthorn Books, 1972.

# 18

## The Black Role in American Politics:
## Part II, The Past

### G. James Fleming

It is a common belief that the black man in America secured the first vestiges of citizenship only when Lincoln pronounced the Emancipation Proclamation. There are also those who see this citizenship made firm and universal with the passage of the Thirteenth, Fourteenth, and Fifteenth Amendments. To these persons the black American first began to be a factor in politics only during the Reconstruction period. Neither of these observations, however, is the fact; and neither singly nor together do they tell the whole story.

Black Americans figured in political decisions long before they were citizens. Many laws and actions of the colonies and of the later Confederation governments were influenced by the presence of black men in the population. The Black Codes, the wording of the Articles of Confederation and of the Constitution, and court decisions, as in the *Dred Scott* case, were all political acts and decisions which followed the patterns they did at least in part because of the presence of blacks—although the latter had no part in the making of any of these decisions. This was true for both "free" and slave, for nowhere was the free black man as free as the white man.

The exclusion of blacks from politics and the privileges of citizenship was not monolithic and absolute. At least on paper, several of the constitutions of the new post-Revolution states extended the suffrage to free blacks by not including any restrictions based on race. Accordingly, blacks voted, but several states disfranchised them in later revisions of their constitutions.

### Earliest Right to Vote

The New Jersey constitution of 1776 extended the suffrage to all residents of the colony, "of full age who were worth fifty pounds proclamation money." Not only were there no restrictions based on race or condition of servitude, but there was no restriction based on sex or place of birth; aliens could also vote. In 1807, however, New Jersey passed a "clarifying act" limiting the ballot to free, white, male citizens. There was protest, but this restrictive measure was reaffirmed in 1820.

In New York in the late 1700s, free blacks could vote if they owned land to the value of twenty pounds or showed financial substance in other ways. The first constitution, adopted in 1777, gave the right to vote for members of the State Assembly to "every male inhabitant of full age" who satisfied residence and property requirements, the latter being ownership of real property (a freehold) to the value of twenty pounds or the leasing of a property for forty shillings. To vote for the Senate the property requirement was one hundred pounds.[1] There was equality in the law as far as suffrage was concerned. These property requirements were nevertheless exorbitant for the rank and file of eighteenth-century Americans and more so for black men, who were the marginal workers.

Enough blacks took to voting, however, to thereby irritate some politicians and their followers into devising ways and means of restricting or eliminating the black vote. This opposition first took the form of an act "to prevent frauds at elections." Section III of this act stated "that whenever any black person or person of color shall present himself to vote... , he shall produce to the inspectors or persons conducting such election a certificate of his freedom under the hand and seal of one of the clerks of the county of this state, or under the hand of any clerk with this state."[2]

Several objections were raised in the legislature to this bill, which set up prerequisites for voting that few blacks could meet—prerequisites much more difficult to attain than the property requirement. Wesley presents the objections that were sent to the Senate as follows:

> These were summarized as (1) the bill was "dangerous in precedent and against the public good"; (2) the description of a person of color was too vague; (3) many persons were born free and would find it difficult to secure freedom certificates; (4) the right to vote was subjected to the pleasure of others who in many cases would be interested in withholding the vote; (5) many Negroes lived and were far removed from their place of birth or manumission; (6) provisions necessary to qualify for the vote were impossible to secure before the election date of April 30, 1811; (7) there was no justification for the passing of an act which disfranchised a portion of the electors, even for a year; (8) there was no precedent for such a radical change in the election laws so close to an election.[3]

Nonetheless, this so-called antifraud act became law on April 9, 1811, shortly before a state election.

One of the reasons for the opposition to black voting was the logical contention that blacks tended to give their support to the Federalists, their aristocratic employers. This pro-Federalist alignment of blacks is credited with providing the "balance of power" which kept the Federalists in power. The anti-Federalists and others were afraid that the growing black population would play an increasingly larger role in determining the outcome of New York's elections. Wesley notes that "In the election of 1800, it was extravagantly said that 'the political character of the national government was changed by the vote of a single Negro ward in the city of New York.' "[4] The opposition party to the Federalists, the Democratic-Republicans, also bellowed a campaign song whose theme was "Federalists with Blacks Unite."[5]

Despite the attempts to restrict black voting, black men could still vote if they met the stringent and discriminatory requirements of 1811. But they were to be restricted even more by the constitutional convention of 1821, in which black suffrage was a central argument. The convention was divided between those who urged equal suffrage for all citizens and those who were obsessed with the idea that the black vote was a bloc vote which could be manipulated against what these opponents considered the public good. In the legislature there were charges that blacks were inferior, lacked intelligence and discretion, and were given to crime—and those who made these charges called on the Bible to help prove their points.

Blacks petitioned the New York legislature to protect their voting rights, and white men such as Peter Jay stressed that although there were some 30,000 black voters in the state, they constituted only one-fortieth of the total vote and represented no threat to the body politic. Several other voices of non-blacks were raised against restrictions on the black vote.

The proposal to limit the vote to white males only was lost, but a new plan was made into law which required of whites ownership of a 40-pound freehold, while setting a 250-pound freehold as the property requirement of blacks. In addition, the law also set different residence requirements for whites and blacks, with an unfavorable differential for blacks. Whites could vote after a residence of only one year, while blacks had to reside in the state three years. Furthermore, black voters had to have paid taxes, while whites could substitute highway or military service for money taxes.

In 1846 another constitutional convention retained all discriminatory differentials against blacks, after vituperative argument and after attempts both to strike out racial distinction and to deny the franchise to blacks altogether were defeated.

While there were assertions that blacks, voting as a bloc, could control New York City politics, Hirsch found that according to the 1820 census, of 10,886 black voters registered in the city only 100 voted in 1819 and only 612 voted in 1820.[6] This was probably due to the restrictive law passed in 1811 and to the other obstacles raised by voting inspectors to keep blacks from voting.

In addition to internal action by the state legislature, proposals to amend the New York constitution so as to strike down the discrimination against black voters were also put before the people in referenda—in 1846, 1849, 1860, and 1869. In every instance the liberalizing proposal was voted down. As late as 1869 the proposal was defeated, statewide, by 249,802 to 282,403. The temper of the majority-group citizens (at least of their representatives) is also shown by the fact that the New York legislature, which had ratified the Fifteenth Amendment to the Federal Constitution, rescinded its ratification in 1870, following the 1869 defeat of the local referendum. It took the ratification of the Fifteenth Amendment by three-fourths of the states to abolish racial discrimination in New York's suffrage laws.

New York furnishes the fullest example of the pattern of politics as far as black suffrage was concerned, prior to the Emancipation Proclamation and the Reconstruction period amendments to the U. S. Constitution. But there were other states in which blacks enjoyed the suffrage, more or less, and for a shorter or longer period of time.

Vermont, Kentucky, and Tennessee, in their constitutions of the 1790s, according to Wesley "made no provision in their constitutions concerning the exclusion of Negroes from the ballot." The Pennsylvania constitution of 1790 did not, on paper, exclude blacks from the suffrage after the word "white" had been deleted in an earlier draft. The constitution adopted in Ohio in 1802 also granted the right of the ballot to blacks, but intermittent objections to the inclusion of blacks came to a head in the constitutional convention of 1850 and a resolution to limit the suffrage to white males was carried by a vote of 66 to 12.

In further reference to Pennsylvania, there is no evidence that blacks voted in that state before 1790, although they could own property and were taxed. "From different arguments in the state legislature over several years there are also indications that the state constitution was interpreted differently in different parts of the state and at different times as to whether Negroes could vote or not." One interesting example of this occurred nearly twenty years before the Dred Scott Decision (1857), when the Pennsylvania Supreme Court held that the black man was not a freeman and therefore not entitled to vote. The case came before the highest court when "a candidate for office in Bucks County, who was defeated, claimed his opponent's seat because Negroes had been permitted to vote for him [the opponent]. . . contrary to law."[7] This case aroused the pent-up ill will of black voters but the Pennsylvania constitution was amended in 1838 to make it clear that the suffrage was limited to whites.

Tennessee, Kentucky, and North Carolina permitted blacks to vote at first, but after some years each amended its constitution to limit the suffrage to white males.

During the period between the Philadelphia conventions of 1787 and 1865, only Maine, New Hampshire, Vermont, Rhode Island, and Massachusetts permitted blacks to vote on equal terms with whites. All other states, at some time, have barred black Americans from the suffrage.[8]

Since citizen group activity is also political, it must be noted that free blacks in New York, Ohio, Pennsylvania, and the other states protested loudly against encroachment on their voting. They called *ad hoc* meetings, established numbers of organizations, filed petitions, and made every effort to arouse sentiment favorable to the proposition that the ballot should be available to black men on the same terms as to whites. Some of the noted names of black history were in the forefront, including the black orator Joseph Sidney of New York; Robert and James E. Forten, the inventors, of Philadelphia; and John M. Langston of Ohio, later a member of Congress.

## The Civil War and Reconstruction

Despite the fact that blacks enjoyed some right to vote before the Emancipation Proclamation and the related Fifteenth Amendment, no black was elected to any important office, although John M. Langston was elected a township clerk in Ohio. But with the Civil War over and the principal slave states brought under a federal reconstruction plan, there was not only expansion of the suffrage, but blacks also had an opportunity to fill high elective and appointive office.

The Reconstruction, as designed by the "Radical Republicans" in Congress (the Reconstruction Act of 1867), divided the rebel states, except Tennessee, into five military districts, and called for new state constitutions, promulgated by constitutional conventions elected by loyal male citizens "of whatever race, color or previous condition." Black men now could vote; and they helped to select delegates to the conventions and later to ratify the resulting constitutions and to elect the first postwar legislatures. Although all the constitutional conventions had black delegates, only one (South Carolina's) had a majority of blacks. Louisiana's convention was equally divided between whites and blacks. The other conventions had only a small number of blacks. The racial composition of these conventions was as follows:[9]

TABLE I—RACIAL COMPOSITION OF STATE
CONSTITUTIONAL CONVENTIONS

| State | Whites | Blacks |
|---|---|---|
| Alabama | 83 | 17 |
| Arkansas | 68 | 7 |
| Florida | 29 | 17 |
| Georgia | 133 | 33 |
| Louisiana | 49 | 49 |
| Mississippi | 68 | 17 |
| North Carolina | 107 | 13 |
| South Carolina | 34 | 63 |
| Texas | 81 | 9 |
| Virginia | 80 | 25 |
| Total | 732 | 250 |

The Reconstruction Act of 1867 came two years after the ratification of the Thirteenth Amendment and while the Fourteenth Amendment was waiting for ratification. It preceded the Fifteenth Amendment (legalizing the right to vote regardless of race, color, or previous condition of servitude) by three years. While aimed at the South, the post-Civil War actions by Congress affected, or were to affect, the entire nation politically, for in 1867 there were several northern states which denied blacks the right to vote.

According to whom one reads, the Reconstruction conventions were (1) composed of and dominated by illiterate ex-slaves who scarcely knew how to conduct themselves; or (2) not dominated by blacks but only included some blacks (among them former "freemen"), many of whom had some schooling and much worldly experience, and several of whom had returned from the North when slavery had been outlawed. The most responsible commentators take the latter view. There is also much support for the position that the constitutions which were drafted by these conventions were progressive, far-seeing, people-centered, aimed at improving the lot of whites as well as blacks, and restrained in reference to former Confederates. Blacks, for instance, took the lead in giving constitutional authorization to publicly supported education, perhaps because they knew so well the need for learning.

By the time Reconstruction began, over 20 percent of the ex-slaves had had some schooling. At the Texas constitutional convention, it has been found that the delegates, "for the most part . . . were able to read and write. At least 30 percent of them had some college training."[10] North Carolina would make as good, or better, a showing in this area. Thus the membership of the state conventions, the membership of the new state legislatures, and the candidates for national office included Negroes of several levels of schooling and experience, as was the case with white office-seekers. Woodson and Wesley note that, "in some of the legislatures more than half of the black members could scarcely read or write," but the authors also hold that "the charge that all black officers were illiterate, ignorant of the science of government, cannot be sustained."[11]

Blacks filled many local elective and appointive offices during the Reconstruction years, but the total number of these offices and their incumbents is not as easy to ascertain as for the higher state and national offices. Two blacks served for some time in the United States Senate: Hiram R. Revels, 1870–71 (an unexpired term), and B.K. Bruce, 1875–81 (a full term). Both were elected from Mississippi. Twenty blacks served in the House of Representatives, from the 41st through the 56th Congress, 1868–95. They were elected from eight states: Alabama, Florida, Georgia, Louisiana, Mississippi, North Carolina, South Carolina, and Virginia. Eleven served a single full term (two years); six served two full terms each; two served three terms, and one, Joseph H. Rainey of South Carolina, served five terms. The largest number of Representatives, eight, came from South Carolina, followed by four from North Carolina; three from Alabama; and one each from Florida, Georgia, Virginia, Louisiana, and Mississippi. The Negroes elected to the House and Senate served a total of seventy-one years.[12]

It should be noted that the blacks elected to Congress were residents of states which were part of the military districts created by Congress in the Reconstruction Act of 1867. No black was elected from Tennessee, which was not subject to the act and to postwar federal "reconstruction." Similarly, during this same period no black was elected to the Congress from any northern congressional district. Prior to the establishment of federal Reconstruction, the former Confederate states voted against extending the suffrage to the emancipated blacks; so also (during 1865–68) did the states of Michigan, New York, Connecticut, Wisconsin, Minnesota, Kansas, and Ohio. In 1866, however, the suffrage was extended by Congress to blacks in all the territories and the District of Columbia.

Blacks were also elected to the state legislatures during the Reconstruction period; but they did not control the former Confederacy. Except in South Carolina, black legislators were always a minority. For example, during 1870–71, the racial distribution in the lower houses was as follows (all the senates were heavily white):[13]

TABLE II—RACIAL DISTRIBUTION IN LOWER HOUSES
OF STATE LEGISLATURES, 1870–1871

| State | Whites | Blacks |
|-------|--------|--------|
| Alabama | 73 | 27 |
| Arkansas | 71 | 9 |
| Georgia | 149 | 26 |
| Mississippi | 77 | 30 |
| North Carolina | 101 | 1 |
| South Carolina | 49 | 75 |
| Texas | 82 | 8 |
| Virginia | 116 | 21 |

In a review entitled *Race and Conscience in America*, prepared by the American Friends Service Committee for its Quaker and Quaker-minded following, it is observed of the Reconstruction period:

> Bills to establish or improve the public school system, to counteract political corruption and extravagance, to establish a homestead law, and to provide relief for the needy were introduced by Negroes. Some former slave states, while condemning political participation by Negroes in the state governments, have continued to function under constitutions which Negroes helped to write.[14]

There was another area in which the black members of Reconstruction legislatures made a contribution. They were of one mind in working for the ratification of the post-Civil War amendments that came before them (the Fourteenth and Fifteenth), making the Constitution protective of rights which, to this very day, might never have come under the purview of constitutional authority if, for instance, the Fourteenth Amendment had not been ratified by the necessary three-fourths majority of the states.

The blacks who went to Congress and those who filled high administrative office in the state and national governments acquitted themselves as men usually do in a world where there are relatively few mental giants. That is not to say, however, that Senators Bruce and Revels would not measure up very favorably to most national lawmakers today, as would John M. Langston (Virginia), H. M. Cheatham (North Carolina), John R. Lynch (Mississippi), Joseph H. Rainey and Robert Smalls (South Carolina), all of whom served in the United States House of Representatives. Men such as Francis L. Cardozo, who served South Carolina as secretary of state and later as treasurer; P. B. S. Pinchback, one of three black lieutenant governors of Louisiana; and T. W. Cardozo, Mississippi's superintendent of education, would stand muster well. Francis Cardozo was educated at the University of Glasgow; Langston was graduated from Oberlin College; Senator Revels studied at Knox College.

One proof of the ability of Reconstruction period black leaders and office-holders is that when the period came to an end or when they left their offices, they went on to show competence as teachers, church leaders, lawyers, administrators, diplomats, and the like.

When white southerners could permit themselves to do so, there were those who did not see everything in Reconstruction government as undeserving of praise. Some publicly lauded the "dignity" and "behavior" of the black state legislators; others, out of respect for certain Negroes, protested the passage of the first Jim Crow laws following the assumption of home rule.

## Reconstruction Ends

While black Americans were enjoying their new political opportunities, year by year the former Confederates were showing that they knew practical politics and respected the doctrine of "if you can't lick 'em, join 'em." The Confederates submitted to the side in power just enough to be politically able to recapture their state governments. This they did gradually, as their leaders were pardoned individually or amnesties were declared. This led first to border states being able to return Democratic majorities in county elections, and to the resurrection of the southern wing of the Democratic party. By the mid-1870s the Confederate Democrats, officially purged, were on the march, with the blessings of their former enemies-in-war. They were taking over their South to reconvert it to lily-whitism, both by right of law and outside the law. What ballots could not do, or would not do fast enough, was done with the aid of the Ku Klux Klan and similar groups.

The final blow to Reconstruction was the withdrawal of federal troops and other federal supports from the Reconstruction states on orders of President Rutherford B. Hayes, with the backing of both parties in Congress. This withdrawal of federal troops was part of Hayes's "Southern Strategy," growing out of the Hayes-Tilden Compromise. This famous or infamous "compromise" was occasioned by the election of 1876, in which Samuel Tilden had 4,300,590 popular votes to Hayes's 4,036,298, but where neither could, at first, reach a majority in the Electoral College. By a number of steps, including the appointment of a special congressional commission, the situation was resolved, with Hayes winning the presidency by one electoral vote. This victory for Hayes instead of Tilden was in exchange for Hayes's pledge to southern states that he would remove federal troops from the former Confederate states and return their governments back to the South, meaning the lily-white South. Hayes kept his word upon reaching the White House. This Hayes-Tilden episode and the period following has been labelled by historian Rayford W. Logan as "the nadir" of the black experience.

By 1902 there was not a single black person in a state legislature and not one in the national Congress. In addition, the southern states adopted numerous devices to prevent blacks from voting: intimidation, laws setting up property and poll-tax requirements, the famous "grandfather clause" (which denied suffrage to anyone whose grandfather could not vote prior to 1876), and the "lily-white" primary. These political measures were followed by the resegregation of those institutions which had been desegregated during Reconstruction, including state universities and other public facilities. All this happened despite the Civil Rights Act of 1875.[15] Of all that was done and would be done to destroy Reconstruction, preventing Negroes from voting was considered the most calamitous.[16]

It took nearly ninety years, countless lawsuits carried from lower courts to the United States Supreme Court, the passage of four Federal Civil Rights Acts (1957, 1960, 1964, 1965), and ratification of the Anti-Poll Tax Amendment (1963), to correct the imbalance somewhat and establish more equal treatment under law. This imbalance began when "home rule" was returned to the former rebel states. In the mid-1960s there were still blacks who were not permitted to register and vote. There was not one black person representing a southern state in the Congress; but there were blacks in the legislatures of former Confederate states—Georgia, Florida, Louisiana, Mississippi, Texas, and Virginia.[17]

## Politics in the North

During the years that the defeated former Confederacy was represented by blacks on the several levels of politics and government, there were almost no blacks similarly situated in the North, with the exception of Massachusetts. In fact, Massachusetts was the first state to elect blacks to its legislature. This it did in 1866; those elected were Edward G. Walker and Charles L. Mitchell.[18] Since that time the North has done better, but mostly in recent years.

When Oscar DePriest of Chicago entered the U. S. House of Representatives in 1929, it had been twenty-eight years since the last black American sat as a member of Congress. Since then there have been altogether nineteen, including Edward W. Brooke, elected to the Senate from Massachusetts (1966)—a state with only about 3 percent black population. Brooke had formerly been Attorney General of Massachusetts.

Some observers have said that the blacks in Congress during Reconstruction made no notable contribution. This cannot be said of the more recent group. For instance, Oscar DePriest of Chicago worked consistently to include in every bill possible a clause insuring no racial discrimination against blacks. He held to this formula especially in reference to the emergency projects of the depression years. Representative William L. Dawson of Chicago, although not known as a "race fighter" in the open, attained high office in his party, thus putting him in the position to elevate black Americans because of his post as a vice president of the Democratic National Committee and chairman of the important House Committee on Government Operations. The late Representative Adam Clayton Powell of New York, a minister by profession, was a racial protagonist, seldom being "polite" to those he suspected of doing or planning anything inimical to blacks. He rubbed many people the wrong way, but his constituents considered him "our man," and in the 88th Congress he demonstrated spectacular leadership in carrying President Johnson's welfare program through the House as chairman of the House Committee on Education and Labor. Representative Charles C. Diggs, Jr., of Detroit, has addressed himself especially to discrimination in the armed forces at home and abroad. Senator Brooke played a key role in keeping anti-black nominees to the Supreme Court from being confirmed by the Senate.

Seniority has played an effective part in the kind of contribution present-day Congressmen can and do make; in addition, Negro candidates for higher office have increasingly had relatively wide previous experience in other public or private responsibilities. For instance, Representative Augustus F. Hawkins of Los Angeles was a member of the California legislature for twenty-eight years and Diggs and Dawson served, respectively, in the Michigan legislature and on the Chicago Board of Aldermen.

It is not as easy to keep track of the membership in state legislatures and city councils. The most recent count shows thirty-three states having 236 Negro members in their legislatures. Little Nebraska and Vermont were in the list, Nebraska having boasted a black legislator for many years. Illinois, New York, Pennsylvania, and Missouri have had black lawmakers for years, New York since shortly after World War I.

Los Angeles elected its first city councilman in 1962, but many other cities have had councilmen over a much longer period, going back again to World War I. George W. Harris and Fred R. Moore of New York were among the earliest, in the 1920s. Oscar DePriest and others were members of the Chicago Board of Aldermen. Some smaller cities, such as Evanston, Illinois, had city councilmen from time to time. Since World War II a number of cities in the South also elected blacks to their city councils. These include Durham, Winston-Salem, Fayetteville, and Greensboro in North Carolina; Oak Ridge, Tennessee, which has since joined Nashville; Louisville, Kentucky; and others. St. Louis and the Kansas Citys have had councilmen for some time.

George D. Carroll was elected mayor of Richmond, California, by his fellow councilmen in 1964. Perhaps the most illustrious municipal post which has been regularly held by a black person since the 1950s is that of President of the Borough of Manhattan (in New York City). Partly administrative, this position is an important political "plum." The highest purely political decision-making position to be held by a black man has been that of "leader of Tammany Hall," more formally chairman of the Democratic County Committee of New York County. J. Raymond Jones, a practicing politician for nearly forty years, was elected to the post in 1965; he is now retired from politics.

Getting elected to state-wide office is seldom attempted by any serious black officeholder. Occasionally an independent runs, but with little chance of election. Exceptions to the rule were the election of Edward W. Brooke as Attorney General of Massachusetts and later, U. S. Senator, and of Gerald Lamb as treasurer of Connecticut. (Mr. Lamb is now senior vice-president of a Connecticut bank.)

Black members on school boards, North and South, are no longer unusual, although there are still countless school boards that have never had a black member. Election to the school board, in a number of cases, has seemed to present the easiest breakthrough where blacks are seeking their first elective office. Perhaps the power brokers and a good part of the dominant community recognize the rightness of blacks sharing in the determination of policies concerning the education of their children. Then, too, school board positions carry no pay and relatively little patronage.

## Patronage and Party Recognition

Outside the South and in nonelective and party organization politics, the Emancipation meant that thousands of free blacks came North, especially into the nation's capital. In Washington they could find steady, nonmenial or semimenial employment or enjoy the fruits of patronage. The fact that most of them received the lowest-paying jobs was disregarded. Washington was viewed as being out of the South and under the protection of the Federal Government. One price paid for employment in the Government was the frequent turnover as administrations changed. *The Tuskegee Year Book* of 1912 listed "colored officers, clerks, and other employees in the service of the U. S. Government." The number included members of the diplomatic corps, enlistees in the Army, laborers employed by the District of Columbia, post office personnel, and miscellaneous department employees. The list shows:

| | |
|---|---:|
| Diplomatic and consular corps | 11 |
| Enlistees in Army | 2,948 |
| District laborers | 2,824 |
| Post Office personnel | 2,997 |
| Miscellaneous | 14,386 |
| Total | 23,166 |

In addition blacks held some prestige positions such as Register of the Treasury, Recorder of Deeds of the District of Columbia, and minister to all-black nations. Some black consuls served in non-black countries. John Mercer Langston became U. S. Minister to Haiti; Frederick Douglass, ex-slave, greatest of the abolitionist orators and frequent advisor to Lincoln, became Minister to Haiti and also served at other times as assistant secretary of the San Domingo Commission, marshal of the District of Columbia, and Recorder of Deeds. Fred R. Moore, New York political leader and editor (the New York *Age*) was one of a long line of black ministers and ambassadors to the American-sponsored Republic of Liberia. Some blacks became collectors of internal revenue, one serving in Honolulu; others were customs collectors, paymasters for the Army, and receivers of public moneys. John C. Napier was Register of the Treasury; Henry Lincoln Johnson, a national committeeman of the Republican National Committee, once served as Recorder of Deeds of the District of Columbia, a position that has been filled by other blacks down the years.

When Woodrow Wilson ascended to the presidency there were 5,836 blacks in the federal service in Washington, according to the New York *Age*. The paper goes on to complain that after Wilson came into office, twenty-nine of those blacks holding the highest offices were "turned out" and their places "filled by white Democrats."[19] This periodic turnover was regular procedure for political appointees, but it struck black Americans hardest of all because of their limited employment opportunities.

Another area of political opportunity for blacks after emancipation, and for many subsequent years, came through being elected as delegates to the Republican National Convention and as members of the Republican National Committee. But when the former Confederate states took over the state governments again and found ways to disfranchise blacks, these national officers were leaders without an effective following. The last to serve was Perry W. Howard, a lawyer born in Ebeneezer, Mississippi, in 1877 and a graduate of Fisk University with an L.L.B. degree from DePauw University. He was once a special assistant to the Attorney General of the United States, and practiced law from 1905 to the late 1950s. Although national committeeman from Mississippi, he made Washington, D. C. his home for more than half of his adult years. But in his heyday he controlled the federal patronage for Mississippi whenever the Republicans occupied the White House; he served on important committees at national conventions; and he led the Mississippi delegation (called "black and tan" by many in the state because it was racially mixed).

Howard and other black national committeemen were accused by their political opponents of representing "rotten boroughs," of preferring an all-black Republican party in the South, and of selling patronage.[20]

Among other Republican national committeemen were Benjamin J. Davis and Henry L. Johnson, both from Georgia. Roscoe Conklin Simmons of Illinois, Robert R. Church of Tennessee, and William H. McDonald of Texas were also important black Republican leaders.

Benjamin Davis was the outspoken editor of the *Atlanta Independent*. He studied at Atlanta University and had been teacher and secretary of a national fraternal order for which he arranged the building of a block of buildings. In addition to being a member of the Republican National Committee, he served as delegate-at-large to his party's convention for twenty-five years. His son, Benjamin Davis, Jr., later became internationally known as an officer of the Communist party and one of the most knowledgeable critics of the American system. He once served on the City Council of New York City.

Simmons was a journalist but became best known as a "silver-tongued" orator. Among blacks he is remembered for standing under a White House window during the Hoover administration, when black Americans felt they had been forgotten by the Republican party, and appealing: "Speak, Mr. President, speak. Tell us that Lincoln still lives." It is probably because blacks felt they did not receive an answer that so many soon after turned to the Democratic party and Franklin Roosevelt. One writer says of Simmons that his "spell-binding oratory was the Negroes' answer to the fire-eating Vardaman, Bilbo, and Heflin. . . ."[21]

Robert R. Church was a real-estate operator and banker, born in Memphis in 1885 and educated at Oberlin College. He was a member of the Republican State Central Committee of Tennessee and Shelby County Executive and Congressional Committees. He was a delegate to the Republican National Conventions of 1912, 1916, 1920, and 1924. In 1922 he was appointed by Secretary of State Charles Evans Hughes to a special commission to study economic conditions in Haiti. Henry Lincoln Johnson was a noted fraternal leader, and William McDonald was reputedly a "Texas millionaire."

These black Republican leaders were professionals who figured largely as voices of the party and patronage dispensers between 1900 and 1932. They, like Frederick Douglass, believed "the Republican Party to be the ship, all else the sea." Men such as Perry Howard have been called political bosses—bosses over certain groups of party followers in a given area, able to deliver promised or expected votes, having close relations with the greater powers that be in the party, and being in a position to reward friends and punish enemies. But there have been other black bosses, both Republican and Democratic, not occupying offices as high as national committeemen. The bosses were usually allied with a white machine and were permitted to control certain territory, certain patronage, or certain enterprises. Sometimes these enterprises were within the law, sometimes outside it. The enterprises have included, at times, gambling or prostitution. Black bossism has usually been a reflection of white bossism. At the present time, when old-fashioned bossism is no longer holding sway, black bosses as well as white have taken on a new image or disappeared.

Some black bosses, by supporting the "Big City" machines, have been able to increase their patronage and other gains for their districts. One reputed boss thereby secured black policemen in his southern city decades before such employment was being made available to blacks in the rest of the South. Other bosses were able to get new schools and other improvements for their people; still others controlled a share of the patronage jobs. Chicago, San Antonio, Baltimore, Memphis, and New York are cities often mentioned as having had successful bosses. There have been many more sub-bosses and little bosses than top big bosses.

In Baltimore there were Marse Calloway, Republican, and Thomas Smith, Democrat, both of whom are credited with serving white overlords, sometimes even to the extent of "paying off" blacks to prevent them from voting. Nevertheless, Marse Calloway is given credit for introducing one of the most popular and most highly esteemed men into politics—Theodore R. McKeldin, two-term mayor of Baltimore and two-term governor of Maryland.

Most blacks in politics so far described have been Republicans because over the long stretch of history and due to Reconstruction, most political activity by blacks was within that party.

Since 1928, however, blacks have increasingly supported the Democratic party. Many blacks were first attracted to the Democrats through New York's Governor Alfred E. Smith. Later, with the promise of the New Deal, they allied themselves to the Democratic party and the majority have remained there since. American blacks are given credit—election after election—for helping the party carry the fifteen urban industrial centers of the country. In nearly every black urban district, registered Democrats outnumber Republicans by as much as 8 to 1. Some Republican candidates, in fact, have felt it is not worth the trouble to campaign in the Harlems of the country.

In a small number of northern cities, blacks were voting Democratic in some areas even before the time of Al Smith. In fact as early as 1917, the Democratic organization of New York had placed Ferdinand Q. Morton as a member of the Civil Service Commission. In the early 1920s the first black municipal judges were backed by the party and elected. This early involvement of blacks in Democratic politics may be credited to the presence of a large West Indian population in New York City, a group that had no built-in attachment to "the party that freed us." With the coming of the New Deal, blacks received many nontraditional job opportunities, albeit that they were in depression or relief openings. Dr. Mary McLeod Bethune became an important adviser to President and Mrs. Franklin D. Roosevelt. Harold Ickes, Secretary of the Interior, and at one time president of the Chicago NAACP, brought into government such men as William H. Hastie, first as a lawyer in the department, and later as Governor of the Virgin Islands (then under Interior). Dr. Robert C. Weaver, economist, held several high positions in relation to manpower procurement. And there were many others. It should be noted that this entrance into government served as useful experience to which Hastie could point when he was nominated by President Harry S. Truman for the U. S. Court of Appeals, and which Weaver could cite when, in the Johnson administration, he was named to the Cabinet (Housing and Urban Development).

In the recent past Thurgood Marshall, formerly Special Counsel of the NAACP, was named Solicitor-General of the United States, then to the U. S. Court of Appeals and finally to the Supreme Court, the first black person to serve on the nation's highest bench. There are three blacks on the U. S. Customs courts, and a number on other federal district and appeals courts.

Blacks have also been named to the higher levels of the foreign service, to both appointive and career positions. There have been both career men and noncareer ambassadors and ministers. For a list of black ambassadors, see Chapter 12, "The Black Professional."

In the White House President Eisenhower named a Negro to the White House staff in the person of E. Frederic Morrow, an administrative assistant with various important duties during the years he served. President Eisenhower also made other pioneer appointments including that of J. Ernest Wilkins to the post of Assistant Secretary of

Labor. (Wilkins became the first Negro to sit in a White House Cabinet meeting). Mrs. Robert L. Vann of Pennsylvania was named a member of the International Development Advisory Board, and Archibald J. Carey, Jr. of Illinois was made chairman of the President's Committee on Government Employment Policy. Scovel Richardson was appointed a member of the Federal Parole Board (of which he became chairman), and was later named a Judge of the United States Customs Court. Scores of other appointments at lower levels were also made during the Eisenhower administration.

With the inauguration of President John F. Kennedy and the Civil Rights Movement of the 1960s, a new climate developed, and the momentum of political participation reflected rapidly changing aspirations and expectations on the part of both blacks and whites.

The black American has never been able to escape politics. Political policies and practices permitted and maintained slavery; political interests and actions ended slavery; politics delivered the freed slaves back to their masters, then rescued them through congressional Reconstruction and later, killed Reconstruction. Politics also was resorted to, both sides, in the battle that has been going on throughout this century to make the black man a first-class citizen, and will figure in the decisions on whether or not to abolish the Electoral College system of electing Presidents, as set out in the Constitution. The record shows that the blacks have had their share of political ups and downs, that they have been victims, not only of the Hayes-Tilden Compromise, but of many other compromises; that they have been frequent political scapegoats, and often been "sold down the river." But, on balance, the gains seem to outweigh the losses. The very current opposition to such signs of change as school busing and the attempts to retool the one-time liberal Supreme Court are indications of reaction to black political progress. The number of blacks elected to public office, North and South, and with a notable share of white votes in many places, is even more indicative that the recent past has not been the nadir of blacks in politics. But in politics, nothing can be taken for granted. Indeed, one of the questions forward-looking blacks might pose is: "Are blacks facing another Hayes-Tilden Compromise?"

## Notes

1. After Leo H. Hirsch, "The Negro and New York, 1783–1865." *Journal of Negro Education*, XVI, No. 4, October 1931, p. 417.
2. *Journal of the Senate of New York, 1811*, p. 143, as quoted by Charles H. Wesley in "Negro Suffrage in the Period of Construction-Making, 1787–1865." *Journal of Negro Education*, XXXII, No. 2, April 1947, p. 156.
3. *Ibid.*, p. 156.
4. *Ibid.*, p. 155. A new examination of the extent to which the Negro vote in New York might have provided a "balance of power" in New York politics is being made by Dr. Elsie M. Lewis, associate professor of history at Howard University.

5. New York *Spectator*, April 29, 1809, as quoted by Wesley.

6. Hirsch, *op. cit.*, pp. 417–18.

7. Wesley, *op. cit.*, p. 162.

8. *Ibid.*, p. 166.

9. *The Negro Year Book* (Tuskegee Institute: Alabama, 1921–22 edition), p. 176; J. R. Ficklen, *History of Reconstruction in Louisiana* (Gloucester Massachusetts: Peter Smith, 1910), p. 193.

10. John Mason Brewer, *Negro Legislators of Texas* (Dallas, Mathis Publishing Company, 1935), p. 217.

11. Carter G. Woodson and Charles H. Wesley, *The Negro in Our History*, 10th edition (Washington, Associated Publishers, 1962), p. 405.

12. For a full listing of the Negro members of Congress, the years they served, and the states they represented, see Samuel Denby Smith, *The Negro in Congress, 1870–1901* (Chapel Hill, University of North Carolina Press, 1940), pp. 4–5.

13. *The Negro Year Book, op. cit.*, p. 176.

14. By a "working party" of the American Friends Service Committee, including the present writer (Norman, University of Oklahoma Press, 1959), p. 13.

15. This act specifically provided to all citizens regardless of race, creed, color, or previous condition of servitude "full and equal enjoyment of all accommodations at inns, conveyances on land or water, theaters, or other places of public amusement." It established a fine of up to $500 or imprisonment of from thirty days to one year for any person excluding anyone from these accommodations on account of race, etc. It further provided for equality of service on juries and set a penalty of up to a $5,000 fine levied against any person who excluded another from serving on a jury.

16. V. O. Key, Jr., *Southern Politics* (New York, Alfred A. Knopf, 1950), p. 536; after an interpretation by S. S. Calhoun, president, the Mississippi Constitutional Convention of 1890.

17. *The Negro Year Book* (Tuskegee, Alabama, Tuskegee Institute, 1918–19 edition), p. 208.

18. *Ibid.*

19. New York *Age*, October 26, 1916.

20. See Report of the Committee, pp. 718–35.

21. Richard Bardolph, *The Negro Vanguard* (New York, Rinehart and Company, 1959), pp. 149–50.

# 19

## Black Participation in
## U. S. Foreign Relations

### Hugh H. Smythe and Elliott P. Skinner

Both the traditional bias of the American Foreign Service and the nature of United States foreign policy affect the role and position of blacks in American foreign relations.[1] Blacks were in bondage when the Department of State was created in 1789; and discrimination was at a peak when the Foreign Service came into existence in 1924. Thus the white Anglo-Saxon Protestant elite has dominated United States foreign affairs from the start. In addition, American foreign policy has been colored by the racial composition of the countries with which we have relations, generally being positive toward the predominantly white western European nations and negative toward the largely nonwhite part of the world.[2] Today, however, the presence of millions of black Americans and an increasing awareness of Africa, especially since the mid-1950s, are bringing about a change in traditional attitudes.

The ability of any group to influence a country's foreign policy is directly related to its ability to influence that nation's domestic affairs. Because blacks have persistently been excluded from the national elite structure, they have had special difficulty in relating to United States foreign affairs, even over issues of vital concern to them. Consequently, past articulation of the foreign policy concerns of blacks has gone unheeded, a condition which will continue until blacks gain sufficient economic and political strength to have an effective voice in the field of American foreign relations.

Blacks in this country have always had an interest in Africa, and a few have looked beyond to black and other nonwhite peoples in Asia, Europe, Latin America, the Pacific, and elsewhere. But early black leaders had little success persuading white America toward more positive relations with black citizens, much less with influencing our foreign policy. What is significant, however, is that the first recorded involvement of blacks with foreign affairs matters resulted from efforts to ameliorate the plight of their fellows in Colonial America, which led to direct involvement with Africa. An example of this occurred in the 1700s when black Captain Paul Cuffee, of Massachusetts, refused to pay taxes after being denied the right to vote. Subsequent events led him to conclude that racial prejudice in the Colonies was so strong that blacks faced an almost hopeless task in aspiring to respectability and independence, and he advocated that blacks turn to Africa, where incentives and opportunities were better.[3]

However, the American Revolution intervened and Cuffee's post-war efforts were foiled by the new American government as well as by a black freedmen elite, who rejected the colonization schemes of both Cuffee and the American Colonization Society as a solution to their problems. Their position was then, and that of their successors is now, that America is their home and they must struggle to achieve full citizenship on these shores. This attitude generated friction during the pre-Civil War years, typified by a heated controversy between ex-slave Frederick Douglass, a leader in the fight for equality at home, and Martin R. Delany, a champion of emigration to Africa. After the war Douglass used the remaining vestiges of his prestige to persuade President Rutherford B. Hayes to appoint black John Henry Smyth as envoy to Liberia. It was while serving there that Smyth realized that not only did the United States not help Liberia; Africa had no organized and effective constituency in America.[4]

With little prospect of influencing American foreign policy toward Africa through political power or membership in the American elite, blacks began to evolve foreign-policy views of their own and articulated their interest in Africa and its people through missionary and philanthropic agencies. At the turn of the century blacks, like most nonwhites around the world, were virtually powerless, and almost all of their countries—except Haiti, Ethiopia, and Liberia—were still in colonial servitude. Nevertheless, American blacks raised their voices in protest over the cruelty to Africans in the Congo, helping to end Belgian King Leopold's private rule there. About this time the concept of Pan-Africanism emerged, and William Edward Burghardt DuBois advocated the development of the Talented Tenth among blacks—those with higher education—as a strategy for advancement. He also used his influence to get a commission appointed to investigate conditions in Liberia, thus helping to preserve a modicum of her independence at a time when Britain was trying to take over her customs.[5]

But the inability of blacks to have a truly effective voice in United States foreign affairs was increasingly demonstrated by developments in the early 1900s. The American government made it difficult for blacks to go as missionaries to Africa; Monroe Trotter tried (and failed) to place before the Allied Peace Conference in Paris in 1919 the claims of Americans of African descent, while DuBois' Pan-African Congress at the time evoked only slight attention.[6] It was after such efforts failed to make an impact on official international positions that the black elite became fully aware of their impotence to influence the treatment of blacks and other nonwhites, whether at home or overseas. Black leaders then closed ranks and through the National Association for the Advancement of Colored People (NAACP) began a long struggle to achieve equality for darker people everywhere.[7]

DuBois planned a Pan-African Congress in Europe in 1921. Marcus Garvey founded the Universal Negro Improvement Association (UNIA), which was oriented strongly toward Africa. The United States Government quickly became concerned about UNIA activities, which involved both European powers in West Africa and the Liberian Government.[8] DuBois, then already in Liberia, was designated as an envoy to the inauguration of the president of that country.[9] But such symbolic gestures exerted a negligible influence in our foreign relations; and the inability of blacks to influence policy was vividly pointed up again during the Depression years of the 1930s.

When DuBois cautioned America that the Firestone Company was exploiting Liberians, rather than intervening directly the United States joined the British and the Germans to force that small African country to submit to a special committee of the Council of the League of Nations to look into its affairs. Nor were American blacks able to get their Government to take a stand against the Italian invasion of Ethiopia in 1935.[10] Four years later the Council on African Affairs was organized, but otherwise blacks paid scant attention to Africa during World War II. DuBois pointed out that in spite of the sacrifices being made by fighting black men of America and Africa, white world leaders were not considering nonwhite interests at the forthcoming Peace Table. And in 1945, when he attended the organizing meeting of the United Nations in San Francisco as an observer, DuBois was scandalized by the contradictions he encountered there, noting that in spite of their talk of democracy, freedom, and free states, the imperial powers continued maneuvering to hold on to their colonies.[11]

The Korean War and the Joseph McCarthy era diverted the interest of black leaders from the African nations. Yet in the 1950s the United States, through its Assistant Secretary of State for the Near East and Africa, George McGhee, publicly acknowledged the relationship between domestic affairs and our African policy. McGhee pointed out that Africans questioned the sincerity of America's attitude toward their continent because of race discrimination in the United States; but he declared that this country would nevertheless not be pressured into any adventures in Africa.[12] It was significant that a highly placed member of the Department of State would officially state that the domestic race problem had a direct bearing on our African policy. This era also showed an increased consciousness among blacks of African petitions to the United Nations and a new awareness of the steps European powers were taking to grant or deny freedom to African and other nonwhite parts of the world.

A significant milestone in black involvement in American foreign affairs occurred with the emergence of Ghana as a politically independent state in 1957. This motivated the Department of State to create the position of Assistant Secretary of State for Africa in 1958. But President Dwight D. Eisenhower's administration, in the absence of a powerful black voting constituency, made little attempt to hasten Belgium's decolonization of the Congo, or to interfere with Britain's imposition of partnership in the Central African Federation; nor would it advise the Portuguese to loosen their reins in Angola and Mozambique or caution South Africa about apartheid.[13]

In the 1960s increasing racial ferment domestically was accompanied by a rising interest in foreign policy among blacks. However, although the African Studies Association, with a grant from the Ford Foundation, encouraged African studies programs in white universities, black Howard University, which had struggled for years to build an African program, was overlooked. And when a group of Africanists decided to form the Africa League to bring pressure on United States policy, blacks were again left out. But John F. Kennedy and Averell Harriman were quick to recognize the close relationship between the American race problem and African sensitivities. Aware of the domestic repercussions of the colonial and nationalist struggle in Africa, after Africa had for the first time in history been an issue in a presidential election, Kennedy gave serious thought to matters involving the domestic affairs of blacks and to their foreign policy concerns for Africa. His Assistant Secretary of State for Africa, G. Mennen Williams, enunciated the slogan "Africa is for the Africans" with presidential support and began a campaign to woo African leaders.[14]

Some whites, fearing this development, emphasized that we need not take too seriously the linkage between black Americans and Africans.[15] In fact, some whites fostered the idea that Africans would reject American blacks. Blacks tried to counter this contention, but had difficulty finding outlets for articulating their views.[16] Then the black American Society of African Culture (AMSAC) was formed and in May 1961 called a meeting in which it specifically proposed to offset the efforts of whites to divide blacks here and in Africa. The gathering requested that blacks be placed in high positions in the Department of State and discussed the relation of American and African blacks. The following year, considering the climate propitious for influencing American policy toward Africa, a group of responsible and well-placed blacks formed the American Negro Leadership Conference on Africa (ANLC).

The ANLC made a hard appraisal of the relationship between African and American blacks and focused on securing positions within the Foreign Service establishment for blacks both here and abroad. Partly due to their efforts, during the Kennedy and Lyndon B. Johnson administrations eight blacks were appointed as ambassadors to such posts as Niger, Ghana, Dahomey, Senegal, and Upper Volta in Africa, as well as to Syria, Norway, Luxembourg, Finland, and Malta. Also in this period four black Deputy Assistant Secretaries of State came into office, one of them in the African bureau. The number of black Foreign Service Officers increased slightly and efforts were made to increase black recruitment through a Ford Foundation grant to establish a special program to attract and train blacks. Government officials began to heed black voices in foreign affairs and sent to black conferences concerned with foreign affairs such dignitaries as Secretary of State Dean Rusk and Ambassador-at-large Averell Harriman. An Advisory Council on African Affairs, appointed by the Assistant Secretary of State for Africa, included blacks from a variety of backgrounds.[17]

It is obviously difficult to assess the impact of such actions on our foreign policy. AMSAC declared that the activities of ANLC had toughened the American position vis-à-vis the Congo, and helped to bring pressure on Britain to oppose the white minority government in Rhodesia. It proposed to use its own good offices in the Nigerian-Biafran civil strife.

But on the whole, black participation in foreign affairs remained minimal due to several major weaknesses. Traditionally a racial or ethnic group becomes important in national politics and its country's international politics only when it has a high level of identity and can wield actual influence in the larger society, can control that influence, and can gain recognition of its demands by collective action. Our history shows in the actions of the Irish, Germans, Jews, and East-European Americans, for example, how groups can exercise considerable influence on United States policy toward their respective ancestral lands.[18] This has not been true for the blacks, however, who suffered a series of disadvantages with which white ethnic groups were not burdened: the absence of black political power historically because of disenfranchisement in the South, the dilution of black votes in areas of concentration through gerrymandering and other means, and the low esteem accorded to blacks and Africa by the white elite, reinforced by efforts to discourage close links of affection between Africans and black Americans.

Since blacks possess little foreign-policy expertise, they are poorly equipped to combat policy enunciations they disapprove. The late former Secretary of State Dean Acheson, although not a specialist on the subject of African affairs, argued in favor of South Africa and supported Rhodesia's right to *de facto* recognition as a state, declaring that neither Britain, the United States, nor the United Nations should interfere in Rhodesia's internal affairs, regardless of the morality of its minority government or its official circumscription of the rights of the majority black population. When Arthur Goldberg, then United States Ambassador to the United Nations, responded with a rebuttal, no blacks added their voices to his. Similarly, when George Ball, former Undersecretary of State, in his book *The Discipline of Power*[19] argued that we ought to review with Europe the allocation of political and strategical responsibilities, particularly in Africa, no blacks took public issue with him. This situation will be remedied only when blacks gain experience, personal knowledge, and long official or professional service related to Africa in particular and world affairs in general, as foreign policy formulation is a complex and difficult assignment.

A look at areas other than our official foreign service, in which nonwhites are few and bunched below the policy-making level[20] reveals those active in organizations concerned with world affairs are minuscule in number. The United Nations Association of the United States of America, the Council on Foreign Relations, the Foreign Policy Association, and Council on World Affairs are almost lily-white. Blacks are practically nonexistent as members of such foreign-area professional associations as the Middle East Institute, the Asia Society, and the Atlantic Council. They are rarely members of delegations to international conferences and are seldom seen on the staffs, especially in key positions, of the North Atlantic Treaty Organization, Organization for European Economic Cooperation, or Organization of American States. Few are employed—none currently in high posts—in the United Nations Secretariat (when Undersecretary Ralph J. Bunche died in 1971, he was replaced by a white American) or in United Nations-affiliated agencies like the World Health Organization; Food and Agricultural Organization; International Monetary Fund; United Nations Educational Scientific and Cultural

Organization; and United Nations International Children's Emergency Fund. In our university and college foreign area and international relations programs there are almost no black faculty members, and black enrollment is almost zero. Black colleges as a group are bereft of international programs, training facilities, curricula, and personnel in the foreign-area field to prepare their students to become professionals in international affairs, although the Phelps-Stokes African Seminar for Presidents of Black Colleges and Ethnic Heritage Programs have stimulated at least a beginning in this direction for a dozen or so colleges.

The administrations of Presidents Richard M. Nixon and Gerald Ford have set a low priority on world areas of special interest to blacks at a time when the emerging black elite in the United States is particularly sensitive to its weakness and of the implications of our foreign policy in Africa for the condition of blacks in America. Congressman Charles Diggs of Michigan, who as chairman of the House Sub-Committee on Africa regularly holds hearings on United States policy toward Africa, declared that he could not continue to represent this country as a delegate to the 26th General Assembly of the United Nations in 1971 in the face of the administration's adverse policy toward Africa, and became the first American ever to resign from the delegation. The Congressional Black Caucus National Black Political Convention emphasized that it had met on behalf of blacks in Africa, America, and the rest of the Western Hemisphere. This stand reflects an intent to bring the collective influence of caucus leaders to bear on issues of American policy toward Africa. It seems to indicate the formation of a serious pressure group devoted to working constructively on behalf of Africans; blacks, following the lead of whites, are letting the government know that the interests of ethnic and racial groups at home must be considered in the formulation of African policy.[21]

Steps forward such as this are heartening; however, blacks are not yet in a position to make a major contribution in drawing up policy since they have never occupied positions in the hierarchy where the ultimate decisions for foreign policy are made. Although action on the civil rights front during the 1960s lessened the resistance against blacks who wished to enter the foreign service, progress in this area has slowed down and the Office of Equal Employment Opportunity in the Department of State has had little recent stimulation toward effectiveness despite the appointment of some blacks to African posts as ambassadors and one to Sweden, from which he resigned in late 1972. (See "The Black Professional," Chapter 12, for a list of those who have served as ambassadors and for the status of black employment in the Department of State.)

Although theoretically any State Department post, even that of Secretary of State, is open to all, the realities of American life make it extremely difficult for blacks and other minorities to accumulate the kind of experience requisite for the top six positions (Secretary, Deputy Secretary, Undersecretary for Political Affairs, Counselor, Undersecretary for Economic Affairs, and Deputy Undersecretary for Management). It is difficult, as well, to qualify on levels just below the top in foreign service. In the more than

120 embassies and some 360 other overseas posts employing 3,000 Foreign Service Officers, there are still fewer than fifty black career officers and under ten ambassadors.[22] Racial distinctions have not disappeared from the Foreign Service, and it seems unlikely. that the Department of State will soon have a staff totally accustomed to dealing easily and naturally with minority group applicants.

In light of this experience with racial handicaps, it is easy to understand why American blacks have little understanding of the formulation of foreign policy. It takes education and continual inquiry to develop an understanding of the techniques necessary to develop a national program with the desired foreign impact: techniques that involve facility with and capacity to cope with international systems; awareness of approaches, familiarity with analytical tools, and factors of foreign policy behavior; and a fund of information about trends and patterns in international politics. So long as blacks remain outside the sphere of foreign affairs they will continue to have little influence in the making of foreign policy. However, in spite of the struggle involved, some blacks have secured the necessary background and expertise to make themselves heard, and are working to attract others into the field. They know that failure to strive for the opportunity to help formulate valid foreign policy would mean abdication of the right of blacks to an equal voice in an area of vital concern to all Americans.

## Notes

1. Ralph Hilton, *Worldwide Mission: The Story of the United States Foreign Service* (New York, World Publishing Co., 1971).

   Gaillard Hunt, *The Department of State of the United States* (New Haven, Yale University Press, 1914).

   G. H. Stuart, *The Department of State* (New York, Macmillan, 1949).

   Elmer Plischke, *The Conduct of American Diplomacy* (New York, D. Van Nostrand, 1950).

   Tracy H. Lay, *The Foreign Service of the United States* (Englewood Cliffs, Prentice-Hall, 1925).

2. James A. Moss, "The Civil Rights Movement and American Foreign Policy," in George W. Shepherd, Jr., ed., *Racial Influences on American Foreign Policy* (Basic Books, New York, 1970).

   James A. Moss, "Racism: A Consistent Aspect of American Foreign Policy," *Afro-American Studies*, vol. 2, 1972.

   Hugh H. Smythe and James A. Moss, "Racial Images Abroad and Making U. S. Foreign Policy," paper presented to the Conference on Racial Problems in American Foreign Policy, University of Denver, Vail, Colorado, July 1967.

3. Leslie H. Fischel and Benjamin Quarles, eds., *The Black American: A Documentary History* (New York, William Morrow, 1970).

   W. E. B. DuBois, "Africa and the American Negro Intelligentsia," *Présence Africaine*, December 1955–January 1956, no. 5.

   John Hope Franklin, *From Slavery to Freedom* (Knopf, New York, 1947).

4. James M. Gregory, *Frederick Douglass The Orator* (Afro-American Press, Chicago, 1969).

   Victor Ullman, *Martin R. Delany: The Beginnings of Black Nationalism* (Boston, Beacon Press, 1971).

John Hope Franklin, *op. cit.*

5. Emmett J. Scott, "The American Commissioners in Liberia," *The Southern Workman*, Vol. 38, 1909.

    Robert E. Park, "The International Conference on the Negro," *The Southern Workman*, Vol. 41, 1912.

    E. D. Morel, "The Future of Tropical Africa," *The Southern Workman*, Vol. 41, 1912.

    William H. Sheppard, "Yesterday, Today and Tomorrow in Africa," *The Southern Workman*, Vol. 39, 1910.

    S.E.F.C.C. Hamedoe, "The First Pan-African Conference," *The Colored American Magazine*, September 1900.

    W. E. B. DuBois, *The Souls of Black Folk* (Greenwich, Connecticut, Fawcett, 1961).

6. George Padmore, *Pan-Africanism and Communism* (New York, Doubleday, 1971).

    W. E. B. DuBois, *The World and Africa* (Viking, New York, 1947).

    George Padmore, editor, *History of the Pan-African Congress* (Manchester, England, Pan African Federation, 1945).

7. August Meier, Elliott M. Rudwick, and Francis Broderick, *Black Protest Thought in the Twentieth Century*, 2nd edition (New York, Bobbs-Merrill, 1965).

    William B. Hixson, Jr., *Moorfield Storey and the Abolitionist Tradition* (New York, Oxford University Press, 1972).

    Henry Lee Moon, *The Emerging Thought of W. E. B. DuBois* (New York, Simon and Schuster, 1972).

8. Amy Jacques Garvey, *Philosophy and Opinions of Marcus Garvey*, Vol. II (New York, Universal Publishing House, 1923).

    *Memorandum of an Interview Between Liberian Officials and the UNIA Delegates*, March 22, 1921, Department of State Files, 882.00/705, National Archives, Washington, D.C.

    E. D. Cronon, *Black Moses* (Madison, University of Wisconsin Press, 1955).

    Birgit Aron, "The Garvey Movement," *Phylon*, Vol. 8, No. 4, 1947.

9. Elliott M. Rudwick, *W. E. B. DuBois: Propagandist of the Negro Protest* (New York, Atheneum, 1969).

    "DuBois in Liberia As Envoy," *The Crisis*, Vol. 27, April 1924.

10. Brice Harris, *The United States and the Italo-Ethiopian Crisis* (Palo Alto, Stanford University Press, 1964).

    Elliott M. Rudwick, *W. E. B. Dubois: A Study in Minority Group Leadership* (New York, Atheneum, 1960).

    Julius Lester, *The Seventh Son: The Thought and Writings of W. E. B. DuBois* (New York, Random House, 1971).

11. Brice Harris, *op. cit.*

    Elliott M. Rudwick, *W. E. B. DuBois: Propagandist of the Negro Protest, op. cit.*

12. "Mr. McGhee's Statement," *Department of State Bulletin*, Vol. 22, No. 572, June 19, 1950.

13. Adelaide C. Hill and Martin Kilson, eds., *Apropos of Africa* (London, Frank Cass & Co., Ltd., 1969).

    The American Assembly, *The United States and Africa* (New York, Columbia University, June 1958).

    Statement by Joseph Palmer II, *Department of State Bulletin*, January 1958.

14. Averell Harriman, "What the Africans Expect of the U. S.," *The New York Times Magazine*, October 9, 1960.

    Henry L. Bretton, "United States Foreign Policy Toward the Newly Independent States," in Peter Judd, ed., *African Independence* (New York, Dell, 1963).

15. Herschelle S. Challenor, "American Relations with Africa: The Evolution of the National Interests," Paper presented before the Africa Study Group of The Adlai Stevenson Institute of International Affairs, The Palmer House, Chicago, Illinois, November 11, 1971.

    Harold Isaacs, "Back to Africa," *The New Yorker*, May 13, 1961.

16. James Baldwin, "A Negro Assays the Negro Mood," *The New York Times Magazine*, March 12, 1961.

John A. Davis, "Black Americans and United States Policy Towards Africa," *Journal of International Affairs*, Vol. 23, No. 2, 1969.

Robert S. Browne, *Race Relations in International Affairs* (Washington, D.C., Public Affairs Press, 1961).

John A. Davis, ed., *Africa As Seen by American Negroes* (Présence Africaine, Paris, 1959).

*Resolutions*, American Negro Leadership Conference on Africa, Harriman, New York, November 23–25, 1962.

17. *Report of African Attitudes Towards the American Negro and the American Negro Attitude Towards Africa*, New York: Special meeting called by the American Society on African Culture, May 27, 1961, Part III.

*Report of the Utilization of Negroes in the State Department and USIA As Overseas Representatives, Especially in Africa*, New York: AMSAC, May 27, 1961, Part I.

18. Louis L. Gerson, *The Hyphenate in Recent American Politics* (Lawrence, University of Kansas Press, 1964).

L. H. Fuchs, *American Ethnic Politics* (New York, Harper & Row Torchbooks, 1968).

George W. Shepherd, Jr., editor, *Racial Influences on American Foreign Policy* (New York, Basic Books, 1970).

Locksley Edmondson, "Race and International Politics Since Versailles," *International Journal*, Autumn 1969.

Peter Rose, *They and We* (Random House, New York, 1964).

Alfred O. Hero, Jr., "Southern Jews, Race Relations, and Foreign Policy," *Jewish Social Studies*, Vol. 27, October 1965.

19. *The Discipline of Power*, George Ball, (Boston, Little Brown, 1968).

Dean Acheson, "On South Africa," *The New York Times*, April 21, 1971.

"Dean Acheson on South Africa," Letter to the Editor, *The New York Times*, May 5, 1971.

Dean Acheson, Letter to the Editor, the Washington *Post*, December 11, 1966.

Arthur Goldberg, Letter to the Editor, the Washington *Post*, January 8, 1967.

20. Foreign policy is made essentially by the President with the help of the Secretary of State and his top two or three aides, and Cabinet Secretaries, especially the Secretary of Defense, whose operations are tied into foreign affairs. The President's National Security Council, particularly his Assistant for National Security Affairs, also plays a role in this process, with Congress being an adjunct factor, particularly the Senate.

21. *Policy Toward Africa for the Seventies;* Hearings Before the Sub-Committee on Africa, of the Committee on Foreign Affairs, House of Representatives, 91st Congress, 2nd session, March 17, 18, 19, 23, 24, May 19, 20, 21, June 4, September 30, October 1, November 18, and December 3, 1970, U. S. Government Printing Office, Washington, D.C., 1970.

Terence Smith, "U. S. Widening Ties to African Whites," *The New York Times*, April 2, 1972.

"U. S. Policy Toward Africa," Hon. Charles C. Diggs, Jr., House of Representatives, *Congressional Record*, Proceedings and Debates of the 92nd Congress, Vol. 118, No. 1, January 18, 1972.

Statement of Representative Charles C. Diggs, Jr., before the Senate Foreign Relations Committee in support of Senate Resolution 214, Washington, February 3, 1972.

Stephan S. Rosenfeld, "Blacks Signal Turn in Foreign Policy," the Washington *Post*, March 17, 1972.

Gerald Fraser, "American Blacks Seeking to Influence the African Policy of the U. S.," *The New York Times*, February 13, 1972.

"Hatcher Reviews Parley of Blacks," *The New York Times*, March 16, 1972.

22. Equal Employment Opportunity Program, *Minority Employment in The Department of State* (as of November 30, 1970), Department of State, Washington, D.C., June 1971.

R. Peter Straus, "Is The State Department Color-blind?" *Saturday Review*, January 2, 1971.

# BIBLIOGRAPHY

Almond, Gabriel, *The American People and Foreign Policy*. New York, Frederick Praeger, 1960.

Arkhurst, Frederick S., ed., *U. S. Policy Toward Africa*. New York, Praeger Publishers, Inc., 1975.

Bailey, Thomas, *A Diplomatic History of the American People*. 6th ed., New York, Appleton-Century-Crofts, 1958.

Browne, Robert S., *Race Relations in International Affairs*. Washington, D. C., Public Affairs Press, 1961.

Cronon, E. D., *Black Moses*. Madison, University of Wisconsin Press, 1955.

Fischel, Leslie H. and Quarles, Benjamin, *The Black American: A Documentary History*. New York, William Morrow, 1970.

Gerson, Louis L., *The Hyphenate in Recent American Politics and Diplomacy*. Lawrence, University of Kansas Press, 1964.

Hilton, Ralph, *Worldwide Mission: The Story of the United States Foreign Service*. New York, World Publishing Co., 1971.

Judd, Peter, ed., *African Independence*. New York, Dell, 1963.

Padmore, George, ed., *History of the Pan-African Congress*. Manchester, England, Pan African Federation, 1945.

Rosenau, James, *Domestic Sources of Foreign Policy*. New York, The Free Press, 1967.

Rudwick, Elliott M., *W. E. B. DuBois: Propagandist of the Negro Protest*. New York, Atheneum, 1969.

Shepherd, George W., Jr., *The Study of Race in American Foreign Policy and International Relations*. Denver, Colorado, Center on International Race Relations, the Graduate School of International Studies, University of Denver, 1969.

Shepherd, George W., Jr., ed., *Racial Influences on American Foreign Policy*. New York, Basic Books, 1970.

Straus, R. Peter, "Is The State Department Color-blind?" *Saturday Review*, January 2, 1971.

Stuart, G. H., *The Department of State*. New York, Macmillan, 1949.

# 20

## Black Americans
## and Africa

### Inez Smith Reid

Black Americans have never completely turned their backs on the African continent. But the nature, degree, and expression of the "African interest" has varied greatly over the years. Stemming initially from a religious-civilizing orientation, it moved on to propound a more egalitarian philosophy grounded in the desire to assist in the liberation and developmental phases of the continent.

Expounders of involvement in Africa have had many obstacles to overcome, however. Chief among these was the fact that from the 1800s to the mid-twentieth century, many black Americans seemed caught up in the negative and very derogatory image which American society had painted of Africa. Some Afro-Americans were openly apologetic about the "backwardness" of Africa at the same time that others were bent on seeing that some "light" seeped into the continent.

This attitude is not surprising when one considers that as recently as 1967 Harold Cruse could write:". . . deep down in the soul of many American Negroes is ingrained the conviction that the African has just barely emerged out of his primitive-tribal past!"[1] In the same vein, Adelaide Hill more diplomatically pointed out:

> In all candor it should be admitted that American Negroes as a group were not at an early date enthusiastic in their desire for knowledge about Africa. For too long Africa and things African seemed to them to relate to their position of inferiority in American life.[2]

And Rayford Logan has written:

> Equally important, and concomitant with the growth of imperialism, was the intensification of campaigns to portray "black Africa" as a land of heathens, savages, and cannibals. As a result, some American Negroes were ambivalent about their identity as Negroes in America and rejected any association with the "dark continent."[3]

Even the noted black historian George Washington Williams succumbed to the American tendency to paint Africans with a negative sweep of the brush. While acknowledging the "importance and worth of the Negro" in early history, Williams nonetheless concluded around 1882:

> The Negro type is the result of degradation. It is nothing more than the lowest strata of the African race. Pouring over the venerable mountain terraces, an abundant stream from an abundant and unknown source, into the malarial districts, the genuine African has gradually degenerated into the typical Negro. His blood infected with the poison of his low habitation, his body shrivelled by disease, his intellect veiled in pagan superstitions, the noblest yearnings of his soul strangled at birth by the savage passions of a nature abandoned to sensuality—the poor Negro of Africa deserves more our pity than our contempt.[4]

Williams was obviously ambivalent in his attitude toward Africa and Africans, however, for he remarked favorably on the governmental system adopted in certain of the African empires and revealed an admiration for the African soldier:

> The Negro empires to which we have called attention are an argument against the theory that he is without government; and his career as a soldier would not disgrace the uniform of an American soldier.[5]

Yet he resorted to such negative connotations about Africa as "languishing Africa" and "savage tribes of Africans."[6]

Little wonder, then, that black Americans were ripe to swallow much of the propaganda on Africa disseminated by whites reputed to be men of letters and science. Louis Agassiz, for example, a Harvard scientist and anthropologist, was not atypically American or scholarly when he described Africans as "indolent, playful, sensual, imitative, subservient, goodnatured, versatile, unsteady in their purpose, devoted, and affectionate."[7]

With the circulation of such writings, interest in Africa was bound to dim. W. E. B. DuBois correlates the flagging black American interest in Africa in the nineteenth century to the rise of the cotton industry and to a simultaneous effort on the part of the church and American society in general to degrade African culture and history. As he pointed out: "When the cotton kingdom of the nineteenth century built on black slavery led to a campaign in church and society to discount Africa, its culture and history, American Negroes shrank from any ties with Africa and accepted in part the color line."[8] As late as 1955 DuBois bemoaned the lack of interest in African affairs among black Americans when he asserted: " . . . it is tragic that American Negroes today are not only doing little to help Africa in its hour of supreme need, but have no way of really knowing what is happening in Africa."[9]

This was all to change, however, with the new emphasis on black pride and beauty which flowered as the 1960s drew to a close. Increasing numbers of black Americans began to identify more readily with Africa by stressing African cultural survivals and expressing empathy for the struggles of Africa—especially those against neocolonialism. This new surge of feeling was accompanied by a strong antipathy to the continued presence of Portugal in Africa as well as criticism of the odious domination of blacks by white minority governments in Rhodesia (Zimbabwe), Southwest Africa (Namibia), and South Africa (Azania).

# EARLY BLACK AMERICAN INTEREST
# IN AFRICA

During the period 1800–1957 black American interest in Africa manifested itself in several areas. These included: 1) missionary and religious endeavors, 2) colonization and emigration schemes, 3) educational projects, 4) a special interest in the Belgian Congo, Ethiopia, and Liberia, 5) self-determination efforts, 6) organizational interests.

## Missionary and Religious Endeavors

In 1895 a Congress on Africa was convened at the Gammon Theological Seminary in Atlanta, Georgia. Participants included Alexander Crummell, John Smyth, and Bishop Henry McNeal Turner. A strong religious flavor pervaded the meeting as black participants repeatedly stressed the need to concentrate on a religious and civilizing mission to Africans. The tone of the gathering was set in a paper delivered by Bishop Turner entitled: "Essay: The American Negro and the Fatherland." In his paper the eminent clergyman asserted: "The heathen Africans, to my certain knowledge, I care not what others may say, eagerly yearn for that civilization which they believe will elevate them and make them potential for good."[10] Also reflecting a deep-seated conviction in the righteousness of a religious enterprise in Africa by Americans was E. W. S. Hammond, editor of the *Southwestern Christian Advocate* in New Orleans. As he spoke on the subject "Africa and Its Relation to Christian Civilization," Hammond maintained:

> I hazard nothing when I say that Africa is now the most practical enterprise open to Christian civilization. . . . The Christian world owes to Africa its highest and best forms and types of Christian civilization. . . . In my humble judgment, our own native land is providentially prepared to play a most conspicuous part in the redemption of Africa.[11]

An examination of two prize-winning hymns composed by black Americans and sung during the Congress gives further indication of the feeling in the air. Rev. Joseph Wheeler of Harrisburg, Pennsylvania, had been awarded first prize in the 1895 Hymn from the Churches competition for his "Missionary Hymn for Africa." The last two stanzas piously urged:

> Arise, O Afric's children,
>   Enter your fatherland,
> Take ye the Gospel banner,
>   Go forth at God's command;
> Remember, Christ is with you,
>   His arm will you defend,
> Remember Jesus' promise:
>   I'm with you to the end.

> O, God of grace and mercy,
>   Look from thy throne above,
> On Africa whose millions
>   Have never known Thy love;
> Grant that the Spirit's power
>   On them may now descend;
> Grant Thou our prayer in mercy,
>   As at Thy throne we bend.[12]

In a similar vein was Alexander P. Camphor's "Hymn of Sympathy and Prayer for Africa," for which he won Gammon's first prize in 1894 during the Hymns from the Seminary competition. A member of Gammon's class of 1895, Camphor, in his middle stanzas, portrayed Africa as the "dark land" in which "heathenism roams":

> Africa, 'tis named, that country,
>   Far away from this bright shore,
> Far removed from light and knowledge,
>   Far remote from Christian lore;
> There, for many, many ages,
>   Ling'ring still in blackest night,
> Africa, dark land of hist'ry,
>   Void of light, is void of light.
>
> How can we remain contented
>   In illuminated homes,
> While our brother gropes in darkness,
>   And in heathenism roams?
> Should not his complete salvation
>   Be our earnest, prayerful plea,
> Till that long-neglected country ·
>   Shall be free, yes, wholly free?[13]

Several American Negroes gained prominence in the 1800s as a result of their missionary endeavors in Africa. Although Paul Cuffee combined a career as a sailor and shipbuilder with his religious convictions, it was as a minister in the Society of Friends that his impact on Africa was felt. Born in 1759 on an island near Massachusetts, Cuffee made several trips to Sierra Leone in 1810–11 and again in 1815. It was in 1815 that he transported some thirty-six or thirty-eight free Negroes to Sierra Leone with his own private funds, on his own private boat, *The Traveller*.[14] Cuffee's writings about Africa and to Africans had definite religious overtones. For example, in one statement describing what he had discovered about Africans, Cuffee declared:

> . . . I have cause to rejoice in having found many who are inclined to listen and attend to the precepts of our holy religion. Nevertheless, I am convinced that further help will be requisite to establish them in the true and vital spirit of devotion.[15]

And, in an address "to my scattered brethren and fellow countrymen at Sierra Leone," Cuffee said:

> I earnestly recommend to you the propriety of assembling yourselves together for the purpose of worshipping the Lord your God. God is a spirit, and they that worship him acceptably must worship him in spirit and in truth; in so doing you will find a living hope which will be as an anchor to the soul and support under afflictions. In this hope may Ethiopia stretch out her hand unto God. Come, my African brethren and fellow countrymen, let us work together in the light of the Lord—that pure light which bringeth salvation into the world, hath appeared unto all men to profit withall. . . .[16]

Another notable Negro clergyman with a missionary spirit was Bishop Henry McNeal Turner, the same bishop who had helped set the tone for the Gammon Congress on Africa. Bishop Turner was devoted not only to a religious "crusade" toward Africa but also to colonization schemes. Born in 1834 in South Carolina, he became a minister in the African Methodist Episcopalian (AME) Church, helped set up AME Churches in Sierra Leone and Liberia, traveled to Capetown, South Africa, to ordain African ministers, and even served as vice president of the American Colonization Society. Alexander Crummell, another participant in the Gammon congress, spent twenty years in Africa as a minister and teacher. An Episcopal minister educated at Queen's College in Cambridge, Crummell was born in New York in 1819. During his lifetime he wrote two books on Africa: *The Future of Africa* in 1862 and *Africa and America* in 1891. Another noted black missionary of the nineteenth century was John Wesley Gilbert, a Georgian born in 1865, who founded a Methodist mission in the Congo (now the Zaire Republic). Named Wembo-Nyama, the mission was the same in which former Prime Minister Patrice Lumumba received his early education. Gilbert coupled his religious interest in Africa with a more practical, service-oriented attitude. Thus while he contended that the "foremost" obligation "that we American Negroes are under to Africa" was "the giving to the African Negro an ideal of all that is best in Christianity," he also insisted on the need to teach Africans pride in their history and concluded that:

> He [the American Negro] ought to carry to his own "Brother in Black" industrial training. . . . God is calling for the Christian Negro physicians of the South to go to Africa. . . . Then Africa is calling for teachers—especially those possessing linguistic ability. . . .[17]

Other important black missionaries included H.W. Sheppard, who after a frustrated first attempt finally managed to establish a Presbyterian mission at Luebo in the Upper Kasai, Congo, in 1891[18] and Francis Burns and John Roberts, both of whom rose to become bishops of the Methodist Episcopal Church in Liberia.[19] Although the role of black American missionaries has not been studied comprehensively, it is clear that they were active on the African continent in behalf of the Christian faith and in many respects did not differ from white Christian missionaries, who often were castigated for their deceptive approach to Africans—taking land and leaving Bibles. Yet some colonial governments feared the black American missionary. Even though black American missionaries seemed bent solely on propagating the tenets of the Christian faith in Africa, this did not calm the fears of colonial governments that their presence might lead to unrest and disturbances directed toward colonial administrations. The English historian

George Shepperson traces the emergence of such a fear on the part of the South African government—showing how it linked early contacts between Bishop Turner and the Africans to two violent phenomena which erupted in South Africa in 1906 and 1921. Wrote Shepperson:

> The phenomenon of "Ethiopianism" in South Africa went back to 1896–8 when separatist South African churches had sought affiliation with the pioneer Negro American independent church, the African Methodist Episcopal church, and its fiery Bishop, H. M. Turner, had made his trip to Africa. Through such connexions, numbers of Africans from South Africa were to visit the United States, often in search of an education which seemed to them easier to obtain in Negro American colleges than at home. Three names stand out in this process: John L. Dube, Solomon Plaatje, and D. D. T. Jabavu, all of whom played important roles in the growth of the South African Native National Congress. The list could be extended considerably until a pattern emerges which makes intelligible the South African Government's fear that Negro Americans were inflaming Bantu racial consciousness. This fear reached unreasonable heights at the time of the 1906 Natal Zulu Rebellion and flamed up again in the 1920s, not only because of Garveyism but also because of the 1921 "Bullhoek Massacre" episode, for Enoch Mgijima, the leading figure in the affair, was known to have been in communion once with the primitive communistic Negro American Church of God and Saints of Christ.[20]

Not all black Americans were staunch believers in an exclusively religious orientation toward Africa. Notable among the dissenters were George Washington Williams and Alain Locke. Williams was born in 1849, attended Newton Theological Seminary, became a Baptist minister, and also studied law. In 1889–90 he was sent by the U. S. Government to investigate conditions in the Belgian Congo. Despite his religious background,[21] Williams obviously did not appreciate the religious-civilizing mission of the Belgian monarchy. This lack of appreciation is apparent in a rather long letter which Williams sent to Leopold II deploring conditions in the Congo. In part Williams wrote:

> I was anxious to see to what extent the natives had "adopted the fostering care" of your majesty's "benevolent enterprise" (?), and I was doomed to bitter disappointment. Instead of the natives of the Congo "adopting the fostering care" of your Majesty's Government, they everywhere complain that their land has been taken from them by force; that the Government is cruel and arbitrary, and declare that they neither love nor respect the Government and its flag. Your Majesty's Government has sequestered their land, burned their towns, stolen their property, enslaved their women and children, and committed other crimes too numerous to mention in detail. It is natural that they everywhere shrink from the "fostering care" your Majesty's Government so eagerly proffers them.[22]

But it remained for Alain Locke, Rhodes scholar, philosopher, professor, writer, and critic to speak out firmly in 1924 against an overconcentration of missionary and spiritual involvement in Africa by black Americans:

> . . . We now see that the missionary condescension of the past generations in their attitude toward Africa was a pious but sad mistake. In taking it, we have fallen into the snare of enemies and have given grievous offence to our brothers. We must realize that

> in some respects we need what Africa has to give us as much as, or even more than what we in turn have to give her.... We need to be the first of all Westerners to rid ourselves of the insulting prejudice, the insufferable bias of the attitude of "civilizing Africa"—for she is not only our mother but in light of the most recent science is beginning to appear as the mother of civilization in general. . . .[23]

No doubt Locke is correct in his conclusion that black Americans overemphasized religion with respect to Africa. Nevertheless it is equally true, as Rayford Logan has reminded us, that "American Negroes who grew up in the early part of the century probably first heard about Africa when a minister, priest, or missionary appealed for funds to support missions there."[24]

## Colonization and Emigration Schemes

Around 1902, toward the end of his career, Bishop Turner urged American Negroes to return to Africa. After his long years of service as chaplain, pastor, and missionary, Bishop Turner concluded:

> But for the Negro as a whole, I see nothing here for him to aspire after. He can return to Africa, especially to Liberia where a Negro government is already in existence, and learn the elements of civilization in fact; for human life is there sacred and no man is deprived of it or any other thing that involves manhood, without due process of law. So my decision is that there is nothing in the United States for the Negro to learn or try to attain to.[25]

A more personal statement was that of Lott Carey, who just before he emigrated to Liberia in 1815 said simply: "I wish to go to a country where I shall be estimated by my merits, not by my complexion."[26]

While not all black Americans voiced such despair over their fate in the United States, several nevertheless did lean toward migration to Africa. Thus while the American Colonization Society, existent in the mid-nineteenth century, did not favor a "general emigration" to Africa, it could not totally escape the movement toward religious-civilizing missions and stated its intention to transport to Africa "such persons as may be practically qualified and suited to promote the development of Christianity, morality, education, mechanical arts, agriculture, commerce, and general improvement." It insisted, however, that those who migrated to the continent "must always be carefully selected and well-recommended" so "that the progress of civilization may not be obstructed."[27]

Martin Delany may be singled out as a black American who had both grandiose and serious concerns about emigration to Africa. Delany, a physician educated at Harvard, had an extraordinarily interesting career during his 73 years (1812-1885). In addition to his medical practice, Delany was a journalist, having established a newspaper called *The Mystery*. In 1854 he decided to lead an emigration to Africa, and finally in 1859 headed an exploring party to the Niger River Valley area in Nigeria. His objective was to discover whether he could obtain land on which Negro Americans could settle. With the help of Henry Highland Garnet, about whom we shall hear more later, Delany hoped to secure enough property to grow sufficient cotton to be placed on the world market at prices low enough to cripple the southerners engaged in the cotton industry.[28] In his own writings, however, Delany maintained that "I had but one object in view—the moral, social, and political elevation of ourselves, and the Regeneration of Africa. . . ."[29]

Elitist in outlook, Delany repeatedly stressed the necessity of assembling "a true representation of the intelligence and wisdom of the colored freemen." For him the black masses could not be recruited to his venture because "it will be futile and an utter failure to attempt such a project without the highest grade of intelligence" since "no great project was ever devised without the consultation of the most mature intelligence, and discreet discernment and precaution. . . ."[30] Delany did manage to reach Africa, but failed ultimately in his mission and allegedly left after creating bitter feelings among some Africans who thought he had tried to trick them out of their land.

## Educational Projects

Black Americans during the period 1800–1957 essayed not only to provide education for Africans but also to inform Afro-Americans about their African heritage. Perhaps the most striking single illustration of the black American role in African education was the part played by John Chilembwe. Brought to the United States in 1897 by Joseph Booth, a white missionary, Chilembwe soon came under the influence of L. G. Jordan, Foreign Mission Secretary of the Negro American Baptist Convention.[31] Gregory Willis Hayes, principal of Virginia Theological Seminary and College in Lynchburg, Virginia, was another important figure in the educational formation of Chilembwe.[32] It was through the help of black Americans that Chilembwe was able to purchase land in Nyasaland for his Providence Industrial Mission. Returning to Nyasaland (now Malawi) in 1901, Chilembwe, after preaching Christianity for a decade or so, became influenced by the activism of John Brown and went on to lead a 1915 uprising in Nyasaland against the policies of the colonial government.[33]

Aside from this isolated example of American Negro assistance in the formation of an African leader, one can point to the extensive role played by black universities in the education of Africans, particularly such institutions as Lincoln, Wilberforce, Howard, Tuskegee, Morehouse, and Fisk. Although Leo Hansberry and Alain Locke accomplished much in this area at Howard University, the work of Lincoln University has been best documented. When he visited Africa in 1949 Horace Mann Bond, who served as president of Lincoln during the most influential period of that university's concern with the education of Africans, found "that there was magic in the name of Lincoln University."[34] This was true because Africans who received their training at Lincoln returned to Africa to relate their enthusiasm for the educational experience they had enjoyed. Bond recalls that from its creation in 1854 to 1954 some 161 Africans graduated from Lincoln University, including two prime ministers—Nkrumah of Ghana and Azikiwe of the Eastern Region of Nigeria, four other Ghanaian and Nigerian Cabinet members, a Sierra Leone legislator, "public health officials of distinction in Sierra Leone and Nigeria," "lecturers at the University Colleges in Sierra Leone, Liberia, Ghana," and "directors of important civil-service bureaus throughout West Africa."[35] During Bond's tenure as president of Lincoln (1945–1957), the institution annually received "more than a thousand" applications from Africans. This to Bond indicated that "Throughout Africa, the name of Lincoln University symbolizes 'Free-dom!'; it is the lodestone for ambitious youth everywhere on the continent."[36] From a concentration of Liberian students in its early days Lincoln moved on to recruit young South Africans, and then turned its attention to a more diverse West African representation.[37] Clearly, Lincoln University played a crucial role in the education of future African leaders and bureaucrats.

Yet there is some evidence pointing to a lack of respect on the part of black American students at Lincoln toward Africans. During a series of interviews conducted at the university by Harold Isaacs, one young respondent reported:

> At college there were African students. They were victims of our rabble. We respected their scholarship but we made fun of them. Lincoln . . . was a rough place and the Africans were the butts of many jokes.[38]

In contrast, another respondent recalled that while "most students" at Lincoln were "indifferent to Africa," some ". . . formed a group called 'Sons of Radical Africa.'" The same student further stated: "I had a sense of Africans being my brothers, part of my family, so it became my imperative duty to resent any ill done to them. . . ."[39]

The role of Tuskegee Institute in the development and education of Africa is not as well known as that of Lincoln. Tuskegee probably made its greatest impact through its two missions to Africa rather than from its education of African students in America. In 1900, at the invitation of Germany, a group of Tuskegee graduates sailed to Togoland to instruct Africans in cotton production. And in 1906 a mission was dispatched to the Sudan. During a 1912 International Conference on the Negro held at Tuskegee, Booker T. Washington stressed the potential educative role of black Americans in behalf of Africa.[40]

According to Shepperson, Booker T. Washington's "self-help educational ideal for coloured people had profound effects on African nationalism, particularly through its influence on James Aggrey of Achimota and John L. Dube of the Ohlange Institute, Natal."[41] As part of this "ideal," Booker T. Washington believed that black Americans could play a substantial role in the education of African teachers and technical assistants. Washington also championed business ventures in Africa such as that of the Africa Union Company, which was "a carefully organized scheme for promoting trade between Negro America and the Gold Coast that was destroyed by the 1914 war's interruption of Atlantic commerce."[42]

While some Afro-Americans were attempting to supply formal education and technical assistance to Africans, others were anxious to inform Afro-Americans about their heritage. Central to this effort was Carter G. Woodson, born in 1875 and educated at Chicago (B.A. and M.A.) and Harvard (Ph.D.). Rayford Logan has written: "I would venture to say that Dr. Carter G. Woodson popularized interest in Africa among American Negroes more than did DuBois or Garvey. Woodson had a following among scholars and the general public."[43] Two of Woodson's works were instrumental in augmenting Afro-American interest in Africa. Both were simply written but highly informative. One took the form of a manual for the study of Africa; the other was a text designed to capture the attention and immediate interest of junior high and high school students. In the first of these, *The African Background Outlined or Handbook for the Study of the Negro* (Washington, D.C., Association for the Study of Negro Life and History, Inc., 1936) Dr. Woodson included chapters on "Ethiopia and Egypt," "Ghana," "Songhay Empire," "Mossi States," "African Survivals in America," "The Partition of Africa," and "African Culture." In the second, *African Heroes and Heroines* (Washington, D.C., Associated Publishers, Inc., 1939, 1944), he brought alive such key African figures as Chaka, Moshesh, Khama, Sonni Ali, and Askia Mohammed. In another work, *The Negro in Our History* (Associated Publishers, 1922), Woodson affirmed and illustrated the African origins of black Americans by commencing his text with three African-oriented chapters: "The Unknown African Origin," "African Institutions: A Background," and "Africans In History With Others." Woodson also forged greater Afro-American interest in Africa through his participation in the Association of Negro Life and History, and his articles in the *Journal of Negro History* and the *Negro History Bulletin*.

Although his contributions to the education of black Americans were not as prolific as Woodson's, John Edward Bruce also deserves credit for his efforts to improve black American knowledge of Africa through the Negro Society for Historical Research, which he founded in 1911 with Arthur Schomburg. Bruce, a newspaperman by occupation, sought not only to arouse Afro-American interest in Africa but also managed to exert considerable influence on certain Africans. For example, Bruce and Schomburg were able to attract key Africans as "honorary presidents," "vice presidents," and "members" of the Negro Society for Historical Research. These included Casely Hayford of Ghana and Duse Mohammed Effendi. In assessing the importance of Bruce, George Shepperson writes:

> ... numerous ... Africans who visited America or who wrote to Bruce bear witness to his influence on their thought about the African past and their desire to gain from it a pride in their blackness. Bruce's own pride in his colour was shown when he acted as American agent for Casely Hayford's *Ethiopia Unbound*. To Aggrey, Bruce was "Daddy." Furthermore, he maintained close relations with Majola Agbebi, Baptist Yoruba founder of what has been called "the first independent Native African church in West Africa," who was introduced to Bruce by Edward Blyden during a visit to America in 1903.[44]

It was Agbebi, Shepperson indicates, who affirmed during a sermon in Lagos: "I am a Negro and all Negro. I am black all over, and proud of my beautiful black skin. . . ." In response to this cry of pride Bruce mobilized a group of black Americans to work for the creation of a "Majola Agbebi Day" in order "to immortalize in him an African personality."[45]

George Washington Williams also sought to enlighten black Americans about Africa. In his classic *History of the Negro Race in America, 1619–1880* (New York, Arno Press and *The New York Times*, 1968), first published in 1883, Williams added chapters entitled "Negro Kingdoms of Africa" (Benin, Dahomey, and Yoruba), "The Ashantee Empire," "African Idiosyncracies," "Sierra Leone," and "The Republic of Liberia."

## Special Interest in the Belgian Congo, Ethiopia, and Liberia

Black Americans took particular interest in three areas of Africa during the nineteenth and early twentieth centuries: the Belgian Congo, Ethiopia, and Liberia.

Probably due to the exploits of Livingstone and Stanley, black Americans assumed a posture of curiosity about the strangeness and adventure of the Congo. Many had heard or read stories dealing with Stanley's explorations. Harold Isaacs has recorded the recollections of several Afro-Americans about their childhood encounters with tales involving the two Englishmen. As three of his respondents recalled:

> When I was a little boy and could first read, I had books on Stanley, Livingstone and things like that. . . .
>
> I knew about Livingstone; we had Stanley's book illustrated, a fat brown book. . . .
>
> I remember my father reading to us, when I was seven or eight, from a book called *With Stanley in Africa*. He used to read it to us and talk about Africa, about Stanley, what they had done to Africa, and tell us that Negroes had been kings when white men were savages.[46]

Gradually, word of Belgian atrocities spread through the black communities. As George Shepperson points out: ". . . by the 1890s . . . a critical attitude was developing amongst the Negro American intelligentsia toward the Leopold regime."[47] Details of Congolese sufferings at the hands of the Belgians filtered down largely through accounts of the Presbyterian missionary William Henry Sheppard, who eventually was incarcerated for eight months in 1908 as a result of his severe and persistent denunciations of "Leopold's Congo."[48] Through the Boston *Guardian*, edited by Monroe Trotter, a contemporary of W. E. B. DuBois, and the *Crisis*, the official journal of the NAACP, Negro Americans were alerted to the mutilations taking place in the Congo. That Sheppard, the *Crisis*, and the *Guardian* all helped reshape black American attitudes toward the Congo is apparent from more of Isaacs' interviews. Said three respondents:

We heard of the Belgian Congo, the crimes of Leopold. I remember my mother talking about how they chopped people's ears off. She read about it, either in Trotter's *Guardian*, or in *Crisis*. . . .

I heard old Rev. Sheppard talk about the Congo, Leopold cutting people's hands off. . . .

The conduct of the Belgian King Leopold, the mutilation of people in the Congo. . . . We had a Negro missionary named Sheppard who came to Morehouse, or to the church in my home town, I forget which, and described all this. It made an indelible impression on me . . .[49]

The Belgian Government's policy led several black Americans to become active in the Congo Reform Association. A prominent member of the group was Booker T. Washington, who felt that once positive changes were made in the Congo for the benefit of Congolese, black Americans should play an instrumental role in the growth of the Congo. W. E. B. DuBois, too, proselytized the Congo case. During his address to the 1900 Pan-African Congress, for example, DuBois asserted: "Let the Congo Free State become a great central Negro state of the world, and let its prosperity be counted not simply in cash and commerce, but in the happiness and true advancement of its black people."[50] In the course of the 1919 Pan-African Congress, Dr. George Jackson summarized his stay in the Congo and indicated that "as a colored American he also had often had cause to blush for America."[51] And of course the mission of George Washington Williams to the Congo, mentioned earlier, cannot be overlooked as an important molder of black American opinion concerning the Congo.

Ethiopia was another area that aroused special interest on the part of black Americans. As early as 1903 the stockbroker William Henry Ellis headed an expedition to that African nation. But black Americans were lukewarm about Ethiopia at first because of a belief that Ethiopians did not identify with Negro Americans.[52] A greater degree of empathy evolved with the violation of Ethiopia's sovereignty.[53] In fact, Rayford Logan detected "an outburst of sympathetic interest" on the part of the Negro American community after the 1935 Italian invasion of Ethiopia.[54] This "outburst" may have been attributable to an identification with a black independent country and a feeling that the integrity of that nation must be maintained at all costs—especially in the face of a white attempt to eliminate a black sovereign state. As John Hope Franklin has written: "Ethiopia was a Negro nation, and its destruction would symbolize the final victory of the white man over the Negro," and "almost overnight, even the most provincial among American Negroes became international-minded."[55]

Isaacs' respondents also noted their sometimes total involvement and anxiety over the Italian-Ethiopian war:

I was up to my gills in the Ethiopian war. I followed every tiny step of it. "Ethiopia shall stretch forth her hands. . . ." You knew what the Bible had predicted. And you knew about Adowa in 1896 and here were the Italians back again. It was a great spectacle.

The *Courier* sent J. A. Rogers to Ethiopia and gained 23,000 circulation with an interview with Haile Selassie. . . .

The Ethiopian war made me bitter; it frightened me. We had Italian neighbors and I fought that war every day. My mother was very excited about it. I just knew the Ethiopians were black and therefore we were for them. . . .[56]

Thus black Americans found themselves paying close attention to developments in Ethiopia, fearful that this illustrious Negro state would find its demise at the hands of an audacious white power.

Although black Americans showed episodic frenzies of interest regarding events in the Belgian Congo and Ethiopia, it was for Liberia that black Americans reserved their greatest degree of "special interest" and involvement during the period from the nineteenth through the mid-twentieth century. Ever since March 1820 when the first black Americans sailed for Liberia, Afro-Americans had maintained at least a passing interest in that country. Much romanticism surrounded its creation. Around 1859, for example, Martin Delany referred to Liberians as a "noble band of brothers" and on his journey to Liberia in July 1859 he described plans for Liberian College as "a grand stride in the march of African Regeneration and Negro Nationality."[57] Even more eloquent was George Washington Williams, who wrote:

The circumstances that led to the founding of the Negro republic in the wilds of Africa perished in the fires of civil war. The Negro is free everywhere; but the Republic of Liberia stands, and should stand until its light shall have penetrated the gloom of Africa, and until the heathen shall gather to the brightness of its shining. May it stand through the ages as a Christian republic, as a faithful lighthouse along the dark and trackless sea of African paganism![58]

Concomitant with such romanticism, however, was a more critical attitude toward Liberia. For Rayford Logan it was "difficult for most American Negroes to avoid a myopic view of Liberia." This was true, asserted Logan, not only because some black Americans were upset when Raymond Leslie Buell revealed "the onerous terms of the Firestone contract," but also because some were disturbed by and apparently believed in the validity of a 1930 League of Nations Commission report which pointed to the existence of "forced labor and peonage" in Liberia. Thus Logan concludes, "American Negroes' view of Liberia vacillates between pride and chagrin."[59]

A long list of black Americans served as ministers to Liberia. One of the first of these was J. Milton Turner of Missouri, who was designated as minister and consul general to the African nation on March 1, 1871.[60] At the close of Turner's term, John Henry Smyth succeeded to the post in 1878. Smyth, who became a close friend of Edward Blyden, then Liberian minister to the Court of St. James, "was not only interested in the commercial relations with Liberia, but he was most profuse in his praise of the resources of the country."[61] Henry Highland Garnet, who had quarreled with Frederick Douglass over the question of black American emigration to Africa, had collaborated with Martin Delany, and whose grandfather was a Mandingo chief, capped an impressive career by serving as minister to Liberia for about two months before his untimely death in Monrovia on February 13, 1882.[62] Then, after John Smyth had served a second term as minister to Liberia, came Moses Aaron Hopkins of North Carolina, who was appointed to the post on September 11, 1885. He was described as "of unmixed African blood and very much interested in the elevation of his race and the redemption of Africa."[63] The list of ministers continued through the years. In addition to the post of minister to Liberia, at least one black American, George W. Ellis, served as Secretary of the United States Legation in Liberia from 1901–1910. After his tenure had ended Ellis wrote a book in 1914 entitled *Negro Culture in West Africa*.[64]

Black Americans, too, traditionally have headed the American Embassy in Liberia. The post was held by Samuel Westerfield from 1968 until his death in 1972.

## Self-Determination Efforts

Early black American efforts to arouse a greater degree of black political consciousness concerning Africa probably began with W. E. B. DuBois. But the impact of the Universal Negro Improvement Association (UNIA) cannot be overlooked. Although headed by the Jamaican Marcus Garvey, the association appealed to a number of black Americans. Organized first in 1914 in Jamaica as the Universal Negro Improvement and Conservation Association and African Communities League, the group claimed by 1919 to have some thirty branches and two million black American adherents.[65] In the early twenties numerous black Americans listened to Marcus Garvey's speech on the occasion of his election as provisional president of Africa. Although riddled with egotistical overtones, Garvey's message did emphasize the political nature of the task ahead in terms of work to be done on the African continent:

> The signal honor of being provisional president of Africa is mine. . . . It is a political calling for me to redeem Africa. It is like asking Napoleon to take the world. . . . He failed and died at St. Helena. But may I not say that the lessons of Napoleon are but stepping-stones by which we shall guide ourselves to African liberation?[66]

Through such simple slogans as "Africa for the Africans," "Renaissance of the black race," and "Africa must be free," Garvey helped immensely to raise the black American's level of consciousness concerning Africa. And even though his scheme to transport black Americans to Liberia ultimately failed, Garvey did manage, according to George Padmore, to make "a marked contribution to the struggle for African awakening."[67]

Yet Garvey and W. E. B. DuBois never really saw eye to eye. In describing Garvey in his *Dusk of Dawn*, DuBois revealed ambivalent attitudes—describing the UNIA both as a "grandiose and bombastic scheme, utterly impracticable as a whole" and as "sincere" and with "some practical features." DuBois went on to label Garvey "an astonishing popular leader" and "a master of propaganda."[68] DuBois seems to have resented the negative effect which UNIA had on the building and organizing of his Pan-African Congress. As he pointed out: "The unfortunate debacle of [Garvey's] over-advertised schemes naturally hurt and made difficult further effective development of the Pan-African Congress idea."[69]

Perhaps no single black American has had as much of a sustained impact upon the development of Africa as W. E. B. DuBois. Scholar, activist, and "diplomat," DuBois essayed not only to help propel Africans along the road to self-determination but also to shape their thinking about the philosophical doctrines which would guide them during the march from dependence to "independence," and "independence" to viable statehood.

DuBois traces the beginning of his interest in Africa to his student days at Fisk University, but it was not until after the turn of the century that he became truly preoccupied with that continent. As he pointed out:

> Africa was not a major thing in my thought or any part of my experience. My first real acquisition of any of this was at Fisk, where they had the beginnings of an African museum. . . . But Africa still never came to the center of my thought. It was something in the background. There was always a lack of interest, a neglect, a resentment at being classed as Africans when Negroes felt that they were Americans. Interest in Africa did not begin with anyone until after 1880 or so. . . . I did not myself begin actively to study Africa until 1908 or 1910. Franz Boas really influenced me to begin studying this subject and I began really to get into it only after 1915.[70]

By 1915 DuBois' emotional involvement with Africa was crystal clear. It poured forth, for example, during a series of speeches on the origins of World War I. In a summarization of these speeches printed in the *Atlantic Monthly*, in May 1915, DuBois remarked:

> The methods by which this continent has been stolen have been contemptible and dishonest beyond expression. Lying treaties, rivers of rum, murder, assassination, mutilation, rape, and torture have marked the progress of Englishman, German, Frenchman, and Belgian on the Dark Continent. The only way in which the world has been able to endure the horrible tale is by deliberately stopping its ears and changing the subject of conversation while the devilry went on.[71]

From that point on the exploitation of Africa by Europeans became one of DuBois' constant themes. Hence he wrote as early as 1919: "What Europe, and indeed only a small group in Europe wants in Africa is not a field for the spread of European civilization, but a field for exploitation."[72]

Yet although DuBois recognized in 1915 the "theft" of Africa's "land and natural resources" and the need to spread "the principle of home rule" throughout Africa, nonetheless he too stressed a kind of "civilizing mission" to Africa when he asserted: ". . . we must train native races in modern civilization."[73] His theme of "civilization and intelligence," consistent with his concept of the "talented tenth,"[74] carried over to 1919 when he revealed his platform for the future of Africa in January during an NAACP-organized mass meeting in Carnegie Hall, part of which read:

While the principle of self-determination, which has been recognized as fundamental by allies, cannot be wholly applied to semicivilized peoples, yet as the English prime minister has acknowledged, it can be partially applied.

The public opinion which . . . should have the decisive voice is composed of:
a) The chiefs and intelligent Negroes among the twelve and one-half million natives of German Africa, especially those trained in the government and mission schools.
b) The twelve million civilized Negroes of the United States.
c) Educated persons of Negro descent in South America and the West Indies.[75]

These themes obviously were consistent with DuBois' overall philosophy of the "talented tenth." For while DuBois clearly opposed wholesale black American emigration to Africa, nevertheless he was convinced that black Americans ought to play a leadership role in behalf of Africans. Thus he insisted at one point: "It is absurd to talk of a return to Africa merely because that was our home 300 years ago, as it would be to expect the members of the Caucasian race to return to the vastness of the Caucasus Mountains from which, it is reputed, they sprang."[76] But DuBois, according to Isaacs, "thought that as far as the black men were concerned, the American Negro, rising steadily in education and attainment despite all obstacles, had to take the lead. He had to speak for the more slowly awakening masses of Africa. . . ."[77]

DuBois' writings on Africa are vast. They include several books and pamphlets: e.g., *Suppression of the African Slave Trade to the United States of America, 1638–1870* (1896), *The Negro* (1915), *Africa, Its Geography, People and Products* (1930), *Africa, Its Place in Modern History* (1930), *The World and Africa* (1947), and *Africa in Battle Against Colonialism, Racism, Imperialism* (1960). DuBois also dashed off countless articles about Africa during his lifetime, many of which were written during his later years when his interest in Africa sharpened. Comments on Ghana, Nigeria, the Congo, and Kenya are prevalent.[78]

In 1909 DuBois tried to initiate an *Encyclopedia Africana* with an international board of advisors but was unable to secure adequate funds.[79] The idea of such an encyclopedia was embraced by the Phelps-Stokes Fund in 1931, and DuBois and Guy B. Johnson were selected to be editors of the *Encyclopedia of the Negro*, a preliminary volume of which was published by the fund in 1945. DuBois was able to obtain "cooperation from many scholars, white and black, in America, Europe, and Africa"; but the "necessary funds," as was the case with the *Encyclopedia Africana*, ware not available.[80] DuBois persisted in his dream of an encyclopedia, however; and when he moved to Ghana in 1961 he headed the staff of the *Encyclopedia Africana* project there. After his death in 1963, project headquarters remained in Ghana, where work on the project is still under way.

Dubois' most notable role, however, in relationship to self-determination, was played in various Pan-African Congresses held periodically from 1900 to 1945. Even though DuBois did not convene the first Pan-African Congress in London in 1900 (that role was played by the lawyer Henry Sylvester Williams of Trinidad) he took an active part in it as a result of his appointment as chairman of the Committee on Address to the Nations of the World. It was in his address that DuBois coined his famous phrase, "The problem of the twentieth century is the problem of the color line. . . . " His introductory thoughts in the address were as follows:

> In the metropolis of the modern world, in this closing year of the nineteenth century, there has been assembled a congress of men and women of African blood, to deliberate solemnly upon the present situation and outlook of the darker races of mankind. The problem of the twentieth century is the problem of the color line, the question as to how far differences of race—which show themselves chiefly in the color of the skin and the texture of the hair—will hereafter be made the basis of denying to over half the world the right of sharing to their utmost ability the opportunities and privileges of modern civilization.[81]

After the death of Henry Sylvester Williams, DuBois gathered up the reins of leadership and himself organized five Pan-African Congresses between 1919 and 1945. (Pan-African initiatives, naturally, were not confined to American blacks; African sentiment in favor of cooperative action had an independent as well as associated growth.) The 1919 conference, held in Paris, was attended by sixteen Afro-Americans, twenty West Indians, and twelve Africans.[82] DuBois was joined in the Paris session by Blaise Diagne, deputy to the French Assembly from Senegal who served as president of the 1919 conference while DuBois held the position of secretary. This congress stressed the general theme of "protection of nations of Africa" and the need to establish a permanent bureau of the League of Nations "to insure observance of . . . an international code of law for the protection of the nations of Africa" and to "further the racial, political, and economic interest of the natives."[83] Many black Americans were unable to secure visas to journey to the Paris conference since colonial governments and the United States apparently found the idea rather unsettling.[84]

The 1921 conference, held in both London and Paris, drew some 113 delegates: 41 Africans, 35 black Americans, 24 "Negroes living in Europe," and 7 West Indians.[85] The London gathering awakened the ire of Belgium when it attempted to pass a resolution highly critical of Belgian colonial policies. The Paris resolutions of 1921, like those of London, tended to stress the concept of the "equality of man" and the need to reject attitudes which pictured African civilization as inferior.[86] Both of the two following conferences, one in London and Lisbon in 1923 and the other in New York in 1927, failed to measure up to the earlier or later Pan-African Congresses. Both had relatively small attendance and even the New York conference did not attract many Afro-Americans.[87] Interestingly, however, the New York conference was financed mainly by "a group of colored American women."[88]

It is the 1945 conference, however, which has gone down in history as the most significant of all the Pan-African Congresses. Participating in this session in Manchester, England, were some 200 delegates including many Africans—Nkrumah, Kenyatta, Wallace Johnson of Sierra Leone, and Peter Abrahams of South Africa. This conference, with its many representatives drawn from the ranks of the political, trade union, and agricultural worlds, had the air of a mass movement. The evils of colonialism were underscored repeatedly; among them the economic exploitation of Africa, the political pretensions of imperialist powers, and the discouragement of industrialization which could benefit Africans as opposed to Europeans. This 1945 Pan-African Congress resolved that complete and absolute independence for the peoples of Africa was the only solution to their problem. Moreover, it led to positive action against colonial powers in the form of strikes, boycotts, and other types of active protest.

DuBois' involvement with Africa carried over into the independence struggle and the battle for an emerging and viable nationhood. Ghana and Nkrumah in particular were of special interest to DuBois. His support of Nkrumah no doubt stems from the days of the 1945 Manchester Pan-African Congress in which Nkrumah played a pivotal role—so pivotal that the 1954 Pan-African Congress was held at Kumasi, Gold Coast (now Ghana). At first DuBois doubted that "Nkrumah had the stamina and patience" to lead Ghana to independence. Yet by 1956, when Nkrumah achieved a significant legislative victory, DuBois did not hesitate to wire his "congratulations."[89] When Ghana became independent DuBois was anxious to accept Nkrumah's invitation to attend the inauguration but was unable to do so when the United States denied him a passport. Nonetheless DuBois dispatched a rather lengthy philosophical and emotional message to the African leader which he concluded by bestowing the title "President of the Pan-African Congress" on Nkrumah.[90] In 1958 DuBois once again had to pass up an opportunity to journey to Ghana, this time for the All-African People's Conference. Battling an illness in Moscow, DuBois was represented instead by his wife, Shirley Graham. In 1960 he had both the necessary papers and the good health to make the voyage to Ghana, where he helped celebrate "Ghana Republic Day" in July. And in 1961, after having formally applied for membership in the Communist party on October 1, DuBois left the United States permanently and became a citizen of Ghana, where he died in 1963.[91]

In summary, DuBois made at least two long-lasting contributions to Africa. The first was his insistence on the need for self-determination or self-government and the need for the immersion of Africans in the Pan-African movement. The second was his attempt to prove that African countries must be guided by an ideology of socialism and cooperative economy. In a memorial issue on DuBois compiled by *Freedomways**** in 1965, both Nkrumah and Nnamdi Azikiwe testified to the importance of Dubois' contribution to the growth of Africa.

Said Nkrumah:

> We in Ghana remember Dr. DuBois as a brilliant scholar, a great champion in the struggle for the rights of man, and an undaunted fighter against racial inequality, discrimination, and injustice. . . . He was not only a champion of the oppressed, but also a source of inspiration in our struggle for freedom and the right of the African to govern himself (p.3).

*Black Titan; an Anthology by the Editors of *Freedomways*, Boston, Beacon Press, 1965.

And commented Azikiwe:

> Dr. DuBois was a pioneer reformer who dreamt dreams of a free Africa. His efforts from the beginning of this century until his death in 1963 have distinguished him as a hero and prophet of his age. . . . His founding of the Pan-African Congress in 1919, in Paris, was a signal for the historic struggle by African nationalists which led ultimately to the political emancipation of this continent.

## Organizational Interests

Several organizations with a clearly African orientation or emphasis came into prominence during the period of early Afro-American interest in Africa. One, the Phelps-Stokes Fund, was chartered to contribute to the educational development of Africans; it has enjoyed an excellent reputation for being able to grant assistance to African students at critical moments in their educational experiences. As early as 1921 J. K. Aggrey, a citizen of the Gold Coast, received support from the fund during his student days at Livingstone College. In turn Aggrey joined the Phelps-Stokes team and traveled to Africa on two different missions with Dr. Thomas Jesse Jones, Phelps-Stokes Educational Director, in order to examine ways in which the fund could be instrumental in educational programs for Africans. In 1929 the Booker Washington Institute was established in Liberia through the auspices and support of the Phelps-Stokes Fund.

Many Africans were recruited to study in the United States under Phelps-Stokes grants. Among them were Robert Gardiner (who today is a respected and admired international civil servant concerned with some of Africa's most pressing developmental problems), Nkrumah, and Azikiwe. Perhaps as a token of appreciation for its assistance to African students, Nkrumah not only permitted the fund to convene its 1961 annual meeting in Ghana but also personally attended it.[92]

The NAACP, as the result of continuing pressure from W. E. B. DuBois, added an interest in Africa to its domestic preoccupation.[93] In 1916 DuBois discussed his research on Africa with the NAACP and suggested the compilation of the aforementioned *Encyclopedia Africana*. When DuBois traveled to Paris to the 1919 Pan-African Congress, he did so as a representative of both the NAACP and the *Crisis*. It was the NAACP which convened a Carnegie Hall meeting in 1919 under the theme "Africa and World Democracy." A telegram to President Woodrow Wilson outlined the hopes of the Carnegie Hall participants and the NAACP that the League of Nations would pay heed to the "development of the peoples of middle Africa."[94] It was thanks to a $3,000 Pan-Africa Fund established by the NAACP that DuBois and Walter White made their way to the 1921 Pan-African Congress.

The *Crisis* was the source of much information about Africa. As James W. Ivy pointed out: "Between 1918 and 1927, the *Crisis* championed African freedom and independence in ringing editorials, which were in most instances simply titled 'Pan-Africa.' "[95]

Ivy went on to indicate that the *Crisis* printed "the facts of African history, geography, religion, art, literature, labor, and tribal life. It raised a voice of indignation at colonial exploitation while making its readers aware of the grinding misery and the persecution hidden behind the façades of the 'white man's burden' and '*la mission civilisatrice*.' "[96]

A third African-oriented organization, the Association for the Study of Negro Life and History, founded in 1915 by Carter G. Woodson and four other individuals, increased black American awareness of Africa not only through periodic association meetings but also through the *Journal of Negro History* and the *Negro History Bulletin*. According to Ulysses Lee the *Journal* contained: 1) general articles on "broad aspects of African civilization and cultures," 2) material concerning "African relations with the New World and with Europe through the slave and other forms of trade," 3) pieces on "Liberian political and social history," 4) anthropological writings on "tribal life and customs," 5) studies of colonialism, 6) treatises on "international relations and the political history of Africa."[97] A fourth organization of note was the Council on African Affairs, whose broad outlines were laid down in London in 1939. Max Yergan, who had spent time in South Africa as a YMCA secretary, was the first to advance the idea and then collaborated with Paul Robeson in actually creating the council in New York. In 1943 Alpheus Hunton, professor of English at Howard University and later author of *Decision in Africa* (New York, International Publishers, 1960) joined Yergan and Robeson as a guiding force of the council. The council not only raised funds for "starving people in South Africa and striking miners in West Africa,"[98] but also conducted lectures on Africa and made contact with various African visitors.

Hard times fell upon the council when it was labeled as "subversive" by the United States Attorney General. Robeson and Yergan differed on how to react to the label "subversive." While Yergan thought that an immediate attack on communist members should be made, Robeson believed that the emphasis should be placed upon the "needed" and valuable work of the council, and that "the political or religious opinions of its members or officials were their own business, so long as the actions of the organization as such were legal."[99] Yergan and Robeson never managed to reach a compromise. Eventually Yergan was relieved of his duties.

In 1948 DuBois was tendered the honorary office of vice chairman of the council, which he no doubt welcomed as he had just been dismissed from the NAACP. By now the council was relatively destitute and in 1950 scholars such as E. Franklin Frazier aided in the planning of a fund-raising dinner built around the celebration of DuBois' eighty-third birthday. But when DuBois was indicted "for not registering as an agent of a foreign power in the Peace Movement"[100] in 1951, this substantially affected plans for the birthday celebration. Many, committed previously to participating in the celebration and its organization, dropped by the wayside. These included Mordecai Johnson, president of Howard University. E. Franklin Frazier, however, "stood firm" and insisted that "the dinner must and would go on."[101] The dinner eventually was held at Small's Paradise, a famous Harlem nightclub, but soon after the council all but collapsed.

The American Council on African Education came into existence toward the end of the 1940s. Organized by two Nigerians, D. O. Mbadiwe and M. Ojike, the council included in its ranks notable Afro-Americans like Roy Wilkins, Mary McLeod Bethune, Mordecai Johnson, Adam Clayton Powell, George Schuyler, and Alain Locke.

In 1953 two additional organizations were founded in which black Americans initially played key decision-making roles: the American Committee on Africa, for which A. Philip Randolph served as co-chairman, and the African-American Institute, launched by the aforementioned Professor Leo Hansberry of Howard University. Since their inception both organizations have functioned under white leadership although black Americans have been accorded supporting leadership roles.

In 1957 Dr. James Robinson, a New York City pastor, unveiled his then unique idea of a student work-study program in Africa, Operation Crossroads Africa. While black American interest and participation in the program lagged during the relatively early years of its existence, it snowballed in the latter part of 1966 as black Americans identified more and more readily with their African heritage.

## AFRO-AMERICAN INTEREST IN AFRICA: POST-1957

With the granting of independence to Ghana in the late 1950s and the emergence of an American Black Power movement toward the end of the 1960s, a noticeable shift in black American attitudes toward Africa occurred. While some remnants of shame and colonial mentality remained with respect to Africa, many black Americans began to point to African cultural survivals, develop new pride in their African heritage, and regard with concern developments in still nonliberated southern Africa.

### African Cultural Survivals

In 1941 Melville Herskovits, an anthropologist, penned his rather comprehensive *Myth of the Negro Past* (Boston, Beacon Press, 1941, 1958) in which he outlined how African cultural traits had been retained by black Americans. In 1958 Lorenzo Turner, then head of the department of English at Howard University, picked up the theme of African cultural survivals and wrote:

> The aspects of African culture which have been most tenacious throughout the New World are survivals in languages, folk literature, religion, art, the dance, and music, but some survivals from the economic and social life of the Africans can also be found in the New World.[102]

Along the coast of South Carolina and Georgia, Turner found "nearly six thousand words of African origin that represent approximately thirty West African languages."[103] Furthermore, Turner pointed to several rhythms allegedly of African origin—the Charleston, "derived from the rhythm of Oshun, the Yoruba goddess of rivers"; "the Juba from that of Iyanjan, the wife of the Yoruba god of thunder (Shango); and the Malaguenha, from that of Oshala, the chief of the Yoruba deities."[104]

When the cry of Black Power was popularized in the late 1960s, increasing numbers of black Americans stressed their African origins by adopting life styles deemed to be African in nature. Thus dashikis displaced sports coats, naturals were substituted for processed hair, and decorative beads and bracelets became fashionable. Scholars such as Professor Johnnetta B. Cole once again advanced the postulate of the persistence of at least some African cultural traits in black America.[105]

Though black Americans were willing to recognize and accept these African cultural traits, interest in Africa remained limited among both the masses and certain segments of the intellectual elite. This changed, however, when black Americans, particularly those who espoused the rhetoric of the Black Power movement, discovered the writings of the West Indian Frantz Fanon—especially the *Wretched of the Earth* (New York, Grove Press, 1963) in which Fanon set forth his philosophical ideas about "liberation" struggles in light of his own experiences as a doctor in Algeria during the long and bloody Algerian war with the French. Due in part to Fanon's influence as well as a greater flux of propaganda and news from southern Africa, black Americans increasingly expressed concern for the still nonliberated territories of Africa: Rhodesia (Zimbabwe), Southwest Africa (Namibia), Angola, Mozambique, Guinea Bissau, and South Africa (Azania). Efforts were made to develop a black constituency designed both to reverse a perceived passive American policy toward these areas and to give more assistance—at least medical and nutritional—to liberation movements. There were even demonstrations, such as the one that took place in Burnside, Louisiana, in early spring 1972. These demonstrations were organized by blacks and proved to be relatively successful since they had the support of black longshoremen.

Then, too, select areas of Africa began to attract black Americans. Outside of the isolated cases of "voluntary" exile—to Algeria by Eldridge Cleaver of the Black Panther party and "voluntary" exile to Guinea by Stokely Carmichael, former head of SNCC—black Americans began to look more closely at countries like Guinea and Tanzania, especially the latter. For example, the Committee for Unified Newark, headed by Imamu Baraka, adopted the model of the Tanganyika African Union (the ruling political party on the mainland of Tanzania) for its organizational structure, while the women's division of the committee emulated the Umoja Wa Wanawake Wa Tanzania (United Women of Tanzania). The Center for Black Education in Washington, D.C., headed by James Garrett, actually took teams to Tanzania to work on specific developmental projects; and the Africana Research Center at Cornell University, directed by Professor

James Turner, sponsored student trips there. With respect to Guinea, Professor Leonard Jeffries, head of Black Studies at San Jose State College in California, organized journeys to that African nation as well as to others. Large numbers of black Americans have journeyed to Africa for summer study and travel since 1965.

Another move forward has been the increase in the number of black Americans who have secured fellowships for research in Africa, mainly through the Ford Foundation Fellowship Program for Black Americans, which concerns itself with developmental problems in Africa and the Middle East. Most recently black Americans, Africans, and other scholars have been given the opportunity to conduct research in Africa under grants made by the African American Scholars Council.

Black American ambassadors to Africa have been more numerous since 1957. Among them have been Elliott Skinner (Upper Volta), Samuel Adams, Assistant Administrator Africa Bureau, AID (Niger); Clinton Knox, Ambassador to Haiti (Dahomey); Clyde Ferguson (Uganda); Samuel Westerfield (Liberia); John Reinhardt (Nigeria); Mercer Cook (Niger, Senegal); and Franklin Williams, President of the Phelps-Stokes Fund (Ghana).

Books by Afro-American scholars have appeared in greater frequency in the post-1957 period. The works of Elliott Skinner, Martin Kilson, Hugh and Mabel Smythe, Joseph Harris, William Shack, John H. Clarke, James Gibbs, Willard Johnson, and Sylvester Whittaker are but a few of the black American writings on Africa. Many journal and periodical articles by younger black scholars have also been published.

It is not too easy to keep abreast of or to document completely all the activities of black Americans with respect to Africa in the post-1957 period. What follows, then, is a brief and necessarily incomplete account of some of the groups and organizations which have emerged in the post-1957 period.

## The American Society of African Culture

Created in 1957 as an outgrowth of the First International Congress of Negro Writers and Artists, AMSAC was extremely active in African affairs until it was rocked by accusations of a CIA link. Black American presence at the 1957 Paris meeting occurred primarily as a result of Richard Wright's 1956 letter to Roy Wilkins, who had been elected Executive Director of the NAACP in 1955, expressing grave concern that black Americans were not responsive to the *Présence Africaine's** call for a world conference of black writers.[106] Due to the NAACP's World War I and post-World War I experience with African affairs, Wilkins did not want to commit the NAACP proper to the congress. Instead he placed the matter in the hands of Professor John A. Davis, of

*Présence Africaine*, founded in 1947 by Alioune Diop, a Senegalese, is a journal devoted to African culture.

the City College of New York, who asked four other prominent black Americans to join him in participating in the Paris meeting. Besides Professor Davis the delegates were Horace Mann Bond, then president of Lincoln University; Professor Mercer Cook of Howard University, who had studied at the Sorbonne with Aimé Césaire, Alioune Diop, and Léopold Senghor; William T. Fontaine, a professor of philosophy at the University of Pennsylvania and former roommate of Nnamdi Azikiwe; and James Ivy, then editor of the *Crisis*.

Out of the Paris conference grew the Society of African Culture. The American delegation was urged to form an American Society of African Culture. Thus, upon his return to the United States Professor Davis formally organized AMSAC. In addition to the American delegates to Paris, AMSAC's founding members included Thurgood Marshall, then counsel for the NAACP Legal Defense Fund; Edward K. (Duke) Ellington; and Langston Hughes. Its first officers were John A. Davis, Executive Director; Horace Mann Bond, President; Mercer Cook, Chairman of the Executive Council; and James Theodore Harris, Assistant Executive Director. Over 250 black American writers, scholars, artists, and librarians participated in the work of AMSAC.[107]

The aim of AMSAC was "to promote greater knowledge and understanding of the African heritage through art exhibitions, conferences, publications, and cultural exchange programs.[108] It sponsored several lecture series, hosted many visitors from abroad, and produced some publications. One of its early publications was Mercer Cook's translations of Senghor's *African Socialism*, and it eventually introduced a journal of its own, *African Forum*.

An AMSAC delegation was sent to the 1958 All-African Peoples Conference in Ghana. It included Etta Moten and Claude Barnett, Horace Mann Bond, Marguerite Cartwright, Mercer Cook, John Davis, St. Clair Drake, George McCray, Maida Springer, and Camilla Williams. President Nkrumah met privately with three members of the group: Horace Mann Bond, Mercer Cook, and John Davis.[109]

In June 1958 Professor Kenneth O. Dike, then at the University College in Ibadan, and Davidson Nicol, then Principal of Fourah Bay College in Sierra Leone, addressed an AMSAC conference on the economic, political, and social problems of Africa. The second AMSAC international conference, which convened in June 1959 in New York, concentrated on a wide variety of topics including education, leadership, economic and social development, history, literature, and press. The banquet address was given by Dr. J. Gikonyo Kiano, then a member of parliament in Kenya. The third AMSAC international conference was held under the theme "African Unities and Pan-African-ism." Out of this grew the publication *Pan-Africanism Reconsidered*. A regional confer-ence, which took place at UCLA in 1960, concentrated on "The Image of Africa." Present to address the conference were Kenneth Kaunda, Ronald Ngala, and John Akar. Howard University hosted the fourth international AMSAC conference devoted to "Southern Africa in Transition." Among those presenting papers were: Eduardo

Mondlane,* "The Struggle for Independence in Mozambique"; Oliver Tambo, "Passive Resistance in South Africa"; Arthur Wina (Zambia), "Theories of Multiracialism: Problems of Political Equality and Economic Opportunity"; and Angie Brooks,** "Southwest Africa: Current United Nations Position and Projection."

In December 1961 AMSAC sponsored a conference and festival in Lagos to celebrate the inauguration of an AMSAC cultural center there. Nnamdi Azikiwe, then Nigerian Governor-General, spoke to the delegates. A banquet in honor of President Sékou Touré of Guinea was given by AMSAC in 1960.

The aforementioned allegations that some of the funding, unknown to the membership, was linked to the CIA, brought an end to the prestige and leadership AMSAC enjoyed during the late fifties and early sixties.

## The Stuggle to Regroup After AMSAC

In the period following the decline of AMSAC black Americans with a special interest in Africa sought to create viable organizations. Disenchantment with the African Studies Association (ASA) spilled over at the Montreal ASA Conference in October 1969. After immobilizing the proceedings, black Americans rallied to the support of the African Heritage Studies Association (AHSA), which had been informally launched the previous year at the 1968 ASA annual meeting in Los Angeles and formally in June 1969 in Washington, D.C.[110] The first officers of the association were John H. Clarke, President; Nicholas D. U. Onyewu, Secretary General; Leonard Jeffries, Vice President; Shelby Lewis Smith, Treasurer; and Maina Kagombe, Publicity Secretary. AHSA indicated that its primary interests lay in:

1. Reconstruction of African history and cultural studies along Afrocentric lines while effecting an intellectual union among black scholars the world over.
2. Acting as a clearing house of information in the establishment and evaluation of a more realistic African or black studies program.
3. Presenting papers at seminars and symposiums where any aspect of the life and culture of the African peoples is discussed.
4. Relating, interpreting, and disseminating African materials to elementary and secondary schools, colleges, and universities.[111]

The popularity of AHSA skyrocketed during 1970 when its second annual meeting, convened at Howard University, drew a crowd of some 2,000 people, all expressing enthusiasm for their African cultural heritage and a desire to obtain more concrete knowledge of Africa. The third annual meeting, held in Baton Rouge, Louisiana, was a working conference designed to increase black American awareness and knowledge of Africa. The fourth conference took place in Chicago in April 1972.

*Eduardo Mondlane was killed in 1969.
**Angie Brooks served as President of the General Assembly in 1969.

Afro-American desires to help shape American foreign policy in Africa surfaced both in 1970 when selected black Americans traveled to Jamaica, West Indies, under the leadership of Professor Adelaide Hill to discuss common concerns about Africa, and again at a meeting scheduled at Airlie House in April 1971 in which black scholars, black congressional members and staff, black State Department and AID personnel, and black journalists participated. Out of Airlie House grew the African-American Scholars Council (AASC) in fall 1971, which was funded initially with a grant from AID for the purpose of supporting research into developmental problems on the African continent. Chaired by Dr. Elliott Skinner, the council is a small working group whose other officers are Hezekiah Jackson of Southern University, vice chairman; Adelaide Hill of Boston University, secretary; and Cleveland Dennard, president of Washington (D.C.) Technical Institute, treasurer. The council intends, through grants to individual African, black American, and other scholars, to build up a greater body of knowledge about Africa which will be useful in helping to resolve African developmental problems.

An *ad hoc* group on Africa whose membership was taken from the ranks of AHSA, Airlie House, the Jamaica group, and the AASC, retreated to Puerto Rico in January 1972 to map out plans for molding American foreign policy on Africa. This meeting, in which Professors Herschelle Challenor, Johnnetta Cole, Adelaide Hill, and Willard Johnson played key organizing roles, resulted in the creation of an autonomous appendage to AHSA—initially labeled the AHSA Positive Action Committee. Professors James Turner of Cornell, Leonard Jeffries of San Jose State, Ron Walters of Howard University, Willard Johnson of MIT, and Herschelle Challenor of Brooklyn College, City University of New York, have helped in the evolution of the AHSA Positive Action Committee.

Collaboration between AHSA, AASC, and other *ad hoc* groups on the one hand and the Congressional Black Caucus on the other have taken place. Congressman Charles Diggs of Michigan has been the key spokesman for the Black Caucus on Africa and has traveled widely in Africa. On one such trip, for example, he headed a delegation to Zambia which thoroughly criticized policies in South Africa that perpetuate the oppression of African peoples. A major conference on Africa sponsored by the Black Caucus with the assistance of several black Americans involved in organizations like AHSA and AASC took place in May 1972.

Southern Africa has received the attention of numerous other black Americans including a Committee of Concerned Black Americans, the National Conference of Black Churchmen, and the African Liberation Day Coordinating Committee. The latter, chaired by Owusu Sadaukai (Howard Fuller), president of Malcolm X Liberation University, consisted of a wide cross section of Afro-Americans including Rev. Ralph Abernathy, Imamu Baraka, Julian Bond, Charles Diggs, Richard Hatcher, Don L. Lee, Huey P. Newton, Betty Shabazz, Rev. Lucius Walker, and Rev. Jesse Jackson. To call attention to liberation struggles in southern Africa and to obtain a greater black American interest in that struggle, the committee coordinated demonstrations in the United States, Canada, and the West Indies to coincide with the celebration of "World Solidarity Day with the Peoples of Africa" designated by the Organization of African Unity (OAU). The demonstrations took place in late May 1972.

Other groups which have concerned themselves with Africa in the post-1957 period are the American Negro Leadership Conference on Africa headed by Ted Brown (which represented a coalition of church, civil-rights, and sorority groups and held several meetings on Africa, sent a delegation to Nigeria during the civil war, and complained to President Johnson about developments in Stanleyville, Congo), the Washington Task Force on African Affairs (WTFAA), an interracial research and action group headed by Daniel Matthews, Director of the African Bibliographic Center, the African-American Repatriation Association, the Pan-African Solidarity Committee, the International African Chamber of Commerce, CORE, the Southern Christian Leadership Council, the Federation of Pan-African Educational Institutions, and many church groups including Rev. Smallwood E. Williams' Bible Way Church.

There are now numerous black-oriented journals, papers, and pamphlets which print articles on Africa. Notable are *Muhammad Speaks, Freedomways,* the *Black Scholar,* the *Amsterdam News,* and a host of student-created publications including the official organ of Youth Organization for Black Unity (YOBU).

A summary of the development and nature of the black American interest in Africa over the past 150 years can be found in the following words of E. U. Essien-Udom, professor of political science at the University of Ibadan, Nigeria:

> ... during the last century and the present, the most articulate among American Negroes in asserting their dignity and integrity in America were by necessity compelled to address themselves to their relationship to Africa, and to articulate and defend the dignity of the African people.
>
> By defending the honor and integrity of the African through their literary endeavors, by generously opening their institutions of higher learning to Africans and by supporting their training, by sending missionaries, educators, and technical assistance to Africa, by assisting in the development of African national consciousness and Pan-Africanism particularly, by demonstrating through the arts and civil struggle their love of liberty and the capacities of the African heritage, Negroes have contributed profoundly to the projection of the African personality. To this extent they were the vanguard of modern African nationalism, of the philosophers of "negritude," of Pan-Africanism, and of Africa's rise to self-assertion in the contemporary world.[112]

As the decade of the seventies progressed, Afro-American involvement with African affairs took an interesting but divergent turn. In the early 1970s various Afro-American groups and individuals worked feverishly to arouse wider opposition to the oppression in Southern Africa. In the summer of 1971, Owusu Sadaukai, then president of Malcolm X Liberation University in North Carolina, and Robert Van Lierop, a black attorney, managed to get into Mozambique and to travel with leaders of FRELIMO as they fought for majority control of that Portuguese territory. Reports of their adventures not only aroused the curiosity of a number of blacks, young and middle-aged, but prompted a more visible black response to the battle against continued minority rule in Southern Africa.

Blacks sensitive to developments on the African continent became incensed when the Congress of the United States passed the Byrd Amendment in the fall of 1971. The amendment, attached to the Military Procurement Act of 1971, permitted "importation into the United States of any material determined to be strategic and critical. . . ."[113] In effect the United States lifted its boycott of chrome and ferrochrome from Rhodesia. By the summer of 1972 blacks were sufficiently organized to make a two-pronged assault on American cooperation with oppressive minority governments in Southern Africa. First came the African-American National Conference on Africa, sponsored by the Congressional Black Caucus.[114] This two-day conference, held on May 25 and 26, 1972, heard speeches from Africans, Afro-Americans, and West Indians on political and economic concerns in Africa. Second came the massive African Liberation Day on May 27, 1972, when more than 50,000 black Americans from all parts of the United States traveled to Washington, D.C., and walked from Malcolm X Park (Meridian Hill Park) to the Washington monument to demonstrate support for African Liberation movements and protest racism in Southern African minority governments. The 1972 African Liberation Day marked the assumption of a leadership role in issues regarding Southern Africa by the African Liberation Support Committee (ALSC). Not only did ALSC launch a fight against the Byrd Amendment; it also raised funds for freedom fighters in Africa. These funds were hand carried to Africa by ALSC members who took the opportunity to meet with liberation leaders. In Angola, ALSC representatives spent three months attempting to clarify reasons for a three-way split in the Angolan liberation movement, a split which had divided Afro-Americans concerning which group, if any, to support.

In addition to activities by ALSC, black Americans became more involved in efforts to keep Rhodesian products out of the United States and to boycott companies doing business in Southern Africa. Black longshoremen, students, professors, and others in Louisiana mounted actions against the entry of Rhodesian chrome into Louisiana ports. In Boston black workers spoke out against Polaroid in South Africa; through the Pan African Liberation Committee, Afro-Americans joined in the boycott against the Gulf Oil Corporation which, in 1970, invested an estimated $20 million in Angola; and black scholars, black church and church-related organizations such as IFCO (Inter-Religious Foundation For Community Organization), the Black Affairs Council of the Unitarian Church, and the Executive Council of the Episcopal Church began to raise their voices on African issues, especially American policy on Southern Africa.

In 1973 the tragic and pernicious effects of the West African drought sent Afro-

Americans into a flurry of activity. The drought, centered in the Sahelian states of Senegal, Mali, Mauritania, Upper Volta, Niger, and Chad, brought death and starvation to literally millions of Africans and virtually wiped out livestock in several of the countries as it devastated vegetation. Later it became evident that the drought had taken its toll on Ethiopia and parts of other countries as well.

Afro-American scholars, writers, and politically concerned entertainers, through the Afro-Americans Against the Famine and the Black Women's Community Development Foundation, began a massive campaign to educate the public (including black journalists) about the African famine. Africare, a Washington, D.C., based group, started a public campaign to collect funds for the drought- and famine-stricken countries. People United to Save Humanity (PUSH) also joined the effort to collect funds for the Sahel. RAINS, a coalition of black organizations which appeared in 1973, had as its primary focus a political effort to urge the U.S. Congress to allocate more funds for the Sahel and to step up its technical aid programs in this area. Using IFCO headquarters, RAINS also raised substantial funds for the Inter-State Committee of the Six Sahelian states.[115] In the fall of 1973, at the Westerfield Conference on economic development in Atlanta, Georgia, sponsored jointly by the Friends of Sam Westerfield (late American Ambassador to Liberia and a black career diplomat) and the African-American Scholars Council, Dr. Samuel C. Adams, Assistant Administrator for Africa, Agency for International Development, announced that the campaign had been most successful.

Between ALSC and other group efforts on behalf of African famine relief, by the end of 1973 blacks had generated funds in excess of $350,000 for the African continent.[116] Perhaps this marked the first time Afro-Americans were able to spearhead an organized monetary commitment to Africa. Even though the funds sent to Africa by Afro-Americans were small in terms of the enormous need, still the effort demonstrated that blacks were ready to give more than lip service to Africa.

If 1972 and 1973 marked the height of Afro-American dedication to the struggle in Africa, 1974 emerged as the year of unrest and confusion. As Portugal released its stranglehold on its Portuguese territories, the issue of liberation for Guinea-Bissau, Angola, and Mozambique faded away and left blacks bereft of at least one unifying issue. Yet the unrest and confusion were not centered in the absence of African issues; rather, they developed out of ideological conflict on the part of several key individuals and organizations concerned with Africa—a conflict which emerged in 1973 and grew until it reached the public eye in 1974.

In July 1974 the Congress of African People, headed by Amiri Baraka, convened an Afrikan [sic] Women's Conference. At that conference it became obvious that the Congress of African People had switched its ideology from a staunch advocacy of cultural nationalism to a feverish advocacy of revolutionary nationalism, pan-Africanism, and scientific socialism. Of the three doctrines socialism was viewed as most important by Chairman Baraka:

> Our nationalism, and PanAfrikanism [sic] merely point to the struggle for socialism. We
> are nationalists only insofar as we struggle for national liberation and the freeing up of
> our productive forces, in order to make socialist revolution.[117]

At the same time that the Chairman championed his socialist position he excoriated
those with whom he had worked closely in earlier years but with whom he now differed
vehemently on "correct" ideology.[118]

Chairman Baraka's speech merely summarized an ideological conflict which had
been growing since plans were unveiled in April 1971 for a Sixth Pan African Congress;
a comprehensive discussion of the early planning stages for the Congress is found elsewhere.[119] Called as part of "one of the greatest movements toward human freedom that
the world has ever known," the Sixth Pan African Congress was convened in Tanzania
June 19–27, 1974.[120]

Numerous problems had to be overcome in order for more than a thousand delegates, observers, and official guests representing black people from all over the world
to gather in Tanzania. Early concern was voiced by President Julius Nyerere that the
Congress should be representative of as wide a segment of the black world as possible.
This concern sent the small cadre of Afro-American organizers back to the drawing
board to secure a more representative delegation, especially from the U.S.A. The
American delegation also faced an agonizing problem in securing transportation for the
trip to Tanzania, complicated by a sudden change in dates from June 3–13, 1974, because
of OAU events. More significant, however, was the report that the Federal Bureau of
Investigation approached Capitol Airways, the airline that had after some difficulty
agreed to fly the American delegation to Tanzania, and inquired whether Capitol Airways "knew the kind of organization they were dealing with in this Sixth Pan African
Congress."[121] That inquiry led Capitol Airways to renege on its agreement to provide
transport. Air India offered its services. A small tragi-comedy threatened the Air India
flight just prior to takeoff when ". . . one delegate refused to board . . . proclaiming that
the whole affair smelled like a plot of the Indian government, which hated Africans, to
destroy us all over the Atlantic Ocean."[122] Eventually the flight took off.

American governmental opposition to the American delegation and perhaps to the
Sixth Pan African Congress itself no doubt could be traced to the presumed ideological
stance of the Congress. The Sixth PAC had announced clearly that "the deepening crisis
in capitalism necessitated a world conference of Africans." Then, too, the fact that
Amiri Baraka and Owusu Sadaukai were openly espousing some form of socialism
obviously had not escaped the attention of American authorities. To have those men go
on foreign soil to advocate socialism and to work closely with Guinea and FRELIMO
to obtain a "strong Marxist rhetoric in the general statement of the Congress"[123] would
have proved embarrassing to the American government, to say the least.

The American delegation itself was deeply divided. Some delegates were irate at the infiltration of a Marxist line; still others resented the fact that "integrationists" were part of the delegation. This internal struggle marked the beginning of a collapse, or at least weakened the base, of some organizations which had devoted long hours to the African movement. As the Sixth Pan African Congress Report put it: "The major evidences of the battle between revolutionary nationalists and Marxists to date have been the disintegration of the Congress of African People, the National Black Assembly, and the African Liberation Support Committee."[124]

Despite the clash of ideologies and other problems, the Sixth PAC managed to talk about political, economic, and scientific issues. Among the political issues considered was the "urgent need" of the "revolutionary Pan African movement" to: "put an end to foreign domination in Africa, get rid of neocolonialism, liquidate foreign military bases in African states, consolidate the unity between peoples of Africa and of African descent and all peoples, define a strategy of revolutionary Pan Africanism in terms of the antiimperialist, anticolonialist, antineo-colonialist, anticapitalist, and antiracist struggle, to exclude all racial, tribal, ethnic, religious, or national chauvinistic considerations for Pan Africanism," etc.[125] If the latter point were adopted, however, Pan Africanism would become a dead issue.

On the economic front the Congress discussed "economic development through self-reliance, democratization of international institutions, the struggle against economic imperialism with special reference to multinational corporations, economic organization in liberation areas, use of African resources, and drought and famine in Africa."[126] One of the significant economic recommendations called for cooperation among the Organization of African Trade Union Unity (OATUU), Coalition of Black Trade Unionists (CBTU), Caribbean Congress of Labour (CCL), The Arab Trade Union Federation (ATUF), and the Pacific Labor Organization. The science, technology, education, and culture discussion seemed to provoke hardly any dissension as the delegates focused on pan African skills, technology and development of natural resources, health, and nutrition.[127]

After the Sixth PAC terminated, 14 delegates (from the U.S. and Brazil) accepted invitations to visit the Somali Republic and Uganda. Ugandan citizenship was conferred on members of the group. These invitations signaled some African attempts to move toward closer contact with Afro-Americans and other world blacks. Notable, too, is the fact that President Julius Nyerere of Tanzania accepted invitations to visit several Caribbean countries and, in fact, did journey to Cuba, Jamaica, Trinidad, and Guyana in September 1974.

What the future will hold for Afro-Americans in terms of their interest in Africa remains to be seen. It can be predicted, though, that blacks in organizations like the African-American Institute, the Phelps-Stokes Fund, the African Heritage Studies Association, and the African-American Scholars Council will continue their concern for African issues, especially at the foreign policy, development, and scholarly levels.

They will also increase their contacts with Africans and their travels to Africa and the Caribbean. It can also be prophesied that those blacks with a clearly Marxist ideology will be isolated from the mainstream of black thought and actions, but will nonetheless make some gains through those Africans and West Indians who share their ideology.

## NOTES

1. Harold Cruse, *The Crisis of the Negro Intellectual* (New York, William Morrow & Co., Inc., 1967), p. 434.
2. Adelaide Cromwell Hill, "African Studies Programs in the United States," in *Présence Africaine, Africa Seen By American Negroes*, Paris, 1958, p. 363.
3. Rayford W. Logan and Michael R. Winston, *The Negro in the United States*, Vol. 2, *The Ordeal of Democracy* (New York, Van Nostrand Reinhold Co., 1971), pp. 92–93.
4. George Washington Williams, *History of the Negro Race in America from 1619–1880* (New York, Arno Press and *The New York Times*, 1968), p. 109.
5. *Ibid.*, p. 110.
6. *Ibid.*
7. Sterling Stuckey, "Twilight of Our Past: Reflections on the Origin of Black History," in John A. Williams and Charles F. Harris, eds., *Amistad 2* (New York, Vintage Books, 1971), p. 276. For a more detailed glimpse into some prevailing negative attitudes toward Africa and Africans see Joseph Harris, "Myths and Stereotypes Regarding Africa and Africans," in Inez Reid, ed., *The Black Prism: Perspectives on the Black Experience* (New York, Faculty Press, 1970), pp. 31–36.
8. Julius Lester, ed., *The Seventh Son*, Volume 2 (New York, Vintage Books, 1971), p. 620.
9. *Ibid.*, pp. 619–620.
10. J. W. E. Bowen, ed., *Africa and the American Negro . . . Addresses and Proceedings of the Congress on Africa held under the auspices of the Stewart Missionary Foundation for Africa of Gammon Theological Seminary in Connection with the Cotton States and International Exposition*, December 13–15, 1895 (Atlanta, Gammon Theological Seminary, 1896).
11. *Ibid.*, pp. 207–209.
12. *Ibid.*, p. 237.
13. *Ibid.*, p. 236.
14. Adelaide Hill and Martin Kilson, eds., *Apropos of Africa* (London, Frank Cass and Co., Ltd., 1969), p. 10; and Bradford Chambers, ed., *Chronicles of Black Protest* (New York, New American Library, 1968), p. 50.
15. *Ibid.*, p. 15.
16. *Ibid.*, p. 18.
17. *Ibid.*, pp. 118–120.
18. C. P. Groves, *The Planting of Christianity in Africa*, Volume 3, 1878–1914 (London, Lutterworth Press, 1955), p. 120–121. Sheppard soon found it necessary to publicize and inveigh against the atrocities being heaped upon the Congolese by Belgians. Still he found time to record information about the Bakuba and some African folk tales. Dorothy B. Porter, "A Bibliographic Checklist of American Negro Writers About Africa," in *Présence Africaine, op. cit.*, p. 380.
19. C. P. Groves, *The Planting of Christianity in Africa*, Vol. 2, 1840–1878 (London, Lutterworth Press, 1954), p. 222.
20. George Shepperson, "Notes on Negro American Influences on the Emergence of African Nationalism," as reprinted in Melvin Drimmer, ed., *Black History* (Anchor Books, Garden City, New York, 1969) pp. 499–501.

21. In his *History of the Negro Race in America*, 1883, Williams had admonished: ". . . we must redeem by the power of the gospel, with all its attending blessings, the savage tribes of Africans who have never heard the beautiful song of the angels: 'Glory to God in the highest, and on earth peace, good-will toward men.' That this work will be done we do not doubt. We have great faith in the outcome of the missionary work going on now in Africa; and we are especially encouraged by the wide and kindly interest awakened on behalf of Africa by the noble lifework of Dr. David Livingstone and the thrilling narrative of Mr. Henry M. Stanley." Williams, *op. cit.*, p. 110.

22. Hill and Kilson, *op. cit.*, pp. 100–101.

23. *Ibid.*, p. 352.

24. Rayford W. Logan, "The American Negro's View of Africa," in *Présence Africaine, Africa Seen By American Negroes*, Paris, 1958, p. 217.

25. Hill and Kilson, *op. cit.*, p. 47.

26. Lucius E. Smith, ed., *Heroes and Martyrs of the Modern Missionary Enterprise* (Toronto, R. Dick, 1857).

27. Hill and Kilson, *op. cit.*, p. 160; see also August Meier, *Negro Thought in America, 1880–1915: Racial Ideologies in the Age of Booker T. Washington* (Ann Arbor, University of Michigan Press, 1963), pp. 59–68.

28. *Cf.* Martin Delany, *Official Report of the Niger Valley Exploring Party* (New York, T. Hamilton, 1861); William M. Brewer, "Henry Highland Garnet," *Journal of Negro History*, Volume XIII, January 1928, pp. 36–52.

29. Hill and Kilson, *op. cit.*, p. 28.

30. *Ibid.*, pp. 22–23.

31. Shepperson, *op. cit.*, p. 505.

32. *Ibid.*, p. 509.

33. For a full treatment of Chilembwe see George Shepperson and Thomas Price, *Independent African, John Chilembwe and the Origins, Settling and Significance of the Nyasaland Native Uprising of 1915* (Edinburgh, Edinburgh University Press, 1958).

34. Horace Mann Bond, "Forming African Youth: A Philosophy of Education," in *Présence Africaine*, *op. cit.*, p. 247.

35. *Ibid.*, p. 248.

36. *Ibid.*, pp. 248–9.

37. *Ibid.*, pp. 251–4.

38. Harold R. Isaacs, *The New World of Negro Americans* (New York, John Day, 1963), p. 180.

39. *Ibid.*, p. 193.

40. See St. Clair Drake, "Negro Americans and the Africa Interest," in Davis, John, ed., *The American Negro Reference Book* (Englewood Cliffs, Prentice-Hall, 1966), pp. 679–684, including footnotes pp. 38–40, 42.

41. Shepperson, *op. cit.*, p. 509.

42. *Ibid.*, p. 510.

43. Logan, *op. cit.*, p. 220.

44. Shepperson, *op. cit.*, pp. 507–8.

45. *Ibid.*, p. 508.

46. Harold Isaacs, *op. cit.*, pp. 146–147.

47. Shepperson, *op. cit.*, p. 502.

48. *Ibid.*, pp. 492, 502.

49. Isaacs, *op. cit.*, pp. 147–148.

50. Philip Foner, ed., *W. E. B. DuBois Speaks, Speeches and Addresses 1890–1919* (New York, Pathfinder Press, 1970), p. 127.

51. Lester, *op. cit.*, p. 193.

52. Isaacs, *op. cit.*, p. 152.

53. See Richard B. Moore, "Africa-Conscious Harlem" in *Freedomways*, Vol. 3, No. 3, Summer 1963, pp. 315–334.

54. Logan, *American Negro's View of Africa, op. cit.*, pp. 221–2.

55. John Hope Franklin, *From Slavery to Freedom* (New York, Knopf, 1947), p. 558.

56. Isaacs, *op. cit.*, pp. 150–151.

57. Shepperson, *Notes, op. cit.*, p. 496.

58. Williams, *op. cit.*, p. 107.

59. Logan, *op. cit.*, p. 222.

60. James A. Padgett, "Ministers to Liberia and Their Diplomacy," *Journal of Negro History*, Vol. 22, No. 1, January 1937, pp. 50–92, 58.

61. *Ibid.*, p. 60–61.

62. *Ibid.*, pp. 64, 68.

63. *Ibid.*, p. 73.

64. Shepperson, *op. cit.*, p. 509.

65. Edmund David Cronon, *Black Moses* (Madison, University of Wisconsin Press, 1955), p. 44.

66. *Ibid.*, p. 185.

67. George Padmore, *Pan-Africanism or Communism* (London, Dobson, 1956).

68. W. E. B. DuBois, *Dusk of Dawn* (New York, Harcourt Brace, 1940), p. 277.

69. *Ibid.*, p. 278.

70. Harold Isaacs, "Pan-Africanism As 'Romantic Racism'," pp. 210–248 in Rayford Logan, ed., *W. E. B. DuBois* (New York, Hill and Wang, 1971), pp. 223–4.

71. Foner, *op. cit.*, p. 246.

72. *Crisis*, February 1919 as reprinted in Lester, *op. cit.*, p. 189.

73. Foner, *op. cit.*, p. 254.

74. For DuBois the "talented tenth" represented the "intelligentsia" of black Americans as he explained it: "I believed in the higher education of a Talented Tenth who through their knowledge of modern culture could guide the American Negro into a higher civilization." W. E. B. DuBois, *Autobiography* (New York, International Publishers, 1968), p. 236.

75. Foner, *op. cit.*, p. 273.

76. Isaacs, *op. cit.*, p. 239–40.

77. *Ibid.*, p. 239.

78. Lester, *op. cit.*, pp. 740–760.

79. DuBois, *op. cit.*, pp. 219–220.

80. *Ibid.*, p. 302.

81. Foner, *op. cit.*, p. 125.

82. DuBois, *Dusk*, p. 262.

83. Hill and Kilson, *op. cit.*, p. 312.

84. DuBois comments on the difficulties of getting blacks passports: "Meantime our State Department chuckled and announced that there would be no Congress and refused Negroes passports." Lester, *op. cit.*, p. 197; for a more detailed synopsis of the 1919 Conference, see *Ibid.*, pp. 190–196.

85. Hill and Kilson, *op. cit.*, pp. 312–313.

86. Hill and Kilson, *op. cit.*, p. 313; for the "Manifesto of the Second Pan-African Congress," see Lester, *op. cit.*, pp. 199–205.

87. See Hill and Kilson, *op. cit.*, pp. 314–5.

88. Logan, *op. cit.*, p. 219.

89. Lester, *op. cit.*, pp. 636–8.

90. *Ibid.*, pp. 647–650.

91. See Isaacs, *New World*, pp. 224–5 and Lester, *op. cit.*, pp. 721–723.

92. For further information on the Phelps-Stokes Fund, see *Educational Adaptations—Report of Ten Years' Work of the Phelps-Stokes Fund, 1910–1920* (1920); *Twenty Year Report of the Phelps-Stokes Fund, 1911–1931* (1932); *Progress in Negro Status and Race Relations in the United States, 1911–1946: The Thirty-Five-Year Report of the Phelps-Stokes Fund* (1948); *Education in Africa* (New York, Phelps-Stokes Fund, 1922); *Education in Africa* (New York, Phelps-Stokes Fund, 1925).

93. See James W. Ivy, "Traditional NAACP Interest in Africa As Reflected in the Pages of 'The Crisis,'" in *Présence Africaine, op. cit.*, pp. 229–246.

94. *Ibid.*, p. 232.

95. *Ibid.*, p. 236.

96. *Ibid.*, p. 238.

97. Ulysses Lee, "The ASNLH, the *Journal of Negro History* and African Scholarly Interest in Africa," in *Présence Africaine, op. cit.*, pp. 401–418.

98. DuBois, *op. cit.*, p. 345.

99. *Ibid.*, p. 345.

100. *Ibid.*, p. 347.

101. *Ibid.*, p. 368.

102. Lorenzo D. Turner, "African Survivals in the New World With Special Emphasis on the Arts," in *Présence Africaine, op. cit.*, pp. 101–116.

103. *Ibid.*, p. 107.

104. *Ibid.*, p. 115.

105. Johnnetta B. Cole, "Culture: Negro, Black and Nigger," in *The Black Scholar*, Vol. 1, No. 8, June 1970, pp. 40–44.

106. Much of the background data on AMSAC was provided by Professor John A. Davis.

107. Active in AMSAC were many outstanding black Americans including Saunders Redding (AMSAC's second president), Calvin Raullerson (AMSAC's second executive director), Adelaide Hill, R. O'Hara Lanier (former Ambassador to Liberia), Mabel Smythe, Hugh Smythe, St. Clair Drake, Maida Springer, George Carter, Zelma George, Willis James, Jacob Lawrence, Julian Mayfield, Ernest Crichlow, Elton Fax, Loften Mitchell, Lorraine Hansberry, John H. Clarke, Fred O'Neal, John Killens, William Scheeler, William Branch, Rosalind Cash, James Porter, J. Newton Hill, E. Franklin Frazier, and Charles Wesley.

108. See Program for AMSAC Fourth International Conference, 1963.

109. *AMSAC Newsletter*, Vol. 1, No. 3, December 30, 1958.

110. At Montreal the black position against ASA was supported initially by Gabriel D'Arboussier of Senegal who has enjoyed a fruitful career first as a Senegalese nationalist and then diplomat; Robert Gardiner, director of the United Nations Commission on Africa; Leon Damas of French Guiana, one of the forerunners of the negritude movement; Abdou Moumouni of Niger; Ali Mazrui of Makerere College; Samir Amin of the University of Dakar, and Joachim Bony of the University of Abidjan. For an analysis of the steps leading to AHSA's creation and the Montreal confrontation see Herschelle Sullivan Challenor, "No Longer at Ease: Confrontation at the 12th Annual African Studies Association Meeting at Montreal" in *Africa Today*, Vol. 16, Nos. 5 and 6, October, November, December 1969, pp. 4–7. For other analyses of the implications of Montreal see articles in *Africa Report*, Vol. 14, No. 8, December 1969.

111. See "Statement of the Executive Committee of the African Heritage Association Presented to the 12th Annual Convention of the African Studies Association, Montreal, Canada, October 15–18, 1969," reprinted in *Africa Today*, Vol. 16, Nos. 5 and 6, October, November, December, 1969, p. 24.

112. E. U. Essien-Udom, "The Relationship of Afro-Americans to African Nationalism," in *Freedomways*, Vol. 2, No. 4, Fall 1962, pp. 391–407, 395, 404.

113. Carnegie Endowment For International Peace, *Irony In Chrome: The Byrd Amendment Two Years Later*, 1973, p. 4.

114. See *From Gammon To Howard. Proceedings of the African-American National Conference on Africa*, edited by Inez Smith Reid and Ronald Walters, 1973.

115. For a summary of early black American involvement in the Sahel crisis, see *Binding Ties*, Vol. 1, No. 3, September 1973, published by the Black Women's Community Development Foundation.

116. This sum represents an estimate based on data provided by the organizations mentioned.

117. Amiri Baraka, "Afrikan Women Unite . . . to Struggle," p. 5.

118. *Ibid.*, p. 10.

119. See James Garrett, "A Historical Sketch: The Sixth Pan African Congress," *Black World*, March 1975, pp. 4–20.

120. See Sixth Pan African Congress, "The Call," p. 1.

121. "The Sixth Pan African Congress: Report of the North American Secretariat," March 21, 1975, condensed version prepared by Julian Ellison for the African Heritage Studies Association Meeting on April 4, 1975, p. 9.
122. *Ibid.*, p. 10.
123. *Ibid.*, p. 13.
124. *Ibid.*, p. 30.
125. *Ibid.*, p. 22.
126. *Ibid.*, p. 25.
127. *Ibid.*, p. 26.

# BIBLIOGRAPHY

DuBois, W. E. B., *Autobiography*. New York, International Publishers, 1968.

DuBois, W. E. B., *Dusk of Dawn*. New York, Harcourt Brace, 1940.

Essien-Udom, E. U., "The Relationship of Afro-Americans to African Nationalism." *Freedomways*, Vol. 2, No. 4, Fall 1962, pp. 391–407.

Groves, C. P., *The Planting of Christianity in Africa,* Vol. 2: 1840–1878; Vol. 3: 1878–1914. London, Lutterworth Press, 1954, 1955.

Hill, Adelaide and Martin Kilson, eds., *Apropos of Africa*. London, Frank Cass & Co. Ltd., 1969.

Isaacs, Harold, *The New World of Negro Americans*. New York, John Day, 1963.

Lester, Julius, ed., *The Seventh Son*, Vol. 2. New York, Vintage Books, 1971.

Logan, Rayford, ed., *W. E. B. DuBois*. New York, Hill and Wang, 1971.

Moore, Richard B., "Africa-Conscious Harlem." *Freedomways*, Vol. 3, No. 3, Summer 1963, pp. 315–334.

Padmore, George, *Pan-Africanism Or Communism*. London, Dobson, 1956.

Présence Africaine, *Africa Seen By American Negroes*. Paris, Présence Africaine, 1958.

Shepperson, George, "Notes on Negro American Influences on the Emergence of African Nationalism." Reprinted in Melvin Drimmer, ed., *Black History*. Garden City, New York, Anchor Books, 1969.

# 21

## Black Influences in the American Theater: Part I

### Langston Hughes*

"The Negro singers, as always, make opera credible. And, as always, they make music shine. They have a physical beauty of movement, natural distinction and grace. Musically they have rhythm, real resonance, excellent pitch, superb enunciation, and full understanding of the operatic convention. They never look bored or out-of-place on the stage or seem inappropriately cast for any musical style," so wrote in 1943 the distinguished composer and critic, Virgil Thomson, in commenting on the Broadway scene. Many before and since have confirmed his opinions.

The logs of slave ships crossing the Atlantic do not reveal African captives willingly singing for the pleasure of others during the long voyage under sail to the Americas. But in *A Journal of a Voyage Made in the Hannibal of London, Ann. 1693–1694* it is recorded, "We often at sea in the evenings would let the slaves come up into the sun to air themselves, and make them jump and dance for an hour or two to our bagpipes, harp, and fiddle, by which exercise to preserve them in health." And *An Account of the Slave Trade on the Coast of Africa* published in England in 1788 states concerning captives during the Middle Passage, "Exercise being deemed necessary for the preservation of their health, they are sometimes obliged to dance, when the weather will permit their coming on deck. . . . The poor wretches are frequently compelled to sing also; but when they do so, their songs are generally, as may naturally be expected, melancholy lamentations of their exile from their native country." Those Africans who revolted with Cinque aboard the *Amistad* off Cuba, and themselves brought their ship to northern waters, reported during their trial for murder and piracy in New Haven in 1839 that sometimes on the decks of that runaway slaver men in chains chanted songs of Africa and black mothers in shackles crooned to their children. On the shores of Colonial America, very early records of life on the plantations and in the cities, as well, report whites as being entertained by the singing and dancing of their black chattels.

*Editorial note:* In keeping with the author's deep identification with the people about whom he wrote, his terminology has been changed and updated, with "black" replacing older forms of nomenclature in a number of instances. Several typographical errors and inaccuracies in names, dates, etc., have been corrected. Otherwise, the chapter remains unchanged from its initial appearance in *The American Negro Reference Book* (1966).

In the early 1800s in New Orleans on Sunday afternoons when the slaves were allowed a few hours of "freedom" to rest and play, the bamboula drums throbbed on Congo Square. There the whites often gathered to watch the blacks sing and dance in African fashion. Many of the newly imported slaves spoke neither French nor English, and their music was as yet uninfluenced by the European. There and then, say the chroniclers of jazz, the rhythms of Africa began to seep into America's musical heritage. Scarcely had the slaves set foot on our shores than their influence on American entertainment began.

Wealthy slave owners soon developed the habit of sending for their most musical slaves to sing and dance for them as they sat on their wide verandas of a summer evening. And some plantations permitted their more talented blacks to travel from plantation to plantation to entertain other wealthy masters and their guests. There were in these slave troupes field hands who could crack jokes, others who shook the bones of spareribs or sheep in syncopated rhythms or played the comb or the banjo or the saw or the cornstalk fiddle and could do the buck-and-wing or the *danse calinda*.

Slaves sometimes became name performers and their masters were in effect their booking agents. The following advertisement on behalf of Toler and Cook appeared on June 27, 1853, in the Richmond *Daily Enquirer:* "FOR HIRE, either for the remainder of the year, or by the month, week, or job, the celebrated musician and fiddler, GEORGE WALKER. All persons desiring the services of George are notified that they must contract for them with us, and in no case pay to him or any other person the amount of his hire, without a written order from us. George Walker is admitted, by common consent, to be the best leader of a band in all eastern and middle Virginia." And in his slave memoirs of life on a Louisiana cotton plantation in the mid-1850s Solomon Northrup wrote, "My master often received letters, sometimes from a distance of ten miles, requesting him to send me to play at a ball or festival of the whites. He received his compensation, and usually I also returned with many picayunes jingling in my pockets ... and secured the loudest and heartiest welcome of them all at the Christmas dance."

The escaped slave Frederick Douglass, in his *Life and Times*, wrote that on the plantations during the Christmas holidays, "fiddling, dancing, and jubilee beating was carried on in all directions." This latter performance was strictly southern. It supplied the place of the violin or other musical instruments and was played so easily that almost every farm had its juba beater. The performer improvised as he beat the instrument, marking the words as he sang so as to have them fall pat with the movement of his hands. Once in a while among a mass of nonsense and wild frolic a sharp hit was given to the meanness of the slaveholders. Take the following example:

> We raise the wheat,
> Dey gib us de corn,
> We bake de bread,
> Dey gib us de crust.

> We sif de meal,
> Dey gib us de huss.
> We peel de meat,
> Dey gib us de skin—
> And dats de way
> Dey take us in.

Thus were born, under the guise of entertainment, the first black protest songs. Others grew out of religious meetings and developed into such great antebellum spirituals as *Go Down, Moses; Oh, Freedom;* and *God's Gonna Cut You Down.* Using the spiritual for entertainment purposes, seven singers born in slavery went on to form the major part of a group known as the Fisk Jubilee Singers. In 1871, eight years after Emancipation, this ensemble began a concert tour of America and Europe that brought the spirituals to international attention. Since then these plantation songs have become world-famous. The black factor in American entertainment can thus be traced back to the plantation singers, dancers, and jesters who, in entertaining themselves, entertained their masters. Booker T. Washington in his *Up From Slavery* says that even after freedom came, when he went to Alabama in 1881 to found Tuskegee Institute, the customs of slave Christmases still continued on the nearby plantations. Each night the field hands "usually had what they called a 'frolic.' "

At least one slave, Blind Tom, became nationally famous before Emancipation as a professional entertainer under the management of his master, Colonel Bethune. Tom became known as a concert headliner, and continued to be booked as a moneymaking attraction long after slavery ended. Billed as the "MUSICAL PRODIGY—with wonder Powers as a Pianist," it was said that Tom could reproduce any piece of music, no matter how difficult, upon hearing it only once. It was also advertised that Tom could "perform with his back to the piano." Blind Tom had a highly successful run in New York City, appearing in Irving Place both matinees and nights in the spring of 1868—and playing on a Steinway, no less.

Before the Civil War the nation's most popular form of entertainment was the all-male blackface minstrel show. In these performances, direct outgrowths of the singing and dancing of the plantation slaves, white men imitated the singing, dancing, speech, and humor of the southern blacks. Their sketches were often dramatized plantation stories. And popular American performers have been borrowing from blacks ever since. It was in 1830 in Cincinnati that the white minstrel Dan Rice saw a little black street urchin dancing to a ditty that went:

> Step first upon yo' heel
> An' den upon yo' toe,
> An' ebry time you turns around
> You jump Jim Crow.
> Next fall upon yo' knees
> Then jump up and bow low

An' ebry time you turn around
You jump Jim Crow.

Rice copied the song, learned the boy's dance steps, and made a fortune from them.

*The Virginia Minstrels,* headed by Dan Emmett, the composer of *Dixie,* was the first of such attractions to perform in New York. It opened on the Bowery in 1843. For more than fifty years thereafter minstrels were in vogue all over the country and in Europe. They played in theaters where the blacks whom the performers imitated could not even buy a ticket, and on whose stages black men were not allowed to perform. The earliest widespread discrimination against blacks in the American theater, as both spectator and performer, began with the minstrels. This is an irony, if there ever was one, since the minstrels derived their entertainment values solely from blacks—black rhythms, black dance steps, plantation melodies, and a bold-faced blackface imitation of black speech and humor.

The white minstrel performers developed so broad a burlesque of what the general public took to be "Negro life" that their shows created a stereotyped concept of black Americans which is with us to this day. The sooty burnt-cork makeup, the exaggeratedly wide lips, the gold teeth, the gaudy clothing, the loud jokes, the fantastic dialect, the watermelon and razor props, and the dice that continue right down to *Porgy and Bess,* became so much a part of commercial theater in the United States that black performers themselves, in order to be successful, felt impelled to imitate these blackface whites. As a result, Bert Williams, in the *Ziegfeld Follies,* made himself twelve shades darker than he really was and spoke a dialect he never heard except from white performers. Later Miller and Lyles imitated the white performers Moran and Mack so well that the white actors who played Amos and Andy in turn imitated Miller and Lyles. Then Rochester imitated all of them put together.

These performers as well as white Al Jolson and black Stepin Fetchit, white Eddie Cantor and black Mantan Moreland, all stemmed from the minstrel tradition. For a long time most black comedians felt that in order to be funny, they had to work under cork. The strangest paradox of all was Pigmeat Markham, one of the funniest and most popular of black comedians. For years on stage his makeup was burnt cork. When changing times after the second world war caused him to stop blacking himself up, his audiences were amazed to discover that in reality Pigmeat was himself darker than the burnt cork he had been using. For neither rhyme nor reason, some black performers continued to perpetuate the minstrel stereotype long after the minstrel era was over.

On the positive side, however, the white blackface minstrels introduced to the American public the entertainment values inherent in black material—before blacks themselves could appear on Jim Crow stages. Thus when *genuine* Negro minstrels did make their appearance, they had a public waiting for them, and in some cases were welcomed into theaters where blacks had not formerly played. In 1865 a black, Charles Hicks, organized *The Georgia Minstrels,* which later came under white management and toured America and Europe. In 1882 this troupe became a part of *Callender's Consolidated Spectacular Colored Minstrels* and toured the United States, as did other Negro minstrel shows, the largest being the *Richards and Pringle Minstrels*. Comedians Sam Lucas[1] and Billy Kersands, who could put a cup and saucer in his mouth, became famous black names in minstrelsy. But the black performer of those days whose work will live—because not only did he appear on stages at home and abroad but was a great songwriter as well—is James Bland, composer of *In The Evening By The Moonlight* and *Carry Me Back To Old Virginny*, now the official song of the State of Virginia.

The first successful breakaway from all-masculine blackface minstrels came in 1891 with the opening in Boston of *The Creole Show*, which featured a singing and dancing chorus of sixteen beautiful girls. In 1893 this show played a full season at the Chicago World's Fair and toured for several years thereafter. During the Gay Nineties other successful black shows were *The South Before the War*, *The Octoroons*, and *Oriental America*. The latter was the first all-black company to appear on Broadway, as well as the first to include operatic selections among its musical numbers and to feature in its cast trained musicians such as J. Rosamond Johnson. The success of these shows led at the turn of the century to the great era of Negro musical comedy in which not only performers but black composers and writers gained a foothold in the commercial theater, and beauty became a part of the brown-skinned world of make-believe.

Sissieretta Jones, a statuesque woman with a glorious voice, made such a hit in the Jubilee Spectacle at Madison Square Garden in the spring of 1892 that in the autumn she was invited to sing at the White House. Billed as Black Patti, Sissieretta Jones with her company of Troubadours toured for many years. Dora Dean, another beautiful woman of color, was such a gorgeous cakewalker that a song called "Dora Dean" was written about her and her dancing. Belle Davis, Ada Overton, Abbie Mitchell, all golden-brown and talented, smartly dressed on stage and off, became the early leading ladies of the black theater. Abbie Mitchell's career spanned more than a half century, from star billing in turn-of-the-century musicals to featured roles on Broadway in such contemporary dramas as Lillian Hellman's *The Little Foxes*. While still in her teens, Abbie Mitchell married the brilliant composer Will Marion Cook, appeared in his *Clorindy*, the first ragtime musical, and later bore him a son, Mercer Cook, who became American ambassador to Niger and Senegal.

The Cakewalk was the first dance of black origin to sweep the country and become a popular favorite, as did other black steps much later: the Charleston, the Lindy Hop, the Jitterbug, and more recently the Twist. Derived from the plantation frolics, and popularized as a comic burlesque in the minstrels, the real charm of the Cakewalk with its high-stepping grace did not reach the stage until 1898 when Cook's *Clorindy: The Origin of the Cakewalk* was produced at the Casino Roof in New York, with book and lyrics by Paul Laurence Dunbar. Performed by handsome couples, the women gorgeously gowned, and nobody in blackface, the dance was a joy. The team of Williams and Walker first came to fame as exponents of the Cakewalk. And it was the Williams and

Walker musicals that in the early 1900s had great success in the theaters. Their *Sons of Ham* played for two years. *In Dahomey* was a Broadway hit, repeated by a long run in London, with a command performance in 1903 at Buckingham Palace. In New York *Abyssinia* and *Bandana Land* followed, with Will Marion Cook and Will Vodery as composers, Alex Rogers, lyricist of *Nobody*, as librettist, and a largely black staff in the production end of these popular musicals. In 1910 Bert Williams graduated to the *Ziegfeld Follies* and became Broadway's first black star in an otherwise all-white show. His burnt-cork comedy, which stemmed from the minstrel tradition, and his droll songs kept him a star until his death in 1922. Williams and Walker, Cole and Johnson (*The Shoofly Regiment*, *Red Moon*), and Will Marion Cook were the musical pioneers who first opened the doors of Broadway to black entertainment.

But on the dramatic stage it took almost a hundred years for black actors to attain success anywhere near that of the singers, dancers, and comics. It was not for lack of trying. On Bleecker Street in New York City from 1821 to 1832 a group of free blacks with James Hewlett as leading man performed Shakespeare's *Othello*, *Richard the Third*, and other classics. The players were known as the African Company and their playhouse was called the African Grove—where, according to a chronicle of the times, the breeze had "free access through the crevices of the boards." White hoodlums who came to laugh and jeer eventually forced this earliest of black dramatic theaters to close, but not before it had posted a sign which read: WHITE PEOPLE DO NOT KNOW HOW TO BEHAVE THEMSELVES AT ENTERTAINMENT DESIGNED FOR LADIES AND GENTLEMEN.

Before the African Grove closed, among its supers who helped create the illusion of a crowd on stage was a youngster from the nearby African Free School whose name was Ira Aldridge. His love for serious drama eventually made young Ira one of the greatest Shakespearean actors of his day—but not in the United States. He came to fame in Europe where, among other classic roles he played Othello in London to Edmund Keane's Iago, performed to acclaim in all the great capitals of the Continent, and never came home. When Théophile Gautier saw Ira Aldridge as King Lear in 1858 in a crowded Russian theater, the French journalist wrote that so convincing was his performance in Caucasian makeup—silver locks, flowing white beard, sallow cheeks—that "Cordelia would never have suspected that her father was a Negro." After forty years of European successes, America's first international star of color died in Poland in 1867. Today at Stratford-on-Avon there is an Ira Aldridge Chair designated in his honor at the Shakespeare Memorial Theatre.[2]

After the demise of the African Grove, it was over a half-century before black dramatic actors had access to theaters of any permanency in which they might perform with regularity. In some sections of the country, however, small stock companies began springing up which sometimes presented plays as well as musical entertainments. Such a company headed by Bob Cole became a part of Worth's Museum in New York for several years, with a number of young black apprentices involved. In the later days of the play's popularity, various companies of *Uncle Tom's Cabin* employed black actors instead of whites blacked up for the slave roles. But it was not until the formation of the Lafayette Stock Company in Harlem by Lester Walton in 1914 that the black performer found himself able to work for a full season in straight dramatic plays ranging from the classics to revivals of Broadway hits—sometimes tailored to the taste of black audiences. From the all-black Harlem productions of *Othello*, *Madame X*, *The Count of Monte Cristo*, and *On Trial*, a number of talented players eventually reached Broadway and Hollywood—among them Charles Gilpin, Evelyn Ellis, Frank Wilson, Edna Thomas, and Clarence Muse. Muse, a very dark young man from Baltimore, became a great favorite with Harlem audiences. At the Lafayette he pulled a complete switch from the days of the minstrels. Instead of appearing in blackface in such plays as *Within the Law*, Clarence Muse appeared in whiteface, complete with a blond toupee. A quarter of a century later in *The Duchess of Malfi*, the late Canada Lee played the brother to Elisabeth Bergner on Broadway in white makeup. The Lincoln Theatre in Harlem, the Pekin Theatre in Chicago, the Standard in Philadelphia, and the Howard in Washington also had, from time to time, stock companies, often borrowing stars from the Lafayette, whose production standards were high.

The Harlem chronicler James Weldon Johnson terms April 5, 1917, the most important date in the history of the black in the American theater. On that evening at the Garden Theatre in downtown New York there opened a bill of three one-act plays, *The Rider of Dreams*, *Granny Maumee*, and *Simon the Cyrenian*, by the poet Ridgeley Torrence. There was entr'acte music by a singing orchestra of Clef Club members conducted by J. Rosamond Johnson, and the show was a great success. Its presentation marked "the first time anywhere in the United States for black actors in the dramatic theater to command the serious attention of the critics and the general press and public." Three years later at the Provincetown Theatre in the Village, Eugene O'Neill's first hit opened: *The Emperor Jones*, with Charles Gilpin in the title role. Gilpin was acclaimed one of the ten best actors of the year, Eugene O'Neill began his ascent to fame, and from that time on the black performer in serious drama became an accepted part of the national scene.

Paul Green's earliest and greatest successes were also with plays cast largely with blacks, among them *In Abraham's Bosom*, a Pulitzer Prize winner in 1926, in which Rose McClendon, Jules Bledsoe, and Abbie Mitchell were featured. Commercially the most successful plays in the twenties concerned with black life were all written by whites, but a number of them furnished excellent vehicles for colored actors to achieve outstanding performances. Notable presentations included O'Neill's *All God's Chillun Got Wings* with Paul Robeson in 1924, David Belasco's production of *Lulu Belle* that same year, Laurence Stallings' *Deep River* in which Rose McClendon won nightly applause merely by her wordless descent of a winding staircase, Jim Tully's *Black Boy* with lovely Freddie Washington, and finally the Theatre Guild's *Porgy*[3] with Frank Wilson, Evelyn Ellis, and Georgette Harvey. Then in 1930, rounding off a decade of almost continuous Broadway activity for blacks, came *The Green Pastures* with Richard B. Harrison as De

Lawd. This folk fantasy by Marc Connelly with a singing orchestra under Hall Johnson achieved one of the longest runs in Negro theatrical history. It opened at the end of a delightful ten-year period of Harlem creativity in the arts known as the Negro Renaissance.[4] Unfortunately along with *The Green Pastures* came the Depression and things artistic went downhill for blacks. There were lean years to come both in the theater and elsewhere for black men and women.

The black playwright hardly entered the picture during the rich decade of the twenties although it was a good era for white playwrights and black actors. Negro playwrights existed, but they seldom got a hearing. With little chance even to see plays in many parts of the country because of Jim Crow, and with almost no chance to gain any technical knowledge of theater craft, the black playwright had a hard row to hoe. In the old days his scripts seldom got from the typed page to even the amateur stage, although perhaps a church might sponsor a reading. This was true of the earliest known American black playwright, William Wells Brown, who gave one-man readings of his own plays in churches. In those days almost all plays had double titles. Wells's first play, completed about 1856, was called *Experience, or How to Give a Northern Man a Backbone*,[5] his second was *The Escape, or Leap for Freedom*, and the library shelf rather than the stage was their fate.

Almost fifty years were to pass before another black playwright attracted any attention whatsoever. Then in 1903 the poet Joseph S. Cotter, Sr. of Louisville published a drama, *Caleb, The Degenerate*, concerned with the racial theories of Booker T. Washington. Some ten years later, Angelina Grimké wrote *Rachel*, which the NAACP produced at the Neighborhood Theatre in New York. But in general, other than functioning as sketch writers and occasional librettists for musical shows, blacks attempted little creative writing for the theater and they found no market for what little they did if it was of a serious nature. Until as recently as 1966, that commercial center of the theater, Broadway, had displayed the work of less than a dozen black playwrights. When Wallace Thurman wrote the play *Harlem* which opened on Broadway in 1929, it seemed advantageous for production purposes to accept the coauthorship of his white agent, William Jordan Rapp—so the program credit reads *Harlem*, by Wallace Thurman and William Jordan Rapp. Other black playwrights and many popular songwriters and composers have accepted the coauthorship of whites on their creative work in order to achieve publication or production, but oftentimes the black work is damaged rather than improved by what few white additions are added. Such collaboration helps the work to get published or produced, however, which has often been a difficult thing for a black to achieve alone. It takes a great deal of black integrity to prefer anonymity to publication—even if with an unwelcome collaborator.

In the thirty-five-year period following Wallace Thurman's *Harlem*, only ten black playwrights were produced on Broadway. In 1929 there was Garland Anderson's *Appearances*; in 1933 Hall Johnson's *Run, Little Chillun*; the following year *Brother Mose* (retitled *Meek Mose*) by Frank Wilson; in 1935 *Mulatto* by Langston Hughes; in 1941

Richard Wright's *Native Son*; in 1947 Theodore Ward's *Our Lan'*; in 1953 *Take A Giant Step* by Louis Peterson; in 1954 *Mrs. Patterson* by Charles Sebree; in 1957 *Simply Heavenly* by Langston Hughes; Lorraine Hansberry's *A Raisin in the Sun* in 1959; *Purlie Victorious* by Ossie Davis in 1961; in 1963 *Tambourines to Glory* by Langston Hughes; *Blues For Mister Charlie* by James Baldwin, and Lorraine Hansberry's *The Sign In Sidney Brustein's Window* in 1964. Only Lorraine Hansberry and Langston Hughes had had more than one production on Broadway. Their plays (*Mulatto* in the first instance, and *A Raisin in the Sun* produced a quarter of a century later) enjoyed the longest runs of any vehicles by black authors, each playing for over a year in New York followed by extensive cross-country tours. Both plays have also been translated and performed abroad, and *A Raisin in the Sun* became a Hollywood picture.

Some of the most interesting work by black playwrights has been produced off-Broadway. The Federal Theatre of the thirties in Harlem did Rudolph Fisher's *Conjur Man Dies*, *Turpentine* by J. A. Smith and Peter Morell, and in Chicago *Big White Fog* by Theodore Ward. The American Negro Theatre under Abram Hill's direction sent its *Anna Lucasta* from Harlem to Broadway, and in its uptown productions such talented young actors as Sidney Poitier, Harry Belafonte, and Hilda Simms gained experience. The record run for any play in Harlem is that of the Suitcase Theatre's *Don't You Want To Be Free?* by Langston Hughes, which had 135 performances. Ruth Jett's production of the Alice Childress *Just A Little Simple* had a considerable run at the Club Baron on Lenox Avenue in 1951, as did *A Medal for Willie* by William Branch. The most hospitable theater in New York to the black playwright has been the Greenwich Mews under the direction of Stella Holt, dean of off-Broadway producers.[6] In 1954 Miss Holt presented Branch's drama on John Brown and Frederick Douglass, *In Splendid Error*; in 1955 a hilarious comedy by Alice Childress, *Trouble in Mind*; and in 1956 Loften Mitchell's moving *A Land Beyond the River* about integration in the South.[7] In 1963 the Mews produced William Hairston's *Walk in Darkness*; in 1964 *Jerico Jim Crow*, a freedom song-play by Langston Hughes, and in 1965 his *The Prodigal Son*.

If the black performer had had to depend entirely on Broadway for sustenance over the years, he would have fared badly indeed. Fortunately, between the first world war and the second, there existed for about twenty years a booking agency for southern Negro theaters, known as the Theatre Owners Booking Association[8]—the TOBA—or TOBY as performers called it. It booked some northern theaters, too: the Lincoln in New York, the Monogram and the Grand in Chicago, the Gibson in Philadelphia; and its circuit supplied work for hundreds of Negro entertainers whose offerings ranged from blackface comedy and blues to one-act plays, opera arias, adagio dancing, and magic—for the black performers' talents were many and varied. There have been tumblers like the Crackerjacks, ventriloquists like Wee Johnny Woods, magicians like the Great Gowongo, comics like Butterbeans and Susie, divas like Madame Fannie Wise, dancers like Eddie Rector, and of course great blues singers from Ma Rainey to Bessie Smith and the unforgettable Virginia Liston singing *The Titanic Blues*. Ethel Waters worked the TOBA circuit long before her name went up in lights at the Winter Garden in *As Thousands Cheer* or over the marquee of the Empire in *The Member of the Wedding*.

TOBA was essentially a vaudeville circuit, but it also booked entire companies such as Tutt's *Smart Set*,[9] S. J. Dudley and Company with his mule, and the famous Whitman Sisters. The Whitman Sisters, four singers and dancers who began as a church trio in Kansas, produced tabloid musicals of a very lively nature, usually with two blackface comedians, a blues singer, a pretty leading lady, and a high-stepping chorus line. For several seasons their comedy team consisted of a tall lanky young man who did not wear burnt cork; a midget, Willie Bryant; and Princess Wee Wee. TOBA was both a proving ground and a meal ticket for the Negro performer as well as a source of living theater to millions of Negroes barred from other playhouses. Touring black tent shows along the lines of Silas Green of New Orleans, the Florida Cotton Blossoms, and later Flournoy Miller's *The Smart Set* were profitable for many years—until television made its inroads into all live entertainment, black and white, indoors and out. Popular favorites of big-time vaudeville like the Mills Brothers, the Deep River Boys, and the Ink Spots turned almost entirely to nightclubs, records, and spot appearances on radio or television for a livelihood, whereas Palace headliners like Bojangles, the late great dancer, and featured acts like Glenn and Jenkins, Moss and Frye, and Hamtree Harrington sought refuge in revues, cabarets, or foreign tours. Billy Banks went to Tokyo where he became a television favorite, the Nicholas Brothers to Mexico, South America, and Paris, and Adelaide Hall to the London nightclubs.

Nightclubs from the Barbary Coast of San Francisco earthquake days to Harlem of the present have been lively showcases for Negro entertainers. It was via the Cotton Club (where she was a chorus girl) that Lena Horne came to Broadway. By way of TOBA and the Harlem nightclubs, Ethel Waters rose to fame. Duke Ellington, Cab Calloway, Fats Waller, and Fletcher Henderson first attracted attention in Harlem cabarets[10] before moving on to Broadway, Carnegie Hall, and the world. During the twenties, Small's Paradise, Baron's, the Nest, and later Minton's acted as midnight havens for Negro entertainers, a slew of Billies among them—Billie Holliday, Billy Daniels, Billy Eckstine, Billy Banks, Billy Mitchell. Minton's is credited as the birthplace of bebop music. In more recent years, Small's Paradise popularized the Madison and the Twist. For more than ten years the Club Baby Grand showcased Nipsey Russell, Harlem's favorite comedian and seemingly a permanent fixture there until his hilarious integration jokes caught the ear of downtown listeners and he moved on to the Playboy Clubs and the national TV screens.

It is a long step from the dialect comedy of Bert Williams in grotesque makeup, oversized coat, and funny shoes[11] to the social satire of dapper young comics like Nipsey Russell or Dick Gregory, cool, well-dressed and impudent. If the race problem got even a remote mention in the comedy routines of the TOBA, vaudeville, or nightclub performers in the old days, its mention would usually be in terms unintelligible to white listeners. Even at the Apollo Theatre in Harlem with a 90 percent Negro audience, race problems were seldom a part of the comedy monologue. Jackie "Moms" Mabley alone of all the old comics might slip in a racial wallop once in a while. Racial references, I think, were discouraged by the white owners and managers of most of the theaters and nightclubs where Negroes performed. Nipsey Russell and the Supreme Court were pioneers in changing all this. The school desegregation decrees of 1954 and the subsequent front-page explosions placed the race problem so squarely in the news that it would have been difficult for even a nightclub comic to ignore it. Nipsey Russell in his routines had *never* been ignoring it. At the Baby Grand he had long had free reign and just the right audience for his satire—an audience that would roar with laughter at the mention of the words *Little Rock* if uttered with proper recognition of their absurdity.

"You nine Negro boys and girls about to enter Little Rock High School for the first time," said Nipsey Russell, impersonating a big race leader, "must uphold the honor of the Negro people when you go into that white school. I do not want you young people to go in there all belligerent and ignorant—like they expect Negroes to be. No! Don't go in that school carrying bricks, knives, razors, or guns. Go in there *civilized*—throwing atom bombs!"

Jackie "Moms" Mabley, the grandmother of all Negro comediennes, who once performed in blackface but was later content with toothlessness and a red wig, invented a great Cindy Ella story about the little black girl who was invited by magic to the senior ball at the University of Mississippi—but at the stroke of midnight was changed back into her original little black self. Its telling and its denouement was one of the funniest and saddest bits to be heard on the American stage. Dick Gregory's entire nightclub act is composed of social material—something unheard of for a black comedian in the early fifties—and Godfrey Cambridge thoroughly ribs all forms of segregation in front of the most fashionable audiences in clubs where cover charges are high. The current crop of black comics, unlike the late Lenny Bruce and some other whites, have not as yet resorted to dirty words to add pungency to their comedy. Young black playwrights, in contrast to the comedians, are great users of strong language. Perhaps influenced by Genêt's *The Blacks* and the avant-garde trend in Paris, London, and New York, Adrienne Kennedy's *The Funny House of A Negro*, LeRoi Jones's *Dutchman*, *The Toilet*, and *The Slave*, and James Baldwin's *Blues For Mister Charlie* to name a few productions of the sixties, abound in what used to be called profanity. If a black Lenny Bruce appears on the scene as a social comic, the freedom movement can go no further.

That the black has a great forte for comedy and music cannot be denied. The playbills for the last hundred years prove it so—from the minstrel comics of the 1860s to Ossie Davis and Pearl Bailey now; in song from Elizabeth Taylor Greenfield, known as the Black Swan in 1854 when she sang for Queen Victoria, to Leontyne Price whose recordings are now in many a royal record collection.

Some of the sweetest voices in the world have been black voices—the liquid voice of Camilla Williams, the mighty yet gentle baritone of William Warfield, the cool fountain of sound of Mattiwilda Dobbs, of Adele Addison. (And there is always the memory of the incomparable Roland Hayes, who was still singing in concert at the age of 75; Marian Anderson announcing her farewell tour after a quarter of a century of great performances; and Dorothy Maynor, whose *Depuis le Jour* was pure delight.) Later singers of outstanding ability in concert and opera have included Margaret Tynes, George Shirley, Grace Bumbry, Reri Grist, Betty Allen, Shirley Verrett, Martha Flowers, and Billie Lynn Daniels. La Scala, the Metropolitan, and all the great opera houses of the world have opened their doors to black Americans, beginning with the pioneers of the twenties and thirties, Lillian Evanti and Caterina Jarboro, divas who achieved success abroad.

The loudest singers in the world today, in concert halls or out, are gospel singers, products of the Negro church, and capable of raising at all times "a joyous noise unto the Lord." (See Chapter 25, Afro-American Music.) They are America's last uncontaminated source of pure folk singing. The most famous exponent of gospel singing was the late Mahalia Jackson. Not far behind are Clara Ward, the Davis Sisters, James Cleveland, Princess Stewart, and the Caravans. Alex Bradford and Marion Williams have taken gospel singing from off-Broadway to the Philharmonic, to Europe, Asia, and around the world in the song play *Black Nativity* by Langston Hughes. They sang in 1963 in Coventry Cathedral in England, and their television film of *Black Nativity* received the Catholic Dove Award at Cannes. Since the advent of Josephine Baker* and the *Revue Nègre* in 1926, no group of American black artists received such opening night acclaim in Paris as did the *Black Nativity* company at the Champs Elysées, with the press hailing Marion Williams as a dynamic new star. It was in that same theater that Josephine Baker made her Parisian debut some thirty-five years before.

Josephine Baker ranked among the world's most famous international stars. She drew capacity audiences in the great cities of the world, singing in several languages, and wearing the most expensively elegant wardrobes to be seen anywhere, especially designed for her by the great couturiers. That so beautiful and talented a woman happened to be black seemed not to have affected her career adversely except for an interim period in her own homeland where, when she refused to accept segregation in New York or Miami Beach during appearances there, important columnists attacked her with false charges of radicalism—for which Miss Baker filed libel suits. Subsequent American appearances were highly successful, and Miss Baker's performances in her 60s were as sparkling, as joyous and as heartwarming as ever.

If one were to be asked to name the twelve great personalities of the Negro music and entertainment field in the twentieth century regardless of categories, it would be impossible to omit Josephine Baker. Bert Williams, of course, would have to be included, as would Marian Anderson and Roland Hayes, Paul Robeson, Bojangles Bill Robinson, Rose McClendon, who could move an audience emotionally without saying a word, Jackie "Moms" Mabley, who was one of the funniest women on earth, and Louis Arm-

---

*Josephine Baker, who died in 1975, retained the aura of international celebrity throughout her life.

strong, Sidney Poitier, Harry Belafonte, and Katherine Dunham. Certainly there are others that should be included. But a dozen is only twelve. If a baker's dozen were allowed, the thirteenth would have to be Pearl Bailey. Or did somebody say Billie Holliday? Florence Mills? Bessie Smith? Ethel Waters? Canada Lee? Alvin Ailey? Lena Horne? Eartha Kitt? Except for Louis Armstrong as a singer, we are omitting entirely the field of jazz, pop, and folk—the great Ray Charles, Nina Simone, Lionel Hampton, Jackie Wilson, Chubby Checker, Odetta, Sonny Terry, and Brownie McGhee— performing artists as well as jazzmen, personalities in the theatrical sense of the word as well as musicians—Duke Ellington, Charlie Mingus, Max Roach.

As we saw earlier, one of the most creatively productive periods for blacks in the dramatic arts was the years spanning the 1920s. This decade-long black Renaissance was also called by literary commentators the period of the New Negro. Its center was Harlem where poetry, prose, and painting took a new lease on life, and in whose productivity the downtown white world vouched a more than passing interest. For a few years Harlem was in vogue, and the black in the arts was fashionable. This happy period began with the success in 1921 of an infectious musical called *Shuffle Along*.

It opened in Boston, went to the Howard Theatre in Washington, moved on to Philadelphia, then ended up in a rather out-of-the-way New York playhouse, the 63rd Street Theatre off Broadway, where it suddenly became the talk of the town and ran for nearly two years. It was the kind of joyous little show that people liked to see again and again. It exuded good nature. Its songs were catchy, its comedy easygoing, its girls prancingly pretty, and the overall effect one of happy, syncopated fun. The book for *Shuffle Along* was by Flournoy Miller and Aubrey Lyles, who performed the comedy routines. The songs were by Sissle and Blake, who sang most of them. The show was produced on a shoestring.

This ebullient musical had some wonderful people in it, most of them quite un-known at that time: Josephine Baker at the end of the chorus line, Hall Johnson and William Grant Still in the orchestra, the diva-to-be Caterina Jarboro among the singers. Lottie Gee was the leading lady, substituting for Gertrude Saunders, who after opening had gotten a better-paying job in burlesque. Florence Mills became the star and *Shuffle Along* a milestone in Negro theater. It created a vogue for black musicals that lasted until the Depression. By that time white writers had realized the profits inherent in Negro materials so they began to write shows especially for black casts. It then became diffi-cult for black writers to achieve commercial production. Lew Leslie's *Blackbirds* with a white score made Florence Mills and, in a later edition, Ethel Waters Broadway head-liners.

Following *Shuffle Along* came *Liza*, then late in 1923 *Runnin' Wild*, which featured the Charleston, a foot-flinging, hand-clapping dance that swept the world. Other lively black shows within the next few years were *Africana* and *Dinah*, other Miller and Lyles shows; *Rang Tang* and *Hot Chocolates* with lyrics by Andy Razaf and music by Fats

Waller; *Brown Buddies, Sugar Hill, Hot Rhythm, Fast and Furious* and *Rhapsody in Black*, featuring Valaida Snow and the Berry Brothers. *The Plantation Revue* starred Florence Mills, who then went to London and returned in *Dixie to Broadway*. At the time of her death in 1927, Florence Mills was one of the most beloved of Broadway performers. "I'm just a little blackbird looking for a bluebird" became her theme song; and as her funeral cortege went through Harlem an airplane overhead released a flock of blackbirds.

The big all-black musicals after the thirties were for two decades almost all written by whites—Jimmy McHugh and Dorothy Fields, Vernon Duke, John LaTouche, Rodgers and Hammerstein, and others. These included (besides various editions of *Blackbirds*) *Swinging The Blues, Swinging the Dream, The Hot Mikado, Cabin in the Sky, Carmen Jones,* and *The House of Flowers*. Then *Shinbone Alley* with Eartha Kitt, *Jamaica* with Lena Horne, *Mr. Wonderful* and later *Golden Boy* both starring Sammy Davis, and *No Strings* with Diahann Carroll began a trend away from all-Negro casts toward integrated shows built around Negro stars. Duke Ellington's *Beggar's Holiday* was an early integrated musical starring Alfred Drake, with sets by Broadway's lone black designer, Perry Watkins. It marked the black composer's return to Broadway after a considerable absence. A black lyricist, Langston Hughes, in 1947 wrote the songs for what was termed the "first Broadway opera" *Street Scene*, with a score by Kurt Weill and book by Elmer Rice. Three years later, with a Hughes libretto and music by Jan Meyerowitz, *The Barrier* opened on Broadway, starring Lawrence Tibbett and Muriel Rahn.

In the integrated musical theater, appearing with primarily white casts, Jules Bledsoe in New York and later Paul Robeson in London came to fame singing "Ole Man River" in *Show Boat*. Ethel Waters starred in *As Thousands Cheer*, and later in *At Home Abroad* with Bea Lillie. Juanita Hall sang the haunting "Bali Hai" in *South Pacific*, and was a leading performer in *Flower Drum Song*. Todd Duncan was featured in *Lost in the Stars*; Thelma Carpenter in *The Seven Lively Arts*; Dooley Wilson and Richard Huey in *Bloomer Girl*; William Dillard in *My Darlin' Aida*; Pearl Bailey in *Arms and the Girl*; and Mae Barnes in *By the Beautiful Sea*. The all-Negro cast in the Harold Arlen-Johnny Mercer musical, *St. Louis Woman*, with a book by Arna Bontemps and Countee Cullen from the former's novel, *God Sends Sunday*, again brought black writers to Broadway, and gave Pearl Bailey her first big role. Another showcase for topnotch Negro talent was Virgil Thomson's *Four Saints in Three Acts* by Gertrude Stein, with Edward Matthews and a glorious group of singers. *Carmen Jones* first brought Muriel Smith to fame. *Simply Heavenly* established Claudia McNeil. Black performers had bit roles in *Finian's Rainbow* as well as being in the chorus. And from the late 1940s, Broadway musicals have increasingly included black boys and girls in their singing and dancing choruses, and black musicians in the pit.

While musical integration was gaining a foothold on the Broadway scene, the dramatic stage only infrequently offered effective starring or featured roles to blacks: Ethel Waters in *Mamba's Daughters*, followed years later by *The Member of the Wedding*;

Paul Robeson's triumphant *Othello*; Ruth Attaway in *You Can't Take It With You*; Canada Lee in *Native Son*; Jane White in *Strange Fruit* and later, off-Broadway, *Once Upon a Mattress*, Iphegenia in *Aulis*, and *The Trojan Women*; Gordon Heath in *Deep Are the Roots*; Ellen Holly in *Too Late the Phalarope*; Abbie Mitchell in *On Whitman Avenue*; Zelma Watson George in a powerful wheelchair revival of *The Medium*; Earle Hyman in *Mister Johnson*; Eartha Kitt in *Jolly's Progress*; Chita Rivera and Reri Grist in *West Side Story*; Lawrence Winters in *The Long Dream*; Billy Dee Williams in *The Cool World*; and Claudia McNeil in *Tiger, Tiger, Burning Bright*. Since World War II, more and more black performers have been able to gain professional experience, theatrical discipline, and even earn a living at their craft. For a professional actor, certainly the stage should be his breadbasket.

The biggest single breadbasket for blacks in the history of the American stage has been *Porgy and Bess*. If ever black performers erect a monument to a musician outside their race, it should be to George Gershwin, the composer of that melodic perennial based on the play *Porgy*, by DuBose Heyward, concerning life in Catfish Row. The musical version has been performed all over the now-known world. The moon is yet to see it, but it will in time. *Porgy and Bess* possesses great theatricality. It entertains. Commercially, it is a well-woven theater basket, as durable as baskets come, and filled with a variegated kettle of fish. Its charms are many. Its songs, the melodies derived from the folk blues and spirituals of the black people, are beautiful. There is prancing and dancing. Its argot is quaint. Its characters are colorful and broadly drawn. There are children in the show, a goat, and a marching band. It has almost everything capable of drawing money into the box office. In other words, it is a good show. And it has fed, over long periods of time in many cities and many countries, a great many black performers.

If it were not for the racial complications in American life, one might forego any further discussion of *Porgy and Bess*, and accept it simply as an excellent theater piece and a helpful dinner basket. Unfortunately its basket has been a trap, a steel-toothed trap leaving its marks upon the wrists of the black people who reached therein to touch its fish. And the fish themselves are tainted with racism. Art aside, it is an axiom in the American theater that the cheapest shows to stage are black shows. Their cast budgets are always the lowest of any. If a black show is a hit, a great deal of money may be made. The bulk of this money does not go to Negroes. They are seldom if ever in the top echelons of management or production. Financially the whites get the caviar, the blacks get the porgies. A porgy is a fish, and *Porgy and Bess* concerns fishermen and their women. The character, Porgy, is a cripple, an almost-emasculated man. His Bess is a whore. The denizens (as the critics term them) of Catfish Row are childlike ignorant blackamoors given to dice, razors, and singing at the drop of a hat. In other words, they are stereotypes in (to sensitive blacks) the worst sense of the word. The long shadow of the blackface minstrel coarsens the charm of *Porgy* and darkens its grace notes. Those notes themselves are lifted from black people. Borrowed is a more polite word; "derived from" an acceptable phrase.

Hall Johnson, in *Opportunity*, the journal of the National Urban League, wrote in his review of the original production:

> The informing spirit of Negro music is not to be caught and understood merely by listening to the tunes, and Mr. Gershwin's much-publicized visits to Charleston for local color do not amount even to a matriculation in the preparatory school that he needed for his work. Nothing can be more misleading, especially to an alien musician, than a few visits to Negro revivals and funerals. Here one encounters the "outside" at its most external. The obvious sights and sounds are only the foam, which has no meaning without the beer. And here let it be said that it is not the color nor the aloofness of the white investigator which keeps him on the outside. It is the powerful tang and thrill of the "foam" which excites him prematurely and makes him rush away too soon—to write books and music on a subject of which he has not even begun to scratch the surface.... What we are to consider then is not a Negro opera by Gershwin, but Gershwin's idea of what a Negro opera should be.... Artistically, we darker Americans are in a most peculiar situation with regard to what we have to give the world. In our several hundred years of enforced isolation in this country we have had plenty of time and plenty of reason to sing each other songs and tell each other tales. These songs and stories have a hidden depth of meaning as well as a simple and sincere external beauty. But the same wall which forced them into existence has closed in tight upon their *meaning* and allows only their beauty to escape through the chinks. So that our folk culture is like the growth of some hardy yet exotic shrub whose fragrance never fails to delight discriminating nostrils even when there is no interest in the depths of its roots.

Following the four-year-long tour of *Porgy and Bess* throughout Europe and South America, initiated under State Department auspices, Paul Henry Lang in 1956 wrote in the New York *Herald Tribune*:

> Foreign audiences are seldom aware that *Porgy* does not deal with the present. They do not know that the music is not genuine Negro art.... What they do believe is that this is the sad life of the oppressed Negro everywhere in America, a sordid life riddled with vice and crime in the black ghetto. While I was in Europe last summer, I had many heated discussions on the subject but could not explain away the "authenticity" of life as depicted in *Porgy*.... They cannot realize that the world of Catfish Row, created and set to music by white men, is a view from the outside focused on the Negro only for their entertainment value and as a group apart rather than as members of society. *Porgy and Bess* is indeed an excellent show, but it is no American folk opera.

"Unfortunately, the people in other countries don't think they are acting. They think they are giving a realistic portrayal of actual Negro life," the composer William Grant Still said in *Tones and Overtones*, backing up his contention with quotations from overseas papers. A review in the Spanish music magazine *Ritmo* declared: "*Porgy* is a strong emotional document of the life of the Negro in North America, depicting the humiliation and misery of his way of living, the violent sensuality and passion of his psychology, his crude and spontaneous reactions. All of this constitutes the substance and soul of the Negro, his character, and his tragi-comic life amidst sordid surroundings." The *Australian Music News* called "the whole libretto typically Negro." Which caused

Mr. Still to ask, "Is that the impression we would like to have foreigners get of us, of our life here in America?"

"The ignorant, happy-foot, lust-loving, crap-shooting clown—*Porgy* has them all," wrote black journalist James Hicks. "The presentation of *Porgy* could not happen to any other race in America but the colored race. The Jewish People have their Anti-Defamation League which sees to it that the role of the 'Sheenie' no longer walks the American stage. Catholic groups each week police the theaters and movie houses and order death by boycott to any theatrical presentation which dares depict them in any other light but good."

In black America's Pittsburgh *Courier*, J. A. Rogers observed, "While this stereotype gives joy to whites, it is to thinking Negroes like the frogs in Aesop's fable. To the boys who were having so much fun throwing stones into a pond, the frogs said, "What is fun to you, is *death* to us."

When Samuel Goldwyn was casting the motion picture version of *Porgy and Bess* in 1957, Harlem's *Amsterdam News* ran a front page story to the effect that actor Sidney Poitier turned down a $75,000 offer to play the leading role. It quoted him as saying, "As a Negro I have a certain sensitiveness, and as an artist I have certain responsibilities. Certain things I will play, but they must be constructive to my life as a Negro. *Porgy and Bess* is always played within a restricted range for the actor. There is simply one crap game too many in it." Praising Poitier editorially, the *Amsterdam News* declared, "We think this is a ringing answer to those who say that Negroes are not willing to pay for their self-respect and freedom. . . . The Negro race has been dignified by his creed." But less than a month later, the wire services from Hollywood transmitted to the world Samuel Goldwyn's announcement of acceptance by Sidney Poitier of the role of Porgy. The *Amsterdam News* never informed Harlemites as to just what happened, so they were left wondering if Goldwyn's price went up, or Poitier's pride went down. Yet nobody faulted him much. Blacks are familiar with baskets that are also traps.

Backstage one cold day that winter at Harlem's Apollo Theatre, some of the actors were discussing another high-salaried black artist who had also accepted a part in the Goldwyn opus, but who felt impelled for the record to register a protest. After seeing the script she imperiously told Mr. Goldwyn, "I demands you remove them *dats* and *dis-es* from my role."

To which Mr. Goldwyn is said to have replied, "Why not, darling? Just talk like you are—and everything'll be all right."

So, "I loves you, Porgy" and "Bess, you is ma woman now—you *is*, you *is*, you *is*!" reached the screen intact, dialect and all, as did, "Oh, Lawd, I'm on ma way!" And a Todd-AO Technicolor wide-screen million-dollar production of *Porgy and Bess* went out to the whole wide world singing, "I got plenty o' nuttin', an' nuttin's plenty fo' me." Fortunately the junkie, Sporting Life, in the person of Sammy Davis, Jr., sang, "It ain't necessarily so."

## RETURN OF A CLASSIC
### Porgy and Bess Comes Home From Europe

headlined *The New York Times* in the lead article by Brooks Atkinson on the front page of its theater section for March 15, 1953, when after its tour abroad the Robert Breen production came home. "Now that *Porgy and Bess* has settled down in New York," wrote Mr. Atkinson, "the people who last September opposed the project of sending it abroad ought to feel ashamed of themselves. . . . In the realm of art, nothing matters so much as the quality of the art, which in the case of the Gershwin opera is magnificent. . . . The zeal for outward respectability is a sign of inner uncertainty, and it should not be resolved at the expense of people who know what they are doing." Brooks Atkinson could hardly be accused of ill will or insincerity. And zeal for outward respectability might well be a sign of inner uncertainty. But Mr. Atkinson himself would probably be filled with uncertainty had he been born black, segregated most of his life, denied a job on the *Times* and even tickets to many American attractions, laughed at and ridiculed from minstrel days to the Ziegfeld Theatre, and then chided for not liking make-believe porgies in a Broadway basket—when you have had almost nothing but porgies all your life. Almost nothing but porgies—nothing but porgies, porgies, porgies.

Balance is what America has long needed in relation to the Negro and entertainment. There would be nothing greatly wrong with the U. S. State Department sponsoring *Porgy and Bess* abroad, if at the same time (or before or after) it also sent abroad other equally effective spectacles in which blacks were not portrayed solely as childish darkies, crap shooters, dope addicts, ladies of little virtue, and quaint purveyors of "You *is*, you *is*, you *is*." From the days of the minstrels a hundred years ago, through the half-century of Hollywood movies with their Stepin Fetchits and Butterfly McQueens and the Amos and Andys of radio and television, right up to *The Cool World* with its juvenile delinquents, the "you is" school has by and large prevailed in white versions of black theatrics. It has, with few exceptions, planted its concept of the black on the minds of the world. Always servants or clowns—and not just clowns or servants, but *burlesques* of clowns and servants. Certainly there are servants in the world, so why should they not be portrayed in pictures? The late Hattie McDaniel once said, when attacked for her Hollywood roles as a domestic, "It is better getting $7,000 a week playing a servant, than $7.00 a week *being* one." Being an artist of ability, Miss McDaniel was capable of humanizing even the burlesque concepts of Hollywood directors.

A standard form of direction for black actors playing chauffeur's roles in Hollywood, so an old-time performer told me, ran something like this. Upon opening the car door for one's white employer in any film, the director would command: "Jump to ground . . . Remove cap . . . Open car door . . . Step back and bow . . . Come up smiling . . . Now bow again . . . Now straighten up and grin."

The darkest actors with the widest mouths and the whitest teeth were the ones who until recent years got the best bit parts in Hollywood. There have been some decent, even charming films about Negroes—the early *Hallelujah* and *Hearts in Dixie*, much later *Bright Road* based on Mary Elizabeth Vroman's lovely little story; Maidie Norman in *The Well*; James Edwards in *Home of the Brave*; the moving semidocumentary *The Quiet One*; Belafonte's *A Man Is Ten Feet Tall*; Sidney Poitier in *Lilies of the Field*; and Bernie Hamilton in *One Potato, Two Potato* and also *Nothing But a Man*. And from Brazil via France came *Black Orpheus* with the beautiful black American star, Marpessa Dawn, who came to fame abroad.

In the theater, one must note, 90 percent of the plays about blacks drop their final curtain on defeat—usually death. A serious drama about blacks simply cannot end happily, it seems. From *Uncle Tom's Cabin* to *Blues for Mister Charlie*, if every Negro who has died impotent and defeated on stage were to be buried end to end, their assembled corpses would reach around the world. Shakespeare started it with *Othello*. LeRoi Jones continues it with *Dutchman*, where a white floozie stabs an Ivy Leaguish black boy in the belly and has his body thrown between two subway cars. The stereotype of the black drama is the unhappy ending—spiritually and physically defeated, lynched, dead—gotten rid of, to the relief of the dramatist and the audience, in time for a late supper. O'Neill's *Emperor Jones*, stone-cold dead in the jungle; *Mulatto*'s young hero a suicide; *Native Son* on his way to the electric chair; the young African in *Mister Johnson* begging the white man to shoot him, rather than snatching the gun from the white man and firing a few shots himself; Fishbelly in Richard Wright's *The Long Dream* as dramatized by Ketti Frings should also have shot first—but no! Like the Indians in the old westerns, Fish bites the dust instead of his white enemy; likewise Richard Henry in *Blues for Mister Charlie*. One would have thought the militant Negro in the Baldwin plays being such a bad, bad man, might have shot first. But on Broadway black characters do *not* shoot first. They merely get shot.

A white dramatist, once asked why the black hero in his play did not kill his white adversary, replied, "Why, that wouldn't be tragic!" Maybe his attitude explains why so many of the "serious" plays about blacks ring hollow. Somebody's concept of tragedy is askew. Warren Miller's sociological study of Harlem delinquents reached the stage with all the nuances explaining how the delinquents got that way gone by the wayside. In a letter to the New York *Herald Tribune* Ellen Holly wrote, "*The Cool World* is about as concerned with sociology as an exposé magazine is concerned with morality. Such magazines leer endlessly through keyholes, then tack on a sanctimonious conclusion in a pretense of respectability. To reiterate that a jungle produces animals tells us nothing new and brings us no closer to understanding. It is merely an excuse to ogle at that jungle." Ogling at the jungle, many blacks feel, is about all Broadway drama in the past has been able to do in regard to black themes.

"The constant whine of knives being sharpened is the predominant sound of *The Cool World*. Indeed, by the end of the ninth scene at the Eugene O'Neill, what seems like the entire juvenile delinquent population of Harlem is hard at work honing machetes, switchblades, and stolen kitchen utensils," wrote Walter Kerr in his review which termed it a "distressingly dreary play about the street-corner jungle that turns schoolboys into heroin addicts, schoolgirls into dollar-and-a-half prostitutes, and a random assortment of the group into corpses."

"Somebody is trying to pin their own defeatism, their mind sickness and their death wishes on the Negro," wrote Arna Bontemps. "They haven't stopped to think that Negroes are too black and ugly for that stuff. Look at any of the Negro athletes on TV. They ain't fixin' to quit. Neither are those knotty-headed Africans around Lake Victoria and such places. Something *else* has got to give, not their skulls." In the U.S.A. if blacks had accepted defeat as fatalistically as their counterparts on the Broadway stage, there would not have been twenty million of them alive in the sixties from coast to coast. White Broadway by and large simply fails to reflect the Negro with any degree of basic truth no matter how famous the playwright, how skilled the director, or who designs the sets.

Perhaps it is good that more than one hundred years after Emancipation integration is coming apace in the arts—that Leontyne Price now stars at the Metropolitan in Italian roles; that Lynn Hamilton plays the Queen in *A Midsummer Night's Dream* in Manhattan parks; that Mabel Mercer is a favorite in East Side night spots; that Eartha Kitt not only performs in, but lives at the Plaza when she is in New York; that Frederick O'Neal is president of Actor's Equity; that Katherine Dunham choreographed *Aida* at the Met and *The Bible* in Rome; and Donald McKayle and Talley Beatty direct non-Negro dances; that Anne Bancroft in Hollywood, in full sight of eighty million television viewers, kissed Sidney Poitier when he received his Academy Award as the Best Actor of the Year; that Lorraine Hansberry's *Sign in Sidney Brustein's Window* is cast with white actors; that Diana Sands played a nonracial role as the leading lady in *The Owl and the Pussy Cat*; that black director Lloyd Richards is chosen to direct all-white casts; that white folk singers are singing Negro gospel songs; that the great Martha Graham company, once all white, has leading black dancers; and Arthur Mitchell is one of the stars of the New York City Ballet.[12]

The formerly all-black Alvin Ailey Dance Theater took a white ballerina and a Japanese one with its company to Paris. The ballet people sail happily through the international air with no regard whatsoever for racial problems or stereotypes. Such is the glory of the modern dance. May the Broadway theater eventually acquire a similar glory. The black American has given great joy to the fields of light entertainment. He can add great understanding to the areas of serious make-believe as well. All he needs is playwrights, plays, and a reevaluation of what constitutes tragedy.

## Notes

1. Lucas appeared in white shows rather than those written by blacks.
2. The Ira Aldridge Chair was donated by an American.
3. On this occasion Leigh Whipper first caught the public eye.

4. It was also known as The Harlem Renaissance.
5. There were, however, theatrical materials of African origin available before this date.
6. For a more recent assessment of the contemporary black theater see Chapter 22, Black Influences in the American Theater: Part 11, 1960 and After.
7. Its subject matter is specifically concerned with Clarendon County, South Carolina, site of one of the School Segregation Cases.
8. This organization was known among actors as a demanding and unsympathetic task master.
9. The second version of this show was called Tutt's *Smarter Set.*
10. Noble Sissle's band also followed this route.
11. His costume also featured white gloves.
12. He founded the well-received Dance Theater of Harlem.

# 22

## Black Influences in the American Theater: Part II, 1960 and After

### Helen Armstead Johnson

The current ferment in black theater has energized the whole of American theater in much the same way that it was stimulated and influenced during the Harlem Renaissance. Indeed one might say, as Gilda Gray sang then, "It's getting mighty dark along [and off] Broadway." That this is so is good. What is not good, however, is the appalling lack of knowledge about the black influences which have helped to shape the American stage. Both blacks and whites in the theater and classroom are, in general, either largely uninformed or misinformed about these forces. One must acknowledge, nevertheless, that the fault is not entirely theirs. The traditional lack of respect for the black man in American society has been paralleled in the academic world. If scholars have not been ferreting out the facts on one level, reliable information was certainly not available to the general reader on another. Fortunately, however, this state of affairs is being rectified today. The powerful thrust of black theater since 1960 has been accompanied by the development of new black playwrights, performers, critics, historians, and producers, as well as by an infinite number of theater companies—amateur, semiprofessional, and professional—along with an ever-growing and varied black audience. Moreover, many white playwrights are turning to black themes following a precedent set by such dramatists as Dion Boucicault, Ridgely Torrence, Eugene O'Neill, and Paul Green.

The turning point of the 1960s came with the dynamic emergence of LeRoi Jones, now Imamu Amiri Baraka, whose brilliance and style in *The Slave*, *The Toilet*, *The Baptism*, and *The Dutchman* influenced a whole generation of playwrights, black and white alike. Indeed, in their *Black Writers of America*, Richard Barksdale and Keneth [sic] Kinnamon assert that "It is not too much to say that Baraka has established the tone and pointed the direction for most black writing of the 1970s."[1] Yale professor Larry Neal refers to "the theater of LeRoi Jones" as "a radical alternative to the sterility of the American theater—primarily a theater of the Spirit, confronting the black man in his interaction with his brothers and the white thing." It is this interaction which provides one of the bases for the consistency in LeRoi Jones's thought. In his plays the theme of exorcism recurs constantly, because he believes that the conditions which exist in this country, to which he is most sensitive, are those which call for radical solutions.

Although Jones speaks of murder with great frequency, it is clearly symbolic murder. He says specifically: "We've got to change America as we know it now." He does talk of killing people, and there is a symbolic bloodletting to which he returns again and again, as the title *Experimental Death Unit #1* suggests. Unfortunately, however, far too many people under Jones's political and artistic influence fail to perceive the level and shape of his thought. When he talks about not being a slave to Western culture, he knows the culture of which he speaks; the allusions in his writing attest to this. Those who insist upon rejecting all aspects of Western culture before even identifying them might consider the Picasso-like quality of LeRoi Jones: like Picasso, he is first of all a master draftsman who knows precisely what it is that he is abstracting from any culture. In "Technology and Ethos," in *Amistad 2*, and writing as Imamu Amiri Baraka he illustrates this: "The so-called fine artist realizes, those of us who have *freed* ourselves, that our creations need not emulate the white man's, but it is time the engineers, architects, chemists, electronics craftsmen, i.e. . . . . film, radio, sound etc. [sic], that learning Western technology must not be the end of our understanding of the particular discipline we're involved in." This considered attack upon Western culture concludes with the use of the word *most*: "Most of that West-shaped information is like mud and sand when you're panning for gold!"[2] Since all of it is not, Jones wants to save that which is like gold and change that which is not. It is to this wish for change that he directs his plays.

Along with those of method and theme, one of the changes which took place in the plays of Baraka was in the audience to which they were addressed. This was a change which exerted one of the most powerful influences upon the new black playwrights, freeing them to select a black audience without regard for white sensibilities, if they so chose. Baraka's point of view, however, is not without overtones of Langston Hughes's often-quoted "declaration of independence" in *The Nation* (June 23, 1926): "To my mind, it is the duty of the younger Negro artist . . . to change through the force of his art that old whispering 'I want to be white,' hidden in the aspirations of his people, to 'Why should I want to be white? I am a Negro—and beautiful!'" He continues his declaration by saying: "We younger Negro artists who create now intend to express our individual dark-skinned selves without fear or shame. If white people are pleased we are glad. If they are not, it doesn't matter." He ends by saying that Negro artists should "stand on top of the mountain, free within ourselves."

It is to this kind of freedom and purity that such playwrights as Lonne Elder III and Douglas Turner Ward have addressed themselves. Elder, in a *New York Times* interview with Patricia Bosworth on February 16, 1969, approached it this way:

> Whereas black writers have a very particular frame of reference. [sic] They can't avoid the ghetto or the terrible deprivation or the experience of bigotry and racism. They are in the midst of it all and they have to fight to get on top of it. There is an awful kind of purity in this kind of experience. LeRoi, Ed Bullins, Ralph Ellison, Douglas Turner Ward, we all express ourselves differently as artists but we all create from the same basic need—we are men and we want to be listened to.

Douglas Turner Ward, with his own angle of vision, adds dimension to a 1966 assertion by Saunders Redding that the black writer can now write "without being either false to one audience or subservient to another" when he states: "For a Negro playwright committed to examining the contours, contexts, and depths of his experience from an unfettered, unimaginative, Negro angle of vision, the screaming need is for a sufficient audience of *other Negroes*, better informed through commonly shared experience to readily understand, debate, confirm, or reject the truth or falsity of his creative explorations, not necessarily an all-black audience to the exclusion of whites, but, for the playwright, certainly his primary audience, the first persons of his address, potentially the most advanced, the most responsive, or most critical. Only through their initial and continuous participation can his content and purpose be best conceived by others."[3] A black audience, however, in no way assures positive response.

A review of Ed Bullins's *In the Wine Time* is a case in point. S. E. Anderson asks in *Black Culture Weekly* if the play is really necessary and clearly implies that it is not:

> It attempts to reflect what is happening with the grass-roots brother and sister, telling it like it is, but not like it is *and* like it should be. What is needed in our community is a black theater that will produce black plays: plays that will create positive images of brothers and sisters . . . plays that move brothers and sisters from spending their lives drinking rot-gut and rot-mind wine and becoming warriors that have a revolutionary task at hand and a new world to create.[4]

Anderson concludes his rejection of Bullins's play by virtually denying its blackness altogether:

> Generally speaking, *In the Wine Time*, is not a Black play. It is a militant negro [sic] entertainment for negroes who feel lost and guilty about their middle-class economic status and want to get down with the nitty-gritty folk. This may be of a psychological necessity for some black folk, but it is not sufficient. Let us hope that Brother Bullins will get the "rainbow sign": no more wine; the fire this time!

## Major Themes in Contemporary Black Drama

Any consideration of black drama must deal with its themes. Some of the major themes of Afro-American writing are these: 1) the folk experience; 2) double consciousness; 3) alienation from self, from race, from country, from society in general, from family, and from God and other gods; 4) the substance of Negro life, including middle-class life; 5) a mystical sense of race, which is a kind of Afro-American negritude.[5] 6) miscegenation and the mulatto experience; 7) religion and the church; 8) personal, inner group, and cultural identity; 9) black-white relationships of multiple kinds and nuances (here integration and the love-hate ambivalence should be singled out because of a tendency in the 1970s to ignore them); 10) the jazz experience; 11) migration and the urban experience; 12) patriotism; 13) nationalism; 14) the black American dream; 15) love; 16) the ghetto as experience; 17) freedom, and 18) revolution. Arthur P.

Davis and Saunders Redding cite the following as themes which appear most frequently in the writing of young blacks: 1) the frequent social and political emasculation of the black male; 2) the corruptive influence of white value systems; 3) the emancipating power of militant black racism; 4) black lover/white mistress relationship; and 5) white lover/black mistress liaison—one frequently used in black novels.[6]

There are many powerful variations on the freedom theme. In John F. Matheus's *Tambour* (1929), set in Haiti, Gros John, a full-blooded Negro, protests that he will never go to Port au Prince, where everybody is forced to surrender personal dignity in obeisance to a tyrannical black head of state. He says he "can't be molested that way." In Langston Hughes's *Emperor of Haiti* (1938), Stenio asserts that the mulattoes "are to strike the blow that will break the shackles of submission forever" and "put an end to the presumptuous Negro who dares call himself 'His Majesty.'" The protest against slavery goes on because slavery is still with us. LeRoi Jones's *Slave Ship*, for example, protests the chaining of our minds and spirits.

Lonne Elder's *Ceremonies in Dark Old Men* does the same thing. Mr. Parker, the father of Adele and her two brothers, goes through the ceremony of opening his one-chair barber shop every day, even though all he does in it is play checkers. Just as Gros John said, "I can't be molested that way," Mr. Parker tells Adele that he cannot go downtown to work. "... You're down there every day, and you oughta know by now that I'm too old a man to ever dream I could overcome the dirt and filth they got waiting for me down there."[7] Elder's more graphic protest against the chaining of men's minds and bodies comes as Mr. Parker describes serving his time on the chain gang in Macon, Georgia—the result of being a passenger in a car whose driver was accused of running a red light. Elder's sense of scale here, the size of a deed not even committed, set beside the magnitude of man's peculiar inhumanity makes the protest implicit rather than explicit. Parker transcends his painful memory with a sense of humor which dramatizes the absurdity of it all. He tells his son Theo that all of the men were "hooked up to one big long chain." "You turn over on *this* chain gang in your sleep, and your behind was shot! But if you had to, you would have to wake up, announce that you was turning over, and then you go back to sleep!"[8] The trouble here was that one turn made all the other chains rattle, and each convict would have to sing out his number. It is by resorting to humor as a means of transcendence that the playwright has dealt with the absurdities of existence as have the people he writes about. The black playwright's celebration of the unfettered mind and body is accompanied by an intense yearning for equality that goes beyond the simple right and opportunity to survive. We see this in Charles Gordone's Pulitzer Prize-winning *No Place to Be Somebody*. Mary Lou says to Johnny: "You don't have to make the world any worse," to which Johnny replies wryly, "Never had no chance to make it no better, neither."

Just as freedom has been an important theme in the black theater, so has religion, and one of the most significant plays of the sixties was James Baldwin's *The Amen Corner*

(1964). In his introduction, Baldwin makes it clear that not all people simply turn to the church; some are driven to it.

> Sister Margaret's dilemma: how to treat her husband and son as men and at the same time protect them from the bloody consequences of trying to be a man in this society. . . . She is in the church because her society has left her no other place to go. Her sense of reality is dictated by the society's assumption, which also becomes her own, of her inferiority. Her need for human affirmation, and also for vengeance, expresses itself in her merciless piety; and her love, which is real but which is also at the mercy of her genuine and absolutely justifiable terror, turns her into a tyrannical matriarch.[9]

The most moving speech in Baldwin's *Blues for Mr. Charlie,* however structurally unclear the play may be, is Juanita's outburst after Richard Henry's death: "Oh. Oh. Oh. Mama was frightened. Frightened because little Juanita brought her first real lover to this house. I suppose God does for Mama what Richard did for me. Juanita! I don't care! I don't care! Yes, I want a lover made of flesh and blood, of flesh and blood, like me, [sic] I don't want to be God's mother! He can *have* His icy, snow-white heaven! If He is somewhere around this fearful planet, if I ever see Him, I will spit in His face! In God's face! How *dare* He presume to judge a living soul! A living soul."[10] Black playwrights, as well as white ones, deal not only with the intervention of God in human affairs, but with his failure to intervene as well.

## "Protest" and the Contemporary Theater

For many years the label "protest" was attached to black writing with such facility and special connotation that the degree to which black writers were, like other writers, responding to untenable aspects of the human condition was largely obscured or grossly distorted. Elements of such "protest," evident in works of poetry and fiction, were particularly apparent in the field of drama. As black playwrights sought to project their personal vision of life, patterns of protest began to appear in a variety of forms, including romance and satire, comedy and tragedy, and other modes of dramatic structure. They appeared, too, in the themes which black playwrights treated in common with other black writers. Moreover, by selecting and intensifying the elements of his own experience, the black playwright emphasizes the dominant patterns and essential qualities of all human experience. When a writer feels strongly enough to use an art form to say, "This is the way things are, but I don't think they should be," he is protesting. The problem in speaking of protest is its implied political coloring and restriction. The patterns of protest within the broader definition reveal much about the makeup of the world of the black playwright and the experience of his characters.

There is indeed protest, although nonviolent in nature, in Douglas Turner Ward's humorously satirical *Happy Ending* and *Day of Absence,* and in Ossie Davis's *Purlie Victorious.* In fact LeRoi Jones's *The Dutchman* comes within the broader definition of protest, although his purely revolutionary plays would not. In *The Dutchman* the white girl listens to all that the black man says, although it is she, the protagonist, who is triumphant, the one who takes action. When the black man dies, another gets on the train, and we know that he too will die. The play ends up being a statement about the triumph of whites, one frequently made in black plays, no matter what the object of protest or how noble the aspirations of the characters.

We see another example of this triumph in Adrienne Kennedy's *The Owl Answers* (1965), a very strange play in which the characters veer back and forth from fantasy to reality, as well as in and out of full-length masks. Some indication of the work's strangeness is revealed in the description of the principal character: "She *who is* Clara Passmore *who is the* Virgin Mary *who is the* Bastard *who is the* Owl." The owl is explained in a speech by Bastard's Black Mother: "Clara, you were conceived by your Goddamn Father who was the Richest White Man in the Town and somebody that cooked for him. That's why you are an owl. (laughs). That's why when I see you, Mary, I cry. I cry when I see Marys, cry for their deaths. . . ."[11] The author establishes a line of descent from the symbolic common mother, Mary, who was white. A reference to Ann Boleyn raises the question of who Clara's white ancestors really were. Inasmuch as she can establish them only in maddening fantasy, she reaches back to royal blood because it is the best, and in this case because it flows in the veins of one to whose ill-fated life she can relate her own. Her mother's loss of purity was a symbolic death, and because she herself knows white men so well, the mother predicts her daughter's symbolic death. Thus it is that the mother cries for all virtuous black girls, all derivative Marys. The owl symbolizes the terrible loneliness in Clara's racial limbo and the unanswered question every owl asks repeatedly: "Who?"

## The Expanding Theater of the Sixties

One of the developments of the sixties was the increase in opportunity for black performers, both on Broadway and off, as well as in other media. The trade paper *Show Business* contained such ads as these with weekly frequency: "A black, militant male, bitter type, 25 to 30, attractive, magnetic, masculine, on order Rap Brown, Stokely, or Buck White. Ability to improvise." Or, "Casting girls, preteens to late teens, Negro, white, or Orientals." William Hanley's *Slow Dance on the Killing Ground* first appeared on Broadway in 1964, starring Billy Dee Williams, praised for giving "a fascinating complexity to a flamboyantly brilliant and violent young black." *The Great White Hope*, based upon Howard Sackler's "free dramatization" of the life of Jack Johnson, the first black world heavyweight champion, starred James Earl Jones and won multiple awards. Such musicals as *Promises, Promises*[12] and the revolutionary rock musical *Hair* featured black singers and dancers. Lauren Jones was featured in *Does a Tiger Wear a Necktie?* Another long-running sensation was Pearl Bailey's title role in

*Hello, Dolly.* Although the play continued, Pearl brought the sixties to a symbolic end by leaving the show on December 20, 1969.

Just as LeRoi Jones marked the turn of the 1960s, his disciple Ed Bullins has been "chosen" by the white publishers and producers as the black playwright of today. Evidence that he seems to believe his publicity exists in the introduction which he wrote for *New Plays from the Black Theatre* (1969): "If people say that I'm the greatest American playwright, then they must also admit and acknowledge that LeRoi Jones is one of the most significant figures in American, world, and Black theater." Such condescension is hardly justified by the quality of Bullins's plays. In *Clara's Ole Man* there is dramatic intensity of the early Eugene O'Neill type; as Owen Dodson has observed, it is similar to that found in *The Moon of the Caribees* (1918) and *The Dreamy Kid* (1919). After *Clara's Ole Man*, the rest of Bullins's plays, such as *In New England Winter, Goin' a Buffalo, Dialect Determinism, The Duplex,* and *Death List* are exercises in diminishing returns. In fact, the last of these is no more than a listing of distinguished black leaders to be destroyed by a revolutionary firing squad. Among them are the late Raymond Pace Alexander; Congressmen Clay, Conyers, Diggs, Hawkins; and Congresswoman Shirley Chisholm: "Super Nigger woman traitor to the Black nation of America and our Third World brothers and allies . . . Black People had such hopes for you . . . you Goldberg-lover . . . and you'll not even know why you'll die." Vernon Jordan, John H. Johnson, the late Jackie Robinson, and the late Whitney Young were also to have been among the victims.

When *We Righteous Bombers*, by Kingsley B. Bass, Jr., opened at The New Lafayette Theatre where Bullins was playwright-in-residence, the play was so controversial that a symposium was arranged because of it. Participating in the discussion were LeRoi Jones, Askia Toure, Marvin X, Ernie Mkalimoto, Robert Macbeth, and Larry Neal. According to the biographical information in *New Plays from the Black Theatre*, "Kingsley B. Bass, Jr. was a 24-year-old black man murdered by Detroit police during the uprising." Later an announcement was made that "Kingsley B. Bass, Jr. has recently been awarded The Harriet Webster Updike Theater Award for literary excellence." At the symposium, Marvin X made the opening statement: "Before we begin the discussion, I want to clarify one thing. First of all, Brother Ed Bullins is the author of *We Righteous Bombers.*" Marvin X then quoted Bullins: "Brother Ed wrote the play, he said, in an attempt to suggest the type of play that a brother killed in the Detroit Revolution would have written. And he wrote it in an attempt to suggest some of the rhetoric that is used, you know, among so-called revolutionaries." The report of the symposium appears in *Black Theatre #4*, of which Bullins is the editor.

A paper by Sara Fogg of Indiana University, comparing the play with Camus' *Les Justes*, says: "There can be no doubt that the play, *We Righteous Bombers* . . . is more than a close adaptation of Albert Camus' *Les Justes*. It is an example of wholesale takeover. The setting and names of characters have been changed, but most of the ideas, indeed the very words themselves, have not been." Miss Fogg's supporting evidence, an example of which follows, is unquestionably convincing. The italicized words are those of Camus which appear in *We Righteous Bombers.*

> *And what if the* Black *people at large don't want the revolution?*[13] . . . *Yeah, I, too, have thought of that. There's something missing about dying on the spot. While between the moment the bomb is thrown and the scaffold, there is an eternity, perhaps the only eternity a man can know."*[14]

The play, directed by Robert Macbeth, opened for a six-week run at The New Lafayette Theatre on April 18, 1969. It was hardly what the black community deserved, and a four-hour talkathon was what it clearly did not want.

Another view of Bullins's work comes from the black critic, Clayton Riley. In the introduction to *A Black Quartet,* he gives the following assessment of the popular playwright:

> Ed Bullins created, during the sixties, a roster of dramatic figures best described as street-nigger royalty. This remarkable artist elevated to the averted eyes of Negro America all the uncool, incorrect, funky Black urban field-hand life style we had always imagined could have no practical serviceability in the design of our new truths, our reconstructed myth-dynamic.
>
> Like Milner, Bullins clearly stated just where he was coming from at all times. His naturalism contained, however, a dimension of menace, the imminence of events heavy with deadly probabilities. Death, the knife, and the gun seem, in all his world, scarcely out of view at all times . . . in a pocket, beyond a doorway, around the street corner. His form of theatrical experience is physically draining, an exhaustive encounter which allows only rare opportunities to relax. . . . Bullins manages to terrify by implication; . . . he weaves possibilities into the spectator's imagination, makes audiences believe in the unavoidable arrival of disaster, a crashing, all-inclusive horror dwelling somewhere behind the grim faces of the street folks peopling the stage in his dramas.
>
> . . . Bullins has created as ideology and a supportive framework for the most basic element of Black society—the street culture.[15]

Riley surely damns with faint praise. Ultimately Bullins's reputation must be credited, in large measure, to forces—including force itself—other than his skill as a fine craftsman. Most to be deplored is that he offers nothing for the spirit to soar by.

In September 1972 The Ford Foundation announced it had made a terminal grant to The New Lafayette Theatre for production activities and educational services to other black theater groups outside Harlem. From the initial grant in 1967 to the terminal one in 1972 of $333,725, The New Lafayette Theatre received $1.5 million from Ford. As of early 1973, The New Lafayette had at least temporarily joined the ranks of theaters of the past.

Meanwhile, Bullins was named playwright-in-residence at the membership theater club, the American Place Theater. At the same time, he ventured into producing with his Obie-winning *The Fabulous Miss Marie.*

Just as The New Lafayette Theatre was financed with large grants from major foundations, so was the Negro Ensemble Company, better known as NEC. In 1967 The Ford Foundation made a grant of $434,000 so that the company could be established in 1968. The seeds of the company had been planted in 1965. NEC's organizers were Douglas Turner Ward, artistic director; Robert Hooks, executive director; and Gerald Krone, administrative director. Only Ward remains in his initial position. Hooks is currently Executive Director of the D. C. Black Repertory Company, and the present coordinator of administration is Jim Porter, a black. Sam Zolotow, writing in *The New York Times*, May 15, 1967, quoted Ward on the meaning of the grant to the company: "Until now . . . the theater has more or less defined, created, and controlled the possibilities of Negro stage activity. The Negro Ensemble Company is an example of Negroes' controlling their own possibilities."

NEC's program was ambitious. It included a training program directed by the following: John Blair, Lonne Elder III, Margaret Harris, Luther James, Louis Johnson, Kristin Linklater, Ron Mack, Paul Mann, Lloyd Richards, Michael Schultz, and Charles Vincent. Lloyd Richards directed *A Raisin in the Sun* on Broadway, Margaret Harris directed the orchestra for *Hair*, and Louis Johnson choreographed *Purlie*. (Johnson is now co-director, along with Mike Malone, of the D. C. Black Repertory Dance Company and divides his time between Washington and New York.) Edmund Cambridge was NEC's Project Coordinator. The training program also included publicity, and Irene Gandy worked out of Howard Atlee's Broadway office on NEC projects. Atlee himself was the National Press Representative.

Some of NEC's productions have been outstanding ones, and among them are Douglas Turner Ward's own plays, *Happy Ending* and *Day of Absence* (1966). The first one is an autobiographical work about two aunts who were domestic servants. When Ward discovered them literally weeping about the domestic affairs of their employers, his immediate reaction was to ask: "Goddamn, haven't we really gotten beyond that point of worrying about what's happening to Miss Ann?" The play, to use Ward's word, is an "objectification" of that experience. Its companion piece was an unintentionally prophetic one. Black people have often wondered what white ones would do if all the blacks disappeared, as they do for one day in *Day of Absence*. Stimulated to action by the play, Carlos Russell of Brooklyn College created Black Solidarity Day, and since 1968 has been urging all blacks to stay home on November 5.

*Happy Ending* and *Day of Absence* were awarded the Drama Desk-Vernon Rice Award in 1968, along with an Obie—the off-Broadway award—and Lambda Kappa Mu Citation. The following year they received a special Tony Award and the Brandeis University Creative Arts Award for outstanding achievement and contribution to the theater. *Day of Absence* has been televised, and both plays now appear in numerous anthologies. They have also been published separately, as has Ward's *The Reckoning*. Less well known, this is another treatment of the master-servant relationship, an ancient formula treated metaphorically from the black angle of vision.

Certainly one of the most celebrated NEC productions was Lonne Elder's aforementioned *Ceremonies in Dark Old Men* (1965). Patricia Bosworth, in an eight-column spread in *The New York Times*, February 16, 1969, gives us an indication of the extent of its success:

> Two mornings after his play *Ceremonies in Dark Old Men* opened Off-Broadway to unanimous raves, Lonne Elder III sat in the office of the Negro Ensemble Company and tried to talk about himself and his writing. It wasn't easy because the phones kept ringing on his desk: each call was either a TV or movie bid for *Ceremonies*. Big-name producers who had originally turned down his eloquent drama of a decent Harlem family caught up in the rackets now wanted to take it over for Broadway. Still other producers were offering him huge sums of money for his next play—which he hasn't yet written.

The *Times'* ubiquitous—and often iniquitous—Clive Barnes opened his literally joyous column with this very white observation: "We've known for decades that Negroes were natural actors; we are now discovering that they are natural playwrights." It was this kind of critique that led many blacks to firmly assert that whites could not review black plays. An ironic dimension to Barnes's assertion is the fact that at the time, Lonne Elder was a student in The Yale School of Drama's film-making division.

## Trends in the 1970s

The "blackest" plays seem frequently to suffer from a fault common among young revolutionary playwrights: a concentration on subject matter at the expense of craft—a matter of refusing to learn it. In this writer's review of Joseph Walker's *Ododo* in *Black World* (April 1971), which also mentioned Afolabi Ajayi's *Akokawe*, attention was called to certain weaknesses:

> That they suffer from many of the same flaws is attributable, in large part, to the failure of both playwrights to let go of their material [at a reasonable point] once they had written it. Ajayi assumed the roles of writer, director, and arranger, and Walker those of writer, director, and choreographer. The sense of Black pride which should grow out of Walker's use of his materials—and thus involve the viewer, does not; rather, it is heavily imposed upon them and the viewer remains nearly static, denied the kind of emotional involvement which should be his as he perceives the meaning in—and has feelings about—the playwright's illuminations.[16]

Such criticism, unfortunately, is applicable to far too many plays of the black seventies.

One phenomenon of the seventies has been the proliferation of theater companies. There are literally hundreds spread throughout the country, and their mortality rate is extremely high. There is, of course, a wide range of them in New York, which remains the country's cultural center. Consequently one finds a concentration of talent in all of the arts and crafts of the theater. Partly because of these groups and talent, the Black Theatre Alliance was formed in New York about 1970 and is coordinated by John Sandler. It was the coming together of sixteen theater companies, all of whom share the worthy aims of attacking common problems and developing common services. Among the problems in question are audience development and communication, and the services involved include developing an equipment-lending pool and making technical training available to member companies.

Because of the wide range of companies in New York, one runs considerable risk in going beyond NEC and The New Lafayette for further illustration of the contemporary scene. Some of the best-known are not necessarily the ones which attain or even strive for the highest artistic standards, in spite of assertions to the contrary. One of the groups that falls into this category is Barbara Ann Teer's National Black Theatre, a purely local group. According to Jessica B. Harris in *The Drama Review* (December 1972), "The five Cycles of Evolution are at the base of the technique of the actors of the National Black Theatre. They are:

> I—The Nigger
> II—The Negro
> III—The Militant
> IV—The Nationalist
> V—The Revolutionary"[17]

For a long time the National Black Theatre concentrated on ritual as a means of creating a spiritual base. When this form grew too static to permit artistic expansion, dialogue was added and "revival" came into being. Professor Harris continues as follows: "The Five Cycles of Evolution are at the basis of the rituals and revivals presented at the National Black Theatre. All of the characters are representative of the people of the Harlem community. The characters can move up or down the vertical standard of five cycles. . . . Ms. Teer's Theater is about nation building."[18] Miss Teer's conception of art and its relative importance to these goals is not revealed.

On the other hand, artistic principles of high order are clearly part of Vinnette Carroll's Urban Arts Corps, which she established with the aid of the New York State Council on the Arts in 1968. Its purpose was "to develop the professional skills of minority performers, writers, and composers." Miss Carroll's credits are indeed impressive and provide brilliant illumination of the professionalism with which she guides her Corps. It was she who adapted James Weldon Johnson's poetic sermons, *God's Trombones*, for the stage as *Trumpets of the Lord*. It premiered under her direction at the White Barn Theatre in Westport. Miss Carroll also directed Langston Hughes's *The Prodigal Son* in its off-Broadway run, as well as in Paris, London, Holland, and Brussels. In London she was the star of Carson McCullers' *The Member of the Wedding* on television and Errol John's *Moon on a Rainbow Shawl* on the stage. In New York she was awarded an Obie by the *Village Voice* for her off-Broadway performance in *Shawl*.

It was from the Urban Arts Corps' May 1971 production of Irwin Shaw's *Bury the Dead* that Jonelle Allen went to Broadway in December 1971 as the star of *Two Gentlemen of Verona*, adapted by John Guare and Mel Shapiro, with music by Gault MacDermott. Clive Barnes said of her, "Jonelle Allen is sensational." Those who had seen her under Miss Carroll's direction were already aware of this fact. Upon leaving the Broadway company for the touring one, Miss Allen was replaced by Hattie Winston. The latter had starred in *The Me Nobody Knows*, an adaptation of Stephen Joseph's book by the same title—a collection of writing by ghetto children set to music by Gary Friedman.

In April 1972 Micki Grant literally lighted up Broadway as the composer and star of her own revue, *Don't Bother Me, I Can't Cope*, a musical collage produced by Norman Keen and directed by Vinnette Carroll. Opening at the Playhouse Theatre, it moved to the Edison Theatre on June 13, 1972. Its list of awards is a testimony to excellence: 1972 Outer Critics Circle Awards; 1972 Obie Awards; 1972 NAACP Image Award for Best Musical; 1972 Drama Desk Awards: Music and Lyrics—Micki Grant, Performance—Alex Bradford, Direction—Vinnette Carroll; 1972 Grammy Award for "The Best Broadway Musical Album," produced for Polydore Records by Jerry Ragavoy. A high tribute to Miss Grant's personal achievement was her selection by *Mademoiselle* as one of the ten "Super Woman Achievers" of 1972.

Still in motion, Miss Grant collaborated with Vinnette Carroll on *Step Lively Boys*, an extension of their earlier production of Irwin Shaw's *Bury the Dead* (1971), an antiwar celebration of life in which the dead soldiers refused to stay buried. *Step Lively Boys* premiered at the Urban Arts Corps on February 7, 1973, bringing well-deserved attention to the splendid work of Maryce Carter and Marie Thomas, veterans of the Corps, and to Salome Bey, an outstanding newcomer. With fine artistry, Glory Van Scott performs the role Jonelle Allen created in the original *Bury the Dead*.

Another of the highly professional groups has been Dorothy Maynor's Harlem School of the Arts Community Theatre, which opened officially in 1964. Its statement of belief is explicit:

> The Harlem School of the Arts Community Theatre believes that without a core of playwrights and an acting company it will be incapable of surviving. We are actively working toward that goal. We also believe that the community must be served with the highest artistic performances we can achieve, that the theater must relate to the audience in the most purposeful and enjoyable way possible . . . that portraying life as it is and as it should be and has been is not unattainable if we pursue our objectives with determination.

Actively assisting in the pursuit of the above objectives was a distinguished board: Osceola Archer, Alice Childress, St. Clair Christmas, Chuck Davis, Owen Dodson, James Earl Jones, Earle Hyman, Robert Lewis, Ming Cho Lee, Dorothy Maynor, Dorothy Ross, Perry Watkins, and Richard White. The company was able to attract fine performers such as Marilyn Berry, Georgia Gowan, and the white husband-wife team of Mary Haden and Tom McDermott. McDermott was in Katharine Cornell's company of Chekhov's *The Three Sisters* and was in the 1973 Broadway musical production of *Much Ado About Nothing*. Osceola Archer directed him in her version of John

Galsworthy's *The Silver Box*, in which only the rich family remains white. Plays directed by Artistic Director Dodson included his adaptation of Countee Cullen's *Medea in Africa*, Martin Duberman's *In White America*, and Edgar White's *The Mummer's Play*. He also directed *Run Away People*, written in his playwriting class by 17-year-old Norman Riley, brother of critic Clayton Riley. The young playwright's insight and skill belied his age.

This fine company also produced *Contribution* and *Shoes* by Ted Shine, one of the best of the newer black playwrights. Shine has subjected himself to the discipline of the craft: he is on the faculty of Prairie View A & M College in Texas and received a Ph.D. in theater from the University of California at Santa Barbara in 1973. His *Contribution* was also staged by NEC and had a short life on Broadway with Claudia McNeil as the black grandmother whose expertise was dissimulation and camouflage and whose contribution was arsenic. Miss McNeil's failure to convey a transcendent sense of humor seemed to have much to do with the demise of the play. The play was also produced at Spelman College under the direction of Carlton Molette II. Molette himself is a playwright, the author of *Doctor B. S. Black*, an adaptation of Molière's *The Doctor In Spite of Himself*.[19] With his wife, Barbara, a costumer, he has written *Rosalie Pritchett*, which was seen in New York at the NEC in January 1972. The play is a devastating satire on the southern Negro upper class.

Only a lack of funds forced the closing out of the Community Theatre part of The Harlem School of the Arts. The actors received stipends equal to the off-Broadway union minimum wage, and the high cost of a resident company and staff and mounting productions could not be sustained without major support from the outside.

One of the very busy centers of theatrical activity is the Henry Street Settlement on the lower East Side of New York, where Woodie King and Dick Williams are the producers for the Settlement's two theaters, the Henry Street Playhouse and the New Federal Theatre. The latter was originally a group which was housed in St. Augustine's Church opposite the Settlement's administrative offices. In September 1970 the group moved to the Henry Street Playhouse, and early in 1971 acquired the old Ellen Stewart Theatre as the New Federal Theatre, which opened in 1972.

The first King productions for the New Federal at St. Augustine's were *Willie Big Nigger* and *The Chimpanzee* (1970), plays by Charles Oyamo Gordon. In the same year Dick Williams directed Ed Bullins's *In New England Winter* at the Henry Street Playhouse. Williams's wife, Gloria, was featured in it. Later that year she appeared in J. E. Franklin's play, *Black Girl*, which opened at the Playhouse, moved to Theatre de Lys, and was subsequently sold to Cinerama Releases.

Williams himself came to New York from Watts as the protagonist and director of *Big Time Buck White*, a satire on the poverty program. In it he created a character whose appearance established a prototype for casting and was widely imitated by young black men everywhere. The play, written by Joseph Dolan Tuotti and "adapted" by Williams, was first performed in Budd Schulberg's Writer's Workshop in Watts,

Los Angeles, and premiered in New York at the Village South Theatre on December 8, 1968. Others who arrived with the play and remained a part of the New York theater scene were Kirk Kirksey, Van Kirksey, David Moody, Ron Rich, and Arnold Williams.

Both *Black Girl* and J. E. "Sonny Jim" Gaines's *Don't Let It Go to Your Head* (1971), Playhouse Productions, won Drama Desk awards. The first Playhouse production of 1972 was *In My Many Names and Days*, Charles Fuller's seven-cycle play which traces a black Philadelphia family from the founding of the NAACP (1909) to 1970. Fuller's play on interracial marriage, *Perfect Party* (1969) had a short-lived run off-Broadway at Tambellini's Gate Theatre. Woodie King was one of the performers in this play about five interracial couples having a party in the community which they created to escape racism. Nick, played by Moses Gunn, arrives at his surprise birthday party only to tell his wife that he has decided to leave her for a black woman and a black identity. To prevent his doing this, his friends kill him. As Catherine Hughes wrote in *Show Business* (March 29, 1969), "The party in *Perfect Party* turns out far from perfect, and so does the play Charles H. Fuller, Jr. has written about it."

After Fuller's play at the Playhouse came Martie Evans-Charles's *Jamimma*, in which Dick Williams and Marcella Lowery had the leading roles. It was directed by another of the black female directors, Shauneille Perry, who directed Phillip Hayes Dean's *Sty of the Blind Pig*, the Molettes' *Rosalie Pritchett* at NEC, and many other productions.

What will undoubtedly prove to be of historical importance was the King-Williams premiere on January 26, 1973, of Jones-Baraka's first full-length play, *A Recent Killing*. According to Baraka's office, the play was written in 1963. The New Federal production, however, was based upon a 1967 version of the work. Clearly a semiautobiographical drama about Jones as an airman/aspiring poet, *A Recent Killing* is set at the "Strategic Air Command Base on Caribbean Island of Loca" in the mid-1950s. The central theme is explicitly stated by the Jones-like character, Airman Lennie Pearson: "Man is a hostage of reality," and because evil is so much a part of it, "reality must be changed." The poet, Pearson says, has a role in changing it, primarily because what he wants from poetry is "something more than reality, something poetry makes real."

Baraka's central character alternates between the realms of fantasy and reality, driven in turn by his sexuality and his intellect. Nijinski, Leopold Bloom, and T. S. Eliot wander on and off stage as part of the fantasies, but the bullets, prostitutes, and sexual acts—including those between a black sergeant's wife and his white officer—are unabashedly naturalistic. At one point director Irving Vincent has three couples on stage at the same time simulating copulation and at another point bullets are still arriving from offstage directed at characters who have been replaced by stagehands removing furniture.

The airman's penchant for books and poetry disturbed not only the white officers in the play but the New York *Post's* Jerry Tallmer as well. According to him, Nijinski, Bloom, and Eliot "kept flitting through otherwise naturalistic scenes and messing up the dialogue with poetic nonsense, as some sort of proof that a young black enlisted man or a young black playwright—can have as much of a headful of Whitey's culture as Whitey himself" (January 29, 1973). At the end of the play, the killing of his two intoxicated roommates converts the poet with startling suddenness from dreamer to activist. Most of the concerns of the early Jones appear in *A Recent Killing*: homosexuality, the love-hate ambivalence in black-white relationships, the importance of ideas, and even the toilet.

Gary Bolling, as the poet Lennie Pearson, gave a compelling performance; moreover, he bears a striking resemblance to the author. Jones-Baraka was in the opening night audience and saw a professional but oppressively long performance. The twenty-two scenes consumed three and one-half hours playing time. Eleven of the twenty-three members of the cast appeared "through courtesy of Actors Equity Association."

Many other groups are worthy of attention, although it is impossible to mention all of them here. The important thing is to give some indication of the range and scope of black theater since 1960. A look at Al Fann's Theatrical Ensemble helps to do this. Fann's own play, *King Heroin*, first appeared in community facilities in the Bedford-Stuyvesant section of Brooklyn. The "theater" sites included schools, hospitals, community centers, and the streets themselves. In all, about one dozen performances were given, and various honors and honorary appointments have come to Fann because of his community approach. An actor of impressive talent, Fann captured a role in the film *Cotton Comes to Harlem*, as well as in its sequel, *Come back Charleston Blue*, which he also co-produced. He recently completed a film script, *Sweet Jesus*, for which Barbra Streisand's co-star Danny Meehan wrote the music. Set in Harlem, it focuses on a 14-year-old black mute who performs miracles. Subsequently renamed *The Boy*, Fann directed it but it has yet to be released. Fann's multifaceted role in the film and theater world makes it possible for him to cast performers whom he has trained in his own Theatrical Ensemble.

The diversity and energy in the New York climate is further reflected in the work of Roger Furman. His New Heritage Repertory Theatre was established in 1964 with Office of Economic Opportunity funds. New Heritage opened originally in the YWCA, but since many of its activities were not in harmony with those of the YWCA, it has since moved to its present site on East 125th Street, a high-crime area. This new location has made it difficult to develop a following outside the perimeters of Harlem. Furman's approach to this problem was to initiate subsequent runs in downtown off-Broadway theaters. The first production was his own play, *The Long Black Block*, which ran four months at the New Heritage, playing to a full house of 110 people each night. The play's central theme is a frequent one: the emasculation of black men—this time by drugs. When one considers the traditional African and African-American respect for elders, he is severely jolted by the junkie's treatment of an old tenement woman. The next production at the New Heritage Theatre was a comedy by Lou Rivers, "*A Madam Odum Special on the Rocks*," which satirizes an aging diva who teaches in a small southern college. It is a sharp departure from a large number of recent plays, which have been characterized by an unrelieved absence of comic vision.

Outside his own theater, Furman directed a revival of the Brecht-Weill *The Three-Penny Opera* at the WPA Theatre. An actor's showcase, it starred Geraldine Fitzgerald and David Downing, the latter as Mack the Knife. Downing, an original member of NEC, co-starred with Paul Winfield in *Sounder*, and appeared in *Gordon's War*, which Ossie Davis directed on location in Harlem.

The scope of theatrical activity is broadened as well by such innovative groups as the Soul and Latin Theater (SALT), which is street theater in Harlem. Begun by a white teacher, Maryat Lee, then an instructor in street theater at The New School for Social Research, its first performance was July 1, 1968, on the back of a truck. Three cheerleaders at an East Harlem school wanted to do something concrete about the effect of drugs upon the school's athletes. The result was *Day to Day*, written by Miss Lee, who, "with other uprooted rural people," had written the street play *Dope* in 1951. Other SALT productions for black and Puerto Rican street audiences were *After the Fashion Show*, *The Classroom*, and *Luba*. All of these have been published by Samuel French, including *Dope*. Although Maryat Lee has returned to Appalachia, the theater is still very active, run now, as Miss Lee says, by "insiders."[20]

At the forefront of avant-garde theater in New York is Ellen Stewart's La MaMa, a theater-club complex of several companies. A black woman, Miss Stewart has achieved an international reputation as a producer, and the work of her various companies, such as the Experimental Theatre Co. (ETC) and the Playhouse of the Ridiculous, accounts in part for this. Miss Stewart's all-black company, The Caterina Jarboro Company, is named for the celebrated diva who made opera history in the 1930s in such roles as Aida, Inez in *L'Africaine*, and Balkis in *Queen of Sheba*. Miss Stewart bestowed this honor upon Miss Jarboro at the annual Harold Jackman Collection dinner in 1971.[21] In October 1972 The Jarboro Company appeared at La Biennale Festival in Venice, presenting five one-act plays of Bullins, along with Richard Wesley's *Black Terror*. During the same month, the company played the Al Teatro Lirico in Milan.

Although La MaMa ETC is a complex of companies with individual identities, the companies and performers frequently mesh. As part of a Playhouse of the Ridiculous production, the Jarboro players performed in *Elegy for a Down Queen*, a drama of homosexuality. A mixed cast was also used in Joe Renard's adaptation of Molière's *George Dandin, ou le mari confondu*. Renard's version, with a Caribbean setting, makes the upper class black and the lower one white. In *Thoughts*, too, there is a thoroughly integrated cast. This theater piece is a sparkling musical with book and music by black composer-pianist Lamar Alford, with additional lyrics by José Topia and playwright Megan Terry. *Thoughts* is a retrospective look at a black boy's childhood, and Alford reaches high satirical heights as he follows the boy from his Alabama birth to his arrival as one of the ultra-chic in the arty-party society world of New York.

One of the featured players in *Thoughts* is Bob Molock, a fine character actor who is rarely "at liberty." His dedication to the theater allows him to accept roles, regardless of size, both in plays themselves and in the mounting of them. He is constantly polishing his craft this way, much in the manner of great European actors. The emphasis at La MaMa is on the works of new playwrights, and, as Ellen Stewart says, on "[improving] the caliber of the acting and directing techniques of those who work for us, for go they must, eventually, to the professional stage."[22] The record shows that many have indeed gone, and many have stayed. Molock himself has been with such touring companies as *No Place to Be Somebody* and *The Great White Hope*.

Another kind of theater complex in New York is popularly known as Joe Papp's theater, although its proper title is the New York Shakespeare Festival Public Theater, and it is really four theaters. Joseph Papp, the founder, consistently produced plays by black playwrights, including Adrienne Kennedy's surrealistic *Cities in Bezique* and Gordone's *No Place to Be Somebody*. Chekhov's *Cherry Orchard* opened at the Public Anspacher with a black director, Michael Schultz, and all black principals: Gloria Foster, Ellen Holly, Josephine Premice, Earle Hyman, and James Earl Jones. Walter Kerr rightly said: "The Public Theater could scarcely have assembled a more gifted group." Running simultaneously with this production was the *Wedding Band* of Alice Childress, highlighted by the performance of the gifted Ruby Dee.

A special position at the Public Theater is held by Novella Nelson, once of *Purlie*. Her official title is Consultant to the Producer. It is reliably reported that her position was created in response to pressure exerted by a small but powerful group of black militant theater people to force Papp to share with blacks a larger portion of the considerable sums of money granted his theater. Cast in this liaison role, in 1972 Miss Nelson conducted a black summer festival of Sunday afternoon gospel and jazz programs, and at the Public/Other Stage directed Walter Jones's *Nigger Nightmare*, which closed June 27, 1972, after a limited run of four performances. At the Public Theater Annex, Miss Nelson directed *Sister Son/ji* by Sonia Sanchez, as one of four one-act plays staged as *Black Visions*. The others were *Players Inn* and *Cop and Blow* by Neil Harris, directed by Kris Keiser, and *Getting It Together* by Richard Wesley, also directed by Kris Keiser. *Black Visions* played sixty-four performances and closed April 30, 1972.

In a special category of its own in New York theater is Vinie Burrows's one-woman show: *Walk Together Children*, subtitled "the Black journey from auction block to new-nation time!" On November 1, 1968, Miss Burrows opened at the Greenwich Mews Theater in New York to instant and ecstatic acclaim. Even the diffident Clive Barnes called her "a magnificent performer," and the *Post* said she was "funny, gutsy, diverse, and colorful, ironic, apocalyptic." In 1969 she performed in Algiers at the First Pan-African Cultural Festival, on television in Bucharest and Amsterdam, and before 10,000 people in Stockholm. Vinie Burrows has appeared in seven Broadway shows, beginning with Helen Hayes in *The Wisteria Trees*. She attributes the creation of her one-woman show to the fact that: "As a Black actress whose talents have never been fully used in American culture, I have turned to solo performances, tapping a rich vein from my own Black culture and heritage. . . . Most importantly," she continues, "I have grown to understand that the function of the Black artist is to assist in the psychic, political, and economic liberation of African peoples, whether they be in the United States, the Caribbean, South America, or in the motherland, Africa." Here Miss Burrows enunciates clearly her artistic conception of pan-Africanism. She is a graduate of New York University, and in private life is the wife of Dean Kenneth Harrison, an administrator with the City University of New York. Her daughter's name is Sojourner.

In places other than New York there are serious approaches to good community theater. One of these has been made by Jim Mapp with his Playward Bus Theatre Co., Inc., in Philadelphia. In 1958 Mapp began to implement the first part of a three-phase plan by bringing bus loads of potential theater patrons to New York. Coming from such widely separated places as Massachusetts and Illinois, they saw more than thirty off-Broadway plays as part of Mapp's effort to create black theater audiences. Playing supporting roles in this effort were Diana Sands and Hilda Simms, who served as hostesses. It was they who discussed the play to be seen, and it was Hilda Simms who suggested the word play on Steinbeck's *The Wayward Bus* as the name for the project.

Mapp himself is an actor-director-producer with solid professional training from the Wolter School of Speech and Drama at Carnegie Hall, the Cambridge School of Radio Broadcasting, and Fannie Bradshaw, the Shakespearean coach who is on the board of directors at Stratford-on-Avon. He is also a member of Actor's Equity. Such a background accounts for the professionalism which he has adapted to the needs of a black semiprofessional repertory company. In 1965 Mapp reached the second stage of his plan by forming his own company in Philadelphia, and groups from surrounding areas now go there to see his productions, especially his adaptation of James Weldon Johnson's *God's Trombones*. This production has been in the company's repertory for seven years. Recently a distinguished group of makers of black-theater history went as a group to Philadelphia to see a performance of *God's Trombones*: Caterina Jarboro; Noble Sissle (then 83) and Eubie Blake (89), writers of *Shuffle Along* in 1921; Leigh Whipper (95), veteran actor of more than forty plays and sixty films; and Owen Dodson, whose volume of poetry, *Powerful Long Ladder*, and whose play, *Divine Comedy*, a satire on Father Divine, are among the finest writing in Afro-American literature. Mapp and his company are in the film *Trick Baby*, shot on location in Philadelphia in 1972. In a (Philadelphia) *Sunday Bulletin* interview (December 3, 1972), Mapp said that he wanted "to help mold people to follow in the footsteps of Leigh Whipper." To this he added that there are only two kinds of theater, good and bad, and he wants no part of the bad.[23]

Even the most cursory sweep around the country reveals a tremendous spread of activity. In Boston, Elma Lewis has built the National Center for Afro-American artists, an enormous complex which includes a three-part theater program: drama, a technical center, and the Elma Lewis Playhouse in the Park. For her contributions to the arts, Harvard awarded Elma Lewis an honorary doctorate in 1972. On the West Coast, the diversity of theaters is the subject of an article by Margaret Wilkerson, "Black Theatre in California."[24] It is a report on eight groups from the Los Angeles and San Francisco Bay areas that were active during the late sixties and early seventies: The Ebony Showcase Theatre, The Inner City Cultural Center, The Arts Society of Los Angeles, The Watts Writers Workshop, The Group, North Richmond Theatre Workshop, Aldridge Players West, and Dialogue Black/White. The last two are no longer active. Margaret Wilkerson focuses sharply on one of the main causes of the black-audience problem in all major cities:

> Most of these black theaters, however, in an effort to bring more Afro-Americans into their audiences, particularly those who seldom attend theatrical productions, are located near small shopping areas and homes in predominantly black areas in the belief that the black community should look to its own area for entertainment and enrichment and should support its own enterprises. Presenting their productions in the black community is one way of demonstrating this faith. [The ]Aldridge Players realized that a certain class of blacks was not likely to attend a play in the Western Addition, then a poor section of San Francisco, yet they persisted in their location. On the other hand, Dialogue Black/White traded on the attraction of a "downtown play" by using the Committee Theatre in San Francisco's entertainment district, while maintaining an office and rehearsal studio in the black Fillmore district.[25]

One of the most popular plays of Dialogue Black/White was Loften Mitchell's *Tell Pharaoh*. This documentary drama, along with Mitchell's historical play, *A Land Beyond the River*, was also seen at the Black Drama Festival of 1968 held at the University of California at Santa Barbara.

In another section of the country, one of the best-known groups has been the Free Southern Theater in New Orleans. After a brief demise it was restored to life. Much of its story is told in *The Free Southern Theater by the Free Southern Theater*, a documentary edited by Thomas C. Dent, Richard Schechner, and Gil Moses. Moses' play, *Roots*, is included among the journals, essays, letters, and poetry which comprise the book. The original intent of the founders of the group was to take theater into the rural areas of the South, such places as West Point and Greenville, Mississippi. One of the Free Theater's accomplishments was the creation of a Golden Age drama group in New Orleans. A 1969 report describes its members as an "out-of-sight group of blk [black] actors . . . who have been knocking the community out with a one-act comedy which they have been performing at various community centers and churches." In 1969 Gil Moses was the group's artistic director, and in the same year he directed the Chelsea Theater's production of LeRoi Jones's *Slave Ship* in New York.

A clear picture of the kind of devastating animosity which exists among certain competitive groups comes into focus from Detroit. *Black Theatre* #4 (April 1970), contains the following scathing critique from a representative of the Crescent Moon

Cultural Center:

> The Detroit Repertory Theatre is at present using the same old stereotyped, nothing negro [sic] plays to fill the gap in representing Detroit Black Theatre. The Black, revolutionary, culturally conscious folk of Detroit don't even patronize the DRT. The DRT's patrons are 95 percent white—the so-called "new, hip, white America." The other 5 percent are negro-colored-ignorant-unconscious veterans of that old cabin-in-the-sky cultural status of yesteryear; but almost unjustifiably so by gross ignorance.
> The Detroit Repertory Theatre: Heart of white cultural America, standing on the last leg of an off-off-white American theater, using whatever means necessary to survive . . . even *Black Theatre* magazine.[26]

It is this kind of divisiveness which has led to the early collapse of many theater companies. The existence of the majority of these groups is at best precarious: nearly all of them are financially insecure and many of them are artistically insecure as well. The need is for positive mutual support, not mutual destruction.

The long-established Karamu House in Cleveland, founded by Russell and Rowena Jelliffe in 1916, is still operating but with a difference. When the Jelliffes retired in 1963, blacks moved into policy-making positions which they had not previously held. Leatrice Emeruwa, writing in sympathy about Karamu in *Black World* (January 1973) says that only since 1970 has the institution announced that it has a "Black center of gravity." Yet "it is caught between a financial Scylla. If it appeals too much to the taste of the Black masses, it will probably lose the financial support of its white liberal benefactors. . . ."[27] When the Jelliffes retired, they left behind them a debt-free million-and-a-half dollar complex, and an endowment of almost that much.

The "move to radiate Blackness" to which Emeruwa also refers seems to be the appearance of new plays by local black playwrights: Lois McGuire, Margaret Taylor, Norman Jordan, and L. A. Gatewood. It was at Karamu that Langston Hughes began working while yet a high-school student, and it was for Karamu's Gilpin Players that he wrote *Mulatto*. It was Charles Gilpin, creator of the title role in Eugene O'Neill's *Emperor Jones*, who urged the Karamu Players to "take [themselves] seriously" and make Karamu "a real Negro theater." Many of those whose names are now in lights emerged from Karamu, including Roscoe Lee Browne, Ruby Dee, Greg Morris, and Gilbert Moses. They are part of the fulfillment of the Jelliffes' dream about which Langston Hughes wrote, upon the couple's retirement: "And so the seed/Becomes a flower."

## The Role of Educational Theater

Any survey of black theater as a whole must necessarily include educational theater. The black college has always been the heartbeat of black drama, keeping it alive when no one else would. The names of some of the directors most responsible for this support come easily to mind: Felicia D. Anderson, Fannin Belcher, Sterling Brown, Baldwin Burroughs, James W. Butcher, Anne M. Cook, Owen Dodson, Randolph Edmonds,

Monroe Gregory, William H. Owens, Thomas D. Pawley, and Waters Turpin.[28] To these illustrious names must be added that of Alain Locke, Howard University's philosopher and the spiritual godfather of all black art. Without these educators, some of the most important work of black playwrights would never have been staged, and many black people would never have seen a play. Moreover, an impressive number of performers and playwrights in the contemporary theater have been taught and inspired by those whose class rosters once included such names as N. R. Davidson, Jr., Ossie Davis, Gordon Heath, Earle Hyman, LeRoi Jones, Ted Shine, Hilda Simms, and Joseph Walker.

It was in the black colleges that student actors had the chance to be cast in all roles for which they qualified. This is in distinct contrast to the problem they invariably encounter in white theater departments: a paucity of roles. On the other hand, few of the traditional Negro colleges actually offered courses in theater, and existing programs of any kind were rarely independent of English departments. Moreover, Negro college administrators were notoriously unsupportive: many rehearsal sets had to be broken nightly to accommodate daily chapel services. These facts make all the more important the dedication of those black directors who literally refused to unhitch their wagons from their stars. A useful amplification of this whole problem of drama in black colleges is included in *The Black Teacher and the Dramatic Arts: A Dialogue, Bibliography, and Anthology*, edited by William R. Reardon and Thomas D. Pawley, a report of the Institute in Black Repertory Theatre held on the Santa Barbara campus of the University of California in the summer of 1968.

The institute itself is indicative of the spread of black theater to predominately white institutions, where it arrives in many forms. Much of the momentum, of course, is generated by black students. At York College of the City University of New York, for example, there is a completely amateur group called The Black Students' Players Guild, whose director is a counselor in a special program for inadequately prepared students. Unfortunately, what the Guild has produced thus far has also been inadequately prepared. At the opposite end of the collegiate pole is the University of Iowa's 1973 summer seminar, "The Black Scene: The Afro-American on Stage and Film." Sponsored by the Afro-American Studies Program, it is under the direction of Robert Corrigan and Darwin Turner, the latter a distinguished black drama critic. Among those scheduled as guest lecturers were Imamu Amiri Baraka, Ossie Davis, Owen Dodson, and Helen Armstead Johnson.

Playwright Loften Mitchell is professor of black drama at the State University of New York at Binghamton, and Roger Furman teaches a course in black theater history at New York University. William B. Branch—author of *In Splendid Error* and *A Medal for Willie*—spent a week at Smith College in 1971, where Jeffrey Tucker (MFA Smith, 1971), was then director of the Black Theatre Workshop. In 1970 Tucker directed scenes which included the work of Alice Childress, Langston Hughes, William Mackey, LeRoi Jones, Jimmy Garrett, and Lonne Elder. The *Daily Hampshire Gazette* of Northampton,

Massachusetts (March 7, 1970) made this observation about them: "Last weekend the Hallie Flanagan Studio Theater was the scene of a production by the Black Theatre Workshop that was worthy of note by the community—an entertainment at low cost and high reward that deserved a larger stage and a longer run."

Also working in New England are Archie Shepp and Paul Carter Harrison at the University of Massachusetts at Amherst. Shepp, a graduate of Goddard College in Vermont, is author of *Junebug Graduates Tonight*. Harrison, playwright and director, has had exposure at such institutions as Sacramento State College, Kent State University, and the University of Buffalo, as well as Howard University. His new book, *The Drama of Nommo*, "essays an aesthetic for the Black Theater based upon African retentions in African/American Life." Harrison's new play, *Top Hat*, was on a double bill at Player's Workshop in New York along with William Wellington Mackey's *Requiem for Brother X* (January 1973). Here in New York, too, novelist John Oliver Killens conducts a Creative Writing Workshop in the School of Arts at Columbia University. Its emphasis is on student work in progress, including drama and the screen play. Killens also conducts a similar workshop at Howard University.

At Brockport State College in New York is Dr. William H. Owens, who headed the drama program at South Carolina State College in Orangeburg for twelve years. A graduate of the University of Denver, Owens heads the speech department at Brockport and specializes in the oral interpretation of black drama for the classroom. He has conducted several workshops for in-service teachers in this area. Out in California, actor William Marshall teaches black drama in the Pan-African Studies Department at San Fernando Valley State College at Northridge. Using another approach, at Indiana University at Bloomington the Afro-American Studies Department and the Department of Theatre share the services of Dr. Winona Fletcher, who has been on extended leave from Kentucky State College. Unrelated to these programs was a graduate seminar in "Afro-American Drama: History and Criticism" offered in the summer of 1972 by Indiana's prestigious school of literary criticism, The School of Letters. Seminar students included persons with doctorates in ethnomusicology, theater history, comparative literature, and African drama.

There is growing emphasis on African drama in black colleges. Baldwin Burroughs at the Atlanta University Center, long an outstanding director, is also a specialist in African drama and has done much of his research in Africa. Howard University English department's Dr. John Lovell has been deeply involved in research for a book on African drama. Before going to Africa in 1972, he compiled more than 2,000 references and corresponded with more than 200 people on that continent. He followed up these activities by research in twelve countries located in all four sections of Africa.

Programs of high caliber continue in black colleges that have always had them and new promise comes from those institutions of learning that have recently entered the field. The availability of scripts, the number of anthologies, the increased supply of critical supporting materials, the stimulus of revolutionary theater, the support of foundations, and more enlightened administrators have all contributed to this promise. It is impossible to catalogue here all the people and places that have played a part, but even this brief survey shows that there has been expansion in educational theater similar to that in community and professional theater. As a matter of fact, the American Theater Association, formerly the American Educational Theater Association, has a Black Theater Project headed by scholar-playwright Errol Hill, chairman of the department of drama at Dartmouth College.

## Expansion in Allied Fields

One of the beneficent results of theatrical activity by and about Afro-Americans is the increased number of opportunities which have opened up or expanded in allied areas. Arthur Mitchell, Alvin Ailey, and Louis Johnson are all important black choreographers. Mitchell's Dance Theatre of Harlem has received a $1,250,000 three-year grant from The Ford Foundation, according to the latter's February 1, 1973, report.

> Founded in 1968 by Arthur Mitchell, the Dance Theatre was the first primarily black classical ballet company in the country. Enrolling approximately 1,000 students, the school offers classes in different forms of dance, as well as in theater-production techniques, for fees ranging from $2 to $20 a month. The company recently acquired and renovated a building in Harlem and has toured extensively in the United States, the Caribbean, and Europe.[29]

Alvin Ailey, choreographer, heads his own company. His *Revelations* is an artistically sensational plunge into the recesses of black and white life, and its star, Judith Jamison, is sheer magnificence. Her portrait was on the cover of *Dance Magazine* for November 1972. In the article, by Olga Maynard, the description of Jamison is worth noting:

> She appears on stage, larger than life, more an apparition than a performer, compelling us to look upon her as we might a temple dancer—with a sense of religiosity, of awe. Judith Jamison is the prototype of countless carven and sculptured goddesses, ancient priestesses of the dance. She resembles most, in her elegant, archaic beauty, the images that are consecrated to Yemanja, the dancing goddess of the Yoruba. Subtract any part of her almost six feet of height, color her any hue save her own, and she would cease to be Judith Jamison. She is unique because she is a gifted dancer, because she is female, and because she is black.[30]

The last of the above artists, Louis Johnson, was the choreographer for *Purlie* as mentioned previously, as well as for one of the most beautiful shows of the whole 1960-and-after period, *Lost in the Stars*, starring Brock Peters, with Gilbert Price as his son. The play caused even white men to cry, which circumstance undoubtedly led to the early closing of the show. Virgil Thomson, with tears in his own eyes, told Eubie Blake and Joe Jordan forty years ago: "White people don't like to go to the theater to cry about Negroes." They still do not. John Willis, in his 1973 *Theatre World* (p. 6), described

*Lost in the Stars* as "poignantly performed by Brock Peters and Gilbert Price," and listed it among productions that deserved greater support.

Johnson also choreographed the *Poetic Suite on Sojourner Truth*, written and performed by Glory Van Scott, in which the Louis Johnson Dance Theatre appeared. This was an NEC works-in-progress production of January 1972. It was called "Sojourner Truth Piece" when it appeared on CBS Repertoire Workshop television in July 1971. As a "Poetic Suite," it premiered at Lincoln Center's Library and Museum of the Performing Arts. Miss Scott is a dancer herself and has appeared with the American Ballet Theatre and the Katharine Dunham Company. Her acting credits, including her aforementioned role in *Bury the Dead*, are extensive. She, like Archie Shepps, is a graduate of Goddard College.

Opportunities have opened up as well for black directors, costumers, and musical directors. Edmund Cambridge, Vinnette Carroll, Ossie Davis, Al Fann, Woodie King, Robert Macbeth, Ernie McClintock, Gilbert Moses, Shauneille Perry, Lloyd Richards, Delano Stewart, Barbara Ann Teer, Douglas Turner Ward, and Dick Williams are all well-known directors. Their inclusion in this list is no comment upon quality. It is simply a demonstration of the expansion of opportunity that makes it easily possible to list so many names in the field and provides new stimulus for training and development as directors.

One of black theater's most talked-about costume designers is Bernard Johnson, whose maxicoats were early trend setters. His credits attest to his demand: Lennox Brown's *A Ballet Behind the Bridge* (NEC, 1972), Peebles' *Ain't Supposed to Die a Natural Death* and *Don't Play Us Cheap*, NEC's *Song of the Lusitanian Bogey* and *God Is a (Guess What?)*. For Melba Moore's March 1973 show at the Copacabana, he designed her gowns as well as her show. Also a costume designer, painter and gallery owner Robert Tadlock has been at work periodically off- and off-off-Broadway since the 1950s. One of his shows of this period was *The Egg and I*, for which Diana Sands won an Obie. To his credit are at least six plays, including the WPA production of Ed Bullins's *Goin' a Buffalo*. In February 1973 he designed the costumes for Robert Patrick's *Mercy Drop*. Gertha Brock is a woman with considerable reputation in the field also. Perhaps her biggest triumph was Elder's *Ceremonies In Dark Old Men*.

There has also been a growth of opportunity for blacks in set designing, lighting, and music. Whitney LeBlanc, Edward Burbridge, and Perry Bradford are noted set designers. Marshall Williams has done lighting for both NEC and the Owen Dodson production of *Medea in Africa*. One of the busiest of the current composers and conductors is Coleridge-Taylor Perkinson, who has written extensively for the theater. Evidence of his thorough musicianship was underlined by his appearance as guest conductor of the Symphony of the New World at Philharmonic Hall in February 1973. Margaret Harris, former music director for NEC, and Joyce Brown have made history as musical directors for Broadway hits: Harris for *Hair* and *Two Gentlemen of Verona*, and Brown for *Purlie*.

New critics have appeared too. In general, there are far more reviewers who write immediate analyses than critics who write later and more reflectively from a broad knowledge of drama and theater. Drama as used here refers to the play on a printed page which does not become theater until all the necessary forces have been brought to bear upon it: director, actors, set designer, costumer, lighting designer, choreographer, audience, and, when needed, music and musicians.

Long before black theater became a kind of community commodity, Dr. Darwin Turner, now of the University of Iowa, was a serious academic critic. His essays, noted in the bibliography for this chapter, are among the most valuable in an area largely ignored by black scholars, often for obvious reasons. Most of them attended universities where white drama professors either lacked knowledge or had antagonistic attitudes toward the truths of American theater history. In March 1973 a university professor in New York was still asking if there was really enough black drama for a whole course in it.

In *The Drama Review's* 1968 special issue on Black Drama, the aforementioned Larry Neal—now teaching at Yale—struggled with the dimensions of "a new Black Aesthetic" and tried to organize the popular and muddled rhetoric about an aesthetic for black theater. His judgment has matured since then, and the nature of its growth can be seen in his essay, "Into Nationalism, out of Parochialism," in *Performance* (April 1972). In 1968 he presented the case for rejection of Western art. In 1972 he was able to write: "Our theater should challenge the establishment theater; black artists must confront Western art, not withdraw from it." After reminding the reader how black sound dominates American musical sensibility, he suggests that "Part of what we should do now is take on the American theater sensibility and replace it with ours. Or, at least, place our statement in the arena" (p. 38).

Among others on the academic scene today are Toni Cade Bambara, a short-story writer at Rutgers, who contributed "Black Drama" to Addison Gayle's *The Crisis of the Intellectual* (1967), and Harold Cruse at the University of Michigan, who deals extensively—if not always clearly—with criticism and the playwright as an intellectual.

Fortunately for all Afro-American literature, very often good and frequently brilliant criticism of it in general emerges from the campus. Critical writing which explicates Afro-American aesthetics in general and prose and poetry specifically provides illuminating insights and supports for Afro-American drama. This is especially true when the body of work by James Baldwin or LeRoi Jones-Imamu Baraka, for example, is being considered. When it is, the critical approach to drama is direct. Among the scholars who provide brilliant illumination are Houston Baker, University of Virginia; Richard K. Barksdale, University of Illinois; Wilfred Cartey, Brooklyn College and Columbia University; John Henrik Clarke, Hunter College; Eugenia Collier, Baltimore Community College; Arthur P. Davis, Howard University; Stephen Henderson, Howard University; Blyden Jackson, University of North Carolina; Lance Jeffers,

Bowie State College; George Kent, University of Chicago; Richard A. Long, Atlanta University; Charles A. Ray, North Carolina Central University; and Saunders Redding, Cornell University.

Among those writing for general public consumption are Peter Bailey, an associate editor of *Ebony*, whose work also appears in *The New York Times*. Another who writes occasionally for the *Times* is Clayton Riley, formerly of the New York *Amsterdam News*. James P. Murray, current film critic for the *Amsterdam News*, according to that paper (March 17, 1973), became "the first black man to be elected to membership in the New York Film Critics Circle. . . ." The paper also refers to a statement attributed to Hollywood columnist Walter Burrell, in which he describes Murray as the "finest Black writer working today in the film industry." Among those who appear frequently in *Black World* is Carolyn Rodgers. Theater is highlighted each April in *Black World*'s annual theater issue.

The most spectacular phenomenon of the theater world is Melvin Van Peebles, whose activities have provided opportunities for countless others, including Afro-American publicity agents. Van Peebles received full cover treatment in *The New York Times Magazine*, August 20, 1972. Using profits from films he had produced successfully, Van Peebles was able to put two of his own shows on Broadway at the same time, a second one opening during the successful run of the first. This was indeed a "first"; it had never happened before in the whole history of the Great White Way. *Ain't Supposed to Die a Natural Death* played 325 performances between October 1971 and July 30, 1972, making it the fifth longest-running show of the season. The second show was *Don't Play Us Cheap*.

Van Peebles' films include *The Story of a Three Day Pass*, his first one; *Watermelon Man*, in which Godfrey Cambridge, made up as a white man, turned black mysteriously; and *Sweet Sweetback's Baadasss Song*, in which Van Peebles also starred. (He directed it, too.) The film established the vogue for the current wave of black films which celebrate their "baad" heroes. As *The New York Times*' Mel Gussow said of him, "Melvin Van Peebles is a phenomenon. He is the first black man in show business to beat the white man at his own game." Gene Wolsk, co-producer of *Ain't Supposed to Die a Natural Death*, says that as a businessman, "Melvin is in a class with John Paul Getty and the Rockefeller family." To himself, according to Gussow, Van Peebles is "a one-man conglomerate." It seems highly appropriate, then, that his one-man show at Philharmonic Hall, February 25, 1973, was called "Out There By Your Lonesome."

The growth of the black theater has also been marked by the emergence of a number of exciting new stars. Melba Moore literally soared to fame in *Purlie*, the musical adaptation of Ossie Davis's *Purlie Victorious*. Cleavon Little also achieved stardom in that show. Jonelle Allen, who began as a child professional on television, as mentioned earlier, achieved rank in *Two Gentlemen of Verona*, first in Joe Papp's Shakespeare-in-the-Park productions in Central Park, and later on Broadway where she captured a

1972 Theater World Award. Rosalyn Cash, now playing film leads, got the full media treatment for her NEC role in *Ceremonies in Dark Old Men*. People stood in line on Broadway to see her in Elder's *Melinda*. Cicely Tyson received super-star treatment from all directions, as well as awards, for her role in Elder's film, *Sounder*, and Ernest Gaines's television presentation, *The Autobiography of Miss Jane Pittman*. Like many others, she began on the stage. She was especially effective in the 1969 Cherry Lane Theatre production of *To Be Young, Gifted and Black*, Robert Nemiroff's collage of Lorraine Hansberry's assorted writing, including letters to him, her former husband.

Moses Gunn is another important new actor. Among his many fine performances is his *Othello* of 1970 for ANTA Theatre. The often caustic Richard Watts actually called him "the finest Othello of our time." The late Diana Sands was also a major figure on the stage—*The Owl and the Pussy Cat*; in film, *Doctor's Wives*; and she had her own Westinghouse television special. Her photograph even appeared in New York subway cars: "A beautiful woman is a voting woman." Yaphet Kotto, who replaced James Earl Jones in *The Great White Hope*, later starred in *Across 110th Street*, a film. Robert Guillaume had a long run in the even longer-running Village Gate's *Jacques Brel Is Alive and Well and Living in Paris*. It remained at the Village Gate for five years. One might also mention Ben Vereen, in training for the stage since childhood, able co-star with John Rubinstein (son of famed concert pianist Artur Rubinstein) in *Pippin*, a musical. Vereen had previously scored in *Hair* and as Judas Iscariot in the original cast of *Jesus Christ Superstar* (October 1971), for which he received a Theater World Award. His top award, however, came in March 1973, when he won a coveted Tony award for having been voted "Best Actor in a Musical" (*Pippin*). Another award-winning performance was given by Linda Hopkins in *Inner City*, an adaptation of Eve Merrian's *The Inner City Mother Goose*, which opened at the Ethel Barrymore Theatre on December 19, 1971. Her coveted Tony was for the "Best Supporting Actress in a Musical." The show was short-lived—ninety-seven performances excluding previews, but it catapulted her onto major television shows and back to Broadway for a one-woman show as Bessie Smith.

Although Ruby Dee cannot be called a new star, she added new dimensions to her career when she and James Earl Jones were acclaimed by critics in Athol Fugard's *Boesman and Lena* at Circle in the Square in September 1970. Tom Prideaux of *Life* said, "James Earl Jones and Ruby Dee are doing one of the finest acting jobs I have ever seen in the American theater." Clive Barnes had this to say: "Ruby Dee as Lena is giving one of the finest performances I have ever seen. It is complete—it has the quickness of life about it. You have no sense of someone portraying a role; her frail-sparrow figure, her frail unsubdued eyes, her voice, her manner, her entire being have a quality of wholeness that is rarely encountered in the theater." Of Jones he said, "James Earl Jones is remarkable as Boesman. His coarseness, bestiality, his abject lack of courage, are all somehow transfigured into a kind of reality that encompasses not only the brutalized facts of the character but also demonstrates the forces that produced him." This was Jones's first role after *The Great White Hope*. He has since won acclaim at the Anspacher Theater of the Shakespeare Festival, where Ruby Dee has earned high praise in *Wedding Band*. Leonard Harris of WCBS-TV called it "a marvelous play, superbly acted."

Although space does not permit mention of all the fresh new faces to appear on the acting scene, special note should be made of the following two people, who fall into categories all their own: the first of these is the previously mentioned, multitalented Micki Grant. Her *Don't Bother Me, I Can't Cope* flourished and was simultaneously performed at the Edison Theatre in New York, the Happy Medium Theatre in Chicago, and the Huntington Hartford Theatre in Los Angeles. The second person is actor Frederick O'Neal, who served three terms as president of Actor's Equity, having succeeded Ralph Bellamy in this position in 1964. In 1969 O'Neal succeeded Conrad Nagel as president of the international Association of Actors and Artists of America (AAAA). The eight unions of which it is formed are: Actors' Equity, Screen Actors Guild, Screen Actors Extras Guild, American Federation of Television and Radio Artists, the American Guild of Musical Artists, the American Guild of Variety Artists, the Hebrew Actors Union, and the Italian Actors Union. In 1975 O'Neal was still doing an occasional performance. In 1968 he was Joe Mott in Eugene O'Neill's *The Ice Man Cometh* at the Arena Stage in Washington, D. C. In 1970 he played in Blanche Yurka's production of *The Mad Woman of Chaillot*. Most recently he appeared in Yonkers, New York, along with Hilda Simms, in a local 1972 production of Loften Mitchell's *Tell Pharaoh*.

Many other names come to mind, but the above selections, each of which notes a dramatic personality with a nuance all its own, have been made primarily to demonstrate that the day of the one famous black actor is no longer with us. Solid, well-merited, outstanding reputations are being made on all levels, and the opportunities to make them now reach into all media and every type of theater. Such success, however, cannot alter the fact that survival in the world of theater has been historically precarious and remains so. An analysis of the most successful black people in the theater in any capacity reveals that they have two things in common: knowledge and control of their craft.

## Modern Drama and "the Black Experience"

A careful analysis of the subject matter of recent black plays inevitably leads to an analogy between the former, misleading, all-pervasive minstrel images and what is now being projected from the stage as "*the* black experience," an expression which in a different way also denies the varieties of black life. Audiences come to believe that all black families have junkie brothers, prostitute mothers and sisters, and rats as house guests, even bed mates. These are indeed truths for some families, and it is valid for naturalistic drama to deal with them. But to ignore the varieties of black experience is to turn one's back on the truth, artistically and otherwise.

Many of the newer plays, especially the revolutionary ones, seem to have a number of characteristics in common: 1) although they are purportedly addressed to black audiences, they actually address themselves to white ones. The "I hate Whitey" mono-logue has become not only a cliché, but a bore; 2) there is little compassion or love shown—sometimes none at all—even for other black people. One simply does not find the kind of love which exists between the boy and his grandmother in Louis Peterson's *Take A Giant Step*, and the two boys in Jones's *The Toilet* never discover that love and brotherhood could have saved them, even if it were scented with urine; 3) too many of the plays depict all blacks as monsters because they have been the victims of a monstrous society; 4) the plays, with exceptions of course, tend to deny the validity of middle-class existence, while making all lower-class experience brutal and savage, which it may or may not be; 5) the plays seldom become larger than life, and even unsophisti-cated audiences realize this. In his review of Bullins' *In the Wine Time* quoted earlier, S. E. Anderson wrote: "So what if the play doesn't move from being a reflection of Negroes doing their self-defeating thing. Ed Bullins does not offer black people any way out of the negative environment he depicts";[31] 6) they are self-flagellating because of obvious self-hate; 7) they suffer from an absence of art, whatever the individual playwright's conception of that may be. Although art form must not be dictated, it should be perceivable that the playwright, through his personal vision, must impose order on that which was random and chaotic. Many plays, however, seem to remain just that: random and chaotic.

## Problem Areas in Black Theater Today

A study of the evolution of the black theater from 1960 on leads to negative as well as positive conclusions. One of these is that without the assistance of foundations, there would be no black theater as we know it today. The various state councils on the arts, the private foundations, and corporate arms have together formed a theatrical *sine qua non*. The Ford Foundation, for example, in early 1973 gave NEC an additional $343,000 for two years, bringing its total support to $2,237,498 since the initial grant in 1967. On the national level, Vantile Whitfield is the director of the Expansion Arts Program, an arm of the National Endowment for the Arts. Expansion Arts supports community-based programs, which include black theater as well as other arts programs. Whitfield was the founder and artistic director of the Performing Arts Society of Los Angeles (PASLA) from 1966 to 1971, when he came to Washington, D. C. in his present capacity.

Funding problems create a multiplicity of other problems for black directors. Few of them can actually plan the traditional "season." Everything is contingent upon money, and many plays simply open whenever money makes it possible. Because of a combina-tion of money and personnel problems, many directors are literally one-man shows—playing all major roles from janitor to producer. Moreover, they often teach as they direct, or even before they can direct—something unheard-of in commercial theater.

Another problem facing black directors has been a dearth of material, in spite of the increase in the number of scripts available. Some directors are not aware of much of the existing material and the quality of many available scripts is poor. Moreover, most black plays have only one act. This may, at least in part, be attributed to the tendency to fashion a play from a single event, especially a current one. The emphasis, therefore, is on a dramatization which will be realistic and have immediate impact. Mounting three of these successfully in one night, with severely limited resources, depends upon the pliability of the director, and many who are now calling themselves directors are indeed directors in name only. (When one was mentioned recently, an actor said he would not let the man direct him across the street.) Even good directors, however, are hampered by a shortage of technical personnel and their production problems are sometimes enormously complex and occasionally unsolvable. The situation is aggravated by the fact that in spite of common problems, theater groups often have such abrasive relationships that the few resources they do have are dissipated rather than pooled, a fact to which the theatrical "obituary" columns attest.

An immense problem for black theater groups is location. Having decided that they should locate in ghetto areas, they offered themselves to people without a theater-going tradition. The effort to create one has been seriously eroded by the dual competition of television and black film. The other side of the coin is that those Afro-Americans who are theatergoers—and many are—are reluctant to go at night into slum neighborhoods.

A final and particularly unfortunate problem is posed by the fact that many blacks in the theater are still floundering in search of identity. This is not only lamentable but also ironic, since the American stage was shaped by the gifts of Afro-Americans and their pervasive influences. In return for their contribution, whites have made blacks ashamed of their native gifts, while continuing to earn riches and fame by adapting them. Blacks have long wished to reject their image as singers, dancers, and comedians. Thus most black playwrights have now turned their backs upon basic black contributions and comic vision, instead of adapting and building upon them. Perhaps more research, followed by more books for the general reader, will help young people in the theater act and react with greater pride. No other ethnic group has exerted as much influence upon the American stage.

That Afro-Americans continue to exert positive influence is seen in the following excerpt from John Willis's "The Season In Review: June 1, 1971–May 31, 1972," in his encyclopedic *Theatre World*.

> The healthiest aspect of the season was the increased number of "Black Theater" productions—by and with black talent. They are not only evolving into a commercial art, but also developing new talent. For the first time in Broadway's history, three black musicals were presented—two by the multitalented Melvin Van Peebles. His first production, *Ain't Supposed to Die a Natural Death*, had an approach that for some was too angry, and drove patrons from the theater. Succeeding productions, however, did not assault their audiences with messages, but provided pleasant entertainment. They also initiated new audiences to the magic of live theater—a vitally necessary project if the stage is to survive television and inferior films with lower admission prices.[32]

Even though Willis is totally incorrect about black musicals on Broadway—the Harlem Renaissance provided a whole decade of them, beginning with *Shuffle Along* in 1921 (see Chapter 21, *Black Influences in the American Theater:* Part I), the fact that an assessment was even made is significant testimony in itself. Whereas once theater and literary chroniclers were able to keep black writers and performers invisible, it is now impossible for them to do so, even those for whom integrity has never been a matter of conscience when truth was black. It is an unquestionable fact that over the past decade, as in earlier years, black achievement in the dramatic arts has not only profoundly enriched the American theater but has contributed to American culture as a whole.

## Notes

1. Richard Barksdale and Keneth Kinnamon, *Black Writers of America* (Macmillan, New York, 1972) pp. 320–21.
2. Charles F. Harris and John A. Williams, eds., *Amistad 2* (Vintage Books, New York, 1971).
3. As quoted in Helen Armstead Johnson, "Playwrights, Critics, and Audiences," *Negro Digest*, April 1968, pp. 18–19.
4. S. E. Anderson, *Black Culture Weekly*, January 27, 1967, p. 4. Anderson is identified in the journal's acknowledgments as "mathematician, essayist, poet."
5. "The loss consequent on colonialism and the alienation deriving from the movement away from rural traditions to urban political realities are reflected in one way or another in the thesis of the Negritude poets. To return symbolically to the source, to abnegate the loss, the alienation, the confusion, will be the prime intention and motive of the Negritude poets as they search through their single selves for a communal African authenticity. Thus things remembered, that had been lost—the entry into infancy, something long past—will link them, even as they seek a rebirth, to the beginnings of things. And since the child is, in African ontology, akin to the ancestor, the recalling of ancestors will be but a short step away from the plunging into those elements that lie at the beginning, at the birth. Infancy and ancestry, recalling and reidentifying, exile and return, will all color the poetry of the Negritude poets." Wilfred Cartey, "Exile and Return . . . Negritude," *Whispers from a Continent: The Literature of Contemporary Black Africa* (Random House, New York, 1969) pp. 217–18.
6. Arthur P. Davis and Saunders Redding, *Cavalcade* (Houghton Mifflin, New York, 1949) p. 569.
7. Lonne Elder, *Ceremonies in Dark Old Men*, in *New Black Playwrights*, William Couch, ed., (LSU Press, Baton Rouge, 1968), p. 111.
8. *Ibid.*, p, 124.
9. James Baldwin, Introduction to *The Amen Corner* (Dial Press, New York, 1968), p. xvi.
10. James Baldwin, *Blues for Mr. Charlie* (Dial Press, New York, 1964), p. 94.
11. Adrienne Kennedy, *The Owl Answers in New American Plays*, William M. Hoffman, ed. (Hill and Wang, New York, 1968), p. 254.
12. Produced by Neil Simon and written by Simon, Burt Bacharach, and Hal David.
13. Sara Fogg, unpublished thesis, p. 5. Translated from Albert Camus, *Les Justes* (Librairie Gallimard, Paris, 1950) and compared with *We Righteous Bombers* in *Black Drama in America*, Darwin Turner, ed. (Fawcett Publications, Greenwich, 1971), pp. 559–625. Comparison made at request of Helen A. Johnson as Fellow of the School of Letters, Indiana University.
14. Fogg, *op. cit.*, p. 7.
15. Clayton Riley, Introduction to *A Black Quartet: Four New Black Plays*, Ben Caldwell et al. (New Library, New York, 1970), pp. xx–xxi.

16. Helen Armstead Johnson, "Ododo," *Black World*, April 1971, p. 48.
17. Jessica B. Harris, "The National Black Theatre," *The Drama Review*, December 1972, p. 41.
18. *Ibid.*, p. 42.
19. Carlton Molette II, *Doctor B. S. Black* in *Encore*, XIV, 1970, pp. 28–57. The journal is the official publication of The National Association of Dramatic and Speech Arts founded by Randolph Edmonds. *Encore* is published at Spelman College.
20. Maryat Lee, "Street Theater in Harlem: Soul and Latin Theater—SALT," *Theatre Quarterly*, II, No. 8 (October–December 1972), pp. 35–43.
21. Harold Jackman, a devotee of the arts, was an especially close friend of Countee Cullen, Langston Hughes, Owen Dodson, and other writers. He established a collection in his own name at Atlanta University but later renamed it the Countee Cullen Collection after Cullen's death in 1946. The Harold Jackman Committee in New York continues to add to this collection. Ivie Jackman, sister of the late Harold, is chairman of that committee, and Edith Dodson, sister of Owen Dodson, is an active member of it. Each year the committee has an annual banquet at which it honors an outstanding person in the arts.
22. Ellen Stewart, "La Mama, ETC," *Theatre I: American Theater 1967–1968* (International Theater Institute of the United States, New York, 1969), p. 57. The other performers in *Thoughts* were Mary Alice, Jean Andalman, Martha Flowers, Robin Lamont, Baruk Levi, Barbara Montgomery, Jeffrey Mylett, Howard Porter, Sarallen, and E. H. Wright. The off-Broadway Theater DeLys premiere date for *Thoughts* was March 18, 1973.
23. *The Sunday Bulletin*, Philadelphia, December 3, 1972, Section 5.
24. Margaret Wilkerson, "Black Theatre in California," *The Drama Review*, December 1972, pp. 25–38.
25. *Ibid.*, p. 27.
26. *Black Theatre* #4, p. 3.
27. Leatrice W. Emeruwa, "Black Art and Artists in Cleveland," *Black World*, January 1973, pp. 23–33. This is a survey article which gives further perspective on Karamu House, especially current attitudes toward it.
28. Anderson, Virginia State College; Belcher, West Virginia State College; Brown, Howard University; Burroughs, Spelman; Butcher, Howard University; Cook, Howard University; Dodson, Howard University; Edmonds, Florida A & M in Tallahassee; Gregory, Howard University; Owens, South Carolina State College; Pawley, Lincoln University, Missouri; Turpin, Morgan State College.
29. *Ford Foundation LETTER*, February 1, 1973.
30. *Dance Magazine*, William Como, ed. "Judith Jamison," text by Olga Maynard and photos by Herbert Migdall, including cover. November 1972, p. 24.
31. Anderson, *op. cit.*, p. 7.
32. John Willis, ed., *Theatre World, 1971–1972 Season*, Vol. 28 (Crown Publishers, Inc., New York, 1973), p. 6.

# BIBLIOGRAPHY

Abramson, Doris E., *Negro Playwrights in the American Theatre, 1925–1959*. New York, Columbia University Press, 1969.

*American Playwrights on Drama* ed. Horst Frenz. New York, Hill and Wang, 1965.

Amis, Lola Jones, *Three Plays*. New York, Exposition Press, 1965.

*Anger and Beyond: The Negro Writer in the United States*, ed. Herbert Hill. New York, Harper and Row, 1966.

*Annotated Bibliography of New Publications in the Performing Arts*, Nos. 4 & 5. New York, The Drama Book Shop, January-June 1971.

*Annotated Bibliography of New Publications in the Performing Arts*, No. 6. New York, The Drama Book Shop, July-September 1971.

*Annotated Bibliography of New Publications in the Performing Arts*, Nos. 8 & 9. New York, The Drama Book Shop, January-June 1972.

Baldwin, James, *Blues for Mr. Charlie*. New York, Dial Press, 1964.

————, *The Amen Corner*. New York, Dial Press, 1968.

*Beyond the Angry Black*, ed. John A. Williams. New York, The New American Library, 1966.

*Black Arts: An Anthology of Black Creations*, ed. Ahmed Alhamisi and Harun Kofi Wangara. Detroit, Black Arts Publications, 1969.

*Black Drama: An Anthology*, eds. William Brasmer and Dominick Consolo. Columbus, Charles E. Merrill Publishing Co., 1970.

*Black Drama Anthology*, eds. Woodie King and Ron Milner. New York, Columbia University Press, 1972.

*Black Expression*, ed. Addison Gayle. New York, Weybright and Talley, 1969.

*Black Fire: An Anthology of Afro-American Writing*, eds. LeRoi Jones and Larry Neal. New York, William Morrow and Co., Inc., 1969.

*Black Theatre*, Nos. 1–6(1969–1972), ed. Ed Bullins. New York, The New Lafayette Theater.

Bolcom, William and Robert Kimball, *Reminiscing with Sissle and Blake*. New York, Viking, 1973.

Brawley, Benjamin, *The Negro Genius: A New Appraisal of the Achievement of the American Negro In Literature and the Fine Arts*. New York, Dodd, Mead, & Co., 1937.

Brown, Sterling, *Negro Poetry and Drama and The Negro In American Fiction*. New York, Atheneum, 1969.

Bullins, Ed, *Five Plays by Ed Bullins*. New York, The Bobbs-Merrill Co., 1968.

————, *Four Dynamite Plays*. New York, William Morrow & Co., Inc., 1972.

————, *The Duplex: A Black Love Fable in Four Movements*. New York, William Morrow & Co., Inc., 1971.

————, *The Theme is Blackness: The Corner and Other Plays*. New York, William Morrow & Co., Inc., 1973.

Caldwell, Ben, et. al., *A Black Quartet: Four New Black Plays*. New York, New Library, 1970.

Childress, Alice, *Mojo* and *String*. New York, Dramatists Play Service, Inc., 1971.

————, *Wine in the Wilderness*. New York, Dramatists Play Service, Inc., 1969.

*CLA Journal*, XI, No. 4 (June 1968), ed. Thermon O'Daniel. [Special Langston Hughes Number] Baltimore, The College Language Association, Morgan State College, 1968.

Connelly, Marc, *The Green Pastures*. New York, Court Book Co., 1929.

*Contemporary Black Drama*, eds. Clinton F. Oliver and Stephanie Sills. New York, Charles Scribner's Sons, 1971.

Cook, Mercer and Henderson, Stephen E., *The Militant Black Writer in Africa and The United States*. Madison, The University of Wisconsin Press, 1969.

Couch, William, *New Black Playwrights: An Anthology*. Baton Rouge, Louisiana State University Press, 1968.

Cruse, Harold, *The Crisis of the Negro Intellectual*. New York, William Morrow & Co., Inc., 1967.

Dean, Phillip Hayes, *American Night Cry*. New York, Dramatists Play Service, Inc., 1972.

————, *The Sty Of The Blind Pig*. New York, Dramatists Play Service, Inc., 1972.

————, *This Bird of Dawning Singeth All Night Long*. New York, Dramatists Play Service, Inc., 1971.

Douglas, Rodney K., *Voice of the Ghetto*. New York, Samuel French, Inc., 1968.

Duberman, Martin B., *In White America*. New York, The New American Library, 1964.

Ellison, Ralph, *Shadow and Act*. New York, Random House, 1964.

Emanuel, James, *Langston Hughes*. New Haven, College and University Press, 1967.

Emery, Lynne Fauley, *Black Dance in the United States from 1619 to 1970*. Palo Alto, Cal., National Press Books, 1972.

Farrison, William Edward, *William Wells Brown: Author and Reformer*. Chicago, The University of Chicago Press, 1969.

*Five Black Writers*, ed. Donald B. Gibson. New York, New York University Press, 1970.

Flanagan, Hallie, *Arena*. 1st ed. 1940; reprint New York, Benjamin Blom, Inc., 1965.

Fletcher, Tom, *The Tom Fletcher Story: 100 Years of the Negro in Show Business*. New York, Burdge & Co., Ltd., 1954.

Fox, Charles, *The Jazz Scene*. New York, Hamlyn, 1972.

Franklin, J. E., *Black Girl*. New York, Dramatists Play Service, Inc., 1971.

Frazier, E. Franklin, *Black Bourgeoisie*. New York, The Free Press, 1962.

————, *The Negro Church in America*. New York, Schocken Books, Inc., 1963.

*From the Ashes: Voices of Watts*, ed. Budd Schulberg. New York, The World Publishing Co., 1969.

Funke, Lewis, *The Curtain Rises: the Story of Ossie Davis*. New York, Grosset, 1971.

Gordone, Charles, *No Place to Be Somebody*. New York, The Bobbs-Merrill Co., Inc., 1969.

Green, Paul, *Out of the South: The Life of a People in Dramatic Form*. New York, Harper & Brothers, 1939.

Grimke, Angelina, *Rachael*. College Park, Md., McGrath Publishing Co., 1969.

Hansberry, Lorraine, *A Raisin in the Sun* and *The Sign in Sidney Brustein's Window*. New York, The New American Library, 1966.

*Harlem, USA*, ed. John Henrik Clarke. Berlin, Seven Seas Publishers, 1964.

Hatch, James V., *Black Image on the American Stage: A Bibliography of Plays and Musicals 1770–1970*. New York, DBS Publications, Inc., 1970.

Hatch, James V. and Shine, Ted, *Black Theatre USA, 1847–1972*. New York, The Free Press, 1973.

Hughes, Langston, *Five Plays by Langston Hughes*, ed. Webster Smalley. Bloomington, Indiana University Press, 1963.

Hughes, Langston and Meltzer, Milton, *Black Magic*. Englewood Cliffs, Prentice-Hall, 1967.

*Images of the Negro in American Literature*, eds. Seymour L. Gross and John Edward Hardy. Chicago, The University of Chicago Press, 1966.

Isaacs, Edith J. R., *The Negro in the American Theatre*. College Park, Md., McGrath Publishing Company, 1968.

John, Errol, *Moon on a Rainbow Shawl*. Evergreen Playscript. New York, Grove Press, Inc., 1958.

Jones, LeRoi, *Four Black Revolutionary Plays*. New York, Bobbs-Merrill Co., Inc., 1969.

———, *Slave Ship*. Newark, Jihad Productions, 1969.

———, *Home: Social Essays*. New York, William Morrow & Co., Inc., 1966.

———, *The Baptism* and *The Toilet*. Evergreen Playscript. New York, Grove Press.

———, *The Dutchman* and *The Slave*. New York, William Morrow & Co., Inc., 1964.

Knight, Etheridge, *Black Voices from Prison*. New York, Pathfinder Press, 1970.

*Langston Hughes, Black Genius: A Critical Evaluation*, ed. Thermon B. O'Daniel. [For the College Language Association] New York, William Morrow & Co., Inc., 1971.

Lewis, Allan, *American Plays and Playwrights of the Contemporary Theatre*. Revised edition. New York, Crown Publishers, 1970.

Locke, Alain, *The Negro and His Music/ Negro Art: Past and Present*. New York, Arno Press and *The New York Times*, 1969.

Margolies, Edward, *The Art of Richard Wright*. Carbondale, Southern Illinois University Press, 1969.

Marshall, Herbert and Stock, Mildred, *Ira Aldridge*. Carbondale, Southern Illinois University Press, 1968.

Mays, Benjamin E., *The Negro's God as Reflected in His Literature*. New York, Atheneum, 1968.

Miller, Elizabeth W., *The Negro in America: A Bibliography*. 2nd edition revised & enlarged by Mary L. Fisher. Cambridge, Harvard University Press, 1972.

Nathan, Hans, *Dan Emmett and the Rise of Early Negro Minstrelsy*. Norman, University of Oklahoma Press, 1962.

*New Plays from The Black Theatre*, ed. Ed Bullins. New York, Bantam Books, 1969.

Noble, Peter, *The Negro in Films*. 1st ed. 1948; reprint Port Washington, N.Y., Arno, 1969.

Patterson, Lindsay, *Black Theater*. New York, Dodd, Mead & Co., 1971.

Piro, Richard, *Black Fiddler*. New York, William Morrow and Co., Inc., 1971.

Richardson, Willis, *Plays and Pageants from The Life of the Negro*. Washington, D.C., The Associated Publishers, Inc., 1930.

Rollins, Charlemae H., *Black Troubadour: Langston Hughes*. New York, Rand McNally, 1971.

Russell, Charlie L., *Five on the Black Hand Side*. New York, Samuel French, Inc., 1969.

Shine, Ted, *Contributions: Three One-Act Plays*. New York, Dramatists Play Service Inc., 1970.

Sobel, Bernard, *A Pictorial History of Vaudeville*. New York, The Citadel Press, 1961.

Springer, John, *All Talking! All Singing! All Dancing!: A Pictorial History of the Movie Musical*. 2nd ed. paperbound. New York, The Citadel Press, 1970.

*Stereo Review*, Vol. 29, No. 5, November 1972 [on Sissle and Blake].

*The American Negro Reference Book*, ed. John P. Davis. Englewood Cliffs, Prentice-Hall, 1966.

*Theatre 1: American Theatre 1967–1968.* New York, International Theatre Institute, 1969.

*Theatre 3: The American Theatre 1969–1970.* New York, International Theatre Institute, 1970.

*Theatre 4: The American Theatre 1970–1971.* New York, International Theatre Institute, 1972.

*Theatre Quarterly,* II, No. I, 1972.

*Theatre World, 1971–1972 Season,* Vol. 28, ed. John Willis. New York, Crown Publishers, Inc., 1973.

*The Black Teacher and the Dramatic Arts,* eds. William R. Reardon and Thomas D. Pawley. Westport, Negro Universities Press, 1970.

*The Drama Review: Black Theatre Issue,* Vol. 16, No. 4, December 1972.

*The Drama Review: Black Theatre,* Vol. 12, No. 4, Summer 1968.

*The Free Southern Theater by The Free Southern Theater,* eds. Thomas C. Dent, Richard Schechner, and Gilbert Moses. New York, The Bobbs-Merrill Co., 1969.

*The Negro Caravan,* eds. Sterling A. Brown, Arthur P. Davis, and Ulysses Lee. New York, The Arno Press and *The New York Times,* 1969.

*The New Negro,* ed. Alain Locke. New York, Atheneum, 1970.

*The Oxford Companion to the Theatre,* ed. Phyllis Hartnell. New York, Oxford University Press, 1951.

Turner, Darwin T., *Afro-American Writers.* Goldentree Bibliographies. New York, Appleton-Century-Crofts, 1970.

Walcott, Derek, *Dream on Monkey Mountain and Other Plays.* New York, Farrar, Straus and Giroux, 1970.

Ward, Douglas Turner, *Two Plays: Happy Ending* and *Day of Absence.* New York, The Third Press, 1972.

———, *The Reckoning.* New York, Dramatists Play Service, Inc., 1970.

White, Edgar, *The Rastifarian* and *Dija: Two Black Children's Plays,* in *Scripts,* I, October 1972, pp. 12–17.

———, *Underground: Four Plays.* New York, Farrar, Straus and Giroux, 1970.

Zeidman, Irving, *The American Burlesque Show.* New York, Hawthorn Books, Inc. 1967.

# 23

## *The Black Contribution to American Letters: Part I*

### *Arna Bontemps*

**Poetry**

Early in the nineteenth century Americans of African descent, still somewhat bewildered by the experience which had brought them into bondage in the New World, began to find a strangely satisfying expression for their thoughts and feelings in music. The songs which resulted, now known as Negro spirituals, have not only been a powerful musical influence on the nation as a whole but have been accepted with approval, even acclaim, throughout most of the world. It is well to remember, however, that the spirituals owe as much to their words as to their music. They mark a beginning of poetic expression as influential on subsequent poets as the music has been on later composers.

Actually, the lyrics of songs like "Roll, Jordan, Roll" and "Swing Low, Sweet Chariot" were not the first attempts at verse by Afro-Americans in the United States. An Indian raid on the little Massachusetts town of Deerfield in 1746 is commemorated in couplets by a semiliterate slave girl named Lucy Terry. She called her account "Bars Fight" and began it with these lines:

> August 'twas the twenty fifth
> Seventeen hundred forty-six
> The Indians did in ambush lay
> Some very valiant men to slay
> The names of whom I'll not leave out.
> Samuel Allen like a hero fout
> And though he was so brave and bold
> His face no more shall we behold.

Though nothing more by her survives and no more is known of her interest in verse, Lucy Terry may have been still alive in Massachusetts when the child who became Phillis Wheatley was brought from Senegal in 1761, and when a decade later, "A Poem by Phillis, A Negro Girl in Boston, on the Death of the Reverend George Whitefield" was published. Phillis was 17 at the time, and this poem marked the beginning of a unique writing career.

Writing by slaves was not entirely an American phenomenon, as anyone familiar with the works of Terence and Epictetus, in Rome and Greece respectively, may recall.

741

Nor did all of them, despite their talents, succeed in winning freedom by their writing. Both Terence and Phillis Wheatley did, however, and when Phillis's health failed, she was advised by Boston doctors to take an ocean voyage. She embarked for England and there her *Poems on Various Subjects: Religious and Moral* was first published in 1773. The reception this volume received made her for a time, it has been said, the best-known of living American poets. Written in the spirit of John Calvin and in the manner of her English and American contemporaries, Phillis's poems were commended by George Washington and other prominent figures. But on the whole the poetry written in the American colonies in 1773, including that by Phillis, is of limited interest to poetry lovers in the twentieth century. The same can be said of the poetic composition by Jupiter Hammon which appeared as a broadside in 1760 under the title "An Evening Thought: Salvation by Christ, with Penitential Cries." A slave preacher on Long Island, Hammon appears to have been the first Negro American ever to see in print lines he had himself written.

Legal restrictions on the education of slaves were introduced in the American colonies after the period of Phillis Wheatley and Jupiter Hammon. Their purpose was to keep from the slave news and propaganda likely to incite a lust for freedom. During the French Revolution and the Haitian Insurrections possible rebellion was regarded as a serious matter, and slave uprisings in Virginia, South Carolina, and elsewhere added to the anxiety. Penalties were imposed on owners or other persons who violated the restrictions on learning. Escaped slaves who later wrote autobiographies have left records of the mental anguish this intellectual deprivation caused them.

Denied the ABC's, slave poetry went underground, so to speak. Self-expression was obliged to become oral—as it had been for so many of the black Americans' ancestors in Africa. Whether or not this was a blessing in disguise is a matter of opinion, but one fact is clear. The suppression of book learning by slaves coincided with the earliest musical and lyrical expression in the form which became known later as spirituals. The survival of "Roll, Jordan, Roll," for example, among the slaves from the United States isolated on a Caribbean island since 1824, would seem to place the beginnings of these songs very early in the nineteenth century or late in the eighteenth, allowing for the time it usually took such songs to develop and become generally known. Thus the elegies, commemorations, and devotional poems of Phillis Wheatley and Jupiter Hammon gave way to laments from the slave quarters such as:

> I know moonlight, I know starlight
>   I lay this body down
> I walk in the graveyard, I walk through the graveyard
>   To lay this body down.
>
> I lay in the grave and stretch out my arms,
>   I lay this body down,

I go to the judgment in the evening of the day
   When I lay this body down,
And my soul and your soul will meet the day
   I lay this body down.

or

Bright sparkles in the churchyard
   Give light unto the tomb;
Bright summer, spring's lover—
   Sweet flowers in their bloom.

My mother once, my mother twice, my mother, she'll rejoice,
In the Heaven once, in the Heaven twice, she'll rejoice.
May the Lord, He will be glad of me
In the Heaven, He'll rejoice.

    This, then, was the kind of oral expression that replaced written poetry by Negro Americans during the abolitionist campaign, the Civil War, and the Reconstruction. Of course there were minor exceptions, and at least one that must be considered major. Among the free men of color, as they were called in Louisiana, a strong French influence persisted and stimulated many broad cultural interests. Young black men of talent were sent to Paris to be educated. Among them were poets like Armand Lanusse, Pierre Dalcour, and most important, Victor Sejour, who later became a successful French dramatist and moved in literary circles in which Alexandre Dumas was prominent. In their youth in New Orleans these three Louisiana poets, with a group of their associates, produced a collection called *Les Cenelles*, published in 1845, the first anthology of American Negro poetry. Included was "Epigram" by Lanusse which, as translated by Langston Hughes, shows how far the *Les Cenelles* poets and the free men of color of Louisiana were, culturally, from the slaves who created spirituals:

"Do you not wish to renounce the Devil!"
Asked a good priest of a woman of evil
Who had so many sins that every year
They cost her endless remorse and fear.

"I wish to renounce him forever," she said,
"But that I may lose every urge to be bad,
Before pure grace takes me in hand,
Shouldn't I show my daughter how to get a man?"

    Meanwhile, farther north, George Moses Horton, a slave who had somehow become known to the editor of the *Raleigh Register* in North Carolina, Weston R. Gales, published in 1829 a slender volume of verse under the title *Hope of Liberty*. Gales judged Horton to be about 32 at the time. Already, it seems, the slave poet had become a well-known figure among the college students at Chapel Hill, where he may have been employed, and found it possible to realize a bit of income from his verses. The nature of this writing can only be guessed at, since none of it appears to have survived, but circumstances would not lead one to think that it was passionate antislavery propaganda. Many of the students for whom Horton wrote and who evidently paid him were children of slaveholding families. Moreover, Horton retained in later life a noticeable capacity for humor, and it has been surmised that the poems with which he entertained the students at the University of North Carolina may have been in this vein.

As the title of his first collection indicates, Horton hoped to earn from the sale of his poetry enough money to buy his freedom. He did not succeed, and his attitude changed.

> Alas! and am I born for this,
>   To wear this slavish chain?
> Deprived of all created bliss,
>   Through hardship, toil, and pain?
>
> How long have I in bondage lain,
>   And languished to be free?
> Alas! and must I still complain,
>   Deprived of liberty?

In 1865, after the Union armies had won for him the emancipation his poems had failed to achieve, a second volume of Horton's verses was published in Raleigh under the title *Naked Genius*. By then, however, he was living in Philadelphia, where he seems to have been regarded more as a "character" than as a natural-born poet. In any case, his second and last book contains stanzas which throw a certain light on his early reputation at Chapel Hill.

> My duck bill boots would look as bright,
> Had you in justice served me right;
> Like you, I then could step as light,
>   Before a flaunting maid.
> As nicely could I clear my throat,
> And to my tights my eyes devote;
> But I'd leave you bare, without the coat
>   For which you have not paid.
>
> Then boast and bear the crack,
> With the sheriff at your back,
> Huzzah for dandy Jack,
> My jolly fop, my Jo!

A contemporary of Horton's in Philadelphia was Frances Ellen (Watkins) Harper, whose *Poems on Miscellaneous Subjects* had been published in that city in 1854, when she was 29 years old. Widely popular as an "elocutionist," Mrs. Harper's readings of her poems undoubtedly helped the sales of her book. Ten thousand copies were sold in the first five years, and it was reprinted three times thereafter before her second work, *Moses, a Story of the Nile*, appeared in 1869. Devoted to the cause of freedom, as most poets in the middle of the nineteenth century were, especially black Americans, she promptly came to grips with this theme:

> I ask no monument, proud and high,
> To arrest the gaze of the passer-by;
> All that my yearning spirit craves
> Is bury me not in a land of slaves.

Seven years after the publication of her first little volume, the war of liberation having begun and Mrs. Harper having established herself very favorably in the public eye as a Negro poet and a shining example (along with Frederick Douglass and other platform personalities) of what the black American might become in freedom, she began to contemplate a provocative subject, about which she wrote to Thomas Hamilton, editor of the *Anglo-African*, a recently established monthly magazine: "If our talents are to be recognized we must write less of issues that are particular and more of feelings that are general. We are blessed with hearts and brains that compass more than ourselves in our present plight. . . . We must look to the future which, God willing, will be better than the present or the past, and delve into the heart of the world."

Where she had conceived the notion that slavery was "particular" and not to be equated with the "general" craving of mankind for freedom is not indicated, but the point she raised has now been debated for more than a century and still remains crucial in any consideration of the place of the Afro-American in the arts, in American culture, as creator or as subject. It is therefore worth a moment to contemplate some of the themes Frances Ellen Harper favored when not writing about the specific problem that confronted her people. The evils of strong drink was one of these. Another was childhood, its innocence and blessedness. In "The Double Standard" she treats still another:

> Crime has no sex and yet today
>  I wear the brand of shame;
> Whilst he amid the gay and proud
>  Still bears an honest name.
>
>
> . . . .
>
> Yes blame me for my downward course,
>  But Oh! remember well,
> Within your homes you press the hand
>  That led me down to hell.
>
>
> . . . .
>
> No golden weights can turn the scale
>  Of Justice in His sight;
> And what is wrong in woman's life
>  In man's cannot be right.

*Sketches of Southern Life*, Mrs. Harper's third book, was published in 1873 and is notable for the language it put into the mouths of its black characters. While avoiding dialect, as it was later to be used and popularized by Paul Laurence Dunbar, she nevertheless sought to suggest the flavor of Afro-American speech through characteristic patterns, phrases, and nuances, a technique not unrelated to those used in the twentieth century by such writers as James Weldon Johnson and Langston Hughes.

Mrs. Harper was a frequent contributor to *Godey's Lady's Book* and other periodicals of the day. Understandably, she showed a fondness for the ballad in its most sentimental form, and it may be assumed that these pleased audiences who came to hear her public readings, especially one such as "The Dying Bondman," which began:

> By his bedside stood the master
> Gazing on the dying one,
> Knowing by the dull gray shadows
> That life's sands were almost run.
>
> "Master," said the dying bondman,
> "Home and friends I soon shall see;
> But before I reach my country,
> Master write that I am free."

and ended some stanzas later with:

> Eagerly he grasped the writing;
> "I am free!" at last he said.
> Backward fell upon the pillow.
> He was free among the dead.

Her final collection of poems was *The Sparrow's Fall and Other Poems*, but she continued to write prose, though on the whole less successfully.

Of her contemporaries and immediate successors among black American poets at least three are remembered. James Madison Bell's collected *Poetical Works* was published in 1904. John Wesley Holloway, a member of the famous Jubilee Singers of Fisk University and one of the first black schoolteachers in Georgia, anticipated Dunbar in the writing and publishing of poems in Negro dialect. George Marion McClellan, whose background was somewhat similar to Holloway's, appeared frequently in periodicals during the same period, though his volume *The Path of Dreams* was not collected until 1916. All told, more than thirty volumes of poetry by black Americans were published between Phillis Wheatley's collection and Dunbar's first.

The routine and format as well as the substance of minstrel-show entertainment originated with Afro-American slaves in the United States around 1820. Constance Rourke noted in her *American Humor* (1931), "Every plantation had its talented band that could crack jokes, and sing and dance to the accompaniment of banjo and bones." She added, significantly, "There is a record of at least one of these bands that became semiprofessional and traveled from plantation to plantation giving performances." After emancipation the steps from semiprofessionalism to professionalism were completed, with the results that are now familiar. Paul Laurence Dunbar's lyrics came at the high tide of minstrel popularity.

A son of former slaves, Paul Laurence Dunbar greeted the twentieth century with *Lyrics of a Lowly Life* (1896), a book which won for him a national reputation and enabled him to pursue a literary career for the rest of his life. Undoubtedly helped by the minstrel tradition, his popularity was at first based mainly on poems written in the broad dialect of plantation folk.

In another sense, however, his writing is in the tradition of Robert Burns, a poet dear to literate black Americans who emerged from plantation slavery. Dunbar's life was short, 1872 to 1906, and marred by declining health and personal problems. Other volumes of his verses preceded and followed the *Lyrics*. *Oak and Ivy*, his first published work, was privately printed in 1893 while he was employed as an elevator operator in Dayton, Ohio. Dunbar had graduated from high school in that city and written the class poem, but he had been unable to attend college. A second volume, *Majors and Minors*, followed in 1895. Neither of these attracted wide attention but they won enough approval to provoke a strong and influential introduction by William Dean Howells to *Lyrics of a Lowly Life*. His subsequent books of verse include *Lyrics of Love and Laughter* (1903), *Lyrics of Sunshine and Shadow* (1905), and *Complete Poems* (1913). The latter has never been out of print, and it is found to contain, along with the dialect poems that made him famous, many poems in standard English, some of which provide the lyrics for songs which remain well-known and loved. "Dawn" is an example:

> An angel, robed in spotless white.
> Bent down and kissed the sleeping Night.
> Night woke to blush; the sprite was gone.
> Men saw the blush and called it Dawn.

Another is "Who Knows?"

> Thou art the soul of a summer's day,
> Thou art the breath of the rose.
>   But the summer is fled
>   And the rose is dead
> Where are they gone, who knows,
>   who knows?
>
> Thou art the blood of my heart o' hearts,
> Thou art my soul's repose,
>   But my heart grows numb
>   And my soul is dumb.
> Where art thou, love, who knows,
>   who knows?

Thou art the hope of my after years—
Sun of my winter snows,
    But the years go by
    'Neath a clouded sky.
Where shall we meet, who knows,
    who knows?

A contemporary of Dunbar's was James Weldon Johnson, but Johnson's first collection of poems was not published until eleven years after Dunbar's death. In the days when the two were acquainted, Johnson was known mainly for his popular song lyrics, including one, "Lift Every Voice and Sing," which since its composition in 1900 has become a kind of national anthem for black Americans. His *Fifty Years and Other Poems* (1917), ended what had begun to seem like a mournful silence by black poets in the wake of Dunbar's passing.

True, during the early 1900s, Fenton Johnson of Chicago made occasional contributions to magazines like *Others* and *Poetry: A Magazine of Verse*, and three women poets, Angelina W. Grimké, Anne Spencer, and Georgia Douglas Johnson were writing though not being published; but William Stanley Braithwaite, the only black poet to emerge in this period in the United States, was unrecognized as a Negro American either in his book reviews for the *Boston Transcript*, his yearly anthologies of magazine verse, or his two early volumes of poetry, *Lyrics of Life and Love* (1904), and *The House of Falling Leaves* (1908).

James Weldon Johnson's "Fiftieth Anniversary Ode" in 1913 commemorating the Emancipation Proclamation, was seen by Braithwaite as the first move by a black poet to disengage from whatever it was that had recently held him in thrall. The poem's reappearance in Johnson's *Fifty Years and Other Poems* was confirmation. While Braithwaite seems to have picked the right year for the first sign of the "disengagement," it is now possible to question his estimate of the influence of this particular book. Actually, Johnson's most significant poetic achievement was still a decade in the future, when his collection of folk sermons in verse was to be published as *God's Trombones* in 1927.

The year 1917 is also noteworthy in the field of black American poetry as the year in which Claude McKay's poem "The Harlem Dancer" appeared in *The Seven Arts* magazine under the pen name of Eli Edwards. When this poem reappeared in McKay's *Harlem Shadows* (1922), along with others so warm and fragrant they almost drugged the senses, things immediately began to happen. A chorus of new voices,* led by McKay, Jean Toomer, Langston Hughes, Countee Cullen, and some half-dozen others, helped to turn the twenties into a golden decade for black letters, known as the Harlem Renaissance.

Interestingly, although Braithwaite recognized McKay as the first of these new voices, he regarded him as "a genius meshed in [a] dilemma." It bothered Braithwaite

---

*To these names most certainly must be added that of Arna Bontemps himself, who won the *Crisis* magazine poetry prize in 1926 with his poem "Nocturne at Bethesda."—M. M. S.

that McKay seemed to "waver between the racial and the universal notes." At one time he seemed to be "contemplating life and nature with a wistful sympathetic passion." At another he was a "strident propagandist, using his poetic gifts to clothe arrogant and defiant thoughts." His "Spring in New Hampshire" and "The Harlem Dancer" were instances of the former, his "If We Must Die" of the latter. But a generation later it was "If We Must Die" that Winston Churchill quoted as climax and conclusion of his oration before the joint houses of the American Congress when he was seeking to draw this nation into the common effort in World War II. McKay had written it as the black American's defiant answer to lynching and mob violence in the southern states. Churchill made it the voice of the embattled Allies as he read:

> If we must die—let it not be like hogs
> Hunted and penned in an inglorious spot,
> While round us bark the mad and hungry dogs,
> Making their mock at our accursed lot.
> If we must die—oh, let us nobly die,
> So that our precious blood may not be shed
> In vain; then even the monsters we defy
> Shall be constrained to honor us though dead!
> Oh, Kinsmen! We must meet the common foe;
> Though far outnumbered, let us show us brave,
> And for their thousand blows deal one deathblow!
> What though before us lies the open grave?
> Like men we'll face the murderous, cowardly pack,
> Pressed to the wall, dying, but fighting back!

Obviously neither Churchill nor McKay had at that time considered the possibilities of nonviolence. The poem does show, however, how a short span of years and certain historical events can alter the meaning of a literary work, as well as the risk involved in prematurely trying to separate the local or special subject from the universal.

McKay had come to the United States from his native Jamaica, British West Indies, to study agriculture at Tuskegee Institute and later at Kansas State University. He had already published his first book, *Songs of Jamaica* (1911), mainly in the Jamaican dialect, while serving in the island constabulary, and followed it with another, *Constab Ballads* (1912). It took him less than three years to change his mind about agriculture as a career and head for New York and the literary life. In the course of a trip abroad he published in England in 1920 a small collection of lyrics under the title *Spring in New Hampshire*. On his return to America he became associate editor of the *Liberator* under Max Eastman. *Harlem Shadows* (1922), was his first American publication. It contained most of the poems in the British collection as well as a number of new ones. For long periods thereafter McKay traveled and lived abroad, writing mostly prose. Not until his death in 1948 was another volume of his poems published, and this was the *Selected Poems* (1953), bringing together the best of his early work and adding some poems written after his final homecoming to the United States and conversion to Roman Catholicism.

But the critic Braithwaite, who in his annual *Anthologies of Magazine Verse* had published Spoon River poems by Edgar Lee Masters, chants by Vachel Lindsey, free verse by Carl Sandburg, and early work by many other important American poets before they appeared in other books, reserved his highest praise for Jean Toomer, among the poets of the black Renaissance. Of him he wrote:

> ... In Jean Toomer, the author of *Cane*, we come upon the very first artist of the race, who with all an artist's passion and sympathy for life, its hurts, its sympathies, its desires, its joys, its defeats and strange yearnings, can write about the Negro without the surrender or compromise of the artist's vision. So objective is it, that we feel that it is a mere accident that birth or association has thrown him into contact with the life he has written about. He would write just as well, just as poignantly, just as transmutingly, about the peasants of Russia, or the peasants of Ireland, had experience brought him in touch with their existence. *Cane* is a book of gold and bronze, of dusk and flame, of ecstasy and pain, and Jean Toomer is a bright morning star of a new day of the race in literature.

Despite such reverberations, however, both Toomer and McKay were soon to be eclipsed by the twin stars among the younger Harlem poets of the twenties, Langston Hughes and Countee Cullen, who appeared almost simultaneously and achieved national recognition for their role in the Harlem Renaissance.

Hughes's career as a writer may be said to have begun when he was a high-school student in Cleveland, Ohio. His first poem in a national magazine appeared in *The Crisis* in 1921. It had been written the summer following his graduation, and he called it "The Negro Speaks of Rivers":

> I've known rivers:
> I've known rivers ancient as the world and
>    older than the flow of human blood in
>    human veins.
>
> My soul has grown deep like the rivers.
>
> I bathed in the Euphrates when dawns were young.
> I built my hut near the Congo and it lulled me to sleep.
> I looked upon the Nile and raised the pyramids above it.
> I heard the singing of the Mississippi when
>    Abe Lincoln went down to New Orleans,
>    and I've seen its muddy bosom turn all
>    golden in the sunset.
>
> I've known rivers:
> Ancient, dusky rivers.
>
> My soul has grown deep like the rivers.

This poem by a recent high-school graduate did more than launch a writing career. Among the poems written in the United States since 1921 there are few, if any, that have been more widely read. It has been reprinted scores and scores of times and translated into so many languages the author has been unable to keep up with them. *The Weary Blues*, Hughes's first book of poems, appeared five years later, and many volumes have followed, all of them marked by an ease of expression and a naturalness of feeling that make them seem almost as if they had never been composed at all. Hughes's art can be likened to that of the creators of jazz. His sources are street music. His language is Harlemese. In his way he is an American original.

Countee Cullen was in many ways quite different. Educated in the public schools of New York City, he turned to standard models for his poetry, from John Keats to E. A. Robinson. But if the forms were old, the ideas that went into Cullen's sonnets and quatrains were brand new in American poetry. This poem, one of his earliest, is an indication:

> I doubt not God is good, well-meaning, kind,
> And did He stoop to quibble could tell why
> The little buried mole continues blind,
> Why flesh that mirrors Him must someday die,
> Make plain the reason tortured Tantalus
> Is baited by the fickle fruit, declare
> If merely brute caprice dooms Sisyphus
> To struggle up a never-ending stair.
> Inscrutable His ways are, and immune
> To catechism by a mind too strewn
> With petty cares to slightly understand
> What awful brain compels His awful hand.
> Yet do I marvel at this curious thing:
> To make a poet black, and bid him sing!

He was a student at New York University when he wrote the above work, and *Color* (1925), his first collection of poems, was published by Harper and Brothers in his senior year, after many individual poems had first appeared in leading American magazines. The book won him a Gold Award for literature from the Harmon Foundation as well as widespread critical approval. Cullen received a master's degree from Harvard the following year, and won a John Simon Guggenheim Fellowship for creative writing which enabled him to spend two years in France. Meanwhile, in 1927 his *The Ballad of the Brown Girl* and *Copper Sun* were published. Returning to New York City, he became and remained a public school teacher for the rest of his life. Two books of prose and two more collections of his poems were issued before his death in 1946. A year later his own selections from all his poems (*The Black Christ* [1929] and *The Medea and Other Poems* [1935]) were brought together posthumously in *On These I Stand*.

Frank Horne, Helene Johnson, Gwendolyn Bennett, Donald Jeffrey Hayes, and Waring Cuney were among the contemporaries of Hughes and Cullen in the Harlem Renaissance whose poems continue to reappear in anthologies such as *American Negro Poetry* (edited with an Introduction and Biographical Notes on the poets by Arna Bontemps, Hill and Wang, 1963), in schoolbooks and elsewhere. Sterling Brown's poetry also began appearing in this period, but it became better known in 1934 when his *Southern Road* was published. By then the Renaissance was over in Harlem. Its poets had been scattered, and it was at once apparent that Brown's folk values, authentic and deeply felt, drew more from the rural environment surrounding the colleges in which he had been teaching than from the Harlem haunts that inspired Langston Hughes and Waring Cuney.

Since the Harlem period, black poets in the United States have appeared in procession rather than in groups, bands, or clutches; but though thin, the line has remained unbroken. Margaret Walker won the Yale University Younger Poets award in 1942 with her volume *For My People*, the title poem of which has become a favorite of black speakers and readers. Her "Molly Means" has been popular with verse choirs, but neither has received warmer critical approval than her "October Journey." Gwendolyn Brooks' first book was *A Street in Bronzeville* (1945). Her *Annie Allen*, which followed in 1949, was awarded the Pulitzer Prize for poetry, the first time this honor had been accorded to a black American writer. A collection for children called *Bronzeville Boys and Girls* (1956), was followed by a book of fiction and another book of poems, *The Bean Eaters* (1960), and these in turn led to *Selected Poems* in 1963.

Meanwhile, Owen Dodson's poems were published in 1946 under the title *Powerful Long Ladder*. Despite the implication of the title, these clearly showed the influence of the New Poetry on a black poet. The two books of Melvin B. Tolson's poetry represent both traditional and contemporary attitudes toward his material. *Rendezvous With America* (1944) shows the influence of Langston Hughes and Afro-American folklore. Tolson's *Libretto for the Republic of Liberia* (1953), while treating a black theme, is an exercise in new poetics. It won its author honors from the government of Liberia.

More recent black poets include Robert Hayden (*A Ballad of Remembrance* [1962]), M. Carl Holman, Margaret Danner, Gloria C. Oden (*The Naked Frame* [1962]), Russell Atkins, James A. Emanuel, Samuel Allen, and Conrad Kent Rivers. As we shall see in the following chapter, a new generation, sparked by LeRoi Jones (*Preface to a Twenty-Volume Suicide Note* [1961]) has since the sixties become preoccupied by experimentation in verse and the use of subject matter close to the heart of black Americans and their cause.

## Prose

Whatever else may be said of it, black American writing in the United States has been from first to last, as Saunders Redding once observed, a "literature of necessity." In what sense and to what extent this statement might be applied to all American writing need not detain us here. It is useful to recall, nevertheless, that the cause of the slave, his crying need for human freedom, became as intimate a part of the romantic movement as were the surge of democratic ideals in the nation as a whole and the growing assurance of the perfectibility of the individual.

Slave narratives, a most significant body of literature, offer a starting point and a key to the study of black prose. Just as a kind of poetic tradition stemmed from the lyrics of the spirituals, the work songs, and the playtime rhymes of slave folk, so a prose tradition influential on later black writers appears to have originated with the slave narrative. Two unpublished Ph.D. theses should be noted at this point: Marion Wilson Starling, *The Slave Narrative: Its Place in American Literary History* (New York University, 1946), and Charles H. Nichols, *A Study of the Slave Narrative* (Brown University, 1948). More recently Richard Wright, Ralph Ellison and James Baldwin have drawn effectively from these sources.

The first of the genre, *A Narrative of the Uncommon Sufferings and Surprising Deliverance of Briton Hammon, A Negro Man*, appeared in Boston in 1760. Another, a far more remarkable piece of writing, and one still worth reading, was first published in London in 1789. Its author was Olaudah Equiano; its title, *The Interesting Narrative of the Life of Gustavus Vassa, the African*. Another edition, published in Leeds in 1814, was called *The Interesting Narrative of the Life of Olaudah Equiano, or Gustavus Vassa, The African, Written by Himself.*

Meanwhile, in the United States the slave's necessity provoked further expression. The slave-poet preacher Jupiter Hammon had published and circulated a prose writing called *An Address to the Negroes in the State of New York*. The point of view it reflected was in sharp contrast to the tenor of the slave narratives and may be read as a commentary on his own favored position as the literate slave of a Long Island master. In contrast to the "splendid folly," as Redding describes it, of the authors of the narratives who "burned themselves out in revolt," Jupiter Hammon was resigned to a life of servitude. These are his words:

> Respecting obedience to masters. Now whether it is right and lawful in the sight of God, for them to make slaves of us or not, I am certain that while we are slaves, it is our duty to obey our masters in all their lawful commands, and mind them. . . . As we depend upon our masters for what we eat and drink and wear, we cannot be happy unless we obey them.

Before he is condemned out of hand, it is necessary to remember that Hammon probably could not have gotten a stronger attack on slavery published, and he did add the following:

> Now I acknowledge that liberty is a great thing, and worth seeking for, if we can get it honestly; and by our good conduct prevail upon our masters to set us free: though for my own part I do not wish to be free, yet I should be glad if others, especially the young negroes, were to be free; for many of us who are grown up slaves, and have always had masters to take care of us, should hardly know how to take care of themselves. . . . That liberty is a great thing we may know from our own feelings, and we may likewise judge so from the conduct of the white people in the late war. How much money has been spent and how many lives have been lost to defend their liberty! I must say that I have hoped that God would open their eyes, when they were so engaged for liberty, to think of the state of the poor blacks, and to pity us.

It should be remembered here that this *Address* does not belong to the great period of the flowering and fulfillment of the slave narrative. This coincided with the abolitionist campaign, 1830 to 1861.

Some of the narratives were presented as autobiographies. *Scenes in the Life of Harriet Tubman* (1869), and *Memoirs of Elleanor Eldridge* (1838) belong in this category. Charles Ball's *Slavery in the United States* (1836) and others like it have been regarded as fictionized truth, while still others, like Emily Pierson's *The Fugitive* and Mattie Griffith's *Autobiography of a Female Slave* are out-and-out fiction. Many were "told-to" accounts, and these included *The Confession of Nat Turner* (1831), *The Narrative of Solomon Northrup* (1857), and *The Narrative of James Williams* (1838), dictated to John Greenleaf Whittier. Interestingly, the Williams narrative was branded a fraud by the editor of the *Alabama Beacon*, whereupon the Antislavery Society, its publishers, suppressed it. Harriet Jacobs' *Incidents in the Life of a Slave Girl* was presented as edited and "arranged" by Lydia Maria Child.

It is the genuine slave narratives, authentic autobiographies recalling the bondage and freedom of gifted black men and mulattoes who happened to be born under the peculiar institution, that give significance to this body of writing and justify its place in American literary and cultural history. *Narrative of the Life of Frederick Douglass, an American Slave, Written by Himself* (Boston, 1845) is one of these. *Narrative of the Life of William W. Brown, a Fugitive Slave, Written by Himself* (Boston, 1848) is another. Still others include *The Fugitive Blacksmith, or Events in the History of James W. C. Pennington, Pastor of a Presbyterian Church, New York, Formerly a Slave in the State of Maryland, United States* (London, 1849); *Autobiography of a Fugitive Negro: His Anti-Slavery Labors in the United States, Canada, and England,* by Samuel Ringgold Ward (London, 1855); and *Running a Thousand Miles for Freedom: or The Escape of William and Ellen Craft from Slavery* (London, 1860).

A passage from the Douglass *Narrative* suggests the flavor and quality of this type of writing, as well as the intellectual capacity of the runaways themselves. He wrote the book during the summer of 1844, less than five years after his escape, and the following is typical of the writing as a whole:

> The heart-rending incidents, related in the foregoing chapter, led me, thus early, to inquire into the nature and history of slavery. *Why am I a slave? Why are some people slaves, and others masters? Was there ever a time when this was not so? How did the relation commence?* These were the perplexing questions which began now to claim my thoughts, and to exercise the weak powers of my mind, for I was still but a child, and knew less than children of the same age in the free states. As my questions concerning these things were only put to children a little older, and a little better informed than myself, I was not rapid in reaching a solid footing. By some means I learned from these inquiries, that "God, up in the sky," made everybody; and that He made *white* people to be masters and mistresses, and *black* people to be slaves. This did not satisfy me, nor lessen my interest in the subject. I was told, too, that God was good, and that He knew what was best for me,

and best for everybody. This was less satisfactory than the first statement; because it came, point blank, against all my notions of goodness. It was not good to let old master cut the flesh off Esther, and make her cry so. Besides, how did people know that God made black people to be slaves? Did they go up in the sky and learn it? or, did He come down and tell them so? All was dark here. It was some relief to my hard notions of the goodness of God, that, although He made white men to be slaveholders, He did not make them to be *bad* slaveholders, and that, in due time, He would punish the bad slaveholders; that He would, when they died, send them to the bad place, where they would be "burned up." Nevertheless, I could not reconcile the relation of slavery with my crude notions of goodness.

Then, too, I found that there were puzzling exceptions to this theory of slavery on both sides, and in the middle. I knew of blacks who were *not* slaves; I knew of whites who were *not* slaveholders; and I knew of persons who were *nearly* white, who were slaves. *Color*, therefore, was a very unsatisfactory basis for slavery.

Once, however, engaged in the inquiry, I was not very long in finding out the true solution of the matter. It was not *color*, but *crime*, not *God*, but *man*, that afforded the true explanation of the existence of slavery; nor was I long in finding out another important truth, viz: what man can make, man can unmake. The appalling darkness faded away, and I was master of the subject.

A second and updated version of Douglass' *Narrative* was published ten years later under the title *My Bondage and My Freedom* and subdivided into Part I, "Life as a Slave" and Part II, "Life as a Freeman." In later years Douglass brought out a third version, again revised, updated, and greatly expanded, and given a more standardized biographical title: *The Life and Times of Frederick Douglass, Written by Himself* (1882).

Special interest attaches to *The Life of Josiah Henson, Formerly a Slave Now an Inhabitant of Canada, as Narrated by Himself to Samuel Eliot* (Boston, 1849), because Henson came to be regarded as the original of Harriet Beecher Stowe's Uncle Tom. Both the American and the British editions of this narrative had satisfactory, if not spectacular, sales from the start, but a later version, 1858, with an introduction by Mrs. Stowe, and retitled *Truth Stranger than Fiction, Father Henson's Story of His Own Life*, had an advance sale of 5,000 copies and did even better. The book was still going strong in 1879 when it came out again as *An Autobiography of the Rev. Josiah Henson* (*Mrs. Harriet Beecher Stowe's "Uncle Tom"*) *from 1789–1879*. By then introductory notes by Wendell Phillips and John Greenleaf Whittier had been added to Mrs. Stowe's preface, and the publishers stated that 100,000 copies of the book had already been sold. There were French and Dutch translations as well.

As a matter of fact, good sales had become the rule for slave narratives. *Twelve Years a Slave: The Narrative of Solomon Northrup* (1853), for example, sold 27,000 copies in its first two years. William Wells Brown's *Narrative* went through four editions in its first year. Frederick Douglass' achieved seven in this country alone, according to Ephraim Peabody, writing in the *Christian Examiner* of July 1849. Meanwhile earlier narratives, such as those by Gustavus Vassa and Moses Roper, continued to sell, reaching ten and eleven English-language editions respectively, not to mention translations. By the late 1850s the slave narrative had clearly caught on as a reading vogue. The number published ran into the hundreds.

Their popularity in the nineteenth century, all things considered, was not unlike the vogue of the Western story in the twentieth. The narratives evoked the setting and conditions of slavery, to be sure, but they also created a parable of the human condition, showing mankind in shackles and his yearning for freedom. The perils of escape and the long journey toward the North Star retained their exciting quality until times changed and a new parable, or myth—the Western—replaced the earlier one.

The period in which the slave narrative flourished was synonymous with the period in which the Negro spiritual reached its flowering. Although one was poetry and the other prose, words from the spirituals are often quoted in the narratives. But the connection between the narratives and the subsequent literary expression they stimulated is more direct and immediate than that between the spirituals and the music they came eventually to influence.

William Wells Brown is the link. One of the three men who, in Saunders Redding's judgment, best reflected "the temper and opinion of the Negro in those years," Brown is elected as "the most representative Negro of the age." Of the other two, Charles Remond and Frederick Douglass, Remond's otherwise brilliant career as an antislavery exponent was marred by jealousy of Douglass, and Douglass seemed too exceptional to stand as "representative." All three devoted their lives to the cause of abolition, and only Remond did not leave an autobiography. All three could write effectively when the need arose, but only Brown's writing evolved into what might be called a literary career.

Like many black Americans before and since, indeed like many writers, Brown made maximum use of his personal history as literary material. Some of this can only lead to confusion if the truth is sought, because he gave at least three versions of his parentage and early childhood. In successive versions the details he gave became more exciting. Whether this reflects burgeoning professionalism in letters or merely the shedding of early reticence as he developed, the fact remains that contradictions exist.

Initially, he records that he was born of slave parents in Kentucky and grew up as a slave child working in the fields and the house. His second account introduces a bit of drama which reappears, interestingly, in all the biographies of George Washington Carver. He speaks of being stolen by a slave trader shortly after his birth. Then, in the second revised edition of his *Narrative*, he really lets the chips fall. He was born, he states here, of a white father, scion of the family which owned his mulatto mother in Lexington, Kentucky. The father of his slave mother, "it was said, was the noted Daniel Boon [sic]," according to this account.

The frequent references to white paternity in autobiographical narratives like Brown's, as well as in fictional stories of slaves in that period, have sometimes been branded as propaganda devices by abolitionists wishing to stigmatize slavery by showing the demoralizing effect of the institution on the master class. Photographic evidence in Brown's case, as in many others, moreover, would seem to support the disclosure at least to the extent of the mixed parentage, and apparently no one offered to dispute it while he lived.

Brown got the name by which he became known and by which he is remembered from the Quaker Wells Brown who first befriended him in Ohio after his escape from slavery. Recaptured and passed from owner to owner, he served in turn as cabin boy on riverboats, a slave trader's helper, and eventually a printer's devil in the news office of Elijah P. Lovejoy. These activities are not otherwise documented, but Brown's own story was that he learned to read while working in the St. Louis print shop of the abolitionist journalist who was later mobbed and killed for supporting the cause of freedom.

Constantly on the move as an escaped slave, he supported himself as he could while applying most of his energies to study and gradually made his way to Canada. Later, he states, "I commenced lecturing as an agent of the western New York Anti-Slavery Society, and have ever since devoted my time to the cause of my enslaved countrymen." His antislavery work covered a period of about fifteen years, including five between 1849 and 1854 which were spent in England, and during which he may have made as many as 3,000 public speeches, judging by an estimate of the number he delivered abroad. Indications are that most, if not all, of his speeches were extemporaneous and did not survive the occasions on which they were delivered, but there is evidence that writing of another kind had already become an even more serious interest of his. William Wells Brown was the first creative black prose writer of importance produced in America.

In addition to three successful versions of the *Narrative of William Wells Brown* his abolitionist years yielded also for the cause *Three Years in Europe: or, Places I Have Seen and People I Have Met* (London, 1852); and *St. Domingo: Its Revolutions and Its Patriots* (Boston, 1855). During this period he also wrote and published two novels and two plays, the first pieces of fiction and the first dramas by a black American. As such they may be read either as period pieces of literary Americana or as lineal antecedents of the works of Richard Wright and Lorraine Hansberry.

The first novel, when it appeared in London in 1853, was called *Clotelle; or, The President's Daughter*. Its heroine was a beautiful near-white girl, and there was an implication that it was based on truth, which tied in with gossip then current. The Boston edition was published almost a decade later with a new subtitle: *A Tale of the Southern States*, and was slightly more restrained. According to Saunders Redding, in his study, *To Make a Poet Black* (Chapel Hill, The University of North Carolina Press, 1939), "Brown was driven by the necessity for turning out propaganda in a cause that was too close to him for emotional objectivity and reasonable perspective. He had power without the artist's control, but in spite of this his successes are considerable and of great importance to the history of Negro creative literature. First novelist, first playwright, first historian: the list argues his place."

A quotation from *Clotelle* suggests the mixture. Following a description of a Richmond slave market where a beautiful quadroon girl is offered to bidders, Brown summarizes:

> This was a Virginia slave-auction, at which the bones, sinews, blood, and nerves of a young girl of eighteen were sold for $500: her moral character for $200; her superior intellect for $100; the benefits supposed to accrue from her having been sprinkled and immersed, together with a warranty of her devoted Christianity, for $300; her ability to make a good prayer, for $200; and her chastity for $700 more. This, too, in a city thronged with churches, whose tall spires look like so many signals pointing to heaven, but whose ministers preach that slavery is a God-ordained institution.

The second novel appears to have run in the New York *Anglo-African* as a serial in 1860–61. Its titles seem sufficiently descriptive: *Miralda; or, The Beautiful Quadroon, A Romance of American Slavery, Founded on Fact*. Wells' first play, *Experience; or, How to Give a Northern Man a Backbone*, was completed around 1856, and his second, *The Escape: or, A Leap for Freedom, Drama in Five Acts*, was published in Boston in 1858.

Brown's writings after the Civil War have been described as "more reasonable." With the campaign over and tensions relaxed, he settled down and began to produce histories and narrative essays that still do him credit a hundred years later. *The Negro in the American Rebellion* (1868), *The Rising Son* (1874), and *My Southern Home* (1880) are representative.

Another first, possibly as significant as those he established in fiction, drama, and historical writing, was also recorded by William Wells Brown. He was the first black author in the United States to earn a living by his writing.

A novel by Martin R. Delany, a contemporary of Brown's and like him a stalwart of the antislavery campaign, was announced in the first issue of the *Anglo-African* magazine, January 1859, as "A Tale of the Mississippi Valley, the Southern United States and Cuba." The hero was described as "an educated West Indian black, who deprived of his liberty by fraud when young and brought to the United States, in maturer age, at the instance of his wife being sold from him, sought revenge through the medium of a deep-laid secret organization." The title was *Blake; or, The Huts of America*, and an editorial note promised that the story would run to about eighty chapters or six hundred pages. It apparently did not. Only seven installments followed in the *Anglo-African*, January to August 1859, and decades were to elapse before Paul Laurence Dunbar and Charles Waddell Chesnutt broke the near-silence into which the writing of prose fiction by black Americans seemed to lapse.

However the tradition, or vogue, of the slave narrative did not end abruptly with the conclusion of the war of liberation. In addition to those works which had established themselves as perennials and continued to be reissued (like Douglass' and Henson's), new ones continued to appear. Representative of these were *Incidents in the Life of a Slave Girl* by Harriet Jacobs; *Behind the Scenes by Elizabeth Keckley, Formerly a Slave, but More Recently Modiste and Friend to Mrs. Abraham Lincoln; or Thirty Years a Slave and Four*

*Years in the White House* (1868); *Scenes in the Life of Harriet Tubman, as told by Sarah Bradford* (1869); *Harriet, the Moses of Her People*, also by Sarah Bradford (1886); and finally *Up from Slavery, An Autobiography*, by Booker T. Washington (1900).

*Up from Slavery* promptly established itself as a classic example of the American success story, but it was more than that. It was the last of the great slave narratives and a fitting end to a tradition that had for more than a century disturbed the American conscience by inspiring such books as *Uncle Tom's Cabin*. With this genre out of its system, black writing was at last purged in a way that permitted a fresh start. Dunbar and Chesnutt, both personal friends of Booker T. Washington, but neither sympathetic to his philosophy, were standing by—ready.

Dunbar's prose followed in the wake of his popularity as a poet. Many of his short stories and sketches make use of the same body of folk material. They appeared in *The Saturday Evening Post* and other magazines, and subsequently in such collections as *Folks from Dixie* (1898), *The Strength of Gideon* (1900), *In Old Plantation Days* (1903), and *The Heart of Happy Hollow* (1904). The following sentences from the latter are a fair indication of the substance of all four:

> Wherever Negroes colonize in the cities or villages, North or South, wherever the hod-carrier, the porter, and the waiter are the society men of the town; wherever the picnic and the excursion are the chief summer diversion, and the revival the winter-time of repentance. . . . Wherever laughter and tears rub elbows by day, and the spirit of labour and laziness shake hands, there—there—is Happy Hollow.

At least one of the stories, however, stands out from the others. Called "The Trustfulness of Polly," it is notable for at least three reasons: Dunbar handles the short story form with greater technical assurance here than elsewhere; he ventures into the lower strata of black American life in New York for his material; and in his dealing with the policy game, he anticipates by twenty-five years settings and subject matter that were later to fascinate nearly a whole generation of black writers in Harlem.

Three of the four novels Dunbar wrote, interestingly, differ from the stories and sketches much in the same way that his poems in standard English differ from those in dialect verse. *The Uncalled* (1898), *The Love of Landry* (1900), and *The Fanatics* (1901), were black novels only in the sense that their author was a black American. All three were mediocre but even in *The Sport of the Gods* (1902), when it would seem he was on surer ground with black characters and a setting with which he was presumably more familiar, Dunbar was still not a very good novelist. However, at least one astute critic, Sterling Brown, has detected an improvement in the latter part of that novel over the first and suggested that had he lived longer and worked conscientiously at the art, Dunbar might eventually have mastered the fiction form.

Charles Waddell Chesnutt did work and did gain a certain mastery over his materials. While Dunbar's dialect stories were appearing in *The Saturday Evening Post* around the turn of the century, Chesnutt's were being published in the *Atlantic Monthly*. A cultivated man practicing law in Cleveland, he attained an objectivity of vision in keeping with his technical skills, while at the same time facing up to the sociological realities. He has been called a pioneer of the color line by both his biographers and the critics who have studied his works.

*The Wife of His Youth and Other Stories of the Color Line* and *The Conjure Woman*, his two short-story collections, were both published by Houghton-Mifflin in 1899. His first novel, *The House Behind the Cedars*, was published in 1900; and *The Marrow of Tradition* came out the following year, all from the same publisher. His final novel, *The Colonel's Dream*, was published by Doubleday-Page in 1905.

While Chesnutt always wrote as a prose artist, mindful of aesthetic values, his novels must be regarded as problem novels, and the problems stressed reappear in a good many of his stories. In each of these aspects of his craft he was the first of his race to achieve clear-cut recognition.

Interestingly, from the point of view of his editors and readers he was not at first recognized as a "Negro." This is not only a clearcut commentary on the objectivity of his writing, but Chesnutt the man was similarly unrecognizable as black. In this respect he was, like Jean Toomer and Walter White after him, what has sometimes been called a voluntary Negro. Only in America would he have been so classified, the actual racial mixture in his case being so preponderantly Caucasian, but if this was of any personal distress to him, he showed it only in his preoccupation with stories growing out of such relationships as this unique dilemma can produce. Some aspect of this situation unfolds in each of his fictional works except *The Conjure Woman*, a collection of seven tales based on Negro superstition but departing sharply from the Uncle Remus and the Uncle Billy retelling of black folk stories. Chesnutt also wrote a short biography of Frederick Douglass.

Contemporary with Chesnutt, Dunbar, and Booker T. Washington was a young black writer somewhat harder to classify in a purely literary context, but whose varied writings in that same period were to prove even more influential. Esteemed mainly as a brilliant scholar, W. E. B. DuBois was the first black American to earn a Ph.D. from Harvard (1895). By 1897 he was contributing essays to *The Atlantic Monthly* and other American magazines that can still be read with amazement for their literary quality and insight. These were collected and, with others added, were published in 1903 as *The Souls of Black Folk*, a book which is still in print and which continues to hold its ground as the definitive response to *Up From Slavery* and equally as prologue (more than half a century earlier) and first projection of some of the most arresting ideas and angles of vision in the writings of such essayists and novelists as Ralph Ellison and James Baldwin.

DuBois' writing took many turns after *The Souls of Black Folk*, much that was excellent going into *The Crisis*, a magazine he founded and edited from 1911 to 1933, and resulting in other collections of his short pieces, novels, histories, biographies, and the autobiographical *Dusk of Dawn* (1942). Due recognitions were sometimes tardy, but he lived long enough to reap and eventually enjoy them all.

Meanwhile the first prose work of James Weldon Johnson was published anonymously in 1912, a novel titled *The Autobiography of an Ex-Coloured Man*. It did not make a great impression. In fact, it seemed to usher in a period of relative silence by black American writers in general. Fifteen years later, when it was rediscovered and reissued under his own name, it was as a part of the Harlem Renaissance led by the poets Toomer, McKay, Hughes, and Cullen. By then Johnson was serving the National Association for the Advancement of Colored People.

By then, too, the body of prose writing by black Americans had reached a point where some general observations could be made, though more profound critical studies were still a generation away. What were the suitable subjects for black writers? Was it fitting to delve into "low" life? "Excepting now (and only quite recently) the Russian and the German, no group imposes upon its artists demands as great as does the Negro," Saunders Redding sighed with dismay. Should black writers use dialect? Should they concentrate on black characters or white? To all these questions the Harlem group formulated their own lively answers. In an article called "The Negro Artist and the Racial Mountain," published in *The Nation* in 1926, when the author of this chapter was still in his early twenties, he wrote:

> We younger Negro artists who create now intend to express our individual dark-skinned selves without fear or shame. If white people are pleased we are glad. If they are not, it doesn't matter. We know we are beautiful. And ugly too. The tom-tom cries and the tom-tom laughs. If colored people are pleased we are glad. If they are not, their displeasure doesn't matter either. We build our temples for tomorrow, strong as we know how, and we stand on top of the mountain free within ourselves.

The outburst of creative expression that occasioned this manifesto was called by Alain Locke and other participants or close observers a renaissance and a coming of age. According to Charles S. Johnson, sociologist and editor of the Urban League's influential *Opportunity: A Journal of Negro Life*, "A brief ten years have developed more confident self-expression, more widespread efforts in the direction of art than the long, dreary two centuries before" for the black American.

If the Renaissance had done no more than rediscover and bring back into print a book like *The Autobiography of an Ex-Coloured Man* and inspired its author to project more black folk sermons as poetry for his book *God's Trombones*, it would have earned its name. Actually, however, a good many other positive results followed that happy awakening. Suddenly Roland Hayes was singing in Carnegie Hall, the first concert artist of his race to receive unqualified acceptance in the United States in his generation. Duke Ellington began playing his indigos at the Cotton Club. Late at night and in small underground places the voices of Bessie Smith and Ethel Waters were heard. W. C. Handy arrived from Memphis, and presently the poets caught the beat.

Works of fiction took somewhat longer to establish themselves, and when they did appear, the first of them were greeted with almost embarrassing fanfare. In perspective the short stories by Jean Toomer, collected with his early poems in *Cane* (1923), do not seem to have been over-praised. Although the four novels by Jessie Fauset and the two by Walter White, one suspects, belong exclusively to the period in which they were written, such books as *There Is Confusion* (1924), and *The Fire in the Flint* (1924) made a significant contribution to the development of the writing impulse among young black Americans. Claude McKay's *Home to Harlem* (1928) became a best seller. Eric Walrond's *Tropic Death* (1926) seemed more than promising, as did Wallace Thurman's *The Blacker the Berry* (1929). Rudolph Fisher showed talent in his short stories in the *Atlantic Monthly* and other magazines; but this talent was not quite sustained in his novel *The Walls of Jericho* (1928). In 1930 the first novel by Langston Hughes, *Not Without Laughter*, was published. It was followed four years later by a collection of his short stories, *The Ways of White Folks* (1934). Both survived the period of the Renaissance, as did his poetry.

The Great Depression scattered the Harlem group of writers. It was as if an earthquake had struck, and the effect was intensified with the deaths of Thurman and Fisher, both under thirty, which seemed to pinpoint the ending of an era. Zora Neale Hurston, whose story-telling had become a legend, returned to her native Florida and began turning out books like *Jonah's Gourd Vine* (1934), *Men and Mules* (1935), and *Their Eyes Were Watching God* (1937). Arna Bontemps, author of the light-hearted novel *God Sends Sunday* (1931), found a hiding place in Alabama and began writing, fearfully, *Black Thunder* (1936), a tragic account of slave insurrection in another century.

Whatever else may be said of their achievements, the Renaissance writers succeeded in putting an end to the novelty of the black American as a writer in the United States. Fiction by George Wylie Henderson, George W. Lee, Mercedes Gilbert, Waters Edward Turpin, William Attaway, and Dorothy West, as well as work by the original Harlem group which appeared in the decade that followed, both suffered and profited from this fact.

But the Depression that sent the Harlem writers scurrying more than compensated for this damage by the opportunities it provided for the next wave of literary expression by black Americans. Into the Writers Projects of WPA wandered old defeated writers like the poet Fenton Johnson, to be sure, but the projects also drew the likes of Richard Wright, Ralph Ellison, Frank Yerby, and Willard Motley, and began to create an environment in which the black writer could at last stretch himself full-length. Wright ascended rapidly to major rank among American writers, regardless of race.

Here was a novelist powerful enough to break out of the narrow compartment previously occupied by black writers. For one thing, Wright was acutely aware of his prison, and it did not take him long to conclude, as some critics have done, that the novel as he knew it was and had been for generations a projection of the value system of the dominant class in the society. Taking advantage of the panic into which that society had been thrown by the Depression, he allied himself with the critics of its basic assumptions and demanded that society hear him out. The consensus of intelligent readers was that he made sense, that he handled his themes with authority, expressed himself with power and eloquence, and was entitled to the place he had won in the literary firmament of the Depression years.

*Uncle Tom's Children*, the first in sequence of Wright's major works, was a collection of four short novels written while he was employed by the Illinois Writers Project. Drawn from memories of his Mississippi boyhood, the stories were almost unbearable evocations of cruel realities which the nation and the world had in the past been unable or unwilling to face. Wright's purpose, his determination as a prose writer, was to force open closed eyes, to compel America to look at what it had done to the black peasantry into which he was born. In a competition offered by a publisher for the best fiction book submitted by a writer on WPA in 1938, *Uncle Tom's Children* was judged the winner. The critical reception was enthusiastic, and its author was launched.

The same critics were more than surprised, indeed bowled over, when *Native Son* appeared two years later as a Book-of-the-Month Club selection and actually, as one of them said, "dwarfed" its powerful predecessor. From the Mississippi locale Wright had moved his setting to Chicago, and the narrative vigor which had impressed readers of the four novellas had been intensified by a deeper probing into the society that spawned the characters and produced the grim tragedy. The author had confirmed his own insights by a new acquaintance with the discipline of sociology.

That Wright's was the most impressive literary talent yet produced by black America was only rarely disputed in his time, and this same high estimate of his stature was concurred with by critics and readers abroad. Nearly fifty translations and foreign editions of his books followed in the next fifteen years as his writings became known in the major countries around the world. His name was bracketed with the small handful of America's foremost writers, and interest in him as a personality began to spread.

The latter development was aided, no doubt, by his third book, the autobiographical *Black Boy*, in 1945, which not only repeated the success of *Native Son* when it too became a Book-of-the-Month Club selection but also impressed a number of critics as being in some ways an even more remarkable accomplishment. Certainly *Black Boy* gave evidence that the range of its author, like his standing among his contemporaries, was still expanding. Relating Wright's personal history to the quests of his mind, the book showed the influence of another intellectual discovery. Where his first book had been sparked by Wright's conversion to communism, his second by an embrace of sociology, *Black Boy* reflected Wright's encounter with the mysteries of psychoanalysis.

At this point Richard Wright moved his family to Paris and promptly became one of the most celebrated American expatriates in Europe. He did not publish another book for eight years, and when he did, *The Outsider* (1953), his second full-length novel, showed him bringing to bear on his writing the attitudes of French existentialism of the post–World War II era. But *The Outsider* was not quite up to Wright's earlier books. Something was missing. Perhaps it was anger. His new French friends had made the suffering, alienated author feel at home. He had given them his love in return. The anguish and outrage that made his early books memorable faded in the fiction he wrote in the remaining years of his life. *The Long Dream* (1956) was a dim echo of the Mississippi stories written while he was still bleeding. *Savage Holiday* (1954) was a paperback potboiler. Some of the stories collected in the volume *Eight Men* (1961) had been written years earlier and properly belong beside the novellas. *Lawd Today* was a fledgling work, apparently antedating *Uncle Tom's Children*, but salvaged posthumously in 1963 from Wright's unpublished manuscripts.

The Paris years that added nothing to Richard Wright's stature as a novelist stimulated considerable writing of another kind, however. In 1941, between *Native Son* and *Black Boy*, Wright had written a deeply felt text for *Twelve Million Black Voices*, described as both a folk history of the black American and "a broad picture of the processes of Negro life." *Black Power* (1954) was also nonfiction but in another vein. Wright's account of his sojourn in West Africa was effective personal journalism. The formula was repeated in *The Color Curtain* (1956), based on the author's attendance at the Bandung Conference of 1955 on the Island of Java, and again in *Pagan Spain* (1957). *White Man, Listen* (1957) brought together a series of lectures delivered in Europe under impressive auspices between 1950 and 1956, years when any statement by Richard Wright was likely to be regarded as important in France, Italy, Germany, or Scandinavia. The papers show that he took his responsibilities as spokesman seriously.

Wright was singing the praises of young Ralph Ellison a number of years before the latter's *Invisible Man* was published in 1952. A painstaking worker, Ellison had evidently been chipping away at his sculptured novel for at least a decade. No one who knew him was likely to doubt Ellison's seriousness or even, perhaps, his prospects, and Wright knew him well; the question was one of endurance. When the book finally appeared, it was hailed as a major contribution to American literature. Surprisingly, it bore little or no resemblance to the work of Wright, whom some had mistakenly assumed to have been Ellison's mentor.

Ellison's first novel was strikingly original. His aims as a storyteller were as different from Richard Wright's as his methods. Where Wright had associated himself with the tradition of Dostoevski and Dreiser, Ellison had been influenced by T. S. Eliot and James Joyce. Complexity of form, layers of meaning, point and counterpoint could be seen as elements of Ellison's deliberate concern as well as a possible explanation of his novel-a-decade rate of composition.

The American Booksellers gave their fiction award to *Invisible Man* in the year following its publication, and seemed thereby to confirm the claims of its publishers that the book was not only a great triumph of storytelling and characterization but also a profound and uncompromising interpretation of the black American's anomalous position in society. The claim has not been withdrawn. The novel has had tremendous success both here and abroad in a variety of translations.

While Wright and Ellison made their direct assaults at winning a place in American literature with the kind of material they knew best, Yerby and Motley sought to "emancipate" themselves from what some have felt to be the limitations of "black" subjects and became the first "popular" writers among black Americans. Together, it now seems fair to say, these four gave the black writer a new image, and ushered in a new era.

Ann Petry, Chester Himes, and Roi Ottley were among the first to profit from the change. They were followed by a host of young writers. Such names as William Demby, Owen Dodson, Alden Bland, William Gardner Smith, Lloyd Brown, and Willard Savoy appeared in publishers' lists as routinely as if novels by new black writers were to be expected. The emergence of Saunders Redding in this period was neither routine nor expected, but his essays and literary criticism link him uniquely with the writers of the era and their mood. No one has understood them better.

Redding's essays, however, despite their brilliance, did not strike fire when they first appeared in the way that James Baldwin's did a decade or more later. In between, the black rebellion—or revolution, if that is preferred—occurred in the United States, and young black writers were among the first beneficiaries, Baldwin most prominently.

After writing a good but unspectacular novel in *Go Tell It on the Mountain* (1953), Baldwin began to produce personal essays so arresting as to convince some readers that he might succeed in reviving interest in what they had begun to think of as an old and possibly outdated literary form. The first collection of his essays, as if to establish a link with Richard Wright, was published as *Notes of a Native Son* (1955). The essays were provocative, and the title did no harm, but their reception was modest and remained within bounds. Another volume, subtitled *More Notes of a Native Son*, was published in 1961 as *Nobody Knows My Name*. This was followed in 1963 by *The Fire Next Time*, consisting of two pieces previously published in magazines: "Letter to My Nephew on the One Hundredth Anniversary of the Emancipation" (*The Progressive*) and "Letter from a Region in My Mind" (*The New Yorker*). The latter two volumes became national best-sellers, thanks in part, no doubt, to a favorable conjunction with the surge of the black protest movement in the United States. Astonishingly articulate on platform as well as printed page, calling on old skills in public address acquired as a boy preacher in store-front churches between the ages of 14 and 17, Baldwin did not hesitate to speak out amid the storm. To nearly everyone's surprise, he was given rapt attention.

Meanwhile his novels, treating subjects which previously might have been considered taboo, and certainly not in the mainstream of the black revolt, leaped to vast popularity. *Giovianni's Room* came out in 1956, *Another Country* in 1962. Baldwin's first published play was *Blues for Mister Charlie* (1964).

During this period, temporarily eclipsed by the Baldwin phenomenon, a brilliant new wave of younger fiction writers stood waiting in the wings. They included Alston Anderson, Frank London Brown, William Melvin Kelley, John Oliver Killens, Paule Marshall, Julian Mayfield, Herbert Simmons, and John A. Williams. To their ranks were soon added such innovative and arresting talents as James Alan McPherson, Ishmael Reed, and John Edgar White, as well as the bright promise of Rose Struthers and Alice Walker. Significantly, they arrived on the scene at a moment when revivals of interest in the poetry and stories of Paul Lawrence Dunbar and the surge of the Harlem Renaissance were simultaneously being manifested. The emergence of names and personalities such as Maya Angelou, Nikki Giovanni, and a bevy of women scholars suggested, as some have observed, a kind of reemergence of the black woman as author. The continuing popularity of the poet Margaret Walker's novel, *Jubilee*, seems symbolic of this period, which paved the way for the dramatic output of the midsixties and after.

# 24

# *The Black Contribution*
# *to American Letters: Part II*
# *The Writer as Activist—1960 and After*

## *Larry Neal*

### Attitudes Toward Tradition

All literature exists in the context of both a public and a private field of language. The writer brings his creative sensibility to bear on the tradition inherited from his literary forebears. Implicit in the writer's situation is the cumulative effect of that tradition upon the culture of his times. One could claim that the writer is essentially a creation of the books he has read.

Ralph Ellison uses the term "literary ancestors" to describe the writer's relationship to tradition. In an article published in *Dissent* (Autumn 1963), editor Irving Howe accused James Baldwin and Ralph Ellison of abdicating the tradition of protest literature exemplified by Richard Wright. Ellison retorted: "But perhaps you [Howe] will understand when I say [Richard Wright] did not influence me. If I point out that while one can do nothing about choosing one's relatives, one can, as artist, choose one's 'ancestors.' Wright was, in this sense, a 'relative'; Hemingway, an 'ancestor.' Langston Hughes, whose work I knew in grade school and whom I knew before I knew Wright, was a 'relative'; Eliot, whom I was to meet only many years later, and Malraux and Dostoevski and Faulkner, were 'ancestors'—if you please or don't please!"[1]

What we have here is a clash between the private and public aspects of literary performance. As a Marxist, Howe leans toward the idea of literature as basically a public performance, one whose essential function is to bring about a revolution in social consciousness. According to Marxist canon literature must speak to public needs. Thus Howe envisions literature as a political tool to be used as a militant voice of change.

Because the decade of the sixties was so intensely political, a great deal of Afro-American literature leaned decidedly in the direction of public encounter. The writer, then and since, however private his concerns, has been compelled to function in an atmosphere of speech-making—particularly when much of this speech-making concerns his very function as an artist. Thus the black writer finds himself torn between the arena and his study. He may, on the one hand, develop a sense of guilt concerning his lack of public commitment to the political struggle. Or he may, like Malraux in *Man's Fate*, attempt to distill the militant language of struggle and liberation into a self-contained work of art. Whatever his choice, some faction lies in wait to decry his decision; such is the nature of critical debate.

The turbulent arena of political encounter presents the black writer with a highly charged field of expression. (Note, for example, the political speeches in Ralph Ellison's novel, *Invisible Man*). In the sixties, expressive language sprang mainly from the sermonistic style of the black church, and from that of urban street speakers like Harlem's Ed "Pork Chop" Davis. This style is characterized by the traditional format of call and response. It is also characterized by the modulated repetition of key phrases, images, hyperbole, and biblical allusions.

The sermonistic style is especially associated with leaders like the late Reverend Martin Luther King, Jr., whose speeches gesture toward the high forensic. It is a style we readily associate with great moments in history and with partiotic fervor. It is the messianic voice of the social revolutionary who sees himself as projecting into the world a truer vision of human possibilities. Speeches like King's could arise only at a time of acknowledged social conflict. It is as if the nation is at war. The images employed strongly convey the idea of unity against oppression, while laying the basis for a strategy of moral confrontation.

Although Adam Clayton Powell's, Malcolm X's, and H. Rap Brown's rhetorical styles also derive, in part, from the tradition of the church sermon, we most readily associate their styles with the vernacular language of the black urban communities. When this rhetoric is vitriolic it bears close affinities to the language of the "dozens,"[2] and is highly influenced by jazz rhythms, slang, and jive talk:

> . . . I heard Bobby Kennedy charge, publicity is the Freedom
>     Riders' cause.
>     And his finger popped!
> His daddy is well-known exploiter, a thief—dig?
>     And their fingers popped loud!
> And all around fingers were popping and gum-chewing white
>     liberals were encouraging youth, white and black, to fill
>     the jails while they paid off their mortgages and Hi-Fi
>     payments.
>     And their fingers popped too!
> I was spinning with Earth and a foul wind was blowing.
>     Finger pop! . . .[3]

The numerous aesthetic and political issues black writers were forced to confront during the sixties were hardly new. Some of them grew out of the historic struggle to obliterate racism in America. Others sprang from the general dilemma of identity which haunts American cultural history. Still others seemed to stem from an overall crisis in modern intellectual thought in Western society, where values are being assaulted by a new generation of youth around the world as it searches for new standards and ideals. Black literature reflects this search, complete with its uncertainties and ambivalence.

The emergence of a distinctly chauvinistic and increasingly nationalistic tendency among the more vociferous of the young black writers of the past decade cannot be summarily dismissed as a historical aberration. Given the highly political character of the sixties, it was inevitable that some kind of literary voice should emerge to address itself, if only obliquely, to the complex of tensions underlying the demands for social equality. At one end of the literary/political spectrum, we have the example of the Christian James Baldwin eloquently defending King's philosophy of love and nonviolence, while at the other extremity stands Malcolm X, the Muslim. Symbolically clustered around Malcolm X are such writers as LeRoi Jones, Eldridge Cleaver, Don L. Lee, and Welton Smith. It is only natural that the more militant writers of the decade should tend toward Malcolm X's rhetorical style. He was a man of the city; and most of these writers had been born or reared in the black communities of the urban North. Since many of them had been forced to cope with the implicit violence of the urban community, they could not countenance the concept of nonviolence. Many of these writers may even have been former members of the warring street gangs of the fifties.

These street gangs were very much like traditional warrior societies. They had definite codes of conduct. Some of them were structured like small nations: there might be a minister of information or a minister of war. They claimed a turf with definite boundaries; and sometimes there were even "treaties" concerning these boundaries. Great stress was put on *machismo* and the ability to defend oneself against an adversary.

The street gangs brought to black literature a distinct and varied oral tradition. This function is of special importance. We have already alluded to the "dozens" in the context of political and artistic speech. But the "dozens" are just a minor aspect of a larger urban folk-narrative tradition. In this tradition, we find a pantheon of culture heroes. First, there is the finely attired Signifying Monkey, a trickster figure who uses words to bring about ordered chaos. Then there is Shine, who according to folk legend was the only black on the Titanic when it sank.

Shine is working down in the kitchen when he notices that the ship is leaking. He informs the captain of the ship's impending catastrophe, but the captain rebukes Shine, saying that the ship is well equipped with enough pumps to keep it afloat. After repeatedly trying to warn the captain that the ship is sinking, Shine jumps overboard into the ocean. The captain, finally realizing that Shine is right, implores Shine to save him:

> . . . Just then the captain said, "Shine, Shine, save poor me;
> I'll give you more money than a nigger ever did see."
> Shine said to the captain: "Money is good on land and on sea,
> but the money on land is the money for me."
> And Shine swam on. . . .

Along the way Shine encounters a whale and a later a shark. The shark says: "Shine, Shine, you swim so fine; you miss one stroke and your black ass is mine." Shine replies:

"You may be king of the ocean, king of the sea; but you gotta be a swimmin' mother-fucker to outswim me." And Shine swims on. Shine traditionally ends up safely back home in the United States, usually in the vicinity of the raconteur's home.

Other folk heroes of the urban narrative include the foul-talking bad men of the gun. Folk characters like Big Bad Bill, Stagger Lee, and Billy Lyons wear their meanness as a badge of honor. Undoubtedly the folk speech that springs from these street narratives has influenced the style of much contemporary black literature. Playwrights like Ed Bullins, Ronald Milner, Douglas Turner Ward, and Joseph Walker utilize these modes of black urban speech in their dramatic works. Much of the tone here is frankly aggressive.

This brings us to another feature of some of the new literature, its scatological content. The conscious use of scatological language and imagery is a deliberate attempt to shake the language loose from its genteel moorings. There are several possible lines of literary precedence here. Black writers are familiar with the works of James Joyce, Henry Miller, Jean Genet, and Allen Ginsberg. Furthermore, scatology is as old as the English language itself. In black poetry, scatology functions to release tension, invoke laughter, or to heighten the sense of outrage against the forces of injustice.

Scatology can be an embarrassing device in the hands of an unskilled poet, but when modulated carefully, as in Welton Smith's suite of poems entitled "Malcolm,"[4] it operates as a unit of energy. There are six movements to this work. The first movement is lyrical; the voice is somewhat withdrawn and contemplative as it speaks to the private memory of Malcolm X.

> i cannot move
> from your voice.
> there is no peace
> where i am. the wind
> cannot move
> hard enough to clear the trash
> and far away i hear my screams.

Then the poet invokes the memory of Sister Betty Shabazz, the widow of the assassinated leader:

> the lean, hard-bone face
> a rich copper color.
> the smile. the
> thin nose and broad
> nostrils. Betty—in the quiet
> after midnight. your hand
> soft on her back. you kiss
> her neck softly
> she would turn
> to face you and arch up—
> her head moving to your chest.

her arms sliding
round your neck. you breathe deeply.
it is quiet. in this moment
you know
what it was all about.

your voice
is inside me; i loaned
my heart in exchange
for your voice. . . .

This section continues with an overall poetic design of Malcolm's life and sense of mission. Finally the section ends in something of an elegiac tone:

now you pace the regions
of my heart. you know
my blood and see
where my tears are made.
i see the beast
and hold my frenzy;
you are not lonely—
in my heart there are many
unmarked graves.

The "beast" referred to is the one mentioned in the biblical book of Revelations. In the iconography of many black writers the beast symbolizes the evils of white Western civilization. This apocalyptic image lays the ground for the next poem in the suite. Entitled "The Nigga Section," it is an outraged invective directed against Malcolm's Afro-American assassins.

slimy obscene creatures. insane
creations of a beast. you
have murdered a man. you
have devoured me. you
have done it with precision
like the way you stand green
in the dark sucking pus
and slicing your penis
into quarters—stuffing
shit through your noses.
you rotten motherfuckin bastards. . . .

The scatology seems to be functioning here as a precisely directed burst of tension-releasing images. Heard aloud, this poem takes on the characteristics of a contemporary saxophone solo by a John Coltrane or an Albert Ayler.

Very few of the writers of the sixties were as successful as Welton Smith in the utilization of scatological invective. A great deal of the writing in this vein descended to the level of obscene sloganeering. What are we to make of a phrase like; "Up against the wall motherfucker this is a stickup"? This line appears in a poem by LeRoi Jones,[5] and was the subject of legal discourse during Jones's trial for weapons charges at the time of the Newark rebellion in the summer of 1967. Subsequent to the court case, in which Jones was acquitted, the lines appeared on the placards of white youth protesting the war in Southeast Asia.

However significant the above factors are to the understanding of some aspects of the black literary revival of the sixties, they did not affect the work of all black writers with the same degree of intensity. Nevertheless, the general sociopolitical climate was also reflected to some extent in the work of more established Afro-American writers like the poet Gwendolyn Brooks or the novelist Ernest Gaines, whose *Autobiography of Miss Jane Pittman* is both one of the best novels of the sixties and a highly significant American novel (in 1974 it was made into a prize-winning television feature presentation starring Cicely Tyson in the title role). Here again we see evidence of the inevitable tension between the private and public character of the writer. In a sense the work of art, the novel, the poem, or the play, is the dialectical working-out of this tension. A literary work may evolve as a private dialogue with one's literary ancestors, but its survival depends upon whether or not it speaks to some significant segment of the contemporary reading public. And in fact, the new black literature, even when parochial and pedestrian, has raised questions of such compelling *emotional* significance that writers like Richard Gilman, William Styron, Albert Murray, and Ralph Ellison could not ignore them.

## Nonviolence and its Aftermath

The struggle for civil rights was essentially directed outward, against the most obvious symbols of racism. The emphasis was on acquiring the rights presumably guaranteed by the United States Constitution with its amendments. The struggle of the 1960s emerged at first as an assault against the social custom of segregated public facilities. There were sit-ins, marches, and picketing. These activities began as uncomplicated nonviolent demonstrations, but white resistance gradually forced a change of tactics. Organizations like the Student Nonviolent Coordinating Committee (SNCC) began to conduct voter-registration drives in the deep South. Subtly, the simple demand for fair treatment in a restaurant or on a bus was escalated into a bid for political power.

But there was also an *inward* direction to this process which took place on the psychic level, affecting both those who participated physically in the movement and the audience, who with the aid of mass media, witnessed the conflict as if it were taking place on a gigantic television screen. The civil rights struggle, when directed inward, sought to convince Afro-Americans of the righteousness of their cause.

King's constant insistence that the movement remain nonviolent assumed that there was an overriding extralegal moral principle behind the struggle for civil rights. It also assumed that dramatization of this principle would have the positive effect of winning the racist adversary over to the righteous cause of the oppressed. This is what King meant when he enjoined his followers to refrain from violence, thus maintaining the struggle on a "high plane of dignity." In the now-famous March on Washington speech of August 28, 1963, he admonished his predominantly Afro-American audience:

> Again and again we must rise to the majestic heights of meeting physical force with *soul force* [our italics]. The marvelous new militancy which has engulfed the *colored community* [our italics] must not lead to a distrust of all white people, for many of our white brothers, evidenced by their presence here today, have come to realize that their destiny is tied up with our destiny and their freedom is inextricably bound to our freedom. . . .[6]

Here King set forth values which were basically independent of the rights guaranteed by the Constitution. These values centered around what might be called the public-relations aspect of the struggle. But he was to find himself faced with an opposition which eschewed public relations and tended to see the movement in more parochial terms. In the summer of 1964, for example, a year after the March on Washington, there was a proliferation of middle-class white youth in the movement. Civil rights tradition up to that point would have ordinarily considered this development a blessing. It would bring needed allies into the movement and would perhaps lead to the politicization of a significant segment of the white community. But the presence of white youth created problems for some of the nationalistic black activists. Proceeding from an orientation different from that of their more liberal elders, they viewed the increased participation of whites as a threat to *independent* black leadership.

This philosophy led to a backlash—a distinct reaction against interracial organization and cooperation. Black activists suddenly demanded racial autonomy in the running of their organizations. The new will toward self-determination as expressed in all of its cultural variations, from controlling the institutions in the black community to the way one dressed or wore one's hair came to be called the Black Power movement. It is important to understand that this movement is not a historical accident. There has been a subterranean history of nationalism operative throughout the whole of Afro-American cultural history. It has not always expressed itself in radical political terms, but nevertheless, nineteenth-century nationalists like Martin Delany, David Walker, and Wilmot Blyden are as clearly a part of this nation's history as Frederick Douglass or Booker T. Washington. In fact, many black writers and intellectuals suddenly discovered themselves to be in closer sympathy with Marcus Garvey than with Walter White. They compared their militant zeal for liberation with that of men like Nat Turner and Denmark Vesey. Some writers of the sixties identified themselves as descendents of militant heroes, very much in the manner of men reciting their biological genealogy. Here is a character in *The Reluctant Rapist*, a novel by Ed Bullins:

> He spoke of black intellectuals in a historical context. "Before me was Richard Wright, DuBois . . . " he continued. He read off the names of negroes I had read about, negroes I had heard of briefly. It was like returning to a place that I had abandoned once, a place of my childhood that I longed for but feared. Marcus Garvey, Frederick Douglass.

Names from history and modern personalities spilled from the pages, all connected by the color of the characters' black skins and the dark history that they influenced. Len had his name intermingled with theirs, but where did I stand?[7]

## Nationalism and the Search for Self

As we have seen, black writers of the midsixties and after increasingly shaped their ideologies along nationalistic lines. They were not concerned with linking hands with their "white brothers." Rather they demanded a separate orientation, a movement whose essential thrust was internal, directed toward the realization of a separated identity, a separate set of values, and even a separate ontology. They were seeking a break with Western cultural and political values. What cultural compulsives lay behind this quest for alternative values?

On one level, there is the natural tendency of the modern artist to seek innovative forms. But in the context of political insurgency, the quest for new forms becomes an aspect of the larger quest for freedom and identity. In this respect, black writers and artists have much in common with their white avant-garde colleagues, who themselves have a special attitude toward tradition. For example, T. S. Eliot, indisputably a major voice in contemporary poetry, longed for a deeply rooted cultural tradition. We can make an analogy between his migration to England and subsequent change of citizenship, and that of a similarly alienated black writer who sets up shop in Nigeria or Marrakesh. Both have in common an aversion to what they see as the spiritual bankruptcy of American culture.

In like manner, the African or Caribbean writer seeks a more profound identity—one that is firmly rooted in his native culture. Tensions and contradictions arise here from the fact that he must find his own voice within an enslaving colonial linguistic structure. He could, of course, attempt to step out of the Western frame altogether. In Haiti, this might mean that the poet shuns French, choosing instead to recite his poetry in Creole on the streets of Port-au-Prince. Similarly, a poet like Leopold Senghor might try to continue his poetry in the oral traditions of the Senegalese Griots, the African tribal poets. But such an approach would seem almost impossible for men like Senghor, the poet-president of Senegal, or Aimé Césaire, the Martinican father of the term "Negritude."[8] These men have firm ties to the formal literature and philosophical systems of the West. Like the concepts of Black Power and the Black Aesthetic,* Negritude is a defensive frame, the purpose of which is the resolution of the cultural and psychological identity crises brought on by the Africans' contact with the West. Both colonialism and slavery confront the black writer with such crises. Consistently in these encounters we find the writer trying to arrive at some kind of *rapprochement* between his native culture and that of the enslaving force.

*See "The Black Arts Movement," later in this chapter.

As previously stated, this identity problem is not confined simply to black writers. Rabindranath Tagore faced it as an Indian writing in English. The poets and playwrights of the Irish Renaissance—even the perpetually alienated James Joyce—felt compelled to modulate the influence of English literature on their works by plunging into their own Celtic mythology and folklore.

To writers influenced by the ideology of Frantz Fanon, the West was a dying place. It was perceived as dying because its philosophical and cultural values seemed to have produced nothing but chaos. To paraphrase a metaphor Reverend King used in his famous March on Washington speech, America had defaulted on her promissory note; the freedom promised by the Constitution and the Declaration of Independence had been denied to Americans of African descent.

The so-called moderates and militants were in accord on this point, but they differed in essential matters of strategy and tactics. As a result, they projected different rhetorical styles. One style assumes the voice of traditional Western reasoning; the other, often violent in tone, attacks that tradition at its very roots. For example, what are we to make of an orientation that sees the totality of Western culture as demonic? Where King spoke of reaching out for "our white brother," to the Muslims "the white man was the Devil."

Indeed, for some black writers, America, with its rapid technological development, its material values, and its history of racism, emerges as the ultimate symbol of decadence. One of the first young black writers to project this tendency was Askia Muhammed Touré, who in 1963 founded *Umbra* magazine on New York's Lower East Side. The *Umbra* group included such writers as Ishmael Reed, David Henderson, Albert Haynes, Tom Dent, and the volatile Calvin Hernton. According to Ishmael Reed, it was Touré, known as Rolland Snellings before his conversion to orthodox Islam, who spearheaded the movement.

Touré, from the beginning of his literary career, called for the rejection of Western values:

> ... Like a nurseryman prunes a tree or a jeweler fashions an uncut stone, so must we prune and fashion our minds and spirits; we must strive to develop a revolutionary soul— total psychic unity with the masses of our people. We must become the very embodiment of their hopes, dreams, consciences, and desires for justice. We must develop into mental and spiritual fighting machines of Black America, instruments of the people ... Yes we must know, absorb, and value our cultural heritage, but not as a shield for inferiority complexes; rather, to become one with Self, with Blackness—embracing the Universal in man. Brothers and Sisters, this is the only sure way that militants, intellectuals, and potential leaders can begin their inevitable triumph over the West. By becoming so determined, so dedicated, so full of faith in a greater future, the materialistic hedonism of White America becomes the undesirable trait of a dying civilization.[9]

A complex of strategies is at work here. First, the statement is addressed specifically to a black audience. Second, it calls for the development of a "revolutionary soul." The unity it demands is not political, but "psychic." It sees as essential the development of "spiritual fighting machines." The function of the "cultural heritage" (tradition) is the development of a Self that is one with itself and with Blackness. And Blackness itself is perceived as "embracing the Universal in man."

There is a decidedly religious impulse operative through the above statement, as well as distinct echoes of the writings of Garvey, DuBois, Malcolm X, Senghor, and the Marxist critic Christopher Caulwell. In his willed drive toward righteousness, Touré suggests the profound debt the New Militancy owes to the language of religious reform. The Idea of Blackness (Self) as presented here seems to indicate some kind of religious transcendence. Most obviously, it portends a profound shift in poetic symbology and iconography. It clearly eschews the traditional Western metaphysical attitude toward Blackness as a symbol of evil and sin and forms the symbolic context for the emergence, later in the decade, of the counterslogan "Black Is Beautiful."

The quest for Self has a ritualistic dimension as well. This can be clearly seen in the ritual divesting of the so-called slave names;[10] e.g., Malcolm Little becomes Malcolm X; Rolland Snellings becomes Askia Muhammad Touré; and LeRoi Jones becomes Imamu Amiri Baraka. But this renaming process is only one aspect of a larger historical myth/ritual construct.

The names adopted derive from all parts of the African world. Their very diversity is indicative of the complex and often confused manner in which large segments of the black community view the African past. For example, some of the names stem from Arabic sources. This is especially ironic, given the historical relationship between slavery and the spread of militant Islam in Africa. The same is true of Swahili, a language so intimately connected with the East African slave trade that it owes its very existence to the commerce between the Bantu-speaking tribes of East Africa and Arab merchants.

This is not in any way meant as a denigration of any particular orientation toward names, but rather as an indication of the intricate value system which gave rise to such actions.

Ralph Ellison was one of the first Afro-American writers to isolate the particular complex of emotions surrounding the black American's attitude toward his name:

> And when we are reminded so constantly that we bear, as Negroes, names originally possessed by those who owned our enslaved grandparents, we are apt, especially if we are potential writers, to be more than ordinarily concerned with the veiled and mysterious events, the fusions of blood, the furtive couplings, the business transactions, the violations of faith and loyalty, the assaults; yes, and the unrecognized and unrecognizable loves through which our names were handed down unto us.[11]

Ellison goes on to cite the examples of the followers of Father Divine and Elijah Muhammad. For Ellison the discarding of their original names symbolized a "rejection of the bloodstained, the brutal, the sinful images of the past. Thus they would declare new identities, would clarify a new program of intention and destroy the verbal evidence of a willed and ritualized discontinuity of blood and human intercourse."[12] In this kind of emotional approach to history, the acquisition of a new name designates not only a change of identity in the present, but the possibility of some prior existence in a state of what Baraka calls "former glory." The study of black history is an essential part of the new religiously inspired nationalism . . . a nationalism which, although perhaps excessively brutal at times, springs from a profound and fervent need among a group of Afro-Americans to claim something in the world that deepens the *collective humanity* of black people everywhere.

## The Black Arts Movement

It is quite possible that this romantic search for a "former glory" provided the psychic backdrop for the emergence of the Black Arts Movement. The Movement may also have arisen from the compulsive need of the literary artist to address himself to the spiritual and philosophical implications of the freedom struggle. Although the Movement is closely associated with the opening of Imamu Baraka's Black Arts Theatre/School in the spring of 1965, shortly after the assassination of Malcolm X, its beginnings coincide with those of other literary groups—particularly the aforementioned *Umbra* group.

Politically oriented magazines such as the quarterly *Freedomways* also played an integral part in the creation of the Movement. *Liberator* magazine, founded like *Freedomways* in 1961 and edited by Daniel H. Watts, operated as an important source of news concerning the African liberation struggles and the Third World revolutionary movements. Then came the revolutionary nationalist journals like the Revolutionary Action Movement's (RAM) *Black America*, founded in 1963 by Max Stanford. RAM was one of the first organizations in the sixties to advocate the principle of armed struggle which later became so prominent a part of the political ideology of the Black Panther Party. Closely associated with *Black America* was *Soulbook*, which also had a Third World orientation. It was founded in the mid-1960s by Ken Freeman and Bobb Hamilton.

On the West Coast, the Movement was marked by the appearance of two especially significant magazines. The first and most important was the *Journal of Black Poetry*, founded in late 1964 by Joe Goncalves, who is still its editor. The *Journal's* creative orientation is essentially a blend of traditional black nationalism and revolutionary Pan-Africanism. It has been instrumental in introducing black American writers to the works of the Chilean poet Pablo Neruda, and the Afro-Cuban Nicolas Guillen. It has also published translations of such African poets as David Diop, Birago Diop, and Leopold Senghor. The second of these West Coast publications, *Black Dialogue*, first appeared in 1966. Its editor was Abdul Karim. *Black Dialogue* published such writers as Eldridge Cleaver, Marvin X, and the playwright Ed Bullins.

But the magazine that has probably had the most consistent effect on contemporary black letters is *Black World*, originally published as *Negro Digest* in 1941 by John H. Johnson, who is also the publisher of *Ebony* magazine. Some of the most significant questions concerning the role of the black writer were first raised in *Black World*. It was Hoyt Fuller, the magazine's editor, who started the relatively recent controversy concerning the possibility of developing a Black Aesthetic. This controversy originally stemmed from a survey of the artistic and ideological views of thirty-eight black writers. The flurry of critical and/or ideological debate this engendered has persisted into the seventies. *Black World's* strong influence on the new literary movement derives from the fact that it is the most stable and widely read of the magazines concerned with the full range of issues confronting the black artistic community. It is significant that the home office of Johnson Publications is located in Chicago, since it was here that Richard Wright got his start as a writer with the John Reed club in the early thirties.

Chicago is also the home of the previously mentioned Gwendolyn Brooks, a long-time established voice in contemporary American poetry. Together with Fuller she helped to spark a literary movement in Chicago which brought writers and poets like Don L. Lee, Sam Greenlee, Carolyn Rodgers, and Johari Amini (Jewel Latimore) to the attention of a newly conscious black reading public.

Another factor contributing to the growth of the Black Arts Movement was the creation of independent publishing houses like Dudley Randall's Broadside Press in Detroit, Don L. Lee's Third World Press in Chicago, and Baraka's Jihad Press in Newark.

The above developments and trends, along with the flowering of black theaters and the proliferation of black bookstores around the nation, helped to define the literary personality of the politically active sixties. They do not tell the entire story of Afro-American writing during the decade, however. There are and were significant writers like Margaret Danner, Mari Evans, Alston Anderson, Alice Walker, Charles Wright, William Melvin Kelley, Stanley Crouch, Paule Marshall, Ronald Fair, and Barry Beckham who, although thematically related to the tradition of Afro-American letters, chose to concentrate upon the private aspects of language and deal essentially with the problems of literary craftsmanship on its own terms.

## Nationalism and the Folk Spirit

One of the most influential aspects of the new nationalism on black writers has been its emphasis on the study of African and Afro-American culture. This has deeply affected writers like Henry Dumas, Stanley Crouch, Paul Carter Harrison, Ishmael Reed, Imamu Baraka, James Stewart, and Charles Fuller, who became especially interested in the aesthetic use of African and Afro-American cosmologies and mythological systems.

Even more important, there developed among these writers a profound respect for the power and dignity of black music. In *Blues People*, a book on Afro-American music, LeRoi Jones wrote:

... I am saying that if the music of the Negro in America, in all its permutations, is subjected to a socio-anthropological as well as musical scrutiny, something about the essential nature of the Negro's existence in this country ought to be revealed, as well as something about the essential nature of this country, *i.e.*, society as a whole.[13]

Here is a hint that a specific set of cultural characteristics can be found embedded in the music; that the music, in its numerous manifestations, is the expression of the black American's collective ethos. This is Jones's variation on the theme of the nineteenth century folk spirit.

This same emphasis on folk spirit is seen in the research undertaken by such German scholars as Johann von Herder and the Grimm Brothers. It is also evident toward the end of the nineteenth century in the Irish literary Renaissance. Yeats, O'Casey, Synge, and even that ultimate exile, James Joyce, are products of this kind of orientation. Variations on the theme of folk spirit also occur in the writings of such nineteenth century colorists as John Greenleaf Whittier, Ralph Waldo Emerson, Bret Harte, and Joel Chandler Harris. Folk themes reach their apogee in American fiction in the work of Mark Twain. Whitman's *Leaves of Grass* also owes something to this essentially romantic tradition.

In a sense, the new nationalism can be compared to an earlier flowering of "black consciousness" during the Harlem Renaissance of the twenties. This first wave of literary nationalism announced its entry into the American cultural scene with the publication of Alain Locke's anthology, *The New Negro* (1925). This seminal anthology contained the works of such writers and poets as Langston Hughes, Zora Neale Hurston, Claude McKay, Jean Toomer, and Arna Bontemps. Locke described the new sensibility as being characterized by a "deep feeling toward race." Further, he stated, there was among these writers a "consciousness of acting as the advance guard of the African peoples in their contact with twentieth-century civilization." Harlem, he reasoned, was the home of Negro "Zionism," the symbolic crossroads of black people in the diaspora. Anticipating the Pan-Africanism of the sixties, he wrote: " ... In terms of the race question as a world problem, the Negro mind has leapt, so to speak, upon the parapets of prejudice and extended its cramped horizons. In doing so it has linked up with the growing group consciousness of the dark peoples and is gradually learning their common interest."[14]

This persistent strain of nationalism could never have become a significant factor in Afro-American intellectual history if it were not somehow rooted in folk tradition. For example, what are we to make of the high premium many black communities, particularly in the South, put on self-reliance? A northern black American, upon visiting relatives in the South, will ritualistically inquire as to the status of the attempt of the community to gain economic and political power. His relatives will give him the latest news: Black contractors have developed a new tract of land; the church mortgage is paid up; the local black college has a new science building; and one of the local high-school students has been accepted at a prestigious eastern college. And what of the symbolic importance in popular black consciousness of such folk heroes as Jack Johnson,

Joe Louis, Bessie Smith, Adam Clayton Powell, Aretha Franklin, and James Brown? Are not these persons, and others too numerous to cite, in fact being conceived of as living embodiments of the soul of the race?

Again, given the nature of the particularly brutal oppression Africans experienced during the Middle Passage and slave period, is it not logical that many black people would develop a special view of history? Accordingly, a novel like Ralph Ellison's *Invisible Man* (1952) derives much of its tension from the nameless narrator's encounter with various attitudes toward tradition and history. At one end of the spectrum of the novel is the folk-consciousness of the narrator's grandfather. At the other is the romantic nationalism of Ras, the Exhorter, whose view of history swings back to the "former glory" of Africa, while gesturing toward a world controlled by black men:

> You *my* brother, mahn. Brothers are the same color; how the hell you call these white men *brother*? Shit, mahn. That's shit! Brothers the same color. We sons of Mama Africa, you done forgot? You black, BLACK! . . . You got bahd *hair*! You got thick *lips*! They say you *stink*! They hate you, mahn. You African. AFRICAN! . . .[15]

This speech occurs in the midst of a physical clash between representatives of two opposing Harlem political factions. Each claims to have the valid view of history. Ras's orientation is derived symbolically from the racial view of history as promulgated by Garvey, while the narrator and Tod Clifton represent the pseudoscientific attitudes of the Marxist-oriented brotherhood. At one point in Ras's eloquent appeal to the African racial memory a plane passes over:

> His chest was heaving and a note of pleading had come into the harsh voice. He was an exhorter, all right, and I was caught in the crude, insane eloquence of his plea. He stood there, awaiting an answer [from Tod Clifton]. And suddenly a big transport plane came low over the buildings and I looked up to see the firing of its engine, *and we were all three silent, watching* [our italics]. Suddenly the Exhorter shook his fist toward the plane and yelled, "*Hell with him, some day we have them too!* [our italics] Hell with him!"[16]

This is a typical Ellisonian epiphany. At this moment of stillness, in the midst of conflict, three black men are confronted with the awesome force of the twentieth century's technologial realities, realities which on one level exclude black people from exercising control over their destinies, while on another presenting them with a set of new possibilities. Thus the broadening horizon of experience represents, for some, a possibility for creative endeavor; while for others it serves only to deepen a sense of collective alienation and frustration.

Afro-Americans have traditionally played a complex role in the folklore of the nation. On the one hand, they represent the perpetual servant and buffoon—a singing, dancing, laughing clown. In another context they are seen as soulless beasts. In the theater they have been the object of dramatic satire. Their folkways have been burlesqued by white men in blackface. Their songs have been copied by white entertainers and composers, many of whom went on to build famous careers on the basis of white interpretations of Afro-American music, dance, humor, and oral style.

But this does not tell the whole story. There are other attitudes toward the Negro American as well. Some of them revolve around the perception that the Afro-American presence in the United States permeates the entire range of the nation's culture, coloring white attitudes toward all forms of aesthetic activities from lovemaking to writing novels. There is what Albert Murray called a "blues sensibility" present in much of American cultural life as well as a sense that the black American symbolizes something of the essential truth about America as a whole. Thus despite a long history of social injustice and the subsequent brutalization which sprang from that injustice, the Afro-American often appears in popular American culture as the quintessence of the American man of feeling. This is so because Afro-American culture adds a unique emotional dimension to the overall texture of American life, and is what Murray is getting at in his book, *The Omni-Americans*, when he makes the following statement:

> ... But the United States is in actuality not a nation of black people and white people. It is a nation of multicolored people. There are white Americans so to speak. But any fool can see that the white people are not really white, and that black people are not black. They are all interrelated in one way or another. . . .[17]

To illustrate the soundness of Murray's thesis, one has only to trace the history of cultural exchange and interaction between black and white Americans. Constance O'Rourke, in *American Humor*, has designated some of the ways in which the image of the black American impinges on the popular and folk consciousness. This thesis is further supported when we study the history of popular and dance music in America. Humanists like Murray and Ellison rejoice in this fusion of cultures, but nationalists must *of necessity* maintain their antagonism toward cultural exchange, since the overall aim of nationalism is the conservation of group cultural values. Nationalism is essentially a defensive frame aimed at providing a nation or an ethnic group with a common sense of history and purpose.

## Nationalism and the Black Aesthetic

Among black Americans today, the nationalistic impulse gives rise to a romantic longing for the pastoral innocence of the African past. Increasingly writers and artists are turning to the folk culture for inspiration and new formal ideas. The central purpose here is the revitalization of memory. The nationalist artist explains that this resurrection of the African and folk past is necessary for the collective uplifting of the race. One of Garvey's most famous slogans was: "Up, You Mighty Race; You Can Accomplish What You Will!" Behind this exhortation lies the idea of an Edenic Africa where black men built the pyramids, explored the sciences, and engaged in philosophical discourse. Given the circumstances of racial oppression in America, it should be easy to understand how this kind of romantic orientation can foster emotional bombast.

Typically the American writer's sensibility has been torn between Europe and America. The Afro-American writer, however, experiences an added tension, that of his romantic "allegiance" for Africa. The resulting conflicts underlie much of the writing about Africa which emerged in the twenties and which reemerged with renewed fervor in the militant struggles of the sixties. Furthermore nationalism, wherever it occurs in the modern world, must legitimize itself by evoking the muse of history. This is an especially necessary step where the nation or group feels that its social oppression is inextricably bound up with the destruction of its traditional culture and with the suppression of that culture's achievements in the intellectual sphere.

This latter attitude accounts for the defensive posture some contemporary black writers have assumed toward Afro-American culture. Some critics like Hoyt Fuller, Addison Gayle, and Don L. Lee have expressed the idea that white critics are not qualified to judge black literature. They maintain that the criticism of black creative arts should be the special province of the black writer himself. These critics assume that black people have a special history, a special set of artistic values which can be understood only within a black-aesthetic frame of reference. The obvious pitfalls of this kind of critical position do not concern us here. What must be understood, however, is that positions of this kind spring from a specific set of attitudes toward tradition and history. Obviously Afro-American writers and intellectuals who hold such positions are expressing their ideas in the context of a particular cultural nationalist history. What is being manifested here is a fear of the destruction of black culture; a position that perceives Western culture as an aggressive and alien force. This posture accounts for the strident tone of much of the literature of the sixties:

> Poems are bullshit unless they are
> teeth or trees or lemons piled
> on a step. Or black ladies dying
> of men leaving nickel hearts. . . . Fuck poems
> and they are useful, they shoot
> come at you . . .
> we want poems like fists beating niggers
> out of Jocks. . . .[18]

These lines are from the famous Baraka poem entitled "Black Art," which weaves together several significant themes. First, poetry is perceived as having a decidedly revolutionary function. Second, the poem is specifically addressed to black people; this point is of utmost importance, because one of the things the nationalist literary artist attempts to do is to envelop his art in what he perceives to be the exclusive spirit of his people:

> Let Black People understand
> that they are lovers and the sons
> of lovers and warriors and sons
> of warriors Are poems & poets &
> all the loveliness here in the world. . . .[19]

In this context, the poet sees himself as functioning as the voice of the nation. Such aesthetic orientation arises as a response to the struggles taking place in the political arena. Advocates of this viewpoint, a species of Marxist literary thought, hold that the role of the artist is to foment revolution. Ron Karenga, chairman of the cultural-nationalist organization US, expresses this position in the following terms:

> Black art, like everything in the black community, must respond positively to the reality of revolution. It must become and remain a part of the revolutionary machinery that moves us to change quickly and creatively. We have always said, and continue to say, that the battle we are waging now is the battle for the minds of Black people. . . . It becomes very important, then, that art plays the role it should play in black survival and not bog itself down in the meaningless madness of the Western world wasted. In order to avoid this madness, black artists and those who wish to be artistic must accept the fact that what is needed is an aesthetic, a black aesthetic, that is a criteria for the validity and/or beauty of a work of art.[20]

What Karenga means by a "black aesthetic" is not clear. Nowhere in any of his work is the concept outlined or described. However, the main thrust of his ideas seems to indicate that a black aesthetic is, in fact, implicit in artistic works that champion the cause of racial solidarity and black liberation. A similar view is expressed in the critical writings of Addison Gayle and Don L. Lee, now known as Haki R. Mahubuti; upon close examination, however, these ideas turn out to be updated versions of Marxist literary theory in which the concept of race is substituted for the Marxist idea of class. In his book, *Dynamite Voices*, a critical study of contemporary black poetry, Lee (Mahubuti) makes the statement several times that the "critic is first and foremost a blackman, redman, yellowman or whiteman who writes. And as a critic, he must stem from the roots that produced him." What he is stressing here is the belief that the black critic owes a special allegiance to the Afro-American community and its problems, and further, that his special experiences as a black man must somehow interact positively with his critical role, which is to aid in the psychological and spiritual liberation of black people. Lee's (Mahubuti's) critical orientation places a great deal of emphasis on the idea of art as *experience* instead of *method*.

What this amounts to is an attack against the tendency of modern critics to concern themselves with questions of form, structure, and genre (what Northrup Frye calls "modes"). (Actually, the hub of much so-called contemporary black criticism revolves around the question of form over content.) Black critics who stress the importance of content over form are usually trying to get the edge on white critics whose social backgrounds often differ radically from those of black artists. To stress content over form, structure, texture, and conscious craftsmanship is simply a way of stressing questions of social morality over those of abstract aesthetics. (This critical method, as we have noted, has its roots in Marxian proletarian literary criticism.) Hence any writer who evinces a persistent concern for artistic "method" is looked upon as engaging in art for art's sake.

This approach to literary art as experience is problematic at best. As Kenneth Burke points out in *Counter-Statement*: "When the appeal of art as method is eliminated and the appeal of art as experience is stressed, art seems futile indeed. Experience is less the *aim* of art than the *subject* of art; art is not *experience*, but something added to experience. But by making art and experience synonymous, a critic provides an unanswerable reason why a man of spirit should renounce art forever."[21] In other words, if a man can make real physical love to a woman, what's the sense in writing a love poem?

The critical positions advocated by Addison Gayle, Don Lee (Mahubuti), and Ron Karenga are finally attempts to apply the ideology of race to artistic creation. Only on the level of emotional rhetoric do these propositions make sense. Afro-Americans do have a distinctive culture and, as Albert Murray points out, a distinctive blues-oriented attitude toward experience. However, in a larger sense, their experiences ramify throughout the whole of human existence. The task of the contemporary black writer, as of any serious writer, is to project the accumulated weight of the world's aesthetic, intellectual, and historical experience. To do so he must utilize his artistry to the fullest, distilling his experience through the creative process into a form that best projects his personality and what he conceives to be the ethos of his national or ethnic group.

Writers like the late Henry Dumas and Ishamel Reed were able, by dint of craftsmanship and study, to create literary works which are uncompromising in their quest for Pan-African forms, yet refuse to sacrifice anything in the way of artistic integrity. Dumas, killed by a white policeman in a Harlem subway station, was a student of both African and Afro-American mythology and folklore. His poetry and fiction clearly illustrate the possibilities of a Pan-African approach to literary expression in the English language. Similarly, we find an analogous synthesis in the voodoo novels and poetry of Ishmael Reed.

In summary, it is clear that many contemporary literary attitudes toward tradition stem from highly emotional evaluations of the meaning of life in Western society. Literature is, after all, an attempt to define creatively man's place in the world and in doing so to aid him in the discovery of his profoundest self. The historical problem of black literature is that it has in a sense been perpetually hamstrung by its need to address itself to the question of racism in America. Unlike black music, it has rarely been allowed to exist on its own terms, but rather been utilized as a means of public relations in the struggle for human rights. Literature can indeed make excellent propaganda, but through propaganda alone the black writer can never perform the highest function of his art: that of revealing to man his most enduring human possibilities and limitations.

### Notes

1. Ralph Ellison, *Shadow and Act* (New York, Random House, 1964), p. 140.
2. The "dozens" are sometimes called the "dirty dozen." This is a verbal context in which the contestants ritually insult one another in rhymed scatological doggerel. The object of insult is usually the respective combatant's mother. The point of the game is to defeat an opponent with sheer verbal dexterity. For a study of the dozens see Roger Abrahams, *Deep Down in the Jungle* (New York, Folklore Associates, 1964).
3. Charles Anderson, "Finger Pop'n" in *Black Fire*, ed. LeRoi Jones and Larry Neal (New York, Morrow, 1968), p. 189.

4. Welton Smith in *Ibid.*, pp. 283–91.

5. LeRoi Jones, *Evergreen Review*, December 1967, pp. 48–9.

6. Marcus Hanna Boulware, *The Oratory of Negro Leaders: 1900–1968* (Westport, Conn., Negro Universities Press, 1969), pp. 272–3.

7. Ed Bullins, *The Reluctant Rapist* (New York, Harper and Row, 1973), pp. 154–5.

8. Negritude is a concept developed in Paris during the thirties by African and Afro-Caribbean writers while they studied in French universities. Negritude is an outgrowth of, or a reaction to the psychological consequences of colonialism. It is a defensive frame whose essential function, like a talisman, is to ward off the presumed evils of assimilation. Leopold Senghor, Leon Damas, and Aimé Césaire, the acknowledged creator of the term, all felt psychologically threatened by a formidable French culture. They felt that they were becoming black Frenchman. Negritude was the attempt of these writers to return to the psychic roots of their native cultures. See Leopold Senghor's *Liberté 1: Negritude et Humanisme* (Paris, Editions du Seuil, 1964). Also see, Irving Leonard Markovitz, *Leopold Sedar Senghor and The Politics of Negritude* (New York, Atheneum, 1969).

9. Rolland Snellings, *Liberator*, November 1964, p. 26.

10. This change of names also relates to a rejection of Christianity as an operational mythology. Christianity is rejected by many of the new nationalists who see it as the religion of the oppressor. On the aesthetic level, there is a tendency to probe African religious systems in search of new motifs and symbols. In some of the fiction, drama, and poetry of the sixties we find allusions to Yoruba deities like Shango and Yemaya. There are in the work of Henry Dumas, for example, allusions to tree spirits and ancestor worship. And two of Ishmael Reed's novels, *Yellow Back Radio Broke Down* (1969), and *Mumbo Jumbo* (1972), revolve around ideas derived from Haitian voodoo and New Orleans-style Hoodoo. Jahneinz Jahn's *Muntu* (1961) is one critical source for some of the neo-African experiments in Afro-American writing during the late sixties.

11. Ellison, *op. cit.*, p. 148.

12. *Ibid.*

13. LeRoi Jones, *Blues People* (New York, Morrow, 1963), p. ix.

14. Alain Locke, *New Negro* (New York, Atheneum edition, 1968), p. 14.

15. Ralph Ellison, *Invisible Man* (New York, Modern Library, Random House, 1952), p. 280.

16. *Ibid.*, p. 282.

17. Albert Murray, *The Omni-Americans* (New York, Outerbridge and Dienstfrey, 1970), p. 3.

18. Jones, *Black Fire*, p. 302.

19. *Ibid.*, p. 303.

20. Ron Karenga, *The Black Aesthetic* (New York, Doubleday, 1972), p. 31.

21. Kenneth Burke, *Counter-Statement* (Berkeley, University of California Press, 1968), p. 77.

## SOURCES AND BIBLIOGRAPHY

### An Ideological Overview

Baldwin, James, *Notes of a Native Son.* Boston, Beacon, 1955.

———, *Nobody Knows My Name.* New York, Dial Press, 1961.

Baraka, Imamu (LeRoi Jones), *Home: Social Essays.* New York, Morrow, 1966. Contains political and critical essays covering the period from 1960 to 1965. Key essays are "Myth of A Negro Literature," "Black Writing," and "The Legacy of Malcolm X, and the Coming of the Black Nation."

———, *African Congress: A Documentary of the First Modern Pan-African Congress.* New York, Morrow, 1972.

Brown, H. Rap, *Die Nigger Die*. New York, Dial Press, 1969. This is a political autobiography of one of the most militant activist spokesmen of the sixties.

Clarke, John Henrik, ed., *Malcolm X: The Man and His Times*. New York City, Collier, 1969. Essays by twenty-one black writers about Malcolm X. They cover such topics as "The Meaning of Malcolm X," C. Eric Lincoln; "The Influence of Malcolm X on the Political Consciousness of Black Americans," James Boggs; "Malcolm X: An International Man," Ruby M. and E. U. Essien-Udom.

Cleaver, Eldridge, *Soul On Ice*. New York, McGraw-Hill, 1968. Much of this was written while Cleaver was incarcerated in Folsom Prison. Prison writing, or writings by ex-prisoners, is a new genre of Afro-American writing. The general theme of the prison genre is the convict's discription of how he arrived at certain ideological conclusions.

Davis, Angela Y., *If They Come in the Morning*. New York, Third Press, 1971. A miscellany of prison writing centering around Miss Davis, the most famous female political activist of this period. The significant thing about most of the new prison writing is its projection of the idea of convicted criminal as political prisoner.

Essien-Udom, E.U., *Black Nationalism*. New York, Dell edition, 1964. This is one of the key sources on the historical role of black nationalism in Afro-American history. Discusses such topics as the nationalist tradition, the Nation of Islam, Black Zionism, and the eschatology of the Nation of Islam.

Foner, Philip S., ed., *The Black Panthers Speak; The Manifesto of the Party: The First Complete Documentary Record of the Panthers Program*. Philadelphia,

Lippincott, 1970. Compare to Baraka's Pan-African entry cited above. The Panthers represent an attempt to merge nationalism and Marxism. In the late sixties, there were ideological squabbles between Pan-Africanist nationalists like Ron Karenga and Marxist-oriented nationalists like Eldridge Cleaver. These squabbles resulted in the deaths of two Panthers, allegedly at the hands of Pan-African nationalists.

Frazier, E. Franklin, *Black Bourgeoisie*. Riverside, N.J., Free Press, 1957. This book was a major influence on the generation of black college students who initiated the civil rights movement of the early sixties.

Hernton, Calvin C., *White Papers for White Americans*. Garden City, N.Y., Doubleday, 1966. Essays on literature and politics by one of the founders of the *Umbra* group.

Holt, Len, *The Summer That Didn't End*. New York, Morrow, 1965. This is an activist lawyer's account of the Mississippi civil rights project of 1964. In the South, that was an especially traumatic summer. Three civil rights workers were lynched, and several churches were bombed. That summer also marked the end of formal interracial cooperation between black youth and white youth in the civil rights struggle.

Jackson, George, *The Prison Letters of George Jackson* (Introduction by Jean Genet). New York, Bantam Books, 1970.

Lacy, Leslie, *The Rise and Fall of a Proper Negro*. New York, Macmillan, 1970. The dust jacket reads: "The awakening of a black bourgeois and his search for a new identity and Black Manhood."

Lester, Julius. *Look Out Whitey! Black Power's Gon' Get Your Mama*. New York, Dial Press, 1968.

———, *Revolutionary Notes*. New York, Grove Press, 1970.

———, *Search for the New Land*. New York, Dial Press, 1969. An attempt to describe the sixties in terms of a journalistic collage.

New York 21, *Look For Me in the Whirlwind: The Collective Autobiography of the New York 21*. New York, Random House, 1971.

Seale, Bobby, *Seize The Time: The Story of the Black Panther Party and Huey P.*

*Newton*. New York, Random House, 1970.

Shabazz, Malik(Malcolm X), *The Autobiography of Malcolm X*. New York, Grove Press, 1965.

———, *Malcolm X Speaks*. New York, Grove Press, 1965. Contains the speeches of Malcolm X.

United States Riot Commission Report, *Report of the National Advisory Commission On Civil Disorders*. New York, Bantam Books, 1968.

## Some Sources for a Poetic Framework

Baraka, Imamu (LeRoi Jones), *Blues People*. New York, Morrow, 1963. A seminal work. Black music is described as the purest expression of what it means to be a Negro American. Jones maintains that the music, unlike black literature, survives mainly because it drew its strength and beauty from traditions that were carried by the "lowest classes." Herderian idea has had a profound impact on the recent generation of black writers. See Ellison's rebuttal to *Blues People* in *Shadow and Act*.

Deren, Maya, *Divine Horsemen: The Voodoo Gods of Haiti*. (Introduction by Joseph Campbell) New York, Chelsea House, 1970.

Diop, Cheikh Anta, "The Cultural Unity of Negro Africa. Paris, *Présence Africaine*, 1959.

DuBois, W. E. B., *The World and Africa*. New York, International Publishers, 1965.

Higgins, Godfrey, Esq., *Anacalypsis* (in two volumes). Secaucus, N.J., University Books, 1829, 1965. Higgins subtitles this compendium of myths, religious ideas, and inquiries into the roots of man's primary consciousness, "an attempt to Draw Aside the Veil of the Saitic Isis; or an Inquiry into the Origin of Languages, Nations, and Religions."

Jahn, Janheinz, *Neo-African Literature: A History of Black Writing*. New York, Grove Press, 1968.

Rainwater, Lee, ed., *Soul*. New Brunswick, N.J., Rutgers University, Trans-action Books, 1970. Discusses such topics as the significance of soul, rapping in the black community, and the making of a Black Muslim.

## General Readings

Aaron, Daniel, *Writers On the Left*. New York, Harcourt, Brace & World, 1961.

Bluestein, Gene, *The Voice of the Folk*. Amherst, University of Massachusetts Press, 1972.

Burke, Kenneth, *Attitudes Towards History*. Albuquerque, N.M., Hermes Pub., 1959.

———, *Counter-Statement*. Berkeley, University of California Press, 1968.

———, *A Grammar of Motives*. Berkeley, University Of California Press, 1969.

Cooke, Mercer and Henderson, Stephen, *The Militant Black Writer*. Madison, University of Wisconsin Press, 1969.

Ellison, Ralph, *Shadow and Act*. New York, Random House, 1964.

Frye, Northrup, *Anatomy of Criticism*. Princeton, Princeton University, 1957.

Gayle, Addison, *The Black Situation*. New York, Dell, 1970.

———, *The Black Aesthetic*. New York, Doubleday, 1972.

Gilman, Richard, *The Confusion of Realms*. New York, Random House, 1969.

Harrison, Paul Carter, *The Drama of Nommo*. New York, Grove Press, 1973.

Jahn, Janheinz, *Muntu: The New African Culture*. New York, Grove Press, 1961.

Mphahlele, Ezekiel, *Voices In the Whirlwind*. New York, Hill & Wang, 1972.

Murray, Albert, *The Omni-Americans*. New York, Outerbridge & Dienstfrey, 1970.

———, *South to a Very Old Place*. New York, McGraw-Hill, 1971.

## Some Representative Fiction

Bambara, Toni Cade, *Gorilla, My Love*. New York, Random House, 1972.

Baraka, Imamu, *Tales*. New York, Grove Press, 1967.

Barrett, Lindsay, *Song For MuMu*. London, Longmans, Green and Co., Ltd., 1967.

Beckham, Barry, *My Main Mother*. New York, Walker and Co., 1969.

Brown, Cecil, *The Life and Loves of Mr. Jiveass Nigger*. New York, Farrar, Straus & Giroux, 1969.

Cain, George, *Blueschild Baby*. New York, McGraw-Hill, 1970.

Davis, George, *Coming Home*. New York, Random House, 1971.

Dumas, Henry, *Ark of Bones and Other Stories*. Carbondale, Southern Illinois University Press, 1970. (The importance of this writer cannot be emphasized enough.)

Fair, Ronald, *Many Thousand Gone*. New York, Harcourt, Brace & World, 1965.

———, *Hog Butcher*. New York, Harcourt, Brace & World, 1966.

Heard, Nathan C., *Howard Street*. New York, Dial Press, 1968.

Kelly, William Melvin, *Dem*. Garden City, N.Y., Doubleday, 1967.

Major, Clarence, *All-Night Visitors*. New York, Olympia Press, 1969.

Marshall, Paule, *Soul Clap Hands and Sing*. New York, Atheneum, 1961.

McPherson, James Alan, *Hue and Cry*. Boston, Atlantic-Little Brown, 1969.

Reed, Ishmael, *Mumbo Jumbo*. Garden City, N.Y., Doubleday, 1972.

Williams, John A., *The Man Who Cried I Am*. Boston, Little, Brown, 1967.

Wright, Sarah, *This Child's Gonna Live*. New York, Delacorte Press, 1969.

Young, Al, *Snakes*. New York, Holt, Rinehart and Winston, 1970.

## Poetry of the Sixties

Angelou, Maya, *Just Give Me a Cool Drink of Water 'fore I Diiie*. New York, Random House, 1971.

Baraka, Imamu (LeRoi Jones), *Black Magic Poetry 1961–1967*. Indianapolis, Bobbs-Merrill, 1969. An important volume of poetry by one of the major voices of the sixties.

Cortez, Jayne, *Pissstained Stairs and the Monkey Man's Wares*. New York, Phrase Text, 1969. This hard-to-find volume is strongly influenced by contemporary black music and blues.

Crouch, Stanley, *Ain't No Ambulances For No Nigguhs Tonight*. New York, Baron/ E. P. Dutton, 1973. Clearly one of the best poets writing today. Has an interesting understanding of the relation between poetry and music.

Cruz, Victor Hernandez, *Snaps*. New York, Random House, 1969. Cruz is from the Puerto Rican community of El Barrio, but has been closely associated with the Black Arts Movement. These poems are excellently crafted, making use of street rhythms and incisive urban imagery.

Dumas, Henry, *Poetry For My People*. Carbondale, Southern Illinois University Press, 1970. This volume contains perhaps some of the best poetry of the last decade. Dumas, more than any writer of the sixties, had effected a brilliant synthesis of Afro-American and African folk-and-myth ideas. There is also in this volume an excellent critical essay on Dumas by his friend, poet Jay Wright. This book was published after Dumas' untimely death.

Henderson, David, *De Mayor of Harlem*. New York, E. P. Dutton & Co, 1970. Henderson's career began with the *Umbra* poets in 1963. He is the master, and the natural voice, of the long line.

Knight, Etheridge, *Poems From Prison*. Detroit, Broadside Press, 1968. Knight's work first began appearing in the *Negro Digest* (now *Black World*) during the midsixties. He was an inmate in the Indiana State Prison when many of these poems were written. As a result, many of them exude the bleakness of the prison environment.

Joans, Ted, *Black Pow-wow Jazz Poems*. New York, Hill & Wang, 1969. Ted Joans, ex-Village Bohemian, turns "Black."

Jordon, June, *Some Changes*. New York, Baron/E. P. Dutton, 1971.

Latimore, Jewel C., *Let's Go Some Where*. Chicago, Third World Press, 1970. Representative of the group of female poets like Carolyn Rodgers, Nikki Giovanni, and Mae Jackson. This kind of poetry is often interesting when read aloud, but it sometimes fails to encounter the private self.

Lee, Don, *Selected and New Poems*. Detroit, Broadside Press, 1971. Lee is an important poet if only for his impact on the black college generation of the sixties. His work is uneven, however. The propagandistic thrust often dilutes the main emotional thrust of his lines.

Sanchez, Sonia, *Home Coming*. Detroit, Broadside Press, 1969.

## Anthologies of New Black Poetry and Literature

Chapman, Abraham, ed., *New Black Voices*. New York, Mentor, 1972. Contains an excellent introduction by the editor. This collection embraces the work of several generations of contemporary Afro-American writers, including such writers as John O. Killens, Ralph Ellison, Quincy Troupe, Gerald W. Barrax, and a strange, exciting poet by the name of "Conyus."

King, Woodie, ed., *Black Spirits*. New York, Random House, 1972. Much of the material here is duplicated in other anthologies. But the thrust of this collection is contained in Amus Mor's classic poem on growing up in Chicago, "We are The Hip Men."

Randall, Dudley and Burroughs, Margaret, *For Malcolm*. Detroit, Broadside Press, 1967. This is one of the seminal anthologies of the sixties. The poems here are dedicated to the life and death of Malcolm X.

## Anthologies Containing Critical Essays on Afro-American Writings.

Barbour, Floyd B., ed., *The Black Seventies*. Boston, Porter Sargeant Publications, 1970.

Bigsby, C. W. E., ed., *The Black American Writer*, Volumes I and II. DeLand, Florida, Everett/Edwards, 1969.

Bone, Robert, *The Negro Novel In America*, rev. ed. New Haven, Yale University Press, 1965.

Gayle, Addison, ed., *Black Expression*. New York, Weybright & Talley, 1969.

Hill, Herbert, ed., *Anger and Beyond*. New York, Harper & Row, 1966.

Henderson, Stephen, *Understanding Black Poetry*. New York, Morrow, 1973.

Contains an excellent selection of the New Poetry, along with an intensive critique of black aesthetics.

Jones, LeRoi and Neal, Larry, eds., *Black Fire*. New York, Morrow, 1968.

Margolies, Edward, *Native Sons: A Critical Study of Twentieth-Century Negro-American Authors*. Philadelphia, Lippincott, 1969.

Redding, J. Saunders, and Davis, Arthur P., eds., *Cavalcade: Negro American Writing From 1760 to the Present*. Boston, Houghton Mifflin, 1971.

—p.826

# 25

## *Afro-American Music*

### *Wendell Whalum, David Baker, and Richard A. Long*\*

It is convenient to consider the musical activity of the Afro-American as flowing in three streams: Folk, Jazz, and European. In the first two the Afro-American dominates as creator and performer. In the third he participates only marginally as creator, as do Americans generally, and as a performer, as fully as American conditions have permitted.

Each of the streams may be thought of as having a specific locus. Folk music has its roots in the rural experience and is associated with work, socials, and the church. Jazz is urban and is the music of the cabaret and the vaudeville house. European music is that of the drawing room and the concert hall. There have been points of contact among the three streams, but it is best to consider them separately.

## THE FOLK STREAM

The oldest collection of Afro-American songs, which provides a foundation for the study of most of the music discovered since its publication, is *Slave Songs of the United States* (Allen *et al.*, eds., 1867). Henry E. Krehbiel used it in his pioneer study of 1914; James Weldon Johnson studied it carefully for his two-volume collection, which includes detailed prefaces; John W. Work was thoroughly familiar with its contents when he published his *American Negro Songs* in 1940 with a lengthy and important discussion of the background of the music. Miles Mark Fisher's book, *Negro Slave Songs in the United States* (1953) is almost entirely devoted to an analysis of its contents.

Over the years, scholars in general and Johnson and Work in particular have supplemented this original material with the fruits of their research, providing not only additional information about the music itself but historical data as well. Such data was beyond the grasp of the 1867 collection. Its editors were white northerners who were attracted by the beauty and unfamiliarity of the music, but who were unfamiliar with

\*Material on the *The Folk Stream* was prepared by Professor Whalum; material on *The Jazz Stream* by Professor Baker. Other material and editing done by Professor Long.

the conditions that produced it. This prevented them from fully appreciating the music's extraordinary overtones, expressed in textual implications, topical references, and double meanings.

This early music originated with the individual and proceeded from the individual to the group. This was a logical sequence because the experiences of the individual could be and often were the experiences of any member of the group. Group singing thus became a form of testimony or endorsement by the members of the community, and the music which evolved lives on today, both as a form of communication and as a memorial to the conditions out of which it was born. The music has been called by various names including jubilees, mellows, melodies, plantation melodies, and slave songs.

Groupings of Afro-American music are difficult to construct, primarily because its dominant factor is rhythm. Since much of the music has a basic rhythmic similarity, we are forced to rely heavily on textual differences when assigning a song to a particular category. The categories to be used in this discussion are:

> Spirituals (including sacred sorrow songs)
> Work Songs
> Social Songs (including love, game, and/or play songs)
> Hymn Tunes (linear)
> Blues (including secular sorrow songs)
> Gospel Music

## Spirituals

The ever-popular spiritual makes use of scriptural fragments and phrases expressing religious ideas. Its mood is dignified and reverent. That spirituals are the largest group of songs collected to date is not surprising. Most of the collectors in the years after 1865 were Christians who felt a sympathetic attraction to the black man's concept of God. They marveled at his music, and commended him for his faith. The popularity of the spiritual, however, must not overshadow the fact that the slave had other music as well, music more expressive of his lot. A natural fear of punishment for doing that which was not looked upon with favor by his overseers probably prevented the slave from revealing this music to his white masters. Although we cannot know for sure, there is reason to question whether the spiritual was as popular with the slave in the eighteenth century as it was with collectors in the nineteenth.

The second collection of Afro-American music, which was also the first to contain spirituals exclusively, was G. D. Pike's *The Jubilee Singers* (1874). Of the sixty-one songs included, the majority are sorrowful in text and mood. A sampling of the titles clearly indicates their religious nature:

> Nobody Knows the Trouble I See, Lord!
> Swing Low, Sweet Chariot
> From Every Graveyard

Children, We All Shall Be Free
I'm a Rolling thro' an Unfriendly World
Didn't My Lord Deliver Daniel
I'll Hear the Trumpet Sound in That Morning
We'll Die in the Field
Give Me Jesus (you may have all this world)
Go Down, Moses
Keep Me from Sinking Down
I'm a Trav'ling to the Grave

Credit for our awareness of this type of music goes largely to the original group of Jubilee Singers from Fisk University, whose tours through America and Europe, lasting from 1871 to 1878, provided the opportunity to expose the world to the music that their parents and relatives sang during slavery. Yet in spite of what we have learned from *Slave Songs of the United States*, *The Jubilee Singers*, and subsequent scholarship, we still know relatively little about the origins of these songs. How they were actually created remains a matter of speculation. In the preface to *Slave Songs* two possible explanations are given:

As to the composition of these songs, "I always wondered," says Col. Higginson, "whether they had always a conscious and definite origin in some leading mind, or whether they grew by gradual accretion, in an almost unconscious way. On this point I could get no information, though I asked many questions, until at last, one day when I was being rowed across from Beaufort to Ladies' Island, I found myself, with delight, on the actual trail of a song. One of the oarsmen, a brisk young fellow, not a soldier, on being asked for his theory of the matter, dropped out a coy confession. 'Some good spirituals,' he said, 'are start jess out o' curiosity. I been a-raise a sing, myself, once.'

"My dream was fulfilled, and I had traced out, not the poem alone, but the poet. I implored him to proceed.

" 'Once we boys,' he said, 'went for tote some rice, and de nigger-driver, he keep a-callin' on us; and I say, "O, de ole nigger-driver!" Den annuder said, "Fust ting my mammy told me was, notin' so bad as nigger-drivers." Den I made a sing, just puttin' a word, and den anudder word.'

"Then he began singing, and the men, after listening a moment, joined in the chorus as if it were an old acquaintance, though they evidently had never heard it before. I saw how easily a new 'sing' took root among them."

A not inconsistent explanation is that given on page 12 of an "Address delivered by J. Miller McKin, in Samson Hall, Philadelphia, July 9, 1862."

"I asked one of these blacks— one of the most intelligent of them (Prince Rivers, Sergeant 1st Reg. S.C.V.)— where they got these songs. 'Dey make 'em, sah.' 'How do they make them?' After a pause, evidently casting about for an explanation, he said: 'I'll tell you, it's dis way. My master call me up, and order me a short peck of corn and a hundred lash. My friends see it, and is sorry for me.

> When dey come to de praise meeting dat night dey sing about it. Some's very good singers and know how; and dey work it in— work it in, you know, till they get it right; and dat's de way.'"

James Weldon Johnson, in describing a camp meeting, relates how, during a meeting, there would be at least one participant who was "a leader of singing, a maker of songs, who could improvise at the moment lines to fit the occasion." Too, states Johnson, "committing to memory the leading lines of all the Negro spiritual songs is no easy task, for they run up into the hundreds. But the accomplished leader must know them all, because the congregation sings only the refrains and repeats; every ear in the church is fixed upon him, and if he becomes mixed in his lines or forgets them, the responsibility falls directly on his shoulders."[1]

The spiritual may be classified according to the differences found in the musical arrangement. Some contain short melodies, others long. Some have a solo line which is immediately answered by the group. Others make use of strong syncopation. John Work, in *Papers of the Hymn Society of America*, states it this way: "Musically, spirituals may be classified into three large groups or types: the 'call and response' chant; the slow, sustained lone-phrase melody; the syncopated, segmented melody." Almost all the old spirituals extant can be fitted into one of these categories. The few that do not conform resemble folk tunes from other lands with which the slave was no doubt familiar, and for which he changed the text to fit his own needs without altering the music. While the rendition may closely resemble the spiritual, careful scrutiny reveals its failure to adhere to the spiritual's basic patterns.

Work elaborates on the three types of spirituals as follows:

> The first of these, the "call and response" chant, may be identified by the alternation of a solo verse line with a choral response of a short phrase or word. The leader's call changes from line to line but the choral response rarely changes, though it may be in two parts and on occasion may have an ending phrase which serves as a release. These songs usually are characterized by a rapid tempo and a pounding rhythm although the best-loved and best-known of all spirituals, and one which illustrates the form well, "Swing Low, Sweet Chariot," is sung in the opposite manner. Answering the leader who sings many lines beginning with "Swing Low, Sweet Chariot" the chorus responds with the line "coming for to carry me home." The well known song "Go Down, Moses" uses the choral response "Let my people go" to answer the leader's varying call line. Another striking example of this type of song is "Walk Together, Children."

> "Deep River," "Lord, I Want to Be a Christian," "O the Rocks and the Mountains Shall All Flee Away," "My Lord, What a Morning," and "There Is a Balm in Gilead to Heal the Sin-sick Soul" are good examples of the second type of spiritual, having slow, sustained, long-phrase melodies.

In general the best-liked of the spirituals are those with the episodic, segmented melodies and the syncopated rhythms. These are the third type of spirituals. Such songs as "Little David, Play on Your Harp," "O Give Me Your Hand," "Got Religion All Around the World," "Oh Bye and Bye I'm A-going to Lay Down My Heavy Load," "Ain't Goin' to Study War No More," and "Ain't I Glad I Got Out of the Wilderness" are good examples.[2]

The exact meaning of the words used in spirituals presents another interesting problem, though not a new one. Dr. Newman White included textual analysis in his *American Negro Folk Songs* (1928), and John W. Work, Sr., tackled the problem in his *Folk Songs of the American Negro* (1915), as did Miles Mark Fisher, referred to above. These texts, however, do not readily lend themselves to analysis. The slave did not know literary English and his use of English developed in the milieu of his peers, hence it is not surprising that a special language resulted. That the texts of the spirituals are sometimes banal, that there is often no logical connection between verses and refrain, and that there are seemingly excessive repetitions of words and phrases is hardly surprising. But the slave well understood what he sang about and the texts usually make good poetry. In transcribing scriptural thoughts into song form, the slave showed a thorough comprehension of his material:

> You read in the Bible and understand,
> Methuselah was de oldest man.
> He lived 900 and 69,
> Died and went to heaven in due time.
> Who'll be a witness?

or,

> O, wasn't that a wide river?
> River of Jordan
> Wide River!
> There's one more river to cross.

In 1969 Sister Savannah Morgan, an 80-odd-year-old member of Allen Temple African Methodist Episcopal Church in Atlanta, Georgia, recalling her grandparents singing in Hamilton County, Georgia, sang the following song for this writer:

> I wish I was in heaven today
> I wish I was at home.
> I wish I was in heaven today
> I'd hear my mother when she moaned.

This, she stated, was sung one night as the family sat around reminiscing about "old times." Her grandmother related how the old slave preacher "sho' made heaven a beautiful place where all the members gone on are just like they were here. After the sermon, the preacher, he lead the song."

One favorite technique when using a biblical text for singing spirituals was to have the leader ask a question and have the group or congregation answer it. Famous in this genre are the following:

> Leader:   Have You Got Good Religion?
> Response:   Cert'ny Lord.
> Leader:   Have You Got Good Religion?
> Response:   Cert'ny Lord.
> Leader:   Have You Got Good Religion?
> Response:   Cert'ny Lord. Cert'ny, Cert'ny, Cert'ny Lord!

Or the famous passage from Jeremiah 8, which concludes with "Is there no balm in Gilead? Is there no physician there?" The spiritual answers the question with "There is a balm in Gilead, to make the wounded whole, to heal the sin-sick soul!" Two more examples will suffice: The spirituals embracing the suffering and death of Christ are immediately related to a slave's own suffering. "Mumbalin' Word" is a familiar one. But the question asked in "Did you hear that Jesus rose?" is answered "Yes He rose, rose on Easter Day." And what of the question posed in "Didn't My Lord Deliver Daniel?" It is answered, "Well, why not every man?" Another version concludes with "why not deliver po' me?"

There are several lines in spirituals that recall the Last Supper. "Break Bread," "Drinking of the Wine," "It Was the Blood." These are in use in the current black church.

The above songs and many, many others like them developed the fullness of the drama in the scriptural texts. But the one that best sums up the whole matter of the slaves' looking toward a better day is "In That Great Gettin' Up Mornin'," which is also a good example of the "sermon in song" spiritual. This song which bids goodbye to all earthly toils and cares, heralds the great day. It begins with a prologue, "I'm going to tell you 'bout the comin' of the Savior" and the response "fare ye well" is the same throughout the song. It was possibly first sung by a very musical preacher, for its twenty-odd verses follow exactly the pattern of the folk sermon, coupling scriptures with an immediate interpretation. The verse on Gabriel is an excellent example:

> De Lord spoke to Gabriel, Fare Ye Well, Fare Ye Well;
> Go look behind de altar, Fare ye well, Fare ye well.
> Take down the Silvah trumpet, Fare ye well, Fare ye well,
> Blow your trumpet, Gabriel; Fare ye well, Fare ye well.

(Gabriel): Lord, how loud shall I blow it, Fare ye well, Fare ye well;
(Lord): Blow it right calm and easy, Fare ye well, Fare ye well.
Do not alarm my people, Fare ye well, Fare ye well.
Tell 'em to come to judgement; Fare ye well, Fare ye well.

One hears from time to time certain statements regarding the double and hidden meanings of the texts of spirituals. Musical scholars have even suggested that the spirituals were *never* intended to underscore a real and abiding faith in Christianity, but were intended to confuse the white man. Miles Mark Fisher, for one, dwells on this point at length. One thing is clear, however: once institutional Christianity claimed the mind of the slave the spirituals found a solid anchor. Whatever the original meaning of "Steal Away," or "There's a Meetin' Here Tonight," or "Walk Together, Children" or

Where you goin' my sister?
Where you goin' now?
I'm goin' on down by the river of Jordan
Where you can't cross there, in the morning.

Christianity was broad enough to absorb and redirect that meaning. This is not to suggest that texts originally did not contain hidden and double meanings, but to judge them properly we must keep in mind the ambiguity that was an inevitable part of the slave mentality and outlook.

The spirituals that one hears from the concert stage or from trained choirs today lack much of their original sound. This has been true since the days of the Jubilee Singers, whose songs were not as authentically Afro-American as one might initially suspect but had been harmonized European-style. The spiritual's true sound is one that does not reveal predetermined harmony or harmony that adheres to the rules of music theory. The singer of this music traditionally sang additional notes which are not represented in conventional notation. He frequently overlapped cadences and added notes whenever he desired, or whenever the "spirit moved him" to do so. In the old-time spiritual, the leader is always expected to anticipate the coming lines and to fill in any felt gaps in the rhythm. The pentatonic scale is very often employed and minor intervals frequently appear in otherwise major songs. The flatted third and seventh are characteristic tones that are found.

Harmony is rare in the music. Occasionally one will hear the bass voice singing the melody an octave lower, but more often one finds a unison line and when there is harmony it is in two parts in parallel motion.

The following is sung frequently at the Bethlehem Church of God, Holiness, in Georgia. Recently, Aneedra Bolton, a 12-year-old, led it during devotions for the morning worship and the harmonies were as follows:

The spiritual is unaccompanied. The patting of feet (rarely the clapping of hands outside the Holiness Churches), and the vocal embellishment make for a stunning rendition.

Whereas church choirs and college choirs utilize four-part harmony in singing spirituals, their performance by congregations, both in the early church and in rural churches today, has been confined almost exclusively to unison or two-part singing. Additional voices are a rarity.

A few writers on the subject have attempted to deny that the spiritual is wholly a product of the black people. Richard Wallaschek, in his book, *Primitive Music* (1893) and George Pullen Jackson, in *White Spirituals of the Southern Uplands* (1933) and in *Spiritual Folk Songs of Early America* (1937), attempted to establish Euro-American origins for these songs. Later research, such as that done in Alan Lomax's Columbia University Cantometrics project, shows the flaws in such arguments and successfully refutes them.

## Work Songs

Just as the spiritual filled a particular need in his life, so did the black man turn to the work song for companionship and as a means of easing his back-breaking labors. Recognized and documented as a unique song form in post-Civil War years, a study of the music's rhythmical structure offers the best approach to understanding its makeup. The texts as well have an important role to play.

These songs sing of the white boss and his mean ways, or deal with incidents and persons with whom the workmen were familiar. Several of the songs that have come down to us today have texts dealing with living conditions, despicable persons in the community, and "pretty gals." The most prevalent pattern in these songs is the call and response form in which questions raised by the singing black foreman are answered by the work crew. Laying cross ties on a railroad, driving spikes, digging ditches, breaking rock, carrying bales of cotton, loading timber, laying rails—all formed a part of the kind of heavy labor that was the black man's lot, especially after the war when living conditions began to depend on what he could earn.

The musicologist Willis Lawrence James found the following call and response song during his years of musical collection:

> Leader:   Hey, can't you line 'em?
> Response:   Bigboy
> Leader:   Hey, can't you line 'em?
> Response:   Bigboy
> Laader:   Hey, can't you line 'em?
> Response:   Bigboy
> Leader:   Hey, can't you line 'em right?
> Verse:   Jack, the rabbit, Joe, the bear,
>               Can't you move it, just a hair?

The white boss was generally addressed as "captain." The next song was sung while laying rails and driving in spikes:

> Leader:   Oh, the cap'tin can't read.
> Response:   No, he can't.
> Leader:   The cap'tin can't tell.
> Response:   No, he can't.
> Leader:   If he catch you,
> Response:   No, he can't.
> Leader:   Jes' run like hell.
> Response:   No, he can't.
>
> Leader:   Pull it to the right,
> Response:   Uh, huh.
> Leader:   Pull it to the left,
> Response:   Uh, huh.
> Leader:   Turn around
> Response:   Uh, huh.
> Leader:   Touch the ground.
> Response:   Uh, huh.
> Leader:   Now let's move on, on, on,
>               Let's move on.

In studying the two songs quoted above there is more to observe than the tune, rhythm, and text. The work song acted as a sure means to organize the work team. The leader was in command, second only to the white boss. It was his duty to keep the men working busily in unison until the job got done. He paced the song according to the rhythm best suited to accomplish the task at hand. In his way he was as much a leader as the leader of spirituals in the church or the song leader at a camp meeting.

In some of the songs, especially those about the legendary John Henry, the leader's part consists of long stanzas to which the workers respond with the sound made by the fall of the hammer, or the breath exhaled while pulling the crowbar. The "Hammer Song," reprinted in the *Negro Caravan*, is an excellent example:

> Well she ask me— hunh—
> In de parlor— hunh—
> And she cooled me— hunh—
> Wid her fan— hunh—
> And she whispered— hunh—
> To her mother— hunh—
> "Mamma, I love dat— hunh—
> Dark-eyed man"— hunh—
>
> Well I ask her— hunh—
> Mother for her— hunh—
> And she said she— hunh—
> Was too young— hunh—
> Lord, I wished I'd— hunh—
> Never seen her— hunh—
> And I wished she— hunh—
> Never been born— hunh—
>
> Well I led her— hunh—
> To de altar— hunh—
> And de preacher— hunh—
> Give his command— hunh—
> And she swore by— hunh—
> God that made her— hunh—
> That she'd never— hunh—
> Love another man— hunh—

The work song was primarily a man's song, a song of muscle and sinew. Women, as they worked at washing, ironing, cleaning, cooking, and sewing, sang the old meter hymns of the church or hummed melodies reminiscent of the blues or sorrow song. There is much use of music by the individual at work, but the individual might or might not adhere to a rhythmic scheme as tenaciously as would be imperative for a leader and his group. Field hands, while plowing, for example, did not do work that calls for a strong rhythm, and therefore would sing either old meter ("conventional") hymns, the blues, a love song, or the like. The following song could be performed either by an individual or by a group with a leader. In the latter case, the group would respond with some kind of answer that was coordinated with its work.

### It Sound Like Thunder[3]

I'm a man tall like a mountain
I'm a man steady like a fountain
Folks all wonder what makes it thunder
When dey hear, Lawd, my hammer fall.

#### Chorus

An' hit sound like thunder
Lawd, hit sound like thunder
When my hammer fall.

Did you read it in de paper
'Bout de gov'nor and his family,
Dey am 'cided to come to de new road
Jes' to hear, Lawd, my hammer fall.

Boss got money— mo den de government
Come to town ridin' a chariot
Drivin' forty big, fine racehorses
Jes' to hear, Lawd, my hammer fall.

## Social Songs

As the black man moved more and more toward the development of his own community following the Civil War, certain forms of entertainment grew with him. With his increasing freedom, he could adapt to his own needs forms of pleasure formerly denied him, but with which he was nevertheless familiar. Dancing, playing instruments, and the celebration of holidays and great feast days were to receive new appreciation and new interpretation in the postwar period.

Music was everywhere. At the close of the day, work camps reverberated with the sound of all kinds of musical instruments as the workmen sought relaxation. Any old rhythm-keeping instrument or tool would do. Bones, boxes, tin cans, saws, pipes, jugs, and the like all played a part in the group's musical equipment as they played, danced, and sang the evenings away.

Back home in the communities, the approach was slightly more sophisticated. Here blacks taught themselves to play European-designed instruments, infusing their music with their own artistic concepts and techniques. Children, too, had a role to play, composing play songs as they engaged in new, creative games. All of this activity had existed in the slave communities in some form or other but now the black had a far greater say in choosing the type of music and involvement he enjoyed.

The black man's use of improvisation and extemporization is rooted in these years, which mark the development of the social songs of love, gambling, fun, and play. It was now, as well, that the so-called blues was born—out of contrast with happier moments and in moments of full realization of the nature of the times.

By the early 1930s the social song had run its course and was engulfed by the fast-growing popularity of commercial blues and jazz. The recording companies had triumphed with the Mamie Smith recording of Perry Bradford's "Crazy Blues" on August 10, 1920, and other "race records," and the black jazz bands were fast becoming staples in the entertainment world.

John Work analyzes the social song as follows:

> The social songs can hardly be considered as rich and distinctive in melodic content as the spirituals or the blues, although the improvised accompaniment showed harmonic feeling superior to the spirituals and a development in rhythmic figures comparable only to that shown in the blues.
>
> The melodies are not as interesting in structure and design as those of the other types of folk song. We do not find such fine melodies among them as "Deep River," and "You May Bury Me in the East," among the spirituals; or as "Little Low Mamma Blues," or "Arkansas Blues." This is due, probably, to the fact that they did not spring from deep emotional experience nor, originally, from serious attempts at description of events. Instead, they were created for dance purposes, and that fact explains the highly developed rhythm of the accompaniment. I have not found a song of this class in waltz time. All of those I have encountered have been in duple and quadruple time, slow and fast, distinguished by rhythmic figures.[4]

## Hymn Tunes

Hymn tunes entered black religion via the institutional church, whose traditional forms of worship called for specifics in the order of service. Along with scriptures, prayer, and sermon, hymns were an integral part of the Methodist and Baptist denominational services.

Blacks were introduced to this type of music by the white churches to which they were taken as slaves. (It was customary for slaves on many plantations to attend church on Sunday afternoons for worship, although some plantations did not grant their slaves the right of worship.) During these services the blacks were preached to by white preachers or occasionally by another slave who had been granted this privilege, and participated in the singing.

It is generally felt, therefore, that hymns do not really "belong" to the black man, at least in the same creative sense that spirituals do. They are in another way, however, profoundly his—in the sense that any Christian feels ownership over his aids to worship.

Viewed from a strictly musical point of view, the hymns of early white America were relatively cut-and-dried. The black church "rearranged" them and gave them a flavor that is much more moving and, to this writer, more musical. It is largely the manner in which they are sung that transforms the traditional Christian hymns into black music. The most popular method involves the "lining out"[5] of the text by a deacon or pastor. This is followed by the singing of the "lined" phrases by the congregation. The old "Dr. Watts"[6] hymns and psalms, typical of this approach, still form a part of the devotional phase of many black Baptist churches.

In performing this music the singers take all the freedom that they feel is necessary in order to truly "raise the hymn." Willis James has observed that the singers actually add space to the music. And space is indeed created, space that is then filled with all kinds of embellishments. The rhythm is relaxed and meters are elongated to their farthest points by pressing each word syllable to its musical height.

In some of these hymn tunes the melody is so embellished that it is almost impossible to recognize it. At Allen Temple A. M. E. Church, in Atlanta, "Amazin' Grace" is an excellent example of this kind of embellishment. The result is a new tune, one capable of being appreciated on its own merit rather than through the awareness of the more familiar melody.

The hymns are sung in one of two ways: (1) in unison with the bass voices doubling at the lower octave, when necessary, or (2) in parallel fourths and fifths.

Hymns of this type survive in many churches today. They may be sung, as already mentioned, in the "prayer service"; and they are sung, in addition, at moments such as the "right hand of fellowship," communion, or a break during the sermon.

## Blues

The blues, a mature secular sorrow song, has its roots in early slave laments. These songs of sorrow belong to the individual and depict his slave and postslavery experiences. The music we have been discussing up until now proceeded from the individual to the group. The blues, however, begins with the individual and is finally taken over by other individuals, remaining thereby a solo song. A strong secular form, it is concerned with worldly thoughts and concrete ideas rather than notions of heaven and the spiritual life to come. It is a reflective form, the cry of a man who has nothing, seems unable to get anything no matter how hard he tries, and whose life appears without hope. It is, too, a state of mind voiced by men or women, often in sad and penetrating phrases.

In the blues form, the text is as important as the music. The usual textual pattern is to repeat the first line, add an antecedent phrase, then follow with a third line.

> I feel like running, running way away
> I feel like running, running way away
> Ain't got nobody, an' no where to stay.
>
> Ain't got no mother, daddy been long gone,
> Ain't got no mother, daddy been long gone,
> Ain't got no money, an' I ain't got no home.
>
> My man left dis mornin' and didn't leave no tracks behin'
> My man left dis mornin' and didn't leave no tracks behin'
> I know I can't make it, all I got is one thin dim'.
>
> I heard the whistle blowin' 'bout de break of day,
> I heard the whistle blowin' 'bout de break of day,
> Sound like it tell me, he gotta be on his way.
>
> Ef anybody see him, sen' him home to me
> Ef anybody see him, sen' him home to me
> Tell him I'm worried, broke as I can be.

The blues is reflective of a human condition, hence has a wide appeal. It is not unusual to hear people interpret blues that they have heard on a recording in such a personal manner that it appears that they were made up on the spot by the singer.

The blues of which we have been speaking is rural music, music anchored in the world of experience associated with the levees and Delta section of the Mississippi, and extending on to the river-connected Southwest. It is here that the blues form began and from here that it slowly developed with the eventual help of both black and white recording artists.

A study of the blues in *The Negro Caravan* suggests that "Jelly Roll" Morton and "Ma" Rainey were among the first to popularize the blues. Then too there was W. C. Handy:

> [Handy] recognized [the blues'] value, and in 1909 wrote "Memphis Blues," and in 1912, the most widely known blues of all, "St. Louis Blues." Handy is called the "Father of the Blues." As the first musician of creative and analytical powers to appreciate the possibilities of the blues, and the writer of the first published blues, Handy is credited by Abbe Niles with "commencing a revolution in the popular tunes of this land comparable only to that brought about by the introduction of ragtime."
>
> The blues is recognized as indubitably the Negro's. Many songs that have come out of Tin Pan Alley are called blues with very dubious warrant. Irving Berlin's "Schoolhouse Blues," Jerome Kern's "Left All Alone Again Blues," Braham's "Limehouse Blues," Hess's "Homesickness Blues" and "Blues My Naughty Sweetie Gave to Me" are examples of these pseudo blues. As one critic summarizes it, in the blues by Tin Pan Alley composers the grief is feigned, but in genuine Negro blues the gaiety is feigned. The musical influence upon jazz of the genuine blues is great; the "blue note" is one of the most significant developments in jazz, and it is entering "serious" American music. Certain bands are advertised as bands that play the blues as it should be played; certain white singers, such as Dinah Shore and Jack Teagarden, are famous for the way they sing the blues. One music critic points to a hillbilly's singing of a Negro blues with Swiss yodeling added, as a good instance of the hybridization of American popular music. The blues is now an inseparable part of that music. But it is still, almost entirely, of Negro origin, and at its best is close to folk sources.
>
> Because of the enormous popularity on phonograph records of women blues singers such as Ma Rainey, Mamie Smith, Bessie Smith (the "Blues Empress"), Clara Smith, Trixie Smith, Ida Cox, and Billie Holliday, the blues is frequently thought of as a woman's plaint for her departed or departing lover. Not so widely known to America are the many male blues singers such as Jim Jackson, Lonnie Johnson, Leroy Carr, Leroy's Buddy (Bill Gaither), Peetie Wheatstraw, Hound Head Henry, Big Bill, and Huddie Ledbetter (Leadbelly), but they are enthusiastically received by the Negro masses. (pp. 427–28)

## Gospel Music

A definite resuscitation of interest in Afro-American music for religious purposes became apparent in the second decade of the twentieth century. This followed a period in which the black church had "experimented" with hymns, anthems, and even gospel hymns derived from the white evangelical movements of the closing years of the nineteenth century. With the emergence of the Holiness, Sanctified, and other black cults, however, black music regained a position of top priority as an accompaniment to a variety of forms of worship.

Of all the bodies that came into being between 1890 and 1920, it was primarily the Church of God in Christ that most consistently sang and created music that stemmed from or reflected the black man's slave experiences. These churches, and there were many, literally followed Psalm 150—"praise God with the instruments . . . ," permitting tambourines, drums, wind instruments, washboards, and the like to join in the praising. It was not and is not rare to find a nineteenth-century unaccompanied spiritual being sung in the Church of God in Christ to the accompaniment of a band of instruments and a percussion group. The rendition more often than not will also include clapping, dancing, and shouting. It is also frequent practice to make up new songs during the service, songs that grow out of the sermon or out of an experience of the maker. Such music continues to follow the traditional pattern of "call and response."

A few years ago at the Pentecostal Church of God in Christ in Memphis, Tennessee, a healthy, big-voiced lady musically aroused the church with the stirring question: "What do you think about Jesus?" The response was "He's all right." From this there developed a twelve-minute song that stirred the entire body of worshipers.

Gospel music is, in a sense, the twentieth-century spiritual. It came to the fore after the decade of the 1920s when the Depression weighed heavily on a meager existence, and found its initial reception greatest among black women, the keepers of the home and the church. The gospel is not as deeply rooted in the black experience as the spiritual, however. Neither is its text as meaningful, although it does emanate from the same lower-economic, undereducated bracket of blacks that gave birth to the spiritual. Gospel music is a music that achieves its success not by what is sung, textually, but through the singing itself, the beat, or the effects. It takes the shape sometimes of blues, sometimes of rock, and sometimes of jazz.

One of the primary forces in the development of gospel music was Thomas A. Dorsey. He began playing jazz on the piano at an early age and as a teenager found himself accompanying, among others, The Syncopaters, Les Hite, and "Ma" Rainey. Following some serious self-examination and a few chastening family encounters, he went on to devote his attention to the church. By the early thirties, at the beginning of the Depression, he was projecting a music that has since achieved a wide appeal.

Gospel music takes many shapes. Some of it reflects wholesale borrowing from known hymnody: "I Heard the Voice of Jesus Say," "Praise God from Whom All Blessings Flow," "Blessed Assurance," "Amazin' Grace," "I Surrender All," and "Draw Me Nearer." Some simply take one or two phrases from an existing song: "O Happy Day," "Leaning on the Lord," "Where He Leads Me," "Standin' on the Promises." Most gospel music, however, is formally composed, with carefully phrased, thoughtful texts that deal with the more melancholy aspects of human experience.

The main difference between spiritual and gospel music is the obligatory accompaniment of the piano and/or other instruments in rendering the latter. Gospel music, for example, has capitalized on the electric organ with all its effects. Another difference is that the musical intensity of gospel music is much slighter than that of the spiritual.

It is quite obvious that gospel singers and the audience to whom they appeal get more from the actual sound of the voices and the effects of the loud notes, high notes, and "juicy" harmonies they employ, than from what is being sung. Gospel music has an all-important emotional factor that must be taken into account by all singers of the music. Its harmonies are simple, with frequent sequences of secondary seventh chords, and its melodies are characteristically weaker in shape and logic than those of the nineteenth-century spiritual. Where the rhythm in the older music is a constant marvel, the gospel has a stereotyped beat, borrowed from the swinging secular music of the black people.

The phonograph recording has done much to hurt the creative aspect of gospel music. Groups prefer to imitate each other rather than develop their own creative potential, and this they do via recordings. A choir will not sing the famous "O Happy Day" unless it can get a contralto soloist of the same quality as the soloist on the recording that made the work famous. In other words innovation has been replaced by the carbon copy, and gospel groups, at rehearsal, listen and imitate rather than explore and learn.

Gospel groups have found it necessary to develop colorful and often outlandish choir robes for their use in the performance of the music, and it is often difficult to get a group to perform unless it can put on such robes. The robe is used as an identifying agent rather than a garment that makes the group part of the clergy.

The typical gospel voice has a hoarse, coarse, loud quality and the groups rock, dip, jump, and shout while putting a song across. The truest gospels stem from the older, original groups: the Martin Singers, the Davis Sisters, the early Ward Singers, Brother Joe May, and Sister Rosetta Tharpe, among others.

The gospel's chords, harmonies, and effects are very similar to those used in secular music. Riffs, ostinatos, call and response, obbligatos, effects from singing on the syllables of "woo" and "ah," rocking in time, and the like, are usual accompanying aids. Here is a typical gospel of the 1940s:

> There is a great change in me,
> A great change in me,
> I am so happy, I am so free,
> Since Jesus brought me out of the darkness
> Into His marvelous light, and
> Oh, oh, oh, There's a great change in me.
>
> Oh well I stepped on the rock
> And the rock was sound,
> The love of God came streaming down.
> Since Jesus brought me out of the darkness
> Into His marvelous light, and
> Oh, oh, oh, There's a great change in me.

Some gospel composers consider themselves as creators, taking pride in their ability to dash off any number of new works. Such artistry is of little value, however, when we realize that none of the gospels are performed as they are printed. It is perfectly permissible to improvise on these scores, adding or reharmonizing at will.

Thomas Dorsey has called "Precious Lord, Take My Hand" one of his best. It may very well be. But when performed by Ben Branch or Mahalia Jackson it is definitely different from what is taken to be the original. And it is regrettable to find that by reducing "Precious Lord" to its original notes, what one ends up with is "Must Jesus Bear the Cross Alone?" with a few displaced notes:

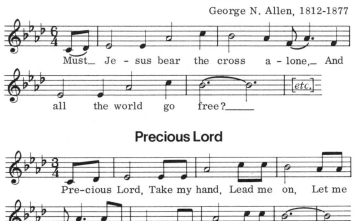

### Must Jesus Bear the Cross Alone?

George N. Allen, 1812-1877

Must_ Je - sus bear the cross a - lone,_ And all the world go free?_____ [etc.]

### Precious Lord

Pre-cious Lord, Take my hand, Lead me on, Let me stand,_ I am tired, I am weak, I am worn,_____

Gospel music has performed a valuable service by providing its audience with a musical vehicle by which to transform earth's sorrows to heaven's joys, as well as allowing for the musical participation of the talented but largely untrained group of black people who continue to popularize it. But in spite of such merits, its products are short-lived; most gospels die the death of popular songs. A group may continue to sing the song that made it famous over a long period of time, but other old songs are quickly abandoned in favor of new ones with fresh appeal.


## THE JAZZ STREAM

Much has been written about jazz, its composers, performers, genesis, and relative importance. But unfortunately the literature of jazz contains many fabrications, half-truths, and general misconceptions.

In any serious consideration of jazz it must above all be remembered that jazz is black music. It is the black man who gave this musical idiom its language, vocabulary, syntax, and heart, and he is the one who is responsible for every significant advancement and major innovation in the field.

The popular conception of jazz is that it springs from the meeting of African rhythms and European harmonies. This idea has given rise to the notion that whatever dignity and worth jazz has, comes from the European half of the equation. It explains, in part, why when jazz is performed as concert music, it is generally presented in a watered-down form. Much of this "acceptable" jazz is testimony to a serious effort to neutralize the music's African elements.

Jazz music has its roots in the social, racial, economic, and cultural conditions of the South. New Orleans has been made famous in song and story as the cradle and the nursery of jazz. Indeed, its geographic, economic, demographic, and social factors provided a favorable cultural climate for this new music. Jazz existed for many years as a multifaceted idiom whose character depended largely on the social and racial constitution of its audience. Developing out of nineteenth-century folk music, it drew on a variety of materials from a multiplicity of external sources and synthesized them into a new music.

New Orleans, the largest city in the South at the turn of the century, was also perhaps the most liberal southern city. The city's residents, true to their French-Spanish heritage, winked at what their rural neighbors, predominantly white Anglo-Saxon Protestants, would have found immoral and unlawful, In this easy-going atmosphere, blacks enjoyed more latitude culturally, socially, and otherwise than anywhere else in the South. This factor, combined with the lure of the higher wages to be found in a large port city, served as a strong attraction for southern blacks. New Orleans' tradition of using music for practically all occasions was another major drawing card. (The city had a tradition of Negro music in the early and middle 1800s, with blacks gathering regularly in Congo Square to perform African music.)

Other elements, both musical and social, contributed to the birth of this remarkable music. The blues, brass bands, and the stimulating effect of piano rags all had their parts to play. The opening of Storyville, with its bordellos and cabarets, also gave an unexpected boost to this new uninhibited music, despised by the arbiters of culture and later castigated in the press.[7]

It can not be definitively stated that jazz was born in New Orleans. But there is very little doubt that by 1900 the city was the center of black musical activity in the South, and that part of this musical activity was the playing of what later was to be called jazz. It should be kept in mind, however, that not all music played by Negroes in New Orleans or elsewhere was jazz. Both the folk stream and the Euro-American stream were represented.

Other important factors that helped jazz to flower were the creation of certain musical groups, later to serve as models; such practical matters as available sources for instruments and musical materials; and the emergence of a psychological need to create a music that is essentially protest music.

For although jazz can express feelings like ebullience, *joie de vivre*, happiness, etc., the fact remains that it was and remains protest music. It could only have been born after the downtrodden black lost his obsession with the "striving-to-be-white" attitude of the Creole of color and the pseudo-aristocrats of New Orleans.

The first jazz bands were created in the image of brass bands. These "hot brass" bands marked the beginning of a revolution in popular music, acting as cultural catalysts. Their ensemble playing was basically more heterophonic than polyphonic and the common denominator that linked them to the first jazz bands was the blues. Instrumental jazz developed from the merging of the traditions of the New Orleans brass band with those of the urban blues. The art of group improvisation (although early improvisation was more often melodic embellishment than real improvisation) like the blues was associated with the uptown section of New Orleans. In general the instrumentation and function of each instrument was the same in the brass band and the early jazz band; the cornet usually carried the lead, upon which the clarinet embroidered, and the trombone supported the other wind instruments by fulfilling a rhythmic-melodic function. The rhythm section (drums, tuba, and, for nonmarching occasions, banjo or guitar, string bass, and later piano) provided the supporting background.

New Orleans between 1870 and the turn of the century had an abundance of marching bands which played for street parades, funerals, wakes, and so forth, as well as bands attached to labor organizations and Negro fraternal benevolent associations including the YMCA, Elks, and Moose.

Despite its debt to the brass and marching bands, jazz emerged as a decidedly different idiom from its predecessors. This difference stemmed mainly from the fact that jazz men were usually forced to improvise rather than read their music, and that the music itself came from more diverse sources: marches, blues, popular songs, rags—virtually every source with which the enterprising black bandsmen came into contact. While the street bands imitated the Europeanized military music they heard, the jazz bands "ragged" the same music rhythmically and treated the tunes in improvisatory folk-heterophony.

As to instruments, the Negroes found that Confederate military bands had left them a legacy of secondhand conventional instruments. All over the South decrepit military instruments survived among the vestiges of the Civil War, and these the blacks appropriated for their own use. Bandsmen supplemented these European instruments with such *ad hoc* additions as fly swatters, jugs, washboards, buckets, spoons, and pie pans.

The first jazz bands played mostly ensemble music, collectively improvised for the most part, with each man contributing almost equally to the total sound of the band. The emphasis on ensemble was, on the surface, an imitation of brass-band technique, but the real reasons for the emphasis on ensemble work actually went much deeper than that if one considers the music from a social and psychological point of view. For although the United States was starting to change from a rural to an urban society during the first decade of the twentieth century, a strong sense of community still existed throughout the land, particularly among blacks. A person belonged first and foremost to a group—to his family, his lodge or club, or his profession—so it comes as no surprise that jazz stemmed from a musical tradition whose cornerstone was community song.

True to the tradition of oral music and African precedents, the early jazz men infused their music with special vocal music qualities—growls, pitch variations, smears, slurs, and the cadence of conversation. This particular phenomenon, which is a facet of a much larger attitude diametrically opposed to Western tradition, with its emphasis on regularity of pitch, timbre, vibrato, and other musical components, needs some comment.

The African and Afro-American strived for the negation of many of the European traits mentioned above. All through black American music we therefore find a unique and dynamic use of smears, slurs, timbre alterations, and the introduction of various physical techniques that subtly or drastically alter the basic sound of European instruments. We witness time and time again the many different approaches to sound production and the multiplicity of resultant sounds. There is in jazz no concept of a universal jazz sound. This is of course very much an African retention because in African society obliquity and ellipsis, wide latitude of interpretation, pitch, meaning, and so on are the rule.

Perhaps the best-known figure from this first period of jazz is Joe "King" Oliver. The classic form of the New Orleans band was crystallized by his ensemble, The Creole Jazz Band, which produced the quintessence of early jazz. According to Gunther Schuller the following things characterize his music:

1. King Oliver's music had a warmth of expression, a relaxed easy swing, lovely instrumental textures, and a remarkable discipline and logic.
2. His musicians used referential improvisation (they used the melody as a point of departure for improvising). King Oliver was the master of thematic transformation.
3. His band was the apex of intuitive coordination.
4. The role of each musician (as in the brass bands) was clearly defined.
5. He conceived of the band as a single instrument.
6. In his music heterophonic homophony established the four-beat harmonic basis for collective improvisation.
7. There was in his band an extraordinary unity which was exacted at the price of renouncing all stylistic progress.
8. The whole philosophy of Oliver's approach is based on the perfect rendition of a completely predictable result.
9. The performance excitement engendered by his band derives from the perfected rendition of certain traditional devices and patterns.
10. The only real surprises tolerated in the New Orleans style were in the "breaks." (The excitement generated in the "breaks" was a strong factor in eventually expanding the solo break into a bona fide solo.)[8]

Despite the greatness of King Oliver's music, jazz, as all great art must do, continued to evolve. Several factors contributed to the demise or at least the evolution of Oliver's music. Perhaps the most important was the fact, as Schuller puts it, that "once a single player could hold the listeners' attention, the collective ensemble became unnecessary."

Louis Armstrong, a King Oliver sideman, was to be that first "single player." Along with the emergence of Armstrong as the first great jazz soloist came certain changes, structural and musical, in the jazz ensemble. Composition assumes a place of greater importance, thus providing a vehicle for a soloist. (It is an aphorism that inventive composition stimulates improvisational invention.) The guitar replaces the banjo and the piano is given a more or less independent role. The introduction of stepwise movement into basically chordal structures produces real melody lines. The drums are counterpointed against a melodic line which is still marking the time, and finally percussion techniques grow more sophisticated, leaving behind the military two-step and moving toward an approximation of the polyrhythms of African and Caribbean music.

Louis Armstrong was the apotheosis of the musician of this second period in jazz. His technical prowess and fertile imagination mark his recorded work as the most artistic achievement of jazz in the twenties. His was to be the dominant jazz voice for nearly twenty years. Other important figures of this era include Freddie Keppard, Bunk Johnson, Kid Ory, and Mutt Carey.

## Ragtime (1900–1920)

The characteristics of ragtime, which emerged from and went on to influence jazz may be listed as follows:

1. Multitheme (usually four themes grouped either ABACD or ABCD).
2. Harmonic orthodoxy (a carry-over from jazz).
3. Simple syncopation, rarely rhythmically complicated.
4. An interest in key relationships that reflects its affinity to European music. This means simply that certain traditions were established regarding how each section related to the other sections vis-à-vis key.
5. Mandatory recapitulation (return to the theme statement).
6. Usually the compositions observed a sixteen-bar limit divided into four equal parts.
7. The left hand was supportive and never syncopated.
8. The changes were essentially from tonic to dominant.
9. This was essentially a piano music.
10. It descended from the cakewalk.
11. The music was hard, bright, cheerful, and machinelike.

Despite some of the negative traits of ragtime, this music did suggest for the first time in jazz that formal organization might not be incompatible with instinctive utterance. A handful of black artists were able to transcend the music's limitations and to effect a rebirth of much of this music by interjecting personal creative talent. In a short time the folk themes, ring shouts,[9] and church themes were transmogrified into a unique, identifiable body of pianistic music.

The important ragtime players were Scott Joplin, who wrote two ragtime operas, "A Guest of Honor" and "Treemonisha," James Scott, Joseph Lamb, Artie Matthews, Tom Turpin, Charles Hunter, Charles Johnson, Henry Lodge, Paul Pratt, and Louis Chauvin.

## The Jazz Age

Jazz music at the outset of World War I was no longer primarily confined to New Orleans. In 1917 a group of white jazz musicians calling themselves the Original Dixieland Jazz Band made the first jazz record. The record was a success and so was the group. This and subsequent records did much to spread the word of this new music to a wide public. All over the United States jazz bands of varying degrees of competence sprang up. A consequence of this was an abundance of job opportunities in the North.

Many Negro jazz musicians took advantage of job offers from the North. The increasing popularity of jazz and its widespread dissemination via records and radio had led to the creation of large audiences for the music in places like Chicago, which had one of the largest Negro populations in the country. Many of these blacks were recent immigrants from the South who came North because of the possibilities of good jobs created by war industries. Most of these recent arrivals were overjoyed with the prospects of a music from "down home." By 1922 Chicago had replaced New Orleans as the center of jazz development. Black musicians had little trouble finding work in the many cabarets on the South Side and in the recording studios.

In the early 1920s Chicago boasted two bands of major importance: one was King Oliver's Creole Jazz Band (discussed earlier) and the other was the New Orleans Rhythm Kings. The Rhythm Kings was a band of five young white musicians who were to have a great influence on the group known as the Austin High Gang, which included the famous cornetist Bix Beiderbecke.

The era known as the Jazz Age was a period of rebellion, prohibition, lawlessness, gangsters, gaiety, and ruthlessness, a time in which youth was characterized by the title the "Lost Generation." It was also a time of great and rapid change, a phenomenon which extended into the field of music. Some characteristics of jazz music of the 1920s were:

1. A true polyphony (tension between melodic direction and the fundamentals of harmony and metrical time.)
2. Harmonic phraseology, with the soloist needing the hand of the arranger to supplant collective improvisation.
3. An increased importance in the role of the arranger (see above).
4. The extension of blues melodies and the cumulative excitement of riffs, leading to a true polyphony.

In the fragmented social milieu of the North, particularly Chicago, jazz had begun to divest itself of many of its rural characteristics. Composition began to assume a place of growing importance. It was the Chicago of the twenties that spawned Jelly Roll Morton, the most significant composer among the New Orleans musicians. Jelly Roll, according to Martin Williams:

> . . . combined the melodic-compositional emphasis in rags and the improvisational-variational emphasis in blues. It was an almost brilliant stroke, for it combined and developed the virtues of both forms, the dangers of neither. It made variation meaningful, but channeled and controlled it; it kept the music fresh and alive, but gave it order and purpose. It also opened up many possibilities for future developments. Later conceptions might have allowed more freedom, but at this stage, and with polyphonic structures, it was precisely this discipline of Morton's that helped immeasurably in transforming impulse and craft into art. He was part of a movement which saved Afro-American music from degeneration at the hands of pseudo and second-rate ragtimers and continued its development.[10]

In the early twenties two large bands of vital importance to jazz were being born in the East—those led by Fletcher Henderson and Duke Ellington. Along with Armstrong, their music proved to be apocalyptic. Both Ellington and Henderson were products of the Negro middle class, an important sociological factor when one considers their music in relationship to that of Armstrong and the other New Orleans jazz men from the lower economic stratum. It is not without significance that both Henderson and Ellington played the piano, a considerably more sophisticated instrument than the trumpet, the main jazz voice of the early twenties.

The most important soloist to develop within the Henderson band was tenor-saxophonist Coleman Hawkins. Hawkins developed a pianistic, vertical (chord-running) approach that was to influence legions of players.

The impact of Henderson's band on the course of jazz was largely shaped by the quality of its arrangements. These were the work of Don Redmon and Fletcher Henderson himself.

Redmon's arranging style, while essentially a refinement of brass-band writing, was a formalization of the improvised elements of the smaller New Orleans bands. He was very much concerned with the sound of instruments in a group. His innovations center around:

1. The use of reeds (a new mobility).
2. Introduction of the saxophone trio.
3. Development of reed writing.
4. Adaptation of dance-band material to jazz.

The Redmon-Henderson solution to writing for large jazz ensembles is still the dominant one today.

Duke Ellington completely transformed the aesthetic of jazz. He is the most important composer produced by the world of jazz and perhaps by the United States. The style he developed served to broaden the entire spectrum of orchestral color, and his vivid imagination in the area of orchestration has rarely been paralleled. Unlike Henderson, Ellington wrote idiomatically and idiosyncratically for specific soloists whose individual characteristics he used to enhance his total musical scheme of thematic development.

## The Thirties

By the 1930s the foundations had been laid for a new expansion of the jazz idiom. Technical facility was remarkably improved and solos were on a par with ensemble work; the harmonic framework had been expanded and enriched; the two basic approaches to improvisation (vertical and horizontal) were in evidence; composition, thanks to such composers as Ellington, had matured considerably; and the basic methods of writing for the large ensemble had been established.

The 1930s saw many changes in the jazz scene. New York became the center of jazz music; jazz began to evolve away from polyphony; a new breed of musician, schooled and trained, emerged; and the role of the jazz soloist began to decline. It was this period, as well, that marked the birth of a new concept of harmonic direction resulting from the new guiding force of the composer-arranger, who was beginning to exert considerable control over the soloist. Ensembles became more cohesive and solos took on a greater degree of stylistic unity. The string bass replaced the tuba; the guitar replaced the banjo; rigid formats were the musical rule; and sweet music threatened to become the order of the day. The main tune types were blues and popular tunes.

By the thirties, virtually every city outside of the Deep South with a sizable black population had a big band. In 1937 alone there were 18,000 musicians employed in traveling bands, playing in the prevailing jazz style.

In the Southwest Benny Moten, Walter Page, and Count Basie led some of the important bands. The typical band from the Southwest was comprised of three trumpets, three trombones, four reeds, and four rhythm instruments. After 1930 the antiphony of the southern Negro church was adapted by these bands. Basie demonstrated the importance of relaxation in ensemble playing and stressed the role of the blues. The popularity of these blues-based bands was concomitant with the breakthrough of the blues into the middle-class urban realm.

While these bands were important as entities, it was a handful of improvisors who made the truly lasting impression on the music of their day, not only thanks to the high caliber of their work, but also because of the impact they had on young musicians who were just beginning to find themselves in the early forties and who were to carry jazz on into its next era. Their numbers included Lester Young, Coleman Hawkins, Roy Eldridge, Benny Carter, Teddy Wilson, Art Tatum, J. C. Higgenbotham, Charlie Christian, Jimmy Blanton, Joe Jones, and Sid Catlett.

The first of the above, tenor-saxophonist Lester Young, was to have a far-ranging influence on jazz. A Count Basie soloist and one of the first of the great instrumental blues players, Young's tone and style were to set the stage for bebop. He was largely responsible for the reestablishment of rhythmic priorities in jazz, and his concept of sound and of horizontal line had far-reaching effects on the next generation of jazz men.

### The Forties

By the early forties a change in jazz direction was inevitable. There were many reasons for this change, which was to prove an even greater departure from the past than was Louis Armstrong's or that of the big bands.

Much of the development of the new jazz idiom—bebop, as it came to be known—took place in New York City, by then the center of the music business. Members of the various big bands, when in New York, congregated at various clubs in Harlem, places like Minton's and Monroe's Uptown House, to jam after hours. The experimentation and much of the groundwork that went into creating the new style stemmed from these sessions.

As Ross Russell described it:

> Bebop is a music of revolt: revolt against big bands, arrangers, vertical harmonies, soggy rhythms, non-playing orchestra leaders, tin-pan alley—against commercialized music in general. It reasserts the individuality of the jazz musician as a creative artist playing spontaneous and melodic music within the framework of jazz, but with new tools, sounds, and concepts.[11]

The bebop rhythm section was one of the most functional in jazz history. Duplication was dispensed with and each instrument was assigned a basic and essential role. The spirit of bebop was one of simplification, reducing jazz to its most functional aspects. Bebop attempted to build complex patterns with a simple structure and with a minimum of materials. To achieve this end it drew on jazz skills that had been developed over several generations of instrumental experimentation.

Despite the accusations against bebop musicians that the demanding framework of bebop called more for clever minds and nimble fingers than for true creativity, virtuosity and harmonic erudition were used strictly as tools by the revolutionaries and never, except for the untalented and imitative, as ends in themselves. The main emphasis was on a tireless reexamination of the basic problems of polyrhythmics, collective improvisation, and jazz intonation. The function of the rhythm section was drastically altered during the bebop era as follows:

*Piano*—The piano player ceased striving to imitate an orchestra. He no longer played stride piano, chords became sparse, and the instrument became much more percussive. The "comping" (composition) became fragmented and jagged.

*Bass*—Repeated notes in the line were dispersed and the line became melodic and diatonic through the use of leading tones and scales. The time-keeping role shifted to the bass.

*Drums*—The rhythmic ostinato shifted from the bass drum to the ride cymbal, producing a much more legato sound. Bass drum dropped "bombs," played accents, commented on the time. Accompaniment became more and more fragmented. Polyrhythms were reintroduced into the music.

Bebop brought with it many changes in attitude vis-à-vis society and the role of the artist in society. In the midforties America was in the midst of a cataclysmic upheaval. The second world war, with its heavy demand for men and production, ended forever the provincialism lingering in our society. Rootlessness became a way of life.

Young Negro artists were rebelling against decades of exploitation and disfranchisement. Consciously and subconsciously the revolutionaries set out to create a music of such complexity as to discourage its appropriation by white imitators. The black musician thought of himself as an artist rather than an entertainer. Increased consideration was given to the music's artistic qualities—form and structure, thematic and harmonic development.

Bebop served as an intellectual and artistic awakening for jazz musicians. It led to an unparalleled rise in basic musicianship according to Western standards. (*i.e.*, basic technique, precision, intonation, etc.). It opened the doors to greater rhythmic and metric choices and above all it established a vocabulary and syntax that is still in use today.

Among the important musicians of the era were Dizzy Gillespie, Kenny Clarke, Bud Powell, J. J. Johnson, Fats Navarro, Charlie Mingus, Max Roach, Oscar Pettiford, and the famed Charlie Parker.

Parker was one of the most influential figures in modern jazz. His influence extended into all areas and media of jazz expression, including composition. It is no surprise to the jazz intelligentsia that Parker's influence has not been limited to jazz alone. Virtually every commercial, jingle, and TV background owes some demonstrable debt to his innovations. Charlie Mingus has said, "If Charlie Parker were alive he would think he was in a house of mirrors."

## Since Parker

Never before in its brief history have there been so many divergent schools of jazz coexisting and enjoying concurrent popularity—blues, big band music traditional, avant-garde, thirdstream, eclectics, and myriad offshoots of these.

These schools can be divided into five broad overlapping categories:

1. Mainstream
2. Jazz influenced by other ethnic musics
3. Avant-garde
4. Thirdstream
5. Liturgical jazz

The mainstream includes primarily postbebop and soul jazz. The postbeboppers comprise the largest contingent of any of the aforementioned schools. In the postbeboppers the style is melodically, harmonically, and rhythmically more complex than any previous jazz style. The innovations and techniques pioneered in the late forties by Charlie Parker, Dizzy Gillespie, and their confreres have been brought to fruition in this segment of contemporary jazz. The men who actually pioneered this music make up the bulk of the present generation of players.

Soul jazz (funky, blues, down-home, etc.) derives from the rhythmic music of the rural black church. Until the recent surge of black nationalism and black pride this type of jazz was viewed rather condescendingly by black jazz musicians. This music, like rhythm and blues, offered a revitalization, a recovery of the basic, primitive, emotional drive characteristic of early folk-rooted jazz. It incorporates the technical advances of bebop, particularly its melodic and rhythmic complexities, while reverting to a more traditional harmonic framework.

Some of the representative figures of this music are Cannonball Adderly*, Wes Montgomery, Charlie Mingus, Slide Hampton, Horace Silver, Tommy Turrentine, Ramsey Lewis, Les McCann, and Jimmy Smith. The music of the next category, jazz influenced by other ethnic musics, is enjoying an unparalleled popularity today. Its diverse sources include Spanish, Latin American, African, Indian, Gypsy, and Eastern music as well as others. Some of the characteristics of this type of music are:

1. A heavy drawing upon identifiable musical characteristics of other ethnic groups.
2. The utilization of rhythmic, harmonic, and melodic characteristics of foreign music.
3. A liberal use of the compositions of the foreign culture.
4. Employment of the instruments, instrumental concepts, and often the musical philosophy of foreign music.

Some of the players actively involved in this segment of contemporary music are Miles Davis, Dizzy Gillespie, Herbie Mann, Gil Evans, Charlie Mariano, Don Ellis, and Gerald Wilson.

The next category, which many people deem the most important of all, is the avant-garde. This music springs from vastly disparate experiences. All of the important players in this category are black and most align themselves implicitly or explicitly with the movement toward black consciousness. Many black jazz men, in their fierce protectiveness of the music, refuse even to call the music jazz, preferring to label it simply black music.

Much of this music is self-consciously nationalistic and laden with social import. Much of it strives to divest itself of those things which can be construed as Western or European. The call is for a return to Africa, both philosophically and musically. Freedom, with all of its implications and ramifications, becomes the battle cry.

The chief practitioners of the avant-garde are George Russell, Ornette Coleman, Archie Shepp, Don Cherry, Albert and Don Ayler, John Coltrane, and Cecil Taylor.

The thirdstream (a term coined by Gunther Schuller) is ostensibly a marriage between western European concert music and jazz. Its characteristics include:

*Adderly died in 1975.

1. Emphasis on composition.
2. The use of instruments not normally associated with jazz (strings, woodwinds, French horns, harps, etc.).
3. The use of voices in something other than the traditional manner in which they have been used in jazz.
4. The use of techniques and devices generally considered the domain of the European classical composer. These include tone rows; classical forms like sonata, allegro, ternary, fugue, passacaglia, etc.; computer techniques, the "classical orchestra" combined with various jazz combinations; extended developmental forms; and other twentieth-century classical devices such as pointillism, indeterminacy, chance music, aleatory devices, sets, etc.
5. A music usually much closer to Western art forms than any other type of jazz.

In this area of contemporary jazz, an uneasy symbiosis exists, at best, or as LeRoi Jones so perceptively observes:

> There is no doubt in my mind that the techniques of European classical music can be utilized by jazz musicians, but in ways that will not subject the philosophy of Negro music to the less indigenously personal attitudes of European-derived music. Taylor and Coleman know the music of Anton Webern and are responsible to it intellectually, as they would be to any stimulating art form. But they are not responsible to it emotionally, as an extra-musical catalytic form. The emotional significance of most Negro music has been its separation from the emotional and philosophical attitudes of classical music. In order for the jazz musician to utilize most expressively any formal classical techniques, it is certainly necessary that these techniques be subjected to the emotional and philosophical attitudes of Afro-American music; that these techniques be used, not canonized. Most thirdstream jazz, it seems, has tended to canonize classical techniques rather than use them to shape the expressive fabric of a "new" jazz music.[12]

Some of the writers in the thirdstream are Gunther Schuller, Larry Austin, John Lewis, J. J. Johnson, and David Baker.

The final area of contemporary jazz concerns itself with a relatively new phenomenon which to many people seems a contradiction in terms, liturgical jazz. The characteristics of this new genre are:

1. A jazz music for use in the church or with church-related activities.
2. The use of religious or spiritual text.
3. A merging of harmonic, melodic, and rhythmic elements of jazz with liturgical forms (mass, oratories, cantatas, etc.)
4. The incidental use of jazz music in both formal and informal religious ceremonies.
5. A music functionally appropriate to the church and yet faithful to the jazz genre.
6. Tune sources which include original composition, musical materials from the liturgy and secular sources, and extant jazz types (blues, rhythm, etc.).

The late Duke Ellington, Mary Lou Williams, John Coltrane, Lalo Schifrin, and David Baker are among those composers who have worked to establish this new genre.

John Coltrane was perhaps the most influential jazz performer of the contemporary period. His influence is felt in the playing of virtually every jazz voice today. Coltrane enriched the harmonic vocabulary (*i.e.*, "Giant Steps," "Count Down") expanded the tonal technical resources of the saxophone, and was instrumental in changing the basic unit of the jazz solo from the eighth notes to the sixteenth note. But above all it is for his relentless pioneer spirit that continues to light the way for young jazz musicians today that Coltrane will be remembered.

## THE EUROPEAN STREAM

Two important studies of the Afro-American in music are Maud Cuney Hare's *Negro Musicians and Their Music* (Washington, 1936) and Alain Locke's *The Negro and His Music* (Washington, 1936). Both books give valuable surveys of the period leading up to their publication. Maud Cuney Hare's book treats the European stream as a norm, but Alain Locke's book presents the three streams on conditions of relative parity.

While it has been primarily as performers that Afro-Americans have participated in the European stream, some have achieved distinction as composers, suffering more than other American composers, however, from the limited opportunities available for performance. Composers mentioned in Alain Locke's study include Harry T. Burleigh, best known as an arranger of spirituals; R. Nathaniel Dett, composer of effective program music for the piano; and William Grant Still, whose *Afro-American Symphony* has had many performances. Locke also mentions the work of William Dawson and his *Negro Folk Symphony*. Of the host of composers who have emerged since then, only a few can be mentioned here. The best known of those to come to prominence after World War II are Howard Swanson, Ulysses Kay, and Margaret Bonds. Others include George Walker, T. J. Anderson, Coleridge-Taylor Perkinson, and Arthur Cunningham.

It is above all in the field of singing that, after the international triumphs of Roland Hayes, Paul Robeson, and Marian Anderson, a more general acceptance of the Afro-American as recital artist and finally as opera singer has occurred. Among those singers to achieve international reputations are Anne Wiggins Brown and Todd Duncan, the original leading artists of George Gershwin's opera *Porgy and Bess*. Other singers who concertized in the thirties include Caterina Jarboro, Lillian Evanti, and Etta Moten. Appearing slightly later were two great singers—Dorothy Maynor and Carol Brice—as well as Laurence Winters, who gained a considerable reputation in Germany. More recently, Mattiwilda Dobbs, Leontyne Price, and William Warfield have risen to fame, to be joined on the international scene by such singers as Grace Bumbry, George Shirley, Martina Arroyo, Reri Grist, and Shirley Verrett.

Afro-Americans have had little encouragement as classical instrumentalists. Exceptions are the noted pianist Hazel Harrison, long a professor at Howard University, and Philippa Duke Schuyler, who achieved fame as a child prodigy in the thirties and early forties. Pianists of great ability in the period since World War II have been George Walker, Eugene Haynes, Natalie Hinderas, and Robert Pritchard. More recently, the young virtuoso André Watts has had the distinction of being able to develop a full concert career.

In the conducting field, pioneer choral conductors included John W. Work, R. Nathaniel Dett, Hall Johnson, and Eva Jessye. Other conductors are Leonard de Paur, who has been forced to confine himself to choruses of his own formation; the widely acclaimed Dean Dixon and Everett Lee, both of whom have had to seek posts as conductors in Europe; James De Priest, who as winner of a Mitropoulos Award served as assistant conductor of the New York Philharmonic for a year and conducted the Philadelphia Orchestra in a subscription series; and Henry Lewis, who has managed a breakthrough with an American orchestra.

Unfortunately, the presence of the Afro-American in the European stream has been a peripheral adjunct to the American presence, itself marginal. Americans are outnumbered by Europeans on the list of concert-hall composers, conductors, and instrumentalists throughout the world. Only as singers have Americans fully challenged the Europeans on their own ground, and here the Afro-American achievement is enviable.

## Notes

1. James Weldon Johnson, *Autobiography of an Ex-Colored Man* (New York, Alfred A. Knopf, 1927) Chapter X.
2. John Work, "The Negro Spiritual," in *The Papers of the Hymn Society of America*, XXIV (1962), p. 24.
3. Willis Laurence James, "Work Songs and Social Songs," *The Negro Caravan*, ed. by Sterling A. Brown, Arthur P. Davis, and Ulysses Lee (New York, The Citadel Press, 1941), pp. 468–69.
4. John Work, *American Negro Songs and Spirituals* (New York, Howell, Soskin, 1940).
5. The method of "lining" by the deacon or pastor is usually to read off two lines, lead in their singing, read two more lines, etc. Lining originally insured that the hymn could be followed by those members of the congregation unable to read. Hymns like the following are lined and have remained favorites among the congregations: "A Charge to Keep I Have," "Come, We That Love the Lord," "I Love the Lord, He Heard My Cry," "Dark Was the Night," "What a Friend," "Amazin' Grace," and many more.
6. Dr. Isaac Watts (1674–1748) is one of the great writers on whom the black church has depended for much of its hymnody. His output numbered around 454 hymns and versions of psalms. The black churches frequently use them in services where they hold an honored place. They are referred to as "Dr. Watts's hymns." In some Baptist churches there are even Dr. Watts's choirs.
7. Charles Edward Smith, "New Orleans and Traditions in Jazz," in Nat Hentoff and Albert J. McCarthy, editors, *Jazz* (New York, Grove Press, First Evergreen Edition, 1961), pp. 29–30.
8. Gunther Schuller, *Early Jazz* (New York, Oxford University Press, 1968), pp. 77–88 (*passim*).
9. Songs which accompany a dancelike ritual.
10. Martin Williams, *Jelly Roll Morton* (New York, A. S. Barnes, 1962), pp. 67–68.
11. Ross Russell, "Bebop," in Martin Williams, editor, *The Art of Jazz* (New York, Oxford University Prsss, 1959), pp. 187–217.
12. LeRoi Jones, *Blues People* (New York, Wm. Morrow & Co., Inc., 1963), pp. 229–230.

# BIBLIOGRAPHY

Allen, William Francis; Ware, Charles P.; and Garrison, Lucy M., *Slave Songs of the United States*. New York, A. Simpson & Co., 1867.

Barton, William E., *Old Plantation Hymns: A Collection of Hitherto Unpublished Melodies of the Slave and the Freedman, with Historical and Critical Notes*. Boston, Wolfe & Co., 1899.

Boatner, Edward and Townsend, Willa, *Spirituals Triumphant*. Nashville, Sunday School Publishing Board, National Baptist Convention, 1927.

Brown, Sterling A., Davis, Arthur P., and Lee, Ulysses, eds., *The Negro Caravan*. New York, The Citadel Press, 1941.

Brown, William Wells, *The Anti-Slavery Harp*, 2nd ed. Boston, B. Marsh, 1849.

Christy, E. P., *Christy's Plantation Melodies*. Philadelphia, Fisher, 1851.

Clark, George W., *The Liberty Minstrel*. New York, Leavitt & Alden, 1844.

Coleridge-Taylor, Samuel, *Twenty-four Negro Melodies: Transcribed for Piano*. Boston, Oliver Ditson Co., 1905.

Curtis, Natalie Burlin, ed., *Negro Folk Songs*, Book I. New York, G. Schirmer, Inc., 1918.

———, *Songs and Tales from the Dark Continent*. New York, G. Schirmer, 1920.

Dett, R. N., ed., *Religious Folk Songs of the Negro*. Hampton, Hampton Institute Press, 1919.

———, *Religious Sacred Song Book*. 1919.

Fisher, Miles Mark, *Negro Slave Songs*. New York, Cornell University Press, 1953.

Fisher, William Arms, *Seventy Negro Spirituals*. Boston, Oliver Ditson Company, 1926.

Handy, W. C. and Niles, Abbe, *Blues: An Anthology*. New York, Albert and Charles Boni, 1926.

Hare, Maud Cuney, *Negro Musicians and Their Music*. Washington, D.C., The Associated Publishers, Inc., 1936.

Hayes, Roland, *My Songs*. Boston, Little, Brown and Co., 1948.

Higginson, Thomas Wentworth, *Army Life in a Black Regiment*. Boston, Atlantic Monthly, 1867.

Jackson, George Pullen, *Down-East Spirituals and Others*. New York, J.J. Augustin, 1943.

———, *Spirituals, Folk Songs of Early America*. New York, J.J. Augustin, 1937.

———, *White and Negro Spirituals, Their Life Span and Kinship*. New York, J.J. Augustin, 1944.

———, *White Spirituals in the Southern Uplands*. Chapel Hill, The University of North Carolina Press, 1933.

Jackson, Marylou I., *Negro Spirituals and Hymns*. New York, J. Fisher and Brothers, 1935.

James, Willis Laurence, "Romance of the Negro Folk Cry." *Phylon*, XVI (Atlanta University, First Quarter, 1955), pp. 15–30.

Jessye, Eva, *My Spirituals*. New York, Robbins-Engle, 1927.

Johnson, Charles S., "Jazz Poetry and Blues," *Carolina Magazine*. Chapel Hill, 1928.

Johnson, Guy B., *John Henry*. Chapel Hill, The University of North Carolina Press, 1929.

Johnson, J. Rosamond and Johnson, James Weldon, *The Book of American Negro Spirituals*. New York, The Viking Press, 1925.

———, *The Second Book of Negro Spirituals*. New York, The Viking Press, 1925.

———, "Negro Folk Songs and Spirituals," *Mentor*, XVII. (February 1929) pp. 50–52.

Jones, LeRoi, *Blues People*. New York, Apollo Editions, Wm. Morrow and Co., Inc., 1963.

Kemble, Frances A., *Journal of a Residence on a Georgia Plantation in 1838*. New York, Harper and Brothers, 1863.

King, Edward, *Negro Songs and Singers— The Great South*. Hartford, The American Publishing Co., 1875.

Knapp, William, "An Interview with H. T. Burleigh," *Baton*, V. (March 1926) p. 2.

Krehbiel, Henry Edward, *Afro-American Folksongs*. New York, (c. 1914).

Leiding, Harriette Kershaw, *Street Cries of an Old Southern City*. Charleston S. C., 1910 (self-published).

Locke, Alain, "The Negro and His Music," *Bronze Booklet*, No. 2. Washington, 1936.

———, *The New Negro*. New York, Albert & Charles Boni, 1925.

Lomax, John A., "Sinful Songs of the Southern Negro," *The Music Quarterly*, Vol. XX. New York, 1934.

Marsh, J.B.T., *The Story of the Jubilee Singers With Their Songs*. Boston, Houghton, Mifflin & Company, 1875.

Mellers, Wilfred, *Music in a New Found Land*. New York, Alfred A. Knopf, 1967.

Murphy, Jeanette Robinson, *Southern Thoughts for Northern Thinkers and African Music in America*. New York, Bandana Publishing Company, 1904.

Odum, Howard W. and Johnson, Guy B., *The Negro and His Songs*. Chapel Hill, The University of North Carolina Press, 1925.

———, *Negro Workday Songs*. Chapel Hill, The University of North Carolina Press, 1926.

Parrish, Lydia, *Slave Songs of Georgia Sea Islands*. New York, Creative Age Press, Inc., 1942.

Pike, G. G., *Jubilee Singers*. Boston, Lee and Shepard, 1873.

———, *The Jubilee Singers of Fisk University*. Boston, Lee and Shepard, 1874.

Ryder, C. J., *The Theology of Plantation Songs*. New York, American Missionary Association Bible House, 1891.

Schuller, Gunther, *Early Jazz*. New York, Oxford University Press, 1968.

Stearns, Marshall W., *The Story of Jazz*. New York, Oxford University Press, 1958.

Talley, Thomas W., *Negro Folk Rhymes*. New York, The Macmillan Company, 1922.

Thurman, Howard, *Deep River: An Interpretation of Negro Spirituals*. California, Mills College Press, 1945.

Wallascheck, Richard, *Primitive Music: An Inquiry into the Origin and Development of Music, Songs, Instruments, Dances, and Pantomimes of Slave Races*. London, Longmans, Green, 1893.

Washington, Joseph R., *Black Religion*. Boston, Beacon Press, 1964.

White, Clarence Cameron, "The Musical Genius of the American Negro." *Etude Musical Magazine*, XLII (May 1924), p. 305f.

Williams, Martin T., ed., *The Art of Jazz*. New York, Evergreen E272, Grove Press, 1959.

Woodson, Carter G., *The History of the Negro Church*. Washington, D. C., The Associated Publishers, 1945.

Work, John W., *American Negro Songs: A Comprehensive Collection of 230 Folk Songs, Religious and Secular*. New York, Crown Press, 1940.

————, *The Folk Songs of the American Negro*. Nashville, Fisk University Press, 1915.

————, and Work, Frederick J., *Folk Songs of the American Negro*. Nashville, Work Brothers, 1907.

————, *New Jubilee Songs*. Nashville, Work Brothers, 1901.

## Recommended Reading

Blesh, Rudi, *Shining Trumpets; A History of Jazz*. New York, Alfred A. Knopf, 1946.

————, *They All Played Ragtime*. New York, Alfred A. Knopf, 1950.

Bradford, Perry, *Born With the Blues*. New York, Oak Publications, 1965.

Butcher, Margaret Just, *The Negro in American Culture*. New York, Alfred A. Knopf, 1956.

Charters, Samuel Barclay, *Jazz: New Orleans, 1885–1963*. New York, Oak Publications, 1963.

Davis, Frank Marshall, *Black Voices (Robert Whitmore)*, ed. by Abraham Chapman. New York and Toronto, Mentor Books, New American Library, 1968.

de Lerma, Dominique-René, ed., *Black Music in Our Society*. Kent, Kent State University Press, 1970. If not entire book, at least John Hammond's "An Experience in Jazz History."

Dexter, Dave Jr., *The Jazz Story*. Englewood Cliffs, N. J., Prentice-Hall, Inc., 1964.

*Downbeat Magazine*. Maher Publications, 222 W. Adams, Chicago, Ill. 60606.

Feather, Leonard, *The Book of Jazz*. New York, Horizon Press, 1957.

————, *The Encyclopedia of Jazz in the Sixties*. New York, Horizon Press, 1966.

Garland, Phyl, *The Sound of Soul*. Chicago, Henry Regnery Co., 1969.

Handy, William C., *Father of the Blues*. New York, Macmillan, 1942.

Hodeir, Andre, *Jazz: Its Evolution and Essence*. New York, Grove Press, 1956.

Jones, LeRoi, *Black Music*. New York, Apollo Editions, Wm. Morrow & Co., Inc., 1967.

Keil, Charles, *Urban Blues*. Chicago, University of Chicago Press, 1966.

Leonard, Neil, *Jazz and the White American*. Chicago, University of Chicago Press, 1962.

*The New Jazz Book; A History and Guide*. New York, Hill & Wang, 1962.

Pleasants, Henry, *Serious Music and All That Jazz*. New York, Simon and Schuster, 1969.

Shapiro, Nat, and Hentoff, Nat, *The Jazz Makers*. New York, Reinhart, 1957.

Stearns, Marshall W., *The Story of Jazz*. New York, Oxford University Press, 1970.

Ulanov, Barry, *A History of Jazz in America*. New York, Viking Press, 1955.

## Recommended Listening

**Bebop**

| | |
|---|---|
| Historical Masterpieces, Charlie Parker | Charlie Parker Record PLP 701 |
| The Charlie Parker Story | Verve M6V 8001 |
| Study in Brown, Clifford Brown and Max Roach | Emarcy Mo 36037 |

**Mainstream: Post-Bebop**

| | |
|---|---|
| Milestones, Miles Davis | Columbia CS 9428 |
| A Touch of Satin, J. J. Johnson | CL 1737 |
| Sonny Rollins, Sonny Rollins | Blue Note 1558 |
| The John Lewis Piano | Atlantic 1272 |
| Giant Steps, John Coltrane | Atlantic 1311 |

**Soul Jazz**

| | |
|---|---|
| Blowin' the Blues Away, Horace Silver | Blue Note 4017 |
| The Cannonball Adderley Quintet at the Lighthouse | Riverside RLP 344 |
| Going Out of My Head, Wes Montgomery | Verve V8 8642 |

**Ethnic Jazz**

| | |
|---|---|
| Sketches of Spain, Miles Davis & Gil Evans | Columbia CS 8271 |
| Ole Coltrane, John Coltrane | Atlantic 1373 |

**Thirdstream**

| | |
|---|---|
| City of Glass, Stan Kenton | Capitol W736 |
| Outstanding Jazz Compositions of the Twentieth Century | Columbia C2S831 |
| The Golden Striker, John Lewis | Atlantic 1334 |
| Intents and Purposes, Bill Dixon Orchestra | RCA—LSP 3844 |

**Avant-Garde**

| | |
|---|---|
| Eastern Man Alone, Charles Tyler | ESP 1059 |
| Unit Structures, Cecil Taylor | BLP 4237 |
| Change of the Century, Ornette Coleman | Atlantic SD 1327 |
| Outward Bound, Eric Dolphy | NJLP 8236 |
| Ezzthetics, George Russell | Riverside 375 |
| Ascension, John Coltrane | Impulse A95 |

**Liturgical Jazz**

| | |
|---|---|
| A Love Supreme, John Coltrane | Impulse A77 |
| Jazz Suite on the Mass Texts, Paul Horn and Lalo Schifrin | RCA Victor LPM 3414 |
| Prodigal Son, Phil Wilson Quartet | Freeform Records No. 101 |

**Recommended Additional Listening**

| | |
|---|---|
| Glenn Miller Concert | RCA Victor, LPM 1193 |
| Big Band and Quartet in Concert, T. Monk | Columbia CS 8964 |

| | |
|---|---|
| Wonderland, Charles Mingus | Solid State Stereo SS18019 |
| The Band of Distinction, Count Basie | Clef Records, M6 C-722 |
| Change of the Century, Ornette Coleman | At SD 1327 |
| Great Jazz Pianists | Camden Cal. 328 |
| Giants of Boogie Woogie | Riverside 12–106 |
| Hub Tones, Freddie Hubbard | Blue Note 4115 |
| Sliding Easy, Curtis Fuller | UAL 4041 |
| Stratusphunk, George Russell | Riverside 341 |
| Point of Departure, Andrew Hill | Blue Note 4167 |
| Porgy and Bess, Miles Davis | CL 1274 |
| Heavy Sounds, Elvin Jones | Impulse A-9161 |

# 26

## Afro-American Art

### Edmund B. Gaither

From his African past, the slave or indentured servant brought with him a rich artistic heritage. Dance, music, art, legend, and folklore had all been facets of his everyday experience and integral parts of his social, religious, and political world. But with the shock of transfer to the New World and the subsequent process of Americanization, his African world view was shattered and his art forms, severed from their traditional context, quickly lost their vigor. Gradually, however, black artists began to reassemble the pieces and look for a new creative direction. The black American's contribution to the visual arts is one of the fruits of this search.

The assessment of the character of Afro-American participation in the visual arts is still in its infancy. In attempting to reconstruct the events making up Afro-American art history, the scholar is faced with large informational gaps; hence, few studies of individual artists or specific creative trends have been completed. Nevertheless Alain LeRoy Locke (1886–1954) and James Amos Porter (1905–1969) have suggested approaches to, as well as outlines for, the study of Afro-American art history.

Locke and Porter, both black scholars, had clear commitments toward advancing the Afro-American artist and his art although their methods differed significantly. Locke was graduated from Harvard College and subsequently studied at Oxford as a Rhodes Scholar, at the University of Berlin, and again at Harvard University. He distinguished himself as an aesthete, patron, critic, and writer, as well as the architect of the New Negro Movement, a movement based around the explosion of artistic talent and opportunity that erupted in the 1920s in the newly developed urban centers of the North.

As an intellectual and part of the generation of W. E. B. DuBois and Pan-Africanism, Locke saw Negro art as international; united across political boundaries by its common African base. Whether it originated in the United States, the Caribbean, or South America, Locke fought for the presentation of Negro art in a worldwide context.

Porter, educated at New York University and the Sorbonne, was a historian born of the generation of E. Franklin Frazier. He was more cautious, more scientific in his approval and less given to generalizations than Locke. Without turning his back on African traditions, Porter evaluated the efforts of Afro-American artists within the context of American art. He was more a historian than a philosopher. Comments such as "the American Negro has no pictorial or plastic art" spurred him on in his researches and increased his conviction concerning the ". . . neglect and deliberate indifference with which Negro effort in the field of art was received."[1] Porter's *Modern Negro Art*, which remains the best existing volume on Afro-American art, was an apologia for Afro-American artists. In it, he attempted to write them into American art history for, in his view, they worked within the social and historical traditions of America.

The essential differences in the two scholars' approaches are evident in their evaluations of early Afro-American art. Locke, with his emphasis on African tradition and the interpretation of art on the basis of racial experience, found early Afro-American art disappointing. He believed that racial experiences engraved themselves into the collective consciousness of a group and that such experiences, however remote, provided a reservoir on which artists belonging to the group had a natural monopoly, and on which they should draw for their art. He thus disparaged early Afro-American art as a ". . . halting and somewhat over-ambitious imitation of the arts of the white man's culture."[2] Porter, on the other hand, viewed the same art as a heroic and healthy struggle to draw from and merge into the American mainstream. He looked for traits in this work which might hark back to Africa, especially in the crafts and ironwork, but he saw no value in a self-conscious return to African forms as models, seeing such a return as overly academic. Moreover, he felt that African forms might well be  inappropriate to the new situation of Afro-American artists.

In an effort to explain his disappointment with the black American art of his day, Locke advanced his theory of artistic reversal. The central tenet of this theory was that the art of the Afro-American did not reflect the true art of the Negro, that it was ". . . neither characteristically African nor to be explained by ancestral heritage," and that its mediocre quality resulted from the Afro-American's peculiar experience in America with its attendant emotional upheaval, trials, and ordeals. Afro-American artistic expression owed its shortcomings to ". . . the working of environmental forces rather than the outcropping of race psychology; . . . the acquired [rather than] the original artistic temperament."[3]

Locke's theory further stated that this reversal stemmed from the physical transplantation of the Negro which cut him off from his cultural roots, robbed him of his language, and reduced him to "cultural zero." In the ensuing process of assimilation, he lost his sense of discipline, of subtlety, of quiet harmony, and of tradition—all earmarks, in Locke's view, of the finest African art.

A believer in the concept of racial memory, Locke prescribed as a cure for the Afro-American artist renewed exposure to, and study of, traditional African art. "There is the need to, at the outset, establish a historical perspective in order to get at the true values of the Negro as artist,"[4] Locke wrote. The Negro artist would then be able to create valid racial art in America because he would understand his African past; his art would demonstrate the "formal revival of historical memory" and would reveal "race through the subtle elements of rhythm, color, and atmosphere."[5] When the Afro-American artist became sufficiently immersed in his artistic past, he would be able to eclipse Picasso and Brancusi in the contemporary extension of African ideas in Western art. Moreover, he would be able to consistently project the racial dimension of his art irrespective of subject matter. Negro art would be coequal with the great creative traditions of the West.

Porter, in contrast, took a more pragmatic approach. Seeking out for discussion individual artists who had achieved a certain level of proficiency in their craft, he compared them to their white peers and raised the question, "Why aren't they in the art books?" He went on to emphasize that those black artists who had gained success had done so in spite of the unfavorable circumstances which had blocked and sometimes nearly defeated them.

Just as Locke and Porter, both of whom loved African art, differed with respect to how black American artists should draw from it, so they differed in their theories of how the African artistic heritage had been crushed in America. Locke leaned toward the view that the trauma of slavery had delivered the *coup de grâce* to African plastic arts, while Porter emphasized the destructive impact of the loss of African religion and institutions. He illustrated his point by citing how African art and thought flourished in Catholic countries, (*e.g.*, Haiti, Brazil, Cuba) whereas in the Protestant United States neither fared well. As we shall see, however, Catholic and Protestant influences may have had less to do with it than did the greater survival of African culture in the countries named.

## Art as Social History

Cedric Dover, in his book *American Negro Art*, reviews the work and thinking of both Porter and Locke. A study of Dover's book, as well as several years spent studying Afro-American art, has led to the conclusion that the visual-arts tradition of black America can be most fully appreciated if the art is approached in terms of social history.

The social approach seems particularly applicable to Afro-American art because the dilemma of being black in America has given the work of the Afro-American artist a special flavor. Social circumstances have affected his ability to participate in the mainstream of American art much more than they have his white counterparts. Subject matter, style, patronage, and work arena have at every point been affected by his dubious standing as an artist, an American, and a human being.

The approach to art through social history assumes that there is a necessary connection between the art object and its sociopolitical matrix; that a work of art is not a neutral statement but reflects a point of view related to larger social interests, and that to fully understand an artistic creation, social as well as aesthetic factors must be taken into account.[6] Thus art must be analyzed in terms of: 1) relevant artistic traditions, 2) the psychology of the individual artist, and 3) the impact of the sociopolitical context on the work in question. From an examination of the sociopolitical context, one gains an appreciation of the limitations and possibilities confronting the artist. From a psychological study of the artist one gains a sense of how he has come to grips with the dynamic historical forces of his times. And from the analysis of the artistic work in the context of a given artistic tradition one is able to judge the success or failure of the work.

If this approach is applied to art history, it becomes immediately apparent that the same possibilities do not exist for every artist at every point in time. The Afro-American artist, caught in a sometimes hostile, sometimes patronizing setting, has found his horizons circumscribed accordingly, and any discussion that does not take into consideration the limitations imposed upon him by history cannot appreciate the art forms which he has created. Nor must it be forgotten that the stifling of the Afro-American artist was an integral part of the sociopolitical realities of American cultural life. If an artist such as the twentieth-century muralist Aaron Douglass never reached his full potential, it may not have been because he lacked talent; it was more probably because his historical context forced him to choose between martyrdom or a sublimated, hence potentially limited, output.

The social-history approach serves to explain the dynamics of the conflict between Locke and Porter as part of the larger growth of the intellectual tradition in black America vis-à-vis the visual arts. Their differences, like those of the artists they studied, reflect the tensions in the black experience caused by conflicting pulls toward racial nationalism and assimilationism. The social-history approach also provides the framework for a clearer understanding of the reasons behind Locke's emphasis on African continuities and racial self-image, Porter's insistent projection of the Afro-American into the existing spectrum of American art, and the broad range of influences and attitudes to which the style and subject matter of this art was exposed.

## THE HISTORY

### The African Background

Afro-Americans, like all other New World blacks, are children of Africa; but it should be kept in mind that of all the areas in the Americas and the Caribbean, the United States probably suffered the sharpest break with the mother continent. To be sure, the split was not so complete as it was once thought to be—it was not a return to "cultural zero." Yet compared to the situation in Cuba, Haiti, Surinam, and Brazil, it was considerable. In the aforementioned countries, black people retained much that was undeniably African in their religion (Yoruba cults, voodoo, etc.), in their language, in their social institutions, and in their art.[7] Wherever the drums remained, the arts, whether decorative, functional, or ceremonial, persisted. Leopold Society dance regalia was found in

Cuba until the revolution; Akan- and Ashanti-derived woodwork and stools are currently produced in Surinam and Bahia. The images of the gods Danballah and Shango are still found in Haiti and Brazil. Almost everywhere in the West Indies the ancient art of African basketry is still being practiced. Unquestionably, the nonurban populations of blacks in the Caribbean and South American nations are providing a creative reservoir from which their artists draw the strength and inspiration to express their African heritage.

By contrast, the circumstances under which blacks lived in the United States systematically destroyed those elements which could have fostered the growth of things African in America. The outlawing of the drum, the separation of those slaves sharing a common language and culture, the conversion of slaves to iconoclastic Protestantism, all these factors led to the decimation of the heritage which would have provided a wellspring of inspiration for the African plastic arts. Yet in spite of the careful surveillance of blacks by their overlords, they still managed to wed at least part of their cultural past to the new traditions which they were forced to accept. Jazz, gospel, poetry, dance— all were products of this marriage to the culture of white America, the process by which Africans became Afro-Americans. The above forms had the great advantage over the visual arts of requiring no physical material from which to create them, and thus undoubtedly had great bearing on the comparative development of the plastic arts vis-à-vis music, dance, and theater. Moreover, the church, as it became the new institutional center of black life in America, assumed the role of patron and sponsor in the fields of music, dance, and theater, while remaining indifferent to the plastic arts. Whereas in Africa the plastic artist had traditionally served religion and society, in America he found himself disinherited and without a *raison d'être*.

African crafts traditions fared only slightly better than the plastic arts in the United States. There is limited evidence of craft contributions in America. Among the crafts objects documented are a large Ashanti drum collected in Virginia; a group of grotesque clay jugs collected in the nineteenth century at Bath, South Carolina; some carved walking canes collected in Missouri in the midnineteenth century; and a number of African baskets found in the South Carolina Sea Island area. Additionally, some clay pipes have been discovered in the Deep South which are similar to pipes produced in Cameroons.[8]

The Ashanti drum from Virginia was so clearly in the tradition of the Ashanti that no question of its origin could be raised. The grotesque jugs were early shown by Porter to be African-inspired, although Dover discussed them more cautiously, preferring to call them "slave pottery." The recent research of Robert F. Thompson,[9] noted scholar on African and Afro-Caribbean art, however, convincingly shows a parallel between these works and art from the Congo and Angola, areas well represented in the slave population of South Carolina. Additional credence is given to the African origins of the jugs when one considers that slaves directly from Africa were still being smuggled into South Carolina in the midnineteenth century. The carved "conjur" canes decorated with snake and other reptile motifs have a relationship to African medicinal staffs, and have been found in other black communities in the Americas, notably Jamaica.

The African, like other craft traditions, had been in constant decline since the eighteenth century. This decline has been inversely proportionate to the rise of consumerism and urbanism. But in the more remote southern communities, where crafts objects were made for personal or intragroup use, there remained an intragroup aesthetic and technical craft tradition. The objects produced in these locales were outside the mainstream of the American crafts traditions and reaffirmed to what extent the black family unit retained some of its pre-Americanization standards. With time, however, such craft objects came to be regarded as primitive, as rural or "country," and thus as undesirable. And with the rush to become urban in the twentieth century, there was a rejection of all things handmade—or in the case of these particular objects "mammy made." One had to be a consumer. The full impact of this attitude, accelerated by compulsory public education, could be seen in the South by World War II. By the sixties, even in such areas as the Sea Islands, African-based crafts traditions had all but vanished.

## The Mechanical and Industrial Arts

Most writers on Afro-American art have given considerable attention to the role of the Afro-American in the mechanical and industrial arts. Porter, Dover, and more recently art historian Judith Chase cite a number of black men employed before the twentieth century in the manufacture of clothing, cloth, furniture, tools, etc. Additional figures such as Thomas Fleet, the Afro-American engraver, and others in similarly creative but mechanical arts are singled out. It is important to note the participation of blacks in these areas, although their contributions are best seen as part of the history of American industrial and mechanical arts. With the exception of ironsmiths, they will not be considered here.

Black ironsmiths were given an important place by Locke, Porter, and Judith Chase, and they provide a good example not only of the prowess, but also of the problems of black workmen in the mechanical arts. Porter saw in the ironworks-embellished houses in Charleston, South Carolina; Mobile, Alabama; and New Orleans (Le Vieux Carré) "solid and tangible proof that the Negro brought with him into his slavery the ancient art tendencies of Africa."[10] Dover expressed himself in more cautious terms, however, observing that "actually proofs of the extent to which Negroes participated in forging the wrought iron of the Deep South [were] circumstantial rather than documentary; and that it was stretching the evidence to call it a Negro art arising from African heritage."[11]

Probably Dover's position relative to the handsome iron balconies is more nearly valid. One must remember that the technology surrounding iron production and smithing in the United States was new to the Afro-American. To be sure, he had a long acquaintance with the working of iron; but in his tradition, the blacksmith had had social and religious associations—sometimes even quasi-magical roles—none of which was relevant in the United States. In the Deep South the slave artisan was made to adhere to Euro-American standards, both aesthetically and technically. He was merely the means by which the architectural, mechanical, and industrial plans were realized, working under the direct supervision of whites to realize the task set before him. While he may have had a degree of artistic freedom, assuredly it was small. To consider the iron-workers of Charleston as the direct heirs of ancient African artists of Benin and Ife is to ignore the difference between creating for oneself and creating for others. In the former case, interpretation is desirable; in the latter, the artisan is limited by the desires of his patron-consumer. Slave labor was a cheap way to approximate the elegance, beauty, and comforts of Europe in America. White America knew what it wanted; it was ready to impose the necessary aesthetical and technical standards, and depended on labor solely to yield the coveted product. In brief, although black artisans were talented, adaptable men, they did no more than render the product that white society demanded.

## The Fine Arts Tradition

Scipio Moorhead, a late eighteenth-century painter, is regarded traditionally as the earliest Afro-American artist working in the fine arts tradition.[12] Although it is doubtful whether he was, in fact, the first, it is certain that he played a significant role in the creative life of his times.

Moorhead and the black poet Phillis Wheatley, his contemporary and counterpart in the field of Afro-American formal verse, had much in common. Both were essentially apologists for black America. Both sought to prove that Afro-Americans could be ladies and gentlemen, and that they could produce art like white people. Both adopted class and cultural values generally denied to their group, modeling their standards on the white ethic. Witness the embrace of the Euro-American point of view in Wheatley's poem, "To S. M. An African Painter:"

> Twas mercy brought me from my Pagan land
> Taught my benighted soul to understand
> That there's a God, that there's a saviour
>   too
> Once I redemption neither sought nor knew.
> Some view our race with scornful eye,
> "Their color is a diabolic die"
> Remember, Christians, Negroes, Black as
>   Cain,
> May be refined, and join th'angelic train.[13]

No works of Moorhead's are known firsthand. Knowledge of his *oeuvre* rests almost entirely on the poetic tribute paid to him by Phillis Wheatley in the above-quoted work. The poem suggests that Moorhead was working at the time on portraying an episode from the story of Damon in Greco-Roman mythology. The treatment of such lofty subject matter—in the genre of "history painting"—seems to indicate Moorhead's desire to join the company of Leonardo da Vinci, Raphael, Poussin, and other masters of the Western fine-arts tradition, for until the nineteenth century history painting was regarded as the highest form of painting to which an artist could aspire. Drawing its subject matter from Christian and classical mythology, it served as a vehicle for the expression of moral and political values in contrast to such "lower" art forms as landscape, genre, still-life, and portraiture. Thus Scipio Moorhead seemed bent not on building an Afro-American tradition, but on associating himself with the best of the prevailing artistic trends. Aspiring to the company of those whose erudition and culture would predispose them to appreciate his work, he hoped to be viewed as a special case, an exception, a man above the crowd.

Thus the fine-arts tradition of the Afro-American began as a parallel movement bent on approximating existing Western painting, sculpture, and graphics through the use of European standards and techniques. Like all endeavors that are defensive in nature, this parallel tradition was deeply conservative, attempting in subject matter and style to out-European the European.

The values set forth in Scipio Moorhead's art found support in the small mulatto and free black communities. In spite of their concern with the overall plight of black people, these communities were basically elitist and welcomed Moorhead's basically bourgeois idiom as a counterbalance to the coarseness of the slave majority. Thus the early black community, like the early Afro-American artist, worked from a defensive posture, regarding established European values as the only ones worthy of pursuit.

Considerable emphasis has been given here to the conceptual embrace among Afro-Americans of Euro-American standards, since battles are won or lost at the level of ideas. It must also be remembered, however, that with the assimilation of the European fine-arts tradition came mastery of European technology. It was with oil paints, brushes, canvas, burin, and the lithographers' stone that Afro-American artists created their work. Learning to work with these tools helped the artist to expand his technical potential, but at the same time the imposition of traditional subject matter dictated by a conservative sociopolitical matrix blunted his expressive power.

Joshua Johnston (c. 1770–1825) is the earliest Afro-American artist to leave a large body of works for our examination. A painter in the tradition of the American limner or early portrait painter, it is not known who taught him. His work, however, attests to the fact that he was a relatively talented though provincial artist. His subjects are, by and large, white planters and merchants from the Baltimore area. Johnston presents them in a flat, linear style emphasizing such decorative details as bouquets, silk cuffs and collars, and the careful rendering of upholstery tacks. Little psychological interpretation of the subject was achieved.

Not much is known of Johnston's life. Possibly slave-born, he is generally associated with Colonel John Moale, but his ownership is contested by the families of James

McCormick, General Samuel Smith, and General John Stricker. Whatever his origins, it is clear that Johnston was by the early nineteenth century a "free householder of color" who made his living as a painter and seemed to have only a marginal relationship with the black community. There is no known painting by Johnston of a Negro sitter in spite of the number of eminent blacks in Baltimore at the time.[14]

Another black American who worked in the fine arts tradition was Robert S. Duncanson (1822–1872). Active in Detroit and Cincinnati, Duncanson was an exponent of the Hudson River School of landscape painting. His life typifies the dilemma of the nineteenth-century Afro-American artist. Like most members of this group, he was a mulatto who had received an unusually good education, who lived outside the South and in a city, and who was determined to become a painter in spite of his racial handicap. Like most he found himself faced with the irresolvable conflict that sprang from being both an artist and a black man.

As an artist, Duncanson produced large-scale decorations, illustrations, and easel works. Although he executed a small number of uneven portraits, he preferred to paint landscapes with literary themes. "Flood Waters, Blue Hole, Little Miami River" (1851), and a small group of related works dating from the late forties and fifties are Hudson River landscapes *par excellence*. Duncanson's later landscapes, particularly those done after his travels in Europe with William Sonntag, a landscapist also active in the Midwest, are more romantic in mood and almost without exception inspired by poems of Tennyson and Sir Walter Scott, whose sentimentality obviously appealed to the painter. These canvases testify to Duncanson's interest in the painting of Claude Lorrain and Poussin, whose works set the standard for the pastoral landscape.

Duncanson seems never to have coped effectively with the pressure exerted upon him because of his race. In the United States he could not escape the tug-of-war between the antislavery and the proslavery forces nor the atmosphere of prejudice which hampered him in the free exercise of his profession. Although he gained acceptance in Western art circles, he felt more at home in Canada than in the United States. Undoubtedly part of the reason for his love of England and Scotland was their lesser stress upon race.

It is alleged that Duncanson, when asked about his race and art, answered that he was concerned with "paint, not color"; nevertheless, the historical setting in which he lived made such a neutral viewpoint impossible and probably contributed to the nervous breakdown the artist suffered before his death.

Edward Mitchell Bannister (1829–1901) was a more original painter than were any of his predecessors. After studying in Boston with William Rimmer and possibly William Brackett, he settled in Providence, where, after a brief exposure to works by Americans associated with the Barbizon School, he developed an extremely free style of landscape painting which was stylistically ahead of the contemporary American norm. Bannister painted small, lyrical scenes distinguished by an intimacy of viewpoint and an increasingly less representational visual language. His nature works seemed almost like studies in their abbreviated descriptiveness when compared to the ponderous realism of most late nineteenth-century landscapes. Far in advance of his conservative peers, it is no wonder that his painting "Under the Oaks" won the bronze medal in its class at the Philadelphia Centennial Exposition of 1876.

In spite of Bannister's outstanding work, the racial prejudice which nearly excluded him from the Centennial Exposition building when he went there to receive his award has prevented his inclusion in books dealing with the history of American painting in the nineteenth century.

Henry O. Tanner (1859–1937), internationally decorated and respected, stands as the giant among Afro-American artists. But in spite of a distinguished career which eclipsed that of most nineteenth-century American artists, he, like Bannister, has not been assured of a place in the history and teaching of American art.

Trained at the Pennsylvania Academy of Fine Arts under Thomas Eakins, Tanner was undoubtedly the most technically prepared of the early Afro-American artists. After two years at the academy, Tanner worked and traveled in the South, where he also tried his hand at photography, known in those days as daguerrotype. Out of these travels came "Banjo Lesson," Tanner's most famous early painting. Completed in 1892, "Banjo Lesson," because of its sympathetic portrayal of black life, was regarded by Booker T. Washington and others as the beginning of a school of Afro-American art that would reveal the true beauty of the black man to the world. The poignancy of this hope is particularly evident when seen against the background of the nonracial subject matter of other important nineteenth-century Afro-American artists. Tanner had both the emotional and the artistic power to launch a new genre; however, after a period of simultaneously coping with being black and an artist in America, he succumbed to the almost universal desire of every American artist of the nineteenth century to study abroad. By the mid-1890s he had settled permanently in France, returning to the United States only for an occasional visit.

Tanner's early works are largely genre subjects; but his interest in surfaces permeated by light was evident from the first. This interest was to form the basis for the central stylistic trait of his mature works. In "Banjo Lesson," for example, the light comes from behind the figures and gently molds them.

In France, where Tanner drew favorable attention from Gérôme and other salon painters, his style became increasingly descriptive, e.g., the "Young Sabot Makers." Shortly thereafter (c. 1897–98) he, like Moorhead before him, turned to history painting with its explicitly realistic style. Works of this period, such as "Annunciation" and "Daniel in the Lion's Den," brought him praise, recognition, and salon prizes. Having distinguished himself in Europe as few Americans had before him, Tanner now felt free to develop his own personal style. By the early twentieth century, he was working characteristically with religious themes and painting in blue-green glazes. These works evoke a nocturnal world testifying to a deeply spiritual vision in which concrete physical reality is only sketchily recalled. Tanner's quiet, reverent paintings suggest an associa-tion with Ralph Blakelock and Albert P. Ryder, his contemporaries, who also developed highly personal, nocturnal styles. But in comparison to Tanner's work, Blakelock's and Ryder's paintings seem darker and more somber, with an inclination toward morbidity.

If Johnston, Duncanson, Bannister, and Tanner avoided black subjects in their work, preferring socially neutral themes, the same cannot be said of Patrick Reason and Edmonia Lewis.

Patrick Reason, a minor graphic artist of the midnineteenth century, was active as a teacher and lithographer in New York City. His significance lies in the fact that he put his art to the service of the antislavery cause, evidencing a degree of social commitment without precedent in his age among Afro-American artists. His interest in ameliorating the lot of the black masses and his deliberately political art places him at the beginning of self-conscious black social art in America.

Reason's contemporary, Edmonia Lewis (1845–1890), a sculptress in the neoclassical tradition, lived and worked in Italy. In her marble works she sought for a thematic balance between the American Indian and black strains in her background. Lewis produced a number of portraits of abolitionists, but her most interesting treatment of a racial theme is found in "Forever Free," a marble figurative group executed during the 1870s. The work is intended to commemorate the emancipation of black slaves in the United States. It shows a couple, the woman bowed at her husband's side as he purposefully raises his hand to show his broken chains. Significantly, however, the figures have been given the features of Italian peasants. (Before Tanner's genre-works of the late 1880s, there are no examples of works other than portraits in which the black physiognomy is treated.)

Reflecting on the nineteenth-century Afro-American art scene, one is struck by an absence of group spirit. Rather, there were a handful of individual artists working in widely separated centers, each searching for his own way to accommodate to the existing artistic mainstream, and each finding his career to some degree shaped by the racial stresses of his day. Because of the individual nature of the nineteenth-century Afro-American artist's struggle for survival, his twentieth-century counterparts had little sense of a common tradition before the 1920s.


## THE TWENTIETH CENTURY

The period of the late teens and early twenties marked the first significant departure of black artists from the independence and isolation which had been their accustomed lot in the nineteenth century. Several important social and political developments precipitated this change.

With the heavy northward migration and the birth of large black urban communities came a remarkable sense of self-discovery which manifested itself in all areas of black life. This new personal awareness was stimulated by the very diversity of the city colonies. The transition from a southern hamlet of 1,000 inhabitants to a city block with the same population represented no small change. Thus the movement North, although fundamentally an effort to realize economic gains, occasioned tremendous intellectual and cultural ferment among both the elite and the masses. Poets, writers, musicians, historians, and painters sprang up in response to the potential of the new urban centers. An artist now had not only the hope of an audience to spur him on but also an abundance of subject matter and the possibility of patrons. As we have seen, Locke dubbed this important development the New Negro Movement. Change, growth, expansion, and creativity were the watchwords of the day.

Swept up in this surge of self-expression, Afro-American artists began to discover the beauty and richness of things black. Black themes suddenly became not only attractive but respectable. The Afro-American artist found guidance and intellectual support for his new direction in such figures as Alain Locke, while his financial support sprang from a growing involvement with the American left.

At the same time that the urban ghettos of the North were rocked with cultural explosions, they were pregnant with social discontent. Jobs were hard to find. Living conditions were bad. Exploitation by white America had not abated. The rise of eloquent leaders such as Garvey heightened the political consciousness of the populace; conditions were ripe for political agitation. The American Socialist party and the recently organized Communist party were making their bid for black support and saw artists as natural allies in their effort. Thus it was that the left became the economic supporter of much Afro-American art, particularly the work of artists inclined toward social themes. This association between the American left and Afro-American artists was to continue until the second world war.

The New Negro Movement sought to inculcate the plastic artist with Locke's ideas concerning racial art. On the one hand, artists were encouraged to reexamine African art; on the other, they were urged toward the sympathetic treatment of portraits and genre scenes drawn from black life and attempting to capture its unique flavor.

Among the black artists who gave serious attention to African art in the twenties were Aaron Douglass and Sargent Johnson. Douglass created small graphic designs as well as large murals using ideas taken from African designs. Sargent Johnson is particularly noted for his creative use of formal elements taken from the African mask. The most outstanding example of this technique is seen in his work of 1931 titled "Copper Mask," in which the stylization is unmistakably African. Unfortunately, there was not a sufficient bulk of material available to Afro-American artists during this period to allow them to explore more deeply into African art.

The black genre subject in painting and sculpture was thriving admirably, however. Edmonia Lewis's idealized marble freedmen group of the 1870s had given way to sculptress Meta Warrick Fuller's semi-idealized "Ethiopia Awakening" (an Egyptian-inspired salute to the rise of black people), which in turn had given way to May Howard Jackson's realistic busts of such important Afro-American figures as Dean Kelley Miller of Howard University. This progression toward acceptance of the black physiognomy culminated in the late twenties in the work of such painters as Edward Harleston, William E. Scott, Lois Mailou Jones, Richmond Barthe, and Augusta Savage. Archibald Motley was a contemporary of this group, but he was given to satire and caricature of black people in his art.

An event of much importance in the development of Afro-American art occurred in the late twenties with the establishment of the Harmon Foundation in New York City. Before the appearance in 1927 of this foundation, with its commitment to the support of minority artists, the Afro-American artist had been largely without any regular exhibition outlet.

In its early years the Harmon Foundation presented the public with the works of almost every significant Afro-American artist in the nation. These exhibitions were accompanied by catalogues reproducing some of the works shown as well as news of artistic interest. In later years the foundation was often attacked for its critical naïveté, but it did play an extremely important role at a time when the professional art world had no dealing with Afro-American artists. Unfortunately, the Harmon Foundation did not seek to become an intermediary between professional arts institutions and Afro-American artists. Instead it settled for presenting exhibitions at the YMCA or other civic centers where blacks already had entrée.

Interest in the visual arts abounded in the twenties and this interest bore fruit in the early 1930s in the form of art programs at the black colleges. (Traditionally, music had been the favorite child of the black college; art was associated with academic failure.) Fisk University and Howard University led the way in the new move to establish effective study programs in the arts. It was at Howard that James V. Herring opened in 1930 what may well have been the first college gallery at a black school. By World War II most of the land-grant colleges had art departments. In 1941 Hale Woodruff and Atlanta University inaugurated the Atlanta Annual, which exhibited Afro-American artists throughout the Southeast. Unfortunately, most of the departments were sorely understaffed and underbudgeted; and it is a tribute to their tenacity that any of them survived to blossom forth in more recent years.

As the colleges joined the ranks of the Harmon Foundation and such community art centers as Karamu House in Cleveland and the Southside Art Center in Chicago to promote the cause of Afro-American art, what was perhaps the single most important impetus to the furtherance of such art was coming into being. This was the Works Progress Administration (WPA) program of art projects. The WPA projects included easel, mural, graphic, and sculpture workshops; and artists were paid to teach and to produce art for public buildings. Under the WPA more Afro-American artists were at work than at any previous point in history. In the larger cities, mature artists ran art workshops for their communities. In New York, for example, Charles Alston and Henry Bannarn were in charge of art workshops in Harlem. Numerous young painters such as

Jacob Lawrence, Charles White, Romare Bearden, and Hughie Lee-Smith began their careers under the WPA, often receiving their initial training from other Afro-American artists paid with WPA funds. In addition to being able to both paint and eat, Afro-American artists associated with the WPA found their horizons widened through their increased contact with white artists. Common professional problems as well as common social philosophies became the bases for friendships between the races which would probably never have developed otherwise. And although fair play was not yet the rule of the day, useful contacts were sometimes made between the official art world and the black artist.

Most Afro-American artists who began working in the thirties found themselves under the influence of social realism, whether in graphics, painting, or murals. Even those whose styles were relatively abstract, such as Jacob Lawrence, were bound up in social narrative art. Hale Woodruff, who worked in a midwestern regional style, and Charles White, whose work had the flavor of Mexican social art, were exponents of social commentary focusing on ethnic mores and customs, tragic events, and hard times. Their work depicts lynchings, Jim Crow, sharecropping scenes, and floods. Sometimes they chose to illustrate history with an eye to ennobling the black past. Lawrence's "Toussaint Series," Woodruff's Amistad murals, and White's "Five Famous Negroes" illustrate this narrative tendency.

Not all Afro-American artists in the twenties and thirties were swept up in these larger movements, however, although most did share a sense of community that had not existed before World War I. Some Afro-American artists of the period were devoted to the pursuit of academic directions, particularly with the increase in students attending art schools. These artists, whether of the generation of William Harper, William A. Johnson, or Lois Mailou Jones, were part of a related and parallel movement to that discussed above. They generally reflected a more technical and sophisticated approach in their art, tending toward either the depiction of neutral subject matter, such as land-scapes, still lifes, and city views, or subjects of a highly personal nature. These artists were not in creative conflict with their more politically- and socially-oriented peers; rather, they gave testimony to the new diversity of Afro-American art.

More commercially successful than the sophisticated Afro-American painters of the thirties and forties were the primitives. Horace Pippin, a man of remarkable simplicity, was exhibiting at the Museum of Modern Art well before that institution would acknowledge his academically trained peers. His success with New York critics may well have been due to the fact that the white world was able to accept the black man as a simple, happy, noncritical animal but not as a skilled, intelligent human being. Jacob Lawrence's work, though not primitive, was a logical next step in the adjustment of the white world to conceptually more powerful Afro-American artists. Lawrence's work is visually direct and simple, but it is informed by history. Pippin, together with Lawrence, whose works were shown at the Downtown Gallery, formed the spearhead for the Afro-American artist's breakthrough into the American cultural mainstream.

## The Aftermath of World War II

The first decade after World War II was a quiet one for the Afro-American artist. Those able to survive without WPA support continued to produce art—often under appalling conditions. Some Afro-American artists worked in styles parallel to those of their white peers in the hope of integrating into the mainstream art world. Others followed individual directions and achieved individual successes. A small number of Afro-American artists were now handled by galleries, but often through arrangements which compromised their integrity. Many were forced to stand by and see themselves eclipsed by lesser white artists.

The decade of the sixties brought unprecedented growth, development, and consolidation for the Afro-American artist; and as in the twenties and thirties, the forces making for the new burst of activity were directly related to the sociopolitical matrix in which the artist found himself.

As the old civil rights movement, with its pro-integration stance, lost energy, a new nationalism appeared in the American black community. The doctrine of non-violent resistance and redemptive suffering, as advanced by Dr. Martin Luther King, Jr., gave way to the more pragmatic political realism of the Mississippi Democratic party and the Student Nonviolent Coordinating Committee in the South, and the Panther party in the North.

Having witnessed the establishment of the fact that one could be an artist, militant, and black (as shown by James Baldwin), poets such as LeRoi Jones metamorphasized into Imamu Barakas. At the same time, arts groups such as Spiral[15] disappeared and those of the character of the Black Emergency Cultural Coalition began to take form. Simultaneously the seething black inner city took things into its own hands and exploded with riots. Before long, black people were America's number-one problem. No institutions were secure from their attack—be they schools, churches, or museums. The powers that be swiftly moved to contain and co-opt this new burst of energy. Studies were commissioned, repressive forces were put to the ready, money for "art" was made available. To quiet the general furor, greater mobility and attention was granted to Afro-Americans on a number of fronts.

Afro-American art and the artist benefited from the new climate of thought in two ways: both enjoyed a heightened visibility as all aspects of black culture became "of interest" to white America, and both received money and concessions not previously forthcoming. The money was intended to create situations which would lend constructive form to black aggression, but many people, aware of the pendulum swing of American racial stress, opted to use these "peace offerings" to build genuinely needed institutions.

During this period the Afro-American artist gained a new sense of his value as an artist and felt himself called upon to speak for the first time in a long while. Thus a number of nationalist and pronationalist art groups sprang up. Other less-voluble

artists simply adjusted their styles to harmonize more closely with the historical movement. The desire to be "artists of the people" characterized a number of new social artists,
such as Dana Chandler.

The new black social artists of the later sixties, who were rooted in nationalistic
political ideology and pro-African sentiment, led in the fight to take art to the community, to make it affordable, to find a basis for mass appreciation of art, and to make
art the servant of a larger political world view. These artists worked primarily with the
print and the mural as public art forms. An excellent example of such a group of artists
is AFRICOBRA in Chicago. In 1967 OBAC (Organization of Black American Culture)
created the "Wall of Respect" in Chicago's South Side. The mural was a fresh and potent
concept. It depicted such heroes as Malcolm X and Aretha Franklin, whom black people
knew and loved. The figures were presented in an informal manner on the wall of an
old building. Within two years Chicago's "Wall of Respect" had inspired more than
thirty such walls in other cities. The OBAC groups, after having created the wall,
evolved in much the same fashion as did LeRoi Jones. First there was OBAC, which
became COBRA (Coalition of Black Relevant Artists), and still later turned into
AFRICOBRA (The African Commune of Bad Relevant Artists). The group now
produces large, high-quality prints which it sells very cheaply. These are an expression
of its ongoing commitment to art for the "African" community in America.

Other black artists are committed to achieving the integration of American museums
in terms of their staffs and services. These artists and their groups have precipitated the
naming of blacks to posts in museum administrations, curatorial staffs, etc., and have
forced the use of black art historians in the organization and presentation of black
shows.

The "black show," an exhibition of works by artists whose skins are black, came
into its own late in the 1960s. Such shows were a response to pressures growing out of
America's racial stresses. They rarely had an art historical or stylistic common denominator, being defined more by sociology than by art history.

Precedents for the black show date back to the Harmon Foundation Annual. Other
early significant black shows were the 1940 American Negro Exposition at Chicago, a
product of the WPA and the Harmon Foundation, and "The Negro Artists Come of
Age," presented at the Albany Institute of History and Art in 1945. The latter was an
outgrowth of the 1940 exposition.

"The Evolution of Afro-American Artists: 1800–1950" (1967), organized by
Romare Bearden and Carroll Greene, set the tone for such later black shows as
"Counterpoint," "Afro-American Art since 1950," and "Six Black Artists." "Afro-
American Artists, New York and Boston," presented by the Museum of the National
Center of Afro-American Artists and the Museum of Fine Arts, Boston, and organized
by Edmund B. Gaither and Barnet Rubinstein, stands as the largest and most successful
exhibition of contemporary black art to date. Other large black shows include "Black
Art—1971," organized by Robert Glauber and sponsored by Illinois Bell Telephone
Company; "Harlem on My Mind," presented by the Metropolitan Museum of Art;

and "Contemporary Black Artists in America," organized by the Whitney Museum of American Art. Both the Metropolitan and the Whitney exhibitions were the objects of considerable protest. Much of the adverse criticism resulted from the absence of significant black input into exhibitions which presumed to represent an aspect of black creative life.

In the early seventies, as more museums began to hire Afro-Americans, the black show promised to become an academic issue. But one cannot doubt the impact these shows have had in presenting black America to the larger public, thereby achieving greater recognition of the quality, beauty, and power of black cultural life.

Afro-American artists and their supporters have recently joined together in an effort to develop professional teaching and commercial arts institutions, institutions operated by and committed to Afro-Americans. These institutions, if well built, will provide a much-needed platform for the promotion, preservation, and criticism of Afro-American art on a continuous basis. In the forefront of this movement are the Studio Museum in Harlem, the Museum of the National Center of Afro-American Artists, the Brockman Gallery, and the Acts of Art Gallery. Institutions such as the above are potentially the most important development of recent years. In spite of such steps forward, however, Afro-American art is faced today with serious problems. These include:

1. The absence of a developed art history.
2. The lack of an appropriate body of criticism.
3. A serious shortage of committed advocates.
4. The failure to have created professional art institutions which would assure its survival.

The absence of a developed art history and the lack of an appropriate body of criticism stem from the failure of black scholars and thinkers to focus attention on the visual arts. Intellectuals interested in working on specific art historical and critical problems are sorely needed. A comprehensive volume on Afro-American art must be preceded by the publication of more narrowly defined works of basic research such as monographs and critical essays. These would provide the basis for broader discussion. The quarterly journal, *Affairs of Black Artists*, was formed to help sponsor such informed dialogues.

Recent years have seen a small growth in the ranks of black art historians and museum and gallery personnel. These natural advocates of the Afro-American artist should by their very presence help to free the artist to devote himself to his art. In the past the Afro-American artist had to serve as his own defender, advocate, and critic.

The consolidation of strong and ongoing institutions is the surest way to insure abiding support for the Afro-American visual artist. Such institutions can serve not only as vehicles to preserve the artist's works and provide a place to show them, but can sponsor his advocates, enlarge his public, and use their institutional strength to defend his interests in the cultural arena. As we have seen, important work currently being accomplished in this field should help to guarantee the black artist a place in the American art world commensurate with his contribution.

## Notes

1. James A. Porter, *Modern Negro Art* (New York, Arno Press, 1969), Preface.
2. Alain L. Locke, "Negro Art, Past and Present," *The American Negro: His History and Literature* (New York, Arno Press, 1969), p. 119.
3. Alain Locke, "The Legacy of Ancestral Arts," *The New Negro: An Interpretation* (New York, Albert and Charles Boni, 1925), pp. 254–255.
4. *Ibid.*
5. *Ibid.*
6. The author's thinking on social art is much influenced by Arnold Hauser's *The Philosophy of Art History* (New York, Meridian Books, 1963).
7. James A. Porter, "Transcultural Affinities in African Art," *Africa Seen by American Negro Scholars* (New York, Standard Press and Graphics, Inc., 1963).
8. Judith Chase, *Afro-American Art and Craft* (New York, Van Nostrand Reinhold, 1971).
9. Robert Farris Thompson, "From Africa," *Yale Alumni Magazine*, New Haven, 1970.
10. *The New York Times*, August 8, 1926.
11. Cedric Dover, *American Negro Art* (Greenwich, Conn., New York Graphics Society, 1960).
12. The fine-arts tradition should be distinguished from the African crafts tradition and the American mechanical- and industrial-arts tradition. The fine-arts tradition is rooted in the formal pursuit of painting, sculpture, and graphics within the aesthetic and technical guidelines of the West.
13. William H. Robinson, *Early Black American Poets* (Dubuque, Iowa, William C. Brown, Co., 1969), p. 100.
14. "The Black Cleric," a painting in the collection of Bowdoin College, Brunswick, Maine, is attributed to Johnston. The author does not believe the attribution to be correct.
15. Spiral was a group of older New York artists who sought to find a way to make their art reinforce the civil rights movement.

# BIBLIOGRAPHY

## Books

*Affairs of Black Artists.* Museum of the National Center of Afro-American Artists, Boston, 1971.

*Art Gallery Magazine.* Ivoryton, Special Issue, April 1970.

*The Art of Henry O. Tanner.* Washington, D. C. National Collection of Fine Arts, 1969.

*Black Art Notes*, ed. by Tom Lloyd. New York, National Collection of Fine Arts, 1971.

*Black Dimensions in Contemporary American Art*, ed. by Edward Atkinson. New York, New American Library, 1971.

Bearden, Romare and Henderson, Harry, *Six Black Masters of American Art.* New York, Doubleday and Company, 1972.

Chase, Judith, *Afro-American Art and Craft.* New York, Van Nostrand Reinhold, 1971.

*Contemporary Black Artists in America.* New York, Whitney Museum of American Art, 1971.

Dover, Cedric, *American Negro Art*. Greenwich, Conn., New York Graphic Society, 1960.

*Edward Mitchel Bannister, Providence Artist*. Providence, R. I., Museum of Art, Rhode Island School of Design, 1966.

*The Evolution of Afro-American Artists, 1800–1950*. New York, City College of New York, 1967.

Fax, Elton, *Seventeen Black Artists*. New York, Dodd, Mead & Company, 1972.

Gaither, Edmund B. *Afro-American Artists, New York and Boston*. Museum of Fine Arts and National Center of Afro-American Artists, Boston, 1970.

*Images of Dignity*. New York, Ward Ritchie Press, 1967.

Locke, Alain L., *The New Negro*. New York, Albert and Charles Boni, 1925.

———, *The Negro in Art*. Washington, D.C., Associates in Negro Folk Education, 1940.
———, *Negro Art, Past and Present*. Washington, D. C., Associates in Negro History, 1936.

Matthews, Marcia M., *Henry O. Tanner: American Artist*. Chicago, University of Chicago Press, 1969.

Metropolitan Museum Bulletin, Special Summer Issue. New York, Metropolitan Museum of Art, 1969.

Perkins, Marion, *Problems of the Black Artists*. Chicago, Free Black Press, 1971.

Porter, James A., *Modern Negro Art*. New York, Dryden Press, 1943.

*Robert S. Duncanson: Centennial Exhibition*. Cincinnati, Cincinnati Art Museum, 1972.

Rodman, Seldon, *Horace Pippin*. New York, Quadrangle Press, 1942.

Saarinen, Aline, *Jacob Lawrence*. New York, American Artists Association, 1960.

*Sargent Johnson*. Oakland, California, Oakland Museum, 1971.

*Ten Afro-American Artists of the Nineteenth Century*. Washington, D. C., Howard University, 1967.

*William H. Johnson*. Washington, D. C., National Collection of Fine Arts, 1971.

## Articles

Bearden, Romare, "Rectangular Structure in My Montage Paintings." *Leonardo*, Vol. 2. Pergamon Press, 1969.

Pleasant, J. Hall, "Joshua Johnston, First Negro Portrait Painter." *Maryland Historical Magazine*, Vol. 37, 1942.

Porter, James A., "Robert Duncanson, Midwestern Romantic Realist." *Art in America*, Vol. 34, 1951.

———, "Versatile Interest of Early Negro Artists." *Art in America*, 1936.

———, "Transcultural Affinities in African Art," *Africa Seen by American Negro Scholars*. New York, Standard Press and Graphic, Inc., 1963.

Whatley, JoAnn, "Meeting the BEEC," *Affairs of Black Artists*. Boston, Museum of National Center of Afro-American Artists, 1971.

# 27

## *The Popular Media: Part I*
## *The Mission of Black Newsmen*

### *Luther P. Jackson, Jr.*

In the spring of 1972 when some of the faculty of the Columbia University School of Journalism informally considered naming the Summer Program for Members of Minority Groups* after a black newsman, they resurrected T. Thomas Fortune (1856–1928), the editor of the old New York *Age*. Fortune's name, however, was quickly reinterred as being so seldom remembered that it might be connected with the Fortune Society, the modern rights organization of ex-convicts.

Like many latter-day protesters for civil rights, Fortune spent a few hours in jail in 1890 for a "sit-in" at a Manhattan saloon that refused to serve him a glass of beer. The reason for the refusal is one of the many obscure facts of his life. (Since he was fair-skinned, with a shock of wild stringy hair, was the refusal due to something other than his race? Was it because he had already drunk too much?) It is known of Fortune that his series of three newspapers—the *Globe*, the *Freeman*, as well as the *Age*—were easily the best of the late nineteenth-century black publications, and that his later life was wracked by alcohol, mental depression, and poverty.

If ever a man was misnamed, it was Fortune. And from a historical standpoint, his greatest misfortune was that from the time in 1895 when Booker T. Washington raised his hand at the Atlanta Exposition and cried, "In all things that are purely social we can be as separate as the fingers, yet one as the hand in all things essential to mutual progress," Fortune has been mainly identified with him.

The fate of all early black journalists, like that of Fortune, is that they have become adjuncts to history; that their lives and times have been overshadowed by the preoccupation of students and their professors with Washington and two other black leaders—Frederick Douglass and W. E. B. DuBois.[1] In reality, black journalists have had a distinctive history; in addition to the trials and tribulations of blacks of any calling, they have endured some that are uniquely their own.

Fortune would have received high marks from latter-day black students for his 1885 pamphlet, *The Negro in Politics*, which challenged Douglass' dictum that "the

---

*The program was ultimately named the Michele Clark Fellowship Program for Minority Journalists; Ms. Clark was a black graduate of the program and a reporter for the Columbia Broadcasting System before she died in an airplane crash in 1973.

846

Republican party is the ship, all else the open sea." And Fortune's cry of "Race first, then party!" would surely have gained supporters at the 1972 black political convention in Gary, Indiana. Again, activist journalists, as well as nationalist politicians, would have applauded Fortune's design for his 1887 protest organization, The Afro-American League. He envisioned a national all-black coalition of local chapters with thousands of black "feeder" organizations—churches and lodges—serving as "preparatory schools." Its members, Fortune declared, should not be afraid to die in an all-out fight against disenfranchisement, lynch and mob law, unequal school funding, the chain gang and convict lease system, and Jim-Crowed transportation and public facilities. Fortune's later explanation for his preference of "Afro-American" would surely draw enthusiastic "Right ons!" from modern rhetoricians:

> You can take your choice of names, but I am an "Afro-American." All of the white newspapers of this country regard you as "negroes" and write Negro with a little *n*. . . . They regard you as a common noun. . . . Now I get around that undesirable title by adopting "Afro-American," which calls for the use of two big capital *A*'s. I AM A PROPER NOUN, NOT A COMMON NOUN![2]

But the parallels of history, as well as its verdicts, are often tricky. Things are the same, yet different. In the first place, given the current inflated economic costs and emphasis on academic credentials, no young journalist could emulate the 24-year-old Fortune by coming to New York and getting financial backing for a newspaper with only a printer's apprenticeship and two years at Howard University behind him. And from a style standpoint, no young journalist could demand the serious attention of his elders if he essayed the high-flown language of much of Fortune's early writings. Fairly typical was his description of the 1877 Republican compromise that sacrificed the freedmen's constitutional rights to gain the presidency for Rutherford B. Hayes as the "last grand master stroke of villainy and perfidy." While ornate language flourished in that era of personal journalism, the pen of today's young writer would be stayed by professionalism, principally the standards of objectivity that gradually took hold in the twentieth century. But behind Fortune's windy rhetoric—unfettered by the "ifs," "buts," and "on the other hands" of modern journalism and scholarship—lay a hard nut of moral courage.

As the years passed into the twentieth century, the crusading Fortune was tumbled from his black charger by still another journalistic circumstance of the time: most small newspaper editors, white and black, depended upon political advertising and patronage as their main source of income. And among blacks, membership in the southern-dominated Democratic party was nothing short of heresy. So when Fortune branded himself a political maverick early in his career he immediately closed the door on Republican largesse in the form of a job or as advertising for his newspaper. Thus Fortune became increasingly dependent upon small sums from Booker Washington, who needed the voice of the best black newspaper, as well as the lesser ones, to effectively present his views to black folk.

Secretly, Washington later took financial control of the *Age*, but it cannot be said that he ever "bought" its editor. Fortune differed with his benefactor on many issues and found subtle ways of maintaining a measure of independence. He even went so far as to take Washington's position in one editorial and his own in another. In 1906, for example, when Theodore Roosevelt summarily and dishonorably discharged three companies of black troops at Brownsville, Texas, for allegedly "shooting up" the town without identifying any specific culprits, Washington persuaded Fortune to write an editorial pointing out the dangers of abusing the President. But in the same issue another editorial appeared declaring that Roosevelt's Brownsville order had evoked the ecstatic approval of the white South. Emma Lou Thornbrough, in her 1972 biography, reasoned that in the years of Fortune's and Washington's "uneasy" alliance a "pragmatic, accommodationist stance seemed to be the only way for black people to survive," adding that Fortune's "personal misfortune" was his inability to fully accept this arrangement. She continued:

> ... He lacked Washington's capacity to rationalize, to accept and adjust, and insist that things were getting better when they were in reality getting worse. Fortune had always been more skeptical than Washington about the good will and cooperation of whites, and he had never gone to the lengths to which the Tuskegeean had gone to placate and conciliate. He was simply unable to adopt a patient, compromising, pragmatic position on questions of human rights and human dignity. Whatever his other vagaries and inconsistencies, on this fundamental question he was consistent throughout his long career. This is the reason that what he wrote and said remains relevant to a later generation—but it was also his personal curse. . . .[3]

Fortune's "personal curse" was that he succumbed to his inner torment as well as to age and alcohol. In 1907—the year before the Afro-American League finally expired—he lost the editorship of the *Age* to Fred R. Moore and was reduced to a wage hand. By 1913, after recovering from a mental breakdown, the 57-year-old Fortune was struggling to keep his home at Red Bank, New Jersey, and help his son through college by freelancing on a wage of ten dollars a week; and the *Age* was $193.50 in arrears. His desperation was shown in a plaintive letter to Emmett J. Scott, Washington's personal secretary: "What am I to do? The Negro papers are not able to pay for extra work and the daily papers do not care for Negro productions of any kind. Under such circumstances I face the future with $5 in hand and 57 years as handicap."

In his final years, Fortune's problems became those of simple survival; of how to sustain himself and his family on a pitifully irregular income. "Unable to bend," Professor Thornbrough wrote, "as Washington had, he was broken." But the broader implications of Fortune's dilemma are not quite as black or white as the allusion to "bend or be broken" suggests. All people "bend," but how much? When does one stop bending and with what priorities? Race first, country first, party first, or self and family first? That human beings usually come down on the side of self does not preclude selfless goals. This ageless and universal conflict particularly affects black newsmen, whose calling to journalism often stems from the altruistic desire to make the black press a free voice for an oppressed people.

"We wish to plead our own cause," John B. Russwurm wrote in the first black newspaper, aptly titled *Freedom's Journal*. "Too long have others spoken for us." Thus the black press was born with a mission.

The same high calling was demonstrated by Frederick Douglass in 1847 when he founded *The North Star* after deciding that William Lloyd Garrison's *Liberator* had spoken for him long enough.

Fortune's very act of founding the Afro-American League in 1887 presents black journalists of the 1970s with an additional historical challenge. By this action, Fortune implied by deed as well as words that the black press should be an activist press. But Fortune's goals, like his life, were fraught with contradictions, and given the imperatives of a far more complex society for "credibility," if not "objectivity," his activism is perhaps too big a burden for young journalists to shoulder. Yet given the ambivalence of the white media on racial matters of the 1970s, black journalists willing to risk historical parallels might ponder these words from Fortune's *Freeman* calling for an Afro-American League:

> It is a remarkable state of the case that the entire press of the North has ceased to dwell upon the state of affairs in the South in other than a wishy-washy way, chronicling such outrages as cannot well be passed over in silence as news matter, but putting such matters in such shape as invariably to make the colored person guilty of all that is charged upon him and excusing those who constitute themselves judge and jury in the execution of the mob's decree; while it is in exceedingly rare instances that the misdeeds of individual offenders ever find a voice in the press. The people suffer in silence. This should not be. They should have a voice.[4]

In sum, black newsmen, even in their historical infancy, had the explicit goal of serving black people. "Race first!"—then party, as Fortune cried, or then country or self. As self-appointed spokesmen of the race, black journalists have since called the black press a "protest" press; yea, a "fighting!" press. Yet in the face of implacable white racism, Fortune, his contemporaries, and his heirs have all had to lower their voices.

## THE AGE OF THE EDITOR AND PROPRIETOR, 1880–1910

During the Fortune years of 1880 to 1910 the voice of the black press was muted, largely due to the simple fact that relatively few blacks knew how to read. Further, nine out of ten blacks lived in the South, where speaking out was not long tolerated. In 1890, half of some 130 black newspapers were located there, but with few exceptions such as John Mitchell, Jr.'s Richmond *Planet*, they rarely raised their voices above a whisper. Though some northern-based city newsmen—such as Edward E. Cooper and his successor, George L. Knox, of the Indianapolis *Freeman*, and H. C. Smith of the Cleveland *Gazette*—claimed "national" circulations, these never exceeded a few thousand and their accounts of southern outrages were second- and third-hand reports.

In fact, editors and proprietors, black or white, of one-man weekly publications seldom engaged in routine reporting. As much as two or three pages of their four-paged newspapers were filled with preprinted columns of general news features and advertising (mostly for patent medicines), sold by news syndicates. These "patent insides" or "boiler plate" frequently reflected the racial prejudices and stereotypes that black editors hoped to combat. Most of the remaining columns contained editorial opinions and commentaries, including "exchanges" written by editors in other cities and obtained through the mailed exchange of newspapers. "Locals" consisted of short paragraphs of social news, often interlaced with kind words for a handful of local advertisers.

Then, as now, social news was the bread and butter of the black press. Aside from the "locals," each issue contained columns from out-of-town agent-correspondents, so named because they doubled as solicitors and collectors. Accounts of a weekly round of teas, parties, meetings, and funerals were crammed into articles by women and young men with social or literary ambitions, such as those written for Fortune in the early 1880s by a teen-aged W. E. B. ("Willie") DuBois under the heading "Great Barrington (Mass.) Notes." Another persisting characteristic of the black press was what Gunnar Myrdal described as its function as an "additional" newspaper. Black editors rightly or wrongly assumed that their readers also bought white daily newspapers, so their emphasis was on black news or general news with a race-relations "angle."

With little advertising income and a subscription rate of only one or two dollars a year, the black press of Fortune's *Age* was a subsidized press. Unlike Fortune, few black editors were full-time newsmen. They were lawyers, ministers, teachers, and printers first; journalists second. Most newspapers were short-lived, some appearing during political campaigns and vanishing after elections. They were supported by the editors themselves or through white philanthropy or political patronage, which came to be dispensed by Booker T. Washington. Some part-time politicians, like lawyer Ferdinand L. Barnett of the Chicago *Conservator*, gained professional appointments, but most were consigned to the dregs of Republican patronage, working in city halls, county buildings, and statehouses as clerks, doorkeepers, and messengers.

Christopher J. Perry of the Philadelphia *Tribune*, for example, worked for fifteen years as a sheriff's office clerk, yet in his case the political subsidy paid off not only for him and his newspaper but also for other blacks. At a time when blacks were not allowed to ride on the horse-drawn trolleys of Philadelphia, Perry successfully campaigned for a black driver of a black trolley and for other jobs and better working conditions. Although his circulation never exceeded a few hundred copies, Perry's efforts contributed mainly to the *Tribune's* present distinction as the oldest black general circulation newspaper. It has been in continuous publication since 1884.

The black press not only survived; its voice grew stronger. Perhaps the strongest voice among black "newsmen" was that of the wife of the *Conservator's* Ferdinand Barnett. Before marrying and rearing four children, Ida B. Wells shared the title of "editor and proprietor" with two men because she refused to join their Memphis *Free Speech and Headlight* unless she was made "equal to themselves." In 1892, on a trip East, Miss Wells was met by Fortune in Jersey City with the news that her Memphis printing press had been destroyed and her life threatened by white hoodlums because of editorials she had written supporting a boycott of white businesses as a protest against lynching, and denouncing white women who provoked mobs by yelling "Rape!" when caught in the arms of black lovers. Miss Wells's information was based partly on her own investigation of several lynchings in Mississippi's Delta. Exiled from Memphis, Miss Wells briefly acquired a one-fourth interest in the *Age* in exchange for her subscription lists. Also in that year of 1892, recorded U. S. lynchings reached an all-time peak of 226, including 155 black victims.

It was the January 31, 1893, lynching of Henry Smith at Paris, Texas, that led to Miss Wells's fame as a journalist-crusader, perhaps one of the greatest of any age. Then lecturing in Washington, D. C., on the subject of lynchings, Miss Wells used $150 in fees to dispatch a Kansas City Pinkerton detective to the Texas scene, only for the agency to send her a batch of newspaper clippings. But for the purpose of Miss Wells's crusade those clippings told enough, for many white newsmen were among the lynching's 10,000 witnesses. Most had come to the lynching by special trains. The event was so flagrantly public that it could not be suppressed, minimized, or rationalized by the white press as was usually the case among many of the most liberal northern newspapers.[5]

In two Great Britain lecture tours and in her pamphlet, *The Red Record*, Miss Wells told about Smith's grisly death. A mental retardee, he had been accused of raping and killing a 5-year-old white girl. As he protested his innocence, Smith was hauled to a platform—so that the throng could better view the proceedings. Red-hot pokers pierced his body and were shoved down his throat; his eyes were burned out; and after nearly an hour of such torture he was set afire. After his body had turned to ashes, men, women, and children poked through them for bones, buttons, and teeth for souvenirs. By Miss Wells's accounts, the story did not end then; a year later a traveler through Texas reported this exchange between an 8-year-old white girl and her mother:

"I saw them burn the nigger, didn't I, Mama?"

"Yes, darling, you saw them burn the nigger."

By that time the yearly lynching rate had dropped below 200, and largely because of Miss Wells's voice, rarely would America's most barbaric crime again be condoned by the northern white press.

Another vigorous black voice was that of William Monroe Trotter, whose Boston *Guardian* challenged Booker T. Washington's accommodationist views. In 1903 Trotter was jailed after he led a group of early-day militants who disrupted a Washington speech and all but chased the speaker from Boston's Symphony Hall. Drawing no race distinctions, Trotter later incurred President Woodrow Wilson's ire by personally criticizing him for introducing Jim Crow into Washington's federal office buildings.

But whether their voices were muted or strong, the black editors and proprietors spoke mainly as individuals. Fortune's Afro-American League was a forerunner of all national protest organizations, ranging from Trotter's National Rights League to the National Association for the Advancement of Colored People (NAACP) to the 1972 Black Political Convention, but by and large black newsmen confined their organizational efforts to national and regional press associations. Another characteristic of the period was the professional decorum of black newsmen. At a time when Joseph Pulitzer and William Randolph Hearst were introducing "yellow" journalism to receptive white immigrants, the black press was aimed at staid black families. "It refused to print anything," Fortune commented, "that would damage the good name or morals of the race, and kept all scandal and personalities, however sensational the news might be, in the background."[6]

This would soon change. In the next period of the black press, the age of the publisher, black newsmen would pitch their voices in screaming 72-point headline type at the masses of newly literate blacks. With the support of mass circulations, black newsmen would build an institution that would be called "the single most powerful" in black America. For these institution builders, Robert S. Abbott would lay the cornerstone, and though he adapted some of the worst techniques of yellow journalism, his newspaper was aptly named the Chicago *Defender*.

## THE AGE OF THE PUBLISHER, 1910–1954

Robert S. Abbott neither looked nor acted like a man who could defend himself, much less his race. Only 5 feet 6 inches or so, his long legs and short torso gave him a top-heavy look, and his shyness approached cowardice. He never could speak or—by modest journalistic standards—write very well, yet his name and those of Robert L. Vann of the Pittsburgh *Courier* and Carl Murphy of the Baltimore *Afro-American* stand out as boldly in the history of black publishing as the headlines that emblazoned their nationally circulated newspapers.[7]

Abbott's genius, like that of all great publishers, was his ability to get others to speak and write for him or even risk their lives for a story or a cause. While Abbott, for example, visited his native southland only under heavy disguise and the cover of darkness, two of his agent-correspondents were killed and others routed from their homes because they wrote for or distributed the *Defender*. And once, when a beefy Georgia sheriff confronted Abbott in his office with papers charging him with libeling a southern judge, the publisher flatly denied being Abbott, and called on an associate to remind the sheriff that he was in the Black Belt of Chicago, not in the clay hills of Georgia.

The sheriff's nemesis, Dr. George C. Hall, wrote a health column for the newspaper and was an early director of the Chicago Urban League. Just as Abbott called a personal defender to his rescue, he commissioned Ida B. Wells, the inveterate crusader, to investigate race riots in Springfield and East St. Louis, Illinois, and paid Roscoe Conkling Simmons, the supreme orator of the day, the then munificent sum of $125 a week to tour the country for the sole purpose of promoting the *Defender*.

No politician like Robert Vann, or scholar like Carl Murphy, the *Defender* publisher revolutionized the black press, first because he was in the right place, the Black Belt of Chicago, at the right time, the 1910 decade. The Black Belt was then a prototype of what the sprawling ghettos of Baltimore and Pittsburgh—as well as Detroit, Philadelphia, Cleveland, Newark, and Washington, D. C.—were to become in the 1950s, 1960s, and 1970s. In 1910, Chicago's 44,103 blacks were concentrated within a few South Side blocks; so few, in fact, that in 1905 Abbott could cover the community on foot, solicit advertising, and hand-deliver 300 copies all by himself. With each passing decade, Chicago's black population, like none in any other city, would grow in quantum leaps, jumping southward from 31st Street to 47th by 1920 to 63rd by 1930, adding twenty blocks or so in each of the later decennials. Although the Black Belt, so named because it was once girded by railroad tracks, would give Chicago its reputation as being the nation's most segregated city, in newspaper business terms, this meant a large and accessible black circulation base.

It was circulation, mass black circulation, that freed many black newsmen from dependence on political handouts. Unlike white publishers, they could not rely on advertising for profits and priced their newspapers accordingly. Even during the Depression years, for example, when a dime could buy six Monday-through-Saturday copies of most daily newspapers, black publishers charged as much for a single weekly copy. And with one cent from each dime Abbott became a millionaire.

Of all the statistics that might help explain this Abbott Age phenomenon, the most telling one is that by 1910 seven out of ten blacks over 10 years old could read; within four decades, the black illiteracy rate had tumbled from 80 percent to 30 percent. These newly literate blacks were hungry for status and for information about themselves that no white newspaper provided. They wanted to be called Mister and Miss or Mrs.; not "darky" or "auntie" or "burly black beast." They wanted news of their schools, churches, and lodges; of their small achievements and institutions; their weddings and funerals; not their presumed shiftlessness and crime. And even if no one listened, they needed a voice that would talk back to their oppressors in no uncertain terms because they—as Howard University's E. Franklin Frazier explained—"were not interested in the dignified and theoretical discussion of their rights." In simple *Defender* headline terms, they needed a loud and "sassy" voice.

At the *Defender*'s peak in 1920, Abbott claimed a circulation of 283,571, but even that high figure does not reflect the readership and the listenership, if you will, of the *Defender* and other black newspapers.[8] In churches, lodges, and barber shops, these publications were often posted and read aloud. Furthermore, some copies were passed from hand to hand so frequently that one mailed back to the Chicago *Enterprise* was described by Frederick Detweiler as being "so thumbed and worn as to be scarcely recognizable even to its publishers." The writer had requested a duplicate copy.

In a 1920 report on Mississippi migration, Charles S. Johnson wrote that in Gulfport a man was regarded as "intelligent" if he read the *Defender*, and in Laurel, "old men who did not know how to read would buy it because it was regarded as precious." Further, a black Mississippian was quoted as saying that "Negroes grab the *Defender* like a hungry mule grabs fodder." Johnson, later a Fisk University sociologist, had a Freudian explanation for the *Defender*'s popularity among oppressed Mississippi blacks:

> . . . Negroes could read the things they wanted to hear most, expressed in a manner in which they would dare not express them. It voiced the unexpressed thoughts of many and made the accusations for which they themselves would have been severely handled. Freud's theory of the suppressed wish finds a happy illustration in this rage over the Chicago *Defender*.[9]

This writer's less scholarly guess is that the "suppressed wish" theory might well be applied to the *Defender*'s publisher. Though outwardly shy, even humble, his psychic rages might have been vented through his newspaper. The complex story of the quiet man behind the screaming headlines was revealed in a posthumous biography, *The Lonely Warrior*, by the late Roi Ottley, a former editor of the New York *Amsterdam News*. Unlke the fair-skinned Robert Vann or the brown-skinned Carl Murphy, Abbott was black, almost literally so, at a time when black was definitely not regarded as beautiful. His blackness cost Abbott the hand of a dearly loved Savannah, Georgia, boyhood sweetheart; troubled him during four years at Hampton Institute; and after he had obtained a law degree at Chicago's Kent School, forbade a legal career. He was told by the equally dark Nick Chiles of the Topeka *Plaindealer* that he would "starve to death" if he attempted to practice in Topeka and by a fair-skinned and prosperous Illinois lawyer that he was "a little too dark to make any impression on the courts of Chicago."[10] It took great patience and tenacity on the part of "Black Abbott," as he was called, to become accepted in the circle of Chicago's black society. But when he became a millionaire, he gained that acceptance.

Unlike T. Thomas Fortune, whose "personal curse" was his liquor-fed emotional instability, Abbott never drank; and he, inadvertently perhaps, turned his blackness into strengths. But they were a long time in coming. Unmarried at 37 and having given up a part-time job as a printer's helper, Abbott issued the first *Defender* on May 5, 1905, as "The Only Two-Cent Weekly in the City." If so, that was probably its only distinction. The earliest extant copy, dated the following September 16, was staid, dreary, and boiler-plated: a four-page, handbill-sized sheet, unredeemed by the brilliant writing of a Fortune or the courageous reporting of an Ida B. Wells. In contrast with Abbott's later sensationalism, his lead story was about his friend Dr. Hall and another physician attending a convention in Richmond, Virginia. Each week Abbott paid a printer $13.75

to produce 300 copies, but he performed every other task, including the previously mentioned one of being a 37-year-old newsboy. As Ottley described it:

> Rain or snow, slush or mud, he carried a load (of newspapers) the length and breadth of the community, ringing doorbells and peddling the paper. Nights he visited every South Side barber shop, poolroom, nightclub, saloon, drugstore, and church, indeed anywhere Negroes assembled, selling papers and gathering news and advertising. He often was made the butt of coarse jokes, but he merely turned his head aside.[11]

Yet "Black Abbott"—as he padded his shoe soles with cardboard and dined on fish sandwiches and soda pop—came to know his fellow "Georgia boys," as he called them, and what they wanted to read. His first crusade, in 1909, was against prostitution on the South Side. Being against sin afforded this headline: "MOTHER TAKES INNOCENT DAUGHTER TO HOUSES OF ILL FAME," adding in small type, "to play the piano." Yet Abbott almost gave up on journalism. He tried, through Dr. Hall's acquaintance with Booker Washington, to land a political job as Assistant U. S. Recorder of Deeds. But fortunately for Abbott, he was turned down and thus did not become indebted to Washington as Fortune had been. While ideological battle lines were being drawn between Washington and W. E. B. DuBois, Abbott managed to chart his own course. While Washington in Atlanta had urged blacks to "cast down your buckets" in the South, Abbott cried, "Come North!" And while DuBois had called for a "talented tenth" of black leaders, Abbott declared for "the masses, not the classes."

To that hoary phrase, Abbott gave meaning. By 1910 Abbott was no longer groping to touch the masses; in that year he reached them. It was the same year that Vann incorporated the *Courier*. Also in 1910, P. B. Young, Sr. converted a fraternal organ into his Norfolk *Journal & Guide*, later praised as the most objective of black newspapers. Although it was not a newspaper, the *Crisis* also was launched in 1910, for the masses, perhaps, but read mainly by the classes.

If any one incident could possibly pinpoint the beginning of the black press revolution, it might be Abbott's 1910 hiring of the handlebar-moustached J. Hockley Smiley, described by Ottley as a "prodigious drinker" and a "a slender brownskin dandy troubled with hacking coughs." Before Smiley, the first paid *Defender* employee, Abbott had kept his newspaper afloat strictly through the volunteer help of friends and acquaintances, including his landlady, Harriet Plummer Lee, who provided rent-free office space. Ten years or so after Smiley's appointment, Abbott's Chicago staff alone would be large enough to occupy a plant whose value he announced at $475,000, debt-free. One of Smiley's miracles was wrought practically overnight, according to Ottley:

> Utilizing Abbott's ideas, [Smiley] began by frankly copying the front-page styles of the Chicago daily newspapers, especially introducing something of Hearst's techniques of yellow journalism. Then the publisher had him change the format; second, adopt banner headlines; third, treat the news sensationally; and fourth, lay emphasis on the concerns, fears, and aspirations of the rank-and-file, which were dear to his heart. . . .[12]

Thus from the Chicago *Tribune's* "World's Greatest Newspaper" Smiley adapted "World's Greatest Weekly." The *Tribune* apparently did not protest, but Hearst's lawyers sued some years later because newsstand buyers were mistaking the *Defender* for Hearst's two Chicago newspapers. And no wonder: Smiley's imitations included an exact duplicate of the American standard and eagle that flew from the Hearst mastheads. Flattered yet alarmed by the suit, Abbott satisfied the court by replacing America's symbols with Egypt's sphinx.

But the new *Defender* was hardly as silent. Smiley raised the decibel level of the newspaper's headlines from 18-point to 72-point volume, matching Hearst's racist headlines with screaming red ones of his own: "100 NEGROES MURDERED WEEKLY IN THE UNITED STATES BY WHITE AMERICANS; JIM CROW CARS RUNNING OUT OF CHICAGO DEPOT; WHITE MAN TURNS BLACK IN ST. LOUIS." When reproached for his strident tone—even by some black publishers who later copied the *Defender*—Abbott gave an explanation similar to that provided by white publishers in their successful attempts to reach poor immigrants: The *Defender*, as Ottley wrote, was trying to acquire the largest possible number of readers, thereby improving and advancing the Negro race as well as the nation.

Such explanations might be challenged by Smiley's excesses; for instance, he was not above making up a story on a slow news week, and once he reminded Roscoe Simmons, the orator, of a debt he owed to Abbott with this front-page streamer: "COL. ROSCOE CONKLING SIMMONS DIED [sic] SUDDENLY IN ST. LOUIS." When the traveling Simmons read his obituary, he hurried back to Chicago. Abbott gradually drew in the reins on Smiley and his growing staff as he became increasingly sensitive to the criticism of middle-class blacks. When he knew reporters' facts to be inaccurate, he sent them clippings of the offending stories with cryptic marginal notes, such as "Don't put this trash in my paper!" And for all the *Defender's* scare headlines, Abbott had not abandoned the American dream or the golden rule. "If we act like decent people," he noted, "the chances are we shall be treated decently." More characteristically, his notes were simple aphorisms: "Elevation of the race is our job!"

Shy Abbott's habit of writing notes helped keep his staff loyal to him. According to Ottley, he never chastised an employee publicly. Another key to Abbott's success as a black journalist, rather than a Hearst in blackface, was suggested by one staffer's tribute: "Imbued as he was with a passion for the rights of Negroes, a passion bordering on fanaticism, he was able to transmit this passion to his associates." Here is Ottley's own assessment of Abbott's relations with his staff:

> As a group, these people embraced Abbott and his ideas, and though emerging from varied backgrounds, they seemingly had a talent for the give and take of teamwork. Abbott himself was gifted at teamwork, for he had the necessary self-control. Consequently, the *Defender* developed an atmosphere of camaraderie, in which each one assumed personal responsibility for the progress and success of the paper.

Still on the subject of teamwork, Ottley pictured this scene at Abbott's first office—Mrs. Lee's rooming house—to elucidate the point:

> Nights when they were correcting galley proofs, they often chipped in ten cents apiece to buy meat and vegetables for supper. Fay Young did the cooking, using Mrs. Lee's gas range, pots, and dishes. If Abbott happened to be out while the cooking was in progress, they always prepared enough for him. Bessie Boykin often brewed tea to wash down the vittles. Upon Abbott's return they would all sit down like one family to eat. Afterwards they would gather around the potbellied stove and discuss the *Defender*.[13]

When Smiley died in 1915, the *Defender* was ready to expand into a full-sized eight-page newspaper. Abbott memorialized Smiley as "a man who never watched the clock," but a more fitting tribute would have been recognition of an original Smiley idea that had helped make the *Defender* a national newspaper. Seeking a way to overcome thorny distribution problems, Smiley had reasoned that since Chicago was the nation's railroad center, why not press into service hundreds of porters and waiters as *Defender* salesmen and distributors? They came and went daily and were, in fact, the only blacks who traveled from place to place on regular schedules. Through word-of-mouth porters and waiters got Smiley's message and scores of them quickly accepted his offer. So did road-show entertainers and itinerant jazz musicians. Profit was their original motive, Ottley wrote, but as the *Defender* "became more and more vigorous in espousing the Negro's cause, these people felt it a 'race duty' to help distribute the paper and even became couriers bringing back the news."

Wider circulation brought a sharp southern reaction. Abbott complained of attempts to bar the *Defender* from the mails, threats on his life, and abuses to his agent-correspondents. As World War I progressed, the support of the Allies in the black press was diminished when the Army hanged eighteen black troops for allegedly inciting a 1917 race riot in Houston, Texas, in which twenty persons—eighteen white, two black—had been killed.[14] When the United States entered the war "to make the world safe for democracy," the black press attacked abuses of black troops so vigorously that it was accused of being disloyal. Queried by the War Department, Abbott laid the charge to his "enemies" in the South.

The South's dispute with Abbott was mainly due to his "Great Northern Drive." Its urgent imperative, "The *Defender* Says Come!" was draining southern plantations and households of their black man and woman power. When the campaign began on May 15, 1918, many blacks—as in the Douglas Turner Ward play, *Day of Absence*—simply vanished. Blacks came North on foot, by wagon, and on excursion train. The migration did not subside until the end of the war, but that May 15 and the week thereafter was marked by Charles S. Johnson as "the date of the heaviest rush to the North, the periods of greatest temporary congestion, and the wakening of the North to the presence of their guests."

Thus the Age of the Black Publisher, as personified by Abbott, was marked by the second so-called "exodus" of blacks from the South. The first had been a trickle of some 40,000 to Kansas in 1879 and 1880; the second a floodtide of more than 300,000 to the cities of the industrial North, including 50,000 to Chicago. The strongest lure was wages ranging from fifty cents to one dollar an hour for common labor, as much as could be earned for a full day's work in the South. And just as Kansas and Oklahoma newspapers had beckoned blacks West, Abbott's *Defender* sounded the call to the North. But while such western papers as Edward P. McCabe's Langston, Oklahoma, *Herald* cautioned blacks to "come prepared or not at all," the *Defender* welcomed "all you folks—the *Defender* says come!"

As blacks flocked into Chicago, many of those turned away by employers and agencies at least had the *Defender*'s ear. "Let us be your spokesman and defender," the newspaper urged. "In defending you, we defend ourselves. Consult our legal and health editors. Their advice is free. Bring your troubles to us!" Not only did the many migrants visit Abbott's office, they stopped him on the street, and he was flattered by the attention of his fellow "Georgia boys." Ottley quotes Abbott's associate, Phil A. Jones, as saying that the publisher's "greatest pleasure in life came in being able to stand on the corner of 35th and State Streets, with a fat cigar in his mouth, and discuss the race problem with anyone."

Following the war, the "Red Summer" of 1919—so-called because of its racial clashes—saw seven major race riots, in two of which the *Defender* was involved. According to the historian Arthur I. Waskow, the Longview, Texas, riot erupted when Samuel L. Jones, a schoolteacher and *Defender* agent-correspondent, was beaten with iron rods and gun butts because he was suspected of writing a *Defender* story claiming that a lynch victim of four months before had been a white woman's lover, not a rapist. The second riot involving the *Defender* raged for a week in Chicago, leaving fifteen whites and twenty-three blacks dead. The *Defender*'s early statistical reports of the dead and injured, identified as "white" and "Negro," appeared like box scores. According to Ottley, it was as though "the score must be kept even—that is, on an eye-for-an-eye basis." Later, however, Abbott became alarmed and issued an "extra" urging Chicagoans "to make things peaceful." As a member of the Chicago Commission on Race Relations that explored the causes of the riot, Abbott signed a 1922 report recommending that the Negro press exercise more "care and accuracy" in handling racial subjects.

Abbott's new civic interests gave him less time for the "Georgia boys" at 35th and State; and the *Defender*, meanwhile, was losing its reputation as a "fighting" newspaper along with its war-inflated circulation. Moreover, Abbott's sensitivity about his blackness took many twists and turns, not all good for staff morale or his image in the black community. For instance, his first wife, whom he married at 50, was nearly white, and after two grand trips abroad and a stormy divorce, he took on a second wife of the same complexion. Then in the middle of the Depression, when millions of blacks were jobless and hungry, he made the mistake of writing a series of twenty articles about the race's need for culture and refinement. Abbott's illnesses and absentee management also contributed to the *Defender*'s decline, but at his death in 1940, perhaps the main reason for its downfall was that the newspaper did not grow with its readers as they became better educated and more urbanized.

While time passed Abbott's *Defender* by, Robert Vann's *Courier* was aimed at the second generation of black urbanites. Its headlines were sometimes as outrageous as the *Defender*'s in the latter's J. Hockley Smiley days, but were more thoroughly buttressed by facts. And although the *Courier*'s editorials on such moralistic subjects as honesty, justice, and kindness were traced by historian G. James Fleming to the sermonettes of Arthur Brisbane (the best-known of Hearst's editors), the *Courier* was essentially its own creation. Rather than use red ink to attract the eyes of readers, the *Courier* employed a salmon-colored front page, clear body type, and photography. Its reportorial style and its sparkling society, entertainment, and sports pages were more like a stroll down Harlem's Seventh Avenue or Chicago's South Parkway than Pittsburgh's Wylie Avenue. The *Courier* was promoted as a national urban newspaper partly because Pittsburgh's black circulation base never approached that of Chicago or a score of other cities, North and South. During World War II the *Courier* printed some twenty editions, competing with the *Defender* and the New York *Amsterdam News* on their own turf and becoming the number-one black newspaper in Washington, D. C., Birmingham, Miami, and dozens of other black-population centers.

When Vann died in October 1940, six months after Abbott, the *Courier*'s circulation had reached 147,000. With Vann's widow, Mrs. Jessie L. Vann, leaving the newspaper's direction to Executive Editor P. L. Prattis and Business Manager Ira F. Lewis, the *Courier* and the other black newspapers during World War II spotlighted many of the same racial injustices of the first global war. Again, there was employment discrimination, military Jim Crow of black troops and a failure to recognize their heroism. But this time the black journalists, wary of promises, were on guard, warning their readers that they could not expect concessions from the white society once the fighting ended. The black press, amid renewed cries of disloyalty, uncovered abuses in Army camps and Army towns. It also deployed thirty-six war correspondents, including eight from the *Courier*, whose dispatches were pooled and circulated by the National Negro Publishers Association (NNPA) and Claude A. Barnett's Chicago-based Associated Negro Press.

Feature articles about the day-to-day activities as well as the heroics of black troops were sent to such newspapers as William O. Walker's Cleveland *Call and Post*, Loren Miller's Los Angeles *Sentinel* and Frank L. Stanley's Louisville *Defender*. Almost all of the war dispatches were mailed to weekly subscribers without fear of having the news dated by stories appearing first in white dailies. White publishers, editors, and news services generally ignored events among blacks in their segregated military units.

Eager for black news were wartime readers who could afford to buy. The *Courier*'s circulation reached an all-time peak of 257,000; the *Defender* bounced back from the

Depression with 202,000; and the *Afro-American*'s five newspapers totaled 137,000. More important, the *Courier*'s "Double V" campaign for "victory abroad and victory at home" provided the rallying cry for a phalanx of black institutions, especially the NAACP and A. Philip Randolph's Brotherhood of Sleeping Car Porters, to score legal and fair employment victories. As this movement gathered momentum, Gunnar Myrdal hailed the black press as the race's "single most important power." After the war, the black press backed successful suits for equal teachers' salaries and school facilities, and the desegregation of the Armed Forces. Such efforts culminated in the 1954 Supreme Court decision in the School Desegregation Cases.

With victory presumably in sight, and with integration as a clear goal, the NNPA symbolically substituted "newspaper" for the "Negro" in its title, as explained editorially by the Louisville *Defender:* "The change in the name of the NNPA will enable the more democratic-thinking publishers to eliminate some of the glaring inconsistencies in their papers and will permit them to go ahead with the fight for full integration and full participation of Negroes in the American way of life."[15] But the "fight" of black newspapers had presumably become that of the nation, so when the best black reporters were hired by the white press, black publishers wished them luck. Black readers were flattered by the sudden attention they received in the white press, and many stopped buying black newspapers even on an "additional" basis. Black publishers rationalized these losses by pointing to significant gains in white advertising revenue, and in the process became less radical than some white newspapers on racial issues. In other words, the black press had gone full circle from a dependency on white politics to a dependency on white advertising. Meanwhile, the black press was losing the mass circulation base that had given it, in the Age of Abbott, its loudest and most irrepressible voice.

Carl Murphy's *Afro-American*, however, was still published in Baltimore, Washington, Philadelphia, Newark, and Richmond. At times, the revered "Mr. Carl" was America First in his editorials and news columns, yet in the early 1950s he stood by Paul Robeson and W. E. B. DuBois while they were being shunned and excoriated by whites and blacks for their associations with communists. Murphy took his stand during the era of U. S. Senator Joseph McCarthy when the white press, including *The New York Times*, was quaking in its boots. And later when reporter William Worthy was forbidden by the U. S. Department of State to visit Red China, he went there as a correspondent for Murphy's *Afro*.

Carl Murphy did not die until 1967, but the Age of the Publisher had ended long before that. Again the United States was at war, but no black newspaper sent a correspondent to Southeast Asia. Once again blacks were flowing into the cities, but black barber shops no longer stocked black newspapers; they offered their customers *Life* and *Playboy* and perhaps *Ebony* and *Jet*. And as black communities again were being torn by upheavals, these events were covered by black reporters who worked for the white press.

## THE AGE OF THE REPORTER, 1954 TO THE PRESENT

The history of black newsmen employed by the white press dates at least as far back as the 1880s, when few newspapers, black or white, could afford salaried reporters.[16] When T. Thomas Fortune, for example, sought a job at the New York *Evening Sun* he was told that reporters were paid only if their stories were accepted for publication. Under this hit-and-miss arrangement, Fortune and other blacks sold articles to all of New York's Democratic and Independent newspapers. This fact prompted Fortune's wry comment that though the Republican newspapers "had done the most preaching about the equality of colored men," they were "the last to put their preaching into practice."

The early twentieth century marked the growth of the white press from a craft into an industry, yet fewer and fewer newspapers were "preaching" about racial equality or hiring black newsmen under any conditions. In New York, for example, where news staffs had grown ten- and twenty-fold, editors no longer used blacks such as Fortune and John Edward Bruce as regular free-lance contributors. It was not until the 1920s that the *World* broke the New York barrier against full-time employment of black newsmen by hiring Lester A. Walton. The next breakthrough did not occur until the late 1940s, with the hiring of George Streator by the *Times*, Edgar T. Rozeau by the *Herald Tribune*, and Theodore R. Poston by the *Post*. All had worked for the black press.

In the 1950s white newspapers in cities with large black populations hired black reporters at a rate of one, two, or three per city. In Chicago, for instance, three of the four dailies hired Lestre Brownlee from the *Defender*, Wendell Smith from the *Courier*, and Fletcher Martin from the Louisville *Defender*. The 1954 Supreme Court school segregation decision did not alter the employment pattern. A year later, *Ebony* counted only thirty-one blacks on white newspapers; black newsmen were so few in broadcasting that no counts were taken. The employment "blackout" lasted until the late 1960s, when in the aftermath of Watts, Newark, and Detroit, white media managers deemed that black reporters were needed to cover such rebellions, if nothing else. The need for black newsmen was given a fuller dimension by the 1968 Report of the National Advisory Commission on Civil Disorders. Better known as the Kerner Commission Report, it chided white media for their tendency to "report and write from the white man's world." Many media managers sought to change this all-white image by following these guidelines from Chapter XV of the Report:

> The media have not communicated to whites a feeling for the difficulties and frustrations of being a Negro in the United States. They have not shown understanding or appreciation of—and thus have not communicated a sense of—Negro culture, thought or history.

> When the white press does refer to Negroes and Negro problems it frequently does so as if Negroes were not a part of the audience. . . . such attitudes, in an area as sensitive and inflammatory as this, feed Negro alienation and intensify white prejudices.

> News organizations must employ enough Negroes in significant responsibility to estab-lish an effective link to Negro actions and ideas and to meet legitimate expectations. Tokenism—the hiring of one Negro reporter, or even two or three—is no longer enough.

> It would be a contribution of inestimable importance to race relations in the United States to treat ordinary news about Negroes as news of other groups is now treated. Specifically, newspapers should integrate Negroes and Negro activities into all parts of the paper, from the news, society, and club pages to the comic strips. Television should develop programming which integrates Negroes into all aspects of televised produc-tions. . . . For example, Negro reporters and performers should appear more frequently— and at prime time—in news broadcasts, on weather shows, in documentaries, and in advertisements.

With the Kerner Report as gospel, the nation's white media and journalism schools began "plotting infinite growth from zero," as the University of Wisconsin's Lionel C. Barrow later phrased it. Not quite zero, but almost. The black student population at the Columbia Graduate School of Journalism, for example, rose from two in the gradu-ating class of 1968 to twenty in the class of 1972, almost one-fifth of the entire student population. In the course of seven summers the special Columbia program for Members of Minority Groups trained and provided jobs for about 225 black broadcast and news-paper journalists, as well as other minority group members, or more than four times the number counted by *Ebony* in 1955. Moreover, such black colleges and universities as Hampton, Shaw, and Bishop began either programs or departments of communica-tions where only a single course, if any, had previously existed. In the 1971–72 academic term, Howard and Atlanta joined Lincoln (Missouri) and Texas Southern as black uni-versities with schools of journalism or communications. Eventually these universities would graduate scores of journalists along with film and speech communicators yearly.

The flurry of training programs posed a crucial question: Who would hire all of these graduates? And as a corollary to that, who *has* hired them? Employment figures filed by fifteen TV stations owned by the three major networks showed 100 black "professionals" out of a total of 777, or 12.8 percent, but the classification was so broad that working journalists could not be separated from such categories as "trainees," "researchers," and "entertainment staffers," so that these figures were hardly meaning-ful.[17] Perhaps more significant was a 1972 report by the American Society of Newspaper Editors showing an employment figure for black editorial workers including editors, reporters, and photographers of less than 1 percent.[18]

One inevitable result of plotting "infinite growth" in a five-year period was that many young blacks were attracted to broadcasting, especially, with only the foggiest notion of what they might contribute to it. Some rightly assessed television news pro-grams, for example, as part journalism and part show business, but wrongly reasoned that their good looks or their melodious voices would see them through. Not fully understanding the white media managers' disposition to apply a double standard of professionalism when it suits the purpose, say, of covering a ghetto riot, and a single standard when it does not, the summers of 1972 and after found the ghettos cool and a number of black newsmen and women among the swelling ranks of the black unemployed.

This joblessness occurred in spite of the fact that many broadcasting stations, as well as other media, had carried out some of the Kerner Commissions's guidelines to the letter. Black newsmen, as well as entertainers and fashion models, were more visible than ever. Predictably, though, the television industry was more responsive to changes affecting its image than to those involving substance. Regardless of whether the faces on the television screen, for example, were white, black, or both, the commercials were as puerile and unrelated to the black experience as ever. Nor did the mere substitution of a black newscaster such as NBC's Carl Stokes, the ex-Mayor of Cleveland, for a white newscaster alter the fact that almost all radio and television news stories amounted to little more than an audio-visual account of information contained in the first paragraphs of articles destined to appear in the next morning's newspaper. Moreover, black oriented news programs and documentaries had tended to vanish from the air. Some of the reasons for this turn of events since the Kerner Report were explained by Washington newswoman Dorothy Gilliam:

> . . . White illiberalism has grown, the civil rights movement has died, and large segments of the population are in a touchy mood. And [the media]—reflecting this conservation as well as the economic recession—have lost their enthusiasm for hiring blacks. Some have delayed fulfilling promises to upgrade blacks already on their staffs. And the press has continued to concentrate primarily on conflicts at a time when black power and unity have become black-community themes, and antibusing and Law and Order, whites' themes.
>
> Caught in the dilemma is the black professional in the general media. However you view it, he has problems. He is penned into a situation where whites, refusing to see that they have as great a stake as he in racial harmony in the U. S., push all "racial" stories upon him, all the while doubting his "objectivity." Or, on the other hand, he shies away from these stories altogether and festers quietly, seeing himself—literally—misrepresented. Further, the black community, which has been burned so often that it is crusty, often doesn't trust him. Nor does it grasp the hierarchical gamut the black must run to get news about the black community into print.[19]

The sad irony was that while blacks were being trained by the hundreds to work in the white media, many of those "in" were intensely dissatisfied because of their positions at the bottom of the decision-making ladder, where they had little control over their assignments, and once assigned had no say over how their stories would be presented, if they were presented all. Dramatic evidence of this discontent was shown in 1972 at the Washington *Post*. The *Post* and *The New York Times* had been singled out as being ultra-liberal by the Nixon Administration, yet eight of the *Post*'s black city-staff reporters sued the newspaper for racial discrimination under the District of Columbia's equal employment opportunity law. This action would not have been so noteworthy if the *Post* were not the acknowledged leader among all news organizations in hiring blacks and promoting them from the lower ranks. At various times, *Post* blacks had held such positions as assistant city editor, foreign correspondent, editorial writer, and columnist. But this record did not seem impressive in a city where the population was nearly three-quarters black and blacks occupied the highest positions in city government.

Other expressions of discontent were fully aired in March 1972, when the Congressional Black Caucus convened hearings on the plight of blacks in the media. High on the agenda was the case of *United States v. Caldwell.* A San Francisco correspondent for *The New York Times*, Earl Caldwell was subpoenaed in 1970 by a California Federal Grand Jury investigating the Black Panther Party and ordered to turn over his notes and tapes of interviews with Panther officials. Caldwell refused and retained his own counsel to fight the case, with lawyers of the *Times* providing administrative support. When ordered by a Federal District Court to appear before the Grand Jury, Caldwell appealed on the grounds that his testimony would be behind closed doors, creating doubts among blacks, generally, and the Black Panther Party, specifically, as to the nature of the testimony. At this point, the *Times* dropped out as a party to the case, though filing an *amicus curiae* brief in Caldwell's behalf. Then the appellate court unanimously nullified the subpoena, saying that it would "convert the reporter into an investigative agent of the government."

At the Black Caucus hearings the above facts were presented by Ernest Dunbar, a *Look* editor before that magazine ceased publication in September 1971. As later summarized by Dunbar, the case had "great significance for black reporters everywhere." He added:

> The point of all this is that Caldwell was subpoenaed, as an individual, and the *Times* was not. As a black reporter, he was on that firing line. Before his courageous stand, *Newsweek*, *Life*, CBS, NBC, and other media giants had meekly turned over their files to requesting agencies. After the Caldwell case, these organizations discovered their backbones and began to resist. . . . The important issue in *U.S. v. Caldwell* is that black newsmen bear a special burden as gatherers of information that whites frequently cannot obtain, and that to require a black reporter to testify either about material in confidence or to give any testimony behind closed doors does irreparable harm to his ability to continue to function in the black community, which is where black reporters are. . . .[20]

Finally on June 29, 1972, the Supreme Court of the United States, by a five-to-four vote, ruled that the power of a grand jury took precedence over the First Amendment in handing down decisions against Caldwell and two white reporters. But unlike Caldwell, Paul Branzburg of the Louisville *Courier-Journal* and Paul Pappas of WTEV-TV in New Bedford, Massachusetts, were not stripped of the rationale for their being hired in the first place; namely, to "function in the black community." In a despairing *Saturday*

*Review* article, Caldwell recalled that the Black Panther Party's Eldridge Cleaver had once asked him: "What good do you do, anyhow?" And after the decision, Caldwell's comment was this: "I wrestled with the question then; it is more difficult to answer now."

The frustrations of black newsmen have been further compounded by the conviction of many that they have the capacity for doing good; that they, as Dunbar wrote, "have a special and valuable input to make because of where [they] stand in the society." He continued:

> We saw the folly of Vietnam long before our white colleagues found it fashionable to oppose the war. We know something about narcotics because dope has been in the black community for four decades. . . . We do not go into other countries to report with frozen American attitudes because we have seen our own contributions denigrated by ugly Americans. In short, we do not have the standard white male superiority notions through which to view the rest of the world.[21]

Skilled and sensitive black newsmen have a special capacity, as a white editor once told this writer, for "building bridges between the races." But in 1972 the role of goodwill ambassador did not fit into black communities. Blacks were no longer flattered by the attention of the media, as they had been in the 1950s and early 1960s. While professional blacks who had been the major beneficiaries of the so-called black revolution commiserated about their problems in their urban and suburban enclaves, the masses of poor blacks were left to fester among the remains of their dying communities and institutions and ask the white media and their black agents, *What good do you do, anyhow?*

## TOWARD REALIZING A MISSION

*What good do you do, anyhow?* T. Thomas Fortune might have asked himself this question during his "uneasy alliance" with the pragmatic Booker T. Washington. Fortune could not follow a path of racial idealism and solidarity and still "get along" within a racist society. Yet he survived his ordeal by selling editorials and columns in the 1920s to black publications as diverse as Marcus Garvey's *Negro World* and the Norfolk *Journal & Guide*. In other words, Fortune's survival until his death at age 72 was made possible through the viability of the black press. Aside from the black press, what options were available to his heirs in attempting to make the white-controlled media more responsive to the needs of black people?

It would seem that "unity, not uniformity"—as Mrs. Martin Luther King expressed it—was essential in the 1970s, as it was in 1887 when Fortune formed his Afro-American League. Even though unity was still an elusive goal, two New York groups, Black Perspective and Second Front, helped fight the Caldwell case and rallied behind William Artis, whose 1970 charge of discrimination against the New York *Post* was upheld by the State Division of Human Rights, only to be overturned in 1972 by a two-to-one vote of the division's appeal board. But except in periods of crisis such professional groups in New York and other cities were sustained only through irregular meetings and mailings and occasional newsletters.

Although black newsmen saw the need for stronger pressures upon their employers, the events of 1972 indicated that white media producers would be more responsive to demands by blacks who were not dependent upon them, namely the masses of consumers within black communities. Just as the riots in the late 1960s had set off a flurry of hiring, the organization of community-based "media watchdog committees" in the 1970s offered the greatest hope of obtaining new concessions. These committees monitored TV and radio programs for the purpose of using discrimination as grounds for challenging the renewal of station licenses. Under the threat of such challenges by a group known as Black Citizens for Fair Media, New York's local ABC and NBC stations agreed, according to *TV Guide*, to generate "an ongoing input by blacks into the decision-making process." This would include black committees and consultants on programming and hiring, and the running of black-created, black-written, and black-produced programs on black subjects in prime time; but black newsmen doubted that the networks would honor the agreement. In Philadelphia, a Communications Coalition of fifty-seven black and Spanish-speaking organizations challenged the license renewals of seven TV and seventeen radio stations on discriminatory hiring and programming grounds, declaring that in a city with a 40 percent minority population, at least one-third of the employees should come from minority groups.

Yet in the broadcasting arena, as well as in the cases of Caldwell and Artis, 1972 was a bad year for black newsmen in the courts and other public tribunals. In Washington, D. C. the Court of Appeals ruled against sixteen black community leaders who had presented a challenge to the Federal Communications Commission in a case involving WMAL-TV. The court held that criticism of WMAL's programming "ran the risk of turning the FCC into a censorship board," that charges of racism cannot be made on employment figures, and that there need not be any correlation between public-service broadcast time and the needs of any percentage of the viewing public.

*TV Guide* reported that some white media managers had hailed the District of Columbia decision as a "landmark"—the same term, ironically, that they had applied to the civil rights decisions of the recent past. This reaction may have been colored by the fact that in 1972 white newsmen in the lower echelons felt their own job security threatened, causing the media managers to characterize the black demands as "blackmail." As in the days of Fortune, there were still conflicts, of course, between personal and racial concerns. One anonymous black newsman agreed with the "blackmail" accusation, but pointedly told *TV Guide* that the media managers "won't do anything unless they *are* blackmailed."

Blackmail or not, many black newsmen agreed that pressure tactics were necessary, not only to gain further concessions but in order to consolidate previous gains. Tony

Brown, a public-television producer and then dean of the Communications School of Howard University, told the March 1972 Black Caucus that his program was saved by a host of letter writers—organized as "Friends of 'Black Journal.'" Such incidents suggested that blacks, like Alice in Wonderland, had to run faster to stay in the same place.

One reason for mail campaigns and "watchdog" activities is that blacks neither own television stations nor serve in decision-making positions. Yet blacks *watch* television, according to Mr. Brown's Black Caucus testimony, on an average of twenty-five hours a week, nine hours longer than whites. The ratio between black and white radio listeners may be even greater; yet only 16 out of some 7,000 commercial radio stations were owned by blacks. In Chicago, where one of four black-oriented stations is black-owned, a black editor was quoted by journalist L. F. Palmer as saying that the four stations "reach more listeners in an hour than the black newspaper has readers in a month."[22] With radio and TV so pervasive in black communities, the black struggle for greater access to the electronic media was seen by Philadelphia newswoman Justine J. Rector as "a battle for our children's minds."

In the 1970s, it was perfectly clear to black newsmen that the electronic media were the wave of the present, as well as the future, but they were faced with the economic reality that TV and radio licenses were highly profitable, and whites were unlikely to relinquish them, even if blacks could afford to buy. Further, even as white media managers sharply questioned the "qualifications" of many black newsmen, the network news directors, bemused by ABC's jovial "Eyewitness" programs, were bent on disguising bad news as good news, reducing the profession of journalism to fun and games. Meanwhile, Lou Potter, a former CBS producer, advised a meeting sponsored by Black Perspective and the New York NAACP to avoid such professional pratfalls. "Black people have suffered far too long at the hands of incompetent white newsmen," he said. "They have the right to demand excellence from us and we have the responsibility to deliver it."

The likelihood of delivering excellence, if only on a small scale, in a strong black voice might be still greater in the black press than in the white-controlled media. Since the Age of the Publisher, the strength of that press had shifted from newspapers to magazines, led by the empire (*Ebony, Jet, Black World, Black Stars*) of Chicago's John H. Johnson with a circulation of two million. In addition, such new magazines as *Black Enterprise, Black Sports, Encore, Essence*, and *Soul Illustrated* were providing black newsmen with markets that Fortune might envy. The old "Big Three" newspapers were now two. The *Afro-American* had lost circulation and influence since Carl Murphy's death. But Abbott's *Defender* heir, John H. Sengstacke, had acquired the *Courier* newspapers to add to a growing chain with a circulation of nearly one-half million.

Black newspapers and magazines were still under attack by young newsmen for not being "relevant," and for looking and reading too much like white publications. But this view in 1972 seemed short-sighted, given John H. Johnson's success. For all of *Ebony*'s articles on parties and cotillions, eligible bachelors and fashionable women that were aimed at white advertisers, as well as status-seeking black readers, Johnson still provided the black power base for eloquent black voices, especially that of Senior Editor Lerone Bennett. White publishers, for instance, would be most squeamish about permitting a Thomas A. Johnson of *The New York Times* or a Robert Maynard of the Washington *Post* to raise the question, as Bennett did: "Was Abe Lincoln a White Supremacist?" and answer it in the affirmative. Furthermore, Johnson's profits from *Ebony* enabled him to rename and recast his old *Negro Digest* into *Black World*, a publication of fresh literary and cultural expression.

This departure into popular and literary magazines suggested that black newsmen should not restrict their thinking of "news" to topical issues and events. If Bennett, for instance, could bring fresh information and insights to bear on Abraham Lincoln, then this would be news, even though the facts would be a century old. In other words, black newsmen needed to be innovative, like blacks in music and the arts. And though individual reportorial talents abounded, black newsmen needed orchestrators like Duke Ellington more than they needed virtuosos. They also needed many more business-minded John H. Johnsons, and, drawing from the past, they needed more Abbotts whose patience and persistence and capacity for getting people to work together were more valuable than Fortune's brilliant rhetoric. But most of all, as many were fond of saying, they needed to be professionally and financially able to "do their own thing," rather than slavishly imitate the old New York *Sun* like Fortune, or the old Chicago *American* like Abbott, or *Life* and *Readers Digest* like Johnson. If nothing else, the attacks in the 1970s on the white media by the Government and all manner of dissident groups decisively demonstrated that white was no longer right in the media as well as other institutions.

The 1970s may be the time to rejuvenate a black press that can both draw on those virtues that remain in the white media, and profit from the lessons of Abbott and Fortune. A valuable lesson that might be learned from the previous ages of black newsmen was that for all their faults, Abbott and Fortune and their contemporaries wielded more influence among blacks than the later generation of newsmen. At his peak, Abbott's great virtue was that his strength came from the black masses below rather than whites above. And it was the profits obtained from the dimes paid by many thousands of black readers that enabled the black press to provide the cutting edge for the black and white coalitions of the civil rights movement. In the 1970s, historical reflection suggested that if such coalitions were to be renewed they must again spring from a black power base, that black newsmen cannot yet trust their manhood and their destiny to whites and their media, and that they will be unable to gain the full confidence of the black community if their power derives solely from white sources. The painful United States record of assassination and repression recalls a question raised in Fortune's 1891 description of a black editor's mission: *Can we reasonably expect other men to use their lungs to cry out for us when we are wronged and outraged and murdered?*

In the 1970s, as in the 1890s or any other age or time, it is to the task of fulfilling his mission—to voice outrage and to right wrongs—that the black newsman must turn. Clearly, fresh instruments are needed to speak for black communities and institutions which have suffered as much from the failure of the white community to live up to its promises of civil rights and urban renewal, as they have from poverty and crime. What forms might these instruments take? Surely they should not be daily metropolitan newspapers. The distribution and labor problems of white dailies had become so heavy by 1972 that New York was the only city left with more than two competing newspaper managements. Before the end of summer, Boston had lost its *Herald Traveler*, Washington its *Daily News*, and Newark its *Evening News*. Foreseeing the end for New Jersey's best newspaper, Newark's black mayor, Kenneth Gibson, launched a city hall publication, *Information*, to supplement the meager coverage of the city's only remaining daily, the *Star Ledger*.

But whether the mayor is black or white, black newsmen should not entrust their mission to city hall. They require an independent voice equipped to reach a city-wide audience in cities like Newark and Washington, D. C., where blacks are in a majority, or one large community such as Chicago's South Side or New York's Harlem or Bedford-Stuyvesant. In sum, fresh approaches and higher standards are needed in the 1970s to make black voices heard through the din of radio and television; a multi-organed approach is needed to heighten the volume of black voices in the white media as well as in the black press. In his Black Perspective talk, Lou Potter made these demands on black broadcast journalists, but they could as well be adapted for those in other media:

> We must continually press for change within the shops where we work. We must fight for promotion into the hierarchy where the reins of power lie. We must become voices for the democratization of the industry on every level. We must fight against the racist labor unions that continue to arrogantly exclude blacks from the technical side of the industry. We must work with the community on license challenges where they are feasible strategies. We must not be afraid to join together to make our voices heard on these and other issues on which as a group, we have been too silent for too long.

## Notes

1. As editors of *The North Star* and *The Crisis*, the NAACP magazine, respectively, Douglass and DuBois are sometimes identified as journalists. But their journalism was not their chief historical contribution, so they will not be considered here as black newsmen.
2. Emma Lou Thornbrough, *T. Thomas Fortune, Militant Journalist* (Chicago, University of Chicago, 1972), p. 134. As evidenced in Professor Thornbrough's biography, Fortune rejected the term "colored" even though he sometimes used it. During his long career he apparently used "Negro" most often. Along with Roi Ottley's *The Lonely Warrior*, the biography of Robert S. Abbott, the Thornbrough volume was indispensable to the development of this article.
3. *Ibid*, pp. 369–370.

4. Martin E. Dann, ed., *The Black Press 1827–1890* (New York, Putnam, 1971), p. 371.

5. The old Chicago *Tribune* was a notable exception, publishing annual compilations of lynchings from 1885 to 1912 when the practice was adopted by the NAACP and a year later by Tuskegee Institute. See the NAACP's *Thirty Years of Lynching in the United States* and the numerous editions of Tuskegee's *The Negro Year Book*. The introduction to Miss Wells's posthumous *Crusade for Justice* (1972), p. xxii, contains an excerpt from her *A Red Record* (1895) noting that the lynchings cited therein were "vouched for" by the *Tribune*. However, the bulk of information here on lynching and Miss Wells was drawn from *Crusade for Justice*.

6. Frederick G. Detweiler, *The Negro Press in the United States* (Chicago, University of Chicago, 1922), pp. 60–61.

7. L. F. Palmer, for instance, calls the *Defender, Courier,* and *Afro* the "big three" of the black press. Some writers add a fourth, P. B. Young Sr.'s Norfolk *Journal & Guide*, but their reference is to the newspaper's quality. Young's *Guide* was never a national newspaper.

8. The circulation claim was made in a promotion pamphlet. It was scaled down by Roi Ottley to an estimated 230,000, and by Frederick Detweiler to 150,000. In his 1922 book the latter estimated the 1920 total circulation of black newspapers as "over one million." At the time, only four out of the 217 publications listed in Ayer's *Newspaper Directory* provided sworn circulation figures. Historically, estimates of the numbers and circulations of black newspapers at any given time have always shown wide variations. In addition to relying on publisher's estimates, some writers on the black press have not only counted magazines, scholarly journals, and religious publications, but also obvious propaganda organs and promotional sheets. The 1971 Editor and Publisher Yearbook's "Black Newspapers in America" is a case in point. On the basis of secondary sources and telephone interviews, the researcher, Henry G. LaBrie III, found 173 newspapers with a combined circulation of 3,589,103 "paid and free distributed." But from this writer's knowledge of some of the "free distributed" sheets, they could not be classified as newspapers by any journalistic standard.

9. Charles S. Johnson, "Stimulation of the Movement," Chapter 3 from Emmett J. Scott, ed., *Negro Migration During the War, 1920* (New York, Arno Press Edition, 1969), p. 30. Johnson, along with Monroe Work and Scott's friend T. Thomas Fortune, are cited as investigators for the study in the editor's foreword. Johnson is not specifically credited with the authorship of any chapter, but "Stimulation of the Movement" is apparently adapted from an earlier work, "Report on the Negro Migration from Mississippi."

10. Under the caption "Topeka's New Lawyer," the *Plaindealer* of July 19, 1901, pictured a pince-nez-wearing Abbott and reported that he had "opened an office" with James Guy, an established Kansas lawyer. Ottley wrote that Abbott did not pass the Illinois bar and does not mention his practicing anywhere. In any case, the evidence showed that Abbott spent no more than a few months in Topeka as a "traveling agent" for Nick Chiles's newspaper.

11. Roi Ottley, *The Lonely Warrior: The Life and Times of Robert S. Abbott* (Chicago, Regnery, 1955), p. 93.

12. *Ibid.*, p. 106.

13. *Ibid.*, p. 118.

14. Monroe Work, *Negro Year Book, 1918–1919* (Tuskegee, Ala., Negro Year Book Publishing Co., 1919), pp. 51–52.

15. Jessie P. Guzman, ed., *1952 Negro Year Book* (New York, Wm. H. Wise and Co., 1952), p. 36.

16. For six months in 1894, the crusading Ida B. Wells, on her second tour of the British Isles, was a paid correspondent for the Chicago *Inter-Ocean*. Other early staff members of white newspapers included Ralph W. Tyler of the Columbus, Ohio, *Evening Dispatch* and John S. Durham of the Philadelphia *Evening Bulletin*.

17. "Blacks in Broadcasting," *TV Guide*, August 19–25, 1972, p. 22.

18. Cited by Robert G. Maynard, "A Black Journalist Looks at White Newsrooms," Washington *Post*, April 26, 1972.

19. *Columbia Journalism Review*, May/June 1972, p. 48.

20. (MORE) *A Journalism Review*, April 1972, p. 15.
21. *Ibid.*, p. 17.
22. L. F. Palmer, Jr., "The Black Press in Transition," *Columbia Journalism Review*, Spring 1970.

# BIBLIOGRAPHY

## General

Detweiler, Frederick G., *The Negro Press in the United States*. Chicago, University of Chicago, 1922.

Frazier, E. Franklin, *The Negro in the United States*. New York, Macmillan, 1949.

Guzman, Jessie P., *et al.*, eds., *Negro Year Book, 1941–1946*. Tuskegee Institute, Ala., The Department of Records and Research, 1947.

———, *1952 Negro Year Book*. New York, Wm. H. Wise & Co., 1952.

Myrdal, Gunnar, *An American Dilemma*, 2 vols. New York, Harper Torchbooks, 1966. Chapter 42 of this 1944 study is about the Negro press.

Palmer, L. F. Jr., "The Black Press in Transition," *Columbia Journalism Review*, Spring 1970.

Pride, Armistead S., "The Black Press: A Bibliography," prepared for Association for Education in Journalism Ad Hoc Committee on Minority Education, mimeo., December 1968.

U. S. Library of Congress, "Negro Newspapers on Microfilm: A Selected List," Washington, D. C., 1953.

Wolseley, Roland E., *The Black Press, U. S. A.* Ames, Iowa, Iowa State University, 1971.

## The Age of the Editor and Proprietor, 1880–1910

Dann, Martin E., ed., *The Black Press 1827–1890*. New York, Putnam, 1971. Documentary includes T. Thomas Fortune's 1887 proposals for an Afro-American League.

Fortune, T. Thomas, *The Negro in Politics: Some Pertinent Reflections on the Past and Present Political Status of the Afro-American, Together With a Cursory Investigation into the Motives Which Actuate Partisan Organizations*. New York, Ogilvie & Rowntree, 1885.

———, *Black and White: Land, Labor, and Politics in The South*. New York, Arno Press Edition, 1968.

Fox, Stephen R., *The Guardian of Boston: William Monroe Trotter*. New York, Atheneum, 1970.

Penn, I. Garland, *The Afro-American Press and Its Editors*. Springfield, Mass., Wiley, 1891. New York, Arno Press Edition, 1969. Includes a brief essay by T. Thomas Fortune on the "mission" of black editors.

Thornbrough, Emma Lou, *T. Thomas Fortune: Militant Journalist*. Chicago, University of Chicago, 1972.

———, "American Negro Newspapers, 1880–1914," *Business History Review*, Vol. 40, 1966.

Wells, Ida B., *Crusade for Justice: The Autobiography of Ida B. Wells*, ed. by Alfreda M. Duster. Chicago, University of Chicago, 1970.

———, "Lynching at Memphis, 1893," taken from her pamphlet, *A Red Record*

(1895), Richard Hofstadter and Michael Wallace, eds., *American Violence*. New York, Vintage Books, 1971. This documentary also gives a brief account of the 1893 lynching at Paris, Texas.

## The Age of the Publisher, 1910–1954

Baltimore *Afro-American*, "Carl Murphy Dies," February 28, 1967.

Brewer, James H., "Robert Lee Vann, Democrat or Republican: An Exponent of Loose Leaf Politics," *Negro History Bulletin*, February 1958.

Drake, St. Clair and Cayton, Horace R., *Black Metropolis*, 2 Vols., New York, Harper Torchbooks, 1962. Study of Chicago's Black Belt discusses the World War I migration and the Chicago *Defender*.

Fleming, G. James, "Negro Press Research Memorandum." Mimeo., September 1, 1940; Schomburg Center, New York Public Library. Investigation for Myrdal's *An American Dilemma* contains sections on the Baltimore *Afro-American* and the Pittsburgh *Courier*.

Harris, Genevieve C., "Classmate Recalls Early Days of Afro Publisher," Washington *Afro-American*, March 2, 1968. A tribute to Carl Murphy on the anniversary of his death.

*Headlines and Pictures*, "An American Family: The Youngs of Norfolk," January 1946. The *Journal & Guide*'s P. B. Young, Sr. is profiled.

Johnson, Charles S., "Stimulation of the Movement." Chapter 3 from Emmett J. Scott, ed., *Negro Migration During the War, 1920*. New York, Arno Press Edition, 1969.

Jones, Dewey R., "Effect of the Negro Press on Race Relationships in the South." New York, Columbia University Graduate School of Journalism master's thesis, 1932.

Norfolk (Va.) *Journal & Guide*, "Final Rites for P. B. Young, Sr." October 13, 1962.

Ottley, Roi, *The Lonely Warrior: The Life and Times of Robert S. Abbott*. Chicago, Regnery, 1955.

Prattis, P. L., "Racial Segregation and Negro Journalism." *Phylon*, Fourth Quarter, 1947.

*Time*, "How to Interview MacArthur." June 11, 1951. Pittsburgh *Courier* reporter Stanley Roberts scoops the white press.

Vann, Robert L., 1934–1936 clippings from the Pittsburgh *Courier*, Washington *Tribune*, Norfolk *Journal & Guide* and *Saturday Evening Post;* Schomburg Center, New York Public Library.

Waskow, Arthur I., *From Race Riot to Sit-In, 1919 and the 1960s*, Garden City, N. Y., Doubleday Anchor Books, 1967. Gives account of riot involving Chicago *Defender* agent in Longview, Texas, and other racial clashes for the "Red Summer" of 1919.

## The Age of the Reporter, 1954 to the Present

Aronson, James, "Mediations." *Antioch Review*, Fall 1971. Discusses role of black reporters and possible emergence of a "new" black press.

Bagdikian, Ben, H., "The Washington *Post* and Blacks on Its News Staff." Washington *Post*, March 22, 1972.

Caldwell, Earl, "Ask Me. I Know. I Was the Test Case." *Saturday Review*, August 5, 1972.

Daniels, George, "New Prosperity for The Black Press as Readership, Revenue Move Up." *Black Enterprise*, May 1971.

Dunbar, Ernest, "Notes From The Belly of a Whale." *(MORE) A Journalism Review*, April 1972. Discusses problems of blacks working for white media.

*Ebony*, "Negroes on White Newspapers," November 1955.

Efron, Edith, "What Is Happening to Blacks in Broadcasting?" A three-part series, *TV Guide*, August 19, 26, September 2, 1972.

Gilliam, Dorothy, "What Do Black Journalists Want?" *Columbia Journalism Review*, May/June 1972.

Hamilton, Charles V., "Blacks and Mass Media." *The Columbia Forum*, New York, Winter 1971.

Hill, Robert B., *et al.*, "Coverage of Minority Group Affairs in the New York News Media and the Black Evaluation: A Pilot Study." Mimeo., Columbia University Bureau of Applied Social Research, June 1969.

Jackson, Luther P. Jr., "The Sound of a Different Drum: Race in the News."

Patricia W. Romero, ed., *In Black America, 1968: The Year of Awakening*. Washington, D. C., United Publishing, 1969.

———, "The Problem of Telling It Like It Is." *Negro History Bulletin*, April 1966. Discusses the time pressures on newsmen as the "first draftsmen" of history.

LaBrie, Henry G. III, "Plotting Infinite Growth From Zero: Distinguished Black Journalists Review the Mass Media's Recent Interest in Minority Affairs." Mimeo.; for Minority News Subcommittee, American Press Managing Editors Association National Convention, Philadelphia, October 19–22, 1972.

Maynard, Robert G., "A Black Journalist Looks at White Newsrooms." Washington *Post*, April 26, 1972.

Mencher, Melvin, "Recruiting and Training Black Newsmen." *Quill*, September 1969.

*National Association of Educational Broadcasters*, "Minority Employment Practices of Public Television Stations." Washington, D. C., 1971.

*Our World*, "The Black Newshawks." March 1952.

Potter, Lou, "Demands on the Black Broadcast Journalist." Mimeo., speech delivered at Forum on Black Journalism sponsored by Black Perspective and the New York NAACP, May 14, 1972.

Pride, Armistead S., "Low Man on the Totem Pole." *Nieman Reports*, April 1955. Cites blacks employed by white newspapers.

*Report of the National Advisory Commission on Civil Disorders*. New York, Bantam Books, 1968.

*Time*, "The Press: Beyond Ghetto Sniffing." From special issue, "Black America, 1970," April 6, 1970.

West, Hollie I., "Howard's 'Black Journalism'" and "Activist Dean Tony Brown." Washington *Post*, January 30, 1972.

Williams, Roger M., "Journalism Expands on Black Campuses." *Columbia Journalism Review*, July/August 1971.

Work, Monroe, *Negro Year Book, 1918–1919*. Tuskegee, Ala, Negro Year Book Publishing Co., 1919.

# 28

## The Popular Media: Part II
## The Black Role
## in Radio and Television

### George E. Norford

The electronic media—radio and television, but especially television—are by far the most pervasive and persuasive instruments of mass communication ever developed by man. At the end of 1971 both radio and television were in more than 62 million homes across the nation, served by over 7,000 commercial and nearly 700 educational stations. Just about half of the 62 million TV-owning homes possessed color sets. Cable TV, which enjoys a potential for an unlimited number of channels, is already serving at least six million viewers.[1] Total viewing time daily per home, for TV of all kinds, is now estimated to run well over six hours. In truth, the United States is fast becoming a wired nation.

With the dawning of the satellite age in the early 1970s, TV began not only uniting countries but linking nations as well. Thanks to the new advances in communication technology, the world is fast shrinking into the "global village" foreseen by many.

In addition to its tremendous reach and unifying qualities, television has great credibility. Since 1961 it has led steadily as the most believable news medium, and by 1968 it had established a two-to-one lead over newspapers in this respect. Nothing has happened since to narrow the margin. On the contrary, television's percentage has increased while the figure for newspaper believability has remained constant. The concept of "seeing is believing" obviously is a major factor here. The Roper organization, an independent public-opinion research group, provides an interesting table on the development of this attitude since 1959. The question was asked: "If you got conflicting or different reports of the same news story from radio, television, the magazines, and the newspapers, which of the four versions would you be most inclined to believe—the one on radio or television or magazines or newspapers?" The answers were as follows:[2]

| Most believable | 12/59 % | 11/61 % | 11/63 % | 11/64 % | 1/67 % | 11/68 % | 1/71 % |
|---|---|---|---|---|---|---|---|
| Television | 29 | 39 | 36 | 41 | 41 | 44 | 49 |
| Newspapers | 32 | 24 | 24 | 23 | 24 | 21 | 20 |
| Radio | 12 | 12 | 12 | 8 | 7 | 8 | 10 |
| Magazines | 10 | 10 | 10 | 10 | 8 | 11 | 9 |
| Don't know or no answer | 17 | 17 | 18 | 18 | 20 | 16 | 12 |

In 1960, television provided a showcase for John F. Kennedy that helped to secure his election as the first Catholic president in the United States, long before the country had thought this was possible. In the presidential campaign of 1972, when Shirley Chisholm sought the presidential nomination of a major political party (the Democrats), television brought her into many homes across the nation as she campaigned for the nomination.

During the late 1950s and early 1960s, television served to raise the consciousness of blacks and whites alike. Starting with the sit-in at a Woolworth's lunch counter in North Carolina of four black freshmen in 1960 and continuing through the March on Washington in 1963 and the riots in Watts in 1965 and in Newark, New Jersey, and Detroit in 1967, it helped to generate a deeper sense of awareness which undoubtedly added substance and momentum to the civil rights revolution.

At the same time that it affected the political perceptiveness and involvement of many Americans, television played an important role in heightening the level of expectation of the black population, which before it had had access to a "window on the world" had seen little of the affluent society that is America and from which it has been excluded. This in turn led to a feeling of frustration and bitterness among blacks as it became increasingly clear that this new medium, which possesses the power to alter individual lives and the social climate, as well as shaping images and attitudes, rigidly excluded them.

Only when Negroes made "news" with sit-ins, wade-ins, marches, confrontations, demonstrations, acts of violence, or flaming rhetoric; or when their super-athletes performed in track and field, on the baseball diamond or in the prize-fight ring, were they likely to be granted exposure.

As late as the end of the 1960s, the National Advisory Commission on Civil Disorders, commonly called the Kerner Report, noted:

> The disorders in our cities are only one aspect of the dilemmas and difficulties of race relations in America. In defining, explaining, and reporting this broader, more complex, and ultimately far more fundamental subject, the communications media ironically have failed to communicate. Media have not yet turned to this task with the wisdom, the sensitivity, and the expertise it demands.

It was clear that in spite of its vast technological reach the electronic media lagged woefully far behind in its social grasp, particularly in its relationship to black Americans and other identifiable minorities. This led Negroes to draw an inevitable conclusion: If their story was to be told with the necessary "expertise and sensitivity," they would have to have a hand in the telling.

The opportunity for black Americans to participate in radio and television was a long time in coming, however. The first radio station in America was licensed to go on the air on September 15, 1921,[3] but if the thought of acquiring stations of their own ever occurred to Negroes in those early years, when radio frequencies were available, it was rapidly dismissed. There were several reasons for this. It took sizable sums of money to put a station on the air. It took trained technicians to operate it, expert salesmen to make and keep it profitable, creative personnel skilled in the craft of program development to make it appealing. It took Government examination and sanction before licenses would be granted.

If the world of radio was new to whites, it was even newer to Negroes. Moreover, the whites had the money and the blacks did not. The result was that the stations went to the large corporations, financiers, major publishers, and individuals who were able to assemble the funds, legal counsel, and influence in Government circles to acquire them.

It was not until 1945, therefore, that the first radio station, WERD in Atlanta, Georgia, was acquired by a black businessman, Jesse B. Blayton.[4] As late as 1972 black Americans owned and operated only sixteen commercial stations out of the total of 7,131 then on the air.[5] Three additional stations, all FM, were being operated at predominantly black colleges.[6]

In January of 1972, 339 radio stations carried "black" programs beamed to Negro communities. Thirty-four were programmed 100 percent for black audiences, twenty-four hours a day. The remainder carried programs of interest to Negroes for from one to twenty-three hours daily. All but eight with 100 percent Negro programming were in the South.[7] Negroes exercised little or no control over these stations, their content, or their administration, since they were all white-owned. Music—sometimes gospel, sometimes "soul," infrequently jazz, pop, and rock—constituted their staple fare. Quite often they were referred to as "soul" stations or "rhythm and blues" stations, because of the preponderance of such music. They did little to educate, inform, or raise the cultural consciousness of their black listeners.

Before the 1960s, Negroes were seldom heard on the general-market radio stations. Rare exceptions included a pioneering CBS Radio Network series which appeared in 1929 called the "Negro Achievement Hour," and performances by the Fisk Jubilee Singers beginning in 1945 on CBS in a Sunday morning time period commonly referred to in the trade as "the Cultural Ghetto."

There was little on the general-market stations that was edifying to the Negro's image. Black Americans were generally presented as porters, maids, waiters, and valets, easily distinguishable by their accents, their names, and their happy-go-lucky view of life. Nor did these stations contribute significantly to the Negro's financial well-being, since many of the "black" radio roles were played by white actors. The most famous examples of this type of casting were the stars of the weekly "Amos 'n' Andy" weekly comedy series, which first came on the air in 1939.

Leonard Evans was the first black to produce a radio series. Entitled "Ruby Valentine," it starred Juanita Hall and Sara Lou Harris.[8] After its completion in 1954 Evans tried to market the series, but with little success.

Few statistics were kept of the number of blacks appearing on radio in the early days or of the income derived from their appearances. To most black Americans it remained a magical kind of medium, remote from the reality of their day-to-day lives, and decidedly the "white man's" private preserve.

The above was also true of television, which emerged from the experimental stage shortly after World War II. This new medium offered little or nothing to improve the Negro's economic position or to advance his cause.

As had been the case with radio, the idea of acquiring television channels in the early days was discarded by Negroes for financial and other reasons. As late as 1971, among America's existing 904 television stations, 205 of which were noncommercial, not one was black-owned.

If only a few authentic black voices were heard on radio, even fewer were seen or heard on television. Anyone from abroad watching American television would have been hard put to believe that the society it supposedly reflected was multiracial.

In the 1950s, when black Americans did begin to appear, it was in the traditional guise of song-and-dance performers, musicians, and servants. Outstanding examples of this kind of type-casting included Eddie "Rochester" Anderson, who was valet to Jack Benny in his long-run weekly show on CBS-TV (1950–1963) and Lillian Randolph, who played the maid, Birdie, on "The Great Gildersleeve" on NBC-TV during 1955. (This latter show had run on radio from 1952 to 1955.) Miss Randolph also replaced another black maid played by Hattie McDaniel on the short-run "Beulah" show on ABC-TV from 1950 to 1953. The part of the domestic, Beulah, central to the plot, had originally belonged to Ethel Waters and later to Louise Beavers. These four ladies represented the sum total of the black "dramatic" actresses seen with any regularity on early television.

In the television variety programs, black entertainers fared better. However, they were usually pictured alone, as isolated from the white performers as possible so that if there was any objection from stations in the South about their appearance they could easily be eliminated without disturbing the program's overall continuity. How many times the performances of Negro stars such as Lena Horne, Dorothy Dandridge, William Warfield, Harry Belafonte, Nat "King" Cole, the Mills Brothers, Louis Armstrong, "Buck and Bubbles," the Nicholas Brothers, and Bill "Bojangles" Robinson ended up on the cutting-room floor of southern television studios, no one will ever know.

Ed Sullivan was the first to star black performers with any regularity. This occurred on his Sunday variety show on CBS-TV.[9] Just as Ed Sullivan opened the door to black performers on CBS-TV, Arthur Godfrey was instrumental in doing so on CBS radio. He signed the Mariners, a singing quartet who had met in the service during World War II, as regular guests on his three programs, "Arthur Godfrey Time," "Arthur Godfrey's Talent Scouts," and "Arthur Godfrey and His Friends."

The 1950s were marked by the emergence of four major black talents, provided through the medium of television with spectacular network platforms. The first of these was Sidney Poitier, who made his television debut in 1955 in his first major dramatic role in Robert Alan Aurthur's "A Man Is Ten Feet Tall." The play appeared on NBC's "Philco Television Theater." There was no fear that the company would cancel the series or that viewers' reaction would hurt it because it was the last show of the series. In 1955, as well, NBC's "Opera Television Theater" brought Leontyne Price, the second of these new talents, to national prominence in the opera *Tosca*. She played the title role, the only Negro in an otherwise all-white cast. That year also saw the appearance of a third new talent, Harry Belafonte, who did a series of shows on the NBC "Colgate Variety Hour" that capitalized on the calypso craze of the day.

The last of the eminent foursome was Nat King Cole, who was signed up in 1956 by NBC for a regular weekly variety series. This was a bold move on the part of the network, which kept the show on the air sustaining in prime time for over a year.[10] When it finally became evident that no sponsor would underwrite the show nationally, despite attempts of many high-priced stars to keep it going by appearing without remuneration, NBC threw in the sponge and cancelled it.

Recent years, however, have seen the emergence of several top-rated weekly television series with black stars. One of the first of these was "Julia," starring Diahann Carroll. It made its debut on the NBC Television Network on September 17, 1968, and continued through May of 1971. This would be considered a long run by any standard.

It was a simple story of widow Julia Baker making a new life for herself and her little boy in a big city. Her old life had ended with the death of her husband, an Air Force captain who was killed in Vietnam.

To face her new life, the subject matter of the series, Julia had the following assets, according to an NBC promotion piece: "(1) her beauty, brains, and personality; (2) her 'little-man' son, Corey, age 7; (3) a comfortable apartment in an integrated apartment house; (4) a friendly white neighbor, and her own little 7-year-old redheaded son, Corey's friend; (5) a good job as a registered nurse."

"Julia" was criticized by many members of the black community as being slick, unrealistic, and matriarchal. But it made money for Miss Carroll, NBC, and its white creator, producer, and sometime writer Hal Kanter, as well as chalking up high rating points.

Another top-rated series was the spectacularly successful "Flip Wilson Show," which began its fourth season on the NBC Television Network, in September 1973.

The hour, built around the popular comedian and his many alter egos, Geraldine Jones, Sonny the janitor, Charley the chef, Freddy the playboy, and Herbie the ice-cream man, was for four years running among the leading ten shows on television.

Top name entertainers such as Jack Benny, Pearl Bailey, Diana Sands, Carol Channing, and Ed Sullivan made guest appearances on the show regularly. According to a study released by the A.C. Nielsen Company in February 1972, forty million viewers watched the show during an average week. Mr. Wilson was asked what the results of this survey meant to him: "It means I have to work as hard as I can to entertain those forty million people," he replied. "Work" has been Flip Wilson's byword since he made his debut as a comic at the age of 9.

His show was as popular among blacks as it was among whites, though some blacks disparage the Geraldine character as being loud, lazy, insolent, and a stereotype of the white man's conception of a black.

"Sanford and Son," a third successful NBC Television Network series starring blacks, premiered on January 14, 1972, featuring veteran comedian Redd Foxx and Demond Wilson, a relative newcomer to television, as Fred and Lamont Sanford, two junk dealers living in Los Angeles. It is based on the long-running British Broadcasting Company hit about two Cockneys, "Steptoe and Son." Adapting the material for the American viewer presented no problem, according to NBC-TV, since the relationship of father and son is universal whether they are black and living in South Central Los Angeles or Cockney and living in England.

Fred Sanford is 65 years old. He will do whatever is necessary to keep his son from leaving him. This includes faking heart attacks and calling to his deceased wife, Elizabeth, to witness his travails.

Although most of the first season's scripts were rewrites of "Steptoe and Son" scripts, they were then followed by original contributions from outside writers. In its first season, "Sanford and Son" was listed among the prized top ten television shows.

Two new variety shows hosted by black performers went on TV toward the end of 1972: "The George Kirby Show," which was syndicated, and "The New Bill Cosby Show," which premiered on the CBS-TV network in September 1972.

The TV action was not limited to the commercial stations, however. "Soul," a talk variety hour-long program, one of the first all-black shows to be produced by WNET, the New York City flagship station of the National Educational Television, was aired in 1968 as a local entry and has been seen nationally since that time.

According to its black executive producer, Ellis Haizlip, "the primary function of 'Soul' is to give alienated black people a voice. . . . black people turn us on every week because they know they will see an undiluted black show. . . . since television is probably the most popular medium, 'Soul' tries to fill the void of those who are not turned on by any other media."

"Black Journal" began as an educational television program in 1968. Its first producer was white. Its second was black, and in 1969, under his direction, the show won a television Emmy award (Academy of Television Arts and Sciences). Its third producer,

Tony Brown, also a black man, continued to move it toward the front of programs of its kind when he took over in June 1969.

He saw "Black Journal" as a show "produced by black people, to black people, for the liberation of black people."

If the number of Negroes appearing on radio and television in the 1950s was small, the number of those behind the scenes in the administration, programming, sales, and technical departments was minuscule. Not only are these the areas which employ 92 percent of those involved in commercial broadcasting, but it is here as well that programs are developed and policies and decisions made.

This state of affairs continued well into the 1960s, leading Dr. Everett Parker, Director of the Office of Communications, United Church of Christ, to testify before the New York City Commission on Human Rights in March 1968, that "six black musicians or clerks don't counterbalance the lack of script writers, commercial announcers, directors, and other creative personnel. Minority groups must be represented at every level. Our mass-communications media must lead the way; they cannot be permitted to be last to adapt to change."[11]

In 1964 the Office of Communications petitioned the Federal Communications Commission to deny renewal of the license to television station WLBT in Jackson, Mississippi, on the grounds that "it systematically discriminated against the Negro population in its viewing area." After several years of hearings, the challenge was upheld and the license revoked in 1968. The license was then assigned to a new licensee on an interim basis, and the new licensee went on to initiate personnel and programming practices satisfactory to the FCC and the black citizens of Jackson.[12] By 1972 the station had a Negro, William Dilday, in the top administrative post as station manager.[13] Throughout the 1960s, the United Church of Christ gave guidance to a variety of community-based coalitions organized to challenge renewal of licenses on the grounds that the stations were not responsive to the needs of their communities or fair in their employment practices. In most instances these coalitions, which sprang up across the country from Boston to Los Angeles, represented a wide spectrum of community organizations.[14]

Many community groups, such as the Black Broadcasting Coalition of the Youngstown metropolitan area, Youngstown, Ohio, before challenging licenses, did exhaustive research on the Negro programming, the number of Negroes employed by stations, and the type of work they were assigned.

A survey of this kind conducted by the Youngstown area Urban League in 1969 to study the hiring practices and programming of AM-FM radio and television stations in the Mahoning-Shenango Valley (Youngstown, Ohio; Warren, Ohio; Niles, Ohio; and Sharon, Farrell, and Newcastle, Pennsylvania) produced the following statistics:

| Station | Hours Per Week | Black Programming | Black Employment |
|---------|----------------|-------------------|------------------|
| WKBN AM | 168 | 0 | 2 (janitors) |
| WKBN FM | 87 | 00 | |
| WKBN TV | 124 | 0 | |
| | 379 | 0 | 2 |
| WFMJ AM | 133 | 0 | 1 (secretary) |
| WFMJ TV | 124 | 0 | 0 |
| | 257 | 0 | 1 |
| WBBW AM | 140 | 20 min. (gospel) | 1 (janitor) |
| WBBW FM | 112 | 0 | 1 (part-time announcer) |
| | 252 | 20 minutes | 2 |
| WHOT AM | 168 | 1 hr. (gospel) | 0 |
| WHOT FM | 136 | 0 | 0 |
| | 304 | 1 | 0 |
| WNIO AM | 84 (average) | 2 hrs. (gospel) | 0 |
| WHHH AM | 126 | 1 hr. (gospel) | 0 |
| WYTV | 119 | 1-1/2 hrs. | 2 (photographer, announcer) |
| WKST AM | 126 | 0 | 0 |
| WJZY | 84 (average) | 0 | 0 |
| WPIC AM | 84 (average) | 0 | 0 |
| WPIC FM | 126 | 0 | 0 |
| | 210 | 0 | 0 |
| WFAR AM | 126 | 1 | 0 |
| TOTAL | 2067 | 6 hours 50 minutes | 7 employees |

As black Americans became increasingly aware both of the enormous power of radio and television and of the media's indifference to black aims and aspirations, they grew more and more discontented with their limited role in these fields. The 1960s began with the slogan "jobs for the jobless." Toward the end of the decade, this became "a voice for the voiceless," with black organizations demonstrating an unusual unanimity in their demands. The issue was no longer moral—the seeking of jobs and participation through appeal to the goodwill of white owners and station managers. Blacks now turned to the law, seeking jobs and participation through the edicts of the courts.

In June 1972 *Newsweek* magazine noted in a story "Blacks vs. Broadcasting" that "the black community is at last discovering a powerful source of legal leverage over television stations—the license challenge. The FCC, which must reconsider a station's license every three years, is currently processing more than 100 license challenges—90 percent of which have been filed by predominantly black coalitions. The organization credited with the largest role in mobilizing such campaigns is the Washington-based Black Efforts for Soul in Television (BEST). Financed by the Unitarian-Universalist Association, BEST operates as a sort of how-to-do-it agency for minority groups struggling to master the intricacies of license-challenge procedures. To disseminate that knowledge, BEST director William Wright has conducted 'media workshops' in more than forty U. S. cities." Wright is convinced that black power will really come to broadcasting only with the establishment of a nationwide network of black television stations. That goal will be hard to reach in mass-audience television, but the notion of an all-black network is already being experimented with in radio. Mutual Black Network (MBN), a newly formed service of the Mutual Broadcasting System, began beaming 100 five-minute news and sports programs each week to about forty Mutual stations coast to coast.

This type of new awareness and leadership sparked, in June 1972, the appointment of Judge Benjamin L. Hooks of Memphis as the first black commissioner to the seven-man FCC, which oversees the operation of the broadcast industry.[15] In 1973 the FCC appointed Lionel J. Monagas as chief of the newly created Equal Employment Opportunity Unit.

An opening move in the effort to achieve equal job opportunities and advancement in the industry through Government assistance was made in New York in 1962. To determine how this could be accomplished, George Norford, the first Negro to produce television network programs and an executive in the Standards and Practices department of NBC-TV, was given a leave of absence at the request of New York's Governor Nelson Rockefeller, to serve as a consultant on broadcasting to the State Commission for Human Rights. His first report to the commission minimized fears expressed by many broadcasters that there would be reprisals from sponsors, the South, and certain sectors of the overall public if more Negroes appeared on the air or were hired in such sensitive jobs as sales or account executives, which provide the most direct route in the industry to management positions.

In 1965 Norford, who by now had joined Group W (Westinghouse Broadcasting Company) as a general executive, set up the Broadcast Skills Bank with the support of Group W chairman Donald H. McGannon in conjunction with the Urban League's National Skills Bank.[16] The purpose of the bank—part of an "affirmative action" program—was to seek out, employ, and advance minority-group members in the Westinghouse Broadcasting Company organization. Within a year the bank had proved itself successful and the program became industry-wide, with the networks, ABC, CBS, and NBC, and other group organizations lending their sizable weight to its implementation. As many as twenty-five banks sprang up in major cities across the country. From 1966 to 1972, the banks were able to place over 2,000 minority-group men and women in professional positions in the industry.

The sixties saw the formation of other organizations to accomplish similar objectives. One of these, the Full Employment Committee of the New York branch of the Academy of TV Arts and Sciences, had as its chairman the noted television, stage, and screen actor, Ossie Davis. Another, the Community Film Workshop, which concentrated on training black film technicians for television, was headed by Cliff Frazier and was also based in New York. Equivalent organizations developed in other major cities across the country but it was New York City which provided the cutting edge in the thrust for black involvement.

It is in New York, for example, that the commissions, including the Federal Equal Employment Opportunity Commission (EEOC), held their hearings into industry practices. It is here that the headquarters of all the major networks are located, and where decisions having to do with hiring practices, programming, and everything else, are made. Sixth Avenue in New York City, between 49th and 54th streets, is called by those in the trade "broadcast boulevard"; within these blocks lie the corporate head-quarters of NBC, CBS, ABC, Time-Life Broadcasting, McGraw-Hill Broadcasting, and the Mutual Broadcasting System.

During the sixties formal hearings were conducted in New York not only by the Federal EEOC but by the city and state Commissions on Human Rights as well. The findings of these commissions generally corroborated the fact that minorities were greatly underrepresented in the industry, especially in management and policy-making positions.

In January 1968 the Federal EEOC, following its New York hearings on discrimi-nation in white-collar employment, released a report stating that "Negroes are repre-sented in white-collar jobs in New York City's communications industries at rates substantially below their proportion to the city's population. . . ."[17] [N]ewspaper publish-ing is generally laggard among communication industries and radio/television [is] the leader [in hiring], closely followed by book publishing."

|  | Percent Black Office and Clerical | Percent Black Officials and Managers | Percent Black Professionals |
|---|---|---|---|
| Radio-TV | 7.6 | 0.9 | 1.9 |
| Book Publishing | 5.2 | 1.0 | 2.4 |
| Periodical Publishing | 5.2 | 0.7 | 1.0 |
| Newspaper Publishers | 4.2 | less than 0.1 | 1.2 |

Though the above statistics show that the policies of the radio and television industry left much to be desired, their record in the employment of Negroes was better than that of the other media. This was mainly because of their use of the "public's air," which gave them a greater obligation to operate in the "public's interest" than print media, which, since it is privately owned and not subject to Government regulations, has no such responsibility to remain nonpartisan in nature.

Another area in which blacks were faced with difficulties was in the field of script writing. If radio/television was not inhospitable to black American writers it was certainly indifferent to their submissions. As late as the sixties, considered a decade of transition, there were no black writers regularly employed on any series or other pro-gram. Breakthroughs were few and far between. Bill Branch wrote one drama for NBC's "Frontiers of Faith" in 1958, and two others for "Look Up and Live" and

"Lamp Unto My Feet" on CBS-TV; Ossie Davis, John Killens, and Alice Childress wrote a token script or two; and the late playwright Lorraine Hansberry was commissioned to write a television drama for CBS which was never produced. Louis Peterson, Bob Goodwin, and Harry Dolan wrote occasional scripts for series such as NBC's aforementioned "Julia."

Dolan was a product of the Writers Workshop started in Watts, Los Angeles, by the noted author Budd Schulberg shortly after the 1965 riots there. NBC produced his first play for television, "Losers Weepers." It focused public attention on the Watts experiment and on Dolan personally, who continues to write an occasional television script and now heads the Writers Workshop.

Negro directors fared no better than did black writers. Two managed to surface, however, during the sixties: Mark Warren and Bill Greaves. Both had to go to Canada, where they spent several years apprenticing and directing before returning to the U. S. and a changing racial climate. Greaves directed and produced independently while hosting and directing "Black Journal." His independent company began making its mark commercially and artistically in the 1970s. Warren directed a top-rated weekly variety series on NBC-TV, "Laugh-In," before going on to direct films.

It was not until the late 1960s and early 1970s that Negroes began appearing at the decision-making levels of broadcasting companies. In 1968 George Norford was elected a Vice President-General Executive of Group W. In 1970 he was elected to the company's board of directors. From 1970 to 1972, other networks and groups followed the example of Group W, but still on a "token" basis. In 1973 CBS became the first network organization to elect a Negro to its board. The director in question, Franklin A. Thomas, is president of the Bedford-Stuyvesant Restoration Corporation.[18] The same year saw the appointment of Mamie Phipps Clark to the board of ABC,[19] and Richard J. Kennedy, III to the boards of both RCA and NBC.[20]

Two other major group organizations appointed Negro vice-presidents in 1971 and 1972. Capital Cities Broadcasting Corp. in 1971 named Andrew Jackson, a seasoned broadcaster, as vice-president for community relations; and in 1972 the Post-Newsweek stations appointed Tyrone Brown vice-president for legal affairs and a member of its board. In 1971 NBC-TV made Stanley Robertson a vice-president of its film-producing division on the West Coast. Other appointments to vice-presidencies were made by such local stations as WOR-TV in New York City, which appointed John Murray vice-president for public affairs, and WNEW-TV (also in New York) which named David Hepburn vice-president of community affairs. Minorities were yet to enter the meaningful areas of programming, sales, news, and station management, however, despite the growing visibility of black newscasters in major cities.

In the field of television commercials, blacks were almost nonexistent before the 1960s. In 1967 Lawrence Plotkin, professor of psychology at the City College of New York and consultant on media to the Metropolitan Applied Research Corporation (MARC), prepared a report on the frequency of black appearances in television commercials for the Legal Defense Fund of the NAACP. Dr. Plotkin's study showed that in 1962 there were only "two instances of Negroes reported on commercials and public-service announcements. By 1964 the number had risen to thirty-six."

In testifying before the New York City Commission on Human Rights hearings on television, March 1968, Dr. Plotkin stated:

> In 1966, the Legal Defense Fund of the NAACP received complaints from Negro professional athletes that they were discriminated against in advertising and industrial fees. We decided to monitor televised sports events and related programs (interviews, pre-game programs, and game highlights). It was our feeling that sports audiences might be more receptive to commercials featuring Negroes because of the high incidence of Negroes in professional sports. Furthermore, the popularity of televised sporting events, particularly professional football, is proof that the viewing audience will not tune out black faces on the home screen. Ironically, we found that Negroes appeared in only 5 percent of the commercials; most of these appearances were in supporting roles and as momentary flashes. In only 1 percent of the monitored commercials was a Negro the "star." Further evidence of the infrequent use of Negroes in commercials was found when personal endorsements were considered. Of the eight reported in the Legal Defense Fund survey, only one featured a Negro (Louis Armstrong and his trumpet) while white athletes were featured in five of the other seven personal endorsements. It is surprising that not one Negro athlete was featured in commercials on programs where there are so many Negro stars. In 1967 the Joint Equality Committee monitored commercials on all programs.[21] The Negro rate of appearance was 2 percent and the overall minority rate was 2.3 percent.[22] In both surveys, repeated commercials were counted. We can conclude that the rate of Negro appearance in commercials is even lower than that in television programs. In both cases, however, the token rates reflect a limited economic and employment opportunity for Negro actors, entertainers, and athletes.

The television picture has been changing, however, albeit not rapidly enough. Greater Negro participation in the media is attested to by the following table of percentages of those employed at the three major networks, ABC, NBC, and CBS:[23]

| Title | 1967 Black Percentage | Minority Percentage[24] 1971 | | |
|---|---|---|---|---|
| | Network[25] | A | B | C |
| Managerial and Executive | 1 | 5.7 | 7.0 | 4.5 |
| Sales | 2 | 4.0 | 9.1 | 10.3 |
| Crafts | 3 | 12.8 | 11.1 | 8.0 |
| Office Employees | 9 | 18.0 | 24.5 | 30.3 |

By the early 1970s, the new possibilities for involvement had brought about a significant alteration in the Negro's attitude toward television, which he considered the prime communications medium. This is shown in a 1971 poll conducted by Louis Harris, one of the nation's leading pollsters, in which a national cross section of Negroes was asked about U. S. institutions generally. Only television and the U. S. Supreme Court emerged among pluralities of blacks as clearly committed to black equality, while

Congress was viewed with ambivalence and newspapers, corporations, and white churches were judged to be relatively indifferent or actively hostile to black aspirations.[26] Although there is still a long way to go, television is working to broaden its "public" obligation to include the best interests and participation of *all* Americans.

## Notes

1. It is predicted that the cable-TV (CATV) audience will top 23 million by 1980, according to a study made by Frost and Sullivan Inc., New York market researchers.
2. Source: Booklet entitled "An Extended View of Public Attitudes toward Television and Other Mass Media, 1959–1971," by The Roper Organization, Inc.
3. WBZ, Springfield, Mass. WBZ is now assigned to Boston (*Broadcasting Yearbook, 1972*).
4. It was sold in 1968 to a white group, RadioAd, Inc., and its call letters were changed in January 1972, to WXAT.
5. WEUP, Huntsville, Ala., Leroy Garrett, owner
   WRDW, Augusta, Ga., James Brown Broadcasting
   WMPP, Chicago Heights, Ill., Seaway Broadcasting, Inc.
   WTLC (FM), Indianapolis, Ind., Calojay Broadcasting, Inc.
   WEEB, Baltimore, Md., James Brown Broadcasting WEBB, Inc.
   WCHD (FM), Detroit, Mich., Bell Broadcasting Company
   WGPR (FM), Detroit Mich
   WCHB, Inkster, Mich., Bell Broadcasting Company
   WWWS (FM), Saginaw, Mich., Clark Broadcasting Company
   WORV, Hattiesburg, Miss., Circuit Broadcasting Company
   KPRS, Kansas City, Mo., KPRS Broadcasting Company
   KWK, St. Louis, Mo., Vic-Way Broadcasting Company
   WVOE, Chadbourn, N. C., Ebony Enterprises, Inc.
   WJBE, Knoxville, Tenn., James Brown Broadcasting
   WKLH, Compton, Calif., John Lamarr Hill, owner
   WSOK, Savannah, Ga., Black Communication Corporation
6. WSHA, Raleigh, N. C., Shaw University School of Communications
   WAOV, Hampton, Va., Hampton Institute Mass Media Arts Dept.
   WHUR-FM, Washington, D. C., Howard University Radio (School of Communications)
7. WKND, Hartford, Conn.; WOL, Washington, D.C.; WVON, Cicero, Ill. (with a black president); WTLC (FM) Indianapolis, Ind.; WWWS (FM), Saginaw, Mich.; WNJR, Newark, N. J.; WLIB (FM), New York; WVKO, Columbus, Ohio (*Broadcasting Yearbook, 1972*).
8. Evans is now a successful publisher of Tuesday Publications. Sarah Lou Harris is now Lady Carter, wife of Sir John Carter, Ambassador from Guyana in the West Indies to the Court of St. James. Juanita Hall is dead.
9. "Toast of the Town" premiered on CBS-TV on June 20, 1948. Later it became the Ed Sullivan Show, one of the longest running variety programs in the medium's history. The last performance was June 6, 1971.
10. Sustaining: unsponsored, paid for by the network.
11. The United Church of Christ is a union of the Congregational Christian Churches and the Evangelical and Reform Church. The Office of Communications carries on a ministry in mass communication through press relations, motion pictures, and television and radio.
12. Communications Improvement Corporation.
13. Dilday was formerly director of personnel, radio station WHDH in Boston, Mass.

14. Organizations supporting Black Broadcasting Coalition goals
    Youngstown Area Urban League
    District 26 United Steel Workers
    Eastern Ohio Baptist Association
    Youngstown 2nd Ward Councilman
    Freedom, Incorporated
    Greater AFL-CIO Council
    Covington P. T. A.
    Ministerial Alliance
    Youngstown Community Action Council
    Youngstown Leadership Conference
    Saint Patrick Catholic Church
    Mahoning County Deputy Coroner
    Mahoning County Legal Assistance Director
    Youngstown City Law Director
    Warren, Ohio NAACP
    Trumbull County Human Relations Director

15. Judge Hooks, the first black man to be named to any federal regulatory agency, is a minister-lawyer and vice-president of a bank.

16. A group broadcasting organization like a network can own from two to fourteen stations: five television, seven AM radio, and two FM radio. The difference between the group organization, of which there are over 100, and the networks, of which there are only three, is that networks can have stations affiliated with them on a contractual basis to take their prime time—7: 30 to 10: 30 p. m.—programs.

17. White collar employment in New York City's communications industry is defined to include five segments: (1) advertising agencies; (2) book publishers; (3) newspaper publishers; (4) periodical publishers and (5) radio/television broadcasters.

18. A local community organization which develops and implements programs in housing, economic development and manpower to improve living conditions and create employment opportunities in central Brooklyn.

19. Dr. Clark is director of the Northside Center for Child Development.

20. Mr. Kennedy is president of the North Carolina Mutual Life Insurance Co. of Durham, N. C.

21. The Joint Equality Committee is composed of delegates from the American Federation of Television and Radio Artists (AFTRA), the Screen Actors Guild, the Directors Guild, and the Writers Guild.

22. Orientals, Puerto Ricans, and Indians, as well as Negroes.

23. Source: National Association of Broadcasters.

24. Black employees constitute 89.2 percent of minority percentages according to Television Information Office. In 1971 minorities custodial workers were 38.3 percent of the total employed, which was only twenty-nine.

25. Networks are identified as A, B, and C, at the request of the Government agency releasing the figures.

26. Source: The New York *Post*, August 20, 1971.

# 29

## Black Participation in the Armed Forces

### Richard J. Stillman, II

Paradoxically, within the last decade the U. S. Armed Forces have been subject simultaneously to enthusiastic praise and sharp criticism over their racial policies. Supporters of the military have pointed with considerable pride to the fact that the Defense Department was the first and only American institution to integrate blacks and whites thoroughly—even prior to the 1954 Brown Supreme Court Decision. The Armed Services, they contend, have proved that integration can and does work successfully in real life. Moreover, supporters of the military argue that today the services give many ghetto youth their only real opportunity to escape poverty and pursue a worthy, lifetime career. They point out as well that recent national daily exposure to blacks fighting in Vietnam alongside whites has given Negroes new status and prestige at home.

True, say the critics of the Armed Forces' racial policies, the services were the first to integrate, but now they have gone on to become overly integrated! Too many blacks were in the front combat ranks in Vietnam doing more than their fair share of the fighting and sustaining a proportionately higher percentage of the combat fatalities. And although official military policy does preach equality and equal opportunity regardless of race, in fact military life is shot through with discrimination and racism—one need only look at the token number of senior black officers, the few Negro National Guardsmen, and the high percentage of blacks serving prison terms in military stockades.

What then is the current status of blacks in the U. S. Armed Forces? Does military policy, as some contend, reflect the most advanced form of racial equality in America today? Or, as others argue, is it in truth less color-blind than it pretends?

In order to gain some perspective on the present racial orientation of the defense establishment, it is first necessary to step back into history and examine how service racial policies evolved into their present form. The history of race relations in the Armed Services conveniently divides into three periods: pre-1940, when segregation and exclusion were frequently—but not always—standard military policy; 1940 to 1954, an epoch that witnessed the integration of the Defense Department; and the present era, in which Vietnam and racial unrest at home have added new complexities to the problems of military race relations.

# THE PRE-1940 ERA: UNSTABLE BLACK-MILITARY RELATIONS

Even the most cursory assessment of military-black relations from the American Revolution until World War II demonstrates that black Americans were for the most part loyal citizens who served their country in uniform in every major American war—showing their share of the valor under fire and suffering their share of the combat losses—yet the defense establishment has more often than not predicated its use for black personnel on the immediate demands for manpower by battlefield commanders rather than any consistent open-door policy for black servicemen. In short, when there was a pressing need for men, blacks saw service in uniform, but when the pressure for manpower was not acute, standard military policies were frequently restrictive and segregationist.

## The American Revolution

Blacks can point to their role in the American Revolution to prove their long-time identification with their national heritage. At one time or another 5,000 blacks served in the Colonial army (out of a total of 300,000 Americans who fought in the Revolutionary War) and they participated in almost every engagement, North and South, on land and sea. None served as officers but several became legendary heroes. The first American to die in the Boston Massacre, March 5, 1770, was Crispus Attucks, a runaway slave turned seaman. Lemuel Haynes, Peter Salem, Barzillai Lew, and Prince Estabrook were among the minutemen who responded to Paul Revere's alarm to face the British Grenadiers at Lexington and Concord on April 19, 1775. Salem Poor was cited as "a brave and gallant soldier" by fourteen of his comrades who fought at Concord, and Peter Salem's presence at Bunker Hill was depicted in the famous contemporary painting of that battle.[1]

Washington's headquarters, however, made early attempts to exclude blacks from the Army. In 1775 several policy directives—on July 9, September 26, October 8, and November 12—prevented black enlistments.[2] These orders were issued mainly because southern slave-holding interests claimed that their property was disappearing into the army. However, these efforts to exclude blacks from the military were repealed by the Continental Congress on January 16, 1776, at General Washington's request.

Three factors prompted this policy reversal. First, the free blacks in the Continental Army, many of whom had served since Bunker Hill, bitterly protested to Washington that they were being rejected after several months of faithful military service. Second, the Americans soon found themselves bidding against the British for the black fighting man. In November the British Governor of Virginia, Lord Dunmore, organized 300 slaves into a regiment to suppress the rebellious colonists. Although these units were never effectively used in combat and were disbanded by June, the colonists became alarmed at the possibility that blacks who comprised nearly half of the southern colonies would join the side of the Crown if barred from the Continental Army. Some 14,000 blacks did in fact eventually join the British side and many of them subsequently gained their liberty in the West Indies.[3] A third factor that caused the Americans to abandon their exclusionary enlistment policies was the shortage of manpower. As the war progressed, the colonies became increasingly hard-pressed for recruits and hence willing to take any volunteers to maintain the strength of the state militia. Several states even offered both freedom and substantial bonuses to black recruits. Georgia and South Carolina alone refused black enlistments; but even these two states utilized slave manpower for logistical support. In only three colonies—Connecticut, Rhode Island, and Massachusetts—were separate black units formed. These units were small and short-lived; they participated in few engagements.[4] Essentially during the American Revolution, blacks fought side by side with whites, taking part in every major battle, mostly as common foot soldiers.

## The War of 1812

After the Revolution, in 1792 Congress barred blacks from joining the state militia, and in 1798 the first Secretary of the Navy, Benjamin Stoddert, prohibited blacks and mulattoes from entering the Navy or Marines. Despite these new restrictions, several hundred blacks served as sailors in the naval war with France (1798–1800). The War of 1812 also saw blacks in uniform. Approximately 100 were with Oliver Hazard Perry's ships which won a decisive naval battle against Lord Nelson on the Great Lakes. Said Perry of his own sailors: "I have fifty blacks on board this ship and many of them are my best men. . . . "[5] More than 500 Negroes, including black commanding line officers, fought with General Andrew Jackson in the critical Battle of New Orleans which stopped Major General Edward Parkenham's advance on that city.

## 1813–1860: An Era of Exclusion

After the battle of New Orleans, opportunities for blacks to serve in their country's Armed Forces came to a near end. Between the War of 1812 and the Civil War, the South developed its rigid institution of slavery and the North as well sanctioned segregation in many of its public and private institutions.[6] U. S. Attorney General William Wirt in 1823 succinctly stated the government's policy that "it was not the intention of Congress to incorporate Negroes and people of color with the Army any more than with the militia."[7] Southerners were especially vocal on this subject and significantly influenced the exclusionary policy of the military. Senator John C. Calhoun in 1842 asked Congress to exclude blacks from the Navy except as cooks, stewards, and servants, stating: "It was wrong to bring those who have sustained the honor and glory of the country down to a footing of the Negro race—to be degraded by being mingled and mixed up with that inferior race."[8] His bill passed the Senate but was defeated in the House of Representatives.

Only a handful of blacks participated in the Mexican-American War; and from 1850 until the Civil War, the country's professional peacetime Army and Navy were all white.

## The Civil War: The North

At the outbreak of the Civil War, President Lincoln's policy toward blacks in uniform was governed by his overriding political objective of maintaining the union. During the beginning of hostilities, Lincoln refrained from using black troops out of a reasonable fear that such an action would alienate the border states. When the President issued his first call for 75,000 volunteers, a large number of blacks from urban centers in the North responded with enthusiasm, but Secretary of War Cameron's reply to their attempts to enlist was: "I have to say this department has no intention to call into service any colored soldiers."[9] However, as was the case in the American Revolution, the critical manpower shortages that developed as the war progressed caused individual field commanders to use black troops. In 1862, generals commanding three areas—Port Royal, South Carolina; New Orleans, Louisiana; and Bates County, Missouri—hard-pressed for men and situated near large groups of blacks sympathetic to the Union cause, recruited blacks into separate units to protect their positions. Due to the increasing need for men, a quiet change in official policy was made at the end of April 1862 when Gideon Welles, Secretary of the Navy, proclaimed to flag officers of the southern squadron that they might enlist blacks "freely in the Navy with their consent rating them as boys at eight, nine, ten dollars a month and one ration."[10] In the summer of 1862 Secretary of War Stanton permitted up to 50,000 black volunteers to be assigned to labor units in the Quartermaster Corps.

The Emancipation Proclamation, issued January 1, 1863, ended Union efforts to keep blacks out of uniform. Blacks joined the military readily, and Union commanders were eager by now to have the extra men. Eventually 163 black federal regiments and two state regiments were raised, totaling 178,985 men. Black units participated in 449 engagements and suffered 36,847 casualties. Few black soldiers were in mixed units and most black regiments were officered by whites. A total of 7,122 blacks were commissioned as officers, mainly as doctors and chaplains.[11] The expansion of the Navy, from 76 vessels in 1861 to 671 ships in 1865, created a persistent shortage of manpower, and by the war's end, in many ships frequently one-quarter of the crews were black.

## The Civil War: The Confederacy

In 1860 three-quarters of the nation's 4,441,830 blacks lived in the South, comprising a third of the population of the Confederate States. Although President Jefferson Davis strongly censured Lincoln's use of black troops in combat, from 1863 onward there was considerable discussion in the South about using slaves in battle. However, the idea of putting slaves in uniform was too sharp a contradiction in the southern mind with its basic belief in black inferiority. It was not until March 15, 1865, that a desperate Confederate Congress finally passed a last-ditch law allowing black enlistments. On April 2, however, Lee surrendered, and no blacks were ever inducted into the Confederate States Army (C. S. A.).[12] Nevertheless slaves provided invaluable logistical support for southern armies throughout the entire war effort.

Perhaps one of the most tragic chapters in the war's history was the Confederate policy that no black Union soldier had the right to be treated as a prisoner of war. The Fort Pillow Massacre, April 12, 1864, at Fort Pillow, Tennessee, saw the wholesale slaughter of four companies of black Union troops by C. S. A. General Nathan B. Forrest, even after all resistance by the northern soldiers had ceased.[13] Black Union soldiers thus lived under double jeopardy while in combat—they could be killed in the fighting, or, if captured by the enemy, they faced the bleak prospect of enslavement or death.

## Post-Civil War Period

At the close of the Civil War the U. S. Congress legally established the right of the black man to serve in the military by enacting legislation on July 28, 1866, which set up six black units at an authorized troop strength totaling 12,500 men—the 9th and 10th Cavalry Regiments and the 38th, 39th, 40th, and 41st Infantry Regiments. The shortage of defense funds later reduced the black infantry regiments to two units—the 24th and 25th regiments. Until the Spanish-American War these troopers patrolled the frontier regions of the country and fought in frequent skirmishes with the Indians. The black cavalry regiments were nicknamed "The Buffalo Soldiers" by the Indians because they wore coats of buffalo hides during the winter months.

The 9th and 10th Cavalry units were with Colonel Theodore Roosevelt's famous "Rough Riders" as they stormed up San Juan Hill in the Spanish American War. Roosevelt later wrote of his black troopers: "I want no better men beside me in battle than these colored troops showed themselves to be."[14] The 24th and 25th Infantry Regiments fought at Siboney and El Caney, Cuba, and were later assigned to the Philippines to suppress the Filipino insurrection.

## World War I

On April 6, 1917, when the United States declared war on Germany, there were four black regiments in the regular Army and several such units in the Army National Guard. During the war the number of black servicemen rose to 371, 710 or 10.7 percent of all troops, and over 200,000 of these saw service overseas—three-quarters of them serving in the tough labor and stevedore battalions. Most of the overseas combat soldiers were part of the 92nd and 93rd Divisions. After considerable delay and controversy, the Army began commissioning black officers at Camp Des Moines, Iowa, and 1,353 were eventually commissioned at the camp. Throughout the war the U. S. Navy restricted black enlistments to its messmen's branch, in which approximately 10,000 Negroes served. No blacks were permitted to join the Marine Corps.[15]

World War I saw official Armed Forces policy toward blacks at its worst—rigid segregation, partial exclusion, and open and virulent racism on the part of numerous white commanders of black units. As Charles Houston, a black Army lieutenant in the 368th Regiment of the 92nd Division and later dean of Howard University Law School, wrote of his experience in World War I:

> The hate and scorn heaped upon us as Negro officers by Americans at Camp Mencou and Vannes in France, convinced me there was no sense in dying in a world ruled by them. . . . They boarded us off from our fellow white officers. They made us eat on benches in order to maintain segregation and they destroyed our prestige in front of French officers.[16]

After inspecting the conditions of the 92nd Division in France, William E. B. DuBois, the editor of *Crisis* and the first black Ph.D. from Harvard University, observed in print:

> It seemed that instead of trying to increase morale of his division, it was General Ballou's [the 92nd Division Commander] intention to discourage the men as much as possible. His action in censuring officers in the presence of enlisted men was an act that tended toward breaking down the confidence that the men had in their officers, and he pursued this method on innumerable occasions. On one occasion he referred to his division, in talking to another officer, as the "rapist division"; he constantly cast aspersions on the work of the colored officers and permitted other officers to do the same in his presence.[17]

It was small wonder that with this sort of leadership, the 92nd's combat record was often unsatisfactory and that racial clashes were frequent between blacks and whites. When the 93rd Division arrived in France in May 1917, it was immediately broken up and each of its four regiments—369th, 370th, 371st, and 372nd—fought beside French combat units. With French leadership, which was at least less openly racist, there was a marked difference in the combat performance of these latter black units. One highly decorated black unit, the 370th Regiment, with all-black company commanders, held a sector of the Allied Front before St. Mihiel and later a sector in the Meuse-Argonne from June 22 to August 15, 1918. It then went on with the French 59th Division to drive the Germans north of the Oise-Aisne. The men of the 370th suffered 665 casualties in the offensive and received 75 Croix de Guerre and 75 Distinguished Service Crosses.[18]

## The Postwar Period

Unfortunately, the faulty performance of the 92nd Division dominated military policy considerations in the postwar period. Policy studies conducted by the War

Department Personnel Division in 1922, 1927, 1933, and 1937 restated a basic theme: that blacks must be kept in segregated units with only limited numbers permitted into the combat arms. The Army banned blacks from the air corps, the artillery, engineers, signal, and tank corps while the Navy and Marines excluded them from all except messmen's units. An Army War College report, "Use of Negro Manpower" (November 12, 1936), reflected the strong racist sentiment prevalent in post-World War I military thinking:

> As an individual, the Negro is docile, tractable, light-hearted, carefree, and good-natured. If unjustly treated, he is likely to become surly and stubborn, though this is a temporary phase. He is careless, shiftless, irresponsible, and secretive. He resents censure and is best handled with praise and ridicule.[19]

## FROM SEGREGATION TO INTEGRATION: 1940–1954

At the outbreak of World War II, the U. S. Armed Forces racial policies showed many similarities to those of World War I. The services once again excluded Negroes from many job categories and they were barred from the Marine Corps. In 1941 all of the Navy's 5,026 black seamen served in the messmen's branch. Later, in 1943, nineteen black seabee (construction battalion) units totalling 18,600 men were organized for building port facilities and coastal roads for the Navy. At the start of the war the Army still maintained its restrictions on blacks entering the air corps, artillery, engineers, signal, and tank corps.[20]

Large segregated units were once again activated as they had been in World War I with the reactivation of the 92nd Division, numbering 12,000 enlisted men and 500 black officers, in October 1942 at Fort Huachuca, Arizona. In May 1942 the 93rd Division, also with the above number of men and officers, was reactivated at Camp Clipper, California. Later, a third all-black division, the 2nd Cavalry, was formed at Fort Clark, Texas, in February 1943. After considerable protest and effort on the part of several prominent Negro leaders, an all-black 99th Fighter Squadron was activated October 2, 1942; in Italy during 1943 this unit was expanded to the 332nd Fighter Group. Segregation applied not only to combat units but off-duty hours as well. The USO, NCO, and Officer Clubs were segregated. The Red Cross established a separate Jim Crow blood bank—even though it was a black physician, Dr. Charles R. Drew, who along with Dr. John Scudder had first developed the use of blood plasma.

Besides exclusion and segregation, another characteristic of Armed Service racial policies in World War II was the placing of blacks primarily in "supportive" rather than "combat" positions. The Army assigned one out of every five blacks to manual-labor units which built such facilities as Anzio Beach Port, landing fields in Europe and the Far East, and the Ledo Road, a vital supply link from India to China. In port units 77 percent of the men were black; in the transportation corps, the figure was 69 percent. More than three-fourths of the Red Ball Express, which supplied the critical Allied Drive into Germany during 1944 was staffed by black soldiers.[21] Even black combat divisions often spent little time up front fighting and much time in reserve. For example, the 93rd Division throughout the war was mainly restricted to housekeeping and mopping-up exercises in the South Pacific. As Walter White, the National Secretary of the NAACP, wrote after an inspection of the 2nd Cavalry Division:

> The unit had been trained for combat and shipped overseas a few weeks before I encountered them in Oran. But they had arrived in North Africa at a time when port battalions were needed to unload ships. Though there were many Italian prisoners of war available for such manual labor and large numbers of American solders who had been inactive at Oran for some time, who might have served as port battalions, the decision had been made to transform this outfit from combat to service status. The sudden transition had driven morale to the vanishing point.[22]

But this is not to say that black GI's never saw combat. To the contrary, one of the most decorated units for bravery in combat was the 99th Fighter Squadron (later the 332nd Fighter Group) which flew missions from North Africa and Italy. By V-E Day, the unit had flown 1,575 missions, 15,533 sorties, and received 865 awards, including 95 Distinguished Flying Crosses. It produced a number of air-combat heroes, including its commander, Benjamin O. Davis, Jr. (later the first black major general), Jack D. Holdsclaw, George S. Roberts, and Clarence D. Lester. In March 1945 the 332nd Fighter Group was decorated with the Distinguished Unit Citation (the highest unit decoration) for a 1600-mile round-trip air attack on Berlin with Colonel Davis in command. The 92nd Army Division, although it did not arrive in Italy until August 1944, fought as part of General Mark Clark's Fifth Army, taking heavy losses while crossing the Arno River, occupying the Lucca Canal, and engaging in mountain combat in northern Italy. In battle the 92nd sustained 25 percent casualties and received 12,098 military decorations. The 761st Tank Battalion—the first black armored unit committed to battle—fought with Patton's 3rd Army and spent almost 183 days in continuous combat. Patton, speaking of this unit, said:

> Men, you're the first Negro tankers ever to fight in the American Army. I would never have asked for you if you weren't good. I don't care what color you are as long as you go up there and kill those kraut sonsabitches.[23]

In the Navy as well, even though restricted to the messmen's branch, blacks showed a capability for combat. Three won the Navy Cross, the Navy's highest military decoration for bravery in action—Dorie Miller while aboard the U. S. S. *Arizona* at Pearl Harbor; Leonard R. Harmon on the U. S. S. *San Francisco* in the Solomons; and William Pinckney, at sea on the U. S. S. *Enterprise*.[24]

## Changes in Military Racial Policy During World War II

The general exclusionary and segregationist policies of the Armed Forces caused considerable black discontent within and without the defense establishment. Hardly a month went by without some report of racial unrest, frequently because blacks felt they were unfairly treated by white military leaders. Open riots broke out at Army posts in Hawaii, Louisiana, and Georgia; and the Navy experienced similar serious racial clashes at ports in San Francisco and Guam. Sammy Davis, Jr.'s autobiography, *Yes I Can*, vividly describes his difficulties in World War II as a soldier:

> I had been drafted into the Army to fight, and I did. We were loaded with southerners and southwesterners who got their kicks out of needling me, and Jennings [his sergeant] and his guys never let up. I must have had a knockdown, drag-out fight every day. . . .[25]

Nevertheless, despite the open disenchantment in many quarters with the Armed Services racial policies, civilian leadership supported the status quo. Secretary of the Navy Frank Knox stated that "the policy of not enlisting men of the colored race for any branch of naval service but the mess-men's branch was adopted to meet the best interests of general ship efficiency."[26] John J. McCloy, Assistant Secretary of War, felt that winning the war had every priority over improving race relations: "Frankly, I do not think that the basic issues of this war are involved in the question of whether colored troops serve in segregated units or in mixed units, and I doubt whether you can convince the people of the United States that the basic issues of freedom are involved in such a question. If the United States does not win this war the lot of the Negro is going to be far, far worse than it is today."[27]

However, despite such official civilian policies, integration efforts began in 1944 due to acute manpower shortages in the Army and Navy. By the end of 1944 there was a dearth of infantry riflemen in the European theater of operations due to the German offensive, the Battle of the Bulge. This manpower shortage threatened to grind to a halt any effective counterattack upon the enemy. Lt. General John C. H. Lee, Eisenhower's Commander of Service Forces in Europe, proposed retraining 20,000 men in his command for service as infantrymen at the front and extending this program to include black servicemen. While there was some reluctance on the part of senior staff officers to accept this innovative idea, the pressure for men overrode their objections and 20,000 volunteers along with 4,562 black GI's were assembled in Noyons, France, on January 10, 1945, for a six-week retraining program. Beginning in March blacks fought side-by-side with whites in these volunteer combat units until V-E Day. Colonel John R. Achor of the 99th Infantry Division later reported: "These men were courageous fighters and never once did they fail to accomplish their assigned mission."[28]

A moving force behind the integration of the Navy was James Forrestal. Early in 1944 he succeeded Frank Knox as Secretary of the Navy. Pressed like the Army for more men, in July 1944 Forrestal forced the Navy to abandon its segregated advanced-training facilities for black NCO's and early in 1945 basic-training facilities were also integrated. In August 1944 the Navy organized twenty-five auxiliary ships (oilers, tankers, and cargo vessels) manned by crews which were 10 percent black. In October 1944 the WAVES permitted blacks to enlist as officers and NCO's. In March 1944 twelve black officers and one warrant officer were graduated from the Great Lakes Naval Training Station—the first black naval officers in the history of the United States. These were the first among fifty-eight black naval officers commissioned during World War II (the Army commissioned 28,300 black officers, or 11.4 percent of its officer ranks). In the same year the Marines opened their enlistments to blacks and eventually 16,900 served in the Marine Corps. Nevertheless, 85 percent of the Navy's 165,000 black sailors were in the messmen's branch when the war ended.[29]

## The Postwar Period

Shortly after World War II the Army Chief of Staff, Dwight D. Eisenhower, established a board of senior military officers headed by General Alvar C. Gillem to examine how Negro troops should be utilized in the peacetime Army. The Gillem Board Report, entitled "The Utilization of Negro Manpower in the Postwar Army," was published March 4, 1946, and emphasized several points: 1) the maintenance of a 10 percent quota for black enlistments; 2) the future employment of black soldiers in segregated regimental-sized units or smaller; 3) the necessity to encourage an increase in the number of black officers; 4) the utilization of skilled black NCO's in white overhead and special units, thus permitting a limited amount of integration in noncombat units; 5) the assignment of black units to areas where sentiments were favorable to black troops; 6) the integration of on-base buses, recreational facilities, and officer messes, but only where this policy would not infringe on local customs.[30]

Despite the Gillem Board Report, which was hardly a revolutionary document, there was no appreciable change in the speed of military integration, in the pace of black officer recruitment, nor in the numbers of senior skilled black NCO's who found jobs in all-white units. And while both the 24th and 25th black Infantry Regiments were stationed in Japan, several smaller training units were posted in the South, a locale that caused many problems for black GI's.

In the postwar Navy, Secretary Forrestal was seriously convinced that integration was the right course for his department to follow and vigorously pushed it despite the doubts of senior naval officers. In December 1945 he issued an unequivocal policy statement to all ships and stations: "In the administration of naval personnel, no differentiation shall be made on the basis of race or color. This applies also to authorized personnel of all Armed Forces aboard Navy ships."[31] Despite Forrestal's deep personal commitment to a program of racial equality in the Navy, the hard fact remained that as of April 1946, out of the Navy's 19,102 blacks, 83 percent were still in the messmen's branch, only twenty-four were chief petty officers, and three were officers.

## Executive Order 9981 and the Fahy Committee

A major turning point in the Armed Forces racial policy came in 1948. After considerable black protest over the segregationist policies of the services[32] and after a strong civil rights plank had been written into the 1948 Democratic Convention (pushed through largely by the efforts of the young mayor of Minneapolis, Hubert H. Humphrey), President Harry Truman returned to the White House after the mid-July Democratic Convention and signed Executive Order 9981, July 26, 1948, which stated in the first paragraph:

> It is hereby declared to be the policy of the President that there shall be equality of treatment and opportunity for all persons in the armed services without regard to race, color, religion, or national origin. This policy shall be put into effect as rapidly as possible, having due regard to the time required to effectuate any necessary changes without impairing efficiency or morale.[33]

Official civilian policy thus for the first time in American history stood squarely behind an integrated defense establishment, but it was to take more than six years to implement the President's Order 9981. This important task was left to the President's Committee on Equality of Treatment and Opportunity in the Armed Forces (the Fahy Committee), chaired by Charles H. Fahy, a former U. S. Solicitor General.[34] Through the support of Louis B. Johnson, then Secretary of Defense, the Fahy Committee received detailed proposals from each of the Armed Services in 1949 for ending racial segregation and deadlines for implementing their integration plans.

The newly organized Department of the Air Force made the speediest response. After one meeting with the Fahy Committee, the Air Force on May 11, 1949, submitted its plan for integration including: 1) the breaking up of the major black unit, the 332nd Fighter Group at Lockbourne Field within ten days; 2) disbanding the few smaller black support units as soon as possible; 3) the elimination of the 10 percent ceiling on black enlistments; 4) the notification of all field commanders of the department's new policy with emphasis on the department's strong desire to have it carried out speedily; 5) a close monitoring of the progress of integration with completion of the integration process within one year. True to its word, the Air Force completed its program in less than twelve months.[35]

Although the Navy had been the first service to support an official policy of integration in 1945 under James Forrestal's leadership, four years later the department still had too many black stewards and too few black officers. Its report to the Fahy Committee on June 7 called for 1) the issuance of a clear policy statement on racial equality in the Navy for minorities; 2) a better-publicized effort to attract black officer and skilled NCO recruits; 3) an effort to encourage more black applicants for NROTC; 4) permission for men to transfer easily from the messmen's branch; 5) changing the rank of chief of stewards to the rank of chief petty officer; 6) elimination of segregated Marine Corps and Navy basic-training units. By May 1950, a year later, when the Fahy Committee completed its work, 52 percent of black sailors were serving outside the mess-men's branch and the number of Negro naval officers had quadrupled from four to seventeen. E. W. Kenworthy, the secretary to the Fahy Committee, wrote in *The New York Times* that the Navy's "obligation to make fair words good continues."[36]

The Army's five-point proposal for racial integration was not submitted to the Fahy Committee until October 1, 1949. It promised to: 1) abolish the 10 percent quota for blacks in the Army; 2) develop a new promotion system based upon competition without regard to race; 3) conduct ROTC summer-camp training on an integrated basis; 4) establish a board of Army officers to review policies toward blacks; 5) retain segregated units but give blacks an opportunity to attain skills and skilled positions in white units. Despite the efforts of the Fahy Committee and President Truman's Executive Order 9981, in May 1950 when the committee finished its work, the 60,000 black Army personnel were still for the most part in segregated units. Several of the Fahy Committee members despaired of ever being able to alter the Army's segregationist position,[37] though with the advent of the Korean War, the situation quickly changed.

### The Korean War

In 1949 as we saw above, the Army promised the Fahy Committee that it would abolish its racial quota of 10 percent for blacks. Thus at the start of the Korean War, black enlistments shot up to 25 percent of the total enlistments for July 1950 (in March the percentage had been 8.2). This rapid influx meant that the only way to maintain segregation was to place blacks in their own units, which were already over-manned, while white units were desperate for men. This hardly seemed logical. Thus one by one, local commanders—frequently at their own initiative and without decisive Pentagon guidance on the matter—integrated their units out of practical necessity to equalize the strength of their units. In August 1950 this situation first developed at Fort Jackson, South Carolina. Here the basic training unit found that it was "totally impractical to sort men out by race" and so integration proceeded as a pragmatic expedient. Soon all basic-training units were following Fort Jackson's example.[38]

The same pattern for integration developed in Korea. With the absence of racial quotas and the flood of new black soldiers, black units were staffed at overstrength while white regiments were begging for reinforcements. Furthermore, because there were comparatively few black combat units, whites were suffering a proportionately higher percentage of combat fatalities, which in turn increased the pressure both at the front and at home to equalize the fighting effort.[39] Thus by January 1951 the Eighth Army Headquarters in Korea had adopted an unofficial policy of integrating Negroes into understaffed white units. As historian S. L. A. Marshall, who witnessed these newly integrated units in action during the retreat from the Yalu River, observed: "In my opinion those integrated companies handled themselves as effectively and courageously as any companies in the war."[40]

Despite the successful performance of the integrated units in combat, it took considerable deliberation by senior Army officers and a major research effort under the direction of the Operations Research Office at Johns Hopkins University in 1951 (with the code name of Project CLEAR) to persuade the Army permanently to alter its official policy.[41] Finally on July 26, 1951, the Army announced publicly that it would integrate its entire Far Eastern Command in six months and that the black 24th Infantry Regiment was being disbanded. In December 1951 the U. S. Army commanders in Alaska and the United States were ordered by the Pentagon to proceed with orderly integration of their units, and on April 1, 1952, the same order was issued to U. S. commanders in Europe. By September 1953 90 percent of black personnel were serving in integrated units—and the number of black units had dropped from a high of 385 in June 1950 to 88. By October 31, 1954, integration of the U. S. Armed Services was officially completed—six years, three months, and five days after President Truman issued Executive Order 9981. As Richard Dalfiume noted, "A quiet racial revolution had occurred with practically no violence, bloodshed, or conflict."[42]

## BLACK AMERICANS IN THE U.S. ARMED FORCES: THE PRESENT

Historically, the black citizen in the U. S. Armed Forces has made the greatest progress in periods when strong civilian-defense leadership and wartime expansion of the military have been reinforced by effective black political action. The late 1940s and early 1950s saw such a period with the simultaneous emergence of commitment by the strong-minded Truman, Forrestal, and the Fahy Committee to a progressive racial policy; the rapid rise of troops during the Korean conflict; plus the decisive role the black community played in Truman's 1948 election victory. Conversely, during the eight years of the Eisenhower Administration (1952–60) these factors were absent; consequently there was relatively little serious effort to evaluate the remaining problems of race relations in the Armed Services.

The 1960s once again saw a juxtaposition of these three critical elements. First, President Kennedy's election was won by a hair's breadth in 1960. Kennedy received 49.7 percent of the popular vote as opposed to 46.6 percent for Richard Nixon. The Democratic victory largely depended upon carrying the major northern industrial states of New York, Pennsylvania, Ohio, Michigan, and Illinois. In all these states the black vote was crucial and Kennedy throughout his campaign made frequent promises to these voters that if elected he would make strong efforts in the civil rights field in their behalf. Similar pledges were made by President Lyndon Johnson four years later when he was swept into the White House with more than four-fifths of the black vote in his favor.

## The Gesell Committee

The important black support at the polls given to two Democratic Presidents brought in return strong initiatives in the field of military civil rights. In 1962 President Kennedy appointed Gerhard A. Gesell as chairman of the President's Committee on Equal Opportunity in the Armed Forces (the Gesell Committee).[43] After a year of careful investigation, the Gesell Committee discovered that black servicemen faced severe difficulties in finding adequate housing and integrated schools for their children near many military bases. Only half of the married servicemen could find on-base housing and the other half were therefore forced to live off-base. For black GI's, the Gesell Committee reported, off-base living frequently meant segregated quarters—often the most expensive, distant, and dilapidated. Furthermore, especially in the South, the children of black soldiers usually attended segregated and inferior schools. The *Initial Report* of the committee suggested that the Department of Defense use its full powers to eliminate the problems of segregated housing and schools near military posts. The *Final Report* further stressed that the Department of Defense must take the necessary steps to eliminate the final vestiges of segregation in the National Guard. The Gesell Committee had found several states, especially in the South, where there were either restrictions on black participation in National Guard units or token forms of integration. The *Final Report* emphasized that since 90 percent of Guard support came from the Federal Government, funds should be withdrawn from units that failed to comply with full integration. The Gesell Committee's recommendations were later repeated by the President's Commission on Civil Disorders (1968), which publicly lamented the fact that only 1.15 percent of the Army National Guard and 0.6 percent of the Air National Guard (the Navy has no Guard units) were black. Their conclusion was that urban racial unrest could have been better handled by a more racially representative National Guard.

## Secretary of Defense Robert McNamara

The seven-year tenure (1961–68) of Robert S. McNamara as Secretary of Defense proved him to be one of the strongest and perhaps most innovative men to hold that office since James Forrestal. McNamara, much like Forrestal, had a deep commitment to racial equality in the U. S. Armed Services and, particularly after the issuance of the Gesell Report, several policy statements emanated from his office underscoring this commitment. On July 26, 1963, for instance, one directive emphasized that: "Every military commander has the responsibility to oppose discriminatory practices affecting his own men and their dependents and to foster equal opportunity, not only in his own areas under his command but also in nearby communities where men live or gather in off-duty hours."[44] In order to stress the importance he placed on providing equal opportunity for all races in the military, McNamara set up the Office of Deputy Assistant Secretary of Defense for Civil Rights and Industrial Relations to oversee and monitor racial integration in the Armed Forces.[45]

Following the recommendations of the Gesell Committee, McNamara further moved to use the powers of the Department of Defense to eliminate segregated housing patterns from around Andrews Air Force Base in Washington, D. C. On July 1, 1967, the Secretary of Defense declared off limits all segregated housing in the area and ordered all military personnel at Andrews not to live or rent in segregated buildings within three miles of the base. The ban was later extended to the entire Washington, D. C. area and still later by Defense Secretary Clark Clifford to the entire United States and overseas.

In another bold move, McNamara introduced Project 100,000 on August 24, 1966, aimed at "salvaging" 100,000 men per year over a three-year period. These men had failed the Army Qualification Test and were rejected by the military as unfit for service, with the classification of 1-Y. McNamara's argument was that the defense establishment should use its educational facilities to train educationally disadvantaged youths in skills that could be beneficial to them as well as to the military.[46] Initially the "salvaging concept" met with considerable criticism from several quarters of the black community who saw it as a military ploy to fill the combat ranks in Vietnam with black troops. Said William Booth, chairman of the New York City Human Rights Commission: "The salvaging move was another attempt to get more Negroes in the Vietnam Conflict."[47] The late Congressman Adam Clayton Powell charged: "It's brutal. It's nothing more than killing off human beings that are not members of the elite."[48]

While the ultimate results of Project 100,000 are still being evaluated, one report has observed that between October 1966 and September 1969 246,000 men were inducted into the program—92 percent had previously been rejected for low mental test scores and 8 percent due to medical problems (mainly over- or underweight). Forty-one percent of these men were nonwhite. Statistics have shown that of those men participating in Project 100,000, 94.6 percent graduated from basic training; 90 percent received "good" or "excellent" supervisory ratings while in uniform; 12 percent were separated from the service for a variety of reasons; 6 percent signed on for another tour of duty; and of those with educational deficiencies, 80 percent completed a course to improve their reading skills and on the average advanced approximately two grade levels in reading ability (from the fourth to sixth grades). In a rather guarded statement on the results of the program, the report on the results of Project 100,000 concluded:

> As could be expected, the men brought in under reduced mental standards do not perform as well as a cross section of men with higher test scores and educational abilities. This is true on all measures—training attrition, promotion, supervisory ratings, disciplinary record, and attrition from service. The differences are not large and we feel they are acceptable when balanced against the military and social goals of the program.[49]

## The Vietnam War

If the actions of McNamara and the Gesell Committee reflected renewed commitment to the goals of racial equality on the part of defense leadership, their program was reinforced by the advent of the Vietnam War, which proved to be a major catalyst in stimulating black participation in all areas of military life. In contrast to World War II and Korea, black servicemen in Vietnam served in every type of unit and fought in every major battle, on land, on sea, and in the air. Vietnam was the first totally integrated war America fought, but perhaps, charge the critics, the war has been too integrated! As Stokely Carmichael of the Student Nonviolent Coordinating Committee and Floyd McKissick of the Congress of Racial Equality emphasized in 1967: "Black mercenaries of a white government are fighting against their colored brothers in Vietnam." They called on young blacks to resist the draft.[50]

Indeed at the start of the escalation of the Vietnam conflict in 1965–66, due largely to the local draft-board system and student deferments by which a disproportionate number of whites were exempted from the draft, black inductions rose to 16.5 percent while the casualty rate grew to 22.3 percent during the same period.[51] In several front-line combat units, blacks numbered from 30 to 60 percent of the ranks. However, after the introduction of the draft's lottery system, yearly black inductions fell to a figure representing their approximate percentage in the total population, 12.9 percent; and the total death rate for blacks in Vietnam (combat and noncombat) between 1961 and March 1972 similarly dropped to 12.7 percent.[52] Nevertheless, black representation in many elite combat units remained disproportionately high; some authorities have speculated that the special bonuses received for volunteering for these units as well as the extra pay awarded for reenlistments results in inducing more blacks, particularly from low-income backgrounds, to join up. Whether or not this is their true motivation, the distribution of Negroes throughout the Armed Forces today is clearly uneven.

## The Distribution of Black Servicemen

Compared to many civilian professions, statistics place the Armed Forces in a favorable position in providing career opportunities for blacks. While blacks make up about 2 percent of America's practicing physicians, 1 percent of lawyers, and less than 1 percent of engineers, they currently represent 2.3 percent of the officer ranks and 12.1 percent of the enlisted men in the Armed Forces (see Tables I, II, and III). During the last two decades their percentage in all the services has steadily climbed. In 1949 only 7.5 percent of the enlisted ranks and 0.9 of the officers were black. Between 1949 and 1971 the percentage of black officers in the Navy rose from almost 0.0 percent to 0.8 percent (1.33 percent in 1975); in the Marines from 0.0 percent to 1.3 percent; in the Air Force from 0.6 to 1.7 percent; and in the Army from 1.8 to 4.2 percent. The enlisted ranks have experienced a similar increase during the last twenty years: the Navy from 4.7 to 5.7 percent; Marines from 2.1 to 12.3 percent; Air Force from 5.1 to 12.5 percent and the Army from 12.4 to 15.6 percent. As Table IV points out, the reenlistment rates for career-enlisted personnel have with minor exceptions consistently been higher for black NCO's and the first-term reenlistment rates have been normally two to three times higher for blacks compared to white soldiers[53]—good indicators of a higher sustained interest by Negroes in pursuing military careers.

### TABLE I—BLACK PARTICIPATION IN THE ARMED FORCES BY GRADE
(Enlisted)
1949, 1965, 1971
ALL SERVICES

| Grade | 1949 | | | 1965 | | | 1971 | | |
|---|---|---|---|---|---|---|---|---|---|
| | Total | Black | % | Total | Black | % | Total | Black | % |
| E-9 | | | | 14,041 | 289 | 2.1 | 15,165 | 638 | 4.2 |
| E-8 | | | | 36,082 | 1,443 | 4.0 | 38,800 | 3,065 | 7.9 |
| E-7 | 99,271 | 2,149 | 2.2 | 114,621 | 6,218 | 5.4 | 147,761 | 17,037 | 11.5 |
| E-6 | 93,599 | 3,703 | 4.0 | 230,463 | 20,773 | 9.0 | 264,826 | 37,662 | 14.2 |
| E-5 | 150,444 | 8,677 | 5.8 | 406,091 | 51,706 | 12.7 | 402,945 | 48,302 | 12.0 |
| E-4 | 212,581 | 16,867 | 7.9 | 460,653 | 54,030 | 11.7 | 529,694 | 53,910 | 10.2 |
| E-3 | 314,258 | 31,165 | 9.9 | 535,530 | 56,963 | 10.6 | 391,306 | 44,109 | 11.3 |
| E-2 | 436,258 | 30,033 | 6.9 | 376,555 | 40,627 | 10.8 | 225,470 | 34,809 | 15.4 |
| E-1 | 109,604 | 12,901 | 11.8 | 304,767 | 28,703 | 9.4 | 129,060 | 19,497 | 15.1 |
| Total | 1,416,051 | 105,495 | 7.5 | 2,478,803 | 260,752 | 10.5 | 2,145,027 | 259,029 | 12.1 |

Source: Office of Equal Opportunity, U. S. Department of Defense, Washington, D.C.

### TABLE II—BLACK PARTICIPATION IN THE ARMED FORCES BY GRADE
(Officer)
1949, 1965, 1971
ALL SERVICES

| Grade | 1949 | | | 1965 | | | 1971 | | |
|---|---|---|---|---|---|---|---|---|---|
| | Total | Black | % | Total | Black | % | Total | Black | % |
| 0-7 and above (General or Flag) | 864 | 0 | 0.0 | 1,310 | 1 | .1 | 1,336 | 11 | .8 |
| 0-6 (Colonel) | 7,816 | 2 | 0.02 | 16,430 | 25 | .2 | 17,349 | 119 | .7 |
| 0-5 (Lt. Colonel) | 17,392 | 14 | 0.1 | 34,743 | 238 | .7 | 39,607 | 941 | 2.4 |
| 0-4 (Major) | 25,955 | 56 | 0.2 | 57,697 | 1,050 | 1.8 | 62,764 | 1,567 | 2.5 |
| 0-3 (Captain) | 52,112 | 333 | 0.6 | 105,742 | 2,634 | 2.5 | 124,314 | 2,998 | 2.4 |
| 0-2 (1st Lieutenant) | 59,523 | 919 | 1.5 | 59,124 | 1,112 | 1.9 | 56,329 | 1,026 | 1.8 |
| 0-1 (2nd Lieutenant) | 15,987 | 250 | 1.6 | 46,783 | 951 | 2.0 | 33,251 | 605 | 1.8 |
| WO (Warrant Officer) | 10,699 | 63 | 0.7 | 16,178 | 340 | 2.1 | 23,876 | 881 | 3.7 |
| Total | 190,348 | 1,637 | 0.9 | 337,998 | 6,351 | 1.9 | 358,826 | 8,141 | 2.3 |

Source: Office of Equal Opportunity, U. S. Department of Defense, Washington, D.C.

**TABLE III—NUMBER AND PERCENTAGE OF BLACKS IN THE ARMED FORCES**
As of December 31, 1971

### Air Force

| Officers | | Enlisted | |
|---|---|---|---|
| Total | 125,214 | Total | 624,595 |
| Black | 2,137 | Black | 78,070 |
| Percent Black | 1.7 | Percent Black | 12.5 |

### Army

| Officers | | Enlisted | |
|---|---|---|---|
| Total | 138,706 | Total | 823,741 |
| Black | 5,161 | Black | 129,146 |
| Percent Black | 4.2 | Percent Black | 15.6 |

### Navy

| Officers | | Enlisted | |
|---|---|---|---|
| Total | 74,885 | Total | 520,048 |
| Black | 576 | Black | 30,043 |
| Percent Black | 0.8* | Percent Black | 5.7** |

### Marine Corps

| Officers | | Enlisted | |
|---|---|---|---|
| Total | 20,022 | Total | 176,643 |
| Black | 267 | Black | 21,769 |
| Percent Black | 1.3 | Percent Black | 12.3 |

*This figure was 1.3 percent in March, 1975, according to the Assistant Chief of Naval Personnel for Human Goals.
**This percentage had risen to 8.6 by early 1975.

Source:   Office of Equal Opportunity, U.S. Department of Defense, Washington, D.C.

**TABLE IV—REENLISTMENT RATE FOR CAREER ENLISTED PERSONNEL**
As of the end of each Calendar Year

| Year* | Air Force | | Army | | Navy | | Marine Corps | |
|---|---|---|---|---|---|---|---|---|
| | White | Black | White | Black | White | Black | White | Black |
| 1965 | 88.9 | 92.2 | 80.7 | 96.9 | 89.6 | 93.4 | 87.7 | 92.3 |
| 1966 | 88.3 | 91.4 | 74.1 | 92.2 | 85.1 | 82.7 | 80.7 | 80.1 |
| 1967 | 86.8 | 88.8 | 69.3 | 83.0 | 78.2 | 85.1 | 77.7 | 83.3 |
| 1968 | 87.5 | 88.7 | 66.4 | 71.7 | 79.5 | 85.8 | 78.1 | 81.8 |
| 1969 | 86.6 | 87.9 | 62.9 | 72.9 | 77.0 | 83.1 | 73.5 | 80.9 |
| 1970 | 87.5 | 88.4 | 38.3 | 42.6 | 87.2 | 93.8 | 80.7 | 83.3 |
| 1971 | 92.5 | 93.4 | 32.5 | 39.1 | 89.9 | 94.4 | 78.0 | 80.2 |

*Reenlistment rates by race are not available prior to 1965.

Source:   Office of Equal Opportunity, U. S. Department of Defense, Washington, D.C.

However, the pattern of distribution of black service personnel presents a less favorable picture. As Tables II and V illustrate, there are only 11 (or 0.8 percent) black officers of general or flag rank. The services point out, however, that this is a substantial jump from even six years ago, when there was only one black general, Brigadier General Benjamin O. Davis, Jr. of the Air Force. Curiously, at the captain, major, and lieutenant colonel ranks an average of 2.5 percent are black while the percentage dips noticeably to 1.8 among lieutenants. Some knowledgeable observers attribute this decline in junior officers to the unpopularity of the military and the Vietnam War among black college youth. Similarly, in the NCO ranks there is a shortage of blacks at the E-9 grade (see Table I) but a strong representation at all other levels, E-1 through E-8.

### TABLE V—BLACK GENERAL OFFICERS IN THE ARMED FORCES

| Army | Date of Rank |
| --- | --- |
| Major General Frederic Davison | October 1, 1968 |
| Brigadier General Roscoe Cartwright | July 28, 1971 |
| Brigadier General Oliver Dillard | January 19, 1972 |
| Brigadier General James Hamlet | August 23, 1971 |
| Brigadier General George M. Shuffer, Jr. | June 7, 1972 |
| Brigadier General Harry W. Brooks, Jr. | June 7, 1972 |
| Brigadier General Edward Greer | June 7, 1972 |
| Brigadier General Julius W. Becton, Jr. | June 7, 1972 |
| Brigadier General Arthur J. Gregg | June 7, 1972 |
| Air Force | |
| Brigadier General Daniel James, Jr. | |
| Nominated to Four-Star General on: | July 16, 1975 |
| Colonel Lucius Theus | |
| Nominated to Brigadier General on: | January 27, 1972 |
| Navy | |
| Rear Admiral Samuel Gravely | July 1, 1971 |
| Marine Corps | |
| Lieutenant Colonel Frank E. Peterson, Jr. | October 1, 1967 |
| Highest ranking Marine Corps black officer. | |

### HIGHEST RANKING BLACK WOMEN IN THE ARMED FORCES

| Army | |
| --- | --- |
| Colonel Martha E. Cleveland | January 1, 1972 |
| Navy | |
| Commander Hazel T. McCree | January 1, 1968 |
| Air Force | |
| Lieutenant Colonel Joyce E. Summers | May 9, 1968 |
| Marine Corps | |
| Captain Gloria E. Smith | March 1, 1971 |

Source:   Office of Equal Opportunity, U. S. Department of Defense, Washington, D.C.

A prime means of increasing the number of professional black officers is through the service academies. There are approximately 9,800 cadets at these schools (3,000 at West Point; 4,000 at Annapolis; and 2,800 at the Air Force Academy), but among the 1972 graduating classes at the three schools there were only twenty-four blacks, less than 1 percent of the total graduates. As Table VI indicates, the numbers of black graduates have remained fairly constant during the last decade with the marked exception of the

1972 Naval Academy class which jumped to thirteen after an intensive recruiting drive in recent years was inaugurated by the Department of Defense. It should be noted that the entering classes in 1973 and 1974 each had 7.0 percent black members, as contrasted with 1.7 percent in 1970. However, since 1966 the service academies have graduated a total of 103 blacks, or more than half of the total number of blacks to complete their education at these schools (189 since 1887). Hence the trend is decidedly upward and should continue to increase, particularly as the number of black Congressmen continues to grow (four-fifths of service-academy appointments come from individual Congressmen).

#### TABLE VI—BLACK GRADUATES FROM MILITARY ACADEMIES

| Year | U. S. Military Academy | U. S. Naval Academy | U. S. Air Force Academy |
|------|------------------------|---------------------|-------------------------|
| 1960 | 1 | 0 | 0 |
| 1961 | 2 | 3 | 0 |
| 1962 | 1 | 2 | 0 |
| 1963 | 4 | 1 | 3 |
| 1964 | 2 | 4 | 1 |
| 1965 | 4 | 3 | 4 |
| 1966 | 3 | 0 | 0 |
| 1967 | 2 | 2 | 1 |
| 1968 | 9 | 4 | 6 |
| 1969 | 8 | 2 | 6 |
| 1970 | 7 | 6 | 8 |
| 1971 | 3 | 3 | 9 |
| 1972 | 8 | 13 | 3 |

Source :    Office of Equal Opportunity, U. S. Department of Defense, Washington, D.C.

Another important source of black officer recruitment is through ROTC training programs on college campuses. The Army and Air Force each operates fifteen ROTC units at predominantly black colleges, and the Navy has opened five since 1968.[54] In 1971 the Department of Defense undertook a major effort to attract more black officers by encouraging several black colleges to start ROTC programs; by setting up minority officer-recruiting offices in several major urban areas; by establishing several new junior ROTC programs in nonwhite high schools and by granting seventy-five three-year senior ROTC scholarships to underprivileged youths in colleges.[55] It is too early to evaluate the impact of this intensive minority officer-recruitment program, but if the program is vigorously pursued, the next five years should clearly witness a further increase of nonwhite officers.

Despite the upward trend in percentages of black officers, the problems of keeping young Negroes in the officer ranks will nevertheless remain a serious one for the Defense Department, particularly because of the keen talent hunt for qualified blacks by private industry. As was previously pointed out, there has been a marked drop in the percentages of junior black officers, attributable in part to the current unpopularity of the military but also to the better opportunities open to young blacks with skills in civilian life. As one black Air Force major recently emphasized: "Blacks just aren't coming in, because the opportunities are better on the outside—better chances for advancement. Yesterday the military was where it was at. It is the reverse now."[56] Perhaps with the end of the Vietnam conflict, plus an increase in the number of black college graduates and a general tightening of the American economy, the near future will see a reversal of this downward trend of junior-officer recruitment. However, the conversion to a peacetime military will put serious pressure on the services to reduce the numbers of senior positions, thus slowing down advancement of blacks and whites alike, which would be a further incentive for skilled nonwhites to leave the military.

As Table I indicates, nonwhites are fairly well represented in the NCO ranks from the E-1 to E-8 levels; however, there is a significant imbalance of black NCO's in the "combat arms and supply branches" and "the technical specialties." A 1971 Defense Department survey reported (see Table VII) that of black NCO's with 19 to 24 months of service, 36 percent are in the infantry and 20.8 percent in service and supply units, while only 1.1 percent are found in technical or allied fields, 5.5 percent in communications and intelligence, and 3.6 percent in medical and dental units. As Frank Render, former Deputy Assistant Secretary of Defense, pointed out: "Statistics indicate that there are some obvious discrepancies in numbers and percentages of blacks and their distribution at various levels, even when comparing individuals with similar records and equal time in service."[57]

**TABLE VII—ARMY ENLISTED PERSONNEL BY OCCUPATIONAL SPECIALTY AND BY RACE**

| | Personnel with: | | | |
| --- | --- | --- | --- | --- |
| | 19-24 Months Service | | 34-36 Months Service | |
| Army Occupational Area | % White | % Black | % White | % Black |
| 0 Infantry | 29.7 | 36.0 | 12.0 | 22.1 |
| 1 Elec. Equip. Repair | 3.2 | 2.5 | 12.3 | 6.9 |
| 2 Comm. & Intell. | 9.2 | 5.5 | 5.9 | 4.6 |
| 3 Medical & Dental | 5.0 | 3.6 | 4.2 | 4.4 |
| 4 Tech. & Allied | 2.4 | 1.1 | 3.1 | 1.1 |
| 5 Admin. | 18.6 | 15.5 | 24.4 | 27.3 |
| 6 Elec./Mech. Repair | 12.0 | 11.8 | 22.8 | 17.8 |
| 7 Craftsmen | 3.1 | 3.2 | 6.0 | 3.9 |
| 8 Service and Supply | 16.8 | 20.8 | 9.3 | 11.9 |
| | 100.0 | 100.0 | 100.0 | 100.0 |

Source:   Office of Equal Opportunity, U. S. Department of Defense, Washington, D.C.

The chief difficulty in remedying this imbalance is that assignments in NCO occupational specialties are based upon scores on the Armed Forces Qualifications Test (AFQT). Among military NCO's with 19 to 24 months of service, about 23 percent of whites had scores of 30 or below on the AFQT while 72 percent of black recruits in 1971 fell into the same category. A high percentage of low scorers end up in the "soft-core fields," such as infantry, administration, and supply, while the "hard-core areas," or technical occupations, attract the higher-scoring individuals. This selection system helps to explain why a higher percentage of blacks wind up in the combat arms, hence in the front lines in Vietnam. Since higher pay and swifter promotions normally go along with the "hard-core specialties," there has in recent years been significant disenchantment in progressive circles with the AFQT.

In an interesting analysis of this problem by a special NAACP study committee, it was recommended that the Armed Services adopt a "Philadelphia Plan" that would retrain numbers of black servicemen for the "hard-core fields" as well as thoroughly reexamining the AFQT.[58] A recent Congressional Black Caucus Report on the problem made similar recommendations.[59] At present the Defense Department is in fact involved in such a reexamination with a view to initiating reforms in testing procedures in the near future.

A serious problem for black prospective enlisted men in the early 1970s was the trend toward increasing selectivity on the part of the armed services, which turned down men who in years past would have been granted moral waivers to enlist. In April 1971, for example, 6 percent of the Army enlistees for that month had moral waivers as compared with less than 1 percent for April 1972. For the youth from the ghetto who runs a higher risk of some involvement with the law, it appeared that this selectivity would close off career opportunities for many young blacks. However, as the armed services were transformed into an all-volunteer military, this trend was reversed, thus keeping military career possibilities available for the disadvantaged.

## The National Guard

The Army and Air National Guard operates under the command of the fifty state governors and adjutants general (the District of Columbia also has a Guard unit), except in times of war or national emergency, when the President is authorized to take control of the Guard. Thus normally the Guard is a state responsibility, fulfilling state needs in times of civil disorders or natural disasters. However, the Guard has quasi-federal responsibilities as well, since it can be placed under the President's authority in emergencies. Also, Article I of the U. S. Constitution authorizes Congress to help finance Guard units; presently approximately 90 percent of funds for Guard operations comes from the federal treasury to support the 404,000 men in the Army National Guard and 77,000 men in the Air National Guard.

As of 1970 there were 5,487 blacks in the Army and Air Guard or about 1.15 percent of its total strength, a slight drop from 1.18 percent in 1969. The Army Guard in 1970 was 1.24 percent black compared to 0.76 percent in the Air Guard. Unlike the Regular Army and Air Force with their high overall black participation, the National Guard has been criticized by both the Gesell Committee and the National Commission on Civil Disorders for its traditionally low black participation, its token numbers of black officers (fewer than thirty states have black Guard officers), and its especially small number of blacks in southern Guard units (in the eleven states of the Deep South, only 0.4 percent of the 122,000 Guardsmen are black). Generally, northern industrial states have the largest representation of blacks in their units, while rural southern and midwestern regions have the lowest percentages. The eight Guard units with the highest percentages of black participation (in descending order) are the District of Columbia (26 percent), Illinois (6 percent), New Jersey (5 percent), Maryland (4 percent), Delaware (2 percent), New York (2 percent), Pennsylvania (2 percent), and California (2 percent).

Much like the regular Armed Services, many states barred blacks from Guard service until after World War II, and it was not until 1963 that the last state, North Carolina, removed its ban on black participation. This still recent exclusionist stand on the part of many southern states helps to explain why so few nonwhites are found today in the ranks of their units. In addition, a 1968 survey of 1,052 blacks in fifty-three areas of the country showed that minorities have a generally adverse image of the Guard, partly because of its role in riots and demonstrations and partly from a feeling that National Guard units are discriminatory.[60] This attitude differs sharply from the sentiment toward the regular Armed Forces in the black community. William Brink and Louis Harris in 1966 asked a representative cross section of 1,059 blacks, "How would you rate the Army, Navy, Marine Corps, and Air Force as a place for a young man to serve?"[61] An average of 50 to 60 percent rated the services either "excellent" or "very good" while less than 5 percent saw them as "a poor place."

From time to time it has been suggested that federal funds should be withheld from Guard units that display "tokenism" or "discrimination" in their recruitment and promotion practices. However logical this proposal may sound, the realities of the powerful political influence of the National Guard in Washington, D. C. makes such budget cuts difficult, if not impossible.[62] A more promising approach to increasing black enlistments in the Guard was exhibited by New Jersey four years ago. After a summer of bloody urban riots, the New Jersey Guard in 1968 was authorized at a temporary overstrength of 5 percent—865 vacancies—and made an intensive drive for black recruits, giving them special priorities for enlistment despite the long waiting lists for spaces in Guard units due to the Vietnam conflict. The results of this intensive effort were that the New Jersey Guard in three months nearly tripled its number of blacks in uniform from 315 to 850 (or a percentage increase from 2.5 to 6.4 of its total strength).

The success of the New Jersey experiment prompted the Department of Defense in 1968 to propose a similar program for the entire National Guard. It was estimated that raising the percentage of Negroes in the Guard to 11 percent by 1971 would cost $177 million; but the proposal was trimmed to a modest 4 percent increase costing $20 million over three years. Congress, however, was reluctant to accept the proposal because of the expenditures involved as well as the concern that such an action might be seen as "discrimination in reverse." Nevertheless, the New Jersey experiment did seem to prove that an intensive recruiting drive for blacks could quickly raise their percentages in Guard units—despite the generally negative image of the Guard in the black community.

## On-Base Racial Tensions

Like American society in general, the U. S. Armed Forces in the last decade have been troubled by racial incidents. These have occurred both in overseas assignments such as Tiensha and Longbinh, Vietnam; Heidelberg, Germany; Rota, Spain; and in stateside areas including Fort Bragg, North Carolina; Fort Knox, Kentucky; Kaneohe Marine Air Station in Honolulu; and Camp Lejeune, North Carolina; as well as aboard ships at sea as on the U. S. S. *Kitty Hawk* and U. S. S. *Constellation*. Both the July 20, 1969, Marine Corps Camp Lejeune disturbances and those aboard the U. S. S. *Kitty Hawk* and U. S. S. *Constellation* (which took place October 12, 1972, and November 3–4, 1972, respectively) received considerable public attention and ultimately warranted in both cases special congressional investigations.

In the case of the Camp Lejeune unrest, while drinking and competition for women at an evening party were the immediate causes of the disturbances that left fifteen Marines injured and one dead, as a special House Subcommittee that later investigated the situation pointed out, the new awareness of black identity and the striving for self-determination on the part of young blacks was also a major contributing cause of the troubles.[63] Racial slurs and evidence of prejudice were no longer likely to go unchallenged by young black Marines. Another important factor that precipitated the trouble was a general breakdown in communications, leadership, and discipline at the camp—particularly at the junior officer and senior NCO levels. As the House Subcommittee discovered:

> There was some tendency to shy away from leadership and disciplinary problems when race was a consideration. On occasion, it was overreaction to a fear of being labeled a racist or being charged with discrimination. In other cases, the white NCO or junior officer would refer a matter involving race to a black Marine or to a black NCO or officer. Of course, this reaction is unfortunate and does dilute leadership and shows inexperience in leadership.[64]

The House Subcommittee further cited the general laxity of security around the post despite the repeated warnings of a possible riot.

Three years later racial disturbances which injured nearly 100 sailors aboard the U. S. S. *Kitty Hawk* and U. S. S. *Constellation* made news headlines and once again a special House Subcommittee investigation was undertaken. The House Subcommittee report found many of the same causes for racial troubles that had been discovered in the earlier Lejeune report. Both shipboard incidents were sparked by a small minority of sailors, particularly militant young blacks, who had "perceived" flagrant racial discrimination on the part of their white comrades and superiors. The House Subcommittee found a breakdown in communications, especially in terms of adequate counseling for new recruits:

> Once a new seaman reports to a division, there is too little individual contact between him and his immediate supervisors, the petty officers and junior officers assigned to that division. Too frequently the seaman is not counseled regarding his performance ratings, even if they are low. There is also a failure to effectively explain to him any opportunities he has for advancement and the steps he should take to achieve promotions. As a result, the young seaman sometimes becomes frustrated concerning his future as he performs unskilled laborers' jobs on a continuing basis.

This frustration is exacerbated by the tendency of Navy recruiting advertisements "to promise more than the Navy is able to deliver." Similar to the Lejeune investigations, the report on the *Kitty Hawk* and *Constellation* disturbances detected "a failure in the middle management area in that there has been a reluctance to utilize the command authority inherent in those positions." Nor was there, in the words of the special House Subcommittee, "proper precautionary action to prevent their [the racial disturbances] occurrence or to deal with such actions when they occurred."

Through several, often bold, approaches, since 1969 the Armed Forces have attempted to reduce the likelihood of racial tensions on bases. On September 3, 1969, General Leonard F. Chapman, the Marine Corps Commandant, issued a message to all Marine commands calling for an end to racial violence and a renewed effort to end discrimination against Negroes. The message contained several concessions to black soldiers: the Afro haircut was permitted if neatly trimmed, and blacks would be allowed to give the "black power clenched fist salute" as long as it did not "suggest direct defiance of duly constituted authority."[65] Soul music, soul food, ethnic literature and cosmetics were to be provided at PX's and service clubs,[66] and promotion and grievance procedures were to be reviewed to insure that no unfair treatment was exhibited against blacks. Shortly after General Chapman's order, the Army, Navy, and Air Force issued similar statements permitting concessions to the rights of blacks, thus paving the way for greater cultural diversity within the services. Some units like the Americal Division set up "hot lines" and "watch committees" for rapid communication of grievances between black NCO's and senior staff officers and others have established human relations committees, human rights officers, and sensitivity training sessions for black and white NCO's and junior officers. A number of military commanders, such as Major General Ryan at Camp Lejeune, have issued direct orders banning all racial slurs and have prepared pamphlets for unit leaders on ways to cope with racial problems in their commands. The recent appointment of a black general, Frederic Davison, as commander of U. S. Army forces in Europe was also a very important step in emphasizing the military commitment to racial equality.

Perhaps the most obvious symbol of a renewed emphasis on dealing with on-post racial tensions came May 11, 1972, at Patrick Air Force Base, Florida, where Secretary of Defense Melvin Laird dedicated the Defense Race Relations Institute. The institute, with 44 civilian and military faculty members, is designed to train 1,400 instructors for the Armed Services in six-week sessions, with 100 students per session. These instructors in turn are to teach and train others to teach the six-semester-hour course in race relations required for all personnel in uniform (a yearly six-hour refresher course in the subject is also obligatory). As L. Howard Bennett, former Deputy Assistant Secretary for Civil Rights and Industrial Relations, predicted:

> We will have some 2.5 million Americans in the military undergoing repeated study of how to solve racial problems. This must have some impact on the civilian society because there has never before been a widespread systematic educational attack on America's most pressing problems.[67]

Another strong measure designed to attack military racism was announced in May 1971. Thereafter, future Army, Navy, and Air Force officer fitness reports will include ratings on the individual's racial attitudes and his commitment to equal treatment for minorities.[68]

### Off-Post Housing Discrimination

A recent NAACP report called housing "without question, the most pervasive problem confronting black soldiers. At every installation we visited," the study group indicated, "black soldiers of all ranks mentioned housing as a major grievance."[69]

Finding suitable housing at the average military post is indeed a problem for non-whites. At the average base, one-half of the married personnel live off-post because of the shortage of on-base housing. Until the 1960s the traditional military policy was one of accommodation to the discriminatory housing patterns of local communities. This policy changed in 1963 when the Gesell Committee documented the extent of discriminatory housing near military bases and showed how, in turn, local segregation impinged upon internal base operations. Yet a later study in 1967 reported that only 31 percent of housing surrounding military bases was certified in writing as "open to all races."

Thus in April 1967 the Defense Department began a concerted attack on this problem. The Pentagon ordered all commanders to take a census of multiple dwelling units in their areas and to submit monthly status reports of their efforts to end housing discrimination. Metropolitan Washington, D. C. was selected as a "model area" for intensified housing efforts; and on July 1, 1967, Secretary McNamara banned all military personnel from entering into any new contracts or rental arrangements with landlords who practice discrimination. Secretary Clark Clifford later extended these sanctions to the entire United States and abroad. As of January 1, 1972, of the more than two million rental facilities surveyed by the Defense Department, statistics show that 98 percent are "listed" in the base housing referral service—meaning that the facility has produced written assurance of an open-housing policy, or a signed certificate has been issued by the post commander that adequate assurance of nondiscriminatory policies was received. Individual state-by-state breakdowns show a uniformly high percentage of such listings, even in Deep South states like Alabama, with 98.9 percent of rental units "listed"; Georgia, with 97.8 percent; and Mississippi, with 98.4 percent. Nineteen states rate 100 percent "listed."[70]

Unfortunately, despite the impressive effort and array of statistics frequently cited by the Defense Department to back their claim of having opened up housing for non-white soldiers and their families, in reality off-post housing patterns have not substantially been altered since 1967. The Department of Defense can show few instances where its actions have made significant progress in integrating civilian communities. There are several reasons for the failure of its housing program: first, signed or verbal promises from landlords can be and are easily broken in practice. As David Sutton in his perceptive essay on this problem has pointed out:

> At a base in Georgia which has reported 100 percent open housing in off-base housing facilities, the housing officer said that although the housing program had been in effect about a year, he did not know of any Negro airmen who had moved into a previously all-white housing area or facility. In the adjacent host community, a major real estate dealer told this writer he would not rent or sell a place in a white neighborhood to a Negro even though he had signed the open housing pledges.[71]

There are simply too many ways landlords can evade selling to nonwhite servicemen —even if they are "listed" with the base housing office—as a recent NAACP report pointed out:

> Several soldiers told us how they had arranged by phone to see vacant apartments listed at the Housing Office. When they appeared in person, the landlord told them that the apartment had been rented. Subsequently, they would continue to see the apartment listed at the housing office.[72]

Furthermore, there is no necessity for local real estate agents to be "listed" with the base housing office. In fact, in many areas of the country and overseas, housing is already so scarce that military business is not of great importance to these firms. Thus if they want to discriminate openly, they can simply bypass the base housing office altogether, knowing full well that there will still be abundant demand for their services.

Finally, even if a landlord who has signed an "open housing pledge" clearly breaks his agreement, placing such housing on an "off limits" list involves a lengthy bureaucratic process—a process that few military commanders are willing to undertake for fear of jeopardizing relationships in the neighboring community. Again to quote Sutton:

> While local leaders may assist a commander in receiving a promotion or a job after retirement they may also cost him his position or adversely affect his career if he upsets them, since a harmonious base-community relationship is often taken as a sign of an effective and successful tour of duty without "disturbances." Further, they know that complaints by local people to their congressional representatives may cause reverberations throughout the command and possibly result in [the officer's] being sacrificed even though the trouble arose because [he was] carrying out official policy.[73]

Sutton's analysis helps to explain why few requests have ever been received or processed by the Defense Department for sanctioning unfair treatment by landlords. The Pentagon's program of "listing" open housing is backed up by few tangible punishments for violators—a fact of which many landlords are aware.

Today adequate housing remains the issue that hits the black serviceman and his family the hardest, and although the Department of Defense has since 1967 put considerable effort into issuing directives and guidelines to make its "listing" program workable, tangible results have been slow to come, and the question needs careful reconsideration. Indeed, a wiser policy for the Pentagon to pursue might be simply to build more on-base housing units—particularly in areas where many families are presently forced to live off-post. Doubling the quarters allowances for officers and enlisted personnel living off-base might also serve as an effective incentive for home-building firms situated near military bases to construct new—and hopefully integrated—homes for servicemen. However, neither of these alternatives is likely in the post-Vietnam days of declining defense appropriations.

## The Military Judicial System

The military system of justice is so complex that it is really understood only by the relatively few who are experts in military law. Nevertheless, its essential framework can be grasped by the layman. Basically, the military system of justice operates on two levels: judicial and nonjudicial action. Judicial action embraces primarily the military court system and court-martial process while the nonjudicial system—where most military justice is dispensed—involves the administration of discipline at the company level by military officers. Both judicial and nonjudicial punishments are prescribed in the regulations set forth under the Uniform Code of Military Justice in the Manual for Courts-Martial, and with minor exceptions these regulations are the same for all five uniformed services—Army, Navy, Air Force, Marines, and Coast Guard.

Judicial punishments consist of either confinement or less-than-honorable discharges or frequently a combination of the two types of punishments such as a short or suspended sentence along with a less-than-honorable discharge. There are three types of administrative discharges, of which two are less than honorable, and two types of punitive discharges, both of which are less than honorable. The administrative discharges include 1) an "honorable discharge" for individuals who perform well in uniform and are therefore entitled to all veterans' benefits; 2) a "general discharge" issued for adequate though undistinguished job performance, which entitles the holder to normal veterans' benefits; and 3) an "undesirable discharge" or a discharge under other than honorable conditions which prevents reenlistment into the service and, depending on the cause and severity of the crime, can disqualify an individual for veterans' benefits. These three types of administrative action can be undertaken by military authorities without convening formal judicial hearings, although new regulations which are expected to take effect in

1976 will require more stringent procedures governing military commanders' issuance of other than honorable discharges. The requirement of convening a hearing board, allowing defendants to have the right of counsel, and permitting defendants to cross examine and to submit depositions, are among these new procedures.

The two types of punitive discharges are given by convening courts-martial and include both a discharge for "bad conduct" and a "dishonorable discharge." The difference between these two sentences in reality turns very much on the particular judgment of the individual court involving what they regard to be the degree of severity of the effense; for example, desertion in peacetime may merit only a "bad conduct" court-martial while desertion under fire in wartime would very likely be cause for a dishonorable court-martial. The two types of punitive discharges are given only by conviction by a court-martial, a formal and rather complex judicial proceeding which normally results in separation from service without the right to receive veterans' benefits. Increasingly, however, those convicted by a court-martial of less severe crimes either serve a suspended sentence, are sent to a rehabilitation unit, or both.

Officially, the rules governing the military judicial systems do not consider pretrial confinement as a form of punishment, but as simply a convenient means for holding for trial a serviceman who has committed an offense in order to prevent him from going AWOL; nevertheless, in practice, it is frequently used as a means of punishment. Individuals placed in pretrial confinement can be held up to thirty days without the filing of any formal charges against them; if authorities wish to hold a man longer his confinement can be extended another thirty days by a request from the commanding officer, with no need to serve formal notice to the prisoner. Recent surveys of military disciplinary barracks and stockades show that pretrial confinement is a fairly common form of punishment, since nearly one-third of those released from stockades in 1971 had had no formal charges filed against them.

The criticism of the military system of justice by blacks—both inside and outside the military—tends to center on the disproportionate share of punishments that they receive in comparison to whites, under both the judicial and nonjudicial processes. Statistics show that between 25 and 33 percent of those receiving nonjudicial punishment are nonwhite; about half held under pretrial confinement are black; and in terms of judicial punishments, Air Force figures for the first six months of 1972 show that 28.9 percent of those discharged under less-than-honorable conditions were black and that in 1971 between 33 and 63 percent serving in military prisons for specific offenses were black (see Table VIII).

After a careful investigation of these problems, an NAACP Study Group in 1971 recommended that the military tighten its present rather informal standards of issuing nonjudicial punishment and pretrial confinements for exacting punishments, so as better to protect the civil liberties of both white and nonwhite servicemen. In particular, they emphasized that the Armed Services should guarantee its men the right to counsel when facing judicial or nonjudicial punishment. The Study Group further noted that only one of the forty full-time military judges serving in Europe was black and that in 1971 there was not one nonwhite JAG Captain (Army law officer). The NAACP recommended an intensive program to increase black representation among military judges and JAG officers; also that the services contract for individual lawyers and law students to provide legal counsel to minority servicemen, both abroad and at home.[74] On May 15, 1972, a Congressional Black Caucus Report made similar recommendations concerning the reform of the Uniform Code of Military Justice as well as the expansion of minority legal services in the Armed Forces.[75]

TABLE VIII—BLACK SERVICEMEN CONFINED FOR MAJOR OFFENSES, 1971

| Category of Offense | Percent of offenders in each category who are black |
|---|---|
| Willful disobedience | 63 |
| Assault | 62 |
| Desertion | 45 |
| AWOL | 41 |
| Article 134* | 37 |
| Larceny | 33 |

*"Conduct of a nature to bring discredit upon the Armed Forces" and "disorders to the prejudice of good order and discipline in the Armed Forces."

Source:   U. S. Department of Defense

In view of the recent criticisms of the military judicial system, former Secretary of Defense Melvin Laird on April 5, 1972, appointed a Department of Defense Task Force on the Administration of Military Justice composed of ranking civilian and military experts in the field.[76] This high-level Task Force was charged with the responsibility:

> ... To make such recommendations to the Secretary of Defense as may be deemed appropriate to eliminate existing deficiencies and/or enhance the opportunity for equal justice for every American serviceman and servicewoman.[77]

With this Task Force investigation now underway, new reforms in the Uniform Code of Military Justice as well as the general system of dispensing military justice should shortly be implemented.

## In Conclusion

As we have seen, there is no simple answer to the question, What is the current status of blacks in the U. S. Armed Forces? On the one hand, from the perspective of history, nonwhite status is much improved from a generation ago, when segregation was still very evident within the military.[78] Even by comparison today with other professions—law, medicine, politics, or engineering—or other institutions in American life, such as business and higher education, the record of the Armed Services in fostering positive race relations presents a dramatic contrast (though perhaps not quite as dramatic a contrast as it seemed to be a decade ago). Still, the Armed Forces have not as yet achieved the status of being "the model employer" due to remaining fundamental problems of black-white relationships in the area of the distribution of black servicemen, the National Guard, on-base racial tension, off-post housing, and the military system of justice. The defense establishment is not as perfect as its ardent admirers tend to believe, nor is it as imperfect in its performance on the racial front as its critics claim. The truth, as usual, lies between the two points of view.

However, this is not meant to conclude that the Department of Defense should rest on its laurels; rather, the Armed Services must consciously continue to strive toward improved race relations in its ranks. In particular, the services should exercise caution in making bold promises to minorities and let programs for improvement demonstrate the quality of human relations policies. At the same time, black criticisms of the Armed Services have sometimes been excessively pessimistic; negative predictions concerning Project 100,000, for example, were not borne out in terms of its significant success in raising the educational levels of nearly 100,000 nonwhites from deprived backgrounds.[79] Similarly, the 1971 program set forth by Admiral Elmo R. Zumwalt, then Chief of Naval Operations, to raise the proportion of black officers and men in the Navy to 12 percent by 1976 has significantly increased enlistments as well as black enrollees at the Naval Academy, although it is highly unlikely that the goal will be realized by 1976. The recruitment and training of black officer candidates must be given strong and unremitting support if full and equal black participation is to become a reality.[80]

In short, the solutions to the complexities of racial problems in the Armed Forces today will not be found in either stroke-of-the-pen reforms or unreflective statements of intentions. Serious thought and hard work are required in the years ahead.

## Notes

*Note*: The author wishes to thank the following individuals for their assistance in the preparation of this chapter: Dr. Mabel M. Smythe, Vice-President, Phelps-Stokes Fund; Professor Todd LaPort, Acting Director, Institute of Governmental Studies, University of California, Berkeley; and James C. Evans, L. Howard Bennett, Colonel George R. Hovey Johnson, and Major Fernandez of the Office of the Deputy Assistant Secretary of Defense (Equal Opportunity), Department of Defense; Professor Samuel P. Huntington, Harvard University.

1. John P. Davis, "The Negro in the Armed Forces of America," in John P. Davis, ed., *The American Negro Reference Book* (Englewood Cliffs, N. J., Prentice-Hall, 1966), p. 593. Also refer to Benjamin A. Quarles, *The Negro in the American Revolution* (Chapel Hill, University of North Carolina Press, 1961).
2. Peter Force, compiler, *American Archives*, 4th series, Vol. 2 (United States Congress, Washington, D. C. 1837–1846), p. 1630.
3. Henry Steele Commager and Richard B. Morris, *The Spirit of Seventy-Six* (Indianapolis, Bobbs-Merrill Co., 1958), Vol. 1, p. 111. *Also see* George Washington Williams, *The Negro In American History 1619–1880* (New York, G. P. Putnam's Sons, 1888), Vol. 1, p. 340.

4. John Hope Franklin, *From Slavery to Freedom: A History of the American Negro* (New York, Alfred A. Knopf, 1956), pp. 130–40.

5. George Washington Williams, *op. cit.*, vol. 2, p. 23.

6. For three excellent descriptions of southern slavery and northern segregation prior to the Civil War, read Kenneth M. Stampp, *The Peculiar Institution* (New York, Alfred A. Knopf, 1956); Leon F. Litwack, *North of Slavery: The Negro in the Free States, 1790–1860* (Chicago, University of Chicago Press, 1961); and Richard C. Wade, *Slavery in the Cities: The South, 1820–1860* (New York, Oxford Books, 1964).

7. Leon F. Litwack, *op. cit.*, p. 32. *Also see*, Lorenzo J. Greene, "Negroes in the Armed Forces of the United States to 1865," *Negro History Bulletin*, XIV, 1951.

8. Leon F. Litwack, *op. cit.*, p. 33. It should be noted that a small number of Negroes remained in the Navy throughout this era but they were limited to one-twentieth part of the crew of any vessel.

9. John P. Davis, *op. cit.*, p. 600.

10. *Ibid.*, p. 602.

11. For two outstanding studies of Negroes in the Civil War, *see*: Dudley Taylor Cornish, *The Sable Arm: Negro Troops in the Union Army, 1861–1865* (New York, Longmans, Green, 1956) and Benjamin Quarles, *The Negro in the Civil War* (Boston, Little, Brown & Co., 1953).

12. In February 1864, President Jefferson Davis sent a message to the Confederate Congress calling for the impressment into service of the C. S. A. Army of 20,000 slaves for duty as cooks, teamsters, and hospital attendants.

13. Dudley T. Cornish, *op. cit.*, pp. 157–180 and John Hope Franklin, *The Emancipation Proclamation* (Garden City, Doubleday & Co., 1963), p. 149.

14. For a discussion of the part played by Negro troopers in the Spanish-American War, *see*: Frank B. Freidal, *The Splendid Little War* (Boston, Little, Brown & Co., 1958); Herschel V. Cashin, *Under Fire with the Tenth U. S. Cavalry* (New York, F. T. Neely, 1899); S. E. Whitman, *The Troopers* (New York, Hastings House, 1962); William G. Muller, *The Twenty-Fourth Infantry, Past and Present* (privately printed, 1922); and John H. Nankivell, *History of the Twenty-Fifth Regiment United States Infantry, 1869–1926* (privately printed, 1926). For a description of the tragic racial tensions in Brownsville, Texas, where the 25th Infantry was stationed in 1906, read: E. L. Thornbrough, "The Brownsville Episode and the Negro Vote," *Mississippi Valley Historical Review*, December 1957, pp. 469–93.

15. These data have been drawn from Emmett J. Scott, *The American Negro in the World War* (Chicago, Homewood Press, 1919). Unfortunately, an adequate history of black participation in World War I has not yet been written.

16. The Pittsburgh *Courier*, March 19, 1960 (reprinted from an earlier edition).

17. W. E. B. DuBois, "An Essay Toward a History of the Black Man in the Great War," *Crisis*, June 1919, p. 70.

18. *Crisis*, September 1918, p. 238.

19. For a good analysis of pre-World War II military racial policies, read: Ulysses G. Lee, *U. S. Army in World War II: The Employment of Negro Troops*, (Washington, D. C., USGPO, 1966), ch. 1; and Richard Dalfiume, *Desegregation of the U. S. Armed Forces* (Columbia, University of Missouri Press, 1969), Chapters 1 and 2. Perhaps it should be emphasized that Jim Crowism in the military during the first half of the twentieth century was probably no worse than it was in the general American society. For an excellent account of the origins and rise of Jim Crow in this era, read: C. Van Woodward, *The Strange Career of Jim Crow*, 2nd edition (New York, Oxford University Press, 1966).

20. *Ibid.*

21. "Occupational Distribution of Uniformed Negro and White Personnel in World War II as of January 1, 1943" as cited in Richard J. Stillman, II, *Integration of the Negro In the U. S. Armed Forces* (New York, Praeger Publishers, 1968), p. 24.

22. Walter Francis White, *A Rising Wind* (New York, Doubleday, 1945), p. 76.

23. Trezzvant W. Anderson, *Come Out Fighting: The Epic Tale of the of the 761st Tank Battalion, 1942–1945* (Salzburg, Salzburger Druckerei und Verlag, 1945), p. 15.

24. Dennis D. Nelson, *The Integration of the Negro into the U. S. Navy, 1776–1947* (Washington, D. C., Department of the Navy, 1948), pp. 24–26.

25. Sammy Davis, Jr. and Jane and Burt Boyar, *Yes I Can* (New York, Farrar, Straus, 1965); excerpts quoted from "The Military Ordeal of Sammy Davis, Jr." *Ebony*, December 1965, p. 157.

26. The Fahy Committee Report, *Freedom To Serve* (Washington, D. C., USGPO, 1950), p. 17.

27. John J. McCloy, *Memo*, July 2, 1942, as cited in Ulysses G. Lee, *op. cit.*

28. Jean Byers, *A Study of the Negro in Military Service*, unpublished. Manuscript available in the U. S. Army Library in the Pentagon (Washington, D. C., June 1947), pp. 164–82. Also refer to Ulysses G. Lee, *op. cit.*, pp. 689–95; Richard Dalfiume, *op. cit.*, pp. 99–100; John Davis, *op. cit.*, pp. 645–647; and Lee Nichols, *Breakthrough on the Color Front* (New York, Random House, 1954), pp. 68–69.

29. U. S. Department of the Navy, *A Guide to the Command of Navy Personnel* (Washington, D. C., NavPers. 15092, 1944); Jean Byers, *op. cit.*, pp. 213–260; and Dennis Nelson, *op. cit.*, pp. 94–141.

30. U. S. War Department, "Utilization of Negro Manpower in the Postwar Army," *Circular 124* (Washington, D. C., Department of War, April 27, 1946). Also see The President's Committee on Civil Rights, *To Secure These Rights* (Washington, D. C., USGPO, 1947).

31. Dennis Nelson, *op. cit.*, p. 20.

32. For an excellent discussion of the vigorous Negro political effort that prodded Truman to issue Executive Order 9981, read Richard Dalfiume, *op. cit.*, ch. 8, pp. 148–174; and Richard Stillman, II, *op. cit.*, pp. 32–42.

33. Executive Order 9981 as cited in Richard Stillman, II, *op. cit.*, pp. 41–42.

34. Other members of the Fahy Committee included: Alphonsus J. Donahue, a prominent Catholic layman; Lester Granger, executive director of the National Urban League; John Sengstacke, publisher of the Chicago *Defender*; William E. Stevenson, president of Oberlin College; Dwight G. Palmer, board chairman of General Cable Corporation; and Charles Luckman of Lever Brothers (Donahue died before the committee made its report; Luckman was inactive). Working closely with the Fahy Committee and its staff was James C. Evans, who has served nearly thirty years in the Department of Defense.

35. It should be noted that the Air Force had several advantages over the other services which permitted it to integrate at a faster rate, namely, a lower percentage of colored personnel as well as a higher proportion of skilled Negroes which permitted an easier transfer to other jobs within the organizational structure; refer to, Richard Stillman, II, *op. cit.*, p. 46.

36. E. W. Kenworthy, "Taps for Jim Crow," *The New York Times*, May 23, 1950, p. 12.

37. Perhaps the Army's resistance to integration can best be explained by the fact that in the postwar era, senior military officers exercised an unusual degree of freedom in making military policy. As Professor Samuel P. Huntington has hypothesized, the vertical structure of the Army made the civilian Army Secretary highly dependent upon the advice of his Chief of Staff, who was in the direct chain of command. Both the logistical-support branches and the field commanders were directly responsible to the Chief of Staff. The Navy's structure permitted more direct civilian authority over naval operations. Each bureau chief reported directly to the civilian secretary as well as the Chief of Naval Operations. The Navy's balanced organization permitted the secretary to hear more officer viewpoints than the Army's vertical-organizational hierarchy, which permitted the Chief of Staff to speak for the entire military body; Samuel P. Huntington, *The Soldier and the State* (Cambridge, Harvard University Press, 1957), p. 429.

38. Richard Dalfiume, *op. cit.*, pp. 201–219; and Lee Nichols, *op. cit.*, pp. 109–113.

39. Richard Dalfiume, *op. cit.*

40. Lee Nichols, *op. cit.*; for a rather derogatory comment on the fighting capability of the 24th Infantry, see Roy E. Appleman, *The United States Army in the Korean War, South to Naktong, North to Yalu* (Washington, D. C., Department of the Army, 1961), and for a commentary on Appleman's views, read John P. Davis, *op. cit.*, pp. 649–52.

41. For the text of Project Clear and an interesting background commentary on the origins of this study, see Leo Bogart, ed., *Social Research and the Desegregation of the U. S. Army* (Chicago, Markham Publishing Co., 1969).

42. Richard Dalfiume, *op. cit.*, p. 219.

43. Other members of the committee were Nathaniel S. Colley, Abe Fortas, Louis J. Hector, Benjamin Muse, John H. Sengstacke, and Whitney M. Young, Jr. The *Initial Report* was issued June 21, 1963, and the *Final Report* in November 1964.

44. *The New York Times*, July 27, 1963, p. 1. Similar policy statements have been made by a number of senior civilian and Defense Department leaders in the last decade. Most recently Secretary of Defense Melvin R. Laird emphasized: "The Department of Defense is committed to the goal of making military and civilian service in the department a model of equal opportunity for all." *Commanders Digest*, May 18, 1972, p. 1. For students of black military history, it does indeed seem somewhat paradoxical that the most rapid racial progress in the Armed Services has come during the tenure of Defense Secretaries (Forrestal and McNamara) who were products of conservative, business backgrounds.

45. Since it was established more than a decade ago, this office has suffered from a high turnover of Deputy Assistant Secretaries (six in ten years) as well as being rather remote from the centers of Pentagon power. Under McNamara the office was staffed largely by civilians, while under Laird military men dominated the staff. Perhaps the chief function of this office during the last decade has been as a source of research and data collection on the problems of race relations in the Armed Services. For an interesting study of the problems of collecting racial information in the Federal Government, *see*: Albert Mindlin, "The Designation of Race or Color on Forms," *Public Administration Review*, June 1966, pp. 110–118.

46. *The New York Times*, August 25, 1966, p. 1.

47. *The New York Times*, August 26, 1966, p. 3.

48. *Ibid.*

49. *Project One Hundred Thousand: Characteristics and Performance of "New Standards" Men* (Washington, D. C., Office of the Secretary of Defense, December 1969), mimeographed. Even though Project 100,000 was one of the most interesting Defense Department experiments in the last decade, little has been written on it. Certainly this project deserves a careful investigation by scholars of defense policy.

50. For representative statements of Carmichael and McKissick, see *The New York Times*, July 2, 26, and August 22, 1966. Cassius Clay's refusal to be inducted into the Army and Martin Luther King's campaign against the Vietnam War in April 1967 publicized black protest against the war. Also refer to: *The Black Scholar*, November 1970, pp. 7–18 and 40–46. However, Gallup surveys in 1968 showed a majority of Negroes still favoring the President's war policy, which may indicate that the bulk of nonwhites are more conservative than either the statements of civil rights leaders or newspaper headlines tend to reflect. Perhaps it is safest to conclude that blacks, like whites, were deeply divided over the war issue during the 1960s.

51. *The New York Times*, March 10, 1966, p. 4. For Negro reaction to the inequities of the draft system, read: *The New York Times*, November 3, 1966, p. 29; and August 26, p. 16. Indeed, perhaps it was largely because of black criticism of the draft that the lottery system was introduced.

52. Based upon Defense Department statistics as of March 30, 1972.

53. In 1966 Army statistics showed first-term reenlistment rates for blacks were 66.5 percent, compared to 20.0 for whites. While the consistently higher first- and second-term reenlistment rates do tend to reflect a higher sustained interest among blacks as compared to whites for military service, attitude surveys of black soldiers get mixed reactions. Charles Moskos found in a sampling of black soldiers in the midsixties that 84 percent thought the military offered more racial equality than civilian life, in his book, *The American Enlisted Man* (New York, Russell Sage Foundation, 1970), p. 223; while a *Time* Magazine survey (September 19, 1969, p. 22) found considerable disenchantment with military life among black NCO's.

54. The Navy opened its first three NROTC units at Prairie View A & M College, Texas; Savannah State College, Georgia; and Southern University, Louisiana. Later North Carolina Central University and Florida A & M University were added. Information regarding NROTC programs supplied by Rear Admiral Charles F. Rauch, Assistant Chief of Naval Personnel for Human Goals, March 13, 1975. The Navy also operates the U. S. Merchant Marine Academy at Kings

Point, New York, which trains midshipmen for the American merchant marine. Approximately 9 percent of the entering class of July 1972 was made up of minority candidates—a considerable increase over previous years. *Navy Times*, May 17, 1972, pp. 20 and 44–48.

55. *The New York Times*, February 16, 1971, p. 21; and April 1, 1971, p. 29.

56. *The Search for Military Justice: Report of an NAACP Inquiry into the Problems of the Negro Serviceman in West Germany* (New York, NAACP, 1971), p. 5.

57. *Ibid.*, p. 4.

58. *Ibid.*, p. 20.

59. *The Congressional Black Caucus Report on Racism in the Military: A New System for Rewards and Punishments*, May 15, 1972, mimeographed, p. 21.

60. *The New York Times*, April 30, 1968, p. 33.

61. William Brink and Louis Harris, *Black and White: A Study of U. S. Racial Attitudes Today* (Simon and Schuster, New York, 1967), pp. 270–72. For a critical study of discriminatory habits of many Guard units, read: William A. McWhirter, "The National Guard—Awake or Asleep?" *Life*, October 27, 1967, pp. 83–98.

62. For an excellent account of the general political influence of the National Guard in Washington, read Martha Dethick, *The National Guard in Politics* (Cambridge, Harvard University Press, 1965).

63. Committee on Armed Services, House of Representatives, *Inquiry into the Disturbances at Marine Corps Base, Camp Lejeune, North Carolina, on July 20, 1969* (Washington, D.C., USGPO, December 15, 1969), p. 5056.

64. *Ibid.*, p. 5057. For other interesting assessments of general military race relations, read: Charles C. Moskos, Jr. "Racial Integration in the Armed Forces," *American Journal of Sociology*, September 1967, pp. 132–48; Gene Grove, "The Army and the Negro," *The New York Times Magazine*, July 24, 1966, p. 4ff; Whitney M. Young, Jr., "When the Negroes in Vietnam Come Home," *Harpers*, June 1967, pp. 63–69; David Parks, *GI Diary* (New York, Harper and Row, 1968); and "The Black Soldier," *Ebony*, August 1968, entire issue.

65. *The New York Times*, September 4, 1969, p. 39; and October 14, 1969, p. 27.

66. Since 1970 when the Armed Services introduced ethnic foods, music, and literature in their PX's and commissary facilities, sales for these items have been in excess of four million dollars—an indication of the demand for these goods among servicemen.

67. *The New York Times*, March 6, 1971, p. 1.

68. *The New York Times*, May 22, 1971, p. 18. It is still too early to evaluate this reform as well as the establishment of the Defense Race Relations Institute; nevertheless, if all that it brings about is more understanding and discussion of existing problems within the services, this in itself will be beneficial. It is this author's belief, however, that the military could take further steps to establish a regularized channel for servicemen complaints regarding race relations and other matters by setting up an independent office of military ombudsman which would receive and investigate such grievances. Presently the Office of Inspector General serves this function; however, because the Inspector General is so closely tied to the military chain of command, servicemen are frequently reluctant to formally express their grievances. Perhaps a military ombudsman appointed by and reporting to Congress would serve as a valuable independent channel for investigating GI complaints in the Department of Defense.

69. NAACP Report, *op. cit.*, p. 24.

70. Department of Defense statistics as of January 1, 1972.

71. David Sutton, "The Military Mission Against Off-Base Discrimination," in Charles C. Moskos, Jr., ed., *Public Opinion and the Military Establishment* (New York, Russell Sage Foundation, 1971), p. 164.

72. NAACP Report, *op. cit.*, p. 18.

73. David Sutton, *op. cit.*, p. 170. *Also see*: Adam Yarmolinsky, *The Military Establishment* (New York, Harper and Row, 1971), pp. 351–52.

74. NAACP Report, *op. cit.*, pp. 21–23.

75. Congressional Black Caucus Report, *op. cit.*, pp. 14–29.

76. Members of the task force include: Mr. James V. Bennett, former director of federal prisons; Mr. W. Haywood Burns, director of the National Conference of Black Lawyers; Honorable C. Stanley Blair, United States District Judge; Honorable John Carro, New York City Criminal Court Judge; Mr. Adolph Holmes, deputy executive director of the National Urban League; Honorable Joseph C. Howard, Baltimore City Court Judge; Mr. Nathaniel R. Jones, NAACP general counsel; Lt. General Claire E. Hutchins, Jr., First U. S. Army Commander; Miss Patricia A. King, Office for Civil Rights, H. E. W.; Major General George S. Prugh, Judge Advocate General, U. S. Army; Rear Admiral Merlin Staring, Judge Advocate General, U. S. Navy; Major General James S. Cheney, Judge Advocate General, U.S. Air Force; and Brigadier General Clyde R. Mann, director, Judge Advocate Division, U. S. Marine Corps.

77. "Charter of the Task Force on the Administration of Military Justice in the Armed Forces," Office of the Secretary of Defense, April 5, 1972, p. 2.

78. An example of the improvement in race relations in the military was indicated by World War II veteran Sammy Davis, Jr., after returning from entertaining the troops in Vietnam: "It's just 152 percent better. I mean the effort they are making on black and white relationships. They're bending some rules these days; they're regarding men as individuals. For example? Well, when I was in the Army, I was on a post where a colored guy couldn't get his hair cut. Now you can. There are a thousand little things like that that make things better now." *The New York Times*, February 24, 1972, p. 45. Also see Sammy Davis, Jr., "Why I Went to the Troops," *Ebony*, June 1972, pp. 144–48. For an interesting contrasting view of race relations in Vietnam by a young black GI, see David Parks, *op. cit.*

79. *Project One Hundred Thousand*, *op. cit.*

80. *The New York Times*, April 1, 1971, p. 29.

# BIBLIOGRAPHY

## Books

Bogart, Leo, ed., *Social Research and the Desegregation of the U. S. Army: Two Original 1951 Field Reports*. Chicago, Markham Publishing, 1969.

Brink, William and Harris, Louis, *Black and White: A Study of U. S. Racial Attitudes Today*. New York, Simon and Schuster, 1967.

Byers, Jean, *The Study of the Negro in the Military Service*. Unpublished, 1947.

Cashin, Herschel V., *Under Fire with the Tenth U.S. Cavalry*. New York, F. T. Neely, 1899.

Cornish, Dudley T., *The Sable Arm: Negro Troops in the Union Army, 1861–1865*. New York, Longmans, Green and Co., 1956.

Dalfiume, Richard M., *Desegregation of the U. S. Armed Forces: Fighting on Two Fronts, 1939–1953*. Columbia, University of Missouri Press, 1969.

Dethick, Martha, *The National Guard in Politics*. Cambridge, Harvard University Press, 1965.

Higginson, Thomas Wentworth, *Army Life in a Black Regiment*. New York, Collier Books, 1962.

Huntington, Samuel P., *The Soldier and the State: The Theory and Politics of Civil Military Relations*. Cambridge, Harvard University Press, 1957.

Janowitz, Morris, *The Professional Soldier: A Social and Political Portrait*. Glencoe, Free Press, 1960.

Lee, Ulysses G., *The United States Army in World War II: Special Studies: The Employment of Negro Troops*. Washington, D.C., USGPO, 1966.

Little, Arthur W., *From Harlem to the Rhine: The Story of New York's Colored Volunteers*. New York, Covici, Friede, Inc., 1936.

Moskos, Charles, Jr., *The American Enlisted Man*. New York, Russell Sage Foundation, 1970.

Murray, Florence, ed., *The Negro Handbook, 1949*. New York, Macmillan Company, 1949.

Nelson, Dennis D., *The Integration of the Negro into the United States Navy, 1776–1947*. Washington, D.C., Department of the Navy, 1948.

Nichols, Lee, *Breakthrough on the Color Front*. New York, Random House, 1954.

Parks, David, *GI Diary*. New York, Harper and Row, 1968.

Quarles, Benjamin, *The Negro in the American Revolution*. Chapel Hill, University of North Carolina Press, 1961.

———, *The Negro in the Civil War*. Boston, Little, Brown and Co., 1953.

Scott, Emmett J., *The American Negro in the World War*. Chicago, Homewood Press, 1919.

Stouffer, Samuel A. *et al.*, *The American Soldier*. Princeton, Princeton University Press, 1949, three vols.

Stillman, Richard J., II, *The Integration of the Negro in the U.S. Armed Forces*. New York, Frederick A. Praeger, Publisher, 1968.

White, Walter, *A Man Called White*. New York, The Viking Press, 1948.

Yarmolinsky, Adam, *The Military Establishment*. New York, Harper and Row, 1971.

## Public Documents

"The Congressional Black Caucus Report on Racism in the Military: A New System for Rewards and Punishments," Washington, D.C., Congressional Black Caucus Office, 1972, mimeographed.

The President's Committee on Civil Rights, *To Secure These Rights*. Washington, D.C., USGPO, 1947.

The President's Committee on Equal Opportunity in the Armed Forces, *Initial Report*. June 1963; and *Final Report*. November 1964, mimeographed.

The President's Committee on Equality of Treatment and Opportunity in the Armed Services, *Freedom to Serve*. Washington, D.C., USGPO, 1950.

*Project One Hundred Thousand: Characteristics and Performance of "New Standards" Men*. Washington, D.C., Department of Defense, December 1969.

"Report by the Special Subcommittee on Disciplinary Problems in the U.S. Navy." (Washington, D.C., USGPO), issued January 2, 1973.

*Report* of the Special Subcommittee to Probe Disturbances on Military Bases of the Committee on Armed Services, House of Representatives, "Inquiry into the Disturbances at Marine Corps Base, Camp Lejeune, N.C., on July 20, 1969." Washington, D.C., USGPO, 1969.

*The Search for Military Justice: Report of an NAACP Inquiry into the Problems of the Negro Serviceman in West Germany*. New York, NAACP, 1971.

## Articles

"The Black Soldier." *Ebony*, August 1968, entire issue.

Bennett, L. Howard, "Command Leadership and the Black Serviceman." *U. S. Naval Institute Proceedings*, April 1971, pp. 42–47.

Boyd, George M., "A Look at Racial Polarity in the Armed Forces," *Air University Review*, Sept./Oct. 1970, pp. 42–50.

Davis, John P., "The Negro in the Armed Forces of America," in John P. Davis, ed., *The American Negro Reference Book*. Englewood Cliffs, N.J., Prentice-Hall, 1966.

DuBois, W. E. B., "The Black Man in the Revolution of 1914–1918." *Crisis*, March 1919, pp. 218–23.

———, "An Essay Toward a History of the Black Man in the Great War." *Crisis*, June 1919, pp. 63–87.

Gibson, Colonel James M., "Seminar on Racial Relations." *Military Review*, July 1970, pp. 13–19.

Grove, Gene, "The Army and the Negro." *The New York Times Magazine*, July 24, 1966, pp. 4–5 and 49–51.

McWhirter, William A., "The National Guard—Awake or Asleep?" *Life*, October 27, 1967, pp. 83–98.

Moskos, Charles C., Jr., "Racial Integration in the Armed Forces." *American Journal of Sociology*, September 1967, pp. 132–148.

Newton, Isham G., "The Negro in the National Guard." *Phylon*, Spring 1962, pp. 18–28.

Stern, Sol, "When the Black GI Comes Home." *The New York Times Magazine*, March 24, 1968, pp. 26ff.

Stillman, Richard J., II, "The Negro in the U. S. Armed Forces." *Phylon*, Summer 1969, pp. 139–59.

Sutton, David, "The Military Mission Against Off-Base Discrimination." in Charles C. Moskos, Jr., ed., *Public Opinion and the Military Establishment*. Beverly Hills, Sage Publications, 1971, pp. 149–184.

White, James S., "Race Relations in the Army." *Military Review*, July 1970, pp. 3–12.

Young, Whitney M., "When the Negroes in Vietnam Come Home." *Harper's Magazine*, June 1967, pp. 63–69.

## TV Programs

"The Anderson Platoon," July 4, 1967, CBS-TV.

"Negroes in the U. S. Military," CBS-TV, April 3, 1966, narrated by Walter Cronkite.

"Same Mud, Same Blood," NBC-TV, December 11, 1967, narrated by Frank McGee.

## Newspapers

Johnson, Thomas A., "The U. S. Negro in Vietnam." *The New York Times*, April 29, April 30, May 1, 1968, pp. 1ff.

Watson, Mark S., "Guard Commands All Units to End Bias." Baltimore *Sun*, March 31, 1964, pp. 1ff.

# 30

## The Black American in Sports[*]

### Edwin B. Henderson

## HISTORICAL BACKGROUND

Among the most striking developments in recent years have been the growing pride of blacks in their heritage, their achievement in ever-increasing numbers of fields of endeavor, and the fact that the world now recognizes this achievement. Black prowess in athletics has been a particular source of inspiration to the youth of America. The voluminous amount of printed matter devoted to sporting events, as well as the generous sports coverage by the popular media, has made available an unprecedented fund of knowledge and communication concerning black excellence in the sports world. The urgency of the demand for such information, heightened by the marked increase in black studies in schools and colleges throughout the country, has generated a variety of published material on black sportsmen, both past and present.

Before the turn of the century there were almost no books available on the Negro American athlete, except for a few "ghost"-written accounts, such as *The Story of Marshall "Major" Taylor*, a world champion bicycle rider, published around 1900. Perhaps the first attempt at recording the history of blacks in sports appeared in a Spalding handbook on athletics entitled *The Official Handbook of The Inter-Scholastic Athletic Association of Middle Atlantic States*, published yearly from 1910 through 1913. It contained the first accumulation of athletic records for high schools, colleges, and athletic clubs in the nation and detailed the beginnings of basketball in eastern schools and clubs. In 1937 Carter G. Woodson, the black historian, persuaded this writer to attempt the story of the black American in sports. The result, *The Negro in Sports*,[1] which appeared in 1939, was the first authentic history to record the widespread participation of black athletes in track and field, and in team sports and varied athletic events.

In 1949 *The Negro in Sports* was revised and amplified to include records of such black-dominated sports as boxing and horse racing; it also contained records of the American Tennis Association, the National Golf Tournament, national bowling events, women's track and field events, and college sports.

[*]The editor wishes to acknowledge with appreciation the research assistance of Judith Miles and Toni T. Parker of the staff of the Phelps-Stokes Fund.

The tenth volume of *The International Library of Negro Life and History*, published in 1969, was entitled *The Black Athlete*. This book details the life stories of current and past black athletes. Since publication of the earlier editions of *The Negro in Sports* and the story of "Major" Taylor, dozens of books have been written dealing with black participation in sports and the lives of individual athletes. *Black Sports*,[2] a recently published magazine, is devoted to this subject. The proceedings of a 1971 Big Ten symposium on the history of physical education and athletics, published by the Athletic Institute of Chicago, includes a chapter on blacks in sports.

Prior to 1904 blacks as athletes received scant notice in the press; this lack of exposure applied as well to the early radio programs where they went unmentioned except when competing with white opponents in prize fights. In such cases, however, their race was seldom mentioned; they were usually described as "giant" or "freak" contestants.

With the development of television, the increasing role of blacks in the sports world has become much more obvious. Black announcers of ability now appear on network sports programs; Bill White, former Giant first-baseman, and O. J. Simpson, Buffalo Bills back, are examples. Others include Bob Teague, who played halfback for the University of Wisconsin and now is a newscaster in New York City, and Don Perkins, who retired from the Dallas Cowboys to take a broadcasting job with CBS.

The first attempt to organize competing teams among black schools and colleges was initiated by Howard University, Morgan State College, and the high schools of metropolitan Washington, D. C. This led to the formation in 1906 of the Inter-Scholastic Athletic Association of the Middle Atlantic States. The first college athletic conference was formed in 1912 and consisted of colleges in Washington, D. C., Maryland, Pennsylvania, Virginia, and North Carolina.

Along with the development of conferences, athletic enthusiasts have organized "officials," groups designed to train and assign umpires, referees, and the like for athletic contests. The oldest of these is the Eastern Board of Officials, organized in 1915 in Washington, D. C., and still operating mainly in the Middle Atlantic States. Black officials are gradually appearing in major college and professional contests. One of them, Emmett Ashford, recently retired from the American Baseball League.

Another development in the course of the past half-century has been the rise to fame of a number of coaches and physical-education directors. These include Edward P. Hurt and Talmadge Hill of Morgan State College; Charles H. Williams of Hampton Institute; the late Cleveland Abbott of Tuskegee Institute; A. S. Gaither of Florida A. & M. College; Edward S. Temple, formerly of Tennessee State A. & I. University; and Eddie Robinson of Grambling.

Prior to 1900 physical education was not included in the curriculum of all-black schools. The first such program appeared in 1902 in Baltimore and Washington, D. C. high schools. Thereafter, courses were gradually set up in health teaching and physical training, and athletic coaches became a part of the faculty. Eventually athletics became an integral part of the curriculum in most black high schools. Today college coaches scan the high-school playing field for potential material.

The first recognized physical education director on the collegiate level was Abraham Molineaux Hewlett at Harvard University. Although few outstanding black athletes are recorded prior to the early 1890s, it is significant that Hewlett was a black man. He was employed as an instructor and director of the first gymnasium, built in 1859, and remained in charge until his death in 1871.

As mentioned earlier, prior to 1950 an athlete's race was rarely mentioned in the press or on the radio; consequently, the American public was not generally aware of the activities of black athletes. Not only were the 1950s marked by increased exposure for the black athlete, but also by striking performances on his part in a variety of fields.

For many years following the end of slavery, blacks were not accorded the right to compete in athletics with whites in most of the United States. Gradually their abilities, combined with the sense of fair play that underlies the concept of democracy, caused this situation to change. Track and field athletics offered the first area of acceptance of black Americans in sports. Evidence of superiority in these events lies in standard measurement, and any track coach was glad to get an athlete who could consistently excel. Gradually black Americans were accepted for other athletic teams as well, not only because they enhanced the chances of winning but also because they attracted black paying customers. The United States domination of track and field sports since 1932 could not have happened without its splendid black athletes.

In the 1956 Bowl games, five black players appeared in the Shrine, Orange, and Cotton Bowl games played in the South. Six Negro Americans were on teams in that year's Rose Bowl game. Six black players participated in the East-West professional game played on January 13, 1957, at Los Angeles.

A black tennis player, Althea Gibson, won twelve overseas tennis tournaments in 1956 and was ranked as the second-best women's tennis player in the world. A black woman, Mildred McDaniels from Tuskegee Institute, established a new world record for the high jump in the 1956 Olympic Games.

At the close of 1956, black boxers held five of the six weight-class championships held by American prizefighters.

In the 1956 Olympic Games black athletes from America won seventeen of the thirty-nine gold, silver, and bronze medals awarded to American athletes in the track and field events. Black competitors won ten and white twelve first-place medals. The star of the world championship Olympic basketball team, Bill Russell, was black, as was one of the two American winners in the boxing events, James Boyd of Rocky Mount, North Carolina.

In 1959, of the eleven All-American football players selected as the best by experts, two were Negroes. Two of the best five college basketball players in the season ending in 1956, Bill Russell and K. C. Jones, were black. In professional baseball, by the end of the 1950s black Americans led the National League in hitting, had been named "Rookie of the Year," and had been voted "Most Valuable Player."

The ever-increasing recognition accorded to black athletes in recent decades is evidenced by the creation in 1973 of a National Black Sports Hall of Fame. The thirty-eight athletes chosen in June of that year by the editors of *Black Sports* magazine include:

*Football:* Jim Brown, Dr. Brud Holland, Henry McDonald, Marion Motley, Fritz Pollard, Paul Robeson, Buddy Young.

*Baseball:* Roy Campanella, Roberto Clemente, Martin Dihigo, Larry Doby, Monte Irvin, Willie Mays, Minnie Minoso, Satchel Paige, Jackie Robinson.

*Basketball:* Elgin Baylor, Wilt Chamberlain, Chuck Cooper, Edwin B. Henderson, Bill Russell.

*Track and Field:* Cleveland Abbot, Bob Beamon, Harrison Dillard, Rafer Johnson, Ralph Metcalfe, Jesse Owens, Eulace Peacock, Wilma Rudolph, Willye White.

*Boxing:* Muhammad Ali, Henry Armstrong, Joe Louis, Ray Robinson, José Torres.

*Tennis:* Althea Gibson, Dr. Robert Johnson.

*Golf:* Charlie Sifford.

# TEAM SPORTS

## Baseball

Baseball became a popular pastime in the United States during and following the Civil War. The first college game was between teams representing Amherst and Williams Colleges in 1859. Professional-league baseball began with the formation of the National League in 1876; the American League was organized in 1882. However, after Welday and Moses Fleetwood Walker played for Toledo (in the American Association) in 1884, black players were not permitted to participate in major-league baseball until 1947.

Negroes began to play baseball as members of hotel teams, community teams, and occasionally college teams. Two early college players who were widely acclaimed were Clarence Matthews at Harvard University in 1902 and J. Francis Gregory at Amherst and Yale Divinity School about 1898 to 1900. Others included Merton P. Robinson at Oberlin; Watkins and Williams at the University of Vermont, 1905; Oscar Brown at Syracuse in 1908; William Kindle at Springfield, 1914; Service Chandler of Middlebury College, Leslie Simms at Northeastern and the redoubtable Paul Robeson at Rutgers around 1918; Harry Thompson at Dartmouth, 1919; George Crossen at Boston University, 1922; Charlie Ray at Bates; Earl Brown at Harvard around 1923; Harold Martin at Norwich University; F.M. Sheffield and John Copeland, captain of the Oberlin College team; Sam Taylor at Northwestern; and Booker T. Spencer at Western Reserve.

Because of segregation there were no integrated teams in the South; when teams of the North played colleges in the South, their black players did not participate. However, black college baseball teams were active except for a brief period when football became king.

The first attempt to organize all-black professional leagues was in 1887, but the leagues did not become successful until between 1906 and 1920, when the Eastern and Western Leagues were formed. These leagues recruited players from the sand lots and colleges. It has been estimated that many of their members would have held their own on the organized white teams of the day.

Black immortals chosen from among pre-1947 professional players are:

*Catchers:* Joshua Gibson, "Biz" Mackey, and Clarence Williams.

*Pitchers:* Joseph Williams, Richard Redding, David Brown, Rube Foster, William Foster, and Satchel Paige (see below).

*First Base:* Ben Taylor, Buck Leonard, and Leroy Grant.

*Second Base:* Samuel Hughes.

*Third Base:* Jud Wilson and Andrew Jackson.

*Shortstop:* John Henry Lloyd and "Home Run" Johnson.

*Center Field:* Oscar Charleston.

*Right Field:* Peter Hill.

*Left Field:* G. Patterson and L. Torrienti.

*Utility:* Richard Lundy and Fred Grant, infield; Dixon and Chester Brooks, outfield.

*Manager:* Rube Foster.

Those deserving honorable mention include:

*Pitchers:* Andres "String Bean" Williams, Frank Wickware, "Bullet" Rogan, John Donaldson.

*Infielders:* Frank Warfield, Bingo Demoss, Henry Blackman, William Monroe, Eddie Douglass, John Beckwith, Jim Taylor, Oliver Marcelle.

*Outfielders:* J. Lyons, Spotswood Poles, Jesse Barbour, Peter Washington, Clinton Thomas, "Jap" Payne, McNair and Clarence "Fats" Jenkins.

Special mention should be made of the versatile Martin Dihigo. Dihigo first played in the United States in 1923 with Alex Perripez's Cuban Stars. He was about 15 years old at the time and was used at first base, as a pitcher, and on second base. In subsequent years Dihigo, who had exceptional speed and immensely powerful arms, was used at *every* position by the Cubans, Hilldale, and the Homestead Grays. Buck Leonard, among others, had called him the greatest ball player of all time.

In 1971, the previously mentioned Leroy (Satchel) Paige, former pitching star of the Kansas City Monarchs, became the first black baseball star of the Negro Leagues to enter the Hall of Fame at Cooperstown, New York. To be eligible for the Hall of Fame a player must have participated in the big leagues for at least ten years. A new wing honors those who have played in the Negro leagues for at least ten years. The setting up of this separate facility has evoked criticism.

Because of racial barriers, Paige played in the majors for only a short time toward the end of his career when he joined the Cleveland Indians in 1948. However, in 1968 the Atlanta Braves recruited the 60-year-old Paige; he did not play but his position helped him to qualify for pension benefits.

Monte Irvin, former New York Giants star, later an assistant to Baseball Commissioner Bowie Kuhn, was named to the Baseball Hall of Fame in February 1973. Irvin was the fourth black player selected by the Special Committee on the Negro Leagues, joining Paige, Joshua Gibson, and Buck Leonard. And in 1975, William "Judy" Johnson, a star of the Negro League, became the fifth black member to be inducted into the Baseball Hall of Fame.

Branch Rickey, who headed the Brooklyn farm system of baseball teams, can be thanked for introducing black players into major-league baseball. In 1946 he signed on the late Jackie Robinson as a trial player with the Montreal team of the Brooklyn system. Robinson, who had been a four-letter man at UCLA and a member of one of the black professional teams, played a year with the Montreal outfit and then was called to play with the Brooklyn Dodgers in April 1947.

At the close of the year, he was named "Rookie of the Year," an award made for excellence by a player in his first year. Brooklyn won the National League pennant in 1947 with Robinson leading the league in stolen bases as well as batting .296, one of the highest scores of that year. For ten years Robinson was a stellar player for the Brooklyn team, which won several pennants as well as a world championship. When Robinson was traded to the New York Giants team in 1957, he elected to end his baseball career. In 1962, Robinson was the first black player to be elected to the Baseball Hall of Fame. Honored at the 1972 World Series, he soon suffered a heart attack and died in October 1972.

Shortly after the admission of Robinson to organized baseball, other black players were signed by the big-league teams. Between 1947 and 1956, seventy-one black players joined the two major-league teams.

Outstanding black players since the Jackie Robinson era include:

*Roy Campanella, catcher.* In one of his best years, 1953, Campanella batted .325, hit 33 homers, drove in 108 runs, and won his first MVP (Most Valuable Player) Award. His baseball career ended in 1958, when he suffered a broken neck in a traffic accident and became disabled. He is a member of the Baseball Hall of Fame.

*Elston Howard, catcher.* After tours in black baseball Howard became a member of the Yankee organization in 1950, succeeding the famous Yogi Berra as number-one catcher in 1960. In 1961 he became the first American League black winner of the MVP Award.

*Don Newcombe, pitcher.* Newcombe helped the Brooklyn Dodgers win the pennant in 1956 and hurled his way that year to a 27-7 record.

*Ernie Banks, shortstop.* Banks hit more home runs in the 1955–1960 seasons than any other major-leaguer. He won the MVP Award in 1958 and became the first National League player to win this award in two consecutive years.

*Maury Wills, shortstop.* Wills, a member of the Dodgers' team, became known for his base-stealing. In 1962 he stole 104 bases and won the MVP Award.

*Ritchie Allen, first base.* In the 1964 season Allen had twenty-nine homers, ninety-one runs batted in and a .318 batting average. This performance led to his designation as Rookie of the Year by the National League. In the same year, Minnesota Twins outfielder Tony Oliva was named Rookie of the Year in the American League—the first time in baseball history that black players received this award in both major leagues.

*Hank Aaron, outfielder.* While with the Atlanta Braves, Aaron broke the home run record of Babe Ruth in April 1974 when he hit his 715th major league home run.

*Bob Gibson, pitcher.* Gibson, who hurled for the St. Louis Cardinals in the 1967 World Series, won three complete game victories and was voted the outstanding player of that Series. Gibson led the Cardinals to first place in the National League in 1968, winning his league's MVP and Cy Young Awards. Another Cardinals player, Curt Flood, ranked in fifth place in the National League that year with a .301 batting average.

*Frank Robinson, outfielder and manager.* Robinson led the Cincinnati Redlegs to the pennant in 1961; the Baltimore Orioles to four pennants in 1966, '69, '70, and '71, and two World Series playoffs in 1966 and '70. He was one of the outstanding black hitters of the 1970 season. As of this writing he is the only player in baseball history to have won the MVP award for outstanding performances in both leagues. He was named, in October 1974, as manager-player of the Cleveland Indians, the first black man to hold this position.

*Willie Mays, outfielder.* Mays is sure to become a legendary figure in baseball. He is one of very few players ever to hit four home runs in one game. As of 1968 Willie Mays, with the San Francisco Giants at this writing, had a total of 587 home runs, a record higher than any National League player and any right-handed batter in history. He became a coach/consultant to the New York Mets after the 1973 season.

*Willie McCovey, infielder.* McCovey, with the San Francisco Giants, won the National League's MVP Award in 1969. He led the league that year for home runs (forty-five) and achieved a .320 batting average for the season. New York Mets outfielder Cleon Jones, with a batting average of .342, and Dodger outfielder Willie Davis were other outstanding National League players in 1969. Davis achieved a .311 batting average in addition to a thirty-one-game hitting streak, a record in baseball history.

*Rico Carty, fielder.* In 1970 Carty, of the Atlanta Braves, was named the league's batting champion with an average of .366. That same year in the American League, Alex Johnson of the California Angels led with a batting average of .329. Reggie Smith of the Boston Red Sox was among the outstanding black hitters of the 1970 season.

*Fergie Jenkins, pitcher.* Jenkins, of the Chicago Cubs, has consistently been ranked among the National League leaders, setting records in both innings pitched and strike-outs. He won twenty games four seasons in a row. Finally in 1971 he was named winner of the Cy Young Award as the top pitcher in his league.

*Vida Blue, pitcher.* Blue, of the Oakland Athletics, was the winner of both the MVP Award and the Cy Young Award in 1971.

*Dick Allen, third base.* Allen, of the White Sox, ended his last days of the 1972 season among the American League's top ten hitters. He had more home runs and runs batted in to his credit than any other player.

*Joe Morgan, second base.* Morgan, of the Cincinnati Reds, was voted MVP in 1975 by the greatest margin in baseball history.

## Football

American football did not become popular until after the Civil War. In 1869 Rutgers College and Princeton University teams met in what was the forerunner of the game as we know it today. Negroes first participated in football as members of college teams. The first black college game was played between teams representing Biddle and Livingstone colleges in 1890.

Black players made their appearance on the elevens of predominantly white colleges in 1891. One of the eleven best players in the nation selected by Walter Camp of Yale, who began to pick all-star teams in 1889 and continued through 1918, was William H. Lewis who, with another black player, William Jackson, was on the varsity team at Amherst in 1889, and played center on the Harvard University team in 1892 and 1893. Both of these years Lewis was named to Camp's All-American team. As late as 1900, Lewis was considered the best center player that had appeared up to that time. Lewis, who died in recent years, became a lawyer of national repute in Boston, and was at one time an Assistant Attorney General of the United States.

Noteworthy black college football players during the first half of the twentieth century include William Chauncy Matthews of Harvard; Edward Morrison and William F. Brown of Tufts; Fritz Pollard of Brown University; Matthew Bullock of Dartmouth; Paul Robeson of Rutgers; Bill Bell of Ohio State University; Capt. Homer Harris of Iowa; Horace Bell and Bob Marshall of Minnesota; Duke Slater and Archie Alexander of Iowa; Sam Taylor, Tom Verdell, and Bernard Jefferson of Northwestern; Walter A. Gordon and Brice Taylor of the University of California; Edward Trigg and Sidat Singh of Syracuse; Brud Holland of Cornell; Kenney Washington and Woodrow Strode of UCLA; Chester Pierce of Harvard University; and Captain Levi Jackson of the Yale University football team.

Blacks have played an increasingly important role in college football. Two black Americans, Leroy Keyes and Orenthal James (O.J.) Simpson were the stars of the 1967 college football season. Rarely have two runners turned in such spectacular performances in a single season. In 1966, Keyes, at Purdue, was a good sophomore defensive back.

He shifted to offense in 1967 and wound up that year as the highest scorer in college football and everybody's All-American.

O. J. Simpson was All-American at Southern California. He led Southern Cal to the number-one-ranked football team in the nation and scored twice as Southern Cal beat Indiana 14 to 3 in the 1967 Rose Bowl.

The 1968 consensus All-American football team, comprised of top college players named in all of the polls, included the following black athletes: Paul Gibson of Houston, Joe Green of North Texas State, Ron Johnson of Michigan, Leroy Keyes of Purdue, and Jerry Levias of Southern Methodist University.

Bobby Mitchell, another noteworthy black player, was brilliant at the University of Illinois. The Cleveland Browns' Coach, Paul Brown, teamed Mitchell next to his star back, Jim Brown. As a rookie Mitchell gained 500 yards rushing while Jim Brown ran for 1,527 and led the league in rushing. Later Mitchell became a star on the Redskins in Washington, D.C.

For some time the black quarterback was a rarity in integrated college football, but in recent years Jimmy Jones at Southern California (1971–72), Eddie McAshan at Georgia Tech (1970–72), and Cliff Brown at Notre Dame (1971–73), have proven their ability to engineer the play of the team. The presence of talented undergraduate quarterbacks at Harvard, Princeton, and Columbia may indicate that talented young black athletes may be more concerned with academic benefits than with football alone.

A highlight of the 1969 college football season was the game between the Florida A. & M. and the University of Tampa football teams, in which the Negro conference team won 34 to 28. Although there was much competition in the area of the game at the Tampa stadium, a crowd of 46,471 witnessed the first contest between a top black and a top white university team in the South. Jake Gaither, a coach of twenty-five years at Florida A. & M., said after the game, "The old days are gone; from now on I invite the best team, whether it is black, white, yellow, or brown."

In 1971, as a tribute to their outstanding athletic performances that year in college football, *Black Sports* magazine named the following players to its first annual All-American Football Team:

*Offensive Team*

| | |
|---|---|
| Tight End: Jerome Barkum | Jackson State University |
| Tackle: Lionel Antoine | Southern Illinois University |
| Guard: Robert Penchion | Alcorn State University |
| Center: Orderia Mitchell | Air Force Academy |
| Running Back: Greg Pruitt | University of Oklahoma |
| Quarterback: Chuck Ealey | University of Toledo |
| Guard: Reggie McKenzie | University of Michigan |
| Tackle: Daryl White | University of Nebraska |
| Wide Receiver: Tom Gatewood | University of Notre Dame |
| Running back: Bobby Moore | University of Oregon |

*Defensive Team:*

| | |
|---|---|
| Defensive Back: Cliff Brooks | Tennessee State University |
| Linebacker: Mel Long | University of Toledo |
| Defensive End: Willie Hall | University of Southern California |
| Defensive Tackle: Tab Bennett | University of Illinois |
| Defensive Back: Leon Gannon | Alcorn State University |
| Defensive Tackle: Sherman White | University of California |
| Defensive End: Willie Harper | University of Nebraska |
| Linebacker: Richard Glover | University of Nebraska |
| Linebacker: Mike Taylor | University of Michigan |
| Defensive Back: Craig Clemons | University of Iowa |
| Defensive Back: Tom Darden | University of Michigan |

In 1972 Tom Gatewood became the first black to captain Notre Dame's football team. Gatewood is also the first black college player to be named as Academic All-American in both his junior and senior years. That same year, Chuck Ealey was named as *Black Sports* choice for Player of the Year. Ealey, quarterback for the University of Toledo, through 1972 had never played in a losing game. He was voted best back in the Mid-American Conference in 1970, '71, and '72.

The year 1972 saw the Heisman Trophy for outstanding football go to Johnny Rodgers, running back of the University of Nebraska. In 1975 the Ohio State University back, Archie Griffin, who set a new national four-year college career rushing record of 5176 yards, became the first player ever voted the Heisman Trophy twice. (He had won it in 1974.)

The Southeastern Conference (SEC), whose football teams ranked among the best in the nation, was the last college football league to integrate its teams, beginning in 1960. In 1966 Tennessee broke the color bar by signing defensive back Lester McLain. During the 1972 season, blacks comprised about 10 percent of the roughly 1,000 players in the conference.

In spite of the extensive black participation in college football today (blacks now star at dozens of colleges and are named to all-star teams of every description), in the years preceding the formation of the professional leagues (the National Football League [NFL] in 1919 and the American Football League [AFL] in 1946) only a handful of black athletes were playing on the teams of the major colleges. The establishment of the leagues, however, especially the AFL (see Figure 1) which actively sought out black talent, gave a tremendous boost to black participation in the sport, both on the college and professional levels, since many college players go on to make their mark in the professional leagues. The first black man to play professional football was Henry McDonald, who played with the Rochester Jeffersons.

So many blacks have played professional football through the years that it is possible here to name only a few of those heralded as the best. Among the early stars were:

Marion Motley, fullback for the Browns from 1946 to 1953. During those years the Cleveland Browns won the NFL championship four straight times. Coach Paul

**FIGURE 1**—BLACK PARTICIPATION IN PROFESSIONAL FOOTBALL, 1949–1971

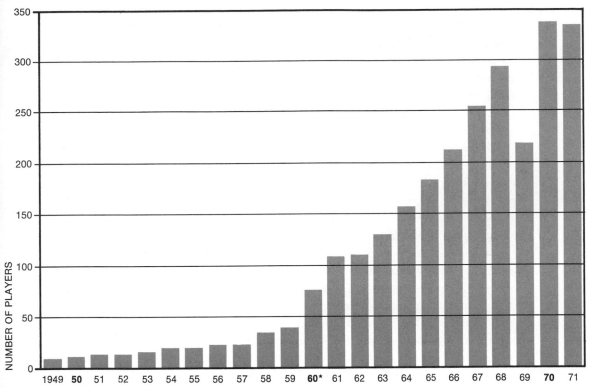

*Formation of American Football League

Source: *Black Sports,* May–June 1972.

Brown, formerly of the Browns, considers Motley the finest back ever to play for him.

Ollie Matson, an Olympic sprinter in the 1952 games, won the silver medal in the 400-meter run. He decided to play football and joined the Chicago Cardinals. After a tour in the Army, he returned to the Cardinals for the third game in 1954, and immediately ripped off two long runs to help the Cardinals beat Pittsburgh 17–14. His best year's rushing effort was in 1956 with 924 yards.

Lenny Moore, ex-Penn State star, became a member of the Baltimore Colts in 1956. He won the Jim Thorpe Memorial Trophy as the NFL's most valuable player for 1964.

Claude "Buddy" Young was only 5 feet, $4\frac{1}{2}$ inches tall and weighed 166 pounds in his prime, but he had a brilliant career with the Baltimore Colts. When he retired, his jersey number, 22, was retired. He then joined the Colts organization as a public relations representative, and today is an assistant to Pete Rozelle, Commissioner of Football. He was elected to the Football Hall of Fame in 1968 along with Marion Motley. Paul Robeson is also a member of the Hall of Fame.

Undoubtedly the greatest runner in football history was Jim Brown, who starred on the Cleveland Browns. He led the NFL in rushing in eight of his nine seasons of professional play, beginning in 1957. He carried the ball for a record of 12,312 yards, averaging 5.2 yards in every game he played.

Another potential "great," Ernie Davis, a Syracuse University football player, was listed for the Cleveland Browns but never played for them. In the 1959 college football season, he was listed as the number-one back in the nation, and in 1961 he became the first black to win the Heisman Trophy. But Davis contracted leukemia and died at the age of 23 in 1963.

The first two black stars in the AFL were Abner Haynes and Paul Lowe. Haynes, who starred with the Dallas Texans in the early sixties, was the first black player for a major Texas college when he enrolled at North Texas State. He led his school to win two Missouri Valley Conference titles and twice was named League Back of the Year.

Paul Lowe, a former high-school star, was signed in 1962 by the newly formed Los Angeles team of the AFL, then desperate for players. Lowe sat around for a year waiting to play, but when he did start, he became a star. In 1963 he broke loose for 1,010 yards, and in 1965 he gained 1,121 yards and was named the AFL's Player of the Year.

Haynes and Lowe, the AFL's first super ball carriers, were followed by Mike Garrett and Jim Nance as the new glamor runners in the league. Garrett, winner of the 1965 Heisman Trophy, was an All-American from Southern California. The Boston Patriot fullback Jim Nance, from Syracuse, in 1966 rushed 1,458 yards on the ground for an AFL record and was named Player of the Year.

Halfback Charley Taylor from Arizona State was named 1964 Rookie of the Year on the Redskins' team and established himself as a player long to be remembered.

Otis Taylor, from Prairie View A. & M., was a flanker on the Kansas City Chiefs; Bob Brown was all-pro tackle for the Philadelphia Eagles; Roosevelt Brown became the first black captain of the Giants' team and joined the coaching staff when he no longer was an active player.

Herb Adderley and Willie Woods of the Green Bay Packers combined nicely to become the most efficient defense in the AFL.

Jim Parker from Ohio State was a front-line star in the Colts' team. "Deacon" Jones, Lamar Lundy, Meslin Olseu (the only white man on the line), and Roosevelt Grier were popular on the Los Angeles Rams team. Willie Davis and Buck Buchanan out of Grambling starred in the AFL. (Special note should be made here of the role of Grambling College in furthering black participation in professional football. Grambling, founded in 1936, sent into the major professional ranks such standouts as Willie Davis of the Green Bay Packers, Buck Buchanan and Ernie Ladd of the Kansas City Chiefs, Sam Horrell of the Philadelphia Eagles, Willie Young of the New York Giants, Rosey Taylor and Frank Cornish of the Chicago Bears. Since 1948 more than sixty Grambling men have played football in the United States and Canada; in 1968 alone twenty-two Grambling graduates reported to pro-football training camps. Young men from Florida A. & M, Jackson State, Prairie View A. & M., Morgan State, Maryland State, Tennessee, Tuskegee, and other black colleges have become successful pro-grid players, but Grambling remains a unique phenomenon.)

More recent black professional stars include the following:

Leroy Kelly in 1966 was a starter on the Cleveland Browns' team. He scored fifteen touchdowns and finished second to Gayle Sayers (see below) in rushing. His carry average was 5.5 yards, the league's best in 1966; in 1968 he led the NFL in rushing. As of 1972 Kelly had gained more yards (6074) and scored more touchdowns (67) than any other active player in the AFL. That same year, Clifton McNeil of San Francisco ranked first in pass receiving and scoring.

Gayle Sayers of the Chicago Bears was considered one of the fastest and shiftiest backs in the game. Sayers announced his retirement from professional football in 1972 during a preseason game. A knee injury and repeated surgery had forced Sayers to miss the last two seasons. Sayers' career, although brief, was outstanding. He played in only sixty-eight games yet he holds the NFL record for touchdowns in one game (six) and in one season (twenty-two). He led the league in rushing for two years.

In January 1968, the New York Jets won the Super Bowl in a 16-7 upset over the Baltimore Colts. Jets player Matt Snell emerged from the game as the leading runner, covering 121 yards in 30 carries. Randy Beverly and Johnny Sample played outstanding defensive ball in the game, helping their team to victory.

That same year the Cleveland Browns won the Century Division title aided by the fine playing of Leroy Kelly, quarterback Bill Nelsen, and Paul Warfield. The Browns beat the Dallas Cowboys in the NFL playoffs, despite the superb playing skills of fullback Don Perkins and split end Bob Hayes.

Also in 1968, Marlin Briscoe became the first black quarterback in the AFL, playing that position for the Denver Broncos; and the naming of Paul Robinson, halfback for Cincinnati, as Rookie of the Year. Detroit Lions' Earl McCulloch was the offensive Rookie of the Year; Atlanta's Claude Humphrey won that award for the NFL.

Many black athletes gave outstanding performances during the 1972 professional football season. Larry Brown, Washington Redskin halfback, was named NFL offensive Player of the Year. The title of Rookie of the Year was given to Pittsburgh Steeler running back Franco Harris.

Floyd Little of the Denver Broncos, 1971 NFL rushing champion, gained more than 700 yards during the 1972 season. Frenchy Fuqua of the Pittsburgh Steelers, Willie Ellison of the Los Angeles Rams, and Leroy Kelley of the Cleveland Browns were among the top pro-football running backs. Green Bay Packers player John Brockington ran 1,105 yards in 216 carries for a 5.1-yard gain average, the highest record for a rookie in NFL history.

On the business side of football, all of the franchise owners are white, with the exception of two blacks from New Orleans, Norman Francis and C. C. Dejoie, who have invested in the National Football League's New Orleans Saints. (Nine black Detroiters invested in the now defunct Detroit Wheels of the World Football League.)

## Basketball

Basketball was invented in 1891 by Dr. James Naismith, an instructor at the YMCA Training School at Springfield, Massachusetts. Shortly thereafter black teams began to crop up in various sections of the nation. Basketball requires a large indoor space, however, and few places outside of metropolitan cities had such playing facilities at the turn of the century.

New York, Brooklyn, and Pittsburgh had excellent teams of black players from the start, some of whom competed with white teams. Among the first black teams to achieve a reputation were the Smart Set of Brooklyn; the St. Christophers, the Alphas, and the Spartans of New York; and the Leondi team of Pittsburgh—all appeared between 1900 and 1915. A decade later the Renaissance Five and the Incorporators of New York figured among the top black teams.

As owner and coach of the Renaissance Five, West Indies-born Bob Douglas, now in his late eighties, was recently elected to the Basketball Hall of Fame. His team, which was named to the Hall of Fame in 1964, won eighty-eight consecutive games in 1933.

Black colleges began to have basketball teams about 1909, and many of the best players started there. The game has increased in popularity by leaps and bounds until today it ranks second only to football as the major national team sport. Most of the black conferences stage championships and tournaments.

A few of the black players who established fame at some of the bigger colleges in the late 1950s were Paul Robeson at Rutgers, Whittaker at Dartmouth, Wilmeth Sidat

Singh at Syracuse, George Gregory at Columbia University, William "Dolly" King at Long Island University, Don Barksdale of the Pacific Coast, and Chuck Cooper at Duquesne.

During the past decade black players have been sought by the larger universities and colleges throughout the land. Today it is difficult for a black college to bid successfully for a player who has made a national reputation during his high school days, especially when professional teams may start recruiting high school students as in the case of Moses Malone, the seventeen-year-old who signed a three million dollar contract with the Utah Stars.

For the past several years at least one and occasionally two black athletes have been selected by the experts as the best players of five so designated. Maurice Stokes of St. Francis College was selected as the top rookie of the 1956 season. In 1956, as mentioned earlier, Bill Russell and K. C. Jones, both of the University of San Francisco, were considered by many as the two top players of the year. These two players were selected as members of the Olympic team that won the world championship in the Olympic Games. Carl Cain of the University of Iowa was also a member of that Olympic team. On Russell's return to the United States, he was offered a salary of $30,000 to play with the Harlem Globetrotters, but elected to play with the Celtics team. Jones, after starring with the Celtics, went on to San Diego. He became the sole black coach in the ABA, in the 1972–73 season.

The continued success of blacks in college basketball is shown by the fact that black Americans made up the entire first college All-American team for the 1966–67 season and three of the top five the next season. In the college world, one of the greatest seasons for black players was in 1965–66 when the University of Kentucky team, which ranked first in the polls all season with not one black on the squad, faced little Texas Western College, which did not use a single white player in the entire contest. Underdog Texas Western won the title.

In 1968 the following black stars were included in the consensus All-American team for that year, compiled from teams chosen by AP, UPI, NBA coaches, and Basketball Writers Association:

Lew Alcindor (Kareem Abdul-Jabbar), UCLA
Lucius Allen, UCLA
Elvin Hayes, Houston
Merv Jackson, Utah
Bob Lanier, St. Bonaventure
Calvin Murphy, Niagara
Don Smith, Iowa State
Westley Unseld, Louisville
Mike Warren, UCLA
Jo Jo White, Kansas

Kareem Abdul-Jabbar was named 1968 Player of the Year by the Helms Foundation, while UPI and AP designated Elvin Hayes as their choice for the honor.

In 1970, 7 foot, 2 inch Tom Payne became the first black man to play on the University of Kentucky basketball team. There are blacks playing in the SEC, breaking down the racial barriers of the past. Although the number of blacks participating in the SEC is small (forty-one athletes in eight sports at ten schools), their presence indicates an advance over past policies.[3]

In 1971 Florida State University reached the finals against UCLA using all black players.

Black players have dominated professional basketball more than any other sport. During the 1967-68 season, of the 139 players in the National Basketball Association (NBA), 71 were black. The establishment of the American Basketball Association (ABA) in 1967 by a group of California sportsmen provided increased opportunity for black participation in the game (see Figure 2). The ABA was avid for talent and willing to pay for it, and scoured the black schools for players. By 1972 out of approximately 110 ABA league players, 63 were black.

One of the basketball teams that has elicited more comment than any other professional organization is the Harlem Globetrotters organization. In 1927 the late Abe Saperstein selected five excellent players and at first named them the Savoy Big Five in honor of their playing court, the Savoy Ballroom in Chicago. After losing the use of the ballroom to a roller-skating arena, the team became the Harlem Globetrotters. It enjoyed a phenomenal success. To save the energies of the players, Saperstein had the players play hard for ten minutes and clown the rest of the game.

In 1943 the Globetrotters won the championship in a tournament that was labeled a world championship event. Until 1970 the Globetrotters had won 9,200 victories of 9,600 games played. They have performed all over the world, from the cow fields of Morocco to white-tie audiences in London's Wimbledon Stadium, before Pope Pius XII, and again for the largest crowd in history—75,000—in Berlin's Olympic Stadium.

Since 1953 a new group of stellar players has emerged, formed by Marques Oreol Haynes, an ex-top player on the Globetrotters, and "Goose" Tatum. The group is called the Fabulous Magicians. Both Haynes, noted for his dribbling, and Tatum, dubbed the Clown Prince of basketball, had become dissatisfied with Saperstein. Leaving the Globetrotters, where his yearly top salary had been $10,000, Haynes soon became an entrepreneur with real estate holdings and earning $75,000 annually. His partner, "Goose" Tatum, died in 1967, one year after the death of Saperstein. Both the Globetrotters and the Magicians continue to entertain millions and serve as goodwill ambassadors all over the world.

The literature covering basketball is replete with stories of great black players and games during the last half-century. Here are some of the recent players who have been widely publicized (space does not permit mention of all the stars).

**FIGURE 2**—PERCENTAGE OF BLACK BASKETBALL PLAYERS IN THE NATIONAL
AND AMERICAN BASKETBALL ASSOCIATIONS. 1959–1972

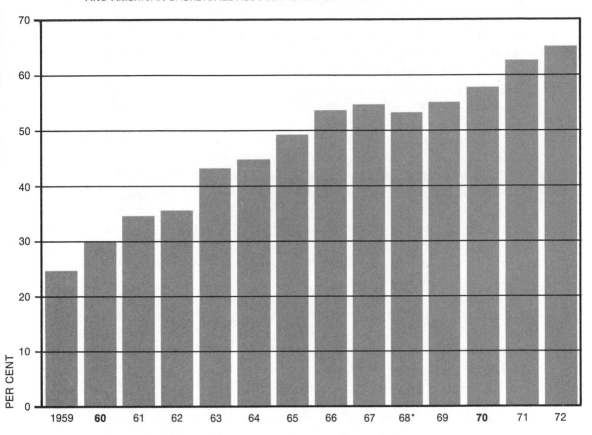

*Founding of American Basketball Association

Source : *Black Sports,* May–June 1972.

Kareem Abdul-Jabbar's (Lew Alcindor's) fame is worldwide. At the University of California at Los Angeles, he established a variety of records and helped the team win many championships. As a professional, he is indomitable. Star player for the Milwaukee Bucks in the 1970–71 season, he was the top scorer with a total of 2,596 points, an average of 31.7 points per game. Jabbar led the Bucks to victory over the New York Knicks in the NBA championship playoff games. He was the top individual scoring leader of the 1971–72 season with 2,822 points, an average of 34.8 per game. As a tribute to his outstanding abilities, Jabbar was awarded the Podoloff Trophy as the Most Valuable Player of the 1971–72 season.

Wilt Chamberlain is often regarded as the greatest offensive threat in the history of basketball. Chamberlain, 7 feet, 2 inches tall and 265 pounds, was a track and field star in Philadelphia. He gained notoriety in basketball while a student at the University of Kansas. As a professional he led the NBA in scoring for six straight seasons. At the start of the 1970–71 season, Chamberlain ranked first in the all-time NBA basketball scoring. Formerly the captain of the Los Angeles Lakers, he earned the rebounding title for the league, the tenth such title of his career, as well as leading in field-goal percentage during the 1971–72 season. He is now retired from basketball and has organized a women's volleyball team.

Bill Russell led the Boston Celtics to world championship titles for several years. He later became coach and manager of the Celtics—a first for a black player. Russell was elected to the Basketball Hall of Fame early in 1975, but he refused to accept the election, in protest against earlier discrimination which excluded many illustrious black predecessors from the Hall of Fame.

Nate Thurmond, who played for the San Francisco Warriors in the mid-1960s, was considered by many experts to be a better defensive player than Wilt Chamberlain and a better offensive player than Bill Russell—high tribute, indeed.

Elvin Hayes was the first black to play for the University of Houston. In his senior year he broke the major college record by scoring 1,214 points for a single year, five more than a previous senior had scored fourteen years earlier. While at Houston, he broke every basketball record. His most notable performance was during the 1967–68 season, when his team defeated Jabbar and his UCLA team 71–69. Hayes, now playing with San Diego, has been listed among the top professional basketball players.

Notre Dame's Austin Carr was ranked as the second-highest individual scoring leader at the beginning of the 1971–72 college basketball season. Carr, who was also listed among the all-time college scoring leaders, accumulated 1,101 points, averaging 38.0 per game. Carr is now playing pro ball with the Cleveland Cavaliers.

Other top rebound leaders included Wes Unseld of Baltimore, Jabbar, Nate Thurmond, E. Smith of Buffalo, and Elvin Hayes, Bob Lanier, and William Bridges of Philadelphia. Named as assistant leaders were Sonny Wilkens of Seattle, Nate Archibald, Archie Clark of Baltimore, Norm Van Lier of Chicago, and Walt Frazier and Walt Hazzard of Buffalo.

The NBA in 1975 had several black basketball coaches. Earl Lloyd had been with the Detroit Pistons since the 1971–72 season; Al Attles, former player with the Golden State Warriors (San Francisco), was coaching the team. Other black basketball coaches in 1975 were K. C. Jones (Washington Bullets); Ray Scott (Detroit Pistons); Lenny Wilkins (Portland Trailblazers). Bill Russell had moved over to the Seattle Supersonics.

As for managers, the record was even less impressive. Wayne Embry, appointed general manager by the Milwaukee Bucks in 1970, was still the only black holder of such a position in 1975.

## Hockey

It is interesting to note that in spite of the ever-increasing popularity of American hockey, this is a sport in which blacks are yet to make a significant mark. The New York Raiders of the World Hockey Association have recently drafted Alton White, one of two black hockey players competing in the United States. The other black player on the circuit is Willie O'Ree of the Western Hockey League's San Diego team. O'Ree, who played briefly with the Boston Bruins, was the first black player in National Hockey League history.

## Soccer

Blacks from other countries have distinguished themselves as soccer players at many colleges, particularly Howard and Lincoln among the black colleges.

Perhaps the surprise of the 1971 season was the winning of the NCAA National Soccer Championship by the Howard University soccer team, playing before a crowd of 5,800 in the Orange Bowl in Miami. The Howard team defeated the strong University of St. Louis team, which had won the National Soccer Championship for three successive years. Howard, by a score of 3 goals to 2, thus became the first black university to win a national sports title. The man behind the victorious Howard University soccer team was Lincoln Phillips, a native of Trinidad, who was a star in the American Soccer League and later in the North American Soccer League. Soccer is played in numerous countries throughout the world, but has only in recent decades assumed major proportions in the United States.

## Rowing

There have been several black members of college rowing crews. In 1915 the great Syracuse crew of that year included a black, Joseph Edward Trigg, who rowed number-four oar.

## INDIVIDUAL SPORTS

### Boxing

Black boxers have been prominent since the earliest years of the republic. Slave owners often pitted their hands against the slaves of other plantations. Some Negro Americans won their freedom by winning for their masters. (It was not until 1816 that the first prizefight between white and black men took place in America.) The first black pugilist to attain distinction in the "ring" was Bill Richmond, who was born on Staten Island and taken to England by Lord Percy, Duke of Northumberland, in 1777. There he fought many memorable battles between 1800 and 1818, including a match with the redoubtable English champion Tom Cribb, which Richmond lost by a decision.

The first American champion to fight in an international bout was Tom Molyneaux, a former slave from Virginia who had won his freedom by his athletic prowess. He began boxing in the old Catherine Markets in New York City in 1809 and was later taken in tow by Bill Richmond. Molyneaux won several matches in England and was eventually matched with Tom Cribb. This fight, which took place on December 18, 1810, was the first great "battle of the century." It was a monumental struggle and had it not been for the trickery of the Cribb seconds, Molyneaux would have been judged the winner. In the twenty-third round Cribb was unable to continue, but the seconds delayed the time beyond the thirty-second limit until Cribb could get himself together. At the end of the fortieth round Molyneaux was unable to continue, and Cribb was declared the winner.

After Molyneaux, a steady flow of black pugilists appeared on the American scene. One of them, Bob Travers, engaged in more contests in the ring than any American fighter before him; his best-known fights were with Jem Mace, who won the world championship in 1840. George Godfrey of Boston was the first recognized black heavyweight champion of America; he lost his championship to Peter Jackson, the famous heavyweight champion of the latter part of the nineteenth century. Neither Jackson nor Godfrey was able to coax John L. Sullivan into meeting them in the ring because of their race. Peter Jackson was considered the best heavyweight in the world; but not until he was over 30 years old and had survived at least 100 battles did he get a chance to meet the leading white boxer, James J. Corbett. They met on May 21, 1891, at the California Athletic Club, and after sixty rounds of fighting, neither boxer was able to carry on and the event was declared a draw.

One of the most famous bantam and featherweight boxers of all times was black George Dixon. He defeated the English featherweight champion, Nunc Wallace, at the Pelican Club in London in June 27, 1890, for the title, and held the featherweight championship for the years 1892 through 1900.

The most talked-of fighter in the early part of the twentieth century was Joe Gans, a lightweight who not only held the lightweight championship from 1902 through 1908, but also battled heavier men in all classes. Another prominent black boxer was Joe Walcott,* a native of Barbados, who did most of his fighting as an American citizen. Walcott held the title of welterweight champion of the world from 1901 through 1906.

Practically all prizefighters have lacked college training, whereas football and basketball players and track and field athletes traditionally are the products of college participation in athletics. The boxer, like the sprinter, needs to have a natural endowment of neuromuscular skills and coordination, courage, and a will to win against all odds. For this reason many black men have looked on boxing as a "natural" sport. Ever since the color line was abandoned in boxing, as in many other sports, black Americans have entered the lists and have dominated the championships.

Black Americans have astounded the athletic world by the number of championships they have held in professional boxing. In amateur contests they have exceeded the number of white American and world champions in titles held during the past decade. Looking at the record of professional champions, we find the following data.

Black fighters who have held heavyweight championships are: Jack Johnson from 1903 to 1915; Joe Louis from 1937 to 1949; Ezzard Charles in 1949 and 1950; "Jersey Joe" Walcott for 1951; Floyd Patterson, 1956–59 and 1960–62; Charles "Sonny" Liston, 1962–64. As 1956 ended, blacks held five of six weight-class championships held by Americans. Floyd Patterson was the heavyweight champion (and of the ten ranking contenders, nine were black). Archie Moore was the recognized light-heavyweight; Ray Robinson the middleweight; Joe Brown of New Orleans the lightweight; and Sandy Sadler the featherweight champion.

Perhaps the most colorful heavyweight of recent years is Muhammad Ali, born Cassius Clay, who fought his way through the Golden Gloves tournaments in Louisville, Kentucky, in the mid-1950s to become Golden Gloves and AAU Champion. He went on to earn the title of Olympic light-heavyweight champion in Rome in 1960. He began his professional career by knocking out Doug Jones, Andre Moore, and Henry Cooper, then looked to the heavyweight championship held by Sonny Liston. After much publicity in the press and antics on TV, he was finally matched with Liston in 1964. Ali defeated Liston by a technical knockout in the seventh round, becoming the twenty-fourth World Heavyweight Champion. Liston attempted to regain his title in 1965, but Ali triumphed with a first-round knockout in what was one of the quickest boxing matches in the history of the sport.

In 1967 Ali refused induction into the Army on the grounds of his Muslim faith. A Houston jury, unconvinced of his claim to exemption as a conscientious objector, sentenced him to five years in federal prison. After Ali lost an appeal on the verdict in 1968, he brought the case before the Supreme Court, which reversed the ruling of the lower court in an 8–0 decision in 1971. During the three-and-a-half years of court pro-

*Not to be confused with "Jersey Joe" Walcott of later fame.

ceedings, however, the New York State Athletic Commission revoked Ali's heavyweight title; boxing officials throughout the country kept Ali from the ring, even though his case was being appealed.

In September 1972 Ali defeated former two-time heavyweight champion Floyd Patterson in the seventh round of the Madison Square Garden match. Ali, then 30 years old, had won thirty-eight out of thirty-nine scheduled bouts.

In 1971 Ali lost the world championship title to Joe Frazier of Beaufort, South Carolina. Frazier had achieved fame as a Golden Gloves champion in 1962, 1963, and 1964, and had won the Olympic heavyweight crown in the Tokyo Olympics. Frazier held the championship until January 1973, when he was knocked out by fellow black George Foreman. And in October 1974, in Kinshasa, Zaïre, Ali regained the heavyweight title in a fight against Foreman that was televised around the world.

In the lower-weight divisions, John Henry Lewis was light-heavyweight champion from 1935 to 1939. Archie Moore held the light-heavyweight title from 1953 to 1961. During 1965-66 the crown was held by José Torres. Among the middleweight champions have been Tiger Flowers for 1920 to 1923, "Gorilla" Jones for 1931 and 1932, and Ray Robinson from 1951 to 1952 and again for 1955 and 1956. Welterweight champions have been the aforementioned Joe Walcott from 1901 through 1906; Young Jack Thompson for 1930 and 1931; Henry Armstrong from 1938 through 1940; Ray Robinson for 1947 through 1951; Johnny Bratton for 1951; Kid Gavilan from 1951 through 1954; and Johnny Saxton for 1954, 1955, and 1956.

Probably the most versatile of all the lesser-weight champions was Henry Armstrong, who in 1937 and 1938 won and held championships in three weight classes: the featherweight, lightweight, and welterweight divisions.

Among the lightweight champions have been Joe Gans from 1902 to 1908; Henry Armstrong for 1938 and 1939; Beau Jack and Bob Montgomery in the years 1943 and 1944; Bob Montgomery and Ike Williams in 1946 and 1947; James Carter in 1951, 1952, 1954, and 1955; and Joe Brown in 1956. Featherweight champions have been George Dixon from 1892 to 1900; Kid Chocolate in 1932; Henry Armstrong for 1937 and 1938; Chalky Wright in 1941 and 1942; and Sandy Sadler for 1948, 1949, and 1950. Bantamweight titleholders have been George Dixon from 1890 to 1892 and Al Brown from 1929 to 1935. No black American professional has held a championship in the flyweight division, and seldom does any American win in this lightest weight class.

Of the twenty-one boxing victories the United States has won in the Olympic Games since 1904, six were won by black fighters. In the 1952 Olympics, blacks won five first places in boxing events and for the first time the United States won the boxing-point championship. All of the five winners were black: Nathan Brooks, flyweight champion; Charles Adkins, lightweight; Floyd Patterson, middleweight; Norval Lee, light-heavyweight; and Hayes E. Sanders, heavyweight. Norval Lee was judged the best boxer in the Olympic series. The tally of the boxing events was the deciding margin of the unofficial point score which led America to victory over the Russians. In 1956, as previously mentioned, one of the two Americans who won Olympic boxing medals, James Boyd, was black.

## Track and Field

In national competition, black track and field athletes began to show their mettle in the broad-jump event in 1920, when Sol Johnson of Dubuque, Iowa, won the national American Athletic Union (AAU) title. In thirty-six national contests, black broad jumpers have won twenty-six national championships, with Dehart Hubbard of Cincinnati winning for six consecutive years. Ned Gourdin of Harvard University was the first man in the world to jump more than 25 feet in 1921; Dehart Hubbard followed and raised the mark to 25 feet, 10 inches. Haitian Silvio Cator was the first broad jumper in the world to surpass 26 feet. For over thirty years Jesse Owens held the world record with a jump of 26 feet, $8\frac{1}{4}$ inches, made at Ann Arbor, Michigan, on May 25, 1935.

Black supremacy in the sprint races has been as notable as in the broad jump. Howard Drew was the first of the great black sprinters. He won the national title in 1912 and 1913 in the 100-yard dash, won the 220-yard dash in 1913 and 1914 for the University of Southern California, and for a time held the 100-yard record of 9.6 seconds. Not until the early thirties, however, did black sprint champions become the rule rather than the exception. Eddie Tolan won sprint honors in the 1932 Olympics, and others could claim victories in over seventeen AAU championships by 1960. In some of these annual competitive events they have taken first, second, and third places; occasionally all six finalists have been black. Black sprinters have also dominated the 200-meter and 220-yard events since the early thirties. Eddie Tolan, Ralph Metcalfe, Mack Robinson (brother to Jackie Robinson), Barney Ewell, Elmore Harris, Andrew Stanfield, Robert Tyler, Lloyd LaBeach, James Ford, and Arthur Bragg were winners between 1940 and 1960.

Middle-distance runners have been less numerous. Prominent among them have been Archie Williams, Elmore Harris, Phil Edwards, James Herbert, Dave Bolen, Reginald Pearman, John Woodruff, Mal Whitfield, Cecil Cooke, and Robert Kelly.

One of the greatest black middle-distance runners was John Borican of Virginia State College and of Columbia University, who died in the prime of life. He was national 1,000-yard champion from 1939 to 1941, and was the first man in the United States to win both the pentathlon and the decathlon in the same year (1941).

High jumping is another event in which black Americans have excelled. A black high jumper, Charles Dumas of Compton College in California, broke the world record in 1956 with a leap of over 7 feet. Dumas also won the Olympic high jump with an Olympic record jump of 6 feet, $11\frac{1}{2}$ inches. Two black women have won Olympic high-jump titles: Alice Coachman, formerly of Tuskegee, and Mildred McDaniels of Tuskegee. Miss Coachman won in London in 1948 and Miss McDaniels won in 1956 with a world-record jump of 5 feet, $9\frac{1}{2}$ inches. The first black high jumper to win an

Olympic medal was Cornelius Johnson, who won the national championship while still a high school student in 1936 and went on to win the Olympic championship in that year. Other great jumpers have been Melvin Walker of Ohio State University, Joshua Williamson of Xavier University, Adam Berry of Southern University, and Ed Burke of Marquette University, all of whom cleared 6 feet, 8 inches. Between 1932 and 1948, this group won or tied in twelve national championships, and in one of those years there were five black contenders among the six finalists.

Several outstanding hurdlers have been black. One of the early black stars was Charles R. Brookins, who was national champion in the low hurdles for 1923 and 1925. Elmore Harris of Long Branch, New Jersey, was the 1944 champion low hurdler. In 1946 and 1947 Harrison Dillard was both national low-hurdles champion and national high-hurdles champion. The longer hurdle race, 440 yards, has had only one black champion, Josh Culbreath of Morgan State College in Maryland, who won the national title in 1953 and 1954.

Only two black Americans have won the hop-step-jump event: Dehart Hubbard in 1922 and 1923, and Don Barksdale in 1944. No black athlete has won a national championship in the pole vault, hammer throw, or javelin throw, although some have won in college competition. Archie Harris won the national discus-hurling championship in 1941.

Only a handful of black runners have won championships in distance running. R. E. Johnson of Pittsburgh was national champion for the five-mile run in 1921, 1922, and 1923, and also won the ten-mile championship for 1921 and 1924. Gus Moore of New York won national honors for the ten-mile race in 1930 and was national cross-country champion in 1928 and 1929. Frank Dixon was collegiate mile champion in 1942 and won the cross-country championship the same year. In 1954 Theodore Corbitt of the Pioneer Club of New York won the American Marathon championship. No black track man has yet won a national mile championship.

Negroes have been outstanding in the more grueling multiple-performance events, the pentathlon and the decathlon. In 1956 Rafer Johnson of the University of Southern California was runner-up to Milton Campbell, who won the Olympic decathlon with a score of 7,937 points. In Moscow's "Little Olympics" of 1958 Johnson set a new world record in decathlon by defeating Russia's Vasily Kuznetsov. Johnson held the world decathlon record after winning a gold medal in the 1960 Olympics and setting a new record with a total of 8,392 points. Other black winners of the national pentathlon titles have been Edwin Gourdin in 1921 and 1922, and Eulace Peacock of Asbury Park, New Jersey, in 1933, 1934, 1937, 1943, 1944, and 1945. John Borican won this event in 1938, 1939, and 1941. Decathlon winners of national honors were William Watson of the University of Michigan in 1940 and 1943, John Borican in 1941, and Milton Campbell in 1953.

The Olympic records in the period from 1956 to 1968 can be seen in the accompanying listing of winners in the following Olympic games: 1960, 1964, 1968.

**TABLE I—BLACK AMERICAN OLYMPIC WINNERS: 1960, 1964, 1968**

| | | | |
|---|---|---|---|
| Les Carney | 200-Meter Dash | Second—20.6 | Rome, 1960 |
| Lee Calhoun | 110-Meter Hurdles | First—13.8 | Rome, 1960 |
| Willie May | 110-Meter Hurdles | Second—13.8 | Rome, 1960 |
| Hayes Jones | 110-Meter Hurdles | Third—14.0 | Rome, 1960 |
| John Thomas | High Jump | First—7'¼'' | Rome, 1960 |
| Ralph Boston | Running Broad Jump | First—26'7¾'' | Rome, 1960 |
| Irv Roberson | Running Broad Jump | Second—26'7⅜'' | Rome, 1960 |
| Otis Davis (member of team) | 1600-Meter Relay (each runner does 400 meters) | First—3.02.2 | Rome, 1960 |
| Rafer Johnson | Decathlon | First—8.392 points | Rome, 1960 |
| Wilma Rudolph | Women's 100-Meter Dash | First—11.0 | Rome, 1960 |
| Wilma Rudolph | Women's 200-Meter Dash | First—24.0 | Rome, 1960 |
| Earlene Brown | Women's shotput | Third—53'10⅝'' | Rome, 1960 |
| Martha Judson Barbara Jones Lucinda Williams Wilma Rudolph (members of team) | Women's 400-Meter Relay (each runner does 100 meters) | First—44.5 | Rome, 1960 |
| Robert Hayes | 100-Meter Dash | First—9.9 | Tokyo, 1964 |
| Henry Carr | 200-Meter Dash | First—20.3 | Tokyo, 1964 |
| Paul Drayton | 200-Meter Dash | Second—20.5 | Tokyo, 1964 |
| Hayes Jones | 110-Meter Hurdles | First—13.6 | Tokyo, 1964 |
| Paul Drayton Robert Hayes (members of team) | 400-Meter Relay (each runner does 100 meters) | First—39.0 | Tokyo, 1964 |
| John Thomas | High Jump | Second—7'1¾'' | Tokyo, 1964 |
| John Rambo | High Jump | Third—7'1'' | Tokyo, 1964 |
| Ralph Boston | Running Broad Jump | Second—26'4'' | Tokyo, 1964 |
| Wyomia Tyus | Women's 100-Meter Dash | First—11.4 | Tokyo, 1964 |
| Edith McGuire | Women's 100 Meter-Dash | Second—11.4 | Tokyo, 1964 |
| Marilyn White | Women's 100-Meter Dash | Third—11.6 | Tokyo, 1964 |
| Willye White Wyomia Tyus Marilyn White Edith McGuire (members of team) | Women's 400-Meter Relay (each runner does 100 meters) | Second—43.9 | Tokyo, 1964 |
| Jim Hines | 100-Meter Dash | First—9.9 | Mexico City, 1968 |
| Charlie Greene | 100-Meter Dash | Third—10.0 | Mexico City, 1968 |
| Tommie Smith | 200-Meter Dash | First—19.8 | Mexico City, 1968 |
| John Carlos | 200-Meter Dash | Third—20.0 | Mexico City, 1968 |
| Lee Evans | 400-Meter Dash | First—43.8 | Mexico City, 1968 |
| Larry James | 400-Meter Dash | Second—43.9 | Mexico City, 1968 |
| Ron Freeman | 400-Meter Dash | Third—44.4 | Mexico City, 1968 |
| Willie Davenport | 110-High Hurdles | First—13.3 | Mexico City, 1968 |
| Erv Hall | 110-High Hurdles | Second—13.4 | Mexico City, 1968 |

BLACK AMERICAN OLYMPIC WINNERS: 1960, 1964, 1968 (Cont.)

| Ed Caruthers | High Jump | Second—7'3⅜'' | Mexico City, 1968 |
|---|---|---|---|
| Bob Beamon | Long Jump | First—29'2½'' | Mexico City, 1968 |
| Ralph Boston | Long Jump | Third—26'9½'' | Mexico City, 1968 |
| Jim Hines<br>Charlie Greene<br>Ronnie Ray Smith<br>Mel Pender | 400-Meter Relay | First—38.2 | Mexico City, 1968 |
| Lee Evans<br>Ron Freeman<br>Larry James<br>Vince Matthews | 1600-Meter Relay | First—2:56.1 | Mexico City, 1968 |
| Wyomia Tyus | Women's 100-Meter Dash | First—11.00 | Mexico City, 1968 |
| Barbara Ferrell | Women's 100-Meter Dash | Second—11.1 | Mexico City, 1968 |
| Madline Manning | Women's 800-Meter Dash | First—2:00.9 | Mexico City, 1968 |
| Wyomia Tyus<br>Barbara Ferrell<br>Margaret Bailes<br>Mildred Netter<br>(members of team) | Women's 400-Meter Relay (each runner does 100 meters) | First—42.8 | Mexico City, 1968 |

Source:  *Black Sports,* May/June 1972.

TABLE II—BLACK AMERICAN OLYMPIC WINNERS AT MUNICH, 1972

| Ray Seals | Light welterweight | |
|---|---|---|
| Vincent Matthews | 400-meter run | First Place |
| Rod Milburn | 110-meter hurdle | First Place |
| Randy Williams | Long jump | First Place |
| Larry Black | 200-meter run | Second Place |
| Wayne Collett | 400-meter run | Second Place |
| Tom Hill | 110-meter hurdle | Second Place |

In the 1956 Olympic Games at Melbourne, black athletes won six gold medals and white athletes eight, of the fourteen first places in track and field events won by Americans. Charles Jenkins of Villanova won the 400-meter race, Charles Dumas of California won the high jump, Gregory Bell won the broad jump, Lee Calhoun of North Carolina College for Negroes (now North Carolina Central University) won the high hurdles, Milton Campbell won the grueling decathlon and the aforementioned Mildred McDaniels of Tuskegee won the high jump for women. Other medal winners were Andy Stanfield, second in the 200 meters; Josh Culbreath of Morgan State College, third in the 400-meter hurdles; Rafer Johnson, second in the decathlon; Willye White of Tennessee State College, second in the broad jump for women. Ira Murchison of the U. S. Army and Leamon King of the University of California were members of the winning 400-

meter relay team, and Lou Jones of the U. S. Army and Charles Jenkins of Villanova were on the winning 1500-meter relay team.

In the period extending from the Olympic Games held in San Francisco in 1932, up to the 1956 games, black athletes won ten of the twenty first-place medals in the flat races (100, 200, 400, and 800 meters). In 1932 Eddie Tolan won the 100- and 200-meter races. In 1936 Jesse Owens won both sprint races; Archie Williams won the 400-meter and John Woodruff won the 800-meter run; Cornelius Johnson won the high jump; Jesse Owens the broad jump. In the London games of 1948 Harrison Dillard won the 100-meter dash; Malvin Whitfield won the 800-meter run; Willie Steele won the broad jump, and Alice Coachman the high jump for women. At Helsinki in 1952 Andrew Stanfield won the 200-meter dash, Malvin Whitfield the 800-meter run, Harrison Dillard the 110-meter high hurdles, and Jerome Biffle the broad jump.

Looking back it becomes apparent that since World War II the Olympics would have meant little to America had it not been for black competitors in the sprints, relays, hurdles, broad jump, high jump, and triple jump. The earlier-mentioned Olympic games of 1948 in London and 1952 in Helsinki were the games of Harrison Dillard and Mal Whitfield; those of 1956 featured Milt Campbell; 1960 produced Otis Davis, Ralph Boston, and Rafer Johnson; and the 1964 games starred Hayes Jones, Henry Carr, Bob Hayes and many others.

Although few U. S. white women did well in the track and field events in the Olympics, American black women were the stars in the sprints. In 1960 Wilma Rudolph easily won the 100 and 200 meters and the winning leg on the mile relay. In 1964, Wyomia Tyus was Olympic sprint champion. Both of these women athletes and many others were trained by Edward Temple of Tennessee State A. & I. University, who grew famous as a track coach of teams which dominated women's championships for many years. In the 1968 Olympic competitions Madline Manning won a gold medal for the 800-meter dash and Wyomia Tyus finished first in the 100-meter dash, setting a new world's record. Tyus teamed up with Barbara Ferrell, Margaret Bailes, and Mildred Netter to win the 400-meter relay event.

Preparation for the Munich Olympics produced new champions as records were made and broken in the process.

The 1968 Olympic Games was the scene of record-breaking performances by black track and field athletes. Jim Hines won the 100-meter event in 9.9 seconds, setting an Olympic record and equaling the world record. Tommie Smith set a world record in the 200 meters, Lee Evans won the 400 meters in record-breaking 43.8 time, while teammates Larry James and Ron Freeman finished second and third. Willie Davenport finished in first place in the 110-meter high hurdles, setting an Olympic record. U. S. relay teams in the 400 meters and 1,600 meters set new world records by their victories. In the long jump, Bob Beamon leaped 29 feet, $2\frac{1}{2}$ inches, establishing a new record.

In the 1972 Olympics, Vince Matthews finished first in the 400-meter competition, outrunning teammate Wayne Collett, who finished a close second in the race. The stadium crowds reacted negatively to Matthews' and Collett's attitude on the victory podium during the playing of the U. S. National Anthem. The two winners chatted briefly during the anthem and the crowd, interpreting their inattention as a black-power protest, booed their behavior. Both athletes denied the charge and claimed that the crowd had misinterpreted their actions. Despite their denials, the International Olympic Committee barred Matthews and Collett from all future Olympic events, including the 1600-meter relay scheduled for the Munich Games.

The scene was reminiscent of the 1968 Olympics, where runners John Carlos and Tommie Smith raised black-gloved fists in the black-power sign on the victory stand. The two players were suspended from the team amid much controversy.

## Tennis

Tennis was introduced in America in 1873. It began as a game reserved for the social elite. Philadelphia and Chicago had courts as far back as 1874, but black Americans did not enter the sport until 1890. Among the first black tennis players were Emmett J. Scott, S. E. Courtney, and E. T. Atwell, who later became prominent as an official of the American Recreation Association. Tournaments for black players began around 1899 with pioneers like Reverend W. W. Walker and Professor Charles Cook of Howard University popularizing the game.

For a long time, as with many other branches of sport, prejudice against black players barred them from entering competition with white players under the auspices of the United States Lawn Tennis Association. In November 1916 the black American Tennis Association was formed. (Whenever a national sports organization excluded black members and called itself an "American," "National," or "United States" association, black organizations also adopted a name signifying a national organization, usually using one of the above terms: for example, if the white group used the term "American," the black group took the name "National.")

Among the black tennis players who achieved some fame in competition for national honors were H. S. McCard, William H. Wright, B. M. Rhetta, and Ralph Cook of Baltimore; Henry Freeman, John F. N. Wilkinson, James Walker, Sylvester Smith, and Tally Holmes of Washington, D. C.; Gerald K. Norman and Kinckle Jones of New York; "Ma" Semmes and Edgar Brown of Chicago.

Black colleges have done much to spur tennis competition. Several excellent black tennis players have emerged from the predominantly white colleges as well. Richard Hudlin of Chicago in 1927 was the first black captain of a collegiate tennis team in the Big Ten universities. Douglass Turner was a letter man in tennis at the University of Illinois and was runner-up for the Big Ten title in 1929. Reginald Weir was captain of the 1928 New York City College team. Weir was at first rejected as an entry in the indoor national championships but later played in outdoor national championships.

In 1956 the woman tennis player who ranked second best in the world was the earlier-mentioned Althea Gibson of New York. She first attracted the attention of black sponsors of tennis by her performances in black tournament play. Coached by the late Dr. Walter "Whirlwind" Johnson of Lynchburg and helped by others, she emerged a seasoned player capable of taking on the best in the game. After winning top honors in contests with black women players, she was accepted in national tournaments. As previously mentioned, in 1956 she went abroad and in the course of her travels through Scandinavia, Egypt, Italy, France, and England, won twelve tournaments, including championship matches in Rome, Naples, Genoa, Palermo, Cologne, and Nice; Adelaide and Sydney, Australia; Dakar, West Africa; Paris; and Manchester and Birmingham, England. In her own country she won the Pennsylvania State Open, the Eastern Open, Midwestern, and Southern Pacific tournaments. She lost at both Forest Hills and Wimbledon to Shirley Fry, whom she had beaten in other tournaments, but won the women's singles title and the doubles championship (with Darlene Hard) at Wimbledon in 1957. In 1957 and 1958 she won the U. S. women's singles championship at Forest Hills, becoming the first black named as the top-ranked woman tennis player in the United States.

Arthur Ashe was the first black American named to the Davis Cup Team (1964), and by 1965 he had swept through the best players in Australia. There, in one hour and fifteen minutes he disposed of the tough Fred Stolle, 6-4, 6-4, 6-4. Then in the semifinals Ashe defeated John Newcombe, 6-4, 6-4, 6-3. Ashe won the final grueling match in this Australia Tournament against the great Roy Emerson, 3-6, 6-2, 6-3, 3-6, and 6-1.

Ashe was the first black American to win the men's U. S. National Title by defeating Tom Okker of the Netherlands in the first National Open matches held at Forest Hills in 1968. And in the same year he won the Australian Open Title. Rated top tennis player in the country, he won a total of thirty matches in a row in 1968.

In 1975 Ashe won the men's singles title at Wimbledon, defeating Jimmy Connors, the top-rated American tennis player, 6-1, 6-1, 5-7, 6-4. He was the first black man to take the Wimbledon title; in the same year he also won the World Championship Tennis Crown.

Ashe began to play tennis at age 7, with a borrowed racket, under the auspices of the black Richmond Racquet Club in Virginia. It was not long before he came under the tutelage of Dr. Robert Johnson of Lynchburg, Virginia, who kept Ashe under his eye on a private court at his home.

Ashe enrolled at UCLA, where the weather favored a long season of play and he had access to the good coaching of J. D. Morgan. Under Morgan's direction Ashe climbed in national ranking from twenty-eight to eighteen, from eighteen to six, then from six to one. Since then he has become a professional, leaving no black stars on the integrated amateur circuit, although there are some making great progress in black circles.

An activist in civil rights, Arthur Ashe succeeded in forcing the racial issue in South African tennis when he requested a South African visa to compete in the South African

Open championship. His request for a visa was denied, and South Africa was barred from participation in the 1970 Davis Cup competition as a result.

## Golf

Shortly after golf was introduced to America in 1888, black Americans began to play. Because of the expense of owning and maintaining golf courses, however, black players found it difficult to find playing sites. Many of the black men who were employed as "caddies" on private courses solved this problem by practicing the game on the spot during their off periods, and some of these men attained excellence. With the advent of public golf courses, supported and maintained by taxes, thousands of blacks have taken up the game. Over a dozen good golf clubs have been organized by blacks throughout the nation; a national all-black tournament has been held since 1926. Some of the notable exponents of golf include John Shippen, champion in 1926; Robert "Pat" Ball of Chicago, who was black champion in 1927, 1929, 1934, and 1941; Howard Wheeler of Atlanta, Georgia, who was champion for 1933, 1938, 1946, and 1947; and John Dendy of Asheville, North Carolina, who was champion for 1936 and 1937.

The late Cleve Abbott of Tuskegee sponsored the first black college competition in 1938. Golf has been encouraged in many black colleges, largely through the efforts of the athletic departments. Some black Americans have competed in sectional golf meets, where the color line is dropped; Bill Spiller and Ted Rhodes have scored well in some of these open meets. George Roddy of Greensboro, North Carolina, was captain of the Iowa State golf team and twice won the black amateur national title.

Black golfers have been slow in appearing on the scene largely because of the above mentioned inability to find suitable places to play, which in some cases is linked with their failure to become members of the prestigious clubs which have splendid grounds and facilities. Few black colleges have golf teams to develop through competition. The few outstanding golfers of today are one-time caddies, developed through the black clubs and tournaments, or who played on the grounds of city recreation or public parks.

In recent years Harold Donovant, the first black pro to work at a New York City municipal course, has organized the United Association of Professional Golfers in an attempt to give blacks a chance to play tournament golf in preparation for the P.G.A. circuit.

Lee Elder was the first black to qualify for the Masters Tournament (April 1975). His appearance on the Augusta green brought to a close another tradition of black exclusion from formerly all-white tournaments.

Such other leading black golfers as Pete Brown, Ray Botts, Chuck Thome, Charles and Curtis Sifford, and George Johnson are among the handful of black golfers playing on the P.G.A. tours today. The versatile Althea Gibson has also proved her excellence on the links.

## Horse Racing[4]

Blacks were vital participants in the early days of horse racing. Not only did they work in the stables, grooming and training horses, but black jockeys were the stars of the races. In the first Kentucky Derby held in May 1875, fourteen of the fifteen starters were ridden by black jockeys. The winner was ridden by black Oliver Lewis. Perhaps the most illustrious figure of his time was Isaac Murphy, who rode at the same time as Oliver Lewis. He established the record of three Kentucky Derby victories—in 1885, 1886, and 1888—a record which stood for nearly a century. Other black jockeys who achieved success in the late nineteenth century were Erskine Henderson, Garrett Lewis, James Perkins, and Willie Simms. Simms was the first black jockey to achieve international fame.

Gradually, black jockeys were replaced with white riders; 1911 was the last year for the Kentucky Derby to have a black jockey. However, with the increase in civil rights activities of the 1960s, there has been a resurgence of black jockeys. Alfred Johnson and Ronnie Tanner rode in New York State races during that decade. James Long was the first black to win first place at Saratoga Springs (1974). A black woman, Cheryl White, is one of the few women jockeys to race.

## Fencing

Fencing has only recently become popular in the United States. Over the years the United States has won only two silver and three bronze medals in Olympic fencing competition. Olympic officials in America have considered giving up in fencing. However, in the 1972 Martini and Rossi International Fencing Tournament in New York, two fencers, both black college students, emerged as favorites to win in the Munich Olympics. Ruth White, then a New York University senior, took up fencing at a Baltimore YWCA while in high school; Tyrone Simmons, National Collegiate Foil champion, attended Franklin High School in Philadelphia and continued his studies at the University of Detroit. Although neither, in fact, participated in the 1972 Olympic Games, their emergence on the sports scene is a hopeful sign for American fencing as a whole.

## Billiards

Although not an athletic sport per se, billiards is second to none of the so-called social sports in the need for body fitness, mental training, and motor coordination.

The greatest black pool player in the nation is Cicero Murphy, who helped to crack the color line in this sport. Murphy has won the New York City championship, the state title, and the Eastern States title, as well as the Metropolitan Summer League

Tournament. He was apparently maneuvered away from a chance at the 1965 world crown, but a group of Californians subsequently held a special session of the world championship with every major player participating. Murphy won that title; he finished fourth in the New York version of the world championship.

## Marksmanship

Negro Americans are making a mark in many of the less popular sports. In the eastern part of the United States there are more than a score of Rod and Gun Clubs. Hundreds of members of these clubs go in for skeet and clay pigeon competitive shooting, game hunting, and deep sea fishing. Dr. and Mrs. Ernest B. Wetmore, a black couple from Morristown, New Jersey, have achieved notable recognition as expert shooters in skeet contests. Before the color bar was written into the bylaws of the Amateur Trapshooting Association of America in 1944, Dr. Wetmore became one of the best marksmen in the nation. In 1936 he retired the Governor Hoffman of New Jersey Trophy by winning the state championship for three consecutive years. In 1933, his last year at registered targets, he made 97.6 percent hits out of 4,000 targets. He is also a member of the Century Club, whose members have scored 100 hits out of 100 chances. His best run was 487 scores before a single miss.

## Weight Lifting

Some black athletes go in for weight lifting, and some have become American champions. Two of the six members of the weight-lifting team that competed in the world weight-lifting championship held in Vienna in 1948 were black. John Davis of Brooklyn was winner in the light-heavyweight class; John Terry of New York was fourth in the featherweight class and the maker of a new world snatch record for his weight. In 1938 Terry held the American record for the two-hand lift. He won the lightweight championship in 1940 and 1941. In 1941 John Davis won the world championship in the heavyweight class with a lift of 1,005 pounds in three lifts. He broke the fourteenth Olympic record with a hoist of $999\frac{1}{2}$ pounds to become for that year the strongest man in the world Olympic competition. Davis won the Olympic heavyweight championship in 1948 and 1952. James Bradshaw of Washington, D. C. was judged second-strongest man in the 1952 Olympics.

As we have seen, black Americans have competed against all challengers in many sports, but none has yet attained national reputation in archery, bowling, canoeing, casting, chess, curling, fencing, lacrosse, lawn bowling, polo, rackets, squash tennis, swimming, table tennis, wrestling, and yachting, although some have been capable contenders in several of these sports.

## WOMEN ATHLETES

Black women athletes have paralleled the feats of their racial brothers in track and field, tennis, and golf. The attitude in America toward athletic competition for women, however, soft-pedals interschool competition for women and girls, puts more restrictions through rules on other athletic events, and plays down the importance of competition in gymnastics and track and field sports. Except for swimming, American women athletes have tended to be outclassed in Olympic competition by women athletes from other nations.

Only a few colleges, mainly black, and scattered athletic clubs like the Police Athletic Clubs in New York and the Catholic Youth Organizations in Chicago, were encouraging track and field competition for girls in the mid-1960s, but there is an increasing trend among black girls today to compete in track and field, although not as representatives of their schools. The black schools have not increased their support of athletic programs for girls to the same extent as white colleges and universities, therefore most of the competition is among AAU club teams. The Atoms Track Club team from Brooklyn, a black club, is outstanding among the current AAU club groups.

Until the demise of Coach Cleve Abbott, the Tuskegee-trained women's track and field teams excelled others in the nation and in the Olympic Games. Since 1950, however, Tennessee State University's excellent women's team has been the strongest contender for national honors in track and field. Alcorn A & M College has perhaps the next best of the college teams competing in the AAU meets. Other colleges participating in AAU competition are Prairie View A. & M. and Texas Southern University. These schools do not compete in the Division of Girls' and Womens' Sports (DGWS) Section of the American Association for Physical Education and Recreation intercollegiate championships, however, because of a rule forbidding athletic scholarships, which black colleges offer.

Of nineteen track and field meets for seniors under the auspices of the AAU since 1936, Tuskegee women's teams have won thirteen championships. Two Tuskegee women have won Olympic championships (see section on **Track and Field**). Both indoor and outdoor national championship track and field meets were won by the team representing Tennessee State A. & I. (now Tennessee State University) in 1955.

More recent achievements by young black women athletes include the following:

1972 National Indoor Track and Field Championships, New York, N.Y.

Long jump : first, second, third, and fourth places
60-yard hurdles (finals) : second and third places
220-yard dash (finals) : first, second, and third places
880-yard run (finals) : first place

Fourth DGWS National Intercollegiate Track and Field Championships May, 1972

High jump: first place
200-meter hurdles: first place
100-yard dash: first and third places
220-yard dash: first and fourth places
440-yard dash: second place

## CHANGING ATTITUDES IN
## AMERICAN SPORTS

The militancy of black athletes is increasing in areas throughout the nation in such widely dispersed schools as the Universities of Florida, Notre Dame, Texas, and Washington. As mentioned earlier, in the 1968 Olympic Games the black-gloved fist was raised in protest against racism in America. Most recently at Stanford, protest brought about the hiring of a black coach, Bill Moultrie, who now coaches a freshman football team. At the University of Indiana ten of fourteen black football players were suspended for boycotting practice in protest against the way black players were being treated. At the University of Washington four black players were suspended from the team for failing to show "a 100 percent commitment" to football; eight other players refused to play in the next day's football game with U.C.L.A in protest of the suspension. At Notre Dame black basketball players demanded and received a public apology for "booing" when five black players entered the game against Michigan State in 1969. Similar protest against racial prejudice has taken place in many colleges.

In 1967 eleven black track men at the University of Texas at El Paso refused to compete against Mormon-sponsored Brigham Young University (BYU), because of Mormon restrictions on the role of blacks in the church, and their athletic scholarships were cancelled. Bob Beamon, star of the 1968 Olympic Games, was one of the eleven. Again in 1969 fourteen black football players at the University of Wyoming were dismissed for wearing black arm bands in protest against playing BYU. This action was followed by half a dozen protests by Western Athletic Conference athletes.

In 1969 black basketball players at the University of New Mexico sought to protest BYU's religious bias by wearing black-ribbon arm bands, but were denied this addition to the regular uniforms.

One of the newer signs of militance among black athletes was the attempt of Curt Flood of the Philadelphia Phillies to challenge in court the "reserve clause" in contracts made with players which, in effect, limits the player to the will of the team with which he initially signed a contract. Flood, who was traded by the St. Louis Cardinals in 1968 to the Philadelphia team without his consent, brought a suit for $3 million in damages; meanwhile, he refused to play. The Supreme Court, in June 1972 refused to disturb the fifty-year-old practice in baseball, in language which suggested that it may soon be curtailed. At the same time, the Court indicated that such a clause is limited to baseball.

Oscar Robertson of the Milwaukee Bucks, representing basketball players, testified before Senator Ervin's Antitrust Committee in the United States Senate, opposing the merger of the ABA and NBA Associations, largely on the grounds that freedom of choice and leverage for increased salaries would be reduced.

In 1970, because of world protest, South Africa was barred from any further Olympic competitions because of its apartheid policy by a vote in the Olympic Committee of 35 to 28, and similar pressures resulted in the elimination of Rhodesia on a technicality in 1972.

Another cause of black dissatisfaction is the fact that few black Americans have found a place in the front office of major professional sports, although a few have been used as assistant coaches as their playing days ended. A break-through was made when Bill Russell became coach-manager of the Boston Celtics and Wayne Embry became a general manager in 1972 of the Milwaukee Bucks, the NBA champions. As mentioned earlier, Frank Robinson became the first black manager/player in professional baseball.

Formerly a bulky center with the Cincinnati Royals, second to Bill Russell, then the first black coach in major league sports, Embry was instrumental in the trade for Oscar Robertson, his Royals teammate for six seasons. When Ray Patterson, club president, resigned, the eleven directors on the Bucks' board voted unanimously for Wayne Embry.

Black Americans have shown capabilities as managers, especially in baseball in South America and the Caribbean islands. Among those whom most sports writers adjudge capable of managing major-league teams are Elston Howard, Maury Wills, Jim Gilliam, Willie Mays, Ernie Banks, and Bill White.

## The Mystique of the Black Athlete

The enormous success of blacks in team sports as well as in track and field has raised the question, Is the black athlete any different from the white man that he should so excel? In 1968 the question was put to a group of men qualified to make judgments. Some of their comments are as follows:

The late Vince Lombardi said, "I think the Negro is more naturally endowed. They have more quickness; they're built differently. Their muscles are not as bunched. . . . This gives them greater spring and more quickness."

A. S. "Jake" Gaither, winning coach at Florida A. & M. University, answered, "I can't prove it scientifically, but it apparently is a fact that the Negro is faster. He apparently has better natural coordination."

Bill Rigney, who managed both the San Francisco Giants and California Angels, thinks blacks are a little stronger and have more stamina. He also thinks they are "wound a little tighter."

Bernie Casey, black star pass catcher in the NFL replied, "I have formed some of my own conclusions which I could not substantiate medically. First, the Negro was brought to this country as a physical specimen, a physical thing to work the land. He was right away involved in physical labor (for nearly 300 years). Also, the Negro evolved in a warm climate—conducive to being outdoors most of the time. . . ."

Tom Hawkins, of the Los Angeles Lakers, said, "From an early age, you identify with people who have been successful. The Negro sees such idols in sports and entertainment."

Generally speaking, because of the way he is treated in the United States, and the barriers that are set in his way in many fields of endeavor, the black American tends to be more anxious to succeed in athletics. In the annals of sports, "the Negro is hungrier."

Back in 1904, when John Taylor of the University of Pennsylvania became national quarter-miler and a member of the Olympic squad, some reasoned that because Taylor's legs were proportioned like those of a typical white runner, he was more able. Later some claimed that anatomical differences such as a peculiar patella or a longer heel bone were responsible.

After Jesse Owens' remarkable performance in the 1936 Olympics, and the preceding victories of Tolan, Metcalfe, Gourdin, and others, Dr. W. Montague Cobb of the Department of Anatomy at Howard University, was called upon in 1936 to study the characteristics that seemed to account for the greatness of black sprinters and jumpers. Dr. Cobb concluded in the summary of his studies:

> There is not a single physical characteristic which all the Negro stars have in common which would definitely identify them as Negroes. There is nothing to indicate [that their] physical characteristics explain the domination of Negro sprinters and jumpers.[5]

Whatever the reasons may be, it is certain that black achievement in sports is a source of pride to young and old alike and a stepping-stone in the struggle of the black American for full recognition as a citizen.

### Notes

1. Edwin B. Henderson, *The Negro in Sports* (Washington, D. C., Associated Publishers, Inc., 1939; Revised edition, 1949).
2. The first issue of *Black Sports*, a monthly magazine edited and published by Allan Barron, appeared in April 1971.
3. Edwin B. Henderson and the editors of *Sport Magazine*, *The Black Athlete—Emergence and Arrival*, United Publishing Corp., Philadelphia, 1970.
4. D. Evans Saunders, "When Negro Jockeys Ruled the Sport of Kings," *Negro Digest*, June 1961, pp. 42–45.
5. Henderson, *op. cit.*

# BIBLIOGRAPHY

Amdur, Neil, "Black Power in Sports: From Protest to Perspective." *The New York Times*, March 12, 1971, section 5, p. 1.

*Black Sports*, a monthly magazine edited and published by Allan Barron.

Edwards, Harry, *The Revolt of the Black Athlete*. New York, The Free Press, 1969.

Flood, Curt and Carter, Richard, *The Way It Is*. New York, Trident Press, 1971.

Henderson, Edwin B., *The Negro in Sports*. Washington, D.C., Associated Publishers, Inc., 1939; Revised edition, 1949.

Mandell, Richard D., *The Nazi Olympics*. New York, Macmillan, 1971.

Peterson, Robert W., *Only the Ball Was White*. Englewood Cliffs, N.J., Prentice-Hall, Inc., 1970.

Robinson, Sugar Ray with Anderson, Dave, *Sugar Ray*. New York, Viking Press, 1970.

Sample, Johnny, *Confessions of a Dirty Ballplayer*. New York, The Dial Press, 1970.

Scott, Jack, *The Athletic Revolution*. New York, The Free Press, 1971.

Toback, James, *Jim: The Author's Self-Centered Memoir on the Great Jim Brown*. New York, Doubleday, 1971.